PRAISE FOR *WAGNERISM*

Named a best book of the year by *The New York Times,*
Chicago Tribune, NPR, *Rolling Stone*, and *Financial Times*

"Readers who let Ross lead them anew through the twentieth century in 2007's *The Rest Is Noise* will find familiar comforts in his sure guidance and musical prose. But they'll find dazzling new dimensions in his scholarship, as adept with large swaths of history as attentive to small crannies of expertise."
—Michael Andor Brodeur, *The Washington Post*

"Magnificent . . . Every culture has its own issues with Wagner, and Ross' even hand is especially impressive when taking on the Big One. His explication of Hitler's rise and the legacy of Wagner's anti-Semitism is a moving lamentation . . . In the end, the inconsistencies are what made Wagner matter, and what make Ross today's perfect Wagnerite."
—Mark Swed, *Los Angeles Times*

"Suavely brilliant . . . [This] magnum opus more than a decade in the making . . . sets out to do nothing less than chart the entire scope of Wagner's influence in Western history and culture, including everything from French Symbolist poetry to *Star Wars*. That capsule description conveys the work's jaw-dropping blend of ambition and erudition, but downplays its easy accessibility."   —Joshua Kosman, *San Francisco Chronicle*

"Here is cultural history that ties together politics, philosophy, sex, war and race . . . You'll see your world differently."
—Christopher Borrelli, *Chicago Tribune*

"One of the many beauties of this incomparably rich book is that it refuses to engage in any simplistic analysis of its subject, who emerges in his full bewildering complexity. It is one of the most valuable books about Wagner I know of, compelling one to engage not merely with the composer and his legacy but with music itself, how it works on us, what it is . . . The miracle of Ross's book is that it is so fresh and so personal; his intellectual stamina, though prodigious, is never flaunted."   —Simon Callow, *Air Mail*

"Reading *Wagnerism* took me two weeks, and once through with it I felt as if I'd spent a fortnight in Bayreuth among affable and highly informed friends. It's a magnificent, eminently readable and often entertaining fund of knowledge and I recommend it unreservedly."

—Rob Cowan, *Gramophone*

"What I love best about *Wagnerism* is Ross's effort to show the teeming floods of fans and their different fandoms, their efforts to grapple with these matters—and their failures—and their adaptations of other failures, and other successes—and above all, the creation, dissolution, and re-creation of communities around the art. That, ultimately, is why he gives us this flood of stories, lives, artworks, anecdotes, conflicts, and creations: to show us not Wagner's triumphs and failures, but those of our living, ongoing world of culture and belief."

—Alison Kinney, *VAN Magazine*

"It's always cause for rejoicing when *New Yorker* music critic Ross publishes a book . . . It's a tribute to the thoughtful and accessible Ross that his conclusions seem both valid and inevitable . . . With this multifaceted jewel of a book, Ross has produced a monumental study of Wagner's legacy. Eighteen out of eighteen anvils."

—Bill Baars, *Library Journal* (starred review)

"Capacious, fascinating . . . A deeply informed history as vigorous as Wagner's music."

—*Kirkus Reviews* (starred review)

"Richard Wagner (1813–1883) is all things to all people in this sweeping cultural history . . . Ross manages to tame the sprawl with incisive analysis and elegant prose that casts Wagner's music as 'an aesthetic war zone' . . . The result is a fascinating study of the impact that emotionally intense music and drama can have on the human mind."

—*Publishers Weekly* (starred review)

"An absolutely masterly work . . . A miraculous synthesis. Ross's writing is an art that conceals art, propelling the reader on and on."

—Stephen Fry, actor and author of *Mythos* and *Heroes*

"*Wagnerism* is as magnificently realized as it is monumentally ambitious—a cultural history of the modern world that Wagner and his protean art helped mightily to create, and equally a brilliantly synthetic mapping of the infinitely multiplying, antagonistic, and cross-pollinating readings and misreadings, transformations and transmogrifications that the world has wrought in its unceasing, ongoing grapplings with Wagner. Alex Ross has assembled a vast convocation of the artists, proponents, and prophets of realism and hallucination, psychology and mythification, avant-gardism and populism, democracy and fascism, cosmopolitanism and racism, and collectively they offer us an epic account of the progress of modernity through the mazes of aesthetics, ideology, and consciousness. It's a journey for which Ross is the ideal guide: lucid, astoundingly erudite, scrupulous, generous, profound, objective, and engaged, and enormously entertaining."

—Tony Kushner, playwright

"In this epic, extraordinary book, Alex Ross contends with the 'infernal logic' of Wagner's legacy, through the centuries and across poetry, literature, art, philosophy, architecture, politics, war, film. *Wagnerism* is a hugely exhilarating read, and a virtuoso feat of scholarship and supple writing. Ross is such a companionable guide, connecting ideas so casually and unspooling stories so fluidly that you can almost lose sight of the ferocious erudition that undergirds every page. I can't think of a better or more profound work about the long, complicated shadow of cultural influence."

—Patrick Radden Keefe, author of *Say Nothing*

"For those who love Wagner, this book is obviously heaven. But *Wagnerism* goes far beyond the man himself, using its subject to springboard into a breathlessly entertaining and dizzyingly diverse survey of art, politics, and culture over the past century and a half. Ultimately, it's a book about how humans are inspired by art, and like all of Alex Ross's writing, it bottles that strange lightning and inspires us in turn."

—Rian Johnson, director of *Knives Out* and *The Last Jedi*

"Until now, what I didn't know about Wagner and his influence on culture could have filled a book. Fortunately, Alex Ross's brilliant evocation of the composer's world more than elucidates Wagner's various mysteries—it gives voice to why and how he came to be such a significant political and aesthetic influence on the world stage. Masterfully written and researched, *Wagnerism* is itself a masterpiece—a breathtaking achievement."

—Hilton Als, author of *White Girls*

"*Wagnerism* is monumental not only in scale but in accomplishment. Wagner casts a vast shadow over modern culture, and it takes an incandescent critical intelligence to illuminate this legacy in its full complexity, distorted by neither hagiography nor demonology. Afro-Wagnerians jostle with Nazis, Gilded Age feminists share the stage with Zionists, gay Wagnerians consort with modernist litterateurs. The result is a singular achievement of scholarship, sensibility, and storytelling."

—Kwame Anthony Appiah, author of *The Lies That Bind*

"In this prodigious interdisciplinary opus, encompassing the visual arts, literature, and philosophy, Ross deftly teases out the tremendous and often polarizing impact that Wagner's music and theories had on modern culture and history, parsing those luminaries who celebrated the composer and those who reviled him. In doing so—in this prismatic examination conducted through a Wagnerian lens—Ross underscores a paradox at the heart of modernism itself: the tension between the retrograde and the avant-garde and, thus, the political right and left, themes of even greater relevance in our present times."

—Vivien Greene, senior curator of nineteenth-
and early twentieth-century art at the Guggenheim Museum

"A masterpiece—massive and magnificent. A book I've been waiting fifty years to read. It turns lights on in regions where I have humbled in murk."

—Peter Schjeldahl, author of *Hot, Cold, Heavy, Light,*
100 Art Writings 1988–2018

"Attention: a masterpiece! *Wagnerism* is extraordinary for the richness of references and testimonies drawn from literature, philosophy, the visual arts, musicology, and cinema. It is probably the most informed work on Wagner and his aesthetic and cultural significance that I have ever read."

—Jean-Jacques Nattiez, author of *Wagner Androgyne*

ALEX ROSS

WAGNERISM

Alex Ross has been the music critic of *The New Yorker* since 1996. His first book, the international bestseller *The Rest Is Noise: Listening to the Twentieth Century*, was a finalist for the Pulitzer Prize and won a National Book Critics Circle Award. His second book, the essay collection *Listen to This*, received an ASCAP Deems Taylor Award. He was named a MacArthur Fellow in 2008 and a Guggenheim Fellow in 2015.

WAGNERISM

ART AND POLITICS IN THE SHADOW OF MUSIC

ALEX ROSS

PICADOR

FARRAR, STRAUS AND GIROUX

NEW YORK

In memory of And   Patner

Wagner *sums up* modernity. It can't be helped,
one must first become a Wagnerian.

—FRIEDRICH NIETZSCHE

The best in this kind are but shadows;
and the worst are no worse, if imagination amend them.

—*A MIDSUMMER NIGHT'S DREAM*

CONTENTS

■ ■

For an audiovisual companion,
a guide to Wagner's works,
a glossary, and other auxiliary materials,
go to www.therestisnoise.com/wagnerism.

WAGNERISM

■ ■

DEATH IN VENICE

Only down deep
is it trusty and true;
false and base
is the revelry above!

At the end of *Das Rheingold*, the first part of Richard Wagner's operatic cycle *The Ring of the Nibelung*, the gods are entering the newly built palace of Valhalla and the Rhinemaidens are singing in dismay. The river nymphs know that Valhalla rests on a corrupt foundation, its laborers paid in gold extracted from the water's depths.

On the evening of February 12, 1883, some three decades after *Rheingold* was finished and seven years after the *Ring* was first performed complete, Wagner played the Rhinemaidens' lament on the piano. As he got into bed, he remarked, "I am fond of them, these subordinate beings of the deep, with their yearning."

Wagner was sixty-nine years old, and in poor health. Since September 1882, he had been living with his family in a side wing of the Palazzo Vendramin Calergi, on the Grand Canal, in Venice. Sequestered in what he called his "blue grotto"—a chamber decorated in multicolored satin fabrics and white lace—he was writing an article titled "On the Womanly in the Human." When it was done, he had said, he would begin composing symphonies.

The next day, clad in a pink dressing gown, Wagner continued to work on his essay. In a corner of a blank page, he wrote: "Nonetheless, the process of the emancipation of women goes ahead only amid ecstatic convulsions. Love—tragedy." Elsewhere in the family suite, Cosima Wagner, the composer's second wife, was playing Schubert's song "Lob der Tränen" ("In Praise of Tears") at the piano, in an arrangement by her father, Franz Liszt.

Sometime after two, Wagner cried out, asking for Cosima and his doctor, Friedrich Keppler. He was found writhing in pain, a hand clutched to his heart. A maid and a valet carried him to a settee, next to a window facing the Grand Canal. When the valet tried to remove the gown, something fell to the floor, and Wagner uttered his apparent last words: "My watch!" At around 3 p.m., Dr. Keppler entered, and established that the Meister, the Sorcerer of Bayreuth, the creator of the *Ring*, *Tristan und Isolde*, and *Parsifal*, the man whom Friedrich Nietzsche described as "a volcanic eruption of the total undivided artistic capacity of nature itself," whom Thomas Mann called "probably the greatest talent in the entire history of art," was dead.

By late afternoon, a crowd had gathered at the street entrance of the Palazzo Vendramin. Dr. Keppler came to the door and said, "Richard Wagner died an hour ago, following a heart attack." Murmurs went up: "Richard Wagner dead, dead." The news spread through a city drenched in rain: "*Riccardo Wagner il famoso tedesco, Riccardo Wagner il gran Maëstro del Vendramin è morto!*" John W. Barker's book *Wagner and Venice* quotes the first obituary, which ran the next morning in *La Venezia*:

Deceased yesterday in our city was the musical genius of Germany.
The composer of *Lohengrin* was for some months among us with his

wife and his delightful children, hoping that the mild air of our heaven
might have served to restore him in health, delicate for some time . . .

Last evening we went to the Palazzo Vendramin Calergi to have
news.

—Riccardo Wagner is dead—there it was told—and his widow, kneeling before his corpse, crazed with grief, hardly believing that her beloved
companion sleeps the eternal repose!

How many memories crowd upon our mind—the bold struggles that
he sustained, the sublime victories that he achieved—the art that he
created—the bitter enemies he had—the fanatical partisans that idolized him as a God—the crowned kings who knelt down before him!

No more—a corpse!

But from him rises a voice that will not die—and perhaps will become in time more powerful, more hearkened to, more beloved.

Five thousand telegrams were reportedly dispatched from Venice in a
twenty-four-hour period. The news traveled as far as Dunedin, New Zealand, where Fergus Hume composed a sonnet hailing Wagner's "Æschylean
music."

Voluminous obituaries reviewed the composer's epic life: his middle-
class origins; his early struggles in provincial posts; his failed first stab
at Parisian fame; his years as a progressive opera director in Dresden;
his participation in the revolutions of 1848–49; his Swiss exile; his
quarter-century of work, with long interruptions, on the *Ring*; his disorderly private life, including two marriages and interminable financial
crises; his miraculous rescue by King Ludwig II of Bavaria; the building of a festival theater in Bayreuth, Germany; the premiere there of the
Ring, in 1876, with two emperors and two kings in attendance; and the
mystical farewell of *Parsifal*, in 1882. "The life of Richard Wagner affords
a remarkable illustration of the results of persistent effort in carrying out
to its conclusion the inspiration of genius," the *New York Times* intoned.
The more unsavory aspects of Wagner's character were usually omitted.
The *New York Daily Tribune*, in an obituary that consumed more than
a page of fine newsprint, gave only one sentence to his vicious attacks
on Jews.

Radical-minded Wagnerites thought that the mainstream tributes had
got it all wrong. The American firebrand Benjamin Tucker wrote in his

journal *Liberty*: "None of the newspapers, in their obituaries of Richard Wagner, the greatest musical composer the world has yet seen, mention the fact that he was an Anarchist. Such, however, is the truth. For a long time he was intimately associated with Michael Bakounine, and imbibed the Russian reformer's enthusiasm for the destruction of the old order and the creation of the new." Moncure Conway, a freethinker, abolitionist, and pacifist from the American South, made a similar argument in a memorial sermon in London. Through artists like Wagner, Conway said, "the old order has become unreal."

Fellow composers, whatever their opinion of the man, were shocked by his departure. "*Vagner è morto!!!*" wrote Giuseppe Verdi, Wagner's Italian antipode. "Reading the news yesterday, I was horror-struck, I can tell you! There is no question. It is a great personality that has disappeared! A name that leaves a most powerful imprint on the History of Art!!!" Johannes Brahms, seen as Wagner's chief German adversary, sent a large laurel wreath to the funeral. Young zealots were in despair. Gustav Mahler ran through the streets in tears, crying, "The Master has died!" Pietro Mascagni secluded himself for several days, writing at high speed the *Elegia per orchestra in morte di R. Wagner*. Liszt memorialized his son-in-law in a strange piano sketch that wavered between emphatic assertions of major-key tonality and meanderings in harmonic limbo. It was titled *R. W.— Venezia*. A few months later, Liszt produced a still gloomier, eerier piece called *At the Grave of Richard Wagner*.

There was a flurry of memorial poems. "He hath ascended in the Magic Car," wrote the American educator William Henry Venable, in "Wagner Dead." Algernon Charles Swinburne rose above the rest with an elegy titled "The Death of Richard Wagner," its alliterations echoing the composer's bardic manner:

> Mourning on earth, as when dark hours descend,
> Wide-winged with plagues, from heaven; when hope and mirth
> Wane, and no lips rebuke or reprehend
>   Mourning on earth.
> The soul wherein her songs of death and birth,
> Darkness and light, were wont to sound and blend,
> Now silent, leaves the whole world less in worth.

The thirty-eight-year-old Friedrich Nietzsche was in Rapallo, completing the first part of *Thus Spoke Zarathustra*, which proclaims the death of all gods and the coming of the *Übermensch*. Nietzsche later noted that he had finished his task "in that sacred hour in which Richard Wagner died in Venice." After seeing the newspapers the following day, he spent several days ill in bed, stupefied. Nietzsche's brother-in-law, Bernhard Förster, heard the news in Asunción, Paraguay, where he was making plans to establish an Aryan colony. "What a thunderbolt it is to hear that Wagner has gone to Nirvana," Förster wrote to a friend, unaware that the composer had cast doubt on the Paraguay scheme a few days before his death.

Commemorative concerts took place on both sides of the Atlantic. "All the world there," said Mary Gladstone, William Gladstone's daughter, of an all-Wagner event at the Crystal Palace, in London. Four days after the composer's death, the Boston Symphony discarded its scheduled program in favor of a "Wagner Night." Various institutions in New York City—the New York Academy of Music, the Philharmonic Society, the Brooklyn Philharmonic, and the New York Chorus Society—paid homage. In Paris, the Colonne and Lamoureux orchestras mounted impromptu festivals. The most extravagant tribute was held, fittingly, in Venice, on April 19. Outside the Palazzo Vendramin, the conductor Anton Seidl led an orchestra arrayed in *bissone*, Venice's ornate ceremonial boats, with hundreds of people observing from gondolas. Siegfried's Funeral Music, the orchestral epitaph from *Götterdämmerung*, resounded on the Grand Canal.

The American essayist Sarah Butler Wister attended one of the Paris memorials, her interest perhaps piqued by her musically inclined son Owen, who later wrote the classic Western novel *The Virginian*. The following year, in *The Atlantic Monthly*, Wister gave a vivid account of the occasion, recording not only the adoration of progressive factions but also the hatred of conservative patriots, who had not forgotten Wagner's chauvinistic agitation during the Franco-Prussian War of 1870–71:

> The music had swallowed us alive, like a gulf. The excitable audience
> was wrought into a frenzy, in which other passions than melomania
> had a share. There was in some hearers real antipathy to the composer,
> in others animosity to him as a German, and these prejudices struggled
> fiercely against the dominating power of the music and the rapturous

enthusiasm of the majority. The grandeur of the Tannhäuser, the charm of the spinning chorus from the Flying Dutchman, the gravity and interest of the prelude to Parsifal, kept the dissidents in check until the wild gallop of the Valkyrie began. The stern daughters of Odin rode on the whirlwind above the din of the battle-field, sweeping mortals with them on their breathless course; and then the storm burst in hisses, hooting, stamping, shrill whistles, calls, cries, and counter-cries: "That's not music!" "Bravo! bravo! bravissimo!" "If the Germans want to hear it, let them go hear it at home!" "Bis! bis!" (Again, again.) "You sha'n't have it!" "Superb! Magnificent!" "Stop it!" "Turn out the blackbirds!" (the men with the whistles.) "Down with the circus-riders!"

Memorials in German-speaking lands were impassioned and frequently politicized. In Austria, an attachment to Wagner was common among youthful pan-Germanists—those who advocated the unification of Germanic peoples under one national banner. According to the author Hermann Bahr, young Viennese would declare themselves Wagnerites before they had heard a bar of the music. A friend of Bahr's once camped out for three days at a train station in the mistaken belief that the Meister was due to arrive.

On March 5, Vienna's German student association organized a tribute in the Sophiensaal, where the Strausses once held waltz evenings. Several thousand attended. Pan-German rhetoric mounted as the event went on, with antisemitic slurs becoming audible. Bahr, then a member of the Albia fraternity, delivered a fiery oration. At the climax, he employed a metaphor derived from *Parsifal*, comparing Germany to Wagner's chaste hero and Austria to the outcast Kundry. The Reich was implored to "have mercy and no longer forget the sorely penitent Kundry, still waiting yearningly on the other side of the border for her Redeemer!" The phrase touched off a commotion, with the students singing "Die Wacht am Rhein" and the Deutschlandlied. The police intervened. Decades later, Bahr remembered Georg von Schönerer, the pro-German, anti-Jewish rabble-rouser, swinging a club and sputtering with anger.

The incident drove one Jewish alumnus of Albia to resign from the society in protest. Expressing his sorrow that a Wagner memorial had "developed into an antisemitic demonstration," he wrote: "I would not think of polemicizing here against this retrograde fashion of the day; I will mention

Wagner's coffin arriving in Munich

only in passing that even as a non-Jew I would have condemned, from the standpoint of the love of freedom, this movement to which my fraternity has to all appearances been connected. To all appearances; for if one does not audibly protest against actions of this kind, one is bound in solidarity to them. Qui tacet, consentire videtur! [Silence gives consent!]" This was Theodor Herzl, the future architect of the Zionist state. Herzl, too, felt drawn to Wagner, and the composer's antisemitism did not discourage him. While he was writing *The Jewish State*, in Paris in 1895, he often attended performances of *Tannhäuser*, Wagner's tale of a wanderer seeking redemption. "Only on the evenings when no opera was performed," Herzl later recalled, "did I doubt the rightness of my ideas."

As news of Wagner's death rippled outward, his remains journeyed back to Bayreuth, the Franconian town where he had established his festival and home. The casket was brought by water from the Palazzo Vendramin to the Venice railway station, whence it traveled in a mortuary car across Austria to Germany, arriving in Bayreuth on the evening of February 17. Three additional railway carriages were filled with wreaths. Twenty-seven firemen kept watch at the station overnight. The funeral began at four the following day, with a regimental band playing Siegfried's Funeral Music. After speeches were delivered, a long procession moved slowly through the city, toward the villa that Wagner had christened Wahnfried—"peace from delusion." The deceased was placed in a tomb that had been built in the yard behind Wahnfried, next to the grave of a favorite dog, a Newfoundland named Russ.

La Venezia did not exaggerate when it said that Cosima Wagner was "crazed with grief." Once the guests had departed, the Meisterin, as she would now be known, climbed down into the grave and lay next to the casket. She had ordered her daughters to cut off all her hair, and a velvet cushion containing the shorn locks was placed on the dead man's breast. She seemed to want to die with him. Eventually, Siegfried, her thirteen-year-old son, persuaded her to return to the house. She would live until 1930, having remade Bayreuth as a cultural monument.

Wagner's resting place became a site of homage. One sonneteer took note of a "wondering band / Of loitering pilgrims who entrancèd stand." John Philip Sousa, the American March King, went to some trouble to gain entrance, persuading the Wahnfried housekeeper to let him in when Cosima was away. Often, visitors left with a souvenir. The Boston arts patron Isabella Stewart Gardner took a leaf from the ivy that covered the grave and pressed it into her scrapbook. The composers Anton Bruckner and Emmanuel Chabrier also collected vegetation; Chabrier displayed his Wagner ivy in a box in his office. Rev. H. R. Haweis, the author of the bestselling tract *Music and Morals*, helped himself to a branch of a fir tree that was hanging overhead. A character in Upton Sinclair's novel *King Midas* brings home a pebble.

Some pilgrimages were less sentimental. The African-American writer and activist W. E. B. Du Bois, when attending the festival in 1936, walked past the grave twice a day. Mindful of the composer's racist legacy, Du Bois could still write, "The musical dramas of Wagner tell of human life as he lived it, and no human being, white or black, can afford not to know them, if he would know life." When Leonard Bernstein stopped at the site, he joked that the slab was big enough that you could dance on it. Bernstein was undoubtedly thinking not only of Wagner but also of Adolf Hitler, who, on his first visit, in 1923, stood at the grave for a long time, alone.

Wahnfried is now the site of the Richard Wagner Museum. The sofa on which the Meister died—the *Sterbesofa*—can be seen in an upstairs room. The Palazzo Vendramin is occupied by the Casinò di Venezia, which offers poker, blackjack, and roulette under the slogan "An Infinite Emotion." Facing the Grand Canal is a commemorative plaque, for which the poet-politician Gabriele d'Annunzio composed a suitably elusive text, in 1910:

In this palace
the souls hear
the final breath of Riccardo Wagner
perpetuated like the tide
which laps the marble stones.

The global ceremonies of mourning in 1883 showed how immense a shadow Wagner cast on the world in which he lived. The truly extraordinary thing is that after his death the shadow grew still larger. The chaotic posthumous cult that came to be known as Wagnerism was by no means a purely or even primarily musical event. It traversed the entire sphere of the arts—poetry, the novel, painting, theater, dance, architecture, film. It also breached the realm of politics: both the Bolsheviks in Russia and the Nazis in Germany used Wagner's music as a soundtrack for their attempted reengineerings of humanity. The composer came to represent the cultural-political unconscious of modernity—an aesthetic war zone in which the Western world struggled with its raging contradictions, its longings for creation and destruction, its inclinations toward beauty and violence. Wagner was arguably the presiding spirit of the bourgeois century that achieved its highest splendor around 1900 and then went to its doom.

He became the Leviathan of the fin de siècle in large part because he was never merely a composer. An idiosyncratic but potent dramatist, he wrote

Wagner's grave at Wahnfried

the texts for all of his operas, combining spectacular action sequences with intricate psychological studies. He was a prolific, all-too-prolific essayist and polemicist, whose menagerie of concepts—Gesamtkunstwerk ("total work of art"), leitmotif, "endless melody," "artwork of the future"—overran intellectual discourse for several generations. He was a theater director and theorist who reshaped the modern stage. Productions at his Festspielhaus in Bayreuth anticipated the advent of the cinema, conjuring legends in the dark. Finally, and fatally, he dabbled in politics, helping to popularize a pseudoscientific form of antisemitism. The sum of all these energies cannot be fixed. "The essence of reality lies in its endless *multiplicity*," Wagner wrote in 1854. "Only what changes is real."

When the term "Wagnerian" first surfaced, it had an ironic ring. In 1847, a critic in the German city of Chemnitz wrote of the "triumph of the Wagnerians, of which we are lucky to have several fine specimens here." Early on, the word denoted a follower or fan. Later, it marked an artistic quality, an aesthetic tendency, a cultural symptom. The social critic Max Nordau, in his 1892 polemic *Degeneration*, called Wagnerism "the most widespread, and therefore the most significant, of all present-day aberrations." Eventually, it became a synonym for grandiose, bombastic, overbearing, or, simply, very long. Things that have been described as Wagnerian include the film *Fight Club*; the sound of ice breaking; the All-Ireland Gaelic football championship of 1956; the feud between Boeing and the European Aeronautic Defence and Space Company over a $35 billion tanker deal; servings of sausage and schnitzel in German-speaking Switzerland; the roar of a Lamborghini V10; and the monsoon in Mumbai. Similar lists could be made for "leitmotif" and "Gesamtkunstwerk." The currency of such terms, however spurious their application, testifies to Wagner's lasting grip.

Even when Wagnerism is defined more narrowly, its meanings multiply. In these pages, it may mean a modern art grounded in myth, after Wagner's example. It may mean imitating aspects of his musical and poetic language. It may involve combining genres in pursuit of a total artwork. It may take the form of what I call "Wagner Scenes"—tableaux in novels, paintings, and films in which the music is played, discussed, or heard in the background of an interaction, often a seduction. Despite Wagner's identification with German nationalism, he lived much of his life as a

European nomad, and his impact was international in scope. Circa 1900, the composer was like a massive object in space, drawing some entities into its orbit, making others bend just a little as they moved along independent paths. Violent apostasy from Wagner can be Wagnerism inverted, as Nietzsche was the first to demonstrate. Among modernists of the early twentieth century, the agon with Wagner was so widespread as to be almost a distinguishing trait.

This is a book about a musician's influence on non-musicians—resonances and reverberations of one art form into others. Wagner's effect on music was enormous, but it did not exceed that of Monteverdi, Bach, or Beethoven. His effect on neighboring arts was, however, unprecedented, and it has not been equaled since, even in the popular arena. He cast his strongest spell on the artists of silence—novelists, poets, and painters who envied the collective storms of feeling that he could unleash in sound.

Dialogues between genres are not always persuasive or coherent. The theatrical visionary Adolphe Appia wrote, "Any attempt to transfer the Wagnerian idea into a work which is not based on music is a contradiction of that very idea." In a way, this book is a story of failed analogies; the field of Wagnerism is rich in mistranslation, and those ubiquitous Gesamt- and leit- words long ago took on lives of their own. (Wagner used the term "Gesamtkunstwerk" a handful of times in 1849, then set it aside, exclaiming, "Enough of that!") Yet misreadings can themselves be imaginative acts, as Harold Bloom showed in *The Anxiety of Influence*. To a surprising degree, an allegedly tyrannical artist becomes a blank screen on which spectators project themselves. Charles Baudelaire wrote to the composer: "You returned me to myself." Nietzsche, reviewing his youthful effusions, said, "All the psychologically decisive passages speak only of me."

The salient element of such experiences is that Wagner creates ambiguity and certitude in equal measure. Whatever is flitting through the subject's mind is amplified and reinforced by a deep engagement with the music. The behemoth whispers a different secret in each listener's ear. Although Wagner had strong ideas about what his work meant, those ideas were far from consistent, and, in any case, ambiguity was a necessary outcome of his dramatic method, which ultimately rested on the manipulation of myth. "The incomparable thing about myth," he wrote, "is that it is always true, and its content, through utmost compression, is inexhaustible for all time." His hoard of borrowed, modified, and reinvented archetypes—the wanderer on his ghost ship, the savior with no name, the cursed ring, the sword in the tree, the sword reforged, the novice with unsuspected powers, and so on—is his most durable legacy.

Early chapters of *Wagnerism* show a proliferation of mythologies, whether in Nietzsche's fable of the *Übermensch*, the poetical arcana of Symbolist Paris, the neo-medieval conceits of the Pre-Raphaelites, or Thomas Mann's tales of bourgeois decline. The mania gathers momentum not only in opera houses but also in occult shrines and anarchist cells. The middle third explores questions of race, gender, and sexuality. We roam the Wagnerian prairies of Willa Cather and gauge the equivocal responses of modernist writers like James Joyce, Marcel Proust, T. S. Eliot, and Virginia Woolf. The last section crosses the bloodlands of the twentieth century and enters the dreamscape of Hollywood, from *The Birth of a Nation* to *Apocalypse Now*. Some of these artists knew the work intimately; others had only glancing knowledge of it. The point is that for several consecutive generations it was omnipresent. The historian Nicholas Vazsonyi writes: "There is no path into the twentieth century—for good or evil—that bypasses Wagner."

Of the Wagnerisms, the Nazi version is by far the best known. "The term 'proto-fascist' was virtually invented to describe Wagner," the philosopher Alain Badiou has said. The association is not a random accident. Emphasis on "Hitler's Wagner" in recent decades has been a necessary corrective to the silence that Wagnerites long maintained, whether because of lingering Nazi sympathies or because of a simple wish to avoid the subject. The composer's worldview, despite its inner conflicts, contained seeds of Nazi ideology. At the same time, the Wagner-to-Hitler narrative has its shortcomings. It is prone to what the literary critic Michael André Bernstein called "backshadowing"—the habit of reading German history as an irreversible march into the abyss. Contemplating the literature of the Holocaust, Bernstein wrote: "We try to make sense of a historical disaster by interpreting it, according to the strictest teleological model, as the climax of a bitter trajectory whose inevitable outcome it must be." One danger inherent in the incessant linking of Wagner to Hitler is that it hands the Führer a belated cultural victory—exclusive possession of the composer he loved. As early as 1943, the great leftist theater critic Eric Bentley was asking, "Is Hitler always right about Wagner?"

Whatever the merits of the "proto-Nazi" framing, Wagner's afterlife assumes a tragic shape. An artist who had within his reach the kind of universality attained by Aeschylus and Shakespeare was effectively reduced to a cultural atrocity—the Muzak of genocide. Still, Wagnerism survived the ruination of the Nazi era. In the postwar era, radical directors reinvented the operas onstage. Fantasy epics like *The Lord of the Rings*, *Star Wars*, and *Game of Thrones* rejuvenated Wagner's mythic devices, consciously or not. The mysticism of *Parsifal* wafted through the later novels of Philip K. Dick. Musicologists and historians have excavated half-forgotten understandings of the composer, and those alternative Wagnerisms are at the heart of my story: socialist Wagner, feminist Wagner, gay Wagner, black Wagner, Theosophical Wagner, satanic Wagner, Dadaist Wagner, sci-fi Wagner, *Wagnerismus*, *Wagnerismo*, *Wagnérisme*. I am conscious of my limits, in both expertise and language. Nietzsche accused Wagner of dilettantism: in fact, the composer's legacy is so multifarious that anyone who studies it is a dilettante by default. Writing this book has been the great education of my life.

You need not love Wagner or his music to register the staggering dimensions of the phenomenon. Even lifelong admirers sometimes become exasperated or disgusted with him. As George Bernard Shaw said, in his classic study *The Perfect Wagnerite*: "To be devoted to Wagner merely as a dog is devoted to his master . . . is no true Wagnerism." You can sympathize with Stéphane Mallarmé, who spoke of "*le dieu Richard Wagner*," and also accept W. H. Auden's description of the man as "an absolute shit." Wagner's divisiveness, his undiminished capacity to enrage and confuse, is part of his allure. He would have puzzled over the majority of artistic responses to his work, not to mention latter-day styles of opera production. Most of all, though, he would have marveled at the persistence of his music in a world grown alien. Cosima Wagner wrote in her diary: "He believes that after his death they will drop his works entirely, and he will live on in human memory only as a phantom." In this respect, as in many others, he has been proved triumphantly wrong.

RHEINGOLD

Wagner, Nietzsche, and the *Ring*

In the beginning was the tone: octave E-flats in the double basses, sustained in a barely audible rumble. Five bars in, bassoons add a pair of B-flats, five steps higher. Together, these notes form the interval of the perfect fifth. Like the fifth that glimmers at the start of Beethoven's Ninth Symphony, it is an emanation of primordial nature, the hum of the cosmos at rest. Then eight horns enter one after another, in upward-wheeling patterns, which resemble the natural harmonic series generated by a vibrating string. Other instruments add their voices, in gradually quickening pulses. As the mass of sound gathers and swirls and billows in the air, the underlying tonality of E-flat does not budge. Only after 136 bars—four to five minutes in performance—does the harmony change, tilting toward A-flat. The prolonged stasis engenders a new sense of time, although it is difficult to say what kind of time it is: perhaps an instant passing in slow motion, perhaps eons passing in a blur.

This is the prelude to *Das Rheingold*, which is itself the *Vorabend*, the preliminary evening, to the *Ring*. The orchestra represents the river Rhine, the repository of the magic gold from which a ring of unimaginable power can be forged. In his autobiography, *My Life*, Wagner relates how the opening came to him while he was staying in La Spezia, on the Ligurian Sea, in September 1853. Resting at his hotel, he fell into "a kind of somnambulistic state," and the prelude began sounding in his head. Although biographers doubt that it happened exactly that way, we can surmise that the river is not purely German, that it flows from deeper, warmer waters.

"It is, so to speak, the world's lullaby," Wagner said. Out of the rocking cradle a universe emerges. The golden triads of Western harmony gestate from a fundamental tone; then language gestates from music. The Rhinemaidens swim up from the depths, singing a mixture of nonsense syllables and German words. Wagner told Nietzsche he had in mind the phrase "*Eia popeia*," sung for centuries by mothers to lull their babies.

Weia! Waga!
Woge, du Welle,   Welter, you wave,
walle zur Wiege!   surge around the cradle!
Wagalaweia!
Wallala weiala weia!

Wagner is employing a highly stylized version of the old Germanic verse scheme of Stabreim, which is structured around internal alliteration. The affect is epic, the language abstract. The modernists paid heed: T. S. Eliot quotes the Rhinemaidens in *The Waste Land*, and Joyce has them swim in the river of *Finnegans Wake*.

The prelapsarian bliss lasts for only twenty-one more bars before the harmony darkens to C minor and Flosshilde warns her fellow maidens that they are neglecting their guardian duties. The Rhine tries to resume its course in the key of B-flat, but it is again tugged into the relative minor. The double basses, having ceased their cosmic drone, play a loping pizzicato. Alberich, the Nibelung dwarf, has entered, his eyes fixed first on the maidens and then on the gold. Wagner sets up a clear duality between the beauty of nature and the malevolent energy of a subhuman outsider. Alberich is the chief antagonist of the *Ring*, although not necessarily its chief villain. Wotan, the chief of the gods, also lusts after the gold and falls prey to its illusions.

In 1876, in advance of the *Ring* premiere, Nietzsche, then a kind of intellectual publicist for the composer, issued a pamphlet titled "Richard Wagner in Bayreuth." Amid much flummery, Nietzsche devises as succinct a synopsis of the cycle as can be found: "The tragic hero is a god who thirsts for power and who, after pursuing all paths to gain it, binds himself through contracts, loses his freedom, and becomes entangled in the curse that is inseparable from power." Needless to say, the topic is eternally relevant. The story of the fatal ring can always speak to the latest soul-stealing technological marvel, the latest swearing of vengeance, the latest rotting empire. The contradiction at the heart of the project is that the *Ring* is itself an assertion of power—huge in size, huge in volume, huge in ambition. Wagner criticized monumentality as an artistic value, calling for a vital folk art that spoke to its time instead of gesturing toward posterity. Nonetheless, the monumental and the Wagnerian were fated to become synonymous.

When, in the wake of the *Ring*, Nietzsche broke with Wagner, he thought of himself as a fugitive slave. Although he disavowed the man, he could not disavow the work. During the twelve years of philosophical activity left to him, he continued to wrestle with the composer's shadow. In *Ecce Homo*, he writes: "*I* actually have it on my conscience that such a high estimation of the *cultural value* of this movement arose." The movement is *Wagnerei*—Wagnerism. Nietzsche is referring to his early gushing on the Meister's behalf, but it is the later, ostensibly anti-Wagnerian writing that shows the movement in full flower. The rejection of Wagner results only in a new interpretation of Wagner. Such is the infernal logic of his protean presence at the dawn of the twentieth century. As Nietzsche eventually admitted: "Wagner *sums up* modernity. It can't be helped, one must first become a Wagnerian."

THE *RING* AND REVOLUTION

The revolutionary year 1848, which gave rise to the *Ring*, shook the old European order but failed to bring it down. In Paris, three days of street protests in February brought about the abdication of King Louis-Philippe and the proclamation of the Second Republic. Similar revolts took place in German-speaking lands, and a national parliament attempted to form in Frankfurt. Karl Marx and Friedrich Engels published *The Communist Manifesto* in London in February; communist, socialist, and anarchist groups organized across the continent. Amid the tumult, counterrevolutionary

The Dresden uprising of 1849, with the soprano
Wilhelmine Schröder-Devrient exhorting the crowd from a window

forces regained the upper hand. The culminating moment—famously described by Marx as historical tragedy repeating itself as farce—was the dissolution of the Second Republic by Louis-Napoléon, Bonaparte's nephew, at the end of 1851.

Wagner, then in his mid-thirties, charged into the melee. Since 1843, he had been serving as the Royal Saxon Hofkapellmeister in Dresden, his reputation founded on his sprawling grand opera *Rienzi*, a dramatization of populist rebellion in fourteenth-century Rome. Over the course of his Dresden tenure, Wagner became increasingly attuned to leftist politics. By June 1848, he was writing poetry about cries of freedom resounding from France. In a fiery speech before the Vaterlandsverein, a democratic-nationalist association, he demanded the obliteration of the aristocracy, the imposition of universal suffrage, the elimination of usury, an enlightened German colonization of the world, and, somehow, the self-reform of the king of Saxony into the "first of the folk, the freest of the free." Except for the German-nationalist element, these proposals resembled the philosophy of Pierre-Joseph Proudhon, who envisioned a society made up of communal units, free of state control but traditional in character.

In the same period, Wagner was delving into old Germanic tales of the hero Siegfried, who slays the dragon Fafnir, wins the dragon's gold hoard, and dies with a spear in his back. Politics plainly motivated this turn: the gold represents the capitalist enemy, Siegfried a new German nation. More broadly, Wagner became engrossed by the evolution and function of myth. Sometime in 1848, he began writing "The Wibelungs," an impressively convoluted essay in comparative mythology, which muses on the inter-relationship of pagan legends, Christian lore, the Nibelung treasure, the Holy Grail, and historical personalities such as Charlemagne and Emperor Friedrich Barbarossa. What fascinated the composer was how the same stories keep getting told in different guises: light against dark, warmth against cold, hero against dragon.

Wagner's subsequent interweaving of mythic stories in operatic form caused him to be described—by none other than the anthropologist Claude Lévi-Strauss—as "the incontestable father of the structural analy-sis of myths." The extension of ancient cycles into the present day brings with it an unsettling implication: the same dark, cold, dragon-like adver-saries will be present in modern Germany. Ominously, Wagner compares the murder of Siegfried to the Crucifixion, remarking that "we still avenge Christ on the Jews today."

In the fall of 1848, Wagner emerged with a prose sketch titled "The Nibelung Myth," outlining a plot roughly equivalent to that of *Götterdäm-merung*. It includes an elaborate backstory of gods, giants, dwarves, heroes, and Walkyrien essentially the whole of the *Ring* in a few dense pages. The scenario combines material from various Nordic and Germanic sources—the Poetic Edda, the Prose Edda, and the *Vǫlsunga saga* of Iceland; the Old Norwegian *Þiðreks saga*; the German *Nibelungenlied*; Jacob Grimm's *German Mythology*—into an inspired mishmash that owes as much to the composer's unruly imagination as to the extant sources.

The Ring itself is a new contraption. The old stories make mention of hoards and magic rings, but only in Wagner's version does the gold yield a weapon of absolute omnipotence. The one vague antecedent is Plato's Ring of Gyges, which makes the wearer invisible and thereby endows him with "the powers of a god." Even a just man might misbehave with such a device at his command, Plato suggests. Likewise, Wagner's Ring bends all to its will. Its companion gadget, the Tarnhelm, enables one to disappear, change shape, or travel far in an instant. It is surely no accident that such magic lore found new life in the late nineteenth century, when technolo-gies of mass manipulation and mass destruction were coming into view.

"The Nibelung Myth" begins not with an image of natural splendor, as in the finished cycle, but with a sinister picture of an infested earth:

> Out of the womb of night and death there germinated a people, which lives in Nibelheim (Mist-Home), that is, in gloomy underground chasms and caves: they are called *Nibelungs*; with shifty, restless activity they burrow (like worms in a dead body) in the bowels of the earth . . . *Alberich* seized the bright and noble Rhinegold, abducted it from the water's depths, and with great and cunning art forged from it a ring, which gave him supreme power over his entire kin . . . Alberich strove for domination of the world and everything contained in it.

The good-versus-evil duality breaks down, though, when Wagner makes the noble gods complicit in the general corruption. "The peace by which they achieved domination is not grounded in reconciliation; it is accomplished through force and cunning. The intent of their higher world order is moral consciousness, but the wrong they are pursuing adheres to themselves." In this early version, Wotan survives the upheaval, like the reformed monarch in Wagner's Vaterlandsverein speech, and Alberich is set free with the rest of humanity.

Wagner fleshed out the story in a prose draft titled *Siegfried's Death*. He then set the project aside and engaged in the most intense political activity of his life. In May 1849, Dresden revolutionaries rose up in protest of anti-constitutional actions by the Saxon king, and Wagner joined them, generating propaganda, helping to obtain arms, and sending signals from the tower of the Kreuzkirche. He was often at the side of the future anarchist Mikhail Bakunin, who had long-standing ties to German radical circles. According to one witness, Wagner fell into a paroxysm of rage, shouting, "War and always war." The day after the Dresden opera house was set ablaze, a street fighter supposedly called out, "Herr Kapellmeister, the beautiful divine spark of joy has ignited." This was an allusion to the "Ode to Joy" in Beethoven's Ninth, which Wagner had conducted a few weeks earlier: "*Freude, schöner Götterfunken.*"

In the aftermath, both Bakunin and Wagner's friend August Röckel were captured, convicted, and condemned to death, though the sentences were later commuted to prison terms. Wagner would probably have met the same fate if he had not eluded the authorities and made his way to

Zurich, where he remained until 1858. For several years, he all but stopped composing and threw himself into the writing of essays, manifestos, and dramatic texts. In "Art and Revolution," he assails commercial interests, saying, "Our god is money, our religion is making money." Because of the false collectivity of capitalist society, artists must join the revolutionary opposition. In "The Artwork of the Future," he upholds ancient Greek theater as a model for an amalgamation of the arts—the fabled Gesamtkunstwerk. And in the book-length treatise *Opera and Drama* he sets out the principles that underpin the *Ring*: a clear, uncluttered projection of the text; the use of recurring motifs to illustrate characters, concepts, and psychological states; the deployment of the orchestra as a medium of foreboding and remembrance.

Wagner's antagonism toward the other, toward an elemental Alberich-like foe, comes to the fore in "Das Judenthum in der Musik," or "Jewishness in Music," published under a pseudonym in 1850. That essay contends that Jews have no culture of their own and that leading Jewish composers like Felix Mendelssohn and Giacomo Meyerbeer are stale imitators of tradition and/or agents of capitalist greed. Chillingly, the analogy of a worm-ridden corpse recurs, purporting to evoke Jews' presence in German society. Relatively few people read this odious document at the time: the *Neue Zeitschrift für Musik*, where it appeared, had a circulation of about eight hundred. Almost two decades later, Wagner republished the essay under his own name, ensuring that it could never be forgotten or excused.

The violence of Wagner's language in this period is still startling to behold. He writes to his supporter Theodor Uhlig: "Works of art cannot be created at present, they can only be prepared for by means of revolutionary activity, by destroying and crushing everything that is worth destroying and crushing." He tells Liszt, his most steadfast musical ally, that he has an "enormous desire to commit acts of artistic terrorism."

Having delivered a kind of polemical artillery barrage—a preview of the assaultive manifesto culture of the early twentieth-century avant-gardes—Wagner returned to his Nibelung material, greatly expanding its scope. First he drafted a prequel to *Siegfried's Death*, titled *The Young Siegfried*. Then he went back further and wrote texts for what became *Das Rheingold* and *Die Walküre* (*The Valkyrie*). The two Siegfried librettos were revised as *Siegfried* and *Götterdämmerung*. In the final scenario, Wotan and the gods, representative of a failed monarchical order, are consumed in flames. Wagner told Uhlig that he could conceive of a performance of the entire work "only *after the revolution*; only the revolution can offer me the artists and listeners I need." A "great dramatic festival," in a theater erected on the banks of the Rhine, would "make clear to the people of the revolution the *meaning* of that revolution, in its noblest sense. *This audience* will understand me: present-day audiences cannot." The revolution he has in mind is a future one—the "great *revolution of humanity.*"

The *Ring* is grounded not only in politics but also in philosophy. The young Nietzsche called the cycle "an immense system of thought without the conceptual form of thought." The *Rheingold* prelude is itself a kind of cosmological proposition. The upwelling of E-flat major is not a creation myth that depends upon a godlike spark, a shout of "Let there be light." Instead, a world materializes in evolutionary fashion, as in the transmuting organisms studied by Jean-Baptiste Lamarck or the nebularly cohering galactic systems theorized by Immanuel Kant. Early in his career, Kant speculated that the solar system had germinated from a mass of gas and dust. Friedrich Engels saw social implications in that hypothesis: humanity, too, should be seen no longer as a system of fixed relations but as an organism undergoing continual evolution.

The revolutionaries of 1848 leaned heavily on the German philosophical tradition, which, since Kant's writings of the 1780s, had transformed how thinking beings viewed themselves and the world. As old certainties trembled—monarchic government, religious morality, hierarchies of class—German idealism put forward a new intellectual faith. Kant had enshrined the principle of autonomous reason, of "always thinking for oneself," as the essence of the Enlightenment. G. W. F. Hegel, Kant's commanding successor, unveiled a grandiose theory of progress, in which a World Spirit guides history toward a utopian future. To those disconcerted by the condition of evolution and flux, Hegel extended the promise that a perfected world was near.

In the 1830s and '40s, another wave of thinkers, the Young Hegelians, appropriated the master's schema, determined to accelerate the World Spirit's progress. They took aim at religious pieties (David Strauss's *The Life of Jesus Critically Examined*, Ludwig Feuerbach's *The Essence of Chris-*

tianity) and at social inequality (the early economic thought of Marx and Engels). Wagner especially prized Feuerbach's notion of the "philosophy of the future," which, the composer later said, promised a "ruthlessly radical liberation of the individual from the bondage of conceptions associated with the belief in traditional authority." This fixation on futurity—Wagner spoke variously of the artwork of the future, the drama of the future, the theater of the future, the artist of the future, the actor of the future, the religion of the future, the woman of the future, the humanity of the future, and the life of the future—became a favorite target of satirists, but it was a calculated rhetorical device that moved art out of the domain of upper-class entertainment and into the main sociopolitical arena.

Wagner also absorbed the Romantic precept that art should fill the void left by the retreat of traditional religion. Friedrich Schiller, in his 1795 treatise *On the Aesthetic Education of Man*, declared that humanity achieves freedom through the perception of beauty, that communities find unity through shared aesthetic experience. Schiller saw the advent of an "aesthetic state," a "joyous realm of play and of appearance." Friedrich Hölderlin, Friedrich Schlegel, and Friedrich Schelling all held that artistic mythologies could give new spiritual direction to what Max Weber would later call the disenchanted modern world. When Schlegel spoke of a reversion to the "primordial chaos of human nature, for which I know of no lovelier symbol than the motley throng of the ancient gods," he might have been dreaming of the *Ring*, even if he had Greek gods in mind. The musicologist Richard Klein summarizes the Wagnerian synthesis: Romantic art-religion is bound to Hegel's dialectic of progress, creating an aesthetic juggernaut.

Nationalism was a complicating factor. Hegel came to believe that the Spirit would find fulfillment in the modern state, and many shared his view. Johann Gottfried Herder, a member of the Weimar Classical circle that also included Schiller and Goethe, had codified modern nationalism with his thesis that humanity necessarily divides itself into distinct peoples, defined by language and folk traditions. One of philosophy's great pluralists, Herder had no wish to aggrandize the German *Volk* at the expense of others. Wagner sounds like Herder when he says, in "Art and Revolution," that the artist must transcend borders, exhibiting national features merely as a "charm of individual diversity." More aggressive definitions of Germanness followed. Johann Gottlieb Fichte, in his *Addresses to the German Nation* (1807–1808), upheld the superiority of German culture, saying that it could bring about a worldwide renewal. The later Wagner fell in with the militant chauvinism that flourished in Fichte's wake, although the imperial state ultimately disappointed him. Dieter Borchmeyer, in his book *What Is German?*, describes how nineteenth-century Germany wavered between cosmopolitan and nationalist answers to the titular question. Wagner raised the issue himself and never gave a clear answer.

The metaphysical bravado of German philosophy masked a host of insecurities and fears. Why had the "land of poets and thinkers" failed to form a nation in the political sense? Was Germany's backwardness a condition to be overcome, or did it preserve premodern values amid dizzying change? Many Romantics, Wagner included, recoiled from nineteenth-century modernity—industrialization, urbanization, mass politics, mass media, the collective onslaught of the age of steam and speed. In the *Ring*, the Rhine is a resource in danger of exploitation and despoliation. The composer's urge to heal the break with nature culminates in *Parsifal*, where the hero says, "Only the spear that inflicted the wound can close it." In a way, that formula captures Wagner's own method. His critique of industrial society employs advanced stagecraft and tools of promotion—a culture of spectacle that looks ahead to Hollywood as much as it looks back to ancient Greece. What is modern in his work is intended to heal modernity's wounds.

Awesome as it is, the *Rheingold* prelude is something other than an idyll of natural innocence. As Mark Berry argues in *Treacherous Bonds and Laughing Fire*, a study of the *Ring*'s political philosophy, the cycle carries no naïve message about the loss of paradise. Wotan's world is compromised from the start. The motif of the Rheingold—a C-major trumpet fanfare amid shimmering strings—may seem to possess the same triadic purity as the immemorial rushing of the river, but it gives off an illusory, deceitful sheen. And while the Rhinemaidens make a primeval first impression with their watery sound poetry, in Alberich's vicinity they become sneering sophisticates, mocking the ugly interloper. In *The Perfect Wagnerite*, Shaw compares them to denizens of high society who disdain a "poor, rough, vulgar, coarse fellow." Modern productions often depict them as aloof party girls. Their humiliation of the dwarf is cruel, and breeds a resentment that many in the audience may find sympathetic.

In revenge, Alberich takes the gold and fashions the Ring. Significantly, he does not win the prize by force. Wagner has given the Rheingold a peculiar feature, which is not to be found in the medieval sources:

Only he who renounces love's power,
only he who spurns love's pleasure,
only he can attain the magic
to wrest the ring from the gold.

In short, power and love are incompatible. If you have one, you cannot have the other. Alberich is willing to make the trade: "Thus I curse love!"

When the gods enter, in the second scene of *Rheingold*, they present a handsomer picture of the same ugly contradiction. Wotan is locked in a loveless marriage, with Fricka. Inscribed on his spear are the treaties that keep warring factions at bay and preserve his own preeminence. As we later learn, he cut this spear from the World Ash Tree, which withered as a result. Here is more evidence that shadows fell on the *Ring* universe long before Alberich shuffled in. Wotan has undertaken a massive construction project, Valhalla, which he can ill afford. The giants Fasolt and Fafner have yet to be paid for their work in building it, and they want compensation in the form of Freia, keeper of the apples of eternal youth. When Wotan hears of the Ring, he realizes he can use it to pay off the giants. With Loge, the demigod of fire, Wotan descends to Nibelheim, Alberich's world, intending to trick the dwarf into giving up the hoard.

During the transition to Nibelheim, Wagner unleashes a gigantic percussion section that includes eighteen anvils—a frightening, futuristic sonority, far removed from the idyll of the Rhine. Shaw seizes on the industrial modernity of the Nibelung domain: "This gloomy place need not be a mine; it might just as well be a match-factory, with yellow phosphorus, phossy jaw, a large dividend, and plenty of clergymen shareholders." Alberich has multiplied the gold into vast wealth; like Marx's potentates, he is captive to his capital and takes no pleasure in it. Yet—to adapt an American politician's quip about the Panama Canal—he stole the gold fair and square, by renouncing love. Wotan makes no such sacrifice, at least consciously, and is therefore a thief of a higher order. As Wagner makes clear in his initial sketch of the Nibelung story, Alberich is "right in his complaints against the gods." In the final scene of *Rheingold*, the dwarf delivers his terrible curse upon the Ring, which is also a curse upon Wotan:

> Am I free now?
> *laughing angrily*
> Truly free?
> Then receive my freedom's
> first greeting!
> As it came to me through a curse,
> so shall this ring be cursed in turn! . . .
> Let all covet
> its acquisition,
> let none enjoy
> its benefit! . . .
> Forfeit to death,
> let the coward be fettered by fear:
> as long as he lives,
> let him die away craving,
> the lord of the ring
> as the slave of the ring:
> till I hold the spoils
> in my hand again!

Wotan and Loge try to laugh away this diatribe—"Did you hear his love greeting?"—but the curse kicks in when Fafner kills his brother, Fasolt, in a dispute over possession of the Ring. Wotan begins to realize that his dealings rest on an "evil wage."

The terms of the political analogy are clear. Wotan is a ruler in the modern mode, willing to allow limited freedoms but prepared to resort to violence. In his mania for treaties, he resembles Klemens von Metternich, the master of the old order. The lesser gods are the aristocracy; the giants are the restless proletariat; Alberich is a self-made capitalist. Loge is like a renegade philosopher-politician who has joined Wotan's coalition for pragmatic reasons. Many commentators have likened Loge to Bakunin, who, according to Wagner, imagined a world conflagration arising from peasant rebellion. At the end of *Rheingold*, Loge is tempted to torch Valhalla earlier than scheduled: "They're hurrying on towards their end, though they think they will last forever . . . I feel a seductive desire to turn myself into guttering flame." The fall of the gods is the necessary prelude to a true uprising. *"Alles, was besteht, muß untergehen,"* Wagner wrote in his 1849 essay "Revolution"—"All that exists must go under." The words parallel the prophecy of the earth goddess Erda, who warns Wotan, "All that is, ends."

Rheingold closes with the degraded majesty of the gods' entrance into Valhalla. Just as Wotan and his clan set foot on the rainbow bridge that leads to their new home, the Rhinemaidens are heard pleading for the return of the gold ("Only down deep is it trusty and true"). Wotan scowls to Loge: "Put an end to their teasing." Fergus Hume, in his memorial sonnet of 1883, was right to call Wagner "Æschylean": the scene resembles the ending of *Agamemnon*. As Clytemnestra and Aegisthus enter the palace of the murdered king, the chorus chants, "Have your way, gorge and grow fat, soil justice, while the power is yours," to which Clytemnestra replies, "Do not heed their empty yappings." Both processions are hollow triumphs. False and base is the revelry above. The challenge is to hear the irony in Wagner's wall of sound: the thrill of the sonority, with its seventeen blaring brass, can trick us into taking the bombast at face value.

DIE WALKÜRE AND METAPHYSICS

In the summer of 1854, Wagner arrived at *Walküre*, the first full-length opera of the *Ring*. Settled in Zurich, he composed at a manic pace. By September, he had churned his way through the first act, in which Siegmund and Sieglinde, Wotan's twin offspring, fall in love without knowing each other's identity. Despite the scandalousness of the situation, or perhaps because of it, nineteenth-century audiences found these scenes as rousing as any popular romance of the day. The climactic cascade of sensations—Siegmund's ardent song of love and spring ("Winter's storms have waned"); Sieglinde's equally ardent answer ("You are the spring for which I longed"); Siegmund's drawing of the sword from the tree ("Nothung! Nothung!"); the final orgasmic embrace—is a tour de force of hot-blooded Romantic entertainment.

Wagner in Zurich, from Thomas Mann's picture collection

In the second act, the emotional temperature plummets. Wotan enters in a buoyant mood, convinced that he has found a way to regain the Ring. Having surrendered the gold to Fafner, Wotan cannot revoke the deal, on account of the contracts etched into his spear. Yet the wild human Siegmund would appear to be free of his father's will and of godly commitments. Surely he can win the Ring from Fafner, who has taken the precaution of turning himself into a dragon. Fricka, Wotan's disgruntled spouse, proceeds to pick the plan apart. Incestuous love is an outrage, she says, and Siegmund's independence is a sham: the free man is transparently a pawn. Fricka demands that Wotan stand aside when Sieglinde's husband, Hunding, comes seeking satisfaction. Wotan descends into a twenty-minute monologue of anguish. The chief of the gods comes to understand his own powerlessness and, beyond that, the inevitability of his end.

Wagner wrote of this scene: "If it is presented as I require—and if all my intentions are fully understood—it is bound to produce a sense of shock beyond anything previously experienced." First, downward-crawling bassoons, cellos, and a bass clarinet suggest Wotan's dejection. When his Valkyrie daughter Brünnhilde asks what is wrong, he howls:

O heilige Schmach!	O righteous shame!
O schmählicher Harm!	O shameful sorrow!
Götternoth!	Gods' distress!
Götternoth!	Gods' distress!
Endloser Grimm!	Infinite rage!
Ewiger Gram!	Eternal grief!
Der Traurigste bin ich von Allen!	I am the saddest of all living things!

The alliterations of Stabreim here follow a subtler function, of a kind that Wagner discusses in *Opera and Drama*. When our ears detect consonant patterns—say, "*hei*lig" ("holy/righteous") and "*Ha*rm" ("sorrow")—we recognize a bond between seemingly opposed emotions.

The music is titanic. The vocal line dives down jagged intervals— octave, major seventh, minor seventh. The orchestra piles on monolithic dissonances over a cavernous C. The bass note keeps moving down, one false bottom giving way to another, until we reach the basement of the world. Wotan now retells the story of the *Ring* with a clear view of his own guilt: "I longed in my heart for power . . . I acted unfairly . . . I did not return the ring to the Rhine . . . The curse that I fled will not flee from me now . . . Let all that I raised now fall in ruins!" Finally, he emits two cries of "*Das Ende!*"—the first stentorian, the second a whispered gasp. In a bitter epilogue, Wotan bequeaths to Alberich the "worthless splendor of the gods."

Just before Wagner wrote this music, he made a discovery that reshaped his intellectual landscape. A fellow exile in Zurich was the revolutionary poet Georg Herwegh, who, in 1848, had led an expeditionary force into the Grand Duchy of Baden in support of attempts to found a republic there. Herwegh recommended that Wagner read Arthur Schopenhauer's *The World as Will and Representation*. First published in 1818, this lyrical masterpiece of philosophical pessimism initially attracted little attention. In the years when Hegel's vision of historical progress held sway, Schopenhauer of-fered a far darker picture of a pain-filled world spinning toward no definite goal. By the early fifties, the pessimist had come into fashion, his world-weariness matching the depleted mood of the postrevolutionary era. At first, Schopenhauer's imperative of self-abnegation alarmed Wagner, but Herwegh made him realize that all tragedy rests on an awareness of the "nothingness of the world of appearances."

The World as Will appealed to Wagner not least because it elevated music to a place of preeminence among the arts. In Schopenhauer's thought, the Will is not simply the striving of the individual but a drive inherent in the universe—an endless need that never finds satisfaction. Music, Schopenhauer says, is the one art form that, rather than copying the outer shell of representation, mimics the operation of the Will itself. The composer reveals the "innermost nature of the world," and his work "gives the innermost kernel preceding all form, or the heart of things." The great boon of aesthetic experience, Schopenhauer elsewhere says, is that in replicating the activity of the Will it grants the spectator relief from the Will's insatiable pressure, by letting him imagine that he has stepped outside of it. "We celebrate the Sabbath of the penal servitude of willing; the wheel of Ixion stands still."

Nietzsche later smirked that Wagner's embrace of Schopenhauer was no surprise, given the superpowers that this philosophy bestows on the musician: "Henceforth he became an oracle, a priest, indeed more than a priest, a sort of mouthpiece of the 'in itself' of things, a telephone of the beyond." But the appeal was not simply narcissistic. Wagner saw striking resemblances between Schopenhauer's work and the *Ring* in progress. One passage in *The World as Will* reads like a précis of the opening of *Rheingold*: "I recognize in the deepest tones of harmony, in the ground-bass, the lowest grades of the will's objectification, inorganic nature, the mass of the planet." The ethic of self-abnegation matches Wotan's acceptance of his powerlessness. Schopenhauer says that only a denial of worldly appearances, a denial of the will to live, can bring peace to the suffering individual. He who overcomes the self will "change his whole nature, rise above himself and above all suffering . . . and gladly welcome death." The Wotan of *Walküre* begins to attain such wisdom, although his behavior lags behind his understanding: "What I love, I must relinquish."

These ideas had sources older than Schopenhauer. To expose the unreality of the outer world, the philosopher drew not only on the Western intellectual tradition—Plato's shadows in the cave, Kant's world of phenomena—but also on Christian asceticism, Buddhism, and Hinduism. The Hindu concept of *māyā*, the veil of illusion, was paramount. Feuerbach, in his *Thoughts on Death and Immortality*, had taught that the lust for life is also the lust for death, that "only nothingness can cure being." True heaven is the "better I of another humanity" that comes into being when the ego withers. The Romantics had long sung in praise of death, dissolution, self-annihilation. Wagner seemed especially open to such thinking after 1848, when his alienation from both political and artistic life became profound. The world is "evil, *evil, fundamentally evil,*" he wrote to Liszt. "It belongs to *Alberich.*" Bryan Magee, in his philosophical study *The Tristan Chord,* proposes that Wagner's apparent conservative turn resulted from this deeper philosophical transformation: "His significant movement was not from left to right but from politics to metaphysics." Music itself becomes the metaphysical agent, the way to a "trusty and true" world beyond the veil.

In December 1854, Wagner sent Schopenhauer the text of the *Ring,* no doubt hoping that the philosopher would recognize it as the work of a kindred spirit. Schopenhauer, who preferred Mozart and Rossini to more modern music, made biting notes in the margins. "Wodan under the slipper!" he wrote next to Fricka's critique of her husband in Act II of *Walküre.* The goings-on between the twins caused him obvious distress. Next to the stage instruction that ends the love scene in Act I—"The curtain falls quickly"—Schopenhauer added, "And it's high time."

SIEGFRIED DIONYSUS

Siegfried's theme, from Wolzogen's guide to Ring *leitmotifs*

At first, Siegfried, the blond hero born of Siegmund and Sieglinde, loomed almost erotically large in Wagner's imagination. In 1851, he spoke of "the beautiful young man in the shapeliest freshness of his power . . . the real, naked man, in whom I was able to discern every throbbing of his pulse, every twitch of his powerful muscles." The strapping youth also has the appearance of a revolutionary, free of sentimental attachments to the extant world. Nietzsche wrote: "His origin already amounts to a declaration of war on morality—he comes into the world through adultery, through incest . . . He overthrew all tradition, all respect, all *fear*. He strikes down whatever he does not like." Shaw called Siegfried "a totally unmoral person, a born anarchist . . . an anticipation of the 'overman' of Nietzsche."

Siegfried receded in importance as the *Ring* grew in scope and Wotan moved into the foreground. The god "resembles *us* to a tee," Wagner wrote in 1854. Siegfried is more abstract—"the man of the future whom we desire and long for but who cannot be made by us since he must create himself on the basis of *our own annihilation*." At times, the composer sounded almost disillusioned with Siegfried, even though his only son bore the hero's name. "The best part of him is the stupid boy," Wagner said in 1870. "The man is awful." Indeed, Siegfried is the most problematic character in the cycle. By design, he lacks complexity: he can seem like an action-movie figure barging into a psychological novel. Stupidity is his tragic flaw. Nonetheless, the entire drama hinges on him.

In 1856, Wagner set about composing *Siegfried*—the "stupid boy" part of the cycle. It is the archetypal tale of a budding superhero discovering powers he does not yet understand. Siegfried is in the care of Mime, Alberich's brother, who intends to use the boy to slay the dragon and take the Ring. Siegfried reforges Nothung, Siegmund's shattered sword, and does the deed. When he tastes the dragon's blood, he can suddenly understand the discourse of a magical Woodbird, who tells him of Mime's treacherous nature. Siegfried kills the dwarf and moves on to his next mission: winning a Valkyrie maiden who sleeps within a ring of fire. In the final act, he finds his way blocked by Wotan, who is now disguised as the shadowy Wanderer, his one-eyed face concealed beneath a broad-brimmed hat. The hero breaks the Wanderer's staff, prances through the magic fire, and meets his destined mate, Brünnhilde.

In the summer of 1857, with two acts of *Siegfried* drafted, Wagner set the *Ring* aside in favor of a new project: the romantic tragedy *Tristan und Isolde*. He was in the throes of an infatuation with the author Mathilde Wesendonck, who was married to his Zurich patron Otto Wesendonck. The love triangle of *Tristan* mirrored his personal situation. Relations with the Wesendoncks and with his first wife, the actor Minna Planer, reached a point of crisis, and in 1858 he decamped to Venice, rented rooms in a canal-side palace, and buried himself in *Tristan*. His intention was to produce a more manageable score, one that could earn him the money he needed to finish the *Ring*. The opera that emerged was so radical in its musical language that it was at first deemed unperformable. After *Tristan* came *Die Meistersinger von Nürnberg*, a comedy of colossal dimensions. In 1864, work resumed on the first two acts of *Siegfried*, but not until 1869 did Wagner take up Act III. In the interim, his style had been transformed. At any performance, you feel a jolt when the curtain rises on Act III and the enriched technique of *Tristan* and *Meistersinger* comes flooding in, with nine distinct *Ring* leitmotifs superimposed.

The word "leitmotif" has sown much confusion over the years. Hans von Wolzogen, one of Wagner's most militant young followers, popularized the term, against the composer's own wishes. Although Wagner referred to "melodic moments" and "basic motifs" in his work, he criticized Wolzogen for treating such motifs purely as dramatic devices, overlooking their musical logic. In the simplest definition, leitmotifs are identifying sonic tags: when someone talks about the sword, you hear the sword's theme. Leitmotifs certainly function this way in the *Ring*, but they are less finished melodies than charged fragments, which transcend their context and gesture forward or backward in time. They not only illustrate the action but indicate what characters are thinking or sensing—or even what they are unable to perceive.

As the *Ring* proceeds, Wagner handles his leitmotifs in increasingly cavalier, even subversive ways. The motif commonly called "Renunciation of Love" first sounds in *Rheingold*, as the Rhinemaiden Woglinde explains how the gold can be won. It is heard again in *Walküre*, when Siegmund is preparing to pull the sword Nothung from the tree. There its purpose is more obscure, and has stirred much speculation. It implies some concealed identity between the lusty hero and the loveless dwarf—and the identity of opposites is a favorite Wagner theme. Even more tellingly, the motif sounds in *Götterdämmerung* when Brünnhilde tells her sister Waltraute that she will not give up the Ring, because it symbolizes her bond with Siegfried. The Ring's power has advanced to the stage that love and lovelessness serve its purposes equally.

A psychological study has concluded that neither general musical training nor command of German is necessary for subjects to be able to recognize and recall the leitmotifs. They are superbly designed to lodge in the memory of a broad public, orienting listeners in large-scale compositional structures. Eric Prieto, in his book *Listening In*, writes that the leitmotif is "not a musical technique at all" but instead a device "borrowed from drama, and dependent on that eminently linguistic procedure, the attribution of a referent to a sound symbol." Because of its literary nature, the leitmotif has affected literature in turn. Wagnerian authors create networks of phrases that recur across a wide span. Visual artists and filmmakers, likewise, introduce motifs of pattern and color. Although the analogy can become vague to the point of vanishing, artists in many disciplines have respected Wagner's way of giving continuity to extended forms.

What no artist can imitate with complete success—though Thomas Mann and Proust come close—is the uncanny way leitmotifs operate in later stages of the *Ring*, bridging expanses of time. The music of previous days resurfaces, as if from another life. From Act III of *Siegfried* forward, the old motifs are, indeed, the voice of Wagner's younger self intruding on his mature style. When Siegfried breaks the Wanderer's staff, the mighty descending figure of Wotan's spear undergoes a harmonic fracture, breaking into whole-tone intervals. The Spear motif will recur in *Götterdämmerung*; there it falls into the hands of Alberich's demonic son Hagen, who dispatches Siegfried with a stab in the back. Having helped to establish identity and personality, leitmotifs also suggest the loss of identity, death itself.

By the time he returned to *Siegfried*, Wagner had settled in a lakeside house in Tribschen, outside Lucerne. Living with him was Cosima von Bülow, his lover since 1863. The couple remained unmarried until 1870, when Hans von Bülow, Cosima's first husband, agreed to a divorce. (Minna Wagner had died in 1866.) In the meantime, Cosima had given birth to two illegitimate children, Isolde and Eva. Although she performed the role of helpmate, Cosima was a woman of high intelligence and broad culture, anything but meek in her opinions. That the Bayreuth Festival survived Wagner's death and became a permanent institution owed everything to Cosima's skill as a theatrical director, her flair for administration, and her half-ethereal, half-steely charisma. Few women of the period achieved comparable authority. She was also politically reactionary, and, if anything, even more antisemitic than her husband. In 1869, she began keeping a diary, in which she recorded Wagner's daily utterances and depicted him as a German sage. That formidable document—twenty-one volumes, nearly a million words—is both a rich fund of biographical data and a masterly exercise in image control.

Wagner in Lucerne

"At lunch a philologist, Professor Nietzsche," Cosima wrote on May 17, 1869. Nietzsche had first met Wagner the previous November, in Leipzig and succumbed at once to the composer's personality. "Wagner played all the important parts of *Meistersinger*, imitating all the voices in very boisterous fashion," Nietzsche reported. "He is indeed a fabulously lively and fiery man, who speaks very rapidly, is very funny, and makes an intimate party of this sort a total joy." In private, the glowering Meister of official portraits was antic, ebullient, even clownish. He liked nothing more than to cavort with his dogs, who ruled the household.

In the spring of 1869, the twenty-four-year-old Nietzsche had been appointed professor of classical philology at the University of Basel, which was several hours from Lucerne by train. He came to Tribschen in the hope of renewing his acquaintance with the Meister. It was the eve of Pentecost, Nietzsche recalled—the day the Holy Spirit visits the Apostles. He lingered outside the villa, listening as Wagner tried out chords at the piano. Later, he determined that he had heard the passage of *Siegfried* in which Brünnhilde sings, "He who woke me has wounded me!" It is a telling moment. Brünnhilde has been confined to the ring of fire for disobeying Wotan's commands. When Siegfried enters her domain, she initially resists his advances and laments the loss of her Valkyrie powers. She is no helpless maiden awaiting rescue; her pride and intellect remain. When she yields, she does so in the knowledge that this relationship is not a personal matter but a means of world transformation. "Twilight of the gods, darken above," she sings—the one time that the word *"Götterdämmerung"* is uttered in the *Ring*.

When Nietzsche mustered the courage to announce himself, Wagner sent word that he did not wish to be disturbed. The young man was, however, invited for lunch the following Monday. "A quiet and pleasant visit," Cosima wrote. In early June, Nietzsche returned and spent the night— not any night, but the night that Cosima gave birth to Siegfried Wagner. During Wagner's remaining years in Tribschen—he moved to Bayreuth in 1872—Nietzsche visited so often that he was given his own room in the house. The friendship deepened into something like a father-son connection. "Strictly speaking, you are, aside from my wife, the one prize I have received in life," Wagner wrote to his disciple in 1872. Later, in a draft of the preface to the second part of *Human, All Too Human*, Nietzsche described the relationship as "my only love-affair," before striking the phrase from his proofs.

Nietzsche grew up in a Lutheran household that cherished the German musical tradition. His father, the pastor of Röcken, a village not far from Leipzig, played the piano and organ in a style that his son characterized as "free variation." Nietzsche took up piano at an early age, studying repertory from Bach to Schumann. He also composed, in an indistinct Classical-Romantic idiom, and later made the mistake of showing his efforts to the Wagners and their circle. In 1872, Hans von Bülow passed lacerating judgment on Nietzsche's talent: "From the musical standpoint, your 'Meditation' is tantamount to a crime in the moral world. I could discover no trace of Apollonian elements, and as for the Dionysian, I was frankly reminded more of the morning after a bacchanal than of a bacchanal per se."

At first, Nietzsche regarded the "music of the future" with suspicion. When, in 1866, he studied the score of *Walküre*, he found "great deformities and defects" alongside "great beauties." By 1868, though, his interest had intensified into an obsession, as he praised Wagner for possessing qualities that he also attributed to Schopenhauer: "the ethical air, the Faustian scent, cross, death, and grave, etc." The material of the *Ring*, and especially the figure of Siegfried, transfixed him. On hearing the preludes to *Tristan* and *Meistersinger*, he wrote, "Every fiber, every nerve in me is quivering." Later, he would compare the experience to taking hashish. Many Wagnerites felt the music to be intoxicating or narcotic in effect. Baudelaire likened it to opium, others to alcohol, morphine, and absinthe.

Nietzsche promptly took on a role that others filled before and after him: that of companion, propagandist, factotum. He stayed at Tribschen during the holidays and carried out duties elsewhere. On one occasion, he was sent to procure caramels and other desserts in Strasbourg; on another, he fetched silk underwear in Basel. There was an element of calculation on both sides. Nietzsche seized the chance to align himself with a star of European culture. Wagner, who lacked strong support in the academic world, knew the value of having a gifted and impassioned young scholar as an ally.

Fulfilling Wagner's request for a "longer and more comprehensive work," Nietzsche published his first book, *The Birth of Tragedy from the Spirit of Music*, in 1872. Its central idea, the duality of the Apollonian and the Dionysian, is one that he had been pondering for a while, but he surely discussed it with the composer, who had his own notions about the Greek gods. In "Art and Revolution," Wagner associates Apollo with the perfection of the male form, the ordered harmony of Greek architecture, and the swinging rhythm of music. In passing, Wagner comments that Dionysus inspires the tragic poet as he brings forth drama under Apollo's gaze. A synergy of the two is implied. Hanging in Tribschen was a watercolor of Bonaventura Genelli's neo-classical painting *Bacchus Among the Muses*; Nietzsche thought of the picture as he worked on his book. In 1871, Wagner told Nietzsche that the painting, *The Birth of Tragedy*, and his own work came together in a "remarkable, even miraculous connection."

Nietzsche also echoes his mentor when he proposes that Greek tragedy gestated in the musical utterance of the chorus. In *Opera and Drama*, Wagner compares the modern orchestra to the Greek chorus, using the metaphor of the *Mutterschooß*, the mother's womb, to describe the function of orchestra and chorus alike. In his 1870 essay on Beethoven, he writes that "out of choral song the drama projected itself onto the stage"— that "out of the spirit of music" the entire Greek order arose. The last phrase passed into the title of *The Birth of Tragedy*, and the womb image is replicated in the text: "The choral passages that are woven into the tragedy are, in a certain sense, the womb of all of the so-called dialogue, i.e., of the total stage world, the actual drama."

At almost every turn, however, Nietzsche pushes Wagnerian thought to new rhetorical extremes. His emphasis on Dionysian revelry outpaces the composer's warier engagement with orgiastic states. His claims on behalf of art are fanatical: "Only as an *aesthetic phenomenon* is existence and the world eternally *justified*." Master and follower diverge most conspicuously on the question of slavery. For Wagner, slavery was a flagrant flaw of Hellenic culture; a Greek revival would require a different social structure, one that would make beauty available to all. Nietzsche repeats certain of these sentiments but never strongly affirms them. In the grip of the Dionysian rite, the slave can achieve freedom, anyone can feel like a god; yet his permanent liberation seems neither possible nor desirable. In an essay on the Greek state, which was dropped from *The Birth of Tragedy* in its final form, Nietzsche declares that "slavery belongs to the essence of a culture," its logic binding the masses to the service of a superior, art-creating minority. The intellectual historian Martin Ruehl speculates that Wagner persuaded Nietzsche to omit this material when they discussed the manuscript.

In the last part of *The Birth of Tragedy*, Nietzsche writes that German music will incarnate "*the gradual awakening of the Dionysian spirit*." Amid the degeneracy of contemporary life, one can take comfort in the fact that

> the German spirit rests and dreams in an inaccessible abyss, like a knight sunk in slumber, its splendid health, profundity, and Dionysian strength intact; and from that abyss the Dionysian song is wafting up our way, to let us know that this German knight still dreams even now his age-old Dionysian myth in blissfully serious visions. Let no one believe that the German spirit has forever lost its mythical homeland, if it can still understand so clearly the bird voices which tell that homeland's tale. One day it will find itself awake, in the morning freshness of a tremendous sleep; then it will slay dragons, destroy the spiteful dwarfs, and awaken Brünnhilde—and Wotan's spear itself shall be unable to block its way!

It is a polemical account of the *Ring*. Not only Brünnhilde but also Siegfried are cast as sleepers waiting to be awoken. The hero becomes like Friedrich Barbarossa, the Holy Roman Emperor, who was said to lie beneath the Kyffhäuser hills in Thuringia, waiting to rise again. As Benedict Anderson shows in his classic study *Imagined Communities*, the metaphor of awakening is a commonplace in nationalist discourse, recasting a newly invented entity as a resurrected one. German readers would have related such imagery to the Franco-Prussian War of 1870–71 and the crowning of Wilhelm I as Kaiser of a unified Reich. In fact, Nietzsche, who witnessed the war's carnage as a medical orderly, felt that militarism was eroding the German soul, and argued the point with Wagner, who was in a jingoistic phase. Nietzsche aired those reservations in his 1873 essay on David Strauss, but not in *The Birth of Tragedy.*

Wagner pronounced himself pleased. "This is the book I have been longing for," he told Cosima. But it may have impressed him more as a feat of publicity than as a faithful picture of his ideas. Nietzsche thought that Wagner "did not recognize himself in the text." What is missing is an awareness of Siegfried's flaws—his gullibility, his rashness, his obliviousness—and a sense of Brünnhilde's redeeming wisdom. Nietzsche effectively jettisons the *Ring*'s critique of power. He would later say that Wagner went astray when he lost touch with Siegfried's vitality and gave in to Wotan's pessimism: "Everything goes wrong, everything is a disaster, the new world is just as bad as the old one:—*Nothingness*, the Indian Circe beckons." The disjunction between Nietzsche and Wagner is visible from the start.

BAYREUTH 1876

"The chief feature of the Wagner district is a great lunatic asylum," George Bernard Shaw wrote in 1889. "It is a desperately stupid little town." To call it stupid is unjust, but Bayreuth is certainly a quiet place—a typical provincial

German city, with a quaint old center and a fine Baroque opera house. There are no fast trains from metropolitan centers; most travelers must change to a local in Nuremberg, about fifty miles to the southwest. For Wagner, the relative dullness of Bayreuth was a boon. He wanted to locate his festival in a city large enough to accommodate an influx of visitors but not so large as to possess a well-heeled, prejudiced art public of its own. The site had to exist outside of extant cultural networks; it had to be a blank slate.

Wagner had long wished for a new kind of festival experience, through which his audience could escape urban distractions and enter a more receptive frame of mind. There were precedents for such a ritual, such as the Passion Play at Oberammergau, which has been reenacting Jesus Christ's trial and death at ten-year intervals since 1634. The ultimate model was the Great Dionysia, the civic festival of ancient Athens, which revolved around dramatic performances in the form of tetralogies—three tragedies followed by a satyr play. Wagner set forth his plan in an 1850 letter to Uhlig:

> I would erect, in a beautiful meadow near the town, a crude theater of boards and beams, built to my specifications and equipped only with such decor and machinery as is necessary for the performance of *Siegfried* . . . At the new year, announcements and invitations to all friends of the musical drama would go out to all the German newspapers, with the offer of a visit to the proposed dramatic musical festival: anyone who responds and travels for this purpose to Zurich would be assured an entrée—naturally, like all the entrées, gratis! In addition, I would invite the young people here, university, choral societies, etc. When everything was in order, I would arrange, under these conditions, three performances of *Siegfried* in one week. After the third, the theater would be torn down and my score burnt. To those who had enjoyed the thing I would then say: "Now go do the same!"

It would cost ten thousand thalers, Wagner added. Although he soon set aside the immolation of the score, he stuck to this initial scheme for a long time. He often spoke of his theater as a temporary structure, made of light materials. Even at a late stage, he hoped to offer free tickets, so that the experience would be open to all. To be sure, the expense of traveling to Bayreuth would still have been more than most people could bear.

By the later sixties, Wagner was a figure of international renown, his insurgent aura fast dissipating. In 1864, Ludwig II, the teenaged monarch of Bavaria, had come to the composer's rescue. The king adored Wagner's music but had his own ideas about architecture, and was not inclined to underwrite a temporary theater in a meadow. When the Romantic-Classical master Gottfried Semper drew up plans for a massive theater in Munich, Wagner called it "nonsensical," although he approved of Semper's design for the auditorium itself. The projected cost of the building provoked criticism, adding to the cloud of controversy that surrounded Wagner in Bavaria. Court intrigues and press campaigns forced a retreat to Switzerland. Still, Ludwig sought to make Munich the Wagner capital. Between 1865 and 1870, *Tristan*, *Meistersinger*, *Rheingold*, and *Walküre* all had their premieres there. Wagner disliked the manner of presentation, and expressed relief when the Munich project came to naught.

Finally, in 1870, Wagner's eye landed on Bayreuth. The Festspielhaus that rose there, on a hill above the town, was a compromise between the austere 1850 plan and Ludwig's penchant for luxury. It was a real theater, not a provisional one, yet it was an unostentatious building in an out-of-the-way place. Reviewing the blueprints, Wagner asked for more simplicity, more functionality. "Away with the ornaments!" he wrote on one design. The structure, he said, should be "no more solid than is necessary to prevent it from collapsing." Seen from the train station, the Festspielhaus looks like a graceful industrial facility rather than a temple of culture. A "rambling, no-style building," one critic said. The novelist Colette compared it to a gasometer. But it has aged well—a stately pile of brick and wood, framed by stands of trees. Veteran Bayreuthians call the festival complex the Green Hill, as if it were an outgrowth of the park that surrounds it.

The interior was even more jarring to nineteenth-century sensibilities. Traditional opera houses conform to a horseshoe shape, with many of the boxes facing one another—an arrangement conducive to social display. Bayreuth has a fan-shaped array of steeply raked rows, like a section lifted from a Greek amphitheater, so that every seat is angled toward the stage. Two proscenia are nested inside each other, drawing all eyes forward. The pit is set unusually deep, removing the musicians and the conductor from the field of vision. In an acoustical miracle that has never been fully explained, the orchestral sound diffuses richly through the auditorium, even though it must pass through an aperture in front of the stage. Modestly adorned columns line the sides of the auditorium. Hard-backed seats keep the listener awake and alert. In an 1873 essay, Wagner headily summarized the intended effect on the spectator:

> Once he has taken his seat, he finds himself in a veritable "Theatron"— that is, a space designed for nothing other than looking, and looking where his position points him. Nothing distinctly perceptible comes between him and the image to be looked at—instead only a sense of hovering distance, which results from the architectural arrangement of the two proscenia; in this way, the abstracted image assumes the unapproachability of a dream vision, while the music, sounding spectrally from the "mystic abyss," like vapors arising from the sacred *Ur*-womb of Gaia beneath the seat of Pythia, carries him into that inspired state of clairvoyance in which the scenic picture becomes for him the truest reflection of life itself.

This essay bears the imprint of Schopenhauer's analysis of occult phenomena—clairvoyance, prophetic dreams, encounters with ghosts. The philosopher says that the dreaming or mesmerized mind can find a shortcut to the sphere of the will, where artificial constructs of space and time melt away and glimpses of the future intrude upon the present. Wagner is likewise suggesting that his theater will send its audience into a state of *Hellsehen*, or clairvoyance. The Pythia was the oracle at Delphi; Bayreuth has a similar function.

In all, Bayreuth was intended to foster a new level of seriousness in the theater public. Spectators should feel themselves disappearing into the work at hand. To assist in that illusion, Wagner planned to have the lights in the auditorium dimmed—again defying an operagoing culture that saw its own finery as part of the spectacle. At the first *Ring*, adjustable gas lamps failed to operate as planned, resulting in near-total darkness. Although the system was fixed, the idea of Wagnerian gloom took hold. The darkening of theaters actually dates back centuries, but Bayreuth popularized the practice in opera.

Wagner was also keen to discourage the bursts of applause that interrupted standard opera presentations. He did not, however, mandate worshipful silence, as is often claimed. In 1882, at the premiere of *Parsifal*, he requested that there be no curtain calls after Act II, so as not to "impinge on

The view from the "mystic abyss"

the impression," as Cosima wrote. The crowd took this to mean that there should be no applause at all, and total silence greeted the final curtain. Wagner plaintively asked, "Did the audience like it or not?" At a later performance, someone shouted, "Bravo!" during the chorus of the Flower Maidens, and was hissed. That someone turned out to be the composer. Here was an early sign that Wagnerism was taking on a life independent of its creator.

Nietzsche hoped that Bayreuth would be the fulfillment of his Greco-German dreams—a modern festival along Hellenic lines, fusing Apollonian and Dionysian elements, presented before an audience of elite aesthetes. Wagner, for his part, clung to his fantasy of a great popular festival, open to people of all backgrounds. Supporters were building up an international network of Wagner Societies, whose members made advance contributions in exchange for tickets. Through their patronage, Wagner hoped to keep admission free. By 1873, fund-raising was lagging, especially among German notables. Two of the biggest donors were, reputedly, Abdülaziz, the sultan of the Ottoman Empire, and Isma'il Pasha, the khedive of Egypt.

To Nietzsche fell the task of writing an "Exhortation to the Germans," urging native support. As promotional literature, it left much to be desired, its arguments bending toward the tortured and the delusional: "The German will appear honorable and beneficial to other nations only when he has shown that he is terrifying, and yet *through the exertion of his highest and noblest artistic and cultural powers he will make one want to forget that he was terrifying.*" Delegates from the Wagner Societies rejected Nietzsche's work on account of its "bold language," according to Cosima, though she considered it "very fine."

Nietzsche's culminating publicity effort, "Richard Wagner in Bayreuth," was published in July 1876, just before the festival opened. The tone is portentous, at times preposterous: "When on that day in May 1872, in pouring rain and under dark skies, the cornerstone was laid on that hill in Bayreuth, Wagner rode back to the city with some of us; he was silent and for a long time turned his gaze inward with a look that would be impossible to describe in words." We are told that Wagner breathes in the "sublime and the ultra-sublime," that he provides "the supreme model for all art in the grand manner," that *Tristan* is "the true *opus metaphysicum* of all art." Bayreuth was to be a gathering of chosen apostles, as on that rainy day in 1872, which, Nietzsche solemnly recorded in his notebooks, also fell in the period of Pentecost. At the same time, somehow, the festival would welcome the masses, since Wagner's art "no longer even recognizes the distinction between cultivated or uncultivated."

Even as he was manufacturing hype, Nietzsche was inwardly pulling away. The Wagners' move to Bayreuth led to emotional as well as physical distance. The bustle of the nascent festival made for a dispiriting contrast to the otherworldly idyll on Lake Lucerne. Initial notes for the Bayreuth essay, from 1874, show smoldering skepticism:

If Goethe is a displaced painter and Schiller a displaced orator, then Wagner is a displaced actor.

W.'s youth is that of a many-sided dilettante who seems destined to come to nothing. In an absurd way, I often have doubted whether W. has musical talent.

W. has a domineering character, only then is he in his element . . . the inhibition of this drive makes him immoderate, eccentric, obstreperous.

W. gets rid of all his weaknesses by imputing them to his age and his adversaries.

Nietzsche remains admiring of the musical achievement, its *"unity in diversity,"* but he is hostile to the public, theatrical nature of Wagner's enterprise. The 1876 festival drew many glittering names. Kaiser Wilhelm I greeted Wagner by saying, "I *never* thought you'd pull it off." Dom Pedro II of Brazil, who once expressed interest in becoming Wagner's patron, made the long journey from Rio de Janeiro. Various dukes, princes, and counts attended—more than two hundred members of the German and Austro-Hungarian aristocracy. Such leading composers as Liszt, Bruckner, Tchaikovsky, Grieg, and Saint-Saëns were present, though Brahms and Verdi stayed away. The crowd included some eminent painters and writers: Hans Makart, Franz von Lenbach, Henri Fantin-Latour, Catulle Mendès. For the most part, though, well-to-do curiosity-seekers set the tone. Joseph Bennett, one of a hundred or more journalists present, spotted American women "in a chronic state of ecstasy about 'darling Liszt'" and Frenchmen "meditating epigrams of a withering character." Tchaikovsky noted that the visitors looked preoccupied, "as if in search of something." That something turned out to be food, which was in short supply: "Cutlets, baked potatoes, omelettes—all are discussed much more eagerly than Wagner's music." Shops were full of tacky merchandise, with Wagner's face emblazoned on beer mugs, pipe bowls, cigar boxes, and sundry toiletries.

In the end, a festival that professed to shun consumerism all but wallowed in commercial values. As Nicholas Vazsonyi demonstrates in *Richard Wagner: Self-Promotion and the Making of a Brand*, the composer helped to pioneer modern techniques of mass dissemination and publicity. Wolzogen's leitmotif guide appeared ahead of the festival. Press releases provided behind-the-scenes anecdotes. The fund-raising system resembled a stock company, a network of investors; the Wagner Societies operated like fan clubs. The buzz of scandal that followed Wagner kept his name in the news—a crucial component of the machinery of celebrity. Somehow, the *Ring* itself, that radical monument, rose above the noise. Vazsonyi writes: "Wagner's special skill was the ability to preserve the artistic integrity of his towering works amidst the blaze of commodification to which he in the first place had subjected them."

Wagner knickknacks at the Reuter Wagner Museum in Eisenach

Nietzsche was appalled. "I no longer recognized anything, I scarcely recognized Wagner," he wrote in *Ecce Homo*, remembering the "profound alienation" he felt when he arrived for the final rehearsals of the *Ring*. "*What had happened?*—Wagner had been translated into German! The Wagnerian had become the master of Wagner!—*German* art! The *German* master! *German* beer! . . . Enough; in the middle of it all I left for a couple of weeks."

The biographical reality is somewhat different. Nietzsche indeed fled to the mountain forest resort of Klingenbrunn, but he was there for only about a week. He went mainly because of his chronic ill health, which included eye problems, piercing headaches, and attacks of vomiting. Sitting for extended periods in a theater was all but unbearable for him. Most likely, he was suffering from a hereditary neurological or vascular disorder; his father, who died at the age of thirty-six, showed similar symptoms. Nonetheless, Nietzsche could not stay away from what he called the "liquid gold" of Wagner's orchestra, and he returned to Bayreuth in time for the first public performances, August 13–17.

If Nietzsche exaggerated his flight from Bayreuth, there is no doubt that he felt estranged from the festivities. Throughout his life, he believed that a philosopher must wage war on existing forms and conventions— "overcome his time in himself." Bayreuth made it plain that the former pariah Wagner was now an adornment of the age. A crowd of "bored, unmusical" patrons and "idle European riff-raff" traipsed about, using the place for sport. On a personal level, Nietzsche's intimacy with the composer was slipping away. The French author Édouard Schuré recalled that

Wagner displayed "fantastic gaiety" and "exuberant humor" in gatherings at Haus Wahnfried, putting on his customary one-man performances. Nietzsche, in contrast, seemed deflated—"timid, embarrassed, almost always silent," Schuré wrote.

Once the festival was over, Wagner, too, lapsed into a state of dejection. Despite all of his ingenious promotional tactics, he had lost a great deal of money, and in many ways the productions failed to satisfy him. Cosima wrote: "R. is very sad, says he wishes he could die!" The next time, he told her, everything would be done differently. In blacker moods, he thought to himself, "Never again, never again!" There was even talk of "giving up the festival entirely and disappearing." Did Wagner sense that he had fallen far short of his old dream of a free festival in a meadow? In any event, he fled south, as if to recapture the Mediterranean glow in which he had first glimpsed his treacherous gold.

NIETZSCHE'S BREAK

Prof. Dr. Friedr. Nietzsche.

The last meeting between Nietzsche and Wagner took place in the fall of 1876, in Sorrento, on the Amalfi Coast. The Wagners were ensconced at the Grand Hotel Vittoria, which looks out at the sea. Nietzsche was staying in humbler quarters a few minutes away, in the company of his former pupil Albert Brenner and the writers Malwida von Meysenbug and Paul Rée. Relations with Richard and Cosima remained outwardly cordial, but the mood was strained. For one thing, the Wagners were suspicious of Rée, because of his Jewish heritage. They also took an intrusive interest in their friend's medical issues. To Otto Eiser, Nietzsche's doctor, Wagner later offered the observation that he had seen other "young men of great intellectual ability" cut down by similar problems, and that these were often the result of masturbation. Eiser replied with polite skepticism, saying that his patient displayed no such abnormalities. At some subsequent date, word of Wagner's amateur diagnosis got back to Nietzsche, who was left with the impression that his idol suspected him of "unnatural excesses, with hints of pederasty."

The immediate cause of the break, however, was a brazen display of independence on Nietzsche's part. During his stay In Klingenbrunn, in the summer of 1876, he had begun making notes for the book that became *Human, All Too Human*. The style departs markedly from his earlier published writing. In place of spacious paragraphs and ornate sentences, it proceeds by way of aphorisms and polemics, pithy strikes and sudden swerves.

> *Sleep of virtue.*—When virtue has slept, it will arise refreshed.

> *Luke 18:14 improved.*—He who humbles himself wants to be exalted.

> *Against originals.*—When art clothes itself in the most worn-out materials, we most readily recognize it as art.

This change of voice, inspired in part by Rée's brisk positivist philosophy, goes hand in hand with an attack on metaphysics. Wagner, after the *Ring*, turned toward the mystical ritual of *Parsifal*—a staging of the Schopenhauerian ethic of self-abnegation, with elements culled from the great world religions. Nietzsche veered in more or less the opposite direction.

Human, All Too Human begins with a sweeping refutation of the Romantic sublime. All attempts to grasp some fundamental truth behind the veneer of existence—the *Ding an sich*, the "thing in itself"—result from a false duality; reality consists of a tangled but ultimately graspable web of historically fluctuating relationships. Later sections pick at the moral pieties that underpin so much of Wagner's work. *Parsifal*, following Schopenhauer's philosophy of compassion, sets forth an ethic of "knowing through compassion"—"*durch Mitleid wissend*." Nietzsche, who had read Wagner's prose draft for the opera as early as 1869, hammers away at that word *Mitleid*, considering it a badge of weakness. Instead he praises animal urges, the flexing of strength, the exercise of force, even to the point of cruelty. "Culture simply cannot do without passions, vices, and acts of malice." He goes so far as to say that "temporary relapses into barbarism" can rejuvenate an aging civilization. Wagner and Schopenhauer exude sickness and decadence; Nietzsche stands for power and health.

Wagner goes unnamed in *Human, All Too Human*, but a number of passages take clear shots at him. "Any degree of levity or melancholy is better than a romantic turn to the past and desertion, an accommodation with any form of Christianity whatsoever": this is a preemptive critique of *Parsifal*. "It is in any case a dangerous sign when an awe of oneself comes over any human being": this is a slap at the Wagner cult. There is even a swipe at Cosima, under the heading "*Voluntary sacrifice*": "Nothing that women of significance do for their husbands, if they are men of renown and greatness, does more to make their lives easier than becoming the receptacle, as it were, for the general disfavor and occasional ill humor of other people." That Nietzsche felt a strong attraction to Cosima had long been a complicating factor.

Nietzsche hoped that Wagner would take the book's challenge in stride, as part of a back-and-forth between equals. Two copies of *Human, All Too Human* were sent to Bayreuth in April 1878, with a playful dedicatory poem from "Friedrich the Free-minded of Basel" to "the Meister and the Meisterin." Cosima wrote: "At noon arrival of a new book by friend Nietzsche—feelings of apprehension after a short glance through it." On subsequent days she described it as "strangely perverse," "sad," and "pitiful," insisting all the while that she was not reading it. "Evil has triumphed here," she wrote to a friend.

Wagner was no less dismayed, but he kept on reading, and even gave a lyrical recitation of the book's ending—the ode to the wanderer, who sees "swarms of muses dancing past him in the mist of the mountains." Did he feel a lingering fondness for Nietzsche's thought, foreign as it now seemed? One day Wagner thought of sending Nietzsche a congratulatory telegram on the birthday of Voltaire, who is lionized in *Human, All Too Human*. This might have been the kind of large-spirited gesture that Nietzsche sought. Cosima talked her husband out of it. Bayreuth maintained a cold façade, and Nietzsche felt a "great excommunication."

That summer, Wagner published the third part of an essay titled "Public and Popularity." This work and other writings of his last years appeared in the *Bayreuther Blätter*, the newly founded magazine of the Bayreuth circle. (Wagner had originally wanted Nietzsche to edit the publication; Wolzogen, the labeler of leitmotifs, took the post instead.) Amid a typically rambling disquisition, Wagner refers to certain philologists and philosophers who have achieved "unbounded progress in the field of criticism of all things human and inhuman." These individuals enact "pitiless" sacrifices of noble victims; they renounce the worship of genius; they are "astonished that Sunday-morning bells still ring today for a Jew crucified two thousand years ago." (This answers one of Nietzsche's jabs at Christianity.) Cosima wrote that her husband had taken on Nietzsche "in such a way that a reader who is not fully in the know will not notice." The ploy was hardly as subtle as that. The excommunication was now official.

Wagner took special umbrage at Nietzsche's critique of compassion, which directly contradicted his own philosophy. In the course of stewing over *Human, All Too Human*, he remarked that the chief characteristic of the Devil was "malice, pleasure in the misfortune of others." Nietzsche appeared to be extolling such pleasure; Wagner thought himself to be taking the side of the weak, in a Christian spirit. If Nietzsche had been able to debate the question face to face, he might have responded that he was concerned chiefly with the hypocrisy of the compassionate; the ones taking pity find selfish delight in a display of emotion and a sense of power. He might also have noted the limits of Wagner's love of humanity, particularly with regard to Jews.

In the end, both men harbored impulses that look ominous from the vantage point of the post-Holocaust era. What Wagner disliked in Nietzsche—the pitilessness, the exaltation of power—and what Nietzsche disliked in Wagner—the Teutonic chauvinism, the antisemitism—added up to an approximation of the fascist mentality. Once the better angels of their natures are set aside, Wagner and Nietzsche darkly complete each other in the Nazi mind. Of the two, only Nietzsche had an inkling of what the future held. "I know my lot," he wrote in *Ecce Homo*. "One day my name will be linked to the memory of something monstrous—to a crisis like none there has been on earth . . ."

SIEGFRIED ZARATHUSTRA

Wagner had no direct contact with his former acolyte in his final years. The last chance for a reunion would have been at the premiere of *Parsifal*, in 1882. Nietzsche told friends that he would go to the festival if he received a personal invitation, but none came. It is likely that Wagner regretted the demise of the friendship. Nietzsche's sister Elisabeth, who was at Bayreuth that summer, claimed that the composer said to her, "Tell your brother that since he left me I am alone." But public concessions were not in Wagner's nature. Nietzsche was reduced to monitoring events through intermediaries. "The old sorcerer [*Zauberer*] has had another tremendous success, with old men sobbing, etc.," he wrote to his amanuensis Heinrich Köselitz. Nietzsche is presumably the source of the epithet "Sorcerer of Bayreuth."

Any attempted reconciliation would have been spoiled by the publication that summer of *The Joyful Science*, which sets aside indirect sniping in favor of frontal assault. Nietzsche accuses Wagner of having misunderstood the philosophy implicit in his own art. Schopenhauer has beguiled him into anti-Jewish blather, into a dubious conflation of Christianity and Buddhism, into an overweening concern for the well being of animals. (The last shot was carefully aimed, given Wagner's adoration of his pets.) What is the true philosophy? "The innocence of the highest selfishness; belief in the great passion as a good in itself; in one word, what is Siegfried-like in the countenance of his heroes." In the next part of *The Joyful Science*, Nietzsche announces the death of God. Wagner is a fallen Wotan, his staff broken by his substitute son.

The stage is set for the most troublesome of Nietzschean beings, the *Übermensch*. The word had surfaced in the philosopher's earlier writings, but usually in a negative sense. The critique of the "cult of the genius" in *Human, All Too Human*—unmistakably directed at Wagner—isolates the crisis moment when the genius begins to "take himself for something superhuman." Then, in *The Joyful Science*, the term acquires a positive connotation. In the section headed "The greatest advantage of polytheism," Nietzsche advocates a *"plurality of norms,"* and in so doing mentions "gods, heroes, and superhumans of all kinds, as well as near-humans and sub-humans, dwarves, fairies, centaurs, satyrs, demons, and devils." It sounds like the dramatis personae of the *Ring*, augmented by Greek and Christian guests. The translation of "*Übermensch*" as "superman," popularized by Shaw in his 1903 play *Man and Superman*, is problematic not only because "*Mensch*" is gender-neutral but because the word now makes readers think of the brawny comic-book character. Nietzsche's overman is no caped hero, although he is clearly a superior sort of being, almost a new species.

The *Übermensch* makes a formal entrance in *Thus Spoke Zarathustra*, which Nietzsche was writing at the time of Wagner's death. Zarathustra, the *Übermensch*'s prophet, appears toward the end of *The Joyful Science*, preparing to descend from his mountain and undertake his *Untergang*, his "going under." The word "*Untergang*," which can mean descent, decline, downfall, dissolution, or destruction, is one that Wagner uses repeatedly and indiscriminately. He speaks of the downfall variously of the state, of the gods, of history, of the world, of himself, and, notoriously, of Jews. He wrote to Liszt in 1853: "Mark well my new poem—it contains the world's beginning and its downfall!" *Untergang* also has a philosophical history; Hegel's *Logic* states that the highest stage of human understanding is that in which its *Untergang* begins. So Zarathustra's going under is also a going over (*Übergang*) to new life, to the world of the *Übermensch*. The words are paired in one of the book's most celebrated passages:

> Mankind is a rope fastened between animal and *Übermensch*—a rope over an abyss . . . What is great about human beings is that they are a bridge and not a purpose: what is lovable about human beings is that they are an *Übergang* and an *Untergang*.

Roger Hollinrake, in *Nietzsche, Wagner, and the Philosophy of Pessimism*, argues that both Zarathustra and the *Übermensch* stem from Wagner. In one passage, Zarathustra sounds very much like the Wanderer of *Siegfried*—Wotan in disguise—in dialogue with the earth goddess:

> WANDERER: Awake! Vala! Vala, awake! From your long sleep I awaken you, slumberer. I summon you forth: Up! Up! Up from the misty chasm, from the depth of night! Erda! Erda! Eternal woman!

ZARATHUSTRA: Up, abysmal thought, out of my depths! I am your
rooster and dawn, you sleepy worm: Up! Up! . . . And once you
are awake, you shall remain awake eternally. It is not *my* manner
to wake great-grandmothers from their sleep only to tell them—go
back to sleep! . . . My abyss *speaks*, I have unfolded my ultimate depth
to the light!

Yet the *Übermensch* is something other than a fearless, boyish hero. (Nietzsche's misogyny makes a female *Übermensch* unlikely.) In fact, he eludes
any kind of brief description. His mastery is rooted in tremendous struggle, not only with the outer world but with himself. Nietzsche melts down
the materials of the *Ring* as he forges his own creation.

In the last book of *Zarathustra*, the protagonist meets the *Zauberer*, the
Sorcerer, one of several tempters who try to lure him from his path. Even if
we hadn't read Nietzsche's prior references to the "old sorcerer," we would
recognize Wagner's personality in this restless, twitching, frantically gesturing figure, who babbles self-pitying monologues and dubs himself "the
greatest person living today." Zarathustra exposes him as an actor, a coun-
terfeiter. After spluttering in protest, the Sorcerer gives in: "I am weary of
and nauseated by my arts, I am not *great*, why do I pretend!" A conciliatory
dialogue follows, and the Sorcerer hails Zarathustra as "a vessel of wisdom,
a saint of knowledge, a great human being." This seems pure fantasy on
Nietzsche's part, an imaginary victory over his mentor turned oppressor
although he claims in his notebooks that when he confronted Wagner in
private the composer accepted the criticism. "I wish that he would also do
it publicly. For what constitutes the greatness of a character other than that
he is capable, for the sake of truth, of also taking sides *against himself*?"

The Sorcerer later stages a momentary comeback. In a pseudo-Christian
supper scene, he strums his harp and sings mumbo-jumbo redolent of the
Tristan libretto. The assembled company is hypnotized. Before long, all
turn religious, kneeling before an ass and chanting Parsifalian pieties.
Zarathustra responds with a string of contemptuous rebuttals, leading to
another make-believe dialogue with Wagner's ghost:

"And you," said Zarathustra, "you wicked old sorcerer, what have you
done! Who in these liberated times is supposed to believe in you any-
more, if *you* believe in such asinine divinities?

"What you did was a stupidity; how could you, you clever one, commit such a stupidity!"

"Oh Zarathustra," replied the clever Sorcerer, "you're right, it was a stupidity—and it's been hard enough for me."

The pious mood gives way to roguish laughter, and it is in this spirit that the book ends: learning to laugh, to love the earth, to love what is fated, to be willing, under the doctrine of eternal recurrence, to relive the same life in every excruciating detail.

BECOMING WAGNER

Nietzsche writes to Cosima Wagner, January 1889

On February 3, 1883, Wagner glanced at an article about *The Joyful Science*, and, according to Cosima, responded with "utter disgust." He died ten days later. It was not the ending that Nietzsche had pictured for a friendship that remained active in his mind. He was distraught but also relieved. The tension with Wagner had become unbearable. He wrote to Köselitz: "In the end, it was the aged Wagner against whom I had to defend myself; as far as the real Wagner is concerned, I intend in good measure to become his *heir*."

In the major works of his last years of sanity, from 1885 to the end of 1888, Nietzsche brings his diatribe against conventional morality to its highest pitch. *Beyond Good and Evil* provisionally endorses "harshness, violence, slavery, danger in the streets and in the heart, concealment, stoicism, the art of seduction, and devilry of every kind . . . everything evil, horrible, tyrannical, predatory, and snakelike in humanity." All this "serves to elevate the species 'humanity' as well as its opposite." *On the Genealogy of Morality* relates the good and noble to the innocent conscience of the predator, the "magnificent *blond beast* roaming about lustily after prey and victory." Modern European civilization, meek and effeminate, has lost touch with the voluptuous cruelty once exhibited by Germanic tribes. *The Antichrist* continues the theme: "What is good? Everything that heightens in man the feeling of power, the will to power, power itself." What is bad? Weakness, tolerance, forgiveness, compassion—*Mitleid* again.

Nietzsche is still looking for a savior figure, an unfettered Siegfried. In the *Genealogy*, he dreams of a future hero of "sublime malice," a *"redeeming* man of great love and contempt." Insinuating italics differentiate this redeemer from the ascetic hero of *Parsifal*. Redemption will entail not a flight from reality but a close embrace of the true nature of humanity. Nietzsche's latter-day defenders posit that he is not actively praising war, aggression, and the rest. Rather, he is acknowledging that human beings will invariably be vicious to one another and to the world around them. Nietzsche's critique of morality posits that moral language is not the same as moral action, and, indeed, that moral language can serve as a cover for actions that are immoral in the extreme. We must accept the reality of human nature and the vicissitudes of fate. The Dionysian urge is a "triumphal yes to life over and above all death and change."

The Case of Wagner, written in the spring of 1888, promises to be the ultimate act of apostasy. In a style of high intellectual comedy, Nietzsche pillories German gigantism ("the *lie* of the grand style"); diagnoses the composer as a pan-European neurosis ("*Wagner est une névrose*"); coins deft one-sentence summaries of the operas ("You should never be too sure who you are really married to" is *Lohengrin*); praises Bizet's *Carmen* at Wagner's expense ("Music must be mediterraneanized"); and inserts a cackling footnote to the effect that the author of "Jewishness in Music" might himself have been Jewish. Yet the entire exercise is undercut by a preface that places Wagner at the very heart of modern life. The "case" is especially indispensable to the philosopher, for

where would he find a more knowledgeable guide to the labyrinth of the modern soul, a more articulate connoisseur of souls, than Wagner? Modernity speaks its most *intimate* language in Wagner: it hides neither its good nor its evil, it has forgotten any sense of shame. And conversely:

when one is clear about the good and evil in Wagner, one is close to a reckoning of the *value* of the modern.—I understand perfectly when a musician says today: "I hate Wagner, but I cannot stand any other music." But I would also understand if a philosopher were to declare: "Wagner *sums up* modernity. It can't be helped, one must first become a Wagnerian . . ."

What does Nietzsche mean by "modernity"? Competing definitions of the word exist in different intellectual spheres. In philosophy, it is often associated with the formation of a free, self-determined consciousness in the Renaissance and Enlightenment eras. In sociology, it applies more often to nineteenth-century modernization—the economic and social upheaval analyzed by Marx, Weber, and Émile Durkheim. In cultural criticism, the "modern" denotes a radicalization of the arts, culminating in the modernist movements of the early twentieth century. Nietzsche defines modernity more narrowly, as the culture of decadence—overripe, indecisive, weak, detached from primal instincts, premised on false ideas of freedom. He must have known, however, that such an untethered abstraction would strike his readers in various ways. Broader understandings of modernity crowd into our minds. *The Case of Wagner* is more the opening of a case than the settling of one: it provokes a debate about what it means to be "modern" just as the word is coming into vogue.

Toward the end of his career, Nietzsche drops the pretense of being anti-Wagnerian and confesses his vestigial adoration. In *Ecce Homo*, a paragraph on *Tristan* lapses back into the rhapsodic mode of *The Birth of Tragedy* and "Richard Wagner in Bayreuth":

To this day I am still searching for a work of such dangerous fascination, of such shuddering sweet infinity, as *Tristan*—I am searching all the arts in vain . . . I think that I know better than anyone what tremendous things Wagner was capable of, the fifty worlds of foreign ecstasies that only he had wings to reach; and being what I am, strong enough to turn what is most questionable and dangerous to my advantage and thus become even stronger, I name Wagner the greatest benefactor of my life. That which relates us—the fact that we have suffered more deeply, also from each other, than people of this century are capable of suffering—will reunite our names eternally . . .

Such passages support Thomas Mann's belief that Nietzsche's polemic against Wagner is really a "panegyric with the sign reversed, another form of glorification," serving more to "goad one's enthusiasm than to cripple it."

Most of Nietzsche's public commentary on Wagner takes the form of propaganda, positive or negative. In the more considered passages of his writings and notebooks, he finds his way to a clear-eyed, nuanced understanding. *The Joyful Science* dismantles clichés about Wagnerian hugeness and loudness, even before such clichés had fully taken hold. The composer may think of himself as a maker of "great walls and brazen murals," but he is really a master of psychological moments, an "Orpheus of all secret misery." *The Case of Wagner* scorns the cycle's popular showpieces as so much "noise about nothing." Instead, we should marvel at the "wealth of colors, of half shadows, of the secrets of dying light . . . glances, tendernesses, and comforting words." Wagner is "our greatest *miniaturist* in music, who can urge an infinity of meaning and sweetness into the smallest spaces."

Nietzsche also works to rescue Wagner from the triumphalism of the new Reich. In his 1878 notebooks, he sees the Bayreuth ritual as both a self-aggrandizement and a self-enslavement on the part of the German public. The resulting psychological contradiction could lead, he speculates, to a scapegoating of outsiders, such as Jews. One project of the later writings is to separate Wagner from bad national mythologies and guide him toward the Nietzschean ideal of the "good European," who has no fatherland or motherland. The Teutonic culture-hero venerated in imperial Germany is a "phantom," unrelated to the immoralist-atheist whom Nietzsche knew in private. The true Wagner is a "*foreign country*," a "living protest against all 'German virtues.'" Nietzsche's joke about Wagner being translated into German makes the same point. The composer's unforgivable mistake was that he "*condescended* to the Germans—that he became *reichsdeutsch*."

Most impressively, Nietzsche exposes the neurosis that his own excessive fandom has generated—a dynamic that is by no means unique to Wagnerism. "Wholesale love for Wagner's art is precisely as *unjust* as wholesale rejection," he writes in 1878. "I revenged myself on Wagner for my deceived expectations," he says. Tellingly, in the midst of such musings, he quotes the passage from *Siegfried* that Wagner was composing when the two men met in Tribschen: "He who woke me has wounded me!" Nietzsche would appear to be Brünnhilde, sleeping within the ring of fire until the arrogant, flawed hero makes his entrance.

This furiously conflicted relationship is best understood in terms of the Greek agon—the contest between worthy adversaries, in athletics or the arts. Nietzsche wrote about the agon in his 1872 essay "Homer's Contest," saying that the Greeks abhorred the predominance of a single figure and desired, "as a *means of protection* against genius—a second genius." It is not far-fetched to guess that Nietzsche was thinking of himself and Wagner. As the philosopher Christa Davis Acampora emphasizes, the aim of the agon is not the destruction of the other but the elevation of the self, through a sublimation of the ineradicable human instinct toward aggression and violence. "Richard Wagner in Bayreuth" shows that the composer's battles with contemporaries were the crucible in which he "became what he is"—an early version of a favorite formula. Likewise, Nietzsche's agon with Wagner is part of a process of self-formation. In fact, this contest benefits both participants, defining the one and redefining the other. The ritual of going up against Wagner, the dialectic of love and hate, often recurs in the annals of Wagnerism.

Around Christmastime 1888, while staying in Turin, Nietzsche sent a copy of *Ecce Homo* to Cosima. A draft for the accompanying letter is addressed to "the only woman I have ever revered," and is signed "The Antichrist." In the first days of the new year, Nietzsche broke down in the streets of Turin, allegedly after seeing a horse beaten by a coachman. For a few days, he continued to send incoherently stylish correspondence, calling himself "the Crucified" and "Dionysus." Cosima received several more letters; one of them, addressed to "Princess Ariadne," announced that the writer's previous incarnations were Buddha, Dionysus, Alexander, Caesar, Voltaire, Napoleon, and "perhaps also Richard Wagner." Once he was institutionalized, Nietzsche was heard to say, "My wife, Cosima Wagner, brought me here."

Having become himself in the course of his agon with Wagner, Nietzsche fell back under the sorcerer's spell in the end. He lived eleven more years, increasingly blank-eyed, gentle during the day, given to animal groans at night. In fulfillment of his prior prophecies, his work enjoyed an ever-growing vogue, soon to rival Wagnerism in breadth and intensity. But the news of his victory passed him by. In 1900, he was buried by the side of his father's church.

GÖTTERDÄMMERUNG

(When the gods are completely enveloped in flames the curtain falls.)
(Als die Götter von den Flammen gänzlich verhüllt sind, fällt der Vorhang.)
Un poco ritenuto.

On November 21, 1874, Wagner finished the orchestration of *Götter-dämmerung*, ending a project that he had begun twenty-six years earlier. "Thrice sacred, memorable day!" Cosima wrote in her diary. At lunch-time, though, she inadvertently enraged her husband by showing him a letter from her father. Why the letter caused offense is not clear—it seems that Wagner simply found it distracting—but Cosima spiraled into self-castigating despair. "The fact that I dedicated my life in suffering to this work has not earned me the right to celebrate its completion in joy," she wrote. The two were later reconciled, but the dispute was a strange way to mark the realization of a work that affirms the triumph of world-changing love.

George Bernard Shaw accuses Wagner of a sort of backsliding in *Götterdämmerung*—of reverting to such grand-opera clichés as "a magnifi-cent love duet . . . the opera chorus in full parade on the stage . . . theatrical grandiosities that recall Meyerbeer and Verdi . . . romantic death song for the tenor." Shaw neglects the dramatic purpose of such well-worn devices: we have left the realm of the gods and are down on the human plain. Hagen, son of Alberich, is hatching a scheme to defeat Siegfried and win back the Ring. His unwitting ally is his half brother Gunther, the status-seeking chief of the Gibichungs. When Siegfried arrives at the Gibichung court, he is served a memory-erasing potion, so that he forgets Brünnhilde and falls in love with Gunther's sister, Gutrune. It is decided that Gunther should marry the Valkyrie and that Siegfried should disguise himself as Gunther in order to win her hand. This fully operatic web of deceit stirs resentment and vengefulness on all sides. An infuri-ated Brünnhilde tells Hagen of Siegfried's vulnerability—his unprotected back—and Hagen makes fatal use of the information by the waters of the Rhine. Before Siegfried meets his fate, the Rhinemaidens plead one last time for the Ring, their cry of "Weialala leia" grown forlorn.

Siegfried dies, the Funeral Music thunders, and Brünnhilde arrives to deliver her final monologue. "All things, all things, all things I know," she sings, without entirely disclosing what she has learned. Deciding on the right ending gave Wagner considerable trouble. The essential action was fixed early on: Siegfried's funeral pyre blazes; Brünnhilde rides her horse, Grane, into the flames; the Ring falls back into the Rhine. But what conclusion should Brünnhilde draw? In the initial 1848 sketch, with its happy message of liberation for all, she exudes revolutionary fervor: "Rejoice, Grane: soon we will be free!" Soon, though, Wagner's vision darkened. The flames of the pyre consume Valhalla, and the end becomes a *Todeserlösung*, a redemption through death. In the version that was printed in 1853, he added a passage influenced by Feuerbach, in which material society is overcome by the power of love:

> Though the race of gods
> passed away like a breath,
> though I leave behind me
> a world without rulers,
> I now bequeath to that world
> the hoard of my most sacred wisdom.—
> Not goods, not gold,
> nor godly glory;
> not house, not court,
> nor lordly pomp;
> not the treacherous bonds
> of murky treaties
> not the harsh decree
> of dissembling convention:
> blessed in joy and sorrow—
> love alone can be.

The "Feuerbach ending," as it is known, gave way to a "Schopenhauer ending," in which Brünnhilde takes cover in visionary solitude:

I draw away from desire's realm,
I flee forever the realm of delusion;
the open gates
of eternal becoming
I shut behind me . . .
Deepest suffering
of sorrowing love
opened my eyes:
I saw the world end.

This, too, was excised, to the regret of the young Nietzsche. Ultimately, Wagner chose not to delay the denouement with philosophical musings. Brünnhilde proceeds directly to her final lines, in which she urges Grane toward the flames—"Does the laughing fire lure you to him?"—and jubilantly salutes her beloved: "Siegfried! Siegfried! See! In bliss your wife bids you welcome!"

In the orchestra, we hear a reprise of the galloping motif of "The Ride of the Valkyries"—one of the first inspirations that Wagner had for the *Ring*, in the summer of 1850. It is joined to a regal theme that has been heard only once before in the cycle. In Act III of *Walküre*, after Brünnhilde saves Sieglinde and the unborn Siegfried from Wotan's wrath, Sieglinde responds with a hymn of praise addressing the Valkyrie as "*O hehrstes Wunder! Herrliche Maid!*" ("O noblest wonder! Glorious woman!"). The melody for these words turns floridly around the tonic note, as in a bel canto aria, and then dips down a seventh before climbing back up to the tonic. Wagner called it the "glorification of Brünnhilde," although it seems more a glorification of Sieglinde's selfless love. Once Valhalla falls, this theme becomes sovereign, with a stepwise bass line supplying hymnal gravity. The harmonization is almost sentimental: two-chord sequences like Amens, a wistful turn to the subdominant minor. The cycle ends in an incandescence of D-flat major.

Later it became fashionable to regard the ending of *Götterdämmerung* as a disappointment. Shaw said it was "trumpery." Nietzsche thought that Wagner should have stuck with his original ending, in which Brünnhilde "was to say goodbye with a song in honor of free love, leaving the world to the hope of a socialist utopia where 'all will be well.'" Theodor W. Adorno, one of the leading Wagner skeptics of the twentieth century, compared the closing theme to the finale of Gounod's *Faust*, "in which Gretchen hovers as a Christ-angel above the rooftops of a medium-sized German town."

Many modern Wagnerites are inclined to read the ending not as a turnabout but as a continuation of the composer's long struggle with political and personal power. In *Treacherous Bonds and Laughing Fire*—a title derived from the various versions of Brünnhilde's monologue—Mark Berry asserts that the closing theme is no cliché of Love Triumphing over All but a "shift, albeit partial, from erotic to charitable love," positing the basis for a humane political state. Slavoj Žižek, similarly, understands it as "a gesture of supreme freedom and autonomy," the "transformation from *eros* to *agape*." Alain Badiou sees not merely the death of the gods but "the destruction of *all* mythologies."

The final tableau of *Götterdämmerung* includes a silent human chorus, which gathers as the fires consume Valhalla. "Men and women watch with the greatest emotion," Wagner writes in the full score. In Patrice Chéreau's epochal 1976–80 production of the *Ring* at Bayreuth, these citizens of an unknown future turn around as Brünnhilde's melody is unfurled and move to the front of the stage, looking out at the auditorium. They seem to say, in the words of the musicologist Jean-Jacques Nattiez, "It is up to you!" Their implicit message recalls Wagner's early prospectus for a festival at which the theater was to have been torn down and the score burnt: "To those who had enjoyed the thing I would then say: 'Now go do the same!'" The most monumental artwork of the nineteenth century is merely a prelude to future creation. The audience must write the rest.

2

TRISTAN CHORD

Baudelaire and the Symbolists

The Lohengrin *riot of 1887*

I n January and February of 1860, Wagner conducted three concerts of his music in Paris, hoping to conquer a city that had largely shunned him in his youth. He had set his sights on a staging of *Tristan und Isolde*, his latest and boldest creation. To that end, he included the prelude to *Tristan* on his programs, alongside selections from *The Flying Dutchman*, *Tannhäuser*, and *Lohengrin*. Concert performances of the prelude had already taken place in Prague and Leipzig, but the Paris of the Second Empire, crowded as it was with republicans, anarchists, bohemians, and the literary vanguard, promised the ideal audience. In the throng at the Théâtre-Italien was Charles Baudelaire, the dark prince of French poetry, who had won infamy three years earlier with the publication of *Les Fleurs du mal*. "The Death of Lovers," from that collection, already has the air of *Tristan*: "Vying to spend their last heat, / Our two hearts will be two vast torches, / Reflecting their double light / In the twin mirrors of our souls."

To prepare his listeners, Wagner wrote a program note in which he laid out the rudiments of the story. Tristan, the nephew of King Mark of Cornwall, is sailing from Ireland with Princess Isolde, who has been betrothed to Mark as part of a political bargain. Isolde is enraged, because this same Tristan killed her fiancé in battle. During the voyage, she asks Brangäne, her attendant, to prepare a death potion, which she and Tristan will drink together. Brangäne, unwilling to part with her mistress, serves a love potion instead. The prelude gives a preview of the music that accompanies the drinking of the philter, but it stands as an independent orchestral statement, in which we hear

> insatiable longing well up from the shyest confession of the tenderest attraction, through anxious sighs, hopes and hesitations, laments and wishes, raptures and torments, to the mightiest onrush, the most violent effort, to find the breach that shows the infinitely yearning heart the way into the sea of endless loving rapture. In vain! Powerless, the heart sinks back to languish in longing, in longing without attainment, since each attainment leads only to renewed desire, until in final exhaustion the breaking glance catches a glimpse of the attainment of the highest rapture: it is the rapture of dying, of ceasing to be, of the final deliverance into that wondrous realm from which we stray farthest when we try to penetrate it with the stormiest force. Do we call it death? Or is it the nocturnal wonder-world, out of which, the legend tells us, an ivy and a vine once grew in intimate embrace over the grave of Tristan and Isolde?

Wagner chose not to issue this program, apparently because Mathilde Wesendonck, the object of his own Tristan-like affections, deemed it too personal in tone. In a letter to her, he parsed his music in terms of what he described as the Buddhist theory of the origin of the world: "A breath clouds the clear expanse of heaven." As in the *Ring*, Wagner must relive the moment of creation before he can begin his story.

More words may have been spilled about the first three bars of *Tristan*—a rising minor sixth in the cellos, a semitone descent, a pungent chord of cellos and winds—than about any short passage in music, with the possible exception of the opening notes of Beethoven's Fifth. That first chord, named the "Tristan chord," is a nebulous, ambiguous half-diminished seventh. In a well-defined harmonic context, it would be

unremarkable, but in the hazy space delineated by the cellos it assumes
an identity at once sensuous and unstable. The sequence seems to repeat,
departing at a higher pitch, yet the music is not quite the same. The initial
leap in the cellos is wider than before, a major sixth rather than a minor
sixth. We drift deeper into the mist. The third iteration introduces further
irregularities: an extra downward step in the cellos, an extra upward step
in the winds. With such minute variations, Wagner captures the texture
of unconscious, dreaming states. David Michael Hertz, in his book *The
Tuning of the Word*, relates the passage to the literary technique known
as parataxis: phrases appearing one after another, without a clear sense of
connective tissue. Hertz's description of the opening of *Tristan*—"A chain
of fragments, each one freely bonded to the next"—pertains just as well to
Baudelaire or Mallarmé.

All of *Tristan* is a hymn to oblivion. The political realities surrounding
the Irish princess and the Breton-Cornish knight dissipate like a mirage.
When, in Act I, Brangäne announces that their ship is approaching land,
Isolde asks, "Which land?" And when Tristan is told that King Mark is
approaching, he asks, "Which king?" The obliteration of reality is most
pronounced in Act II, much of which is given over to the Liebesnacht, or
Night of Love. After King Mark and his party go out on a hunt, Tristan
and Isolde sing a forty-minute duet that oscillates between extreme sexual
agitation and blissful lassitude. Serene ecstasy settles over the music as the
two foresee their death together:

So starben wir,	Thus we died,
um ungetrennt,	so that, undivided,
ewig einig,	forever one,
ohne End',	without end,
ohn' Erwachen,	without waking,
ohn' Erbangen,	without fearing,
namenlos	namelessly
in Lieb' umfangen,	enveloped in love,
ganz uns selbst gegeben,	given entirely to each other,
der Liebe nur zu leben!	we might live for love alone!

The Gestalt philosopher Christian von Ehrenfels claimed to have found
not one but two places in Act II where "orgasmic ejaculations" occur.

With a crashing orchestral chord, erotic stasis gives way to savage action. The lovers are caught; Tristan is fatally wounded; King Mark launches into an agonized lament. Act III, set at Kareol, Tristan's ancestral castle on the Brittany coast, tracks the encroachment of death: prolonged, fitful, and feverish, in the case of Tristan ("Where—was I? Where—am I?"); becalmed and beatific, for Isolde ("Do I alone hear this melody?"). Isolde has crossed the Channel to heal his wound, but as she approaches Tristan tears off his bandages and lets his life bleed away. He dies in her arms, with a musical phrase that evaporates into silence. Taking charge of the *"So starben wir"* melody, Isolde sings a colossal monologue of farewell—*"Mild und leise wie er lächelt,"* or "How softly and gently he smiles"—and dies by Tristan's side.

How that overwhelming music came to be known as the *"Liebestod"* ("Love-Death") is another curiosity of Wagnerian apocrypha. The composer applied the word "Liebestod" not to the ending but to the opening passage of the prelude, which evokes the switching of the potions. His preferred title for the final monologue was "Isolde's Transfiguration." Then, in 1868, Liszt published a piano paraphrase of the ending, calling it *Isolden's Liebes-Tod.* Because of the popularity of piano transcriptions, Liszt's title supplanted Wagner's own. Originally, the Liebestod was a seeming death that turns into love. It became almost the opposite—love that turns into death.

In fact, the word "death" is missing from Isolde's valediction. Rather, this is a hallucination of life: Tristan's lips forming a smile, his eyes shining, his heart beating, his breath rising, mysterious music emanating from him, sound merging with sight, taste, and smell. And Isolde is desperate to share the mirage with others: "Friends! See! Do you not feel and see it?" A mystical synthesis transpires:

In dem wogenden Schwall,	In the surging swell,
in dem tönenden Schall,	in the ringing sound,
in des Welt-Atems	in the world-breath's
wehendem All,—	wafting vastness—
ertrinken,	to drown,
versinken,—	to sink—
unbewußt,—	unconscious—
höchste Lust!	highest bliss!

Her death is spelled out in the stage directions: "Isolde sinks, as if transfigured, in Brangäne's arms, gently onto Tristan's body." But, as the musicologist Karol Berger writes, it is a mistake to think of the ending as a "glorification of the nihilistic death wish," as he characterizes the common view. The monologue is ultimately concerned with the metamorphosis of the lovers' story into myth, into art. Tellingly, even as the language dissolves into fragments, the music achieves a radiant simplicity, the vocal line becoming fixed almost exclusively on the notes of the B-major scale, with the elemental interval of the octave rising at the end. You have the sense that Isolde is not so much dying as disappearing back into the music that set the tale in motion.

In Paris, it took time for *Tristan*'s potion to kick in. When Wagner conducted the prelude at the Théâtre-Italien, it met with a tepid response. "A sort of chromatic moaning," said the composer-critic Hector Berlioz, a sometime supporter. Baudelaire was bewitched by most of what he heard but had nothing to say about *Tristan*. Wagner had a more difficult time in France than he had hoped; it was not *Tristan* but the more conventional *Tannhäuser* that reached the stage of the Opéra in 1861, and even then a storm of opposition arose. *Tristan* did not arrive at the Palais Garnier until 1904. By century's end, though, Wagner had become a godfather of modern art, his name invoked variously by Baudelaire, Mallarmé, Paul Verlaine, Paul Cézanne, Paul Gauguin, and Vincent van Gogh. The short-lived journal *Revue wagnérienne* facilitated the emergence of the Symbolist movement in literature. *Tristan* set the course for an avant-garde art of dream logic, mental intoxication, formless form, limitless desire.

Wagnérisme, the French cult of Wagner, was an astonishing development, as those who lived through it knew. "You cannot imagine the impression that this music made on those of my age," the novelist Alphonse Daudet said, according to his son Léon. "It truly transformed us. It renewed the atmosphere of art." Camille Mauclair, a devotee of Mallarmé and the Symbolists, remarked that Wagnérisme had the rhythms of a great love affair—"the first stammerings of the Wagnerian revelation; the arguments, the disavowals, and the enthusiasms, all equally furious; the blazing apotheoses and then the restless unease, the god debated . . ." Mauclair's generation felt not only an intemperate love for the god himself but also a "terrible disgust" for everything else. The fervor was all the more notable given the mutual distrust that festered between France and Germany in the decades after the Franco-Prussian War. That so many Parisian intellectuals welcomed the cultural figurehead of a nation that had humbled France on the battlefield never ceased to baffle the patriotic bloc.

Nietzsche monitored the early stages of this national obsession. In *The Case of Wagner*, he links the composer to contemporary France ("Very modern, right? very Parisian! very *décadent!*"). In *Ecce Homo*, he names Baudelaire "the first *intelligent* follower of Wagner." The philosopher cherished French culture, but his ascribing of Parisian manners to the master of Bayreuth had a cutting edge; his goal, surely, was to embarrass those who considered Wagner the most German of artists. The Wagnéristes, though, sincerely believed that their idol belonged in France—that Paris was his "proper *soil*," as Nietzsche said. The early twentieth-century author André Suarès openly declared that France was the place where Wagner had been understood best; the operas had transcended their German milieu and become essential to French intellectual life. Indeed, in a 1916 essay, Suarès wrote, "Wagner at the end of his life is freer of Germany than is Nietzsche, who prides himself on having escaped from it." This proposition would have annoyed Nietzsche no end.

For the French, Wagner was, first and foremost, modern. A notion of *modernité* had become integral to the self-image of the Parisian vanguard. Baudelaire began campaigning for unflinching representations of *la vie moderne* in the 1840s, and he fashioned an axiomatic definition in the 1860 essay "The Painter of Modern Life": "By 'modernity' I mean the ephemeral, the fugitive, the contingent, the half of art whose other half is the eternal and the immutable." The modern artist can find the eternal within the ephemeral, "poetry within history." At first glance, Wagner seems distant from modernity thus defined: the ephemeral is not his subject. But Baudelaire will recognize in the composer another kind of adversarial potential. Wagner's "passionate energy of expression," his "strange superhuman quality," makes him, in fact, the "truest representative of modernity." The last phrase probably inspired Nietzsche's aphorism about Wagner summing up the modern condition. The two comments are, however, very different in spirit. For Nietzsche, Wagner epitomizes a decadent culture that must be overcome. For Baudelaire, decadence is a site of resistance, a source of secret power.

Decadence long had a purely negative connotation: it was the overripe expression of an exhausted civilization. The conservative critic Paul Scudo

found in Wagner's music "the qualities and the defects of an epoch of decadence." Baudelaire took possession of the word in his 1857 essay on Edgar
Allan Poe, saying that any literature labeled "decadent" was almost certain
to be superior to the alternative. In 1881, the novelist and critic Paul Bourget defined decadent style as "one in which the unity of the book breaks
down and gives way to the independence of the page, in which the page
breaks down and gives way to the independence of the sentence, and in
which the sentence breaks down and gives way to the independence of the
word." For some, this atomization of discourse was a misfortune; for others,
it advanced the cause of art. Although Bourget does not mention Wagner,
Nietzsche makes the connection, using the Frenchman's analysis to lament
that life no longer resides in the whole, that discourse is devolving into an
individualist free-for-all. *Tristan*, with its disconnected, groping phrases, is
a case in point—even if Nietzsche cannot stop listening to it.

Wagner was modern; he was decadent; and he was dangerous. Riots
and brawls accompanied French performances of his works until the
end of the century, when the torch of scandal passed to the modernists. Opposition arose not only because of his German nationality but
also because of the perceived difficulty of his music and the undoubted
pugnacity of his prose. His rhetoric of perpetual revolution delighted the
nonconformist artists and writers of Paris. That the conservative wing denounced Wagner and his followers as "terrorists of music" spoke in their
favor. For the Wagnéristes, the composer had little to do with Germany;
rather, he represented an international revolt against the artistic status quo.

Walter Benjamin, in his 1935 essay "Paris, the Capital of the Nineteenth Century," describes the ambivalence that the likes of Baudelaire
felt in the face of an expanding popular marketplace. Recoiling from
commerce, they put a premium on absolute novelty, which was a kind of
market value in itself. In Benjamin's estimation, Wagner's total artwork
became the ultimate expression of the art-for-art's-sake mentality. For that
reason, "Baudelaire succumbs to the Wagner infatuation." Yet Wagnéristes
were by no means blind idolaters, nor did they necessarily retreat from
social questions, as Benjamin's analysis implies. Their relationship with
Wagner was a double-edged exchange, a contest of wills, an agon. Mallarmé directed writers to "take back what is ours" from the rival domain
of music drama. "What a singular challenge Richard Wagner imposes on
poets, whose duty he usurps with the most candid and splendid bravura!"

EARLY WAGNÉRISTES

Wagner's first Parisian foray, from 1839 to 1842, was a humiliating defeat, at least in his own mind. Fleeing creditors in the Baltic city of Riga, where he conducted for two seasons, he and Minna Wagner arrived in the bourgeois metropolis of Louis-Philippe with few friends and no money. For two and a half years, Wagner found work as an arranger and a journalist, but his music received scant notice, and his profligacy nearly landed him in debtor's prison. Ever after, he viewed this experience as the crucible in which his mature self was forged.

Although Paris generally ignored him, Wagner did attract a glimmer of attention when, in advance of a staging of Carl Maria von Weber's Romantic opera *Der Freischütz*, he contributed a two-part article to the *Revue et gazette musicale*, explaining the work's roots in folk legend and identifying supposed differences between German and French taste. Wagner predicted that the supernatural dimension of *Freischütz*—its magic bullets, its enchanted forest, its Wolf's Glen—would mystify Parisian audiences who were accustomed to promenading in the Bois de Boulogne. Only the melancholy, questing German spirit, steeped in the lore of the Black Forest and the Teutoburger Wald, could feel at home in Weber's opera. George Sand, near the height of her fame, read that article and paraphrased it in the introduction to her own diabolically tinged story "Mouny-Robin." The woods of France have their own devilish secrets, Sand retorted.

Interest in Wagner quickened after 1848. The failure of revolutionary hopes impelled a turn away from politics and toward the otherworldly, the bizarre, the visceral, the voluptuous—a distinctively French counterpart to Wagner's turn to metaphysics. The cult got off to a somewhat shaky start when the author and critic Gérard de Nerval, a flickering fixture of Paris bohemia, reviewed the premiere of *Lohengrin* without having attended it. The performance took place in 1850, in Weimar, under Liszt's direction. Nerval fell sick en route but assembled a plausible account using materials that Liszt sent his way. "Lohengrin is one of the knights who go in search of the Holy Grail," Nerval wrote. "Such was the goal of all adventurous expeditions of the Middle Ages, as with the Golden Fleece in ancient times and, today, California . . . This is an original and bold talent which has revealed itself in Germany, one that has as yet said only its first words." Wagner approved of the article, despite its erratic summary of the plot.

Nerval continued to follow the German singularity from afar, writing in 1854 that his own theories were "quite related to those of Richard Wagner"—although he still had not heard any of the operas. He was by then immersed in his unfinished final work, *Aurélia*, which begins with the sentence "Dream is a second life." Nerval's sustained examination of the "overflow of dream into real life" intersects at many points with the Wagner of *Tristan* and the *Ring*. Confined to a clinic, the protagonist imagines being attended by Valkyries and has premonitions of world destruction. In one sequence, he meditates on the origins of the white and black races, the Nibelung hoard, Brünnhilde, Siegfried, Charlemagne, and the Holy Grail—a swirl of topics that overlaps with Wagner's 1848 essay "The Wibelungs." Nerval committed suicide in 1855, but his preoccupations became central to French literature.

The poet, novelist, and critic Théophile Gautier, a comrade of Nerval's from schooldays onward, understood Wagner in terms of the art-for-art's-sake stance that Gautier popularized in his poetry and prose. One of his most famous poems, "Symphonie en blanc majeur" ("Symphony in White Major," 1852), set off a fad for musical titles in poetry and painting. Gautier, who shared Nerval's taste for dream states and the supernatural, first encountered Wagner when the *Tannhäuser* overture was played in Paris in 1850. He judged it "a work full of knowledge, of original instrumental effects," surpassing "those facile banalities that the French public is always ready to applaud." When Gautier saw the complete opera, in Wiesbaden, in 1857, his reaction was more measured, not to say confused. Expecting the music of a "*paroxyste*," he instead professed to hear a formally conservative work "full of fugues"—an analysis that few musicologists have seconded.

The majority of Francophone critics were unremittingly negative. In 1852, the eminent Belgian theorist and critic François-Joseph Fétis wrote a seven-part series of articles disparaging Wagner's music and ideas, yoking the composer to such "aberrations of the spirit" as the realism of Courbet and the radicalism of Proudhon. French listeners could not easily judge for themselves, since almost no one was playing the music. Between 1842 and

1860, Paris heard nothing by Wagner except two isolated renditions of the *Tannhäuser* overture. Then began the "second assault on Paris," in the words of the Wagner biographer Ernest Newman. First came the concert series at the Théâtre-Italien, then the *Tannhäuser* fiasco at the Opéra, which launched Wagnerism as an international event.

THE *TANNHÄUSER* SCANDAL

"The author of the *Tannhäuser* overture! Open all the doors," the poet and critic Auguste de Gasperini wrote to his friend Léon Leroy in September 1859, announcing Wagner's return to Paris. Two years earlier, Gasperini, a former naval surgeon who read German philosophy and espoused radical politics, had heard the *Lohengrin* wedding march in the spa town of Baden-Baden, and found himself "subjugated" by it—a strong reaction to a somewhat innocuous piece. Since then, Gasperini had been proselytizing on Wagner's behalf. Leroy, a musically trained journalist and editor, spread the word in liberal circles.

The political backdrop helps to explain the ensuing battle over Wagner in Paris. Louis-Napoléon was crowned Napoleon III in 1852, and in the

Wagner in Paris, 1861, from Thomas Mann's collection

early years of his regime he exercised an authoritarian grip, effectively suppressing opposition at both ends of the political spectrum—the republican left, adhering to the ideals of the Revolution; and the legitimist right, dedicated to restoring the Bourbon monarchy. By the end of the fifties, though, the left was gathering strength, and the emperor responded with a strategy of partial liberalization. The system of censorship that forced Baudelaire to remove six poems from *Les Fleurs du mal* in 1857 eased modestly in the following decade, giving encouragement to new artistic voices.

Even if Wagner had retreated from politics, his reputation rested in large measure on his revolutionary pamphlets, and he had many fans on the left. The ranks of the Wagnéristes grew to include the politicians Jules Ferry and Émile Ollivier (the latter married to Liszt's daughter Blandine); the philosopher and future Third Republic statesman Paul-Armand Challemel-Lacour; the poet and dramatist Théodore de Banville, who greeted Wagner as "a democrat, a new man, wanting to write for everyone and for the people"; the pianist Maria Kalergis, who, by Eugène Delacroix's report, adored the composer "like a fool, as she adores the Republic"; and the author Marie d'Agoult, mother of Blandine Ollivier and Cosima von Bülow, later Cosima Wagner.

When Wagner presented his concerts at the Théâtre-Italien, musical conservatives ratcheted up their opposition to the alleged Marat of composers. Critics mocked the audience as a parade of poseurs: "Dresses of yellow satin with crimson bodices; bouffant skirts held up with belts of gold braid; small amaranth hats with turned-up brims; bundles of cherry pink ribbon intertwined with beads and shells; white plumes perched on the ear; in sum, the hairstyles and *toilettes* of the future." Paul Scudo scowled at the "mediocre writers, painters, sculptors without talent, quasipoets, lawyers, democrats, suspect republicans, deceivers, women without taste, day-dreamers of nothing." According to Baudelaire, Scudo stood at the exit after one rehearsal and laughed maniacally, "like one of those unfortunates in mental institutions who are called *agités*." It was a prophetic aside: the critic died insane four years later.

Wagner was finally famous in Paris, but at a price. Just after his concert series ended, Jacques Offenbach's musical satire *Le Carnaval des revues* opened at the Théâtre des Bouffes-Parisiens, almost next door to the Théâtre-Italien. This entertainment included a scene set in the Elysian Fields, where Gluck, Grétry, Mozart, and Weber pass judgment on a certain "composer of the future" who blends jarring discords with vulgar tunes. When the departed greats hear a pop hit of the Second Empire in the mix, they dismiss the newcomer as a beggar and a brigand. If parody had the power to kill, *Le Figaro* said, "Richard Wagner would be a dead man at this moment."

Being branded a revolutionary was of no help in winning a performance at the Opéra, as Wagner knew. He began hosting a salon on Wednesdays, inviting not only republicans but also legitimists and members of the emperor's circle. His latest commentaries prioritized psychology over politics. For a French translation of his librettos, he wrote an introductory "Lettre sur la musique," which dwelled on myth, dreams, and the unconscious. The mark of a great poet, Wagner says, is his ability to let his public grasp in silence what is left unsaid. In the case of the musician, "the infallible form of his resounding silence is *endless melody*." Music and literature can meet in an ideal space that exists at the outer limits of each discipline. Canny as ever, Wagner sets the stage for a radical literary reception of his work.

"Endless melody" proved to be another inescapable Wagner formula. It stands in seeming contrast—almost in contradiction—to the leitmotif, which entered common parlance after the premiere of the *Ring*. Leitmotifs are crisply defined melodic fragments that play a signifying role; endless melody suggests a continuous, formless flow of consciousness. As the German musicologist Carl Dahlhaus once showed, the two concepts are really complementary. Endless melody consists, in essence, of leitmotivic materials seamlessly interlocking.

In March 1860, Napoleon III commanded a performance of *Tannhäuser* at the Opéra. The historian Gerald Turbow diagrams the politics behind the move: the emperor wished to improve relations with Austria, and Princess Pauline von Metternich, the wife of the Austrian ambassador, was a Wagner champion. At the same time, the gesture seemed intended to win allies among domestic progressives. In a similar liberalizing spirit, Napoleon III would sponsor the 1863 Salon des Refusés, giving his imprimatur to Édouard Manet, James McNeill Whistler, and other painters rejected by the Académie. In the end, the entire scheme backfired. Some leftists who had seen Wagner as a revolutionary stalwart now looked at him askance. The legitimists had even less reason to approve of him. When *Tannhäuser* finally opened, on March 13, 1861, much of the audience was predisposed to dislike it.

The opera was already more than fifteen years old—a landmark of Wagner's early development rather than a harbinger of his mature style. In his first four operas, he had tried his hand at various genres. *Die Feen* is a Romantic fantasy; *Das Liebesverbot* is an Italianate treatment of Shakespeare's *Measure for Measure*; *Rienzi* is a grand opera in French style; *The Flying Dutchman* returns to the Romantic supernatural. *Tannhäuser*, based on a medieval legend that Wagner probably first encountered by way of a retelling by Heinrich Heine, attempts a synthesis, incorporating grand-opera and bel canto features in a German Romantic frame. Wagner was never altogether satisfied with the result, and for the Paris production he extensively reworked the score.

Baudelaire summarized the story thus: "*Tannhäuser* represents the struggle between two principles that have chosen the human heart for their chief battlefield: that is to say, flesh and spirit, hell and heaven, Satan and God." The title character is torn between the debauchery of the goddess Venus, who tempts him into the mountain grotto of the Venusberg, and the more wholesome adoration of Elisabeth, the niece of the Landgrave of Thuringia. The eventual self-sacrificial death of Elisabeth brings about Tannhäuser's redemption, as the hero escapes Venus's clutches. Many of the opera's principal motifs are given a lavish presentation in the overture. The "furious song of the flesh," as Baudelaire heard it, fails to vanquish the stately Pilgrims' Chorus: the two elements are intertwined and reconciled.

When Wagner revised *Tannhäuser* for the Opéra, he gave special attention to the opening scene, in which nymphs, bacchantes, and other revelers enact the Venusberg. With an injection of the advanced harmonic language of *Tristan*, the sequence turns into a matchless orgiastic frenzy. Wagner hoped that the new material would solve an imminent crowd-control problem. Paris audiences were accustomed to seeing a ballet scene not at the beginning of an opera but in the second act. The noblemen of the Jockey Club, who occupied many of the most prominent boxes, were in the habit of skipping the first act, arriving in time to see their favorite ballerinas. Although Wagner refused to supply a ballet in the expected place, he thought that his supercharged Venusberg music and the accompanying dancing would astound everyone into surrender.

He miscalculated, to say the least. The Jockeys, who had ties to the legitimist camp and no great love for Napoleon III, had already decided to ruin the show. They came equipped with hunting whistles and made a mighty noise. The entrance onstage of ten hunting dogs, loaned by the emperor, caused merriment, eliciting cries of "*Bravo les chiens! Bis les chiens!*" The Wagnerites fought back, shouting, "*À bas les Jockeys!*" Fistfights broke out; Princess Metternich attempted to confiscate the Jockeys' noisemakers. At the second performance, the din grew so loud that Nina de Callias, the model for Manet's *Lady with Fans*, compared it to the sound of a dozen locomotives. In the end, *Tannhäuser* seemed to have won over most of the public. But Wagner had had enough. After one more tempestuous performance, he withdrew the work in a fit of pique. The Opéra did not touch his music for another thirty years.

Paris had witnessed such scenes before, and more were to follow. In 1830, at the premiere of Victor Hugo's *Hernani*, the eighteen-year-old Gautier had shouted on behalf of the new Romanticism. The most crucial phase of such aesthetic battles took place not during the performance but afterward in the press. In the case of *Tannhäuser*, the conservatives almost immediately lost the argument. As the musicologist Annegret Fauser notes, Wagner and his allies successfully characterized the opposition as a convocation of imbeciles who were blocking progress. The most effective broadside appeared on April 1, 1861, in the *Revue européenne*: an eleven-thousand-word article titled "Richard Wagner," by Charles Baudelaire.

BAUDELAIRE

Baudelaire, 1863

Eight years younger than Wagner, Baudelaire could hardly have been more different in personality. While the composer came from relatively humble origins, the poet grew up in comfortable bourgeois circumstances, and assumed, with a certain pride, a downward trajectory. Where Wagner refrained from most bohemian habits, Baudelaire indulged in absinthe, opium, hashish, and large quantities of wine. Wagner's love affairs often stopped short of sexual congress; Baudelaire's early and frequent encounters with prostitutes probably gave him the venereal disease that has been linked to his early death. Wagner never lost faith in an ever-evolving conception of God; Baudelaire hailed Satan. Wagner gazed backward to mythic origins; Baudelaire opened his poetry to the seamiest tendencies of contemporary life. Even so, the poet's identification with the composer was profound. Having endured his own scandal on account of *Les Fleurs du mal*, Baudelaire saw the same forces of philistinism conspiring against *Tannhäuser*.

Listening to Wagner's music and reading his texts, Baudelaire felt repeated shocks of familiarity. Both men relied on the rhetoric of the new. "Children! make something *new*!" was one of Wagner's slogans; for Baudelaire, it was "To the bottom of the Unknown to find the *new*!" Both sympathized with wanderers and outcasts. Venus flits through *Fleurs*, which critics have divided into cycles of the "black Venus," the "white Venus," and the "green-eyed Venus." The poet who contrasted muses and Madonnas with temptresses and whores was well prepared for the Elisabeth-Venus duality of *Tannhäuser*. On the purely musical level, Wagner's investigation of unusual harmonies and timbres accorded with Baudelaire's ideas about the beauty of the ugly and the bizarre. Berlioz had accused Wagner of making the horrible beautiful and the beautiful horrible. Baudelaire might have loved the music for exactly this reason.

Although Baudelaire had warmed to Wagner as early as 1849, he was unprepared for the impact of the Théâtre-Italien concerts. His mania on the subject amused his friends, as he told his publisher: "I dare not speak more about Wagner; I'm getting mocked too much. That music has been one of the great pleasures of my life; it has been easily fifteen years since I have felt such ravishment." The following day, Baudelaire sent a letter to the composer, characterizing his experience as one of addiction, infatuation, subjugation. Indeed, he metaphorically placed himself in a passive sexual role:

Before everything, I wish to tell you that I owe to you *the greatest musical pleasure I have ever experienced* . . . It seemed to me that this music was *mine*, and I recognized it as every man recognizes the things he is destined to love . . . I often experienced a sensation of a rather bizarre nature, and this was the pride and pleasure of comprehending, of letting myself be penetrated and invaded, a truly sensual enjoyment, which resembles that of rising in the air or tossing on the sea.

Some artists might have been alarmed to receive such a piece of correspondence, but Wagner was delighted. In his autobiography, he reports the satisfaction of encountering this "extraordinary mind," which expressed itself "with conscious boldness in the most bizarre flights of fantasy." Despite the lack of a return address—Baudelaire had not given one, to avoid the impression he was asking for a favor—Wagner tracked down the poet and invited him to his salon. Baudelaire set to work on his essay, steadily expanding its scope over many months. "I dream continuously of WAGNER and POE," he wrote to his publisher. Only in the wake of the *Tannhäuser* debacle did the article finally appear in print. It was subsequently republished under the title "Richard Wagner et *Tannhäuser* à Paris."

Baudelaire begins in medias res, in the manner of Poe: "I propose, with the reader's permission, to go back some thirteen months, to the beginning of the affair." There follows a withering précis of the Parisian battle over Wagner, which erupted before anyone had had a chance to hear the music. The poet then tells of his own conversion experience. The prelude to *Lohengrin* struck him most strongly. Reproducing passages from Wagner's program note, which describes the apparition of the Holy Grail to a "pious wanderer," Baudelaire italicizes particular phrases: "*plunges into an infinity of space*," "*he yields to a growing feeling of bliss*," "*radiant vision*," "*he is swallowed up in an ecstasy of adoration, as if the whole world has suddenly disappeared*," "*burning flames gradually mitigate their brilliance*," "*into whose hearts the divine essence has flowed*," "*into the infinities of space*." He then summarizes his own impressions, stressing the overlap with Wagner's text:

I remember that from the very first bars I suffered one of those happy impressions that almost all imaginative men have known, through dreams, in sleep. I felt myself released from the *bonds of gravity*, and I rediscovered in memory that extraordinary *thrill of pleasure* which dwells in *high places* . . . Next I found myself imagining the delicious state of a man in the grip of a profound reverie, in an absolute solitude, a solitude with *an immense horizon* and a *wide diffusion of light*; *an immensity with no other decor but itself*. Soon I experienced the sensation of a *brightness* more vivid, *an intensity of light* growing so swiftly that not all the nuances provided by the dictionary would be sufficient to express *this ever-renewing increase of incandescence and heat*. Then I came to the full conception of the idea of a soul moving about in a luminous medium, of an ecstasy *composed of knowledge and joy*, hovering high above the natural world.

The convergence of these associations, which also resemble phrases from Liszt's essay on *Lohengrin*, proves to Baudelaire that "true music evokes analogous ideas in different brains," that verbal images and musical ones are intimately interrelated. They reflect the "complex and indivisible totality" of God's creation. To illustrate the point, Baudelaire inserts, without naming the source, eight lines from his own poem "Correspondances," published in the first edition of *Les Fleurs du mal*:

> Nature is a temple where living pillars
> Let fall at times a confusion of words;
> There man passes through forests of symbols
> Which look at him with knowing eyes.
>
> Like long echoes that distantly lose themselves
> In a shadowy and profound oneness,
> As vast as night, as vast as light,
> Scents, colors, and sounds answer each other.

Baudelaire thus delineates a correspondence between Wagner's goal of reunifying the arts and the poet's own synesthetic command of smell, sight, and sound. The forest imagery deepens the identification: George Sand had questioned Wagner's assumption that only Germans could understand the enchanted woods of *Der Freischütz*, and now Baudelaire places himself in similar terrain, the mystery only heightened by the incomparably spooky vision of symbols with eyes.

As he confesses in his introductory letter—"From the day I heard your music, I have said to myself constantly, especially at bad hours: *If only*

I could hear a little Wagner tonight!"—Baudelaire is responding with the ardor of an addict, an opium dreamer. Wagner's revolutionary politics leave him cold; the adventures of 1848 and 1849 are an "error excusable in a sensitive and excessively nervous mind." What matters is the composer's "absolute, despotic taste for a dramatic ideal." Baudelaire proceeds to quote Wagner's "Lettre sur la musique," which describes myth's capacity to activate powers beneath conscious reason: "The character of the scene and the tone of the legend work together to throw the mind into that dream-state where it is soon brought to the point of full *clairvoyance*, and it discovers a new interrelationship of the phenomena of the world, which the eyes could not perceive in the ordinary waking state."

Delving into the *Tannhäuser* overture, Baudelaire predictably favors the profane over the sacred. The world of Venus exudes "languors, fevered and agonized delights, ceaseless returns towards an ecstasy of pleasure which promises to quench, but never does quench, thirst . . . the whole onomatopoeic dictionary of Love." Indeed, Baudelaire upends the moral scheme of the opera by claiming that the Venusberg music represents "the overflowing of a vigorous nature, pouring into Evil all the energies which should rightly go to the cultivation of Good; it is love unbridled, immense, chaotic, raised to the level of a counter-religion, a satanic religion."

The extravagant vocabulary of the essay's concluding section foreshadows Nietzsche's Dionysian aesthetics. Indeed, Baudelaire comes close to preempting the *Übermensch* when he says that Wagner's passion "adds to everything a je ne sais quoi of the superhuman." One should exult in "these excesses of vigor, these overflowings of the will, which write themselves on works of art like flaming lava on the slopes of a volcano, and which in ordinary life often mark that delicious phase that follows upon a great moral or physical crisis." This superman is not, however, a specifically German quantity. Indeed, Baudelaire ignores Wagner's Germanness and instead criticizes the chauvinistic small-mindedness that has led French crowds to thwart a work of high importance. In an epilogue that he added for the book version of the essay, he asked, "What is Europe going to think of us, and what will they say about Paris in Germany?"

In the end, this apparent submission to Wagner is a wholesale reinvention of him. As the philosopher Philippe Lacoue-Labarthe puts it in his study *Musica Ficta* (*Figures of Wagner*), Baudelaire wards off music's threatened dominance by way of "subjective reappropriation." Music remains stubbornly inarticulate, even in Wagner's word-heavy, emotionally charged incarnation. Baudelaire's declaration that the music "returned me to myself" stealthily reclaims territory that he had seemingly given up in his state of abject wonder. "I myself am the world," the lovers sing in *Tristan*, the opera that Baudelaire never heard. By saying, in effect, "I myself am Wagner," Baudelaire makes the music his own, and forever changes how the world perceives it. In this agon, the one who surrenders is the victor.

Wagner's initial reply to the *Tannhäuser* essay alludes offhandedly to Baudelaire's "very beautiful" words before retailing the usual stories of his woes. Perhaps he only skimmed it, for in a second letter he suddenly sounds almost desperate with gratitude. He has tried several times to call on Baudelaire in order to convey his appreciation for the article, "which honors and encourages me more than anything that has ever been said about my poor talent." Wagner goes on, in passable French: "Would it not be possible to tell you soon, out loud, how intoxicated I felt upon reading these beautiful pages, which related to me—as does the best poem—the impressions I must boast of having produced on a sensibility as superior as yours? A thousand thanks for this blessing you have given me, and believe me proud to call you a friend." Baudelaire reported that Wagner later hugged him, saying, "I would never have believed that a French writer could so easily understand so many things." Did Wagner like the essay that much? Or did he realize that its unorthodox speculations granted him a kind of exegetic immortality?

When "Richard Wagner" was published, Baudelaire had only six years to live. Symptoms of physical and mental decline soon became evident. In 1866, the poet suffered a massive stroke, and spent his final year in a nursing home, incapacitated and effectively unable to speak. Among his regular visitors were Suzanne Manet, the wife of the painter, and the pianist Eléonore-Palmyre Meurice. Both women played Wagner for the invalid. Another friend recalled: "When I spoke of Wagner and Manet, he smiled with happiness."

In 1888, Nietzsche came across Baudelaire's *Œuvres posthumes*, which recounted the poet's last days and quoted Wagner's appreciative letter of 1861. The only other time the composer ever waxed so effusive, Nietzsche claimed, was when he read *The Birth of Tragedy*. Baudelaire's writings show Wagner to be a cosmopolitan, supra-German artist; at the same time, they point up his decadence, his appeal to sick souls. Nietzsche observes that when Baudelaire was "half mad and slowly going under, they applied Wagner's music to him as medicine." Within a year, Nietzsche had himself passed into the beyond, playing his Wagnerian fantasies at the piano.

AXEL'S CASTLE

The Wagner wars raged on. In October 1861, a few months after the *Tannhäuser* scandal, the conductor Jules Pasdeloup instituted a series of low-priced Concerts Populaires in the Cirque Napoléon, now the Cirque d'Hiver, a circular arena that at the time could seat around five thousand people. The following year, Pasdeloup programmed an excerpt from *Tannhäuser*, and added more Wagner as the decade went on. The conductor also led an extended run of performances of *Rienzi* in 1869 and 1870. A decade later, John Singer Sargent painted Pasdeloup's orchestra in rehearsal—a moody tableau of blurry black-clad figures set against white score pages and golden brass.

Paul Verlaine was a regular at the Cirque, arriving early to be assured of a good seat. In his *Épigrammes*, the poet remembers that he had "thrown a punch / For Wagner" in the skirmishes that regularly took place between fans and detractors. Isidore Ducasse, the short-lived proto-Surrealist author who wrote as the Comte de Lautréamont, also had Wagnerite leanings. In the second canto of *Les Chants de Maldoror*, the testament of an apostle of evil, the figure of Lohengrin is seen hurrying down a city street in an anonymous modern guise. Maldoror is tempted to stab him to death, so that the beautiful youth will not "become like other men," but he restrains himself. "I am yours," he says. "I belong to you, I no longer live for myself."

Émile Zola and Paul Cézanne, schoolboy friends from Aix-en-Provence, belonged to the local Wagner Society and joined the ranks of the Wagnerians at the Cirque on moving to Paris. Zola boasted that he had been among the first to shout "*Bis!*" ("Encore!"). Later, having renounced Impressionism in favor of naturalism, he looked back on those adventurous years with a less sentimental eye. Claude Lantier, the failed, doomed painter at the heart of Zola's 1886 novel *L'Œuvre*, is modeled on Cézanne. Among the cast of supporting characters is a painter named Gustave Gagnière, whose soliloquies preserve some of the more unhinged Wagnerite rhetoric of the period:

> Oh! Wagner, the god, in whom centuries of music are incarnated! His work is the mighty ark, all the arts in one, the true humanity of the characters finally achieving expression, the orchestra separately experiencing the life of the drama; and what a massacre of conventions, of inept formulas! what a revolutionary emancipation into the infinite! . . . The overture to *Tannhäuser*, ah! it is the sublime hallelujah of the new epoch . . .

Gagnière defies the hissing ignoramuses at the Cirque and exits one concert with a black eye.

Baudelaire was not the only French author to develop a distinctive vocabulary for Wagner. Another influential advocate was the arch-bohemian writer and critic Champfleury, the nom de plume of Jules Fleury-Husson—a "juggler, a thermometer of enthusiasms," according to the art historian T. J. Clark. While Baudelaire mulled over his Wagner essay for more than a year, the prolific Champfleury dashed off an aphoristic, free-associating pamphlet a few days after the first Théâtre-Italien concert. Seeking "analogies of sensations" to capture the experience, Champfleury first evokes the infinite expanse of the ocean, then looks toward the forest, which had already made a memorable appearance in Baudelaire's "Correspondances." He writes: "There is a religious aspect in the work of Wagner, the religious feeling that you experience in a thick forest, when you traverse it in silence. Then the passions of civilization fall away one by one: the spirit leaves the little cardboard box where it is habitually locked away whenever one ventures out to a soirée, to the theater, in society; it purifies itself, it visibly grows, it breathes contentedly and seems to climb to the tops of tall trees."

Champfleury's essay was published in March 1860. Wagner, buffeted by attacks in the French press, gratefully seized on it and folded some of its images into his "Lettre sur la musique." According to Champfleury, the music is in no way bereft of melody, as conservative critics complain; rather, it is "only one vast melody," indivisible like the sea. Wagner's "Lettre," in turn, takes up the formula of the "endless melody" and spins its own extended forest metaphor, asking the reader to imagine a lonely

traveler who, on a summer evening, leaves behind the noise of the city and goes walking in a beautiful forest. There, he listens to the "endless diversity of voices awakening in the wood" and has the "perception of a silence becoming ever more eloquent." These sounds cannot be separated from one another; they are "but one great forest-melody," religious in character. Wagner is thinking, no doubt, of the shimmering Forest Murmurs music in Act II of *Siegfried*. The influence is circular: forest imagery first appears in Baudelaire and then reappears in Champfleury's ode to Wagner, which Wagner absorbs in turn. No wonder Baudelaire felt a sense of self-recognition on reading the "Lettre."

Wagner, in his youth, had perplexed George Sand with his assertion that French listeners would never be able to penetrate the forests of German folklore. The rising generation of French writers might have led him to rethink his position, if anyone had thought to challenge it. Deep in the Black Forest, a symbol-encrusted magic castle was about to rise, the creation of a stupendous character who could make even Wagner wish for a little peace: Jean-Marie-Mathias-Philippe-Auguste, Comte de Villiers de l'Isle-Adam.

He always brought in a festival," Mallarmé said. "Time annulled itself those nights." The Goncourt brothers recalled the "feverish eyes of a victim of hallucinations, the face of an opium addict or a masturbator, and a crazy, mechanical laugh which came and went in his throat." This absinthe-breathed bohemian was, in fact, the scion of an ancient family, as his page-wide name testifies. Born on the Brittany coast, Villiers could claim proximity to the romance of Tristan: the hero comes from a Breton line, and, in Wagner's version, dies in the family castle. One of Villiers's distant ancestors had been the Grand Master of the Knights of Malta, and family lore held that he left a great treasure buried somewhere. Villiers's father, Joseph, engaged in ill-advised real-estate ventures in order to carry out excavations in Brittany. According to Villiers's biographer, Alan Raitt, the only thing Joseph ever found was a dinner service. His son inherited the fixation on lost glory, transmuting it into literary fantasy. Auguste gained early notoriety for having declared his candidature—seriously or not, no one could be sure—for the throne of Greece.

Villiers's poems, plays, novels, and tales elude the usual literary categories. How to classify *The Future Eve*, a kind of baroque science-fiction novel in which Thomas Alva Edison invents a female android? This author is most approachable, though not necessarily most likable, when he is engaging in vicious satire: his collections *Cruel Tales* and *Tribulat Bonhomet* rail against bourgeois fatuity and callousness. In one story, the insufferable Dr. Bonhomet breaks the necks of swans, because he has heard that the birds sing most beautifully when they die. Villiers suffered from the usual failings of male European writers of the period: antisemitism, misogyny, elitism. William Butler Yeats liked to quote a characteristic line from Villiers's mystical drama *Axël*: "As for living, our servants will do that for us."

Music-mad from youth onward, Villiers was an energetic if eccentric pianist who, like Nietzsche, specialized in improvisations. He met Baudelaire a year or two before the *Tannhäuser* scandal, and a shared regard for Wagner cemented their friendship. "I will play *Tannhäuser* for you once I am settled in your neighborhood," Villiers wrote. He also fell in with Catulle Mendès, a handsome poet and novelist who floated through Paris society beneath waves of Lisztian hair. The son of a Sephardic Jewish father and a Catholic mother, Mendès won early fame—and a brief prison term—by publishing mildly erotic poetry in his *Revue fantaisiste*. That short-lived journal, founded in 1861, was an early organ of the Parnassian movement, which valued formal poise and exquisite precision in the Gautier manner. In 1866, Mendès married Judith Gautier, Théophile's daughter, who was on the verge of her own significant literary and artistic career; the two had met at one of Pasdeloup's concerts.

In 1869, the Mendès couple, having proved their worth as combative Wagnéristes, received an invitation to visit the composer in Tribschen.

Villiers joined them on the pilgrimage. The itinerary also included Munich, where rehearsals for the premiere of *Rheingold* were under way. Beforehand, Villiers had written a story titled "Azraël," which he dedicated to Wagner, "prince of profound music." Oddly, it was on an Old Testament Jewish theme, depicting King Solomon in conversation with the Angel of Death. As the party approached Tribschen, Villiers displayed mounting elation. He gave Wagner the obscure nickname "palmiped of Lucerne," and exclaimed, "He is cubic!"

The palmiped met them on the railway platform, wearing a large straw hat, which made him look like Wotan. Gautier remembered being fixed for a full, silent minute by the soul-scoping intensity of his gaze. In letters home, Villiers described the "fabulous being" in terms suitable for the cruel angels and crazed scientists of his stories: "Something like immortality made visible, the other world rendered transparent, creative power pushed to a fantastic point, and, with that, the sweat and the shining of genius, the impression of the infinite around his head and in the naïve profundity of his eyes. *He is terrifying.*" He is "the very man of whom we have dreamed; he is a genius such as appears upon the earth once every thousand years."

Cosmic ramifications notwithstanding, Wagner acted much of the time like a hyperactive child. Mendès has him throwing his hat in the air, dancing about, gesturing with nervous excitement, and talking without pause. One day, he made a catlike jump from an upper story of the house into the garden. When Villiers was later asked whether the composer was a pleasant conversationalist, he replied, "Do you imagine, sir, that the conversation of Mount Etna is pleasant?" Like Nietzsche and Baudelaire, Villiers experienced Wagner as a human volcano.

The next year, Villiers, Mendès, and Gautier set out on a second Wagner vacation, witnessing the premiere of *Walküre* in Munich and paying another visit to Tribschen. This time, the Franco-Prussian War intervened. Otto von Bismarck had manipulated a diplomatic dispute into a major crisis, and Napoleon III declared war on July 19, just as the French party—now including the composers Camille Saint-Saëns and Henri Duparc—alighted in Lucerne. Despite the news, the company sat enthralled as Wagner and Hans Richter performed excerpts from the *Ring*. "It is the Nibelungen, all the night of time," Villiers wrote. The Nietzsche siblings, Friedrich and Elisabeth, also dropped by, making for a singular constellation of personalities. The French had hoped to stay for Richard and Cosima's wedding, but this was delayed for legal reasons, and tensions were simmering. "R. demands of our friends that they understand how much we hate the French character," Cosima noted. The Wagners became exasperated by Villiers's "bombastic style and theatrical presentation"—a severe reprimand in this household. Russ, the chief family dog, bit Villiers's hand. On July 30, the French departed, announcing their intention to visit a "friend in Avignon," who turned out to be Stéphane Mallarmé.

Villiers never made it to Bayreuth for the *Ring*. Reportedly, he broke down in tears when he realized that he couldn't afford to go. His Wagnermania persisted, reaching its apex in *Axël*, which once loomed over fin-de-siècle literature as a successor to *Faust*. In 1931, the American critic Edmund Wilson honored Villiers's fading fame by giving the title *Axel's Castle* to his history of Symbolist and modernist literature. The play first took shape at the time of Villiers's visits to the Wagners, for whom he may have read aloud an early draft. The euphoric demise of its self-annihilating lovers, Axel d'Auersperg and Sara de Maupers, smacks of *Tristan und Isolde*; its story of fatally alluring gold, meanwhile, recalls the monetary curse of the *Ring*, not to mention the treasure-hunting escapades of Villiers's father. Villiers was still revising and expanding the play when he died, in 1889. It reached the stage only in 1894, in a performance that lasted nearly five hours, about as long as *Tristan* itself. "Seldom has utmost pessimism found a more magnificent expression," said Yeats, who was present for the occasion.

The climax of the play is like *Tristan* and *Götterdämmerung* superimposed. Sara, having fled a convent, arrives in Axel's castle in the Black Forest, led there by a mysterious book. Axel briefly engages her in combat, gazes upon her, and falls in love. He comes to resemble not only Tristan and Siegfried but also Wotan with Brünnhilde ("I will close your eyes of paradise") and Siegmund with Sieglinde ("Sara, my virginal mistress, my eternal sister"). What to do with the sudden onset of passion? Sara wants to flee to a remote locale and "listen to the hummingbirds in some hut in the Floridas." Axel is unconvinced: "Oh! the external world! Let us not be dupes of that old slave." To break the veil of illusion, he says, they should kill themselves at once. After a certain amount of hesitation, Sara agrees. As the humble songs of a village marriage are heard from outside, she draws poison from the ring on her finger. Axel expresses the hope that the rest of the human race will follow suit. After the lovers die, though, the stage directions dictate a different outcome: "Disturbing the silence of the terrible place where two human beings have just dedicated their souls to the exile of Heaven—we hear from outside the distant murmurs of the wind in the vastness of the forests, the vibrations of awakening space, the swell of the plains, the hum of life." The forest murmurs on; the world has not committed suicide at Axel's behest. The ironist in Villiers shows the limits of his characters' transcendent longing.

Lost to history are Villiers's fabled one-man Wagner entertainments. Joris-Karl Huysmans left a memorable description: "After the meal, he sat down at the piano and, lost, out of this world, sang, in his feeble, cracked voice, several pieces by Wagner, among which he interpolated barracks choruses, joining it all together with strident laughter, crazed nonsense, and strange verses. No one possessed in the same degree the power to heighten farce and make it shoot bewildered into the beyond; he always had a punch-bowl flaming in his brain."

MODERN PAINTERS

Cézanne, Pastorale

More than a hundred thousand soldiers were killed during the Franco-Prussian War. One of them was the brilliant young Impressionist painter Frédéric Bazille, who had been a regular at Pasdeloup's concerts and had fantasized about meeting Wagner. After the conflict, the composer's reputation in France slumped again, thanks in part to his genius for insult. In 1873, he dismayed even his most die-hard French fans by publishing a would-be Aristophanic farce titled *A Capitulation*, which made light of the siege of Paris in the fall and winter of 1870. In the hardest days, Parisians resorted to eating rats and other animals. Wagner's play, for which he thankfully wrote no music, calls for a ballet corps of human-sized rats. Catulle Mendès was particularly incensed, though he could not bring himself to cut all ties. A Hungarian Jewish friend of the author's kept a bust of Wagner with a laurel wreath on its head and a cord around its neck. Mendès adopted the same attitude, admiring and despising his old idol in equal measure.

Between 1870 and 1887 there was only one full staging of Wagner in France—a *Lohengrin* in Nice, in 1881. Orchestral concerts and private events became the main conduit for his music. Pasdeloup soon resumed programming the composer in his Concerts Populaires, causing a predictable ruckus. Boos, whistles, and shouts of "*À la porte Wagner!*" mingled with loud cheers. Saint-Saëns, his attitude altered since he visited Tribschen with Villiers and company, accused Pasdeloup of being a German agent. In the eighties, the younger conductors Édouard Colonne and Charles Lamoureux joined the crusade, including heavy doses of Wagner on their series. Lamoureux, the most musically ambitious of the three, began presenting entire acts of the operas. In 1884, he led Act I of *Tristan*, with the audience listening in rapt silence. In the same period, a society called Le Petit Bayreuth, which had been operating partly in secret to avoid hostile demonstrations, offered excerpts from the *Ring* and *Parsifal*.

Supreme among the Wagnéristes was Judith Gautier, who, after separating from Mendès, had developed an intimacy with the composer that probably remained platonic. The author of several finely drawn novels on East Asian themes, Gautier advised Wagner on Eastern thought and culture, contributing to the ambience of *Parsifal*, which she translated into French. In 1880, Gautier organized a series of Wagner lecture-concerts at the Nadar photography studio, and in 1898 she presented a puppet-theater adaptation of *Parsifal*, for which she crafted dozens of figurines. The latter project led to a break with Cosima, who had tolerated Gautier's ambiguous relations with her husband but could not condone a possible breach of copyright. That contretemps did not diminish Gautier's enthusiasm. In later years, she would show visitors her collection of Wagner relics, including a piece of bread into which the Meister had bitten on the day of the first *Parsifal*. Her menagerie of pets featured a raven named Wotan.

If the war had dampened French Wagnerism, the composer's death seemed to ignite it again. "Curious people!" Tchaikovsky wrote from Paris. "It is necessary to die in order to attract their attention." At the Bayreuth Festival of 1886, the number of French visitors exploded, from a few dozen to well over a hundred. Back home, the Wagner contingent could turn rowdy. One evening, the critic Albert Aurier, an early promoter of van Gogh and Gauguin, got into a fracas with the police after marching through the streets with a crowd of friends, singing the melody of "The Ride of the Valkyries" at full volume. "Sir, I was singing Wagner," Aurier told an officer. "And I know of no law that prevents it."

In 1887, *Lohengrin* finally received a full staging in Paris, amid an uproar that almost outdid the *Tannhäuser* affair of 1861. The Opéra-Comique had planned to produce the opera the previous year, but retreated in the face of a patriotic press campaign that cast Wagner as a warmonger rather than an artist. An academic painter threatened to incite a riot by packing the theater with two hundred toga-wearing art students. Lamoureux then entered the fray, giving notice that he would present *Lohengrin* at the Éden-Théâtre. A Franco-German dispute known as the Schnaebelé Affair intensified the inevitable bout of negative publicity, which included a broadsheet called *L'Anti-Wagner*, subtitled *Wagner pédéraste*.

On opening night at the Éden, hundreds of protesters gathered outside the theater to taunt the audience as it arrived. "La Marseillaise" was sung; whistles were blown; a brick crashed through a window; cries of "*À bas Wagner*," "*À bas la Prusse*," and "*Vive la France*" went up. A young blond man who dared to shout "*À bas la France*" was pursued by an angry crowd, though the police prevented outright violence. Further performances were canceled. Politics was invading everything, Mallarmé wrote—"so much so that even I am talking about it."

Shortly after the *Lohengrin* riot, three leading French artists—Pierre-Auguste Renoir, Claude Monet, and Auguste Rodin—attended a banquet in honor of the indomitable Lamoureux. "Your name cannot be missing from this celebration of independent art," Octave Mirbeau wrote to Rodin in advance. The artists, like the writers, shared an enemy with Wagner:

Wagner by Renoir, 1882

conservative, patriotic, "official" France. Anti-Wagnerism was the sign of a backward mind. Gustave Flaubert indicated as much in his sardonic *Dictionary of Received Ideas*, which illustrated the philistine mentality: "Snicker when you hear his name and make jokes about the music of the future." The people who whistled at *Tannhäuser* in 1861 probably also snickered at Manet's *Déjeuner sur l'herbe* and *Olympia*. When, four years later, Champfleury came upon a group of irate bourgeois at the *Olympia* exhibition, he pranked them by exclaiming, "It's Wagner's nephew!" And when Manet complained about the abuse he was receiving, Baudelaire reminded him that Wagner had endured the same.

Therese Dolan's book *Manet, Wagner, and the Musical Culture of Their Time* explores the possible subtext of Manet's 1862 painting *Music in the Tuileries*, which shows a distinguished crowd in the Tuileries Garden, listening to music of unseen origin. On the left-hand side are Baudelaire, Champfleury, Théophile Gautier, and Fantin-Latour, all vocal Wagnéristes. Offenbach, satirist of the "music of the future," is on the right. Faces are occluded in shadow, becoming like masks, and human figures toward the back are almost indistinguishable from trees and vegetation. Dolan surmises that Manet's turn toward abstraction in this canvas was partly a response to the radical sensibility that Baudelaire detected in Wagner and displayed in his own work. Unsurprisingly, *Music in the Tuileries* stirred up the same kind of vituperation that had greeted *Tannhäuser* the previous year. Wagner's music is unlikely to be playing in this placid outdoor setting, yet a certain edginess in the composition makes one wonder. The Wagnéristes, somber and watchful, look ready for a fight.

Partisans of Impressionist and Post-Impressionist painting often used Wagner as a reference point. The poet Jules Laforgue likened the "thousand little dancing strokes" of Monet and Pissarro to "a symphony which is living and changing like the 'forest-voices' of Wagner's theories, competing vitally for the great voice of the forest." The composer himself had conservative taste in the visual arts, and late in life he scoffed at Impressionists who "paint nocturne-symphonies in ten minutes." Nonetheless, in 1882 he consented to sit for a portrait by Renoir—a pallid, ghostlike image, very unlike the stern patriarch seen in German painting. The session took place in Palermo, immediately after the completion of the score of *Parsifal*.

The first avowed Wagnerian among French painters was Henri Fantin-Latour, who won fame for his lustrous still lifes but harbored higher ambitions. Having fallen for the composer even before the Théâtre-Italien concerts of 1860, Fantin spent decades trying to capture the music dramas on canvas and paper. His first efforts depicted the Venusberg: a nude goddess drapes herself over a dour, black-clad Tannhäuser while nymphs gyrate in an almost Monet-like blaze of sunlight. After a visit to Bayreuth in 1876, Fantin set about evoking the *Ring* in various media—at least forty works in all. In the pastel *Les Filles du Rhin*, later redone in oils, the Rhinemaidens are at play in the primeval waters, sunlight filtering down and irradiating their bodies. In *Scène finale de la Walkyrie*, an indistinct, shrouded Wotan towers over a ridge of fire. The art historian Corrinne Chong relates Fantin's "aesthetic of vagueness" to the phantasmagoria of diffused sound and onstage steam that the painter witnessed at Bayreuth.

Cézanne's Wagnerism crested during his "Romantic period" of the sixties, when themes of murder, rape, and decadent coupling preoccupied him. The German musician Heinrich Morstatt, a friend in Marseille, stoked the painter's interest. "You will make our acoustic nerve vibrate with the noble tones of Richard Wagner," Cézanne wrote to Morstatt in 1865. Cézanne's 1868–69 painting *Young Girl at the Piano*, which now hangs in the Hermitage, was originally known as *Overture to "Tannhäuser."* It shows a young woman playing a parlor instrument while an older woman, perhaps her mother, sews reflectively. The picture is outwardly composed and restrained, seemingly at odds with its Wagnerian source. A previous version, now lost, was evidently wilder in style. A friend of Cézanne's spoke of the painting's "overwhelming power" and said that it was "as much about the future as Wagner's music." Scholars and critics have debated this apparent retreat on Cézanne's part. André Dombrowski argues that the painter was commenting on the domestication of music, its reduction to a leisurely pastime on the level of embroidery. Mary Tompkins Lewis sees a residual theatrical heat in the twisting patterns of the wallpaper. Indeed, tonal lurches in the composition give a sense of strong emotions beneath the surface.

If Lewis is right, the Venusberg informs two other Cézanne works from around 1870: *Baigneuses*, an early try at a favorite scene of women bathing; and *Pastorale* (*Idylle*), another tableau of nude female figures by the water. Both paintings are gloomy, obscure, drenched in nocturnal blue. In the first, Lewis sees a near-abstract impression of the Venus grotto, modeled on Fantin-Latour: vertical shapes on the left-hand side could be stalactites. In *Pastorale*, Lewis discerns Tannhäuser dressed in black, reclining in "melancholic reverie." What is arresting about *Pastorale* is that Cézanne introduces two other males, both facing away from the viewer. All three men are fully clothed, as in Manet's *Déjeuner sur l'herbe*. They seem almost indifferent to the female nudity around them. It's as if spectators at a *Tannhäuser* performance have wandered into the mythological orgy, in a posture of jaded arousal.

Where Cézanne reacted to Wagner in muted hues, Vincent van Gogh, a Dutchman who reached his vertiginous zenith in France, associated the composer with explosions of color. In Arles, van Gogh spoke about the resonance he felt between "our color" and Wagner's ripe chords: "By intensifying *all* the colors one again achieves calm and harmony. And something happens as with the Wagner music which, performed by a large orchestra, is no less intimate for that." Van Gogh had heard Wagner performed in Paris and had studied a compilation of his writings. These encounters left the painter with the sense that music had pulled ahead of the other arts. To Gauguin he wrote: "Ah! my dear friend, to make of painting what the music of Berlioz and Wagner has been before us . . . an art of consolation for broken hearts! There are as yet only a few who feel it as you and I do!!!" And to his brother Theo: "What an artist—one like that in painting, now that would be chic. *This will come.*" The brazen yellows of *Sunflowers* and the inundating blues of *Starry Night* proclaim the arrival of just such an art.

For Gauguin, finally, Wagner stood as a paragon of artistic conviction—an empowering example for the artist's quest for pure worlds beyond the reach of civilization and commerce. In 1889–90, Gauguin spent time in the Breton village of Le Pouldu, in the company of Paul Sérusier and Jacob Meyer de Haan. The group decorated their inn with pictures and slogans, ranging in theme from the earthy-folkish to the philosophical-mystical. On one wall, beneath de Haan and Gauguin's frescoes of Breton women scutching flax, Sérusier inscribed a quotation from Wagner, in emerald-green paint: "I believe in a last judgment where all who have dared to profit in this world from sublime and chaste art, all who have soiled and degraded it with the baseness of their sentiments, with their vile greed for material pleasures, will be condemned to terrible suffering." The same passage, an inexact citation of Wagner's 1841 story "An End in Paris," appears in a document known as "*le texte Wagner de Gauguin.*" As for Wagnerian motifs in Gauguin's work, hard evidence is lacking, but art historians have compared his ondines to the Rhinemaidens, the female nude of *The Loss of Virginity* to Brünnhilde on her rock, and the *Flageolet Player on the Cliff* to the shepherd's song in *Tristan.*

By century's end, genuflections toward Wagner were routine among French painters. Georges Seurat is said to have chosen wider, darker frames for his canvases in imitation of the dramatic blackouts at Bayreuth. The teen-aged Paul Signac painted the names "Manet—Zola—Wagner" on the prow of a canoe that he paddled in the Seine. Maurice Denis compared the color contrasts of the *Mona Lisa* to the instrumental effects of the *Tannhäuser* overture. Circa 1900, the scandal around Wagner in France had subsided, but the composer's triumph over opposition did not diminish his legend. Instead, his unstoppable march from the fringe to the center served as the greatest extant demonstration of a successful avant-garde—the victory for which even the most anticommercial artists yearned.

REVUE WAGNÉRIENNE

By 1885, a new phalanx of writers occupied the front lines of French literature. Verlaine and Mallarmé were its leaders, and at least a dozen young poets filled out its ranks. Paris had seen successive waves of romanticism, Parnassianism, and naturalism; this latest vanguard, which had allies in the visual arts and the theater, touched upon uncanny images, spectral apparitions, the world of dreams, clusters of words so dense that they resisted understanding. The poets of the eighties reacted against the naturalist claim to be showing the world as it is, and, more widely, to materialist and evolutionary understandings of the human condition. Here, behind the veil of reality, was the hidden truth of existence, at the edge of the sayable. The unavoidable question arose of what the new movement should be called. One possible term was "decadence," which Bourget codified in 1881, with his theory of the disintegration of language. Two years later, Verlaine published his poem "Langueur," which begins with the line "I am the Empire at the end of the decadence." This usage reached unashamedly for decadence in the old, disreputable sense—excess amid collapse.

For that very reason, though, many young poets rejected the label. In 1885, Jean Moréas replied to an unflattering essay on "decadent poets" by repudiating bohemianism in the Baudelaire-Verlaine vein, preaching instead a devotion to "the pure Concept and the eternal Symbol." In passing, Moréas proposed the word "symbolist." In a subsequent manifesto, he expanded on the term, explaining that the new poetry obeyed an evolutionary logic while revealing "esoteric affinities with primordial Ideas."

That same year, patrons of the Concerts Lamoureux were offered copies of a new magazine called the *Revue wagnérienne*. It was the brainchild of Édouard Dujardin, the twenty-three-year-old son of a sea captain who supported his literary endeavors with a stipend from his parents. Dujardin also worked out a system for winning at the racetrack, which boosted his coffers until he tried to break the bank at Monte Carlo. Dandyish and bemonocled, Dujardin wore a red vest embroidered with tiny swans, in honor of *Lohengrin*. He caught the Wagner virus in May 1882, when he heard the *Ring* in London. That summer, he went to Bayreuth for the premiere of *Parsifal*, and at the following year's festival he greeted French arrivals at the railway station by blowing discordantly on a horn in what he believed to be a Siegfried manner.

In Wagnerian circles in Paris, Dujardin fell in with two other young men who shared his musical and literary passions. One was Téodor de Wyzewa, a Polish émigré critic with a yen for Villiers, Mallarmé, and Jules Laforgue. The other was Houston Stewart Chamberlain, an expatriate Englishman who would eventually marry into the Wagner family and become Bayreuth's resident racist philosopher. In the early eighties, Chamberlain was more liberal in his opinions, and avidly read the latest French literature. A Wagnerite from the late seventies onward, he, too, had attended the first performances of *Parsifal*. Several times he hovered in the Meister's vicinity, too overawed to speak to him. Together, Dujardin, Wyzewa, and Chamberlain decided to found a Wagnerian journal, dedicated not only to the music itself but to the increasingly large number of artists who took it as a model.

At first, the *Revue* looked to be an offshoot of the *Bayreuther Blätter*, the house periodical at Bayreuth. It offered translations of Wagner's writings, analyses of the operas, schedules of performances, and other tidbits. Then, in the third issue, the *Revue* took an unusual turn, with the publication of a prose poem about the *Tannhäuser* overture. This was the work of Joris-Karl Huysmans, who had already written provocatively about Wagner in his popular and scandalous novel *À rebours* (*Against the Grain*). Des Esseintes, that book's protagonist, bemoans the vulgarity of concerts like the Pasdeloup series, where a "man with the aspect of a carpenter beats a sauce in the air and massacres disconnected episodes of Wagner, to the immense delight of an ignorant crowd!" The music is better enjoyed at home, where the mind can roam free. In his *Tannhäuser* piece for the *Revue*, Huysmans focuses on the Venusberg music and its "screams of uncontained desires, cries of strident lecheries, impulses from the carnal beyond." Venus is "the incarnation of the Spirit of Evil, the effigy of omnipotent Lust, the image of the irresistible and magnificent Sataness."

Dujardin's essay "The Theoretical Works of Richard Wagner," which also appeared in the *Revue*'s third issue, ponders the composer's capacity to disclose deep, hidden truths through the medium of art. Renouncing false realism, the poet-artist will "transport men into the ideal and real realm of the Unity." Here was the transubstantiation that so many Symbolists sought. The difference was that, unlike Wagner, they felt little need to reach a wide audience or to speak in a readily accessible way. In the words of Edmund Wilson: "The symbols of the Symbolist school are usually chosen arbitrarily by the poet to stand for special ideas of his own."

Wyzewa contributed a series of visionary essays that tracked Wagnerism in different artistic fields. In an article on literature, the critic writes that "art re-creates life by way of Signs," although one must detach these signs from conventional referents in order to grasp the perpetual flux of emotion. This agenda sounds Nietzschean, and, indeed, Wyzewa helped to introduce French readers to the philosopher. Wagner and his fellow composers have captured that flux in sound; other arts are striving for the same effect. Wyzewa imagines a new kind of novel that would dive into a single consciousness, duplicating the ebb and flow of thought and feeling. In the visual arts, Wagnerism figures not only among the realists but also among adherents of the "Poetry of painting," who combine "contours and nuances in pure fantasy." Recent works by Gustave Moreau, Odilon Redon, and Edgar Degas qualify as "Wagnerian deeds." In the post-Wagnerian music of the future, scores would be read rather than played.

The final issue of the *Revue*'s first year featured a sequence of eight sonnets, under the heading "Hommage à Wagner." The poets were Verlaine, Mallarmé, Wyzewa, Dujardin, René Ghil, Stuart Merrill, Charles Morice, and Charles Vignier. Except for the first two, they were in their early or mid-twenties—foot soldiers of Symbolism. The work is mostly of the second rank, but it colorfully exhibits the symptoms of Wagnérisme as it spread through the Third Republic. Merrill pictures a cavalcade of heroes—Lohengrin, Tannhäuser, and Parsifal the Chaste—in gold armor under purple banners. (Merrill, an American based in Paris, planned a cycle of twenty-two Wagner sonnets, of which he completed only four.) Ghil renders music as a tender virgin set upon by a virile composer. Morice associates Wagner with fiery hordes and bloody tumult. Wyzewa dips into the domain of sleep and waking dreams. Dujardin bows before a Magus, a "Blasphemer of the Ordinary," who unveils the "other universe" beyond the quotidian.

The Symbolists gave much thought to the innate musicality of the raw materials of language. In 1886, Ghil, who was once so thunderstruck by a Lamoureux Wagner concert that he aimlessly wandered the streets of Paris after midnight, produced *Treatise of the Word*, which, to quote Joseph Acquisto, attempts to establish "scientific correspondences among vowels, consonants, colors, orchestral instruments, and emotions." Undoubtedly inspired by Arthur Rimbaud's 1883 poem "Vowels," Ghil devises the following arrangement:

A, black; E, white; I, blue; O, red; U, yellow

A, organs; E, harps; I, violins; O, brass; U, flutes

In a section on Wagner, Ghil pledges that the new musical poet can meet the Meister's challenge: "In the Brass, the Woodwinds, the Strings that ravish him, through the close and subtle relationships of Colors, Timbres, and Vowels, he will seek the least poorly concordant Speech, in words sounding as notes." (Wagnéristes had a tendency toward Germanic capitalization.) According to Francis Vielé-Griffin, another American-born poet who joined this circle, one group of Symbolists was known as the "Symbolistes-Instrumentistes." Seeking to become more musical, they got hold of a harmonium and hoisted it up to the apartment where they gathered. Unfortunately, it turned out that no one knew how to play the instrument, and so "the organ remained perpetually mute, reinforcing by the solitary solemnity of its presence an atmosphere already rather thick with verbal lyricism."

Dujardin, in a poetic cycle titled *Litanies*, went as far as to supply a notated musical realization. Stilted in compositional terms, *Litanies* is of greater significance in French literary history. The stately metrical structures of classical poetry are giving way to *vers libre*, or free verse. Dujardin later testified that Wagner impelled his first thoughts in this direction: "Because the musical phrase had won freedom of rhythm, it was necessary to win an analogous rhythmic freedom for verse." The composer's librettos are already a kind of free verse, liberated from the tight rhyme schemes that had governed most opera before him. In collaboration with Chamberlain, Dujardin concocted a "literal" translation of the opening scene of *Rheingold*. It begins: "*Weia! Waga! vogue, ô la vague, vibre en la vive!*" The language of *Litanies* is nearly the same: "*Les voiles voguent sur les vagues*" ("Sails waft over the waves"). As Vielé-Griffin concluded, "music made symbolist expression possible."

Even bolder is Dujardin's 1887 novel *Les Lauriers sont coupés* (*The Laurels Are Cut Down*), which answered Wyzewa's call for a new kind of Wagnerian fiction, one that would record a single character's ideas, perceptions, and emotions over a short period. *Les Lauriers*—the title comes from an old French children's song, "*Nous n'irons plus au bois*"—describes the inner life of a dandy wandering about Paris one evening. Passages of insistent repetition bring to mind the heaving texture of the *Tristan* prelude:

> The candles on the mantelpiece are lit; here's the white bed, soft, the carpets; I lean against the open window; outside, behind me, I feel the night; black, cold, sad, sinister night; the dark where appearances change; the silence where sands murmur; the tall trees packed black together; the bare walls; and the windows dim with the unknown, and the windows lighted, unknown; in the pallor of the sky, this vibration of the weeping eyes of the stars; the secret of opaque, mysterious shadows, mixed into something fearsome; there, some unknown, fearsome thing . . . I shudder; quickly, I turn round, grip the window, I push it to, I close it, quickly . . . Nothing . . . The window's closed . . . And the curtains? I draw them to, like this . . . Night is abolished.

Dujardin explained his method in a later essay titled "The Interior Monologue." Just as Wagner's music consists of a succession of motifs that suggest psychological states, the interior monologue is a "succession of short sentences, each of which also expresses a movement of the soul, the similarity being that they are related to each other not according to a rational order but according to a purely emotional order, outside of any intellectualized arrangement." At the time, this idea had few imitators, but its moment would arrive in the next century: James Joyce cited *Les Lauriers* as a precedent for *Ulysses*.

VERLAINE AND MALLARMÉ

Mallarmé by Manet

Experiments in endless melody and *vers libre* aside, the most striking tributes in the *Revue wagnérienne* were in sonnet form. Verlaine's "Parsifal" and Mallarmé's "Hommage" both appeared in the "Hommage à Wagner" issue of January 1886. Each poem heralded a distinct new strain of Wagnerism. Verlaine hosted a Wagnerism of the Decadence, spiked with illicit sexuality. Mallarmé augured a modernist Wagner, esoteric and abstract. Such work disconcerted the more conventional-minded supporters of the *Revue wagnérienne*. The magazine's split identity—part fan publication, part avant-garde periodical—proved untenable, and Dujardin shut it down after the third year.

Dujardin had difficulty extracting a sonnet from Verlaine, who was living in squalid conditions in a small room behind a wine shop. The poet had recently served his second prison term, after threatening to strangle his mother; the first was for shooting Rimbaud. (Almost alone among French writers of the period, Rimbaud was indifferent to Wagner. An obscene drawing in one of his letters, showing a man labeled "Wagner" with a bottle of Riesling inserted into his rectum, has been identified as a reference not to the composer but to an unpopular landlord.) The Irish novelist George Moore, who accompanied Dujardin when the editor went to collect Verlaine's poem, recalled that a young man "with a face so rosy that he reminded me of a butcher-boy" opened the door. The sonnet was handed over, but Moore doubted whether it could be published, because of its eyebrow-raising variation on the theme of Parsifal's threatened chastity.

Although the syntax is equivocal, the boy savior seems tempted not only by Kundry and the Flower Maidens but also by a fellow young male.

> Parsifal has conquered the Maidens, their pretty
> Babble and amusing lust, and his inclination
> Toward the Flesh of virgin boy who is enticed
> To love light breasts and pretty babble;
> He has conquered the beautiful Woman of subtle heart,
> Spreading fresh arms and arousing throat;
> Having conquered Hell, he returns to his tent
> With a heavy trophy on his boyish arm—
> The lance that pierced the Flank supreme!
> He has healed the king, is king himself,
> Priest of the most holy essential treasure.
> In robes of gold, he worships, as glory and symbol,
> The pure vessel where the True Blood shines.
> —And, O those children's voices singing in the dome!

The sonnet wavers between sincere religiosity—Verlaine gestured toward Catholicism in his last years—and unrepentant sensualism. The final line, with its slightly too excited intake of breath, has a campy ring. The poem looks ahead to a turn of the century homoerotic culture in which Wagner's works become an emblem of outlaw desire.

Mallarmé, whom Verlaine generously celebrated in his 1884 anthology *Les Poètes maudits*, remade Wagner in his own image: opulent, intricate, ambiguous. This most recondite of nineteenth-century poets took pride in the drabness of his lineage, describing himself as the scion of an "uninterrupted series of functionaries in the Administration and the Registry." Born in Paris in 1842, Mallarmé lost his mother and sister early. He had the feeling of being an orphan, of having come from nowhere. By the time he was twenty, he had decided upon a literary career. He took jobs teaching English in the provinces, and in his spare time worked on his early masterpieces, "Hérodiade" and "The Afternoon of a Faun." Having dabbled in Romantic and Parnassian moods, he found his own strict and strange style. "I am inventing a language," he wrote in 1864, "which must necessarily spring from an entirely new poetics, which I could define in these few words: *Paint not the thing but the effect it produces* . . . All words must efface themselves before the sensation."

Like van Gogh, Mallarmé felt that music had moved ahead of other art forms. Poets, like painters, must catch up. In an 1862 essay insincerely titled "Art for All," Mallarmé begins with a famous proposition—"Everything that is sacred and wishes to remain sacred envelops itself in mystery"—and praises the art of music for holding fast to its secrets. "If we casually open up Mozart, Beethoven, or Wagner and throw an indifferent eye on the first page of their work, we are gripped with a religious astonishment at the sight of these macabre processions of severe, chaste, and unknown signs." Poetry is lacking in such mystery; Mallarmé will restore it. All this harks back to Wagner's theorizing on the untapped potential of musical drama.

The young Mallarmé had few opportunities to hear Wagner's music live, but he surely encountered it in the salons. Heath Lees, in his book *Mallarmé and Wagner*, has found traces of the composer in early poems like "Sainte" and "Hérodiade." Villiers, whom Mallarmé revered, stimulated a deeper interest. When Villiers and Mendès came to stay with the poet in 1870, after their visit to Tribschen, they were undoubtedly full of talk of the "palmiped of Lucerne." Still, Wagnerism remained dormant in Mallarmé's work for some time. Indeed, Mallarmé was somewhat dormant himself; for fifteen years, he published almost nothing. The explosion of so-called decadent or Symbolist art in the mid-eighties revived him. After Verlaine and Huysmans paid tribute, Mallarmé found himself with a bevy of young acolytes. Among them were Dujardin and Wyzewa, of the *Revue wagnérienne*.

In April 1885, Dujardin took Mallarmé to an all-Wagner event at the Concerts Lamoureux, which included the *Tannhäuser* overture, Siegfried's Funeral Music, and the preludes to *Tristan* and *Parsifal*. Mallarmé was riveted by music and audience alike. The word "*foule*," "crowd," occurs often in his writing on Wagner, and it is never entirely free of the shudder of horror that Huysmans's Des Esseintes feels when he visits the Concerts Populaires. From then on, though, Mallarmé seldom missed a Lamoureux event. Even in high summer he would greet his younger followers at the gate in formal attire, an impeccable top hat on his head. He would take notes as he listened, perhaps with ideas for poems hatching in his mind. Paul Valéry, one of the adepts, said that Mallarmé "left the concerts full of sublime jealousy."

Dujardin asked Mallarmé to write for the *Revue*. The result was "Richard Wagner, Reverie of a French Poet," which appeared in August 1885. "Nothing has ever seemed so difficult to me," Mallarmé wrote to Dujardin, very much in the style of a harried working writer. "Just think, I am sick, I am more than ever a slave. I have never seen anything of Wagner's, and I want to create something original and precise, something which is not beside the point. I need more time. I will work on nothing else, you have my word, until this is done."

Mallarmé begins with praise for Wagner's renovation of decrepit theatrical traditions. Music "penetrates and envelops the Drama through its dazzling will." Characters become manifest in the medium of sound: we encounter "a god dressed in the invisible folds of a fabric of chords," we experience the "wave of Passion" that comes pouring through a single hero, so that "Legend is enthroned in the footlights." But Wagner stops short of the true origin of poetic mystery: "Everything refreshes itself in the primitive stream: not to the source." The inhibiting factor is myth, which supposedly speaks to people of many traditions but in fact falls prey to parochialism. The exacting French mind cannot accept it. We need a new universal fable, "virgin of everything, place, time and known characters," starring a hero with no name. "Everything moves toward some supreme bolt of light, from which awakens the Figure that None is, whose rhythm, taken from the symphony, comes from the mimicking of each musical attitude, and like them it!" Mallarmé envisions a poetry that imitates music, surpasses it, and stages in the theater of the mind the higher drama that Wagner sought in vain.

The "Reverie" ends with a semi-ironic fanfare to the "Genius" and a jibe at the Wagnerites who crowd the pages of the journal in which Mallarmé is writing. "O Wagner," Mallarmé writes, "I suffer and reproach myself, in minutes marked by lassitude, for not numbering myself among those who, bored with everything in order to find definitive salvation, go straight to the edifice of your Art, for them the end of the road." In fact, this crowded temple is only halfway up the slope of a holy mountain, at the top of which is the "menacing summit of the absolute." Mallarmé pictures himself pausing at the Meister's shrine, "drinking from your convivial fountain," and gazing up at that cold peak, which no one seems prepared to scale. "No one!" Mallarmé says again. The reader is left to imagine that a solitary climber, having stocked up at the Wagnerian base camp, is set to perform the impossible feat.

The following January, Mallarmé's "Hommage," also known as "Hommage à Wagner," appeared next to Verlaine's sonnet in the *Revue*. Needless to say, the poem is free of misty word-pictures of swan knights and Valkyries. Mallarmé claimed that it was an admission of defeat—"the melancholy of a poet who sees the old poetic front collapse, and the luxury of words grow pale, before the rising of the sun of contemporary Music of which Wagner is the latest god." This faux-pessimism masks an exercise of poetic might. Ensconced in sonnet form, poetic language wraps itself in a new kind of sacred mystery.

> *Le silence déjà funèbre d'une moire*
> *Dispose plus qu'un pli seul sur le mobilier*
> *Que doit un tassement du principal pilier*
> *Précipiter avec le manque de mémoire.*
> *Notre si vieil ébat triomphal du grimoire,*
> *Hiéroglyphes dont s'exalte le millier*
> *À propager de l'aile un frisson familier!*
> *Enfouissez-le moi plutôt dans une armoire.*
> *Du souriant fracas originel haï*
> *Entre elles de clartés maîtresses a jailli*
> *Jusque vers un parvis né pour leur simulacre,*
> *Trompettes tout haut d'or pâmé sur les vélins,*
> *Le dieu Richard Wagner irradiant un sacre*
> *Mal tû par l'encre même en sanglots sibyllins.*

The already funereal silence of a cloth
Places more than a single fold on the furniture,
Which the settling of the central pillar
Must drag down with default of memory.
Our old triumphal revels of the spellbook,
Hieroglyphs exalted by the millions
To spread a familiar shiver of the wing!
Bury it for me in a cupboard.
Out of the original smiling fracas hated
Among the master clarities there has sprung
Up to the square born for their simulation
Gold trumpets swooning aloud on vellum,

The god Richard Wagner, irradiating a rite
Scarcely silenced by the ink itself in sibylline sobs.

The poem defies explication, never mind translation. Some readers, like Wyzewa, took it as a eulogy, seeing the funereal furniture of the first quatrain as a metaphor for a spent literary art and Wagner as a "sovereign of the Scene" who brings renewal. Since the composer had died not long before, he may also be present in the opening lines: he, too, could be a dusty book of spells. Louis Marvick sees the entire sonnet as a critique, those golden trumpets representing the "stridency of Wagner's music."

The meaning of almost every line or phrase is up for grabs. Consider *"Du souriant fracas originel haï."* What is this fracas? Who hates it? Robert Greer Cohn identifies it as the ancient art of "pure Beauty," abhorred by the false artists of the marketplace. Heath Lees relates it to the Wagner scandals of 1860 and 1861. For Gardner Davies, the fracas is the squiggle of musical notation; for Bertrand Marchal, it is the original force of primitive art. Several commentators believe that the final lines suggest some festive Bayreuth scene. Mallarmé never visited the Festspielhaus, but he probably knew of the ritual that summons the audience back to their seats toward the end of each Bayreuth intermission: brass players assemble on the front balcony and intone motifs from the opera of the day. Interpreters more or less agree that the last line pivots toward the musical literature or literary music of Mallarmé's dreams. That art exists in the form of ink, but it is not truly silent (*mal tû*); its music speaks in "sibylline sobs."

To seek a conclusive meaning, though, is to miss the point. Joseph Acquisto remarks that Mallarmé's work "marks the rebirth of poetic language in a performative mode . . . The poem is re-created each time it is read aloud." At the end of his life, Mallarmé took this indeterminate aesthetic even further in his free-form graphic poem *Un coup de dés jamais n'abolira le hasard* ("A roll of the dice will never eliminate chance"). A text of some seven hundred words is scattered across eleven double pages, in staggered lines and in fonts of varying sizes, often with independent sentences juxtaposed. The layout has the look of musical notation, with voices rising and falling amid expectant silences. Mallarmé invokes Wagner in his introductory note: "A sort of general *leitmotiv* that unfolds itself constitutes the unity of the poem: accessory motifs have gathered around it."

But the performance is a private one, taking place on the inner stage of the reader's mind. The Cirque d'Hiver is obsolete.

For all their inscrutability, Mallarmé's writings on Wagner are clear-eyed and judicious. In many ways, the poet is dealing with the same ambivalence that tormented Nietzsche, but he spares himself the oscillations between adulation and disgust. As Lacoue-Labarthe writes, he is "critical, in some sense, but in no way hostile." The tone is "reserved. Measured, even. And thus, again, admiring." When Mallarmé died, a book about Beethoven and Wagner was found on his bedside table.

3

SWAN KNIGHT

Victorian Britain and Gilded Age America

The wedding of Princess Victoria and Prince Friedrich Wilhelm, 1858

I n the past century and a half, countless millions of women have walked down the wedding aisle to the accompaniment of the Bridal Chorus from *Lohengrin*, also known as "Here Comes the Bride." The custom is a little strange, because in its original context the music is a prelude to catastrophe. Marriages in Wagner's world tend to go badly, and the one in *Lohengrin* is no exception. Elsa of Brabant is engaged to a knight from a faraway land, but the groom has imposed a stifling condition: "You must not ever ask me / Nor should you care to know / Whence I made my way / Nor my name and kind." The wedding, with its indelible lilting tune, takes place at the beginning of Act III. Afterward, Elsa cannot refrain from posing the forbidden question. Lohengrin reveals himself to be a Knight of the Holy Grail—the son of Parsifal, no less. Because his secret is out, he must return to the Grail Temple. Before departing, he undoes the evil magic performed by the pagan witch Ortrud, who has trapped Elsa's young brother in the body of a swan. Despite that happy event, Elsa is too bereft to live, and expires.

By the end of the nineteenth century, the Bridal Chorus had become a fixture of the marital ritual around the world. In 1894, the *Nebraska State Journal* carried this account of the wedding of Miss Nell Cochrane and Mr. Frank Woods, in the city of Lincoln:

> At half past six there was a little pause, and then came the first stirring notes of that perfect wedding march of *Lohengrin*. Twenty girls of the Delta Gamma fraternity entered, marching down the left aisle, carrying ropes of smilax and bunches of loose roses, singing the words of the wedding march. Dr. Lasby took his place under the palms before the chancel. The twenty girls came slowly forward and ranged themselves on either side of him. Next came Miss Daisy Cochrane, the maid of honor, dressed in white silk and carrying a bouquet of pink roses. Last came the bride herself, in white ottoman silk, her veil drawn back from her face, carrying bride roses. She came slowly down the aisle, with perfect repose, seeming scarcely to move, but rather to be borne onward by the triumphant tenderness of Wagner that surged from the organ.

The author of this item, a precocious University of Nebraska student named Willa Cather, added a more idiosyncratic perspective in her column the following day: "If people are going to be foolish enough to be married they might as well do it with a glare of torches and a blaze of trumpets, and have a church wedding and give the community the benefit of it. Then they can have Wagner's wedding march on the organ, and it's worth getting married to have that."

The British royal family, arbiters of wedding fashion across the ages, promoted the Bridal Chorus as a marriage anthem. In 1840, Queen Victoria, of the House of Hanover, wed Prince Albert, of Saxe-Coburg and Gotha. The prince loved German music and showed skill as an organist and a composer. The young queen assimilated Albert's taste, and in June 1855 the couple attended one in a series of concerts that Wagner conducted in London, at the invitation of the Philharmonic Society. The program included, by royal request, the *Tannhäuser* overture. "A wonderful composition, quite overpowering, so grand, & in parts wild, striking and descriptive," Victoria wrote in her diary. She received Wagner and found him "very quiet"—possibly the only time he ever made that impression. They spoke about the composer's dog and parrot. In letters home, Wagner reported that the queen was "very small and not at all pretty, with, I am sorry to say, a rather red nose, but there is something uncommonly friendly and confiding about her." Victoria's willingness to associate with a "politically disreputable person wanted for high treason"—Wagner's self-characterization—flattered him deeply.

Three years later, Princess Victoria, the queen's eldest child, wed Prince Friedrich Wilhelm of Prussia, who, in 1888, would briefly reign as Friedrich III, emperor of Germany. A festive concert after the ceremony featured the wedding scene from *Lohengrin*, with a new text for the blessing of the couple: "O ne'er may England's Princess / One hour of sorrow know; / For her may life's rude billows / With gentle current flow." (The lyricist was Thomas Oliphant, best known for the Christmas carol "Deck the Hall with Boughs of Holly.") Music by Meyerbeer and Mendelssohn followed. It is a historical curiosity that the British royals chose to pair Wagner with the two Jewish composers whom he insults in "Jewishness in Music."

Der Meister and Her Majesty met one other time. In 1877, Wagner returned to London for an extended festival of his music, by which time he had become a regal figure in his own right. At the concerts, he sometimes sat in an armchair, facing the audience, while Hans Richter conducted. Victoria wrote in her journal: "After luncheon the great composer Wagner, about whom the people in Germany are really a little mad, was brought into the corridor by Mr. Cusins. I had seen him with dearest Albert in '55, when he directed at the Philharmonic Concert. He has grown old and stout, and has a clever, but not pleasing countenance. He was profuse in expressions of gratitude, and I expressed my regret at having been unable to be present at one of his concerts." If Victoria now looked askance at Wagner, missives from her daughter in Germany may have influenced her. An 1869 letter from the princess reads: "If you want to read anything *perfectly cracked* you should see Richard Wagner's new pamphlet called 'Jewish Influence in Music.' I never read anything so violent, conceited or unfair."

By the end of the century, memories of Victoria's interest in the composer had faded. An 1897 book titled *The Private Life of the Queen* asserted that "Wagner has found little or no favour in her eyes." But anonymous attendants were not privy to all areas of her spirit. When, in 1889, the singers Jean de Reszke and Emma Albani privately performed an excerpt from *Lohengrin* for the queen, she wrote in her diary: "Beyond anything beautiful, so dramatic . . . The music lasted till four, and I could have listened to it much longer. It was indeed a treat."

The incorporation of *Lohengrin* into the royal wedding protocol exposes a gap between French- and English-speaking responses to Wagner. In France, he was a scandal, an incitement, a field of battle. In Britain and the United States, he was a somewhat tamer product—a "treat," in Victoria's graciously belittling formulation. From Buckingham Palace to the Nebraska plains, the former fugitive could serve as an adornment of Victorian and Gilded Age society. His operas became mainstays of the Royal Opera House and the Metropolitan Opera; touring productions drew a diverse public. Popular accounts, including a series of Wagner books for young people, portrayed a noble-minded idealist, one whose industriousness exemplified the Gospel of Work. Cultured clergymen like Alfred Gurney wrote of the "salutary, soothing, and elevating influence" of *Parsifal*.

Historians have long insisted that the decorous surfaces of Victorian life masked a more complex social reality. Wagner's mythology appealed to the burgeoning imperialist mind-set on both sides of the Atlantic, where presumptions of cultural superiority—the White Man's Burden, Manifest Destiny—rested on theories of racial supremacy that Wagner helped to promote. The fetishizing of Anglo-Saxon origins overlapped with the veneration of the Germanic. The British Isles had been ruled by monarchs of German descent since the early eighteenth century, and the Hanoverian dynasty fostered a respect for German music, literature, and philosophy. Thomas Carlyle, the advocate of Hero-Worship, touted Goethe, Schiller, and Fichte; Walter Pater read Hegel; Schopenhauer's rise to international prominence began in Britain. In the United States, an influx of German immigrants meant that musical culture acquired a Teutonic profile. At the end of the nineteenth century, American orchestras were largely German-speaking ensembles.

Most of all, Wagner captured the Victorian imagination because of his proximity to the Matter of Britain—the tales of King Arthur, the Knights of the Round Table, and the Holy Grail. In 1816 and 1817, new editions of Thomas Malory's *Le Morte d'Arthur* were published, helping to spark an Arthurian revival. Alfred Tennyson, Matthew Arnold, Algernon Charles Swinburne, and members of the Pre-Raphaelite Brotherhood occupied themselves with Arthur, Merlin, Lancelot, Guinevere, and the lovers Tristram and Iseult, whose story occupies the middle part of Malory's book. The *Ring* shares with Arthurian legend the motif of the embedded sword: as the young king draws a blade from the stone, Siegmund draws Nothung from the tree. The tale of Venus and Tannhäuser especially mesmerized the Pre-Raphaelites, who, like the agonized knight, were forever torn between the sacred and the profane.

Even as evocations of a mythic past served an imperial agenda, the anticapitalist allegory of the *Ring* warned against the industrial modernization that fueled the mid-century might of the British Empire and the gathering strength of the United States. Wagner's own vision of London was nightmarish: "This is Alberich's dream come true—Nibelheim, world dominion, activity, work, everywhere the oppressive feeling of steam and fog." The Pre-Raphaelites spoke of the contemporary cityscape in similar terms, lamenting the demise of older, more spiritually grounded ways of life. The novels of Charles Dickens, George Eliot, and Thomas Hardy registered the transformation of the social fabric wrought by steamships, railways, and the telegraph. For many Victorian listeners, Wagner provided a kind of secular cathedral space in which they could contemplate tensions between an idyllic past and an industrial present.

Far-seeing Victorian thinkers devised new paradigms through which to comprehend large-scale social change. In 1859 and 1860, George Henry Lewes, George Eliot's partner, published his two-volume *Physiology of Common Life*, which posits a "vast and powerful stream of sensation" as the sum total of our sensibility—a "stream of Consciousness." Lewes's work appeared at the same time as two other epochal books written in the area of London: Darwin's *On the Origin of Species*, which shows the determining power of evolutionary processes; and Marx's *A Contribution to the Critique of Political Economy*, which demonstrates how economic conditions control all human affairs. The reasoning intellect is dethroned from its sovereign position. Jacques Barzun, in his 1941 book *Darwin, Marx, Wagner*, noted that *Tristan*, too, was completed in 1859, and that it posed an equally jarring challenge to the sensibilities of the day: romantic love dissolves into a quasi-biological music of sexual desire. Wagner's courtly tragedy thus becomes another treatise of and against the Victorian Age.

GEORGE ELIOT

Circa 1855, when Wagner crashed into the Victorian world, music had pride of place as the supreme medium of moral uplift among the arts. This was a different primacy from the one described by Schopenhauer, who considered music the embodiment of the restlessly striving Will. For the Victorians, music, especially instrumental music and choral singing, soared above the vulgar sphere of popular entertainment, opera included. It was an art "exempt from the trail of the serpent," wrote the art critic Elizabeth Eastlake. Musical events in spaces like the Crystal Palace and the Royal Albert Hall offered a fantasy of a harmonious, spiritually elevated public, free of class strife and political division.

Some effort was required to make Wagner conform to Victorian ideals. The creator of *Tristan* had meager credentials as a teacher of virtue. Early on, his music met intense resistance in Britain. During the 1855 visit, the *Sunday Times* had trouble deciding whether he was a "desperate charlatan" or a "self-deceived enthusiast." J. W. Davison, the lead critic of the *Times* and of the *Musical World*, derided Wagner as the "Mahomed of modern music," as a "priest of Dagon," and, most obscurely, as a "veritable man-mermaid." *Lohengrin* was "poison—*rank poison.*"

Wagner's British reception was further complicated by awareness of his anti-Jewish feelings. Thanks to a maladroit article by a supporter, Ferdinand Praeger, the English-speaking music world had recently learned of Wagner's authorship of "Jewishness in Music," which otherwise received almost no international notice. The pamphlet's critique of Mendelssohn as a somehow stunted talent was a particular affront to British music-lovers, who revered that composer almost as an honorary Englishman. When Mendelssohn's overture *The Hebrides* appeared on one of Wagner's London programs, Davison pointedly called it a "magnificently Jewish inspiration."

Mary Ann Evans, who wrote under the pen name George Eliot, was one of the first major English-speaking figures to take Wagner seriously.

Born in 1819, she had immersed herself in music from an early age, playing the piano and attending concerts. A close student of German literature and philosophy, she published translations of David Strauss's *The Life of Jesus* and Ludwig Feuerbach's *The Essence of Christianity*—Young Hegelian treatises that left a mark on Wagner.

In the summer of 1854, Eliot left England for an eight-month stay in Germany. With her was George Henry Lewes, with whom she had begun a nonmarital relationship, shocking friends back in London. The arrangement raised fewer eyebrows in the circle around Liszt in Weimar, where they spent three months. With Liszt installed as the Kapellmeister for the Grand Duchy of Saxe-Weimar-Eisenach, Weimar had become the de facto center of Wagnerian activity—part of an attempt to restore the exalted status that the city had enjoyed in the age of Goethe and Schiller. Eliot saw performances of *Tannhäuser*, *The Flying Dutchman*, and *Lohengrin*, and heard Liszt expound on Wagner's theories. She summarized her experiences in an unsigned 1855 article titled "Liszt, Wagner, and Weimar," in which she makes reference to the "propaganda of Wagnerism"—one of the first appearances of that word in English.

Music is evolving: this is the main insight that Eliot gains from Wagner. Opera should become an "organic whole, which grows up like a palm, its earliest portion containing the germ and prevision of all the rest." Pre-Darwinian evolutionary thought affected Eliot's aesthetics, as Delia da Sousa Correa observes in *George Eliot, Music, and Victorian Culture*. Lewes and his colleague Herbert Spencer were examining the interaction of evolution, physiology, psychology, and the arts; Spencer held that music, the language of emotion, had grown out of a more objective spoken language. Eliot, who often attended opera performances with Spencer, sees a similar logic at work in Wagner: "It is just possible that melody, as we conceive it, is only a transitory phase of music . . . We are but in 'the morning of the times,' and must learn to think of ourselves as tadpoles unprescient of the future frog."

Eliot endorses Wagner's progressive ideas, but the music itself gives her trouble. Accustomed to clean-cut classical forms, she finds the endlessness of Wagnerian discourse bewildering. The biological metaphor is given a humorous twist: "The tadpole is limited to tadpole pleasures; and so, in our state of development, we are swayed by melody." *Lohengrin* reminds Eliot of "the whistling of the wind through the keyholes of a cathedral, which has a dreamy charm for a little while, but by and bye you long for the sound even of a street organ to rush in and break the monotony."

These reservations aside, Eliot supplies some of the most positive and perceptive commentary that Wagner had yet received in Britain. She rejects any "cheap ridicule" of the composer, respecting his skill in dramatic construction. Of *Tannhäuser*, she writes: "I never saw an opera which had a more interesting succession of well-contrasted effects." The title character, she writes, "has become weary of hectic sensualism," and "longs once more for the free air of the field and forest under the blue arch of heaven." Tannhauser sounds a bit like Will Ladislaw, the hotheaded young artist of *Middlemarch*, who quits Rome for the Midlands.

Eliot's visit to Weimar left subtle traces on the succession of novels that culminated in *Middlemarch* and *Daniel Deronda*. Monumental in scale, these books discard the episodic, panoramic structure that defined many prior efforts in the form. In the "Prelude" to *Middlemarch*—Wagner preferred that term from *Lohengrin* onward, in place of "overture"—Eliot vows to honor women who have "found for themselves no epic life wherein there was a constant unfolding of far-resonant action." She later speaks of the "roar which lies on the other side of silence"—the storm of feeling behind the façades of ordinary lives, especially those of women. Such a project may seem far removed from Wagner, even opposed to him, yet several contemporaries made the connection. In 1876, Charles Halford Hawkins, a master at Winchester College, argued that Wagner's "minute development of tone and character painting" and his extraordinary demands on the audience made him the "George Eliot of music."

In that same year, Eliot published *Daniel Deronda*, her most deliberate bid for the kind of "organic unity" that she valued in Wagner. She later said that she "meant everything in the book to be related to everything else there." As serial installments were published, readers struggled with the sheer scope of the narrative. Henry James captured the debate around the novel—and his own ambivalence—by publishing a review in which three imaginary readers express a range of opinions. For one, the book is "so vast, so much-embracing"; for another, it is "protracted, pretentious, pedantic." This sounds like a group of operagoers quarreling over Wagner—particularly when the skeptic says, "The tone is not English, it is German."

Eliot all but invites Wagner comparisons by including a character named Julius Klesmer, a beret-wearing composer-teacher who preaches the music of the future. When Gwendolen Harleth, the heroine, sings a bel canto aria by Bellini, Klesmer reproves her:

> You sing in tune, and you have a pretty fair organ. But you produce your notes badly; and that music which you sing is beneath you. It is a form of melody which expresses a puerile state of culture—a dandling, canting, seesaw kind of stuff—the passion and thought of people without any breadth of horizon. There is a sort of self-satisfied folly about every phrase of such melody; no cries of deep, mysterious passion—no conflict—no sense of the universal. It makes men small as they listen to it. Sing now something larger.

Klesmer's rhetoric fairly reeks of Wagner, although his cosmopolitan ideas about the "fusion of races" depart from the party line. As one member of James's critical roundtable says: "And you must not forget that you think Herr Klesmer 'Shakespearian.' Wouldn't 'Wagnerian' be high enough praise?" The character paraphrases Eliot's own 1855 exposition of Wagner's theories, with "puerile state of culture" supplanting "tadpole pleasures." And when Klesmer performs a composition of his own, one listener compares it to a "jar of leeches, where you can never tell either beginnings or endings"—exactly the sort of insult that critics routinely lobbed at Wagner. Klesmer may be a satire on German seriousness, but his exhortation to "sing now something larger" reverberates beyond the situation described on the page. It can almost be heard as a challenge from the author's Wagnerian character to the author herself.

Sing something larger she does. *Daniel Deronda* breaks the frame of the domestic novel. Gwendolen's marriage to the icy, controlling Henleigh Grandcourt at first seems to follow the pattern of *Middlemarch*, where Dorothea Brooke is trapped in an unrewarding union and then finds her way to a happier outcome. Then the tone darkens: Grandcourt is a monster from whom Gwendolen sees no escape. "I think we shall go on always, like the Flying Dutchman," she says. During a dismal Italian holiday, Grandcourt drowns, and Gwendolen accuses herself of having deliberately failed to save him. It is like an ironic inversion of the ending of the *Dutchman*, where Senta leaps to her death to save the cursed mariner.

Meanwhile, Deronda discovers that he is Jewish, triggering meditations on race, religion, and identity. Eliot had no patience for antisemitism, and denounced it in an 1878 essay titled "The Modern Hep! Hep! Hep!" To what extent she knew of Wagner's anti-Jewish writings is unknown, but when she wrote of the muddled thinking of "the prejudiced, the puerile, the spiteful, and the abysmally ignorant," she might have had the author of "Jewishness in Music" in mind.

Nicholas Dames, in his study *The Physiology of the Novel*, conjectures that Eliot bound together her "much-embracing" novel with a version of the leitmotif—a technique that she had perceptively described in "Liszt, Wagner, and Weimar." The motifs include phrases from an accusing letter, objects such as a ring and a necklace, and physical tics and gestures. Such recurrences jog the memory of a reader who may be overwhelmed by the novel's extended span. They organize a flow of material that begins to resemble Lewes's "vast and powerful stream of sensation." In the end, Dames says, the reader of *Daniel Deronda* is not so much searching out significant events as "enduring temporality itself." We read the book as we live a life. In this sense, the arch-Victorian Eliot begins to look ahead to literary modernism, which has its own tangled Wagnerian roots.

WAGNER AMONG THE PRE-RAPHAELITES

The London Wagner Festival of 1877 was a grand affair, consisting of eight concerts at the Royal Albert Hall. The plan was to recoup the deficit created by the first Bayreuth Festival. Although receipts fell short of expectations, the visit was otherwise triumphant. According to the young George Bernard Shaw, Wagner met with "tempestuous applause" at each concert, and at one he received a laurel wreath. The Prince of Wales, more Wagnerian than his mother, attended. Young dandies sought to show that they were "well up in Wagnerism." Young women felt the slightly illicit thrill of "The Ride of the Valkyries"—or the "Walkers' Ride," as Mary Gladstone, the prime minister's daughter, called it. The press amused itself. *Punch* declared that after each concert "special trains will run from the Kensington High Street station to Colney Hatch, Hanwell and Earlswood"—lunatic asylums on the outskirts of London.

It helped that Londoners were finally seeing Wagner's operas complete:

The Flying Dutchman in 1870, *Lohengrin* in 1875, *Tannhäuser* in 1876. (All were sung in Italian, the standard operatic language of the day.) The Carl Rosa Opera Company, founded by a widely traveled German-Jewish conductor and impresario, had great success with an English-language *Dutchman*. The public was learning to listen in a new way, as *The Musical Times* advised: "The Teutonic element in the house had a marvellous effect in teaching the audience that 'Lohengrin' was not to be judged by the ordinary standard; so when the usual round of applause was given for the favourite singers on their entrance . . . a very decided 'hush' convinced the astonished Opera *habitués* that the vocalists must be considered as secondary to the work they were interpreting." Even J. W. Davison cut back on his vitriol. In a report from Bayreuth, he admitted that the *Ring* was an "incontestable success."

Two German immigrants had painstakingly prepared for this breakthrough. One was the pianist and teacher Edward Dannreuther, a native of Strasbourg who spent much of his boyhood in Cincinnati, Ohio, where his father ran a short-lived piano business. He came to London in 1863 and began publishing articles in which he criticized the "phantasmagoria" of French and Italian opera and lauded Wagner's Beethovenian breadth. By invoking Beethoven, the composer's supporters catered to the Victorian regard for the improving properties of instrumental music. Wagner, too, occupied an "ideal sphere," following the "loftiest aspirations."

Dannreuther's co-conspirator was Francis Hueffer, born Franz Hütter, who had arrived in England in 1869, at the age of twenty-four. A classmate of Nietzsche's in Leipzig, Hueffer had spoken for Wagner's merits at a time when Nietzsche still had doubts. In London, Hueffer established himself as a Wagnerite music critic, and within a decade he had replaced Davison at the *Times*. Like Dannreuther, Hueffer had a knack for uncovering Victorian virtues in his subject. His 1874 book *Richard Wagner and the Music of the Future* praises the composer for his "unequalled firmness and presence of mind" and for the "middle-class freedom and intelligence" of the character of Hans Sachs. Where Baudelaire, listening to *Lohengrin*, is swept away in abstract ecstasy, Hueffer thinks of angels in white clouds. Sealing Hueffer's naturalization of Wagner is the dedication of his book *Half a Century of Music*: "TO HER MAJESTY THE QUEEN, THE FRIEND OF MENDELSSOHN, AND THE FIRST ENGLISHWOMAN TO RECOGNISE THE GENIUS OF WAGNER."

Both expatriates formed alliances to the artists and writers of the Pre-Raphaelite circle. In 1871, Dannreuther married Chariclea Ionides, daughter of the Greek merchant Alexander Ionides, who hosted salons in his homes and hired the likes of William Morris to decorate them. During his 1877 visit, Wagner was a contented guest at the Dannreuther-Ionides house. Hueffer married Catherine Madox Brown, younger daughter of the Germanically inclined painter Ford Madox Brown. Their son would find literary fame under the name Ford Madox Ford. Dannreuther and Hueffer also knew Swinburne, and composed songs on his poems.

Part of the émigrés' plan for the 1877 festival was to facilitate meetings between the Wagners and Britain's leading artists and writers. To that end, the painter John Everett Millais and his wife, Effie Gray, organized a dinner in the Meister's honor. They were crestfallen when he failed to appear. Cosima, who spoke fluent English, was more sociable. She sat for a portrait by Edward Burne-Jones and asked to meet Morris, because he "treated the same subjects that her husband had treated in his music."

Cosima also attended a reception for the Grosvenor Gallery, a showplace for Pre-Raphaelitism and Aestheticism, which opened the day the Wagners arrived. The young Oscar Wilde remarked on the conjunction in the *Dublin University Magazine*: "That 'Art is long and life is short' is a truth which everyone feels, or ought to feel; yet surely those who were in London last May, and had in one week the opportunities of hearing Rubinstein play the Sonata Impassionata, of seeing Wagner conduct the Spinning Wheel Chorus from the *Flying Dutchman*, and of studying art at the Grosvenor Gallery, have very little to complain of as regards human existence and art-pleasures." Wagner did not, in fact, conduct the Spinning Chorus, but the point generally holds.

Eliot, who frequented Pre-Raphaelite circles, was a constant presence at the Wagner Festival. The music continued to fascinate her, nagging hesitations notwithstanding. She reportedly wept over the scene between Siegmund and Brünnhilde in *Walküre*. She and Lewes were in attendance when Wagner read aloud his recently completed *Parsifal* libretto at Dannreuther's—a riveting two-hour performance, according to several witnesses. The man himself left Eliot cold. He had the personality of an "*épicier*," a grocer, she said. Cosima, on the other hand, was a "rare person," even a "genius." Cosima returned the admiration, recording in her diary that Eliot had made "a noble and pleasant impression." The two women sat together at rehearsals while Wagner yelled at the orchestra. Lewes later encouraged Cosima to read a pamphlet titled *George Eliot und das Judenthum*, the work of a Jewish theologian.

The hoped-for meeting of minds never quite came about. Wagner's politics and personality may have been stumbling blocks, but the deeper problem was one of cultural ownership. The Pre-Raphaelites saw the stories of Tristan and the Knights of the Grail as their own possession, and tended to look on Wagner as an interloper. Even when they acceded to his power, they did so with a slight grimace. Hence Burne-Jones, in 1884: "I heard Wagner's Parsifal the other day—I nearly forgave him—he knew how to win me. He made sounds that are really and truly (I assure you, and I ought to know) the very sounds that were to be heard in the Sangraal Chapel."

T he Pre-Raphaelite Brotherhood, which sought to revive the hand-crafted aesthetic of the Middle Ages in anticipation of a better world, formed in 1848, in the midst of the pan-European wave of revolutionary agitation that also spawned the *Ring*. The young men at the core of the group—Millais, Dante Gabriel Rossetti, and William Holman Hunt—held back from direct political action, but they sympathized with the working-class Chartist demonstration of April 1848. The first Holman Hunt painting to carry the designation "P.R.B." was *Rienzi Vowing to Obtain Justice*, a brightly austere canvas in which the Roman populist Cola di Rienzo is seen raising a defiant fist over his brother's body. For Holman Hunt, as for Wagner and many other leftists, Rienzi symbolized the long struggle for political liberation. The painter intended an "appeal to Heaven against the tyranny exercised over the poor and helpless . . . 'How long, O Lord!'"

Morris and Burne-Jones gravitated toward the Pre-Raphaelites while studying at Oxford in the mid-fifties. They were disciples of John Ruskin, who prized the craftsmanship of Gothic architecture and decried the "degradation of the operative into a machine." The Pre-Raphaelites, too, believed in the Gospel of Work, but only when workers could take pleasure in their tasks. Morris soon emerged as the most audacious thinker in the Brotherhood, applying himself in a variety of media—painting, poetry, fiction, essays, decorative arts, textiles—in pursuit of social reform. He was the principal force behind the Arts and Crafts movement, which sought to restore wholeness and richness to the drab decor of daily life. "The leading passion of my life has been and is hatred of modern civilisation," Morris later said. Swinburne, a slightly younger Oxfordian, entered the circle around 1857, his tastes more Continental in orientation.

This brand of progressive nostalgia is not unlike Wagner's own blend of revolution and reaction. The composer felt that the lusty expressivity of the late medieval and early Renaissance periods had given way to artifice and mannerism, and that the artwork of the future should bring back lost unities. For the Pre-Raphaelites, too, the revivification of an idealized past implied a direct attack on an ugly, iniquitous present. The vivid color schemes and quasi-photographic perspectives of Pre-Raphaelite painting—the aroused crouch of Holman Hunt's *The Hireling Shepherd*, the blissed-out gaze of Millais's *The Bridesmaid*, the flatly sexual stares of Rossetti's *Venus Verticordia* and *Astarte Syriaca*—bring to mind the hedonistic harmonies of Wagner's Venusberg and his *Tristan* love scene. And the luminous Holy Grail sonorities of *Lohengrin* and *Parsifal* are akin to Burne-Jones's pale knights and prayerful maidens.

The narrative of Tannhäuser and the Venusberg was known to English readers through Carlyle's translation of the Ludwig Tieck poem "The Trusty Eckart," which Wagner also read. But the Pre-Raphaelites happened to take a sudden interest in the material around 1861, the year of *Tannhäuser* in Paris. First, Burne-Jones made a watercolor titled *Laus Veneris* (The Praise of Venus). Not long after, Swinburne set to work on a poem with the same title. Morris began a poem called "The Hill of Venus," which eventually appeared in his 1870 cycle *The Earthly Paradise*. Burne-Jones prepared illustrations for Morris's poem and then revisited the subject in darkly glowing oils. The *Tannhäuser* scandal, together with Baudelaire's impassioned response, probably helped to drive interest across the Channel.

Swinburne may well have learned of Wagner through Baudelaire. He was the first British writer to take serious notice of *Les Fleurs du mal*, reviewing it in 1862. The following year, he traveled to Paris in the hope of meeting his idol. He failed to do so, but happened to see Fantin-Latour's rendering of the Venusberg in Manet's studio. Baudelaire later sent Swinburne a letter of gratitude, in which he repeated what Wagner had said to him about the *Tannhäuser* essay: "I would never have believed that a French writer could so easily understand so many things." In the same spirit, Baudelaire was amazed that an Englishman had comprehended *him*. By a quirk of fate, this letter never reached its destination; the photographer

Nadar neglected to deliver it, and it surfaced only after Swinburne's death. Baudelaire also mailed a copy of his Wagner essay, and this did show up at Swinburne's door—a cryptic message from one poet to another.

Swinburne was already at work on *Laus Veneris*. From the start, his personal obsessions colored his approach to the legend—the pleasure of pain, the pain of pleasure, a queasy eroticism that borders on sadomasochism:

> Asleep or waking is it? for her neck,
> Kissed over close, wears yet a purple speck
> Wherein the pained blood falters and goes out;
> Soft, and stung softly—fairer for a fleck . . .
> Inside the Horsel here the air is hot;
> Right little peace one hath for it, God wot;
> The scented dusty daylight burns the air,
> And my heart chokes me till I hear it not.

The last lines recall Baudelaire's picture of the Venusberg, "breathing a perfumed but stifling atmosphere, lit by a rosy light which came not from the sun." They also echo Swinburne's own description of *Les Fleurs du mal*: "It has the languid lurid beauty of close and threatening weather—a heavy heated temperature, with dangerous hothouse scents in it." Swinburne later recommended that anyone wishing to understand his conception of Venus should read the passage of Baudelaire's *Tannhauser* pamphlet that depicts the "fallen goddess, grown diabolic among ages that would not accept her as divine." This unapologetically erotic, paganistic poem caused a scandal of its own when it appeared in Swinburne's 1866 collection *Poems and Ballads*. Accused of "Greek depravity" and "schoolboy lustfulness," Swinburne cited Baudelaire and Wagner in his defense.

Burne-Jones's *Laus Veneris*, the final version of which showed at the Grosvenor in 1878, is a sumptuous snapshot of Venus in repose. She reclines in a full scarlet gown, her right arm dangled behind her head, her eyes disaffectedly drifting down. Four female attendants prepare to sing for her, music being the preferred mode of seduction in Venusberg tales. On the music stand is an illuminated score titled "Laus Veneris." At the top of the canvas, a window opens to a cool, blue world outside, where five young knights are riding by. The middle one stares in with particular intensity; he might be Tannhäuser. The scene has a hothouse stillness. As

often in Pre-Raphaelite work, a present-tense immediacy burns through
the veneer of the faux-ancient, setting up unstable resonances between
past and present, the imaginary and the real.

Among Pre-Raphaelite visions of the Venusberg, Morris's "The Hill of
Venus" is closest to Wagner in mood. At the outset, the knight wanders
the world in cynical despair. Hope flickers in him when he sees Venus's
grotto, and narcissistic rapture overtakes him: "For this, for this / God
made the world, that I might feel thy kiss!" After a time, though, he wea-
ries of that ever-burning love, and begins to fear the fires of hell. He makes
his pilgrimage to Rome, seeking absolution. Before the Pope, he again
grows defiant, and mercy is denied. At the end comes a finely calibrated
moral twist: after the knight slinks back to the hill, the Pope loses confidence in his judgment and asks whether he has done wrong. Suddenly,
his staff blooms, signaling a miraculous forgiveness that stems from older
powers within the earth. There is a taste of the atmosphere of *Parsifal*:
Christianity and paganism reconciled in a Good Friday Spell.

No wonder Cosima Wagner expressed a desire to meet Morris: his
universe overlapped with her husband's to a remarkable degree. He
wrote of Venus and Tannhäuser; he painted Iseult; he treated the world of
the Grail; he pored over the Icelandic sources that furnished much of the
material of the *Ring*. In the sixties and seventies, Morris studied Old Norse
with the Cambridge-based scholar Eiríkr Magnússon, who collaborated
with him on an English translation of the *Vǫlsunga saga*. Morris saw this
as "the Great Story of the North, which should be to all our race what the
Tale of Troy was to the Greeks."

Yet Morris loathed the very idea of Wagner. On receiving an English
version of *Walküre*, in 1873, he said that it was "nothing short of desecration to bring such a tremendous and world-wide subject under the gas-
lights of an opera." He apparently never heard Wagner's music in person. If
he had, he might have felt the same as Ruskin, who described *Meistersinger*
as "clumsy, blundering, boggling, baboon-blooded . . . sapless, soulless,
beginningless, endless, topless, bottomless." In the same year that the *Ring*
premiered, Morris composed a four-book epic titled *The Story of Sigurd
the Volsung and the Fall of the Niblungs*. Jane Susanna Ennis, in a comparative study of Morris's and Wagner's texts, speculates that *Sigurd* "would

William Morris, La Belle Iseult

have been very different—indeed, may not even have been written at all—had it not been for Wagner's *Ring*."

Every telling of the Siegfried story hinges on the scene in which the young hero discovers Brünnhilde—or Brynhild, in Morris's spelling—within her aerie of fire. Morris and Magnússon, in their version of the *Vǫlsunga saga*, interpolate a passage from the Poetic Edda and translate it fairly faithfully:

Long have I slept
And slumbered long,
Many and long are the woes of mankind . . .
Hail to the day come back!
Hail, sons of the daylight!
Hail to thee, dark night, and thy daughter!

Wagner, too, stays close to the Edda text. It falls to the orchestra to conjure the majesty of the scene—the first harsh glint of the sun (E minor) followed by the warming spread of its rays (harp-caressed C major).

Hail to you, sun!
Hail to you, light!
Hail to you, light-bringing day!
Long was my sleep;
awakened am I;
who is the hero
who woke me?

Morris, in *Sigurd*, casts Brynhild's hymn to the sun in more flowery terms, as if trying to compensate for the orchestral resources of the German rival:

But therewith the sun rose upward and lightened all the earth,
And the light flashed up to the heavens from the rims of the glorious girth;
But they twain arose together, and with both her palms outspread,
And bathed in the light returning, she cried aloud and said:
"All hail, O Day and thy Sons, and thy kin of the coloured things!
Hail, following Night, and thy Daughter that leadeth thy wavering wings!
Look down with unangry eyes on us today alive,
And give us the hearts victorious, and the gain for which we strive! . . ."

Hueffer and Shaw considered *Sigurd* a worthy counterpart to the *Ring*. But the plainer, more pungent language of Morris's earlier translation has aged better.

Wagner and Morris differ most in their valuation of past and present. Morris often frames his legendary world as a lost paradise. *Sigurd* begins: "There was a dwelling of Kings ere the world was waxen old." The same elegiac voices speak at the end of the Brynhild chapter: "They are gone— the lovely, the mighty, the hope of the ancient Earth." In *The Earthly Paradise*, Morris bids the reader to "Forget six counties overhung with smoke, / Forget the snorting steam and piston stroke, / Forget the spreading of the hideous town." Wagner avoids that tone of "Once upon a time." In the preludes to *Tannhäuser*, *Lohengrin*, and the *Ring*, a distant world is materializing out of the mist, yet it is soon overcome by the illusion, exciting and dangerous, of the past bleeding into the present. Wagner removes the gilt border around the stuff of myth.

The tale of Tristram and Iseult is indisputably a property of the British Isles, even if the earliest surviving versions come from twelfth-century France. Iseult the Fair is an Irish princess, her castle thought to lie on the outskirts of Dublin. King Mark, to whom she is betrothed, has a castle in Cornwall, often identified with Tintagel, where King Arthur is said to have been conceived. Tristram, the Breton orphan, is effectively Cornish, because King Mark has adopted him. By the time Wagner took up *Tristan*, in the late fifties, he was a latecomer; Morris was painting a fresco of the lovers on the walls of the Oxford Union, and Matthew Arnold had published a three-part poem called *Tristram and Iseult*. When, many years later, Arnold heard *Tristan* in Munich, he placidly commented, "I have managed the story better than Wagner."

Arnold confines himself to three fragments of the romance. First we see Tristram awaiting his beloved; then the lovers in their last embrace; and, finally, a scene from the lonely life of Iseult of the White Hands, Tristram's wife in the original legend. (That character is absent from Wagner's opera.) Despite Romantic touches, Arnold takes a dim view of "this fool passion . . . an unnatural overheat at best." Tennyson's treatment in "The Last Tournament" (1870–71), the gloomiest chapter of his *Idylls of the King* cycle, is even harsher. Tristram is arrogant and hard-hearted, a player of "broken music," and Isolt is motivated as much by hatred of

Burne-Jones, Tristram and Iseult stained-glass panel

her husband as by desire for her lover. The tale ends with jarring abrupt-ness, as Liebestod is reduced to death pure and simple:

> He rose, he turn'd, and flinging round her neck,
> Claspt it; but while he bow'd himself to lay
> Warm kisses in the hollow of her throat,
> Out of the dark, just as the lips had touch'd,
> Behind him rose a shadow and a shriek—
> "Mark's way," said Mark, and clove him thro' the brain.

The Pre-Raphaelites could never be so unsentimental. In Morris's Oxford Union fresco, Tristram and Iseult clutch each other amid lush vegeta-tion, their love implicitly organic and natural. In the same period, Morris painted *La Belle Iseult*, with Jane Burden, his future wife, appearing as a pensive queen, her gaze fixed on a book. In 1862, the arts-and-crafts firm of Morris and Co. produced a series of Tristram-and-Iseult stained-glass panels, with Burne-Jones, Rossetti, and Ford Madox Brown making con-tributions; a tone of noble suffering prevailed.

Swinburne, who felt that Tennyson had "degraded and debased" the ro-mance, sought to put matters right in his long poem *Tristram of Lyonesse*, begun around 1870 and completed in 1882. Just before embarking on the project, Swinburne studied a collection of Auguste de Gasperini's writing on Wagner, with its extensive treatment of *Tristan*. He also conferred regularly with the wealthy Welsh connoisseur George Powell, a vehement Wagnerite who went to Bayreuth in 1876. (During his visit, Powell had tea with Co-sima and attempted to interest her in Swinburne's poetry, apparently with-out success.) Wagner's connection to Schopenhauer especially interested the poet as he prepared to leap into the ravishing abyss of the Tristan story.

Morris launches his *Sigurd* with an image of time revolving backward. Swinburne, in a more Wagnerian maneuver, begins with an incantatory, forty-four-line sentence in praise of love:

> Love, that is first and last of all things made,
> The light that has the living world for shade,
> The spirit that for temporal veil has on
> The souls of all men woven in unison,
> One fiery raiment with all lives inwrought . . .

Swinburne admits that love has wrecked those in its path, as "soul smote soul and left it ruinous"; but, unlike Arnold and Tennyson, he still insists on love's painful joys. Indeed, repeating a motif from *Laus Veneris*, he proposes that love entails "a better heaven than heaven is." As in *Tristan*, the heat of Tristram and Iseult's ecstasy causes the outer world to dissolve. Binaries break down: day becomes night, night becomes day. When the lovers first kiss, "four lips became one burning mouth." The carnal oblivion extends to the dimension of sound, as the lovers hear an inner music that drowns out the roar of the sea and, later, festive shouts from the nearing shore. It is hard not to hear this self-deifying music as Wagner's *Tristan* score, now swallowed up in poetry's realm:

> Yet fairer now than song may show them stand
> Tristram and Iseult, hand in amorous hand,
> Soul-satisfied, their eyes made great and bright
> With all the love of all the livelong night;
> With all its hours yet singing in their ears
> No mortal music made of thoughts and tears,
> But such a song, past conscience of man's thought,
> As hearing he grows god and knows it not.

At the very end, Swinburne tells of how King Mark, having forgiven the lovers, builds a tomb for them—"a chapel bright like spring / With flower-soft wealth of branching tracery made." (Burne-Jones pictured such a tomb in his contribution to the Pre-Raphaelite stained-glass project, with sculpted lovers lying side by side and two hounds keeping watch.) Swinburne then recalls that according to legend the Kingdom of Lyonesse sank into the sea. So, above the lovers' submerged shrine, the tide "gleams and moves and moans," and they find permanent peace in the "light and sound and darkness of the sea." The obliterating action of the ocean plays much the same role as *Tristan*'s "Transfiguration," where Isolde sinks and drowns in highest bliss.

Swinburne endured two shocks after publishing the poem he considered his best. In October 1882, Powell died suddenly at the age of forty. In February 1883, Wagner expired in Venice. In a poem titled "Autumn and Winter," Swinburne called Powell a "herald soul," flying up in advance of his musical god. There followed "The Death of Richard Wagner," the noblest of the dozens of poems written in commemoration of Wagner's death. It ends with an image of "the rising of doom divine as a sundawn risen to sight / From the depths of the sea." These poems appeared alongside "Two Preludes: Lohengrin and Tristan und Isolde" in the 1883 volume *A Century of Roundels.* The British literary world had resisted Wagner, but it gave way in the end. Tristram became Tristan, Iseult Isolde.

YOUNG ADULT WAGNER

"The Wagner-cultus has grown and spread of late amongst British musical amateurs to an extent that is little short of the phenomenal," a critic said in 1881. The following year brought a Wagner wave to London, encompassing most of his mature output. A touring production of the *Ring,* based on the 1876 Bayreuth staging, presented three complete cycles in London; the Prince of Wales attended most of the performances, having rearranged his schedule to accommodate them. William Gladstone, the giant of British liberalism, also showed approval of Wagner. *Parsifal,* which was still confined to Bayreuth, acquired an especially lofty reputation in the Victorian era. Anne Dzamba Sessa, in *Richard Wagner and the English,* writes that the opera "bathed the listener in a soothing wash of inchoate and luxurious pious emotion."

Later in the decade, the physician and Theosophist William Ashton Ellis launched a journal called *The Meister,* dedicated to the "regenerative life-force of the Spring of Richard Wagner's genius." Ellis also began publishing translations of Wagner's prose writings, making the doubtful claim that even if the Meister had "never composed one bar of music, and never conceived one scene of drama, his prose works alone would have ranked him amongst the foremost thinkers of the day." Regrettably, Ellis's clumsy, literal, borderline-unreadable renderings of Wagner's already intractable prose remain the standard English versions. *The Meister* aimed to be the counterpart to the *Revue wagnérienne*, but it fell on an altogether lower literary level. A few commemorative poems give sufficient flavor of the whole:

> Immortal Master! earthward wing thy flight . . .
>> (Henry Knight, "In Memoriam: R. Wagner")

> I will not call thee dead, for such as thee
> Death is but Life . . .
>> (Clara Grant Duff, "At Richard Wagner's Grave")

> Thou, O Belovëd, O Master,
> Magical child of the spring . . .
>> (Evelyn Pyne, "Anniversary Ode")

> Farewell, Great Spirit! Thou by whom alone,
> Of all the Wonder-doers sent to be
> My signs and sureties Time-ward, unto me
> My inmost self has ceased to be unknown!
>> (Alfred Forman, "The World's Farewell to Richard Wagner")

Forman, a minor poet and scholar who made a living as a paper merchant, prepared the first English translations of the *Ring* and *Tristan*, which rival Ellis's work in their alliterative opacity ("Fitly thy ravens / take to their feathers"). Isolde's Transfiguration lapses into the lilt of a Victorian parlor song: "To drown—/ go down—/ to nameless night—/ last delight!"

Publishers in both Britain and the United States saw a market for explications of Wagner, especially ones oriented toward younger readers. These books naturally highlight the heroes-and-dragons dimension of the music dramas. In keeping with popular sensibilities, they maximize the nobility of Wagner's characters and minimize their sins. *Wonder Tales from Wagner*, by the American author Anna Alice Chapin, begins its account of

Tristan with the words "Once upon a time." Isolde is "tall and very fair, with hair of a deep, brilliant gold, and clear, shining blues." Tristan is a "deeply tanned" lad with "short, curling brown hair." With the onset of the Night of Love, the two show apparent restraint, seating themselves upon a bank of flowers and "satisfying themselves and each other with assurances and proofs of their love and fidelity."

Reticence was obligatory in the genre of Wagner for the Young. The composer's less wholesome goings-on, especially the incest in the *Ring*, necessitated a fair amount of bowdlerization, not to mention outright falsification. The *New York Times*, reviewing William Henry Frost's *The Wagner Story Book: Firelight Tales of the Great Music Dramas*, dryly concluded that "the emotional contents of the Wagner dramas are altogether too stupendous to lend themselves readily to reduction to child literature." The critic noted Frost's "masterly inactivity" on the subject of the brother-sister love in Act I of *Walküre*. Grace Edson Barber, in *Wagner Opera Stories*, omits the entire first act of that opera, saying only that Brünnhilde had defended an unnamed "brave friend" who had "not been true to all the laws." Chapin mentions the twins in *The Story of the Rhinegold*, but slyly disguises their relationship, saying, "They loved each other as much as though they had been really brother and sister."

Götterdämmerung posed another challenge: how could young people be expected to cope with the self-immolation of Brünnhilde and the incineration of Valhalla? In Barber's telling, Brünnhilde manages to return the Ring to the Rhinemaidens without having to ride into the pyre. She exclaims, "The transformation is coming!," whereupon, after a few days of darkness, "the birds awoke and caroled glad songs of love." Florence Akin, a former schoolteacher from Pasadena, California, performs even more drastic surgery in her *Opera Stories from Wagner: A Reader for Primary Grades*, allowing the survival not only of Brünnhilde but also of Siegfried. The lovers deposit the Ring in the Rhine, whereupon "hurry, worry, falsehood, greed, and envy vanished from the earth."

A few contributors to the Wagner youth market delved deeper. Dolores Bacon, in *Operas Every Child Should Know*, briskly confronts the racist question: "Probably no stupider thing was ever said or done than that by Wagner when he wrote a diatribe on the Jew in Art." Constance Maud, the author of *Wagner's Heroes* and *Wagner's Heroines*, hints at Wagnerian feminism, of which more will be said in Chapter 7. The daughter of a British clergyman, Maud was involved in the suffrage movement and, in 1911, published a fiery feminist novel titled *No Surrender*. She makes sure that her young readers register Brünnhilde's "commanding tones," her "tone of queenly authority." Furthermore, she gives glimpses of Wagner's revolutionary agenda. When Valhalla burns, Maud perceives that Wotan has fallen victim to "the love of power and the love of gold." There are few blunter summations of the *Ring*, for adults or children.

WAGNER IN AMERICA

*Herman Matzen's statue of Wagner in
Edgewater Park, Cleveland, erected in 1911*

In his final years, Wagner flirted with the notion of immigrating to the United States, a place he never saw. Reeling from the financial disaster of the first Bayreuth Festival, he spoke of selling Wahnfried and moving with his family to the New World. Cosima wrote in her diary: "America??

Then never again a return to Germany!" In 1879, the *North American Review* published an essay attributed to Wagner, positing the New World as an idyll where the "unconquerable vigor and strength" of the German spirit would find new life. Although the essay was ghostwritten by Hans von Wolzogen, the *Bayreuther Blätter* editor, it reflected Wagner's outlook: his disappointment in the new Reich; his belief in the indestructibility of "holy German art"; his concerns about racial intermixing; and his fantasies of cultural rebirth. In the same period, he described his Bayreuth idea as "a kind of Washington for art"—comparing the festival to the American capital that rose on swampy land by the Potomac River.

By 1880, the American plan had become an idée fixe. Cosima wrote: "Again and again he keeps coming back to America, says it is the only place on the whole map which he can gaze upon with any pleasure." He went so far as to draft a financial prospectus, in consultation with Newell Sill Jenkins, his American-born, German-based dentist. The idea was that American supporters would raise a million dollars—around twenty-five million in today's currency—to resettle Wagner and his family in "some State of the Union with favourable climate." In return, the United States would receive earnings from *Parsifal* and all other future work. "Thus would America have bought me from Europe for all time." The pleasant climate he had in mind was, curiously, Minnesota.

The conceit was not as absurd as it seems. Around a million Germans had immigrated to the United States between 1846 and 1855. They were often called Forty-Eighters, because many had fled after the failed 1848 revolutions, and they played a pivotal role in American politics before the Civil War. Predominantly liberal in their thinking, they tended to support Lincoln and the Union cause. The most illustrious of them was Carl Schurz, who fought as a Union general, became a senator from Missouri, and served as the secretary of the interior under President Rutherford B. Hayes. (Wagner approved of Schurz, saying that he showed "what a proper German can do.") Another significant Forty-Eighter was Hugo Wesendonck, who left Germany under the threat of a death sentence and proceeded to make a fortune in the life-insurance business. His company, Germania, thrives today, under the name Guardian. Wesendonck's brother Otto, who funded Wagner during his Zurich years, was a partner in a textile-import firm that had its headquarters in lower

Manhattan. The money that kept Wagner afloat for a time was American in origin.

The image of Wagner in America is amusing to contemplate—it might make for a lively historical novel—but it never came close to reality. The talk of exile may have been a ploy intended to whip up support from sources closer to home. Ludwig II, among others, took fright when he learned of the scheme, and wrote to the composer: "Your roses cannot thrive in America's stony soil, where self-seeking, callousness, and Mammon reign." With a certain amount of adaptation, Wagner indeed took hold across the Atlantic. In time, a full-blown cultus arose, to the point that streets were named after his characters—at least four American towns have a Parsifal Place—and statues of him were erected in parks in Cleveland and Baltimore. The monuments still stand, despite occasional calls for them to be removed.

Each country saw Wagner through a self-fashioned prism. For the French, he was a torchbearer of the modern; for the British, a messenger of Arthuriana. In the United States, Wagner harmonized with a national love of wilderness sagas, frontier lore, Native American tales, stories of desperadoes searching for gold. Joseph Horowitz, the leading historian of American Wagnerism, cites Frederick Jackson Turner's conception of the frontier, according to which "coarseness and strength combined with acuteness and inquisitiveness" define the nation's self-image. In much the same vein, the New York critic Henry Krehbiel contended that American operagoers saw themselves reflected in the "rude forcefulness" of Wagner's heroes. Siegfried, especially, stirred sympathy with his "unspoiled nature," his freedom from "false and meretricious" habits. Wagnéristes said that France was the composer's true homeland; Yankee Wagnerites made the same claim. The historian and memoirist Henry Adams wrote that the "paroxysms of nervous excitement" surrounding the *Ring* at the Met showed that "New York knew better than Baireuth [*sic*] what Wagner meant."

At the same time, Wagner allowed the young nation to prove itself as a maturing global power. Great American cities such as New York, Boston, and Chicago, aspiring to rival European capitals in cultural richesse, nurtured symphony orchestras and opera houses alongside museums and architectural monuments. Wagner productions, notably the Metropolitan Opera's 1903 staging of *Parsifal*, were among the most opulent entertainments of the American fin de siècle. That program of self-improvement conformed to what the philosopher George Santayana called the "genteel tradition"—the American counterpart to Victorian propriety.

With his usual double-sidedness, Wagner spoke both to the crude vigor of American enterprise and to the yearning for refinement and uplift. The spiritual dimension of his work received special emphasis, joining a national mania for alternative religions and therapies: Theosophy, New Thought, Christian Science, the Chautauqua movement. The agnostic orator Robert Ingersoll loved Wagner, too: "I would rather listen to Tristan and Isolde—that Mississippi of melody—where the great notes, winged like eagles, lift the soul above the cares and griefs of this weary world—than to all the orthodox sermons ever preached."

The American quest for heroic self-definition was caught up in questions of gender and race. Theodore Roosevelt, with his "Rough Rider" persona, epitomized an American masculinity that resisted a supposed European tendency toward effeminacy and degeneracy. Furthermore, the country's striving for global influence and its pursuit of Manifest Destiny coincided all too often with ideologies of Aryan and Anglo-Saxon racial superiority. Herbert Spencer, the theorist of social evolution, visited the United States in 1882 and predicted that its Aryan stock would "produce a finer type of man than has hitherto existed." Roosevelt was vulnerable to this kind of thinking; in 1911, he bemoaned "loose and sloppy talk about the general progress of humanity, the equality and identity of races." Wagner's work and ideas provided fodder for both sides of a battle over American identity that is ongoing.

STAR-SPANGLED WAGNER

GERMANIA MUSICAL SOCIETY.

Wagner's music arrived in the United States in the luggage of the Germania Musical Society—two dozen radical-minded musicians who formed a collective in Berlin in early 1848 and then emigrated en masse. As Nancy Newman relates in her history of the group, the Germania aimed to create a musical-social utopia, a band of free individuals tied together by fellow feeling. Believing that "communism was the most perfect principle of society," they adopted the ideals of "one for all and all for one," of "equal rights, equal duties, and equal rewards." They contrasted this picture of musical leveling with what they saw as the egotistical mannerisms of solo virtuosos in the employ of the upper classes. The Germanians hoped that their performances of composers from Bach to Wagner would "enflame and stimulate in the hearts of these politically free people . . . love for the fine art of music."

In 1852, the Germanians played an excerpt from *Tannhäuser* in Boston. The following year, in the same city, they organized a Grand Wagner Night, augmenting selections from *Rienzi*, *Tannhäuser*, and *Lohengrin* with Rossini and Bellini arias. The New England poet Henry Wadsworth Longfellow, soon to write his Native American epic *The Song of Hiawatha*, was there, and wrote in his diary: "Strange, original, and somewhat barbaric." The Germanians toured widely with this repertory, and news of their activities reached the *Neue Zeitschrift für Musik*, one of whose contributors, Richard Pohl, made this prediction: "Wagner, the man of the liberal arts and the man of the future, will rise anew in the land of freedom and the future, and find a permanent home." The essay ends with the sentence "*Westwards moves the history of art!*" The composer proudly noted, "In *Boston* they are now even presenting *Wagnernights*, evening concerts at which only my own compositions are performed." He did not know about the Rossini and Bellini.

The Germania disbanded in 1854, but its influence lingered, especially in New York City. Carl Bergmann, one of its leaders, began conducting the Philharmonic Society of New York in 1855, causing excitement there with performances of Wagner. Four years later, Bergmann led a full staging of *Tannhäuser* at the Stadttheater, on the Bowery, which catered to German immigrants. Despite less than ideal conditions—the theater was small and grubby, one critic said, with boys selling glasses of beer and chunks of cheese—the opera gained respectful reviews.

Wagner did not lack for critics in the American press, although they were milder than their European counterparts. John Sullivan Dwight, the publisher of *Dwight's Journal of Music*, frequently objected to the composer's ideas, but he did a fair job of explaining them. An idealist with ties to Transcendentalism, Fourierism, and the utopian Brook Farm community, Dwight saw music as a means of moral improvement and social reform. At first, the new import piqued his interest. "Verily here is a deliberate attempt to Wagnerize us," he wrote in advance of the Germania's Wagner Night. "But why shall we not test the new sometimes, by the old?" In the event, Dwight found the music too taxing, and as he got to know Wagner's writings his doubts increased. In 1869, when "Jewishness in Music" was republished, he spent several pages denouncing its "ignoble and small-minded statements" against Jews.

Wagner's most decisive advocate in the post–Civil War years was the German-born conductor Theodore Thomas, who came to the United States with his family in 1845, when he was ten. Thomas was one of the first modern conductors—a strong-willed podium technician in the lineage of Berlioz, Wagner, and Hans von Bülow. Thomas's first orchestral concert, in New York in 1862, began with the *Flying Dutchman* overture. In subsequent years, he led the Philharmonic Society of New York and the Brooklyn Philharmonic, and in 1891 he helped found the Chicago Symphony. Thomas often included Wagner excerpts on the summertime concerts that he led in the Central Park Garden, starting in the late sixties. In 1872, he presented "The Ride of the Valkyries," using a copy of the manuscript. "The people jumped on the chairs and shouted," he wrote in his memoirs. The "Ride" was already a hit in Europe, despite Wagner's intermittent disapproval of the practice of playing excerpts.

In 1876, on the occasion of the hundredth anniversary of American independence, Thomas succeeded in commissioning an *American Centennial March* from Wagner himself. The fee was five thousand dollars—equivalent to more than one hundred thousand dollars today. After haggling over rights, Wagner produced a work of thoroughgoing mediocrity, its most promising musical idea set aside for the Flower Maidens scene in *Parsifal*. The premiere took place at the opening of the Centennial Exhibition, in Philadelphia. Despite the dreariness of the music, the response was generally warm. According to one press report, Wagner had honored the "feminine loveliness, noble natures, and pure mental activity of American women"—the march was dedicated to the Women's Centennial Committee—and evoked "a world of souls communing together in universal concord."

The rising young composer and bandmaster John Philip Sousa added a Wagner twist to his own centennial composition, a medley of national airs titled *International Congress Fantasy*. The piece culminates in a festive orchestration of "The Star-Spangled Banner" in the style of the *Tannhäuser* overture, with stuttering motifs accompanying the principal theme. In a band arrangement, the anthem is marked "à la Wagner." Sousa once told an interviewer, "My two most popular pieces are the 'Tannhaeuser Overture' and the 'Stars and Stripes.'" He added: "Wagner was a brass band man, anyway." When he took charge of the U.S. Marine Band, in 1880, the March King regularly programmed Wagner on official occasions, including that of the inauguration of President Grover Cleveland, in 1885.

Wagner had impinged on the American presidency before. Ulysses S. Grant was present for the premiere of the *American Centennial March*, though he famously had no ear for music. ("I only know two tunes: one is 'Yankee Doodle' and the other isn't," he supposedly once said.) Rutherford B. Hayes, Grant's successor, hosted musicales at the White House, including piano performances by his secretary of the interior, Carl Schurz. On at least one occasion, the First U.S. Cavalry Band serenaded Hayes with a Wagner selection. Cleveland, who served two discontinuous terms as president, apparently liked Wagner, and his young wife, Frances Folsom, was a conspicuous enthusiast. Sousa's Marine Band played the Bridal Chorus at the Clevelands' wedding, in 1886, and later performed selections from *Lohengrin* on the White House lawn, with the First Lady sitting enthralled at a window.

American Wagnerism entered its peak phase in 1884, when Theodore Thomas marshaled a grand tour of seventy-four Wagner concerts in twenty North American cities, employing monster choruses and drawing audiences as large as eight thousand people. The success of that endeavor caught the attention of a fledgling New York company, the Metropolitan Opera, which had opened the previous year and immediately run into financial trouble. For the second season, the Met board, led by James A. Roosevelt, Theodore's uncle, decided to switch from Italian opera to German fare. The émigré conductor Leopold Damrosch, well acquainted with Wagner, was engaged as music director. *Tannhäuser*, *Lohengrin*, and *Walküre* formed the core of the repertory, the last causing a sensation that probably ensured the survival of the house.

When Damrosch died suddenly of pneumonia toward the end of his first season, the Met brought in Anton Seidl, a greatly gifted young conductor who had assisted Wagner in Bayreuth. The company kept to an all-German format until 1891: out of nearly six hundred performances in that period, more than half were of Wagner. In the 1888–89 season, Seidl led the first American *Ring*, and subsequently took the cycle on tour, as he had done with the Bayreuth *Ring* in Europe. In St. Louis, the *Ring* was advertised, in the P. T. Barnum manner, as "THE GREATEST OPERATIC ATTRACTION IN THE WORLD." The Wagner mania reached across the continent to San Francisco, and even penetrated the Francophone bastion of New Orleans, where Rex, the King of Carnival, brought his masked retinue to a gala performance of *Lohengrin*.

Amid growing reverence for Wagner, Seidl became a cult figure, as Joseph Horowitz recounts in *Wagner Nights: An American History*. In 1891, Seidl replaced Thomas at the Philharmonic Society, maintaining a Wagner focus. He also led summertime programs at Brighton Beach, where Wagner was by far the most frequently performed composer. In 1890, in Brooklyn Heights, Seidl presided over a singular event known as the "*Parsifal* Entertainment"—an abridged concert rendition with religious accoutrements, falling on Palm Sunday. The Clevelands attended, libretto in hand. Laura Holloway-Langford, the spiritually inclined head of an organization called the Seidl Society, hoped to launch a summer Wagner festival, a kind of Brooklyn Bayreuth. There were proposals for building exact replicas of the Festspielhaus in the United States—one in Milwaukee, Wisconsin, another on the Hudson River. These went unrealized, despite rumors of support from Cosima.

In 1903, Heinrich Conried, the Met's new general manager, mounted a full production of *Parsifal*, in defiance of Bayreuth's claim of exclusivity. Cosima tried to stop the staging with a lawsuit—*Wagner et al. v. Conried et al.*—but the U.S. Circuit Court ruled against her. Because the United States was not a signatory to the Berne Convention, *Parsifal* fell outside of German copyright. A secondary controversy involved protests from religious quarters, on the grounds that *Parsifal* made inappropriate use of Christian symbolism. Reverend C. H. Parkhurst, of New York, called it "stupid sacrilege." Several American clergymen came to the opera's defense: Washington Gladden, a leader of the liberal-minded Social Gospel movement, crowned Wagner one of the "witnesses of the light," alongside Dante and Michelangelo. Amid the furor, the first run of eleven performances was a major success, generating $186,000 in receipts.

Opening night was Christmas Eve 1903. The *Times* lavished coverage on the fashions of the Golden Horseshoe, as the elite boxes at the Met were known: "Mrs. Vanderbilt was in black velvet and wore a black silk beaver hat, Mrs. Baylies was in black lace pailleted in gold. Her small black hat had a long white plume, and a black and white lace wrap. Mrs. Barney was in her box, and with her was her daughter, Miss Katharine, in pale blue satin. None of the party wore hats." Up in the galleries, the crowd was more diverse: "A colored man wearing a jewel in his necktie which if real was worth nearly $30,000, discussed motifs and movements with a man and his wife from beyond the Bronx who were in evening attire." As in London, the crowd assimilated the Bayreuth ban on intermittent applause: "Even when the wild heroine Kundry, in the person of Mme. Ternina, clad in skins and with dishevelled hair, came galloping madly through the air the silence was as of the grave."

The man then occupying the White House took notice. "Mother came back yesterday, having thoroughly enjoyed Parsifal," Theodore Roosevelt wrote to his son Kermit. The president might be classified as a casual Wagnerian: mentions of the composer dot his correspondence, though he had no time for in-depth exploration. When his friend Senator Henry

Cabot Lodge went to the Wagner shrine, Roosevelt wrote, "I envy you Bayreuth. In a perfectly dumb way I have always admired Wagner's operas and I should like greatly to see them in their own place." In 1904, the president spent nearly an hour inspecting a series of *Parsifal Tone Pictures* by a favorite artist, the expatriate Symbolist painter Pinckney Marcius-Simons, who lived in Bayreuth. In 1906, Alice Roosevelt, the president's oldest child, wed Nicholas Longworth III, and Wagner again resounded at the White House—*Tannhäuser*, not *Lohengrin*—while the president led his daughter down the aisle.

AMERICAN SIEGFRIEDS

Sidney Lanier

One night in 1888, the artist Albert Pinkham Ryder attended a performance of *Götterdämmerung* at the Met. On returning home, he set about painting what he had seen. "I worked for forty-eight hours without sleep or food," Ryder recalled. The resulting picture, *Siegfried and the Rhine Maidens*, is a vision of spirit-shrouded nature, with a gnarled, windswept tree dominating the composition and yellowish moonlight bathing the scene. Siegfried is riding by on a horse; his steed has one leg in the air, as if frightened. The Rhinemaidens wave from the water, their bodies twisted like the branches of the tree. Sometime before 1887, Ryder produced an even wilder, more abstract impression of *The Flying Dutchman*, with paint thickly layered in impasto style. These paintings later made an impression on Jackson

Pollock, who, in the words of the art historian Robert Rosenblum, took them as an image of the "overwhelming energies and velocities of nature."

Ryder's *Siegfried* marks a merger of American and Wagnerian mythologies. It departs from the libretto in setting the scene at night and placing Siegfried on a horse; the background looks more like a Western mountain lake than the Rhine. It's almost the reverse of Mark Twain's *A Connecticut Yankee in King Arthur's Court*: here a lone Wagnerian hero goes riding in the American outback. Similar transpositions appear in Wagner-inspired paintings by Louis Eilshemius and Arthur Bowen Davies, whose dreamlike tableaux represented an American strain of Symbolism. In general, though, Nibelung and Arthurian motifs crop up less often in Gilded Age art than they do among the Pre-Raphaelites. Instead, the Siegfried-like figures who populate the vistas of the American spirit—the frontiersman, the cowboy, the homesteader, the outlaw—are homegrown heroes, denizens of the great wide open.

The "imagined communities" of nineteenth-century nationalism required the invention or elaboration of a deep mythic past. The case of the United States was especially complex because its ruling population had come from Europe. What stories were purely American? Indisputably, the deep past of the North American continent belonged to its native peoples. Longfellow's *The Song of Hiawatha* was one hugely successful attempt at constructing an American epic, even if its metrical pattern imitated the Finnish *Kalevala*. Anton Seidl, at his death, was planning an operatic trilogy on the Hiawatha story, in the hope of creating an "American Nibelungenlied." In the same period, Antonín Dvořák was predicting that African-American spirituals would supply raw material for future compositions. The idea of a national mythology based on the legacies of conquered, murdered, and enslaved peoples was not one for which Wagner provided a precedent.

The American Siegfried strides through the work of the Southern poet Sidney Lanier, who achieved national renown in the late nineteenth century before fading into the literary background. At his best, Lanier created a dense verbal music that has drawn comparisons with the august Victorian poet Gerard Manley Hopkins.

Born in Macon, Georgia, in 1842, Lanier fought for the Confederacy in the Civil War. Disregarding his father's desire that he pursue a career in law, he dedicated himself to poetry and music. In 1873, he took a position as principal flute of the Peabody Orchestra, the resident orchestra of the Peabody Institute, in Baltimore. He also composed several charming pieces for his instrument. In poetry, his chief models were Tennyson and the Pre-Raphaelites. He was fixated on the idea of freeing the English language from classical influences and reestablishing its Saxon roots. In a treatise titled *The Science of English Verse*, he declared that the metrical scheme of an Old English work such as *The Battle of Maldon* was "well-nigh universal in our race."

In 1870, on a visit to New York, Lanier heard a Theodore Thomas performance of the *Tannhäuser* overture. An "unbroken march of beautiful-bodied Triumphs," the poet called it. He obtained a copy of the *Ring* libretto, and, in 1874, began work on a translation. A few effective renderings of passages from *Rheingold* appear in the endpapers of Lanier's German-English dictionary—"Of the Rhine-stream's Gold / Heard I rumors; / Treasure-Runes it / Hides in its crimson gleam"—but the project trailed off. In the end, Lanier came to think that instrumental music was superior to the dramatic kind, that the Gesamtkunstwerk was a retrogression to primitive ritual. Wagner was probably on his mind when he praised the "immeasurable profounds of music" over the "quite measurable shallows of this old Scandinavian godhood."

In 1875, Lanier found fame with "The Symphony"—an anticapitalist poem in which instruments of the orchestra speak out loud and condemn industrial society. That success led to a commission for the American centennial festivities: Lanier collaborated with the New England composer Dudley Buck on a choral cantata titled *Centennial Meditation of Columbia*. Lanier's text takes the form of a monologue by the New World goddess Columbia. The language is knotty and dense, as in the poet's attempted translation of *Rheingold*: ". . . old voices rise and call / Yonder where the to-and-fro / Weltering of my Long-Ago / Moves about the moveless base / Far below my resting-place." The final line is a pseudo-Wagnerian mouthful: "Wave the world's best lover's welcome to the world." The cantata had its premiere on the same program that disgorged Wagner's *American Centennial March*. The music went over well, but the poem caused bafflement and merriment. When Lanier shot back at his critics, Buck said that the ruckus brought to mind "the early Wagner pamphlets in defense of his own ideas."

A year after the centennial, Lanier penned a poem in honor of the composer who filled and troubled his vision. "To Richard Wagner," initially subtitled "A Dream of the Age," recapitulates the antimodern rhetoric of "The Symphony" through an array of Wagnerian motifs. The opening lines paint an American Nibelheim, with the night sky wiped out by the pollution of Trade: "I saw a sky of stars that rolled in grime. / All glory twinkled through some sweat of fight." In a chaotic contemporary landscape, nature is molded anew, creeds collide, art struggles to invent fresh forms. But then a transforming sound is heard, a blast of "old Romance," which rises over the "murk-mad factories" of the present:

> Bright ladies and brave knights of Fatherland;
> Sad mariners, no harbor e'er may hold,
> A Swan soft floating tow'rds a tragic strand;
> Dim ghosts of earth, air, water, fire, steel, gold,
> Wind, care, love, lust; a lewd and lurking band
> Of Powers—dark Conspiracy, Cunning cold,
> Gray Sorcery; magic cloaks and rings and rods;
> Valkyries, heroes, Rhinemaids, giants, gods!

Lanier deserved some sort of prize for summarizing the majority of Wagner's work in a handful of lines. (Anna Alice Chapin quotes them in *Wonder Tales from Wagner*.) In the subsequent stanzas, which were cut from the final version of the poem, Lanier pursues an intricate conceit in which Wagner's myths are woven into contemporary lives—the "modern Last / Explains the antique First." We read of smiths and clerks whose "dull hearts" make manifest the yearning hymns of knights and ladies; of "pale girls by spinning spools in factories" who sing of "Elsa's woes and Brünhild's passionate pleas." Then comes the peroration, which contains a presumably accidental echo of Richard Pohl's 1854 comment about art moving westward:

> O Wagner, westward bring thy heavenly art!
> No trifler thou: Siegfried and Wotan be
> Names for big ballads of the modern heart.
> Thine ears hear deeper than thine eyes can see.
> Voice of the monstrous mill, the shouting mart,

Not less of airy cloud and wave and tree,
Thou, thou, if even to thyself unknown,
Hast power to say the Time in terms of tone!

Lanier seems on the verge of a politicized reading of the *Ring* story, such as Shaw would present in *The Perfect Wagnerite*. At the very least, he is grasping what the Pre-Raphaelites resisted: Wagner wishes to transcend the idyll of the past, not to restore it.

O Wagner, westward bring thy heavenly art!" Owen Wister, another would-be composer who turned to literature, seemed to take the instruction literally, whether or not he ever read Lanier's poem. His 1902 novel *The Virginian*, which established the principal tropes of cowboy literature, was the work of a young man who glorified Wagner and saw the West in explicitly Wagnerian terms. That Wister's writing is shot through with white-supremacist rhetoric brings up the all-too-familiar convergence of Wagnerism and racism, although the likes of Wister had no need to look as far as Bayreuth for inspiration. Scientific theories of racial difference became prevalent in the United States in the years before the Civil War, in the writings of Samuel George Morton, Louis Agassiz, and others.

Wister came from an artistic lineage. His grandmother was the Shakespearean actor Fanny Kemble; his mother was the essayist Sarah Wister, who memorably described a Wagner tribute in Paris in 1883. Henry James was a family friend. Young Owen studied music at Harvard with the composer John Knowles Paine, who disapproved of his student's "indecorous and scandalous explosions of Wagnerian harmony." Wister's obsession had an irreverent strain; parodies of *Rienzi* and other Wagner works figured in the comic operas he helped to concoct at the Hasty Pudding Theatricals, Harvard's long-running revue. Theodore Roosevelt was Wister's classmate. Later, Roosevelt would receive the dedication of *The Virginian*.

In 1882, Wister traveled to Europe to further his studies, and visited Bayreuth. Although he failed to meet Wagner—perhaps fortunately, since Evert Wendell, the Harvard chum with whom he was traveling, reported that the Meister was "looking rather cross"—Wister had a happy encounter at Wahnfried with Liszt, for whom his grandmother had written him a letter of introduction. When Wister played his piece *Merlin and Vivien*,

Liszt called him "*un talent prononcé.*" As in the case of Lanier, Wister's artistic longings ran up against family pressure, as his father pushed him toward a career in banking. In 1885, his health broke down, and he took a restorative trip out west, spending much of the summer at a ranch in Wyoming. (Roosevelt was already a believer in the rugged life.) The West had a galvanizing effect on Wister, and Wagnerian metaphors helped him translate his feelings into words:

> The remains of the moon is giving just enough light to show the waving line of the prairie. Every now and then sheet lightning plays from some new quarter like a surprise. The train steamed away into the night + here we are. We passed this evening the most ominous and forbidding chasm of rocks I ever saw in any country. Deep down below a camp fire was burning. It all looked like Die Walküre.

In the same period, Wister asked his mother to send him his four-hand piano score of *Meistersinger* and also the music for "Wotan's Farewell and Magic Fire," which, he said, should be lying around the drawing room. Some years later, describing Yellowstone National Park, Wister said that the landscape reminded him of those moments in Wagner "when the whole orchestra seems to break into silver fragments of magic—sounds of harps and the violins all away up somewhere sustaining some theme you have heard before, but which now returns twice as magnificent."

In 1891, just after the American frontier had been declared closed, Wister made a first attempt at writing a Western novel—an unfinished story of two Easterners on a hunting trip, titled *The Romance of Chalkeye.* One of the two sounds much like the author on his first trip west: "This extraordinary crystal silence! . . . It's like the opening bars of *Lohengrin.*" His earthier companion dismisses Wagner as "a lot of damned noise." The last line suggests that the experience of the West is leading Wister to become ashamed of his inner Harvard aesthete. Instead, he identifies with the rough male specimens he encounters on his journeys. Most of all, he is enamored of the cowboys—cow-punchers, in the lingo of the day. In his 1895 essay "The Evolution of the Cow-Puncher," which appeared with illustrations by the celebrated Western artist Frederic Remington, Wister compares cowboys to the knights of old: "In personal daring and in skill as to the horse, the knight and the cowboy are nothing but the same Saxon of different environments." Native Americans, he writes elsewhere, are unfortunate members of an "inferior race" who fall before the conquering whites.

The narrator of *The Virginian* is, like the author, a fellow from the East. When the title character is introduced, Wister invents the iconography of the Western loner in a single stroke: "Lounging there at ease against the wall was a slim young giant, more beautiful than pictures. His broad, soft hat was pushed back; a loose-knotted, dull-scarlet handkerchief sagged from his throat; and one casual thumb was hooked in the cartridge-belt that slanted across his hips." This figure exerts an almost erotic appeal, as the narrator admits—"a something potent to be felt, I should think, by man or woman." We are in an American Eden, all history stripped away. As at the beginning of the *Ring*, we relive "creation's first morning."

The Virginian's name is never disclosed. By withholding it and substituting monikers like "trustworthy man," Wister gives his hero a legendary aura. Wagner's nameless knight from a far-off land springs to mind. Like *Lohengrin*, *The Virginian* concerns a relationship between a reticent man and an inquisitive woman, but in this case the alliance has a happy ending: the Virginian gives up his free-roaming ways to marry Molly, a schoolteacher from Vermont. Because he remains unnamed to the end, Molly has avoided Elsa's mistake of asking too many questions about her betrothed. The soul of the Anglo-Saxon male remains pure. The convention of the nameless Western hero would later find its apotheosis in Sergio Leone's trilogy of spaghetti Westerns, in which Clint Eastwood plays the Man with No Name.

Amid the skillful tale-spinning, a more menacing agenda emerges. Wister not only cherishes the West as a land of unlimited possibility but upholds the Virginian as a superior exemplar of a superior race. Wister's narrator lapses into strident editorials: "It was through the Declaration of Independence that we Americans acknowledged the *eternal inequality* of man . . . We decreed that every man should thenceforth have equal liberty to find his own level. By this very decree we acknowledged and gave freedom to true aristocracy, saying, 'Let the best man win, whoever he is.'" Embedded in this founding text of the Western genre is an unusually ugly articulation of the racist social-Darwinist philosophy that underlay so much of the rhetoric of Manifest Destiny. Although there is no evidence that Wagner incited such rants, the music supplied a mental soundtrack for Wister as he spun his cowboy fantasies.

WAGNERIAN SKYSCRAPERS

Adler and Sullivan's Auditorium in Chicago

The American city, too, became Wagnerian. In 1920, the critic Paul Rosenfeld suggested that the nation's urban life might have been molded in the composer's image:

> The very masonry and river-spans, the bursting towns, the fury and expansiveness of existence shed his idiom, shadowed forth his proud processionals, his resonant gold, his tumultuous syncopations and blazing brass and cymbals and volcanically inundating melody . . . American life seemed to be calling for this music in order that its vastness, its madly affluent wealth and multiform power and transcontinental span, its loud, grandiose promise might attain something like eternal being.

In London, Wagner saw "Nibelheim, world dominion, activity, work." He would have thought the same of New York and Chicago, with their crowded streets and jutting skylines. Yet his music spoke loudly to several presiding architects of the American metropolis—particularly to the Chicago School of John Wellborn Root, Daniel Burnham, and Louis Sullivan. The city of the future, as these architects imagined it, would be a place not of soulless functionality but of ever-changing form and color. In Sullivan's view, ancient values, "rhythmical, deep, and eternal," would interpenetrate the modern. Structures such as the Wainwright Building, in St. Louis, and the Bayard Building, in New York, should have the noble mass of Gothic cathedrals, or give the impression of trees in a dense forest. The steel-frame building was "a thing rising from the earth as a unitary utterance, Dionysian in beauty."

Root led the Chicago architects in embracing Wagner. A sometime church organist, he thrilled friends with his lively rendition of "The Ride of the Valkyries." What roused him was not the might of the sound but its internal variety. In an 1883 essay, he called for a future "symphony of color" comparable to the nuances of musical language, in pursuit of the "complete unification of the arts for which Wagner labored." Burnham, too, had musical leanings, and designed a home for Theodore Thomas's Chicago Symphony. When Burnham died, in 1912, the Chicago orchestra responded to the news by playing Siegfried's Funeral Music, as New York had done for Seidl. The Monadnock Building, Root and Burnham's magnum opus, was originally to have been built of many-colored bricks, embodying the visual symphony; in the end, it became a uniform, unadorned purple-brown, heralding twentieth-century modernism. The construction methods underpinning early skyscrapers proved more influential than the semi-Wagnerian aesthetic that the pioneers wished to wrap around their steel skeletons.

Sullivan took nourishment from German philosophy, Transcendentalism, and the Pre-Raphaelites. In his youth, he saw Thomas conduct the Act III prelude of *Lohengrin*, and heard many more Wagner excerpts on arriving in Chicago. To quote his third-person memoir, *Autobiography of an Idea*: "He saw arise a Mighty Personality—a great Free Spirit, a Poet, a Master Craftsman, striding in power through a vast domain that was his own, that imagination and will had bodied forth out of himself. Suffice it—as useless to say—Louis became an ardent Wagnerite . . . his courage was ten-folded in this raw city by the Great Lake in the West." In the late eighties and early nineties, strains of Wagner filled Sullivan's studio, as the young Frank Lloyd Wright, one of Sullivan's apprentices, attested: "He would often try to sing the leitmotifs for me and describe the scenes to which they belonged, as he sat at my drawing board." Wright addressed Sullivan with the Bayreuthian epithet "*Lieber Meister*."

In 1884 and 1885, the Met brought its Wagner to Chicago, setting off the usual hysteria. It was decided that Chicago should have its own major opera house. Sullivan and his partner, the German-Jewish émigré Dankmar Adler, received the commission to design it. The result was the Auditorium, the first major building in which Sullivan had a hand. The driving force behind the project was the progressive-leaning real-estate mogul Ferdinand Peck, who imagined a public space where people of all classes could congregate and imbibe the unifying tonic of great art. (Peck had been horrified by the Haymarket riot of 1886 and other signs of labor unrest.) As Joseph Siry has argued, Peck envisioned the Auditorium as a riposte to the Met, with its horseshoe of elite boxes. After a tour of European theaters, Peck and Adler settled on a more egalitarian fan-shaped seating plan, after the Festspielhaus model. Sullivan handled the ornamentation of the interior, using arching forms, gold-relief patterns, delicate mosaic work, and incandescent lighting to generate an atmosphere of enveloping warmth. Wagner is one of four figures portrayed in medallions to either side of the proscenium; the others are Haydn, Demosthenes, and Shakespeare.

In 1893, Adler and Sullivan unveiled an even more arresting color-symphony at the World's Columbian Exposition, in Chicago. Their Transportation Building, nearly a thousand feet long, was a prominent feature of the White City, the makeshift metropolis that arose on the Exposition grounds. The sea of white was broken by a polychromatic Golden Doorway, its predominantly crimson hues including some forty different tints. As the art historian Lauren Weingarden points out, the color scheme acted to diminish mass, to "dissolve enveloping surfaces," to make the structure seem to hover. A guidebook to the Exposition stated: "The architects of the building have called its vari-colored effects 'Wagnerian,' and we may accept their ideas so far as to name this entrance the wedding-march of a 'Lohengrin'—in other words, an unquestionably beautiful feature in an *ensemble* that is purposely devoid of entertainment and delight."

The Golden Doorway has vanished, along with the rest of the White City, but Sullivan's vari-colored aesthetic persists in the "jewel box" banks that he designed in his later years, when his reputation was in decline and commissions for large-scale projects eluded him. In towns across the Midwest, Sullivan pursued his dream of making buildings that vibrate with color over the course of the day. Echoing Root, he spoke of a "color symphony" or "color tone poem," with "many shades of the strings and the wood winds and the brass."

The exterior of the National Farmers' Bank, in Owatonna, Minnesota, is an imposing red-brick box, its grand arched windows facing the town center. Orange and green hues give the interior an ethereal air, with stained glass filtering light from the sides and above. The Farmers & Merchants Union Bank, in Columbus, Wisconsin, is heavily ornamented on the outside, with eagles and lions standing guard; the interior is again much warmer, its stained-glass windows centered on abstract, swirling discs of many hues. Bank business is still conducted in both buildings; townspeople depositing checks must walk around tourists gazing upward in awe. Wagner's Bayreuth was designed as a respite from capitalist clamor; Sullivan hoped to cast a wholesome light on the daily life of American commerce, as if the unsullied Rheingold were gleaming from the vaults.

DEMOCRATIC VISTAS

By the turn of the century, Wagner loomed large in American life, his operas laden with the neo-Gothic trappings that informed so much American architecture of the period. The master of the Gothic Revival, the Boston-based architect Ralph Adams Cram, identified himself as a "besotted Wagnerite," seeing the composer as a foe of materialist decadence. He and his partner, Bertram Goodhue, built churches that dissented from the teeming sidewalks and streets around them, their interiors giving an exaggerated, almost cinematic sense of space. Goodhue remarked that St. Bartholomew's, a neo-Byzantine church in New York, would "look more like Arabian Nights or the last act of *Parsifal* than any Christian church." One could even hear Wagnerian strains ringing from bell towers. The carillon of Riverside Church, in New York, still marks the passing quarter-hours with a sequence based on the bell motif in *Parsifal*. It was donated by John D. Rockefeller, Jr., son of the Standard Oil tycoon.

Yet the "Wagner fever," as a character in William Dean Howells's 1889 novel *A Hazard of New Fortunes* calls it, spread only so far. The nation's aspiration toward European grandeur, *Parsifal* Entertainments included, clashed with a contrary impulse to shrug off an effete, unmanly European inheritance. American popular culture was in ascendance, seeking its roots in homegrown folk traditions, and Wagner presented himself as an obvious target for insolent jibes. In Victor Herbert and Harry B. Smith's

1905 musical *Miss Dolly Dollars*, a millionaire heiress flouts the *Parsifal* fad
at the Met:

> Oh, I love those songs where "honey"
> Is the only rhyme for "money"
> They are better than old Parsifal to me.

Tin Pan Alley lyrics for Scott Joplin's "Pine Apple Rag" follow a similar
line:

> Some people rave about Wagnerian airs,
> Some say the Spring Song is divine,
> Talk like that is out of season,
> What I like is something pleasin',
> Pine Apple rag for mine . . .

In pop culture, Wagner was both a phenomenon to be emulated—he was,
after all, a master of spectacle—and a rival to be defeated. This American
Wagner complex will play out most obviously in Hollywood movies, but it
is already evident in Owen Wister's attempt to reconcile his love of Wagner and his adulation of cowboys. It also surfaces in the alert ambivalence
of two earthy-minded American authors who repudiated Gilded Age pre
tension: Mark Twain and Walt Whitman.

Twain is often credited with a world-class barb: "Wagner's music is
better than it sounds." In fact, the humorist Bill Nye said it; Twain merely
quoted it. An eager operagoer, Twain had his ups and downs with Wagner, emphasizing the downs for his readers. *A Tramp Abroad*, published
in 1880, relates one encounter: "We went to Mannheim and attended a
shivaree,—otherwise an opera,—the one called Lohengrin. The banging
and slamming and booming and crashing were something beyond belief.
The racking and pitiless pain of it remains stored up in my memory alongside the memory of the time that I had my teeth fixed."

In 1891, Twain trained his gaze on the juiciest high-culture target of
all, undertaking a ten-day visit to Bayreuth. He reported on the experience
in a rippingly funny newspaper article that first appeared under the title
"Mark Twain at Bayreuth" and was later republished as "At the Shrine of
St. Wagner." Selective quotations of its sharpest jabs have made it seem a

merciless takedown. It is, in fact, an oblique expression of embarrassed fandom, nearly as conflicted as Nietzsche's *The Case of Wagner*.

The essay begins with a respectful description of the Festspielhaus, "the model theater of the world." Twain's response to the *Parsifal* prelude is rhapsodic, almost delirious: "Out of darkness and distance and mystery soft rich notes rose upon the stillness, and from his grave the dead magician began to weave his spells about his disciples and steep their souls in his enchantments." The visitor has the impression that Wagner was "conscious in his grave of what was going on here, and that these divine sounds were the clothing of thoughts which were at this moment passing through his brain." The music is "exquisite," "delicious." The problems start with the singing. Twain wishes that he could listen to Wagner with the vocal parts omitted, so that he could bask in the orchestration. Despite the absence of "anything that might with confidence be called rhythm, or tune, or melody," Twain enjoys the first act all the same. Later, he falters. "Seven hours at five dollars a ticket is almost too much for the money."

The next day brings *Tannhäuser*, which, Twain says, "has always driven me mad with ignorant delight." The Pilgrims' Chorus sends him into rhapsodic mode again: "music to make one drunk with pleasure, music to make one take scrip and staff and beg his way round the globe to hear it." *Tristan* is more of a struggle. Twain becomes preoccupied with the almost inhuman attentiveness of the audience around him. The most famous passage ensues:

> This opera of "Tristan and Isolde" last night broke the hearts of all witnesses who were of the faith, and I know of some and have heard of many who could not sleep after it, but cried the night away. I feel strongly out of place here. Sometimes I feel like the one sane person in a community of the mad; sometimes I feel like the one blind man where all others see; the one groping savage in the college of the learned, and always, during service, I feel like a heretic in heaven.

Less widely quoted are the sentences that follow: "But by no means do I ever overlook or minimize the fact that this is one of the most extraordinary experiences of my life. I have never seen anything like this before. I have never seen anything so great and fine and real as this devotion."

When Twain hears *Parsifal* again, he resists no longer. Instead, his disdain falls on those who tell him afterward that second-rate artists had substituted for the first cast. In an abrupt reversal, he announces, "I was the only man out of 3,200 who got his money back on those two operas." In all, the essay is the record of a reluctant conversion—another inverted panegyric, like Nietzsche's. That it has so often been mistaken for a frontal attack indicates the degree to which Twain was hedging his bets on the question of America's relationship with European culture. Even though Bayreuth won him over, he knew which way the native wind was blowing. Some years later, he reverted to an anti-Wagner line, comparing the composer unfavorably to the blackface minstrel shows he saw in his youth. In his autobiography, he wrote: "If I could have the nigger show back again, in its pristine purity and perfection, I should have but little further use for opera." Twain appears unaware of the irony of posing a choice between Wagner's operas and homegrown racist entertainment.

Whitman felt no embarrassment over his love for the European musical tradition, which he considered essential to his American art. "But for the opera I could never have written *Leaves of Grass*," he once said. He was speaking not of Wagner but of Italian bel canto, which was the mainstay of his younger years. By the time the cultus took hold, Whitman was no longer attending opera regularly. He said to Horace Traubel in 1888: "I have got rather off the field—the Wagner opera has had its vogue only in these later years since I got out of the way of going to the theater." But he mentioned hearing "bits here and there at concerts, from orchestras, bands, which have astonished, ravished me, like the discovery of a new world."

Poet and composer had much in common. Whitman's irregular, ever-rolling rhythms seem the American equivalent of "endless melody"; his incantations of signature phrases ring out like leitmotifs; his creed of all-embracingness—"I encompass worlds and volumes of worlds"— resembles Tristan and Isolde's cry of "I myself am the world." For all his rude robustness, Whitman was not immune to Liebestod sentiments. "I am not sure but the high soul of lovers welcomes death most," he wrote in the Calamus section of *Leaves of Grass*. "What indeed is finally beautiful except death and love?"

The elderly Whitman could not help noticing how often his name was paired with Wagner's. He told Traubel: "So many of my friends say Wagner is Leaves of Grass done into music that I begin to suspect there must be something in it." As early as 1860, the freethinker Moncure Conway—who, after the composer's death, would eulogize him as the prophet of a new social order—connected Whitman's line "There was a child went forth every day" with the opening chords of the *Tannhäuser* overture. In Britain, Edward Dannreuther inserted several Whitman references into his 1873 book *Richard Wagner: His Tendencies and Theories.* And William Sloane Kennedy named Whitman the "Wagner of poets": "As Wagner abandoned the cadences of the old sonatas and symphonies,—occurring at the end of every four, eight, or sixteen bars,—so Whitman has abandoned the measured beat of the old rhymed see-saw poetry."

Although Whitman never saw a full Wagner production, he accepted the idea that the operas were "constructed on my lines"—that they "attach themselves to the same theories of art that have been responsible for *Leaves of Grass*." In 1881, he wrote an essay with the Wagnerian title "The Poetry of the Future," in which he bids his colleagues to "arouse and initiate more than to define or finish." Whitman declares, as van Gogh would do later in the same decade, that music has taken the lead: "The music of the present, Wagner's, Gounod's, even the later Verdi's, all tends toward this free expression of poetic emotion." Poetry, by contrast, is stuck in outdated values of "verbal melody, exquisitely clean and pure."

All the same, Whitman hesitated. "Do you figure out Wagner to be a force making for democracy or the opposite?" he asked. His longtime friend William Douglas O'Connor argued for the former. "O'Connor swears to the democracy—swears to it with a big oath. Others have said to me that Wagner's art was distinctly the art of a caste—for the few. What am I to believe?"

4

GRAIL TEMPLE

Esoteric, Decadent, and Satanic Wagner

Reginald Machell, Parsifal

"ere time becomes space," the sage old Gurnemanz says in Act
I of *Parsifal*. A foolish, lawless lad has blundered into the secret
realm of the Holy Grail. Even though he has introduced himself
by senselessly killing a noble swan, his arrival appears to be no accident,
and Gurnemanz offers to lead him to the Grail Temple, where the *Liebes-
mahl*, the communal love feast of the Grail Knights, is about to be held.
No path will show the way to the sacred place. Only one whom the Grail
has chosen can find the route. Parsifal takes a few steps, and says, "I am
hardly moving, yet I already seem to have come far."

There follows an orchestral passage that the libretto designates as *Verwandlungsmusik*, or Transformation Music. As Gurnemanz and Parsifal tread the hidden path to the temple, bells sound repeatedly from the pit—the notes C, G, A, E, as in John D. Rockefeller's Riverside Church carillon. The inaugural *Parsifal* production of 1882 used a memorable device: as the singers walked in place, a panorama unscrolled behind them, giving the illusion of great distances traversed. The illusion is also musical: the hypnotic repetition of the bell figure, through shimmering orchestration, conjures an "immense horizon," as Baudelaire said of the Grail music in *Lohengrin*. The march of industry in the nineteenth century had led to a pervasive feeling of an accelerating, shrinking world. When, in 1838, the steamer *Sirius* crossed the Atlantic in a mere seventeen days, the *New York Morning Herald* famously spoke of the "annihilation of time and space." A similar phrase entered the lexicon of Marx, describing the global grasp of capitalism. *Parsifal* supplied the opposite sensation: time slowing, space expanding, the fleeting moment stretched into eternity.

Victorian odes to *Parsifal* tended to glance over the sheer strangeness of what happens once Gurnemanz and Parsifal reach the temple. First the Knights of the Grail enter, taking their places for the feast. The boys' voices admired by Verlaine float down from the temple dome, delivering unchildlike sentiments: "With joyful heart let my blood now be shed for the redeeming hero." The Grail is brought forth, covered in its shrine. Squires also carry King Amfortas, the suffering ruler wounded by sin. He is a variant on the figure of the Fisher King, whose fertile realm becomes a Waste Land when he falls sick. Wagner's Amfortas awaits the "pure fool" who will cure him—Parsifal, as yet unready for the task.

There is a long, lugubrious silence. Amfortas is weary of the ritual he must perform again and again. Each time he uncovers the Grail, the miracle of the Savior's blood gives sustenance to all, but his own wound bleeds anew. "Let me die," he cries. A sepulchral voice within the temple, sounding "as if from a tomb," commands Amfortas to do his duty. This is Titurel, Amfortas's father and the founder of the order. Hundreds of years old, too feeble to rise from his bed, he relies on his son to lead the ceremony, which prolongs his life. Amfortas sings a monologue of dire lamentation—"Take my inheritance from me, / close the wound"—and then performs his office. Darkness descends. The chalice glows red. Amfortas's blood flows. Titurel cries, "O heavenly rapture!" This grisly sacrament raises the question of what kind of sect the Grail Knights really are. Titurel could be mistaken for a vampire.

In Act II, the evil sorcerer Klingsor, who engineered Amfortas's fall from grace, attempts to ensnare Parsifal as well. When the troupe of Flower Maidens fails to seduce the newcomer, Klingsor presses into service the enigmatic Kundry, who has been wandering the earth for centuries after having laughed at Christ. Kundry, too, falls short, whereupon Parsifal vanquishes Klingsor and reclaims the Holy Spear—"the lance that pierced the Flank supreme," as Verlaine calls it. In Act III, Parsifal reappears in the province of the Grail, clad in black, and finds that the situation has deteriorated further. Amfortas can no longer bear to repeat the Grail rite; Titurel is dead. Nevertheless, Gurnemanz discloses to Parsifal the miraculous vision of the Good Friday Spell, in which "all creation gives thanks, all that blooms and soon fades away." A sinuous melody of grace courses through the strings, then drifts into a harmonic haze.

Suddenly, "as if from far away," the bells of Monsalvat begin to ring. Their fixed tones clash against the diminished chord on which the strings have landed. The bells are thus turned against their nature and made to sound baleful. The Knights stage a second procession, one group bearing Amfortas and the other bearing Titurel's corpse. When the bells ring again, gnashing dissonances in the orchestra crash against them. The Grail music has become funereal, catastrophic, demonic.

Once Parsifal has touched the Spear to Amfortas's wound, a rite of healing unfolds. The opera ends with glowing affirmations of the key of A-flat major, the same in which it began. Yet the shadows of the journey linger in the mind. Wagner's own comments make clear that *Parsifal* is no bland exercise in moral uplift. "The Savior on the Cross, blood everywhere" was his concise summary. The night before the first performance, he is said to have issued this exhortation: "Children, tomorrow it can finally start! Tomorrow the devil is let loose! Therefore, all of you who are taking part, seek that the devil enters into you, and you who are in the audience, seek that you receive him properly." While Wagner was no doubt speaking metaphorically, such tremors of diabolism led the American critic James Huneker, a renegade Nietzschean, to write a story in which a character asks, "What is *Parsifal* but a version of the Black Mass?"

Parsifal is certainly a Mass of a different color. It is a religious work— Wagner called it his "stage consecration festival play"—yet it belongs to no one religion. Indeed, despite the claims of the Anglo-American genteel tradition, it has an adversarial relationship with organized faith, at least in its modern form. Back in 1849, Wagner had dreamed of a "new religion," one that would smash the materialist values that imprisoned art, politics, and spirituality alike. By the time he began composing *Parsifal*, he was no longer remotely a revolutionary, but his antimaterialist slant remained. His 1880 essay "Religion and Art" raises the hope that art can renew worn-out faiths: "One could say that when religion becomes artificial, it falls to art to save the core of religion, by grasping the figurative value of those mythic symbols that religion wants us to believe as literally true, and revealing through an ideal presentation the deep truth hidden in them." Christianity and Buddhism are the greatest of religions, preaching "renunciation of the world and its passions," yet secular society holds them captive. They can regain their original strength only if they recognize the unity of living things under the sign of compassion.

Although the later Nietzsche considered *Parsifal* a capitulation to Christianity, he better explained the composer's stance in an 1875 note: "If Wagner takes up Germanic-Christian myth one moment, seafaring legends another, then Buddhistic myths, then pagan-German ones, then the Protestant bourgeoisie, it is clear that he stands *free* of the *religious* meaning of these myths, and requires the same of his listeners." The Christianity in *Parsifal* is obvious. The ceremony of the Grail in Act I is a Eucharist, and when a penitent Kundry washes Parsifal's feet in Act III she is channeling Mary of Bethany in the New Testament. But elements of other traditions crowd in. "Redemption to the Redeemer," the gnomic motto of the work, recalls the formula "Salvator salvandus," or the Savior saved, in Gnostic teachings. The Good Friday Spell intimates a pagan celebration of nature; the Resurrection carries on age-old cycles of death and rebirth. The no less primordial Kundry earns the nicknames *Urteufelin* ("Arch-she-devil") and *Höllenrose* ("Rose of hell"). "Unfortunately, all of our Christian legends have an external, pagan origin," Wagner wrote in 1859.

Eastern traditions had nearly equal weight in Wagner's thinking. He probably first learned of them through his brother-in-law, the philologist Hermann Brockhaus, who translated Sanskrit and Persian. Schopenhauer's meditations on Eastern concepts pulled Wagner in deeper. In 1856, he began planning a Buddhist drama called *Die Sieger*, or *The Victors*, which would have told of the maiden Prakriti's love for the monk Ananda and her overcoming of desire under the Buddha's guidance—a story mentioned in the essay Wagner was writing the day he died. The theme of lust turned to love, of self-seeking becoming compassion, passed into *Parsifal*. Traces of Hinduism and Islam also surface. Ronald Perlwitz proposes that Parsifal's misdeed in Act I, his killing of the swan, is modeled on a passage in the Sanskrit epic *Ramayana*, which condemns the murder of a crane. Islamic influences reside in the medieval Parzival romance of Wolfram von Eschenbach, the opera's primary source. The Grail there takes the form of a precious stone; Wagner plausibly compared it to the veneration of the Kaaba at Mecca. He erred, though, in thinking that the name Parsifal was derived from the Persian for "pure fool."

The philosopher Ernst Bloch handily summarizes *Parsifal* as "Christian-Buddhist-Rosicrucian art-religion or religious art." Poised between blinding light and devouring night, it rose as a supreme, enigmatic symbol over the epoch of the fin de siècle, when artists everywhere felt that some revelation was at hand. For some, the pilgrimage to Bayreuth—until 1903, the one place where the sacred play of *Parsifal* could be seen—was less about worshipping Wagner than about undertaking a private quest toward hidden worlds. These journeys had many different destinations—Catholic mystery, Gnostic riddle, Buddhist enlightenment, Black Mass—but they began with a departure from the world as it was, an escape from Nibelheim.

It was the age of esotericism, occultism, Satanism, Spiritism, Theosophy, Swedenborgism, Mesmerism, Martinism, and Kabbalism. Reinventions or fabrications of medieval sects multiplied: the Knights Templar, the Hermetic Order of the Golden Dawn, and various Rosicrucian orders, which sought to revive Renaissance alchemical and necromantic lore of obscure origin. Not only fringe gurus but also denizens of high society were dabbling in séances, tarot cards, astrology, and homeopathy. A large number of writers, artists, and musicians took an interest in one or another of these movements; the Symbolists, including the Mallarmé circle, were especially prone. They might have agreed with William Butler Yeats, who saw occult happenings as "metaphors for poetry"—so spirits from the other side told him.

Holbrook Jackson, writing in 1913, associated the mystical revival with a "revolt against rationalism" and a "salvation by sin"—ideas implicit in *Parsifal*. The spiritualist movements were one more face of the resistance to industrial capitalism that manifested itself in the underworld tableaux of Baudelaire, the neo-primitivism of Gauguin, and the archaism of the Pre-Raphaelites. The advent of positivism, social Darwinism, and other mechanistic explanations for human behavior brought a countervailing urge to restore the dimension of the miraculous. The occultists also rejected dualities of good and evil, seeking a more complex balance of darkness and light. Nietzsche's jeremiads against conventional morality were widely read, as was Mikhail Bakunin's posthumous book *God and the State*, which portrays Satan as "the eternal rebel, the first freethinker and the emancipator of worlds."

Wagner blended readily with the mystical milieu. Édouard Schuré, a leading French explicator of arcane practices and non-Western religions, acclaimed him as "a fallen Lucifer" and "the greatest unconscious occultist who ever lived." Gérard Encausse, who took the pseudonym Papus and co-founded the modern Martinist order, said that "the world of enchantments has confided all of its secrets" to Wagner. Rudolf Steiner, the leader of Anthroposophy, declared: "That there is in Wagner and in his works a very large measure of occult power, is something that mankind is gradually learning to realize." In 1901, Aleister Crowley, the British magus, addressed the composer thus:

> O MASTER of the ring of love, O lord
> Of all desires, and king of all the stars,
> O strong magician . . .

Crowley asserted that *Parsifal* had been created at the bidding of the German occultist Theodor Reuss, the Outer Head of the Ordo Templi Orientis, or Order of Oriental Templars. Wagner's name appears on a fantastical list of members of the order, alongside Siddartha, Osiris, Orpheus, Mohammed, Merlin, Dante, Goethe, and Nietzsche.

The quest for mystical truth produced reams of nonsense, but it also inspired thrilling imaginative leaps—indeed, some of the earliest feats of artistic modernism. Michelle Facos and Thor Mednick, in *The Symbolist Roots of Modern Art*, describe how the Symbolists undermined conventional modes of representation in an effort to "access the divine directly." John Bramble, in *Modernism and the Occult*, notes that artistic avant-gardes often patterned themselves on the esoteric orders of the day, sometimes becoming indistinguishable from them. Art in the cultic mode, which would persist deep into the twentieth century, had no greater exemplar than the Sorcerer of Bayreuth.

ROSE + CROIX

Joséphin Péladan

After Wagner's death, Bayreuth faced an uncertain future. *Parsifal* drew less than full houses in 1883 and 1884—a sign the festival could not subsist on one work alone. When Cosima Wagner assumed control, she expanded the repertory, adding *Tristan* in 1886 and *Meistersinger* in 1888. By the end of the decade, the festival had found a steady footing. Cosima, an Italian-born French-Hungarian who spoke fluent German and English, knew that Bayreuth's future depended on an international audience, and she proved adept at obtaining one. The guest lists for 1888 included the composers Giacomo Puccini, Ferruccio Busoni, Max Reger, and Johann Strauss, Jr.; the rising musical revolutionary Claude Debussy, who occasionally visited occult circles; a raft of eminent Bostonians, including

Isabella Stewart Gardner and Bernard Berenson; Édouard Dujardin and Houston Stewart Chamberlain, of the *Revue wagnérienne*; the photographer Alfred Stieglitz; the architect and stage designer Adolphe Appia; and the Symbolist painter Fernand Khnopff.

Conspicuous in the crowd that summer was Joséphin Péladan— novelist, playwright, art critic, and performance artist *avant la lettre*. Péladan habitually went about in a flowing white robe, an azure or black velvet jacket, a lace ruff, and an Astrakhan hat, which, in conjunction with his bushy head of hair and double-pointed beard, gave him the look of a Middle Eastern potentate. Perhaps on account of that costume, he failed to gain admittance to Wahnfried, but he became a fervent Wagnerite all the same. Three hearings of *Parsifal*, he later said, led him to his calling as a Rosicrucian mage: "The renovation of the Rose + Croix was born at Bayreuth, was born of Bayreuth!" Although he had doubts about the festival, he cherished it as a place free of cynicism, where "one goes in search of emotions and not epigrams." If not for the German language, he said, it would be the loveliest place on earth.

Péladan was born in Lyon, in 1858, into a family steeped in esoterica. His father, Louis-Adrien, was a conservative Catholic who tried to establish a Cult of the Wound of the Left Shoulder of Our Savior Jesus Christ. Péladan's older brother, Adrien, wrote a medical text describing how the brain subsists on unused sperm that takes the form of vital fluid. When Adrien died prematurely, of accidental strychnine poisoning, his brother propagated his ideas, arguing that the intellect can thrive only when the sexual impulse is suppressed. The Péladans were reactionary in their politics, detesting democracy and demanding the restoration of the monarchy. Péladan differed from many other occultists in couching his Rosicrucian rhetoric as an extension of authentic Catholic doctrine.

He made his name first as an art critic, inveighing against naturalism and Impressionism, both of which he considered banal. "I believe in the Ideal, in Tradition, in Hierarchy," he said. His model painter was Pierre Puvis de Chavannes, who, in a manner akin to Pre-Raphaelitism, rendered neoclassical subjects in archaic style, flattening perspectives and whitening colors. "What he paints has neither place nor date," Péladan wrote of Puvis. "It is from everywhere and always." At the same time, he had a taste for the lurid, enjoying the nastily glittering Salomé pictures of Gustave Moreau and the gruesome caricatures of Félicien Rops. Péladan singled out for praise Rops's *Les Sataniques*, etchings of visibly aroused demons penetrating and killing women. Such pendulum swings between piety and depravity were typical of the fin-de-siècle milieu.

In 1884, Péladan published his first novel, *Supreme Vice*—the initial installment in what turned out to be a twenty-one-volume cycle titled *La Décadence latine*. A magician named Magus Mérodack is pitted against embodiments of decadent society, notably the domineering, sphinxlike Princess Leonora d'Este. A flagrant misogynist, Péladan often saw women as vessels of satanic energy. He attributed to Rops the saying "Man puppet of woman, woman puppet of the devil." *Supreme Vice* had a considerable success, despite its obscure and inconclusive narrative. Crucially, it caught the eye of the poet Stanislas de Guaita, who began exchanging ideas with Péladan about the restorative capacity of magic. By the time Péladan arrived in Bayreuth, in 1888, he had joined forces with Guaita to form a Rosicrucian society called the Kabbalistic Order of the Rose + Cross.

Mystical circles were prone to constant internecine warfare, and even the smallest sects found ways to subdivide into still tinier ones. By 1890, Péladan and Guaita were parting ways, mainly over Catholic doctrine: the one adhered to strict beliefs, the other inclined more toward Kabbalism, Buddhism, and paganism. (Guaita's thinking was actually closer to the syncretism of *Parsifal*, though he showed little interest in Wagner.) Péladan proceeded to found the Order of the Catholic Rose + Croix of the Temple and the Grail, dubbing himself Le Sâr Péladan, after the Akkadian word for "king." He published a book titled *How One Becomes a Mage*, and let it be known that he had completed the syllabus. He informed Félix Faure, the president of the Republic, that he had the gift of "seeing and hearing at the greatest distance, applicable to enemy councils and suppressing espionage." To the Minister of Public Instruction and Beaux Arts, he wrote that he had "reforged Nothung." He began one lecture by saying, "People of Nîmes, I have only to pronounce a certain formula for the earth to open and swallow you."

Péladan's trip to Bayreuth yielded a novel titled *The Victory of the Husband*, the sixth book in the *Décadence* cycle. The preface offers "greetings and glory to you, Richard Wagner, thaumaturge and discoverer of the third mode, conqueror and emperor of the Western Theater!" The plot concerns the love of Izel and Adar: she, the adopted daughter of a wealthy Avignon priest; he, a young genius aghast at the stupidity of his time. They speak "in Wagner," styling themselves Siegmund and Sieglinde. When they honeymoon at Bayreuth, one of the more stupefying Wagner Scenes in literature ensues. During a performance of *Tristan*, the newlyweds cannot restrain themselves and begin making love. "Tristan! Isolde!" the lovers cry onstage. "Adar! Izel!" the lovers murmur in the audience, possibly to the irritation of their neighbors. As their lips lock together, there is a salty taste of blood.

On the question of *Parsifal*, however, the lovers diverge. For Izel, the opera is too "chaste, sweet, and calm." For Adar, it opens the door to a new mystic consciousness. He goes to study with a sinister Nuremberg sorcerer named Doctor Sexthental and drifts away from his bride. Sexthental, sensing an opportunity, projects himself astrally into Izel's chambers, in the form of an incubus. The initiate defeats this incursion, but marital strife persists. Adar must renounce his magic—"I resign the august pentacle of the Macrocosm"—to regain Izel's love.

Wagner figures in various other Péladan novels. In *Le Panthée*, a starving composer stoops to playing piano at a resort; when he is told that his choice of *Tristan* is agitating the clientele, he defiantly launches into Siegfried's Funeral Music. In *The Androgyne*, an angelically feminine thirteen-year-old boy improvises on Beethoven and Wagner, "sounding the bells of the Grail after a phrase from the *Pathétique* Sonata." And in *The Gynander*, another androgyne, Tammuz, makes it his mission to convert "gynanders"—Péladan's term for lesbians—to heterosexuality. His final triumph comes when he performs the feat of generating replicas of himself, each of whom seduces and marries a wayward lesbian. As an orchestra plays the wedding march from *Lohengrin* and music from *Walküre*, the brides fall to worshipping a giant phallus. Thus summarized, Péladan's writing sounds daft. But it is impressively daft, and had many admirers in its day. Anatole France, Paul Valéry, André Gide, and André Breton read him with pleasure. Verlaine called him "bizarre but of great distinction."

I n 1892, Péladan found a new identity as an artistic impresario, inaugurating the Salons de la Rose + Croix. The intermingling of the arts at these annual affairs—painting, sculpture, theater, music—anticipated the mixed-media happenings of the twentieth and twenty-first centuries. John Bramble goes so far as to say that the Salon pioneered the "religion of modern art." What Péladan took from the "superhuman Wagner" was, above all, the idea that the artist should be "a priest, a king, a magus." At the Salon, Péladan wrote, "there will unfold intellectual rites as noble as the celebrated ones at Bayreuth . . . The Ideal will have its temple and its knights." The opening ceremony was to have taken the form of a Solemn Mass of the Holy Spirit at St.-Germain l'Auxerrois, with excerpts from *Parsifal* sounding on the organ. Wary clerics withheld permission, on the grounds that Wagner was Protestant. So Péladan and his cohort repaired to the Cathedral of Notre-Dame, where they held aloft a rose crossed with a dagger, to the bafflement of ordinary parishioners. At the exhibition itself, which occupied the Galerie Durand-Ruel, brass players intoned the *Parsifal* prelude.

The Salons continued annually until 1897, attracting large crowds and voluminous commentary. Such luminaries as Mallarmé and Verlaine paid their respects. Yet Péladan never won the confidence of the artistic community at large. He alienated several leading figures, including Puvis, by prematurely advertising their participation. The end result was a somewhat indiscriminate mix of stylistic schools and levels of accomplishment. Péladan complicated his task by issuing strenuous restrictions and regulations. He forbade history paintings, still lifes, seascapes, "everything humorous," and "all representations of contemporary life, whether private or public." (Lest anyone miss the anti-naturalist agenda, a poster for a later Salon showed a Perseus-like hero holding up the severed head of Émile Zola.) Architectural entries were discouraged, "that art having died in 1789." Female artists were ostensibly excluded, "following Magical law," although at least five women exhibited under pseudonyms—including the arch-Wagnériste Judith Gautier, who contributed a relief sculpture titled "Kundry, Rose of Hell."

In the midst of the first Salon, Péladan feuded with his chief financial supporter, Antoine de La Rochefoucauld, who held the title of Archonte des Beaux-Arts. The point of contention was Péladan's play *The Son of the Stars*, which told of a shepherd-poet being initiated as a magus. The Montmartre composer Erik Satie wrote astonishing, borderline-atonal music for the premiere—another instance of mystical impulses leading into uncharted regions. When La Rochefoucauld decided to cut back on Salon events, including two performances of *The Son of the Stars*, Péladan proclaimed a schism and arranged a disruption of a concert that remained on the schedule—a Wagner program conducted by Charles Lamoureux. During the *Siegfried Idyll*, an ally of Péladan's, ineffectively disguised by a thick beard, began shouting imprecations, calling the Archonte "a felon, a coward, a thief." The heckler was ejected, causing a glass door to shatter and the musicians to fall silent. Cries of "Vive Péladan!" were drowned out by "Vive La Rochefoucauld!" Somehow, the concert proceeded to its close—the final scene of *Parsifal*.

Péladan's notoriety dwindled as the nineties went on. Satirists reduced him to caricature: Jean de Tinan's 1897 novel *Mistress of Aesthetes* features a Grand Master Sotaukrack, author of *The Sphinx with Mauve Eyes*. By the time of his death, in 1918, Péladan seemed a perfumed relic. Still, he was never forgotten, his influence surfacing in unexpected places. Ezra Pound consulted Péladan's *The Secret of the Troubadours*; Wassily Kandinsky cited Le Sâr's dictum that "the artist is a 'king' . . . not only because he has great power, but also because his responsibility is great." Later in the century, Joseph Beuys read Péladan with interest. What caught these artists' attention was Péladan's faith in the alchemy of the creative act. In 2017, the much-mocked magus received belated vindication in New York, as the Guggenheim Museum, housed in Frank Lloyd Wright's upward-spiraling modernist temple, presented a re-creation of the Salons de la Rose + Croix. Fittingly, *Parsifal* emanated from the loudspeakers.

BRUGES-LA-MORTE

In his headiest moments, Le Sâr imagined that he could make the world of the Grail real. He spoke of a "Monsalvat restored"—some solitary, ruined abbey that would be consecrated for his order, its walls ringing with strains of Aeschylus, the Ninth Symphony, and Titurel's funeral music. During a visit to Belgium, where his ideas intrigued local artists and writers, Péladan was told that a wealthy American had offered to donate an old church as the site for a new Grail Temple. If his account is to be believed, and most likely it is not, Péladan was returning from Brussels to Paris to meet with the supporter, *Parsifal* resounding in his head, when customs inspectors confronted him at the border. They sized up his exotic dress—the hat, the boots, the cloak—and deemed him unhygienic. When an undeclared package of Egyptian cigarettes was found in his luggage, Péladan

Fernand Khnopff, Isolde, *1905*

was detained for some hours, missing the assignation with the mysterious American. "Wagner alone suffered such hatred," he wrote.

Belgium would have been a logical place for a new Monsalvat, since the nation was to some extent an operatic creation. In the summer of 1830, the revolutionary overtones of Daniel Auber's opera *La Muette de Portici*, a work that Wagner appreciated, incited riots during and after a performance at the Théâtre Royal de la Monnaie, the venerable opera house of Brussels; those riots are credited with setting off the Belgian Revolution, which led to independence from Dutch rule. La Monnaie was later the site of one of Europe's staunchest Wagner cults. Performances of *Lohengrin* held particular attraction, since that opera is set in the vicinity of Antwerp. It received its Belgian premiere in 1870, long before it arrived in Paris. In the years when Wagner was still scarce in France—only in the nineties did his operas begin to enter the repertory—intellectuals often traveled to Brussels to hear what they were missing.

As the sinuous lines of Art Nouveau mingled with centuries-old Gothic and Baroque architecture, Belgian cities took on a dreamlike air. By night, they could be mistaken for opera sets. Such is the mood of Georges Rodenbach's 1892 novel *Bruges-la-morte,* or *Bruges the Dead,* in which the paralyzed sorrow of the widowed protagonist is of a piece with the town's ascetic, brooding atmosphere. The Belgian architects and designers who helped to invent Art Nouveau often mined Wagner for ideas. Henry van de Velde, a harbinger of modernist design, set himself the goal of making a Gesamtkunstwerk out of the domestic sphere. The art historian Katherine Kuenzli writes that van de Velde's fastidiously harmonized Bloemenwerf villa, on the outskirts of Brussels, "shifted the setting for aesthetic experience from the mythical stage of Wagner's festival theater at Bayreuth to the realm of everyday life."

An atmosphere of withered medieval romance pervades the work of Maurice Maeterlinck, the most renowned Belgian writer of the period. Although Maeterlinck was confessedly ignorant of music, he knew Wagner's librettos and took Villiers de l'Isle-Adam's *Axël* as a model. Maeterlinck's 1892 play *Pelléas et Mélisande*, immortalized in operatic form by Debussy, shares traits with *Tristan* and *Parsifal*. It is a tale of forbidden love set in a decaying kingdom, with the enigmatic, Kundry-like Mélisande emerging from a Symbolist forest. Maeterlinck's people, in contrast to Wagner's, are aggressively depersonalized, at the mercy of nameless fates. Maeterlinck once wrote: "It may be necessary to remove the living being entirely from the scene."

The leading Belgian art journals, like their French counterparts, named Wagner as a fellow combatant in the war against bourgeois taste. The progressive periodical *L'Art moderne* wrote of a "valiant Wagnerian army" doing battle with ignorance, indifference, and routine. In 1883, the critic Octave Maus, co-founder of *L'Art moderne*, took the lead in organizing Les XX, or the Twenty, an artistic alliance whose original roster included Fernand Khnopff and James Ensor. They were later joined by Rops, van de Velde, and two sympathetic Frenchmen, Paul Signac and Odilon Redon. With the exception of Rops, all were Wagnerites, and Khnopff was the most avid of the lot.

A child of the haute bourgeoisie, Khnopff spent part of his youth in Bruges, absorbing the city's timeless atmosphere. He later provided the frontispiece for *Bruges-la-morte*—an Ophelia-like figure floating amid weeds on a canal. Having made his name as a society portraitist, Khnopff ventured into the Péladan circle in the mid-eighties. *Supreme Vice* enjoyed a Belgian vogue, and Khnopff was one of several XX painters who responded to it. An 1885 drawing based on the novel showed a female nude, representing Leonora d'Este, in the company of a sphinx. This caused a commotion, because Khnopff transposed the face of the soprano Rose Caron—then preparing to sing in *Meistersinger* at La Monnaie—onto the naked figure. When Caron protested, Khnopff destroyed the work, although he later made another on the same theme. The artist went on to illustrate several of Péladan's novels; in the frontispiece of *Istar*, vegetation is entwined around the crotch of a Venus whose hands appear to be bound above her head.

Khnopff first visited Bayreuth in 1888, the same season that gave Péladan his Eureka moment. He later assisted in the design of opera productions at La Monnaie, including its 1914 production of *Parsifal*. The young Austrian composer and pianist Alma Schindler, later to find fame as Alma Mahler-Werfel, met Khnopff in Vienna in 1900 and wrote in her diary that the painter "knows and loves every note of *Tristan*." After Schindler played the "Prelude and Liebestod" at the piano, Khnopff picked up the vocal score of the opera and pointed to his favorite passages. "He dug his fingernails forcefully into the vocal score and shouted like a man possessed," Schindler wrote. "Suddenly he said: 'I must stop, otherwise I'll get depressed.'"

The chief Wagnerian work in Khnopff's catalogue is a 1905 drawing titled *Isolde*, in which the Irish princess tilts her head back and looks out with vacant, lustrous eyes. Alma Schindler's diary affords a clue to its meaning. The passage in *Tristan* that Khnopff raved about occurs just after the lovers have drunk the potion. As it takes hold, in a recapitulation of the prelude, Isolde utters the word "Tristan," over a descending minor-seventh interval. "Khnopff wants to make a free translation of these two notes into color," Schindler writes. "Of Tristan only an arm—of her perhaps just the face—but all expression concentrated in that face—all the torment, pride, love, hate, every nerve-fibre a-tremble." *Isolde* might realize that idea, except that the torment and fury are absent. The heroine is oddly serene, her arched eyebrows and faint smile conveying the hauteur of a woman who knows how men will act. There is something startlingly modern about her: Isolde surveying an urban salon.

If Khnopff partook of Wagnerian esoterica with aristocratic detachment, his younger contemporary Jean Delville, a brash spirit from a poor background, plunged into the thick of the occult, executing hallucinatory visions with almost neoclassical clarity. In 1896, Delville inaugurated the Salons d'Art idéaliste, which he modeled on Péladan's Rosicrucian salons and on the Pre-Raphaelite Brotherhood. The first exhibition featured his own *Treasures of Satan*, in which a muscular Lucifer equipped with a massive head of red hair and elongated tentacles hovers over a writhing mass of nude male and female bodies, their faces more ecstatic than agonized. While Delville, like Péladan, warned of the dangers of uninhibited lust, his version of Hell hints at the Venusian pleasures savored by Baudelaire.

Delville not only idolized the Meister but enlisted him in the battle against naturalism. "The destiny of the Wagnerian work," he wrote, "will be to annihilate once and for all the naturalist muck where Zola has sat for nearly a half-century." Like Péladan, Delville felt that realist art foreclosed the possibility of spiritual growth and locked the viewer in the industrial present. Delville's 1887 drawing *Tristan et Yseult* is more mystical than erotic—an "animastic union of male and female," according to the art historian Brendan Cole. Tristan lies on his back, his body in shadow. Isolde is draped over him, one hand holding aloft an empty cup. The bodies together form an upward-arching, triangular mass. Light streams from behind the chalice. This tableau captures the drinking of the potion in Act I, though it also prefigures the opera's ending: Tristan has a lifeless look, Isolde seems transported. The luminous cup could be mistaken for the Grail.

Odilon Redon, Brünnhilde, *1885*

It fell to Odilon Redon to summon on canvas the sublime menace of *Parsifal*—Delville having fallen short with a kitschy picture of a fleshy youth in curly blond locks. Redon belonged to the Paris vanguard, but he found early recognition among les XX in Brussels. Confronted with the serene severed heads of Redon's lithographic series *In the Dream*, the Belgian critic Jules Destrée, later a leading socialist politician, made reference to certain phrases in Wagner that "leave you shivering and troubled for a long time." In a similar vein, Redon's bouquets, with their seductive explosions of color against vacant backgrounds, reminded the French decadent author Jean Lorrain of the Flower Maidens in *Parsifal*, blooming in oblivion.

Redon once criticized Henri Fantin-Latour for producing "pale and soft sketches on the poems of the musician Wagner." His own Wagner pictures are cryptic, unearthly, and—as Téodor de Wyzewa said in the *Revue wagnérienne*—"terrifying." There are three of Brünnhilde. The first, which appeared in an 1885 issue of the *Revue*, is a lithograph of a boyish Valkyrie amid the fire of battle, her shield raised, her eyes wide with fierce concentration. The second, from 1894, shows a subdued warrior, her hair streaming in more feminine style, her face drawn into a mask of sadness. (Mallarmé owned a copy of this work.) Around 1905, Redon created a turbulent pastel in which Brünnhilde rides a dark purple horse that is rearing up into a sapphire sky. A mass of gold-brown brushwork could be either earth or fire. If this is the climax of *Götterdämmerung*, it is a coolly rapt vision of the world to come.

Redon's two renderings of *Parsifal* are two decades apart and seem to span a lifetime. In a lithograph from 1891, the hero has large, dark eyes, a long, straight nose, and thin, determined lips, his left hand clutching a spear that looks more like a long arrow. The critic Ernest Verlant elaborated on the image: "His head is anointed, his feet sprayed with perfume; he has been crowned King of the Grail, master of august rites, initiate of Christ. Mystical promise is fulfilled in him; he is 'the pure one, the holy soul rendered *voyant* through pity,' and that is why his eyes widen in a supernatural fever and magnetize towards eternity." A 1912 pastel of Parsifal provides a jolting contrast. This seems to be the transformed hero of Act III—the black-clad victor over Klingsor's magic. His face is wrapped in a mass of flattened, brownish hair, with a stringy beard hanging down. There is something misshapen about the visage: the mouth is a sliver across the middle. No spear is visible. The figure seems hunched and tired, as if he is pausing in the middle of an interminable trek. The sky is a skirmish of light above a rocky outcrop. What unites this haunted sage with his younger counterpart is the wide-open sadness of the eyes, staring blankly into the future.

The Symbolists ran up against a quandary that was not unfamiliar to the man who founded the Bayreuth Festival: their excoriation of bourgeois mediocrity did not prevent the bourgeoisie from consuming their art. A vestige of Romantic mystery clung to the work of Khnopff, Delville, and Redon, making it suitable decor for wealthy salons. James Ensor, the chief rebel of Les XX, banished Symbolist aesthetics in favor of a brusque, bristling style that prophesied twentieth-century trends of Expressionism, Cubism, Surrealism, and even Pop Art. Ensor made scathing caricatures of Catholic clergy, military brass, and financiers—the alliance that underpinned the ruthlessly exploitative regime of King Leopold II, the Belgian monarch. As the scholarship of Debora Silverman has made clear, the Art Nouveau splendor of Brussels depended on riches gained from the brutal colonial operation of the Congo Free State.

His habitual nonconformism notwithstanding, Ensor joined in the general veneration of Wagner. "This extraordinary genius influenced and sustained me," he wrote. "I glimpsed a huge and beautiful world." La Monnaie's production of *Walküre* in 1887 apparently led him to paint a *Ride of the Valkyries*, in which the maidens ride over a tumultuously abstract landscape. An 1890 work is titled *Indignant Bourgeois Whistling at Wagner in 1880 in Brussels*. In the 1902 painting *At the Conservatory*, Ensor trains his ire at the bourgeois culture that consumes Wagner without comprehending his deeper meanings. An elegantly attired singer performs from a score whose cover is imprinted with a garbled version of Brünnhilde's cry: "HO.Y.HOTOYO / HO Y HO HO / HAUT Y HAUT / TROP HAUT / TROP PEAU . . ." ("too high, too skin"). She is being pelted with flowers, a cat, a duck, and a pickled herring. In the midst of this fiasco, Wagner himself is seen holding his fingers to his ears.

Ensor's most celebrated work is the enormous—almost Wagnerian—*Christ's Entry into Brussels in 1889*. It is a phantasmagoric vision of the Savior riding a donkey through a carnivalesque throng, with a wooden-soldier brass band at the center and a bloated bishop at the front. In Patricia Berman's reading, the painting condemns Leopold's Belgium for its abuse of

Christian iconography in the service of state violence. Originally, Ensor intended to include Wagner in the nightmare procession: a preparatory drawing from 1885 has at its center a banner reading "PHALANGE WAGNER FRACASSANT," or "Wagner Army Raising a Din." The same legend appears in a later copper etching. Is this a band of anti-Wagnerians, denigrating the Bayreuth master as a purveyor of mere noise? Or are Belgian Wagnéristes themselves the butt of the satire—revering the composer of *Parsifal* while travestying the Redeemer's message? Ensor gave no evidence of his thinking, and in the final painting he omitted the "PHALANGE" banner, probably by painting over it. Wagner is drowned out by the urban din, the savage parade.

SATANIC WAGNER

Péladan spoke of "*sathanisme de l'amour.*" Baudelaire invoked a "satanic religion." Huneker beheld a Black Mass in *Parsifal.* The idea that Wagner's music tapped into devilish forces had wide purchase, both among the composer's detractors and among his wilder-eyed disciples. Fin-de-siècle culture granted mighty powers to artists, and by some accounts Wagner was capable of administering a sort of aural potion of death or derangement.

The supernaturally inclined could point to a string of mishaps that befell people close to Wagner. The tenor Ludwig Schnorr von Carolsfeld dropped dead shortly after creating the title role of *Tristan*, in 1865. His widow, the soprano Malvina Garrigues, who was the first Isolde, received mediumistic messages from Schnorr and accused Cosima of being an "infernal spirit." Alois Ander, who had earlier rehearsed Tristan in Vienna, died insane in 1864. Felix Mottl suffered a fatal heart attack while conducting *Tristan* in 1911. Ludwig II died a watery death in 1886. The Russian-Jewish pianist Joseph Rubinstein, a fanatical follower, killed himself in 1884, supposedly in despair over the Meister's passing. The Polish pianist and composer Carl Tausig, also Jewish, died of typhoid at twenty-nine; some blamed the strain of serving Wagner. Nietzsche crossed the border into madness while raving about Richard and Cosima. On the other hand, Cosima herself lived to the age of ninety-two.

Wagner saw himself as an affirmative artist, preparing humanity for a better world. Yet he, too, sensed danger in his music. While composing

Félicien Rops, frontispiece for Péladan's Le Vice suprême

Tristan, he worried that it would drive people insane. After Schnorr's death, he wrote in his diary: "My Tristan! My beloved! I pushed you to the abyss!" (The salutation quotes Kurwenal, Tristan's friend and servant.) Undeniably, there is a romance of evil in Wagner. Venus, in *Tannhäuser*, bewitches the ears, especially in the Paris version of 1861. Telramund and Ortrud, the malefactors of *Lohengrin*, hatch their plots over jagged, corkscrewing figures that announce Wagner's mature style. Alberich and Hagen, in the *Ring*, stride grandly in the bass regions. Conversely, paeans to goodness in the operas are not always convincing. Siegfried's Funeral Music is more impressive than the man himself. Parsifal's wound-closing monologue often sounds a touch hollow. Suffice to say that evil is necessary in Wagner's world, and the division between evil and good is fluid.

Fin-de-siècle fiction feasted on Wagner's macabre side. An early instance is Élémir Bourges's 1884 novel *Le Crépuscule des dieux*, whose title is the French name for *Götterdämmerung*. Bourges, a member of Péladan's Rose + Croix order, tells of a great old family in decline—a popular story arc of the period. A German notable named Charles d'Este, Duke of Blankenbourg, is introduced as the "son of a race of gods." He is marking his birthday by hosting Wagner in a command performance. During Act I of *Walküre*, the duke learns that Prussian troops have entered his territory, and he is forced to flee. As he departs, the composer solemnly informs him that the *Ring* will end with a *Twilight of the Gods*. Decadence infects the family, sowing death and madness. A scheming Wagner soprano named Giulia Belcredi, having become the duke's mistress, plots to destroy two of the duke's children, the half-siblings Hans Ulric and Christiane. Belcredi convinces the duke to host a domestic performance of *Walküre*, with Hans Ulric and Christiane cast as Siegmund and Sieglinde. She knows, somehow, that Wagner's drama will trigger incestuous love in the real-life pair. When it does, Hans Ulric kills himself and Christiane enters a convent. At the end, the duke falls ill, attends *Götterdämmerung* at Bayreuth, and dies.

As the eighties gave way to the nineties, vampiric, necromantic, and satanic themes proliferated in post-Wagnerian, post-Symbolist literature. Joris-Karl Huysmans set the tone with a series of novels that began with *À rebours*, in 1884, and continued with *En Rade* (1887) and *Là-bas* (1891). Against a backdrop of hyper-refined aestheticism, Huysmans exposed his readers to homosexuality, incubi and succubi, sadism, the child murders of Gilles de Rais, the Black Mass, and, most exotically, a Mass of Sperm. Huysmans adroitly placed this ghastly subject matter in the context of a wide-ranging spiritual search; in the end, he and his protagonists return to traditional Catholicism, "From exalted mysticism to raging Satanism is but a step," a character says in *Là-bas*. "In the beyond, all extremes meet."

"The Succubus," an 1898 story by the Belgian writer Camille Lemonnier, is in the Huysmans mold, and also harks back to Poe and E. T. A. Hoffmann. It opens at a performance of *Tristan* somewhere in Bohemia. The narrator cannot take his eyes off a deathly pale woman in a neighboring box, who, he senses, has some connection to his past life. The sight of this "satanic perversity" harmonizes with Wagner's "torrent of love and sadness," his "symphony of afflictions." During Act III, the narrator remembers what happened. In his youth, when he was bedridden with a near-fatal illness, a woman had visited him, clad only in red and black ribbons.

> This devouring virgin penetrated under my sheets and bit my lips with so fearful a kiss that my blood immediately gushed a large jet. Our bodies

immediately convulsed; mine, in my effort to escape her, writhed like a wounded slow-worm; and at the end I stopped repulsing her deadly thirsty lips. While in small strokes she continued to lick my red substance, I myself drank life at her neck, under the black ribbon, as from a fountain . . . My mother, entering my room in the morning, found me half expired and bathed in my own blood.

When the lights go up, the narrator rushes to the exits, but "the Lady with red headbands, like a lithe phantom, like the vampire that she was, seemed to have dissolved in the air of the street."

In Latin America, the *Modernismo* movement, led by the Nicaraguan poet Rubén Darío, mixed Symbolist, Decadent, and Wagnerian strains, to sometimes creepy effect. Horacio Quiroga, a Uruguayan epigone of Poe, wrote two stories on Wagner subjects: "The Death of Isolde" and "The Flame," also called "Berenice." The second is set largely in Paris in 1842, and features Wagner and Baudelaire as characters. Baudelaire introduces the composer to a wealthy patron and her ten-year-old daughter, Berenice, who shows signs of being enraptured by Wagner's music. The score of *Tristan* is tried out with orchestra. Wagner feels the child throbbing beside him, and is surprised to discover that she has suddenly grown older: "Those twenty minutes of hurricane-force passion had just converted a child into a woman radiant with youth, eyes darkened in mad fatigue." As the opera progresses, the aging process advances at terrifying speed, until Berenice has become a decrepit, cataleptic old woman. She remains in that condition until her death, forty years later. In the face of such poetic license, it seems pointless to add that Wagner did not know Baudelaire in 1842, nor did *Tristan* exist.

The apogee of satanic Wagnerism is, arguably, Marcel Batilliat's 1897 novel *Chair Mystique*, or *Mystic Flesh*. Schooled in Zola and Huysmans, Batilliat adopted a style at once precise and precious. *Mystic Flesh*, which has a notation from *Tristan* as its epigraph, tells of a young woman named Marie-Alice, who, trapped in a provincial life, is drawn to the literature and music of high passion. She dreams of "reviving the divine loves of the Wagnerian heroes," of becoming the "modern Isolde" to a "modern Tristan." Her mother died of tuberculosis, and she is fated to perish of the same disease. Her knight in black armor is an alienated aesthete named Yves. They form a bond as Marie-Alice plays *Tristan* at the piano, the odor of death rising around her. Moving to an isolated forest house, they lose themselves in an oblivion of love. Marie-Alice falls sick, and a doctor friend warns Yves of infection. Instead, Yves hurls himself into prolonged bouts of love-making, in the hope that he will contract the disease. On breaks, the lovers read the Symbolists and "adore above all the sublime pages of *Tristan und Isolde*." A stray cat joins the ménage and acquires the name Klingsor. Eventually, poetry bores them; only music matches their delirium. Marie-Alice dies in Yves's arms, her last throes resembling orgasm. They remain entangled as rigor mortis sets in.

But this is not all. Marie-Alice is buried, and Yves, now falling ill himself, has a dream in which he sees his lover's corpse approaching him. Batilliat abruptly switches stylistic gears, using the kind of hyper-clinical language favored by naturalist writers:

> She was naked as on their nights of love, and all green amid a swarming of parasitic worms! Everywhere, ocher, amber, and slate-gray emphysemes stretched the integuments; a purulent, brownish fluid exuded through the pores, flowed from natural openings which were full of larvae and worms. On the depressed thorax, whose ribs were bursting the skin, serous vesicles contrasted in their paleness with red plaques that marked the place of the intestines, and the ruptured abdominal walls, scarred by a huge wound, gave out their putrid contents, all twitching with the activity of roundworms. The eyes were black holes, where oozing brain matter turned into pus; bared teeth, stained with purulence, laughed a horrible laugh, between saponified muscles and blueish aponeurosis. Alone among all these horrors, the golden hair, flowing like a scarf as on the day of farewell, had remained resplendent, like a streaming of light.

Even in the wake of this magisterially revolting hallucination, the *Tristan* fantasy lingers. At the very end, Yves again salutes the operatic pair, "who loved each other as one must love: to the utmost!" Indeed, with his scene of eroticized decomposition, Yves has set a new outer limit of Wagnerian passion—one that will have no serious rival until the 1960s, when Yukio Mishima filmed an act of seppuku to the tune of *Tristan*.

THEOSOPHY

The Goetheanum, Dornach

Helena Blavatsky, the chief figure in Theosophy, did not care at first for Wagner. In 1883, she had this to say about *Parsifal*: "Such a handling of the 'most sacred truths'—for those for whom those things and names are *truth*—is a sheer debasement, a sacrilege, and a blasphemy." Four years later, Madame Blavatsky, as she was widely known, suffered a near-fatal medical crisis, and formed a good opinion of the doctor who treated her— William Ashton Ellis, the indefatigable and fatiguing English translator of Wagner's prose. Ellis had embraced Theosophy in the mid-eighties, around the time he began writing about the composer. Almost at once, Theo-sophical opinion turned around. In 1888, Blavatsky's magazine *Lucifer*— the title denotes the bringing of light, not Satan—warmly greeted Ellis's Wagner journal, *The Meister*, saying that Wagner was a "mystic as well as a musician" who "penetrated deeply into the inner realms of life."

Ellis was right to see common ground between Wagner and Theoso-phy. Blavatsky's synthesis of West and East resembles the religious fusion of *Parsifal*, although she gives stronger emphasis to Eastern thought, espe-cially Buddhism. The daughter of a Russian military officer, Blavatsky trav-eled widely in her youth, gaining a reputation as a psychic. She claimed to have received telepathic communications from a group calling themselves the Mahatmas, or super-evolved Masters. In 1873, she showed up in New York, where she began to elaborate her Secret Doctrine. Disavowing spiri-tualism, she defined Theosophy not as a religion but as a rational inquiry into religion, a "purely divine ethics." She was not above using cheap tricks to soup up her legend. An 1885 investigation by the Society for Psychical Research concluded that Blavatsky was "one of the most accomplished, ingenious, and interesting imposters of history." She plowed ahead regardless, and by the time of her death, in 1891, Theosophy had become international in scope, its headquarters based in Adyar, India.

In 1888, *Lucifer* published Ellis's essay "A Glance at *Parsifal?*," which interprets Wagner's Grail as "the Divine Wisdom of the ages, the *Theosophia* which has been ever jealously guarded by bands of brothers." It abides in a place "whence Time and Space have fled away." The titular hero "unites in his nature the characteristics of Jesus Christ and Gautama Buddha." Brotherhood heals the world's discords. The message of the opera, Ellis says, is acutely relevant "in these days when each man's hand is turned against his brother, when materialism is rife . . . and each state in Europe, laughing at [religion's] shrill, unmeaning bleat, adds another fifty thousand paid butchers to its bloated armaments!"

Although Ellis soon withdrew from active involvement in Theosophy, other Wagnerites took his place. In 1896, Basil Crump, a barrister who specialized in maritime law, began publishing pamphlets analyzing the Wagner operas as composites of religious traditions. He was soon joined by Alice Leighton Cleather, a clergyman's daughter who belonged to Blavatsky's circle. Together, Crump and Cleather published four studies of the Wagner operas. In *Parsifal*, they write, "the essential elements of the great religions of the Eastern and Western worlds—Christianity and Buddhism—are blended in a form especially adapted to the Western world of to-day." *Tristan*, too, acquires an Eastern tinge. Crump and Cleather label a phrase from the prelude the "Nirvâna motive" and link it to the "redeeming power which shall bring peace and rest in the bosom of the Oversoul." When Cleather visited Bayreuth, she was pleased to see many Eastern texts in the Wahnfried library.

In the mid-nineties, a group of American Theosophists split from Blavatsky's heir apparent, the British socialist and anti-imperialist Annie Besant, to form the Theosophical Society in America. They were under the sway of Katherine Tingley, a social worker from an obscure background, possibly theatrical. Grandiose in manner, habitually wrapped in robes and scarves, Tingley announced a World Crusade, in the hope of gaining a global presence for the American wing. In an essay on Theosophical

Wagnerism, Christopher Scheer notes that excerpts from the music dramas were often heard at Tingley's events. In 1897, the Third Annual Convention of the Theosophical Society in America, at the Madison Square Garden concert hall, opened, Péladan-style, with *Parsifal* on the organ.

For a few years, Crump and Cleather participated in Tingley's movement, perhaps lured by its Wagnerian trappings. In 1897, they traveled to North America and lectured on Wagner and Theosophy, drawing crowds of up to a thousand people in halls bedecked with the flags of Tingley's Crusade. Musical examples were played, though in modestly scaled arrangements. In keeping with the Bayreuth idea of the invisible orchestra, the musicians remained hidden behind a screen. Journalists made much of the duo's penchant for high-tech illustrations: magic-lantern images of Lohengrin, the Flying Dutchman, Parsifal, and other Wagner heroes flickered before audiences' eyes. Crump happily concluded: "The new aspect of Theosophy presented in these musical lectures has proved very attractive and has interested a new section of the public who are ready for the message but needed touching in a different way."

The World Crusade had a destination in view: Point Loma, California, a Theosophical utopia outside San Diego, overlooking the Pacific Ocean. The complex included a Temple of Peace, the Raja Yoga Academy, and an open-air Greek theater. On seeing it, the actor Helena Modjeska exclaimed, "A

Reginald Machell, The Holy Grail

second Bayreuth!" Nellie Melba said that the scene reminded her of her first experience of *Parsifal*. A group of *Parsifal* paintings by the Theosophical artist Reginald Machell, an Englishman who had settled in Point Loma, exemplified the Tingley vision; in two of them a guru-like figure holds the Grail over his head, his arms forming a sacred geometry with the cup. "Every conqueror of himself conquers also for others," Machell explained.

Like the Rosicrucian sects of Paris, branches of Theosophy kept feuding with one another and engaging in doctrinal warfare. When Annie Besant anointed an Indian boy named Jiddu Krishnamurti as a Messiah figure, the German Theosophist leader Rudolf Steiner left the society, taking much of German Theosophy with him. In 1912, he formed his own discipline, Anthroposophy, which has endured longer than most fin-de-siècle spiritual movements. Hundreds of Waldorf schools around the world follow Steiner's philosophy of holistic education, fostering creativity and independence in children. More intellectually rigorous than many in the Theosophical world, Steiner was well grounded in philosophy, science, and socialism. Intolerant of Theosophy's Eastern slant, Steiner focused on the Western mystical heritage, with particular attention to tales of the Grail. He directed Munich productions of Édouard Schuré's spiritual dramas, *The Sacred Drama of Eleusis* and *The Children of Lucifer*, and wrote his own mystery plays, which, in the words of one acolyte, represented "the psychic development of man up to the moment when he is able to pierce the veil and see into the beyond."

Steiner joined Schuré, Ellis, and others in sensing a "strange and deep connection" between Wagner and the new spiritual trends. In the eighties, in Vienna, he encountered rabid young Wagnerites, whom he characterized as "homeless souls," hungry for an alternative to materialist modernity. In 1905, he gave four lectures on the topic "Richard Wagner in Light of Spiritual Science," and two years later, having seen *Parsifal* in Bayreuth, he spoke about Wagner and mysticism. Following Schuré, Steiner framed the operas not as psychological dramas but as treatises on initiation, on the overcoming of mundane reality. Thus, Isolde's Transfiguration evokes the union of souls in an astral world—a "surging ocean of bliss" removed from ordinary sexual desire, indeed from the division of gender itself. Dwelling on *Parsifal*, which he sometimes used as entrance music for his lectures, Steiner predicts that the human reproductive organs of the future "will not be infused with desire, but will be pure and chaste, like the plant-calyx that turns itself toward the love-lance, the ray of sunshine."

In 1912, Steiner said, "We have been thinking about a kind of Bayreuth." A year later, in the Swiss town of Dornach, outside Basel, he laid the foundation stone for a hilltop complex that he called the Goetheanum—a structure defined by two intersecting domes. Some interior features, particularly the stage space underneath the smaller dome, resembled the Grail Temple set in *Parsifal*. After the building burned, in 1922, the Goetheanum was rebuilt in even more inventive style, its undulating forms prophetic of late twentieth-century architectural trends. Many "new Bayreuths" were imagined in the fin-de-siècle years, but few led to tangible results. Not only did Steiner see his vision through, but his temple still stands, serving as the world headquarters of Anthroposophy. To see it rising above Dornach is like glimpsing the Festspielhaus from the Bayreuth train station: the impossible has become real.

YEATS AND THE CELTIC TWILIGHT

"Westward roams the glance / Eastward strikes the ship," sings a young seaman at the outset of *Tristan*. The vessel is bound for King Mark's castle in Cornwall; Isolde is gazing back toward her native Ireland. An injured Celtic pride is implicit in the heroine's rage at the outset of the opera ("Who dares to mock me?"). Such touches undoubtedly boosted Wagner's popularity in Ireland, although he had a following there even before *Tristan* was widely known. Around the turn of the century, Carl Rosa's company performed most of Wagner's operas in Dublin, attracting flocks of writers and artists, including the young James Joyce.

The period of Wagner's ascendancy coincided with the cresting of Irish nationalism. More than a few artists and impresarios looked to the composer as they pondered how to forge their own political identity. The new Irish state, whatever form it took, would need its native myths, legends, heroes, and leitmotifs. Cultural pride mingled easily with an influx of mystical and esoteric movements. The Celtic Revival concerned itself with old Gaelic literature and age-old Irish folktales, resulting in a heightened awareness of faeries, elves, ghosts, and other supernatural entities. Insofar as Wagner functioned as a conduit for such half-forgotten spirit forces, he became an honorary member of the movement that W. B. Yeats called the Celtic Twilight.

Wagnerism wafted around the Irish Literary Theatre, which Yeats co-founded in 1899. The project received backing from Annie Horniman, an English theater maven who went to Bayreuth almost every year and wished to create an equivalent institution in Ireland. As the literary scholar and biographer Adrian Frazier writes, Yeats was Horniman's Wagner, and "the theater was to be his Bayreuth." Horniman also designed costumes for several of the theater's productions; those for Yeats's *The King's Threshold* are said to have looked like the costumes in Bayreuth's *Tristan*.

Edward Martyn and George Moore, two other founders of the theater, were keen Wagnerites who sometimes greeted each other by whistling Siegfried's motif. Martyn, a wealthy landowner who was active as a musician and a dramatist, valued the composer's "cult of liturgical aestheticism." In his 1899 play *The Heather Field*, a deranged landlord has visions of nymphs and faeries, of stories of the Rhine, of a rainbow, of "strange solemn harmonies" of singing boys. Unexpectedly, this Gaelic-Gothic spirit later became the first president of Sinn Féin, which led the drive toward Irish independence in 1921.

Moore, a cousin of Martyn's, spent much of his youth in Paris, where he consorted with Dujardin and Mallarmé. Accompanying Martyn on expeditions to Bayreuth, the musically untrained Moore felt that there was "something in [Wagner's] art for everybody, something in his music for me." Moore's 1898 novel *Evelyn Innes* is an early entry in the small but lively genre of Wagner-soprano fiction, which Willa Cather brought to its zenith. Under the influence of a Wagnerite named Owen Asher, Evelyn pursues an operatic career and achieves great success, winning the approval even of Cosima Wagner—though the Meisterin deems her Brünnhilde too womanly and insufficiently godlike. Evelyn also meets an austere young composer named Ulick Dean, who resists the Wagner craze but is gripped with desire for Evelyn on hearing her sing Isolde. Afterward, "she threw herself upon him, and kissed him as if she would annihilate destiny on his lips." As in Péladan, *Tristan* acts as an aphrodisiac.

Evelyn Innes has potboiler elements, but it also experiments with interior monologue in the Dujardin mode. Evelyn's love life and stage career come into conflict with longings for a pious existence. She mulls over her predicament in bed, ellipses indicating pauses in her thoughts. "It was unendurable to have to tell lies all day long—yes, all day long—of one sort or another. She ought to send them both away . . . But could she remain on the stage without a lover? Could she go to Bayreuth by herself? Could she give up the stage? And then?" She indeed walks away, forgoing the chance to sing Kundry in Bayreuth, and enters a convent, where she carries on singing Wagner all the same. Unusually, the sensual-spiritual division of *Tannhäuser* becomes the concern of a female rather than a male protagonist. For Evelyn, singing Wagner is merely a stage of a larger quest, one that dominates the novel's sequel, *Sister Teresa*.

Ulick Dean's physical appearance is modeled on that of Yeats. Moore writes: "He had one of those long Irish faces, all in a straight line, with flat, slightly hollow cheeks, and a long chin. It was clean shaven, and a heavy lock of black hair was always falling over his eyes. It was his eyes that gave its sombre ecstatic character to his face. They were large, dark, deeply set, singularly shaped, and they seemed to smoulder like fires in caves, leaping and sinking out of the darkness." Certain of Ulick's views sound like Yeats's, as when he says that the Celtic gods are alive for him, or when he extols William Blake. Ulick's operas adapt Irish tales, like Connla and the Fairy Maiden, and Diarmuid and Gráinne. His style is full of "strange, old-world rhythms, recalling in a way the Gregorian she used to read in childhood in the missals, yet modulated as unintermittently as Wagner." And Ulick surely speaks for Yeats when he says, in parting from Evelyn, "God is our quest—you seek him in dogma, I in art."

Yeats's language sings across the page, but his knowledge of music was limited. Moore bluntly called him "unmusical." That lack did not prevent him from citing Wagner and imitating his methods. The cultures in which Yeats moved—the Celtic Revival, London Aestheticism, Parisian Symbolism, Theosophy and its variants—were all sufficiently soaked in Wagner that he could absorb the influence without having tasted it firsthand. After 1902, Yeats also delved into Nietzsche, whose posthumous vogue was well under way. The dispute between the Germanic titans concerned the poet little: both were models of aesthetic imperiousness and heroic force.

For Yeats, as for many others, Wagner showed how folk sources could shape a national consciousness. In his 1898 essay "The Celtic Element in Literature," he wrote of Ireland's connection to the "ancient religion of the world, the ancient worship of Nature." The Celts, he said, were "nearer to ancient chaos." The Scandinavian tradition drew from similar sources. Through the medium of Wagner, the Nordic sagas had become "the most passionate element in the arts of the modern world." Yeats also considered the composer an agent of Symbolism, "the only movement that is saying new things." Like Villiers de l'Isle-Adam, Mallarmé, the Pre-Raphaelites, and Maeterlinck, Wagner had found spiritual intensity in the practice of his art, fighting against materialism and rationalism. In another article, Yeats placed the "ecstasy of *Parsifal*" alongside William Morris's *The Well at the World's End* and Villiers's *Axël* in the category of art that seeks to "bring again the golden age."

Yeats's occult adventures led him first to Theosophy's Esoteric Section and then to the Hermetic Order of the Golden Dawn, which had been co-founded in 1888 by MacGregor Mathers, a charismatic English guru of invented Scots heritage. More insular than Theosophy, the Golden Dawn burrowed into Rosicrucian, Masonic, and Egyptian ritual. In the usual fashion, it underwent schisms and quarrels. Mathers placed his hopes in Aleister Crowley, who progressed from the Golden Dawn to Thelema, a discipline of his own invention. Crowley's Holy Books make heavy use of Wagner; the *Book of Thoth* includes a phallic interpretation of *Parsifal*, saying that the hero "attains to puberty" when he grasps the Holy Spear. Crowley also wrote a Tannhäuser play in which Venus is revealed as Lilith—"The soul of the Obscene / Incarnate in the spirit."

Although Yeats never ventured quite so far afield, his occult activities were a heady brew of poetic ambition, political fantasy, and sexual desire. For many years, the chief object of his romantic longing was the Irish nationalist activist Maud Gonne, another member of the Golden Dawn. A devout Wagnerian, Gonne probably did more than anyone to stir Yeats's interest in the composer, having once told him that *Parsifal* is "worth travelling round the whole world to hear." She was often likened to a Valkyrie, and invited the comparison by wearing a hat adorned with black wings. Her first trip to Bayreuth was in 1886, when she was nineteen. Soon after, she fell in love with Lucien Millevoye, a right-wing French politician who shared her Wagnermania. Gonne bore a child out of wedlock, who died young. In a turn of events that could have been scripted by

Péladan, she came to believe that the boy could be reincarnated if another child were conceived in the vicinity of the corpse. Supposedly, she and Millevoye proceeded to make love at the tomb. Their second child was named, of course, Iseult.

Thanks to informants like Gonne, Moore, and Horniman, Yeats could speak confidently about Bayreuth's sightlines and unified stage picture. He also expertly deployed Wagnerite rhetoric. In 1898, he got into a public debate with the critic John Eglinton on the question of the Irish literary revival. Eglinton rejected the idea of an Irish national literature founded on ancient legend, contending that the latter had no relevance for the modern age. In response, Yeats brought up Ibsen's *Peer Gynt* and the Wagner dramas, which "are becoming to Germany what the Greek Tragedies were to Greece." Eglinton replied, in turn, that Bayreuth did not strike him as a plausible rebirth of Athenian democracy. Yeats shot back that Wagner's impact was hardly limited to the tony crowd at Bayreuth: it stretched across Europe and fired the imaginations of contemporary writers such as Villiers.

The Irish Literary Theatre opened in 1899 with Yeats's *The Countess Cathleen*—a tale of a munificent aristocrat who sacrifices her soul to save her land from famine and demons. The lead character, intended for Gonne, resembles nobly self-obliterating Wagnerian heroines like Senta in *The Flying Dutchman*, Elisabeth in *Tannhäuser*, and Brünnhilde. The premiere production, static and hieratic in style, apparently took inspiration from Bayreuth. The stage directions suggest some mixture of the *Ring* and *Parsifal*: "The darkness is broken by a visionary light. The Peasants seem to be kneeling upon the rocky slope of a mountain, and vapour full of storm and ever-changing light is sweeping above them and behind them . . . A sound of far-off horns seems to come from the heart of the light." *Tristan* lurks behind Yeats's *Diarmuid and Grania*, co-written with Moore between 1899 and 1901, and his *Deirdre*, from 1907. Both plays involve a triangle of two younger lovers and an older man of authority.

Yeats's most consciously Wagnerian work is *The Shadowy Waters*, a short play first conceived when he was a teenager, written and rewritten between 1894 and 1900, and then revised again at intervals in the following decade. In the tradition of *Tristan* and *Axël*, it tells of a pair of doomed lovers, named Forgael and Dectora. The setting is vague, but Yeats specified in one draft that the actors should be "dressed like Wagner's personages, except that the men do not wear winged helmets." The action begins, as in *Tristan*, on the deck of a ship, with the voice of a sailor. Forgael, the sailors' leader, is a mariner-musician on an obscure quest—a cross between Tristan and the Flying Dutchman, the wanderer in search of redemptive love. Dectora enters as a captured queen, very Isolde-like, but Forgael's magic harp makes her lose interest in the world.

During an American trip in 1903 and 1904, Yeats saw the Met's staging of *Parsifal*, and, as he later recounted, objected to its literalism. "*Parsifal* symbolises an action that takes place in the mind alone," he remembers telling the Met director. He wanted a more suggestive, dimly lit production for *The Shadowy Waters*, in Parisian Symbolist style. The 1904 premiere in Dublin went badly, but the play found a more receptive public when the Theosophical Society hosted a performance at its congress in London in 1905. Such eminences as Maeterlinck, Annie Besant, and Rudolf Steiner attended the meeting, and all may have seen *The Shadowy Waters*. Even in that rarefied milieu, though, Yeats was criticized for his lack of dramatic action. He subjected the play to a heavy revision, shedding "needless symbols." After reading Arthur Symons's essay "The Ideas of Richard Wagner," Yeats wrote to the author: "The Wagnerian essay touches my own theories at several points, and enlarges them at one or two." While struggling with one passage, Yeats came upon "that paragraph where Wagner insists that a play must not appeal to the intelligence, but directly to the emotions."

As Yeats entered his maturity, the play took on a harder edge, losing its Celtic Twilight glow. Even so, the debt to Wagner becomes, if anything, more pronounced. In the revised text published in 1906, the sailor's first line is "Has he not led us into these waste seas / For long enough?" This echoes a phrase in *Tristan* that will also be quoted in T. S. Eliot's *The Waste Land*: "Waste and empty the sea." When the lovers meet, they preach to each other a world-liquidating love, looking toward a "country at the end of the world" that seems coterminous with Tristan's "*Wunderreich der Nacht*," the wonder-realm of night:

> I would that there was nothing in the world
> But my beloved—that night and day had perished,
> And all that is and all that is to be,
> All that is not the meeting of our lips.

It is also a mystical transport to a place beyond the material world, a plane
of initiation where eternal knowledge is attained:

> Where the world ends
> The mind is made unchanging, for it finds
> Miracle, ecstasy, the impossible hope,
> The flagstone under all, the fire of fires,
> The roots of the world.

This imagery recurs in Yeats's 1930 poem "Byzantium": "At midnight on
the Emperor's pavement flit / Flames that no faggot feeds, nor steel has lit,
/ Nor storm disturbs, flames begotten of flame . . ."

In the mid-twenties, on a visit to Palermo, Yeats stayed at the Grand
Hotel et des Palmes, where, four decades earlier, Wagner had finished
Parsifal and sat for a portrait by Renoir. One could see the room in which
he stayed and, purportedly, a pen with which he wrote. Visiting Palermo's
Cappella Palatina, with its Byzantine mosaics, Yeats heard a local story to
the effect that the chapel had given rise to the Grail Temple in *Parsifal*.
That claim is biographically doubtful—Wagner mentioned Siena Cathedral as his principal scenic source—yet Yeats seized on it. The path that
leads to Monsalvat points onward to the dream city of Byzantium, where
broken lives are gathered into the artifice of eternity.

5

HOLY GERMAN ART

The Kaiserreich and Fin-de-Siècle Vienna

Unveiling of the Wagner Monument in Berlin, 1903

At the end of *Die Meistersinger von Nürnberg*, Wagner's epic comedy of Renaissance Nuremberg, Hans Sachs, the wisest of the town mastersingers, gives a lecture about the beauty and power of German culture. Nuremberg has held its midsummer singing contest, and Walther von Stolzing, a young singer-knight with a rebellious style, has won the day. But Walther is piqued by the criticism he has received from the more pedantic of the mastersingers—especially from Sixtus Beckmesser, a preening music critic in period garb. Still resentful, Walther threatens to refuse membership in the masters' guild. Sachs proceeds to show Walther the error of his ways.

"Scorn not the masters, I bid you, and honor their art," Sachs says.

They have embraced you, he tells Walther, not because you are highborn or bear splendid arms but because you are a poet—one who is making bold to extend the tradition that they have kept alive in their often bumbling fashion. Some further lines, which appear in an 1862 draft of the libretto but which were not set to music, urge Walther to follow a high artistic path, away from the noisy illusion of reality: "Many a habit and custom wither away, / Crumble to dust, go up in smoke, / Let go of the fight, / neither musket thunder nor gunpowder puffs / will ever bring back what's merely a breath!" Sachs pictures a day when the Holy Roman Empire will have vanished from the earth. What will remain is an empire of the spirit—"holy German art." The earliest draft of Sachs's closing speech, from 1845, has him speaking in a manner "half ironic, half serious."

If Wagner had left it at that, *Meistersinger* might not have become the most politically charged of his operas, the one destined to be entangled in German history. The message of the unused passage is almost pacifist: mastersingers have no need of muskets. But, in January 1867, as Wagner was completing his initial composition draft, he made a drastic change to Sachs's peroration, replacing the "Let go of the fight" material with new lines that he had written in the middle of the night. The changing of gears can be felt in every performance of the opera. Until this point, Sachs has come across as a ruminative, almost Schopenhauerian character. He now mutates into a demagogue warning of enemies all around:

> Beware [*Habt Acht*]! Evil tricks threaten us:
> should the German *Volk und Reich* one day decay
> under false Romance rule [*in fälscher wälscher Majestät*]
> soon no prince would understand his people any longer;
> and Romance mists with Romance vanities
> would be planted in our German land;
> no one would know any longer what is German and true,
> unless it lives on in the honor of German masters.

The trickiest element here is the old German word "*wälsch*." It points toward Romance culture; the historical Hans Sachs, who lived from 1494 to 1576, once applied it to the opulence that accompanied the entry of Emperor Charles V into Nuremberg. Given that *Meistersinger* is a story about music and musicians, the "*Habt Acht!*" passage may prophesy the invasion of French and Italian opera. But "*wälsch*" can also mean "strange" or "foreign," insinuating a threat from within—perhaps Jewish or Jesuit. Tellingly, the music takes a stagily ominous turn, with strings playing tremolos and the brass swelling to nasty, punchy chords.

The text of the original draft resumes, but the meaning of "holy German art" has shifted. It now has the ring of a propaganda slogan:

> Therefore I say to you:
> honor your German masters,
> for then you will conjure up good spirits!
> And if you favor their endeavors,
> then should the Holy Roman Empire
> dissolve in mist
> for us there would still remain
> holy German art!

A festive tone takes over. The townspeople of Nuremberg repeat Sachs's final words. Walther's resistance to the guild gives way. "Heil! Sachs!" the company exclaims, as the opera bustles to a C-major close, with marchlike sounds of drums and brass.

We can no longer hear these lines as nineteenth-century audiences heard them. Echoes of their future, which is now our past, intrude. We think of the young Hitler copying out Sachs's closing speech; of an audience in Bayreuth in 1924 rising to its feet during the monologue and breaking into the Deutschlandlied afterward; of the chorus "*Wach auf, es nahet gen den Tag*" ("Awake, the dawn is drawing near") resounding as a salute to Hitler in 1933; of *Meistersinger* being staged during Nazi Party rallies in Nuremberg; of Joseph Goebbels calling the opera "the incarnation of our folk character"; of the Act III prelude appearing on the soundtrack of Leni Riefenstahl's film *Triumph of the Will*. All of Wagner's operas have political dimensions, but *Meistersinger* is the only one that makes its politics unavoidable. Karol Berger, in his book *Beyond Reason: Wagner contra Nietzsche*, has written: "I can think of no other example of a masterpiece so profoundly wounded by its ending."

The question of how to stage "*Habt Acht!*" bedevils and fascinates latter-day stage directors. Wieland Wagner, the composer's grandson, de-Germanized *Meistersinger* in his 1956 production at Bayreuth, to the point that it was dubbed "Meistersinger without Nuremberg." Peter Konwitschny put history front and center in a 2002 production in Hamburg: the performance came to a halt while the singers debated the meaning of "holy German art" onstage. Katharina Wagner, the composer's great-granddaughter, brought a critical spirit to Bayreuth in 2007. The hapless Beckmesser is made over as an outcast hipster hero, while Sachs is shown in an increasingly unattractive light. During the final monologue, the set design alludes to the Nazi era: soulless statues in the style of Arno Breker, icy lighting à la Albert Speer. Sachs, lit from below, takes on a demonic appearance. He becomes a Fascist conjurer out of Thomas Mann's "Mario and the Magician." Beckmesser watches with growing agitation, and flees in terror.

I am the most German person, I am the German spirit," Wagner wrote in 1865, while composing *Meistersinger*. In the same period, he wrote to the political theorist Constantin Frantz: "My own artistic ideal stands or falls with the salvation of Germany; without Germany's greatness my art was only a dream: if this dream is to find fulfillment, Germany, too, must necessarily attain to her preordained greatness."

Wagner's Germanness has never been in doubt, whatever Nietzsche said. Rather, the question is: which Germany do we mean? The Kaiserreich, the unified German empire that formed under Wilhelm I in 1871, has been subject to a barrage of competing interpretations. In the decades after the Second World War, the dominant paradigm of German history was the *Sonderweg* ("special path") model, according to which the nation's political development had diverged from that of the rest of Western Europe. It was held that Germany had failed to undergo a bourgeois revolution of the kind that modernized other European states. Instead, much of the old feudal order remained, and parliamentary democracy never put down healthy roots. German conservatives longed for a radical alternative to the liberal, bourgeois nation-state, one that would manifest the will of the people in a consolidated autocratic leadership. In this view, the progression toward Nazism was all but foreordained.

In recent decades, many historians have abandoned or greatly modified the *Sonderweg* model—the "deep-cultural teleology of catastrophic exceptionalism," as Geoff Eley calls it. Instead, they assert that the bourgeoisie had a strong cultural-political presence and that public discourse was by no means rigidly controlled. Richard J. Evans writes that Wilhelmine Germany should be seen "not as a static social and political system locked into a preprogrammed authoritarian rigidity, but as a rapidly changing, turbulent society in which new developments of all kinds were possible." In the Kaiserreich, the modern welfare state took hold; unionist, feminist, and gay-rights movements made advances; artistic avant-gardes flourished. At the same time, militarism tightened its grip; antisemitism became endemic; a murderous colonial regime was established in Africa; imperial bombast prevailed. Similar debates revolve around the Austrian Empire, habitually characterized as a decadent culture drifting toward apocalypse. Many historians now see imperial Germany and Austria as ambiguous laboratories of modernity, where reactionary and progressive impulses collide. Wagner shows us much the same.

The odd thing about Wagnerism in German-speaking lands is how limited it was, especially in comparison with developments in France. The number of performances was vast: more than seventeen thousand in Germany between 1901 and 1910. Yet, as Erwin Koppen argues in his book *Decadent Wagnerism*, the hermeneutic daring of the Wagnéristes was largely absent. The German vanguard made sparing use of Wagner, looking elsewhere for inspiration. It's as if the composer were too sacrosanct to undergo creative manhandling. Indeed, because he so quickly became a figurehead of imperial style, satirists and social critics found him a choice target. Theodor Fontane, the chief progenitor of modern German fiction, led the way in deflating Wagner's grandeur; the playwright Frank Wedekind and the novelist Heinrich Mann followed suit. At the center of this confused tableau is the towering, daunting figure of Thomas Mann, whose entire oeuvre is a kind of aftermath of Wagner.

Only in the Germany of the Kaiserreich did Wagner become a predominantly conservative cultural phenomenon—not just an official artist but also a mass-market commodity. He became "Wagnerian" in the pejorative sense: the master of the colossal. In Andreas Huyssen's words, Wagner engendered a "nineteenth-century imaginary of triumphal architecture, stable origins, and mythic groundings of the nation." For the Austrian novelist Hermann Broch, this grandeur concealed an inner emptiness— an emptiness inherent in the Reich itself. "The Wagnerian artwork was great, is great, and is the mirror of the vacuum," Broch wrote. The weight of the object sank down into the unconscious of the German-speaking world. Sigmund Freud, in *The Interpretation of Dreams*, analyzes a dream of a Wagner performance that goes until 7:45 in the morning with a conductor leading his forces atop a tower. The image is symbolic, Freud infers, of a "*distorted* world and an *insane* society." One need not see Wagner's operas as vacuous or insane to grasp how their overwhelming effects, detached from psychological complexity, could empty out into oppressive nationalist kitsch.

WAGNER AND LUDWIG

The Singers' Hall at Neuschwanstein

At first glance, Neuschwanstein, Ludwig II's castle in the foothills of the Bavarian Alps, would seem to be the most Wagnerian place on earth. When the young king began planning it, in the late 1860s, he told Wagner that "the spot is one of the most beautiful to be found, sacred and inaccessible, a worthy temple for the divine friend"—the friend being, of course, the composer. The word "inaccessible" ("*unnahbar*") alludes to Lohengrin's Grail Narration: "In a far-off land, inaccessible to your steps . . ." Inside the walls of this ersatz Grail castle, Wagner settings abound. The Singers' Hall displays scenes from the Lohengrin and Parsifal legends; the Throne Room is Grail-based. The entrance hall features Siegfried, the study Tannhäuser, the drawing room Lohengrin, the dressing room Hans Sachs. The bedroom belongs, fittingly, to Tristan and Isolde. There is also a little

Venusberg grotto—a setting re-created on a bigger scale on the grounds of Ludwig's Linderhof palace, which also offers replicas of Hunding's hut, from *Walküre*, and Gurnemanz's hermitage, from *Parsifal*. Ludwig would enact Wagner fantasies in these surroundings, traversing the grotto lake in a shell boat, with hidden dynamos generating lighting effects.

This strange and lonely man did as much as anyone to give Wagner semi-godlike status in German culture. The composer's career and afterlife would have been far different if Ludwig had never attained the Bavarian throne. As late as 1860, Wagner was still a political fugitive, unable to set foot inside the German Federation, the loose agglomeration of states that had replaced the Holy Roman Empire. In that year, the king of Saxony finally permitted him to travel in German lands, although Saxony itself remained out of bounds until 1862, when a full amnesty was granted. On his first trip back, Wagner felt little emotion, even a certain disdain. "Believe me, we have no fatherland!" he wrote to Liszt. "And if I am 'German,' then be assured I carry my Germany within me." As in the early versions of *Meistersinger*, "holy German art" is framed as a cultural rather than political entity. Thomas Mann would use a similar formula when he arrived in New York in 1938: "Where I am, there is Germany."

Further setbacks accentuated Wagner's feeling of homelessness. He attempted to stage *Tristan* in Vienna, but the project foundered after protracted rehearsals, tenor mishaps, and press controversies. In early 1864, he fled Vienna, under threat of imprisonment for mounting debts. He returned to Switzerland before wandering on to Stuttgart. There he received a visiting card from a man identifying himself as the "Secretary to the King of Bavaria." Under the impression that it was a trick concocted by a creditor, Wagner took evasive action. Franz Pfistermeister, the official in question, eventually delivered the astounding message: the new king, just eighteen years old, adored Wagner, had memorized his writings, and wished to place the resources of the court at the composer's disposal, with an eye toward a production of the *Ring*. This implausible sequence of events is, in fact, one of the better-documented episodes in Wagner's life. It is a fairy tale that Ludwig had the power to make real.

King and composer were in each other's thrall to the end. The attachment began with vows of affection, but within a few years it had grown more distant, mostly on account of Wagner's errant behavior—his prodigal spending, his adulterous affair with Cosima, his attempts to insert himself into Bavarian politics. After Wagner returned to Swiss exile at the end of 1865, he and the king rarely met face to face. Still, their bond of dependency remained. Ludwig could not exist without Wagner's music; Wagner could not exist without Ludwig's money. The landmark premieres of the composer's final period—*Tristan* in 1865, *Meistersinger* in 1868, *Rheingold* in 1869, *Walküre* in 1870, the entire *Ring* in 1876, and *Parsifal* in 1882—relied on Ludwig's support. The Bayreuth Festival stayed afloat on the strength of royal loans.

In the early days, as Wagner positioned himself as an *éminence grise* in Ludwig's court, he resumed the production of political pamphlets, writing chiefly for the king's benefit. For the time being, though, purely national-ist definitions of Germanness remained foreign to him. In the 1864 essay "On State and Religion," he criticizes patriotism as a collective blindness that undercuts human solidarity and promotes perpetual war. *Patriotis-mus* is *Wahn*, madness—the same word that Sachs intones when he rues the riot that overtakes Nuremberg in Act II of *Meistersinger*. In a kind of instructive journal that he wrote for Ludwig in 1865, Wagner denounces "lust for power" and the "yearning after 'German mastery.'" The desire to conquer other lands is "un-German." So is any system of standing armies, which creates a useless military class. The German nature is "defensive-conservative," he says, inclined toward contemplation rather than domi-nation. It was, in fact, in the absence of political power that German art rose to greatness. Imperialism and militarism are blamed on Austrians, Junkers, and Jews.

Wagner's political thinking showed the influence of Constantin Frantz, whose conception of a pan-German "metapolitics" combined illiberal el-ements (antisemitism, anti-French rhetoric, cultural conservatism) with more progressive ones (opposition to Prussian aggression, advocacy of a European federation). To that viewpoint Wagner added his dream of a national aesthetic utopia—an entity that would transcend worldly politics and give itself over to the promotion of art. Essentially, he wanted a Lud-wig for all the Germans.

When Wagner came under Ludwig's protection, Bavaria was a prosper-ous independent kingdom with strong ties to Austria. In 1866, Prussia defeated Austria in the Seven Weeks' War, establishing itself as the chief German power. As a result, Wagner took a new tack. Although Bavaria had fought alongside Austria, he was impressed by the ruthlessness of Bismarck, the Prussian minister-president. Bismarck, for his part, made oblique over-tures toward Wagner, hoping to use him to coax Ludwig away from the Austrians. It occurred to Wagner that a German emperor could replace Lud-wig as his chief patron. In 1869, the composer spoke of sending Bismarck's wife, Johanna von Puttkamer, a copy of "German Art and German Politics": "Perhaps she can influence her husband to take an interest in German art." During the Franco-Prussian War of 1870–71, Wagner indulged in the kind of bellicosity he had warned against just a few years earlier. The conjunc-tion of early performances of *Meistersinger* with the formation of the Reich seemed fateful. He wrote: "It appears that the entire German war is being waged only to help me achieve my goal"—the performance of the *Ring*.

As the years went by, it became clear that the war had been waged with other purposes in mind. Imperial support for Bayreuth failed to material-ize. Yet Wagner's growing disaffection for the new Germany was not simply egotistical. Although he devoted many pages of his late writings to obnox-ious claims of Germanic superiority, he was again recoiling from militarism and making noises of sympathy for the left. In 1879, he said that he felt shame over his former belief in the Kaiser, particularly when he thought back to old leftist comrades like Georg Herwegh. His quasi-anarchism was resurfacing, now wedded to vegetarianism, anti-vivisectionism, tem-perance, and pacifism. In "Religion and Art," he speaks fearfully of the latest technologies of war—"armored Monitors, against which the proud and noble sailing ship can no longer hold its own"—and wonders whether humanity would one day accidentally blow itself up. His final opera decries violence. First, Parsifal is upbraided for his killing of the swan. Later, when the hero lunges for Kundry, Gurnemanz laments, "Violence again?"

In the end, Wagner fell back on Ludwig, who retained his royal title and considerable independence after Bavaria became part of the Kaiser-reich. But the king's taste for kitsch was a source of aggravation. In Janu-ary 1883, just before his death, Wagner shuddered at a news item about Neuschwanstein under construction: "The description of the King's castle in *L'Italie* annoys R., making him feel ashamed of the whole relationship." When *Rheingold* and *Walküre* were produced in Munich, Wagner grew irritated at Ludwig's desire for a pedantically detailed style of Romantic neo-medievalism. As Patrick Carnegy writes: "Ludwig's passion for scenic illusion derived from his need for a personal time-machine in which he could relive the past and visit 'faery-lands forlorn.'" This Wagnerland "had everything to do with Ludwig's dream world and very little to do with the composer's own images of his works."

Ludwig, who was more than thirty years younger than Wagner, survived him by only three years. His still unexplained death—he was found floating in Lake Starnberg, next to the body of his psychiatrist—took place three days after Bavarian ministers had arranged for him to be declared unfit to rule. In his own unreal way, Ludwig represented the conflicting energies of the Kaiserreich. At times, he appeared progressive, advancing the rights of workers and rejecting Wagner's antisemitism. In other respects, he was dangerously out of touch, lost in feudal fantasies. Dieter Borchmeyer remarks that for Ludwig, Wagner's operas were his "private mystery," divulging the nature of his kingship and his inner self. Even the composer's most zealous supporters would probably balk at the idea that his work should be used as a manual for governance.

WAGNER IN THE KAISERREICH

Hans Thoma, Wotan's Head

Cosima Wagner wrote in her diary on November 20, 1870: "A friend of Richter's writes that after the battle at Sedan the military band played the prayer from *Lohengrin* as the King of Prussia appeared!" Sedan was the decisive victory of the Franco-Prussian War, leading to the fall of Napoleon III's regime. Various accounts indicate that some version of King Heinrich's prayer from Act I of the opera, beseeching God to "speak through the sword's victory a verdict that makes clear what is truth and what is deceit," was heard as Wilhelm I, soon to be emperor, toured the battlefield. One French source has the "guttural shouts of these masses of men" mixing with strains of *Lohengrin*. Theodor Fontane, reporting on the German occupation of France, heard the March from *Tannhäuser* played by the Kapelle of the fortieth regiment in Dieppe. The spread of such stories, both at home and abroad, marked a turning point in Wagner's public image: his music now signified the military might of the new German nation.

The emperors themselves—Wilhelm I, Friedrich III, and Wilhelm II— kept a wary eye on Wagner and Bayreuth. Wilhelm I attended the opening of the festival in 1876, reserving no fewer than twenty-six seats for his party, but he absented himself after the first two *Ring* operas to supervise military exercises. Nietzsche claimed that the Kaiser had applauded while barking to his adjutant, "Dreadful! Dreadful!" Friedrich, Princess Victoria's husband, was more culturally attuned: he saw the first *Parsifal* and marveled at the Grail Temple scenes. Wagner's personality pleased him less—"spoiled, pampered, vain." Whether Friedrich could have led the Empire in a more liberal direction remains a matter of historical debate; in any event, he ruled for only ninety-nine days, in 1888, before dying of cancer. His son Wilhelm would be the final occupant of the throne.

The character defects of Wilhelm II were known to his mother, who described him as "*chauvinistic* and *ultra* Prussian to a degree & with a violence wh[ich] is often very painful to me"—this in a letter to Queen Victoria. Wilhelm seemed mildly besotted with Wagner in his youth; like Ludwig, he delighted in the operas' exterior splendors, their brassy fanfares and medieval decor. He allegedly wore his admiral's uniform to performances of *The Flying Dutchman* and outfitted his automobile with a horn that played the thunder motif from *Rheingold*. He first visited Bayreuth in 1886, in the company of his confidant Philipp Eulenburg, and came away convinced that the festival was of national importance. Indeed, he proposed that it should become an annual event, so that its "ennobling effect" could spread. He returned in 1889, as Kaiser, but no official endorsement was forthcoming. By the turn of the century, his interest had waned. "I don't like Wagner, he is too noisy," he said. Bernhard von Bülow, the German chancellor from 1900 to 1909, theorized that Wilhelm liked Wagner mainly in order to antagonize his mother. At heart, he preferred Mozart, Lortzing, Meyerbeer, and Gilbert and Sullivan.

Wagnerian nationalists hardly needed permission from above to glorify their hero. The opening of Bayreuth set loose an avalanche of articles, pamphlets, and books on the theme of Wagner's *Deutschtum*, or Germanness. Hannu Salmi has assembled a list of publications that includes *Richard Wagner and German Culture*, *Richard Wagner and Deutschtum*, *Richard Wagner and the National Idea*, *Richard Wagner and His Meaning for the German People*, and *Richard Wagner as Founder of a German National Style* (the last by Nietzsche's antisemitic brother-in-law, Bernhard Förster). The *völkisch* faction—those who believed that ultimate wisdom resided in the people—was especially receptive. The Patrons' Association that arose in support of Bayreuth favored a nationalist racist program. *Meistersinger* was often the prime exhibit. For the composer Peter Cornelius, the opera represented the "eternal idea of *Deutschtum*," a "glorious, world-conquering" spirit. For the scholar Ludwig Nohl, it marked the end of "an epoch of servitude to a foreign pseudo-civilization."

Wagner "showed us what we were," one pamphleteer wrote. Visual artists underscored the point by projecting the composer backward in time. Franz von Lenbach, the reigning portraitist of Wilhelmine Germany, fashioned what became a more or less official image: head in profile, eyes fixed in the distance, nose and chin cutting into gray space, a large beret leaning to the side. The Rembrandtesque contrast of light and shadow, which also appears in Lenbach's portraits of the German Kaisers, the Austrian emperor Franz Joseph, and Bismarck, creates an Old Master ambience. As the Wagner scholar John Deathridge has observed, the donning of a beret itself has a political slant. Martin Luther wears one in a portrait from the workshop of Cranach the Elder, as does the real-life Hans Sachs in a sixteenth-century engraving. During the Napoleonic Wars, German freethinkers took to wearing berets as an expression of national identity. Wagner took up the trend around 1867, just as he was falling in line with the drive toward unification. He was consciously assuming a symbolic role.

Artistic renderings of scenes from Wagner's operas adapted them to various imperial styles. Hans Thoma, who designed costumes for the 1896 *Ring* in Bayreuth, looked back to the German Renaissance, and certain of his *Ring* pictures have a deliberately antique air: a sketch of Wotan is like a pagan god as seen by Dürer or Cranach. In contrast, Thoma's portrayal of Wotan and Brünnhilde is more in a domestic-naturalist mode. The god comes across as a stern but good-hearted rural patriarch, listening as his daughter pleads for freedom. A Venus and Tannhäuser painted by Gabriel von Max has a somewhat bourgeois appearance, despite the baring of breasts. In 1883, the Austrian painter Hans Makart, whose plush, color-rich style pleased Wagner, exhibited eight canvases based on the *Ring*. In a depiction of Alberich's theft of the gold, the Rhinemaidens writhe about in a manner foreshadowing Gustav Klimt.

The artist most closely identified with Wagner was Franz Stassen, whose illustrations for *Tristan*, *Parsifal*, and the *Ring* were enormously popular in the Wilhelmine years and beyond. Clean-lined, instantly legible, faintly titillating, Stassen's work anticipates the style of classic American comic books. In the *Parsifal* sequence, the journey to Monsalvat is not an initiatory metamorphosis but a climb through picturesque scenery. Many of these projects were aimed at the edification of the young, paralleling the likes of *Wonder Tales from Wagner*. In 1912, Stassen illustrated Rudolf Herzog's *Siegfried the Hero, Told for German Youth*.

Wagner merchandise flooded the market. The Reuter Wagner Museum in Eisenach has a priceless collection of Wagner figurines, Wagner pipes, Bayreuth paperweights, Wagner candlestick holders, Wagner plates and mugs, Siegfried slippers, and Rheingold *sekt*. As Rudolph Sabor records in his book *The Real Wagner*, restaurants served Siegfried Schnitzel, Wotan Ham à la Walhall, and Nibelung Dumplings, and the firm of Moosdorf & Hochhausler marketed a bathtub in which one could rock back and forth while singing "Wagalaweia!" In 1907, the Weinhaus Rheingold opened on Potsdamer Platz in Berlin, with Rhinemaidens cavorting in the decor. Brassy arrangements of Wagner blared in parks, restaurants, and spas: Gottfried Sonntag fashioned a quick-stepping *Nibelungen-Marsch* from Bayreuth's brass fanfares. There were more than five hundred military bands in Wilhelmine Germany, and almost all had Wagner in their repertory. What the composer would have made of this crescendoing din is anyone's guess. Although he wrote marches himself, in 1882 he expressed horror at the idea that his son Siegfried might have to march to a military beat.

The Kaisers were not alone in resisting the deification of Wagner. Until 1900, and even after, the composer remained a contentious figure in Germany, his status disputed on musical, personal, and political grounds. Musical classicists, those faithful to Haydn, Mozart, and Beethoven, felt threatened by his hostility to traditional instrumental forms. Torchbearers of the "other Germany," the one that was racing toward modernity and reveling in urban culture, tended to view him not as the artist of the future but as a musty relic. The split in Wagner's political identity, between the youthful revolutionary and the aging conservative, affected his image on both sides of the divide. To many on the left, he was an apostate. To some on the right, he was a decadent in faux-Teutonic garb. A 1903 publication collected epithets that critics had lobbed at Wagner over the years: Antichrist, Heliogabalus, Beelzebub, Orcus, Moloch, Megatherion.

One camp of authors treated Wagner as an amusing fad. Johannes Scherr's 1858 novel *Michel* describes a certain Herr Schwarbel as a "musical savior and tyrant of the future, of whom musicians say that he is a great writer, and writers that he is a great musician." The Viennese playwright Johann Nestroy parodied *Tannhäuser* in 1857 and *Lohengrin* in 1859. In the one, Tannhäuser is a drunken student and Venus a bierkeller hostess; in the other, Lohengrin enters drawn by a sheep, to which he sings a farewell aria ("Leb wohl, mein gutes Schaf!"). Friedrich Theodor Vischer's

Franz Stassen, "Nothung is lodged in your heart"

1878 satire *Auch einer* (Another One) features a megalomaniacal druid who compels his village to perform his epic poem. It is a garbled version of the *Ring*—"Weia! Waga!" becomes "Pfisala, Pfnisla, Pfeia!"—set to a cacophony of bagpipes and steerhorns. In an odd twist, Vischer, a philosopher and liberal politician, helped beget the *Ring* with an 1844 essay calling for a multipart national opera based on the Nibelung story.

In right-wing circles, the most prominent Wagner skeptic was Paul de Lagarde, a scholar of Near Eastern languages and religion who found a second calling as a social critic and religious philosopher. In his *German Writings* and other publications, Lagarde pilloried Wilhelmine materialism and espoused a pure Germanic-Christian religion. Wagner read Lagarde's work with excitement. Yet Lagarde rebuffed approaches from Bayreuth. He disliked the music—"I was bored to extinction," he said of *Siegfried*— and doubted that it could provide moral guidance. "The *Volk* cannot travel to Bayreuth to become better," Lagarde wrote in 1888.

Even more antipathetic was Julius Langbehn, whose pan-Germanist tract *Rembrandt as Educator* sold in huge quantities in the nineties. For Langbehn, Wagner was an empty showman, lacking the humility and depth of Shakespeare. "He out-Meyerbeered Meyerbeer," Langbehn sneered, implying that Wagner fit the profile of a restless, rootless Jew. Wilhelm Heinrich Riehl, another *völkisch* eminence, wondered whether Wagner could be truly German if he made such a positive impression on the French. Cosima herself did not avoid scrutiny. In 1894, an anonymous critic wrote: "As a half-Magyar, half-French woman, she is hardly called upon to assume a leading position in matters of German art." There were widespread complaints about the *Überfremdung*, or foreign colonization, of Bayreuth, whether in the casting of singers, the makeup of the audience, or the eclectic genealogy of the Wagner family.

Such objections subsided as the nineteenth century gave way to the twentieth. The alignment of Bayreuth with the German right was reinforced by the publication, in 1899, of Houston Stewart Chamberlain's *Foundations of the Nineteenth Century*, which picked up strands from Lagarde and Langbehn but restored Wagner's primacy as a *völkisch* prophet. Antisemitism cemented the bond, as the next chapter will show. Still, the composer was too eccentric to function as an infallible national signifier. As the historian Celia Applegate points out, Bayreuth failed to become a center of national spirit, despite aspirations in that direction. Instead, it was a "kind of limbo, a musical Neverland," in which adepts of various nationalities, faiths, and ideologies glided past one another, under the Wagner spell.

FONTANE

When Theodor Fontane came to Bayreuth in 1889, the summer of Wilhelm II's final visit, he was not among the enraptured. At *Parsifal*, the densely packed auditorium gave him an attack of claustrophobia, and he left as the prelude was ending. He amused his wife, Emilie, by describing what he had done in his free time. He walked back to his hotel; he read; he went out for coffee; he returned to the hotel to write letters; he went out to mail the letters; he went for another walk; he returned to the hotel and read for an hour. "*Parsifal*, though, is still far from over." He took more pleasure in observing the multilingual bustle of the town: visitors from Siam, Shanghai, Bombay, Colorado, Nebraska, Minnesota. "The whole story is staged only for *Lords* and *Bankiers*," he wrote. Despite the waste of a hundred marks, Fontane felt that "to have seen Bayreuth in the midst of the Wagner season and Wagner cult is worth much to me."

Fontane was the leading German exponent of novelistic realism, in the tradition of Balzac, Flaubert, and Turgenev. He came along later than those nineteenth-century masters; perhaps only after the Empire had formed could such sharp-eyed dissections of German society be written. The mature Fontane was by no means a radical: during the wars of unification, he took a patriotic line in his journalistic writing, and remained admiring of Bismarck. But the Kaiserreich did not fulfill his political dreams. In an increasingly antisemitic climate, he wrote with subtle sympathy about Jewish lives. He was, above all, a man of reason—dedicated, in Thomas Mann's words, "not to intoxication but to insight." The all-intoxicating Wagner became for him a symptom of the pretensions and delusions of Wilhelmine society.

Although Fontane generally took a dim view of Wagner's music, he was not insensible to its power. In an 1873 note about *Meistersinger*, he defended the opera against criticism that it had violated dramatic principles; art is often most interesting when it breaks the rules, he wrote. In the early eighties, he studied the *Ring* librettos, chiding them for their "childish, taste-less, pretentious" language while admitting their "mystical, profoundly fairy-tale-like" substance. Fontane later sketched a novel called *Oceane von Parceval*, an interweaving of mythic and contemporary elements. The title character was to have been a "modern Melusine," who glides through the human world and longs to experience the fullness of emotion; she can feel love but not pain. A scholar well versed in Wagner and the Edda suggests that "there are more Wogelindes than you know," and quotes the opening of the *Ring*. Her longings unfulfilled, Oceane goes for a swim and disappears whence she came.

Fontane inserted three major Wagner Scenes into his fiction, with the Wagnerites in them becoming progressively uglier in spirit. In the novella *L'Adultera* (1882), the wealthy banker Ezechiel van der Straaten, a converted Jew, is married to Melanie, a considerably younger woman. He cordially despises Wagner; she is a confirmed devotee. Ezechiel probably speaks for the author when he says: "And *who* is your idol? That knight of Bayreuth, an enchanter if there ever was one. And you stake the salvation of your souls on that Tannhäuser and Venusberg fellow . . . You sing and play the stuff morning, noon, and night . . . It's rotten magic, I tell you." Melanie feels attracted to a young businessman named Ebenezer Rubehn, also Jewish. Noticing that the young man belongs to "that little community whose name and focus I don't even need to mention"—the Wagnerites—Melanie asks Rubehn which of the Master's works he likes the most. The answer: *Die Meistersinger*. Melanie falls in love with the young man, sings with him, and has a child by him in Venice. Nineteenth-century stories of this kind usually end in tragedy, but here the denouement is unexpectedly happy. Van der Straaten magnanimously grants a divorce; Melanie and Rubehn work their way back into society; and they discover a maturer, more selfless form of love, one that has little use for Wagner.

The crux of the 1886 novel *Cécile* is a fatal night at *Tannhäuser*. Robert, an arrogant civil engineer, is in love with Cécile, a sensitive young woman with a soldier husband and a shadowy past. Robert prepares to immerse himself in Wagner, for "he knew every note and followed with understanding and pleasure." The tenor is Albert Niemann, who sang in *Tannhäuser* in Paris. Then Robert sees Cécile sharing a box with another man—a glib liberal, no less—and jealousy overcomes him. That the pair are conspicuously attentive to Wagner's art only makes Robert angrier. He visits their box and engages in formulaic chatter—Niemann "is of course a born Tannhäuser and nobody else comes near him"—but his manner is frosty. Later, he calls on Cécile and berates her, refusing to be a "mere plaything in a woman's hands." When Cécile's husband learns of Robert's visit, he challenges his rival to a duel and kills him. Cécile herself sees no way out but suicide. Fontane gives *Tannhäuser* two functions, neither exalted: first it serves Robert's sententious self-presentation, then it becomes a trigger for his rage.

Effi Briest, Fontane's autumnal masterwork, is anti-Wagnerian in both content and style. Precise, subdued, detached, it thoroughly undermines the values of its time. Here again is a story of a captivating young woman married to a forbidding older man. Geert von Innstetten, an aristocratic civil servant who takes great pride in his acquaintance with Bismarck, marries Effi and drags her to a remote estate. A Wagnerite, he often asks Effi to play him something from *Lohengrin* or *Walküre*. But it is enthusiasm without passion: "Why he had been drawn to this composer was uncertain; some said it was his nerves, for down to earth as he might seem, he was actually of a nervous disposition, others put it down to Wagner's stand on the Jewish question. Probably both were right." For Effi, there is no escape from the ring of fire: when her affair with a major is discovered, her husband kills the lover in a duel, divorces Effi, and takes custody of their child. Despite his high status, he becomes a shell of a man, living one resigned day to the next. Effi dies young, her bright, childish nature systematically destroyed. Her true desire is simply to sleep—a sleep from which, unlike Brünnhilde, she will not awaken.

In each of these novels, characters attempt to apply Wagner to their daily lives, with disastrous results. The lovers in *L'Adultera* discover the hazards of world-defying Tristanoid bliss, and are saved by the compassion of a Wagner-hating Jew. In *Cécile* and *Effi Briest*, men use Wagner to ratify their righteous self-image, while for the women the music is a mirage of a liberated life that is ultimately unattainable. The Fontane scholar Isabel Nottinger describes this as a kind of low-level decadence: not the lurid excesses of French literature, but a subtler corrosion, in which "the artificial takes the place of social reality." Thomas Mann,

Fontane's best disciple, inherits these themes, but he is more forgiving of Wagner's dream-world, having grown up within it as a child of the Reich.

MUNICH MODERNISM

"*München leuchtete*"—"Munich shone." So begins Mann's 1902 story "Gladius Dei." The Bavarian capital was, by the end of the century, a metropolis of aesthetes, home to more than a thousand painters and sculptors and many more writers. "Art is flourishing, art rules the day, art with its rose-entwined scepter holds smiling sway over the city," Mann goes on, with a trace of a smirk. The city was also musical. An ambling pedestrian could hear strains of piano, violin, and cello floating from the windows. And the city was Wagnerian. "Young men whistling the Nothung motif" stroll about with literary periodicals tucked under their arms.

Like the Brussels of Art Nouveau, Munich strove to become the model of a comprehensively designed, beautified city. The aestheticization of the urban space meshed with the spirit of the Münchner Moderne, as the city's vanguard was known. In 1892, ninety-six members of the Munich Artists' Association split off as the Munich Secession, which gravitated toward Symbolism and the integrated decorative ethos of Jugendstil. The latter was the German version of Art Nouveau, taking its name from the lushly illustrated art magazine *Jugend*. As Maria Makela notes in her study of the Secession, two paintings at the Munich Annual Exhibition of 1889 signaled a shift from traditional subjects: Franz von Stuck's *The Guardian of Paradise*, in which a winged youth wields a sword as tall as he is; and Gabriel von Max's *Monkeys as Critics*, in which simians crowd around an unseen painting identified on the back as a rendering of *Tristan und Isolde*. The latter work lashed out at the jurors of the Annual: just as Munich once stymied Wagner, now it was obstructing his successors. Secession painters, like their Parisian counterparts, used the Bayreuth master as a shield against reactionary opposition.

At the head of the Münchner Moderne was the writer and critic Michael Georg Conrad, who made much of the Gesamtkunstwerk. Like Henry van de Velde in Belgium, Conrad applied Wagner's concept not just to freestanding artworks but to the spaces of daily life. In 1898, in his journal *Die Gesellschaft* (*Society*), Conrad wrote: "From the Gesamtkunstwerk of the stage there follows, at a distance, the Gesamtkunstwerk of the house, of the bourgeois residence." The formulation has a chic, cosmopolitan sound, yet it is embedded in a nationalist outlook. Vicious antisemitism surfaced often in the pages of *Die Gesellschaft*. Some two decades later, Conrad was an early convert to Nazism, helping to forge links between Hitler and the Wagner family. Seen darkly, his total art is a kind of aesthetic imperialism.

The secretive high priest of Munich literature was the poet Stefan George, who acquired immense fame in the German-speaking world in the early years of the twentieth century. An early adherent of French Symbolism, George went to Paris in 1889, when he was in his early twenties, and attended Mallarmé's Tuesday salons. A skilled translator, he introduced German readers to Mallarmé, Verlaine, and Rimbaud as well as to Rossetti and Swinburne. Symbolist atmosphere hangs over George's poetry, but it parts to reveal a complex interior landscape in which heroic self-fashioning shares space with despair, doubt, and visions of destruction. "Schweige die klage," from the early collection *Pilgrimages*, begins:

> Lament be silent!
> Which envy too
> Aligned with your gifts.
>
> Seek and bear
> And over suffering
> The song will prevail!

In 1892, George launched the magazine *Blätter für die Kunst*, which resembled the *Revue wagnérienne* and other French Symbolist organs. His inaugural manifesto demoted naturalism in favor of a new form of "spiritual art," unbesmirched by quotidian concerns.

From a distance, George could have been mistaken for a Wagner epigone. Styling himself a Meister surrounded by acolytes, he drew on a vocabulary of rings, heroes, swords, and temples. The early poems are flecked with Wagnerisms. The first phrase of "Schweige die klage" repeats a line from Act II of *Götterdämmerung*—the moment in which Siegfried is urged to swear an oath that he has not betrayed Gunther. The 1892 poetic cycle *Algabal*, a rhapsody on the ultra-decadent Roman emperor Heliogabalus, depicts a Venusberg-like subterranean kingdom filled with artificial flora and fauna. The 1904 poem "Litanei" includes the line "Kill the longing / close the wound / Take love from me / give me your joy!"—an apparent allusion to Amfortas's lament in *Parsifal* ("Take my inheritance from me / close the wound").

Yet the hectic theatricality of the Wagner business grated against the poet's temperament, much as it had alienated Nietzsche. George later condemned the composer as a "bad actor [*Mime*]" and the *Ring* as a "Valhalla-swindle." Bayreuth committed the sin of "dragging the cultish onto the stage." Still, references to Wagner peppered George's conversation: he could not negotiate the terrain of Germanness, legendary history, and esoteric heroism without acknowledging the Meister of the previous generation. Like many artists on the cusp of modernism, George saw Wagner as an influence to be subsumed and overcome. Poetry becomes a forge in which Wagnerian imagery is melted down into new, more abstract forms.

The god Richard Wagner came in for brutal treatment from the more subversive Munich writers and their allies elsewhere. In 1911, Friedrich Huch, a friend of Thomas Mann's, published a trio of short "grotesque comedies," titled *Tristan und Isolde*, *Lohengrin*, and *The Flying Dutchman*, in which Wagner's characters wander into modern milieux and struggle to find their bearings. Tristan and Isolde are confused when King Mark reacts to their forbidden love by running off with Brangäne. An exasperated Elsa says of Lohengrin, "In God's name, let him keep his own name to himself! Nobody is interested!" And the Dutchman seems aware of his operatic nature: "For some time now I have been fixated on the idea that my entire destiny has played out as if on a stage, that I perform my own Passion every seven years." Georg Kaiser's 1913 play *King Cuckold* tells the Tristan story from the point of view of King Mark, now a senile, dirty old man who obtains vicarious arousal through the escapades of the lovers.

Frank Wedekind was in some ways the most brutal of the lot, although his target was less the operas themselves—he found them variously irritating and engrossing—than the culture industry that fed on their allure. His full name, Benjamin Franklin Wedekind, advertises his exotic origins: he was born in Hanover, Germany, but conceived in San Francisco, California. His father, a doctor with a knack for real-estate speculation, had settled in California as part of the wave of Forty-Eighters fleeing counter-revolution. Wedekind's mother, Emilie Kammerer, was singing with a San Francisco opera troupe when she met Dr. Wedekind, who forced her to give up her career. Erika Wedekind, Frank's sister, was able to realize her mother's deferred dream, establishing herself as a coloratura soprano.

With that background, Wedekind knew of the yawning gap between opera's aesthetic fantasy and social reality. In his 1906 play *Music*, a young woman aspiring to sing the Wagner roles goes to study with an eminent teacher, and is smitten by his "irresistibly beautiful 'Flying Dutchman' beard." She sleeps with him and becomes pregnant. Her life is ruined by degrees: first she has an abortion and is jailed on account of it; then she bears a child, who dies. Surveying the wreckage of her hopes, she says, "Love for my art was to me my religion."

Gerardo, the star Wagner singer in Wedekind's 1899 play *Der Kammersänger* (often translated as *The Tenor*), shows the flip side of the opera trade—the wreckage of success. He resides at a grand hotel, where wreaths, laurels, and fan mail testify to his latest triumph. He exclaims to himself: "Good God! I am supposed to sing *Tristan* tomorrow night in Brussels and I don't remember a note!" He sings "Isolde! Geliebte!" in half-voice, then goes to the window, where he finds a young admirer hiding behind the curtain. He fends off her advances, not on moral grounds but because the exertion would strain his voice. He is next inconvenienced by Dr. Dühring, an elderly post-Wagnerian composer who wants Gerardo to perform his would-be chef d'oeuvre. The tenor apologetically explains that he is "under contractual obligations"—a knowing play both on the music business and on Wotan's dilemma in the *Ring*. When Dühring presses him, Gerardo dispenses with politesse and sings a soaring aria of cynicism:

> We artists are a luxury article of the bourgeoisie, who outbid one another in order to pay the bill. If you are right [that there is nothing higher than art], then how, for example, would an opera like *Walküre* be possible, one that deals with matters that the public would find abhorrent to the depths of their being if exposed? Yet when I sing Siegmund, even the most anxious mothers bring along their thirteen- and fourteen-year-old daughters. When I am onstage, I am absolutely certain that not a single person in the auditorium is paying attention to what we are

acting out. If they were paying attention, they would run for the exits. That is what they did when the opera was new.

Finally, we meet the twenty-year-old Helen, with whom Gerardo has been having an affair. In the face of his heartlessness—"Love is a damned bourgeois virtue"—Helen pulls out a revolver and shoots herself. At the end, Gerardo rushes out, shouting, "I must sing *Tristan* tomorrow night in Brussels!" This blackly funny play presents Wagner as a hollowed-out shell, his formerly revolutionary ideas disregarded by the audience that enjoys the noise he makes.

Wedekind's chief works—*Spring Awakening* and the Lulu plays, *Earth Spirit* and *Pandora's Box*—show the tragic consequences of the sensual-spiritual divide that found classic expression in *Tannhäuser*. In the view of Eric Bentley, Lulu, the elemental figure on whom an array of men project their fantasies, is an inversion of Wagner's Venus; although she goes to her doom, she is the demonic queen of love re-empowered. At the end of *Tannhäuser*, the hero is tempted by Venus one last time, but turns away as Elisabeth, his "angel," is said to be pleading his case in heaven. At the end of *Pandora's Box*, Jack the Ripper butchers Lulu's body while Countess Geschwitz, Lulu's lesbian admirer, exclaims, "My angel!" The impulse to divide a woman along lines of sense and spirit ends in a pool of blood.

THE VIENNESE SECESSION

Vienna, the other glittering showplace of the German-speaking art world, was long divided on the Wagner question. At first, the "music of the future" seemed like an assault on the city's classical tradition, the legacy of Haydn, Mozart, Beethoven. *Meistersinger*, the most outwardly conventional of the later operas, turned Viennese opinion in Wagner's favor. Pan-Germanism, the dream of unifying all the German-speaking lands, had many believers across Austria, and Wagner became a focus of that longing, both on the right and on the left. Antisemitic nationalists such as Georg von Schönerer exploited Wagner; so did Victor Adler, the leader of the Social Democrats. Still, as in the Kaiserreich, some pan-Germanists spurned the composer as unworthy of the cause. The Viennese critic Ludwig Speidel had this

Gustav Klimt's Beethoven frieze

to say about the *Ring* in 1876: "No, no, and three times no, the German people have nothing in common with this now evident musical-dramatic *Affenschande* [beastly shame]." That insult joined "Beelzebub" and "Megatherion" in the lexicon of anti-Wagner invective.

Artists of the Viennese fin de siècle, like their Munich counterparts, sought to unite the arts in a comprehensively aestheticized environment. Although such darker spirits as Oskar Kokoschka and Egon Schiele have come to dominate posterity's idea of Vienna, the musicologist Kevin Karnes highlights an optimistic, utopian strain in the city's artistic output—"diverse imaginings of perfected places or states." As in Munich and Brussels, the Gesamtkunstwerk broadens to encompass the spaces of everyday life. "The city was a dream, and the emperor a dream within its dream," Hermann Broch later wrote, in an ironic reminiscence of Vienna circa 1900.

The most explicitly Wagnerian of Viennese dreamers was the architect and city planner Camillo Sitte, who named his first child Siegfried. In 1889, Sitte began to conceive of a different kind of cityscape, one that would resist the trend toward regimented grids, overbearing façades, onrushing traffic, and anonymous crowds. Wagner helped him to imagine an integrated environment in which individuals merge into a harmonious whole. As Carl Schorske writes in his classic book *Fin-de-Siècle Vienna*, Sitte "translated Wagner's idea of the total work of art as social model for the future from the opera house to the city itself." Where Louis Sullivan and the Chicago School sought to beautify the rectilinear lines of modern architecture, Sitte wished to swerve back in time, to the irregular plan of medieval cities. Urban planning would be more spiritual than utilitarian, tied to the cultivation of national mythology. The isolated monads of modern existence would be rejoined, just as Siegfried reforged the fragments of Siegmund's sword. Reactionary as Sitte's vision may sound, it looked ahead to mid- and late twentieth-century urban thinking. Schorske comments that the American activist Jane Jacobs echoed Sitte as she called for the restoration of communal life in an overadministered city.

The Viennese Secession, founded in 1897, had a similar craving for the lived-in Gesamtkunstwerk. Joseph Maria Olbrich's Secession building, with its gilt laurel dome, sought to transfigure the cityscape around it. The painter and sculptor Max Klinger, who had close ties to the Secession, expounded the concept of *Raumkunst*, an integration of architecture, artwork, and interior decor. The most ambitious of the Secession's presentations, the special exhibition of 1902, was built around Klinger's gargantuan sculpture of Beethoven—naked, godlike, enthroned. Karnes and other scholars believe that the welter of Beethoven images produced for the 1902 spectacle reflect Wagner's understanding of the composer. In the 1870 essay "Beethoven," Wagner speaks of music breaking from the "chaos of modern civilization" and uttering the biblical phrase "Our kingdom is not of this world." Gustav Klimt affixed those words to one panel of the gigantic frieze that he created for the exhibition. Beethoven is cast as a knight in golden armor, holding an oversize sword. The composer of the "Ode to Joy" radiates both the ferocity of Siegfried and the gravitas of Wotan.

The Secession's Beethoven exhibition coincided with a revolution in Wagner staging. At a private viewing of the frieze, Gustav Mahler, the fiery young director of the Vienna Court Opera, conducted an excerpt from Beethoven's Ninth. Overlapping artistic circles brought Mahler into contact with the painter Alfred Roller, who criticized extant Wagner production and urged a bolder approach. The following year, Mahler invited Roller to design a new *Tristan*. Roller banished pseudo-realistic clutter and instituted a more suggestive, semi-abstract style. Settings were simplified and stylized. Lighting design took a considerable leap forward, as Roller devised color-coded schemes for various stages of the drama: scorching orange brightness for the first act on board the ship; a violet murk, augmented with twinkling stars, for the nocturnal love scene of Act II; a chilly gray ambience for Tristan's madness and death. The costumes, too, showed intricate patterns of color. The critic Max Graf wrote that when Tristan asks in Act III what flag is flying on Isolde's ship the answer could have been "the flag of the Secession."

Staging Wagner as a symphony of changing light was not a new notion, although it had never been done with such success. Roller probably knew of the theories of Adolphe Appia, who had critiqued traditional Wagner productions and propounded a new art of "sculptured light." Analogous ideas were percolating in France, where the painters known as the Nabis made spare designs for Symbolist theater, and in Italy, where the inadequacies of extant Wagner production spurred the Spanish-born painter and designer Mariano Fortuny y Madrazo to develop new technologies of theatrical lighting. Wagnerism became a kind of feedback loop: the composer impelled experiments in other fields, and those experiments affected perceptions of his work in turn.

For the cultured youth of Vienna, Wagner productions blended with the general dream-consciousness of the city, which promised a realization of Schiller's "aesthetic state." In 1891, the prodigiously gifted teenaged poet Hugo von Hofmannsthal wrote a sonnet called "Music of the Future," in which images from the *Ring*, *Tristan*, and *Parsifal* swirl together in a reverie on musical rapture and the limits of language:

> Rushing waves of sacred pity
> Beat in sound on every heart;
> Words are forms that cannot speak,
> Cannot grasp the glowing spirits.

A decade later, in his "Letter" to Lord Chandos, Hofmannsthal wrote at length about the problem of the unsayable, seeking a "language in which mute things sometimes speak to me." He, too, is confronting the challenge articulated by Mallarmé and Stefan George: poets must now write their own music of the future, in an unknown tongue.

D'ANNUNZIO

D'ANNUNZIO

In 1899, the German publisher Samuel Fischer released a book with the florid title *Der Triumph des Todes*, or *The Triumph of Death*. The following year, Albert Langen, in Munich, published *Feuer*, or *Flame*. Both were translations of novels by Gabriele d'Annunzio, one of the brighter and weirder stars in the firmament of fin-de-siècle literature. Both books allude to Wagner and Nietzsche, who seized d'Annunzio's imagination as he wavered between Continental decadence and Italian nationalism. His work proceeded to make waves in German literature. an altered image of Wagner was projected back across the Alps. More ominously, d'Annunzio adumbrated a fusion of art and politics—Gesamtkunstwerk in the most all-devouring sense. He began as an apostle of aestheticism; by 1920, he had refashioned himself as a proto-Fascist leader, the *comandante* of the city-state of Fiume.

Italians, like Germans, had recently assembled a national unity from a host of older states, relying on cultural heritage as a bonding mechanism. In 1871, the year of the founding of the German Empire, the Risorgimento, the unification of Italy, reached its final stage with the incorporation of Rome. As in Germany, a composer symbolized the new order: Giuseppe Verdi, whose music had served an anthemic role during the drive toward unification, became a national hero, his name read as a cipher of the sovereign (Vittorio Emanuele, Re d'Italia). But for many progressive-minded Italian artists, Wagner's art mattered more than Verdi's: it had the gleam of the modern. The year 1871 also saw a triumphant performance of *Lohengrin* in Bologna, which marked the onset of Italian Wagnerism. In the nineties came a short-lived journal called the *Cronaca Wagneriana*, the Italian equivalent of the *Bayreuther Blätter*, the *Revue wagnérienne*, and *The Meister*.

D'Annunzio found his way to Wagner along the decadent path. His first great success had been the 1889 novel *Il piacere*, an ode to aestheticism in the Huysmans mode. During a stay in Naples in the early nineties, d'Annunzio became enamored of *Tristan*, to the point where he had the composer Niccolò van Westerhout play the entire score some ten times at the piano. A member of his circle recalled: "He wanted to hear the nagging prelude again and again, he took notes, he almost clung with his eyes to the page where the torture of the potion begins." (This is the same musical passage that transfixed Fernand Khnopff.) In 1893, d'Annunzio published a three-part article titled "The Wagner Case," which appropriates the title of Nietzsche's famous broadside but reaches quite different conclusions: "In articulating our need for metaphysics, [Wagner] has revealed to us a hidden part of our interior life." D'Annunzio goes on to savor the *alte Weise*, the sad old shepherd's tune that preoccupies the dying Tristan in Act III of the opera. "For what fate am I born? For what destiny? The old melody tells me once more: TO DESIRE AND TO DIE! TO DIE OF DESIRE!"

D'Annunzio was then at work on *The Triumph of Death*, and his paraphrase of the mad Tristan reappears in the novel, in a scene of climactic Wagnerian frenzy that may have influenced the ghoulish lovemaking of Marcel Batilliat's *Chair mystique*. Giorgio Aurispa, a morbidly narcissistic nobleman of rural origins, is in love with a married woman named Ippolita. Wagnerian-Nietzschean dreams of Dionysiac passion simmer in Giorgio's mind. Troubled by a nameless malady, he feels marked for a dark but fulfilling fate. At first, the affair is thrillingly depleting. The lovers spend two days at the Hotel Danieli in Venice, in a state of "oblivion, supreme intoxication." (Wagner spent his first night in Venice at the Danieli, as d'Annunzio was probably aware.) Then the excess of lust becomes oppressive. Giorgio begins to see Ippolita as the Enemy, as a purely sexual being who is sapping his higher spiritual yearnings. The only apparent solution to this conundrum, which his own misogyny has created, is death.

By the end, the lovers are alone in a house on the cliffs of San Vito Chietino, on the Adriatic coast. A piano arrives, and they play on it for hours, progressing through Schumann, Chopin, and Grieg to *Tristan*. The narrator speaks in praise of Bayreuth, vividly describing its architecture, acoustics, and ambience—a feat on d'Annunzio's part, since he never went to the festival. An almost blow-by-blow account of the opera ensues, refracted through Giorgio's fixations:

> The Mystic Gulf truly became irradiated like a sky. The sonorities of the orchestra seemed to imitate those distant planetary harmonies that, long ago, the souls of vigilant contemplators believed they surprised in the nocturnal silence. Gradually, the long tremblings of restlessness, the long bursts of anguish, the pantings of vain pursuits, and the efforts of the ever-deceived desire, and all the agitations of terrestrial misery, were appeased, became dissipated. Tristan had finally crossed the limit of the "marvelous empire"; he had finally entered into eternal night. And Isolde, bent over the inert shell, felt at last the heavy weight that still crushed her slowly dissolve . . . The Sorceress of Ireland, the formidable mistress of philters . . . the poisoner, the homicide, became transfigured by the power of death into a being of light and of joy, exempt from all impure lust, free from all base attachment, throbbing and respiring in the breast of the diffused soul of the Universe.

It is a pyrotechnic elaboration both of Wagner's text and of his endless melody—but in the service of a hideous twist. Giorgio tries to persuade Ippolita that they should perish together, asking, "Wouldn't you like to die such a death as Isolde's?" She answers: "I would. But on earth, people don't die like that." Atop the cliff, he pulls her toward the edge. She resists, shouting, "Are you mad?" and "I love you! Forgive me!" and, finally, "*Assassino!*" They plunge to their deaths. Isolde cannot imagine life without her lover, and therefore falls dead. Giorgio cannot imagine his lover living on without him, and therefore kills her. Liebestod has become Lustmord—the German term for sexual murder.

When, in 1900, d'Annunzio returned to Wagner in *Il fuoco* (*The Fire*), self-destructive decadence gave way to self-mythologizing heroism. The story is set in Venice, in late 1882 and early 1883. The protagonist, Stelio Effrena, is a poet and composer who admires Wagner and aspires to surpass him. Free of Aurispa's sickliness, Effrena feels at one with the multitude: he believes that poets should pursue not only pure beauty but also "violent action." Early in the novel, he delivers a fiery speech in which he prophesizes the arrival of a new god. The oration is free of normal political content, but the fever it incites in the crowd is charged with revolutionary potential. Effrena dreams of building a theater on the Janiculum in Rome, eclipsing Bayreuth. Wagner is a model insofar as he helped to beget an empire: "His musical figures had contributed as much as the will of the Chancellor, as much as the blood of the soldiers, to the work of exalting and perpetuating the soul of his race." But as an Italian, Effrena must find his own style. His art will be distinguished by the "powerful, sincere simplicity of its lines, by its vigorous grace, by the ardor of its spirit, by the pure force of its harmonies."

When Effrena learns that Wagner is in Venice, he asks a gondolier to take him past the Palazzo Vendramin. "It was there that the great ailing heart was beating. The image of the barbaric creator reappeared, with its blue eyes shining under the vast brow, its lips closing above the robust chin that was armed with sensuality, pride, and disdain." Effrena throws flowers at the door, shouting, "Hail to the victorious one!" Later, he finds himself sharing a boat with the Meister, alongside Liszt and Cosima. Wagner collapses, and they carry him from the boat. Effrena quivers at the touch of "the Revealer" who had brought forth "the essences of the Universe." All the while, he is crystallizing his own ideals. When Wagner dies, Effrena asks Cosima if he can join those who are to bear the casket at the beginning of its journey back to Bayreuth. The Revealer's demise clears space for a new Italian art, whose contours are already visible in the sturdy bodies of two Roman Siegfrieds who assist Effrena with his new theater.

From *The Triumph of Death* to *The Fire*, Wagner imagery undergoes an unsettling slippage. In the one, the hero descends into a hysteria in which homicidal and suicidal impulses become indistinguishable. In the other, the hero forges a new populist art that devolves toward demagoguery. The birth of hyper-nationalism from the spirit of aestheticism presages twentieth-century developments. When, after the First World War, d'Annunzio established his short-lived dictatorship in Fiume, he virtually stepped into the character of Effrena, delivering vehement speeches from the balcony of the Governor's Palace. Mussolini learned much from d'Annunzio's style; Hitler, in turn, learned from Mussolini, while nursing his own Bayreuthian fantasies. D'Annunzio gives evidence of the political dangers inherent in Wagnerism. The Mann brothers, Heinrich and Thomas, studied his case closely.

THE BROTHERS MANN

Heinrich Mann, born in 1871, and Thomas Mann, born in 1875, reached adulthood at the crest of imperial pomp. Their divergent trajectories gave evidence of the Kaiserreich's split nature. Heinrich veered strongly to the political left, lambasting Wilhelmine culture, Wagner included. Thomas stayed aloof from politics, then bent to the right. Although the younger brother freely admitted that Wagner was a "questionable" quantity, renunciation was unthinkable. In 1911, while staying at the Grand Hotel des Bains, on the Lido of Venice, Thomas characterized his relationship with the composer as "an affair—skeptical, pessimistic, clairvoyant, almost testy, and yet full of passion and indescribable joie-de-vivre." The phases of that affair, intersecting with issues of Germanness, Jewishness, sexuality, and politics, extends through the turmoil of the First World War, the Weimar Republic, the rise of Hitler, and Mann's exile in Switzerland and California; the Wilhelmine period is merely the first stage of the saga.

The brothers grew up in the Baltic Sea port of Lübeck, sons of the grain merchant Thomas Johann Heinrich Mann and of the Brazilian-born immigrant Júlia da Silva Bruhns. Lübeck had once been the chief port of the Hanseatic League, but in the later nineteenth century Hamburg displaced it in importance. Although the family grain business was in decline, the brothers still enjoyed the trappings of bourgeois luxury. Music filled the house: Júlia Mann was an opera lover and amateur musician who sang Schubert, Schumann, and Brahms to her children. Lübeck also had its share of Wagnerites. Ludwig Winkelmann, Thomas's violin teacher, was the brother of Hermann Winkelmann, who created the role of Parsifal; one of Thomas's classmates, Franz Sucher, was the son of Rosa Sucher, a noted Isolde. Thomas's first experience of Wagner was sometime in 1892 or 1893, when the tenor Emil Gerhäuser sang in *Tannhäuser*, *Lohengrin*, and *Meistersinger* at the Lübeck Stadttheater. Although Thomas was immediately beguiled, in a piece for his school newspaper he affected disinterest, saying that the Wagner had been "hard to digest" and that an operetta had come as a relief.

The death, in 1891, of Johann Mann, the brothers' father, led to the liquidation of the family firm. Thomas and Heinrich received generous allowances and were able to devote themselves to writing. Heinrich lived variously in Berlin, Switzerland, and Italy, working on his first novel, *In a Family*, a Fontane-like story of frigid marriages and hot-blooded adultery. Thomas finished school and joined his mother in Munich. Michael Georg Conrad's *Gesellschaft* published some of the brothers' earliest work. Of the two, Heinrich was the first to deploy Wagner. *In a Family* has a scene in which the weak-willed, excitable protagonist attends a performance of *Tannhäuser* and becomes inflamed with desire for the young woman seated next to him—confusingly, the second wife of his father-in-law. Heinrich writes: "In the accompaniment of the Venusberg scene, with madly swirling violins struggling to free themselves from the orchestra's roar, heightened ever more massively through invading trumpet motifs, the passion reached a point where, in a strange way, it became unbearable for him."

Early on, Heinrich followed the fin-de-siècle fashion for cultural pessimism. As the editor of the conservative-tending journal *The Twentieth Century*, he wrote articles that contained pro-forma antisemitic slurs. Thomas contributed to the same journal. Both brothers read Nietzsche, though they took different lessons from him: Heinrich emulated Nietzsche's slashing, acerbic mode, while Thomas adopted the philosopher's pervasive skepticism. The brothers also absorbed the latest Continental literature. D'Annunzio caused a division of opinion: Heinrich held him in high regard, while Thomas thought him a "bad little Wagner imitator."

Around the turn of the century, Heinrich turned to social critique. His 1900 novel *Im Schlaraffenland*, translated as *In the Land of Cockaigne*, assailed the Berlin literary scene and the moneyed interests that it served. There followed a trilogy of Renaissance-era novels called *The Goddesses*, redolent of d'Annunzio—fantastical, erotic, espousing a liberal philosophy of freedom. Thomas found all this distasteful. "I have no interest whatsoever in political freedom," he wrote to Heinrich. The younger Mann remained wedded to aestheticism and bourgeois bohemianism. Homosexual longings gave him a sense of separateness, both from the conservative mainstream and from its radical alternative. He held fast to Wagner, seldom missing a chance to hear the operas in performance—particularly *Tristan*.

Thomas's first Wagner Scene occurs in the 1897 story "Little Herr Friedemann." The title character, based on a subsidiary figure in *Effi Briest*, is a hunchbacked young man who renounces love and buries himself in books, music, and the theater. Until the age of thirty, Friedemann avoids entanglements, but then a new commandant comes to town, bringing with him Gerda, his enchanting wife. *Lohengrin* is playing at the city theater, and Herr Friedemann finds himself seated next to Gerda. As in Fontane's *Cécile*, the enjoyment of a favorite score becomes impossible under the pressure of raw emotion: "The violins sang, the trombones blared. Telramund was struck down, the orchestra sounded a general triumph, and little Herr Friedemann sat motionless, pale and silent, with his head drooping right down between his shoulders, one forefinger propped against his mouth and the other hand thrust under his lapel." Friedemann flees the box in mental disarray. Wagner again activates suppressed Dionysian desires. When, at the end, Friedemann realizes that Gerda's flirtatious attentions are meant in jest, he drowns himself. He is like Alberich taunted by the Rhinemaidens, except that he is incapable of exacting revenge.

Buddenbrooks: Decline of a Family, Thomas's debut novel of 1901, evolves from irony in the Fontane manner toward Wagnerism at highest pitch. The scope of the work almost begs for comparison with the *Ring*: as Wagner tells of the fall of the gods, Mann recounts the *Verfall*—decline, decay, downfall—of a German mercantile family, modeled on his own. In a 1901 letter, he sketched the nature of Wagner's influence on the book: "The considerable epic effect of the *leitmotif*. The *Wagnerian* in the effect of this literal reference back over long stretches, in the change of generations."

Later, Mann maintained that, just as Wagner had first conceived *Siegfried's Death* and then developed the earlier parts of the cycle, the final part of *Buddenbrooks* had been imagined first and that the story was then extended backward.

Buddenbrooks begins, like the *Ring*, with the acquisition of real estate. Old Johann Buddenbrook, the son of the founder of the family business, has gathered relatives and friends to celebrate their move into a new home on Meng Strasse. Guests cross the threshold like the gods traversing the Rainbow Bridge. Just as Wotan's Valhalla rests on shady dealings, the new Buddenbrook mansion is haunted by a buried family conflict: a son from a prior marriage is demanding his part of the inheritance. Johann Jr. recommends reconciliation, saying, "There should be no secret crack [*Riss*] running through the building that we have erected with God's gracious help." In the prologue of *Götterdämmerung*, the three Norns, weavers of the rope of fate, find that their thread is fraying, and finally it breaks: "*Es riß!*" The gods' fate is sealed. By analogy, the Buddenbrooks face similar peril. Such portentous references have an undertow of comedy, as Mann pointed out; they underscore the self-aggrandizement of the German bourgeoisie, no less than the neo-Grecian façades of villas like Wahnfried.

Later in the novel, Wagner assumes an active narrative role. Into the Lübeck community comes another Gerda—an elegant, superior young woman from Amsterdam, who plays violin and appreciates Wagner. To the puzzlement of the townspeople, she marries Thomas Buddenbrook, old Johann's grandson, who is himself a mutation of the family line, with his pretensions toward fashion and his propensity to quote Heine. Their little son Hanno is musical, and Edmund Pfühl, a local organist devoted to Bach, is engaged to teach him. At first, Pfühl takes an anti-Wagner line, decrying the composer's "demagoguery, blasphemy, and madness." Gerda persuades him to reconsider. Even the sainted Bach once roiled the public with his dissonances, she observes. While Pfühl never comes around entirely to *Tristan*, he adores *Meistersinger*, happily pounding out its "great, old-fashioned, wonderful, and grandiose march." This is in 1868, the year of *Meistersinger*'s premiere. Pfühl's conversion to Wagner is a token of national unification: the severe North German joins with the sensuous Saxon-Bavarian.

At the same time, Wagner acts as a virus of degeneration. In Thomas Buddenbrook's view, music is preventing his child from becoming a true

Buddenbrook. Hanno drifts into a dream-world, vulnerable to "womanly influences." He spends too much time with a friend named Kai, another artistic lad, who spins tales of rings and magic castles. Like his creator, Hanno undergoes a conversion through *Lohengrin*: "And then the joy had become reality. It had swept over him with ineffable enchantments, secret thrills and shudders, sudden fervent sobs, and a rapture of insatiable ecstasy." Back home, Hanno prolongs the trance with piano improvisations. At times, he seems to be fantasizing on *Ring* motifs: "Was he slaying dragons, scaling mountains, swimming great rivers, walking through fire?" A piece in B major that lingers on an E-minor chord, with a C-sharp delaying resolution, can only be Isolde's Transfiguration. The boy's activity at the keyboard is almost autoerotic: "Not yet . . . not yet! One moment more of delay, of unbearable tension that would make the release all the more precious."

The Liebestod signals Hanno's end. Mann switches to a bloodless medical-textbook style, in the manner of Flaubert, to describe how the boy succumbs to typhoid. A Wagner atmosphere returns as Mann reaches the final stages of the illness, in which the patient "lies in remote, feverish dreams, lost in their heat . . . wandering along strange, hot paths." That mental Venusberg is Hanno's last station on the way to oblivion.

At the fin de siècle, the German bourgeoisie spent a great deal of time at spas and sanatoriums, which had long played a significant role in European society. All manner of health fads and alternative cures took hold, overlapping with spiritual movements such as Theosophy and Anthroposophy. Spa orchestras and bands routinely had Wagner on their playlists, as Auguste de Gasperini's life-changing encounter with *Lohengrin* in Baden-Baden attests. Bayreuth was itself a kind of spa of a higher order, from which harried urban souls could emerge refreshed. For novelists, the spa had long been a convenient laboratory in which to examine social manners and neuroses. Both Mann brothers wrote sanatorium tales; after the First World War, Thomas monumentalized the genre in *The Magic Mountain*.

Heinrich's 1898 story "Doctor Bieber's Temptation" is set at a high-end *Nervenklinik* that offers itself as a respite from a hyperkinetic world of bicycles, automobiles, and telephones. Bieber, its star young doctor, mesmerizes elderly ladies with an array of scientific and occult techniques. He is characterized as a "spiritualist, vegetarian, Jägerian, and communist, a temperance campaigner and Wagnerite—in short, everything a man of correct intentions can be today." (Gustav Jäger promoted the wearing of wool on the skin, to increase vitality.) Doses of Wagner are among his methods of treatment. When Bieber plays Isolde's Transfiguration at the piano, the effect is much the same as when he practices hypnosis: "There were tones no more, it was the wafting of a pair of souls and the whisper of their kisses that went through the room and that the women heard, hands fallen powerless in the lap, the head tilted back, an unconscious, lost smile on the half-open mouth." Bieber explains, in garbled Schopenhauerese, that a work like *Tristan* allows one to "bathe in the absolutely pure will," shedding the dross of personhood. Eventually, he is exposed as a charlatan, and Wagner is discredited with him.

Thomas wrote his own sanatorium tale four years later—the novella *Tristan*. The clinic here is called "Einfried," which suggests an enclosure of peace, with a hint of Wagner's Wahnfried. It is a microcosm of the Kaiserreich, grand and bright and empty. Decadence is embodied in a writer named Detlev Spinell, a cartoon aesthete who exhibits no obvious symptoms and seems mainly to enjoy the lofty unreality of the sanatorium environment. Various clues indicate that he is modeled on the Hungarian-Jewish writer Arthur Holitscher, author of the 1900 novel *The Poisoned Well*, in which a femme fatale styles herself after Venus in *Tannhäuser*. Mann performs the tricky maneuver of mocking a fellow Wagnerite while luxuriating in his own fantasy. Holitscher left a rueful description of how on one occasion, after a convivial visit to Mann's home, he turned around to see his colleague at the window, studying him through opera glasses.

The inevitable Wagner Scene initially plays like a parody of d'Annunzio's *Triumph of Death*. As Detlev makes his rounds at Einfried, he becomes fixated on Gabriele Klöterjahn, the ailing wife of a vulgar merchant. She is a Pre-Raphaelite apparition, pale and ethereal. One winter day, the healthier residents of Einfried go for an excursion on sleighs, leaving Gabriele and Detlev almost alone. As the sleds move away, there is a festive jingling of bells, and then the "merry noise died away." This is like the beginning of Act II of *Tristan*, where the horns of King Mark's hunting party fade in the distance. Detlev, who has heard Gabriele speak of musical evenings with her violin-playing father, encourages her to go to the piano. The aesthete earlier speculated that "an old family, with traditions that are entirely practical, sober, and bourgeois, undergoes in its declining days a kind of artistic transfiguration." Mann is now parodying himself: we are being given a miniature *Buddenbrooks*, with Gabriele taking the place of little Hanno.

In *The Triumph of Death*, the lovers sample Chopin before moving on to Wagner. Gabriele, too, starts with Chopin nocturnes, as a kind of musical foreplay. Detlev rummages around for more music and finds a score that leaves him speechless. "It's not possible . . . It can't be true! . . . And yet there is no doubt of it!" He shows Gabriele the title page. "I wonder how that got here," Gabriele says. In a Wagner-saturated society, the work need not be named, and in any case the title is the same on the novella in one's hands. As Gabriele plays parts of *Tristan*, Mann narrates each excerpt in turn—again following the pattern of *The Triumph of Death*. But the arch tone slips away. In place of d'Annunzio's extravagant paraphrase, Mann remains faithful to Wagner's text, often simply compressing it into prose paragraphs, with musical description appended. The author drops his mask and indulges his adolescent love for the music:

> The Sehnsucht motif, a lonely wandering voice in the night, softly uttered its tremulous question. Silence followed, a silence of waiting. And then the answer: the same hesitant, lonely strain, but higher in pitch, more radiant and tender. Silence again. And then, with that wonderful muted sforzando which is like an upsurging, uprearing impulse of joy and passion, the love motif began: it rose, it climbed ecstatically to a mingling sweetness, reached its climax and fell away, while the deep song of the cellos came into prominence and continued the melody in grave, sorrowful rapture . . .

At the climax of the love duet comes a masterstroke—perhaps the most finely studied Wagner allusion in literature. Gabriele breaks off playing as she sees, on the far side of the room, the spectral figure of Pastorin Höhlenrauch, an ancient, demented patient. This interruption parallels the abrupt entrance of Melot and King Mark, catching the lovers in flagrante. In one sense, the satirical frame is restored, as mundane reality breaks into Detlev's fantasy. Yet the apparition induces a shiver: the Pastorin is a harbinger of death, signaling that Gabriele is not long for the world. As in

Buddenbrooks, Wagner's music acts on two distinct planes—as a playful cultural symbol and as a force of destiny.

I n the years before the First World War, a rift opened between the brothers Mann. Heinrich's leftist convictions became more pronounced, as did his allegiance to French culture. Thomas drifted to the right. Wagner was one point of contention: Heinrich lost interest, while Thomas remained spellbound. Thomas felt free to question Wagner from all angles, even to wonder whether the composer's time had come and gone, but he could not accept contemptuous dismissal. He therefore took offense at Heinrich's most incendiary novel, *Der Untertan*, or *The Underling*. It was serialized in 1914 but did not appear in book form until 1918; the onset of war made its critique of Wilhelmine mores unpublishable.

Diederich Hessling, the underling in question, is a small-town paper manufacturer turned rabble-rouser who worships Wilhelm II to a self-abasing degree. Through a campaign of boasts, slander, and betrayals, he rises in society and wins the hand of a wealthy heiress, Guste. On the eve of their wedding, they go to see *Lohengrin*. Unlike Fontane's Wagnerites, Diederich is an aesthetic idiot who takes pleasure mainly in the "shields and swords, lots of clanking armor, patriotic sentiments, 'Ha!' and 'Hail!' and upraised banners." He wishes that he had "had such music when he gave his speech in the sewer debate." The villainous Ortrud and Telramund remind him of machinating Jews. He is happy when the people cede authority to Lohengrin: the Reichstag should be made to do the same. The wedding scene prompts him to fondle Guste's behind. The lesson of the opera is that women are too inquisitive, that political loyalty trumps all other considerations, that revolution is crime. If the Kaiser required it, Diederich would sacrifice Guste in a flash. "This is the art we need!" he exclaims. "This is German art!" A thousand performances of such a work would unite the nation. He is moved to send the composer a congratulatory telegram, but Guste informs him that unfortunately this is no longer possible.

Wagner stimulates Diederich as he realizes his highest aim, the construction of a town monument in honor of Wilhelm I. At the unveiling of the statue, a regimental band tootles a selection from *Tannhäuser*—the Entry of the Guests at the Wartburg—as dignitaries march in. Diederich has prepared a speech in praise of Germany's military might and "master culture." His parallel attack on French materialism and publicity-mongering reeks of Wagnerian polemic. His voice rises to a shriek as he declares that "the soul of the German being is the veneration of power" and that the enemies of the fatherland must be "exterminated root and branch [*auszurotten bis auf den letzten Stumpf*]." This harangue soon read as a grim prophecy. In 1920, two years after *Der Untertan* was published, Hitler, the virtuoso of the oratorical crescendo, would apply the phrase "*mit Stumpf und Stiel auszurotten*" to the Jews.

Just as Diederich is about to receive a decoration for his efforts, a storm brings a sudden downpour. Amid panic, the band plays on, "like the orchestra on a sinking ship to the accompaniment of terror and dissolution." When the German director Wolfgang Staudte filmed the novel, in 1951, he made the prophecy explicit by jumping forward in time, to the last years of the Second World War. Diederich's town lies in ruins, but the statue of the Kaiser on horseback still stands. In the local opera house, one assumes, Wagner's operas are still playing.

6

NIBELHEIM

Jewish and Black Wagner

W. E. B. Du Bois's ticket to Lohengrin *at Bayreuth*

In 1903, W. E. B. Du Bois published *The Souls of Black Folk*, one of the founding texts of the African-American civil-rights movement. Through a contrapuntal interweaving of history, sociology, memoir, and fiction, Du Bois bore down on the intractable realities of racial inequality, challenging the assimilationist approach of Booker T. Washington, the established black leader of the era. Threaded through the book are two crucial concepts of racial difference: "double consciousness," which Du Bois defines as "this sense of always looking at one's self through the eyes of others"; and the metaphor of the Veil, which expresses a complex web of divisions and connections between the black minority and the white majority.

The one fictional chapter, "Of the Coming of John," is a tale of humiliation and rage—an antecedent to Richard Wright's *Native Son* and Ralph Ellison's *Invisible Man*, landmarks of mid-century African-American fiction. John Jones, a young man who aspires toward racial uplift in the Washington mode, leaves his native Georgia to study at a black school. Back home, his family and friends prepare for his triumphant return.

"When John comes," they say. In childhood, John had a playmate named John Henderson, a white judge's son. That John goes off to Princeton; his family, too, awaits his homecoming. After an initial struggle with school discipline, John Jones applies himself to his studies. With education comes awareness: "He grew slowly to feel almost for the first time the Veil that lay between him and the white world."

One September, John goes to New York, and finds himself swept up in a well-dressed throng of people who, it turns out, are on their way to an orchestral concert. He buys a ticket and is seated next to a young white couple, whose faces he does not see. The elegance of the concert hall mesmerizes him—"a world so different from his." The first work on the program is the prelude to *Lohengrin*, and it sends John into a state of rapture not unlike the one experienced by Baudelaire in 1860:

> A deep longing swelled in all his heart to rise with that clear music out of the dirt and dust of that low life that held him prisoned and befouled. If he could only live up in the free air where birds sang and setting suns had no touch of blood! Who had called him to be the slave and butt of all? And if he had called, what right had he to call when a world like this lay open before men? Then the movement changed, and fuller, mightier harmony swelled away . . . he felt with the music the movement of power within him. If he but had some master-work, some life service, hard,—aye, bitter hard, but without the cringing and sickening servility, without the cruel hurt that hardened his heart and soul. When at last a soft sorrow crept across the violins, there came to him the vision of a far-off home,—the great eyes of his sister, and the dark drawn face of his mother. And his heart sank below the waters, even as the sea-sand sinks by the shores of Altamaha, only to be lifted aloft again with that last ethereal wail of the swan that quivered and faded away into the sky.

There is a tap on John's shoulder. An usher asks: "Will you step this way, please, sir?" The manager of the hall informs John that there has been a mix-up with the seating and that he will have to leave. In reality, the white man has asked for his removal. John realizes with a shock that his neighbor is Henderson, his childhood friend. He goes away crushed and despairing.

When John returns home, his hopes crumble to nothing. He starts up a black school, but it is shuttered when the judge hears that ideas of equality are being taught. The final blow comes when Henderson sexually assaults John's sister. Incensed, John kills his white double. As he awaits the inevitable lynch mob, his mind drifts back to the one moment in his life when the Veil seemed to lift—the time he heard the "faint sweet music" of *Lohengrin*.

> He leaned back and smiled toward the sea, whence rose the strange melody, away from the dark shadows where lay the noise of horses galloping, galloping on. With an effort he roused himself, bent forward, and looked steadily down the pathway, softly humming the "Song of the Bride,"—*"Freudig geführt, ziehet dahin."* Amid the trees in the dim morning twilight he watched their shadows dancing and heard their horses thundering toward him, until at last they came sweeping like a storm, and he saw in front that haggard white-haired man, whose eyes flashed red with fury. Oh, how he pitied him,—pitied him,—and wondered if he had the coiled twisting rope. Then, as the storm burst round him, he rose slowly to his feet and turned his closed eyes toward the Sea. And the world whistled in his ears.

The irony that overhangs this savage ending hardly needs to be spelled out. Wagner was a bigot who expended thousands of words vilifying Jews and other races. Still, *Lohengrin* represented an ideal in Du Bois's mind, one that floated above the bloodland of American racism. Scholars have traced various parallels between the opera and the story. For Russell A. Berman, both are tales of incommensurability, of figures cut off from humanity by impenetrable Veils. Lohengrin withholds his name because he wishes to be treated like everyone else, without regard to "secondary attributes of rank or race." John Jones thinks much the same when he takes his seat in the concert hall and loses himself in the music. In Sieglinde Lemke's reading, Lohengrin's fate shows the "incompatibility of the mortal and the immortal spheres," while John's death shows the "incompatibility of the racial spheres."

What Wagner thought of Jewish people and people of color is an inescapable question, although the answer is not as simple as it seems. Since this is a book about Wagnerism, the even more crucial issue is what

Jews and people of color thought of *him*. When they admire Wagner, they are often accused of self-hatred, as if such admiration annuls their identity. The American comedian Larry David addressed the topic on a 2001 episode of his television show *Curb Your Enthusiasm*—a scene that became instantly legendary among latter-day Wagnerites. Outside a movie theater, David's character finds himself absentmindedly whistling the *Siegfried Idyll*, and proceeds to tell his wife the story of how Wagner wrote it as a birthday present for Cosima. Another patron, overhearing the conversation, labels David a "self-loathing Jew." David responds, "I do hate myself, but it has nothing to do with being Jewish." The man shouts: "Millions of Jews were taken to the concentration camps with Wagner being played in the background!" David retaliates by hiring musicians to play the *Meistersinger* prelude beneath his accuser's window, much as Wagner serenaded Cosima with the *Idyll*.

Persecuted minorities have a long history of internalizing negative images of themselves, and Wagnerism provides more than a few mournful case studies. At the same time, latter-day critiques of Jewish and black Wagnerites easily fall prey to essentialism—the reduction of a complex cultural identity to "one stylized essence," to quote the musicologist Laurence Dreyfus. We should not pretend to know, Dreyfus writes, "how a proper German Jew ought to have behaved or how an opera free from social prejudices ought to have been composed." Complicating matters further is the fact that two towering figures in modern African-American and Jewish history—Du Bois and Theodor Herzl—held Wagner's art in high esteem. Du Bois's intricate definition of "double consciousness" can guide us toward a more sophisticated sense of how Wagner operated in the lives of his conflicted devotees.

These tangled histories raise bigger and tougher questions. In the face of a sacred monster like Wagner, what power do spectators have? Are we necessarily subject to the domination of his works, complicit in their ideology? Or, in embracing them, can we take possession of them and remake them in our own image? In *A Midsummer Night's Dream*, Theseus broaches the latter possibility as he contemplates a particularly problematic theatrical production: "The best in this kind are but shadows; and the worst are no worse, if imagination amend them." The emendation of Wagner in the imagination of the racial other is double consciousness in action.

WAGNER AND JEWS

Darwinistische Entwicklungslehre.

A Viennese cartoon of Wagner as a Jew

Murderous hostility toward Jews had existed in Germany for centuries before Wagner was born. The composer's ugliest utterances pale next to the verbal violence unleashed by Martin Luther in his 1543 pamphlet "On the Jews and Their Lies," which calls for the burning of synagogues and the razing of Jewish homes. A long procession of intellectual luminaries had disparaged Jews and Jewishness, including Kant ("Judaism is not really a religion at all") and Goethe ("We will tolerate no Jew amongst us"). In the nineteenth century, though, anti-Jewish rhetoric underwent a fateful transformation. Formerly, it had had a religious basis, or was tied to critiques of capitalism. When scientific-sounding theories of race took hold, in the final years of Wagner's life, Jews were categorized as biologically different from the rest of humanity. Wagner helped to propagate this racialized hatred, which came to be known as antisemitism. Jean-Jacques Nattiez, in *Wagner antisémite*, declares that the composer has the "sad privilege of being one of the first, perhaps the first," to make the transition between the two forms of anti-Judaism.

Anti-Jewish remarks crept into Wagner's writings in the 1830s, as he began to hold Jews responsible for the cultural marketplace that had failed to capitulate instantly to his genius. The resentment intensified after 1849, when his musical and political ambitions collapsed in tandem. At that time, leftists routinely portrayed Jews as avatars of capitalism. Karl Marx's 1843 essay "On the Jewish Question," responding to a similarly titled work by Bruno Bauer, states that Jewish political activities are founded on egoism and the pursuit of material gain; that the Jewish mentality pervades society; and that liberation from Jewishness will be achieved only through the abolition of capitalism. Wagner may well have read Marx's essay in the

Deutsch-Französische Jahrbücher, where it first appeared. Three decades later, he cited a letter from Arnold Ruge to Marx that was published in the same volume. The Wagner scholar Udo Bermbach notes that the closing argument of "On the Jewish Question"—"The *social* emancipation of the Jew is the *emancipation of society from Judaism*"—anticipates the thrust of "Jewishness in Music," though the tone is far milder.

Paranoia fueled Wagner's obsession, as he came to believe that both Felix Mendelssohn and Giacomo Meyerbeer, Europe's preeminent composers of Jewish descent, were plotting against him. The relationship with Meyerbeer, the German-born master of French grand opera, was particularly fraught. Meyerbeer had generously assisted Wagner in Paris, and *Les Huguenots,* Meyerbeer's towering 1836 opera about religious persecution in France, prefigured the leitmotif system. The prospect of owing multiple debts to a Jewish composer apparently caused Wagner no end of psychic agony. Furthermore, just as his own fortunes were crashing, his older colleague was enjoying renewed success. In 1849, Meyerbeer's latest opera, *Le Prophète,* began a triumphal march across Europe. When Wagner saw it in Paris, in early 1850, he became infuriated. This was the immediate spur for "Jewishness in Music."

Political sentiments and professional jealousies fail to explain the fervency of Wagner's hatred, however. It welled up from deep in his psyche, as he admitted to Liszt: "This rancor is as necessary to my nature as gall is to the blood." Ulrich Drüner has shown how the drafting of the "Judaism" essay coincided with the first sketches for *Siegfried's Death,* the earliest stage of the *Ring.* Hostility toward Jews may in some way have been integral to Wagner's grandest undertaking. He remarked cryptically to Liszt that he was composing the work for the Jews of Frankfurt and Leipzig— "it is all made for them." He implied that the conflagration at the end of the *Ring* would consume a Jewish-dominated world.

"Jewishness in Music" appeared in September 1850, in two issues of the *Neue Zeitschrift für Musik,* under the pseudonym K. Freigedank ("Free Thought"). The *Neue Zeitschrift* had taken an aggressive pro-Wagner stance, and also regularly bashed Meyerbeer. Earlier that year, the Dresden-based musician Theodor Uhlig had accused Meyerbeer of purveying *Judenmusik,* a recognizably and unattractively Jewish manner of composing. The conservative critic Ludwig Bischoff responded by calling Uhlig's concept a "fantasy derived from prejudice." It was at this point that Wagner stepped into the fray. In language of still shocking crudity, he charges Jews with being cultural parasites, feeding off of the healthy artistic material of other peoples. "The Jew has never had an art of his own," Wagner writes. Nevertheless, a composer like Meyerbeer is able to manipulate superficial effects and intermingle styles in a way that wins him popularity. Meyerbeer is never mentioned by name, but it is clear who is meant. "Jewishness in Music" is a work of double cowardice—an anonymous assault on an unnamed target.

The essay's most disquieting passages present a negative physiognomy of Jewishness. As Thomas Grey has written, Wagner is "feeling his way toward the as yet uncodified theory or 'science' of race." First comes a dissection of Jewish speech: "The Jew speaks the language of the nation in which he dwells from generation to generation, but he speaks it always as a foreigner." The Jewish voice is described as a "hissing, shrill, buzzing, grunting" sound, instinctively repugnant to German ears. Wagner then purports to find analogies for such attributes in Mendelssohn's music. He also professes to hear Jewish "melismas and rhythms." These ill-defined traits have spread to the rest of the musical world, leading to the "*Verjüd-ung*," the "Jewification," of modern art. Wagner did not invent this loathsome term, as is sometimes claimed; it had been around for centuries, and appeared in commentaries on the failure of the 1848 revolutions. Still, he helped to ensure that it would have a long life in antisemitic discourse, up to and including *Mein Kampf.*

To close, Wagner considers two exceptions to the alleged worthlessness of Jewish artists. One is Heinrich Heine, who wins praise for exposing artistic deceptions of modern society. The other is Ludwig Börne, who takes the even more honorable path of a "self-annihilating, bloody struggle." The last sentence is infamous: "But remember that one thing alone can be your redemption from the curse that oppresses you, *the redemption of Ahasuerus*: *Der Untergang*!" Ahasuerus is the Wandering Jew, a folk-tale figure who is cursed after taunting Jesus.

The ambiguities of "*Untergang*," the going-down or going-under of a thing or person or idea, animate the philosophical poetry of Nietzsche's *Zarathustra*. In "Jewishness," they create a festering crisis of interpretation. The proximity of the word "annihilating" gives some critics the impression that Wagner has physical destruction in mind. Others insist that he simply means racial assimilation—a folding of Jewishness into Germanness. He suggests as much when, in the revised version from 1869, he changes "self-annihilating, bloody struggle" to "rebirth through self-annihilation." A further complicating factor is that Wagner counts himself among those who must perish and be reborn: "I wish to go under in *Valhalla's blaze.*" Metaphorical or not, *"Untergang"* is a menacing entity. Isolated on the page, it has the ring of finality.

I n the sixties, Wagner continued to blame Jews for the setbacks he encountered, but he now directed his ire mainly at journalists. His chief foe was the influential Viennese music critic Eduard Hanslick, a Catholic of half-Jewish descent. At first, Hanslick had belonged to the pro-Wagner camp, but in 1858 he backed away and joined the opposition. Wagner's first act of retribution was to associate Hanslick with the character of Beckmesser in *Meistersinger*—the obnoxious pedant who performs the role of Merker, or judge, in Mastersinger contests. Although the character had been conceived many years earlier, Hanslick almost certainly affected the end result: in prose drafts from 1861, the Merker bears the name Veit Hanslich.

Given that background, Hanslick gave *Meistersinger* a surprisingly warm review at its 1868 premiere; the soaring Quintet in Act III caused his skepticism to melt away. He was less solicitous toward *Tristan*, saying that the prelude made him think of "the old Italian painting of that martyr whose entrails were slowly unreeled from his body." Wagner suspected, without foundation, that Hanslick had conspired to foil the attempted Viennese premiere of *Tristan*. German antisemitism had abated in the sixties—the emancipation of Jews in the North German Confederation, in 1869, met with little immediate resistance—but the composer's paranoia about Jewish journalism portended the next wave.

> Nehmt rückhaltslos an diesem selbstvernichtenden, blutigen Kampfe Theil, so sind wir einig und untrennbar! Aber bedenkt, daß nur Eines Eure Erlösung von dem auf Euch lastenden Fluche sein kann, die Erlösung Ahasver's:
>
> Der Untergang!

In that same year, Wagner made the enormously consequential decision to reprint "Jewishness in Music" under his own name. His authorship of the essay had been exposed as early as 1851, but memories of it had faded. The 1869 publication, as a freestanding pamphlet, touched off an uproar. Far from restraining his younger self, Wagner wrote an extended afterword in which he piled on new insults. A diatribe against Hanslick makes sneering reference to the critic's "delicately hidden" Jewish background. The darkest new thought is this: "I cannot judge whether the decline of our culture could be halted through the violent expulsion of the corrosive foreign element, because this would require powers whose existence is unknown to me."

An international controversy erupted, and commentaries pro and con flew back and forth. Cosima recorded in her diary that the *Karlsruher Zeitung* faulted Wagner for damaging his own cause by "treating a whole race of people . . . ruthlessly"; that in Paris the article had "stirred up great indignation"; that Wagner's sister Luise was "sad about the Jewish pamphlet." Princess Victoria told her mother it was *"perfectly cracked."* The essay also elicited much ridicule—evidence that Wagner's anti-Judaism was misaligned with elements of German and Austrian opinion circa 1870. A spoof titled *Hepp, hepp! or The Mastersingers of Nürnberg: Grand Sectarian-Social-Democratic Future-Opera in 3 Contemporary Acts* rewrites *Meistersinger* so that Walther is a Jew who passes himself off as a pure German and is exposed by Beckmesser. Fritz Mauthner's 1878 satire *The Unconscious Ahasverus, or The Thing-in-Itself as Will and Representation* lays waste to Wagner's prejudice, prose style, intellectual airs, and need for sycophants, appending the motto "If only you'd written just the score / All this scorn would count no more."

Not long after "Jewishness in Music" resurfaced, the comic writer Moritz Anton Grandjean and the composer Josef Koch von Langentreu, both Viennese, concocted a men's chorus called "Das Judenthum in der Musik," in which passages from the pamphlet are pasted onto Wagner melodies, to ludicrous effect. The lustily singing sailors from *The Flying Dutchman* are made to deliver the rallying cry of the anti-Jewish riots of 1819—

Jewishness here and there!
Jews are found everywhere!
Hepp! Hepp! Hepp! Hepp!

—while the pilgrims from *Tannhäuser* solemnly chant:

> Only in Petersburg, only in Moscow did I find
> The terrain of the musical press still free of Jews . . .

At the end, Wagner is defeated by an infusion of merry Offenbach. To the "Partons" chorus from *Orpheus in the Underworld*, the company sings in praise of "*Judenthum, Judenthum, Judenthum*," declaring that no amount of Wagner can stand in the way.

Cosima's diaries, which began in 1869, record a daily barrage of hateful antisemitic language. According to a survey by Annette Hein, Jews are characterized variously as "a true plague," "calculating predators," "trichinae," "warts," "flies," and "rats and mice." More than once, Wagner appears to condone violence. When he hears that four hundred Jews have died in a theater fire in Vienna, he makes a "ferocious joke to the effect that all Jews should be burned at a performance of *Nathan* [*the Wise*]." He ponders other solutions. In 1879, Adolf Stoecker, the leader of the Christian Social Party, had said that "Israel must give up its claim to become the master of Germany." Cosima wrote: "I read a very good speech by the preacher Stoecker about the Jews. R. is in favor of expelling them entirely. We laugh to think that it really seems as if his article on the Jews marked the beginning of this struggle."

But the conversation was not always so bilious. What to make of the fact that *Nathan the Wise*—Gotthold Ephraim Lessing's parable of interfaith tolerance, with an enlightened Jewish merchant at its center—was considered suitable reading material for the children? In 1874, Wagner took an interest in Jewish mysticism, his thinking shaped by the theologian August Friedrich Gfrörer, who saw continuities between Jewish and Christian belief. Cosima writes: "The seven-day silence before the seat of judgment in the books of the Jewish mystics makes a great impression on him." Wolf-Daniel Hartwich speculated that *Parsifal*'s otherworldly rites are marked by Kabbalistic concepts and practices—"Jewish Theosophy," as he calls it. The ascetic Therapeutae sect of first-century Alexandria might be a prototype for the Grail community.

Wagner's late-period musings on race and spirituality, known as his "regeneration writings," introduce more contradictions. Notoriously, he draws attention to Arthur de Gobineau's *Essay on the Inequality of Human*

Races (1853–55), which gives credence to the theory of polygenesis—
separate evolutionary origins for various human races. In Gobineau's
scheme, which is similar to that of the naturalist Georges Cuvier, the white
race is the loftiest, the black the lowest, the yellow somewhere in between.
Any admixture from another race spells ruination for the white. The *Essay*
almost immediately won admirers among American white supremacists,
two of whom issued an abridged translation in 1856.

Although Wagner found Gobineau's book compelling, he disputed
many of its findings. In "Herodom and Christianity," he questions whether
humanity is fated to degenerate and whether certain races are unalterably
superior to others. Partaking of the blood of Jesus "might raise the very
lowest races to the purity of gods." No such transfiguration features in
Gobineau. And, even though Wagner denies that Christ has Jewish lineage, the question of his race is left unresolved: "The blood of the Savior,
flowing from his head, from his wounds on the cross—who would blas-
phemously ask whether it belonged to the white race or to some other?"

The strangest of the later essays is "Know Thyself." Its most unnerving
line, quoted in Nazi propaganda, describes the Jew as the "plastic demon
of the downfall of humanity, in triumphant certainty." Yet Wagner apparently intended the article as a corrective to the organized antisemitism of
the period—the "present movement against the Jews." It is not enough
to get rid of Jews, he writes, since society is afflicted by a general disease
of which Jews are merely the symptom. That affliction is the "innocence-
strangling demon" of Gold. Forecasting future political stagings of his
work, Wagner says that the cursed hoard of the *Ring* now takes the form of
paper money, of a "stock portfolio." Jews may oversee finance, but "the art
of making money out of nothing was invented by our civilization itself."
Society must awake from the nightmare of political and religious strife.
"Only when the demon that keeps people raging in the madness of party
conflict can no longer find a time and place among us will there be—no
more Jews." Wagner again approaches Marx's formulation in "On the Jewish Question."

The end result is confusion. On the subject of Jews, Wagner oscillates
between fantasies of redemption and fantasies of vengeance. One day he
and Cosima are studying Jewish mystical literature and reading *Nathan
the Wise* to their children; another day, they joke about Jews being burned
alive at a performance of the same play. *Parsifal* preaches compassion, and

the late essays condemn state-sanctioned violence, from wars of aggression to the vivisection of animals. Yet, as Ruth HaCohen observes in her book *The Music Libel Against the Jews*, compassion is withheld from Jews, who are, in Wagner's eyes, "the most heartless of all human beings" and deserve no pity in return. A few early readers followed this logic to its unthinkable endpoint. In 1851, the composer Johann Christian Lobe, a friend of Mendelssohn's, summarized "Jewishness in Music" thus: "I hate the Jews; I hate and envy Mendelssohn and Meyerbeer; I therefore recommend that all Jews be annihilated." Lobe came to the bitterly sardonic conclusion that that the essay must be a satire designed to expose the idiocy of anti-Judaism.

There are no Jews in Wagner's operas—or, at least, no characters identified as Jews. Blatant stereotypes on the order of Fagin in Dickens's *Oliver Twist*, Svengali in George du Maurier's *Trilby*, or the hook-nosed financier in Degas's painting *At the Bourse* do not appear. That absence once enabled liberal Wagnerites to create a kind of firewall between the composer's despicable views and the ostensibly humane content of his works.

After the rise of the Wagner-loving Hitler, that barrier broke down. The philosopher Theodor W. Adorno, whose father was a Jewish-born convert to Protestantism, made an influential claim in his 1939 essay "Fragments on Wagner," later republished in the book *Essay on Wagner*: "The gold-grabbing, invisible-anonymous, exploitative Alberich, the shoulder-shrugging, loquacious, overflowingly self-praising and deceitful Mime, the impotent intellectual critic Hanslick-Beckmesser—all the rejects of Wagner's works are caricatures of Jews." By century's end, scholars were asserting not only that the operas contain antisemitic stereotypes but that they embody, in David Levin's words, an *"aesthetics* of anti-Semitism."

In fact, suspicion about racism in Wagner's operas goes back further than Adorno—further even than Heinrich Mann's *Der Untertan*, where Diederich Hessling compares the villains of *Lohengrin* to Jews. Around 1870, the conjunction of early performances of *Meistersinger* with the republication of "Jewishness in Music" prompted speculation about the opera's anti-Jewish content. One pamphleteer interpreted the essay as a "pendant to the riot scene in *Meistersinger*"—the late-night town brawl that leaves Beckmesser bruised and beaten. In advance of the 1870 Viennese premiere of *Meistersinger*, a rumor went around that Beckmesser's Act II serenade was a burlesque of synagogue melody. At that point in the score, loud hisses went up in the theater, and a noisy war broke out between factions in the audience. Similar incidents were reported in Berlin, where Wagnerians and Jewish protesters engaged in a half-hour-long shouting match, and in Mannheim, where one antisemite silenced the hissing with a cry of "Hepp, hepp!"

These incidents were discussed in the Wagner household. "The J[ews] have put it about that 'Beckmesser's Song' is an old Jewish song, which R. wished to ridicule," Cosima wrote. The phrasing implies that she and Richard found the story doubtful. Nonetheless, many modern commentators accept the hypothesis that Beckmesser is a quasi-Jewish character. Barry Millington, in a pivotal 1991 essay, argued that the Merker's grotesqueries mock Jewish singing, insofar as Wagner perceived it. Further, Beckmesser displays a Jewish physiognomy, insofar as Wagner defined it: he blinks, he shuffles about, he carps. His awkward vocal line, with its misplaced accents and its lapses into nonsense, seems to illustrate Wagner's belief that Jews can never fully absorb the language of the culture they inhabit. Frequent leaps into an uncomfortable upper register force the singer to sound shrill. Finally, Millington proposes that *Meistersinger* alludes to the Grimms' fairy tale "The Jew in the Thornbush," in which a scheming Jew envies a bird singing in a tree, and is subsequently made to dance amid thorns. In Walther's Trial Song in Act I, the spirit of winter hides in a thornbush, consumed with jealousy of spring. The same kind of narrative sadism governs Beckmesser's fate in *Meistersinger*: he is roughed up in the riot of Act II and humiliated in the song contest of Act III.

Millington's theory is heavily disputed. Some scholars protest that Beckmesser's serenade is better understood as a parody of bel canto, or that the character conforms to old comic conventions of the pedant and intriguer. A thorough documentary search by David Dennis uncovered no evidence that German-speaking racists thought of Beckmesser as Jewish, even during the Nazi period. Wagner's final stage direction for Beckmesser has him "disappearing into the crowd [*Volk*]," implying that he comes from the *Volk* and is integral to its fabric—an impossibility if Beckmesser were Jewish. It might be that antisemitic stereotypes were shaped by theatrical clichés, rather than the other way around. In other words, Beckmesser "reads" as Jewish because representations of Jews are modeled on his long-standing theatrical type. But this debatable proposition hardly removes the problem that the character poses for modern audiences. Hans Rudolf Vaget has fashioned a compromise: Wagner "aspired to broad, even universal acceptance, and therefore took pains to keep any overt indication of his very particular anti-Jewish obsession out of his operatic work." In Beckmesser's case, though, that obsession seeps into the libretto and score—perhaps unconsciously, perhaps by design.

The dwarves in the *Ring* also resemble Jewish caricatures. When Alberich sings a line like *"Mir zagt, zuckt und zehrt sich das Herz, / lacht mir so zierliches Lob"*—"My heart quivers, quakes, / and burns with desire / when such sweet praise smiles on me"—the noisy consecutive z's suggest those "hissing, shrill, buzzing" sounds that Wagner attributed to Jewish speech. In his 1848 sketch for the *Ring*, he says that the Nibelung dwarves "burrow with shifty, restless activity (like worms in a dead body) in the bowels of the earth." In the pamphlet, likewise, Jews are a "swarming colony of worms" that take up residence in the body of art. Although Wagner gave no sign that he thought of the dwarves as Jews—Cosima says that she associated them with Mongols—some Jewish listeners of the time saw Alberich and his brother Mime as racial stereotypes. None other than Gustav Mahler once commented that Mime is "intended by Wagner as a persiflage of a Jew," and added: "I know of only *one* Mime, and that is *me*." Alberich and Mime are cast as obviously Jewish bankers in Paul Gisbert's 1877 parody *Der Ring der nie gelungen* (*The Ring That Never Worked*), which transposes the characters of the *Ring* into the milieu of the Kaiserreich. References in *Götterdämmerung* to the mixed, tainted blood of Hagen also fit the implicit racial pattern.

Parsifal, that sacred opera with a spooky heart, emerged from the same muggy atmosphere that precipitated Wagner's regeneration writings, with their musings about race and religion. Kundry, fated to wander eternally for having laughed at Christ, recalls Ahasuerus, the Wandering Jew, who, in some tellings, committed the same sin. Wagner himself made this connection: "Kundry lives an unfathomable life of ever-changing rebirths, in consequence of an ancient curse that condemns her, like the 'eternal Jew,' to inflict on men, in new personae, the suffering of the seduction of love." She can be saved "only if one day the purest and most robust of men could resist her most powerful seduction." Kundry is also said to be the reincarnation of Herodias, mother of Salome, who, in the New Testament, demands the death of John the Baptist. The word "Jew" does not appear in the libretto, but these allusions come close to identifying Kundry as Jewish.

Already in Wagner's time, liberal and Jewish critics felt a certain chill at *Parsifal*, as Paul Lawrence Rose notes in his book *Wagner: Race and Revolution*. The dramatist and novelist Paul Lindau viewed the opera as an extension of "Jewishness in Music." It was, in essence, "Christianity in Music"—"not the Christianity of the German man, which lives and lets live, but rather that of the Spanish Inquisitor, which burns heretics while the pure voices of children praise God's mercy in sensuous song and bells ring from high towers." Max Kalbeck wrote that German antisemites who are "tired of inconvenient evangelical tolerance and love of neighbor may thank Wagner for this blond Christ." Ludwig Speidel, the critic who called the *Ring* an *Affenschande*, wondered whether *Parsifal* might inspire an outbreak of *Judenhetze*, or Jew-baiting. Such critics were hardly being fanciful: several contributors to the *Bayreuther Blätter*, the festival magazine, interpreted *Parsifal* in explicitly antisemitic terms. In 1879, three years in advance of the premiere, the racial theorist Ludwig Schemann, Gobineau's German translator, construed the opera as an exemplar of an "a-Jehovan," de-Judaized Christianity. That article received Wagner's approval.

Some of Wagner's adversaries tried to turn the tables, spreading rumors to the effect that the composer was Jewish or that he displayed Jewish mannerisms. His stepfather, the actor, painter, and playwright Ludwig Geyer, who was possibly his real father, had a name that sounded Jewish to some ears. As Nietzsche wrote in *The Case of Wagner*: "A *Geyer* [vulture] is almost an *Adler* [an eagle, and a common Jewish name]." (Geyer was, in fact, not Jewish, as researchers laboriously demonstrated in the Nazi era.) Cartoonists sketched Wagner with stereotypical Jewish features. The novelist Gustav Freytag said that if Wagner were to be judged against the qualities he assigns to Jewish composers then "he himself appears to be the biggest Jew." The Austrian-Jewish satirist Daniel Spitzer spoke of Wagner's "Talmud-sniffing nose." The *Ring*, Spitzer wrote, "abounds in the drama of question marks, and this continual questioning and answering of a question with a new question is also one of the little Jewish traits of the rabbi of Bayreuth or, as we say in German translation, the Master."

The question remains open. The Jewishness of Beckmesser, Kundry, and Alberich is not settled fact; nor has it been disproved. The debate tends to go in circles because Wagner's operas resist dualities of light and dark, good and evil, high and low. Beckmesser is a nuisance, but viewers may feel a sneaking sympathy for him as the pompous Mastersingers proceed across the stage. Kundry, with her yearning for redemption and release, is an elementally affecting creation. And, as Wagner himself said, Alberich has a just complaint against the gods. He forged his Ring after renouncing love; Wotan took it by guile. At the end of *Götterdämmerung*, the dwarf lord is apparently still alive, poised to play a role in whatever new world arises. Cosima once noted that her husband "felt every sympathy" for Alberich. A little over five feet in height, restless and antic in his movements, Wagner often struck people as a gnomelike personage. Of the leading figures in the *Ring*, Alberich is the one the Meister most resembles.

WAGNERIAN ANTISEMITES

Toward the end of the 1870s, anti-Jewish feeling in Germany coalesced into a political movement. In 1879, Wilhelm Marr, an enthusiastic Wagnerite, founded an organization called the League of Anti-Semites, helping to standardize the term "antisemitism." In the same period, Adolf Stoecker and his Christian Social Party began fulminating against Jewish influence; the historian Heinrich von Treitschke announced that "the Jews are our misfortune"; and Bernhard Förster, Nietzsche's future brother-in-law, circulated a petition demanding severe restrictions on the rights of German Jews. This upsurge in anti-Jewish activity came in the wake of the stock-market crash of 1873, which was widely blamed on Jews. Stoecker, intent on weaning workers away from socialism, included socially progressive policies in his platform. At a time when many socialist leaders were Jewish, Stoecker found antisemitism to be a convenient political weapon. The Nazis would employ the same tactics.

The transition to so-called scientific antisemitism—a mind-set that relied on deep-seated biological definitions of race, and that ruled out the possibility of assimilation—was fitful and incomplete. Several leaders of the new antisemitic politics were inconsistent in their doctrine; Stoecker and Treitschke still claimed to believe that Jews could convert and become

German. Scientific antisemites found it necessary to contemplate more drastic measures: expulsion, resettlement, or something worse. Even as they adopted an essentially eliminationist logic, antisemites continued to fall back on the older, less venomous brand of anti-Jewish discourse. Theodor Fritsch's *Antisemites' Catechism* of 1893, later known as the *Handbook of the Jewish Question*, included several paragraphs from Wagner's "Jewishness in Music" alongside citations from Herder, Goethe, Fichte, Kant, Feuerbach, and Schopenhauer.

Few publications were more implacably racist than the *Bayreuther Blätter*, which, under the leadership of Hans von Wolzogen, dedicated itself to the "purification and re-establishment of the true German culture." To all appearances, the newsletter operated with Wagner's blessing, although the composer sometimes questioned its more dogmatic utterances. He declined to sign Förster's petition against Jewish rights, despite the fact that it had evidently originated at Bayreuth. Cosima gives three reasons for his refusal: "he has already done what he can"; "he dislikes appealing to Bismarck"; and "nothing more can be done in the matter."

The Bayreuth Circle, as associates of the *Bayreuther Blätter* came to be known, departed most conspicuously from the Meister in their glorification of the Kaiserreich. When, in 1884, Wagner's old ally Constantin Frantz floated the hope that Bayreuth could become a model for a peaceful "brotherhood of nations," Wolzogen warned that such high-minded cosmopolitan concepts might frighten away the nationalistic youth who were taking up Wagner in a rush of patriotic feeling. Minimizing the composer's antimilitarist and anti-Prussian leanings, Wolzogen recast him as a prophet of a crusading German spirit that found its full expression in Kaiser Wilhelm II. In the same vein, Carl Friedrich Glasenapp, in a six-volume Wagner hagiography that appeared in stages between 1877 and 1911, portrayed a "pious, patriotic, bourgeois gentleman, lover of children and dogs," to quote David Large.

A slight but measurable gap was opening between Wagner and his followers. Troublesome elements in his worldview—the persistence of revolutionary impulses, the moments of cosmopolitan large-mindedness, the spasms of world-weariness—fell away. An idiosyncratic mass of beliefs and prejudices was hammered into a doctrine. In the last weeks of his life, Wagner took note of that process. He was reading Förster's pamphlet *Parsifal Echoes*, which contained paeans to Aryans and polemics against

Jews. Wagner accepted the argument but complained that his dream of worldwide renewal was being misunderstood. To Cosima he said that whenever he tossed out a thought his acolytes made "something inalienable and fixed out of it—now we know." Four days before his death, he expressed a plaintive concern that the Bayreuth Wagnerites were poised to "make all the ideas he expresses look ridiculous."

Wagner did not approve of all antisemites, nor did all antisemites approve of him. The invective of Paul de Lagarde and Julius Langbehn, two leaders of anti-Jewish agitation, exceeded Wagner's in stridency. Lagarde saw Jews as bacilli to be exterminated; Langbehn considered them poisonous for the German nation. Both thinkers shunned Wagner and Bayreuth. The socialist Eugen Dühring, one of the most vituperative antisemites of the period, was also anti-Wagnerian. Writing from a positivist-atheist position, Dühring derided the composer's religiosity and doubted his motivations, describing him as a sort of magnet that attracted Jewish money with one pole and repulsed Jews with the other. The journal *The Twentieth Century*, a few years before it was edited by the young Heinrich Mann, printed an article by the nationalist, antisemitic, vegetarian, and nudist campaigner Heinrich Pudor, who thought that Wagner exhibited too many foreign, decadent, and Jewish traits to be considered truly German.

Abroad, too, Wagnerism and antisemitism often went their separate ways. In France, Wagnerites fell on both sides of the Dreyfus Affair— the national furor over the conviction and imprisonment of the French-Jewish army officer Alfred Dreyfus, falsely accused of treason. Téodor de Wyzewa, co-founder of the *Revue wagnérienne*, was one of the more splenetic anti-Dreyfusards, circulating antisemitic conspiracy theories. Émile de Saint-Auban, author of a book titled *A Bayreuth Pilgrimage*, belonged to the same camp. But a large number of Wagnéristes came to Dreyfus's defense: René Ghil, Stuart Merrill, Francis Vielé-Griffin, Pierre Bonnier, Félix Fénéon, and Camille Mauclair. Mallarmé applauded Zola when the latter wrote his pro-Dreyfus pamphlet *J'accuse . . . !* Joséphin Péladan, a law unto himself, was capable of denigrating Jewish culture on the one hand and defending Dreyfus on the other.

Conversely, some French antisemites found Wagner useless to their cause, or even antagonistic to it. Édouard Drumont, whose 1886 book *La France juive* became an antisemitic bible, began his career with a small publication on Wagner, but disenchantment later set in. Like Dühring, Drumont doubted the Meister's allegiance to the eternal fight against Jews: "He would have known how to make an alliance with the evil race at the appropriate time." The arch-nationalist and antisemite Léon Daudet felt the same. A committed Wagnériste in his youth, Daudet came to see the Bayreuth brand as a dangerous blend of Germanness and Jewishness. In a 1915 memoir, he gave a startling account of the French premiere of *Walküre* in 1893:

> The German and German-Jewish colony occupied the Opera in full force and seemed to say: "This time, we take Paris." I recognized through my lorgnette the regulars from Territet-Montreux, Vevey and Clarens, the goats, the camels, the stinking *kamerads* of the salons Dreyfus, Lazard, Meyer, Seligmann, etc., each having brought his own Berliner, his own Frankfurter, his own Frankfurter-Viennese, his own Berliner-Triestine, his own Boche named after a Boche city. All these people communed with Wagner and discussed stock prices in German during the intermissions. Prussian and Viennese newspaper correspondents roamed the corridors, stoked enthusiasm, took notes in their notebooks. Under the guise of poetry, music, the god of fire, the theme of sleep, the Germanic invasion settled itself very precisely into the front rows.

Proust's *In Search of Lost Time* gives a glimpse of this perplexing confluence of anti-Wagnerism and antisemitism. We are told that when society women are in the vicinity of Anne de Rochechouart de Mortemart, a prominent anti-Dreyfusard, they must refrain from greeting Odette Swann, because she is "a woman who was perfectly capable of having gone to Bayreuth— by which one meant *faire les cent dix-neuf coups* [going wild]." A passage drafted for *Sodom and Gomorrah* gives this ironic summary of society thinking: "Whenever you find a Dreyfusard, scratch a little. Before long you will find the ghetto, foreignness, inversion, or Wagnermania."

Antisemitic anti-Wagnerites were not a particularly numerous species, but their existence underscores how much the composer's image has changed over the past century. Circa 1900, anti-Jewishness was not widely considered one of his defining characteristics. In part, this was because the prejudice was so widespread: antisemitism was lamentably commonplace in fin-de-siècle culture. Just as important, Wagner's cultural and political influence gyrated in so many different directions that no one ideology could possess him. Wagnerism was a phenomenon still growing in breadth and complexity.

HOUSTON STEWART CHAMBERLAIN

For a decade or so after Wagner's death, the Bayreuth Circle was a relatively inconsequential group. At the turn of the century, the circulation of the *Bayreuther Blätter* averaged around four or five hundred copies. Once Wagner had left the scene, the journal's articles made few waves in the outer world. They tended toward a contorted, at times unreadable style, encumbered with footnotes. Matters changed with the ascent of Houston Stewart Chamberlain, the British botanist turned Symbolist Wagnerite turned German racial ideologue. This remarkable and repellent man, in whom superficial erudition mingled with profound intolerance, is essential to understanding Wagner's fate in the twentieth century. More than any other figure, he forms the bridge between Bayreuth and Nazi Germany. In 1882, he stood in Wagner's presence at the *Parsifal* premiere; four decades later, he hailed Hitler as Parsifal incarnate.

Born in 1855, Chamberlain spent long stretches of his childhood in

France and studied natural sciences in Geneva. He first got to know Wagner's operas in the mid-seventies, through a man named Blumenfeld, first name unknown. In his memoirs, Chamberlain describes how Blumenfeld, an "honest Jew," revered Wagner as the "only great phenomenon of the second half of the nineteenth century." Transfigured by his Bayreuth visit in 1882, Chamberlain threw himself into the *Revue wagnérienne*, and, on further visits to the festival, began burrowing his way into the Bayreuth Circle. His attachment to Symbolism led to awkward moments at Wahnfried. When Chamberlain showed Cosima the poetry of Mallarmé, the Meisterin deemed it an "expression of sterility," and was distressed to hear that it was the work of a Wagner admirer.

Early on, Chamberlain resisted ideological interpretations of the operas, declaring that for any given reading of Wagner there would be an equally plausible opposing view. A shift takes place in the 1895 book *Richard Wagner*, Chamberlain's first major publishing success. Like Glasenapp's biography, it is an airbrushed portrait suitable for the bourgeois home. At the same time, it gives considerable space to the prose writings, and thus to political themes. Insidiously, Chamberlain normalizes Wagner's most extreme late-period views, effacing their eccentricities and contradictions. The section on antisemitism makes a show of reasonableness, conceding that "the Jews themselves, with their gift of astuteness, were almost everywhere among the first to divine Wagner's immense artistic significance." Chamberlain claims that the composer was free of malice and envy—more touches of the airbrush—and that "Jewishness in Music" was merely a defense of German art against injurious influences. The entire unpleasantness could be resolved if Jews were to find a way to "cease to be Jewish," in Wagner's own words.

A similar strategy guides Chamberlain's *Foundations of the Nineteenth Century*, which appeared in 1899. Its principal thesis is that modern Western civilization, manifested most splendidly in the German Empire, is rooted in the "awakening of the Teutonic peoples [*Germanen*] to their world-historical destiny." Chamberlain makes clear that his account of the Teutons' heroic struggle will require scrutiny of the role played by Jews, but he assures his readers that he deplores the "downright ridiculous and outrageous tendency to make the Jew the general scapegoat for all the vices of our time." Instead, in an echo of Wagner's "Know Thyself," he advises that the "'Jewish peril' lies much deeper," that "we created it ourselves and we must overcome it ourselves." Chamberlain seems poised to advance a spiritual rather than biological definition of Jewishness.

This proves deceptive. On page after page, Jews lurk as nemeses of the Teutons, malefactors of the utopia that the superior race is trying to build. Brutal generalizations pin them down: they are willful, grasping, materialistic, idolatrous, formalist, rationalist, humorless, vehement, voluble, usurious, and altogether pernicious. Drawing on then-fashionable scientific vocabulary, Chamberlain reproduces drawings of skulls and speculates on the interaction of different types of blood. Ostensibly positive statements about Jews, about their purity and single-mindedness, merely reinforce their demonic character. Some of the bluntest judgments are reserved for the footnotes, which, rather than supplying scholarly backing for the main text, serve up further bile: "Not just the Jew alone, but everything that emanates from the Jewish spirit is a substance that chews up and destroys the best in us."

In style, Chamberlain's disquisitions seem far removed from gutter antisemitism. In substance, the thought is the same, the learned manner making the content all the more lethal. One of the most eager readers of the *Foundations* was Kaiser Wilhelm II, who began a vigorous correspondence with the author that continued throughout the First World War. Assuming a tutorial role, Chamberlain boosted Wilhelm's sense of himself as an agent of German destiny.

Although Wagner receives only scattered mentions in the *Foundations*, he hovers behind much of its language. Some Bayreuthians felt that Chamberlain had failed to give the Meister proper credit. As Roger Allen establishes in his account of the affair, Cosima remained outwardly friendly but grumbled behind the scenes. The art historian Henry Thode, who was married to Cosima's daughter Daniela von Bülow, took the dispute public, accusing Chamberlain of plagiarism. Chamberlain responded by writing a new preface in which he distinguished his scientific understanding of race from Wagner's "childlike and naive" approach. Indeed, he states that the Meister "never in his whole life concerned himself with racial questions"— not in the systematic way that Chamberlain professed. His summary of the composer's "slapdash" thinking is not inaccurate: "Today Wagner swears by Feuerbach and tomorrow by Schopenhauer; today he is a republican and tomorrow an advocate of the Divine Right of Kings; today the degeneration of humanity stems from diet, tomorrow from racial mixing."

Chamberlain's attention remains fixed on the works themselves and on the "higher truth" they communicate.

The friction with Bayreuth did not last. Chamberlain had long dreamed of grafting himself to the Wagner family tree, having made approaches at various times to Cosima's daughters Blandine and Isolde. In 1908, he succeeded in marrying Eva Wagner, Richard and Cosima's younger daughter. He promptly moved to Bayreuth and made his presence felt. The previous year, an ailing Cosima had withdrawn from daily operations, and Siegfried, her son, had become the head of the festival. Siegfried generally deferred to Chamberlain in intellectual matters, and by the outbreak of the First World War the merger of Wagner's idiosyncratic ideology with the Wilhelmine cult of race, nation, and power was almost complete.

JEWISH WAGNERITES

Otto Weininger

Stationed in the "mystic abyss" at the premiere of *Parsifal* was the conductor Hermann Levi, the Kapellmeister of the Bavarian Court Opera and the scion of a long line of German rabbis. How a Jewish musician came to preside over Wagner's "stage consecration festival play" is a circuitous tale. Ludwig II had lent the Court Opera ensemble to Bayreuth for *Parsifal*, and Levi came with them. Wagner struggled to accept the situation. He lauded Levi's musicianship, describing him as his "alter ego," but found it strange that this supposedly "most Christian of all artworks" should be conducted by a Jew. He proposed to solve the problem by having Levi baptized—an insulting idea that Levi rebuffed. Levi conducted *Parsifal* as a Jew; in subsequent years, he arranged to have kosher food delivered when his father visited Bayreuth.

The novelist and dramatist Paul Heyse once rebuked Levi for pledging himself to "a man who seizes every opportunity to give vent to his fanatical hatred of members of your tribe." Indeed, Levi endured humiliation in Wagner's service, but he kept faith in the man and his music. "He is the best and noblest person," Levi told his father. "Even his struggle against what he calls Jewishness in music and modern literature springs from the noblest motives, and that he harbors no petty *Risches* [a Yiddish word for "malice," applied to antisemitism] . . . is proved by his relationship with me, with Joseph Rubinstein, and his former intimate relationship with Tausig, whom he dearly loved." Levi refers to the pianists Joseph Rubinstein and Carl Tausig, who also had tortured relations with the Meister. Rubinstein, who suffered from mental illness, had introduced himself to Wagner as a Jew who asked for "salvation through participation in the production of the *Nibelungen*," as Cosima put it in her diary.

Many other Jews found places in the Wagner circle. The impresario Angelo Neumann organized the touring production of the *Ring*, which traveled to twenty-five cities in 1882 and 1883. George Davidsohn, editor of the politically liberal *Berliner Börsen-Courier*, was a leader of the pro-Wagner press. Catulle Mendès, Judith Gautier's husband, was a welcome guest before the Franco-Prussian War. That a celebrated antisemite should have so many Jews around him seemed to require explanation, and the composer tried to provide one in a letter to King Ludwig. Few of Wagner's utterances make as little sense as this: "If I have friendly and compassionate dealings with many of these people, it is only because I consider the Jewish race the born enemy of pure humanity and all that is noble in man: there is no doubt that we Germans especially will be destroyed by them, and I may well be the last remaining German who, as an artist, has known how to hold his ground in the face of a Judaism which is now all-powerful." In other words, he cultivated Jews as an act of self-preservation against an unbeatable enemy.

The Jews who surrounded Wagner have long been considered paragons of self-loathing. The philosopher Theodor Lessing, in his 1930 book *Jewish*

Self-Hatred, argued that Levi and others effectively endorsed the composer's antisemitic tirades by failing to contradict them. The historian Peter Gay depicted Wagner and Levi's relationship almost as a sadomasochistic one, in which a victim offers himself to a master. Laurence Dreyfus, though, believes that such pathologizing does Levi an injustice. The conductor was independent in his attitudes, retaining ties to Jewish communities and to the Munich synagogue even as he filled his duties at Bayreuth. Philipp Eulenburg, Wilhelm II's confidant, related in a letter to the Kaiser how Levi fended off the extremist tone of conversation at Bayreuth, breaking into a coughing fit when Cosima railed against foreign influences on German culture. In all, Levi's behavior seems less an instance of pure abjection than a case study in double consciousness—what Howard Winant describes as an internalization of racial difference that also provides a defense mechanism against oppression.

The existence of Jewish Wagnerites first drew wide notice amid the controversy over the reprinting of "Jewishness in Music," when a fair number of Jews remained steadfast in their support of the composer. In 1869, Tausig sent a telegram to Wagner claiming that a Berlin performance of *Lohengrin* had repaired the damage done by the essay: "Huge success of *Lohengrin*, all Jews reconciled." When that telegram was made public, pamphleteers debated whether such a reconciliation was possible. Daniel Spitzer caustically reported that at the 1870 *Meistersinger* in Vienna "one could hear Christian-musical Germans hissing, and, on the other hand, one could see the owners of noses heavily bent by the weight of Semitism applauding." This was the same event at which some Jewish listeners protested Beckmesser as an antisemitic stereotype—a sign that Jews were far from unified on the subject of Wagner.

Jewish operagoers continued the debate through the end of the century and into the next. Some advocated a boycott of Wagner; others reasoned that "we can gain greater revenge by listening to his music." Many simply accepted him as part of the cultural backdrop of the time. Gerson von Bleichröder, Bismarck's banker, arranged for Wagner to be played at parties, as none other than Benjamin Disraeli told Queen Victoria: "There was a gallery for the musicians, who played Wagner, and Wagner only, which I was very glad of, as I have rarely had an opportunity of hearing that master." The Bridal Chorus was heard at Jewish weddings as at

Gentile ones, although it underwent occasional mutations. The *Jewish Criterion*, of Pittsburgh, Pennsylvania, once recorded the playing of "Lowengreen's Wedding March."

For some German Jews, an attachment to Wagner served as a kind of shield, minimizing their otherness and advertising their nationalist bona fides. Adalbert Horawitz, in his 1874 pamphlet *Richard Wagner and the National Idea*, understood Wagnerism as a form of self-cleansing: Jews had much to learn from "Jewishness in Music" as they assimilated themselves to the new German unity that Wagner symbolized. In a few cases, the notion of a penitential pilgrimage was taken literally. In 1882, the Theosophical polymath Friedrich Eckstein performed the feat of walking 280 miles from Vienna to Bayreuth. Gustav Mahler thought of undertaking the same journey.

One of Wagner's most pugnacious Jewish defenders was the Munich mathematician Alfred Pringsheim, who gave early financial support to Bayreuth and propagandized on its behalf. At the 1876 *Ring*, Pringsheim got into a fight with two Jewish anti-Wagnerians and struck one of them with a beer mug. The incident led to a duel, which fortunately resulted in no injury. Ironically, the publicity surrounding this bizarre fracas may have resulted in Pringsheim becoming persona non grata at Haus Wahnfried. Still, he went on fighting for the cause. An amateur musician of considerable skill, he published arrangements of favorite Wagner excerpts, such as a piano trio titled *Sea Voyage*, based on *Tristan*.

In 1905, Pringsheim's daughter, Katia, married Thomas Mann. The author of *Buddenbrooks* had first encountered the Pringsheim family at a Munich Wagner festival and was immediately drawn to their lofty sphere. He noticed not only Katia but her twin brother, Klaus, who hoped to become a conductor. "No thought of Jewishness arises in dealings with these people; one senses only culture," Thomas wrote to his brother.

The marriage had a strange literary sequel. Mann's 1905 story "Blood of the Wälsungs" portrays a high-bourgeois Jewish family called the Aarenholds, plainly patterned on the Pringsheims. The parents, passionate Wagnerites, have named their twin children Siegmund and Sieglind, after the incestuous Wälsung siblings in *Walküre*. Now nineteen, the twins are intimate with each other, prone to kisses and caresses. Sieglind is engaged

Klaus and Katia Pringsheim

to a dull Gentile official named Beckerath, who struggles to keep pace with the Aarenholds' repartee. He stands in for Hunding, Sieglinde's cuck-olded husband in *Walküre*. As the wedding nears, the siblings go to the opera—*Walküre*, naturally—and are overcome with mutual desire. Back home, they engage in an act of "hasty tumbling" on a bearskin rug—like the rug on which Siegmund collapses in *Walküre*. All this recalls Élémir Bourges's novel *Le Crépuscule des dieux*, with its copulating Wagnerian siblings. Even more jarring is Mann's way of indicating the Aarenholds' Jewishness. When Siegmund looks in the mirror, he sees supposed "badges of his blood" in the form of a full lip and a drooping nose. The original version had him dispatching Beckerath with a Yiddish phrase: "*Beganeft haben wir ihn, den Goi*" ("We've robbed him, the goy").

Understandably, this scenario caused consternation in the Pringsheim family. Fearful of scandal, Mann withdrew the work before publication, and when he resuscitated the story, in 1921, he substituted a tamer ending. As so often, his intentions remain obscure. Although the narrative appears to traffic in stereotypes, it may also be exploring the cultural quandary of the Jewish Wagnerite in German society, as Hans Rudolf Vaget sug-gests. The intertwining of musical sensuality with outlaw sexuality points toward private preoccupations that would dominate Mann's most confes-sional Wagnerian tale, *Death in Venice*.

To Jewish satirists of the fin de siècle, the assimilated, self-concealing Wagnerite made for a delectable target. In Daniel Spitzer's 1880 novel *Wagnerians in Love*, a composer named Max Goldschein is at work on a music drama titled *Schwanhilde*. Dressed in silky, multi-hued garb, Goldschein boasts of his de-Judaizing: "I am no longer fasting on the Jewish Day of Atonement, but am doing the only fasting that the Master has prescribed: for years, no melody has passed my lips. I am now ur-Germanic." The Munich playwright Carl Sternheim features an equally risible Wagnerite in his 1911 farce *Die Hose*, or *The Underpants*. In order to rent a room from a bourgeois civil servant, the barber Mandelstam is obliged to deny his Jewishness. He spouts such statements as "Wagner, not Schiller, is the man of our time" and "Every penny that I put aside, all for Wagner. I have heard *Lohengrin* three times."

Satire aside, Sternheim was capable of dissolving into tears after hearing *Meistersinger*. Arthur Schnitzler, an incomparably keen-eyed observer of the Central European Jewish predicament, had the same susceptibility, often playing *Tristan* at the piano. After a performance of *Tannhäuser*, Schnitzler wrote in his diary, "Worries, sickness, death, all sorts of fear, even if they are outside the door, are as trivial as the wind whistling outside or butterflies flying past." His characters find no such innocent escape: Wagner operates as a point of tension. Marc Weiner writes: "Music for Schnitzler had the function of a psychological and social seismograph, a kind of matrix through which he interpreted both himself and the often complex social relations around him."

Schnitzler probed the Wagnerian psyche most deeply in his 1908 novel *The Road into the Open*, set in the Vienna of the late nineties. The central character is an aristocratic Gentile named Georg von Wergenthin—a composer of high ambition and modest talent, who yearns for "a future full of work, fame, and love." His putative music is post-Wagnerian, but he lacks the discipline to write it down. The milieu in which he moves is heavily Jewish, and he acts as a kind of sounding board against which Jews of various backgrounds rehearse their hopes and fears. Georg thinks: "Wherever he went, he encountered only Jews who were ashamed that they were Jews, or else Jews who were proud of it and feared that someone might think them ashamed." Some seek assimilation, whether through Catholicism or Social Democracy. Others gravitate toward Zionism or older forms of

Jewish identity. With a writer named Heinrich Bermann, Georg plans a *Tristan*-esque opera in which a young man loves a princess betrothed to a duke. In a discussion of Jewish issues, Bermann spurns both Zionism and conventional assimilation, preferring solitary "wanderings into the open."

A climactic scene involves a *Tristan* performance at the Vienna Court Opera. Schnitzler expertly lays out the glittering bustle of the bourgeois milieu, in which Jews figure prominently. But, as in so many turn-of-the-century Wagner Scenes, from Péladan to Mann to Du Bois, the opera becomes the backdrop for an interior drama. Georg drifts from the *Tristan* realm—"weary ocean waves breaking on a desolate coast and the aching sighs of a fatally wounded hero vanishing in thin blue air"—into a fantasy of his own future greatness:

> He dreamed of model performances, to which people would necessarily flock from all over; he sat there no longer as a bystander but as one who was quite possibly marked out to become director in the not too distant future. Farther and higher ran his hopes. Perhaps only a few years would pass before his self-discovered harmonies would echo in a wide and festive space; the audience would listen enraptured as they do here today, while somewhere outside a vapid reality would impotently flow by. Impotent? That was the question! . . . Did he know if he had it in him to grip people through his art, like the master who made himself heard here today? To be victorious over the fretfulness and wretchedness and woe of daily life?

Marc Weiner notices that a crucial name goes unuttered in this *Tristan* sequence: that of Gustav Mahler. It was with *Tristan* that Mahler established his authority as a Wagner interpreter in Vienna. That Georg never acknowledges Mahler's existence, instead projecting himself in the conductor's place, points up the strain underlying Georg's outwardly amiable ties to Jews.

The most extreme of Jewish Wagnerites was the Viennese philosopher Otto Weininger, whose brief life unfolded like a particularly merciless Schnitzler story. In the summer of 1903, at the age of twenty-three, Weininger published a tract titled *Sex and Character*, a mélange of proto-Freudian psychology, post-Schopenhauerian philosophy, antisemitism, misogyny, and Wagner. Later that year, Weininger committed suicide. After his death, *Sex and Character*, which had initially attracted little attention, became a cult bestseller, impressing Karl Kraus and Ludwig Wittgenstein, among others. Both Jewish and gay, Weininger seemed almost paralyzed by the psychic burden of his minority identities, although from time to time he stumbled onto striking perceptions.

Weininger's father, Leopold, a renowned goldsmith, was a Wagnerite who took Otto to see *Meistersinger* when the boy was eight. After seeing *Parsifal* in Bayreuth, Leopold wrote: "I am now so overwhelmed I can hardly say a word . . . I go to bed, but for me that does not mean to sleep." Leopold was conflicted about his Judaism, although he is said to have regretted his son's public antisemitism. Otto converted to Protestantism after graduating from the University of Vienna, in 1902. That summer, he went to Bayreuth, just before his father's visit. He, too, was left speechless by *Parsifal*. He later wrote that Wagner's work "leaves behind all other impressions of art," including Michelangelo, Bach, and Goethe.

Sex and Character plots gender and sexuality on a spectrum: some individuals are mostly male, some mostly female, and those between the poles display a mixture of gender characteristics. Weininger's chapter on "Judentum" alleges that race can also be mapped on the same sort of continuum: the Aryan ideal is analogous to masculinity, Jewishness to femininity. Although Weininger worships the Aryans, his thinking diverges from that of most racist philosophers of his period. Judaism, he says, is a "mental direction" rather than a fixed population—Wagner's view, more or less. "There are Aryans who are more Jewish than many Jews, and Jews who are actually more Aryan than certain Aryans," Weininger writes. Those at far ends of the spectrum—entirely Aryan Aryans, entirely Jewish Jews—have no anxieties about race. Those in the middle are disturbed by the fraction of the other that they harbor. "Hatred, like love, is a phenomenon of projection: one hates only that which reminds one uncomfortably of oneself." Thus, strident antisemitism is to be found among Aryans who harbor Jewish habits, as well as among partly Aryan Jews who hope to purify themselves. "The sharpest antisemites are to be found *among the Jews*." Weininger is at once analyzing and exhibiting Jewish self-hatred.

Even though Wagner is said to be "the greatest man since Christ," he falls into the category of the Jewish-seeming Aryan antisemite. A "tinge of

Jewishness" is evident not only in his person but in the "intrusive, noisy, ignoble" quality of some of his music. Compensating for those traits, Wagner creates emblems of pure Germanness. Moreover, the music makes its strongest impression on the in-between types—Jewish antisemites who cannot escape Judaism and antisemitic Aryans who fear being overcome by it. Both groups seize on Wagner as a means of resolving inner conflict. As often with Weininger, these speculations are a blend of genuine insight and malignant gibberish. He hints at intriguing explanations for why listeners of various backgrounds identify with Wagner. Possibly, he catches a glimpse into the composer's own psyche. Yet the terms "Aryan" and "Jewish" devolve into the same racist clichés peddled by Chamberlain.

Weininger was tormented by his Jewishness to the end, as aphorisms from his last days show. One of these declares: "The devil is the one who blames the believer (God). In that sense, Judaism is radical evil. The fool is the one who smiles over the question with a superior air, who recognizes no problem: Parsifal legend." That Weininger also characterized his own work as evil in origin might indicate his feeling of defeat before the interior reality that he tried to overcome. To be sure, he was a young man in the grip of mental illness, and his death should not be imputed to any one source. Still, it is difficult to avoid the sense that he understood Wagner's call for "self-annihilation" literally. His suicide, which happened in the house where Beethoven died, won him the darkest imaginable praise. In 1941, Hitler recalled his mentor Dietrich Eckart saying that Weininger was the one "decent Jew," because "he took his own life when he realized that the Jew thrives on the corrosion of other peoples."

ZIONIST WAGNERISM

In 1911, the Indologist and *völkisch* ideologue Leopold von Schroeder published a book called *The Completion of the Aryan Mystery in Bayreuth*. The rebarbative title encapsulated an article of faith among many German ultranationalists: Wagner was the exclusive property of the Teutonic peoples. Whatever satisfaction the Bayreuth Circle derived from such literature, the increasingly voluminous inventory of international Wagnerism demonstrated otherwise. Whether in the occult guilds of Symbolist Paris, the Celtic Twilight in Ireland, or the architectural studios of Chicago,

Theodor Herzl overlooking the Rhine in Basel, 1901

Wagner's mythic hoard proved readily exportable. Any community that was in the throes of forging its identity could see itself reflected in some aspect of his stories: the self-discovery of the hero; the crusade against massed forces and entrenched beliefs; the unleashing of primordial energies and emotions; the revival of communal theatrical practice; the fusion of art and religion. This process of reverse assimilation—Wagner absorbed into other bodies of *völkisch* mystery— also crossed the boundaries of race.

Theodor Herzl was born in Budapest and moved to Vienna in his late teens. At the University of Vienna, he joined the Albia fraternity—the group he later disavowed when its members uttered antisemitic slurs at a Wagner memorial. After obtaining a doctorate in law, Herzl attempted to make a career as a playwright. He also wrote for the feuilleton pages of the *Neue Freie Presse*, the liberal Viennese paper that published Eduard Hanslick. When, in 1891, Herzl became the *Neue Freie Presse*'s Paris correspondent, he paid close attention to worsening antisemitism in France. He was present for the public humiliation of Alfred Dreyfus, at which the crowd chanted, "Death to the Jews!" Although the effect of the Dreyfus Affair on Herzl has been exaggerated—Austria was always his main concern—the French situation gave him the sense that emancipation and assimilation had failed to solve the antisemitic problem.

For some years, Herzl remained convinced that assimilation was the only way forward. In an 1894 play titled *The New Ghetto*, he confronted the themes that Schnitzler had dealt with in *The Road into the Open*—tensions among assimilated, unconverted, and other-minded Jews. But Herzl took a more polemical approach. He defined the "ghetto" not just as a physical entity but also as a psychological one. Jews had to escape from it by ridding themselves of stereotypically Jewish traits. The lead character, Jacob Samuel, says at the end of the play: "O Jews, my brethren, they won't let you live again until you know how to die." The formulation makes one think of Wagner's demand for the "self-annihilation" of Jews, and even more of what the composer once said of Hermann Levi: "He—as a Jew—has merely to learn to die." When Schnitzler read *The New Ghetto*—Schnitzler and Herzl had attended university together—he objected to that line in particular. "There was a time when thousands of Jews were burned at the stake," Schnitzler wrote to his friend. "They knew how to die. Consequently, they were not allowed to live." The play lacked "strong Jews," Schnitzler said. This criticism might have played a role in Herzl's about-face in 1895, when he rejected assimilation and championed the Zionist idea.

In May and June of that year, Herzl began sketching his manifesto, *The Jewish State*. *Tannhäuser* was playing at the Opéra for the first time since 1861. After attending the dress rehearsal, Herzl sent a dispatch to the *Neue Freie Presse* in which he recounted the 1861 scandal at length, noting that the hunting dogs onstage became restless when members of the Jockey Club blew their whistles. Now, Herzl says, antipathy has given way to adoration, and "Wagner-experts are sprouting like mushrooms." He concludes: "How loved this music is! Who has brought this about? Who? The mysterious, great procurer: success."

The bemused tone masks a deeper engagement with Wagner. In his diaries, Herzl mentions seeing *Tannhäuser* again, and relates it to his vision of a Jewish homeland: "We will also have such magnificent auditoriums, the men in evening dress, the ladies as luxurious as possible. Yes, I want to make use of Jewish luxury, along with everything else . . . I will also cultivate majestic processional marches for great celebrations." Two days later, Herzl is reading Eliot's *Daniel Deronda* and picturing himself as a Moses leading a second Exodus. The Zionist endeavor will be Wagnerian in scale: "The Exodus of Moses has the same relation to this [undertaking] as a Shrovetide Play by Hanns [*sic*] Sachs has to a Wagner opera."

Herzl made no secret of his Wagnerism. In an 1898 autobiographical sketch, he tells of the gestation of *The Jewish State*: "Heine says that he heard an eagle's wings rustling over his head while he was writing down certain verses. I, too, imagined something like a rustling over my head while I was writing this book. I worked on it every day until I was completely exhausted; my only rest in the evening was listening to Wagner's music, particularly to *Tannhäuser*, an opera that I went to hear as often as it was given. Only on the evenings when no opera was performed did I doubt the rightness of my ideas." Music from *Tannhäuser* was played at a concert honoring the Second Zionist Congress in Basel in 1898.

What about *Tannhäuser* appealed to Herzl so strongly? Carl Schorske, in *Fin-de-Siècle Vienna*, took the view that the opera vindicated "the heart against the head, the *Volk* against the mass, the revolt of the young and vital against the old and ossified." Steven Beller underscores a more precise parallel: just as Tannhäuser makes a pilgrimage to the Pope to seek absolution, Herzl once thought of asking for the Pope's protection in return for a mass conversion of Jews. Having abandoned that scheme, Herzl might have registered the Pope's cold words to Tannhäuser: "Redemption can never bloom for you." Tannhäuser finds a different path to salvation, through Elisabeth's sacrifice. Beller contends that Tannhäuser's redemption "becomes an allegory of both Herzl's private crisis and that of the Jewish people as a whole."

Post-Wagnerian Zionism led to some peculiar juxtapositions. The movement's promotion of youthful vitality relied on folkish rhetoric of a kind fashionable in antisemitic circles. In an address to the Second Zionist Congress, Max Nordau, author of *Degeneration*, predicted that a Jewish "folk ideal" would usher in a new generation endowed with "muscle-Jewishness." Zionist-themed illustrations by the Jugendstil artist Ephraim Lilien featured imperious Brünnhilde-like heroines and angels with Siegfried bodies. Wagnerian antisemites, for their part, sometimes upheld Zionist goals, as a few positive mentions in the *Bayreuther Blätter* attest. In 1895, Fritz Lienhard proposed that Zionists could be the "followers and at the same time the destroyers of anti-Semitism." Adolf Wahrmund, a proponent of forced Jewish immigration to Palestine, had kind words for the Zionists in an 1898 article, though he advised them to become serious about their mission, lest they fall victim to an unspecified catastrophe.

Jewish Wagnerites were not confined to the European bourgeoisie.

Arthur Holitscher, visiting America in 1911 and 1912, noted that a portrait of Wagner hung alongside pictures of Zola and Tolstoy in the lobby of the Thalia, a leading New York Yiddish theater. In the wake of the Met *Parsifal* of 1903—engineered by the company's Jewish manager, Heinrich Conried—the actor-singer Boris Thomashefsky mounted a Yiddish-language version of *Parsifal* at the People's Theatre, on the Bowery. As the musicologist Daniela Smolov Levy recounts, Thomashefsky often adapted high-culture works—*Richard III*, *Othello*, and the like—and had no compunction about treating *Parsifal* likewise, assuming the title role himself. The production combined a reduction of Wagner's score with spoken dialogue. Reviews were generally unkind; the orchestra was criticized for being out of tune, and the Yiddish translations sounded silly to some ears. One critic brought up the underlying tension: "Happily the author of 'Das Judenthum in der Musik' is now in the world of spirits, where, no doubt, such trivial incidents as *Parsifal* on the Bowery are overlooked." Nevertheless, Wagner's antisemitism seemed no great obstacle. Levy notes that a 1907 Yiddish-language guide to opera described *Parsifal* as "religious, but not narrowly religious, rather religious in the broadest sense of the word."

Another enterprising scholar, Daniel Jütte, has unearthed Heinrich York-Steiner's 1898 story "Mendele Lohengrin," set in a rural Austrian village. A poor Jewish wedding musician named Mendele Klesmer—is it a coincidence that he has the same last name as the Lisztian-Wagnerian composer in *Daniel Deronda*?—scrapes together money to make a trip to Vienna and attend a performance at the Imperial Court Theater. The opera is, naturally, *Lohengrin*, the gateway drug for Wagnerites. Mendele is at once entranced by the magical high string chords of the prelude, although he hears them in a different way, remarking to himself that Gypsy violinists often play with mutes. Then he drifts into the customary trance:

> What were they playing down there? And why had it taken hold of him so powerfully? He got up, stretched his little head upwards, stood on his toes, as if he wanted to come closer to the notes. They quivered through the air like the wistful prayer of angelic choirs, like the quiet sobbing of God, like the music of cherubs, trying to soothe God's pain. The stirring within him grew, his breath evaded him, his eyes stared transfixed

to the heavens, his hands shook nervously, and when the prelude ended, he set himself down in a daze on the wooden step.

Returning to his village, Mendele swears off traditional Jewish music and insists on playing *Lohengrin* at weddings and other gatherings. This annoys the community, which starts calling him "Mendele Lohengrin" and "Reb Wagner." Finally, someone breaks the news to him that Wagner is an antisemite. Mendele doesn't believe it at first, but when he is faced with the evidence of "Jewishness in Music" he rips the text to shreds. Still, he cannot repudiate Wagner altogether. He turns away from *Lohengrin*, but he also abandons the traditional music to which he has been dedicated. "Wagner is just, he knows the causes of our infirmities, he is no blind hater—he also sees a way out—our dissolution—the Untergang, so it is written in this document." Mendele proceeds to smash his basetla—a cello-like instrument used in Polish klezmer bands. It is an ambiguous ending. Is Mendele a pitiful figure who has been undone by his love of Wagner? Or is he progressing toward some affirmative new Jewish art?

Lohengrin had a special appeal for Jewish listeners, as Jütte observes. The opera romanticizes the figure of the itinerant outsider who stands apart from the "normal" community, much as many Jews perceived themselves within German society. It offers up an image of reconciliation—a wedding not merely of individuals but of social worlds. That promise of wholeness, of the integration of the outsider, appealed not only to Jews. The sounds of the prelude affect Mendele much as they affect John Jones in Du Bois's *The Souls of Black Folk*: "The infinite beauty of the wail lingered and swept through every muscle of his frame, and put it all a-tune . . ." Tellingly, Du Bois's doomed protagonist hums an amended version of the Bridal Chorus (*"Freudig geführt"*) as he prepares to meet his fate. With Mendele and John Jones alike, the failure of that attempted reconciliation is a Wagnerian outcome. *Lohengrin* also ends in tragedy, with the solitary hero withdrawing from the scene. In York-Steiner's tale, however, it is Wagner himself who ruins the dream of reconciliation that his work has fostered.

LURANAH ALDRIDGE

Racism is not a monolithic phenomenon. Doctrines of racial inequality loom large in European and American history in the late nineteenth century, but they do not always neatly align. It makes more sense to speak of a constellation of locally rooted hatreds. Gobineau, in his *Essay on the Inequality of Human Races*, pays scant attention to Jews, and when he does he calls them a "free, strong, and intelligent people," one that unfortunately fell prey to miscegenation. For Wagner, Jews are, of course, a blind obsession. People of color, on the other hand, cause Gobineau to shudder with disgust, while the composer's opinion of them wavers.

Much of the time, Wagner echoed the common prejudice. According to Cosima's diaries, he used "Negro" or "mulatto" as a metaphor for dim-wittedness; hence his description of *Tristan* as "my first Italian opera for an audience of mulattoes." Although he died before the launch of German colonialism in Africa, he took an interest in the ideas of the colonialist agitator Ernst von Weber.

Yet Wagner could also be sympathetic to black people. He criticizes Thomas Carlyle's pamphlet "Occasional Discourse on the Negro Question," expressing surprise over Carlyle's "taking sides against the Negroes." He says that the American Civil War was "the only war whose aim was humane"—presumably meaning the abolition of slavery. He is so upset by a newspaper's "spiteful remark" about the abolitionist author Harriet Beecher Stowe that he threatens to cancel his subscription. On the subject of Native Americans, Wagner seconds Cosima's view that "I would give the whole of discovered America in exchange for the poor natives' not having been burned or persecuted." And he praises Cetshwayo, king of Zululand, who humiliated British forces in the early stages of the Anglo-Zulu War of 1879. The Zulus' military prowess causes Wagner to doubt the prevailing colonial attitude toward non-Western peoples. "Zulus are human beings like ourselves," he says.

European stages were generally closed to people of color, but in the middle of the nineteenth century an African-American performer achieved unprecedented renown, in a way that caught Wagner's attention. The actor Ira Aldridge was a native New Yorker who moved to England in his teenaged years. When he essayed the role of Othello, white audiences were taken aback by his verbal refinement and emotional intensity. A racist press campaign undermined his Covent Garden debut, in 1833, and relegated him to the provinces. In the fifties, though, he began to find success on the Continent, playing not only Othello but also Macbeth, Richard III, Shylock, and King Lear. Théophile Gautier described Aldridge's Othello as "sage, controlled, classical, majestic," and judged his Lear even finer. In Germany, the actor found himself the subject of mass adulation, with full houses greeting him in each town and critics vying with one another to invent superlatives. Friedrich Wilhelm IV, the king of Prussia, conferred on Aldridge a Gold Medal for Art and Science. In Budapest, admirers threw a wreath with the message "Thou doth fascinate a foreign people, the spirit of Shakespeare is with thee."

In 1857, the year in which the U.S. Supreme Court defined black people as a "subordinate and inferior class of beings," Aldridge brought his Othello to Zurich. Gottfried Keller and Georg Herwegh, two of Wagner's associates, were in attendance; Herwegh wrote, "Everything thought through, everything calculated . . . All understanding, all art." Wagner probably joined them, since he had mentioned the performance in advance to Mathilde Wesendonck: "Wednesday: *Othello Ira Aldridge*. Tickets to be booked in a timely fashion." In the period of the Harlem Renaissance, Wagner's apparent interest in Aldridge did not go unnoticed; both James Weldon Johnson and Langston Hughes remarked on it.

Wagner said nothing more about Aldridge, but the name resurfaced at Bayreuth at the end of the century. Three of the actor's children with the Swedish singer Amanda von Brandt pursued musical careers. Ira Frederick showed skill as a pianist, composer, and conductor before dying at the age of twenty-four. Amanda had a long and varied life as a singer, composer, and teacher, giving instruction to Roland Hayes, Marian Anderson, and Paul Robeson, among others. The most gifted was Luranah, who, in the 1890s, seemed on the verge of a major operatic career, until health problems curtailed her appearances. In 1895, Luranah came to the attention of Cosima Wagner, who cast her as one of the Valkyries in the *Ring* at Bayreuth.

Very little documentation exists of Luranah, but she was said to have been a "strong-willed, dominating, and pleasure-loving woman." A French critic reported that she gave the impression of "vigorous masculinity." Born in 1860, educated at a convent school in Gent, she later studied in London, Berlin, and Paris. In 1891, a Hamburg critic noted her "strong, dark-colored, quite well developed" voice. Charles Gounod recommended her to Covent Garden: "Do you want to hear one of the most beautiful voices that exist? Very well! Grant an audition to Mademoiselle Luranah Aldridge." Not surprisingly, she was hired at once.

Wagner figured prominently in Aldridge's repertory. In 1893, she participated in a Grand Wagner Orchestral Concert in London, and in the same year she appeared as a Valkyrie in *Walküre* at the Theatre Royal, which, in a previous incarnation, had seen her father's Othello. She sang Valkyrie roles again in London in 1898 and 1905, the last time with the Bayreuth eminence Hans Richter conducting. At some point, Aldridge took the part of the earth goddess in the *Ring*, for the soprano Félia Litvinne autographed a photo for her with the message "*à mon Erda*." One or another of these notables must have alerted Cosima to the new talent.

Although her assignment at Bayreuth was small, Luranah received unusual treatment. The nineteen-year-old Eva Wagner, the future wife of Houston Stewart Chamberlain, befriended her, and Cosima apparently invited the young singer to stay at Wahnfried in the months before the festival. The Amanda Aldridge papers at Northwestern University contain a stiff piece of cardboard with a picture of the Festspielhaus on the front and a message from Eva on the back: "To dear Miss Aldridge with many thanks and best wishes, enjoying to see her again! Kindest regards from my mother and yours truly, Eva Wagner. Bayreuth, 2 [?] January 96."

Sometime in the spring of 1896, Aldridge fell ill. The Wagners evidently sent her to recover at the Hôtel Kurhaus, in Rupprechtstegen. Eva wrote: "Mama and we all were happy to get good news from you and we hope that every day will be a progress! Mama spoke immediately to Mr. v. Gross"—Adolf von Gross, the financial master of Bayreuth in the Cosima era—"who surely meanwhile will have fulfilled your wish. What say the spirits to the haunted chamber? Here is every day the same. Work and again work! 'Auf gutes Wiedersehen' and best love from all in Wahnfried!" There was still hope that Aldridge would regain her health in time to perform in the *Ring*, for Friedrich Wild's *Practical Handbook for Festival Visitors*, published just in advance of the festival, listed her as a participant and supplied a brief biography:

> A name that may well ring strangely in the ears of even the most observant art-lovers is that of Luranah Aldridge, who will sing one of the eight Valkyries. Of Luranah Aldridge one cannot say that she did not come from far off, as she hails—from Africa. She is the daughter of the African tragedian Ira Aldridge and studied singing in Germany, England and France, and has appeared with great success in operas and concerts outside of Germany. She is praised as the possessor of a true contralto voice with a wide range. In the course of the festival there will be an opportunity to put these statements to the test.

Aldridge's fellow Valkyries would have included Ernestine Schumann-Heink and Olive Fremstad. In the audience were Mahler, Shaw, Diaghilev, Adolphe Appia, Renoir, Romain Rolland, Colette, Albert Schweitzer, and the fourteen-year-old Franklin Delano Roosevelt. But she did not perform.

By the end of 1896, Aldridge had recovered, and in the spring she

Bayreuth.

wrote to Cosima about returning to Bayreuth. The Meisterin dictated the following reply, in her elegant if slightly mannered English:

> My dear Miss Aldridge, I am very sorry indeed to be obliged to tell you that our personelle is complete and that it is now too late to invite you to take a part in our performances. I am very sorry about it, but I was very glad to hear that you are well again and that you can use your fine voice. Only I would advise you to go to a good master in order to learn how to manage this fine voice, and not to destroy it before time. I should have been very glad to have seen you again, dear Miss Aldridge, I assure you, and with best wishes for you, my children and I send you kindest regards. C Wagner May 24 1897.

Did Aldridge take offense at this gentle criticism? Did she make further attempts to reach Bayreuth? Nothing more is known. She continued to give recitals in London until the First World War, her programs ranging from Lieder to chansons to parlor songs by her sister Amanda. On one occasion, she sang Wagner's "Schmerzen" in conjunction with Amanda's *Three African Dances*. But rheumatoid arthritis restricted her movements, and by the 1920s she was bedridden, with Amanda attending to her. On November 20, 1932, at the age of seventy-two, she committed suicide by taking an overdose of aspirin.

It is tempting to wonder what conversations might have taken place at Bayreuth around Aldridge. At the time she was there, Chamberlain was beginning to plan *The Foundations of the Nineteenth Century*, and in early 1896 he sent Cosima an outline of the book. Her response was generally positive, but she raised questions about various points. Amid a series of miscellaneous comments, she said: "The *Negroes* have surprised me. But I am entirely prepared to be convinced." Given that Chamberlain has nothing positive to say about people of color, Cosima seems to be speaking in their defense. The arrival of Ira Aldridge's daughter in Bayreuth may have affected her thinking.

In the end, the case of Luranah Aldridge is too singular to reveal much about the culture that surrounded her. The brief and partial flowering of her career was, like her father's sustained success, an exception to the racist attitudes of the time—the kind of exception that excuses racism by covering it with a veneer of tolerance. At the same time, Aldridge's ghostly presence at Bayreuth indicates the degree to which the festival remained a world unto itself, not yet wholly in the hands of ideologues, still under the spell of the uncategorizable man who founded it. For the time being, Wagner still seemed to speak for all.

BLACK WAGNER

W. E. B. Du Bois

"She is surely happier at last and you have the consciousness of duty well and faithfully done," W. E. B. Du Bois wrote to Amanda Aldridge after Luranah's death. Letters in the Du Bois archive imply that he visited the Aldridges in London once or twice. In the papers can be found a typewritten page detailing Théophile Gautier's praise for Ira Aldridge's Othello. The Aldridge family exemplified the racial vanguard that Du Bois called the "Talented Tenth"—the "aristocracy of talent and character" that would set the pace for the remainder of the African-American population.

Just as Herzl looked to *Tannhäuser* to fortify his Zionist vision, Du Bois took Wagnerian myth as a model for a heroic new African-American spirit, one that would make use of its own legends. This spirit was not nationalist or separatist in nature. As Kwame Anthony Appiah has said, Du Bois adopted a philosophy of "cosmopolitan nationalism," aiming to nurture a Negro consciousness while opening that consciousness to the wider world. In a similar vein, the historian Paul Gilroy links Du Bois to the formation of the "black Atlantic"—a "counterculture of modernity" that draws on German sources as on many others. This ideal of a transnational black identity is not unlike the "holy German art" that preoccupied Wagner while he was writing *Meistersinger*.

African-American Wagnerism did not begin with Du Bois. In 1900, the baritone Theodore Drury formed the earliest successful black opera troupe, the Drury Opera Company. An announcement of his plans in the *Nashville American* noted that Drury would begin with *Carmen* but was looking ahead to the "master of masters—Wagner," with an eye toward singing in *Tristan und Isolde*. The paper added: "The appearance of the Northern hero, Tristan, with a swarthy skin, should be grotesque enough to cause Herr Wagner to turn over in his grave." The composer Harry Lawrence Freeman, born in Cleveland in 1869, heard *Tannhäuser* in Denver when he was eighteen and resolved to create music dramas like it. He became known as the "Colored Wagner," and, in keeping with that title, completed an African tetralogy, titled *Zululand*. This cluster of black Wagnerians has led Samuel Dwinell to speak of a school of "Afro-Wagnerism," with Du Bois at the center.

By the early twentieth century, the composer was a point of reference in African-American culture. Black colleges sometimes presented Wagner evenings, as the musicologist Kira Thurman has discovered. Alain Locke began his 1925 anthology *The New Negro*, a manifesto of the Harlem Renaissance, with a reference to Wagner's Three Norns. In 1942 Langston Hughes placed *Tristan* on a list of personal favorites, alongside "goat's milk, short novels, lyric poems, heat, simple folk, boats, and bullfights." Ralph Ellison studied composition in his youth, especially admiring Wagner; it has been proposed that *Invisible Man* follows a leitmotif system. Even Martin Luther King, Jr., a bel canto fan, was not immune. In a 1957 sermon, King suggested that certain forms of aesthetic reception can approximate the presence of the divine—for example, listening to "a Wagnerian opera or a Beethoven symphony."

Du Bois's investment went considerably deeper, intersecting with a Germanophilia that gripped him early. His commencement address at Fisk University applauded Bismarck for having made a nation out of "bickering peoples." From 1892 to 1894, he studied at the Friedrich Wilhelm University in Berlin (now the Humboldt), attending lectures by the progressive economists Adolph Wagner and Gustav von Schmoller as well as by the nationalist historian Heinrich von Treitschke. In his spare time, Du Bois attended concerts and opera. At a performance of *Götterdämmerung*, he is struck by the sight of a dark-haired woman of lower-class background who begins crying during the performance—"one of the sorrows of Berlin." In later years, this German sojourn gleamed in Du Bois's memory as a liberating experience, one that gave him his first real taste of equality. "I had a very, very interesting time," he said. "I began to realize that white people were human."

German theories of racial superiority horrified Du Bois, but they led him to think about how African-Americans could cultivate their own inheritance. His 1897 speech "The Conservation of Races" appropriates the familiar trope of the mighty *Volk* stirred from slumber: "We are Negroes, members of a vast historic race that from the very dawn of creation has slept, but half awakening in the dark forests of its African fatherland. We are the first fruits of this new nation, the harbinger of that black to-morrow which is yet destined to soften the whiteness of the Teutonic to-day." Generally pro-European in his outlook, the young Du Bois neglected the sinister side of German politics—notably, the Reich's imposition of a colonial regime on what is now Namibia, which led to the genocide of the Herero and Nama peoples. Nor did his later recollections take note of Treitschke's anti-Jewish rhetoric.

Decades after he wrote "Of the Coming of John," Du Bois fulfilled a long-standing dream of going to Bayreuth. He chose a curious time to make his visit: 1936. Several of his colleagues wondered what he was doing in Nazi Germany, but Du Bois knew very well where he was. In a travel column for the *Pittsburgh Courier*, he wrote that German antisemitism "surpasses in vindictive cruelty and public insult anything I have ever seen; and I have seen much." All the same, he felt less conscious of his race than he did at home. He wrote: "I have not suffered from race prejudice . . . I can go to any hotel which I can afford; I can dine where I please and have the head-waiter bow me welcome." That he felt less open hostility in Hitler's Germany than in Roosevelt's America is a devastating verdict on American race relations.

The first of Du Bois's two columns about Bayreuth begins: "Men need places where they can renew their strength; where they can catch again faith in themselves and in their fellow men." His lodgings are on Lisztstrasse, just down the street from Wahnfried, and twice a day he passes close to Wagner's grave, the house where Liszt died, and the former home of the German Romantic writer Jean Paul, where—he is careful to note— Houston Stewart Chamberlain spent his last years. He is well attuned to the contradictions of the place. He regrets the high ticket prices and the presence of obnoxious wealth. Yet Wagner's works rise above petty materialism; they militate against the idea that "Clothes and Show and Extravagance spell Life." In the second column, Du Bois reveals that *Lohengrin* thrills him still: "It is a hymn of Faith. Something in this world man must trust. Not everything—but Something. One cannot live and doubt everybody and everything. Somewhere in this world, and not beyond it, there is Trust, and somehow Trust leads to Joy."

Du Bois proceeds to muse on what the *Ring* might mean to African-Americans. He writes: "It is as though someone of us chose out of the wealth of African folklore a body of poetic material and, with music, scene, and action, re-told for mankind the suffering and triumphs and defeats of a people." In his late-period autobiographical novel *Worlds of Color*, Du Bois revisits the Bayreuth trip in lightly fictionalized form, assuming the alter ego Manuel Mansart. This character, too, pursues an Afro-Wagnerian agenda: "He thought how among American Negroes, legend and fantasy might thus be wed to histrionic ability and imagination, to build a great dramatic tradition."

In the same period, Du Bois was falling in love with a fellow Wagnerite: the writer, composer, and political thinker Shirley Graham. In 1932, Graham had drawn national notice for an African-themed opera titled *Tom-Tom*, which was performed in Cleveland and broadcast on NBC radio. At the time Du Bois went to Bayreuth, Graham was teaching at the Tennessee Agricultural and Industrial State College, where she introduced her class of 150 students to *Götterdämmerung*. She wrote to Du Bois: "Now, that is something—to have the opportunity to lead hungry, young Negroes to Wagner!"

Graham's counterpart to "Of the Coming of John" is the 1939 radio drama *Deep Rivers*, which surveys millennia of black life: Nubian slaves building the pyramids; African villagers dancing; an auction block in New Orleans; excerpts from the spirituals "Deep River" and "Wade in the Water"; a Mississippi flood; and, in an ironic final scene, wealthy white patrons whispering excitedly before a recital by a black contralto who is undoubtedly Marian Anderson. The fixed presence in this diverse scene is the River, which rolls symbolically through so many spirituals. Graham evokes it through a score that combines her own music with preexisting pieces. At the beginning, "Deep River" and the opening bars of *Götter-dämmerung* are heard as a narrator intones Langston Hughes's "The Negro Speaks of Rivers": "I've known rivers: / I've known rivers ancient as the world and older than the flow of human blood in human veins. / My soul has grown deep like the rivers."

The conceit of self-hatred would imply that these black Wagnerians were in some way ashamed of their heritage. Such condescension is just as dubious in the case of civil-rights stalwarts like Du Bois and Graham as it is for Theodor Herzl. Paul Allen Anderson points to a different rationale: Du Bois privileges the Wagner experience precisely because it does not conform to type. Jazz and other popular styles troubled Du Bois because, in Anderson's paraphrase, they "fetishized black racial difference through a fascination with the most ribald and seamy side of African American life." Similarly, Du Bois distrusted the cult of sports, because it perpetuated stereotypes of black people as purely physical beings. (In 1936, he had more to say about Wagner than about Jesse Owens's triumph at the "Nazi" Olympics.) Samuel Dwinell sees Du Bois's "Afro-Wagnerism" as integral to a "nascent practice of black internationalism." Du Bois's vision of a diasporic black culture, which he set forth at the first Pan-African Congress in 1900, echoed pan-Germanism even as it defied German racist thought.

Du Bois's faith in art now has an antiquated air, its aspirational rhetoric undermined by twentieth-century terrors. Even so, Afro-Wagnerism surfaces here and there. Amiri Baraka's 1964 play *Dutchman* restages Wagner's opera as an erotic, violent encounter between a black man and a white woman on the subway. The gay African-American author Samuel Delany nods to *Parsifal* in his science-fiction novels. Singers such as Grace Bumbry, Simon Estes, Jessye Norman, and Eric Owens have realized Aldridge's Wagnerian promise. Sly allusions pop up in jazz: the stride pianist Donald Lambert fashioned a rollicking metamorphosis of the Pilgrims' Chorus in 1941, and Charlie Parker inserted phrases from the Song to the Evening Star into several solos. More recently, the German literary critic Ijoma Mangold has meditated on the peculiarity of being a black Wagnerite in modern Germany. When a far-right author told him to "go back to Africa, in the bush," Mangold thought of Hans Sachs's Act III monologue: "Who will give it its name? It is the old madness . . ."

7

VENUSBERG

Feminist and Gay Wagner

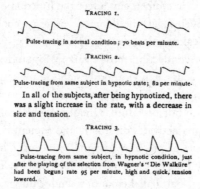

TRACING 1.

Pulse-tracing in normal condition ; 70 beats per minute.

TRACING 2.

Pulse-tracing from same subject in hypnotic state; 82 per minute.

In all of the subjects, after being hypnotized, there
was a slight increase in the rate, with a decrease in
size and tension.

TRACING 3.

Pulse-tracing from same subject, in hypnotic condition, just
after the playing of the selection from Wagner's "Die Walküre"
had been begun; rate 95 per minute, high and quick, tension
lowered.

In 1894, Aldred Scott Warthin, a pathologist at the University of
Michigan, tested the effect of music on hypnotized subjects, and reported the following:

> Wagner's "Ride of the Walküre" was played from the piano-score. The
> subject's pulse became at once more rapid, fuller, and of increased ten-
> sion. As the music continued the pulse-rate rose from 60, his normal rate,
> to 120 per minute, becoming very quick, full, and of low tension; at the
> same time the rate of respiration was increased from 18 to 30 per minute.
> The subject's face showed great mental excitement; his whole body was
> thrown into motion; the legs were drawn up and the arms tossed in the
> air; at the same time the whole body was bathed in a profuse sweat.

What kind of excitement is this, exactly? Warthin cautiously touches on
the topic of arousal. "The Ride of the Valkyries" and passages from *Tristan*

und Isolde prompt "feelings of 'longing,' 'frenzy,' etc.," but not "sexual desire or suggestion." However, "by the aid of word-suggestion, such effect could be produced, and the emotions of 'longing,' etc., could be made identical with the physical desire." Warthin closes by saying that these experiments, if carried too far, could yield "disastrous results."

Warthin's paper is one of a number of turn-of-the-century medical studies that purport to document cases of erotomania, or excessive sexual desire, induced by the music of Wagner. The medical historian James Kennaway has collected various others, including a paper hinting that the composer could incite hysteria in women and affect the function of the ovaries and the uterus. Otto Weininger, the doomed young psychologist of Vienna, believed that musical impulses were wrapped up in sexual ones, and that Wagner made that connection most clear. In his study *Eros and Psyche*, Weininger wrote: "Music can vicariously stand in for sexual intercourse—Wagnerizing [*Wagnerei*] especially is often just a better surrogate for coitus."

Writers of fiction pursued similar inquiries. The brothers Mann liked to show how Wagner activates disorderly and sometimes fatal desires. In Péladan's *The Victory of the Husband*, the sound of *Tristan* compels Izel and Adar to make love in the cane-bottomed seats at Bayreuth. In stories by d'Annunzio, Batilliat, Lemonnier, and Quiroga, Wagner's music drives love to the point of murder, necrophilia, and demonic possession. A sketch by the Viennese writer Peter Altenberg has a man and a woman making love after *Götterdämmerung*, with the woman murmuring, "It is the continuation." Léon Bloy said that the Bayreuth theater was darkened "for the convenience of the gropers and feelers." James Joyce put it most bluntly: "*Wagner puzza di sesso*"—he stinks of sex. All this supports Laurence Dreyfus's thesis in *Wagner and the Erotic Impulse*, a revelatory study of Wagnerian sexuality: that in the late nineteenth century the composer's erotics caused more trouble than his politics, amounting to "a sickness that required a pseudo-clinical diagnosis and moral castigation."

The discourse of Wagnerian sexual degeneracy goes back to Nietzsche, who had a personal reason to dilate on the topic. Wagner had once suspected his acolyte of indulging in excessive masturbation; in *The Case of Wagner* and *Beyond Good and Evil*, Nietzsche exacts revenge, hurling all manner of medical jargon. Wagner's art is sick, Nietzsche writes. It is the work of a hysteric, a neurotic, a decadent. Not only that, it corrupts everything and everyone around it. The Wagnerians are just as sick, if not sicker. The female of the species is fraying her nerves with such pathological and dangerous music, leaving her incapable of fulfilling her "first and last profession, to bear strong children." Doubt is also cast on the morals of the men. "Just look at these youths—stiff, pale, breathless! . . . Wagner becomes master over them." To be a Wagnerian is to have one's masculinity compromised.

The word "degeneration," suggesting a devolution to a primitive mental or moral condition, is a staple of fin-de-siècle discussions of Wagner. The historian Daniel Pick has shown how concepts of a society-wide epidemic of degeneration caught on in the wake of the revolutions of 1848, as liberal thinkers struggled to explain the apparent halt of the march of social progress. The term was not a German invention: it first appeared in an 1857 treatise by the French psychiatrist Bénédict Morel, and was later adopted by the Italian criminologist Cesare Lombroso. Theodor Puschmann's 1872 pamphlet *Richard Wagner: A Psychological Study* presents its subject as a case of "moral degeneration." Max Nordau's 1892 broadside *Degeneration* charges Wagner with megalomania, persecution mania, erotomania, graphomania, sadism, and a "tendency to stupid puns." Nordau's gallery of degenerates also includes Baudelaire, Mallarmé, Verlaine, Tolstoy, Ibsen, Zola, Whitman, Wilde, and, ironically, Nietzsche, whose excoriations of disease do not prevent him from being labeled a disease himself.

Moral crusades in art seldom succeed in felling their targets, and Wagner was no exception. What provoked disgust in one group of people stirred hope in another. Those who identified with the dispositions that the composer was accused of spreading—sexual freedom, unconventional gender roles, homosexuality—saw him as a heroic figure, an enemy of conformity. Feminists found much to like in the musical and dramatic strength of Brünnhilde and Isolde. The boldest moments in Wagner's works seemed to advocate the overturning of norms, the liberation of desire, and the disclosure of one's true self. In *Walküre*, after Fricka censures the behavior of the sibling lovers, Wotan takes exception to her cold morality, which guarantees a world of sham marriages and unfulfilled longings:

> Unholy
> I deem the vow
> that binds unloving hearts . . .
> Age-old custom
> is all you can grasp:

but *my* thoughts seek to encompass
what's never yet come to pass.

Even without verbal messages, the texture of Wagner's music—its uninhibited sensuality, its androgynous merging of opposites—intimated new
ways of living in the world. Small wonder that in certain circles it served
as a kind of password. *The Intersexes*, a 1908 treatise by the gay author
Xavier Mayne, includes a self-diagnostic questionnaire whereby a subject
can identify himself as a "Uranian," or homosexual. One question is "Are
you peculiarly fond of Wagner?"

The undeniable daring of Wagner's approach to sexuality drew interested scrutiny from leading psychologists of the fin de siècle—researchers
working at a higher level than that of Puschmann and Nordau. Such pioneers of psychoanalysis as Carl Jung, Otto Rank, Sabina Spielrein, and,
on occasion, Sigmund Freud himself cited Wagner, zeroing in on topics
of incest, hysteria, and homoeroticism. The sexologist Magnus Hirschfeld,
who effectively launched the modern gay-rights movement, interpreted
the composer's sexual eccentricities in a sympathetic rather than mocking spirit. To the new scientists of sex, Wagner was an essential case study
because he made explicit what the rest of society repressed.

WAGNER AND WOMEN

Although Wagner is noted for his hatreds, almost all of his mature work
turns on the redeeming force of love. The *Ring* stages a contest between
loveless power and selfless love, with the latter triumphing in the end.
Tristan glorifies love to the point of death. *Parsifal* teaches compassion, the
highest form of love. Wagner addressed such themes from the very beginning of his career, when he felt drawn to the sexually rebellious Young
Germany movement. His second opera, *Das Liebesverbot* (*The Love Ban*),
was intended as an attack on "puritanical hypocrisy" and a "glorification
of 'free sensuality.'"

Yet Wagner was no hedonist; he professed to believe in monogamy,
and in *Parsifal* he prizes chastity, though in an eroticized atmosphere. The
ultimate passion is an extreme yearning that goes unconsummated. Even

Cosima Wagner, from Thomas Mann's collection

in Act I of *Walküre* and Act II of *Tristan*, the pinnacles of Wagnerian erotics, arousal is cut off before release. Many of Wagner's own affairs and flirtations probably stopped short of physical intercourse. He seemed to thrive on the indefinite deferral of orgasm, on foreplay without end. Herbert Marcuse, in his book *Eros and Civilization*, writes of Wagner: "The most orgastic *Liebestod* still celebrates the most orgastic renunciation."

Like a great many nineteenth-century male artists, Wagner fits the profile of a misogynist. Although he idealized the female spirit, he imposed subservient roles on the women around him. Cosima's diaries record a string of demeaning comments. For example, Wagner said in 1869: "The father is there to protect mother and child, that is to say, to take care of the external things; woman has nothing to do with the outside world. Of course she has immeasurable influence, but not by voting and trying to turn herself into a man, which she can never do." Cosima put up little resistance to such strictures, berating herself when he expressed displeasure. Wagner's first wife, Minna Planer, withheld abject devotion, and the marriage ended in a bitter separation, which Minna refused to ratify with divorce.

Then again, the composer was hardly conventionally masculine in his habits. He fetishized silk and satin, especially in shades of pink, and spent lavishly on the finest fabrics. These were not only draped in his inner sanctum—such as the room at the Palazzo Vendramin where he died—but also wrapped around his person in the form of gowns, linings, and undergarments. He enjoyed the fragrance of rose perfumes. As Dreyfus observes, this behavior can be considered a form of cross-dressing.

Wagner did not make a display of his proclivities, and in 1877 he suffered an extraordinary public humiliation when his letters to Bertha Goldwag, his Austrian-Jewish costumier and interior designer, fell into the hands of the relentless Daniel Spitzer, who printed them in the *Neue Freie Presse*. One missive describes a house robe in pink and white satin: "This trimming or flounce must be particularly opulent and beautifully worked, and must extend on both sides by a foot in width and then, as it rises to the waist, lose itself in the usual width of the puffed ruche that encloses the waist." Spitzer sniggered that such a design would "create a furor on any lady at court." Cartoonists had a field day with images of "Frou-Frou Wagner." On learning that the letters were to be published, Cosima wrote, "When R. now talks about emigrating to America, I no longer have the courage to speak against it."

Throughout his life, Wagner pursued an ideal of androgyny, a spiritual merger of the sexes. In *Opera and Drama*, he characterized the relationship of words and music in gendered terms, with poetry as the masculine, penetrating element and music as the feminine, receiving organ. Given that Wagner wrote both words and music for his operas, he becomes, as

Abb. 438. Frou-Frou Wagner.

Jean-Jacques Nattiez writes in his 1990 book *Wagner Androgyne*, an "androgynous being"—one who is somehow capable of inseminating himself. In *Parsifal*, androgyny is elevated to the level of religion: the Savior redeems the world by overcoming the duality of gender. Cosima says that the chorus is given the opera's love-feast theme "so that the effect would be neither feminine nor masculine," because "Christ must be entirely sexless, neither woman nor man." Wagner's misogyny, like his racism, can dissipate in the face of an unexplained force that erases distinctions and brings about transcendent unity. This force was music itself—the uncontrollable factor that foils any attempt to sum up what Wagner means, or, indeed, who he was.

B efore Wagner set to work on the *Ring*, Louise Otto-Peters, a pioneer of German feminism, had urged the creation of a great German opera based on the Nibelung legend. In 1845, Otto addressed the subject in a series of essays for the *Neue Zeitschrift für Musik*, elaborating a proposal that Friedrich Theodor Vischer had made the previous year. She also drafted her own libretto, samples of which appeared with her articles. Having seen *Rienzi*, which left her "deadly pale and trembling," she considered Wagner the ideal composer for her Nibelung project. Apparently, an intermediary forwarded Otto's offer to Wagner, who declined, on the grounds that he wrote his own librettos. But if he read Otto's excerpts, he would have seen a pointed characterization of Brunhilde as an independent woman, who seethes at becoming another's property: "My proud freedom is all gone, / I have become the slave of a strange man!" In 1852, Otto, by then the editor of the feminist journal *Frauen-Zeitung*, published a complete *Nibelungen* libretto, and articulated its message for her readers: "In Brunhilde we see the free, bold woman who doesn't want to be a man's slave."

The libretto of the *Ring* stops well short of that progressive ideal. In general, Wagner's female characters comprise a confusing array of archetypes: darkly scheming, dangerously seductive, nobly self-sacrificing, faithful domestic, loving-heroic. Feminist critics have long debated whether these figures conform to misogynist stereotypes or whether they cut against them. Catherine Clément, in her classic 1979 study *Opera, or the Undoing of Women*, argues that opera habitually affirms a patriarchal order by mandating the degradation and deaths of women: their voices are exalted at the price of their eventual silence. Although violence against women is rare in Wagner's operas, his principal female characters have a way of dropping dead for no evident reason. Both Elsa and Kundry collapse lifeless ("*entseelt*," de-souled). Ortrud "sinks with a shriek." Elisabeth walks away and perishes off stage. Isolde, having sung the so-called Liebestod, "sinks, as if transfigured."

In Wagner's early operas, as in much nineteenth-century art, women tend to fall into two distinct and opposing categories. At times, they are selfless exemplars of the eternal feminine; at others, devouring femmes fatales. Senta, in *The Flying Dutchman*, throws herself from a cliff in order to release her beloved from the curse of eternal wandering. She constitutes, in the words of the German musicologist Eva Rieger, a "typically Wagnerian fantasy—to be loved eternally, without interruption, by a woman." In *Tannhäuser*, the angelic Elisabeth goes up against Venus, and wins the contest by offering her life to the Almighty in exchange for Tannhäuser's salvation. According to Rieger, "everything that is actively feminine is confined to the sinful, fear-inducing underworld, while feminine passivity comes across as pure and noble." In *Lohengrin*, Elsa is paired with Ortrud, the vengeful pagan witch who inveigles Elsa into asking her fatal question. Wagner stigmatized Ortrud as a "political woman," in whom the instinct of love is replaced with "murderous fanaticism."

The Danish scholar and dramaturge Nila Parly, in her book *Vocal Victories*, takes a rosier view of Wagner's women. For her, Senta is no servile figure but the opera's driving agent; singing her ballad in Act II, she is a stand-in for the composer, effectively giving birth to the Dutchman as she sings his story. In *Tannhäuser*, Parly is struck by the agitated splendor of Wagner's music for Venus, especially in the 1861 revision. In the wake of *Tristan*, Venus becomes a "deeper and far more complicated, ambiguous being," her state of mind fluctuating through "indignation, calculating manipulation, genuine selflessness, seductive charm, intense anger, distressed entreaties." As for Elsa, Wagner himself supplies a quasi-progressive reading. The character is justified in asking her fatal question of Lohengrin because she is passing from mere worship to the "full essence of love." She forecasts a future revolution in which male egoism destroys itself in the face of a higher, feminine love.

Isolde, Kundry, and Brünnhilde, the imposing women of the later Wagner operas, present the strongest case for a provisional kind of Wagnerian feminism. None of them achieves independence from a male-directed world, yet the sheer potency of the dramatic-soprano voice in the opera house destabilizes whatever hierarchy exists on paper. Brünnhilde is based on the Brunhild of Nordic myth, but she also harks back to Antigone, who defied King Creon by burying her brother Polyneices. In Wagner's eyes, Antigone's ritual of mourning expresses not merely familial love but also a "purely human" love—a blow against a rotten body politic. She performs "self-annihilation out of sympathy," which in the same moment annihilates the state. Brünnhilde, likewise, brings down Valhalla when she rides into the pyre with the Ring on her finger.

Brünnhilde is, after all, a Valkyrie—a "chooser of the slain," governing life and death on the field of battle. Carolyn Abbate, in her book *Unsung Voices*, emphasizes the oldest tales of Brünnhilde, those in which she is an untamed force of nature, possessed of supernatural intelligence. Wagner, in the same spirit, makes her a sibyl figure, a truth-teller and demolisher of false narratives. According to Abbate, Brünnhilde represents not the glorification of Siegfried but an "intoxication or madness" that joins with the flames consuming Valhalla. "She walks by night, brings no solace, no romantic ending, and no feminine or maternal comforts; she offers in the end only laughter itself. She laughs—eternally." The Valkyrie motif was among the first ideas that Wagner sketched for the *Ring* project, even before he decided to introduce Wotan as a character. In a sense, Brünnhilde engendered Wotan, not the other way around.

WOMEN AND WAGNER

In Fernand Khnopff's 1883 painting *Listening to Schumann*, a woman sits in a chair, head bowed down, hand resting on her forehead, while a pianist plays behind her. The hand shields the face from view, giving us no glimpse of whatever emotion is passing over her face. Perhaps the gesture is a sign of the listener being overcome; perhaps it is a signal of intense concentration, as distractions are blotted out; perhaps it is a demand for privacy, a withholding of expression from the painter. That the figure in question is Khnopff's mother, Marie, makes the image all the more arresting. The picture seems to capture the particular value that music held for

Aubrey Beardsley, The Wagnerites

women in nineteenth-century culture. In a patriarchal world that strictly regulated their speech, dress, and behavior, music opened a secret space where they could think and feel freely.

Aubrey Beardsley's 1894 drawing *The Wagnerites* presents a different scene of listening. We are at a performance of *Tristan*, as the lettering on a program indicates. The audience is almost entirely female. Most of the women stare straight, indifferent to the judging gaze. There is an element of caricature: décolletage is low, much flesh is on display, makeup is heavy. Only one male is easily visible, and he displays stereotypically Jewish features. As Emma Sutton writes in *Aubrey Beardsley and British Wagnerism in the 1890s*, the picture could be read either as a lampoon of decadence or as a glorification of it. These brazen women might be a collection of modern Isoldes, ready to enter any room with the heroine's incomparable opening line: "Who dares to mock me?"

Male writers were mesmerized by the spectacle of female Wagnerism, believing that it revealed something essential about the state of womanhood. In Ferdinand von Saar's 1892 novella *Tale of a Viennese Child*, Isolde's Trans- figuration causes one female listener to "writhe on her chair like a snake" and another to shake violently and let out a piercing scream. Such intoxication allegedly left women vulnerable to seduction. Arnold Bennett, in his 1905 novel *Sacred and Profane Love*, relates what happens when a literate young woman sits down to play a *Tristan* duet with a famous pianist:

> I found myself playing strange disturbing chords with the left hand, irregularly repeated, opposing the normal accent of the bar, and becoming stranger and more disturbing. And Diaz was playing an air fragmentary and poignant. The lovers were waiting; the very atmosphere of the garden was drenched with an agonizing and exquisite anticipation . . . "Hear the beating of their hearts," Diaz's whisper floated over the chords. It was too much. The obsession of his presence, reinforced by the vibrating of his wistful, sensuous voice, overcame me suddenly. My hands fell from the keyboard. He looked at me—and with what a glance!

In Eugène Brieux's 1897 play *The Three Daughters of M. Dupont*, an impecunious bourgeois couple pushes Julie, their youngest daughter, to marry Antonin, a wealthy rake. Once the families have negotiated the dowry, a meeting is arranged. Antonin has been tipped off about Julie's love of Wagner, and a score is positioned as a cue for flirtation:

> ANTONIN (*looking at the score on the piano*): You like Wagner, mademoiselle!
> JULIE: Very much.
> ANTONIN: Me, I adore him.
> JULIE: What a genius! Isn't it so?
> ANTONIN: Isn't he?
> JULIE: He is the only musician.
> ANTONIN: The greatest.
> JULIE: No: the only one.
> ANTONIN: The only one, essentially. I am pleased to see we have the same tastes in art.

Later, Antonin tells his mother that he charmed Julie with such topics as "Wagner, children, little blue flowers." Needless to say, the ensuing marriage is unhappy.

The details of the Wagnerian coitus, as Weininger calls it, usually go unspecified, but the poet and novelist Pierre Louÿs, who specialized in erotic writing, spells them out in a sequence of nine sonnets titled *The Trophy of Legendary Vulvas*, each of which depicts a Wagner heroine in unabashedly pornographic terms. The opening of a sonnet to Senta gives the flavor of the whole:

> The handsome Erik is too weak, O Virgin!
> You would swallow him with a jerk of the cunt;
> You want someone who has strong loins,
> Who can push forward a hard ten-inch shaft.

These poems have a burlesque quality, taking aim less at Wagner himself— "the greatest man who ever existed," Louÿs said—than at the solemnity of his cult, including the sonneteering of the *Revue wagnérienne*. Yet their picture of female sexuality is crudely adolescent, tipping over into ugly fantasies of violence, incest, and pedophilia. Above all, they betray a need to reduce Wagner's women to purely sexual creatures, robbing them of their uncanny powers.

O utside of the realm of male reverie, women made Wagner their own. The anarchist Emma Goldman once commented that "more women attend Wagnerian music and understand him than men," and speculated that "the elemental untrammeled spirit of Wagner's music affects the women as the releasing force of the pent-up, stifled and hidden emotions of their souls." The diary of Lucy Lowell, a young woman from Boston, gives anecdotal evidence of this catharsis in action. After attending Theodore Thomas's Wagner Festival in 1884, Lowell wrote: "Utterly unsettled by excitement of the Wagner concerts. I suppose it can't be good for a person to go to things that excite her so that she can't fix her mind on anything for days afterwards." The historian Daniel Cavicchi, who uncovered Lowell's diary, notes that she was still pondering Wagner a year later: "Isa & Edith had a long discussion about the effect of the Walkure, whether it is demoralizing or elevating."

The strength of the female presence in Bayreuth was often remarked upon. In 1897, an observer estimated that "the ratio of tourists is usually one wealthy papa to six daughters and retinue of young ladies, and a fussy but ambitious mamma." Indeed, it had become customary for young women to attend the festival together. In 1887, the British writer R. Milner Barry published a women's travel book geared toward Bayreuth and neighboring destinations—"a plain and unvarnished recital of our adventures, in the hope that it may prove useful to other unprotected females desirous of hearing Wagner's operas performed to perfection in Bayreuth." Hotel guest lists show a preponderance of large female parties from abroad, especially from the United States. In 1912, the Hotel Goldener Anker was commandeered by a group from the American South, including citizens of Macon, Georgia, birthplace of the poet Sidney Lanier.

> English, Miss, Macon Ga. (U. S. A.).
> Hines, Miss, Macon Ga. (U. S. A.).
> Lionigston, Miss, Macon Ga. (U. S. A.).
> Brown, Miss, Anderson (U. S. A.).
> Nimluly, Miss, Macon Ga. (U. S. A.).
> Haley, Miss, Macon Ga. (U. S. A.).
> Nöth, Miss, Spartanburg (S. C.).
> Sirinne, Miss, Grunville (S. C.).
> Jones, Miss, Albany (Ga.).
> Gregory, Miss, Lancaster (S. C.).
> Hicks, Mrs., Macon (Ga.)
> Cates, Mrs., Wayneslow (Ga.).
> Willingham, Mr., Macon (Ga.).
> Murray, Mr., Anderson (S. C.).
> Tift, Me., Tifton (Ga.).
> Woodside, Mr. and Mrs., Greenville (S. C.).
> Callaway, Miss J. P., Leesburg (Ga.).

These expeditions often focused on *Parsifal*, which was thought to be morally improving. "My own impression is that every Christian should see *Parsifal*," wrote Mary Kathleen Lyttelton, the wife of the English Anglican bishop Arthur Lyttelton.

Joseph Horowitz, in his history of American Wagnerism, complicates our picture of such decorous outings. On the surface, Wagner held to traditional ideas of female social roles, as self-sacrificing exemplars of virtue. More covertly, he permitted a form of self-expression that social norms otherwise discouraged. At concerts in New York, women entered into a "secret pact, a shared conspiracy with Wagner," Horowitz writes. He finds evidence of such transport in articles, letters, diaries, and fiction. In 1894, the poet Ella Wheeler Wilcox wrote in praise of *Tristan*:

> A clamorous sea of chords swept o'er my soul,
> Submerging reason. Mutinous desire
> Stood at the helm; the stars were in eclipse . . .

The phrase "mutinous desire" could point either to the world of the opera or to the world of the listener; music erases the difference, at least momentarily.

Female Wagner singers embodied a rare kind of power, which occasionally found a political use. In 1910, the soprano Lillian Nordica declared that her involvement in the suffragist struggle was rooted in her experience on the stage, the "only place where men and women stand on a perfect equality." She said that "our whole social system is founded on conditions that existed in the stone age, when man took what he wanted by force." In 1913, Nordica appeared at two suffragist pageants, both times singing "The Star-Spangled Banner" while attired as Columbia. At the one, a vast outdoor parade in Washington, D.C., the Pilgrims' Chorus from *Tannhäuser* rang out as figures representing Liberty, Justice, Hope, and the like bowed before Nordica. The second rally, at the Metropolitan

Lillian Nordica

Opera House, included a speech by Theodore Roosevelt and an orchestra of professionals and society women playing selections from *Parsifal* and *Lohengrin*.

American fiction of the Gilded Age attests to this genteel mode of Wagnerian feminism. Charlotte Teller, in her 1907 novel *The Cage*, conveys the music's energizing effect on Frederica, a Chicago minister's daughter who is escaping her confined upbringing. In the company of an Austrian-born labor organizer, Frederica attends what appears to be one of Theodore Thomas's Wagner concerts at the Exposition Building in Chicago. "The Ride of the Valkyries," not coincidentally, has the strongest impact: "She felt herself moving, struggling, breathless, to get higher and higher . . . She felt herself strong and vital, astride a horse of Walhalla . . . It was only a war-woman, a Valkyrie, who could bring a man into the home of the gods." Her excitement is to some extent sexual—the Austrian is clutching her hand—but it is also political: she feels solidarity with the immigrant laborers who occupy the cheap seats around her. For Teller, an outspoken socialist and suffragist, Wagner liberates mind and body alike.

Hamlin Garland's 1895 novel *The Rose of Dutcher's Coolly*, the work of an avowed male feminist, tells a similar tale. Rose, a Wisconsin farmer's daughter who shows talent for writing, makes her way to Chicago, where she undergoes a sexual and intellectual awakening. There is another concert-hall epiphany, this time at Adler and Sullivan's Auditorium: "The voice of Wagner came to her for the first time, and shook her and thrilled her and lifted her into wonderful regions where the green trees dripped golden moss, and the grasses were jewelled in very truth." Once again, Wagner stirs hopes of future greatness: "She felt the power to reach out her hand to take fame and fortune . . . She wanted to do some gigantic thing which should enrich the human race." (Compare Du Bois's "Of the Coming of John": "He felt with the music the movement of power within him.") Flushed with feeling, Rose catches the eye of a male admirer—but this one is no Wagnerian predator. "I want you as comrade and lover, not as subject or servant," he says, offering a marriage of equals.

Feminists in the German-speaking world were less inclined to idealize Wagner, perhaps because he was so embedded in the strutting military

culture of the Kaiserreich. Celia Applegate discerns diminishing enthusiasm for the composer in the work of two formidable German intellectuals,
the feminist activist Luise Büchner and the independent-minded author
Ricarda Huch. Büchner had adored Wagner's early work, but the *Ring*
appalled her. "Such crudeness, such lack of any decency is nowhere to
be found as one finds it here," she wrote. Huch got to know the operas
in the nineties and came to see them as superficially exciting, bourgeois, lacking in substance. In Spain, on the other hand, performances
of *Walküre* in the 1890s helped to inspire a long-running cult of the
Nordic Valkyrie type. The feminist anarchist Federica Montseny, who
served in the Popular Front government in 1936, made charged use of
Brünnhilde imagery, as Elena Lindholm Narváez notes in an essay titled
"The Valkyrie in a Bikini."

Sidonie-Gabrielle Colette, one of the most celebrated female authors
of the fin de siècle, trained a piercing eye on Bayreuth at the close of her
quartet of *Claudine* novels (1900–1903), the semi-autobiographical saga of
a young woman who frees herself from bourgeois mores. At the time, Colette was married to the rakish music critic and novelist Henry Gauthier-
Villars, who used the pen name Willy and employed an ensemble of
ghostwriters, his wife included. A lusty Wagnerite, Gauthier-Villars made
regular trips to Bayreuth, befriending Cosima. Colette was more circum-
spect, and her heroines respond in kind. In *Claudine s'en va*, the last of the
series, the focus shifts to Annie, the initially dutiful wife of an overbearing
businessman. The last part of the book is set in Bayreuth, where an amusing menagerie of Wagnéristes circulates. Among them is a writer named
Léon, who is writing his own Bayreuth novel, "as seen by a woman in love,
through the hyperaesthesia of a gratified—and illicit!—passion."

Annie, who narrates *Claudine s'en va*, paints a jaded picture of Bayreuth.
She and her friends glower at the tacky souvenirs—"the postcards, the
Grails in red glass, the color lithographs, the wood carvings, the table
mats, the beer mugs, all bearing the image of the *dieu Wagner*"—and
shudder at "the 'Achs!' and the 'Colossals!' and the 'Sublimes!' and the
whole lot of polyglot exclamations being dispensed by indiscriminate fa-
natics, no, no!" Like Huysmans's Des Esseintes, Annie would rather listen
in an empty theater. To which a friend replies: "You are of the genre of
Ludwig of Bavaria. Look where that morbid fantasy led him."

During *The Flying Dutchman*, Annie has a migraine attack and, like

Nietzsche in 1876, flees the premises. Nonetheless, she is transformed. She has escaped the prison of her marriage, just as Colette was freeing herself of Gauthier-Villars, and her epiphany is couched in Wagnerian terms: "Where has this illumination come from? His absence? . . . Or have I drunk the philtre that restored Siegfried's memory?" At Bayreuth, she has an intimate encounter with Claudine, one that trembles on the edge of sex. "Exalted and wild as a young druidess," Claudine shows Annie a way forward. The cheapened god Wagner still opens a door in her mind.

GAY WAGNER

Fidus [Hugo Höppener], Parzival, *1900*

In *Claudine à Paris*, the second of Colette's *Claudine* novels, the protagonist gets to know a cousin named Marcel—a poised, feminine, cultured, unmistakably gay young man. Colette, no stranger to same-sex attraction, describes the character with a frankness that was revolutionary at the time. Another young man writes Marcel a love letter that is also a manifesto of gay desire. One passage reads: "To confirm my faith and sexual religion, I reread Shakespeare's burning sonnets to the Earl of Pembroke, and

Michelangelo's no less idolatrous poems to Cavalieri; I fortified myself by reviewing passages from Montaigne, Tennyson, Wagner, Walt Whitman, and Carpenter." Claudine, having got hold of the letter, smiles at its over-the-top prose. Certain phrases jog her memory, and she realizes that the lover has plagiarized from Georges Eekhoud's *Escal-Vigor*, a scandalous gay novel of the period, in which a refined count falls in love with a musically gifted shepherd.

Colette was quick to register a somewhat surprising development. By the end of the nineteenth century, campaigners for gay rights had made Wagner part of a self-fashioned cultural genealogy—if not gay himself, then an exceptionally friendly kind of ally. This queering of the Meister drew on the sexually transgressive charge emanating from his works and writings; it also made much of his proximity to Ludwig II, a gay icon of the fin de siècle.

Modern homosexuality was, to some extent, a German invention. In 1867, a lawyer named Karl Heinrich Ulrichs went before the Sixth Congress of German Jurists, in Munich, to urge the repeal of laws forbidding sex between men. With astonishing bravery, Ulrichs declared that those of a "sexual nature opposed to common custom" were being persecuted for impulses that "nature, mysteriously governing and creating, had implanted in them." His preferred term was "Urnings," or "Uranians." In 1869, an Austrian littérateur named Karl Maria Kertbeny, also opposed to sodomy laws, coined the term "homosexuality." By the eighties and nineties, a quasi-legal gay scene had arisen in Berlin, with homosexuals tacitly permitted to gather in bars and organize balls. In 1897, Magnus Hirschfeld founded the Scientific-Humanitarian Committee, the first gay-rights group. The year before, *Der Eigene* ("The Self-Possessed"), the first gay magazine, began publication. Amid such unprecedented openness, homophobic reaction brought down several high-profile figures in the first years of the new century. The most prominent victim was Philipp Eulenburg, a confidant both of the Kaiser and of Cosima Wagner.

The German gay-rights movement grew out of the ethos of Romanticism, with its respect for heroic individuals who vanquish "age-old custom" and live according to their own laws. Schopenhauer was particularly attuned to the complexities of sexuality. In an 1859 addendum to *The World as Will and Representation*, the philosopher took a sanguine view of what he called "pederasty," saying that it arises from human nature and there is no point in opposing it. He cited Horace: "Expel nature with a pitchfork, she still comes back." Karl Heinrich Ulrichs quoted Schopenhauer in a coming-out letter to one of his relatives.

Wagner had a similarly open if befuddled mind about same-sex love. In "The Artwork of the Future," he extols the ancient Greek mode of *Männerliebe*, or love between men, placing it somewhere in the space between spiritual and physical loves:

> This love, in its original purity, makes itself known to us as the noblest and most selfless expression of the human sense of beauty. The love of man for woman is, in its most natural form, an egoistic and pleasure-seeking impulse, in which the man, while finding satisfaction in a definite sensual pleasure, cannot be absorbed into it with his entire being . . . The higher element of this *Männerliebe* resided in the very fact that it excluded the sensual, selfish moment of pleasure. Nonetheless, it did not *only* comprise a purely spiritual bond of friendship; spiritual friendship was the blossom of a consummate enjoyment of sensual friendship, springing directly from the enjoyment of beauty, indeed from the absolutely physical and sensual beauty of the beloved man.

While there is no reason to believe that Wagner acted on such desires, his language sometimes waxes homoerotic, as when he addressed King Ludwig as "my adored and angelic friend" and "my most beautiful, supreme and only consolation." Perhaps he was tailoring his language to suit the king's own *Männerliebe*, although, as Laurence Dreyfus notes, the composer seemed more than a little smitten with his new protector: "I was so gripped by amazement over the miracle of this heavenly royal youth that I was near to sinking to my knees and worshipping him."

Wagner never commented on Ludwig's sexuality, but he noted the gay inclinations of one or two other male friends. The painter Paul von Joukowsky, who designed scenery and costumes for the first production of *Parsifal*, often socialized with the Wagners in the company of his lover, a Neapolitan singer named Pepino. When Cosima called the relationship "silly," Richard replied, "It is something for which I have understanding but no inclination. In any case, with all relationships what matters most is what we ourselves put into them. It is all illusion."

Parsifal, with its imagery of spears, wounds, and fluids, has been inducing giggles among gay listeners for generations. The gash from which Amfortas suffers is implicitly sexual; Wolfram von Eschenbach and Chrétien de Troyes, Wagner's medieval sources, place it in the genital area. Parsifal, who bears the healing spear, is a different kind of hero—chaste, comely, otherworldly. His success in repelling the Flower Maidens could mean that he is simply immune to their charms. The playwright Clyde Fitch, a probable lover of Oscar Wilde, tittered over the character's feyness in an 1897 sketch: "I much prefer Siegfried as a person to Parsifal. He's not such a *very* good boy. There's more an air of athletics, football, rowing, and all that about Siegfried, while Parsifal smacks just a little, I think, of the Young Men's Christian Association."

Klingsor, the villainous sorcerer, is marked as queer. When he sees Parsifal climbing the walls of his magic castle, he exclaims, "Ha! He is beautiful, the boy!" In Wolfram's *Parzival*, Klingsor has suffered castration after having been caught in an adulterous affair. According to Wagner, the sorcerer has emasculated himself, in an attempt to achieve purity and gain admittance to the Grail order. Gurnemanz tells the story to the squires— reluctantly, since they must ask twice before he proceeds:

> I never knew of what sin he was guilty,
> but he then wished to atone, indeed to become holy.
> Powerless to kill the sin within him,
> he laid a wicked hand on himself,
> which he then turned towards the Grail,
> from which its guardian contemptuously drove him.

In an 1865 prose sketch for *Parsifal*, Wagner called Klingsor "the demon of hidden sin, the raging of powerlessness against sin," a man of whom "dark, incomprehensible tales" are told. As it happens, that sketch was written for Ludwig, who was inordinately curious about the projected opera. Is Wagner warning the young king not to lay a wicked hand on himself or on another?

Perhaps—although a subsequent exchange of letters regarding the pivotal seduction scene in Act II suggests a different reading. When Kundry plants a long kiss on Parsifal's lips, the young man recoils, clutches his heart, and cries, "Amfortas!—The wound!—The wound!" In an instant, he has attained the wisdom of compassion. Ludwig asks: Why is this so? Wagner answers: "That is a terrible secret, my beloved!" The composer explains that the kiss awakens in Parsifal an awareness of a sin that he has hitherto been too innocent to comprehend. Wagner then speaks of his own suffering, which, he says, goes deeper than such matters as the *Tannhäuser* scandal or harsh critical reviews. For him, Ludwig is the pure fool who offers compassion. What Wagner presumably did not know was that in his diaries the king invoked Parsifal as he struggled against the temptations of gay desire. In one entry, marking a period in which he was "redeemed" (chaste), he quoted the *Parsifal* sketch: "Strong is the magic of him who desires, stronger is that of him who abstains."

The romantic tinge of the Ludwig-Wagner friendship caused chatter when both men were still alive. When the composer entered Ludwig's circle and began causing trouble in Munich, wits compared him to Lola Montez, the Irish actor whose affair with Ludwig's grandfather Ludwig I had led to the latter's abdication. (The eminent playwright Franz Grillparzer dubbed Wagner "Lolo Montez.") By the nineties, Ludwig's homosexuality was public record: stories of his predilection for soldiers and stable hands reached the press shortly after his death, and an 1891 study by the psychologist Albert Moll included the king in a chapter on "Historical Urnings." Gay men idolized Ludwig as a hero and martyr. Verlaine saluted him as the "virgin king of great heart that beat for man alone." The Parisian aesthete Robert de Montesquiou, in his book-length poem *The Bats*, described Ludwig as a "beautiful hermaphrodite" and "feminine despot" who has become immortal through his association with "the prince, the king, the god Richard Wagner." Montesquiou had a pet bat whom he considered a reincarnation of Ludwig.

The topic of same-sex Wagnerism entered public discourse in the last years of the nineteenth century. In January 1895, an article titled "Bayreuth and Homosexuality" appeared in *Die Gesellschaft*, Michael Georg Conrad's semi-modernist magazine. The author was Oskar Panizza, a Munich polemicist and playwright who managed to outdo even Wedekind in notoriety. Panizza had just published *The Love Council*, a scabrous satire set in Heaven, Hell, and the Vatican, featuring such characters as God the Father, Christ, Mary, the Devil, Salome, and the Borgia Pope. He would soon be convicted of ninety-three counts of blasphemy and thrown in jail.

His *Gesellschaft* article is blasphemy of another sort. It begins with a classified ad that had recently run in a leading German newspaper, shortly before *Parsifal* opened in Bayreuth:

> Seeking young bicyclist, Christian, up to 24 y.o., from v. good family, to join same (foreigner), for a beautiful cycling trip to Tyrol in August. Should be very good-looking, distinguished manners, expressive personality. Answering only applications with photos, which will be returned at once, at "Numa 77" poste restante *Bayreuth*.

As Panizza remarks, the name "Numa" is an unmistakable clue to the ad's purpose, if any is needed; Ulrichs, the gay-rights pioneer, had published his early pamphlets under the pseudonym Numa Numantius. Panizza goes on to consider homosexuality in its various guises, making use of Richard Krafft-Ebing's 1886 sexological study *Psychopathia sexualis*. (Panizza had practiced psychiatry before turning to literature.) With reference to Ludwig II, Panizza speaks of a homosexual love that is more intellectual than physical, particularly when an older man loves a younger one. Behind the façade of aesthetic splendor, the homosexual displays a "powerless, vague, feeble" character, shy of public exposure, cowardly. Panizza tacks on an antisemitic aside, saying that this psychological profile also fits that of the Jew.

Panizza then turns to *Parsifal*, calling it "spiritual nourishment for pederasts." The all-male order of the Grail is set against the sinful temptation of the female. "Young Parsifal is sexually indifferent. That suffices. That makes him *nolens volens* homosexual. He is on the other side. His destiny is to redeem *others*, men." Panizza closes on a bizarrely patriotic note, saying that the German people, who will always remain young, instinctively turn away from the geriatric homosexuality of *Parsifal* and prefer the robust, younger Wagner of *Tannhäuser* and *Lohengrin*. Apparently, that foreign bicyclist seeking an attractive male companion is evidence that *Parsifal* gives pleasure mainly to decadent tourists from abroad.

An unspoken irony attends the essay's ending: the homosexuality of Siegfried Wagner, the composer's only son and the heir of Bayreuth, was an open secret. Commentators like James Huneker portrayed Siegfried as a "feminized" and "almost effeminate" version of his father. Another American critic called Siegfried a "pert and primping imposter." He had a modest reputation as a composer, his fairy-tale style owing more to Engelbert Humperdinck, his principal teacher, than to his towering father. The love of his youth was the dashing English composer Clement Harris, who died in Greece in 1897 while fighting as a volunteer in Greece's war with Turkey—a fate that elicited a memorial poem by the homoerotically inclined Stefan George. Only in 1915 was Siegfried persuaded to marry and produce children. For those in the know, Panizza's evocation of a gay Bayreuth impugns both father and son.

"Bayreuth and Homosexuality" drew a rebuttal from Henry Gauthier-Villars, Colette's husband, who claimed to have visual confirmation of Wagner's heterosexuality: "He was seen backstage at the Bayreuth theater kissing a flower maiden, greedily, *in 1882!*" Panizza's article might have caused further controversy if the furor over *The Love Council* had not pushed it to the side. After serving his sentence, Panizza went into exile and wrote a cycle of poems titled *Parisjana*, which hurl abuse at Kaiser Wilhelm II ("stupid boy"). One section of the poem, describing a performance at the Concerts Lamoureux, casts the composer as a revolutionary enemy of the Kaiserreich: "You in Germany be careful / with Wagner's storm-music." When Panizza returned to Germany, he was again imprisoned, and a mental breakdown followed. His fate was as doleful as any in the annals of Wagnerian decline: in 1905, he was committed to an asylum near Bayreuth.

Panizza's theory about *Parsifal* is sufficiently over-the-top that one suspects him of satirical intent. Still, he was onto something in his subtextual analysis of the opera, and Bayreuth did exude a gay ambience. Krafft-Ebing had taken note of gay Wagnerites in the 1892 edition of *Psychopathia sexualis*, presenting a case history of acute aestheticism:

> In general, my whole sensibility and feeling are feminine. I am vain, coquettish, fond of ornament, and like to please others. I love to dress myself beautifully, and, in cases where I wish to please, I even make use of the arts of the toilet, in which I am quite skilled. While I have but little interest in politics, I am passionately fond of music and an inspired follower of Richard Wagner. I have noticed this preference in the majority of us; I find that this music is perfectly in accord with our nature.

Wagner became part of the syllabus of gay taste. When Magnus Hirschfeld began publishing his researches into gay identity and behavior, he quoted

Krafft-Ebing's case study and cited the classified ad that had so amused Panizza. In Hirschfeld's 1914 book *The Homosexuality of Men and Women*, Bayreuth is described as a "very popular gathering place for Uranians from all over the world." Hirschfeld attended the festival in 1911, and may have witnessed the gay congregation firsthand.

The composer himself qualified as a kindred spirit, a fellow traveler. Edward Carpenter, the British apostle of Walt Whitman who promoted socialism, sexual freedom, and male comradeship, quoted the *Männerliebe* section of "The Artwork of the Future" in his privately circulated 1894 pamphlet *Homogenic Love*. Hirschfeld did the same in his first gay publication, *Sappho and Socrates*, which he published under a pseudonym in 1896. Hirschfeld also mentions Wagner and Ludwig's "love letters" (*Liebesbriefwechsel*). In the next breath, he quotes the famous speech that Oscar Wilde delivered at his first trial in London: "The 'Love that dare not speak its name' in this century is such a great affection of an elder for a younger man as there was between David and Jonathan, such as Plato made the very basis of his philosophy, and such as you find in the sonnets of Michelangelo and Shakespeare." The implication is clear: Wagner and Ludwig belong in the gay pantheon. An extensive selection of the *Liebesbriefwechsel* was published in 1899, and Hirschfeld reprinted many of the letters in his *Yearbook for Intermediate Sexual Types*, the house organ of his Scientific-Humanitarian Committee. A sample: "Heaven is descending to earth for us. O Holy One, I worship you!"

In 1903, a gay-identified author named Hanns Fuchs brought out *Richard Wagner and Homosexuality*, the most thorough treatment of the subject to date. Fuchs classifies the composer as a "spiritual homosexual"—one who adopts gay mannerisms, who values erotically charged friendships with men, but who stops short of having sex with them. Fuchs finds examples of such friendships throughout Wagner's work. *Tristan und Isolde*, for one, features intense bonds between Tristan and his servant, Kurwenal; between Tristan and King Mark; and between Isolde and her maid, Brangäne. But the central exhibit remains *Parsifal*. Fuchs reviews Panizza's essay and accepts many of its propositions. Indeed, he adds a mischievous reading of the Flower Maidens scene: "Doesn't Parsifal bring to mind those homosexuals who very much enjoy the company of women, who enjoy joking and laughing with them, who do not shy away from flirtatious kisses, and who flee only when—more is demanded of them?" Fuchs insists, however, that Parsifal is not gay in the modern sense. When Kundry makes her move, the hero is not seized with the revulsion that a "real" homosexual would display. Instead, Parsifal sets aside temptation in favor of the "ideal male community" of the Grail.

Although Fuchs wrote *Richard Wagner and Homosexuality* at Hirschfeld's behest, he leaned toward another gay-identified group, the one gathered around Adolf Brand's magazine *Der Eigene*. In those circles, the gay male was not an in-between being but the apotheosis of masculinity. Similarly, the sociologist Hans Blüher argued that eroticism was a bonding force in male communities. Blüher made a particular study of the Wandervogel movement, a network of nature-hiking youth. Nationalism, militarism, misogyny, and antisemitism were rampant in the *Eigene* group, and Hirschfeld's Jewishness became a point of contention. The sexologist was deemed too worldly, too womanly, insufficiently enamored of the Aryan ideal. Fuchs's 1909 novel *Eros Between You and Us*, which the musicologist Mitchell Morris has rescued from almost total obscurity, tells of Wagnerian lovers whose pure, manly affection—they clutch hands at a performance of *Tristan* in Bayreuth—outshines the pretensions of effeminate inverts. When one of the lovers reverts to heterosexuality, the other dies in despair, his unfulfilled yearning all too similar to Tristan's—or Isolde's.

The agony of gay masculinity reaches a breaking point in the self-destructive Wagnerism of Otto Weininger. The thesis of *Sex and Character*, that human beings exist on a continuum from the purely masculine to the purely feminine, was relatively progressive for the time; Hirschfeld believed much the same. Furthermore, Weininger thought that gay impulses could not be resisted and that anti-gay laws were inhumane. But he relentlessly favored the masculine over the feminine. Ideally, the male should transcend sexual desire altogether and thus escape the degradation of femininity. *Parsifal*, which Weininger considered the "deepest poetry in world literature," provides a blueprint for this evasion of sex. Parsifal and Klingsor represent "the transsexual and the sexual in man, divided between two persons." In vanquishing Klingsor, Parsifal vanquishes sexuality, thereby releasing Kundry from her torment.

Hirschfeld had a more fluid and inclusive vision of gay identity. In later writings, he focuses less on Wagner's homoeroticism than on his androgyny. The 1910 book *The Transvestites*—a word Hirschfeld invented—includes the composer in a discussion of clothing fetishism and cross-dressing. A close reading of Wagner's letters to his Viennese costumier yields the conclusion that while the Meister undoubtedly had a "feminine element in his psyche" he should not be considered a homosexual, spiritual or otherwise. Nor does he deserve mockery of the kind Spitzer and Nietzsche unleashed. Instead, Wagner's inclination disclosed the "extraordinarily rich and subtle complexity of his inner life"—perhaps the very source of his creativity. No turn-of-the-century interpretation of Wagner offered a more radical or provocative perspective. Hirschfeld had extricated the Meister not only from German nationalist thought but from the patriarchal biases of Western civilization.

GAY WAGNERITES

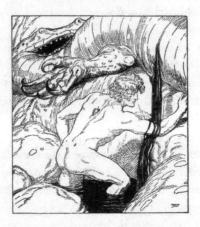

Franz Stassen, Siegfried Bathes in the Dragon's Blood

"It is all metaphysics, music, and pubescent sexuality," Thomas Mann wrote to his brother in 1901, in the throes of an unrequited crush on a young male friend. Implanted in his heart, Mann said, was the image of the "*Wunderreich der Nacht*"—Tristan's words in Act II of Wagner's opera, hailing the potion that converts death to love: "Through the gates of death, whence it flowed to me, it opened wide the wonder-realm of night, where I had awakened only in dreams." The predicament of gay attraction had evidently prompted thoughts of suicide, although Mann assured his brother that he was unlikely to "commit any 'follies.'" Instead, he luxuriated in Wagner as a substitute for love unto death.

Wagner and same-sex desire intermingle in Mann's writing almost from the start. Hanno Buddenbrook's attachment to his classmate Kai has the contours of a romantic friendship, one that arouses suspicion at school: "The teachers tolerated it, but only grudgingly, because they suspected something foul and hostile behind it." The other boys project "crude virility" and revile "effeminacy and dandyism." One sign of Hanno's otherness is his Wagnerian piano-playing. "I should practice my études and sonatas and then stop," he tells Kai. "But I'll probably improvise. I can't seem not to, even though it makes everything worse." Kai replies, "I know what you're improvising about." There is a silence: Kai turns red, and Hanno casts "enigmatic, sidelong glances" toward his friend. Similarly suggestive is Hermann Hesse's first novel, *Peter Camenzind* (1904), where strains of *Meistersinger* stir a romantic atmosphere between two young men: "The music sounded light and vigorous, longing and exuberant, and I felt as though immersed in a warm, effervescent bath. Looking with secret joy at his neck, at the backs of his pale musician's hands, I was overcome by the same feeling of tenderness and respect with which I had once looked at the dark-haired student from my schooldays . . ."

Novelists both gay and straight feasted on the divine friendship of Wagner and Ludwig. Catulle Mendès's 1881 novel *Le Roi vierge*, or *The Virgin King*, is a thinly disguised roman à clef in which a sensitive, unstable monarch named Frédérik hosts an obstreperous composer named Hans Hammer, who is obviously based on the erstwhile "palmiped of Lucerne." Given to rants about "true German art" and late-night banging on the piano, Hammer is "small, lean, tightly wrapped in a coat of brown cloth; and his entire body, frail though perhaps robust—like an assemblage of springs—had the almost convulsive trembling of a hysterical woman." At the end, the king stabs an opera singer, castrates himself, and makes a guest appearance as Jesus in the Oberammergau Passion Play, ordering his servant to pierce his side while he hangs on the cross. The novel was banned in Bavaria, where the real Ludwig had five more years to live. Eekhoud's *Escal-Vigor*, with its nod to Wagner as a herald of sexual freedom, also rang variations on the theme of the gay Mad King. It was sufficiently explicit in its content that it provoked an obscenity trial in Belgium.

The education of the gay neophyte—"Are you peculiarly fond of

Wagner?"—is at the heart of Mikhail Kuzmin's 1906 novel *Wings*, a pioneering example of coming-out literature. When older aesthetes tutor a sexually undecided youth named Vanya, they ply him with *Tristan* and *Tannhäuser*. "It's all like the breath of a new spring, of a new passion, bubbling up from the darkest depths," one gay sage says of the Venusberg. At a performance of *Tristan*, Vanya ignores the antics of the society set and goes pale before the power of the music. Afterward, he puzzles over the conjunction of Wagner's "apotheosis of passion" with the messy reality of sex. Isn't it ridiculous, he asks, that amid such sublime music the lovers have to perform the awkward ceremony of taking off their clothes? He is told that the "most disgraceful act, the most improbable situation," can be elevated by the attitude of the participant. Vanya smiles at his friend Stroop, who, by novel's end, is poised to become his lover.

Oscar Wilde, a connoisseur of disgraceful and improbable situations, had too little patience for unreflective grandiosity to count himself among the Wagnerites. In Wilde's plays and stories, Wagner is most often present as the butt of jokes. Lady Bracknell, the autocratic aunt in *The Importance of Being Earnest*, rings at the door in a "Wagnerian manner," and in *The Picture of Dorian Gray* Lady Henry makes a much-quoted quip: "I like Wagner's music better than any music. It is so loud that one can talk the whole time, without people hearing what one says." Yet the ageless Dorian, an aesthetic cousin of Huysmans's Des Esseintes, takes Wagner more seriously. He objects to Lady Henry's taunts, declaring that he never talks during good music. Later, Dorian is seen "in his box at the Opera, either alone, or with Lord Henry, listening in rapt pleasure to *Tannhäuser*, and seeing in that great work of art a presentation of the Tragedy of his own soul." Wilde's essay "The Critic as Artist" expands on that passing remark, using the *Tannhäuser* overture to argue that spectators shape artworks in their own image, overriding whatever intentions the artist may have had in mind.

> Sometimes, when I listen to the overture to *Tannhäuser*, I seem indeed to see that comely knight treading delicately on the flower-strewn grass, and to hear the voice of Venus calling to him from the caverned hill. But at other times it speaks to me of a thousand different things, of myself, it may be, and my own life, or of the lives of others whom one

has loved and grown weary of loving, or of the passions that man has known, or of the passions that man has not known, and so has sought for. To-night it may fill one with that *ΕΡΩΣ ΤΩΝ ΑΔΥΝΑΤΩΝ*, that *Amour de l'impossible*, which falls like a madness on many who think they live securely and out of reach of harm, so that they sicken suddenly with the poison of unlimited desire, and, in the infinite pursuit of what they may not obtain, grow faint and swoon or stumble. Tomorrow, like the music of which Aristotle and Plato tell us, the noble Dorian music of the Greek, it may perform the office of a physician, and give us an anodyne against pain, and heal the spirit that is wounded, and "bring the soul into harmony with all right things."

The supernatural Victorian TV show *Penny Dreadful* (2014–16), which featured Dorian Gray as a character, provides a delightful addendum to the matter of Wilde and Wagner. In one scene, Dorian plays an Edison cylinder of Isolde's Transfiguration to a masculine American friend. "I'd ask if you had heard of Wagner," Dorian says, "but you'd pretend you hadn't." With the aid of the Liebestod and a few glasses of absinthe, they are soon making love.

Gay artists of the fin de siècle gave Wagner a queer makeover, to the extent that one was needed. Simeon Solomon, who was arrested on moral grounds some years before the Wilde scandal of 1895, pictured Parsifal as a fine-featured young man with tousled hair and full lips. The German illustrators Franz Stassen and Hugo Höppener, the latter using the pseudonym Fidus, lavished attention on the physiques of Parsifal and Siegfried. All were trumped by Beardsley, the high priest of British decadence, who, although predominantly straight in orientation, felt at home in louche gay circles. His impressions of Wagner's heroes are impeccably outré. A slender, waifish Tannhäuser reaches longingly toward the Venusberg with bony hands. Wotan is an ancient wraith with a long white beard, awaiting his end. A picture of Siegfried tasting the dragon's blood borders on the lewd, as Emma Sutton notes: "In his elaborately folded and coyly revealing 'toga,' with his knock-kneed stance, cocked hip, downcast eyes, and daintily arched fingers, he is posed on the edge of an eerie lake, suggesting Narcissus (or a rent-boy touting for business) . . ."

Under the Hill, an illustrated Tannhäuser narrative that Beardsley left unfinished at his death in 1898, crosses the line into high-end pornography—the homoerotic equivalent of Pierre Louÿs's Wagner sonnets. The knight's visit to the Venusberg becomes a riot of decadence, surreally mixing the medieval and the contemporary. In one scene, Tannhäuser, renamed Fanfreluche, is seen in bed reading the score of *Rheingold*, gripped by the "feverish insistent ringing of the hammers at the forge." (Beardsley also planned a comic version of *Rheingold*, casting the gods and dwarves as variously effete and grotesque figures.) In another section, Tannhäuser is attended by a group of serving boys, one of whom takes the motif of Wagnerian penetration literally rather than metaphorically: "As the boy seemed anxious to take up the active attitude, Tannhäuser graciously descended to the passive."

With this unabashed obscenity, Beardsley is sending up the grave rituals of Wagnerism. Yet, like Louÿs, he had a sincere and deep appreciation of the composer; one friend recalled him listening to *Tristan*, "transparent hands clutching the rail in front." These freakish Wagnerites are self-portraits as well as caricatures. A picture of Alberich with a twisted face and a hooked

Aubrey Beardsley, Siegfried, Act II

nose might be considered antisemitic, except that, as Victor Chan points out, it bears a marked resemblance to Frederick Evans's photograph of Beardsley himself.

As gay-male Wagnerites sized up Siegfried and Parsifal, their lesbian counterparts dwelled on Brünnhilde and Isolde, and on the sopranos who portrayed them. Terry Castle, in *The Apparitional Lesbian*, writes about the "unsung history of female diva-worship" in nineteenth- and twentieth-century culture, which flourished in the sexually more permissive environment of the opera house. The opera "was one of only a few public spaces in which a woman could openly admire another woman's body." Aside from the personal attractiveness of a singer like Nordica or Olive Fremstad, Wagner singers modeled an unruly temperament, an independent pride, a defiance of conventional gender roles.

For women, too, Wagner performances gave shelter to "impossible love." The expatriate American author Natalie Barney, a fixture of Paris bohemia, came to Bayreuth in 1904, at a time when she was in love with Pauline Tarn, who wrote poetry under the name Renée Vivien. Their relationship flourished in the low light of the Festspielhaus. Barney wrote: "Captivated by the music, first our eyes then our hands met in the shadows, and each evening found us together." Wagner had a no less aphrodisiac effect on M. Carey Thomas, the founding dean and second president of Bryn Mawr College. In an 1891 letter to her longtime companion Mary Garrett, Thomas wrote a hymn of praise to *Tristan*, "the most glorious of all Wagner's operas, flawless from first to last, the most triumphant rhapsody of love ever th't, rapturous, soaring, heavenly high, winging thro. the Empyrean, without a touch of earth, all human emotion sublimated into godlike passion & longing panting & throbbing . . . I never in a public place came so near to losing my self-control and I never cared so much for an opera of Wagner's."

Lesbian listeners, like gay-male ones, teased out subtexts in the music dramas. Hanns Fuchs was not the only one to suspect a lesbian attachment between Isolde and Brangäne. Katherine Harris Bradley and her niece Edith Cooper, who published under the pen name Michael Field, addressed that pairing in their 1911 drama *The Tragedy of Pardon*. Brangäne says: "I cannot let you go. There is love / Of woman unto woman, in its fibre / Stronger than knits a mother to her child. / There is no lack in it and no defect . . ." A character in Gertrude Stein's early lesbian novella *Q.E.D.* receives a kiss "that seemed to scale the very walls of chastity," and comes to the realization that "like Parsifal a kiss could make me frantic with realisation."

As Stein's Parsifal metaphor suggests, Wagner played a double-sided role for gay and lesbian listeners alike. His apparent openness toward "impossible love" ran up against his agenda of sexual restraint. Indeed, a cathartic release of unorthodox feelings might permit a return to strictly traditional roles. That mechanism helps to explain why so fundamentally prudish and stunted a spirit as Adolf Hitler found as much excitement in Wagner as did the likes of Barney, Beardsley, and Wilde. The latter could have been thinking of Wagner when he wrote, "All excess, as well as all renunciation, brings its own punishment."

DEATHS IN VENICE

Mann's postcard of the Grand Hotel des Bains, in Venice

For nineteenth- and early twentieth-century travelers of the "musical" persuasion, Venice gave off a bright allure. Like other Italian destinations, it had the reputation of being a morally relaxed environment, one in which sexuality was fluid. The fact that Wagner died in Venice added to the city's legend among gay tourists. In 1924, the African-American philosopher Alain Locke took a trip to Venice with a young protégé, Langston Hughes. Locke "knew Venice like a book," Hughes later said. Their tour included the Palazzo Giustiniani, where Wagner worked on *Tristan* and took inspiration from a gondolier's song, and, of course, the Palazzo Vendramin. Locke attempted to seduce Hughes in the course of this Venetian-Wagnerian adventure, but the younger man held back. On the way home, Hughes read Mann's *Death in Venice*.

For some gay men and women, this itinerary of *Tristan*, gondoliers, beaches, sensuality, and freedom threatened a dangerous loss of control. To indulge one's passions might lead to dissolution, degradation, and extinction. This theme receives its classic exposition in *Death in Venice*, but it also runs through stories and novels by Vernon Lee and Henry James, both of whom likely saw Wagner as a hazard to the guarded way of life that came to be known as the "closet." Bayreuth itself was heavily invested in maintaining that protected space: Siegfried Wagner feared being outed by the impudent press of the late-Wilhelmine era.

Vernon Lee was the pen name of the French-born British writer Violet Paget, who presided over lesbian circles in London and Florence. Her 1911 essay "The Religious and Moral Status of Wagner" presents the composer as a kind of Venus flytrap for vulnerable souls:

> Attentive or inattentive, able to follow or not able to follow, your mind is imprisoned in that Wagner performance as in the dark auditorium, and allowed to divagate from the music only to the stage; not the literal stage of indifferently-painted lath and pasteboard, with its stout, be-wigged heroes and heroines brandishing spears and drinking horns, but the inviolable stage of your own emotions, secretly haunted by the vague ghosts of your own past and your own might have been, by the vaguer fatamorgana figures of your own scarce conscious hopes and desires.

Tristan, in particular, triggers unspoken and unspeakable emotion—"inner pantings and faintings . . . languors and orgasms within the human being." Wagner fuels a desire that ordinary life is bound to frustrate.

Lee's story "A Wicked Voice," published in her 1890 collection *Hauntings*, features a conflicted composer named Magnus, who hopes to assume Wagner's mantle with a mythological opera called *Ogier the Dane*. On a trip to Venice, Magnus sinks into the city's "moral malaria," its "miasma of long-dead melodies," and is stalked by the ghost of Zaffirino, an androgynous male castrato singer who can kill people with the beauty of his voice. One of Zaffirino's victims is the Procuratessa Vendramin—a nod to the old Venetian family in whose palazzo Wagner died. Dreaming of his unwritten opera, deep in the "twilight of the heroic world," Magnus ends up "wasted by a strange and deadly disease." The musicologist Carlo Caballero conjectures that Magnus is a stand-in for Wagner himself, receiving his comeuppance. Lee "persecutes Wagner with what he would repress"—the ornate vocal style of bel canto opera.

Henry James brushed against the Meister's gay-leaning ménage in 1880, thanks to his intimate friendship with Paul von Joukowsky, the designer of *Parsifal*. On a visit to Naples, where the Wagners were stationed, James paid Joukowsky a visit, but, as he wrote to a friend, "I did not avail myself of the opportunity offered me to go and see the musician of the future, as I speak no intelligible German and he speaks nothing else." (They could have spoken French.) In another letter, James commented that Joukowsky was "the same impracticable and indeed ridiculous mixture of Nihilism and bric à brac as before," and that the Wagner circle displayed "fantastic immoralities and aesthetics." It would appear that James was unsettled by the composer's friendliness toward openly gay men. It may also be that the man who would become known as the Master did not wish to bow down before the Meister.

Still, James retained a veiled curiosity about Wagnerian doings. When his friend Isabella Stewart Gardner went to Bayreuth in 1892, he asked about her experiences there: "Did Bayreuth come off?" (The Boston patron was a kind of godmother to a circle of gay men, including the architect Ralph Adams Cram, who wrote that visitors "find here in Bayreuth something they have wanted all their lives.") More than once, James sends his characters to a Wagner performance, imbuing the music with a mildly sinister spell. In the 1886 novel *The Bostonians*, which has unmistakable lesbian overtones, the women's rights activist Olive Chancellor and the charismatic young orator Verena Terrant together spend an evening at *Lohengrin*, the older woman worrying that the glamour of the scene will distract the younger. In the 1909 story "The Velvet Glove," a renowned tenor sings Wagner before an elite audience, causing the male protagonist to feel that his consciousness is being "held down as by a hand mailed in silver."

Wagner, death, and Venice glance against one another in James's 1902 novel *The Wings of the Dove*, where the presiding image is of a dove spreading its wings, like the one that hovers in *Lohengrin* and *Parsifal*. The American heiress Milly Theale, suffering from a fatal disease, goes to Italy with a companion to improve her health. The bliss of their voyage is likened to Wagner's orchestration: "The great sustained sea-light had drunk up the rest of the picture, so that for many days other questions and other possibilities sounded with as little effect as a trio of penny whistles might sound in a Wagner overture." In Venice, Milly settles into a palace modeled on the Palazzo Barbaro, which Vernon Lee used as a setting in "A Wicked Voice." But the magical city changes shape and becomes a "Venice all of evil . . . a Venice of cold lashing rain." Milly has walked into a trap laid by the impecunious Kate Croy, whose father has been besmirched by an unspecified scandal of an "odious and vile" nature. Kate plans for her fiancé, Merton Densher, to marry the ailing Milly and thereby gain her wealth. Although Milly learns of the scheme, she still leaves money to Merton when she dies.

A scene of renunciation and redemption follows: Merton, in love with Milly's purity, walks away from the bequest. Thus do Milly's wings "spread themselves for protection," saving him from a compromised life. James deploys another Wagner metaphor in the preface to the novel: he calls Milly a Rhinemaiden, implying that her wealth is like Wagner's fatal gold. Merton, in refusing the money, has effectively thrown it back into the Rhine.

When Thomas Mann married Katia Pringsheim, his *Wagnermanie* temporarily waned. Hans Rudolf Vaget suggests that in distancing himself from the Wagner cult Mann was also extricating himself from the homosexual atmosphere surrounding that cult. (Mann could hardly have avoided the discussion around Bayreuth and same-sex love; one of his poems appeared in the same 1895 issue of *Die Gesellschaft* that contained Panizza's infamous essay.) In 1909, Mann paid his only visit to Bayreuth, in the company of his Jewish brother-in-law Klaus Pringsheim. While he was shaken anew by the music's power of expression, he had the sense that Wagner might have passed into history, "in terms of ambience, tendency, taste."

Two years later, in the spring of 1911, the Viennese magazine *Der Merker*—named after Beckmesser's official title in *Meistersinger*—invited Mann to contribute to a special Wagner issue. He took up the commission while staying at the Grand Hotel des Bains, on the Lido of Venice. The resulting short essay was titled "Auseinandersetzung mit Wagner"—the first word variously meaning analysis, discussion, and dispute. The article must have taken the editors by surprise, for they published it with a disclaimer indicating how little they agreed with it. Mann begins with praise for Wagner's narrative flair, but adds that the composer has always seemed to him "suspect"—"irresistible if also deeply questionable in terms of the nobility, purity, and wholesomeness of his methods." With his "Baroque-colossal" manner, the Meister belongs more to the nineteenth century than to the twentieth. A new classicism is forming, couched in a style "logical, well-formed, and clear." Still, the old affair with Wagner goes on.

As Mann worked on the essay, he found himself distracted. A ten-year-old Polish child named Władysław Moes—Adzio, as his friends called him—played every day on the beach and dined with his family at the hotel. Katia Mann later remembered how her husband kept staring at this "very charming, exceptionally beautiful" boy. Although there is no evidence that Mann ever acted on such pedophilic desires, he felt them and recorded them. Some thoroughly disturbing passages in his diaries reveal that he was aroused by the sight of his adolescent son Klaus. "Obviously someone like me 'should' not bring children into the world," he wrote.

After the Lido, Mann studied the destructive impulse within himself, much as if it were happening to one of those friends whom he surveyed through opera glasses. He imagined what might happen if a writer of his reputation were to surrender to base urges. The homoeroticism that he associated with his love of Wagner passes to an alternative version of himself—older, stuffier, more solitary, trapped in intellect and fame.

Thus was born Gustav von Aschenbach, the central figure of *Death in Venice*, which appeared in 1912. As Mann later said, "nothing is invented" in the story, at least in the scenic setting. A gloomy Adriatic crossing, uncomfortable encounters with an aging fop and a menacing gondolier, a mix-up about luggage, rumors of a cholera epidemic, a boy whose name is misheard as Tadzio—all this comes from Mann's experience. Further, Aschenbach's fictional career is outfitted with various of Mann's abandoned projects. *Death in Venice* diverges from reality in the later chapters, as Aschenbach begins pursuing the Polish boy, at a distance. The threat of cholera turns out to be real, and Aschenbach, desperate to keep Tadzio in sight, fails to warn the boy's family. He dies on the beach, gazing at his beloved.

Wagner is never named, but his shadow falls on an extraordinary paragraph at the heart of the story, one that reconstructs Mann's beachside writing scene of 1911. Sitting under the hot sun, watching Tadzio play on the beach, Aschenbach is seized with the urge to create:

The writer's joy is to let thought become wholly feeling, feeling wholly thought. At that moment, the solitary man had possession and command of such pulsing thought, such precise feeling: namely, that nature trembles with bliss when the spirit bows in homage to beauty. Suddenly, he wanted to write. It is said that Eros loves idleness and is made for that purpose only. But at this point in the crisis, the arousal of the afflicted pointed toward production. The occasion was almost irrelevant. A suggestion, an invitation, to proffer one's views on a certain great and burning issue of culture and taste had been issued in the intellectual sphere and had reached the vacationer. The topic was familiar to him and was within his experience; the desire to shine the light of his language upon it was at once irresistible. What he craved, though, was to work in Tadzio's presence, to take the boy's physique as the model for his writing, to let his style follow the contours of this body which seemed to him divine, to carry its beauty into the realm of the intellect, as the eagle once carried the Trojan shepherd into the ether. Never had the pleasure of words felt sweeter, never had he so known Eros to dwell in words, as in those dangerous and delicious hours when, working on his rough table under the awning, with his idol in sight and the music of his voice in his ears, he crafted his little essay after Tadzio's beauty— that page and a half of exquisite prose whose purity, nobility, and surging expressive tension would soon excite the admiration of many. It is surely for the best that the world knows only the beautiful work and not its origins, not the conditions of its creation; for knowledge of the sources from which the artist's inspiration flowed would perplex and repel the public, and thus supersede the effects of his excellence.

It is a staggering performance, at once narcissistic and self-deprecating, confessional and evasive. The "page and a half of exquisite prose" is, of course, Mann's short piece on Wagner; the coyness with which the subject matter is skirted invites the inquisitive reader to put two and two together. (That he had signed his *Merker* piece with the words "Lido-Venedig, May 1911" gives the game away.) The final sentence mocks itself to death as it exposes, even as it claims to conceal, the secret sources not only of Aschenbach's work but also of Mann's own. Like Poe's purloined letter, the author's sexual secret sits in full view.

Tristan is always in the background. Mann knew of the opera's Venetian associations, which are described at length in *My Life*, the memoir that Wagner wrote for Ludwig's benefit. That book received its first official publication in 1911, and Mann might have noticed Wagner's account of his entry into Venice: "The weather had suddenly become somewhat threatening, and the sight of the gondolas themselves genuinely terrified me; for, as much as I had heard of these peculiar black vessels draped in black, the sight of one of them in nature surprised me in a very unpleasant way. When I had to enter under the awning hung with black cloth, at first I could think of nothing but the cholera scare overcome earlier; I had the decided feeling I was taking part in a funeral procession during a time of plague."

Mann also seamlessly incorporates the Venetian bliss of the early nineteenth-century poet August von Platen, who came as close as any writer of the pre-Hirschfeld era to identifying himself as gay. For Platen, as for many others, Italy provided an escape from punitive social norms. The poet wrote in his diary: "Venice pulls me in, yes, it has made me forget all of my earlier life and activity so that I find myself in a present without a past." The *Sonnets from Venice* (1825) allude to a nameless friend with whom Platen seems to be having a brief but passionate affair. "Venice now exists only in the land of dreams," he writes, pondering the transitoriness of beauty. In the grip of that melancholy understanding, the poet began to plan a drama on the subject of Tristan and Isolde. One fragment of that unrealized project would find fame under the title "Tristan":

He who has beheld beauty with his eyes,
Is already given over to death,
He will be fit for no duty on the earth,
Rather he will tremble before death,
He who has beheld beauty with his eyes!

Aschenbach is seen reciting an unnamed poet's paeans to Venice as he nears the city. As with the hidden Wagner reference, the initiate knows who is meant.

Platen and Wagner were both Hellenists, intent on reawakening the spirit of ancient Greece. *Death in Venice* records the chaos that might ensue if Greek values and customs were revived in literal fashion. Aschenbach initially treats Tadzio as an epitome of lofty Apollonian perfection, but then the Dionysian energies hailed by Nietzsche surge to the fore. In his own work, the fictional author strives toward purity and severity of form—something like the "new classicism" that Mann promoted in his Wagner essay. Yet the attempt to move past Wagnerian romanticism falls short. The language of the story remains hopelessly wedded to *Tristan*-esque word clusters such as "most secret lust of longing" ("*heimlichste Wollust der Sehnsucht*").

Motifs out of Wagner are woven through the novella. In the first paragraphs, a restless Aschenbach, in the course of a Munich constitutional, encounters a mysterious figure who wears a broad-brimmed hat and carries a walking stick. This apparition, with his "imperious, surveying" air, resembles the Wanderer in *Siegfried*, Wotan in disguise. That he might also be an older gay man cruising for sex exemplifies Mann's habit of framing intellectual fantasy in cool naturalism. An even more esoteric reference appears at the very end. Raymond Furness, in his wide-ranging survey *Wagner and Literature*, notes that when a photographer's camera is seen standing on a mostly deserted beach, Mann specifies that "the black cloth draped over it fluttered and flapped in a chilling wind"—an apparent reference to the black flag that is said to fly on Isolde's ship in the original Tristan legend. Wagner omitted the black flag from his opera, but he mentioned it in an often-quoted letter to Liszt, announcing his plan for *Tristan*: "Since I have never in my life enjoyed the actual happiness of love, I intend to erect a further monument to this most beautiful of dreams . . . With the 'black flag' that waves at the end, I shall then cover myself up, in order—to die."

At the end, Aschenbach looks out at Tadzio, who turns back and returns his gaze. "To him it was as if the pale and lovely psychagogue out there were smiling at him, beckoning to him; as if, lifting his hand from his hip, he were pointing outward, hovering ahead, in a vastness full of promise. And, as so often before, he arose to follow him." The language is close to that of *Tristan*: "Where Tristan now parts, / Will you, Isolde, follow him?" Tristan's destination is the *Wunderreich der Nacht*, the wonder-realm of night, which Mann associated with gay desire. Isolde indeed follows her beloved, undergoing transfiguration. Of course, Mann the ironist, the dispassionate chronicler of his own confusion, cannot leave it at that. "Minutes passed before anyone rushed to the aid of the man who had slumped to one side in his chair. They brought him to his room. And later that same day a shocked, respectful world received the news of his death."

Death in Venice was a great success. Far from causing scandal, its gay content became a selling point in the sexually jaded Kaiserreich. "Pederasty is made acceptable for the cultured middle classes," sneered the critic Alfred Kerr. Mann assured readers that the same-sex theme was merely a dramatic device: "I chose homosexual love for my hero only to make the plunge from the summit to the depths seem as fateful as possible." Interestingly, though, the story failed to please the nascent gay vanguard. Kurt Hiller, in an essay on the "homoerotic novel" in Hirschfeld's *Yearbook*, wrote that *Death in Venice* displayed a "moral narrowness" that he would not have expected from the author of *Buddenbrooks*. Healthy gay desire is equated with a "peculiar love for a boy," which arises as a "symptom of decline . . . almost like cholera." This is a notable development. Mann's crypto-Wagnerian novella, at once blatant and elusive, vexes gay critics, who speak aloud what everyone knows but refuses to articulate. They demand, at long last, "knowledge of the sources from which the artist's inspiration flowed."

PSYCHOANALYTIC WAGNER

In *Beyond Good and Evil*, Nietzsche set down an aphorism that Mann took to heart: "The degree and kind of a man's sexuality reach up to the ultimate summit of his spirit." *Death in Venice* is a lesson in that dynamic, exposing the damp roots of Aschenbach's aesthetic. Nietzsche also outlined the process of sublimation, whereby sexual drives not only contribute to the artist's work but are themselves refined into creative impulses. In matters of psychology, as in most other areas, Nietzsche owed much to Wagner, who showed how the fundamental reality of sex underpins worldly power and the most ideal longings. Sexual love is at the core of all other forms of

Sabina Spielrein

love, Wagner said in 1854. That is why the palpable arousal of Kundry's kiss allows Parsifal to grasp the loftier mentality of compassion.

From Nietzsche's psychology of sexuality it is only a few steps to Sigmund Freud's. Mann, as a loyal Wagnerite, emphasized the degree to which the composer of the *Ring* and *Parsifal* had anticipated psychoanalytic theory. In his 1933 essay "Sorrows and Grandeur of Richard Wagner," Mann describes a "very peculiar intuitive affinity" between Wagner and Freud. That insight has been elaborated many times over the past century. Bryan Magee likens Wagner's operas to "animated textbooks of psychoanalysis." Thomas Grey and Adrian Daub write that "Wagnerian music drama was Freudian before there was a Freud." Patrick Süskind, in his 1981 play *The Double Bass*, has his Wagner-hating protagonist say that if psychoanalysis had existed earlier in the nineteenth century "we'd have been spared Wagner."

Although Freud preferred Mozart to all other composers, he paid heed to the Wagner operas, as a young intellectual in late nineteenth-century Vienna was almost required to do. An 1897 performance of *Meistersinger* gave him particular pleasure. He told his colleague Wilhelm Fliess that "real ideas are set to music, as in no other opera," and that "tones of feeling" linger in him afterward. Freud was most struck by Hans Sachs's musings on the significance of dreams. When Walther von Stolzing recounts a beautiful morning dream, Sachs tells his protégé to turn it into song, for "all art of verse and poetry is but the interpretation of true dreams [*Wahrtraumdeuterei*]." On hearing Walther's creation, Sachs labels it the "blessed morning-dream interpretation melody." That moment "moved me sympathetically," Freud said. Two years later, he published *The Inter-pretation of Dreams* (*Die Traumdeutung*).

Freud knew Wagner's operas well enough to quote lines from memory, or slightly misquote them. In *The Interpretation of Dreams*, he approximates a line from the Rome Narration in *Tannhäuser*, in which the hero is damned by the Pope for harboring "evil desire." A letter congratulating Jung on the birth of his son includes a mildly garbled citation of *Tristan* ("My father begot me and died"). Grey and Daub go so far as to suggest that the near-absence of Wagner from Freud's published writings is a kind of repression. The composer's antisemitism was perhaps a contributing factor, but the basic motivation may have been Freud's competitive urge to claim his own intellectual territory. In that sense, his implicit rejection of Wagner is akin to Nietzsche's agon, his Oedipal rebellion.

Much of Freud's 1912 essay "On the Universal Tendency to Debasement in the Sphere of Love" reads like a gloss on *Tannhäuser*. It considers the classic split between sacred and profane loves, as evidenced in bourgeois men who experience impotence in relations with their wives and can become aroused only by "debased sexual objects," namely prostitutes. "Where they love, they do not desire, and where they desire they cannot love," Freud writes. He lays blame on the frustration of sexual instincts in youth. Wagner, too, worried over the bottling-up of sexuality, yet his Venusberg demonstrates the deleterious consequences of unrestrained desire. Freud, likewise, opposes the instant gratification of instincts. The irreconcilability of animal desire and civilized norms is not necessarily a misfortune, since the sublimation of unsatisfied instincts can yield great cultural productions. Freud's finding that "renunciation and sorrow" are social necessities gives his argument a curiously Romantic, Wagnerian flavor. *Death in Venice*, published the same year as Freud's essay, corroborates its findings.

Many of Freud's colleagues and students had no hesitation about addressing Wagner at length. Otto Rank, Freud's right-hand man in the founding of the psychoanalytic movement, specialized in applying the new methodology to artists and artworks; his doctoral thesis, published in 1911, psychoanalyzed the Lohengrin legend, with Wagner's opera as the principal reference point. Rank proposes that the "question ban," the prohibition against asking after Lohengrin's origins, is necessary because Elsa is a mother figure for the hero, in need of being rescued from a rival father. Unsurprisingly, Rank also quotes from the eyebrow-raising passage in *Siegfried* in which the young hero removes the armor of the sleeping Brünnhilde:

> This is no man!
> Burning enchantment
> seizes my heart . . .
> Mother! Mother!
> Remember me!

Modern audiences seldom fail to laugh at this moment. Chronology notwithstanding, it seems a comically literal attempt at putting the Oedipus complex on stage. It also has a homoerotic subtext: before Siegfried discovers that Brünnhilde is a woman, he marvels at the beauty of this sundappled knight (*"Ach! wie schön!"*). Rank's subsequent study of the "incest motif" in myth and literature contains a substantial section on Wagner, locating an Oedipus complex in the composer's childhood. The music and literary critic Max Graf, a follower of Freud's, covers similar terrain in a monograph centered on *The Flying Dutchman*, in which he traces motherly longings and fatherly jealousies through Wagner's dramas and life. Intriguingly, Graf mentions in his foreword some long discussions he had had with Freud on the subject.

Carl Jung, in his 1912 work *Psychology of the Unconscious* (later revised as *Symbols of Transformation*), makes much of the incestuous couples of the *Ring*—the siblings Siegmund and Sieglinde, the nephew-aunt pair Siegfried and Brünnhilde—but he interprets them not in terms of individual sexuality, as Rank and Graf do, but as archetypes of the collective unconscious. Siegfried is depicted as a sun god, a reincarnation of the Egyptian god Horus, whereas Brünnhilde exemplifies the anima, the feminine component of the deity, who is generally representative of the Self. Brünnhilde breaks off from her father, Wotan, and confronts him with manifestations of the feminine drive of which he is not yet conscious. Siegfried's battle with the dragon is his contestation with the "Terrible Mother" who must be overcome. Brünnhilde becomes Siegfried's anima as she was Wotan's—"mother, sister, and wife in one," writes Jean-Jacques Nattiez, in an explication of the Jungian Wagner.

Tristan und Isolde, the most sexually charged of Wagner operas, is oddly neglected in these studies. Sabina Spielrein, the lone woman among the pioneers of psychoanalysis, redressed the balance in a brilliant study of Wagnerian sexuality. In 1904, when Spielrein was eighteen, she received treatment at Jung's Zurich sanatorium, having supposedly undergone a hysterical episode while staying with her family in the city. She recovered, began studying psychology, and fell in love with Jung, who returned the affection, with predictably messy results. After seeing the *Ring*, Spielrein, who was Jewish, couched the relationship in Wagnerian metaphor. In a draft letter to Freud, who played a mediating role in the affair, she reports saying to Jung: "What distinguishes Wagner from previous composers is that his music is profoundly psychological; the moment a certain emotive note occurs, its matching melody appears." The composer "planted the demon in my soul with such terrifying clarity," she says. By "demon," she apparently means the intensity of her passion. She and Jung fantasized about a love child named Siegfried, who visited Spielrein's dreams in various guises, including that of an "Aryan-Semitic minstrel, Aoles."

In the wake of the affair with Jung, which ended in 1909, Spielrein produced a paper titled "Destruction as the Ground for Becoming," in which she studied the age-old nexus of love and death, Eros and Thanatos. This was written before Freud theorized the "death drive"; as Freud admitted in a footnote in *Beyond the Pleasure Principle*, Spielrein influenced his thinking. Unlike Freud, she does not oppose an ego-based death instinct with a sexual instinct toward life. Instead, she sees sex as necessarily destructive in itself, insofar as the lover is losing himself, or more often herself, in the beloved. Her Jungian habit of examining universal drives leads her to conclude that the animal instinct toward self-preservation goes hand in hand with death: one generation must give way to the next. In sadism, this sexual urge to destruction becomes literal. More often, though, the union of lovers involves a figurative, spiritual destruction.

Scanning literature and myth for examples, Spielrein draws liberally on Wagner. The Dutchman, cursed with eternal life, finds redemption in Senta's self-annihilating love. Brünnhilde, preparing to ride into the flames to join Siegfried, sings her great aria of obliteration and rebirth. And, of course, there is Tristan and Isolde's duet of androgynous coalescence: "You Tristan, I Isolde, no more Tristan! You Isolde, I Tristan, no more Isolde!" Spielrein writes: "With Wagner, death is often nothing other than the destroying components of the instinct of becoming." She ends with the image of the Ring falling into the Rhine—"the life power that brought about the downfall [*Untergang*]."

With this ultimately buoyant vision of life and death intertwined, Spielrein thwarts the Liebestod cult that is both solemnized and satirized in *Death in Venice*. At the same time, she grants a new kind of agency to Wagner's women, who no longer sacrifice themselves solely for the sake of redeeming the male. Male and female identities dissolve into a unified subjectivity, "I" into "we." Spielrein's fantasy of an Aryan-Jewish Siegfried child gives a glimpse of an even more radical merger: an androgyny of race, in which ethnicities undergo a mutual dissolution and assimilation.

Later in life, Spielrein returned to Rostov-on-Don, her birthplace, where she studied the psychology of child development. In the summer of 1942, at the height of the Second World War, German forces seized the city. Spielrein, who had assured friends that Germans could not have committed the atrocities attributed to them, failed to flee. During a systematic slaughter of thousands of Jews, Communists, prisoners of war, disabled people, and psychiatric patients, an SS Sonderkommando killed Spielrein and her two daughters. Tragically, her veneration of German culture blinded her to the death drive of the Nazi regime.

8

BRÜNNHILDE'S ROCK

Willa Cather and the Singer-Novel

Olive Fremstad as Isolde

F*ricka knows.*" Thea Kronborg, the magisterial young American singer at the heart of Willa Cather's 1915 novel *The Song of the Lark*, is discussing the role of Wotan's wife, in the *Ring*. Modeled on the turn-of-the-century soprano Olive Fremstad, Kronborg is bound for a starry career as a Wagner soprano, and although she has yet to essay Brünnhilde or Isolde she is winning acclaim as Venus and Elisabeth in *Tannhäuser*, as Sieglinde in *Walküre*, and as Fricka in *Rheingold*. The last role is seemingly the least interesting of the lot. "Fricka is not an alluring part," says Kronborg's friend Fred Ottenburg, who is in love with both Wagner and her.

Kronborg disagrees. "You've never heard it well done," she tells Ottenburg. "Fat German woman scolding her husband, eh? That's not my idea. Wait till you hear my *Fricka*. It's a beautiful part." She describes how her mother, in the Western town of Moonstone, Colorado, used to wear her hair "parted in the middle and done low on her neck behind, so you got the shape of her head and such a calm, white forehead." This is the look Kronborg adopts for Fricka—a picture of maternal forbearance. "It's noble music, Fred, from the first measure. There's nothing lovelier than the *wonniger Hausrath* ["blissful household," a line from *Rheingold*]. It's all such comprehensive sort of music—fateful. Of course, *Fricka knows*."

Cather has gone down in literary history as the bard of the American prairie. Her most popular novels—*O Pioneers!, My Ántonia, Death Comes for the Archbishop*—are set in the Great Plains and in the Southwestern desert, away from large urban centers. Yet Cather was also an acute observer of city culture, and few novelists have so alertly chronicled the world of opera. The backstage and audience chatter in *The Song of the Lark* rings true. Ottenburg's dismissal of Fricka can be heard at performances today, and singers who undertake the role of Fricka still endure it. The mezzo-soprano Stephanie Blythe says: "Whenever somebody asks me what I'm doing next, and I say that I'm doing Fricka, the first thing out of their mouth, ninety percent of the time, is 'God, what a harpy. What a horrible woman.' I have never had to defend a character as much as I've had to defend Fricka. And I am very keen to defend her, because I think she is an extraordinary character. Like all of Wagner's people, she is so beautifully delineated."

What does Fricka know? Kronborg does not say; she soon passes on to more mundane topics. We can surmise, though, that Wotan's wife has foreseen the fate of Valhalla, even if she may not be quite ready to articulate it. When Wotan shows her the splendid new palace of the gods, she urges him, literally and figuratively, to wake up, to see the cost of what he has made. Freia, who ensures the gods' youth, has been promised to the giants as payment. "Give it no thought," Wotan says, shrugging. When Fricka persists, Wotan reminds her that she herself begged him to build it. She confesses that she wanted the new home mainly as a way of preventing him from wandering off. "A glorious dwelling, a blissful household were meant to entice you to tarry and rest." Now the project has become a symbol of Wotan's cold ambition. "What is still sacred and good to your hearts when you men lust for power?"

That searching insight slips away. When Loge enters with news of the Ring, Fricka believes that she can use the trinket to keep her husband in line. In *Walküre*, though, she regains her far-seeingness, as she dismantles Wotan's scheme to save the gods. Her most telling point is purely one of logic: Siegmund, the putatively free hero who would win the Ring, is only an instrument of Wotan's will, and must fail. Emotional, moral, even political arguments are also brought to bear. You have broken your marital vows, Fricka says. The incestuous siblings are the fruit of your depravity. In a passage of the libretto that Wagner chose not to set, she delivers a scathing critique of male hegemony: "If mindless destruction is smashing its way through the world, wild and defiant, who but you, violent Wotan, can bear the blame for the calamity? You never shield the weak, you stand only by the strong."

Fricka enjoys a moment of wistful triumph once her indictment of Wotan is complete. Over a stately triplet rhythm, she sings, "We gods would go to our ruin were my rights not avenged, nobly and gloriously." The formerly titanic motif of Wotan's Spear sounds in quiet resignation. There follows a singular ten-bar passage for orchestra alone. It is in E-flat major, the key in which the *Ring* commenced, the primeval harmony of the Rhine, and it consists of a single upward-arching, gently aching phrase, which ascends two octaves before running into a pang of dissonance and subsiding. Largely unrelated to Wagner's leitmotif system, it appears just this once. What it represents is anyone's guess, but it might be an implicit communication of knowledge to Brünnhilde, who is watching in bewilderment. It is, perhaps, a vision of justice, bound up with a melancholy awareness of what justice will entail.

Brünnhilde's immediate impulse is to defy the gods' command. After trying and failing to save Siegmund, she intervenes successfully on behalf of Sieglinde, who is pregnant with Siegfried. Her disobedience brings down Wotan's wrath, and she loses the godly part of her nature. Through the tribulations of *Götterdämmerung*, she learns of what must come to pass—the end of the gods. The key to Kronborg's enigmatic remark "*Fricka knows*" is perhaps to be found in Brünnhilde's final monologue: "All things, all things, all things I know."

In the annals of literary Wagnerism, Willa Cather occupies a category of her own. Among major authors, only Thomas Mann knew his Wagner better, and he lacked Cather's acumen on the subject of singers. Like Mann, Cather uses the composer both diegetically and non-diegetically, to take terms from the analysis of sound in film. In some cases, we are hearing Wagner "on camera," as part of the milieu of the story. In others, he is felt behind the scenes, providing narrative threads and verbal motifs.

Cather's Wagnerism, like Mann's, intersects with questions of gender and sexuality. The author's passions were directed almost entirely toward women, and for decades she shared a home with the editor and advertising copywriter Edith Lewis, in a "Boston marriage" of the kind depicted in Henry James's *The Bostonians*. Averse to conventional femininity from an early age, she dressed in men's clothes as a teenager and signed her name "William Cather." But she was no feminist in the modern sense. Even as she exalted exceptional women, she often lacked sympathy for ordinary ones, and scorned feminists themselves. Nonetheless, figures like Kronborg, Alexandra in *O Pioneers!*, and the title character of *My Ántonia* show a striking independence of spirit, defining themselves not by their love lives but by their work. Cather's heroines, like Wagner's, radiate power within a male social order.

Mann, in his youth, tended toward the political right. So did Cather throughout her life. Her writing is not free of stereotypical portraits of Jews, African-Americans, and Native Americans. There is racist talk of the "world's masters" and of "beauty-making Latin races . . . rotten at heart." At the turn of the century, the lion of the left was William Jennings Bryan, who wished to overthrow the industrial titans and return government to the people. Bryan was a Nebraskan like Cather, but she preferred William McKinley, the well-padded protector of the moneyed classes. In 1897, Cather applied a lofty adjective to a parade given in President McKinley's honor: "It was so gigantic, this elephantine glee of the multitude, this transcendent passion of patriotism before which everything else is dwarfed and pale. It was like a mighty Wagnerian chorus."

To call Cather a reactionary, though, is to miss the oblique radicalism of her work, which subverts the iconography of the American West even as it rhapsodizes its plains, canyons, and deserts. She resisted the triumphalism of the American Gilded Age, the racially inflamed rhetoric of Manifest Destiny, and instead looked to the land as a refuge from a grasping, devouring present. David Porter notes how often Cather fastened her gaze on towering masses of rock: the mesas occupied by Native American peoples (the Blue Mesa in *The Professor's House*, Acoma in *Death Comes for the Archbishop*), the promontory of Quebec City (*Shadows on the Rock*), the "Enchanted Bluff" that a group of Nebraska boys long to ascend. No wonder she felt such fondness for Brünnhilde, the Valkyrie who sleeps on a high rock within a ring of fire. In Cather's fiction, such isolation is not necessarily tragic: it is the essential condition of the Romantic spirit, incarnated in the ungovernable figure of the author herself.

CATHER ON THE PLAINS

The Willa Cather Memorial Prairie

Red Cloud, Nebraska, where Cather spent much of her youth, is a rural town that retains much of its turn-of-the-century character, mainly because the writer's fame has encouraged the preservation of older homes and commercial buildings. You can tour the one-and-a-half-story frame house where the Cather family lived; you can visit the second-story opera house where she fell in love with the theater; you can drive out to the rural cemetery where her paternal grandparents are buried. A few miles to the south is a patch of land known as the Willa Cather Memorial Prairie, which has been restored to something like its original state. It has the feeling of a place untouched by modern life—an immemorial zone of grass, trees, water, and wind. Such places lingered in Cather's mind, and they took on Wagnerian hues. In *My Ántonia*, she wrote of the sun-soaked atmosphere of late afternoon: "That hour always had the exultation of victory, of triumphant ending, like a hero's death—heroes who died young and gloriously."

Cather was born in 1873, in Back Creek Valley, near Winchester, Virginia. Three of her uncles had fought for the Confederacy in the Civil War, and several of the family's African-American servants had been enslaved in her great-grandparents' household. (Cather brought their histories to life in her final novel, *Sapphira and the Slave Girl*.) Charles Cather, the author's father, managed a sheep farm; when the barn burned, in 1883, the family moved to Nebraska, following other members of the Cather clan. They settled in Red Cloud, on the high plains near the Kansas border. Cather remained there until she graduated from high school, in 1890. She then moved to Lincoln, Nebraska, where she enrolled in the state university.

After the lush gentility of Virginia, Nebraska was a blow to the senses. Cather recalled: "I felt a good deal as if we had come to the end of everything— it was a kind of erasure of personality." Yet she soon made peace with her strange new life: erasure permitted self-reinvention. And Red Cloud was by no means a cultural wasteland. As she rode her pony from farm to farm, she found tenacious clusters of immigrants: Swedes, Danes, Norwegians, Czechs, and Germans. She gained access to European literature through Charles and Fannie Wiener, the one originally from Bohemia and the other from France. Their library had books in French and German, and Mrs. Wiener would read to Willa from them. In the late-period story "Old Mrs. Harris," the Wieners become the Rosens, German Jews whose copy of *Faust* excites a Catheresque young neighbor.

The immigrants brought their music with them. For a year or two, Cather took piano lessons from an eccentric German named Schindelmeisser, who inspired the character of Professor Wunsch, in *The Song of the Lark*—a dissolute but impassioned musician who discovers Thea Kronborg's talent. Cather had little patience for practicing and would instead quiz her teacher about the Old World. "Qvestions! Qvestions! Alvays qvestions!" Schindelmeisser reportedly exclaimed. Cather scholarship has little else to say about him, but the name is one that appears often in the Wagner literature. Louis Schindelmeisser (1811–1864) was a composer, clarinetist, and conductor who met Wagner as a student in Leipzig and promoted his cause in the 1850s, conducting *Tannhäuser*, *Lohengrin*, and *Rienzi* in Wiesbaden and Darmstadt. An examination of newspaper archives, census records, telephone directories, and shipping manifests reveals that Schindelmeisser's son Albert was the one who taught Cather, in the course of a meandering, downward-spiraling American career.

He was born Albert Gustav Balthasar Schindelmeisser, in 1842, in Pest, where his father was then based. He came to America in 1862, just before his father presented *Rienzi*, with Wagner in attendance. By 1867 he had obtained a post teaching music and modern languages at Lawrence University, in Wisconsin. In an article for *The Lawrence Collegian*, Schindelmeisser wrote, "Of all arts music is the most pure and elevated, the most ennobling in its influences." By 1870, however, he had left Lawrence, establishing a pattern of being unwilling or unable to stay in one place for any length of time. He worked in Kansas and Iowa, variously as a musician, teacher, music-store proprietor, and piano tuner; he directed music at the Funke Opera House in Lincoln, Nebraska; and, in 1884 and 1885, he came to Red Cloud. An item about an event at the Baptist church, to which the Cathers belonged, said, "Mr Schindlemeisser, at the piano, showed himself master of the situation and called forth loud applause." By 1886, he was back in Kansas. After that, the trail grows thin. Notices of unclaimed letters suggest that he passed through Kansas City and Macon, Missouri. He is glimpsed in Nashville as late as 1898: "Schindelmeisser A, piano tuner." The name does not appear in the 1900 census.

Cather's sketch of Wunsch in *The Song of the Lark* helps to explain why Schindelmeisser drifted into oblivion. The professor is an unkempt man who "came from God knew where," lacking social graces and often the worse for drink. His flushed face and bloodshot eyes make mothers nervous about placing their children in his care. But something about the motion of his hands seems "alive, impatient, even sympathetic." Wunsch's roughness eases when he speaks of the Old World: he remembers hearing Clara Schumann play and a great Spanish-born contralto sing (almost certainly Pauline Viardot). He does not name Wagner. As a teacher, he is alert to Thea's "power of application, her rugged will," and instills in her ideas of spirit, fantasy, expression. When his alcoholic binges force him to leave town, he gives his pupil a precious score of Gluck's *Orfeo ed Euridice*.

Later, a card arrives from Kansas, signed "A. Wunsch." That is the last anyone hears of him. The Kansas postmark matches Schindelmeisser's itinerary.

Although the Red Cloud Opera House was far too small for Wagner—operettas on the order of *The Bohemian Girl* and *The Mikado* were its usual fare—Cather could have read about the composer in her neighbors' libraries. In *The Song of the Lark*, Kronborg is seen perusing Reverend H. R. Haweis's 1884 book *My Musical Memories*, which heaps praise on Wagner. Later in the novel, Kronborg remembers having learned of the *Ring* from that source. Cather may have done the same. It is noteworthy that Haweis—a liberal-minded Anglican cleric who wrote copiously on music—compares the music dramas to the kind of wilderness scene that Cather loved: "A vista of mountains and valleys is suddenly opened up, and pressing forward you leave far below the murmurs of one world, and raise your enraptured eyes to the black eagle, as he wheels aloft in the golden air beyond the stainless and eternal snows." The critic Philip Kennicott observes that Cather often responds less to Wagner's narratives or his psychological states than to "the place where his dramas transpire"—to his musical evocation of semi-mythic landscapes. That veneration of the land is evident in the early poem "White Birch in Wyoming," where a solitary tree becomes "Brunhilda, girdled by the burning sand."

Cather's early encounters with Wagner made a strong enough impression that she dramatized them in her later fiction. She even wrote about a performance she failed to attend. In the spring of 1895, at the end of her college years, she traveled to Chicago to see the touring company of the Met, which was in residence at the Auditorium, Sullivan and Adler's Bayreuthian palace. Cather got a good helping of Verdi but fell sick with pneumonia before her scheduled *Lohengrin*.

Memories of that expedition inform Cather's 1935 novel *Lucy Gayheart*. The heroine, a naïve, ill-fated young singer, attends the same Met series in Chicago and makes it to the *Lohengrin* that Cather missed. Sitting beside Lucy is Harry, a sturdy Nebraskan who will soon ask for her hand in marriage. In a haze of Wagner, Lucy's thoughts drift instead to her voice teacher, Clement Sebastian, who has an almost vampiric hold on her. "The first measures caught her unaware. Before the first act was half over she was longing to be alone; this wasn't the kind of opera to be hearing with Harry. She found herself leaning away from him as far as possible. The music kept bringing back things she used to feel in Sebastian's studio; belief in an invisible, inviolable world." Here is a variation on the familiar scene of Wagnerian seduction, with the music leading a woman away from a suitable male and toward a dangerous one.

Back in Lincoln, Cather heard Theodore Thomas and the Chicago Symphony in a program that included Dvořák's *New World* Symphony and music from the *Ring*. "It was a great day for me," she later wrote. Thea Kronborg attends more or less the same concert in *The Song of the Lark*. The Dvořák sweeps her away, summoning the "immeasurable yearning of all flat lands." Wagner's Entry of the Gods into Valhalla has less impact, at least consciously. "Too tired to follow the orchestra with much understanding, she crouched down in her seat and closed her eyes. The cold, stately measures of the Walhalla music rang out, far away; the rainbow bridge throbbed out into the air, under it the wailing of the Rhine daughters and the singing of the Rhine. But Thea was sunk in twilight; it was all going on in another world. So it happened that with a dull, almost listless ear she heard for the first time that troubled music, ever-darkening, ever-brightening, which was to flow through so many years of her life."

Cather finally witnessed a full-length Wagner opera in 1897, after moving to Pittsburgh to edit a women's magazine. Walter Damrosch's New York opera company came to town for a week, and Cather, who had proved herself a deft, blunt critic while still in college, had much to say. Her reviews for the *Pittsburgh Daily Reader* and the *Nebraska State Journal* range from pro-forma tributes to Wagner's achievement—"the feeling of the mystical and the supernatural" in *Lohengrin*, the "great ethical conflict" of *Tannhäuser*—to tart remarks about the singing and the staging. Not unlike Mark Twain at Bayreuth, she wonders whether it would be better for the singers to stay silent and "let the eternal conflict of the flesh and the spirit go on in the orchestra, let that never-to-be-satisfied German conscience work out its destiny in music."

A trip to Bayreuth was not in Cather's future, but she heard tell of the festival from Ethelbert Nevin, a Pittsburgh-based composer and pianist who had won fame for sophisticated parlor pieces like *Narcissus* and *The*

Rosary. A onetime student of Hans von Bülow, Nevin adored Wagner and made a sideline of explicating his work. Cather's 1925 story "Uncle Valentine" memorializes Nevin as Valentine Ramsay, a popular composer who is suffering through a broken marriage. One rhapsodic passage suggests the flavor of Wagnerian conversation in Nevin's Pittsburgh circle: "Suddenly, in the low cut between the hills across the river, we saw a luminousness, throbbing and phosphorescent, a ghostly brightness with mists streaming about it and enfolding it, struggling to quench it. We knew it was the moon, but we could see no form, no solid image; it was a flowing, surging, liquid gleaming; now stronger, now softer. 'The Rhinegold!' murmured Valentine and Aunt Charlotte in one breath."

The true revelation came in 1899, when the Met brought its *Lohengrin* and *Walküre* to Pittsburgh. The casts included some of the foremost singers of the day: Lillian Nordica, Jean and Édouard de Reszke, Ernestine Schumann-Heink, Lilli Lehmann, Andreas Dippel, Marie Brema, and Anton van Rooy. Cather found much less to complain about than she had in 1897, and her reviews show that she had been giving more thought to the operas. Having read Shaw's *The Perfect Wagnerite*, she cites his observation that in Act II of *Walküre* Wotan is bound by laws that he knows to be obsolete. "How much more terrible it is to be a helpless god than to be a helpless man," she says. There is an "inexorable law" that "binds and fetters in Walhalla just as it does in Pittsburgh or in Lincoln." The characters of *Lohengrin* are also seen in contemporary terms: "Poor, dull Elsa was a German lady of a philosophical bent of mind and she wanted a name for everything and could not believe in a joy which she could not analyze."

At times, Cather abandons critical discourse for a more novelistic style. She constructs her own dramatic scenes, juxtaposing the grandeur of the performances with glimpses of the singers in mortal guise. After *Walküre*, she sees a familiar face in the streetcar: "His coat collar was turned up, his linen crumpled, the make-up still discolored his eyes, his face was damp with perspiration, and he looked gray and drawn and tired. It was Herr Anton Van Rooy, late of Walhalla, tired as a laborer from the iron mills." Walking outside during an intermission, she hears Brema practicing her "Hi-yo": "The night was murky and starless; only the red lamps of the Hotel Henry and the line of river lights above Mount Washington were visible; on every side rose the tall black buildings that shut out the sounds of the streets. Those free, unfettered notes seemed to cut the blackness and the silence, seemed to pierce the clouds which lay over the city and reach the stars and the blue space of heaven behind, and to carry me up with them."

The charisma of the diva dominated Cather's theatrical vision. She had praised Sarah Bernhardt for "kindling the latent warmth in us, putting around our weary workaday life that brightness and halo which only genius can give." She had imagined from afar the acting duel between Bernhardt and Eleonora Duse, setting the latter's "lofty and spiritualized passions" against the former's more elemental art—"like red lava torn up from the bowels of the earth." Of the soprano Emma Calvé, she said, "You felt as if you should have brought a chaperone . . . The woman can't look at you without flirting atrociously." Such visceral responses back up Terry Castle's concept of "lesbian diva worship," in which "the diva's passion is a mirror: a fluid, silvery form in which desire itself can at times be recognized . . . a poignant, often thrilling token of homoerotic possibility."

WAGNER MATINÉES

Music resounds in Cather's fiction from the start. Her first published story, "Peter," tells of a violinist from Prague who experiences desolation on the prairie, soaking himself in alcohol and wallowing in Old World memories. Before he commits suicide, he smashes his beloved violin, so that his excessively thrifty son won't sell it. The character is based on Francis Sadilek, a Bohemian violinist turned Nebraska farmer, whose suicide was long remembered in Red Cloud. There may also be a trace of the dilapi-

dated Schindelmeisser. Peter once heard Liszt perform in Prague; Schindelmeisser would have had memories of Liszt visiting his father.

Cather's debut collection of stories, *The Troll Garden*, published in
1905, dwells on the pleasures and perils of the artistic life, with Wagner
evidencing both. In "A Death in the Desert," a tubercular soprano who
had once been slated to sing Brünnhilde lives out her last days in a remote
place out west, wistfully remembering her affair with an Ethelbert Nevin–
like composer. In "The Garden Lodge," Caroline Noble, a musically gifted
millionaire's wife, is drawn to a Wagner tenor who has been staying in a
lodge on her property. The possibility of an indiscretion increases markedly when she goes to the piano to accompany him in Act I of *Walküre*.
After the singer has left, Caroline goes alone at night to the lodge and
relives a musical enchantment that had trembled on the brink of physical
consummation:

> Perhaps it was the still heat of the summer night, perhaps it was the
> heavy odours from the garden that came in through the open windows;
> but as she played there grew and grew the feeling that he was there,
> beside her, standing in his accustomed place. In the duet at the end of
> the first act she heard him clearly: "*Thou art the Spring for which I sighed
> in Winter's cold embraces.*" Once as he sang it, he had put his arm about
> her, his one hand under her heart, while with the other he took her right
> from the keyboard, holding her as he always held *Sieglinde* when he
> drew her toward the window.

The Cather scholar John H. Flannigan comments that this solitary re-
enactment of the Siegmund-Sieglinde duet is not so much a woman's
yearning for male potency as an open-ended, ungendered reverie of sexual
possibility—"anything that one chose to believe or to desire," as Caroline
says. Same-sex desire is not far below the surface, and it becomes visible in
"Paul's Case," the most famous of Cather's early stories. Paul is a familiar
fin-de-siècle type: the aesthetic young man for whom art is the sole reality
amid a world of "stupid and ugly things." We can read between the lines
when Paul's night on the town with a college boy begins "in the confiding
warmth of a champagne friendship" and ends with a parting "singularly
cool." Wagner is probably present as Paul gazes rapt upon a portly German
singer who, with an orchestra behind her, becomes a "veritable queen of

Romance." A little like Dorian Gray, Paul lacks understanding of the art he holds dear; he experiences it as atmosphere, luxury. His death by suicide is a hollow Liebestod.

"A Wagner Matinée," which precedes "Paul's Case" in *The Troll Garden*, tells an entirely different story about listening to Wagner—one far removed from the glamour of artists' lives. The tale is a landmark in Cather's early output, bringing together her favorite themes of art and landscape. It is also emblematic of the prewar Wagnerian heyday, attesting to the composer's global reach. Like W. E. B. Du Bois's "Of the Coming of John" and the later chapters of Mann's *Buddenbrooks*, it belongs to a category that might be termed Wagnerian Utopia Revoked. A figure who feels confined or oppressed by society finds in Wagner a momentary sense of liberation that subsequent events foreclose.

The story had its origin in a coincidence. One day in Pittsburgh, Cather received a letter from a woman in western Nebraska and then went to see a Wagner matinée—probably a Pittsburgh Symphony concert in March 1903, under Victor Herbert's direction. "The story was all worked out before I left the hall," Cather wrote. She would picture how that concert might have spoken to a musically attuned person who had been consigned to a harsh existence out on the plains. When "A Wagner Matinée" appeared, Nebraskans accused Cather of exaggerating the deprivations of life in the state, and they had a point, as Cather's own lively childhood shows. In a revised version, she softened her picture of the woman from the plains, making her seem less downtrodden. The original version is starker and more dramatic.

Georgiana, a woman about sixty years old, has made the long journey from Nebraska to Boston in order to settle an inheritance with her nephew, Clark. She had been a Boston music teacher until the age of thirty, when she married a young man who resolved to make his fortune as a Nebraska homesteader. She is now stooped, yellowed, "semi-somnambulant." Startlingly, Clark compares her to "one of those charred, smoked bodies that firemen lift from the *débris* of a burned building." Clark takes her to Symphony Hall for a matinée. As they settle in their seats, he notes that the audience consists chiefly of women—"the color contrast of bodices past counting, the shimmer and shading of fabrics soft and firm, silky and sheer . . . all the colors that an impressionist finds in a sunlit landscape,

with here and there the dead black shadow of a frock-coat." This feminine scene has a touch of decadence—a mild American version of Aubrey
Beardsley's *The Wagnerites*.

When the first strains of the *Tannhäuser* overture are heard, Georgiana
clutches her nephew's sleeve, and a transformation begins:

> For her this singing of basses and stinging frenzy of lighter strings broke
> a silence of thirty years, the inconceivable silence of the plains. With the
> battle between the two motifs, with the bitter frenzy of the Venusberg
> theme and its ripping of strings, came to me an overwhelming sense of
> the waste and wear we are so powerless to combat. I saw again the tall,
> naked house on the prairie, black and grim as a wooden fortress; the black
> pond where I had learned to swim, the rain-gullied clay about the naked
> house; the four dwarf ash-seedlings on which the dishcloths were always
> hung to dry before the kitchen door. The world there is the flat world of
> the ancients; to the east, a cornfield that stretched to daybreak; to the
> west, a corral that stretched to sunset; between, the sordid conquests of
> peace, more merciless than those of war.

Georgiana remains impassive through the next two items, the *Tristan*
prelude and a selection from *The Flying Dutchman*. But the Prize Song
from *Meistersinger* brings tears to her cheeks. During the intermission,
she tells Clark that she had heard that music out on the prairie, from
a young German cow-puncher who had once sung in the chorus at
Bayreuth. Georgiana tried to tame this lad, bringing him into the church
and the choir, but he got into a fight and disappeared. Could Cather have
encountered such a figure around Red Cloud? In Pittsburgh she knew of a
Pastor Baehr, who had been a tutor at Wahnfried.

The second half of the matinée consists of four selections from the
Ring, ending with Siegfried's Funeral Music. The pioneer woman now occupies a Wagnerian infinity:

> The deluge of sound poured on and on; I never knew what she found
> in the shining current of it; I never knew how far it bore her, or past
> what happy islands, or under what skies. From the trembling of her face
> I could well believe that the Siegfried march, at least, carried her out

where the myriad graves are, out into the gray burying-grounds of the sea; or into some world of death vaster yet, where, from the beginning of the world, hope has lain down with hope, and dream with dream and, renouncing, slept.

When the concert is over, Georgiana does not move from her seat. In the revised version of the story, the musicians file out one by one, "leaving the stage to the chairs and music stands, empty as a winter cornfield." Georgiana sobs: "I don't want to go, Clark, I don't want to go!"

Clark thinks he knows what Georgiana is thinking, but Cather honors her female protagonist by pulling a veil over her. Joseph C. Murphy, in an incisive reading of the story, writes that the young man draws a contrast between "Wagner's aesthetic power and Nebraska's cultural vacuity," between "cornfield and concert hall." If we set Clark's skewed perspective aside, we see not an opposition but a confluence of music and landscape. Nebraska "becomes part of the visible image of Wagner's sound worlds," Murphy writes. The fusion seems complete with that arresting final tableau of chairs and music stands as stalks in a cornfield.

Like the inward-turned mother in Fernand Khnopff's *Listening to Schumann*, Georgiana is experiencing music in a way that eludes the male gaze. Such private awakenings were common among Wagner's female listeners. The strength of their understanding resides precisely in their reticence, their avoidance of disclosure. At the intermission, Clark asks, "But do you get it, Aunt Georgiana, the astonishing structure of it all?" She replies: "Who could? Why should one?" The woman whom Clark has compared to a charred corpse skewers the male mania for explanatory mastery. Any attempt to encompass the "astonishing structure of it all" will necessarily reduce the music to ordinary dimensions. Georgiana's Wagner is larger and richer than her nephew's. She doesn't "get" him, and therefore grasps him.

SIEGFRIEDS AND VALKYRIES

Willa Cather liked the writing of Sidney Lanier, and she may have come across his poem in critical praise of the Meister: "O Wagner, westward bring thy heavenly art! / No trifler thou: Siegfried and Wotan be / Names for big ballads of the modern heart." The sentiment resonates with Cather's work. Archetypes of Tristan, Isolde, Siegfried, and Brünnhilde anchor a number of her characters, bearing out her adage that "there are only two or three human stories, and they go on repeating themselves as fiercely as if they had never happened before."

An epic tone elevates Cather's first nationally published story, "Eric Hermannson's Soul," which appeared in 1900. Set in prairie terrain described as "the world's end," it tells of a young Norwegian immigrant who falls under the sway of a born-again sect and gives up his fiddle-playing. Margaret, a young woman from the East, passes through and becomes fixated on the young man, who is variously called a "dragon-slayer," "handsome as young Siegfried," and "Siegfried indeed," his hair as "yellow as the heavy wheat in the ripe of summer." His sister is assigned to the tribe of "young valkyrs." Margaret sets about civilizing him; she also pulls him away from religious rigidity and activates his raw sexual energy. In a way, the Siegfried-Brünnhilde roles are reversed: it is the woman who awakens the man and sets him free. Yet Margaret is alarmed by her "overwhelming longing," by the sense of sap rising, and backs away. Eric, on the other hand, "drew himself up to his full height and looked off to where the new day was gilding the corn-tassels and flooding the uplands with light."

That strapping image calls to mind the Western Wagner fantasies of Owen Wister. Cather never spoke about *The Virginian*, but she knew of it, having given a copy to one of her aunts in 1912. In general, she was no fan of Wister's writing, and she may have satirized him in "Eric Hermannson's Soul," in the form of Wyllis, Margaret's brother, who is sent west to toughen up. Wister, who shot to fame with his 1895 essay "The Evolution of the Cow-Puncher," had made a similar journey. In a 1915 letter, Cather maintains that the "cow-puncher's experience of the West was not the only experience possible there." She looks at the West with a different eye; she has grown up within it. She is, in a way, the true Virginian, the voyager from the East who forms her identity in solitude.

Nor did Cather share Wister's racist vision of the West as an Anglo-Saxon idyll, under threat from immigrants and cosmopolitans. Although she indulged in ethnic stereotyping, she showed generous affection for immigrant communities in Nebraska and, later, for the Hispanic and Native American cultures of the Southwest. According to Susie Thomas, Cather's novels "spoke for the Middlewestern immigrant and the woman, who had hitherto been silent, and they spoke in the language of an old culture taking root in a new land." She thus "created an alternative to the male mythology of the West."

Cather's breakthrough novel, *O Pioneers!*, published in 1913, might in part be a riposte to *The Virginian*, with the male hero displaced in favor of a female loner—the Swedish-American farmer Alexandra. She is introduced as a "tall, strong girl" with a "glance of Amazonian fierceness," her body clothed in a man's coat. While others struggle to make a living on the "wild land," the "wintry waste," Alexandra masters it, guiding her father's farm. After years on her own, she forms a partnership with a man, but marriage is not the necessary completion of her life. At the end, she is seen, as at the beginning, silhouetted against the vastness of the landscape: "She was still gazing into the west, and in her face there was that exalted serenity that sometimes came to her at moments of deep feeling."

Alexandra's brother Emil meets an unhappier fate: he falls in love with a sensuous, flirtatious married woman named Marie, and when Marie's husband discovers the two in flagrante he shoots and kills them. Their tragedy unfolds in a chapter titled "The White Mulberry Tree"—a self-contained, tightly structured narrative within a novel whose rhythms are generally looser and freer. It draws most obviously on Ovid's story of Pyramus and Thisbe, where white mulberries are stained with blood, but the Tristan legend also plays a role. In a preface to a 1925 reissue of Gertrude Hall's book *The Wagnerian Romances*, Cather let drop that she had once imitated a scene from Hall's text in one of her novels. An essay by Mary Jane Humphrey makes the case that the passage in question is Hall's free paraphrase of *Tristan*, and that the story is "The White Mulberry Tree." Emil is Tristan; Marie is Isolde; Frank, her husband, is King Mark. Act II of *Tristan* is set in a garden on a "cloudless summer night," Hall writes; Cather's tale ends in an orchard, on a "warm, breathless" summer night.

Cather's engagement with the Tristan material may go even deeper. By placing the fatal tryst in an orchard, she is following the example of the early Tristan stories. (William Morris's painting *La Belle Iseult* shows the heroine with a bowl of oranges nearby.) Frank's murderous response, likewise, evokes the more brutal King Mark of Malory and Tennyson. To this is added a Romantic fetishism of love and death. Emil is untroubled by the idea that one might lead to the other: "The heart, when it is too much alive, aches for that brown earth, and ecstasy has no fear of death."

The Rhinemaidens swim under Alberich's gaze in Henri Fantin-Latour's *Les Filles du Rhin*, inspired by the premiere of Wagner's *Ring* at Bayreuth in 1876. (© RMN-Grand Palais / Art Resource, NY)

Édouard Manet's *Music in the Tuileries*, 1862, with Charles Baudelaire and other Wagnéristes huddled on the far left (© National Gallery, London / Art Resource, NY)

Paul Cézanne's *Young Girl at the Piano*, 1868–69, originally called *Overture to "Tannhäuser"* (Erich Lessing / Art Resource, NY)

Edward Burne-Jones's *Laus Veneris*, 1873–78: Tannhäuser outside a Pre-Raphaelite Venusberg (Laing Art Gallery, Newcastle-upon-Tyne, UK, © Tyne & Wear Archives & Museums / Bridgeman Images)

LEFT: Albert Pinkham Ryder's *Siegfried and the Rhine Maidens*, 1888–1891 (The National Gallery of Art)

RIGHT: John Singer Sargent's *Rehearsal of the Pasdeloup Orchestra at the Cirque d'Hiver*, circa 1879 (Art Institute of Chicago)

The Bayreuth Festspielhaus as it appeared around 1900. The novelist Colette compared it to a gasometer. (Library of Congress)

The National Farmers' Bank in Owatonna, Minnesota, designed by Louis Sullivan. "He would often try to sing the leitmotifs for me," Frank Lloyd Wright said of Sullivan. (Photograph by author)

Odilon Redon's images of Parsifal, 1891 and 1912: the initiate and the sage
(LEFT: Art Institute of Chicago; RIGHT: Erich Lessing / Art Resource, NY)

Jean Delville's mystically charged *Tristan et Yseult*, 1887 (© Royal Museums of Fine Arts of
Belgium, Brussels; photograph by J. Geleyns—Art Photography / Artists Rights Society)

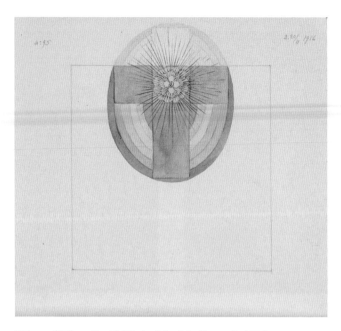

Hilma af Klint, *Parsifal Series*, No. 95, Group 3, 1916 (Moderna Museet, Stockholm)

Franz Marc, *Fate of the Animals*, 1913 (Kunstmuseum Basel)

Vladimir Tatlin's design for *The Flying Dutchman*, 1915–1918
(Erich Lessing / Art Resource, NY)

"O wounding-wonderful holy Spear": the shattered Wagnerism of Anselm Kiefer's
Parsifal III, 1973 (© Tate, London / Art Resource, NY)

Keanu Reeves striking a Parsifalian pose in *The Matrix*, 1999

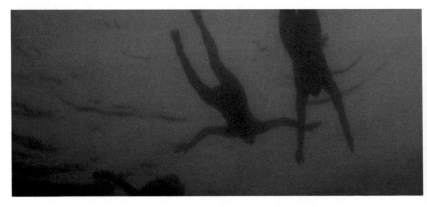

Native American Rhinemaidens in Terrence Malick's *The New World*, 2005

And when Marie's body is found—like Isolde, she briefly survives her beloved, and dies draped across his body—her face has "a look of ineffable content . . . as if in a day-dream or a light slumber." She feels Isolde's "highest bliss" as she expires.

Behind this human catastrophe lies the indifferent natural world: "Two white butterflies from Frank's alfalfa-field were fluttering in and out among the interlacing shadows; diving and soaring, now close together, now far apart; and in the long grass by the fence the last wild roses of the year opened their pink hearts to die." It is the atmosphere of the Good Friday Spell, where all creation gives thanks before fading away. And beyond that is the majestic indifference of the land itself, which humanity occupies, as Alexandra says at the end, "for a little while."

The Wagnerian dimensions of *O Pioneers!* become clear in a letter Cather wrote to her friend Elizabeth Sergeant in 1913, just after she met the soprano who would engender her next novel: "I went up to see Fremstad last week and ever since I've been choked by things unutterable. If one could write all that that battered Swede makes one know, that would be worth while. Lord, but she is like the women on the Divide! The suspicious, defiant, far-seeing pioneer eyes . . . And Oh, Elsie Sergeant, her apartment is just like Alexandra's house!"

FREMSTAD

In 1906, *McClure's*, the most culturally ambitious and politically outspoken American magazine of the day, hired Cather as an editor. She moved to New York, settled in Greenwich Village, and began attending performances at the Met. Her position at *McClure's* afforded access to leading artists, and in 1913 she published an article titled "Three American Singers," profiling Louise Homer, Geraldine Farrar, and Olive Fremstad. Fremstad is by far the most interesting of the trio. She is a "great and highly individual talent" who floats far above the workaday opera business, in the "frozen heights." Her singing deals not just in emotions but also in ideas. She is solitary, obsessive, elusive. She is quoted saying: "We are born alone, we make our way alone, we die alone."

A native of Stockholm, Fremstad came to the United States with her parents when she was a child, and spent part of her youth in the northern prairie town of Saint Peter, Minnesota—a shift hardly less abrupt than Cather's to Nebraska. One passage of Cather's *McClure's* article reads more like oblique autobiography: "Circumstances have never helped Mme. Fremstad. She grew up in a new, crude country where there was neither artistic stimulus nor discriminating taste . . . She fought her own way toward the intellectual centers of the world. She wrung from fortune the one profit which adversity sometimes leaves with strong natures—the power to conquer."

Fremstad's father was a revival preacher, and as a budding musician she led congregations from the organ. In the early nineties, she made her way first to New York and then to Berlin, where she studied with Lilli Lehmann, a veteran of the 1876 *Ring*. Initially cast in lower-lying contralto and mezzo parts, Fremstad made her Bayreuth debut in 1896, as the Rhinemaiden Flosshilde and as the Valkyrie Schwertleite. (She may have met Luranah Aldridge, before the latter fell ill.) Returning to New York in 1903, she caused a sensation as Kundry in the Met's *Parsifal*. She then made a tricky transition to soprano parts, becoming the Met's reigning Brünnhilde and Isolde. She first sang the latter role under Mahler's direction, and later with Toscanini. Those notoriously demanding conductors found a kindred spirit in Fremstad, who spent countless hours studying her parts and plotting how she would move onstage.

In discussing Fremstad's performances, Cather divulges her own understanding of the Wagner heroines. On Kundry: "She is a summary of the history of womankind. [Wagner] sees in her an instrument of temptation, of salvation, and of service; but always an instrument, a thing driven and employed. Like Euripides, he saw her as a disturber of equilibrium, whether on the side of good or evil, an emotional force that continually deflects reason, weary of her activities, yet kept within her orbit by her own nature and the nature of men." On Brünnhilde: "Mme. Fremstad's idea is that the war-maiden in the first opera of the Ring is a girl, not a matron . . . The Valkyr music is restless, turbulent, energetic. The Valkyrs' ride is the music of a pack of wild young things." Cather is alert to gender ambiguity: Brünnhilde's body is "straight and athletic, like a boy's." These interpretations cannot be described as feminist: Cather accepts at face value Kundry's transition to mute subservience, Brünnhilde's evolution toward a more contained womanliness. Still, the girlish-boyish wildness palpably excites her most.

For ordinary mortals, Fremstad was never an easy collaborator. In the 1913–14 season, she quarreled with the Met's general manager, Giulio Gatti-Casazza, who decided that she was worth neither the expense nor the effort. In the spring of 1914, she announced that she would leave the Met roster. Her final performance, in *Lohengrin*, was a legendary occasion, precipitating a twenty-minute ovation. No less fabled was the brief, enigmatic speech that she gave at the curtain. It ended: "My one aim has always been to give you of my best, my very best. May we meet again where there is eternal peace and harmony. Good-bye!" She was only forty-three, and might have gone on singing at least for another decade. But the outbreak of the First World War ruled out a shift to Europe, and a Met comeback never materialized. The abruptness of her exit, and the curtness of her farewell, added to her aura of mystery.

Fremstad's personal life was even more obscure. She married twice, but both relationships were dissolved after a few years. In interviews, she declared that serious artists should remain unattached. Her most stable relationship was with a woman: Mary Watkins, later Mary Watkins Cushing, who became enraptured by Fremstad while still in her teens. Cushing was

Fremstad in Maine

hired as Fremstad's secretary, and soon became her live-in companion. In a memoir with the Wagnerian title *The Rainbow Bridge*, Cushing is candid about her crush on Fremstad. Describing her state of mind before the initial meeting, she says that she "felt like a medieval esquire in vigil on the eve of knighthood." She served, above all, as a "buffer"—Fremstad's word—against the outside world. Isolde now had a Brangäne at her side.

Cather got to know Fremstad better than most. After the *McClure's* article came out, the two women met many times during the singer's final Met season. In June 1914, Cather visited Little Walhalla, Fremstad's summer home in Maine. The novelist watched in amazement as her dream character—"the greatest artist of her time . . . and a Swede off the Divide"—acted exactly as she would have wanted a pioneer Wagnerian to behave. "She fished as if she had no other means of getting food; cleaned all the fish, swam like a walrus, rowed, tramped, cooked, watered her garden . . . It was the grandest show of human vigor and grace I've ever watched." In a letter to Cather, Fremstad wrote of her pleasure in seclusion: "The woods are so strong, peaceful and quiet—so different from this chattering humanity around us." Behind the diva façade, Cather saw a self-sufficient girl from a rural background, not unlike herself.

The Wagner singer, emitting ear-splitting sounds while inhabiting superhuman roles, was irresistible to writers of fin-de-siècle fiction. For those of an idealistic bent, Heldentenors and dramatic sopranos represented a striving at the limit of human possibility. The heroine of George Moore's *Evelyn Innes* makes a smooth transition from the service of Wagner to the service of God. Leonora Brunna, the Spanish Wagner soprano in Vicente Blasco Ibáñez's 1900 novel *Entre naranjos* (*In the Orange Grove*), casts a disconcerting spell on a handsome, callow young man: she is "the arrogant Valkyrie, the strong-minded and valiant female, ready to slap the slightest impudence and handle him like a little boy." Satirists relished the notion of modern people walking off the streets of Berlin or New York and putting on winged helmets. Wedekind's *Kammersänger* is a cynical egoist, leaving human wreckage in his wake. Henry Céard's 1906 novel *Terrains à vendre au bord de la mer* (*Land for Sale by the Sea*) tells of a soprano who hopes to absorb Wagnerian vibrations in a town on the Breton coast, her

attention drawn there by a journalist who has dubbed a local rock formation the Castle of Tristan.

American authors delighted in the strangeness and loucheness of the
Wagner milieu, which allowed them to enter generally forbidden territory. Gertrude Atherton's *Tower of Ivory*, published in 1910, describes the
rise and fall of Margarethe Styr, who leads a life of prostitution before
reinventing herself as a Wagner soprano. Styr has a doomed affair with
a feckless young British diplomat, who, it is clear, has gay longings. Rather
than face a life without her beloved, she arranges that her immolation at the
end of a performance of *Götterdämmerung* be done with real fire. Although
Tower of Ivory seems ludicrous today, Atherton was notable for creating
independent-minded female characters, sometimes with lesbian overtones
attached.

James Huneker, the flamboyant New York critic who christened *Parsifal* a Black Mass, wrote several singer-stories, one of them inspired by
Fremstad. He first heard the singer at Bayreuth in 1896, and wrote in his
review, "Our Olive deserved the crown." His interest was not merely musical: that summer he and Fremstad either had a brief affair or were on the
verge of one. He fictionalized the incident in a story titled "The Last of
the Valkyries," later republished as "Venus or Valkyr," where he represents
himself as a superficial Wagnerite torn between an American singer and a
Romanian sophisticate. (The latter changes tables in a café to avoid having to sit next to an odd-smelling Joséphin Péladan.) In Huneker's later
novel *Painted Veils*, a soprano named Easter Brandes, bewitching to men
and women alike, moves through a decadent milieu in which the names
of Huysmans, Wilde, Nietzsche, and Wagner are dropped with numbing regularity. Although Brandes resembles Fremstad in a few ways—she
studies with Lilli Lehmann, as does Kronborg in *The Song of the Lark*—
her coldly ambitious personality, described as a composite of "harps, anvils, and granite," is very unlike Fremstad's.

Marcia Davenport's 1936 novel *Of Lena Geyer*, a late and sophisticated
entry in the genre, portrays a Fremstad-like diva who approaches her art
with almost comical seriousness. She, too, is a Lehmann pupil, and like
Fremstad she puts her career ahead of any enduring physical relationship.
The way she sings a certain phrase in *Tristan* reveals that "no human love
could touch Lena Geyer; the woman had consecrated herself to a world

of superhuman ideals." She does, however, form a seemingly platonic attachment with a female devotee, Elsie deHaven, who trails Geyer from performance to performance. "The voice poured into me, and from that moment it became the one thing I cared to live for," deHaven says of her first encounter with the singer. Eventually, she becomes Geyer's live-in secretary, as Mary Cushing did for Fremstad. Speaking to the book's narrator, deHaven feels compelled to clarify that this "strange, almost passionate friendship" was, contrary to rumor, a pure and innocent one. In what may be an esoteric inside joke, Geyer is seen weeping over a copy of Cather's *My Ántonia*.

The pitfall of the singer-novel is a tendency toward insiderish chattiness. Cather wrote: "I hate most musical novels—a compound of a story and a lot of musical criticism which never blend." She cites *Evelyn Innes* as one such failure. Although she made no direct comment on Atherton or Huneker's work, she presumably would have disdained their indulgence in potboiler melodrama and overripe decadence, respectively. Her aim was to give a full-length portrait of a singer as artist, and in so doing she accomplished something greater. Joan Acocella describes *The Song of the Lark* as the "first completely serious female *Künstlerroman*, the first portrait-of-an-artist-as-a-young-woman in which the heroine's artistic development is the whole story, with sex an incidental matter."

KRONBORG

The remarkable thing about *The Song of the Lark* is the way Cather seamlessly interweaves Fremstad's early life with her own story. Thea Kronborg, like Fremstad, is a preacher's daughter of Scandinavian descent, who provides musical accompaniment for her father's sermons. But the town of Moonstone is a replica of Red Cloud, down to the little attic room that Thea makes her own. Thea is musical and bookish, but, like the young Cather, she runs free in open land. On a trip to Wyoming, she sees the old trail of the Forty-Niners, the gold-seekers who went west to California in 1849, and finds herself on a virtual stage set for one of her future Wagner performances:

> The road they followed was a wild and beautiful one. It led up and up,
> by granite rocks and stunted pines, around deep ravines and echoing

Jules Breton, The Song of the Lark

gorges. The top of the ridge, when they reached it, was a great flat plain, strewn with white boulders, with the wind howling over it . . . To the west one could see range after range of blue mountains, and at last the snowy range, with its white, windy peaks, the clouds caught here and there on their spurs. Again and again Thea had to hide her face from the cold for a moment. The wind never slept on this plain, the old man said. Every little while eagles flew over.

This grand American prospect doubles as a premonition of Kronborg's upward path.

Professor Wunsch is the first to recognize the extent of her gift—her "nature-voice . . . breathed from the creature and apart from language"— but for some time that gift remains a secret between them. When Wunsch departs, Thea takes over many of his duties, and she seems destined for a career of teaching and occasional performing. Then she has a stroke of luck: a freight train conductor who had hoped to marry her dies in an accident, leaving her money in his will. She uses this money to study piano in Chicago, where a pianist of Hungarian ancestry, Andor Harsanyi, guides her toward singing. Harsanyi proceeds to tell his friend Theodore Thomas about the promising talent he has found. An ordinary novelist would have staged a "star is born" moment, with Thomas crowning Thea the singer of the future. Cather lets the scene hang: the two men veer away to other topics, some of their dialogue drawn from Thomas's memoirs. Thea is left to make her own way, step by halting step.

Cather passes over the technicalities of Thea's development—her studies with a Chicago voice teacher, further work in New York—and instead focuses on the social fabric of high culture that envelops her. She meets the wealthy Fred Ottenburg, who has inherited a love of Wagner from his mother, a bohemian personality with Continental connections. Mrs. Ottenburg is said to be "one of the group of young women who followed Wagner about in his old age, keeping at a respectful distance, but receiving now and then a gracious acknowledgment that he appreciated their homage." When Wagner died, she "took to her bed and saw no one for a week." Fred is a regular at Bayreuth, although his Wagnerian inclinations are counterbalanced by a healthy heterosexual regimen of "ballgames, prizefights, and horse-races."

After two years in Chicago, Thea has failed to make any sort of breakthrough. She is on the point of giving up when Fred invites her to Panther Canyon, Arizona, where remains of Native American cliff dwellings can be found. Thea, having heard tales of the cliff dwellers back home, jumps at the chance. She first goes there alone, with Fred joining her later. She takes shelter in one of the ancient dwellings—"a nest in a high cliff, full of sun." By the end of the summer, a transformation has occurred: she has acquired personality, vision, confidence.

This material has little to do with Fremstad and everything to do with Cather, who had undergone a momentous experience on a trip to Arizona and New Mexico in 1912. The magnificence of the setting seized her at once: "The most beautiful country I have ever seen anywhere . . . The Lord set the stage so splendidly there." The site she calls Panther Canyon in *The Song of the Lark* is actually Walnut Canyon, near Flagstaff, where the Sinagua people built cliff dwellings into the sheer rock walls of a deep and narrow gorge. Enthralled by such places, Cather felt a surge of creative renewal. She decided to quit the magazine world and give herself to fiction full-time.

For Thea, Panther Canyon is the gateway to a new understanding of her art. Music runs through her mind, but it is a wordless, formless kind of music—"much more like a sensation than like an idea." She envisages the lives of the Sinagua and adapts to their rhythms. She thinks about their artistic efforts, their pottery and designs. Bathing in a pool at the bottom of the canyon, she realizes that art is an attempt to capture the flow of life: "In singing, one made a vessel of one's throat and nostrils and held it on one's breath, caught the stream in a scale of natural intervals."

This emphasis on sensation is thoroughly Wagnerian. In *Opera and Drama*, the composer underscores the necessity of pure feeling in the intellectually overfreighted world of art. The cult of emotion, which stems from Feuerbach, is not the same as emotionalism; rather, it envisions an art that follows the free contours of human feeling, refusing to impose the strict controls of intellect. Poetry is liberated when it enters the musical ocean, finding itself reflected in ever-heaving melodic forms. Thea's newly instinctive grasp of musical phrasing becomes the core of her future work. Almost in the same instant, her ambition revives: she forms the plan of going to Germany for further study.

When Fred arrives, they explore the canyon together, entering before sunrise to watch the light pour in: "In a moment the pine trees up on the edge of the rim were flashing with coppery fire." As they eat breakfast, Fred almost jokingly brings up the idea of marriage—"a comfortable flat in Chicago, a summer camp up in the woods, musical evenings, and a family to bring up." Thea answers: "Perfectly hideous!" Fred is undismayed; he knows better than to try to pin her down. They ascend the canyon, and after a while Fred tires and lies down under a pine tree. Thea goes clambering upward and appears in triumph at the top, waving her arm. Fred admires her "muscular energy and audacity," exuding a "personality that carried across big spaces and expanded among big things." He speaks to her, even though she cannot hear him: "You are the sort that used to run wild in Germany, dressed in their hair and a piece of skin."

The image of fire on the canyon's rim alludes to *Walküre*: Wotan placing Brünnhilde beneath a pine tree and igniting impenetrable flames. Fred is an urban Siegfried, breaking Thea's proud solitude on her rock. Tellingly, he hears a woodpecker hammering while he lies by the pine, just as Siegfried listens to the Woodbird while reclining on what Gertrude Hall describes as a "mossy couch." Thea's greeting to an eagle high above also has a Wagnerian grandiloquence: "Endeavor, achievement, desire, glorious striving of human art! From a cleft in the heart of the world she saluted it." The emphasis on will, on youthful ambition, makes one think of Professor Wunsch, whose name means "wish." Wunsch had told her: "There is only one big thing—desire." It has died in him, but he sees its glow in her. She is a "wish-maiden"—the old Icelandic name for a Valkyrie, as Cather noted in her 1899 review of *Walküre*. Wagner uses the words *Wunschmaid* and *Wunschmädchen* repeatedly in *Walküre*, making much of the idea that Brünnhilde fulfills what Wotan wishes but cannot achieve.

Thea's almost occult awareness of the canyon's silenced Native American voices affects her singing. Later, when she is performing Wagner at the Met, Fred thinks back to their time in Arizona: "You're as much at home on the stage as you were down in Panther Canyon—as if you'd just been let out of a cage. Didn't you get some of your ideas down there?" Thea nods. "Oh yes! For heroic parts, at least. Out of the rocks, out of the dead people." She says that the cliff dwellers must have been a "reserved, somber people, with only a muscular language, all their movements for a purpose: simple, strong, as if they were dealing with fate bare-handed." In a letter, Cather confirmed that the cliff dwellings had awakened Thea's "historic imagination—so necessary to a great Wagnerian singer." The composer who had once expressed sympathy for the sufferings of Native American peoples might have welcomed this association.

With Fred's encouragement, Thea embarks for Germany. Cather drafted a section of the novel describing this period, but set it aside, believing that it would "destroy the composition." (She may have been hampered by the fact that she had never been to Germany.) A few glimpses of Thea's time abroad remain: other students are said to have been "mortally afraid" of her rough ways, calling her "*die Wölfin*" (the "she-wolf"). The novel's final chapter leaps ahead a decade, to the singer's first years of stardom. Dr. Archie, the fondly supportive Moonstone town doctor, is struck by the splendor of her voice but disturbed by the sense that the plucky girl he knew exists no longer. "Thea" has become "Kronborg." Fred assures Archie that the master singer-actor they see onstage is the natural extension of the Thea of old. He cites lines of Wagner to convey her force: "*Wie im Traum ich ihn trug, / Wie mein Wille ihn wies.*" These are Wotan's words on seeing Valhalla: "As in my dream I conceived it, / Just as my will decreed it."

Kronborg reaches the apex of her art. When a soprano singing Sieglinde is indisposed, she steps in. On the first night, she "came into full possession of things she had been refining and perfecting for so long." It is not merely a musically or theatrically excellent interpretation but an embodiment of the music's spirit. "She was conscious that every movement was the right movement, that her body was absolutely the instrument of her idea." None other than Mahler is heard to say, "She seems to sing for the idea." Or, as Cather wrote in her profile of Fremstad, "The idea is so intensely experienced that it becomes emotion." Wagner's mandate in *Opera and Drama* has undergone a further modification, almost an inversion. The idea now takes precedence, except that it is indistinguishable from emotion. Kronborg cannot be merely an unthinking conduit of Wagner's music: she must reverse the compositional process, working backward from the level of technique to the inner realm of psychology and myth. Cather thus establishes the fundamental might of the singer's art.

This is also the moment at which Kronborg's understanding of her artistic persona, of her "second self," falls into place. She had long sensed another persona within her: "It was as if she had an appointment to meet the rest of herself sometime, somewhere. It was moving to meet her and she was moving to meet it." As that self comes forward, Cather's story draws to a close. In the wake of the *Walküre* triumph, the narrator announces: "Here we must leave Thea Kronborg . . . The growth of an artist is an intellectual and spiritual development which can scarcely be followed in a personal narrative." A brief epilogue gives glimpses of Kronborg's subsequent career—including her triumphant Isolde—but Cather's attention turns back to the ordinary folk in Moonstone, who marvel that such a phenomenon arose in their midst.

The Song of the Lark is heavily weighted toward Kronborg's childhood and youth. Some critics preferred the first part to the second. The critic H. L. Mencken—who considered Wagner's operas "the most stupendous works of art ever contrived by man"—said as much in his review. Cather responded that the air of anticlimax was deliberate. As an artist develops, the personality is consumed by the art, and "arrives at the vanishing point." Kronborg has gone from the "personal to the impersonal." Cather compares her to Dorian Gray: the person onstage is self-renewing, the person offstage is spent.

Later, though, Cather came to believe that the novel was flawed, and in 1937 she heavily revised it. As Jonathan Goldberg has noticed, Kronborg became a more conventional feminine character in the process. What had formerly been a "virile" voice is now said to be "warm," and the moniker "*die Wölfin*" is dropped. Originally, Fred is heard to say: "No, *that* voice will never betray. *Treulich geführt, treulich bewacht*" ["Faithfully guided, faithfully guarded"—lines from the *Lohengrin* Bridal Chorus]. That remark, suggestive of a woman wedded to her art, disappears; so does the reverberant observation "*Fricka knows.*" Most oddly, Cather cuts references to Kronborg as Isolde and Brünnhilde. To some extent, these changes can be explained as aesthetic choices: Cather is bringing the novel in line with her more oblique later manner. But Goldberg argues that Cather may also be suppressing a fraught relationship of fandom. The changes make Fremstad less recognizable as a model.

Cather's one mistake may have been the title. She wanted people to think of Jules Breton's painting *The Song of the Lark*, in which a peasant girl stares into the distance as a blood-red sun rises behind her—"a young girl's awakening to something beautiful." Unfortunately, many readers took the phrase as a description of Kronborg's vocalism. "Her song was not of the sky-lark order," Cather snapped. A better title might have been *Kronborg*—the single word that stands at the head of the final chapter. In Swedish, the name means something like "mountain fortress." Female figures in the arts have routinely been reduced to their first names, tethered as satellites to a male genius. Such was the fate of Cosima Wagner, earlier Cosima von Bülow, née Cosima Liszt. Thea's surname becomes monumental, equal in weight to those of the masters. We can picture a poster from a tour later in life: KRONBORG SINGS WAGNER.

CATHER IN THE DESERT

After *The Song of the Lark*, Cather still wrote about singers, but her perspective darkened. Awareness of the lonely later lives of performing artists—Fremstad chief among them—matched a deepening preoccupation with themes of loss and regret. *Lucy Gayheart* and "Uncle Valentine" speak of dashed hopes and unfulfilled ambitions. The 1916 story "The Diamond Mine" relates the demise of a diva named Cressida Garnet, who is patterned after Lillian Nordica, the steely feminist soprano. Nordica had died two years earlier, having been married to three men, all of whom treated her poorly. Garnet, likewise, is an exceptional talent surrounded by exploitative men. After her death, her relatives and her last husband attempt

Acoma, New Mexico

to seize a large sum of money that she had bequeathed to her longtime Greek-Jewish coach and pianist. Defeated in court, they are left to haggle over jewels, furs, and gowns—the remnants of the "diamond mine" they saw in her. The narrator sends news of this outcome to the pianist. His sage reply, with which the story ends, consists of the Rhinemaidens' lament: "*Trust and truth / only in the depths are found; / cunning and cowardice / thrive in the sun.*"

Cather's Wagnerism receded after *The Song of the Lark*, but did not disappear. One sign of her abiding interest was her commentary on Hall's *The Wagnerian Romances*. She says that she had first read that book in the "blue air of New Mexico," implying that she brought it with her on her life-changing Southwestern trip of 1912. Perhaps she was replaying Wagner in her mind as she read, for she writes: "Persons who have heard the operas sung, and beautifully sung, many times, but are now living in remote places, will find this book potent in reviving their recollections; the scenes will float before them." She congratulates Hall for reproducing "the emotional effect of one art through the medium of another art"— Wagnerism in a nutshell.

In the summer of 1925, Cather returned to New Mexico, staying in the bohemian colony at Taos. On that trip she came across an account of how two Catholic missionary priests, Jean-Baptiste Lamy and his devoted friend Joseph Machebeuf, founded the archdiocese of New Mexico in the mid-nineteenth century. That discovery led to *Death Comes for the*

Archbishop, Cather's most extraordinary work, wherein Lamy and Machebeuf are renamed Bishop Latour and Father Vaillant. Cather afterward
said: "I had all my life wanted to do something in the style of legend, which
is absolutely the reverse of dramatic treatment." As a model for the fable
style, she cites the frescoes of Puvis de Chavannes, the proto-Symbolist
master. The title comes from Hans Holbein's "Dance of Death" wood-
cuts, which, following a hallowed genre, show Death summoning men
and women both high and low, a bishop among them. Dance-of-death
narratives often have a biting satirical edge, as the pompous and the hypo-
critical are laid low. Latour, however, is an enlightened and compassionate
prelate who looks beyond Catholic dogma to a more ecumenical, multicultural understanding of his Southwestern mission.

If Cather's early novels bear the imprint of the *Ring*, this later one,
fittingly, has the air of *Parsifal*, as several scholars have inferred. Klaus P.
Stich sees in Latour's wanderings an "as yet unconscious Grail quest for
wholeness beyond the Logos that confines his Church and his office." At
one point, Latour and his Native guide take refuge in a cavern that resembles a Gothic chapel and is said to shelter an enormous serpent. The episode is equivalent to the "chapel perilous" stage of Grail quests, in which
the hero finds himself in a place of inexplicable peril. On another occasion,
Father Vaillant speaks of a Native convert whose ancestors had hidden a
"golden chalice" for Mass in a "terrifying canyon of black rock." That image recalls Wagner's Grail Temple, which can be reached only through a
"great portal" in a "granite wall," as Gertrude Hall puts it. The chapter
in which Vaillant tells that story has a Good Friday Spell ambience; it
is spring, Latour's garden is blooming, and a woman named Magdalena,
who has been rescued from a violent husband, is surrounded by doves.

Latour, too, is a hero enlightened through compassion. Unlike Parsifal,
he cherishes nature from the start: where the wild boy heartlessly kills a
swan, Latour is unfailingly tender toward animals, and he stops in awe
before a juniper tree that displays the form of the Cross. He is, as Susan
Rosowski writes in her book *The Voyage Perilous*, another alternative to the
macho cow-puncher. At the same time, Rosowski says, Cather is looking
beyond the mythology of Romanticism, the passionate relationship of subject to object. The divine love that suffuses *Death Comes for the Archbishop*
involves both an acceptance of the physical world and an overcoming of

it. In Rosowski's words, it is "a harmony that defies time and place . . . a magical world in which correspondences link heaven and earth, past and present, history and legend."

The novel is most *Parsifal*-like in its syncretic religiosity. When Father Vaillant finds an Angelus bell, Latour says, "The Templars brought the Angelus back from the Crusades, and it is really an adaptation of a Moslem custom." This melding of West and East is a feature of the Parzival story as told by Wolfram von Eschenbach: Parzival's half-brother Feirefiz is the son of a Moorish queen. Latour also has fruitful contact with Native Americans. "It was the Indian's manner to vanish into the landscape, not to stand out against it," Cather writes. To be sure, the same cannot be said of Latour, who spends his later years supervising the construction of a cathedral in Romanesque style—a building that leaps out of the mountains like an opera set, as its architect says. As Latour lies dying, his Navajo friend Eusabio pays his respects. He is like Death in the etching, come for the archbishop—not in retribution but in reconciliation.

In her 1925 novel *The Professor's House*, Cather has her title character, the solitary-minded academic Godfrey St. Peter, deliver a credo of art's role in the world.

> As long as every man and woman who crowded into the cathedrals on Easter Sunday was a principal in a gorgeous drama with God, glittering angels on one side and the shadows of evil coming and going on the other, life was a rich thing. The king and the beggar had the same chance at miracles and great temptations and revelations. And that's what makes men happy, believing in the mystery and importance of their own little individual lives. It makes us happy to surround our creature needs and bodily instincts with as much pomp and circumstance as possible. Art and religion (they are the same thing, in the end, of course) have given man the only happiness he has ever had.

This formula comes near to Wagner's proposal, in "Religion and Art," that art is destined to "save the core of religion, by grasping the figurative value of those mythic symbols that religion wants us to believe as literally true." Except that Cather gives no hint either of religion itself expiring or of art supplanting it. Rather, religion and art stand side by side, delivering brief, blinding moments of transcendence. Cather was never systematically religious, nor did she entertain lofty ideas about art's ability to change the world. Her achievement was to transpose Wagnerism into an earthier, more generous key. She offered grandeur without grandiosity, heroism without egoism, myth without mythology. Brünnhilde stays on her mountain crag, hailing the sun: no man breaks the ring of fire.

9

MAGIC FIRE

Modernism, 1900 to 1914

Adolphe Appia design for Die Walküre

In the prologue of *Götterdämmerung*, the three Norns stand on the Valkyries' rock, veiled and motionless, the rope of destiny strung through their hands. It is night, and the ring of fire glows in the background. Winds and brass intone the spacious chords that accompany the awakening of Brünnhilde in *Siegfried*—"Hail to you, sun!"—but under them runs a sluggish version of the formerly buoyant music of the Rhine. The Norns tell a new story of earlier days: how Wotan cut his spear from the World Ash Tree, causing it to fester and die. Now, they say, he sits with the gods in Valhalla, waiting for the end, the remains of the ash piled around him as kindling for the final flame. The rope becomes tangled; it frays against the rock; it breaks. The Norns exclaim, "*Es riß!*"—"It tore!"—and sink from sight.

The feeling of a break, of an irreparable tear in the social fabric, all but defined the early twentieth century, both in the sphere of the arts and in the world at large. Virginia Woolf famously wrote that "on or about December 1910 human character changed." Willa Cather found that "the world broke in two in 1922 or thereabouts"—undoubtedly thinking of the twin publication of James Joyce's *Ulysses* and T. S. Eliot's *The Waste Land*. The movement known as modernism rippled across Europe and the Americas, altering the public's understanding of what art is and does. Mass reproduction and broadcast transformed popular culture, fostering new genres and new audiences. The First World War marked an absolute historical rift—and, more or less, the end of Wagnerism as an intellectual phenomenon.

"Wagner *sums up* modernity. It can't be helped, one must first become a Wagnerian." Nietzsche's aphorism predicted the role that the composer would play in the early lives of a number of leading modernist artists. Wassily Kandinsky was swayed toward art after seeing *Lohengrin* in Moscow in 1896. Eliot swooned to *Tristan* when he was at Harvard. Joseph Conrad fell for the same opera in Brussels, shortly after completing his career in the British merchant marine. D. H. Lawrence attended Wagner performances in London after arriving from the Midlands; Joyce absorbed the operas in Dublin. Virginia Woolf grew up in a Wagner-inclined family; E. M. Forster consorted with Wagnerites at Cambridge. And Marcel Proust came of age in the Symbolist-Wagnerian hothouse of Paris. In case after case, Wagnerism turns out to be a kind of larval stage—a metamorphosis from which the mature artistic self emerges. A version of Nietzsche's agon keeps playing out. Emma Sutton, an authority on literary Wagnerism, writes succinctly that Wagner served "both as a model and an antitype for modern art."

The words "modern" and "modernism" are slippery ones, prone to endless disputation. By and large, they indicate a body of work that cuts against prevailing modes of representation, broaches transgressive themes, threatens zones of bourgeois comfort. Circa 1860, Baudelaire defined *modernité* as a pursuit of "the ephemeral, the fugitive, the contingent." Rimbaud declared, "One must be absolutely modern," by which he meant an art of roughness, hardness, assaultive force. The Symbolists gravitated toward the inscrutable and the unsayable; Impressionist and Post-Impressionist painters blurred forms for the sake of perceptual truth. Most of them saw Wagner as an ally, even as they followed independent paths.

Early twentieth-century modernists retained Baudelaire's taste for ephemera—"the spasmodic, the obscure, the fragmentary," in Woolf's words—but they also strove to forge a new order from the shards, as Siegfried reforged his father's sword. The drive toward abstraction, toward the non-representational, served that world-creating ambition. Modernists liked to characterize their work as a reversion to the unadulterated facticity of their chosen medium: paint, language, light, movement, sound. Yet the ideal of self-sufficient abstraction entailed its own kind of mythmaking. When an artwork no longer has a mimetic relationship with the exterior world, it can claim to have shifted from the particular to the universal, from the historical to the eternal. To paraphrase Mallarmé, the modernist Siegfried is a hero with no name.

What modernists respected in Wagner was his will to enact a *future*—and, by extension, to annul the present. Michael Levenson, in his 2011 survey *Modernism*, takes as his point of departure a sentence from Nietzsche's "Richard Wagner in Bayreuth": "For many things the time has come to die out; this new art is a prophet which sees the end approaching for other things than the arts." Modernism's hammering stress on the new, the strange, the unprecedented, the smashing of convention, the imagining of utopias, the reactivation of primitive energies, the fiery scribbling of manifestos, the yoking of artistic change to political, spiritual, even cosmic transformation—all that smacks of Wagner. Ezra Pound's slogan "Make it new" inadvertently echoes the Meister's command to "make something *new*! *new*! and once again *new*!" As it happens, both Wagner and Pound were quoting a saying of the Shang emperor Ch'eng T'ang, as translated by Guillaume Pauthier: "Make it *new*, again *new*, and always *new*."

What modernists had no use for was the Romantic aesthetic that swaddled even Wagner's most adventurous thinking. In place of opulent textures, they put hard lines and harsh colors; in place of a grandiose legendary past, the unadorned present; in place of epic passion, raw desire; in place of "highest bliss," the heart of darkness. The art historian T. J. Clark has explicated modernism in relation to Max Weber's thesis about the "disenchantment of the world"—the banishing of ancestor worship and ritual, the founding of a secular, technocratic, materialist order. Artists felt both "horror and elation" in the face of this new reality, Clark writes. They mimicked its mechanisms while trying to restore a sacred dimension.

Three legacies stand out: the Gesamtkunstwerk; the stream of consciousness; and the juxtaposition of myth and modernity. The first is the most widely cited of Wagner's concepts, and also the most maddeningly vague. Relatively little noticed during the composer's lifetime, it moved to the fore around 1900, in Munich, Vienna, and Brussels. In many ways, the Gesamtkunstwerk is a projection of twentieth-century concerns back onto Wagner. Sound and film technologies allowed for a synthesis of media that went beyond anything a nineteenth-century artist could have pictured. At the same time, as Juliet Koss shows in her book *Modernism After Wagner*, modernists often defined themselves *against* the Gesamtkunstwerk, emphasizing the purity and autonomy of each discipline. Wagner had, in fact, reached the same conclusion: each art form should retain its identity under the Gesamt rubric. (The root German word suggests an aggregation of elements rather than a monolithic totality.) A recurring tic of modernist discourse is to refute a fictional Wagner position in favor of one that is actually closer to what the composer believed.

The stream of consciousness and the interior monologue, leading techniques of modernist literature, are in a clear line of descent from Wagner. It was in the pages of the *Revue wagnérienne* that Téodor de Wyzewa theorized a novel that, after the model of *Tristan*, would plunge the reader into a "sea of emotions," as experienced by a single protagonist in a limited time frame. Édouard Dujardin immediately tried to realize that idea, but it assumed definite form only in the new century, in the work of Woolf, Proust, and Joyce. The challenge is to keep the reader oriented amid the experiential flux. Wagner relied on the leitmotif, and modernist writers often followed his lead. Pushing the technique further, they isolated phrases and patterns within the rush of impressions, using them to create a sense of unity, however fleeting. The tolling of Big Ben in *Mrs. Dalloway*, the uneven cobblestones of *In Search of Lost Time*, the "tap tap tap" of a blind man's cane in *Ulysses* are threads that we grasp as we navigate a space in which conventional narrative structure has been obscured or removed.

As for Wagner's mythic apparatus, it makes itself felt as an implicit allegory, a half-concealed network of correspondences. Even if modernist artists seldom depict sword-wielding heroes in medieval garb, archetypal images of the fallen god, the wounded king, and the untested youth hover

behind contemporary characters and situations. Knightly riders and noble
steeds stride through Expressionist art; the Rheingold is transmuted into a
South American silver mine; a Jewish Dubliner takes on the aspect of the
Flying Dutchman. Wagner remains the unavoidable beast at the heart of
the modern labyrinth.

FIRE DANCES

Loie Fuller was a native of the Chicago suburbs who got her start in burlesque theaters and vaudeville. In 1883, the year of Wagner's death, she was
touring America as part of Buffalo Bill Cody's Wild West Show. Stocky of
build, she began to use swirling fabrics, long canes, and lighting effects to
hide her frame and conjure spectral images—dragons of air, William Butler Yeats called them. After perfecting these techniques in subsidiary roles,
she moved to Paris and launched herself as a solo artist. In 1892, she began
a run at the Folies-Bergère, creating an immediate sensation. Nancy Reynolds and Malcolm McCormick, in their dance history *No Fixed Points*,
write that "on that Paris night, it could fancifully be claimed, dance of the
twentieth century was born." The disappearance of the dancer's body into

a kinesis of light, movement, and material was an early landmark of classic modernism.

Fuller set her most celebrated piece, *La Danse du Feu*, or the Fire Dance, to "The Ride of the Valkyries." She performed in a darkened room on a glass pedestal, with colored lights projected from below. A member of her troupe described the effect:

> As the orchestra began to play, a dim, bluish-reddish flame glimmered at the center of the stage. The edges of the silk stirred gently as the dancer agitated the bottom of the skirt. Then, holding the canes hidden in the sides of the skirt, she crossed her arms before her face and, as the layers of flame seemed to climb higher, for a few seconds, only her eyes showed through. The intensity of the music built up, the veils moved faster, the flames leaped higher—red, blue, orange, purple—the frenzied, glowing silk soared fifteen feet into the darkness. Then, amid a great crescendo of light and sound, the dancer suddenly sank into a heap. A purple ember flickered in a dying gasp.

Electric light had been part of theater technology for decades. The inaugural production of Meyerbeer's *Le Prophète*, in Paris in 1849, used arc light to simulate a sunrise. A few scenes in the first *Ring* at Bayreuth were electrically lit, and a concealed bulb made the Holy Grail in *Parsifal* glow red. Fuller was far more sophisticated in her methods, employing a system of custom lamps, colored glass, and projections, which she designed and patented. She hoped to apply these techniques in the opera house, but that ambition went unfulfilled. Jules Claretie, the director of the Théâtre Français, reported: "She dreams of fantastic new lighting, of projections accompanying the works of a Wagner, adding their harmony to the musical power of the master. Ah! if I could, if I could! . . . At the Opera, 'The Ride of the Valkyries,' lit by me, made to come alive, as I understand it, as I see it!"

Fuller struck awe into artists and writers of the period. Georges Rodenbach, author of *Bruges-la-morte*, saluted her as a Wagnerian goddess: "Brunehilde, it is you, queen of Valkyries / Every man dreams of becoming a god, in order to be your chosen one." (Rodenbach's poem appeared on the eve of the first Parisian production of *Walküre*, in May 1893; the opera was on everyone's mind.) Jean Lorrain wrote: "[She] does not burn . . . she is flame itself . . . She is Herculaneum buried beneath the ashes, she is the Styx and the shores of Hades, she is Vesuvius with its gaping jaws spitting the fire of the earth . . ." Mallarmé saw Fuller's work as a premonition of the abstract, interior theater of his dreams: "Future decor is buried in the orchestra, latent treasure of imagination, to emerge, in flashes, after the image of the idea that the performer now and then puts over the footlights." That sentence plays on Wagner's "mystic abyss," the hidden orchestra in Bayreuth. For Mallarmé, Fuller heralds a post-Wagnerian drama in which word, sound, and gesture are one.

If Fuller disappeared into a frenzy of light and motion, Isadora Duncan made the body itself her instrument, moving in free and simple style. She drew attention for performing in a tunic and bare feet, as if she had stepped off a Grecian urn. "*Isadora Duncan est dionysiaque*," said Joséphin Péladan. Superbly attuned to music, she not only danced to Wagner but grappled with his theories. A native of San Francisco, she came of age in the nascent Californian culture of nondenominational spirituality and back-to-nature mysticism. In the late nineties, in New York, she performed with Ethelbert Nevin, the salon composer who befriended Willa Cather. (Curiously, Cather disliked Duncan's work, despite many similarities in outlook.) In 1899, Duncan went to London, where she won the applause of the later Pre-Raphaelites, and soon after decamped to Paris, where Fuller generously championed her.

Duncan found an eager following in Germany, and she responded by immersing herself in German culture and philosophy—Kant, Schopenhauer, Nietzsche, Wagner. The last she eulogized as the "glorious far-seeing prophet, liberator of the art of the future," whose work "flows through every drop of blood in every artist of the world." In a 1903 lecture in Berlin, under the title "Dance of the Future," Duncan criticizes ballet—it produces "a sterile movement which gives no birth to future movements, but dies as it is made"—and calls for a "return to the original strength and to natural movements of woman's body." She condemns civilized artificiality and reaffirms Greek ideals. The peroration has the excitable quality of Wagner's prose: "This is the mission of the dancer of the future. O, do you not feel that she is near, do you not long for her coming as I do? Let us prepare the place for her."

Wagner, too, deplored the constriction of the body in classical ballet. He dreamed of a "seductively wild and thrilling chaos of groupings and movements" for his *Tannhäuser* Venusberg. But he made no serious attempt to realize these intentions. The Flower Maidens in *Parsifal* were, by all reports, a kitschy bunch. Siegfried Wagner, the Meister's gay son, had somewhat more progressive tastes. After seeing Duncan perform in 1903, Siegfried arranged for her to take part in *Tannhäuser* in Bayreuth the following year. Her assignment was to choreograph the Venusberg Bacchanale and dance the role of the First Grace. David Breckbill believes that this departure from routine had a pragmatic purpose: with *Parsifal* playing at the Met in New York, the Wagners feared that wealthy Americans would no longer bother to make the pilgrimage to Bayreuth, and so Duncan was offered as a lure. She caused chatter on the Green Hill by going around in her usual classical regalia, American companions in tow. The future Hollywood director Preston Sturges, who was there with his mother, Mary Desti, recalled a company decked out in "bare feet, sandals, and little Grecian dresses."

Duncan envisioned a choreographic counterpoint to the tumult of the Venusberg music, as her notes show. In line with Symbolist and early modernist aesthetics, she would make a dance of suggestion, avoiding the futile literalness of a naturalist staging:

> A single gesture of appeal will be able to evoke a thousand extended arms, a single head tossed back will represent a bacchantic tumult which is the expression of burning passion in the blood of Tannhäuser . . . And when these terrible desires arrive at paroxysm, when they attain the point where, breaking all the barriers, they rush forward like an irresistible torrent, I cover the scene with mists so that each one in his own way without seeing, can realise the dénouement in his imagination, which only outstrips any concrete vision.

In an ironic recapitulation of the *Tannhäuser* scandal of 1861, the lack of traditional ballet annoyed the old-time Wagnerites, who felt that Duncan's restrained poses and "chaste Venusberg" made nonsense of the score. Other dancers were apparently much more routine in their movements, resulting in an uncomfortable clash of styles. Duncan did not return.

In 1908, Duncan undertook the first in a series of American tours. "Superwoman in America," the journalist Benjamin De Casseres dubbed her. A 1911 program at Carnegie Hall, with full orchestra, paired selections from Bach with the *Parsifal* Flower Maidens scene and Isolde's Transfiguration. On other occasions, Duncan danced to Siegfried's Funeral Music and Brünnhilde's final monologue. As at Bayreuth, she ignored the turbulence of the Wagner orchestra, embodying the "clear, soft beauty of sensuous rapture," to quote one critic. According to Ernest Newman, her dance to "The Ride of the Valkyries" had a moment of "dead immobility," in which "she gave us an incredible suggestion of the very ecstasy of movement: something in the rapt face, I imagine, carried on the previous joy of the wild flight through the air." In the Transfiguration, André Levinson wrote, she hardly danced at all: "Her legs are motionless: only occasionally does a swift gust carry her ahead a few paces . . . With each crescendo of the orchestra, she shakes her uplifted arms and finally throws them vigorously to and fro." She danced to *Tristan* at her last performance, before a tragic accident took her life in 1927.

Fuller and Duncan entranced fin-de-siècle intellectuals because they seemed to bring the Gesamtkunstwerk to fruition. Yet Duncan had doubts about the concept. As the dance critic Mary Simonson points out, she felt that dance was sufficient in itself, the root of all other artistic endeavors, and need not become one with music and poetry. Duncan said that she once shocked a luncheon at Wahnfried by announcing: "The Master made a mistake, one as great as his genius. Music drama, that is nonsense." She went on: "Man must speak, then sing, then dance. But the speaking is the brain, the thinking man. The singing is the emotion. The dancing is the Dionysian ecstasy which carries away all. It is impossible to mix in any way one with the other. *Musik-Drama kann nie sein* [Music drama can never be]." Cosima stared in icy silence.

The Meisterin might have responded: if dance is self-sufficient, why is Wagner's music needed? All protestations and cavils aside, the Gesamtkunstwerk helplessly fascinated modernist artists. The dispute was really about which art would have pride of place. By dancing to Wagner, Fuller and Duncan effectively demoted him: he became the backdrop against which new audacities were revealed. It may be no accident that both women used "The Ride of the Valkyries" as a favorite foil. The Valkyries have minds of their own.

THE THEATER OF LIGHT

Adolphe Appia, design for Das Rheingold, *1892*

The dances of Fuller and Duncan, with their free gestures in open space, augured a revolution in the theater. By 1900, the age of naturalism was drawing to a close. A new generation of directors and designers wished to discard scenic surplus, eliminate actorly excess, renovate the stage image. For many leaders of this vanguard—Adolphe Appia, Edward Gordon Craig, Georg Fuchs, Max Reinhardt, Mariano Fortuny, and Vsevolod Meyerhold, among others—Wagner was a crucial forebear. Even though the Bayreuth stagings were laden with Romantic bric-a-brac, the works themselves demanded something new. "The Wagnerian contradiction," Appia called it—the disparity between the limitless expressiveness of the music and the confined world of the bourgeois stage.

Wagner was not unaware of this contradiction. He once said to Cosima: "Now that I have created the invisible orchestra, I would also like to invent the invisible theater!" Then again, he remained to the end a man of the theater—a born actor who valued the actor's art, with its larger-than-life projection of personality. Martin Puchner, in his book *Stage Fright*, takes the view that Wagner's unswerving devotion to theatricality explains the conflicted response of the modernist generation: "Almost like a stage diva himself, [Wagner] continues to stand for everything that may be grandiose and compelling, but also dangerous and objectionable, about the theater and theatricality." This discourse began, once again, with Nietzsche, whose great hopes for the *Ring* collapsed when he was forced to confront it as a theatrical presentation.

Of this group, Appia was the most ardent Wagnerite. Born in Geneva in 1862, he was trained in music and became interested in the problem of staging Wagner while still in his teens. He attended the *Parsifal* premiere in 1882 and returned to Bayreuth in 1886 and 1888 for *Tristan* and *Meistersinger*; he also saw the *Ring* in Dresden. These experiences filled him with extreme enthusiasm for the operas—"Wagner has taken the place for him of religion, of love, of *everything*," a relative commented—and with an equal distaste for their presentation. He later defined the prevailing manner thus: "Characters in scrupulously historic costume proudly descend a wooden staircase. In their luxurious and authentic footgear they tread boards cluttered with set pieces, and appear outlined against walls and balustrades which the well-lighted painting indicates to be of marvelously sculptured marble." Bayreuth was a "museum piece, nothing more." He began to work out detailed scenarios for the operas, and published a preliminary study, *Staging Wagnerian Drama*, in 1895. His major early treatise, *Music and the Art of the Theater*, came out in 1899, in German.

For Appia, the score should determine everything that the audience sees. Music controls the flow of time—it *is* time, he insisted—and it also generates a sense of space. Paraphrasing Wagner's definition of his work as "deeds of music made visible," Appia writes: "By means of dramatic representation, music is transported into space and there achieves a material form—in the *mise en scène*—thus satisfying its need for a tangible form, not just illusively in time alone, but quite *actually* in space." The best way to open up space is not through scenery but through lighting. Appia distinguishes between "diffused light," which provides general illumination, and "living light," which is more focused and casts shadows. Such proto-Expressionist painting with light would play out against drastically simplified sets. Appia retained some conventional elements—the Valkyries sport the traditional helmet-and-spear attire—but to fin-de-siècle eyes these pared-down designs would have been wildly unorthodox.

Advances in lighting technology soon allowed Appia's visions to become reality. In 1901, Mariano Fortuny made a crucial contribution by inventing the cyclorama, an overhanging quarter-sphere of fabric onto which light was projected. The Fortuny Dome, as it came to be called, gave the illusion of infinite, ethereally luminous skies—Baudelaire's prose poem on *Lohengrin* come to life. Like Appia, Fortuny formulated his ideas in the wake of several unhappy visits to Bayreuth. For a 1900–1901 production of *Tristan* at La Scala, the artist fashioned the illusion of a prolonged sunset in Act III, with the light changing from yellow to red to purple as it hit the wall and tower of Tristan's castle.

To overcome the "rigid conventions" that impeded an ideal theater, a person of strong will was needed—as strong, perhaps, as Wagner himself. This person was the stage director. The position of *Regisseur*, the word for director in German, had been a lowly one at the beginning of the nineteenth century. Wagner assisted in its elevation by creating works so scenically elaborate that a new wizardry was needed to realize them. Bayreuth's prolonged rehearsal schedule and detailed coaching established a standard that impressed even skeptics like Eduard Hanslick, who named Wagner "the world's foremost *Regisseur*." Appia lobbied for something even more radical. "With the Word-Tone Drama, the person whom we call 'le Régisseur,' whose task currently is to direct the game of fixed conventions, takes the role of a despotic drill instructor, presiding over preparatory exercises for the scenic tableau."

Appia dreamed of working at Bayreuth. Houston Stewart Chamberlain, who had befriended the designer in the early eighties, attempted to interest Cosima in Appia's thinking, but he was no more successful than he had been with Mallarmé's poetry, or than Duncan had been in her efforts to rejuvenate Bayreuth choreography. Appia spent countless hours at Bayreuth, attending performances and observing rehearsals. But when Cosima granted him an interview, she stared at him silently for several long moments and said, "All this has no meaning at all."

Despite the Meisterin's skepticism, Appia's philosophy filtered outward in the early twentieth century. Roller and Mahler's color-saturated *Tristan* in Vienna probably showed his influence. In 1923, Appia himself presided over a *Tristan* at La Scala, with Arturo Toscanini conducting. At the outset of Act II, the audience was almost blinded by the light of the torch that warns Tristan to stay away. When Isolde put it out, the lovers were shrouded in gloom, their bodies almost imperceptible. By the time of Appia's death, in 1928, his theories were gaining traction even in Bayreuth. Siegfried, who had been using a Fortuny cyclorama for a number of years, upset traditionalists with a mildly abstract, light-suffused *Tristan*.

An aesthetic of starkness and spareness also stamped the work of Edward Gordon Craig, one of the chief architects of twentieth-century theater. Craig's early stagings were close enough to Appia's in spirit that he was wrongly considered an imitator: the likeness resulted from a common regard for the Symbolist inheritance. Although Craig never went to Bayreuth, he saw it from afar; when he was a boy, his mother, Ellen Terry, and her lover Henry Irving showed him a book of pictures from the festival. Drawings for Craig's 1903 production of Ibsen's *The Vikings at Helgeland* resemble Bayreuth's Grail Temple, as the theater historian Denis Bablet observes. Later, under the influence of Isadora Duncan, his longtime lover, Craig formed the ideal of the actor as "über-marionette"—the "body in Trance," shorn of theatrical cliché.

Craig soon joined the procession of innovators who tried to persuade Cosima Wagner to modernize Bayreuth. Siegfried, who had brought Duncan to Bayreuth, listened with interest, but Cosima remained intractable. The director reported:

> I said to Frau Cosima that I could not see that the stage trappings at Bayreuth or anywhere else were anything like the visions his music conjured up. And I think I remember her saying 'And what pictures do *you* see, Mr. Craig?' And I described something like the wild pampas of South America, the rushing of the wind, perhaps a prairie fire, and so on. When I looked at Frau Wagner I could hardly see her face, because she had turned the same colour as the table cloth, into which she seemed to be vanishing.

However conservative Cosima may have been, these stories of her obduracy do not do her justice. She was herself a *Regisseur* of strong convictions, inclined toward highly stylized stage gestures and painstaking direction of the chorus. Back in 1887, an American critic had noted that the lighting at Bayreuth was moodier and more atmospheric than elsewhere.

In 1908, Craig inaugurated his magazine *The Mask* with a manifesto titled "The Artists of the Theatre of the Future." He was not the first to deploy such a phrase. In 1905, the German art critic and theatrical manager Georg Fuchs had proclaimed a "stage of the future," in which Wagnerian and Nietzschean ideas would be integrated in pursuit of a more vibrant, vivid stage picture. In order to distinguish himself from his predecessors, Fuchs performed the ritual gesture of repudiating the Gesamtkunstwerk; in place of a synthesis of the arts, he demanded a newly purified articulation of each art form's needs and techniques. Like Duncan, he was closer to Wagner's thinking than he let on, as Juliet Koss makes clear. Fuchs applied his concepts at the Munich Artists' Theater, designed by Max Littmann and opened in 1908. Its steeply raked, unadorned auditorium took after the Festspielhaus. In place of the deep Bayreuth stage, though, actors occupied a shallow platform that pushed the action to the foreground.

The second issue of *The Mask* included an extract from Wagner's essay "The Revolution," in which the spirit of world upheaval vows to "destroy the existing order of things." A commentary ascribed to one Jan Van Holt asks: "I wonder if the ladies and gentlemen who patronize the Opera Houses of Europe and America realise what they are listening to when Wagner lets loose the notes of his soul in the great operas." This was Craig, speaking through a pseudonym. In applauding Wagner, he suggests, the crowned heads are applauding their own imminent extinction. Events in Russia would bring that conceit to life.

ABSTRACTION

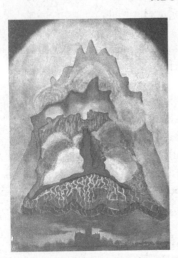 

Wagner *from* Thought-Forms, *and Kandinsky's* Landscape with Red Spots II

The classic chronicle of modernism leaned heavily on rhetoric of purity, autonomy, and freedom. Whether in music, theater, literature, or the visual arts, a quasi-Hegelian spirit of progress guides the artist into uncharted realms. Perhaps the purest of pure images in modernism was the abstract canvas, scrubbed of figurative clutter and at times reduced to a single plane of color. According to the long-reigning explanation advanced by the critic Clement Greenberg, abstraction arises as a logical response to the nature of the medium. Beginning with Manet, painters yield to the flatness of the canvas, to the language of color. Greenberg explicitly pitches his argument against the all-encompassing, medium-transcending aesthetic of the Gesamtkunstwerk, although he does not name Wagner as the malefactor. Irving Babbitt does so in his 1910 book *The New Laokoon: An Essay on the Confusion of the Arts*, on which Greenberg drew. There, Wagner is accused of the "breaking down of all barriers and boundaries."

The fable of modernism inventing itself *ex nihilo*, in an immaculate aesthetic conception, has lost credibility with latter-day art historians, many of whom highlight the fin-de-siècle influences that the likes of Greenberg denied. Occultism once caused embarrassment in scholarly circles; now it has returned to intellectual grace. Around 1900, a new sense of the sacred arose, detached from extant religious practice—ideal forms dwelling behind reality's outer surface. The urge to make such forms visible led at once to experiments with abstraction. Diagrams and dream images in Theosophical texts prefigure the work of Kandinsky, Hilma af Klint, Kazimir Malevich, and Piet Mondrian. "*I* got everything from the 'Secret Doctrine' (Blavatsky)," Mondrian wrote in 1918.

It was primarily through this mystical channel that Wagner—"the greatest unconscious occultist who has ever lived," in Édouard Schuré's words—influenced modernist painters. Kandinsky named two events in his early life that "stamped my whole life and shook me to the depths of my being." One was an exhibition of French Impressionists in Moscow; the other was *Lohengrin* at the Bolshoi Opera. A haystack by Monet, Kandinsky recalled, was no longer recognizable as such, yet its colors gripped him all the more. As for *Lohengrin*, he wrote: "The violins, the deep tones of the basses, and especially the wind instruments at that time embodied for me all the power of that pre-nocturnal hour. I saw all my colors in my mind; they appeared before my eyes. Wild, almost crazy lines outlined themselves in front of me." Kandinsky came away convinced that "painting could develop just such powers as music possesses."

German influences shaped Kandinsky in his youth. He learned the language from his maternal grandmother, who was of Baltic origin, and heard German folktales as a boy. He also studied music, learning cello and piano. At the end of 1896, following his twin epiphanies in Moscow, he moved to Munich to concentrate on painting. There he absorbed Wagnerism, Symbolism, occultism, the "cosmic circle" of Stefan George, and quasi-Nietzschean philosophies of Dionysian paganism and hedonism. Theosophy instilled the idea of art as a conduit for arcane truths, in opposition to materialist culture.

Kandinsky expounded his worldview in *On the Spiritual in Art*, first drafted in German in 1909 and 1910 and subsequently expanded and revised. Decrying the "nightmare of materialistic points of view, which have turned the life of the cosmos into an evil, pointless game," the painter adopts Helena Blavatsky's belief that humanity should turn inward and undergo spiritual revolution. The artist can help to guide that journey. One potent technique is obsessive repetition, whether of a word or phrase in a Maeterlinck play or of a melodic fragment in Wagner. The latter aims to characterize the hero "not only by theatrical machinery, make-up, and lighting effects, but by a certain, precise *motif,* thus by purely *musical means.* This motif is a kind of musically expressed spiritual atmosphere that precedes the hero, so that he emanates spiritually at a distance."

Such ritual patterns course through Kandinsky's work as it progresses from Symbolism toward abstraction. A favorite motif is that of the horse and rider—the hero in motion. In *Der Blaue Reiter*, or *The Blue Rider*, a blue man on a white horse dashes across a green field. In *Farewell*, the tableau of a knight turning away from a maiden could be a nod to *Lohengrin*, except that no swan is in sight. In canvases from the period 1908 to 1913, we see riders ambling across meadows, jousting, or holding golden swords. They are mingled with imagery of the Last Judgment, the Garden of Eden, and Saint George and the Dragon. *Landscape with Red Spots II* is a particularly interesting case. The Finnish art historian Sixten Ringbom once scandalized Kandinsky scholars by pointing out that this painting resembles an illustration in Annie Besant and C. W. Leadbeater's 1905 Theosophical text *Thought-Forms*, which theorizes relationships between sound, emotion, and color. In a section devoted to "Forms Built by Music," Besant and Leadbeater present a visualization of Wagner's music—a bell-shaped mass of color towering above a church. Kandinsky seems to emulate its spiky mountains and splotches of red, though the church has been reduced to an infinite pillar.

Between 1910, when Kandinsky completed the first version of *On the Spiritual in Art*, and 1912, when the essay "On Stage Composition" appeared in the *Blaue Reiter* almanac, Wagner lost some luster in the painter's eyes. The artist-scholar Chris Short finds that Kandinsky's later writings devalue the Gesamtkunstwerk and advocate instead a transcendent theater of music, movement, and color. Wagner may have achieved an impressive monumentality, Kandinsky says, yet the attempt to produce parallel effects in each genre results only in an external unity: "The inner sound of movement does not come into play." The critique recalls that of Mallarmé, who desired a theater of the imagination, detached from the noisy machinery of stage and orchestra.

Kandinsky speaks of "inner necessity" as the way beyond mere spectacle. The phrase has been attributed to Hegel, but Wagner is a likelier source. According to "The Artwork of the Future," man can never realize himself "until his life is the true mirror of nature, consciously complying with the only real necessity, the *inner natural necessity*"—rather than an agenda determined by "religion, nationality, or state." This encapsulates Kandinsky's thinking better than anything in Hegel. Again, a modernist artist rejects Wagner while retaining his ideas.

Inner necessity was just as much a byword of the composer Arnold Schoenberg, who saw his hugely controversial exploration of nontonal harmony—atonality, it came to be called—as a natural extension of the chromaticism of *Tristan*. In 1911, Kandinsky and his partner Gabriele Münter attended a performance of Schoenberg's Second String Quartet and Three Piano Pieces, in which tonality dissolves before one's ears. In the final two movements of the quartet, a soprano joins the ensemble to sing settings of Stefan George's poems "Litanei" and "Entrückung." At the climax of "Litanei," George's apparent allusion to *Parsifal*—"Kill the longing / close the wound"—is joined to a musical echo of Kundry's culminating cry of anguish (her plunge from high B to low C-sharp in Act II). Kandinsky responded to the quartet by painting *Impression III (Concert)*, in which the rough black shape of a piano looms amid blocks of burning color.

Not content to theorize, Kandinsky created dramas of his own. The first of these, originally called *The Giants* and later named *The Yellow Sound*, had a score by Thomas de Hartmann, a Ukrainian-born composer who had worked under the Wagner protégé Felix Mottl. In place of a plot, the drama is all dreamlike tableaux: yellow giants, wordlessly chanting; people waving white flowers in sickly light; a child ringing a bell in a chapel-like space; a dance that ends in chaos and darkness. As in Kandinsky's paintings, we witness a mythic narrative whose specificity has been almost entirely effaced. Schoenberg attempted a similar experiment in his music drama *Die glückliche Hand*, where such Wagnerish elements as a goblet, a sword, an anvil, a piece of gold, and a monster are strewn through a tale of unfulfilled longing.

Such abstracted heroism appealed equally to the Munich-born painter Franz Marc, who joined Kandinsky and Münter in their artists' colony in Murnau. Marc loved Wagner in his youth, citing *Götterdämmerung* as an emblem of the greatness of the age. His manifesto "The Savages of Germany" is a kind of update of Wagnerian art-religion, heralding artists who make "*symbols* for their own time, which belong on the altars of the coming spiritual religion and behind which the technical producer disappears."

Marc's Expressionist eschatology blazes forth in the 1913 painting *Fate of the Animals*, which suffered damage during the First World War and was restored by Paul Klee. It shows a verdant grove consumed by fire, with forest creatures—deer, horses, boars—writhing in terror. At the center is a massive tree, which the art historian Frederick S. Levine has identified as Yggdrasil, the tree of Norse myth. Levine is reminded of *Götterdämmerung*, in which the decay of the World Ash Tree predicts the gods' end. Levine notices, however, that Marc's tree appears to withstand the rain of fire. Four deer have found refuge in the lower right-hand corner of the canvas, and they, too, may survive the inferno. Armageddon could bring about a remaking of the world and a recovery of unity with nature—*Götterdämmerung* as glorious rebirth.

Marc was killed at the Battle of Verdun in 1916. In the same year, the Swedish mystic Hilma af Klint embarked on a cycle of 144 watercolor and graphite pieces that she called the *Parsifal Series*—an emanation from the hidden world toward which so many artists were striving. A long-overlooked pioneer of abstraction, af Klint drew on Theosophy, Rosicrucianism, and Anthroposophy, counting herself a disciple of Rudolf Steiner. Her work tends toward intricate geometrical designs, levitating symbolic forms, and a glowing color palette. The *Parsifal Series* progresses from images of dark confinement—a point of light at the center of a gray-black spiral—to a shimmering chromatic spectrum of squares and circles. The Swedish words for "downward," "backward," "outward," "forward," "upward," and "inward" are inscribed throughout. The series suggests a journey of initiation, like Parsifal's long, fitful progress toward the Grail. It could be the "invisible theater" of which Wagner dreamed.

MODERN NOVELS

"The men and women who began writing novels in 1910 or thereabouts had this great difficulty to face—that there was no English novelist living from whom they could learn their business." So Virginia Woolf wrote in her essay "Mr. Bennett and Mrs. Brown"—the same in which she announced a fundamental change in human character. The novel held sway as the English-language form par excellence: the capacious fictions of Jane Austen, the Brontë sisters, Charles Dickens, and George Eliot were worlds unto themselves, second realities. For Woolf, though, older narrative strategies were failing to comprehend modern life. She criticized Edwardian novelists for their relentless focus on the "fabric of things" and their inability to capture the inner life of characters, especially those who did not match the author's gender or social station. "All human relations have shifted—those between masters and servants, husbands and wives, parents and children." One of Woolf's targets is Arnold Bennett, who whipped up an overheated scene of heterosexual Wagnerian seduction in *Sacred and Profane Love*.

Lacking up-to-date British models, the younger novelists looked to other disciplines: to French poetry, with its leap into free verse; to Impressionist and Post-Impressionist painting, which captured "not the thing but the effect it produces," in Mallarmé's words; to the philosophy of Nietzsche, the psychology of Freud and Jung, the mythography of James Frazer; and to music, where the vogue for Wagner had not yet run its course.

Even as human character changed, it carried forward ancient patterns. The *Ring*, *Tristan*, and *Parsifal* demonstrated the enduring dynamism of mythic material that had been churning through Western culture for many centuries. Literary modernists fashioned narratives in which modern characters fall into archetypal heroic roles, including the retinue that runs from the Flying Dutchman to Parsifal. Thomas Mann had already practiced a kind of Wagnerian doubling in the *Ring* allegory of *Buddenbrooks*, and Willa Cather was reanimating Siegfried and Brünnhilde in her stories of the prairie. Among the British modernists, the relationship tends to be more covert: the reason may be that Wagner had become part of the official culture of the Edwardian era, decor in the bourgeois "fabric of things."

Ford Madox Ford, a chief instigator of English-language modernism, grew up in what may have been the most Wagnerian house in London. His father, Francis Hueffer, was the German émigré critic who preached Wagner to the Victorian masses and the Pre-Raphaelite elite. Ford probably met the Meister in London in 1877; he claimed to remember the "dreadful eyes" of Wagner and other notables in his father's circle, even though he was only three years old. An avid musician, Ford produced his own compositions, in a style suited more to the salon than to Bayreuth. In the nineties, poised to follow his father, he wrote an essay titled "Wagner Educationally Considered."

Instead, Ford turned to fiction. In his first novel, *The Shifting of the Fire*, a rather conventional tale of young love frustrated by financial problems, literary leitmotifs abound, and the male protagonist talks up the "Music of the Future." Ford's debut set a pattern among British modernists: their first or second novel is often the one in which Wagner matters most. The same applies to Lawrence's *The Trespasser*, Forster's *The Longest Journey*, and Woolf's *The Voyage Out*.

After the turn of the century, Ford promoted a new literary manner— hard, clear, anti-Romantic. Defining poetry as "the putting of certain realities in certain aspects," he added an injunction against Wagner: "Even if you wish to sentimentalize, the dustbin is a much safer card to play than the comfrey plant. And, similarly, the anaemic shop-girl at the exhibition, with her bad teeth and her cheap black frock, is safer than Isolde. She is more down to the ground and much more touching." This message got through to Ezra Pound, who, when he met Ford, was weaving medieval conceits, reading Péladan, and, it would appear, listening to *Tristan*. By 1916, Pound had become the perfect anti-Wagnerite, brusque and blunt in style. "Wagner is a bum artist," he wrote. He produced a gnomic Noh play based obliquely on the Tristan tale, as if to dehumidify it. There were two aesthetic philosophies, Pound later decreed: the Wagnerian, in which "you confuse the spectator by smacking as many of his senses as possible at every possible moment"; and the Vorticist, which "aims at focusing the mind on a given definition of form, or rhythm." Only the latter would now do.

In 1898, Ford met Joseph Conrad, né Józef Korzeniowski, a retired Polish sea captain who was now improbably making his way as an English-language novelist. Three years earlier, Conrad had published his first novel, *Almayer's Folly*, which bore the imprint of his formative encounter with *Tristan* in Brussels. In a letter to the Belgian writer Marguerite Poradowska, Conrad said that the book "ends with a long *solo* for Almayer which is almost as long as the solo in Wagner's *Tristan*." He later claimed that the Brussels performance was his only experience of Wagner, and that he otherwise had an "abysmal ignorance" of the music. Conrad's biographer Frederick Karl casts doubt on such claims, noting the novelist's history of passing himself off as a "country boy who stumbled into literature." At the turn of the century, Conrad struck a different pose. In a letter to his publisher, he defended his slow working pace and lack of commercial appeal by placing himself above the herd: "I am *modern*, and I would rather recall Wagner the musician and Rodin the Sculptor who both had to starve a little in their day."

The Conrad style has an insistent, incantatory rhythm. Sentences roll along in heaving waves; ideas recur and evolve in motivic fashion. Consider how a single word burrows through the final section of *Heart of Darkness* (1899), Conrad's nightmarish vision of the Congo under Belgian rule: "The darkness of an impenetrable night . . . the starred darkness . . . the heart of darkness . . . the barren darkness of his heart . . . His was an impenetrable darkness . . . all the hearts that beat in the darkness . . . the heart of a conquering darkness . . . The darkness deepened . . . the threshold of an eternal darkness . . . an unearthly glow in the darkness, in the triumphant darkness . . . the stream of darkness." The last word of the story is foreordained: "The offing was barred by a black bank of clouds, and the tranquil waterway leading to the uttermost ends of the earth flowed sombre under an overcast sky—seemed to lead into the heart of an immense darkness." Did *Tristan* leave its mark on these mesmerizing repetitions? The possibility is intriguing, although, as John DiGaetani writes in *Richard Wagner and the Modern British Novel*, it is safer to speak more generally of an "operatic, staged, and mythic atmosphere."

At times, Conrad makes his references to Wagner unambiguous. In the South Seas tale "Freya of the Seven Isles," the title character, bearing a name out of the *Ring*, plays "fierce Wagner music in the flicker of blinding flashes, with thunderbolts falling all round, enough to make your hair stand on end." The motif of a cursed treasure figures in *Almayer's Folly*, *Heart of Darkness*, and *Victory*. Ford, who served as Conrad's sounding board and part-time stenographer, probably encouraged this allusive pattern. The two authors not only collaborated on a series of novels but participated in the writing of each other's works. In their joint 1909 novella *The Nature of a Crime*, a money-embezzling lawyer goes to see *Tristan* and thinks about how the love potion serves as a metaphor for decisive, sometimes self-destructive acts: "Every human being knows what it is to act, irrationally, under the stress of some passion or other . . . The philtre could do no more than put it in a man's power to do what he would do if he were let loose."

Conrad's 1904 novel *Nostromo*, perhaps his greatest, has the heft of a modern-dress *Ring*. It is set in South America, in the fictional republic of Costaguana, where the San Tomé silver mine is wreaking havoc on the fabric of society. The Conrad scholar Paul Wiley draws the obvious analogy: "The curse attached to the silver is as productive of fatal consequences as that upon the stolen gold in Wagner's *Ring*, for avarice not only defeats the protagonists in the novel but also excludes love as a redeeming force." The master of the mine is a man named Charles Gould, who has come to wield "immense occult influence" over Costaguana's affairs, to the point of installing a dictator friendly to his interests. Gould believes that his wealth can serve civilizing ends; his wife, Emilia, devotes herself to education and charities. They are like Wotan and Fricka, their outward splendor concealing lovelessness. The mine is a new Nibelheim: "Worked in the early days mostly by means of lashes on the backs of slaves, its yield had been paid for in its own weight of human bones." In *Rheingold*, Alberich drives his horde with a whip and Wotan's debt is paid when Freia is measured against the gold. For Wagner, Alberich and Wotan are mirror images: the one gives up love to gain the gold, the other pursues ultimate power to escape a failed marriage. Gould, cold and obsessed, is Wotan and Alberich in one body.

In the face of an attempted coup d'état, Gould threatens to dynamite the mine, preferring to destroy it rather than let it fall into unfriendly hands. With that Götterdämmerung, a more conventional novel might have ended. But the curse has not run its course. The revolt is defeated in part because of the heroism of the charismatic longshoreman Giovanni Battista Fidanza, nicknamed "Nostromo" ("boatswain" or "our man"), who

displaces Gould as the novel's central figure. Nostromo and a scheming journalist, Martin Decoud, are entrusted with a portion of the silver, which they
take out on a cargo lighter. When their boat is struck at night, they decide to
hide the treasure on an island. Decoud, left alone to guard it, goes mad and
commits suicide. Nostromo, having told the authorities that the boat was
lost, prospers for a while, secretly extracting wealth from the trove. In the
closing chapters, though, he becomes the silver's latest victim—a Siegfried
turning into Fafner. Nostromo is described as the "slave of the treasure,"
the "slave of the San Tomé silver," and the "master and slave of the San
Tomé treasure." The last phrase is a near-quotation from Alberich's curse
upon the Ring—"*des Ringes Herr als des Ringes Knecht*" ("the lord of the
ring as the slave of the ring").

Mrs. Gould stands as a beacon of compassion in the capitalist dark.
Nostromo hails her as "Shining! Incorruptible!" When, on the point of
death, he tells her that he knows where the silver is, she chooses to say nothing to her husband or to anyone else. "Let it be lost for ever," she says. Like
Brünnhilde returning the Ring to the Rhine—"I grasp the gold and give it
away"—she is trying to break the curse that has hollowed out her marriage
and all but ravaged her husband. She does not quite succeed. At the very
end, Dr. Monygham, the Goulds' well-meaning but embittered doctor,
pulls up to the island in a boat, "wondering what he would find there." He
seems fated to become the next master-slave of the ruinous hoard.

I n 1908, Ford founded *The English Review*, one of the lively small magazines
in which Anglo-American modernism took shape. One of his aims was
to publish writers from the working classes—"authentic projections of that
type of life which hitherto had gone quite unvoiced," he later said. An
early issue included several poems by David Herbert Lawrence, the son of
a Midlands coal miner. Perhaps Ford imagined that someone from such
a background would be free of Wagnerism and other decadences. Yet the
Midlands were no more insulated from Wagner than was Willa Cather's
Nebraska. Growing up in the vicinity of Nottingham, Lawrence had belonged to an intellectually inclined circle of youths, dubbed the Pagans,
who discussed Wagner, Nietzsche, Darwin, Marx, and the gay socialist
Edward Carpenter. The miners, Ford recalled Lawrence saying, "wanted
their sons to be educated people." The Nottingham Sacred Harmonic

Society had Wagner in its repertory, as did many amateur choruses throughout the coal and iron districts. In 1900, several hundred Welsh singers
delighted London audiences with their rendition of the Pilgrims' Chorus
from *Tannhäuser*.

In 1908, Lawrence took a job teaching in Croydon, on the outskirts of
London. When he went into the city to see Wagner, his feelings were mixed.
Tristan was "long, feeble, a bit hysterical"; *Siegfried* made no great impression. Expressing a preference for Italian opera, he wrote, "Damn Wagner,
and his bellowings at Fate and death." All the same, *The Trespasser*, his
second novel, records an extreme case of Wagner mania, based on a real-
life incident.

A friend of Lawrence's, the teacher and writer Helen Corke, had become
entangled with her violin tutor, a married man named Herbert Macartney, who played in *Ring* cycles at Covent Garden and was swept up in the
"hurricane of music and emotional colour." When Macartney tried to make
love to Corke, she insisted that the relationship remain platonic, probably
because she was lesbian. To mark the spiritual nature of their passion,
Corke renamed herself Sieglinde, and Macartney became Siegmund. A
typical passage from her diary: "Siegmund, in an irresponsible mood, is
whistling the 'Spring Song' from 'Die Walküre.' He is very far away from
me—indeed, I half wonder if I have loved only a dream woven soul, and
no reality." Eventually, Macartney fell into despair and killed himself.

In Lawrence's retelling, the lovers are named Helena and Siegmund.
Like their counterparts in d'Annunzio's *The Triumph of Death* and Batilliat's *Mystic Flesh*, they are addicted to seeing the world through a Wagnerian lens. A foghorn is compared to a sustained pitch in *Tristan*. A sunset
is *Lohengrin*-esque. Siegmund feels lost in dreamland, like Brünnhilde
"sleeping in her large bright halo of fire." The clickety-clack of a train brings
to mind "The Ride of the Valkyries." Just before news of Siegmund's death
reaches her, Helena is roaming Tintagel, the Arthurian castle associated
with King Mark, humming bits of Wagner.

Unlike other *Tristan* scenarios of the period, though, *The Trespasser*
omits the usual Liebestod crack-up. Lawrence, at the outset of his lifelong
campaign against sexual repression, refused to tell stories of the Liebestod
type, of the "ecstasy of the *Untergang*," as Thomas Mann described *Death
in Venice*. (The novella disgusted Lawrence when he read it.) Rather, Siegmund's tragedy is meant to underscore the irreconcilability of passionate

fantasy and humdrum domestic life. The poor man's end—hanging himself on door hooks—has nothing romantic about it. Helena survives, and goes in search of a warmer, earthier mode of existence. Instead of renouncing her musical love, she applies herself to studying German, so that she can "understand Wagner in his own language."

Lawrence's own preoccupation with Germanic culture intensified when, around the time of the publication of *The Trespasser*, he fell in love with Frieda Weekley, née von Richthofen. The couple began frequenting bohemian circles on the Continent, including the artists' colony in Ascona, Switzerland, where occult rituals and naked dances were held on a Parsifal Meadow. For years to come, Lawrence would cultivate the "ancient spirit of pre-historic Germany coming back, at the end of history," as he later wrote.

The famous novels of Lawrence's early maturity feature characters who are Wagnerian in both personality and name. The Brangwen sisters, the artist Gudrun and the teacher Ursula, appear in both *The Rainbow* (1915) and *Women in Love* (1913–16). In *Götterdämmerung*, Gutrune's marriage to Siegfried sets off the final crisis. Likewise, in *Women in Love*, Gudrun's affair with the industrialist Gerald Crich incites a climactic explosion of violence. Gerald, for his part, is a Wagnerian composite. With his blond hair and muscled body, he initially comes across as an Anglo-Saxon Siegfried, but when he goes swimming with the sisters he is said to be "like a Nibelung"—Alberich splashing after the Rhinemaidens. Directing his mines as "God of the machine," Gerald indeed resembles Alberich, not to mention Gould in *Nostromo*. The miners are "blackened, slightly distorted human beings . . . all moving subjugate to his will." Eventually, Gudrun shifts her attention to an effete, sardonic German artist-intellectual named Loerke, whose name recalls Loge, the fixer of the *Ring*. Events move toward disaster as the company takes an Alpine holiday. "One really does feel *übermenschlich*—more than human," Gudrun says. Gerald nearly strangles her in a murderous fury. Stoddard Martin is right to call him a god in decline, seeking *das Ende*. He wanders into the snow and dies.

In the two novels, Ursula emerges as a magnificent Brünnhilde-Isolde figure, although her erotic adventures are as modern as any in the novels of Colette. She enjoys a lesbian romance, and her affair with Rupert Birkin, a stand-in for Lawrence, attains *Tristan*-like levels of nocturnal ecstasy. As Hugh Stevens notes in an essay on Wagner and Lawrence, Ursula undergoes a kind of transfiguration in the closing chapter of *The Rainbow*. Believing that she might be pregnant, she hallucinates fire all around her, as if she were Brünnhilde on her rock: "She let the flames wrap her and destroy her to rest." She also has a vision of a "great flash of hoofs, a bluish, iridescent flash surrounding a hollow of darkness." Finally, a rainbow arches above the Nibelheim of the Midlands, and sensual mysticism takes over:

> And the rainbow stood on the earth. She knew that the sordid people who crept hard-scaled and separate on the face of the world's corruption were living still, that the rainbow was arched in their blood and would quiver to life in their spirit, that they would cast off their horny covering of disintegration, that new, clean, naked bodies would issue to a new germination, to a new growth, rising to the light and the wind and the clean rain of heaven. She saw in the rainbow the earth's new architecture, the old, brittle corruption of houses and factories swept away, the world built up in a living fabric of Truth, fitting to the over-arching heaven.

In *Rheingold*, the rainbow is a false apparition, its splendor betrayed by the greed of the gods. In Lawrence's novel, it is more like the melody that unfurls at the end of *Götterdämmerung*, promising rebirth. A valkyrie stands intact above the flames.

E. M. Forster was the kind of turn-of-century man who couldn't say no to Wagner—gay, cultured, stalked by feelings of social isolation. His father came from wealth but died young, and despite his comfortable upbringing Forster lacked the sense of being born into a high social station. Bullied at school, he took refuge in books, art, and music. At Cambridge University, he joined the elite society of the Apostles and got to know a wider group of young men—Lytton Strachey, Clive Bell, Saxon Sydney-Turner, Leonard Woolf, John Maynard Keynes, and Adrian and Thoby Stephen, Virginia Woolf's brothers—who would form the core of the Bloomsbury set in London. Wagnerism ran rampant in this circle, as did an inclination toward homosexuality, fleeting or permanent.

Forster gives a portrait of the Apostles in *The Longest Journey*, his second novel, which appeared in 1907. A few pages in, an undergraduate is trying to play the prelude to *Rheingold* on the piano. Later, Rickie Elliot, a dreamy and oversensitive writer born with a club foot, experiences a *Rheingold* fantasy, his interior monologue imitating the swelling E-flat-major orchestration of Wagner's fanfare to the *Ring*:

> Music flowed past him like a river. He stood at the springs of creation and heard the primeval monotony. Then an obscure instrument gave out a little phrase. The river continued unheeding. The phrase was repeated, and a listener might know it was a fragment of the Tune of tunes. Nobler instruments accepted it, the clarionet protected, the brass encouraged, and it rose to the surface to the whisper of violins. In full unison was Love born, flame of the flame, flushing the dark river beneath him and the virgin snows above. His wings were infinite, his youth eternal; the sun was a jewel on his finger as he passed it in benediction over the world. Creation, no longer monotonous, acclaimed him, in widening melody, in brighter radiances. Was Love a column of fire? Was he a torrent of song? Was he greater than either—the touch of a man on a woman?

The Apostles scramble Wagner metaphors as they take in the world around them. When Rickie and his philosopher friend Ansell trade letters on the topic of the advisability of marriage, Rickie cites Brünnhilde as a positive example, while Ansell refers skeptically to Elsa in *Lohengrin*. For the musicologist Michelle Fillion, such scenes point up the danger of applying mythology to real life. "Wagner proves a siren song," she writes, "that lures the imaginative mind away from 'the idea of Reality' and 'the ethical idea that reality must be faced'"—convictions central to Forster's trenchantly anti-metaphysical worldview.

The Longest Journey is not merely a satire of collegiate Wagnerism: the operas become doors to understanding. Rickie explicitly sees himself as Amfortas, hobbled by a wound that may be psychosexual as well as physical: he hopes that "his wound might heal as he labour[s] and his eyes recapture the Holy Grail." In later chapters, trapped in a joyless engagement and a school-teaching career, Rickie meets Stephen, a rough-hewn farmer who has the blond locks and blue eyes of a Wagner hero. The erotic spark between the two—"Come with me as a man . . . we're alive together," Stephen says—becomes all the more provocative when it is discovered that they are half-brothers. Wisely, perhaps, Forster dropped his initial plan to name the character Siegfried. As the two friends meander the countryside at dusk, Stephen sets a crumpled piece of paper afloat in a stream and lights it with a match: it becomes a "rose of flame . . . burning as if it would burn for ever." Forster has brought back Rickie's *Rheingold* daydream, with its "column of fire" and "torrent of song." But only a Liebestod is available to this man who yearns for love outside convention. He feels the magic stream slipping away, the dullness of marriage reclaiming him. When Stephen passes out drunk on a railroad track, Rickie rescues him but is killed by an onrushing train. The proletarian Siegfried lives on, transfigured by Rickie's memory.

The Longest Journey lacks the elegant contours and cutting wit of Forster's mature novels. It is, however, a heartfelt work, one that the author cherished. Unlike many of his generation, Forster never swerved away from Wagner; as late as 1954, he visited Bayreuth. Although a few characters in his mature fiction express an aversion to the composer, they are not entirely convincing. In *Howards End* (1910), the practical-minded Margaret Schlegel bemoans the muddling of the arts, as Irving Babbitt did in *The New Laokoon*, published the same year: "Every now and then in history there do come these terrible geniuses, like Wagner, who stir up all the wells of thought at once. For a moment it's splendid. Such a splash as never was. But afterwards—such a lot of mud; and the wells—as it were, they communicate with each other rather too easily now, and not one of them will run quite clear." Her diatribe rings false in the context of a novel that prizes the reconciliation of opposites. Indeed, Margaret later assists in the "building of the rainbow bridge that should connect the prose in us with the passion." That *Rheingold* metaphor reinforces the novel's motto of "Only connect."

STREAMS OF CONSCIOUSNESS

Men dominated the modernist canon, and their work can give off a macho reek: outlaw poses, public melées, acrimonious squabbling over who did what first. Wagner was himself a superb example of the violently insecure male ego. Hilma af Klint found her way to abstraction without recourse to revolutionary bravado, and a parallel path opened in literature, in the field of stream-of-consciousness writing. Virginia Woolf, its most imaginative practitioner, disliked the confrontational stance of her male colleagues—narratives of the "egotistic anti-hero adrift in the modern world," as her biographer Hermione Lee writes. This does not mean that Woolf was timid in her approach. George Eliot had linked women's untold stories to the "roar which lies on the other side of silence." In Woolf's work, the roar becomes gigantic.

George Henry Lewes, Eliot's partner, introduced the term "stream of Consciousness" in 1860, just after Wagner completed *Tristan*, the opera of endless melody. In Lewes's telling, the "vast and powerful stream of sensation" arose from an observer's inward response to the stimuli of the outer world. William James adopted the phrase in his 1890 text *Principles of Psychology*, defining it as a "teeming multiplicity of objects and relations." The term acquired its literary meaning in 1918, when May Sinclair reviewed three novels by Dorothy Richardson—the first installments of what would become Richardson's thirteen-volume *Pilgrimage* cycle. Sinclair wrote: "In this series there is no drama, no situation, no set scene. Nothing happens. It is just life going on and on. It is Miriam Henderson's stream of consciousness going on and on."

Sinclair mentions in the same regard Joyce's *A Portrait of the Artist as a Young Man*, which had appeared in 1914 and 1915. She evidently did not know of the work of Gertrude Stein, whose novel *The Making of Americans* (1902–11), not published until 1925, might have been the first sustained exercise in stream-of-consciousness writing. Nor does she speak of Woolf and Katherine Mansfield. The definition of what constitutes a "stream of consciousness" style has become confused over time. The syntactically broken interior monologues of Joyce's earlier work stand apart from Mansfield's and Woolf's more composed free indirect discourse. Nonetheless, both writers radically evoke the interplay of subjective consciousness and exterior reality.

Music was of paramount importance in this branch of modernism. In the *Pilgrimage* cycle, Richardson comments on the ubiquity of music in Germany, where young women learn to play, and think more deeply about themselves in the process. Mansfield was a serious musician in her youth, studying the cello with an eye toward pursuing a professional career. In

1907, when she was eighteen, she heard a performance of *Walküre* by a touring company, and the experience stayed with her when she went on a camping trip on New Zealand's North Island. In her journal, she wrote: "A bird—large and widely silent—flies from the river right into the flowering sky—There is no other sound except the voice of the passionate river—They climb onto a great black rock & sit huddled up there—alone—fiercely almost brutally thinking—like Wagner." Another note reads: "Oh, the sea and Wagner together—O thank God that I have written five poems." Mansfield was in the throes of an affair with a half-Maori girl named Maata Mahupuku, and her Wagnerian ecstasies may reflect the liberation of her feelings.

In the same period, Mansfield was at work on a novel called *Juliet*, which she left unfinished. Here Wagner plays a different and more sinister role. Instead of freeing up a woman's subjectivity, the music stifles her and exposes her to predatory males. The title character has fallen for a gifted young cellist named David, a Pre-Raphaelite lad with a "dreaming exquisite face." He and his music give Juliet the sense that "her whole soul woke and lived for the first time in her life." David's bohemian London includes a suspect decadent named Rudolf. At the story's fatal turn, Rudolf sits at the piano, plays the *Tannhäuser* overture, and accuses Juliet of being too conventional and fearful:

> He started the Venus motif. "Here am I" he said "reckless, a lover of all that you have desired to love, because my mother was a Danseuse and my father an artist. Also there was no marriage—" He ceased speaking but the music filled the room. He repeated the wonderful Venus call. "Ah, it is divine" he said. "That is what you should be, Juliet. What—how am I for Tannhäuser." The music was flooding Juliet's soul now. The room faded. She heard her hot heavy impassioned voice above the storm of emotion—"Stop, stop" she said, feeling as though some spell was being cast over her. She shook from head to foot with anger & horror.

It is a typical scene of Wagnerian seduction, though with a twist: the male seducer has androgynously assumed the femme fatale role of Venus. The ploy succeeds: when Rudolf grabs Juliet, she surrenders to him. But we are made to feel Juliet's fear and panic as she steps into this erotic-musical trap. A few hours later, David returns, having heard Wagner at a Promenade concert. He finds Rudolf improvising madly at the piano. "I'm still full of Wagner," David says, "& behold I find he is here incarnate in my room." Rudolf responds: "I am Wagner—I'm at the top of the whole world." He lays a hand on David's arm, as if another seduction were beginning.

Mansfield's mature style adapts the stream of consciousness to a clear-eyed realism that often dwells on her New Zealand childhood. Delia da Sousa Correa believes that the writer's musical experiences, not least her brushes with Wagner, shaped her conception of "poetic prose," to take a phrase of Baudelaire's that Mansfield quotes in her notebooks. For Correa, lines from the 1921 story "At the Bay" exemplify that musicality, not only in terms of how they move across the page but in their use of sound as narration:

> Ah-Aah! sounded the sleepy sea. And from the bush there came the sound of little streams flowing, quickly, lightly, slipping between the smooth stones, gushing into ferny basins and out again; and there was the splashing of big drops on large leaves, and something else—what was it?—a faint stirring and shaking, the snapping of a twig and then such silence that it seemed someone was listening.

Shortly before her early death, in 1923, Mansfield made a tantalizing note about a future story: "Aunt Anne. Her life with the Tannhauser Overture." Who Aunt Anne was, or what *Tannhäuser* meant to her, is unknown. Perhaps Mansfield was plotting a tale like Cather's "A Wagner Matinée," in which the music allows an older woman to rediscover a stymied self.

Woolf once said that Mansfield was the only writer who made her feel jealous. She had a harder time making up her mind about Wagner. At times, she seemed as much of a fanatic as her brother Adrian Stephen, and his Cambridge friend Saxon Sydney-Turner. She joined the two on a trip to Bayreuth in 1909, where *Parsifal* stunned her: "I felt within a space of tears. I expect it is the most remarkable of the operas; it slides from music to words almost imperceptibly." In an unsigned essay for the *Times*, she placed the composer in exalted company: "Like Shakespeare, Wagner seems to have attained in the end to such a mastery of technique that he could float and soar in regions where in the beginning he could scarcely breathe." Not long after, she wore a Valkyrie costume to a fancy-dress ball for women's suffrage.

Four years later, though, Wagner has suddenly become intolerable. Woolf writes of a session with the *Ring*: "My eyes are bruised, my ears dulled, my brain a mere pudding of pulp—O the noise and the heat, and the bawling sentimentality, which used once to carry me away, and now leaves me sitting perfectly still." A decade later, she casts her Wagnerism as a phase that men had foisted on her, writing to a younger friend: "I went to Tristan the other night; but the love making bored me. When I was your age I thought it the most beautiful thing in the world—or was it only in deference to Saxon? I told many lies in Covent Garden Opera house." Then again, in the same period she is singing the spring music from *Walküre* as she walks in London, and by the thirties she is enjoying *Meistersinger* at home: "I sit with the book of the score & conduct & I'm furious when they dont follow me." This ambivalence is not of the Nietzsche type—a youthful ardor that gives way to apostasy. Rather, Woolf keeps going back to Wagner, sometimes with enthusiasm and sometimes with skepticism, but always with a sense that the music holds something from which she can learn an aspect of her "business."

Woolf's father, the Victorian man of letters Leslie Stephen, had no great feeling for music, but he impressed upon his children the significance of German culture. Woolf was only sixteen when she first saw a full performance of the *Ring*, in 1898. Wagner references multiply in her correspondence around 1907, when she was living with Adrian in Fitzroy Square, an early site of the Bloomsbury gatherings. For several years, the conductor Hans Richter had been staging Wagner seasons at Covent Garden, and the Bloomsbury contingent went to these almost en masse. Woolf says in letters that she cannot be persuaded to "sacrifice my Richter," that she is about to attend *Meistersinger*, that Adrian is playing Wagner on the piano. During the Richter season of 1908, Woolf reports, "We go almost nightly to the opera, and in the afternoon we have our German." Leonard Woolf, Virginia's future husband, remembers a "Wagner cult," with Sydney-Turner as the high priest. If any composer but Wagner were praised, Sydney-Turner would become irritated.

Bloomsbury Wagnerism peaked in 1909, when Woolf accompanied Adrian and Sydney-Turner to Bayreuth. Thomas Mann made his only visit to the festival at this same time, and it is possible that both writers were present at a *Parsifal* on August 7. In her *Times* essay, titled "Impressions at Bayreuth," Woolf registers feelings that she seems not quite prepared to put into words, that remain "very deep and perhaps indescribable." What strikes her in *Parsifal* is the melding of sensual and spiritual impulses: "Somehow Wagner has conveyed the desire of the Knights for the Grail in such a way that the intense emotion of human beings is combined with the unearthly nature of the things they seek . . . One is fired with emotion and yet possessed with tranquillity at the same time, for the words are continued by the music so that we hardly notice the transition." The acutest passages, though, are those in which Woolf imparts what she experienced when she went outside during the intermissions.

From the hill above the theatre you look over a wide land, smooth and without hedges; it is not beautiful, but it is very large and tranquil. One may sit among rows of turnips and watch a gigantic old woman, with a blue cotton bonnet on her head and a figure like one of Dürer's, swinging her hoe. The sun draws out strong scents from the hay and the pine trees, and if one thinks at all, it is to combine the simple landscape with the landscape of the stage. When the music is silent the mind insensibly slackens and expands, among happy surroundings: heat and the yellow light, and the intermittent but not unmusical noises of insects and leaves smooth out the folds. In the next interval, between seven and eight, there is another act out here also: it is now dusky and perceptibly fresher; the light is thinner, and the roads are no longer crossed by regular bars of shade. The figures in light dresses moving between the trees of the avenue, with depths of blue air behind them, have a curiously decorative effect. Finally, when the opera is over, it is quite late; and half way down the hill one looks back upon a dark torrent of carriages descending, their lamps wavering one above another, like irregular torches.

This tremendous feat of description rivals Willa Cather's early Wagner reviews, with their sketches of singers before and after the performance. Crucially, these are impressions *at* Bayreuth, not *of* Bayreuth. An exact rendering of natural and human surfaces merges with an interior consciousness that seems to flow from *Parsifal* itself. Especially arresting is Woolf's perception of the music of insects and leaves, synaesthetically blending with sights, scents, and sensations. The image of carriages moving in a "dark torrent," as if bearing torches, creates a characteristic Woolfian tableau that is at once beautiful and chilling.

In the same period, Woolf was working on her first novel, which she initially called *Melymbrosia*. She finished a draft in early 1910. Extensive revisions followed, and the novel did not reach its final form until 1913, under the title *The Voyage Out*. The effort precipitated a mental breakdown: in September 1913, Woolf attempted suicide by an overdose of Veronal. Because of her illness, the novel did not see publication until 1915. Like *The Trespasser* and *The Longest Journey*, *The Voyage Out* shows a not entirely successful struggle to absorb ideas from Wagner while attempting to move beyond fin-de-siècle aesthetics. For Woolf, the struggle is peculiarly personal, involving matters of gender, sexuality, and cultural identity. It is a tale of immersion and overcoming, at the end of which the heroine dies and the novelist survives.

The voyage of the title is both geographical and spiritual. Rachel Vinrace, a sensitive young piano-playing Englishwoman, is setting out on a journey to South America from which she will not return. In the second chapter, we see her ensconced in her shipboard cabin, surrounded by books and scores. The room is equipped with a piano, and she likes to "sit for hours playing very difficult music, reading a little German." In both the early and later versions of the novel, she reads lines from one of Isolde's outbursts against Tristan in Act I, as she is dragged from Ireland to Cornwall, where she is to marry King Mark. Below are the German original, a literal translation, and a flowery late-Victorian rendition that Woolf employs:

Der zagend vor dem Streiche	He who, shrinking from the blow,	In shrinking trepidation
sich flüchtet, wo er kann,	takes refuge wherever he can,	His shame he seems to hide
weil eine Braut er als Leiche	because he has won a corpse as bride	While to the king his relation

für seinen Herrn gewann!	for his master!	He brings the corpse-like Bride.
Dünkt es dich dunkel,	Does it seem murky to you,	Seems it so senseless what I say?
mein Gedicht?	my tale?	

In *Melymbrosia*, the first draft, this *Tristan* passage is a cue for reverie. Rachel's mind drifts toward the horizon, into a Conradian "immense vagueness." In *The Voyage Out*, Rachel is considerably more cavalier. She reads the passage with a "shout of laughter," and the line "Seems it so senseless what I say?" gets a catty response: "She cried that it did, and threw down the book." *Tristan* is little more than a Romantic trinket, briefly examined and then tossed aside. Rachel is now more modern, debonair, cheeky.

Before the ship sets out across the Atlantic, Richard Dalloway, a former member of Parliament, and his wife, Clarissa, join the company for a time. They make a pompous, unpleasant first impression; nonetheless, each plays a role in the expansion of Rachel's consciousness. Mrs. Dalloway, hinting at the inner complexities that will require a separate novel to explore, mulls over the futility of "shutting oneself up in a little world of one's own, with pictures and music and everything beautiful." The faces of poor, hungry children make her want to "stop all the painting and writing and music until this kind of thing exists no longer."

When Mrs. Dalloway espies the *Tristan* score, she mimes playing a passage from it and says, "D'you remember this? Isn't it divine? . . . And then Tristan goes like this, and Isolde!" She then luxuriates in memories of Bayreuth: "I shall never forget my first *Parsifal*—a grilling August day, and those fat old German women, come in their stuffy high frocks, and then the dark theatre, and the music beginning, and one couldn't help sobbing." Mrs. Dalloway finishes, though, with the remark "I don't think music's altogether good for people." The implication is that Rachel must break away from her aesthetic cocoon. She soon does so, though presumably not in the way that Mrs. Dalloway meant: in the midst of a storm, Mr. Dalloway plants a kiss on her, an experience she finds at once liberating and horrifying.

Tristan reverberates throughout the novel. At Rachel's side is her aunt, Helen, who, like Brangäne in the opera, idolizes the heroine and feels "presentiments of disaster" on her behalf. On reaching South America, Rachel falls for a well-to-do would-be novelist named Terence Hewet, and their affair is set against a lush, sultry landscape, reminiscent of King Mark's garden. Rachel asks: "Are we on the deck of a steamer on a river in South America? Am I Rachel, are you Terence?" Compare Tristan and Isolde's many moments of ecstatic obliviousness: "Which land?" "Which king?" "You Tristan, I Isolde."

When the company sets out to explore a patch of jungle, Woolf stages a Night of Love, planting some particularly ingenious *Tristan* references. Rachel and Terence go ahead of the party, at which point they confirm their love and decide on marriage. All the while, other members of the party are calling out: "The voices of the others behind them kept floating, now farther, now nearer . . . The shouts were renewed behind, warning them that they were bearing too far to the left . . . Voices crying behind them never reached through the waters in which they were now sunk." The lovers are oblivious, even to their own voices: "So beautiful was the sound of their voices that by degrees they scarcely listened to the words they framed." In Wagner's Liebesnacht, likewise, Brangäne warns the lovers that night will soon give way to day—"Take care!"—only to fade into the orchestral backdrop that represents their bliss. In *Melymbrosia*, the jungle sequence includes a differently charged erotic moment, as Rachel and Helen walk in the jungle alone and roll in the grass. This lesbian subtext, shared with Michael Field's Isolde-Brangäne play *The Tragedy of Pardon*, is mostly absent from the final version, but a touch of it remains as Rachel appreciates Helen's "soft body" and "strong and hospitable arms."

Rachel exits the jungle with a fever and goes into quick decline. Emma Sutton, in *Virginia Woolf and Classical Music*, notes that in this Liebestod the gender roles of *Tristan* are reversed: Rachel suffers and hallucinates before dying, while Terence is left to deliver an elegy over her body. In *Melymbrosia*, we enter Rachel's consciousness as she dies: she feels herself "sinking and sinking," like Isolde. *The Voyage Out* adopts Terence's perspective, and the disparity between this rather dull fellow and the transfigured Isolde makes for ironic comedy. "Tristan! Ah! . . . Isolde!" becomes "Hullo, Terence . . . Well, Rachel." Highest bliss devolves into sentimental cliché: "No two people have ever been so happy as we have been. No one has ever loved as we have loved." Even so, the pathos kicks in: when Terence realizes that "here was a world in which he would never see Rachel again," he begins shrieking her name.

For Emma Sutton, *The Voyage Out* is a feminist critique of *Tristan*. The Wagner spell ultimately entraps the protagonist, lulling her into a wordless state when she should be cultivating and articulating her inner self. It may also be, though, that Rachel is not Wagnerian *enough*—that she has failed to reckon with Isolde's full strength. So argues Louise DeSalvo, who edited *Melymbrosia* for publication. Rachel is made to undergo "the necessary and ineluctable equation of women and caring, of women and loving, of caring and victimization, of loving and madness, of loving and powerlessness, of powerlessness and suicide, of loving and death." Woolf is urging women to "kill this conception of themselves as powerless, as impotent." Rachel should have paid closer attention to Isolde's wrathful, defiant words.

Indeed, early drafts suggest that Woolf initially intended to lament women's loss of potency from the pagan era to the Christian present. In the first act of *Tristan*, Isolde delivers a seething monologue—"*Entartet Geschlecht!*" ("Degenerate people!")—in which she calls for a revival of ancient sorcery and a tempest of retribution. Although Rachel is too weak to summon such forces, a symbolic storm rages through the novel after her death. No damage is done to the hotel where the well-to-do English company is staying, but larger storms may follow.

THE TOTAL WORK OF MARCEL PROUST

In the post-Wagner age, writers tended toward imposing multipart projects. Bookstore shelves sagged under the weight of trilogies, tetralogies, and even longer cycles: Dorothy Richardson's *Pilgrimage* novels, Ford Madox Ford's *Parade's End*, Thomas Mann's *Joseph and His Brothers*, and Romain Rolland's *Jean-Christophe*, itself the saga of a German composer. Grandest of them all was Proust's *In Search of Lost Time*, which appeared in seven parts between 1913 and 1927—the last three posthumous, the author having died in 1922. Although Proust never named the *Ring* as a precedent, it seems clear that the cycle helped him to conceive of a fictional work of vast dimensions, its structure bound together with leitmotifs. *In*

Search of Lost Time is one of the supreme Wagnerian creations, yet it is free of bombast, maintaining an intimate mode of address. Woolf praised Proust for having "solidified what has always escaped—and made it too into this beautiful and perfectly enduring substance."

Like the *Ring*, *In Search of Lost Time* stemmed from a relatively modest initial idea that grew ever larger and subdivided into many parts. Jean-Jacques Nattiez traces this process in his book *Proust as Musician*. Wagner started at the end, with *Siegfried's Death*. Proust began with a sketch for a semi-fictional essay titled *Contre Sainte-Beuve*, which muses on the memories inherent in objects and places—most famously, the childhood-reviving taste of a madeleine. Once *Siegfried's Death* was sketched, Wagner found that he had to tell the earlier parts of the drama in order to give the denouement its necessary weight. Proust, analogously, kept expanding the middle stages of his story, so that chapters became books. The genesis of the *Ring* is itself discussed in *The Captive*, the fifth volume of the *Search*. Marcel, the Proustian narrator, imagines Wagner's sense of wonder as he realizes "all of a sudden that he had written a tetralogy." The composer must have beheld an "ulterior unity," as the piecing together of fragments yields a network of interrelationships. In fact, this précis is a better fit for *In Search of Lost Time* than it is for the *Ring*.

Nattiez also reveals the hidden Wagnerian background of the fictional composer Vinteuil, whose works are heard at pivotal moments throughout the cycle. In the first novel, the Jewish dilettante and collector Charles Swann becomes engrossed by a "little phrase" in Vinteuil's Sonata—music that is threaded through his life and later extends into Marcel's. It acts very much like a leitmotif. Thomas Grey has written that Wagner's motifs are not only a means of labeling but also a "matter of musical memory, of recalling things dimly remembered and seeing what sense we can make of them in a new context." This is precisely how the "little phrase" weaves its way through *In Search of Lost Time*. The delicious complication is that this leitmotif is itself a piece of music: it is, in a way, a metaphor for itself.

In notes from the period 1913–16, Proust wrote: "I shall present the discovery of Time regained in the sensations induced by the spoon, the tea, etc., as an illumination à la Parsifal." What illumination does he have in mind? He may well be thinking of the Good Friday Spell, which is discussed at length in an early draft of *Time Regained*. But he could also mean Parsifal's sexual-spiritual epiphany in Act II: "Amfortas!—The wound!"

The latter had spoken strongly to a number of gay and lesbian readers, from Ludwig II to Gertrude Stein.

B orn in 1871, Proust came of age in a period when aspiring aesthetes were Wagnerites almost by default. He joined the intellectual throng at the Concerts Lamoureux, though he disapproved of how the audience applauded tuneful numbers from Wagner's early operas while failing to acknowledge the transcendence of *Tristan*. Probably by intention, he sounds like Huysmans's impeccably snobbish Des Esseintes. The fact that Proust was coming to terms with his homosexuality made the attachment all the more unsurprising: by the nineties, Wagner was well established as a code of gay taste. Robert de Montesquiou, the worshipper of King Ludwig, was one of Proust's Wagnerian tutors, and received the ambiguous honor of being immortalized as the predatory Baron de Charlus in the *Search*.

The great women of society on whom Proust trained his admiring and dissecting gaze often shared his passion for Wagner. Élisabeth Greffulhe, Montesquiou's fashion-setting cousin, sponsored the French premiere of *Tristan*. The Princesse de Polignac, born Winnaretta Singer, commissioned the sculptor Jean Carriès to produce a colossal door for what was rumored to be a *Parsifal* shrine—the *Porte de Parsifal*, now on display at the Petit Palais in Paris. In some circles, Proust encountered skepticism, and pressed Wagner's case strongly. When the Jewish salonnière Geneviève Straus, Bizet's widow, pronounced the composer "legendary instead of human," Proust responded: "The more legendary Wagner is, the more human I find him." And when the singer and composer Reynaldo Hahn, Proust's sometime lover, lobbed insults at *Lohengrin*, the author responded plaintively: "The Grail; the departure; the giving of the horn, sword, and ring; the prelude; is not all this beautiful?"

In Proust's early stories, fellow Wagnerites come in for light mockery. "Fragments of Commedia dell'Arte" shows us a bourgeois aesthete named Oranthe, who "can read Lamartine only on a snowy night and listen to Wagner only while burning cinnamon." Another youthful piece is an elaboration of *Bouvard et Pécuchet*, Flaubert's satirical encyclopedia of pretensions. In Proust's version, Bouvard, a "revolutionary if ever there was one," declares himself a Wagnerite, although he does not actually know the scores because—again like Des Esseintes—he cannot bear to listen to the music as it is conventionally presented. Pécuchet, by contrast, takes the patriotic stance, saying that for French ears *Walküre* "will always be the most infernal of torments—and the most cacophonous! Not to mention the most humiliating for our national pride." Such were the terms of the Wagner debate in the Paris salons.

The 1893 story "The Melancholy Summer of Mme de Breyves" makes Wagner the key to a character's consciousness. Mme de Breyves is a young widow besotted with the mediocre M. de Laléande. At a soirée, she hears "a phrase from Meistersinger"—the *Fliedermonolog* ("Lilac Monologue"), in which Sachs compares garden scents and birdsong with the strange but fresh music of young Walther von Stolzing. For Mme de Breyves, the phrase becomes a "veritable *leitmotive*" for the beloved. In an almost page-long sentence, she curses the "inexpressible feeling of the mystery of things," the exquisite sinking of the spirit that has "deepened her love, dematerialized it, enlarged it, made it infinite, without having made it any less torturous." She is left with the sense that reality and desire run parallel, never touching: "If, walking on the beach or in the woods, she lets herself be gently overcome by a pleasure in contemplation or reverie, or at least a fragrance, a song that the breeze wafts and mutes, making her forget her sorrow for an instant, suddenly she feels a sorrowful wound in a great blow to the heart." The *Fliedermonolog* speaks of the scent of lilacs, "so gentle, so strong and full."

The idea that a musical phrase can serve as a "veritable *leitmotive*" for a character—or for one character's perception of another—points toward *In Search of Lost Time*. Wagner serves both as a gauge of cultural pretension and as a signpost of fundamental psychological shifts. Early on, in the "Swann in Love" section of *Swann's Way*, the superficial society tone predominates. Mme Verdurin enjoys hosting musical soirées, at which she features young pianists whom she has taken under her wing. About each one, she exclaims, "Really, it oughtn't to be allowed to play Wagner as well as that!" Sometimes, the composer makes "too violent an impression on her." When Swann arrives for his indoctrination into this company, he hears a piano arrangement of a violin sonata by Vinteuil, who, at this stage of the cycle, is a lowly village organist noted mainly for the scandalous lesbian behavior of his daughter.

What jumps out at Swann is a "*petite phrase*" of five notes—"secret, murmuring, detached . . . airy and perfumed." He has heard it before, but failed to catch the composer's name; now he is fully beguiled. The experience coincides with Swann's love for the courtesan Odette, yet the import of the music goes beyond matters of the heart: the refined Parisian aesthete discovers an inner landscape in which his spirit can walk. "After a high note sustained through two whole bars, Swann sensed its approach, stealing forth from beneath that long-drawn sonority, stretched like a curtain of sound to veil the mystery of its incubation." Swann comes out a changed man, his mind absorbing "one of those invisible realities in which he had ceased to believe," to which "he was conscious once again of the desire and almost the strength to consecrate his life." Over the course of the novel, other characters will have epiphanic encounters with the music of Vinteuil, who is eventually acclaimed as a neglected genius.

In early drafts of *Swann's Way*, before the Vinteuil character has come into focus, the little phrase is ascribed to Camille Saint-Saëns. Letters indicate that Proust was also thinking of works by Franck, Fauré, Schubert, and Wagner ("a prelude from *Lohengrin*"). A passage in *Swann's Way* could describe the prelude to Act I of *Lohengrin*, filtered through Baudelaire: "Below the delicate line of the violin-part, slender but robust, compact and commanding, he had suddenly become aware of the mass of the piano-part beginning to emerge in a sort of liquid rippling of sound, multiform but indivisible, smooth yet restless, like the deep blue tumult of the sea, silvered and charmed into a minor key by the moonlight."

The emotional history of the little phrase is an epic in itself. When Odette hears it at the Verdurins', it is the "national anthem" of her love. Elsewhere, it instills in Swann a "thirst for an unknown delight" or serves as a "confidant of his love." When the affair with Odette seems at an end, the phrase is the "specific, volatile essence of that lost happiness." (One sign of the deterioration of the relationship is that Odette brings up the idea of going to Bayreuth while making it clear that she would prefer Swann to stay away—rather like Colette's *Claudine s'en va*.) In *Within a Budding Grove*, with Swann married to Odette, the phrase evokes moments of magical ordinariness, such as the brightness of moonlight in the Bois de Boulogne. "Sound can reflect, like water, like a mirror," Swann says. At this same moment, Marcel takes possession of the phrase. At first, the young man hardly notices it, and considers Vinteuil's music unremarkable; but such initial incomprehension is often the necessary prelude to the understanding of a great work of art. Thea Kronborg experiences something similar when she first hears Wagner.

In *The Captive*, the little phrase has its apotheosis. Marcel first connects Vinteuil's motifs of "the sensual and the anxious" to his own affairs, then addresses the work on its own terms. Rather than serving to remind Marcel of his own life, after the manner of Dorian Gray at *Tannhäuser*, the sonata pulls him into *its* life. He asks: "Was there in art a more profound reality, in which our true personality finds an expression that is not afforded it by the activities of life?" Marcel thinks of *Tristan*, an excerpt of which has just been performed at the Concerts Lamoureux. Dismissing the anti-Wagner faction—"I had none of the scruples of those who, like Nietzsche, are bidden by a sense of duty to shun in art as in life the beauty that tempts them"—Marcel revels in the teeming complexity of Wagner's world, which achieves an organic fullness through the ever-evolving recurrence of leitmotifs. He mentally revisits "those insistent, fleeting themes which visit an act, recede only to return again and again, and, sometimes distant, dormant, almost detached, are at other moments, while remaining vague, so pressing and so close, so internal, so organic, so visceral." There are "so many different strains, each is a person." Some examples are "the song of a bird, the call of a hunter's horn, the air that a shepherd plays upon his pipe, carving its silhouette of sound against the horizon." These are, respectively, the Forest Bird, Siegfried's horn, and the song that haunts the dying Tristan.

If Proust had kept to his original plan, the entire sequence of musical epiphanies would have hinged on *Parsifal*. (Much of the material that appears in *Time Regained*, the final book of the cycle, was sketched in 1910 and 1911.) References to "young girls in flower" bring to mind the Flower Maidens. In *The Guermantes Way*, when Marcel finds himself surrounded by beautiful women of society, he identifies them as "filles-fleurs"—the French name for the *Parsifal* maidens. These allusions would have culminated in a performance of the second act of *Parsifal* at a gathering chez the Princesse de Guermantes. Proust had in mind the Wagner performances that took place in Paris around the turn of the century, hosted by the likes of Judith Gautier, Mathilde Blumenthal, and Élisabeth Greffulhe.

In the early draft, Marcel arrives late at the Princesse's and is asked to wait outside the salon, because the Princesse has forbidden entry once the music has started. Marcel bides his time in the library, meditating on the task of the artist. It is, he thinks, to probe beyond the surface of appearances to a reality that abides far from ordinary life. Any happenstance triggering of memories permits the unveiling of a great reality, in the form of the one, the "only book"—the dream of Mallarmé. "Supernatural beings [*créatures*]" may be the vehicle for such revelations—beings that themselves come from the world of art.

One such being is the motif of the Good Friday music from *Parsifal*, which has floated through the door of the salon. (Proust apparently changed his mind about what music is being played: the Good Friday episode occurs in Act III, not Act II.) It is surely no accident, either, that the word "*créature*" is on Marcel's mind, since Gurnemanz is telling of how "all creation [*alle Kreatur*] rejoices" in springtime—"all that blooms and soon fades away." A meditation on the musical "being" follows:

> What exactly was its clear relationship to the first awakening of spring? Who could have said? It was still there, like an iridescent bubble that had not yet burst, like a rainbow that had faded for a moment only to begin shining again with a livelier brilliance, adding now all the tones of the prism to the mere two colors that had iridesced at the beginning and making them sing. And one remained in a silent ecstasy, as if a single gesture would have imperiled the delicious, frail presence which one wished to go on admiring for as long as it lasted and which would in a moment disappear.

In other words, the Good Friday motif has itself become one of the short-lived flowers that Gurnemanz cherishes. Wagner, too, blooms and fades.

In the final version of this sequence, as it unfolds in *Time Regained*, the Meister vanishes. Marcel still arrives for a musicale at the Princesse's, but with two differences: the Princesse turns out to be Mme Verdurin, newly risen in station; and the music goes unnamed. Is it still *Parsifal*? Perhaps, since the Princesse continues to issue pious Bayreuthian rules about late seating. On the other hand, Marcel speaks of "purely frivolous" pleasures. No Wagnerite would place *Parsifal* in that category.

Marcel's fantasia on the Good Friday Spell does not go to waste. Proust inserts portions of it into the published version of *Swann's Way*, fleshing out Swann's climactic experience of the Vinteuil Sonata. There, the little phrase is said to belong to "an order of supernatural beings whom we have never seen," and it floats through the air in a familiar way:

> It was still there, like an iridescent bubble that floats for a while unbroken. As a rainbow whose brightness is fading seems to subside, then soars again and, before it is extinguished, shines forth with greater splendor that it has ever shown; so to the two colors which the little phrase had hitherto allowed to appear it added others now, chords shot with every hue in the prism, and made them sing. Swann dared not move, and would have liked to compel all the other people in the room to remain still also, as if the slightest movement might imperil the magic presence, supernatural, delicious, frail, that was so soon to vanish.

Both Wagner and Vinteuil generate supernatural presences that fade away the moment they are perceived, like the creatures in the Good Friday Spell. Composers are sorcerers who entice such presences from the realm of hearing into the realm of sight.

The ultimate musical epiphany occurs in *The Captive*, when Marcel marvels over a late work by Vinteuil, his Septet. How noteworthy it is that "the boldest approximation to the bliss of the Beyond should have materialized precisely in the melancholy, respectable little bourgeois." The Septet is, Marcel claims, as great an advance over the Sonata as *Tristan* and *Meistersinger* are over *Tannhäuser*. Vinteuil's nondescript life only augments its aura, as a masterpiece that comes from nowhere. The composer who welds an "indivisible structure" from a "medley of scattered fragments" sounds much like the Wagner who assembles his operas from "insistent, fleeting themes." And once again, a musical phrase is characterized as a "*créature*": "This invisible being whose language I did not know but whom I understood so well . . . is perhaps the only *Inconnue* [unknown woman] that it has ever been my good fortune to meet."

Why does Wagner partly disappear from *In Search of Lost Time*? Nattiez gives a plausible explanation: Proust decided that Marcel should "experience his revelation through an *imaginary* work of art, for according to the logic of the novel a real work always disappoints: attainment of the absolute could only be suggested by a work that was unrealized, unreal, and ideal." The suppression of Wagner is also a displacement, allowing a successor figure to step forward. It is an unobtrusive agon, a quiet coup. Proust reassigns Meisterly authority to a man not unlike himself—a French artist of refined taste and retiring temperament, who rises from obscurity to posthumous triumph. It has not escaped notice that *In Search of Lost Time* is a kind of septet, a piece in seven parts. In the city where Wagnerism began, an equal of the *Ring* has appeared. It has no gods, Valkyries, or dwarves, but, on its final page, it offers an image of memory-laden men as "giants plunged into the years," astride the infinity of time.

10

NOTHUNG

The First World War and Hitler's Youth

Parsifal *in Barcelona, 1914*

Wagnerism reached its zenith in early 1914, on the eve of the First World War. By the terms of the Berne Convention, the copyright on Wagner's works expired at midnight on January 1. *Parsifal*, which had been considered the exclusive property of Bayreuth, entered the public domain, and within a few months it had received stagings in around fifty cities across Europe. On New Year's Day, the opera was mounted in Berlin, Rome, Budapest, Prague, and Madrid. Cosima Wagner had been dreading the moment for years. In 1901, she tried to win a copyright extension from the Reichstag; the bill was derided as a "Lex Cosima" and defeated by a vote of 123 to 107.

First off the mark was the Gran Teatre del Liceu, in Barcelona, whose *Parsifal* was scheduled to begin at 11:00 p.m. on New Year's Eve—midnight Bayreuth time. Catalans felt possessive of the work because local lore held that the Holy Grail once resided at Montserrat, the site of an ancient Benedictine monastery in the mountains northwest of Barcelona. Medieval versions of the Parzival tale placed the Grail in a castle called Montsalvage or Munsalvaesche; Wagner rendered this as Monsalvat, locating it in the "northern mountains of Gothic Spain." The poet Manuel Muntadas y Rovira was particularly keen on the association: he wrote a series of *Balades Wagnerianes*, one of which is titled "Montserrat-Montsalvat," and also delivered a lecture titled "The Probable Catalan Origins of the Legends of the Holy Grail." The sets for the Liceu *Parsifal* were modeled on Montserrat's rock-clinging architecture. The performance, led by Wagner's son-in-law Franz Beidler, actually began at 10:25 p.m., so that the bells of the Grail Temple could ring as midnight struck. It ended at five in the morning.

At the turn of the century, many Catalan artists sought to define themselves in contradistinction to Spanish culture and in solidarity with the rest of Europe. The sensuous Gothic forms of *modernisme*, the Catalan equivalent of Art Nouveau and Jugendstil, manifested that spirit in bravura style. As in Ireland, Wagner was a paragon for the cultivation of native myth—the "interpenetration of the art and the life of each people," as the poet Joan Maragall put it. The proscenium of the Palau de la Música Catalana—the hyper-ornate concert hall designed by the *modernista* architect Lluís Domènech i Montaner—features a relief sculpture, by Didac Masana i Majó and Pau Gargallo, of Valkyries leaping on their horses. At the Liceu, a painted panel shows Wotan and Brünnhilde with WAGNER emblazoned below. Four stained-glass windows depicting scenes from the *Ring* adorn the Cercle del Liceu, a club adjacent to the opera house. The city's most extreme Wagnerites styled themselves as Knights of the Grail in the service of *Parsifal*, which, in one reading, had been dictated by the Holy Spirit.

Antoni Gaudí, the greatest of the *modernistes*, had limited musical interests, preferring the simplicity of medieval chant. Yet his yen for organic grandeur matched Wagnerian aesthetics, particularly when he received commissions from patrons like the industrialist Eusebi Güell, a *Parsifal* fanatic who went to Bayreuth in 1891. Gaudí's Palau Güell could double as a

Wagner set: the massive-pillared subterranean stables have been described as a Nibelung lair, and the central space is capped by a *Parsifal*-like dome with a light-radiating cupola. "It was Gaudí who built the dome of Montsalvat," one of the architect's friends said. A central cupola also figures in the design of the gigantic, unfinished Basílica de la Sagrada Família, on which Gaudí began work in the year of Wagner's death. Robert Hughes writes: "Gaudí's love of extremes, his belief that architecture should deal in ambiguity and gloom, exaltation and anxiety, and theatrically primal spaces—the peak and the cavern—is entirely Wagnerian."

Catalans were not the only ones who felt proprietary about *Parsifal*. The Italians drew attention to Wagner's sojourns on the Amalfi Coast, his encounters with Siena Cathedral and the gardens of Rapallo, his death in Venice. The British gave weight to the story's Arthurian dimension. The French looked to the original *Perceval* romance of Chrétien de Troyes. Portuguese monarchists mythologized the sixteenth-century ruler King Sebastian as a Parsifal figure. Farther afield, Wagner surfaced in Japan, the Arab world, and India. The Sri Lankan Theosophical leader Curuppumullagē Jinarājadāsa hailed *Parsifal* as a true picture of the "struggle of the soul to the Light." Wagner's fame spilled over into the commercial marketplace. The Benz motorcar company manufactured a vehicle called the Parsifal, and a hue known as "Parsifal blue" had a vogue in American fashion.

At Bayreuth itself, cracks were forming in the dynastic façade—tensions that reflected wider political divides. In 1900, Isolde von Bülow, Richard and Cosima Wagner's illegitimate first child, had married Franz Beidler, whose skill as a conductor made him the festival's heir apparent. But the couple was too independent for Cosima's taste. After Houston Stewart Chamberlain entered the family circle, he led a vendetta against the Beidlers, whose expulsion would increase his influence. The family decided to disinherit Isolde on the fallacious grounds that she was not really Wagner's daughter. The ensuing power struggle culminated in a court proceeding that generated headlines in early 1914.

Although Isolde lost the case, and soon fell terminally ill with tuberculosis, the Wagners' reputation suffered lasting damage. On June 27, the day before the assassination of Archduke Franz Ferdinand in Sarajevo, the muckraking journalist Maximilian Harden published a merciless attack on the family, replete with sniggering allusions to homosexuality.

Siegfried Wagner was described as a "savior from a different-colored box" who "cannot wish to be too visible to the eye." Bayreuth's unsuccessful effort to prevent the expiration of the *Parsifal* copyright also dented its image. That campaign took on hyper-nationalist, xenophobic, and anti-semitic overtones.

A semblance of the old cosmopolitan atmosphere still prevailed when the festival opened, on July 22. The hotels were full of international names both great and small: Prince August Wilhelm, the Kaiser's fourth son; the writers Gerhart Hauptmann and Hermann Bahr; Rudolf Steiner, the founder of Anthroposophy; the Comte de Fitz-James and the Fürst zu Hohenlohe-Langenburg; the Finnish composer-conductor Armas Järnefelt; Misses S. F. Mead and W. H. Baxter of Dorset; Countess Annesley of Castlewellan, Ireland; Harry Cake, a piano dealer from Pottsville, Pennsylvania. There were a number of French visitors, though not as many as in earlier years. Among them was Joséphin Péladan, the erstwhile Sâr of Symbolist Paris, now more subdued in manner and dress.

The pilgrims fell into the usual dotty rhythms. The American writer and patron Clare Benedict, who was attending with her mother, read aloud in the woods each day before the stroll up the Green Hill to the Festspielhaus. On entering, she recalled, "we straightway forgot that any other life existed outside!" The Americans were permitted to watch a dress rehearsal. Siegfried Wagner monitored the proceedings from empty rows behind them; Karl Muck, the reigning *Parsifal* conductor, walked back to assess the balances. Once the festival got under way, though, the Benedicts began to notice odd behavior among the higher-ranking figures. Austria-Hungary delivered an ultimatum to Serbia on July 23, and a number of Austrians went home. Before *Siegfried*, Prince August Wilhelm was seen having a tense conversation to the side of the auditorium. Clare Benedict wrote: "The day before, he had been a bright, good-natured boy, today he was an anxious, stern-faced man." Acting on a hunch, the Benedicts booked an early departure, and left after *Götterdämmerung*.

On August 1, Muck conducted *Parsifal*. At 5:00 p.m., around the time the Grail Temple bells were ringing in Act I, the Kaiser ordered a mobilization against Russia. According to Péladan, the news of war raced through the crowd during the intermission before Act III, in which compassion heals a troubled world. There was, he claimed, an immediate transformation of German attitudes: "Glances became insolent, elbows sharp . . . the ears themselves revolted against the accents of our language." German listeners, on their side, probably had the same suspicion. When *Parsifal* ended that night, the festival fell silent for ten years.

WAGNER AT WAR

Franz Stassen, Off to Valhalla!

In his 1880 essay "Religion and Art," Wagner wondered whether bombs, torpedoes, and other military technologies would bring about the end of the world: "One could imagine that all of this—art, science, bravery and honor, life and possessions—could blow up through an unpredictable mistake." It was a vague prophecy of the mass devastation wrought by twentieth-century war. That some of this devastation was done in his name points to the contradiction that has dwelled at the heart of Wagnerism almost from the beginning. Despite the composer's intermittent hostility to the state and his late-period drift toward pacifism, his music often fueled a bellicose mood and, especially in Germany, became a psychological weapon.

When war broke out, German-speaking Wagnerites were already mobilized in spirit. In 1911, Reinhold von Lichtenberg had let it be known that the *Ring* represented the "victorious struggle of the Germanic ideal against foreign, therefore enemy powers." Lichtenberg also contentedly noted that foreigners were no longer in the majority in Bayreuth—indeed, that German attendees counted for 88 percent. Once hostilities began,

Wagner became part of the national arsenal. In the French town of Saint-Quentin, which German forces seized in the first weeks of their lightning assault on the Western Front, a commemorative concert was held for soldiers in the local basilica, and a military newspaper reported that a *Parsifal* excerpt on the organ was the highlight: "The wonderful acoustics of high Gothic spaces, the sanctified music of the noblest motifs and then the occasional dull thump of the distant guns. Gripping! We were all shaken to our core. The events of world history outside were thrust into the holiness of the moment. Here the sounds of the glorification of the pure fool, out there the deeds of the pure sword of the Germans." In August 1914, the illustrated magazine *Kladderadatsch* captioned a wild-eyed Siegfried with the text "Now the strong German spirit / Has forged the old sword anew." The next year, Richard Sternfeld, a conservative Jewish Wagnerite, published a pamphlet titled *Richard Wagner and the Holy German War*, which ended with a citation of Hans Sachs's *"Habt Acht!"* and the words "After the holy German war, holy German art—God grant it!"

Eventually, Wagner became part of military lingo. A defensive bulwark on the Western Front, constructed in 1916, was known as the Siegfried Line; another fortification was called the Wotan Line. In early 1917, when German troops retreated to the Siegfried Line and manned it, they did so under the rubric Operation Alberich. The retreat entailed the razing of houses, the destruction of railways and roads, the poisoning of wells, and the setting of mines and booby traps—an appropriation of Nibelung malevolence in the service of the German cause. In the summer of 1918, the army was preparing a counteroffensive named Plan Hagen, which never went into effect. The German-Jewish industrialist Walther Rathenau, in a 1918 tract titled *To Germany's Youth*, gave an acidulous summary of the reigning mentality: "There is always someone—Lohengrin, Walther, Siegfried, Wotan—who can do everything and beat everyone, who can redeem suffering virtue, punish vice, and bring universal salvation, in a sweeping pose, with fanfares, lighting effects, and scenery."

Back in Bayreuth, Houston Stewart Chamberlain issued essays and pamphlets titled "The German Love of Peace," "German Freedom," "Germany as Leading World Power," "Democratic Delusion," and "Hammer or Anvil." The polemics displayed unrelenting hostility not only toward the foreign enemy but also toward domestic threats of cosmopolitanism, democracy, journalism, and Jewishness. Wilhelm II remained a fervent follower, writing to Chamberlain that he read the essays with "heart-pounding enthusiasm." In a January 1917 letter, the Kaiser described the war as a "struggle between 2 *Weltanschauungen*: the Teutonic-German, for custom, right, loyalty and faith, true humanity, truth and genuine freedom, against the Anglo-Saxon, the worship of Mammon, the power of money, pleasure, land-grabbing, lies, betrayal, deceit, and, not least, treacherous assassination!" One worldview must win, Wilhelm said, and the other must *"go under"*—a presumably inadvertent echo of Wagner's forbidding formula, *der Untergang*.

I n France, Wagner again fell from grace, his name once more synonymous with German aggression. Cartoonists spoofed the Kaiser by costuming him in Wagnerian poses—for example, as Lohengrin riding a swan motorcar. In the fall of 1914, Camille Saint-Saëns launched an anti-Wagner campaign on the front page of *L'Écho de Paris*, warning of a "machine of war against French art." Members of the right-wing Action Française joined the assault. Léon Daudet, who had earlier attacked Wagnerism as a stealth invasion incited by Jews, considered the Great War the antidote to the "German poison" that Wagner had helped to inject into the French bloodstream. Pierre Lasserre insinuated that the composer was of Jewish descent. Charles Maurras, the chief figure of the Action Française, shuddered at the memory of the *Revue wagnérienne* and declared that "the state must de-Germanicize itself." Maurras's reference to "intellectual police" carrying out this cleansing could be taken literally: Louis Aragon recalled gendarmes entering apartments to ask residents to stop playing Wagner.

The anti-Wagner campaign reached the front lines, or at least approached

them. Trucks bringing fresh meat to troops at the front were stamped with an image of a laughing cow, devised by the illustrator Benjamin Rabier. The insignia was dubbed "La Wachkyrie"—"*La vache qui rit*," or "The cow who laughs." The name ridiculed the German habit of giving Wagnerian dimensions to military actions—as in Stassen's picture of Valkyries carrying German soldiers to Valhalla, or Wilhelm Trübner's 1914 lithograph of the Kaiser surrounded by Valkyries on the battlefield. "La Wachkyrie" inspired a fox-trot of the same title and a brand of cheese that remains popular today.

A few loyalists dared to speak up. "Even at the height of the war," the poet and essayist André Suarès wrote, "I want to recognize Richard Wagner as the most beautiful artist of his century." The proper attitude is to remain open to great artists on the enemy side: "One must not be German in French." Suarès goes on to argue that *Parsifal* offers an implicit critique of the philosophy of race and conquest. Péladan takes a similar line in his 1916 book *The War of Ideas*. Although he denounces almost everything German—including the hiring of German maids—he will not hold the Meister responsible for the conflict. Instead, he interprets the *Ring* as an allegory of rising Boche brutality: "*Das Rheingold* begins, like the present war, with contempt for treaties, with the famous scrap of paper." Wotan becomes the Kaiser, a megalomaniac brute. In the end, Péladan writes, the Boches should be "crushed to the rhythm of the Valkyries."

Proust remained a steadfast Wagnériste. Distraught that French artists would deprive themselves of the "prodigious fertilization that is hearing *Tristan*," the novelist called Saint-Saëns's campaign "imbecilic." Robert de Saint-Loup, the liberal-minded cavalry officer of *In Search of Lost Time*, inherits Proust's Germanophilia: "If Saint-Loup had occasion in a letter to mention a song by Schumann, he never gave any but the German title, nor did he use any periphrasis to tell me that, when at dawn on the edge of the forest he had heard the first twittering of a bird, his rapture had been as great as though he had been addressed by the bird in that 'sublime Siegfried' which he so looked forward to hearing after the war." It is not to be; Saint-Loup falls at the front.

When Italy joined the Entente of France, Great Britain, and Russia in 1915, Wagner largely disappeared from Italian opera houses and concert halls. The following year, the conductor Arturo Toscanini placed the Forest Murmurs and Siegfried's Funeral Music on the program of a benefit concert in Rome, precipitating a noisy protest by a band of Futurists. During the Funeral Music, one audience member cried out, "For the dead of Padua!" Ninety-three civilians had recently been killed during an Austrian bombardment of Padua. It turned out that the shout came from a soldier who heard the Wagner as a fitting memorial to his comrades. Musical reprisals were less common among the Central Powers: during the war, Vienna heard Verdi's operas about as often as Wagner's.

The United States declared war on Germany on the afternoon of April 6, 1917. The Met was in the middle of its annual Good Friday *Parsifal*—"that drama of peace and good will among men," as the Met's general manager wryly recalled. The Met board soon began discussing whether Wagner should still be played. The issue reached the desk of President Woodrow Wilson, who wrote that "personally I should hate to see them stop German opera." At first, the Met seemed inclined to keep its Wagner, but by the fall the mood had changed. The Committee on Public Information, Wilson's propaganda outfit, was fomenting a wave of anti-German hysteria. One victim was Karl Muck, Bayreuth's *Parsifal* conductor, who led the Boston Symphony. In October 1917, Muck was falsely accused of having refused to conduct "The Star-Spangled Banner." Wild rumors spread to the effect that he was a German spy. A crowd at a meeting in Baltimore chanted, "Kill Muck! Kill Muck!" Around the same time, the Met board voted against presenting German opera. In March 1918, Muck was arrested on trumped-up charges and sent to an internment camp.

In Britain, the operas stayed in the repertory, although protests were not uncommon. Wagner's staunchest supporter was the unflappably debonair Thomas Beecham, who conducted *Tristan* in Manchester and London in 1916. When a media magnate questioned the endeavor, Beecham pointed out that Wagner was the "favorite composer of that section of the audience which was in khaki." Indeed, a critic reported that British officers had requested Saturday performances so that they could see *Tristan* on leave.

Many Wagnerites on the Entente side believed that the composer not only stood apart from contemporary Germany but could be seen as actively opposing it. Péladan was not the only one who saw the *Ring* as a commentary on German arrogance and comeuppance. Glyn Philpot, a gay British Wagnerite, produced an illustrated pamphlet titled *The Twilight of the Hohenzollerns*, which reconfigured episodes from the *Ring* as a "sub-conscious prophecy of Germany's downfall," with Prussian militarism grasping after world dominion, the maidens of Truth, Liberty, and Justice lodging their protest ("false and base are all who revel above"), and Bismarck issuing Erda-like warnings. At first glance, the piece reads like a satire, but it becomes apparent that Philpot and his literary collaborator, Christopher Sandeman, are in earnest. Philpot's images share in the cult of the sculpted male form that is common in much Wagnerian iconography, but these are bodies marked for death.

Even die-hard Wagnerites had to wonder whether the war had caused the Meister irreparable harm. Camille Mauclair, for one, wrote that German guns had done as much damage to Wagner as they had to Reims Cathedral. "The creation of Empire, with the Empire he will be dead."

WAR FICTION AND POETRY

If, as Thomas Mann said, Wagner epitomized the nineteenth century—its grandeur, its splendor, its faith in progress, its bourgeois materialism, its nationalist mythologies, its moral arrogance, its spiritual longing, and, above all, its veneration of art and artists—then the Great War indeed killed him off, as it did large tracts of the nineteenth-century cultural legacy. To all appearances, the great Romantic liturgy of art-religion, enmeshed with mystical nationalism, had abetted the collective madness of history's deadliest war to date. Meanwhile, new forms of culture were asserting themselves through technologies of broadcast and reproduction. The mobilization of millions of young men helped to popularize genres that could be circulated and consumed quickly. Jazz records, mass-market novels, and nickelodeons not only served the needs of commercial entertainment but fed the appetites of those modernist artists who were turning their attention from metaphysical heights to the everyday. These intersecting forces explain the rapid fading of Wagner's aura from 1914 to 1918—from the *Parsifal* year to Plan Hagen.

Yet the old sorcerer refused to go away, and the twentieth century soon found new uses for him. His music established itself on the newfangled Victrola, the brassy bits breaking through the ambient crackle. The machinery of war fell in sync with Wagnerian myth: aerial combat stimulated thoughts of Valkyries decades before *Apocalypse Now*. The dream of the total artwork underwent radical transformations in the hands of Dadaists and Futurists. At the same time, the day-to-day havoc of war led some Romantic-leaning artists to treasure all the more Wagner's capacity to deliver messages from a buried past or a possible future.

In 1919, Ford Madox Hueffer changed his last name to Ford, thus excising Germanness from his person. Unexpectedly, Ford's major work of the postwar era, the tetralogy *Parade's End*, turned out to be his most Wagnerian creation. A testament to the war's shattering psychic impact, the cycle depends on an elaborate system of leitmotifs to unify its discontinuous, often hallucinatory narrative. Rebekah Lockyer, in an essay on Ford's relationship with Wagner, tracks the recurrence of a particular sonic motif: the clatter of a tea tray falling to the ground. In the prewar scenes of *Some Do Not . . .* , the first novel of the tetralogy, a tea tray drops a short distance, jangling a tense social scene. Then it becomes a simile for an auto accident—"There was a crash and scraping: like twenty tea-trays"—and finally a surreal metaphor for the cacophony of war: "An immense tea-tray, august, its voice filling the black circle of the horizon, thundered to the ground." Ford had served in the British Army, suffering a severe concussion in 1916. *Parade's End* contains many jolting evocations of the soundscape of battle, with fragmentary, at times nonverbal motifs mapping the traumatized consciousness.

In the two war-centered novels at the heart of the cycle, Wagner is deployed with surgical precision, first to suggest the heedlessness of the prewar mind and then to show its crack-up. The central figure is Christopher Tietjens, who has the aspect of an able-bodied Anglo-Saxon hero but is diffident to the point of blankness. His wife, Sylvia, is a cold seductress racked by religious doubts. When Christopher goes off to battle, Sylvia bizarrely decides to visit him in Rouen, just behind the front, in an attempt to win back his alienated affections. Faced with the noise of the male wartime order—guns in the distance, officers carousing, a gramophone blaring—she turns to favorite strains of *Tannhäuser*, and to the Venusberg sequence in particular, explicitly comparing herself to Venus. By extension Valentine Wannop, a young suffragette who has captured Christopher's attention, is likened to Elisabeth, Tannhäuser's pure-hearted savior. As Lockyer notes, the brokenness of the writing displays a "polyphonic simultaneity," as Sylvia senses impending triumph:

> She was humming Venusberg music: she knew music if she knew nothing else . . .
>
> She said: "You call the compounds where you keep the Waacs Venusbergs, don't you? Isn't it queer that Venus should be your own? . . . Think of poor Elisabeth!"
>
> The room where they were dancing was very dark . . . It was queer to be in his arms . . . She had known better dancers . . . He had looked ill . . . Perhaps he was . . . Oh, poor Valentine-Elisabeth . . . What a funny position! . . . The good gramophone played . . . *Destiny!* . . . You see, father! . . . In his arms! Of course, dancing is not really . . . But so near the real thing! So near!" [. . .]
>
> Her gown of gold tissue was like the colobium sindonis the King wore at the coronation . . . As they mounted the stairs she thought what a fat tenor Tannhäuser always was! . . . The Venusberg music was dinning in her ears . . . She said: "Sixty-six inexpressibles! I'm as sober as a judge . . . I need to be!"

In *A Man Could Stand Up—*, Tietjens plunges into the thick of battle, coming face to face with the enemy. The burrowing-out and undermining of trenches occasions a *Ring* analogy: "It was, of course, just like German spooks to go mining by candle-light. Obsoletely Nibelungen-like. Dwarfs probably!" The sounds of war take on the timbres of a Wagnerian orchestra:

> Noise increased. The orchestra was bringing in *all* the brass, *all* the strings, *all* the wood-wind, all the percussion instruments. The performers threw about biscuit tins filled with horse-shoes; they emptied sacks of coal on cracked gongs, they threw down forty-storey iron houses. It

was comic to the extent that an operatic orchestra's crescendo is comic. Crescendo! . . . Crescendo! CRRRRRESC . . . The Hero *must* be coming! He didn't! [. . .]

The Hero arrived. Naturally, he was a Hun. He came over, all legs and arms going, like a catamount; struck the face of the parados, fell into the trench on the dead body, with his hands to his eyes, sprang up again and danced.

Lockyer relates this episode to one of Ford's own wartime experiences. One day the novelist was playing Isolde's Transfiguration at the piano when he looked up to see the Prince of Wales, the future Edward VIII, listening. "Go on playing," said the prince. The swell of sound that accompanies the Hero Hun could be an ironic transcription of the so-called Liebestod, with a "bumpy diminuendo" following. It could also echo Siegfried's Funeral Music in *Götterdämmerung*—a bombastic memorial for a random death.

A poet in the tradition of Stéphane Mallarmé, aloof from the fracas of history, might have been expected to fall silent when the noise of war commenced. Paul Valéry, who had accompanied Mallarmé to the Concerts Lamoureux, somehow found his voice. Like so many members of his generation, Valéry turned to Wagner at an early age, and, unlike many of them, stayed loyal throughout his life, even through two wars with Germany. In 1893, when he was in his early twenties, he had a particularly overwhelming encounter with *Walküre*—so much so that it apparently contributed to his post-adolescent decision to give up writing poetry for some twenty years. He recalled, in the faux-submissive manner of Baudelaire: "I loved the *Walküre* so much, and the Wagnerian conception had so struck me, penetrated me, that the first effect of this action was to make me reject, with the sadness of impotence, everything that was literature." Wagner, he said, filled him with despair. Mallarmé's death also contributed to what became known as Valéry's "Great Silence."

In 1912, at the prompting of his colleague André Gide, Valéry had begun to revisit his adolescent work and shape new material. The project acquired new urgency after 1914: Valéry later said that he felt compelled to produce something from his state of "wartime uselessness." By 1917,

Valéry had produced a five-hundred-line poem titled *La Jeune Parque*, or "The Young Fate," which almost immediately attained masterpiece status. Oddly, having blamed Wagner for his silence, Valéry credited his reawakening to the same source. His experience of *Walküre* was, he said, a "somewhat remarkable case of impregnation," one that eventually led him to produce his own version of Wagnerian "drame lyrique." As he planned the poem, he thought of Wagner as the union of Shakespeare and Beethoven. Such comments are all the more striking given that Valéry made them during the Second World War.

Like Mallarmé's "The Afternoon of a Faun," its obvious model, *La Jeune Parque* is the monologue of a rarefied spirit surveying a sensuous landscape. The image of a solitary Fate who awakens to a new consciousness of the world calls to mind Wagner's women of lonely wisdom—Erda and the Norns in the *Ring*, Kundry in *Parsifal*. The setting is exceedingly vague, yet it has a mythological character. As the Fate examines the nature of her consciousness and its relation to physical reality, she makes reference to gods, mortals, temptations, wounds, rocky gorges, forests, fires, monsters, and gold. One passage, in particular, brings the poem within sight of Wagner's gods and fates:

> This body, I pardon it, and I am tasting ash.
> I am wholly given over to the bliss of descent,
> Open to black witnesses, arms racked,
> Among words without end, without me stammered.
> Sleep, my wisdom, sleep. Shape this absence;
> Turn back to the seed and dark innocence.
> Abandon yourself alive to dragons, to treasures.
> Sleep always! Descend, sleep always! Descend, sleep, sleep!

When Wotan summons Erda in *Siegfried*, he finds her confused by the events swirling around her, even though she has mothered the Norns who hold the rope of fate. Frustrated, Wotan sends her away: "Descend! Descend to eternal sleep!" When the Norns of *Götterdämmerung* discover that the rope of Fate has been broken, they cry, "Down! . . . Down!" And when Brünnhilde prepares to ride into Siegfried's pyre and return the Ring to the Rhine, she gives a consoling message to Wotan: "Rest! Rest, you god!" These descents and slumbers signal in various ways the passing of the gods. Valéry's Fate, though, does not sink into futility or despair; rather, she finds herself on the verge of a purely sensual ecstasy. As she watches the sun rise at the shore of the ocean, she experiences the "sweet and strong return of the delight of birth."

All this is so far distant from the horror of 1917 that Valéry may seem to be fleeing from reality into esoteric purity. Yet, insofar as the poem marks the rebirth of his own poetical instinct, it is really a return to the fray. Where Wagner's gods give way to an unknown human future, Valéry's Fate is more like a god assuming human form. In that sense, she symbolizes a world of art rendered speechless by global catastrophe. Like Wagner, Valéry was something of a conservative anarchist, who felt that art could defy the everyday with images of utopia. Only, he drops the grand-bourgeois pose of mastery: as Theodor W. Adorno observed, this poet makes no effort to dominate readers, but instead opens up an endless dialogue with them, the subject of which is the process by which art comes into being.

T he warring nations justified the slaughter of millions through a cult of martyred heroes, promising them a spot in one Valhalla or another. Willa Cather confronted the hollowness of the noble death when her cousin G. P. Cather was killed at the Battle of Cantigny, the first major action by the American Expeditionary Forces. In 1922, she published a novel titled *One of Ours*, which tells the curtailed life story of a Nebraskan named Claude Wheeler—a sensitive, irresolute youth who seeks glory in war. For a Wagnerian parallel, she looked not to the combative Siegmund or Siegfried but to the peaceable Parsifal. After the novel appeared, the poet Orrick Johns, later a prominent American Communist, asked Cather whether she had Wagner's final opera in mind, to which the author replied: "You wouldn't have made a bad Sherlock Holmes. You are the first sleuth who has dug the Parsifal theme out of Claude Wheeler—and I thought I had buried it so deep—deep! Yet, all through the first part of the book, I kept promising myself that I would put 'The Blameless Fool, by Pity Enlightened' on the title page."

Claude marches out of the same Nebraska landscape that spawned so many Cather characters, but there is pointed emphasis on the Wheelers' German neighbors, on their industriousness and love of music. At college, Claude befriends a cultured German family called the Erlichs, one of whose relations is a redoubtable contralto named Wilhelmina Schroeder-Schatz—a name that Wagnerites would recognize as a variation on Wilhelmine Schröder-Devrient, the vocal idol of Wagner's youth. The advent of war tests these ties. Claude says, "The people that sing all those beautiful songs about women and children went into Belgian villages and—" whereupon his mother cuts him off. Paranoid suspicions fall upon the local Germans, who find that they are no longer free to speak their minds.

Frustrated in love and ambition, Claude feels a surge of purpose as he enlists in the army and prepares to sail to France. In his mind, he is joining a phalanx of pure-hearted soldiers who will "make war without rage, with uncompromising generosity and chivalry." As the boat sails past the Statue of Liberty, Cather comments that the passengers look like "nothing but a crowd of American boys going to a football game somewhere." It is also a replay of an ancient scene: "Youths were sailing away to die for an idea, a sentiment, for the mere sound of a phrase . . . and on their departure they were making vows to a bronze image in the sea."

At about this point, *One of Ours* slips into a stranger, eerier tone. As Claude and company sail to France, influenza claims the lives of several men, including a corporal named Fritz Tannhauser and a lieutenant known mostly as the Virginian—perhaps a joke on Owen Wister. Tannhauser is reduced to feverish babbling; the Virginian gets a nosebleed and dies soon after. Even before the battlefield is reached, young bodies prove too frail for the legendary roles they long to play.

In France, Claude meets an aloof, terse lieutenant named David Gerhardt, who, it turns out, had a distinguished career as a violinist before joining the army. When someone puts on a phonograph record of the Meditation from Massenet's *Thaïs*, Claude notices Gerhardt smiling, and, on looking at the record, sees Gerhardt's name printed on it. An almost romantic friendship develops between the two. (Cather is alert to the all-male energy of soldier communities, and includes the detail that a dead German officer is found with a picture of a young man around his neck, "pale as snow, with blurred forget-me-not eyes.") Claude is allowed a brief epiphany at the church of St. Ouen in Rouen—colors glowing in stained-glass windows, bells ringing from the tower—but cannot grasp the discrepancy between that experience and the clamor of modern war. He goes to the front and happily takes his place among his self-fashioned Knights of the Grail. "With these men he could do anything," he thinks to himself.

"He had learned the mastery of men." A few moments later, he is slain by German bullets. Almost simultaneously, Gerhardt is blown to pieces elsewhere on the battlefield.

Cather's substratum of irony eluded many readers, who saw the novel as a naïve celebration of patriotic sacrifice. Initially, she did view the war in those terms; in a letter written after G. P. Cather had fallen, she named him one of "God's soldiers." By 1922, her perspective had changed, but she avoided inserting antiwar messages. Instead, Claude is allowed to die in the comfort of his illusions. If he is a pure fool in the Parsifal mode— early on he is called a "mortal fool kid," and after his death his mother says that he "was so afraid of being fooled"—his rite of initiation fails. Susan Rosowski writes: "Parsifal heals the wounded, sees and bows before the Grail as a holy light anoints him, then, as others bow before him, raises the Holy Grail in a renewal of consecration. This is very like the destiny Claude *feels* as he leads his men in battle; but Claude's salvation is only in his mind. The holy light he sees is enemy fire . . ."

In 1908, the Hon. Mrs. Assheton Harbord, a pioneering female balloonist, crossed the English Channel in a balloon she named the *Valkyrie*. This may have been the first association between the Valkyries and air travel—a now-familiar trope that testifies to Wagner's near-infinite mal-

leability. With the advent of aerial warfare, the linkage became a cliché almost overnight. In H. G. Wells's 1908 science-fiction novel *The War in the Air*, Asian and German airships do battle over Niagara Falls: "Perhaps a hundred yards above the water, out of the south, riding like Valkyries swiftly through the air on the strange steeds the engineering of Europe had begotten upon the artistic inspiration of Japan, came a long string of Asiatic swordsmen." In 1910, the Aeronautical Syndicate Ltd. introduced a monoplane called the *Valkyrie*, which its designer, Horatio Barber, hoped would be used for military purposes.

The romance of the airman was inseparable from the danger of his mission. William Butler Yeats's 1918 poem "An Irish Airman Foresees His Death" portrays a pilot who has no sympathy for Britain's war on Germany: "Those that I fight I do not hate / Those that I guard I do not love." Nonetheless, he is darkly exhilarated by the prospect of meeting his fate "somewhere among the clouds above." He follows a "lonely impulse of delight" into a liminal condition he describes as "this life, this death." The poem honored the painter-turned-pilot Robert Gregory, Lady Gregory's son, who was shot down in 1918. Gregory shared his mother's liking for Wagner, and had designed Symbolist sets for Yeats's *The Shadowy Waters*. Whether or not Gregory foresaw his death or considered his life a "waste of breath," the figure in the poem articulates a Liebestod of the air.

That *Tristan*-esque longing for oblivion in the sky becomes explicit in the wartime work of Gabriele d'Annunzio, author of the classic Liebestod narrative *The Triumph of Death*. When Italy entered the war, d'Annunzio reinvented himself as "Italy's Hero Airman-Poet," to quote a newsreel of the period. He lost the use of one eye in January 1916, when his plane made an emergency landing. To save his other eye, he lay in bed for weeks, bandaged and in darkness. He began writing a poetic work called *Notturno*, working on thin strips of paper. It is a hymn to night, darkness, and death. D'Annunzio fantasizes his own martyrdom and salutes the martyrdom of comrades: "There is no nobler bond in the world today than this tacit pact that turns two lives and two wings into a single speed, a single prowess, a single death." The bond surpasses "love's most secret, unexpressed shudder"; it is consummated in the glory of the crash. As d'Annunzio recovered from his injury, he listened constantly to music. When a friend played *Tristan* on the piano, he reported that "all my blood trembles." Returning to battle, he wrote one of his girlfriends a farewell letter that "had the rhythm of certain bars of *Tristan*." In the same period he invented a tribal chant for his pilots: "Eia Eia Eia! Alalà!" This was supposed to be a battle cry of the ancient Greeks, though it sounds curiously like the Rhinemaidens' "Wallala weiala weia!" The chant later became part of the rite of Italian Fascism.

Although Proust was more or less the opposite of d'Annunzio in every respect, he indulged in his own romance of the war in the sky. The novelist had taken an interest in flying machines, and, more particularly, in the men who flew them. In 1913, he fell in love with Alfred Agostinelli, who served for a time as his chauffeur and secretary. Agostinelli wanted to become a flier, and enrolled in flying school under the name Marcel Swann. Desperate to win Agostinelli's affections, Proust ordered an airplane for him, proposing to engrave it with lines from Mallarmé—the sonnet "Le vierge, le vivace et le bel aujourd'hui," about a swan trapped in ice. Agostinelli died in a flying accident in May 1914. Albertine, Marcel's chief love object in *In Search of Lost Time*, inherits aspects of Agostinelli's personality, especially his love of speed.

One astounding scene in *Time Regained* depicts a nighttime Zeppelin raid on Paris. Searchlights scan the sky, sirens wail, and fighter planes soar up to do battle with the intruder. Saint-Loup, watching the planes in flight, sees them as a constellation of stars, and then changes his analogy to account for their dizzying descent:

> Just as you have got used to thinking of them as stars, they break away to pursue an enemy or to return to the ground after the all-clear, the moment of *apocalypse*, when even the stars are hurled from their courses . . . One had to ask oneself whether they were indeed pilots and not Valkyries who were sailing upwards . . . That's it, the music of the sirens was a "Ride of the Valkyries"! There's no doubt about it, the Germans have to arrive before you can hear Wagner in Paris.

The composer who served so often as an emblem of artistic power now becomes a metaphor for military aggression. Readers of *In Search of Lost Time* have been subtly prepared for the shift. Earlier in the cycle, the moaning sound of a closing door is compared to instrumental figures accompanying the Pilgrims' Chorus in *Tannhäuser*, and a ringing telephone to the shepherd's pipe in *Tristan*. In *The Captive*, the narrator meditates on Wagner's "Vulcan-like skill," his "industrious toil," and wonders how sublimity can emanate from mere craft. When the music lifts us into the stratosphere, we are winged aloft by

> birds akin not to Lohengrin's swan but to that aeroplane which I had seen at Balbec convert its energy into vertical motion, glide over the sea and vanish in the sky. Perhaps, as the birds that soar highest and fly most swiftly have more powerful wings, one of these frankly material vehicles was needed to explore the infinite, one of these 120 horsepower machines—the Mystère model—in which nevertheless, however high one flies, one is prevented to some extent from enjoying the silence of space by the overpowering roar of the engine!

With this startling analogy, Proust takes the measure not only of the industrial might of Wagner's art but of its posthumous alliance with technology, its dissemination on radio and through recording. Although at the time there was no plane called the Mystère, the French air force began using a fighter-bomber with that name after the Second World War.

WAGNER DADA

Speed, flight, noise, war, chaos, cut-up, collage, the overturning of all artistic norms: these were the values, to different degrees, of Futurism and Dada. On the surface, the avatars of the avant-garde seem the raging antithesis of Wagner and Wagnerism. Indeed, some of them took aim at the Sorcerer of Bayreuth with a venom that Nietzsche might have envied. In January 1914, at the height of the worldwide *Parsifal* craze, the Futurist firebrand Filippo Tommaso Marinetti published a two-page manifesto titled "Down with the Tango and *Parsifal*!," which had the subtitle "A circular letter to some cosmopolitan women friends who give tango tea-dances and who Parsifalize themselves." The tango is dismissed as a sentimental, decadent affair. It is compared to "Tristan and Isolde who withhold their climax to excite King Mark." Marinetti then takes aim at the opera of the moment:

> If the tango is bad enough, *Parsifal* is even worse, as it inoculates the dancers, swaying to and fro, bored and listless, with an incurable musical neurasthenia. How can we avoid *Parsifal*, with its downpours, its puddles, and its floods of mystical tears? *Parsifal* is a systematic devaluation of life! A factory cooperative of sadness and despair. Tuneless stretching and straining for weak stomachs. Poor digestion and heavy breathing of forty-year-old virgins. Whining of flabby and constipated old priests. Wholesaling and retailing of bad consciences and a stylish effeminacy for snobs. Blood deficiency, feebleness of the loins, hysteria, anemia, and greensickness. Prostration, brutalization, and violation of Mankind. Ridiculous scraping of failed, mutilated notes. Snoring of drunken organs sprawling in the vomit of foul-tasting leitmotifs. False tears and pearls flaunted by a Mary Magdalene with a plunging neckline more suited to Maxim's. Polyphonic pus from Amfortas's festering scabs. Worn-out wailings of the Knights of the Holy Grail. Nonsensical Satanism of Kundry . . . Antediluvianism! Antediluvianism! Enough of it!

Guillaume Apollinaire, coiner of the word "surrealism," consigned Wagner to the category "shit," though Dante, Shakespeare, Goethe, and Tolstoy made for good company. The war sharpened such convictions, as strident avant-garde rhetoric mixed with anti-German fervor. Apollinaire declared in 1918: "There is no longer any Wagnerianism among us, and young authors have cast aside all the enchanted hand-me-downs of the colossal romanticism of Germany and Wagner."

Indeed, the classic works of Futurism and Dada—the sound poems of Marinetti and Hugo Ball, Luigi Russolo's noise machines, Marcel Duchamp's urinal, Hans Arp's collages, Kurt Schwitters's assemblages—represent a total break, with Wagner as with all else. Tristan Tzara made mocking reference to the "Wagnerian bouillabaisse." Even so, the manifesto style owes something to the revolutionary-minded composer who wrote of his "enormous desire to commit acts of artistic terrorism." When Marinetti denounces the "unending, futile veneration of the past," he sounds like the

Wagner who wrote, in a letter to Liszt, that "the monumental character of our art will disappear, we shall abandon our habit of clinging firmly to the past, our egotistical concern for permanence and immortality at any price." That Dada originated in Zurich, the site of Wagner's early exile, adds a historical symmetry. The exhibition-performances at Galerie Dada took place a short walk from the Hotel Baur au Lac, where Wagner first read aloud the libretto of the *Ring*.

Peter Bürger's canonical study *Theory of the Avant-Garde* emphasizes the degree to which Futurism and Dada emerged from the fin-de-siècle milieu of Symbolism, Decadence, and Aestheticism. Wagnerism is missing from Bürger's scheme, but it deserves a place. Marinetti shows the dynamic with particular clarity. During his early years as a music and opera critic in turn-of-the-century Italy, he described Wagner as "the greatest decadent genius and therefore the most appropriate artist for our modern souls." In a preview of his future Futurism, he applauded Wagner's "frenetic exuberance," his refusal of "meditation and silence"—language similar to d'Annunzio's. Contemplating the split between Wagner and Nietzsche, Marinetti declined to take sides: he wanted both Wagnerian majesty and Nietzschean clarity.

According to Bürger, Aestheticism's divorce from lived reality sets the stage for the decisive gesture of the historical avant-garde: the socially isolated artist turns back to the public sphere, seeking to "reintegrate art into the praxis of life." The autonomous institution of art is assaulted in the name of an aesthetics that doubles as politics. Arriving at that stage, Marinetti felt the need to cast off bourgeois trappings of "stillness, rapture, and reverie," and Wagner gets jettisoned with the rest. The poet's first Futurist Manifesto of 1909 touts the motorcar, the locomotive, the airplane, the noise of industry. The "Variety Theater" manifesto of 1913 proscribes the "Solemn, the Sacred, the Serious, and the Sublime," and endorses the practice of adapting, compressing, and parodying grand artworks on variety stages: "We support unconditionally a forty-minute performance of *Parsifal*, which is currently in preparation for a great music-hall in London."

Marinetti's tirades against *Parsifal* betray a certain anxiety about whether he has traveled as far from his Wagnerite origins as he wishes us to believe. *Zang Tumb Tuuum*, his 1912 conjuration of the fourth-century Battle of Adrianople, may abandon conventional syntactic logic

and coin phonetic words, but much of the vocabulary is stuck in a grandiose Romantic mode:

> Marcia del cannoneggiamento futurista colosso-leitmotif-maglio-genio-
> novatore-ottimismo fame-ambizione (*TERRIFICO ASSOLUTO SO-
> LENNE EROICO PESANTE IMPLACABILE FECONDANTE*) **zang
> tuumb tumb tumb**

> March of cannonade futurist colossus-leitmotif-hammer-genius-
> innovator-optimism hunger-ambition (*TERRIFYING ABSOLUTE
> SOLEMN HEROIC HEAVY IMPLACABLE FERTILE*) **zang tuumb
> tumb tumb**

Other Futurists admitted a direct debt. Francesco Balilla Pratella, in his
writings on Futurist music, spoke respectfully of "the glorious and revolutionary era dominated by the sublime genius of Wagner," and classified the composer as a Futurist *avant la lettre*. Pratella's opera *L'aviatore
Dro*, first performed in 1920, applied Wagnerian themes and techniques
to the tale of a heroically self-sacrificing aviator, thereby adding to the
subgenre of the aeronautic Wagner. The Spanish avant-gardist Ramón
Gómez de la Serna, writing under the pseudonym Tristán, began his
1910 "Futurist Proclamation to the Spaniards" thus: "Futurism! Insurrection! Clamor! Feast with Wagnerian music! Modernism! Sidereal violence!
Whirling about amid the poisonous pomp and circumstance of life! Anti-
universityism! Cypress bark! Iconoclasm! A stone cast in the nick of time
at the moon!"

The reintegration of art and life is, after all, a Wagnerian project. Futurists seized on the Gesamtkunstwerk, making it newer and louder. In the
prewar years, Georg Fuchs and other theatrical visionaries had called for a
total fusion of artistic disciplines, a final erasure of the boundary between
stage and audience. Kandinsky and Hilma af Klint had brought the total
artwork into an abstract, spiritualized sphere. The Futurists, by contrast,
reveled in a dizzying simultaneity of everyday voices, reflecting the circus,
the music hall, and the variety theater. Futurist spectacles played upon
all the senses, including taste and smell. *Piedigrotta*, a carnivalesque event
that overtook the Futurist Gallery in Rome in 1914, included the odor
of live fireworks. Futurist banquets in the postwar period coordinated

theater, music, interior design, and food. The historian Günter Berghaus writes: "The Futurists wanted to be architects of a new world and to turn life into the ultimate Total Work of Art." Eventually, in the 1933 essay "Total Theater," Marinetti would proclaim that "Futurist theater will synthesize the world."

The Dada historian Peter Dayan has noted Gesamtkunstwerk yearnings among Dada artists as well. Hugo Ball, whose diary *Flight out of Time* makes repeated reference to Wagner, formulated a theory of *Gesamtkunst*, or "total art," from which the element of the "work" has been dropped. The abandonment of the artwork concept, to which even Kandinsky's most radical abstractions stayed true, allowed for the eruption of Dada mayhem. "A Zurich Dada soirée is never a work with a title and a single creator," Dayan writes. Artistic activities in various media transpire concurrently: visual art is on display, music is played, dance is performed, poetry and lectures are recited. But no explicit attempt is made to relate these artistic gestures to one another. The resulting experience is collective only in the sense of juxtaposition and simultaneity—and, perhaps, by way of connections being made in the minds of participants and onlookers alike. Likewise, the art historian Maria Stavrinaki sees the Merz constructions of Kurt Schwitters not as an anarchic activity but as a reunification of dispersed fragments. Schwitters engages in Wagnerian religiosity when he says that artistic rituals, like those of the church, achieve "the liberation of humankind from the worries of everyday life."

The inability of twentieth-century avant-gardes to break entirely with Wagner is more evidence of their nineteenth-century roots. In the words of Alain Badiou, they were "romantic in their conviction that art must be reborn immediately as absolute." Even as they laid siege to a Wagnerian culture, they worked from a Wagnerian script. Indeed, they took the genre of the terroristic manifesto more seriously than did Wagner himself, who, when it came time to putting his outlandish ideas into practice, reverted to pragmatic theatrical principles. For the Futurists and Dadaists, the manifesto was a performance in itself; in a sense, their art could not exist without the ideological armature. Artistic harangues in an apocalyptic register are among Wagner's more dubious gifts to posterity.

THE STAB IN THE BACK

"*Er stösst seinen Speer in Siegfrieds Rücken,*" say the stage directions for *Götterdämmerung*—"He thrusts his spear in Siegfried's back." In the medieval *Nibelungenlied*, Siegfried's only vulnerability is a spot between his shoulder blades: when the hero bathed in the blood of the dragon, a leaf of a linden tree landed on his back, and that area was untouched by the liquid that otherwise made him invincible. There Hagen pierces him. Hence the expression "stab in the back," the byword for betrayal by a seeming friend.

Decades of Wilhelmine triumphalism made the events of 1918 incomprehensible for many Germans. In the spring of that year, as Krupp guns moved within reach of Paris, victory seemed at hand. The rapid reversals of the summer, leading to the Armistice of November 1918, almost required a conspiratorial explanation. Thus arose the "stab-in-the-back legend"—the belief that Germany's certain victory had been stymied by some collusion of evildoers, usually capitalists, socialists, and/or Jews. The metaphor of a *Dolchstoß*, or dagger thrust, originated with military leaders like Erich Ludendorff and Paul Hindenburg, who adopted a mendacious strategy of blaming the political class for a loss they knew to be inevitable. In October 1918, a subordinate wrote of Ludendorff: "A truly beautiful Germanic heroic figure! I had to think of Siegfried, fatally wounded in the back by Hagen's spear." Hindenburg's 1920 memoir extended the metaphor: "We were at the end! Like Siegfried under the treacherous spear-throw of the grim Hagen, so our weary front collapsed." Various cartoons of the postwar period, sometimes antisemitic, show skulking civilians advancing on German soldiers with daggers drawn.

Complicating these Siegfried allegories is the fact that Germans sometimes identified with the hero's killer. In 1918, Plan Hagen was to have been the blow that brought the Entente to its knees. In the medieval *Nibelungenlied*, Hagen is a more ambiguous figure than the black-hearted villain of *Götterdämmerung*: he kills Siegfried, but he also demonstrates the virtue of loyalty, staying true to the oath that binds him to the Burgundian court. And even in Wagner the Nibelungs possess a certain dour nobility: witness Alberich's chant of "Be true! Be true!" In the prewar years, the term *"Nibelungentreue,"* or "Nibelung loyalty," became a token of solidarity unto death. Bernhard von Bülow, the German chancellor, spoke of a *Nibelungentreue* bond with Austria-Hungary. This blood-oath ethic persisted into the Nazi period. The contradictions inherent in the analogy—German heroes being cast as Siegfried and Hagen alike—did not hamper its circulation. The point was that something had gone terribly wrong in the march toward German victory, something that had to be avenged.

How the Great War affected the German psyche is the cause of much debate. In 1990, the historian George Mosse advanced what came to be known as the "brutalization" thesis, contending that the war normalized extreme violence in the period of the Weimar Republic and set the stage for Nazi savagery. More recently, historians have countered that the roots of Nazism lie not in the war itself—it was just as brutal for the French and the British—but in the anarchy that engulfed Germany in late 1918 and early 1919, as the Kaiser fled to the Netherlands, Communist revolutionaries battled right-wing mercenaries in the streets, and politicians fell to assassins' bullets. The swiftness of the collapse encouraged the stab-in-the-back fiction. Soldiers returning from the front were especially prone to conspiracy theories, because they were confronted with a world that had changed beyond recognition. Young men who had indulged in Wagnerian fantasies in the last years of empire now found themselves members of a socialist democracy. For some of them, it was a reality they could not accept.

When the war began, Adolf Hitler was a twenty-five-year-old bohemian painter in Munich, steeped in Wagner, solitary in his habits. Within two years of its end, he had become a rabble-rousing far-right fanatic with

Hitler's sketch of the Alfred Roller production of Tristan

a flair for hysterical antisemitic rhetoric. The nature of that transformation remains central to the almost limitless Hitler literature. Was Hitler brutalized by the war or radicalized in its aftermath? Or did he see himself as Germany's dictatorial savior even before the war began? On such questions the latter-day reputation of Richard Wagner also hangs, since the composer is suspected of having nurtured Hitler's politics of domination and destruction.

From adolescence onward, Hitler was a dreamer and a loner. Averse to joining groups, much less leading them, he spent his days with books, art, and music. Of the Wagner operas, *Lohengrin* caught his attention first. A neighbor in Linz remembers him singing music from it. In *Mein Kampf,* Hitler says that *Lohengrin* was the first opera he saw in the theater. "I was captivated at one stroke," Hitler wrote. "My youthful enthusiasm for the Bayreuth master knew no bounds." Looking back during the Second World War, he said, "We who stood with him were called Wagnerians, the others had no names." The *Lohengrin* performance was probably one that took place in 1901 or 1902, in Linz, where Hitler was attending school. Sebastian Werr notes that both of the *Lohengrin* conductors in Linz in this period were Jewish—as was Julian Wilensky, the Heldentenor who sang the title role.

When Hitler made his first trip to Vienna, in May 1906, he saw *Tristan* and *The Flying Dutchman* at the Court Opera. In a postcard sent to his friend August Kubizek, he conveys the opera house's acoustics: "Powerful waves of sound flood the room, and the murmur of the wind gives way to a terrible rush of surging sound." The language echoes Isolde's Transfiguration, which speaks of surging, rushing waves of tone. The *Tristan* Hitler saw was the renowned production by Alfred Roller, with Mahler conducting. Hitler hoped to study with the painter and designer, but inexplicably failed to make use of a letter of introduction that he obtained. In the mid-twenties, he sketched Roller's *Tristan* set from memory, and when in 1934 he met Roller he could still remember details of the staging, including the "pale light" in the second act. Hitler was also smitten with *Meistersinger*. In 1908, he made a transcription of the first twelve lines of Hans Sachs's final monologue—"Scorn not the masters, I bid you, and honor their art"—and decorated it with a not particularly lifelike drawing of Wagner's face.

The most significant of Hitler's Wagner experiences is said to have taken place a few years earlier, in 1905, at a performance of *Rienzi* in Linz. August Kubizek, an aspiring conductor who shared Hitler's Wagnerism and guided him in musical matters, recounts this occasion at length in his memoir, *Adolf Hitler, Friend of My Youth*. Hitler was supposedly first stunned into silence, and then, in an oratorical flood of words, "conjured up in magnificent, inspiring pictures his own future and that of his people." When Kubizek met Hitler again in 1939, during a visit to Bayreuth, the dictator invoked this *Rienzi* encounter with the portentous words "In that hour it began." Hitler told a similar story to Albert Speer, and mentioned it in his "Table Talk" monologues during the Second World War. He also seems to have spoken of *Rienzi* to his musically inclined friend Ernst Hanfstaengl—or so a document titled "A. H. und Rienzo," to be found in Hanfstaengl's papers, obliquely suggests.

If the *Rienzi* anecdote is true, it is the strongest evidence of Wagner's influence on Hitler's politics. Cola di Rienzo, the "people's tribune" who tried to unify Italy in 1347, was lionized in the nineteenth and early twentieth centuries, especially on the left. Hitler apparently saw Wagner's opera both as an inspiration and as a cautionary tale. In 1930, he told his confidant Otto Wagener that he wished to avoid repeating Rienzi's mistakes: namely, failing to organize a strong party and eliminate his opponents. Yet the anecdote is no Rosetta stone. Hitler liked to project moments of awakening into his childhood and early adulthood, imparting a sense of direction to a largely aimless existence. Kubizek's memoir is unreliable, and problems of chronology have led Sebastian Werr and Jonas Karlsson to conclude that the *Rienzi* story is partly or wholly fabricated. If Hitler thrilled to the opera in his youth, he was more likely impressed by its gaudy pageantry— "hymns, processions, and the musical clash of arms," to quote Wagner's later disparagement of his own work—than by any putative political message.

Hitler had no future as a painter, his technique limited by a want of feeling for human figures. Twice rejected by the Academy of Fine Arts in Vienna, he slipped toward the social margins, residing briefly in a homeless shelter and later in a men's home. His friend Reinhold Hanisch remembers him spouting pan-German views and ranting against Catholics, in the manner of the turn-of-the-century Austrian politician Georg von Schönerer. Hitler also spoke highly of Karl Lueger, the antisemitic mayor of Vienna, who styled himself a "people's tribune," like Rienzi. But the scattered testimony of Hanisch and others gives little evidence of strong antisemitic outbursts on Hitler's part. Indeed, he was apparently friendly with several Jews. This does not mean that he was free of commonplace anti-Jewish prejudice; it does, however, undermine the notion that Wagner had an immediate radicalizing effect.

Nothing about Hitler's development up to this point was notable— especially not his love for Wagner. Instead, to quote Hans Rudolf Vaget, the young man's story is one of "patent normality within the cultural context from which he sprang." The *Rienzi* anecdote belongs to a familiar category of Wagner Scene: the Glimpse of Future Greatness. In Schnitzler's *The Road into the Open*, the young composer Georg von Wergenthin attends Mahler's *Tristan* at the Court Opera and daydreams of hearing his own works performed in a "wide and festive space." In W. E. B. Du Bois's "Of the Coming of John," the African-American protagonist listens to *Lohengrin* and feels "the movement of power within him." Louis Sullivan has his courage "ten-folded." The heroine of Hamlin Garland's *Rose of Dutcher's Coolly* envisions accomplishing "some gigantic thing which should enrich the human race." *Tannhäuser* emboldens Theodor Herzl to pursue his goal of a Jewish state. What is different in Hitler's case is the content of the fantasy. The most ominous precedent is Heinrich Mann's

Der Untertan, where *Lohengrin* leads Diederich to imagine a cleansing of the German spirit.

Hitler claimed that he brought a vocal score of *Tristan* with him when he went off to war in 1914. Allegedly, he would comfort himself by humming the music and envisaging how each moment should be staged. At the beginning, this soldier-aesthete might have seemed a little like Cather's Claude Wheeler, a feckless youth marked for an early death. But the carnage hardened him. Evidence of hard-right nationalist views surfaced around 1915, when Hitler expressed to a Munich friend his hope that the experience of war "will not only smash Germany's enemies abroad but also destroy our inner internationalism."

The classic German account of the war is Ernst Jünger's 1920 memoir *Storm of Steel*, which enthralled many thousands of readers, Hitler among them. Jünger, too, led a bohemian life before entering the army. *Storm of Steel* tells of a man becoming steel himself—fearless, pitiless, machinelike. Although Jünger is too ferociously perceptive a writer to fall into propaganda, he adheres to a proto-Fascist mythology of "ever purer, ever bolder warriordom." At the same time, his vocabulary harks back to Marinetti's Futurist manifestos, aestheticizing war and glamorizing violence. A few casual Wagner references are strewn through the text. A makeshift dugout is named Haus Wahnfried, and soldiers are seen enjoying "pike à la Lohengrin," or fish killed with bombs. These allusions reinforce the sense that Romantic legend has been shorn of sentiment and hammered into a weapon of battle. Wagner is reduced to battle cries and strutting poses.

A disconcerting psychological type was coming to the fore. Harry Kessler, like Thomas Mann and many other cultured Germans, gave in to the initial war fever; later, he had second thoughts. In the course of his military service, he met a man named Klewitz, a petty-dictator chief of staff, who was "very persuaded of his own importance, and yet a plebeian at the same time . . . He does not impose himself on people but rather clobbers them with his position." Kessler calls him a *Schwarzalbe*—a black elf, like Wagner's Alberich. "God save us from being ruled by such people after the war." As Kessler catalogues instances of thuggishness on the front, he is studying Fascism before it has a name.

The military state that devised Operation Alberich and Plan Hagen was internalizing the ethos of hardness that Wagner's philosophy of compassion strove to overcome. It became modish to forswear love, celebrate cruelty, make oneself as hard as steel. The 1848 dream of the overthrow of worldly power gave way to a cult of force: all irony was stripped from the Entry of the Gods into Valhalla. Before this version of Wagner triumphed under Nazism, though, there would be one last pitched battle over the meaning of the composer's name.

RING OF POWER

Revolution and Russia

A Communist Mount Rushmore, from Frank Castorf's
Siegfried at Bayreuth, 2013

I n 1883, the year of Wagner's death, the theater critic William Archer noticed a red-haired, bearded youth who was sitting day after
day in the British Library with two volumes open on his desk: the
French edition of *Das Kapital*, which Karl Marx had written in the library
decades earlier, and the full score of *Tristan und Isolde*. The young man
was George Bernard Shaw, a staunch leftist who saw no conflict between
Wagner's Romantic mythology and Marx's historical materialism. The
descent into Nibelheim is "frightfully real, frightfully present, frightfully
modern," Shaw wrote in *The Perfect Wagnerite*, his anticapitalist reading of
the *Ring*. The drama of the stolen gold is an unmasking of inequity and a
demand for renewal. Both the *Ring* and Marx's writing bear witness to the
"predestined end of our capitalistic-theocratic epoch."

Shaw's perusal of Wagner and Marx must have raised eyebrows in 1883. It seems even more surprising now, given Hitler's success in convincing posterity that the composer belongs exclusively to the extreme right. *The Perfect Wagnerite* was no isolated event, however. In recent decades, scholars have reconstructed a school of Wagnerian leftism, which gained purchase in Europe and America at the end of the nineteenth century. Socialists, communists, social democrats, and anarchists all found sustenance in Wagner's work. The drafting of Siegfried, Hagen, and Alberich into the German war machine dented that idealism, but it persisted after the war's end, achieving a late efflorescence during the Weimar Republic. And, as Wagnerism began to subside in Western Europe, it belatedly surged among Symbolists and avant-gardists in Russia. Alexander Blok, Vyacheslav Ivanov, Andrey Bely, and Vsevolod Meyerhold saw the composer as both an aesthetic and a political model. After the Bolshevik Revolution of 1917, Wagner had a brief vogue as a figurehead of proletarian culture.

Members of the Wagner Left took heart from the composer's 1848-era essays, especially "Art and Revolution," with its admonition that "our god is money." Art, like every other sphere of human activity, has fallen into the clutches of commerce. By breaking the grip of capitalism, Wagner says, artists can guide and elevate the broader struggle for social equality. As it happens, Marxist doctrine had relatively little to say about the political function of art. *The Communist Manifesto* makes passing mention of a "world literature" arising from the erasure of national boundaries, but Marx generally held that economic conditions dictate intellectual life rather than the other way around. "Art and Revolution" spoke to socialists who wanted a more expansive definition of art's role.

The operas themselves mattered just as much. The German literary scholar Frank Trommler has said that the Wagner Left "originated where Wagner had situated the authenticity of his musical mythmaking: in the performance." Trommler argues that the liberated mode of listening delineated by Baudelaire in 1861—abandoning familiar expectations, giving free rein to emotions and impressions—acquired a distinct political meaning. Wagner became a dream theater for the imagination of a future state. Of course, other ideologies exploited the composer in the same way. It would be a mistake to say that Shaw and his fellow leftists found the "true" Wagner. But it would also be a mistake to say they misunderstood him.

SOCIALIST WAGNER

The younger Wagner fascinated the left in large measure because of the emphatic vagueness of his convictions. As he dabbled in various ideologies—socialism, communism, anarchism, democratic liberalism—he created a kind of potpourri of leftist possibilities, which adherents of one camp or another sampled at will. The musicologist James Garratt highlights the composer's vacillation between collectivism and individualism. One part of Wagner longed to join the great popular throng; another could never surrender the artistic independence that stands outside of group definitions. Ultimately, he gravitated toward utopian anarchism, along the lines of Pierre-Joseph Proudhon's vision of a society cleansed of the exploitation of property. But fragments of other ideologies entered his jumble of jargon and concepts—including Marxism.

Although Wagner never mentioned Marx by name, he made scattered references to communism—occasionally positive, more often dismissive. Circumstantial evidence suggests that he read Marx's *On the Jewish Question*, with its brief against Judaism as a cultural-economic condition. Martin Gregor-Dellin, one of several late twentieth-century German writers who tried to repair Wagner's leftist credentials, heard a Marxist echo in notes that the composer made in the summer of 1849: "A tremendous movement is striding through the world: it is the storm of European revolution; everyone is taking part in it, and whoever is not supporting it by pushing forward is strengthening it by pushing back." That fanfare sounds more than a little like *The Communist Manifesto*: "A specter is haunting Europe—the specter of communism." Wagner's picture of isolated art forms reduced to specialization is intriguingly close to Marx's analysis of the alienation of the classes and the division of labor. In both cases, what is needed is a restoration of unity, whether in the form of the Gesamtkunstwerk or the classless society.

Marx's musings on the "perverting power" of money in the *Economic and Philosophic Manuscripts of 1844* line up with the ideology of the *Ring*, as Dieter Borchmeyer has shown. Money, Marx writes, "transforms loyalty into treason, love into hate . . . servant into master, master into servant." The monetary metamorphosis of commodities is analogous to the shape-shifting capabilities of the Ring and the Tarnhelm. When, in *Das Kapital*,

Marx speaks of the hoarding of commodities, he notes that the hoarder "sacrifices the lusts of the flesh to his gold fetish" and adopts "the gospel of renunciation." The word Marx uses here, *"Entsagung,"* is the same that Wagner applies to Alberich's renunciation of love. Only one who refuses love's power, who "renounces sacred love [*der sel'ger Lieb' entsagt*]," can possess the gold. For Marx and Wagner alike, love and power are irreconcilable.

In his last years, after his stint as a Reich nationalist, Wagner again drifted leftward. Bismarck's attempt at outlawing German socialism, in 1878, perturbed him: he and Cosima felt that even if socialist leaders were "muddled people and perhaps intriguers as well . . . the movement itself belongs to the future." A year later, he seemed in favor of overthrowing the capitalist order and dissolving the state: "He is becoming ever more vividly aware of the need for the demise [*Untergang*] of things as they now stand, and finds only the worker entitled to life, as it were." These were the rather abstract sentiments of a man who was living out his life in villas and palaces. Bayreuth had fallen far short of his original dream of a festival open to people of all backgrounds; instead, it had become one more watering hole for the leisure class. Perhaps such thoughts were on Wagner's mind when, a few days before his death, he told Cosima that he wished he had never built Wahnfried, that the "festivals seem absurd."

By a sublime historical coincidence, Marx was traveling through Nuremberg at the time of the first Bayreuth Festival. Unable to find a hotel room in part because of the overflow of festivalgoers from Bayreuth, the co-founder of communism resorted to sleeping on a railway-station bench. In a letter to Friedrich Engels, he heaped scorn on the "Bayreuth fool's festival of the official town-musician Wagner." In another letter, Marx amused his daughter Jenny Longuet with an account of the Wagners' tortuous sexual history, adding, "The activities of this group might also be dramatized, as with the Nibelungs, in a tetralogy." Engels shared Marx's distaste. A long footnote in a later edition of Engels's *The Origin of the Family, Private Property, and the State* expresses alarm over the incest plot in *Walküre*.

Other revolutionaries had a better opinion of Wagner. The anarcho-communist Peter Kropotkin was an admirer; Kropotkin's follower Jean

Grave translated "The Artwork of the Future" into French. The agrarian populist Alexander Herzen endorsed Wagner's revolutionary writings, though not his music. The most committed Wagnerite among Marx's contemporaries was Ferdinand Lassalle, the founder of the General German Workers' Association. Flamboyant, charismatic, fond of silk dressing gowns, prone to scandalous affairs, Lassalle was more than a little Wagnerian himself. After reading the libretto of the *Ring*, he wrote to Hans von Bülow: "I am still in endless excitement like a foaming sea, and days and weeks will pass before I can concentrate the soul sufficiently undivided upon the arid statistical and economic investigations to which my next period is devoted." Lassalle reportedly memorized the text of *Lohengrin* and declaimed it "like a Nordic bard." The appreciation was not reciprocated: Wagner brushed Lassalle aside as a "Germanic-Judaic" type.

In defiance of Marx, Lassalle believed that revolutionaries should engage in parliamentary politics rather than wait for capitalism to collapse from its own contradictions. The Social Democratic Workers' Party (SDAP), the ancestor of the modern Social Democratic Party in Germany, arose from his efforts. Perhaps as a result of Lassalle's legacy, references to Wagner cropped up often among Social Democrats. In general, the party saw music as a useful tool, especially in the form of workers' choirs and bands. Marches from *Rienzi* and *Tannhäuser* blared at a commemoration of the fourth anniversary of Lassalle's death, in 1868.

August Bebel, one of SDAP's founders, lauded Wagner in his popular 1879 tract *Woman and Socialism*, which holds that the "society of the future" would ensure the equality of women and liberate the entire proletariat from menial labor. "Everyone will practice with the like-minded whatever his inclinations and abilities lead him to do," Bebel writes. He then quotes Wagner's prophecy of a postcapitalist utopia in "Art and Revolution": "The purpose of life will be the enjoyment of life . . . every human being will, in some way, truly be an artist." Wagner's formulation, Bebel adds, is "entirely socialistic." Such optimism buoyed German socialists through years of repression. A poster marking the end of Bismarck's anti-socialist law, in 1890, showed Siegfried thrusting his sword into a dragon.

Later socialist literature of the Kaiserreich period held that the "*idea* of the *Ring* tragedy is *socialism*"; that Wagner was an "anticapitalist"; that proletarians should take possession of his art ("The bourgeoisie has not yet managed to grasp the Meister"). A few harder-line Marxists agreed. Clara

Zetkin, who opposed the First World War and went on to become a forceful Communist leader of the Weimar Republic era, argued in 1911 that the "strong, beautiful man" hailed in "Art and Revolution" would be neither a creature of bourgeois individualism nor the "blond beast of the superhuman" but the "harmoniously unfolded personality, inseparable from the whole."

Victor Adler, the leader of the Austrian social democrats, came to Bayreuth for the first performances of the *Ring* and *Parsifal*. He and other Austrian socialist Wagnerites emerged from the Pernerstorfer Circle, a student group that formed in Vienna in the 1860s. Engelbert Pernerstorfer, Heinrich Friedjung, and Adler were the principals; Gustav Mahler attended some meetings, and Sigmund Freud was an interested observer. In the early years, members of the circle combined investigations of socialist thought with readings in Wagner, Schopenhauer, and Nietzsche. Challenging the liberal consensus in Viennese politics, which served the interests of the bourgeoisie, they sought to relight the revolutionary fire of 1848. At the same time, they were pan-German nationalists, advocating a union of Austria and Germany. When the pan-German movement took on a rabidly anti-Jewish tone under Georg von Schönerer, the Pernerstorfer group broke away. Adler founded the Social Democratic Workers' Party in 1889; Pernerstorfer joined him several years later. Adler remained the chairman of the party until his death, in 1918.

The steady crescendo of antisemitic nationalism in the Bayreuth Circle did not discourage the Pernerstorfer group. As the historian William McGrath writes, their call for politics in a "sharper key," infused with Dionysian energy, emulated Wagner's way of eliciting and directing emotion. Adler drew on Wagnerian pageantry for May Day events in Vienna. "For us in Austria the May Day celebration was this waking call [*Weckruf*]," Adler said. He may have been thinking of the choral shout of "Wach auf" in *Meistersinger*. The integration of politics, art, education, and leisure became, in Wolfgang Maderthaner's reading, a political Gesamtkunstwerk, life and art united. For Pernerstorfer, likewise, Wagner was a "man of the people" who worked for freedom and justice. However reactionary and racist the composer may have been in old age, his youthful idealism counted most. Wagnerites betray their master if they are not striving for the liberation of humanity—"and it is not enough to make the pilgrimage to Bayreuth."

Some on the left found the entire notion of "Wagner Social Demo-crats" ridiculous. In 1911, the left-radical journalist Rudolf Franz dismissed Wagner as a *Kleinbürger*, a petit-bourgeois, who "never went to America, but America came to him," in the form of the snobbery of Bayreuth. The Austrian socialist Wilhelm Ellenbogen answered by reaffirming the *Ring*'s anticapitalist credentials, and he ventured to defend the later, mystical Wagner as well. Far from creating rituals of bourgeois distraction, Ellen-bogen says, the music dramas open a path for listeners of all classes to escape into a purely human sphere, that of the ideal future.

Jean Jaurès, the leader of social democracy in France, felt much the same. His 1900 essay "Art and Socialism" asserts that the revolutionary spirit of 1848 "revealed to Wagner the fullness of his genius and the entire meaning of his work . . . It was communism that revealed art to him." *Meistersinger* was Jaurès's favorite Wagner opera—a fusion of ancient tradi-tion and the free play of human instincts, he said, at once deeply traditional and profoundly universal. *Parsifal*, however, left Jaurès cold. It seemed to him an "abdication of the intelligence before the myth of sin and redemp-tion." In general, as the historian Harvey Goldberg has written, Jaurès resisted politics in the mystical mode—"cults of force, faith, and futility." Significantly, Jaurès supported the Dreyfusard cause, even as many fellow socialists shrugged off the Dreyfus Affair as a bourgeois matter irrelevant to fundamental economic problems.

What French leftists valued most in the composer was the sense of solidarity he instilled in his audiences, German or otherwise. In 1903, Romain Rolland issued a manifesto titled *Theater of the People*, in which he named Wagner as the great theatrical personality of the age, one whose "superhuman" characters are poised to stir the emotions of the masses. Un-fortunately, Rolland adds, the music dramas are too complex for an under-educated French public, and they display symptoms of decadence. A more direct, robust form of theater must come forward. In the same period, the theater innovator Firmin Gémier collaborated with Émile Jaques-Dalcroze, the inventor of the eurythmic method of music education, in staging mass festivals inspired by Wagner's "*art totale.*" For Rolland, such productions augur a future utopia in which a professional artistic class would become superfluous. He quotes Wagner to the effect that art might be nothing more than a "confession of our impotence"—that "if we had *life*, we should have no need of *art.*"

Rolland's hope for revolution through the theater seemed plausible to many of his contemporaries because opera and drama played such a central role in nineteenth-century culture. W. B. Yeats quoted Victor Hugo to the effect that the theater is the place where "the mob becomes a people." It can be the staging ground of revolution, where the future goes into rehearsal. As the historian Katerina Clark remarks, Marx's *The Eighteenth Brumaire of Louis Bonaparte* begins with a theatrical metaphor—history as tragedy, then as farce. Marx repeatedly talks about the political stage and about the urban proletariat's inability to hold their place on it. Wagner's "Art and Revolution" offered a tempting shortcut: one magic night, metaphor becomes reality, and the revolution leaps from the theater to the street.

SHAW

Shaw in 1905

In early 1914, the British socialists Sidney and Beatrice Webb, active members of the Fabian Society, attended a performance of *Parsifal* at Covent Garden. They enjoyed the outing chiefly because, as Sidney said, "our seats were just behind Herbert Samuel's and during the interval we had a very interesting discussion on the incidence of sickness during pregnancy." This levelheaded response to Wagner was typical of a group that would adopt the slogan "the inevitability of gradualness." The Fabian Society formed in 1884, its ideology rooted more in radical liberalism than in Marxism.

George Bernard Shaw, who joined the Fabians soon after their founding, tried to win his comrades over to Wagner, with limited success. Social democracy in Britain resisted the Romantic strains of the European left; church hymns and folk songs were more its style.

Shaw was himself a Wagnerite of an unsentimental type, averse to piety. Born in Dublin in 1856, he first encountered the composer in his teenaged years, when a Germanophile neighbor prompted him to buy a vocal score of *Lohengrin*. Shaw moved to London in 1876 and was in the crowd for the Wagner Festival the following year. Between 1888 and 1894, as he was beginning to make his way as a playwright, he worked as a music critic in London, talking up Wagner while dressing down the Wagner cult. In 1889, after his first visit to Bayreuth, Shaw wrote that "the evil of deliberately making the Bayreuth Festival Playhouse a temple of dead traditions, instead of an arena for live impulses, has begun already."

At the outset of his dramatic career, Shaw contemplated making a blatant homage to Wagner. His first play, *Widowers' Houses* (1892), had its origins in an aborted collaboration with William Archer, following their meeting in the British Library. The plan was to write an updated *Rheingold*, with, in the words of the Shaw biographer William Irvine, "a garden scene on the banks of the Rhine, a capitalist villain, tainted gold, and finally a grand gesture of throwing the tainted gold back into the Rhine." In the published play, the setting remains the Rhine and the villain is a sort of Alberich type, but the *Ring* material stays in the background. Scholars have detected half-concealed Wagner allegories in various other Shaw plays. *Heartbreak House* (1913–19) reads like a satire of *Götterdämmerung*, equating the gods with the "cultured, leisured Europe" that faces doom in the First World War. "Come, Alfred," one character says. "There is a moon: it's like the night in Tristan and Isolde." In the last act, the company hears explosions approaching—presumably a Zeppelin raid—and turns on all the lights, inviting the destruction of their Valhalla. Somewhat to their disappointment, they survive.

Perhaps Shaw hung back from direct engagement with Wagner because he wished to avoid placing himself in competition with the Meister. But he also had ideological difficulties with the operas that he so admired as a critic and listener. Those objections become apparent in *Man and Superman* (1901–1903), a comedy of *Meistersinger* proportions, which pits Roebuck Ramsden, a venerable liberal, against the anarchistic Jack Tanner, author of the *Revolutionist's Handbook*. In a long dream scene, Jack is transformed into Don Juan in Hell, conversing with the Devil and the Statue from Mozart's *Don Giovanni*. The Devil gives a report of a posthumous encounter of Wagner and Nietzsche in the lower domain:

> THE DEVIL: Unfortunately he met Wagner here, and had a quarrel with him.
>
> THE STATUE: Quite right, too. Mozart for me!
>
> THE DEVIL: Oh, it was not about music. Wagner once drifted into Life Force worship, and invented a Superman called Siegfried. But he came to his senses afterwards. So when they met here, Nietzsche denounced him as a renegade; and Wagner wrote a pamphlet to prove that Nietzsche was a Jew; and it ended in Nietzsche's going to heaven in a huff. And a good riddance, too.

Shaw is alluding to Nietzsche's critique of the later Wagner, who sets aside Siegfried's heroics in favor of Parsifal's compassion. Shaw sides with Nietzsche: mystical Schopenhauerian moods and decadent longing for death were anathema to him. William Blissett, a pioneering chronicler of literary Wagnerism, sums up the difference neatly: "Wagner is, at least half the time, a poet of the night; with Shaw it is always daylight."

The Perfect Wagnerite, first published in 1898, was Shaw's main gift to literary Wagnerism—a revamping of the *Ring* in the guise of a layperson's introduction. At the outset, Shaw announces his intention to treat the cycle as a "drama of today," so that the proletarian spectator can find in it "an image of the life he is himself fighting his way through." A synopsis of *Rheingold* immediately draws a link between myth and modernity: "Let me assume for a moment that you are a young and good-looking woman. Try to imagine yourself in that character at Klondyke five years ago. The place is teeming with gold." The Klondike gold rush brought tens of thousands of prospectors to the Yukon territory in Canada beginning in 1896. The pretty young woman is a Rhinemaiden; the rough-hewn man who pursues her and then seizes the gold is Alberich.

Shaw goes on to explicate Wagner's allegories of rampant capitalism, the enslavement of working people, and the malfeasance of the nobility and the bourgeoisie. But he claims that the composer could not face the contemporaneity of his story—that "the *Ring* was no longer a Niblung epic, and really demanded modern costumes, tall hats for Tarnhelms, factories for Nibelheims, villas for Valhallas, and so on." Many decades later, that conceit came to life in *Ring* stagings by Joachim Herz and Patrice Chéreau.

In other ways, though, Shaw sticks with nineteenth-century convention. For him, the true hero of the cycle is Siegfried—a "perfectly naïve hero upsetting religion, law and order in all directions, and establishing in their place the unfettered action of Humanity doing exactly what it likes." He is Bakunin's anarchist and Nietzsche's *Übermensch* in one boisterous package. Shaw writes off Brünnhilde as a theatrical cliché of the "majestically savage woman," and her mighty final monologue leaves him longing for the "irrepressible bustle of Siegfried and the revelry of the clansmen." This masculinist action-movie reading of the *Ring* misses the depth of its psychology and the breadth of its critique of power. In later years, Shaw's respect for force would blind him to the true nature of Hitler, Mussolini, and Stalin. In the first version of Shaw's misbegotten League of Nations satire *Geneva*, Hitler appears in the guise of Herr Battler, attired as Lohengrin; it is a comical but by no means negative portrait.

If Shaw had created a fiction based unambiguously on the *Ring*, it might have looked like Upton Sinclair's 1903 novel *Prince Hagen*. The book comes from the early phase of Sinclair's career, before he found his métier exposing the brutal working conditions of American industry. A young poet is camping in the Canadian forest when he stumbles upon Nibelheim, the realm of Wagner's dwarves. Alberich is still alive and scheming in Gilded Age North America, in the company of Prince Hagen, his grandson. The poet undertakes the task of guiding Hagen in the upper world. Before long, the young prince is giving rabble-rousing speeches on the Bowery, calling himself Jimmie O'Hagen, a Democratic Party operative. He then switches to the Republican side, manipulating reformist rhetoric to reactionary ends. The character illustrates Shaw's point about the protean Tarnhelm powers of modern capital. Only the laws of nature can check Hagen's games of deception and subjugation. In a gleeful burlesque of "The Ride of the Valkyries," the prince's imported Persian horses run wild and drag him to his death.

RUSSIAN WAGNERISM

Nicholas Roerich, design for Die Walküre

In 1913, the year of Wagner's centenary, the Russian poet Osip Mandel-stam gave a sardonic picture of a night at the opera on the eve of war and revolution:

> The Valkyries fly, bows sing—
> the cumbersome opera is coming to a close.
> Holding heavy fur coats, servants
> are waiting for their masters on marble stairs.
>
> The curtain is ready to fall firmly;
> A fool is still clapping up in the gods;
> cabbies dance around bonfires . . .
> "So-and-so's carriage!"—Dispersal. The end.

As in Shaw's *Heartbreak House,* fate is stalking an elite public that listens to Wagner for pleasure without thinking through his implications. Here, the upper classes of late-period tsarist Russia are dazzled by the chimera of the *Ring* while their servants kill time outside. The fires around which they dance are ready to consume Valhalla. Although Mandelstam appears to be no great fan of Wagner—so the adjective "cumbersome" suggests—his poem synchronizes with the insurrectionary politics of the *Ring,* which has its own cry of *"Das Ende!"*

Russian Wagnerism, which began later than its counterparts to the west, recapitulates familiar themes and situations. Bernice Glatzer Rosenthal, in an essay on the phenomenon, divides it into three categories: "the aesthetic-cultural, the mystical-religious, and the revolutionary." These phases often blur together, and many personalities pass through each one in quick succession. The pivotal year was 1905, when a massacre of unarmed demonstrators led to protests and strikes against the tsarist regime. The unrest impelled Nicholas II to announce democratic reforms and ease censorship, resulting in the belated publication of Wagner's revolutionary writings. These made a strong impression on Russian artists as they turned toward social radicalism.

Until the end of the nineteenth century, Wagner had limited exposure in Russia. The composer led concerts there in 1863, hoping for elite patronage of his work, but none materialized. The secret police kept him under constant surveillance, having pegged him as a "suspicious and politically suspect person." Only at century's end did the Wagner operas enter the Russian repertory. In 1899, the liberal-minded Sergei Volkonsky took charge of the imperial theaters, launching a Wagner wave. The *Ring* operas began appearing at the Mariinsky Theater in St. Petersburg the following year; the tetralogy was complete by 1905, and annual cycles commenced in 1907, evidently at the command of Nicholas II, whose favorite composers were Wagner and Tchaikovsky.

The great nineteenth-century Russian writers had little use for Wagner, as Rosamund Bartlett makes clear in her definitive study *Wagner and Russia*. Dostoevsky once granted that the composer was "full of noble aims," but elsewhere slighted him as "the most utterly boring German rubbish." Tolstoy was contemptuous, describing *Siegfried* as a "stupid puppet show not even good enough for children." Many pages of Tolstoy's 1897 tract *What Is Art?* are given over to an attempted decimation of the *Ring*, that "model work of counterfeit art." In *Anna Karenina*, Konstantin Levin speaks for Tolstoy when he maintains that "the mistake Wagner and all his followers made was in wanting music to cross over into the sphere of another art form." Nonetheless, Tolstoy shared Wagner's attachment to a religion of compassion, not to mention his penchant for working on a huge, comprehensive canvas. Thomas Mann wrote that the two authors had in common a "naturalistic power in breadth," a "democratic multitudinousness."

At the outset of Russia's Silver Age—the late-tsarist epoch that brought successive waves of Symbolism, Acmeism, and early Futurism—Wagner was suddenly de rigueur. Young Russian artists of the 1890s succumbed to the sort of unrestrained fandom that had swept the West. The artist and designer Alexandre Benois was eighteen when the Angelo Neumann company brought its *Ring* to Petersburg. "The very first chords of *Das Rheingold* made me feel that here was a new elemental force," Benois recalled. Soon he was wandering the woods bellowing themes from *Walküre* and *Siegfried*. Like Adolphe Appia and Edward Gordon Craig, Benois recoiled from the banalities of mainstream Wagner staging. When the Mariinsky mounted *Götterdämmerung* in 1903, Benois took charge of the designs, aiming for a more atmospheric evocation of northern climes.

Serge Diaghilev, the future ringmaster of the Ballets Russes, first heard Wagner's operas in Vienna in 1890, and by the time he reached Bayreuth two years later he was a self-described "Wagner fanatic." To his stepmother he wrote: "Until I've heard all four operas I won't write you my impressions in any detail. I'll only say this: I am certain that people who are disappointed in themselves and their lives, and see no point in living, people who have been put in a difficult situation by life's misfortunes and finally people who despair to the point of bringing their life to an artificial end—all of them should come here." Bayreuth's gay ambience may have affected a young man already acutely aware of his desires. At a concert in 1893, Diaghilev sang some of Amfortas's music from *Parsifal*—material saturated in sexual woundedness. Diaghilev remained a loyal Wagnerite to the end. As he lay dying, in 1929, he sang parts of *Tristan*—in Venice, no less.

In 1898, Diaghilev embarked on a new career as an art impresario. As the editor of the journal *Mir iskusstva*, or *World of Art*, he mobilized an artistic phalanx that included Benois and the painter Léon Bakst. Their philosophy mixed Symbolism, Russian nationalism, and incipient avant-gardism. Early issues of *Mir iskusstva* contained excerpts from Henri Lichtenberger's book *Richard Wagner, poète et penseur*. This was, as Bartlett says, the first time that the composer's theories had been discussed in Russia within a broader cultural context. The magazine also printed a translation of Nietzsche's *Richard Wagner in Bayreuth* and reviews of Wagner performances, including Diaghilev's assessment of the Mariinsky premiere of *Tristan*, in 1899. The following year, thanks to Volkonsky, Diaghilev won a position at the Imperial Theaters. Among the projects he contemplated was a Russian *Parsifal*.

After bureaucratic resistance ended Diaghilev's Mariinsky career, he moved on to Paris, making his name as an importer of Russian trends. An exhibition of visual arts, in 1906, led to seasons of orchestral music, opera, and, by 1909, ballet—the Ballets Russes, a cynosure of early modernism. For collaborators, Diaghilev called on Benois, Bakst, and the choreographer Michel Fokine, as well as Western European luminaries like Picasso, Matisse, and Braque. A violent new physicality came to the fore in the work of two younger artists: Igor Stravinsky, with his rhythmically liberated scores for *The Firebird* and *Petrushka*; and Vaslav Nijinsky, with his hyper-sensual choreography for Debussy's *Prelude to "The Afternoon of a Faun,"* after Mallarmé. In the spring of 1913, Stravinsky, Nijinsky, and the Symbolist painter Nicholas Roerich unleashed the ultimate modernist scandal in the form of *The Rite of Spring*.

Wagner's name floated through the discourse of the Ballets Russes. Benois stated that ballet was the perfect medium for the realization of the Gesamtkunstwerk—"the idea for which our circle was ready to give its soul." Diaghilev likely had the same term in mind when he championed "the very closest fusion of the three elements of dancing, painting, and music." Fokine spoke of the "alliance of dancing with other arts" on terms of mutual respect. Such Gesamtkunstwerk terminology was commonplace at the time, whether in the Vienna Secession, the Nabis, or the Darmstadt Artists' Colony. Yet, as the ballet historian Juliet Bellow argues, the Russian version was more convincing than most: the individual arts retained their identities while contributing to a unified impression.

The infamous premiere of the *Rite*, on May 29, 1913, took place one week after the centennial of Wagner's birth, which received heavy coverage in the French press. The magazine *Montjoie* found the juxtaposition telling: "Periodicals are commemorating this year the centenary of Richard Wagner. We hate how convenient these events ruled by the artistic calendar have become for presenters of all kinds. We render homage to the genius of Richard Wagner by honoring, at its birth, a masterpiece by a young musician whose influence upon the elite is already very great: Igor STRAVINSKY." Inevitably, the ensuing riot at the Théâtre des Champs-Elysées was compared to the *Tannhäuser* uproar of 1861. Annegret Fauser has proposed that Diaghilev was implicitly putting forward Stravinsky as a twentieth-century Wagner.

Each of the *Rite*'s creators had a relationship with the composer. Nijinsky, who could play parts of *Tannhäuser* at the piano, danced the Venusberg at the Mariinsky in 1910, under Fokine's direction. According to his wife, Romola, Nijinsky had ideas for how Wagner should be performed—not only *Tannhäuser* but also *Lohengrin* and *Tristan*—and hoped to work in Bayreuth, like Isadora Duncan. In 1912, Nijinsky joined Diaghilev and Stravinsky on a visit to the festival, where they all saw *Parsifal*. Stravinsky, in later years, insisted that his experience of Bayreuth had been one of extreme discomfort, that he had gone away revolted by the "unseemly and sacrilegious conception of art as religion." At the time, though, the young composer sang a different tune. *Parsifal* interested him sufficiently that he went to see the opera a second time when it was done in Monte Carlo, and in a subsequent letter he wrote respectfully of the "great art of Wagner." A curious feature of Stravinsky's *Rite* score is its use of Wagner tubas—the wide-bore horns that were tailor-made for Bayreuth. They give a tinge of Valhalla to the "Procession of the Sage."

As for Roerich, he not only designed sets and costumes for the *Rite* but co-wrote its scenario. Of Norwegian heritage, Roerich had been besotted with Wagner since the *Ring* came to St. Petersburg in 1889. In 1907, he made sketches for *Walküre*, not on commission but for his own edification. The first of these, showing Hunding's hut, is nothing too unusual, but the following two sketches, for the rocky gorge of Act II and for the ring of fire in Act III, are severe and stylized. The last is dominated by blocks of color: yellow, orange, and red for the fire, deep shades of blue for the mountains. Roerich would give much the same look to the Neolithic world of the *Rite*. In 1912, he made designs for a projected production of *Tristan* by the Zimin Theater; again, the geometric patterning of the costumes parallels the *Rite*. Roerich later said that he wanted to "do the stage setting for Wagner's operas as they had never been done in the world . . . No flames and no smoke. It would be mystery and symbol."

After the war, Roerich launched himself as a Theosophical leader, gaining an international following. On an expedition to the Himalayas, he commented that the rocks seemed to sing Wagner to him. In the United States, he found admirers in high places. Henry Wallace, Franklin Delano Roosevelt's secretary of agriculture and later his vice president, corresponded regularly with the man he called "Guru," casting himself as "Galahad" and, on occasion, "Parsifal." In one letter, Wallace wrote: "Long have I been aware of the occasional fragrance from that other world which is the real world . . . Yes, the Chalice is filling." Rumors about the letters contributed to Wallace's removal from the presidential ticket in 1944; he was thus prevented from succeeding Roosevelt when the latter died the following year. With a different turn of events, Parsifal might have become president of the United States.

Russian Symbolism had its roots in decadent poses and practices that were initially almost indistinguishable from their counterparts in France. The poet and playwright Vyacheslav Ivanov, a leader of the movement, gained notoriety for organizing occult ceremonies, including one at which a goblet supposedly filled with human blood was passed around. Later, Ivanov and his colleagues gravitated toward grandiose mysticism and visions of cataclysmic change. For the Russian Symbolists, as for Mallarmé, Wagner was a kind of halfway station, but in their case the end goal was a ritual that could double as political action. Nietzsche's Dionysian rite merged with Wagner's sacred theater. A favorite word among Russian Symbolists was "theurgy": the belief that divine forces could intervene in and transform human affairs.

In Ivanov's 1905 essay "Wagner and the Dionysian Act," the composer is crowned the "first forerunner of universal myth creation." His greatest gift is his ability to forge a sense of organic concord in his audience—a characteristic that Ivanov links to the Slavophile term *sobornost'*, indicating the unanimity of feeling in Russian Orthodox services. In Ivanov's eyes, though, the audience at Bayreuth plays too passive a role: it stays locked in contemplation while singers act the parts of heroes and the orchestra casts spells of emotion. Influenced by Nietzsche's cult of Dionysian tragedy, Ivanov wants future theatergoers to enter into the dynamics of the drama, like the dithyrambic chorus of ancient Greece: "The spectator must become an actor, a coparticipant in the rite." After 1905, Ivanov turned toward social engagement, propounding with his fellow poet Georgy Chulkov a philosophy of "mystical anarchism"—a conjoining of Symbolist aesthetics and radical politics.

Andrey Bely, the author of the mountainous Symbolist novel *Petersburg*, shared the Wagner obsessions of the Ivanov circle. Born in 1880 as Boris Bugaev—his adopted name means "white"—he fell for music at an early age and hoped to become a composer. His tutor in Wagnerism

was the critic Emil Medtner, a darksome figure who espoused Aryan philosophy and sometimes wrote under the pseudonym Wölfing, Siegmund's
name in *Walküre*. Like Schopenhauer and Walter Pater, Bely felt that music
was the supreme art, the one toward which other forms should aspire. In
his essay "The Forms of Art," he called Wagner "the first musician who
consciously reached out his hand to tragedy as though in an attempt to
facilitate its evolution in the direction of music." Ada Steinberg, in a study
of Bely and music, determines that the author focused less on Dionysian
theater or the Gesamtkunstwerk than on the auditory texture of music
itself. "With phrases as my material, I wanted to do what Wagner did
with the melody," Bely wrote. This brings him close to English-language
stream-of-consciousness writing and its French antecedents.

Between 1899 and 1908, Bely produced a series of prose-poems called
Symphonies: *Pre-Symphony*, *Northern* or *Heroic Symphony*, *Dramatic
Symphony*, *The Return*, and *Fourth Symphony*, later titled *The Goblet of
Blizzards*. These are populated by knights, swans, giants, gnomes, and
dragons, not to mention Siegfried and Brünnhilde. Furthermore, Bely employs an unusually sophisticated leitmotif technique, as Bartlett shows. A
network of repetitions within the literary fabric takes the place of narrative
continuity. Sentences and sections are numbered, giving the work a quasi-
scientific appearance. The *Dramatic Symphony* opens thus:

1. A season of sweltering grind. The roadway gleamed blindingly.
2. Cab-drivers cracked their whips, exposing their worn, blue backs to
   the hot sun.
3. Yard-sweepers raised columns of dust, their grime-browned faces
   loudly exulting, untroubled by grimaces from passers-by.
4. Along the pavements scurried heat-exhausted intellectuals and
   suspicious-looking citizens.
5. All were pale, and over everyone hung the light-blue vault of the sky,
   now deep-blue, now grey, now black, full of musical tedium, eternal
   tedium, with the sun's eye in its midst.

Leitmotifs pile up. Three times we encounter the sentence "The peasants
and horses were different, but what they did was the same." The eternal
recurrence recurs: "Everything returns again and again . . . Everything re-

turns again . . . Everything returns, everything returns again . . . Everything returns . . . Everything returns again."

As the work proceeds, this abstracted ordinary landscape is filled with characteristic fin-de-siècle figures: a philosopher, a liberal democrat, a religious zealot. Glimpsed in the background are Ibsen, Nordau, Maeterlinck, Nietzsche (prophet of the "eternal return"), and even Péladan ("the Parisian magus"). Toward the end, a prophet named Musatov theorizes the fourth dimension and other recondite concepts. At a government office, he inquires after the secrets of the universe, and receives the answer: "But maybe I should just tell you the mystery of mysteries, to put your mind at rest: *there are no mysteries.*" Quotidian life rushes back in, carrying with it the leitmotifs of unchanging nature: springtime, apple trees, sunsets.

Bely's Wagnerism momentarily lapsed around 1906. In the essay "Against Music," he denounced Wagner's "borrowed heroism" and bourgeois pretensions. Bartlett suggests that this reversal was the result of Bely's inability to play the Siegfried role that he had fantasized for himself, especially in his love life. His interest soon rebounded. Around 1909, he began delving into the occult, and *Parsifal* supplied him with esoteric sacred images. Like Yeats, he made a point of staying at the Grand Hotel et des Palmes in Palermo, where Wagner had completed his final opera. By 1913, Bely had become a follower of Rudolf Steiner and Anthroposophy, his interest apparently stirred by a *Götterdämmerung* in Brussels. "We wait for Parsifal," Bely wrote during the war, while living at Steiner's colony in Switzerland.

Petersburg, which Bely drafted in 1911 and 1912 and published in book form in 1916, unfolds in a phantasmagoric city on the verge of upheaval—the Petersburg of October 1905, just before the general strike. Its principal characters are Apollon Apollonovich Ableukhov, a powerful senator of unprepossessing mien and tidy habits; and his son Nikolai Apollonovich, a disaffected aristocrat who joins a cohort of revolutionaries and is eventually ordered to kill his father. Early on, amid a swirl of urban impressions, Bely evokes the Flying Dutchman—flying "from the leaden expanses of the Baltic and German Seas, in order here to erect by illusion his misty estates and to give the wave of amassing clouds the name of islands." The phantom captain becomes a recurring motif, merging with the figure of Peter the Great, who, as it happens, learned shipbuilding at the Dutch East India Company. Peter is also present as the Bronze Horseman—the statue that inspired Pushkin's poem of the same title. The Dutchman, the Horseman, and the sinister stranger all manifest a Dionysian energy that portends an era of destruction and creation.

The upper-crust milieu of *Petersburg* overlaps with that of Bely's Symphonies, as Nikolai moves among Wagnerians, Nietzscheans, Symbolists, and occultists. A salonnière named Sofya Petrovna explains that she "intended to study meloplastics, so as to be able to dance 'The Ride of the Valkyries' neither better nor worse than it was danced in Bayreuth . . . Meanwhile the very pretty maid would bring a gramophone into the little room: and from its red horn the gramophone's tin throat would belch forth 'The Ride of the Valkyries' at the guest." Paranoid chatter about Jews and Freemasons flows through the conversation of the city. There is talk of "healthy barbarism," of a renaissance of pure folk feeling. In one hallucinatory sequence, the Horseman comes to life and flies over Petersburg's rooftops.

A terrorist named Dudkin, known also as the Stranger, leads Nikolai into the heart of the radical cabal, although both men begin to question their mission in the course of a joint spiritual quest. In the end, the bomb intended for Apollon goes off harmlessly. The master bureaucrat retires soon after, having failed utterly to control the tumult of 1905. Nikolai goes off to wander the meadows in a state of solitary contemplation—a Parsifal without temple or Grail. As for Dudkin, we last see him astride the corpse of his malignant superior, in a parody of the Bronze Horseman—or, perhaps, of the Valkyries, bearing the bodies of slain warriors.

Alexander Blok, Bely's exact contemporary, fit the part of the artist-hero Bely aspired to be—a strikingly handsome young man who thought of pursuing an acting career before making his name with Symbolist poems of ecstatic, apocalyptic character. His first experience of Wagner, the Mariinsky's *Walküre* in 1900, inspired a poem in which the meeting of Siegmund and Sieglinde is paraphrased in compressed, heightened language:

Black sword broke against the rocks!
Wälse! Wälse! Where is your sword!

Blok identifies with Wagner's heroes in terms both personal and spiritual. He likens himself to the sword-wielding Siegfried and apostrophizes his ideal love, the "Beautiful Lady," in images suitable for Brünnhilde on her flaming rock: "The whole horizon is on fire—and mercilessly clear. / I wait in silence—*grieving and loving.*" The recurring vision of the red sky, the burning horizon, carries with it a sense of imminent, catastrophic change.

After the turmoil of 1905, in Bartlett's account, Blok sympathized more with Wagner's tragic, flawed heroes: Tristan, Wotan, Siegmund. The 1913 play *The Rose and the Cross* infuses a tale of star-crossed medieval love with Rosicrucian imagery—a belated and stylish echo of Péladan's Rose + Croix. All the while, the poet's attachment to Wagner never wavered. "Every time I hear him," Blok said in 1909, "I am more excited, music is the most influential and dangerous thing." The coming of revolution only intensified his passion. "Wagner is still both alive and new," he wrote in a 1918 essay. "When the Revolution starts sounding in the air, Wagner's Art answers back."

This messianic litany changed surprisingly little as the Bolsheviks laid waste to tsarist society. In his 1919 essay "The Collapse of Humanism," Blok greets Wagner as a "summoner and invoker of ancient chaos"—the chosen one who speaks aloud what humanist thought cannot confront. "The great bell of anti-humanism peals over the earth; the world purifies itself, casting off its old garments; man grows closer to the elemental in nature—he grows more musical . . . Man—human animal, social animal, moral animal—is being reconstructed as an *artist*, speaking in the language of Wagner." The revolution is "born of the spirit of music," and carries the debris of civilization in its torrent. In his diary, Blok quoted the Rhinemaidens: "Only down deep is it trusty and true: false and base is the revelry above!"

BOLSHEVIK WAGNER

Tsar Nicholas II died in a hail of bullets in July 1918, along with his wife and his five children—the climactic event in the Red Terror that followed the Russian Revolution of 1917. Given Nicholas's role in promoting Wagner, performances of the operas might have been expected to grind to a halt once the Bolshevik era began. In fact, the tsar had consigned Wagner

Vladimir Tatlin, design for The Flying Dutchman
and model of the Third International Tower

to enemy status with the onset of the First World War, and his works had already dropped out of the repertory. When the Bolsheviks made a separate peace with Germany at Brest-Litovsk, they effectively made peace with Bayreuth as well. *Rienzi, Tannhäuser, Lohengrin, Rheingold, Walküre, Siegfried,* and *Meistersinger* received stagings in Petrograd, Moscow, and elsewhere. There were even one or two attempts at *Parsifal*, although its religious orientation caused ideological trouble. Some productions displayed Futurist, Constructivist, and other avant-garde features; others revived the turn-of-the-century tsarist style for a new proletarian audience. The general public took advantage of lowered ticket prices to crowd into the old imperial theaters. Bourgeois culture was thus converted into the culture of the masses.

Interest in Wagner reached to the top of the new Soviet hierarchy. Vladimir Lenin was a casual Wagnerite, having been raised in a home that held the composer in high regard. The Bolshevik leader apparently saw no political value in the operas, instead thrilling to their theatrical effects, which sometimes overwhelmed him. "He liked Wagner greatly," Lenin's widow, Nadezhda Krupskaya, recalled. "But he usually left, almost ill, after the first act." He heard the Good Friday music from *Parsifal* in London in

1903; attended Wagner performances while in exile in Zurich; and had three Wagner books in his library at the Kremlin. When, in 1920, he laid a wreath at the Monument to the Victims of the Revolution on the Field of Mars, Siegfried's Funeral Music served as an accompaniment. "It is as if this music was created for this moment," a witness reported.

The same hero's lament rang out at a concert marking Lenin's death, in 1924. Curating that musical memorial was Anatoly Lunacharsky, the People's Commissar of Education and the chief cultural authority in the first years of the regime. Lunacharsky arrived at Bolshevism along a circuitous path that touched on Wagner, Nietzsche, Symbolism, and Theosophy, and his political rhetoric retained a mystical accent. "The Party must be everywhere," he said, "like the biblical spirit of God." Lunacharsky tried to apply his tolerant, eclectic taste to the unsettled world of the Bolshevik arts, where futurists vied with anti-bourgeois proletarians and conservative-leaning academics. Wagner's music and writings seemed to occupy a historically sound middle ground. In 1918, Lunacharsky wrote an introduction for a new edition of "Art and Revolution," in which he made a bold claim of equivalence: "The revolutionary movement of 1848 that gave birth to the great *Communist Manifesto* of our brilliant teachers Marx and Engels was also reflected in the small, lively, deep, and revolutionary brochure of the no less brilliant Richard Wagner." The historian Lars Kleberg calls this 1918 translation of "Art and Revolution" the "first significant publication on theatrical theory to appear in Soviet Russia."

The ideal of a proletarian theater coincided with the more extravagant imaginings of late-tsarist Russia, notably Ivanov's modern dithyrambic chorus. Platon Kerzhentsev, a leader of the Proletkult or proletarian-culture faction, redefined the Gesamtkunstwerk as a "close fraternity between all the arts," where the snobbishly specialized categories of bourgeois culture would cease to apply. Divisions between director and performer, between performer and audience, between participant and onlooker would fall away. More than their counterparts to their west, Russian theorists understood *Gesamt* to mean "communal" or "collective."

The quintessence of the Communist Gesamtkunstwerk was the mass spectacle, which thrived from 1918 to 1920. These pageant-like events involved thousands of people, professional and amateur. The largest of them, *The Storming of the Winter Palace*, recruited soldiers and sailors as performers, with percussive support from the guns of the cruiser *Aurora*.

Around a hundred thousand people are said to have witnessed it. Wagner provided theoretical backing for these occasions, and, sometimes, music as well. *The Mystery of Liberated Labor* reviewed the struggle of the working classes, from the Spartacus Uprising to the present day. Radiant music from *Lohengrin* signaled the advent of the Kingdom of Freedom, the long-sought socialist paradise. (The musical director of this performance was a young pianist named Dimitri Tiomkin, who later had an illustrious career as a composer in Hollywood.) Lunacharsky, reverting again to fin-de-siècle vocabulary, described such affairs as "orgiastic exultation."

Just as *The Storming of the Winter Palace* was unfolding in Petrograd, the artist Vladimir Tatlin unveiled a model of his Monument to the Third International, which, in the unlikely event that it had been built, would have been the ultimate expression of the Bolshevik impulse to fuse art and life. Tatlin envisioned a tower around thirteen hundred feet high, defined by an upward-spiraling twin helix. Within that form were office spaces of various geometric shapes—cube, pyramid, cylinder—each of which slowly rotated at a prescribed speed.

The basic outline of the Monument originated in Cubo-Futurist designs that Tatlin made between 1915 and 1918. The occasion was not architectural but theatrical: a projected production of *The Flying Dutchman*. The Monument's upward-angling tower was originally the mast of the Dutchman's ship, swathed in geometric rigging. Mikhail Kolesnikov has stated that with these designs Tatlin was "the first to break up the surface of the stage, building several planes tilted at different angles and intersecting each other at different levels." Wagner was thus present at the birth of the Constructivist aesthetic.

MEYERHOLD

No Russian artist paid closer attention to the radical strain in Wagner's work than Vsevolod Meyerhold, the tragic hero of Bolshevik theater. Emile Meyergold, the director's father, was a German-Jewish vodka distiller who had immigrated to Russia and converted to Lutheranism. Vsevolod was sufficiently fluent in German that he could tackle Wagner's prose writings, which he read in their entirety. An encounter with Konstantin Stanislavsky's newly founded Moscow Art Theater, in 1898, steered Meyerhold toward a theatrical career. He joined the company, but Stanislavsky's meticulous naturalism failed to satisfy him: he felt that the drama should strike harder and deeper into social reality. "I want to burn with the spirit of the times," Meyerhold wrote to Anton Chekhov in 1901. "The theater can play an enormous part in the transformation of the whole of existence."

Meyerhold established his signature technique of *uslovnost*, or "stylization," around 1905, as he grappled with the challenge of staging Maeterlinck's elliptical plays and other Symbolist works. Early on, the director defined *uslovnost* as an effort to use "convention, generalization, and symbol" to "bring out those hidden features that are deeply rooted in the style of any work of art." In place of florid gestures and tremulous recitations, he demanded statuesque poses and a "cold coining of the words."

When early experiments faltered in Moscow, Meyerhold moved to Petersburg, where the group around Ivanov and Blok offered support. In the same period, he was absorbing the theatrical theories of Appia, Fuchs, and Craig, all of whom shared his antipathy toward naturalist acting and realistic sets. In 1906 Meyerhold collaborated with Blok on *The Puppet Show*, which banished Symbolist atmosphere in favor of a carnival aesthetic. Meyerhold, in the role of the sad clown Pierrot, sat in one scene on the "bench where Venus and Tannhäuser are wont to kiss." At the outset, a trio of Norn-like figures forecast doom, perhaps more for themselves than for the world: "O endless horror, endless dark! . . . The coming is at hand."

The perpetrator of such scandalous entertainments must have seemed an odd candidate to undertake Wagner on the great stage of the Mariinsky, yet Meyerhold was directing *Tristan* there three years later. In preparation, he plunged into extensive research, producing, by Rosamund Bartlett's report, seventy-one pages of notes on Wagner's writings. His preliminary thoughts were set forth in the 1907 essay "First Attempts at a Stylized Theater," which begins with a brusque dismissal of the Gesamtkunstwerk: "The theater is constantly revealing a lack of harmony amongst those engaged in presenting their collective creative work to the public. One never sees an ideal blend of author, director, actor, designer, composer and property-master. For this reason, Wagner's notion of a synthesis of the arts seems to me impossible. Both the artist and the composer should remain in their own fields." Meyerhold goes on to say that Wagner's orchestra does most of the dramatic work and that the singing "lacks the power to express the inner passions of his heroes." What is needed is a "new means of expressing the ineffable." This can be found in the art of "*plastic movement.*" The director wants his actors to perform as orchestral musicians do, virtuosically but "at all costs lacking in individuality."

Meyerhold's investigation of Wagner did not end there. In 1909, in an essay accompanying the finished *Tristan* production, he no longer doubts the potency of the vocal element. "The world of the soul can express itself only through music," he writes. The problem now is the discrepancy between the music of the future and the theater of the present: "The music refuses to harmonize with everyday, automatic gestures." Meyerhold goes on to cite Appia, who had been talking for years about the "Wagnerian contradiction." Quotations from the composer are marshaled to suggest that he foresaw a revolution in the art of direction and design. Meyerhold concludes: "It is clear that the Bayreuth stage could never have satisfied Wagner, because it had yet to sever the final link with the traditions of the Renaissance theater."

The Meyerhold *Tristan* is a legend in the history of Wagner staging, perhaps to an exaggerated degree. As Patrick Carnegy points out, it was less audacious than the prospectus leads one to believe—probably because the Mariinsky was unable to accommodate all of the director's ideas. Meyerhold had wanted the form of a single sail to dominate Act I, with the rest of the ship left to the audience's imagination. A production photograph reveals a fair amount of nautical detail, including rigging, a mast, and furniture for Isolde's cabin. In Act III, where Meyerhold had specified only a vacant horizon and desolate cliffs, the documentation shows props typical of a castle set. Still, Meyerhold defied prevalent styles by pushing the action into the foreground—here Fuchs's influence was apparent—and by employing hangings in place of realistic sets. Above all, he curtailed histrionics. Ironically, his array of frozen attitudes may not have been too different from the hieratic poses of Cosima's Bayreuth.

The director of the Imperial Theaters, Vladimir Telyakovsky, had some reservations—"Tristan and Isolde writhe like worms by the rocks and frequently take on unnatural poses," he wrote in his diary—but the production was ultimately counted a success. The culmination of Meyerhold's activity in the tsarist period came on what was effectively the last day of that era—his staging of Mikhail Lermontov's *Masquerade* on February 25, 1917. The mutiny by members of the Imperial Guard the following day precipitated the fall of the tsar's regime. Katerina Clark, in her book *Petersburg*, explains how the *Masquerade* production fused a Wagnerian-Nietzschean agenda—the tearing away of the masks of commercial theater—with a Marxist concern for working-class voices. A tragedy of an Othello-like nobleman becomes a mirror image of tsarist society on the eve of its downfall. One can only wonder what Meyerhold might have accomplished with a *Ring* staging on the same principle.

Meyerhold's first major work of the Bolshevik period was his agitprop production of Vladimir Mayakovsky's *Mystery-Bouffe*, with designs by Kazimir Malevich. Meyerhold went on to serve as head of Lunacharsky's theater division and to present stagings at a bespoke venue dubbed RSFSR Theater No. 1. His first project at the latter space, in 1920, was Émile Verhaeren's politically charged Symbolist drama *The Dawn*, which culminates in a funeral for a fallen populist tribune. The plot calls to mind the man-of-the-people narrative of *Rienzi*, which appealed to Bolshevik audiences. Meyerhold planned to produce that opera next. Working with his assistant Valery Bebutov, he vowed to bring about the overthrow of operatic convention that he had failed to achieve in his *Tristan*. The scenery, by Georgy Yakulov, was based on sketches originally made for *Mystery-Bouffe*. Singers were to appear in contemporary garb. The libretto was "Bolshevized," with singers and speaking actors slated to double on each part.

The closure of RSFSR Theater No. 1, in response to the cost-cutting agenda of Lenin's New Economic Policy, prevented the full execution of this plan, to Meyerhold's intense regret. Yakulov was, however, able to transfer his scheme of a "symphony of color and light" to his own *Rienzi* of 1923. That production also invoked the circus, with hoops and a trapeze somehow incorporated into the fourteenth-century setting. Constructivist aesthetics figured in several other Wagner productions of the period. Fyodor Komissarzhevsky and Ivan Fedotov's 1918 realization of *Lohengrin*, at the former Zimin Theater in Moscow, included a set made up of conical and cubic forms. A staging of the same opera at the Bolshoi in 1923, with sets by the great Soviet designer Fyodor Fedorovsky, placed the action in a futuristic abstract landscape, with costumes bearing sharp edges and spikes. This production caused excitement among a group of German doctors who were attending to the ailing Lenin.

The Bolshevik arts scene changed drastically after 1921. The governing apparatus was reorganized, and Lunacharsky began to lose his authority. The state was exerting ever greater control over the arts, and a backlash against avant-gardism began. Katerina Clark calls it a "retreat from a more open-ended situation to one where norms prevailed." Meyerholdian reinterpretations of German music drama fell well outside the bounds of those norms. Meyerhold never directed Wagner again.

As the regimentation of Soviet culture proceeded, Wagner's ideological credibility dwindled. Members of the arts bureaucracy criticized *Lohengrin* as "Catholic," "mystical," and "monarchic propaganda." By 1928, the critic Nikolai Malkov was writing that Wagner embodied the "self-affirming aspirations of the bourgeoisie of imperialistic Germany" and was therefore "at variance with our artistic worldview." In 1933, a flurry of events commemorated the fiftieth anniversary of Wagner's death. After that, the Nazification of the composer made him all but untouchable in the Soviet Union. There was one brief resurgence of interest between 1939 and 1941, in the period of the Hitler-Stalin non-aggression pact. Sergei Eisenstein, Meyerhold's protégé, took advantage of that window to direct a production of *Walküre*. Otherwise, Wagner did not return to Soviet stages until after Stalin's death. *Parsifal* was absent until 1997.

Even as Wagner faded from sight in Soviet Russia, Meyerhold's innovations were spreading to the West, and the dream of revolutionary Wagner stagings found a second life in the experimental theaters of the Weimar Republic. Although the effort to wrest the composer from the grip of the *völkisch* right proved a losing battle, the alternative images fashioned in the Weimar years have had a long afterlife. The wildly multifarious Wagner stagings of today are in a direct line of descent from the *Flying Dutchman* that opened at the Kroll Opera, in Berlin, in 1929—a production that restored Wagner's power to shock.

WEIMAR WAGNERISM

The German Empire failed to outlive Cosima Wagner. On November 9, 1918, the Social Democratic leader Philipp Scheidemann shouted from a window of the Reichstag, "Long live the great German Republic!" The long-deferred dream of 1848, that of a free and democratic Germany, was on the

The Kroll Opera's The Flying Dutchman, *1929*

verge of fulfillment. Yet the Social Democratic vision immediately clashed with the ambitions of German Communists, who, under the banner of the Spartacus League, attempted to seize Berlin in January 1919. Friedrich Ebert, the Social Democratic chancellor, made the fateful decision to rely on mercenary forces—the Freikorps—to suppress the uprising. The brutal killing of the Communist leaders Karl Liebknecht and Rosa Luxemburg created a deep rift in the German left, one that may have sealed the fate of the Weimar Republic.

The cult of Wagner survived the political turbulence. Even as the proto-fascist right wing fed on the ideology of the Bayreuth Circle, leftist Wagnerites pressed their case. The Communist stalwart Clara Zetkin kept faith in the composer's revolutionary potential. Luxemburg, her longtime friend, admitted to enjoying *Meistersinger,* and once compared a beautiful June morning to the "Johannistag!" chorus in that opera. Kurt Eisner, who proclaimed the Bavarian Democratic and Social Republic in November 1918, made his name as an interpreter of Nietzsche and was conversant with Wagner's work, although, following Nietzsche's lead, he labeled the composer a "poeticizing dilettante." When Eisner was assassinated, in early 1919, Siegfried's Funeral Music was announced as a selection for his memorial procession—a gesture that pleased Thomas Mann, who thought that Wagner would have "sunk below the horizon" in the new socialist order.

In Weimar Germany, as in Bolshevik Russia, up-to-date versions of the total artwork circulated in progressive artistic spheres. Walter Gropius, the leader of the Bauhaus movement, had absorbed Gesamtkunstwerk philosophies in Munich, Berlin, and Vienna before the war, and his notions of *Einheitskunstwerk* and the *Kunstwerk der Gesamtheit* are variations on a familiar theme. Gropius's Bauhaus manifesto, issued in 1919, contains passages reminiscent of "Art and Revolution" and "The Artwork of the Future":

Today the arts exist in isolation, from which they can be rescued only through the conscious, cooperative effort of all craftsmen. Architects, painters, and sculptors must recognize anew and learn to grasp the composite character of a building both as an entity and in its separate parts . . . Together let us desire, conceive, and create the new structure of the future, which will embrace architecture and sculpture and painting in one unity and which will one day rise toward heaven from the hands of a million workers like the crystal symbol of a new faith.

On the cover of the manifesto is Lyonel Feininger's woodcut *Cathedral*, which fuses Gothic and Cubist sensibilities. Likewise, Gropius's "new structure of the future" combines the Bayreuth idea with industrial cathedrals like the Crystal Palace in London.

A man of Gropius's precisely driven intellect would not permit a mere recycling of Romantic rhetoric. As Matthew Wilson Smith explains in his wide-ranging study *The Total Work of Art*, Gropius's integration of art and society relied not on an "appeal to primordial sentiment," as in Wagner's or William Morris's day, but on "objective organizational and technological power." It is a "total reengineering of the real." Gropius also theorized a revolutionary theater venue—"*Totaltheater*" was his chosen term—that would bring the art form into the electrified twentieth century. Film projections would enhance or replace conventional scenery; stage platforms would be mobile; the audience would be pitched into the middle of the drama. László Moholy-Nagy, similarly, posited a "TOTAL STAGE ACTION," a "Theater of Totality," which would dispense with conventional representation and offer "multifarious complexities of light, space, plane, form, motion, sound, man." Wagner's theories are given the usual straw-man treatment. Moholy-Nagy wrote: "What we need is not the '*Gesamtkunstwerk*,' alongside and separated from which life flows by, but a synthesis of all the vital impulses spontaneously forming itself into the all-embracing *Gesamtwerk* (life) which abolishes all isolation."

The modern-dance movement known as *Ausdruckstanz*, led by Rudolf Laban and Mary Wigman, supplied a more tangible manifestation of total art. Laban's 1921 staging of the *Tannhäuser* Bacchanale at the Mannheim Opera was notable for its free and sensuous movement. In 1925, Laban presented a program of danced scenes from *Tristan*, *Parsifal*, and the *Ring*, passing over detailed characterization and concentrating on fundamental motifs (heroism, dwarfish grotesquerie, and Loge's fire). For the 1930 season in Bayreuth, Laban was invited to choreograph *Tannhäuser*, as Isadora Duncan had done a quarter-century earlier. Many observers felt that Laban's work had an invigorating effect: it prophesied the revolution in Bayreuth staging that would follow the Second World War. At the same time, his affinity for Nordic body culture and his interest in founding a national dance theater made him acceptable to the Nazi regime, at least in the early years. There were more continuities between Weimar and Nazism than the legend of a radical republic lets on.

If, as Wagner and other left-leaning thinkers maintained, the revolution would allow common people to find aesthetic fulfillment in their daily lives, the final frontier was in home decor and fashion. Gertrud Bäumer, a moderate leftist who campaigned for women's rights and "organic democracy," took this line in her book *The Social Idea in the Worldviews of the Nineteenth Century*: "Wagner's program required shifting to the arts of everyday life, literature, and the fine arts—especially arts and crafts—in order to find its full realization." The Austrian-Jewish designer Stella Junker-Weissenberg offered a stylish application of that principle in some sketches from the twenties. For a prospective "Wagner Revue," she imagined a chic retinue of Valkyries, Flower Maidens, and Venusberg denizens: slender, midriff-baring women equipped with spears, shields, and winged headgear.

These flappers of the future never hit the streets, yet Wagner found his way into the Americanized popular culture of the twenties. In the cafés and bars of Berlin and Vienna, one might have heard, along with the hits of the day, Clément Doucet's delicious jazz-adjacent arrangements of *Tannhäuser* ("Wagnéria") and *Tristan* ("Isoldina"). Willy Rosen's cabaret song "Frau Abendstern" incorporates the Song to the Evening Star from

Tannhäuser into a portrait of a heavyset woman who finds herself in vogue with slender young men: "Frau Abendstern, Frau Abendstern / Once again she's *ganz modern* . . ."

In November 1918, just as the German republican experiment began, Heinrich Mann's *Der Untertan*, which had been completed before the war, was finally published in book form. The novel's lacerating critique of Kaiserreich culture, including its takedown of *Lohengrin* as nationalist kitsch, set the tone for literature of the following years. Younger German and Austrian authors, especially those aligned with the left, had difficulty seeing Wagner as anything but a decrepit relic of a national culture that had descended from imperial pomposity into tribal savagery. As in Anglo-American literature, modernist techniques were taking hold—stream of consciousness, leitmotif construction, excavations of everyday culture—and yet Wagner seldom received even glancing credit as a precursor. The mobilization of his work for wartime propaganda probably explains the hostility of the rising generation.

One bellwether of changing attitudes was Hermann Hesse, who had put a homoerotic Wagnerian vignette in his debut novel, *Peter Camenzind*. In the 1919 novella *Klein and Wagner*, Hesse takes a much darker view of the composer's cultural residuum. A bank officer who has embezzled money flees to Italy, his mind fixated on the name Wagner: not only the Meister, but also the real-life figure of Ernst August Wagner, who, in 1913, killed his wife, his four children, and eight residents of the town of Mühlhausen. Klein has a dream in which the two Wagners merge, and he conducts a self-psychoanalysis: "Wagner was himself—Wagner was the murderer and fugitive within him, but Wagner was also the composer, the artist, the genius, the seducer, the inclination toward lust for life and lust for pleasure, luxury—Wagner was the collective name for everything repressed, buried, short-changed in Friedrich Klein, former civil servant. And *Lohengrin*—was not he himself Lohengrin, the knight-errant on the mysterious mission, whose name one cannot ask?" As Hugo Ball wrote in 1927, this doubling of Wagner encapsulates the problem of how a *Volk* that brought forth such transcendent music "plunged berserk into a war and forgot all romanticism, all love."

Franz Werfel, in his 1924 bestseller *Verdi: A Novel of the Opera*, displaces German genius in favor of the Italian equivalent. Having made his name as an Expressionist poet, Werfel was turning toward a more popular idiom, and Verdi's earthy vitality inspired him. Like d'Annunzio in *Il fuoco*, Werfel sets his novel in Venice during the last weeks of Wagner's life, but the Meister now comes across as a vain monologist surrounded by sycophants. In defiance of biographical reality, Verdi skulks around Venice incognito, struggling with feelings of inferiority and obsolescence. The death at the Palazzo Vendramin serves to liberate Verdi from years of self-doubt. Implicit in that ending is the prophecy of a shift from Romantic indulgence to neoclassical clarity—the "mediterraneanizing" of which Nietzsche once spoke.

Perhaps the most pitiless of all Wagner Scenes occurs in *The Man Without Qualities*, Robert Musil's satirical epic of Austria-Hungary on the brink of extinction. Walter, a failed musician and artist, consoles himself by playing themes from the Wagner operas at the piano. Walter's wife, Clarisse, fails to find the music sexually arousing, as her fin-de-siècle predecessors might have done. Indeed, it is now an active turnoff: she goes outside to spend time with Walter's childhood friend Ulrich. Musil writes: "Intermittent waves of random churning sounds reached them. Ulrich knew that Clarisse refused her body to Walter for weeks at a time when he played Wagner. He played Wagner anyway, with a bad conscience, like a schoolboy vice." The last phrase may be an insolent wink at Thomas Mann: Walter is a grown-up, washed-up Hanno Buddenbrook, his Wagnerism indistinguishable from masturbation.

B uried deep in the collective works of Bertolt Brecht is evidence that the future arch-leftist and scourge of Romantic pretension had a weakness for Wagner in his youth. In the anniversary year 1913, when he was fifteen, Brecht wrote an item for his school newspaper calling the music "*herrlich*"—magnificent—and expressing bafflement that audiences ever rejected such a genius. That enthusiasm faded quickly: a list of cultural favorites from three years later specifies "Bach, Mozart (nicht Wagner)." In maturity, Brecht showed unbending disdain for the world of Bayreuth. This public stance concealed a serious engagement with the legacies of leftist and modernist Wagnerism. As a personality, Brecht was hardly the antithesis of the domineering and mercurial Wagner. Both men could be described as scoundrels, callously exploiting those around them. Both experienced exile, and both compromised with power on their return— Wagner in the Kaiserreich, Brecht in East Germany. As Joy Calico writes in *Brecht at the Opera*, the opposing poles of Brecht and Wagner are "bound together by the current flowing between them."

The young Brecht, heavily under the influence of Wedekind, inclined toward themes of criminality and chaotic sexuality. In his first play, *Baal* (1918), a drunken, thuggish poet falls in with a composer, in an erotically charged relationship resembling Rimbaud and Verlaine's. The seedy decadence of their world is established when Baal uses the campy phrase "My dear swan," à la Lohengrin, and when a hurdy-gurdy is heard playing bits of *Tristan*. In the unfinished poem "Siegfried Had Red Hair," Hagen appears to be in love with Siegfried, and kills him when Gunther points this out. With these gay vignettes, Brecht is surely snickering at the well-documented gay atmosphere of Bayreuth, although he had his own history of sexual ambiguity. He admired Hesse's *Peter Camenzind* for its cool detachment from social convention.

In the mid-twenties, as Brecht turned toward social engagement, he seized on the concept of epic theater, which the experimental Berlin director Erwin Piscator was the first to articulate. Borrowing liberally from Meyerhold, the epic theater aimed for stylization, anti-realism, a breaking of the wall between audience and performance. Through "alienation effects"—an adaptation of Viktor Shklovsky's theory of defamiliarization—spectators would think critically about the action onstage and draw political lessons.

Of the various distortions of the Gesamtkunstwerk that circulated in the early twentieth century, Brecht's was the most influential. In the 1930 essay "Notes on the Opera *The Rise and Fall of the City of Mahagonny*," he announces a "radical *separation of the elements*" of the theater—words, music, production—in opposition to a total work in which the arts are muddled together, resulting in a degradation of each element. (Margaret Schlegel makes a similar complaint in *Howards End*.) The Gesamtkunstwerk charade, Brecht goes on, hypnotizes spectators and renders them passive. Such "sordid intoxication" must stop. Wagner makes clear, however, that the arts should *not* dissolve into one another. Nor does he traffic only in mesmerism: at crucial junctures, he breaks the spell that his music has cast, leading to defamiliarization *avant la lettre*. At the end of *Rheingold*, Loge spoils the gods' entry into Valhalla by quipping that they are hurrying to their doom. His manner is like that of a caustic host at a cabaret, as modern productions have emphasized.

Brecht's real target is the popular image of Wagner, especially the Wagner of German nationalism. He means not so much to abolish the Gesamtkunstwerk as to annex it. Matthew Wilson Smith pinpoints the ideological overlap: "Brecht, like Wagner, imagines an artwork that overcomes the fragmentation caused by the division of labor, an artwork inseparable from larger political demands." Brecht wants to present a different kind of unity, one that illustrates connections not by organically smoothing over differences but by accentuating jumps, breaks, discontinuities—an art of "total montage."

The epic theater is bound up with Brecht's idea of Gestus, of "gestic" theater. John Willett defines Gestus as "both gist and gesture; an attitude or a single aspect of an attitude, expressible in words or actions." The formula brings to mind Wagner's interest in *Gebärde*—dramatic and musical gestures that encapsulate the action. Even more, it suggests the unavoidable leitmotif, or *Grundmotiv*, as Wagner sometimes named it. Kurt Weill, the co-creator of *The Threepenny Opera*, was surely thinking of Wagner when he spoke of the *Grundgestus*, the fundamental Gestus. Its function parallels that of the leitmotif: it comments on the action from a distance, manipulating memory. Calico thinks that this focus on gesture recuperates an element of the Wagner drama that Nietzsche had deemed archaic—the "primacy of the body in stylized positions and movements."

Every successful avant-garde movement is fated to become the establishment against which the next vanguard rebels. Brecht follows the Wagnerian strategy of aggressive renaming: as opera was replaced by music drama, so now music drama gives way to epic theater. His critique of opera as a "culinary" form fit for sybaritic tastes recalls Wagner's attacks on the luxuries of French and Italian opera and on the *Schwelger*—hedonists, gourmands—who gobble it up. Wagner's ultimate wish was to overcome the culinary consumption of art and theater; yet Bayreuth quickly became a magnet for crowds consuming bratwurst. The irony awaiting Brecht was that his own work would be subject to the same domesticating process. The ascendancy of "Mack the Knife" as a swanky pop number suitable for Las Vegas acts and Big Mac commercials is another lesson in the decay of ideological purity.

Could Wagner be saved from the ultranationalist parties that claimed him as their prophet? Leftist Wagnerites made the case throughout the twenties. Bernhard Diebold, a Swiss-born progressive, railed against the right-wing appropriation of Wagner in a 1928 pamphlet that had the well-worn title *The Case of Wagner*. At Bayreuth that year, Diebold was distressed to see few liberal Germans in attendance. A wreath bearing Nazi colors rested on Wagner's grave; the black, red, and gold of 1848 was absent. Diebold asks: "Who bears the greatest blame for the political loss of the most popular high art of the past few decades?" The fault, he writes, lies partly with the leftist press, which has surrendered the "immense cultural credit of this world-famous name" to the Houston Stewart Chamberlain faction. Gustav Stresemann, the leading German politician of the mid- and late twenties, also wondered how it was that Bayreuth had "touched up the old democrat Wagner as a modern swastika-type."

Many leftist intellectuals, particularly those with ties to the crusading magazine *Die Weltbühne*, found Diebold's thesis unconvincing. Ludwig Marcuse derided it as "progressive reaction," a wedding of fashionable leftism to aristocratic taste. Kurt Tucholsky amused himself by proposing that Clément Doucet's syncopated hit "Wagnéria" improved on the original. Carl von Ossietzky, *Die Weltbühne*'s fearless editor in its last years, called Wagner "the most brilliant seducer that Germany has known," and added: "No artist has had a more disastrous influence on the mental and emotional disposition of the people, no one has preached more insistently and alluringly the flight from reality, the cult of the beautiful appearance." The music critics Paul Bekker and Alfred Einstein broached the idea that Wagner's works contain antisemitic caricatures.

Whether or not Wagner was inherently leftist or radical, Weimar stage directors remade him in their own image. By the early twenties, the latest innovations in modern theater—abstract set design, photographic projections and film, the distancing effects of Meyerhold and Brecht—were infiltrating Wagner production. For a *Ring* in Duisburg, Saladin Schmitt and Johannes Schröder put into practice what was termed "expressionist color-light-music." Lothar Schenk von Trapp brought stark geometries of light and shadow to *Tannhäuser* and *Lohengrin* in Darmstadt; Leo Pasetti emulated the Expressionist painting of Emil Nolde in designs for *Parsifal* in Munich. Ludwig Sievert's Frankfurt *Ring* had a traditionally outfitted Wotan standing in a jaggedly geometric cleft, more Futurist than Romantic. *Tannhäuser* designs by Karl Moos and Harry Breuer glow with dreamlike color, closer in spirit to Roerich's primal Russian visions.

The real breakthrough took place at the Kroll Opera, in Berlin, which had been charged with developing a working-class audience. Its chief conductor was Otto Klemperer, a headstrong Mahler disciple who followed the latest artistic trends. He brought in the painter, sculptor, and designer Ewald Dülberg, who had progressed from Art Nouveau to Expressionism and Cubism. Caspar Neher, Oskar Schlemmer, and Moholy-Nagy also worked at the Kroll. All this rankled right-wing critics, who labeled it "cultural Bolshevism." Things came to a head when the company turned to Wagner. The Kroll's 1929 production of *The Flying Dutchman*, with designs by Dülberg and direction by Jürgen Fehling, was called "unparalleled cultural shamelessness," an "irresponsible attempt to destroy," an "artistic betrayal of the people."

Dülberg had long been mulling over new images for Wagner. In his 1914 sketches for *Parsifal*, the hero radiates Expressionist ferocity. Dülberg's *Dutchman* projects that harshness and starkness on a large scale. Masts loomed over the stage as semi-abstract forms—geometric cousins to Tatlin's Third International Tower. Both exterior and interior spaces were simplified and stylized. The main characters appeared in modern dress. Senta wore a blue sweater and gray skirt—like a figure from the lithographs of Käthe Kollwitz, as Alfred Einstein said. The seamen looked fresh from a grimy Hamburg pier. The Dutchman, lacking his usual beard and hat, struck Einstein as an "Ibsenesque, almost Strindbergian 'man of the sea.'" But the effect was anything but mundane. Rather, as Wagner's grandson Franz Wilhelm Beidler recalled, "The storm wind that blows against you was felt in this performance as in no other. And also the ghostly, the demonic-ghostly." Bernhard Diebold spoke of "direction [*Regie*] from the spirit of music"—a twist on Nietzsche's most idolatrous text about Wagner.

In conjunction with the Kroll *Dutchman*, Ernst Bloch, part of a young left-intellectual cohort that also included Theodor W. Adorno and Walter Benjamin, wrote a visionary essay titled "Rescuing Wagner Through Surrealistic Colportage." Colportage is cheap, mass-distributed literature—pulp fiction, essentially. The provocative thrust of Bloch's essay is to compare Wagner to Karl May, the prolific German author of Western tales. The comparison is not as outlandish as it sounds: Old Shatterhand, May's German-American hero, is cut from the same rough, noble cloth as Wagner's heroes, or, for that matter, Owen Wister's Virginian. Bloch goes on to make the familiar argument that Wagner has devolved into bourgeois kitsch. But this particular brand of "kitsch-mythology" resists obsolescence: it stands as a "hieroglyph in the hollow space of the nineteenth century," awaiting a new interpretation. Surrealistic techniques—montage, found-object art, fairground aesthetics, colportage—can restore the abrasive vitality of music drama. Bloch even loops in Brecht as he pictures Wagner on board "his pirate ship, with eight sails and fifty cannon"—a reference to "Seeräuber Jenny" from *The Threepenny Opera*.

The time for Wagner's rescue was not at hand. The *Dutchman* and other Kroll stagings agitated not only the right wing but also the more doctrinaire cultural bureaucrats on the left, who thought that a popular opera house should focus on "big singers, big arias, big applause," as Klemperer put it. Decades later, in the 1970s and '80s, directors would attempt what Bloch had in mind—a style of production in which everything questionable in Wagner becomes a "modern question," a question about us.

■ ■

FLYING DUTCHMAN

Ulysses, The Waste Land, The Waves

* * * *

```
Maix   Frisch schwebt der Wind
            Der Heimat zu,
            Mein Irisch' Kind,
            Wo weilest du?
"You gave me hyacinths first a year ago;
"They called me the hyacinth girl".
—Yet when we came back, late, from the hyacinth garden,
Your arms full, and your hair wet, I could not
Speak, and my eyes failed, I was neither
Living nor dead, and I knew nothing,
Looking into the heart of light, the silence.

Madame Sosostris, famous clairvoyant
Had a bad cold, nevertheless
Is known to be the wisest woman in Europe,
With a wicked pack of cards.  Here, said she,
Is your card, the drowned Phoenician Sailor,
(These are pearls that were his eyes.  Look!)
Here is Belladonna, the Lady of the Rocks,
The lady of situations,
```

Manuscript of The Waste Land

N othung! . . . *Frisch weht der Wind . . . Silentium! . . . Fragende Frau . . . Öd' und leer das Meer . . .*" Lines from Wagner are scattered through James Joyce's *Ulysses* and T. S. Eliot's *The Waste Land,* two modernist tours de force that dumbfounded the literary world in 1922. The fugitive German phrases capture the texture of conversation among educated young people of the fin de siècle, many of whom knew their Wagner well enough that they could quote him in apposite situations. "*Nothung!*" is what the aspiring writer Stephen Dedalus shouts at the inebriated climax of *Ulysses,* as he swings his walking stick at a chandelier in a brothel. It is a young man's daydream of heroism, colliding violently and comically with unheroic circumstances.

The very idea of *Ulysses*—a modern Odyssey told through the urban adventures of a Dubliner of Jewish descent—is foreshadowed in Wagner's prose writings. Timothy Martin, in his book *Joyce and Wagner: A Study of Influence*, draws attention to a passage in the 1851 essay "A Communication to My Friends," which names two analogues of the tale of the Flying Dutchman: "the wanderings of Ulysses and his longing after home, house, hearth—and wife"; and "the 'Wandering Jew' . . . forever doomed to a long-since outlived life." This yoking of Ulysses and the Wandering Jew under the sign of the supernatural mariner surely caught Joyce's eye when he read the essay, in the William Ashton Ellis translation. In his copy of the text, he marked a subsequent passage that expands on the longing for home. Eliot's relationship with Wagner is less well documented, but repeated allusions to *Tristan* and *Parsifal* in *The Waste Land* suggest that the composer stands for an internal struggle against disorderly desire.

The dialectic of emulation and rejection that governs early modernist responses to Wagner is redoubled in *Ulysses* and *The Waste Land*. The principal legacies of Wagnerism in the arts—the all-devouring Gesamtkunstwerk structure; the interior upwelling of the stream of consciousness; the imposition of mythic forms on modernity—operate at full force. They exemplify what the philosopher-critic Fredric Jameson calls "the great Work, the Book of the World—secular scripture, sacred text, ultimate ritual mass (Mallarmé's Livre) for an unimaginable new social order." At the same time, modernist techniques atomize the world into fragments. Those snippets of Wagner, alienated from their context, appear as so much cultural flotsam and jetsam that the old century has left in its wake. Both *Ulysses* and *The Waste Land* depict a society that existed before the world war and revolution; both bear the scars of the chaos that followed. Their kaleidoscopic montage techniques and their polyphony of voices mimic the new media technologies of phonograph, film, and radio. Wagner breaks in as if someone were turning a wireless dial, looking for the news. Eliot told Virginia Woolf that *Ulysses* "destroyed the whole of the nineteenth century"—Wagner presumably included.

In 1931, Woolf put her own imprint on the Book of the World, diverging from the self-mythologizing tendencies of her male counterparts. *The Waves*, like *Ulysses*, traces the rhythms of a single day, but entire lives are brought into its current, contours of individual personalities dissolving in the flow. *The Waves* may go further than any literature of its time into the shadowland between words and music. Wagner once defined his work as an "art of transition." Something is always turning into something else: no identity is fully fixed. Tristan becomes Isolde, and vice versa. In *The Waves*, too, the security of self erodes: the ocean of language rises; consciousness swamps reality. Joyce achieves something comparable in his final opus, *Finnegans Wake*, doing away with outer reality almost completely.

Ulysses and *The Waste Land* are works of voluntary exile. Joyce, the renegade Irishman, lived for extended periods in Zurich and Paris, as if following in Wagner's footsteps. Of the Wagner characters, the one who figures most strongly in Joyce's work is the Dutchman, the eternal wanderer. Eliot, the Anglicized American, identified more with Tristan's suffering and with Parsifal's lonely quest for the Grail. Woolf, by contrast, remained in England; her exile was internal, the flight of the mind from the prison of the self. She could see no way out of the state of "self-annihilation" that Wagner romanticized as a space of artistic possibility. Men were freer than women to become restless outcasts in search of redemption.

YOUNG JOYCE

Nora Joyce once said of her husband: "I've always told him he should give up writing and take up singing. To think he was once on the same platform with John McCormack!" Whatever the merits of that judgment, James Joyce had real musical gifts, and in his youth he contemplated pursuing singing as a career. With his light, McCormack-like lyric tenor, he could never have sung Wagner onstage, although he did participate in a concert rendition of the quintet from *Meistersinger*. In *Joyce and Wagner*, Martin plausibly claims that the author was "a more serious and better-trained musician than nearly all the Wagnerites in the literary world." Mann had a deeper knowledge of Wagner's milieu; Cather and Shaw were better acquainted with Wagner in performance. But Joyce approached music with the canniness of an insider.

Joyce's primary allegiance was to bel canto opera. He also treasured Gluck and Mozart, music of the Renaissance and the Baroque, and old Irish airs. It was a determinedly anti-Romantic canon, one in which the heavygoing Wagner seemed to have no place. Indeed, Joyce took many swipes at the composer in later decades, although one informed observer thought him disingenuous. Sylvia Beach, who published *Ulysses*, once commented that Paul Valéry was a Wagnerite—"and, unlike Joyce, owned up to it."

Born on the outskirts of Dublin in 1882, Joyce showed brilliance in literature and languages from an early age. At University College, in Dublin, he unnerved his teachers with his almost devilish learnedness. Such a mind was naturally drawn to the chief provocateurs of the day: Ibsen, d'Annunzio, Wilde, Wagner. Joyce's college friend J. F. Byrne wrote: "As we grew older, it was Wagner who attracted us—especially by such of his music dramas as 'Tristan and Isolde,' and 'Lohengrin.'" According to his brother Stanislaus, Joyce also wrote a long poem "on the Valkyrie."

He probably first heard Wagner courtesy of the Carl Rosa Opera Company, which made annual visits to the Gaiety Theatre, in Dublin. On various tours the company offered *Rienzi*, *Lohengrin*, *Tannhäuser*, *Meistersinger*, *Siegfried*, and *Tristan*. In 1895 and 1896, it revived its production of *The Flying Dutchman*, first seen in the 1870s. These visits drew large enough crowds that a character in *Ulysses* uses them as a benchmark: "God, you've to book ahead, man, you'd think it was for the Carl Rosa." As it happens, the preface to Rosa's libretto for *The Flying Dutchman* calls attention to the "remarkable mixture of the characters of the Wandering Jew and Odysseus." Joyce might have encountered the notion of a Jewish Ulysses at a very young age.

Wagner crops up periodically in Joyce's university-era essays. In an article titled "Drama and Life," he writes, "Every race has made its own myths and it is in these that early drama often finds an outlet. The author of *Parsifal* has recognized this and hence his work is solid as a rock."

This could be the prelude to a nationalist manifesto, but Joyce already had a more cosmopolitan understanding of the artist's role, as another nod to Wagner indicates: "Lohengrin, the drama of which unfolds itself in a scene of seclusion, amid half-lights, is not an Antwerp legend but a world drama." In another early essay, "The Day of the Rabblement," Joyce criticizes the Irish Literary Theatre for purveying popular fables instead of promoting Ibsen, Hauptmann, and Strindberg.

Ibsen was the hero of Joyce's youth. To pair Ibsenism and Wagnerism was not unusual: both terms appear as chapter titles in Shaw's 1908 book *The Sanity of Art*, a riposte to the antimodernist rants of Max Nordau's *Degeneration*. Ibsen and Wagner shared a regard for Nordic myth—the playwright's early work *The Vikings at Helgeland* drew on the *Vǫlsunga saga*—and they sparked controversy for similar reasons. The historian Peter Jelavich writes: "In Wagner's *Ring*, as in Ibsen's plays, the bondage of marriage and the quest for money are trademarks of a bourgeois-capitalist order that can be shattered only by heroic individuals inspired by higher visions." Ibsen's final work, *When We Dead Awaken* (1899), turns in a mystical, possibly Wagnerian direction. Thomas Mann was reminded of the "majestic-sclerotic fatigue" of *Parsifal*; Joyce heard a *Lohengrin* reference in the line "You said I was the swan that drew your boat."

After graduating from university, in 1902, Joyce went to Paris, where he was a regular at the Opéra. One day he wrote to his mother: "Tell Stannie to send me *at once* (so that I may have it by Thursday night) my copy of Wagner's operas." *Siegfried* was playing, and Joyce evidently wanted to refresh his memory of it. The production would have been a considerable advance over Carl Rosa's. The dragon Fafner was nearly forty feet long, with electric lamps simulating fire in its throat. The Siegfried was the tenor Jean de Reszke, whom Willa Cather heard in the same period. Joyce was drawing away from Ireland—he would leave for good in 1904—and Timothy Martin infers that Wagner's musings on the meaning of homeland in exile had a special import for the young author. In "A Communication to My Friends," the composer had written that Germany in the political sense had nothing to offer him, that he sought instead a vaguer kind of *Heimat*, one comprising a "wide community of kindred and familiar souls." This is the passage that Joyce marked when he read the essay. He would find many such communities in his European wanderings.

Wagnerism was all around, sometimes in comical guises. Joyce witnessed

Arthur Symons wallowing in *Parsifal* at the piano and blurting out, "When I play Wagner, I am in another world." *Evelyn Innes* and other novels by George Moore struck Joyce as maddeningly inconsistent, although they affected his development all the same. Through Moore, Joyce learned of Édouard Dujardin, the founder-editor of the *Revue wagnérienne*, and at a railway kiosk in France he picked up a copy of *Les Lauriers sont coupés*, Dujardin's novelistic record of one man's perceptions, thoughts, and emotions over a six-hour period. In later years, Joyce credited Dujardin as the source of his art of "interior monologue." Dujardin returned the praise, declaring that Joyce had finally written the true Wagnerian novel. *Ulysses* gave Dujardin "the sensation of swimming in an ocean of spirituality, the very one I experienced at twenty when I first heard (without knowing German) the four days of *The Ring of the Nibelung*."

Joyce's interior monologues dovetail with his technique of the epiphany. In the posthumously published novel *Stephen Hero*, which was recast as *A Portrait of the Artist as a Young Man*, Joyce's alter ego, Stephen Dedalus (initially Daedalus), defines the epiphany as "a sudden spiritual manifestation, whether in the vulgarity of speech or of gesture or in a memorable phase of the mind itself." The literary scholar Paul Devine has linked Joyce's notion of the epiphany to Wagner's leitmotif, noting that the concepts also intersect in Moore's novels. The leitmotif serves not only as a descriptive tag but also triggers swells of emotion, particularly when it stands for a sudden memory or premonition. In much the same way, Joyce gives a cosmic dimension to a motif as straightforward as the snow that falls outside Gabriel Conroy's window in "The Dead."

The self-styling implicit in the title *Stephen Hero* is fleshed out in the culminating epiphany of *A Portrait of the Artist*, as Stephen metaphorically takes hold of Nothung, sword of Siegmund and Siegfried. Preparing to leave home and undertake his artistic mission, Stephen writes in his journal: "I go to encounter for the millionth time the reality of experience and to forge in the smithy of my soul the uncreated conscience of my race . . . Old father, old artificer, stand me now and ever in good stead." William Blissett notes that Moore used the same metaphor in *Vale*, the third volume of his memoirs, which was published in 1914, as Joyce was completing the *Portrait*. Pondering Ireland's future, Moore asks himself "if I were Siegfried, son of Sigmund slain by Hunding, and if it were my fate to reforge the sword that lay broken in halves in Mimi's cave."

The choice of the word "conscience" is curious. Martin persuasively argues that it is derived from a passage in Wagner's "Art and Revolution"—one that Joyce also marked in his reading copy. In a discussion of the gap between ancient and modern attitudes toward art, Wagner uses the word "*Bewusstsein*," which is usually translated as "consciousness" but which the ever-idiosyncratic William Ashton Ellis renders as "conscience." In the Hellenic world, Wagner writes, art "lived in the public conscience, whereas to-day it lives alone in the conscience of private persons, the public *un*conscience recking nothing of it . . . Grecian Art was *conservative*, because it was a worthy and adequate expression of the public conscience; with us, true Art is *revolutionary*, because its very existence is opposed to the ruling spirit of the community."

Stephen, the budding literary Siegfried, assumes the same heroic stance. With the Irish nation yet to be born, with the multitude mired in abhorrent philistinism, the new conscience or consciousness can be forged only in the soul of the isolated individual. How seriously we are meant to take this swaggering display is unclear. To forge is also to fake, to counterfeit. Joyce may want us to think about the stale, secondhand quality of Stephen's rhetoric.

As Joyce grew older, his relationship with Wagner oscillated between passion and boredom. In Trieste, his primary home from 1905 to 1915, he saw most of the *Ring*, and when *Parsifal* arrived there he attended three or four performances. A friend recalled him singing the Good Friday music, in French. But after hearing *Götterdämmerung* in Rome, he told his brother that "nothing in the opera moved me." On one occasion, he dismissed *Meistersinger* as "pretentious stuff"; on another, he said it was his favorite Wagner opera. A pupil from his years teaching English in language schools reported that Joyce "despised Wagner," though the same pupil remembered him reciting from *Tristan*. His library was well stocked with Wagneriana: in addition to the first volume of the prose works, he owned the librettos for *The Flying Dutchman*, *Rheingold*, *Siegfried*, and *Götterdämmerung*, compilations of Wagner's letters, Shaw's *The Perfect Wagnerite*, Nietzsche's *The Case of Wagner*, May Byron's *A Day with Richard Wagner*, and "Jewishness in Music."

At the end of his time in Trieste, Joyce wrote his only play, *Exiles*. Of his works, it is the one most obviously saturated in Wagner, as his own notes attest. The plot concerns two couples whose ties are complicated by past loves and jealousies: the writer Richard Rowan, a stand-in for Joyce; his common-law wife, Bertha, a version of Nora Joyce; Richard's former lover, the music teacher Beatrice; and her cousin, the journalist Robert. At the heart of the play is an encounter between Bertha and Robert that may or may not amount to infidelity.

Joyce was thinking not only of his own romantic history but also of two Wagnerian love triangles: the composer's affair with Mathilde Wesendonck, conducted under the eyes of her husband, Otto; and the love of Tristan and Isolde, in betrayal of King Mark. Richard plays the cuckold role of Mark, but he finds a strange strength in his humiliation, stage-managing Robert and Bertha's relationship to give himself an ennobling wound. Richard's manipulative masochism averts the kind of disaster that overtakes *Tristan* or d'Annunzio's *The Triumph of Death*, which Robert seems to have read: "To fall from a great high cliff . . . Listening to music and in the arms of the woman I love." (Joyce read both of d'Annunzio's Wagner-themed novels, and particularly liked *Il fuoco*.) The alternative to Liebestod, the Joyce scholar Vicki Mahaffey writes, is the "hard-won acceptance of human difference that was to usher in *Ulysses*."

It was in 1906 that Joyce first conceived of a story about a cuckolded Jew in Dublin. Nothing came of the plan at the time, but he went on gathering material for it—reading Jewish history, learning about Zionism, following news of Dublin's small Jewish community. Personal connections deepened his sympathies. For a time he was smitten with a pupil named Amalia Popper, the daughter of Leopoldo Popper, a Bohemian-Jewish businessman. Later, he befriended Leopoldo, and spent time with him during the years he was writing *Ulysses*. Joyce also formed a bond with the Triestine writer Ettore Schmitz, better known as Italo Svevo, whose 1898 novel *Senilità* contains a memorable Wagner Scene—a brother and sister attending *Walküre*. Svevo may have prompted Joyce to read Otto Weininger, the self-hating gay Jewish Wagnerite. Quotations from Weininger's *On Last Things* appear in the *Ulysses* notebooks starting in 1917.

Joyce must have read "Jewishness in Music," although he made no direct reference to it. Neil Davison, who has studied modernism and Jewishness, guesses at Joyce's attitude toward the pamphlet. In the translation that the novelist owned, Wagner writes: "The Jew converses in the tongue of the people amongst whom he dwells from age to age, but he does this invariably after the manner of a foreigner." This is meant as an insult, but, as Davison says, Joyce may have seen Jewish foreignness as a cultural advantage, comparable to his own status as an Irish writer in an Anglophone literary world. He once said: "The Irish, doomed to express themselves in a language not their own, have stamped it with their genius." He was, in a sense, defamiliarizing English in the name of a universal Irishness.

By making a middle-aged man of Jewish background the chief protagonist of his modernist magnum opus—Bloom is, in fact, a convert from Protestantism to Catholicism—Joyce may have been deliberately pitting himself against Wagner's legacy. There is no question that he felt an intense rivalry with the composer. Ottocaro Weiss told of going with Joyce to see *Walküre* in Zurich, where the author lived from 1915 to 1919. When, at the first intermission, Weiss expressed enthusiasm, Joyce asked, "Don't you find the musical effects of my *Sirens* better than Wagner's?" He was referring to the eleventh chapter of *Ulysses*, a musical swirl of motifs. Weiss answered, "No," whereupon Joyce walked out.

ULYSSES: STEPHEN

In Joyce's mammoth work, mythic correspondences flicker through mundane reality. The story of the Greek hero Odysseus, known to the Romans as Ulysses, is projected onto a Dubliner named Leopold Bloom, who wanders the city on a June day and night in 1904. Joyce did not, of course, invent this way of working. An architecture of myth looms behind Thomas Mann's *Buddenbrooks*, Conrad's *Nostromo*, and D. H. Lawrence's *The Rainbow*, to name a few. The method is, in a way, an inversion of Wagner's, in which modern social questions are embedded in myth. On the subject of Ibsenism and Wagnerism, Eric Bentley once wrote: "Wagner was a fantasist outside, a realist inside; Ibsen was a realist outside, a fantasist inside." The same applies to Wagner and Joyce.

If, as seems possible, *Ulysses* was at least partly inspired by Wagner's conflation of Odysseus and the Wandering Jew, the debt would have placed considerable pressure on an ego as commodious as Joyce's. The theory of the anxiety of influence, as articulated by Harold Bloom, does not suffice to describe the convoluted action that Joyce performs on Wagner: at once a grand inversion and a gleeful burlesque. Perhaps the best term is "*Untergang*," the notorious final word of "Jewishness in Music." In *Ulysses*,

Wagnerism experiences its going-under. The rite of demolition is all the more effective because of Joyce's willingness to scour his own youthful self as a fund of material. Stephen Dedalus, the would-be Siegfried of *A Portrait of the Artist*, runs up against the limits of his uncompromising aestheticism. Joyce's treatment of his alter ego is almost a Wagnerian ritual of self-annihilation.

The first books of the Odyssey center on Telemachus, the hero's son, who is searching for news of his father's fate. Likewise, Stephen dominates the early part of *Ulysses*, unconsciously seeking a figurative father he does not yet know. Throughout the first three chapters, Stephen senses an unknown presence approaching—a vaguely menacing, possibly supernatural being, floating at the edge of his vision, momentarily visible in scattered portents. This turns out to be Bloom, the Jewish Ulysses. Joyce stages Bloom's entrance in the manner of *The Flying Dutchman*, leading to a brilliant comic payoff.

Decadence and mysticism envelop Stephen as the novel begins, with an odor of antisemitism in the air. He has been to Paris, and can drop references to Villiers de l'Isle-Adam, though he forgets the "Adam." He is living with his friend Buck Mulligan in a Martello tower, a small nineteenth-century fort, as Joyce did briefly in 1904. The young men use the tower's cliffside setting as a stage for literary and intellectual poses. Mulligan celebrates a mock Mass, advocates paganism, flirts with homoeroticism, and declares himself a Nietzschean ("I'm the *Übermensch*"). When Stephen hangs back from this carnival mood, Mulligan chants Yeats at him: "And no more turn aside and brood / Upon love's bitter mystery / For Fergus rules the brazen cars." Stephen is indeed brooding: on the recent death of his mother, on his future in or out of Ireland, on the anarchic living conditions of the tower.

The irregular household also includes an Englishman named Haines, who is besotted with Celtic culture and worried about the Jews. Stephen describes himself as a servant of "two masters," the British Empire and the Catholic Church; he then adds, "And a third there is who wants me for odd jobs." He means the Irish national movement, but Haines's mind is elsewhere. "I don't want to see my country fall into the hands of German jews either," the Englishman says. The previous night, we learn, Haines had been "moaning to himself about shooting a black panther." This is based on a real incident: during Joyce's stay at the tower, a man named Trench had a nightmare about a black panther and fired off a revolver. Chaos of this sort induced Joyce to leave. Stephen, too, has had enough: "I will not sleep here tonight. Home also I cannot go."

The figure of the black panther is one of *Ulysses*'s more cryptic motifs, and has spurred much debate among Joyceans. The eccentric animal psychology of Weininger's *On Last Things* provides a clue. Weininger had a fearful obsession with dogs: in a passage sampled in the *Ulysses* Subject Notebook, the philosopher relates that he had experienced a psychological crisis, bordering on suicidal madness, after hearing a dog barking in a peculiar way. He had visions of a "*black* dog" accompanied by a fiery glow. The apparition represented "the annihilation, the punishment, the fate of the evil." Haines's black panther is a related animal, and belongs to the series of omens that betoken an uncanny being drawing near. Another crucial motif is that of the drowned man. After Haines mutters about German Jews, Stephen overhears a conversation between two passersby, concerning a man who drowned some days before and whose body is expected to wash ashore. "There's five fathoms out there," a boatman says. The literate youth will soon think of *The Tempest*: "Full fathom five thy father lies."

Mutterings about a Jewish threat persist in the second chapter, "Nestor," emanating now from Mr. Deasy, the headmaster of a boys' school where Stephen has a temporary job teaching history. "They sinned against the light, Mr Deasy said gravely. And you can see the darkness in their eyes. And that is why they are wanderers on the earth to this day." Stephen proceeds to muse about the Paris Bourse: "The goldskinned men quoting prices on their gemmed fingers. Gabble of geese. They swarmed loud, uncouth, about the temple, their heads thickplotting under maladroit silk hats." The animal metaphor is typical of antisemitic discourse: Wagner, in the translation of "Jewishness in Music" that Joyce read, spoke of the "hissing, shrill-sounding buzzing and grunting mannerisms" of the Jews. At the same time, Stephen shows sympathy for the wandering people, envisioning the "rancours massed about them."

Dujardin's interior monologue has its golden hour in the third chapter, "Proteus," as Stephen goes "walking into eternity along Sandymount strand." Shells crunching beneath his feet, the young man meditates on the theology of Jakob Böhme, the seventeenth-century shoemaker-turned-mystic, who believed that everything in nature is marked with hidden meaning: "Signatures of all things I am here to read, seaspawn and sea-wrack, the nearing tide, that rusty boot." Böhme had a vogue among the German Romantics and again among the Theosophists. If Stephen has been reading Böhme, he may have an at least theoretical interest in esoteri-cism and the occult.

A Germanic mood lingers as Stephen counts his steps and mulls over the words *"nacheinander"* (one after another) and *"nebeneinander"* (side by side). He is referring to G. E. Lessing's essay *Laocoön*, which sets forth a distinction between literature, where words and ideas unfurl in sequence, and the visual arts, where objects and impressions are juxtaposed. *Laocoön* figures in Wagner's discussion of the Gesamtkunstwerk: the composer believed that the dramatic artwork transcends Lessing's distinction, fold-ing the literary and the visual into an integrated whole. Whether or not Stephen has Wagner on his mind, he strikes a Siegfried pose. Wielding his ashplant walking stick, he thinks, "My ash sword hangs at my side." This is subtle preparation for the shout of *"Nothung!"* hundreds of pages later.

The stream of consciousness then carries Stephen back to Paris. He touches on Théophile Gautier, Mallarmé, and, less attractively, Édouard Drumont, the author of the antisemitic tract *La France juive*. Stephen re-calls meeting with an absinthe-drinking Fenian nationalist named Kevin Egan, who said: "M. Drumont, famous journalist, Drumont, know what he called queen Victoria? Old hag with the yellow teeth. *Vieille ogresse* with the *dents jaunes*." The quotation is from Drumont's *Testament of an Antisemite*.

On the beach, two cocklepickers are dragging their bags across the sand. They are Gypsies, and they stir more ruminations on the earth's wanderers, those who trudge from place to place in search of home:

> Across the sands of all the world, followed by the sun's flaming sword, to the west, trekking to evening lands. She trudges, schlepps, trains, drags, trascines her load. A tide westering, moondrawn, in her wake. Tides, myriadislanded, within her, blood not mine, *oinopa ponton*, a winedark sea. Behold the handmaid of the moon. In sleep the wet sign calls her hour, bids her rise. Bridebed, childbed, bed of death, ghostcandled. *Omnis caro ad te veniet.* He comes, pale vampire, through storm his eyes, his bat sails bloodying the sea, mouth to her mouth's kiss.

Stephen scribbles something on a piece of paper. Later in the novel, we find out what it is:

> On swift sail flaming
> From storm and south
> He comes, pale vampire,
> Mouth to my mouth.

The vampire is the last and perhaps most important of Stephen's omen figures, all of which anticipate the coming of Bloom.

In the Joyce literature, the standard explanation for this verse is that Stephen is parodying Douglas Hyde's 1893 poem after an Irish text, "My Grief on the Sea": "And my love came behind me— / He came from the South; / His breast to my bosom, / His mouth to my mouth." An early sketch of "Proteus" points toward a different source: "She dreams him, ~~speeding to her kiss~~ a pale vampire, through storm speeding under bloodred sails, ~~a man's lips~~ mouth to her mouth's kiss." In *The Flying Dutchman*, the title character is called "*der bleiche Mann*," the "pale man," and he enters in the wake of a supernatural storm, in a vessel with "bloodred sails and black masts." Stuart Gilbert first alerted readers to the novel's *Flying Dutchman* atmosphere in his pioneering 1930 study of *Ulysses*, for which Joyce provided guidance. But the opera casts a longer shadow on the novel than has been noticed previously.

The phantom vessel that roves the seas—the French name for *The Flying Dutchman* is *Le Vaisseau fantôme*—is an old superstition among sailors. It took on new life in 1820s Britain, with the publication of a magazine story and then of a melodrama telling of a Dutch sea captain named Vanderdecken, who swears away his soul while trying to make it around the Cape of Good Hope. Heinrich Heine appropriated the tale and added the conceit that the Dutchman, whom he dubbed the "eternal Jew of the ocean," could be redeemed by a faithful woman—a woman who is, in fact, already in love with the mariner, because she has been gazing at an old picture of him in her home. Every seven years, he comes ashore, seeking salvation. Wagner appropriated the Heine version and accentuated its overtones of Ahasuerus, the Wandering Jew, who, in antisemitic folklore, jeered Christ on the road to Calvary and was sentenced to roam the earth until the Second Coming.

Ageless and undead, the Dutchman is a kind of vampire. One of the most popular German operas of the early nineteenth century was Heinrich Marschner's *Der Vampyr*, premiered in 1828. Wagner, cognizant of his story's Gothic roots, took from that work the phrase "*der bleiche Mann*." At the end of the century, Bram Stoker picked up on the same connection. In an early plan for *Dracula*, Jonathan Harker was to have attended a performance of *The Flying Dutchman* before setting off to meet a mysterious Count in Transylvania.

Vampiric trappings aside, Wagner's Dutchman is a charismatic, semi-heroic figure. Disembarking from his vessel, he sings the monologue "*Die Frist ist um*": "The time has come, and seven years have again elapsed." He suspects that his search for the redeeming woman is futile, and that only the "eternal annihilation" of the Day of Judgment will release him. Salvation awaits in the form of Senta, daughter of the sea captain Daland. In Act II, under the spell of the Dutchman's picture, she sings a ballad of his lamentable life:

Traft ihr das Schiff im Meere an,
blutrot die Segel, schwarz der Mast?

Joyce would have known the translation employed by the Carl Rosa company:

Saw ye the ship on the raging deep—
Blood-red the canvas, black the mast?

Stephen's verse about the "pale vampire" fits Wagner's music, especially with the extra quaver that the Carl Rosa version adds to the first line. As it happens, we know that Stephen likes to fool around with Wagner's texts, because later in the novel he devises new words for the blood oath from *Götterdämmerung*, importing the phrase "fragende Frau" from *Walküre*: "Hangende Hunger, / Fragende Frau, / Macht uns alle kaputt" ("Drooping hunger, questioning woman, makes us all kaput").

At the end of the chapter, the drowned man reappears: "Five fathoms out there. Full fathom five thy father lies. At one, he said. Found drowned. High water at Dublin bar. Driving before it a loose drift of rubble, fanshoals of fishes, silly shells. A corpse rising saltwhite from the undertow, bobbing a pace a pace a porpoise landward." Stephen lunges with his ashplant sword, thinks once more of Drumont, and looks back out to sea. "Moving through the air high spars of a threemaster, her sails brailed up on the crosstrees, homing, upstream, silently moving, a silent ship." In *The Flying Dutchman*, when the wraithlike sailors come ashore, they do it *"Stumm und ohne das geringste Geräusch"*—"mute and without the slightest sound." Coincidentally or not, Joyce reproduces this redundancy of silence.

There follows a sublime joke at Stephen's expense—and, perhaps, at Wagner's. We turn the page and read: "Mr Leopold Bloom ate with relish the inner organs of beasts and fowls." Stephen has experienced all manner of forebodings of the Other: the Dutchman, the Wandering Jew, wanderers toward evening lands, darkness shining in brightness, pale vampires, German Jews, French Jews. Now comes Ahasuerus in the flesh, but the ominous fanfares announcing him are made to sound ridiculous. He is a magnificently ordinary man at the outset of his magnificently ordinary day. It is a jest, but a mystical one. As in *The Tempest*, a sea change has taken place: the phantom father wears the face of Bloom.

ULYSSES: BLOOM

With the turning of the page, Bloom's consciousness overtakes Stephen's as the principal medium through which *Ulysses* passes. Fin-de-siècle mists recede, giving way to Bloom's earthier, simpler, but by no means shallower way of life. The chief musical icon is Mozart's *Don Giovanni*, which Bloom sings to himself throughout the day. Stephen remains a substantial presence, his interior monologue periodically resurfacing. In a way, the novel brings about a merger of these two consciousnesses. Given how much of Joyce is in Bloom as well as in Stephen, the *Untergang* of the younger man is also the metamorphosis of the author into the older one. Wagner is adept at such subdivisions of self, especially in *Meistersinger*, where he is present both as the headstrong Walther and as the wise, resigned Hans Sachs.

Once the narrative is centered on Bloom, we realize how often Dubliners reflexively identify him as a darksome stranger. The Dutchman, the Wandering Jew, and the vampire shadow Bloom throughout. In "Scylla and Charybdis," when the two protagonists first brush against each other, Buck Mulligan warns Stephen that Bloom "is Greeker than the Greeks."

This insinuates something queer in Bloom's sexuality—shades of Otto Weininger on the womanliness of Jewish men. Later, Mulligan says, "The wandering jew . . . Did you see his eye? He looked upon you to lust after you. I fear thee, ancient mariner." Coleridge's *Rime of the Ancient Mariner* is another tale of a cursed wanderer of the seas. Stephen observes that Bloom moves with the "step of a pard"—a leopard, a panther, dressed in black.

For others, Bloom has a vaguely Gothic allure. In "Nausicaa," a day-dreaming young woman, Gerty MacDowell, sees Bloom on the beach and filters him through the lens of sensationalist Victorian literature: "The face that met her gaze there in the twilight, wan and strangely drawn, seemed to her the saddest she had ever seen . . . His eyes burned into her as though they would search her through and through, read her very soul." She might have been reading *Dracula*, where the vampire has "positively blazing" eyes and a "deathly pale" face. Bloom also reminds Gerty of a portrait she has at home: "She could see at once by his dark eyes and his pale intellectual face that he was a foreigner, the image of the photo she had of Martin Harvey, the matinée idol, only for the moustache . . . He was in deep mourning, she could see that, and the story of a haunting sorrow was written on his face." This seems a comical replay of Act II of the *Dutchman*, where Senta contemplates her melancholy portrait of the ageless mariner: "Do you feel the grief, the deep sorrow, with which he looks down at me?"

The recurrence of verbal motifs such as the vampire, the panther, and the drowned man suggests that Joyce is using a leitmotif system—much as Andrey Bely does in *Petersburg*, a novel similarly rich in Dutchman lore. The method attains dizzying complexity in the "Sirens" chapter, the one that Joyce considered an improvement on Wagner. Around sixty verbal fragments are laid out at the outset. Matthew Hodgart compares them to the catalogue of leitmotifs that appears at the head of Wagner scores and librettos. "Sirens" is set in the concert room of the Ormond Hotel, where Stephen's father and his friends sing around a piano. Joyce described it as a fugue of many voices, and advised one of his Zurich pupils that it contains a quintet, "as in *Die Meistersinger*, my favorite Wagnerian opera." Gossipy barmaids are like Rhinemaidens, seen in watery light: "By bronze, by gold, in oceangreen of shadow."

The farcical Wagnerism of *Ulysses* culminates in the drunken dreamscape of the "Circe" chapter, which finds Stephen and Bloom at a brothel in the Nighttown district. When prostitutes swirl and warble around Bloom, they reenact the Flower Maidens' attempted seduction of Parsifal, as Martin perceives in *Joyce and Wagner*. Then, in an extended political hallucination, Bloom becomes not only mayor of Dublin but the ruler of something called the "new Bloomusalem." His platform of anarchist populism smacks of the revolutionary Wagner: "Our buccaneering Vanderdeckens in their phantom ship of finance . . . these flying Dutchmen or lying Dutchmen as they recline in their upholstered poop, casting dice, what reck they? Machines is their cry, their chimera, their panacea." In "The Artwork of the Future," Wagner goes on about the ravaging synergy of capitalism, entertainment, and technology—"this industry that kills man in order to use him as a machine." In the same section, Bloom hails a plan for a tramline as "the music of the future." All this pseudo-antique language—the verb "reck," for example—recalls the Wagnerish English of William Ashton Ellis.

As for Stephen, the drunker he gets, the more Wagnerian he becomes. First he lampoons the blood oath from *Götterdämmerung*. Then, confronted by the nightmarish apparition of his dead mother, he shouts, *"Non serviam!"*—I will not serve. "No! No! No! Break my spirit, all of you, if you can! I'll bring you all to heel!" And he delivers his famous Siegfried cry:

STEPHEN

Nothung!

(*He lifts his ashplant high with both hands and smashes the chandelier. Time's livid final flame leaps and, in the following darkness, ruin of all space, shattered glass and toppling masonry.*)

Compare the stage directions at the end of *Götterdämmerung*: "The flames immediately flare up . . the whole stage seems to be engulfed in flames . . . From the ruins of the fallen hall, the men and women watch moved to the very depths of their being." But this apocalypse occurs purely in Stephen's sotted mind. Bloom, on examining the chandelier, finds only minor damage, and gives the madam a shilling to cover the repairs. In contrast to the grandiloquent "smithy of his soul" passage in *A Portrait of the Artist*, Siegfried imagery here functions mainly to make Stephen look silly.

His heroic playacting masks adolescent loneliness and self-absorption. Even so, Wagner has facilitated Stephen's process of self-definition. The jagged gesture in the music—the repeated descent of the octave, which also figures in the Dutchman's monologue—matches the lashing motion of Stephen's thought. His Wagnerism is at once impressive and absurd—typical of a young artist's arrogant identification with towering predecessors.

After the bacchanal, Stephen and Bloom repair to the cabmen's shelter of "Eumaeus," where the *Dutchman* theme finds ironic resolution. A sailor named Murphy reminds Bloom of the Irish baritone William Ludwig, who sang the Dutchman in Carl Rosa's staging. It turns out that Murphy came ashore from the same "silently moving" ship that Stephen had seen that morning off Sandymount Strand. The real Dutchman, in other words, is a boozy sailor telling tall tales. Against that backdrop, Stephen and Bloom form their bond: by the end of the chapter, they are walking arm in arm and talking about music. Bloom describes his taste, and in the process Wagner receives his only direct mention in the novel: "Wagnerian music, though confessedly grand in its way, was a bit too heavy for Bloom and hard to follow at the first go-off but the music of Mercadante's *Huguenots*, Meyerbeer's *Seven Last Words on the Cross* and Mozart's *Twelfth Mass* he simply revelled in, the *Gloria* in that being, to his mind, the acme of first class music as such, literally knocking everything else into a cocked hat." Bloom also names his beloved *Don Giovanni*, Friedrich von Flotow's comic opera *Martha*, and the "severe classical school such as Mendelssohn." Stephen chimes in with favorite Renaissance composers.

An obscure running joke of *Ulysses* is that Bloom keeps confusing the German-Jewish composer Giacomo Meyerbeer, best known for *Les Huguenots*, with the Neapolitan composer Saverio Mercadante, who wrote a setting of the Seven Last Words of Christ on the Cross. Bloom begins ascribing the latter work to Meyerbeer in "Sirens." When Bloom is confronted by barroom slurs in "Cyclops," he exclaims in protest: "Mendelssohn was a jew and Karl Marx and Mercadante and Spinoza. And the Saviour was a jew . . . Christ was a jew like me." Mercadante was not, in fact, Jewish; this time, Bloom means to say Meyerbeer. Mendelssohn and Meyerbeer were the chief targets of "Jewishness in Music," paragons of Jewish rootlessness. So when Bloom inducts the two of them into his musical Valhalla, he is giving an oblique finger to Wagner. Meyerbeer reappears in the last chapter of *Ulysses*, in which Molly Bloom thinks of her husband extolling *Huguenots* and "rigmaroling about religion and persecution." Not incidentally, Meyerbeer's opera tells of the massacre of Huguenot Protestants by Catholics, and ends with a hair-raising chorus containing the line "Let us exterminate the impious race."

Wagner and Wagnerism have effectively been exorcized. The very fact that Bloom mixes up the composers' names undermines the Romantic cult of the genius. Music is music, the two men seem to agree; obscure tunes compete with famous arias, throwaway melodies acquire epiphanic heft, singers outshine the composers they sing. All the same, the vampire Wagner cannot be banished altogether, and he hangs over the book to the end. Molly's monologue might be Joyce's ultimate attempt—at least until *Finnegans Wake*—at "endless melody," at the ever-unspooling rhythm of "and this and this and this and this," which is most ecstatically articulated by Isolde at the end of *Tristan*. Joyce's Wagnerian ambitions, in the fullest sense of that damaged adjective, are unmistakable. They are felt not simply in the scale of *Ulysses*, its mythic-modern fusion, but also in its most intimate moments, in its ever-tightening focus on the phenomenon of love in all its forms.

If *The Flying Dutchman* haunts the early chapters of *Ulysses*, *Parsifal*, with its ethic of "knowing through compassion," might waft over the last ones. Although Stephen and Bloom both gain wisdom from their unexpected bond, Bloom is more like Gurnemanz, the sage elder guiding the pure fool. From Bloom, Stephen learns something of the meaning of love, the word known to all men. This is not just the love of man for woman but the love of man for other men, of woman for other women, of humanity for nature.

Buck Mulligan suspects Bloom of harboring a Wildean love, and Stephen could be thinking the same when he declines Bloom's invitation to spend the night. Perhaps there is some latent physical attraction in Bloom's attachment to Stephen. But the love at issue here is loyalty to friends, kindness toward strangers, equanimity in the face of heartbreak. These are qualities that Bloom displays in quiet profusion, as he plays with his cat, looks after Paddy Dignam's widow, helps a blind man across the street, feeds the gulls, denounces violence at the pub, and feels "with wonder women's woe." Bloom consequently gains a kind of heroic stature. He finds his way to one more Good Friday Spell, where "all creation gives thanks, all that blooms and soon fades away . . ."

YOUNG ELIOT

In a study of modern literary representations of Jews, Bryan Cheyette writes of Joyce: "No writer tried, with more success, to rid his fiction of the strait-jacket of semitic racial oppositions which poisoned the language of the first half of the twentieth century." In ceding *Ulysses* to Leopold Bloom, Cheyette says, Joyce dismantled the familiar duality of Jew and Gentile—or, to trot out Matthew Arnold's infamous distinction, Hebraism and Hellenism. In a way, Joyce was supplying an antidote to a poison that Wagner helped to spread. Bloom is too richly textured a creation to match any stereotype of who a Jew is or how a Jew speaks or thinks—in no small part because the author invests so much of himself in the character. Joyce thus extends the empathetic project of George Eliot's *Daniel Deronda*, another novel in which a Jewish protagonist moves to the center as the story proceeds.

That empathy is entirely absent in the work of Thomas Stearns Eliot, some of whose poems contain antisemitic constructions worthy of the older Wagner and the young Hitler: "The rats are underneath the piles. / The jew is underneath the lot." Similar slights and slurs are found in *Ulysses*, but in Eliot's case the author gives no sign of wanting to separate himself from the bigotry on the page. Lest there be any confusion about his point of view, Eliot said in a 1933 lecture that "reasons of race and religion combine to make any large number of free-thinking Jews undesirable," and that "a spirit of excessive tolerance is to be deprecated." Hitler had come to power three months earlier.

Such cold hatred is hard to reconcile with Eliot's acute sensitivity to the frailty and woundedness of human relations. On the evidence of *The Waste Land*, the poet valued Wagner for his excavations of the agony of desire, which are detached from ceremonies of fulfillment or resolution. The spiritual landscape of the poem, with its juxtaposition of Christian, pagan, and Buddhist elements, has something in common with Wagner's fluid idea of the sacred, his way of stitching together multiple mythic sources and religious traditions. These are quite different qualities from the ones that Joyce prized in the composer—all-embracingness, heroic self-definition, the romance of the wanderer. Eliot's Wagner is Tristan without Isolde, the suffering hero in his dilapidated castle by the sea.

O f Eliot's very few public comments about Wagner, the most revealing is found in the essay "A Dialogue on Dramatic Poetry," from 1928. It stages a kind of internal debate among the author's poetic selves. One voice says to another: "I have also heard you railing at Wagner as 'pernicious.' But you would not willingly resign your experience of Wagner either. Which seems to show that a world in which there was no art that was not morally edifying would be a very poor world indeed." What that experience was remains unknown, but none other than Igor Stravinsky thought that it went deep: "Eliot's Wagner nostalgia was apparent and I think that *Tristan* must have been one of the most passionate experiences in his life."

Although Eliot would have heard Wagner during his youth in St. Louis, Missouri, the passionate encounter in question almost certainly occurred when he was an undergraduate at Harvard, between 1906 and 1909. Like the Cambridge of the Apostles, Harvard was aswarm with Wagnerites: admirers on the faculty included the philosopher George Santayana and the medievalist William Henry Schofield. In the opposite camp, Irving Babbitt inveighed against the Gesamtkunstwerk aesthetic in *The New Laokoon*. In addition, Eliot eagerly read Arthur Symons's *The Symbolist Movement in Literature*, which inflamed his interest in members of the French literary vanguard, so many of whom were Wagnéristes: Nerval, Baudelaire, Villiers, Huysmans, Verlaine, Mallarmé, and the short-lived Franco-Uruguayan poet Jules Laforgue.

The last, a pioneer of free verse who translated Walt Whitman, strongly influenced Eliot's early poetry. Laforgue's attitude to Wagner was neither reverential nor combative; like Aubrey Beardsley, he took an urbane, mischievous approach, bordering on the naughty. In the prose sketch "Lohengrin, Son of Parsifal," from the 1887 collection *Moral Tales*, Elsa comes across as flighty, insipid, and libidinous: "Love me on a low fire, inventory me, massacre me, massacrilege me!" Lohengrin, an effete aesthete, seems unlikely to satisfy her, on account of his preference for "hard and straight hips." Nonetheless, Laforgue's tale attains a kind of surreal grandeur, as an imperial swan carries Lohengrin aloft into the icy altitudes of the Metaphysics of Love. In Eliot's estimation, Laforgue specialized in "the intellectualising of the feeling and the emotionalising of the idea." It is the lyrical equivalent to Schopenhauer's "philosophy of the unconscious and of annihilation," as Wagner is the musical equivalent. A bit cryptically, Eliot adds: "The system of Schopenhauer collapses, but in a different ruin from that of *Tristan und Isolde*."

The likeliest occasion for Eliot's Wagner epiphany was a performance by the Metropolitan Opera on tour, in April 1908, with Olive Fremstad as Isolde and Mahler conducting—"a breadth and power that fairly shook one in his seat," the *Boston Globe* said. The following year, Eliot's classmate Haniel Long reported in his diary that Boston was "crazy over Wagner." This was, after all, the city that offered swan-boat rides on a lake in the Public Garden. That still-flourishing business arose after a nineteenth-century entrepreneur went to see *Lohengrin* and decided to replicate the hero's preferred mode of transportation.

In the fall of 1909, Eliot wrote a *Tristan*-themed poem titled "Opera." It gives little sign of Wagnerian infatuation, instead cocking an eyebrow at Romantic excess:

Tristan and Isolde
And the fatalistic horns
The passionate violins
And ominous clarinet;
And love torturing itself
To emotion for all there is in it,
Writhing in and out
Contorted in paroxysms,
Flinging itself at the last
Limits of self-expression.

We have the tragic? oh no!
Life departs with a feeble smile
Into the indifferent.
These emotional experiences
Do not hold good at all,

And I feel like the ghost of youth
At the undertakers' ball.

The poem is difficult to parse. Are we meant to share in the speaker's flip-pant attitude toward Wagner? Or, with its pursed-lipped tone ("oh no!"), is this a self-satirical display of a shallow collegiate pose? Either way, Eliot is distancing himself from Wagnerian passion. What bothers him most, it seems, is the disparity between precious operatic emotion and the world outside. A similar tableau appears in Osip Mandelstam's *Walküre* poem.

In 1910, Eliot went to Paris to study for a year at the Sorbonne. In that period, he got to know the novelist Henri-Alban Fournier and his brother-in-law Jacques Rivière, future editor of the *Nouvelle Revue Française*. Both were Wagnerites, and in a 1910 essay Rivière described *Tristan* in terms that the future author of *The Waste Land* might have found appealing. The music is a "suffocating cloud," a "black flame," Rivière writes. Act III conveys solitude, desolation, "harrowing lassitude." As for the ending, "never was there a darker, more triumphant entry into nothingness."

During his Parisian year, Eliot befriended a fellow boarder named Jean Verdenal. A medical student by day, Verdenal loved Wagner, admired Mallarmé and Laforgue, knew Rivière, and adhered to the right-wing politics of the Action Française. The relationship was sufficiently close that some scholars believe it was physical in nature. In 1952, the critic John Peter dared to write that *The Waste Land* was an elegy for a young man with whom the poem's speaker had "fallen completely—perhaps the right word is 'irretrievably'—in love." Eliot's response was to demand the pulping of the journal in which the article appeared. James Miller, in his book *T. S. Eliot: The Making of an American Poet*, draws attention to a boat trip that the two friends took together on the Seine, linking that idyll to some suggestive lines in *The Waste Land*: "The boat responded / Gaily, to the hand expert with sail and oar / The sea was calm, your heart would have responded / Gaily, when invited, beating obedient / To controlling hands . . ." But the matter remains as murky as the rest of the poet's emotional life.

In the summer of 1911, Eliot spent time in Munich, where he finished a draft of "The Love Song of J. Alfred Prufrock." Verdenal sent him af-fectionately rambling letters that mixed literary and philosophical specu-lation with gossip and nostalgia. One letter brings up what sounds like a favorite subject: "Try, if possible, to see something by Wagner in Munich. I went the other day to the *Götterdämmerung*, conducted by Nikisch; the end must be one of the highest points ever reached by man." In 1912, once Eliot was back in Cambridge, Verdenal mentions Wagner again, implying that the music is integral to the bond between them:

> I am beginning to find my way in the *Tétralogie*. Each time the plot becomes clearer, and obscure passages take on meaning. Tristan and I., from the first it is agonizingly moving and leaves you prostrate with ecstasy, craving to return to it. But I'm sputtering, all of this is confused and difficult, and impossible to put in words, inevitably (otherwise, one would not have felt the need to express it in music). All the same, I would be happy to know that you too are listening to Wagner in America . . .

The surviving letters trail off at the end of 1912. "I wish so much that you were with me," Verdenal writes in one of the last. Perhaps Eliot ended the correspondence; perhaps it stopped of its own accord. In the spring of 1915, Verdenal was killed in the Gallipoli campaign, felled by a bullet as he was attending to a wounded comrade. Almost immediately, he began to loom large in his friend's imagination. *Prufrock and Other Observations*, Eliot's first collection of poems, is dedicated to Verdenal; its 1925 edition includes a Dantescan epigraph picturing the meeting of Virgil and Statius in Purgatory: "Now can you understand the quantity of love that warms me towards you, so that I forget our vanity, and treat the shadows like the solid thing."

During the war years, Eliot underwent personal crises and wrote little. In 1915, he married the writer Vivienne Haigh-Wood, an alliance that proved calamitous. His productivity rebounded in 1919, when he found a whittled-down new style in "Gerontion," his "thoughts of a dry brain in a dry season." Eliot's terse postwar manner goes hand in hand with bursts of antisemitism, in lines like "the jew is underneath the lot" and "the jew squats on the window sill." This spurt of writing also included a poem called "Dirge," which was probably included in the original version of *The Waste Land*. It takes after the "Proteus" chapter of *Ulysses*, with its image of the drowned man, its allusions to *The Tempest*, and its presentiments of Bloom. In Eliot's hands, though, the spectral figure of a Jewish other becomes merely vicious: "Full fathom five your Bleistein lies / Under the flat-fish and the squids. / Graves' Disease in a dead jew's eyes! / When the crabs have eat the lids."

Anthony Julius, in his study of Eliot's antisemitism, concludes that the poet's prejudice is a compound of American, English, and French paranoias. In comparing Jews to vermin, Eliot sounds like Édouard Drumont, who makes a brief appearance in *Ulysses*. The racial pseudoscience of German antisemitism had less impact. Wagner considered Jews too "repulsive," too "unpleasantly foreign," to be worthy of artistic representation; Eliot, in his high modernist phase, portrays them precisely because of the ugliness he perceives in them. As Julius argues, these assaultive images have a positive function for Eliot: they serve his poetic purposes. In that respect, he is all too close to the Wagner who said that his hatred of Jews was "as necessary to my nature as gall is to the blood." Frighteningly, antisemitism is set so deep in the artist's nature that it becomes indivisible from the creative process.

THE WASTE LAND

In October 1922, Eliot launched a journal called *The Criterion*. The inaugural issue included the first half of a two-part essay by T. Sturge Moore, titled "The Story of Tristram and Isolt in Modern Poetry," in which Swinburne's treatment of the Tristan romance is criticized for excessive verbosity and Matthew Arnold's version is found somewhat wanting next to the "exhilaration and illumination of Wagner's great drama." The next item in the table of contents was *The Waste Land*, receiving its first publication. The juxtaposition is striking, for Eliot's poem is at least in part the interior monologue of an aesthete who came of age in Wagnerism's heyday. In this respect, it is akin to the Stephen Dedalus chapters in *Ulysses*.

Stoddard Martin, in his book *Wagner to "The Waste Land,"* proposes that the personage embodied in the poem—the character who is drawing its references and speaking its lines—is a "synthetic type," modeled on Baudelaire, Verlaine, Nerval, Laforgue, Symons, and Eliot himself: "He is a dispossessed bourgeois tied to a literary tradition but adrift in the physical world; an aesthete attracted to Wagner; a *voyant* preoccupied with modern sex and its futility; a fallen Christian who is attracted to the idea of renunciation, but has a disease of the will which prevents him from developing religious discipline; an unhealthy and incompletely matured man susceptible to catatonic silence, breakdown, madness, and early death." Verdenal must be part of this composite as well. For Martin, the protagonist is Eliot's "cryptic warning to himself," to go no further down the decadent path. Wagner is a danger zone, as he was for Henry James and, intermittently, Thomas Mann. Instead, Eliot makes his way toward a blend of Western and Eastern spirituality, with the legend of the Holy Grail at the center. In a sense, the poet backs away from *Tristan* only to find himself in *Parsifal*.

The Wagnerian content is most obvious at the outset of the poem. Five out of the first forty-two lines of "The Burial of the Dead," the first part of *The Waste Land*, consist of quotations from *Tristan*. First comes the young sailor's song from the opening of Act I, floating down from the mast of the vessel that is taking the enraged Isolde to Cornwall:

Frisch weht der Wind	Fresh blows the wind
der Heimat zu:—	toward the homeland:
mein irisch Kind,	my Irish child,
wo weilest du?	where do you linger?

Eliot changes capitalization and punctuation but otherwise reproduces Wagner's lines intact. A few lines later, he turns to the black-as-night opening of Act III. The wounded, deranged Tristan is lying beneath a lime tree. A shepherd is playing on his pipe, his gestures matched to a mournfully meandering English horn in the orchestra. The shepherd has been told to watch the sea for Isolde's sail. He sees nothing: "*Öd' und leer das Meer*" ("Waste and empty the sea"). Thomas Mann may have been thinking of that same sea when he had Gustav von Aschenbach die before a mostly deserted beach and a wide, flat ocean.

The entire opening section has a German accent. The strangely somber springtime scene—"April is the cruellest month, breeding / Lilacs out of the dead land"—is set in the area of Munich. Showers wash over the Starnberger See, a lake southwest of the city. People drink coffee in the Hofgarten. An aristocratic character named Marie talks of sledding in winter "at the archduke's, / My cousin's." This is Countess Marie Larisch, whom Eliot met in Munich and whose 1913 memoir *My Past* he probably read. She was the niece of Empress Elisabeth of Austria; the cousin of two archdukes who met unfortunate ends (Rudolf and Franz Ferdinand); and a cousin of Wagner's patron Ludwig II, whose body was found in the Starnberger See in 1886. Larisch passes along Elisabeth's account of being visited by Ludwig's ghost, an apparition dripping with water. After Ludwig's death, a popular song lamenting him began, *"Auf den Bergen wohnt die Freiheit"* ("In the mountains lives freedom")—an adaptation of a line of Schiller's. Likewise, Eliot has Marie saying, "In the mountains, there you feel free." These intimations of Ludwig's death introduce the motif of drowning that will overtake the poem.

Between the Marie Larisch scene and the first *Tristan* quotation comes a famous twelve-line passage that is quite different in tone: solemn, prophetic, Eliotic. It begins:

> What are the roots that clutch, what branches grow
> Out of this stony rubbish? Son of man,
> You cannot say, or guess, for you know only
> A heap of broken images, where the sun beats,
> And the dead tree gives no shelter, the cricket no relief,
> And the dry stone no sound of water.

In his notes to the poem, Eliot cites the biblical books of Ezekiel and Ecclesiastes as sources. They may explain "son of man" and "heap of broken images," but not the beating sun. Act III of *Tristan* gives a comparable picture of the desert of the soul:

> O this sun's
> scorching beams,
> how their fiery torment
> burns into my brain!
> Against the swelter
> of this parching heat
> ah, there is no cooling
> shelter of shade!

Against the fearful torture
of my agonies
what balm
could bring me relief?

The wounded Tristan soon collapses, and his loyal friend Kurwenal asks, "Are you now dead? Do you still live?" Eliot inserts a similar limbo just before the citation of "*Öd' und leer das Meer*": "I was neither / Living nor dead, and I knew nothing, / Looking into the heart of light, the silence." Incidentally, "*Öd' und leer das Meer*" was added at a later date; one can see Eliot inserting it into the manuscript by hand. He also adjusted the earlier *Tristan* quotation. Originally, he had written "*Frisch schwebt der Wind*" ("Fresh hovers the wind"); later, he changed it to "*Frisch weht der Wind*," in keeping with the libretto. As William Blissett points out, Eliot apparently cited the lines from memory and then checked them against Wagner's text—"presumptive evidence of first-hand knowledge and more than casual concern."

So far, *The Waste Land* has been mostly free of the disdainful slant of "Opera," Eliot's early *Tristan* poem. Fragments of Wagner are yoked to honest-sounding cries of despair, both from the troubled aesthete at the center of the narrative and from the nameless hordes who tramp through the "Unreal City" of workaday London. The tone changes, though, in the poem's second part, "A Game of Chess." Vernacular voices break in, including Cockney pubgoers and a sample of literary ragtime: "O O O O that Shakespeherian Rag—/ It's so elegant / So intelligent." A Book of the World can catch almost any aspect of experience in its web, unburdened by the need to assimilate found objects into a seamless whole. So it is with *The Waste Land*'s touches of ragtime, the music hall, and jazz. Josh Epstein, in his book *Sublime Noise*, notices that these pop-culture fragments often lapse into a mechanical repeating pattern, like a gramophone stuck in a groove. Undercutting the solemnity of the earlier quotations, they bring about an "implosion of Wagnerian totality into an unstable multimedia text."

When Wagner returns, in "The Fire Sermon," he is a depleted force. Much of this section is given over to a vivid, polyphonic vision of the river Thames, with rats creeping through vegetation on the bank. In the midst of urban grit, we catch a glimpse of Wagner's Rhinemaidens, who take the form of modern women enduring drudgery and indignity. Their pre-verbal song is taken not from the blissful prelude of *Rheingold* but from the darkened, wasted terrain of *Götterdämmerung*:

> The barges wash
> Drifting logs
> Down Greenwich reach
> Past the Isle of Dogs.
>   Weialala leia
>   Wallala leialala

According to Eliot's notes, each of the Rhinemaidens has a brief aria. They sing of "trams and dusty trees," of various neighborhoods in greater London, of the beach at Margate, of "the broken fingernails of dirty hands." By the end, their motto is reduced to a pathetic fragment: "la la." Eliot once told his fellow poet Stephen Spender that he had studied "the whole of the *Ring*" while writing *The Waste Land*. The intricacy of these Rhinemaiden references bears out that report.

The Thames scene is also rife with sexual innuendo, louche behavior, morals loosened in the rolling fog. There is a whiff of a gay come-on when a Smyrna merchant, possibly Jewish, offers a weekend at the Metropole, a fashionable and not entirely reputable seaside hotel. The androgynous Tiresias narrates a mechanical assignation between a young man and woman. In a long satirical passage that was cut at Ezra Pound's behest, a pretentious literary woman is "baptised in a soapy sea / Of Symonds—Walter Pater—Vernon Lee"—all three homosexual. Decadence arrives in glory with a citation of Verlaine's "Parsifal": "*Et, ô ces voix d'enfants chantant dans la coupole!*" (And, O those children's voices singing in the dome!). Recall that Verlaine's hero is tempted not only by the Flower Maidens but by an "inclination / Toward the Flesh of virgin boy."

The Fire Sermon is named after a sermon by the Buddha, one that promises release from the burning suffering of the senses—not least the fire of desire. As the poet seeks such an escape, *Tristan*, the site of youthful passion, is left behind. Wagner himself is still germane: he, too, sampled Buddhism and preached the virtues of renunciation. In *Parsifal*, the hero remains chaste, even as he gains an understanding of Amfortas's sexual wound ("It burns in my heart!"). Although Eliot never made direct mention of *Parsifal*, he could have seen the opera in Boston in 1910 and on many occasions thereafter. A glint of the Grail in the last part of *The Waste Land* leads us once more into the symbolic forest of Wagner's final work.

I n his notes to *The Waste Land*, Eliot writes: "Not only the title, but the plan and a good deal of the incidental symbolism of the poem were suggested by Miss Jessie L. Weston's book on the Grail legend: *From Ritual to Romance*." Eliot later claimed that the footnotes published with the poem were in large part a comedic exercise in "bogus scholarship." Indeed, they mislead as much as they reveal. Still, other sources confirm Eliot's yen for stories of the Grail. In his youth he read Malory's *Morte d'Arthur* and Tennyson's *Idylls of the King*. He could also have taken his title from Wolfram von Eschenbach's *Parzival*, or from Tennyson's "Morte d'Arthur" ("like a wind, that shrills / All night in a waste land"), or from Swinburne's *Tristram of Lyonesse*.

Jessie Weston was a European-educated Englishwoman who took up folkloric studies after visiting Bayreuth in 1892. Four years later, she published a book called *The Legends of the Wagner Drama*. She soon established herself as a leading interpreter of Arthuriana, although she was herself accused of bogus scholarship and occult speculation. *From Ritual to Romance* arose from another trip to Bayreuth. At the 1911 festival, she met the Vienna-based Indologist Leopold von Schroeder, author of *The Completion of the Aryan Mystery in Bayreuth*, an attempt at conjoining Wagner's dramas to Vedic texts. Schroeder was one of many theorists of the period who imagined a lost Aryan homeland from which both Northern European and Indian cultures arose. He was not, however, antisemitic; in his eyes, Aryans and Jews were building modern civilization together. Weston, like Schroeder, saw the romances of Siegfried, Tristan, and Perceval as a shared inheritance of the "great Aryan family."

The other major influence on *From Ritual to Romance* is James Frazer's 1890 study *The Golden Bough*, which groups the ancient stories of Attis, Adonis, Osiris, and Dionysus under the banner of nature or vegetation cults. In legends of this type, a hero dies or is killed and then is reborn. The recurrence of that resurrection cycle in Christian lore, including tales of the Grail, shows the cultic origins of modern religion. Weston theorizes "a close connection between the vitality of a certain King, and the prosperity of his kingdom; the forces of the ruler being weakened or destroyed, by wound, sickness, old age, or death, the land becomes Waste, and the task of the hero is that of restoration." That "divine or semi-divine ruler, at once god and king," is widely known as the Fisher King. Wagner calls him Amfortas.

Fanciful as Weston's ideas are, they do some justice to the multiform spirituality of *Parsifal*. Waste spaces appear throughout the opera: Parsifal is raised in *Öde*, or wilderness; Klingsor's magic garden is conjured from a *Wüste*, or desert, and when Parsifal defeats Klingsor the garden dissolves back into an *Einöde*, another word for desert or wasteland. *Tristan* plays on similar themes: that "waste and empty" ocean under the burning sun is a harsh mirror of Tristan's inner state. *From Ritual to Romance* hardly explains all of *The Waste Land*, but it gives a context for its rites of spring and fertility, its devastated and desiccated landscapes, its repeated references to fishing, and its belated turn toward Indian texts, in the form of the Upanishads.

The final sections of the poem replicate Weston's cycle of death and rebirth. "Death by Water" revisits the motif of the drowned man, which Eliot adapted from *Ulysses*. Apparently, this section was to have included the antisemitic imagery of "Dirge," but Ezra Pound talked Eliot out of it—an ironic turn of events, since Pound later outdid Eliot in anti-Jewish bile. Instead, "Death by Water" consists only of eight coolly mournful lines depicting the watery decay of Phlebas the Phoenician, "who was once handsome and tall as you." Stephen Spender stated that this section crystallizes the hidden elegy that is in *The Waste Land*"—the elegy for Jean Verdenal, Spender elsewhere hints. On April 25, 1915, the first day of the Gallipoli invasion, thousands of soldiers died on the beaches. Although Verdenal was killed a week later and on land, Eliot knew few of the details. He later wrote of an unnamed friend greeting him in Paris "waving a branch of lilac, a friend who was later (so far as I could find out) to be mixed with the mud of Gallipoli." James Miller relates Eliot's discordant memories of Verdenal—springtime, lilacs, death in the mire—not only to the poem's ending but also to its famous first lines: "April is the cruellest month, breeding / Lilacs out of the dead land . . ."

"What the Thunder Said" returns to the rocky desert. Pilgrims traverse a sandy path; the air is full of "dry sterile thunder without rain." The mountains no longer feel free. Images of falling towers intrude. The travelers find themselves in an "empty chapel, only the wind's home"—the Chapel

Perilous of many Grail stories, where the questing hero experiences soul-shaking visions. (*Parsifal* lacks such a chapel, but Titurel's demonic funeral procession produces a similar effect.) Then rains begin to fall, allowing a flicker of hope to steal in—the merest trace of a Good Friday Spell. If the wounded king is not cured, he is at least content: "I sat upon the shore / Fishing, with the arid plain behind me." In the last lines, Eliot turns to the Upanishads: "Datta. Dayadhvam. Damyata. / Shantih shantih shantih." The first three words can be translated as "give, sympathize, control." Eliot relates "shantih" to the phrase "the Peace which passeth understanding," from the Anglican liturgy. Devotion, renunciation, and compassion happen also to be the guiding themes of *Parsifal*.

The last part of *The Waste Land* is like an afterimage of Wagner's syncretic religiosity, as transmitted through French Symbolism. As Stoddard Martin observes, no moment of salvation actually arrives, no holy spear heals the wound. In this respect, Eliot's poem is even further distant from *Ulysses*, with its recuperative celebration of sensual love and spiritual compassion. Instead, the authorial protagonist quivers with unrelieved pain and shame: "My friend, blood shaking my heart / The awful daring of a moment's surrender / Which an age of prudence can never retract." For Wagner, renunciation was not the same thing as repression. Even if desire must go unfulfilled, it can still be felt, even enjoyed. As the composer wrote in the early sketch for *Parsifal*, the one he sent to King Ludwig: "Strong is the magic of him who desires, stronger is that of him who abstains." In *The Waste Land*, desire is a wound that cannot be closed.

Works of post-Wagnerian modernism, *Ulysses* included, superimpose myth and modernity in a way that promises a comprehensive revelation of the world, both its variegated surfaces and its primordial roots. In *The Waste Land*, such correspondences tend to break down. Archetypes float up from the depths of the past, but they ultimately find little lasting resonance in contemporary lives. Instead, they provide a reassuring clutter of allusions for the stranded intellect: "These fragments I have shored against my ruins." In that sense, Eliot's poem is, more than *Ulysses*, an irrevocably anti-Romantic, anti-Wagnerian work.

WOOLF AND *THE WAVES*

Woolf in 1927

Joyce once said that Eliot had put an end to "poetry for ladies." It was not a sentiment that Virginia Woolf would have welcomed. She read Joyce and Eliot with wary fascination, registering both the potency of their technique and the gaps in their vision. When chapters of *Ulysses* began appearing in *The Little Review* in 1918, she wrote in a notebook, "The thing is that he is attempting to do away with the machinery—to extract the marrow." Much later, she recalled reading the book "with spasms of wonder, of discovery, & then again with long lapses of intense boredom"—an ambivalence not unlike her response to Wagner. *Ulysses* struck her as a vulgar display of male ego. She responded more warmly to *The Waste Land*, which had its first book publication by way of her and her husband's boutique press, Hogarth. "It has great beauty & force of phrase: symmetry; & tensity," she wrote. Ultimately, though, Eliot mystified her: she had the sense of a man wearing an unreadable mask.

Woolf's maturing conception of the flow of consciousness assumes a form distinct from the turbulent experimentalism of *Ulysses*. Instead of exposing every corner of her characters' worlds, Woolf maps the hazy boundaries of identity itself, including those of gender. Wagner is one tool she uses to poke beneath the surface of the self. Her 1922 novel *Jacob's*

Room is built around a central character who is not a capacious every-man, as in Joyce, but a cipher: an attractive, unworldly, breezily intellectual youth named Jacob Flanders, who is fated to die in the Great War, as his name portends. Men and women alike encircle Jacob, never breaking his defenses. At the heart of the novel is a night at the opera—*Tristan* at Covent Garden. Woolf paints the doomed splendor of the Empire in half-elegiac, half-mordant tones:

> The autumn season was in full swing. Tristan was twitching his rug up under his armpits twice a week; Isolde waved her scarf in miraculous sympathy with the conductor's baton. In all parts of the house were to be found pink faces and glittering breasts. When a Royal hand attached to an invisible body slipped out and withdrew the red and white bouquet reposing on the scarlet ledge, the Queen of England seemed a name worth dying for.

Then Woolf delineates her characters' disparate reactions to the music, as Forster had done in *Howards End*. But the exercise breaks off abruptly, as if it were too obvious or pointless to be continued:

> Then two thousand hearts in the semi-darkness remembered, anticipated, travelled dark labyrinths; and Clara Durrant said farewell to Jacob Flanders, and tasted the sweetness of death in effigy; and Mrs. Durrant, sitting behind her in the dark of the box, sighed her sharp sigh; and Mr. Wortley, shifting his position behind the Italian Ambassador's wife, thought that Brangaena was a trifle hoarse; and suspended in the gallery many feet above their heads, Edward Whittaker surreptitiously held a torch to his miniature score; and . . . and . . .

> In short, the observer is choked with observations.

In Wagner's thrall, listeners experience a loss of individuality: they conform to type, and "there is no need to distinguish details." Woolf finds the entire spectacle hollow and heartless. She acidly notes that well-dressed patrons leaving the opera are indifferent to the fate of a child thief who is caught in the square. A "man of valour who has ruled the Empire" thinks of bridges and aqueducts as he listens to the lonely music of the shepherd's pipe. That indifference will be writ large when millions of soldiers go to their deaths, Jacob among them.

One figure stands out from the crowd: a "young man with a Wellington nose," sitting up in the cheap seats. He goes away "as if he were still set a little apart from his fellows by the influence of the music." This is Richard Bonamy, quiet, fastidious, bookish, a university friend of Jacob's, and "fonder of Jacob than of anyone in the world." In other words, he fits the profile of the gay Wagnerite, to whom the music whispers secrets. Afterward, Bonamy knocks on Jacob's door, and the gap between them yawns. "About this opera now," Jacob says. "This fellow Wagner . . . I say, Bonamy, what about Beethoven?" As in *The Voyage Out*, Wagner is a divided legacy: some use him as a social prop, others cling to him desperately. Woolf revisits that dynamic in her 1937 novel *The Years*, depicting a performance of *Siegfried* that takes place on the night of King Edward VII's death. Amid the usual glitter, two unattached men sit side by side, one listening "critically, intently" and the other lost in happy oblivion. Again, Wagner is a double image of the Empire in its twilight and of the love that dare not speak its name.

The passing of the age of Wagner is essentially complete in *Mrs. Dalloway*, published in 1925 and set in 1923. When we first met Clarissa Dalloway, in *The Voyage Out*, she raved about the magic of Bayreuth. Now she favors Bach. Whatever remains of Wagnerism is entrusted to another of Woolf's isolated, vulnerable males: Septimus Warren Smith, a shell-shocked war veteran who is on the verge of suicide. Septimus is a strange double of Clarissa, who, beneath her bustling exterior, feels imprisoned. Together, the two characters capture the split world of the author. Jamie McGregor, in a dissertation on Wagnerism in Joyce and Woolf, proposes that Septimus is a meld of Siegfried and Tristan: he is both an unformed being in tune with nature and a wounded warrior yearning for the release of death. In one scene, he sits with his wife in Regent's Park and imagines that a bird is speaking to him, as the Woodbird spoke to Siegfried. Woolf once experienced a similar episode. Another passage weaves a delirious rhapsody around the shepherd's-pipe music from *Tristan*:

> He lay very high, on the back of the world. The earth thrilled beneath him. Red flowers grew through his flesh; their stiff leaves rustled by his head. Music began clanging against the rocks up here. It is a motor horn

down in the street, he muttered; but up here it cannoned from rock to rock, divided, met in shocks of sound which rose in smooth columns (that music should be visible was a discovery) and became an anthem, an anthem twined round now by a shepherd boy's piping (That's an old man playing a penny whistle by the public-house, he muttered) which, as the boy stood still came bubbling from his pipe, and then, as he climbed higher, made its exquisite plaint while the traffic passed beneath . . . He himself remained high on his rock, like a drowned sailor on a rock. I leant over the edge of the boat and fell down, he thought. I went under the sea I have been dead, and yet am now alive, but let me rest still . . .

The dull imperial spectator in *Jacob's Room* hears the shepherd's pipe and lets his mind wander to bridge construction. Septimus does the opposite: amid the noise of the city, he hallucinates the desolate melody that plays against the waste and empty sea.

Woolf's great feminist essay *A Room of One's Own*, published in 1929, heralds a golden age of women's writing. Male fiction has run its course, she says. "Virility has now become self-conscious—men, that is to say, are now writing only with the male side of their brains." Citing Coleridge, Woolf argues that genius is androgynous, fusing male and female traits. She sounds curiously like Wagner when she says that "one must be woman-manly or man-womanly," that in the androgynous mind "some marriage of opposites has to be consummated." *Opera and Drama* defines the ideal of the "purely human" as the loving union of the manly and the womanly, as the fecundation of feeling by understanding. The art of androgyny propels Woolf's 1928 novel *Orlando*, in which the title character changes sex and gender.

In the essays "Phases of Fiction" and "Modern Fiction," Woolf speaks of "some desire still unsatisfied." The novel "can amass details," she writes. "But can it also select? Can it symbolize? Can it give us an epitome as well as an inventory?" *Ulysses* may be the master inventory of modern life, but for Woolf it feels "confined and shut in." She sets her sights on the "common life," the interconnected web of being. In her diary, she writes of her aspiration to "saturate every atom," to eliminate everything extraneous. She would create a "continuous stream, not solely of human thought, but of the ship, the night &c, all flowing together." She would tell "the life of anybody, life in general . . . I am telling myself the story of the world from the beginning." She would show "vast undifferentiated brooding life."

These plans come to fruition in *The Waves*. William Blissett considers it "the most Wagnerian of Virginia Woolf's novels because the most despotically organized, the most 'composite' in its use of musical and painterly, even sculpturesque and ballet-like effects, and the most pervasively leitmotivistic in its structure and symbolism." A half-dozen other commentators—John DiGaetani, Tracey Sherard, Emma Sutton, Gyllian Phillips, Kimberly Fairbrother Canton, and Jamie McGregor—have isolated Wagnerian motifs in the novel. *The Waves* stands as Woolf's chief attempt to match the "overwhelming unity," the "utmost calm and intensity," the "smooth stream at white heat" that she discerned in *Parsifal* in 1909.

The novel follows the lives of seven characters of shared background, very like the Bloomsbury Group in their squabbling intimacy. Each of the nine sections is introduced by an italicized passage describing different stages of a day at the seashore: dawn, various hours of morning, noon, the waning of the day, sunset, night. The characters, meanwhile, proceed from early childhood to school days and on to early adulthood and middle age. The superimposition of two radically different time scales suggests one form of Woolf's desired synthesis: a novel at once microcosmic and epic in scope. The beginning gives a sense of an even grander temporal dimension, one that might reach back to the beginning of the universe:

> The sun had not yet risen. The sea was indistinguishable from the sky, except that the sea was slightly creased as if a cloth had wrinkles in it. Gradually as the sky whitened a dark line lay on the horizon dividing the sea from the sky and the grey cloth became barred with thick strokes moving, one after another, beneath the surface, following each other, pursuing each other, perpetually . . . Gradually the dark bar on the horizon became clear as if the sediment in an old wine-bottle had sunk and left the glass green. Behind it, too, the sky cleared as if the white sediment there had sunk, or as if the arm of a woman crouched

beneath the horizon had raised a lamp . . . Slowly the arm that held the lamp raised it higher and then higher until a broad flame became visible; an arc of fire burnt on the rim of the horizon, and all round it the sea blazed gold.

The slow-gathering power of this passage, ascending from darkness to light and from depth to stratosphere, calls to mind the prelude to *Rheingold*, as well as the first sentence of Katherine Mansfield's "At the Bay" ("Very early morning. The sun was not yet risen"). The initial sentence of the ensuing chapter is this: "'I see a ring,' said Bernard, 'hanging above me. It quivers and hangs in a loop of light.'" The shining of that phantom ring matches the moment in *Rheingold* when the sun beats down into the waters and sets the gold ablaze.

In a series of monologues and dialogues, the novel gives voice to six of the seven characters. One gets to know their attributes—the gregarious Bernard; the melancholy poet Louis; the avid aesthete Neville; the socialite Jinny; the neurotic outsider Rhoda; the domestic-minded Susan—but by design they blur together. "The six characters were supposed to be one," Woolf said. "I wanted to give the sense of continuity." They represent aspects of her own inner world while at the same time mirroring people she knew. Louis is almost certainly a version of T. S. Eliot. He is an outsider in the group, the son of an Australian banker, prim, aloof, unhappy. "My shattered mind is pieced together by some sudden perception," the character says, recalling Eliot's broken images and fragments shored against ruin. Louis also speaks of himself in subterranean terms: "My roots go down to the depths of the world." He wishes to "fix in words, to forge in a ring of steel," a fleeting glimpse of order that the company inspires. Emma Sutton compares him to Alberich, the earth-burrowing forger of the Ring.

The seventh character is the charismatic, enigmatic Percival, who dies young, at the novel's midpoint. The rest of the company revolves around him, both in his presence and his absence. Percival shares characteristics with the Jacob of *Jacob's Room*, and is, by extension, Woolf's final memorial to her brother Thoby. He is also a conspicuously Christlike figure, at once naïve and knowing. One line in the draft—"I then cursed Percival for being such a fool"—makes clear the likeness to Wagner's "pure fool." Percival is described as an emissary from a "pagan universe," a "mediaeval commander." In the novel's central scene, the company bid Percival farewell as he goes off to India, where he will perish in a riding accident. On the table is a vase containing a red carnation; McGregor ingeniously sees this as a stand-in for the blood-filled chalice of the Holy Grail.

It falls to Bernard to articulate the ideal of self-transcendence and mystical communion toward which Woolf has been groping. "I do not believe in separation," he declares. "We are not single." In his closing monologue, an ecstatic sixty-page expanse in which Woolf took particular pride, Bernard says, "Let me cast and throw away this veil of being"—sounding almost like Schopenhauer. He speaks of seeing without being seen, of traversing the world like a ghost. Entering St. Paul's Cathedral, he thinks of dark, dour Louis, "with his neat suit with his cane in his hand and his angular, rather detached gait," who liked to visit the place.

> I am always impressed, as I enter, by the rubbed roses; the polished brasses; the flapping and the chanting, while one boy's voice wails round the dome like some lost and wandering dove . . . I stray and look and wonder, and sometimes, rather furtively, try to rise on the shaft of somebody else's prayer into the dome, out, beyond, wherever they go. But then like the lost and wailing dove, I find myself failing, fluttering, descending and perching upon some curious gargoyle, some battered nose or absurd tombstone, with humour, with wonder, and so again watch the sightseers with their Baedekers shuffling past, while the boy's voice soars in the dome and the organ now and then indulges in a moment of elephantine triumph. How then, I asked, would Louis roof us all in? How would he confine us, make us one, with his red ink, with his very fine nib? The voice petered out in the dome, wailing.

In revisions to the draft, you can almost see Woolf pushing this scene a little more toward Wagner. At first, it is the sound of the organ that reverberates around the dome, but then it changes, more unexpectedly, to the voice of a boy. This evokes not only the chanting boys of Verlaine's "Parsifal" but also Eliot's somewhat jarring quotation of that sonnet in *The Waste Land*. The allusion is augmented by the apparition of a dove. In Act I of *Parsifal*, the boys sing, "The faith lives, the dove hovers," and at the end a white dove flutters over Parsifal's head. McGregor concludes that the "unshakable affirmation of *Parsifal* here proves impossible to recapture." The boy's voice wails, the dove wanders.

Woolf steers clear of the monumental bleakness of Eliot's failed Grail ceremony. In the final paragraphs, the elderly Bernard rouses himself from despair, finding freedom in invisibility and selflessness. At the first flicker of dawn—the day is completing its cycle and is ready to begin again—he catches sight of the "eternal renewal, the incessant rise and fall and fall and rise again." A "new desire" wells up, like a rising wave. Suddenly, he assumes a heroic pose, riding forth on a horse into battle. His enemy is death: "It is death against whom I ride with my spear couched and my hair flying back like a young man's, like Percival's . . ." With that quaintly Romantic-medieval image the novel ends, although an italicized postscript reminds us of the indifferent eternity of nature: "*The waves broke on the shore.*" The last sentence can be joined seamlessly to the first: "*The sun had not yet risen.*"

FINNEGANS WAKE

Woolf wrote in *The Waves*: "One cannot live outside the machine for more perhaps than half an hour." What she admired in Joyce, despite his egotism and vulgarity, was his urge to subdue the machine and expose the disorderly flux of being. Joyce never met Woolf, but he was aware of her. He read *The Voyage Out*, though his reaction is not recorded. He made notes regarding Woolf's commentary on his work, which included a cutting phrase about the "comparative poverty of the writer's mind." The phrase "poverty of mind" duly appears in the omnium gatherum of *Finnegans Wake*.

Joyce almost certainly did not read *The Waves*—his eyesight was too poor by 1931—but his novel-in-progress had elements in common with Woolf's creation. The *Wake* is his novel of night and dream, a transcript not of the stream of consciousness but of the stream of existence itself. It is suffused with references to Wagner, arguably from the first page to the last. Matthew Hodgart and Ruth Bauerle, in *Joyce's Grand Operoar: Opera in Finnegans Wake*, point out that "riverrun," the first word, could be mistaken for "river Rhine," and that the final words, "A way a lone a last a loved a long the," enfold the Rhinemaidens' cry of "Wagalaweia!" In 1937, while staying on the banks of the Rhine, Joyce wrote a letter saying that he could hear the river complaining about being "pressed into service by me."

Wagner was on Joyce's mind from the outset of the project. In early 1923, he began writing prose sketches based on figures from Irish history and folklore. He was interested in the idea of "unconscious memory," of dreams as the "wake thoughts of centuries ago." One sketch, developed from notes headed *Exiles*, was a modern-day send-up of *Tristan und Isolde*, set on the deck of a pleasure boat, with a jazz band playing under the night sky. Tristan is a six-foot-two "rugger and soccer champion"; Isolde is the "belle of Chapelizod," a Dublin suburb associated with the Iseult of Irish legend. The language has the chatty flavor of high-society twits: "The sea looked awfully pretty at that twilight hour . . . It was a just too gorgeous sensation." Isolde says, "I'm so real glad to have met you, Tris, you fascinator, you!" Tristan, who calls her Isy, spouts some sort of Wagnerian-Theosophical gibberish about the "pancosmic urge" and "Allimmanence." Then he thrusts his tongue down Isolde's throat, as if scoring a goal.

When Joyce incorporated the *Tristan* triangle into *Exiles*, he identified most with the King Mark figure. The same sympathy is felt in the *Tristan* sketch. The lovers dismiss Mark as a "tiresome old ourangoutan beaver." They noisily argue—"Curse your stinking putrid soul . . . you bloody bitch"—and then make up with the "big kiss of Trustan with Usolde." But a chorus of seabirds salutes the king with a jaunty song:

> Three quarks for Muster Mark!
> Sure he hasn't got much of a bark
> And sure any he has it's all beside the mark . . .
> Hohohoho, moulty Mark!

The section of the *Wake* known as "Mamalujo" begins with this same poem. In 1963, the physicist Murray Gell-Mann borrowed the word "quark" to describe one of the fundamental constituents of matter.

Why did Joyce return to Wagner at a time when Bach, Stravinsky, and Duke Ellington were the rage? Nora Joyce may have been partly responsible: she went through a phase of listening constantly to Wagner records. Or perhaps, in the wake of the scandalous triumph of *Ulysses*, Joyce could let go of his rivalry with the old sorcerer. Stoddard Martin writes that Joyce's evolving relationship with Wagner "is exactly the behavior, in exactly the pattern, that one would expect the developing Stephen Deda-lus to exhibit towards an 'artist-father': first reverence, then imitation, then competition, then repudiation, finally peaceful coexistence." Harold Bloom, in *The Anxiety of Influence*, calls this apophrades: a poet readmits ancestors that he has previously suppressed, but in a way that preserves his priority and mastery.

Wagner is present in *Finnegans Wake* mainly as a mythic fount—one of those waking beings of the past who now speak in dreams. By Timothy Martin's count, the *Wake* contains 178 allusions to the *Ring* and 242 to *Tristan*. All the other mature Wagner operas are named, plus the early *Die Feen*. Humphrey Chimpden Earwicker (HCE), the fallen patriarch of the *Wake*, is cast both as a Flying Dutchman pariah and as a King Mark cuckold. Again, the wronged husband proves more compelling than the lusty hero. The complication is that both HCE's wife, Anna Livia Plu-rabelle, and his daughter, Issy (Isobel), play Isolde roles, and that Shem and Shaun—HCE and ALP's sons—are rivals in a web of incestuous rela-tions. Furthermore, Joyce draws elements from Wagner's life, especially the affair with Mathilde Wesendonck: one notebook shows him reading Édouard Schuré's book *Woman the Inspirer*, which touches on that rela-tionship. We see Wagnerian struggles between purity and sin, suffering and redemption, night and day.

When Joyce was asked whether the *Wake* was an attempt at combining music and literature, he responded, "No, it's pure music." The transforma-tion of language into music is evident in the proliferation of leitmotifs—at least a thousand of them altogether. More than merely decorative, they are essential to the reader's efforts at comprehension. Only when we see clusters of verbal motifs associated with particular characters do we realize that those characters are present. ALP, for example, is signaled by rhythmically lap-ping phrases that end with "of": "Beside the rivering waters of, hitherand-thithering waters of. Night!" Musicality also takes the form of punning variations. The Wagnerian thesaurus includes Sir Tristram, tristian, Tristis Tristior Tristissimus, Tristy; Issy, Izzy, Isot, Isolade; Wagoner, mudheeldy wheesindonk, Boyrut or Bayroyt ("Fort! Fort! Bayroyt! March!"). The "ev-erlasting ash tree" is "evernasty ashtray"; "Mild und leise" is "Mildew Lisa"; *Götterdämmerung* is "gttrdmmrng"; *Parsifal* is "pussyfours" or "purseyful" or "parciful."

The endless melody of language merges with the master image of the ever-flowing river—the Liffey in Dublin, first and foremost, but also the Wagnerian Rhine. The *Wake* is not merely a dive into the depths of consciousness but a simulacrum of nature itself. In the final pages of the novel, Anna Livia has become the Liffey, coursing toward the obliterating vastness of the ocean—"my cold father, my cold mad father, my cold mad feary father." It is staged as a death, a Liebestod. For Matthew Hodgart, the words "I sink I'd die down over his feet" are a gloss on Isolde's "To drown, to sink'" as well as the lovers' "O sink down, night of love." Once more the modernist mind alights upon the figure of a going-under, an *Untergang*. In *The Waves*, water is the current that carries selves through time. Although Woolf took a dim view of Joyce's *Wake* style, calling it "unintelligible," the sense of confluence with her own work is strong.

"History is a nightmare from which I am trying to awake," Stephen says in *Ulysses*. Joyce felt much the same, striving to rise above the maelstrom of politics, nationalism, and war. History caught him in the end. After Germany invaded France in the spring of 1940, Joyce made plans to flee to Lausanne, only to find that Swiss authorities thought he was Jewish and were refusing a visa for this reason. Savoring the irony, Joyce wrote, "I am thunderstruck! There's a remarkable discovery!" He reached Zurich, but his health collapsed. He died in January 1941, at a time when it seemed very possible that Germany could win the war.

Woolf noted Joyce's passing in her diary, saying that he was "about a fortnight younger than I am." She was at work on a new novel, *Between the Acts*, but the old despair was gnawing at her, and she felt that she was becoming an impossible burden to her husband, Leonard. When, two months later, voices sounded again in her head, she made the decision to end her life, and drowned herself in the river Ouse. "O bitter ending," Joyce wrote in the last pages of the *Wake*. "O Death!" Woolf exclaimed in *The Waves*. For one, death by drowning was a crypto-Romantic metaphor; for the other, it was the final reality.

13

SIEGFRIED'S DEATH

Nazi Germany and Thomas Mann

The Festspielhaus decorated for Hitler's birthday, 1939

On February 13, 1933, fifty years to the day after Wagner's death, Thomas Mann walked onto the stage of the Concertgebouw, in Amsterdam, to deliver his lecture "Sorrows and Grandeur of Richard Wagner." Beforehand, the Concertgebouw Orchestra, under the direction of the Austrian conductor Erich Kleiber, performed Siegfried's Funeral Music and the *Siegfried Idyll*; afterward, they played the *Lohengrin* Act I prelude. The talk was based on an essay that Mann had written for the anniversary—his most ambitious attempt to settle accounts with the "greatest talent in the entire history of art." The Amsterdam engagement was part of a brief series of lectures that Mann had begun three days earlier, in Munich, and continued in Brussels and Paris. As it turned out, his Wagner speaking tour became a permanent exile from Germany. Mann died in Zurich in 1955, and was buried five miles from James Joyce.

Mann had many reasons to leave Germany, where Adolf Hitler had been appointed Reich chancellor on January 30. Beginning in the early 1920s, the formerly conservative author had adopted leftist positions that clashed with Nazi ideology. His wife, Katia, was Jewish, and his children were therefore considered non-Aryan. The Wagner lecture did not improve the family's situation. The *Völkischer Beobachter*, the official Nazi paper, was aghast that a "half-Bolshevik" was purveying a distorted view of Wagner abroad even as Hitler honored the composer at home. This was not unexpected. More shocking to Mann was the "Protest of the Richard Wagner City Munich" that appeared in April 1933, bearing the signatures of such musical eminences as Richard Strauss, Hans Pfitzner, and the gifted Wagner conductor Hans Knappertsbusch, who instigated the action. The document described Mann as not only "cosmopolitan-democratic" but also "unreliable and inexpert"—a jarring demotion for a man who had received the Nobel Prize in Literature four years earlier.

"Sorrows and Grandeur" is more than a political statement. It delves deep into Wagner's warring identities as mythmaker and psychologist, German and European, anarchist and bourgeois, populist and intellectual. But its disgust for the Nazification of Wagner is clear. Mann concedes that "imperialist, demagogic, and crowd-swaying elements" have long been part of the Bayreuth mentality; but these cannot be translated into conventional politics. To interpret Wagner's nationalist gestures in modern terms is to blemish their "romantic purity." The composer is better understood as a utopian socialist who displays a "thoroughly anarchic indifference to governmental structures." Mann recapitulates various fin-de-siècle Wagnerisms, especially the French version, as a way of countering the *völkisch* reading. Baudelaire is again praised as the first true Wagnerian, the one who gave the music a European sheen. Even more pointedly, Mann inverts Nietzsche's critique of the decadent, effeminate Wagner, categorizing apparent vices as hidden virtues. A portrait of the Meister molding the character of Siegfried while attired in "colorful satin robes" is sublimation laid bare:

Thus equipped, he gains the "artistic-voluptuous mood" needed to summon primal Nordic heroics and noble nature-symbolism, to let the golden-blond hero boy forge his sword of victory on the spraying anvil—images that make the breast of German youth swell with lofty feelings of manly glory.

Despite his reactionary streak, Wagner ultimately belongs to the party of "reform, change, liberation"—in other words, to the left. The peroration is brazen:

> This creative spirit, charged with life and stormily progressive despite all spiritual heaviness and attachment to death; this glorifier of a world-destroyer born of the freest love; this audacious musical innovator who in *Tristan* already stands with one foot on atonal terrain, and who today would most certainly be called a *Kulturbolschewist*; this man of the *Volk* who all his life fervently rejected power, money, violence, and war, and who intended his festival theater for a classless society, whatever the age made of it: no spirit of reaction and pious backwardness can claim him—he belongs instead to every future-directed will.

Mann recited this passage almost verbatim in Munich and Amsterdam. He apparently hesitated to brand Wagner with the Nazi buzzword *Kulturbolschewist*, for he crossed out that line in his typescript. Then, as press reports attest, he delivered it anyway.

After the lecture tour, Thomas and Katia Mann went on holiday in Switzerland. They were still planning to return home, but increasingly unsubtle warnings from their children and friends dissuaded them. The weather is bad in Munich, they were told. The house is being cleaned; there is terrible confusion. And finally: "Stay in Switzerland! You would not be safe here."

S orrows and grandeur": even in 1933 it was an old-fashioned phrase, calling forth a Romantic fable of greatness forged from woe. Heard in the present tense, though, it hints at a different narrative: Wagner is again suffering tribulations, and right-minded Germans must act to save him. Mann takes up the mission that Bernhard Diebold had set forth five years earlier—rectifying the "political loss of the most popular high art of the past few decades." This project was, of course, doomed. Wagner would now become the chief cultural ornament of the most destructive political regime in history.

The literature on Hitler and Nazism is prone to what the writer Ron Rosenbaum calls the "single-bullet theory"—simplistic explanations for a complex horror. It has been variously suggested that the key to understanding Hitler is that he had an abusive father; that he was too close to his mother; that he had encephalitis; that he contracted syphilis from a Jewish prostitute; that he blamed a Jewish doctor for his mother's death; that he was missing a testicle; that he underwent a wayward hypnosis treatment; that he was gay; that he was addled by drugs; and, most insidiously, that he himself had Jewish ancestry. To that dubious list can be added the notion that Hitler received posthumous instruction from Wagner. The first definitive statement of the thesis came in 1939, when the poet and historian Peter Viereck identified Wagner as "perhaps the most important single fountainhead of Nazi ideology." An extreme variation occurs in Joachim Köhler's 1997 book *Wagner's Hitler: The Prophet and His Disciple*, where it is said that Hitler's "campaign to exterminate the Jews was part of his love for Wagner."

Hitler stoked such speculation with the claim that a youthful encounter with *Rienzi* propelled him toward a career in politics. Many leading historians of the Third Reich are disinclined to take him at his word, and doubt that Wagner played a significant role in the dictator's political development. Richard J. Evans, in *The Third Reich in Power*, states that "the composer's influence on Hitler has often been exaggerated." Joachim Fest, who had dwelled on the Wagner legacy in his classic biography of Hitler, later concluded that polemics like Köhler's confused the content of the works with the history of their reception, mapping the latter onto the former. (Köhler later accepted the criticism and retracted his thesis.) Wagner was a malignant antisemite, but antisemitism does not amount to a political philosophy. Much about his erratic ideology—the anarchist tendencies, the disapproval of standing armies, the dislike of organized power—is antithetical to the totalitarian mind-set.

Hans Rudolf Vaget takes the view that once we get away from the concept of influence, of some sort of supernatural master-disciple relationship, we can form a more balanced, though still unsettling, picture of the

Wagner-Hitler problem. For Vaget, the question is how Hitler assumed a self-perceived Wagnerian style. "We need a dictator who is a genius," Hitler said in 1920, at the outset of his political career. This "self-styling as genius," in Vaget's words, also preoccupies the historian Wolfram Pyta, for whom "the politician Hitler is unthinkable without the artist Hitler." The porous border between art and politics had been a matter of concern since Walter Benjamin, in his 1935–36 essay "The Work of Art in the Age of Its Technological Reproducibility," wrote of Fascism as the aestheticizing of politics, as the "consummation of l'art pour l'art." Back in 1878, Nietzsche was already linking the "overestimation of genius" to political irrationality. The young aesthete of Linz and Vienna never went away: politics and war became, in a sense, a continuation of art by other means.

The cultural-political apparatus of the Nazi state drew liberally on Wagnerian mythology. The legal and political theorist Carl Schmitt, whose rationalization of dictatorial measures helped to justify Hitler's takeover, was acutely aware of myth's political usefulness—its capacity to direct feeling against real or imaginary adversaries. Schmitt knew his Wagner, and in 1912 wrote an essay for the *Bayreuther Blätter* in which he characterized Hans Sachs's monologue on *Wahn* (madness, delusion) as a discourse on the utility of fiction and illusion. For myths to serve political ends, though, they have to be reduced to easily manipulated iconography—Siegfried forging his sword, Hagen stabbing Siegfried in the back. The political scientist Herfried Münkler writes that when the "narrative context of these evocative images is restored" they can become counterproductive, even "critically destructive," to their political application. Wagner's career in the Third Reich fits that model. He served the Nazi state only when he was shorn of his ambiguities, and even then his presence in mainstream Nazi culture was less pronounced than many accounts let on.

In 1937, Mann visited Tribschen, Wagner's Lucerne refuge. "Horrible oil paintings, utterly Hitler," he wrote. "Ghastly, Hitlerish elements conspicuously visible, even if only latent and prefigured, from histrionic kitsch to Germanic boy-love." In the same year, however, Mann said of Wagner: "The German spirit was everything to him, the German state nothing." The two statements appear to contradict each other, yet Mann never sought a pat formula for the disaster of Germany under Nazism. In a turn of phrase that has not been bettered, he declares that his admiration for Wagner remains undimmed, despite the "malicious abuse to which its great object somewhat lends itself." *Die Handhabe bietet*—Wagner offers a handle for his own exploitation.

BAYREUTH 1924

Franz Stassen's cover design for the 1924 festival guide

In 1924, the Bayreuth Festival reopened, ending the ten-year hiatus caused by the First World War. Visitors from abroad took the opportunity to hear Wagner again on his home ground. Among them were Rose Stein Kirstein, the wife of a Boston department-store owner, and her two teenaged sons. They had made reservations at one of the city's best hotels, but when they arrived they were told that they would be happier staying with a "co-religionist." At a performance of *Meistersinger*, a patriotic demonstration erupted and the audience broke into the Deutschlandlied. A Jesuit priest seated near the Kirsteins began howling in a state of "hysterical rage or joy." Despite the tumult, the festival made a deep impression on Lincoln, the older Kirstein boy. It was, he recalled, "a world wholly, profoundly, dedicated to the realization of the unreal." He went away determined to dedicate his life to such an artistic utopia. More than two decades later, with George Balanchine, he founded the New York City Ballet.

Although Bayreuth had been hospitable to extremist politics since the days of Bernhard Förster, the aggressive chauvinism of 1924 was something new—a trashing of the festival's polyglot past. It exposed not just the radicalization of the German right but also the radicalization of the Wagner family. In 1915, Siegfried Wagner finally married, warding off the danger of being outed as a homosexual. His bride was an eighteen-year-old English orphan named Winifred Williams, who had been adopted by a distant German relative of her mother. Her adoptive father, the pianist and pedagogue Karl Klindworth, was a longtime member of the Wagner circle. From the moment Winifred arrived in Germany, she was breathing an ultranationalist, antisemitic atmosphere, and once settled at the Wahnfried villa she fell in line with the ideology of Houston Stewart Chamberlain. Winifred soon made herself indispensable, not only by producing male heirs—Wieland and Wolfgang—but also by handling business matters.

Hostile to the Weimar Republic from the moment of its inception, the Wagners welcomed various attempts to overthrow it. When the socialist leader Kurt Eisner was murdered, in 1919, Cosima called his killer a martyr. The family first heard of the Nazi Party that same year, just as Hitler began to involve himself in the organization. The intermediaries were Michael Georg Conrad, the former patron of Munich modernism, and the music critic Josef Stolzing-Cerny, who later became the cultural editor of the *Völkischer Beobachter* and helped to edit *Mein Kampf.* The latter's real name was Josef Cerny; the "Stolzing" was an homage to Walther von Stolzing in *Meistersinger.*

Even before Hitler made his presence felt, the fledgling Nazi Party—or the German Workers Party, as it was first known—had Wagnerites in its ranks. Many of the earliest Nazis came out of the Thule Society, which gestated from a national network known as the Germanenorden, or Germanic Order. Drawing mainly on Teutonic lore recorded in Tacitus's *Germania* and other sources, these groups pilfered freely from the Wagner operas; the Thule was the Munich outpost of the Germanenorden Walvater of the Holy Grail. (Walvater, meaning "father of the slain," is an alternate name for Wotan.) The Germanenorden in turn took inspiration from the Austrian pan-German guru Guido von List, who dreamed of reviving a pagan Teutonic religion that he called Wotanism, its rituals to be enacted in a festival amphitheater modeled on Bayreuth. Nicholas Goodrick-Clarke, in *The Occult Roots of Nazism*, summarizes an initiation protocol from around 1912, which found its way into Nazi Party files and is now held at the German Federal Archive in Berlin:

The ceremony began with soft harmonium music, while the brothers sang the Pilgrims' Chorus from Wagner's *Tannhäuser*. The ritual commenced in candlelight with brothers making the sign of the swastika and the Master reciprocating. Then the blindfolded novices, clad in pilgrimage mantles, were ushered by the Master of Ceremonies into the room. Here the Master told them of the Order's Ario-Germanic and aristocratic *Weltanschauung* before the Bard lit the sacred flame in the grove and the novices were divested of their mantles and blindfolds. At this point the Master seized Wotan's spear and held it before him, while the two Knights crossed their swords upon it. A series of calls and responses, accompanied by music from *Lohengrin*, completed the oath of the novices. Their consecration followed with cries from the "forest elves" as the new brothers were led into the grove of the Grail around the Bard's sacred flame.

Paganistic playacting of this kind did not pass muster in Bayreuth, where Chamberlain's ideal of an Aryanized Christianity held sway. Siegfried, for his part, tried to keep up a cosmopolitan veneer, even as he sympathized with the *völkisch* right. When, in the early twenties, the festival began raising funds to resume operations, some Wagnerites proposed limiting subscriptions to non-Jews. Siegfried wrote in protest: "Is that humane? Is that Christian? Is that German? No!" He went on to say, "Whether a person is Chinese, Negro, American, Indian, or Jewish is of absolutely no concern to us." In the period leading up to the 1924 festival, Siegfried attempted to mollify Jewish Wagnerites by writing a letter to Falk Salomon, the rabbi of Bayreuth, in which he made the not exactly reassuring declaration that "we have nothing at all against right-thinking nationalist Jews."

In fact, the 1924 festival pushed a racial-supremacist agenda from the start. The cover of the festival guide bore an illustration by Franz Stassen: a hand gripping a sword hilt, with the Festspielhaus in the background. Surrounding the image is text from *Siegfried*: "Nothung! Nothung! new and made young! I have awakened you to life again." This is a far cry from the "Nothung!" shout that resounds in *Ulysses*. The essays inside dole out tendentious interpretations of the operas. The racist philosopher Hans Alfred Grunsky portrays the dwarf Mime as an intrinsically hateful individual for whom Siegfried, the Nordic archetype, feels "instinctively the most violent racial aversion." The same author sees Parsifal as an avatar of "pure, strong will." Erwin Geck positions Wagner as a bulwark against parliamentary democracy and international capitalism. Professing to avoid party politics, Geck nonetheless makes his affiliations clear when he dubs the composer a "guide toward national socialism."

At the time of the festival of 1924, Hitler was serving a prison term, having attempted the so-called Beer Hall Putsch in Munich the previous year. The guest of honor at the dress rehearsals was, instead, Erich Ludendorff, the World War I general, who had planned to assume military command if the putsch had succeeded. In Ludendorff's honor, Bayreuth flew the old imperial flag, with its colors of black, white, and red, spurning the black-red-gold of the Weimar Republic. Swastikas, Nazi uniforms, and shouts of "Heil!" were in evidence. Ugly incidents occurred, which Winifred regretted: "Here Jews have been spat at, mocked, and verses like the Borkumlied with its 'Throw them out' etc. etc. have been passed around." Leftist Wagnerites put up modest resistance. At the 1927 festival, the Social Democratic Party organized a protest, denouncing would-be Siegfrieds who use "Wagner and his eternal work for political goals that were foreign to the great deceased." Wilhelm Ellenbogen, a leading explicator of Wagner for the working classes, criticized Bayreuth's elite atmosphere and maintained that its legacy should be available to all.

Siegfried made fitful efforts to repair Bayreuth's international reputation. In 1925, a notice asked audiences to refrain from singing at the end of *Meistersinger*, and a quotation from that work underscored the message: "*Hier gilt's der Kunst*" ("Art is what matters here"). When the festival resumed after the Second World War, Wieland and Wolfgang Wagner cited the same formula. The composer's heirs ignored the line's ironic context. In *Meistersinger*, Eva tells Hans Sachs that his age does not matter, because art alone counts. Sachs asks, "Dear Eva, would you mock me?" He is right to doubt Eva's pat little phrase; in the end, her hand goes to the dashing young knight. Wagner was the last person to believe that art could stand apart from reality.

THE MAGIC MOUNTAIN

Circa 1918, the author of *Death in Venice* appeared to be heading down the same path that beguiled so many Wagnerites of his generation—the path

that led, by so many twists and turns, to Fascism. The First World War pushed him toward bellicose nationalism. In his 1914 essay "Thoughts in War," he lauded German might, disparaged French and Mediterranean values, and invoked dark, Dionysian energies. "Civilization and culture are not only not one and the same," he writes, "but they are opposites, they present one of the manifold appearances of the eternal world-opposition and antithesis of spirit and nature," Mann is on the side of *Kultur*, which he defines as a "stylish savagery," not excluding "oracle, magic, pederasty, Vitzliputzli [the Aztec sun god], human sacrifices, orgiastic cultic forms, inquisition," and various other elements. Art, he says, is a "sublimation of the demonic." He upholds the purifying effects of war and declares that only a German victory can ensure long-term peace.

Such bloodthirstiness appalled Heinrich Mann, who had broadcast his loathing for German militarism in *Der Untertan*. In a 1915 essay on Zola, Heinrich inserted a coded dig at his brother, precipitating a wildly disproportionate reaction. For the next three years, Thomas labored over an essayistic work titled *Reflections of a Nonpolitical Man*, in which he scoffs at the democratic views of a character known as the *Zivilisationsliterat*, "civilization's literary man." Thomas's refusal to acknowledge that this person is his own brother makes the *Reflections* a tortured, even deranged document. It is, however, less a diatribe than a painstaking self-examination, especially on the topic of Wagner. As Thomas talks about his beloved composer, he gives notice that his political philosophy is bending in a new direction.

In a chapter titled *"Einkehr,"* or reflection, Mann reconsiders the trinity of Schopenhauer, Wagner, and Nietzsche. He begins with the startling announcement that he is "not a very proper German"—on account of his mother's Latin American heritage. He then claims that his three German heroes are European to the core. The ensuing discussion of Wagner anticipates the liberal slant of "Sorrows and Grandeur"; indeed, several of its passages reappear in the later text. Following Nietzsche, Mann emphasizes Wagner's distance from conventional Germanness; his music has an "unmistakably cosmopolitan cachet." Baudelaire and Maurice Barrès—whose 1903 meditation "The Death of Venice" influenced *Death in Venice*—understood the composer better than his German apologists. Mann confesses that "for the youth who found no place at home and who lived in a sort of voluntary exile in foreign circumstances he did not like, this world of art was literally the homeland of his soul."

In subsequent chapters of *Reflections*, Mann seems to take it all back, insisting that liberal-democratic values are foreign to German culture. The art that Germans prize is inherently amoral, he writes. "It has a basically undependable, treacherous grounding; its joy in scandalous unreason, its tendency to beauty-creating 'barbarism,' cannot be rooted out, yes, one may even call this tendency hysterical, anti-intellectual, immoral to the point of endangering the world." A citation of Baudelaire's *Tannhäuser* essay follows—an uncharacteristic passage in which the poet associates the music with warlike heroes on the march. Despite that reassertion of savage *Kultur*, Mann had exposed his inner vacillation on the subject of Germanness. A turn toward cosmopolitan liberalism was inevitable. His need to be recognized as a European artist ultimately outweighed his need to be recognized as a German one.

The conversion did not happen overnight. During the upheavals of 1919, Mann wavered between moments of revolutionary fervor and a longing for military order. His brother's derision of Wagner could still instill "feelings of hate." (After the war, Heinrich wrote of the "poisoned emotions and falsified spirit" that emanated from the Wagner business.) The diaries contain approving comments about Oswald Spengler's conservative-pessimistic opus *The Decline of the West*, which, without falling into explicit racism, cast doubt on the mixing of global cultures.

Reflections even has a few warm words for Houston Stewart Chamberlain. What jolted Mann awake was the unprecedented viciousness of the far right. In the summer of 1922, militants assassinated Walter Rathenau, then the foreign minister. Mann endorsed the Weimar Republic that fall, in a lecture-essay titled "On the German Republic."

Mann's picture of liberal democracy is an idiosyncratic one, filtered through his erotic fixations. The most unorthodox passage of "On the German Republic" exalts Walt Whitman's conception of American comradeship, describing it as an "all-embracing kingdom of phallically sacred, phallically bursting ardor." Mann had been reading Hans Blüher's studies of homoerotic bonds in all-male organizations, and wished to suggest that such sensual friendships between men could serve peaceful as well as warlike ends. Earlier in the speech, hoping to persuade an imagined audience of restive German youth that democracy is not an alien import, Mann brings Wagner into the discussion:

> Have you heard the *Meistersinger* lately? Well, Nietzsche declares in his sparkling way that they [the Mastersingers] are aimed "against civilization," that they pit "German against French." Even so, they are democracy through and through, democratic in the same degree and in the same exemplary fashion as Shakespeare's *Coriolanus* is aristocratic—they are, I say, German democracy, and they prove, with the sturdiest pomp and in the most romantically heartfelt way, that this compound word, far from being contrary to nature or betraying rigid logic, is instead as organically correct and well-fitting as perhaps only one other could be: "German *Volk*."

How many young Germans were swayed by this quirky gloss of *Meistersinger* is unknown. But the author had found his mature political path.

Casual readers of Mann's fiction might have thought that the author was losing interest in Wagner. The massive novel *The Magic Mountain*, begun in 1913 and finished only in 1924, is set at a Davos sanatorium called the Berghof, but, in contrast to the Einfried clinic of Mann's *Tristan* novella, this facility is almost entirely Wagner-free. Aside from two passing references to *Tannhäuser*, the composer goes unmentioned in a thousand or so pages. Instead, the inmates busy themselves with modern trends: the libido, health fads, séances, the cinema, the phonograph. Hans Castorp, a malleable young man who visits his ailing cousin and ends up staying at the Berghof for seven years, is no great intellectual and lacks the interior depth of other Mann protagonists. The post-Wagnerian culture of the future is arriving.

All the same, no work of Mann's could have escaped Wagner's pull. Vaget notes that the title *Zauberberg* points toward the Venusberg, the *Tannhäuser* pleasure grotto. Indeed, Mann referred to his earliest imagining of the story as the "Hörselberg idea"—the Hörselberg, near Eisenach, being a traditional site of the Venusberg. The Berghof is another Venus flytrap, from which most patients can exit only in a coffin. Its chief lure is the seductive Russian patient Clavdia Chauchat, who vaguely resembles Kundry in her "Asiatic" appearance.

Castorp himself is a Parsifalian pure fool, albeit one who never grows into a hero. He survives the Berghof, but at the end of the novel he vanishes into the battlefields of the Great War, unlikely to emerge intact. We know that *Parsifal* was on Mann's mind as he wrote, because in his diaries he comments on the "domain of sickness" that his novel-in-progress shares with Wagner's opera. In 1939, the American poet Howard Nemerov, then a Harvard undergraduate, sent Mann a copy of his thesis, "The Quester Hero," which interpreted *The Magic Mountain* as a modern Grail quest. Mann replied: "I especially noticed the parallel between the repeatedly emphasized plainness and simplicity of my hero and the motivic title *fool, great fool, guilless fool* [*sic*] of the Quester heroes, and Wagner's 'pure fool' certainly belongs there as well." Castorp is a German cousin of Claude Wheeler, the doomed youth in Willa Cather's *One of Ours*.

At the Berghof, Castorp stands by as two intellectual knights—the Italian liberal humanist Settembrini and the Jewish-Jesuit nihilist Naphta—joust for his soul. The latter character, based partly on the Marxist philosopher Georg Lukács, represents the danger of a slide into charismatic, dictatorial politics, whether on the extreme left or on the extreme right. (The fact that Naphta lives in an apartment draped with brightly colored silks gives him a tinge of Wagner.) Settembrini is to some extent a satirical figure—he has his origins in the *Zivilisationsliterat* figure of *Reflections of a Nonpolitical Man*—but he speaks for the author as he warns of the hazards of Romanticism, aestheticism, morbid pessimism, and, especially, music. Music is "politically suspect," Settembrini says. It can numb us, drug us, send us into a dream-world. Or it can inflame our emotions without properly directing them. "Literature must precede it. By itself, music cannot draw the world forward. By itself, music is dangerous."

No music is specified as the subject of this discussion, but Wagner is obviously the dangerous entity in question. In denying that music alone can draw the world forward, Settembrini is opposing the Schopenhauer-Wagner cult of music. His skepticism about music's opiate effects echoes Nietzsche's critique of decadence. Mann is giving voice to his own misgivings over his Wagnerite youth and over the path he took during the First World War. He is admitting that his brother may have been right all along.

Musical danger flares again in "Fullness of Harmony," one of the novel's closing chapters. A high-quality phonograph arrives at the Berghof, with a treasury of records. Castorp takes control of the device and appoints himself its guardian. The episode reflects Mann's own penchant for home listening; naturally, Wagner dominated his collection. Castorp's taste is more cosmopolitan, favoring Italian and French music over German. His playlist has only one Wagner item—Wolfram's aria *Blick' ich umher in diesem edlen Kreise*" ("When I cast my eye around this noble circle"), from *Tannhäuser*—and when Castorp talks about it he dwells not on the music itself but on the realistic recording of the harp. This multinational selection testifies to Castorp's spiritual progress under Settembrini's tutelage. He has become, Vaget says, a "good European."

Yet Castorp is vulnerable to what Settembrini calls "spiritual backsliding"—the Romantic enticement of "sympathy with death." He listens to "Der Lindenbaum," from Schubert's song cycle *Winterreise*, in which the brokenhearted protagonist passes a linden tree and hears it whispering to him, seducing him toward oblivion: "Come to me, friend / Here you will find rest." The same invitation murmurs to Castorp. He must overcome the *Seelenzauber*, the "enchantment of souls," and affirm his fundamental love of life. A famous passage follows:

> In the solitude of night, Hans Castorp's thoughts, or intuitive half-thoughts, soared high as he sat before his truncated musical coffin—ah, they soared higher than his understanding, were thoughts enhanced, forced upward by alchemy. Oh, it was mighty, this enchantment of the soul. We were all its sons, and we could all do mighty things on earth by serving it. One need not be a genius, all one needed was a great deal more talent than the author of this little song about a linden

tree to become a *Seelenzauberkünstler* [artist of soul enchantment], who would then give the song such vast dimensions that it would subjugate the world. One might even found whole empires upon it, earthly, all-too-earthly empires, very coarse, very progressive, and not in the least nostalgic—his truncated musical coffin, inside which the song decayed into some electrical gramophone music. But the song's best son may yet have been the young man who consumed his life in triumphing over himself and died, a new word on his lips, the word of love, which he did not yet know how to speak. It was truly worth dying for, this song of enchantment [*Zauberlied*]. But he who died for it was no longer really dying for this song and was a hero only because ultimately he died for something new—for the new word of love and for the future in his heart—Those, then, were Hans Castorp's favorite recordings.

What music is really playing here? Schubert's melancholy song is having to carry a rather heavy world-historical burden. And who is this dying young man? The first-time reader will think of Castorp's unlucky cousin Joachim. The return reader will think ahead to Castorp's final fate: in the last paragraphs of the novel, he is seen singing "Der Lindenbaum" amid the chaos of the trenches. But all this is an extended message in code, as Mann scholars have long been aware. The soul-enchanting artist is Wagner; the young man is Nietzsche.

We know this because in November 1924, a few weeks before the publication of *The Magic Mountain*, Mann gave a lecture about Nietzsche's relationship with Wagner. There he explained that if Wagner was the supreme self-glorifier then Nietzsche was the supreme self-overcomer. The philosopher succeeded in transcending his weakness for Wagner's "magic song of death"—the "paradoxical and eternally gripping phenomenon of world-conquering death-drunkenness." Mann then recited, almost word for word, the passage quoted above, though with no mention of Castorp and no indication that his new novel was the source.

When Wagner's name is substituted for Schubert's, the image of an empire founded on music comes into focus. It conjures the Wagnerian Kaiserreich, as Heinrich Mann depicted it in *Der Untertan*. For the modern reader, it also stirs thoughts of Nazi Germany. (In the thirties, émigrés ironically referred to Hitler's Alpine retreat, the Berghof, as the Magic Mountain.) But Mann wrote in an optimistic spirit, not in one of gloomy prophecy. Circa 1924, he had a vision of a peaceful world arising from the ashes of war. The new word of love, the "dream of love," returns in the novel's final sentences, bringing with it a tremor of Whitman's erotic democracy. It is also not unlike the "new idea" that glimmers in Cather's *One of Ours*. As Vaget observes, Mann's innocent phrase seems the verbal equivalent of the so-called "Redemption through Love" melody that gleams above Wagner's twilight of the gods. Still, Mann was prescient enough to end with a question mark: "And out of this worldwide festival of death, this ugly rutting fever that inflames the rainy evening sky all round—will love someday rise up out of this, too?"

HITLER IN BAYREUTH

Hitler with Wagner's grandsons, 1931

Mann knew very well where Hitler came from. In 1938, in American exile, he wrote: "Embarrassingly enough, it is all there: the 'difficulty,' the laziness, the pathetic formlessness in youth; the nowhere-fitting-in; the what-do-you-actually-want?; the half-stupid vegetating in deepest social and spiritual bohemia; the basic arrogance, the basic feeling of being too good for any reasonable, honorable activity—based on what? Based on a vague notion of being reserved for something else, something quite indeterminate, which, if it were named, would cause people to break out laughing." This is from an essay originally titled "Der Bruder"; *Esquire* magazine published a translation as "That Man Is My Brother." Mann recognized Hitler as a malevolent mutation of the dreamer-artist type he so often depicted in his stories.

It is all there—including Wagner. Mann makes more definite the connection, already implicit in *The Magic Mountain*, between Bayreuth sorcery and the fantasy of "subjugating the world." (The essay uses the same phrase as the novel.) He sees Hitler's rise as a twisted fairy tale—the ugly duckling who becomes a swan, the prince who rescues a sleeping beauty, Siegfried awakening Brünnhilde. "The whole thing is Wagnerish, in a debased form, as has long been noticed, and we know of the well-founded, though a bit unauthorized, reverence that the political wonder-worker holds for the artistic enchanter of Europe."

Hitler entered German politics amid the revolutionary and counter-revolutionary turmoil of 1918 and 1919. Because he had remained in the army after the end of the war, he was nominally serving the socialist governments that initially held power in Bavaria. Although he never showed an active inclination toward the socialists, he paid close attention to their tactics and pageantry. In *Mein Kampf*, Hitler writes admiringly of a demonstration he witnessed in Berlin—"a sea of red flags, red scarves, and red flowers . . . a spectacle grandiose in effect." The historian Brigitte Hamann surmised that Hitler might have encountered leftist Wagnerism during his Vienna years: Wilhelm Ellenbogen, author of "Richard Wagner und das Proletariat," was the deputy for Brigittenau, the Viennese district where Hitler lived from 1910 to 1913.

In the summer of 1919, after the ratification of the Treaty of Versailles, Hitler began taking army propaganda classes, which responded to Bolshevism by promoting hard-core pan-Germanism and antisemitism. He was sent out to monitor political activities in Munich, and it was in that capacity that he first attended a meeting of the German Workers' Party. Also present were Alfred Rosenberg, Hans Frank, and Rudolf Hess, future Nazi stalwarts. Hitler drew particularly close to Dietrich Eckart, a poet, playwright, and critic who was best known for his adaptation of Ibsen's *Peer Gynt*. A devout Wagnerite, Eckart had first gone to Bayreuth in 1894 and had written about *Parsifal* for a festival guide. Hitler said in one of his wartime monologues that Eckart had imparted a sense of Bayreuth's "wonderful" atmosphere.

In a 1919 poem titled "Patience," Eckart had pictured a Siegfried-like hero waiting for the "hour of retribution." Hitler stepped into that role at a

February 1920 meeting of the National Socialist German Workers' Party, as it had been renamed. When he recounted his breakthrough speech at the end of the first book of *Mein Kampf*, Hitler employed a Wagner metaphor: "A fire was kindled, from whose glow must come one day the sword that will win back freedom for the Germanic Siegfried and life for the German nation." That August, he delivered the speech "Why We Are Antisemites," confirming his Führer status with a bloodthirsty attack on Jewish "parasites." Wagner was cited twice: first, as a symbol of the "period in which Germany grew from the shame of powerlessness to the unified great German empire"; and, second, as a token of the sacred power of the theater, which elevates the individual from "all wretchedness and misery . . . into purer air." By 1922, Wagner excerpts were introducing Hitler's speeches in Munich. *Meistersinger*'s thunderous chorus of "Wach auf"—"Awake"—blended with the slogan emblazoned on Nazi standards and banners: "*Deutschland erwache!*"

Eyewitnesses report that Hitler's Munich apartment contained a record player, a stack of Wagner records, copies of the composer's writings, and Chamberlain's Wagner biography. Hitler's literacy as a Wagnerite assisted his rise, especially when it came to procuring support from the moneyed classes. He won over Edwin and Helene Bechstein, of the piano-manufacturing firm. He also formed a bond with Ernst Hanfstaengl, a musically gifted German-American whose paternal grandfather had made photographic portraits of Wagner and Ludwig II. Hanfstaengl had attended Harvard, where he knew T. S. Eliot. In 1922, he heard Hitler speak in Munich, and, mesmerized by his oratory, struck up a friendship. At one of their early meetings, Hanfstaengl played *Meistersinger* at the piano, sending Hitler into raptures. "He knew the thing absolutely by heart," Hanfstaengl recalled, "and could whistle every note of it in a curious penetrating vibrato, but completely in tune. He started to march up and down the hall, waving his arms as if he was conducting an orchestra."

In September 1919, Gabriele d'Annunzio led a march on the Adriatic city of Fiume, which had been part of Austria-Hungary and which d'Annunzio now wished to seize for Italy. When Italy rejected his initiative, the author proclaimed himself *il Duce* of an independent republic. The venture lasted little more than a year, but before it ended d'Annunzio had invented much of the iconography of Fascism: blackshirt uniforms, straight-arm salutes, speeches from balconies, paramilitary cadres, chanting crowds of youth, ritualistic symbols and insignia. By the time Benito Mussolini made his March on Rome in 1922, he had appropriated a good part of d'Annunzio's aesthetic.

At the end of September 1923, Hitler arrived in Bayreuth to speak at a "German Day" gathering. There, according to the later recollections of the Bayreuth Nazi leader Hans Schemm, he affirmed that the National Socialist movement was "anchored in the works of Richard Wagner." As paramilitary *Sturmabteilung* (SA) units paraded through the city, Siegfried Wagner offered greetings from outside Wahnfried and received shouts of "Heil!" in return. Chamberlain, who had been debilitated by symptoms resembling those of Parkinson's disease, waved from the veranda of his house, with the frail, eighty-five-year-old Cosima Wagner looking on. After giving a speech, Hitler called on Chamberlain; at a reception at the Hotel Goldener Anker, he met Winifred Wagner, and received an invitation to Wahnfried. He set foot inside the house the following morning, his hands shaking with excitement as he studied relics of the master. He also stood in silence at Wagner's grave. Cosima did not descend.

The awe that Hitler evinced at Wahnfried was undoubtedly sincere, yet it also served a calculated end. Plans for the Beer Hall Putsch were in motion—a coup in Munich, followed by a march on Berlin—and by basking in Bayreuth's aura Hitler could distinguish himself from the thuggish plotters who had preceded him. In a speech in Nuremberg, he said: "We feel the artist Richard Wagner to be so great because in all his works he represented heroic *Volkstum*, Germanness. The heroic is the great. That is what our people desire."

The failure of the putsch should have ended Hitler's political career, but he shrewdly used the subsequent trial to increase his fame and propagate his ideas. Winifred was one of many who fell yet more deeply under his spell. She told local Nazi Party members that Hitler remained the "coming man," the one who would "pull the sword from the German ash tree"— just as Siegmund retrieves his father's sword in *Walküre*. Hitler himself used the Nothung metaphor in a letter he sent to Siegfried Wagner from Landsberg prison, describing Bayreuth as the place where "first through the Master and then through Chamberlain was forged the spiritual sword with which we fight today." While Hitler was in prison, the Wagners, the

Bechsteins, and a distinguished new pair of friends—Hugo Bruckmann, Chamberlain's publisher, and his wife, Elsa—sent care packages that included records and a phonograph. Wagner's music resounded often in Landsberg, with Hitler listening lost in thought, as a comrade recalled. He must have been encouraged when he received a letter from Chamberlain praising his "Parsifal nature."

In early 1924, while Hitler was awaiting trial, Siegfried and Winifred took a fund-raising trip to America. They played a tricky game: on the one hand, they asked American Jews for contributions, and on the other they met with the outspoken antisemite Henry Ford, who had been identified as a potential benefactor of the Nazi Party. Ford, however, was no Wagnerite, and shied away from helping Hitler directly. American Jews, for their part, could not help noticing that Siegfried tended to blurt out antisemitic slurs after he had had too much to drink—so a biting Berlin critic reported. In a subsequent letter to Hitler, Winifred tried to explain the family's tortured logic regarding Jews. Bayreuth transcends politics, she wrote, and cannot become an arm of the *völkisch* movement. Jewish attendees should not be insulted in public, for "the ones who come to Bayreuth are not the Jews who deserve such drastic treatment."

When Hitler first attended performances at Bayreuth, in 1925, he kept a low profile, stealing into the Wagners' box just before the music started. He did not return to the festival until 1933, partly in order to avoid causing a political disruption, although he also objected to the continued presence of Jewish singers. Still, he visited Wahnfried frequently, often arriving after dark. He fawned over the Wagner grandsons and liked to be called "Wolf"—the name that Wotan adopts when he roams the earth and sires the Wälsung twins. Winifred's rapport with Hitler generated rumors that the two might be romantically involved. Although the chatter had no substance, Winifred was clearly infatuated with Hitler to some degree. Hitler, for his part, was smitten with the family, the name, the place, and, above all, the music.

"Hitler, Adolf, writer, Munich," reads the entry in the Bayreuth guest lists for 1925. A few days before he arrived, the first volume of *Mein Kampf* had been published. Several antisemitic passages in that book come exceedingly close to Wagner's formulations about the Jews. Hitler deploys the vile word that the composer popularized—"*Verjudung*," Jewification. As Wagner spoke of the Jewification of art, Hitler speaks of the "inner

Jewification of our people." Wagner wrote, "The Jew has never had an art of his own"; Hitler writes, "The Jew never called a culture his own." For Wagner, Jews were a "swarming colony of worms that takes up residence in the body of art"; for Hitler, they are "a parasite in the body of other peoples."

On at least one occasion, in a 1929 harangue against Jewish Bolshevism, Hitler fashioned antisemitic rhetoric directly from Wagnerian material, warning of an *"Alberichs-Herrschaft"*—a Nibelung empire poised to destroy the German people. Such metaphors were not uncommon in the writings of the most extreme Nazi Wagnerites. For the *Völkischer Beobachter*, Stolzing-Cerny wrote a multipart essay titled "The World War in the *Ring of the Nibelung*," which compares the downfall of the gods to the betrayal of the Reich at the hands of Jews and Bolsheviks, with Wilhelm II's "superficial glory" complicit in the collapse. Alberich is said to embody the "dark spirit of Jewish Mammonism," of "Judeocracy and Social Democracy." A Nazi-era guide to the *Ring* put the allegory most bluntly: "The German people (Siegfried) smashes the power of capitalism (Fafner) and slays Jewishness (Mime)."

Hitler must have read "Jewishness in Music," and he may have perused antisemitic Wagner essays such as Stolzing-Cerny's. Somewhat astonishingly, though, he never directly quoted Wagner on the subject of the Jews. Indeed, as both Saul Friedländer and Dina Porat have established, nowhere in the entire corpus of Hitler's writings, speeches, and recorded utterances is there an unmistakable reference to Wagner's antisemitism. Why is this? The transitional nature of the composer's prejudice may help to explain the silence. Wagner's antisemitism, ferocious as it was, stopped just short of "scientific" or "biological" racism; his conception of Jewishness remained quasi-metaphorical and subject to spiritual transformation. Hitler's worldview had no room for miracles of redemption in the *Parsifal* mode.

No less important, Hitler's relationship with Wagner remained one of musical fandom rather than of ideological fanaticism. His knowledge of the operas was pedantically acute: he impressed artists and fellow music lovers with detailed commentary on tempos, cuts, and matters of interpretation. But he gave no sign of having absorbed Wagner's grander themes—the critique of power in the *Ring*, the consecration of compassion in *Parsifal*. Instead, he indulged in fuzzy speculations: "When I hear Wagner, it seems to me like the rhythms of the primeval world. And I imagine that one day science will discover pulses of creation in the relationships between the physically perceptible sound waves of a Rheingold music." Such breathless rhapsodies, documented during the Second World War, recall the postcards that the teenaged Hitler wrote to his friend Kubizek ("Powerful waves of sound flood the room").

In a paradoxical way, Hitler's uncomplicated, seemingly apolitical devotion to Wagner assisted in the politicization of the composer in the Third Reich. The Meister served the regime better when he was kept away from the specifics of policy. Floating above the fray, enshrined in the German Valhalla, he appeared to look benignly at the work of his disciple.

THE NAZI WAGNER

Benno von Arent's staging of Die Meistersinger

Hitler was named chancellor on January 30, 1933, two weeks before the fiftieth anniversary of Wagner's death. On Hitler's third day in office, his cabinet was already discussing the upcoming Wagner commemorations and what role Party leaders should play in them. On February 12, Hitler appeared at two memorial events in succession. First, in the company of Winifred Wagner and her son Wieland, he attended a morning concert at the Gewandhaus in Leipzig, at which the elderly Karl Muck conducted the *Parsifal* and *Meistersinger* preludes. Later that day, Hitler went to Weimar to see *Tristan*, visiting Elisabeth Förster-Nietzsche in her box. He thus aligned himself with two German titans, eliding their differences in the process.

More elaborate ceremonies unrolled as the year progressed. At the Day of Potsdam on March 21, 1933, the Nazis staged a propaganda spectacle linking the new regime with the heritage of the Prussian state, embodied in President Paul von Hindenburg, who had been present at the founding of the empire. In the same period, Hitler was assuming dictatorial powers—a process made official when the Reichstag passed the Enabling Act two days later. A performance of *Meistersinger*, itself a symbol of the Kaiserreich, capped the day's events. Hitler and his entourage made their way to the Berlin Staatsoper via a torchlight parade, taking their seats in time for the nationalist pomp of Act III. As the chorus sang "Wach auf," they seemed to address the Führer. The *Völkischer Beobachter* evoked "the savior who sat above in his box and followed the performance with a unique light in his eyes and sympathetic understanding."

That summer, Hitler returned to Bayreuth. Perhaps with the demonstrations of 1924 in mind, he ordered the distribution of cards asking audiences not to sing patriotic songs, since "there is no more glorious expression of the German spirit than the immortal works of the Master himself." Still, Bayreuth warped itself around Hitler's presence. Swastikas flew everywhere; in bookstores, *Mein Kampf* was displayed in place of Wagner's *Mein Leben*; members of the SA sang the "Horst Wessel" song in cafés. One performance was delayed while Hitler flew in from Berlin. Walter Legge, reporting for the *Manchester Guardian*, wrote that one could easily have "mistaken this year's Wagner festival for a Hitler festival." When German radio broadcast *Meistersinger* from Bayreuth in August, Joseph Goebbels gave an intermission talk titled "Richard Wagner and the Artistic Taste of Our Time." In the same month, Hitler traveled to Neuschwanstein, Ludwig II's castle, for another Wagner celebration. The castle, Hitler said, was the "protest of a genius against pitiful parliamentary mediocrity." Democracy had blocked German greatness; a new golden age was at hand. Wagner selections were sung, and, according to the *Beobachter*, Hitler listened "leaning forward, his eyes shining and his face serious."

At the end of the summer came the annual Reich Party Days in

Nuremberg—the city of Dürer, of Hans Sachs, of *Meistersinger* itself. Hitler declared that he had chosen Nuremberg as the site of all future rallies because "our movement is nothing less than the continuation not only of German greatness but of German culture." Strains of *Meistersinger* were heard throughout the rally. Trumpets intoned the opera's opening phrase; a children's chorus sang "Wach auf"; an orchestra played the Act I prelude; and, at the end of the first day, Hitler attended a performance of the entire work at the Nuremberg Opera. Leni Riefenstahl was on hand with her cameras, and her half-hour propaganda film *The Victory of Faith* begins with scenes of the old city, accompanied by the brass chorales from the *Meistersinger* Act III prelude. Riefenstahl placed a similar sequence in her full-length film *Triumph of the Will*, based on the 1934 rally. Wagner is heard as an emanation from the past, in pensive contrast to the muscular Nazi present.

This flurry of Wagneriana in the first months of the Nazi regime set a pattern that remained in place until 1939. The composer had a consistent ritual function at the annual Nuremberg rallies. The *Rienzi* overture was played on opening day, and Gottfried Sonntag's *Nibelungen-Marsch* medley set the stage for Hitler's closing speech. The Nuremberg Opera presented gala performances of *Meistersinger*. Party ceremony and stage ceremony merged. The parade of delegates and banners on the rally grounds resembled the meadow scene in *Meistersinger*, while the tall, thin banners lining Benno von Arent's 1935 staging of that scene mimicked Nazi decor. The bass-baritone Wilhelm Rode, an ardent Nazi, gave a vaguely Hitlerian mien to his Hans Sachs. In film footage from the Deutsches Opernhaus in Berlin, Rode is seen raising his arm in a gesture that could be mistaken for a "Hitler greeting."

Wagner and Hitler were often mentioned in the same breath. The critic and composer Siegfried Scheffler wrote of the first Nazi Bayreuth Festival: "*Richard Wagner and Adolf Hitler*—two Führers encounter each other in the fateful year 1933." A writer in the *Bayreuther Blätter* exclaimed: "*Heil dem Führer! Heil dem Meister! Heil Deutschland! Heil Bayreuth!*" Another wrote: "Hitler's spirit is Wagner's spirit [*Hitlergeist ist Wagnergeist*]." Weekly Party posters with inspirational sayings included messages from the Meister: "To be German is to do something for its own sake"; "I am fully myself only when I create." A new edition of "Jewishness in Music" was billed as one of the "nation's most precious documents."

Nazi propaganda sometimes cast Hitler as a knightlike figure in the mode of Lohengrin or Parsifal. In one image, he wore shining armor; in another, he held the pole of a swastika flag as a militaristic dove or eagle hovered overhead. Artistic representations of Wagner bestowed similar godlike properties. In a bronze bust by the sculptor Arno Breker, a favorite of Hitler's, the Meister glowers coldly, his righteous rage interchangeable with that of Beethoven and other German geniuses. In 1940, Goebbels recorded Hitler's remarks about this bust: "It is the art of sculpture to depict the characteristic and enduring traits in a human head, without recourse to photography or mere fantasy." A smaller Breker bust of Wagner occupied a place of honor at Hitler's Berghof refuge, sitting atop a cabinet that contained a speaker system and phonograph records. Wagner's death mask was also on display.

To all appearances, Wagner's position as a Nazi cultural deity was secure. The equation of Meister with Führer found acceptance not only in Germany but also in the outside world. In August 1939, the British humor magazine *Punch* ran a cartoon titled "The Wagnerite," which showed Hitler lost in a reverie at a performance of *Walküre*—an image inoffensive enough that Winifred Wagner pasted a copy into a portfolio of Bayreuth renovation plans that she gave to the dictator. Behind the scenes, though, the composer's complexities caused trouble. He was too strange, too

Arno Breker's Wagner bust

eccentric, to serve as a reliable ideological bulwark. Nor was his work popular enough, in the mass-market sense, to operate as a unifying force. Nazi culture was in large measure a modern, technologically driven, American-style media landscape, and Wagner's place in it was uncertain.

For members of Hitler's inner circle, trips to Bayreuth were all but mandatory. The signatures of Goebbels, Himmler, Göring, and other high-ranking Nazis are visible in the old guestbook of the Hotel Goldener Anker, which, back in 1912, had hosted a party of young American women from Macon, Georgia. (When Thomas Mann passed through Bayreuth in 1949, he looked at the hotel guestbook and noted the names of the "whole devil's brood.") In many cases, the appreciation was genuine. Baldur von Schirach, the head of the Hitler Youth, and Reinhard Heydrich, the chief of the Reich Security Main Office, both came from cultured households. Schirach's father, Carl, had been the Intendant of the National Theater in Weimar; Heydrich's father, Bruno, was a singer, composer, and pedagogue who had success in the major Wagner tenor parts and wrote operas titled *Amen*, *Peace*, and *Chance*. Julius Streicher, the party's chief antisemitic propagandist, quoted from *Meistersinger* when he ordered the razing of Nuremberg's central synagogue: "*Fanget an!*" ("Let us begin!").

Amid the rote praise, doubts about Wagner's real ideological value arose. Alfred Rosenberg, the Party's self-styled philosopher, approved of the composer's outspoken antisemitism, but, in the tradition of *volkisch* thinkers like Paul de Lagarde, Julius Langbehn, and Adolf Bartels, he saw signs of "high decadence" in the Bayreuth operation, to use Bartels's phrase. In his book *The Myth of the Twentieth Century*, a kind of sequel to Chamberlain's *Foundations of the Nineteenth Century*, Rosenberg criticizes *Parsifal* for manifesting a "strongly church-inflected weakening in favor of borrowed values." In his diary, Rosenberg complained about the Wagner cult, saying that the remorseful side of the heroes Tannhäuser and Parsifal contradicted Nazi ethics. Nietzsche deserves to be ranked higher, since Wagner "already had his triumph."

Parsifal, with its ethos of compassion, caused the most trouble. Goebbels, Rosenberg, and Himmler all thought that it should be removed from the repertory because its quasi-Christian message was irreconcilable with Nazi ideology. Hitler thought this criticism foolish, although he had no use for the opera's churchly trappings. He told the Wagner grandsons to think about designing a "timeless Grail Temple"—a setting that "takes us into the mystical, thus into the indefinable and the intangible." Wieland Wagner was nonplussed to hear Hitler saying that he wanted "to have *Parsifal* performed so to speak *against* his own party!!!!"

Certainly, *Parsifal* could be construed as a work in praise of racial purification, as early *Bayreuther Blätter* writers had argued. In 1942, Otto Daube, a Bayreuth musicologist turned youth leader, posited Parsifal as a second Siegfried and Klingsor as the "Jewish-Oriental spirit of decay." Still, *Parsifal*'s overriding message of "knowing through compassion"—*"durch Mitleid wissend"*—diverged from a Nazi culture that all but outlawed sentimental weakness. In December 1941, as the slaughter of Jews, Poles, and Russians coalesced into organized genocide, Hitler expressly directed Germans to suppress feelings of *Mitleid*. Goebbels paraphrased him, saying: "We are not here to feel compassion for the Jews, but only to feel compassion for our German people." A few days later, Hans Frank, the governor-general of occupied Poland, told senior officials: "Gentlemen, I must ask you to steel yourself against all considerations of compassion. We must annihilate the Jews wherever we find them." Hans Stark, the head of the admissions detail at Auschwitz, had a sign over his desk reading *"Mitleid ist Schwäche"*—weakness. The Nazis liked to cite Nietzsche as a source of such bloodless sayings, and indeed one finds the following in *The Antichrist*: "People have ventured to call *Mitleid* a virtue (—in every *noble* morality it counts as *Schwäche*—)."

For most rank-and-file Nazis, such debates were of remote interest. They had little appetite for Hitler's Wagner-appreciation exercises and often fled from them. One party-rally *Meistersinger* turned into a fiasco when, according to Albert Speer, Hitler arrived at the Nuremberg opera house and was vexed to find it almost empty:

> He had patrols sent out to fetch high Party functionaries from their quarters, beer halls, and wine bars to the opera house; but this effort did not succeed in filling the auditorium . . . The next year Hitler expressly ordered theater-averse Party leaders to attend the gala. They appeared bored, and many were visibly overwhelmed by sleep. In Hitler's opinion, the thinly scattered applause was far from appropriate to the brilliant performance.

At the 1936 *Meistersinger*, it was observed that places reserved for important guests were instead occupied by "1. the wife of the dentist Eckerlein

2. a typist from police headquarters 3. the proprietress of the Kakadu cabaret." Evidently, tickets were being given away or sold on the side. Hitler subsequently ordered that *Meistersinger* should be attended "only by those visitors who have a genuine interest in it." To that end, the distribution of free tickets was stopped. Still, the problem persisted: in 1938, guests at a nearby hotel were ordered to fill empty seats. Hitler was also heard to complain that his underlings regularly fell asleep at Berlin performances of *Tristan und Isolde*, and that he had to wake them up to stop their snoring.

Hitler wished to foster a culture in which Wagner and the rest of the classical-music legacy would no longer be limited to the elites. Opera houses should hold more people, and tickets should be cheaper. Nonetheless, Wagner's popularity on German stages actually declined during the Nazi era. In the 1932–33 season, there were 1,837 performances of the operas; in 1939–40, there were 1,154. The same period saw an increase in performances of Verdi, Puccini, and Lortzing. Wagnerites sometimes lamented a dwindling of interest in the music dramas among the young. A contributor to the 1936 Bayreuth Festival guide noted the case of a young female Nazi Party member who had written off Wagner as a "typical agent of liberalism." Christian von Ehrenfels, the philosopher who once counted up the orgasms in *Tristan*, had written in 1931 that "a large proportion of a-Semitic [non-Jewish] German youth take a position against Wagner." In some Hitler Youth circles, Wagner was considered unwholesome, excessively sensual, pessimistic, lacking in Nordic purity.

As Goebbels knew, the general public was most avid for hit songs, dance music, operetta melodies, and light classics. The historian Michael Kater finds that radio programming of Wagner and other so-called serious composers fluctuated in accordance with the political situation: there was more of it when Goebbels was worried about foreign perceptions, less when he wished to firm up domestic opinion. Once the war began, some young conscripts showed active distaste for classical music. "The soldier who is fighting at the battle-front wants light music, dance, and jazz," a respondent to a Wehrmacht survey wrote. American-style pop, especially jazz, had thrived during the Weimar Republic. Although the Nazis denounced jazz at every opportunity, they never formally banned it nationwide, and later found it expedient to give the public what it wanted. Records by Duke Ellington, Louis Armstrong, and Benny Goodman were played, but with the titles changed and the names suppressed. Anti-American propaganda notwithstanding, the Third Reich was to some extent a Fascist makeover of American consumer society, with mass culture, sports, and high-tech gadgetry predominating.

In 1930, Ernst Jünger, author of *Storm of Steel*, stated in his essay "Total Mobilization" that America had won the First World War because it mobilized the entire nation—politically, technologically, culturally. The Central Powers, by contrast, were hidebound by a "proclivity for the employment of outmoded trappings, for a late-Romantic style, especially that of the Wagner operas." The ruling classes, with their high-flown talk of *Nibelungentreue*, could not relate to the new mass public. Culture makes for poor propaganda: it neglects the "primal power of the *Volk*." This popular orientation, which was the core of the Goebbels strategy, displaced Hitler's Wagnerism in the later years of the regime.

B ayreuth was a protected zone within the totalitarian state. Hitler's patronage meant that the festival was beyond the grasp of such warring authorities as Goebbels, Göring, and Rosenberg. The Führer stepped half outside his dictatorial role when he arrived in Bayreuth each summer. For a little while, he would revert to his younger bohemian self—"free of the pressure to display power," Albert Speer said. Staying at the Siegfried Wagner house, next to Wahnfried, Hitler adopted the Wagners as a surrogate family, showering favors on Wieland, the heir apparent. The young man was given a Mercedes, and Hitler's chauffeur monitored his first long-distance drive. During the war, when Hitler stopped going to the opera, he wistfully recalled his visits: "The ten days of Bayreuth have always been the most beautiful time for me, and how I look forward to the first moment when we return!" The day after the festival reminded him of the sad moment when ornaments are removed from the Christmas tree. He spoke of retiring to Bayreuth in old age.

With Hitler's backing, Winifred Wagner set about modernizing Bayreuth's productions. By 1933, she had brought in the conductor and stage director Heinz Tietjen, who had prospered in the Weimar era, and the designer Emil Preetorius, who had fashioned book covers for Thomas Mann. The simplified decor and expressive lighting in Preetorius's work represented a cautious move toward the modernist theater of Adolphe Appia and Edward Gordon Craig. (Hitler's fascination with theater history led him to purchase the personal archive of Craig, who was stranded in Paris during the Occupation.) When Winifred announced that the old *Parsifal* staging would be replaced in the 1934 festival, a phalanx of old-time Wagnerites led by Daniela Thode and Eva Chamberlain rose up in protest. Despite their Nazi leanings, the half-sisters shrank from what Thode termed the "politicization" of Bayreuth. Winifred prevailed. Hitler proposed that Alfred Roller, whose *Tristan* had so struck him in his youth, should direct the new production—an idea Winifred and Tietjen happily accepted. The Grail Temple became a forest of pillars with a semi-secular appearance.

Ironically, though, Hitler's assumption of power sent Bayreuth into financial crisis. Foreign and Jewish visitors, who had remained a crucial part of the festival's audience even after the hyper-nationalist debacle of 1924, grew scarce: in 1933, thousands of tickets remained unsold within weeks of opening day. Hitler stepped in to save the festival. Government agencies bought up tickets and gave them to Party members, students, and the like, even supplying free travel and accommodations. Increasingly, Bayreuth played to a fictitious audience, assembled to validate Hitler's belief that he was bringing Wagner to the masses.

For some years, Winifred retained enough independence that she was able to maintain the foundational Wagnerian hypocrisy of holding anti-Jewish views while employing Jewish artists. As Brigitte Hamann's biography makes clear, Winifred periodically agitated against official policy, working to protect Jewish friends and acquaintances as well as religious figures, homosexuals, Freemasons, and other undesirables. Among those who benefited from her efforts were Alfred and Hedwig Pringsheim, Thomas Mann's parents-in-law. The gay Heldentenor Max Lorenz was shielded from prosecution, and Aryan papers were obtained for Charlotte Appel, his Jewish wife. At the 1943 festival, the sight of Lorenz socializing with Appel aroused indignation, according to an intelligence report. Despite all these gestures, Winifred's allegiance to Hitler remained absolute.

The choicest irony that haunted Bayreuth in the Nazi era was the revival of the old rumor about Wagner's concealed Jewishness. The newly founded Richard Wagner Research Center went to considerable trouble to disprove that tale, which Nietzsche had helped to spread, but it kept circulating all the same. In 1942, as the musicologist Sebastian Werr has discovered, Winifred became incensed over reports that a racial-political training course in Würzburg had included a lecture on "Jewish Kinship of the

Wagner Family," and that in local Hitler Youth groups the Wagner festival was regarded as a "Jewish concern," unsuitable for boys in uniform. Winifred had turned against the Hitler Youth some years before, when she heard people saying, "Well, we'll just have to let the Führer have his Wagner fixation." She wrote a letter to Himmler, begging him to put a stop to such talk. The family feared that in a putative post-Hitler Nazi state the festival would fall by the wayside. This was one problem the Wagners did not have to face.

MANN IN EXILE

Mann near his home in Pacific Palisades, Los Angeles

"Where I am, there is Germany," Thomas Mann said in 1938, on disembarking from the RMS *Queen Mary* in New York Harbor. When the Nazis took power, Mann at first hesitated to denounce the regime, in the hope that his books could stay on the German market. Only in 1936 did he clarify his position, and by the end of the year his writings had been banned and his citizenship revoked. Mann believed that he could protect the best of German culture, Wagner included, from Nazism. His great work of the thirties was *Joseph and His Brothers*, a novelistic tetralogy that took sixteen years to write and offered itself both as a counterpart and as a corrective to the *Ring*. In place of Teutonic mythology, Mann turned to the Old Testament, honoring Jewish heritage at a time when the Nazis were desecrating it. Joseph, son of Jacob, is analogous to Siegfried or

Parsifal, a hero who discovers and develops his extraordinary abilities. As Georg Lukács wrote in a 1936 essay, this tactic of posing a "good" myth against a "bad" one is not without risk: Fascists were better at exploiting myth to political ends.

Mann advertised the Wagnerian heft of the *Joseph* novels in an autobiographical essay that he wrote for a one-volume American edition of the cycle in 1948. He narrates the entire span of his career from the late twenties to the early forties, stressing the traumatic caesura of his Wagner lecture tour of 1933. Mann says that his desire to finish the project

> was only strengthened by certain mythic memories, playful parallels not inappropriate to the subject matter. I stood where Wagner had once stood when, after the grand interpolation of *Tristan* and *Meistersinger*, he again took up work on his dramatic epic, the vast fairy tale of *The Ring of the Nibelung*. True, my method of dealing with myth was in essence closer to the humor of Goethe's "Classic Walpurgis Night" than to Wagnerian pathos; but the unanticipated evolution that the story of Joseph had taken had, I am certain, always been secretly influenced by memories of Wagner's grand edifice of motifs, was a successor to its intentions.

The crucial word is "playful" (*verspielte*). Mann's sense of himself as a latter-day Wagner operates on at least three levels of irony: a Wagner-loving dictator was responsible for the interruption of the cycle; the Jewish subject matter tweaks the antisemitic preoccupations of Wagner and Hitler alike; and this weighty saga has a sly, self-aware tone that is generally absent from the *Ring*. As Mann grew older, he became more unguarded in his approach to sexuality, and young Joseph is given an erotic glow. Just as impish are the interludes portraying God in heaven, surrounded by a disputatious angelic hierarchy. Dignified, evasive, ambivalent, determined to plot the destiny of man in His own oblique, at times perverse fashion, the Almighty is the spitting image of Thomas Mann.

Like the *Ring*, the *Joseph* cycle begins with a Prelude (*Vorspiel*), and its first words return to the beginning of time: "Deep is the well of the past. Should we not call it bottomless?" Because this deep past takes a mythic form, it can speak directly to the present: "The essence of life is presentness, and only by means of myth does it represent its mystery in past and future tenses . . . For it *is*, always *is*, though the common phrase may be: It *was*. That is how myth speaks, for it is merely the garment of the mystery." Or, as Wagner says in *Opera and Drama*: "The incomparable thing about myth is that it is always true." Mann extends Wagner's experiments in comparative mythology and syncretic religion. Joseph's rise from the pit is likened to the stories of Tammuz, Adonis, Gilgamesh, and Christ. Joseph is himself a master of multiple tongues, weaving Hebraic thought into tales that a wider audience can grasp.

The *Joseph* text contains dozens of Wagner allusions, as Eckhard Heftrich and other scholars have documented. When Jacob, Joseph's father, is beset by shame after the apparent death of his favorite son, he is like the downcast Wotan of *Walküre*. In *Joseph in Egypt*, Huya and Tuya, the brother-and-sister parents of Joseph's employer and protector Potiphar, parody the incestuous love of Siegmund and Sieglinde. Bickering dwarfs recall Mime and Alberich, as Mann himself pointed out. The bravura sequence in which Potiphar's Wife falls desperately in love with Joseph borrows from *Tristan* and *Parsifal* as well as from *Death in Venice*. The final installment, *Joseph the Provider*, introduces the unconventional young pharaoh Amenhotep IV, later Akhenaten, who summons Joseph from prison, dubs him the "Unique Friend of the Great King," and grants him enormous administrative powers. The pharaoh's aestheticism, sensitivity, odd habits, and worshipful attraction to Joseph make him a kind of backward projection of King Ludwig.

Nazi commentators took a predictable dislike to the *Joseph* undertaking. One critic asserted that "the racial instinct rebels" against Mann's humanization of a fundamentally Jewish world. Another stated that the Old Testament had been "psychologically smeared with the problems of a decadent time." Outside of Germany, readers were at times bewildered by the scale of Mann's project and fatigued by his innumerable digressions. But the impression that he had created a kind of counter-monument to Nazi culture took hold.

Mann's American publisher, Alfred A. Knopf, Sr., also published Willa Cather. In the thirties, Knopf arranged for the two authors to meet, perhaps sensing that these outwardly conservative, inwardly radical writers had much in common. Cather had not warmed to Mann's previous work, but *Joseph and His Brothers* captivated her, and in 1936 she wrote an essay praising the cycle as it then stood. "Mann has made something like an orchestral arrangement of all the Semitic religions and philosophies," she remarked. At a dinner in 1938, Mann and Cather talked about *Joseph* face to face; on another occasion, they went to Knopf's home to listen to records and drink champagne. Whether Wagner was on the playlist is not recorded.

Mann finished *Joseph* at the beginning of 1943, in his newly built hilltop villa in Pacific Palisades, Los Angeles. He could see the Pacific Ocean from his study; scents wafted in from a grove of eucalyptus; the prospect of a life after Hitler was in sight. Nonetheless, Mann brooded over his country's fate—its "spiritual backsliding," its descent from civilization to barbarism. Within a few months, he was at work on a new book, far darker and more personal in tone. Four years later, the literary world was confronted with *Doctor Faustus: The Life of the German Composer Adrian Leverkühn, Told by a Friend*. It was the book Mann had been preparing all his life to write: the biography of a Faustian artist as an allegory of Germany's spiritual crisis. "It will be my *Parsifal*," Mann wrote to his son Klaus.

Leverkühn belongs to the modernist generation, his advanced idiom similar to that of Schoenberg and Berg, or, at times, Stravinsky. As a personality, he is far removed from the antic, sensuous Wagner: he is cold, intellectual, enigmatic, perverse. He reacts against Wagnerian values by writing music that is at once terse and dense, tragic and ironic, archaic and futuristic. Still, he is cast in a Teutonic mold. The crux of the book is a mysterious encounter with a figure who appears to be the Devil: Leverkühn gives up his soul in exchange for four-and-twenty years of esoteric mastery. Mann had long sensed something devilish at the heart of the Wagnerian pandemic, and Leverkühn, despite his anti-Romantic aesthetic, is a belated exposition of the theme.

Mann's great trick in structuring the novel is to delegate the narration to a fussy, upright, loquacious, conservative-minded spirit named Serenus Zeitblom, Leverkühn's lifelong friend. Like Aschenbach, Zeitblom is an ersatz Mann, an exercise in self-parody. He begins telling his story toward the end of May 1943—the period in which Mann set to work on the novel. Zeitblom is not in exile, however. He belongs to the so-called inner emigration—the cohort of intellectuals who professed to oppose Nazism from within. Mann rejected the concept of inner emigration when it surfaced after the war, and Zeitblom, with his ineffectual reservations about the regime, seems to stand in for such compromised figures as Gerhart Hauptmann, Gottfried Benn, Martin Heidegger, and Ernst Jünger. Although Zeitblom favors older music, he inserts occasional Wagner references into his prose, and even turns them against Nazi culture. Echoing Mann's writings on the misuse of Wagner, Zeitblom deplores the "sordid abuse and cheap peddling of what was old and genuine, faithful and familiar, of what was fundamentally German [*des Treulich-Traulichen, des Ur-Deutschen*] . . ." The last phrase nods to the Rhinemaidens' lament: "Only down deep is it trusty and true [*traulich und treu*]."

Leverkühn comes from a conservative Lutheran town named Kaisersaschern, which is modeled partly on the Naumburg of Nietzsche's youth. Nietzsche inspired many aspects of the character, including his eventual descent into insanity. Leverkühn's principal teacher is Wendell Kretzschmar, an American-born organist of German extraction. Like his predecessor Edmund Pfühl in *Buddenbrooks*, Kretzschmar casts a cool eye on Wagner, that "skilled rabble-rouser." Leverkühn, too, is a skeptic. "His long-range plan was as un-Wagnerian as possible," Zeitblom says. Yet, like Nietzsche, he cannot slip the grasp of the old sorcerer. In a draft of a letter to his teacher, Leverkühn declares that his "quickly sated intellect" has no patience for conventional beauty. He gives an example:

> This, then, is how beauty happens: The cellos intone all by themselves a somber, pensive theme that questions the world's folly in a forthright and highly expressive philosophical "why" addressed to our hustle and bustle, our hounding and harrying. The cellos enlarge on this for a while, shaking their wise heads in regret over this riddle, and at a given, carefully considered point in their comments, the wind instruments, after a preparatory deep breath that causes shoulders to rise and fall again, enter with a chorale, stirringly solemn, splendidly harmonized, and played with all the muted dignity and gently constrained power of brass . . .

Leverkühn continues in that vein for many more sentences. Then he writes: "Dear friend, why does this make me laugh? . . . I, the outcast, must laugh, especially at all those supporting grunts from the bombardon—*boom, boom, boom—bang!* I may perhaps have tears in my eyes, but at the same time the urge to laugh is overwhelming." Mann later revealed that this passage is a blow-by-blow account of the Act III prelude of *Meistersinger*—the same music that Riefenstahl had employed in her Nazi propaganda films. The "world's folly" lamented by the cellos is a paraphrase of the "*Wahn! Wahn!*" that Hans Sachs will bemoan in Act III. Mann is again practicing his peculiar tic of talking at length about Wagner without letting on that he is doing so. When Mann read this section to Theodor W. Adorno, who assisted him with musical matters, the latter failed to recognize the reference.

The Devil promises Leverkühn a total liberation of the imagination, in contrast to conventional art of a "bourgeois-moderate, Nurembergish sort." The advanced works that ensue are contrasted with the "fusty Wagnerism" of Munich, where Leverkühn spends time before the First World War. His marionette theater piece *Gesta Romanorum*, a setting of Latin medieval tales, approaches mythic subject matter "in an utterly destructive fashion," in a spirit of "bizarre whimsy." Leverkühn rants against Wagnerian-Romantic views of redemption and art-religion. Emulating Nietzsche, he calls for a new vitality, lightness, healthiness—art "on a first-name basis with humanity."

In *The Magic Mountain*, Mann advocated Nietzschean values as a way beyond Wagnerian "sympathy for death." By the forties, he was losing faith in that philosophy. Leverkühn's modernism begins to seem less humane than the creaky Wagnerian apparatus that it wishes to supplant. The composer's later works exhibit diabolical strains. The *Apocalipsis cum figuris* supplies sonic visions of the Last Judgment, including a howlingly dissonant "pandemonium of laughter" that represents the entrance of the damned into Hell. The *Lamentation of Dr. Faustus* progresses from a hellish "choral scherzo" to a desolate Adagio lamentoso. The *Lamentation* is also described, chillingly, as a "taking back" of the "Ode to Joy." In place of choral shouts for brotherhood—"Be embraced, millions!"—Leverkühn paints a picture of terminal decay, one instrument after another dying out. If Beethoven's Ninth is revoked, so too is the rationale underlying the life's work of Wagner, for whom the entrance of voices in the Ninth marked the beginning of music drama. The synthesis of the *Ring* is no longer possible. Only the hollowed-out Wagnerism of Nazi Germany remains.

In 1943, around the time that Mann began writing *Doctor Faustus*, the artist George Grosz, a radical Berliner exiled in New York, painted a picture called *The Wanderer*—a self-portrait in the guise of the itinerant, incognito Wotan of *Siegfried*. The fallen god is striding into the cold, his coat drawn tight around his neck, his spear reduced to a walking-stick. Ravens fly overhead; fire rises in the distance. We don't see the man's face clearly: he could be mistaken for Wagner himself.

HITLERIZING WAGNER

Program for a 1944 Red Cross benefit conducted by Toscanini

Thomas Mann's bombastic claim that he was carrying Germany's cultural legacy with him into exile found wide acceptance in the Western democracies where the brothers Mann and so many other eminences took refuge. During the First World War, everything German had been demonized. This time, the Allied countries made a point of extolling the "good Germany"—an intellectual and artistic community that could reconstitute itself abroad. The United States, in particular, congratulated itself on having saved the best of Europe from ruin, even though xenophobic immigration laws prevented hundreds of thousands of German-Jewish refugees from entering the country.

For most cultural arbiters, the "good Germany" still included Wagner, who kept his place in the opera and concert repertories of Allied countries. British and American music lovers tended to follow the line taken by Willa Cather when she spoke of *Parsifal* in 1945: "I still love the opera and the legend—though so much of Wagner has been rather spoiled for us by being boisterously played for very un-musical purposes." When E. M. Forster wrote an essay defending democracy against the Fascist cult of force—"the strong are so stupid"—he looked to the *Ring* to reinforce his case: "Fafnir, coiled round his hoard, grumbles and grunts; we can hear him under Europe to-day; the leaves of the wood already tremble, and the Bird calls its warnings uselessly." The Valkyries are countervailing voices of courage and intelligence: Brünnhilde sings of the "love which is eternally triumphant and feeds upon Freedom." The children's author Elizabeth Enright felt no compunction about sending a character in her 1941 novel *The Saturdays* to a performance of *Siegfried*: the boy calls it "swell."

Arturo Toscanini, the most widely acclaimed classical musician of the era, managed to make Wagner a symbol of the anti-Fascist struggle. The maestro was idolized everywhere from Bayreuth, where he conducted in 1930 and 1931, to New York, where he led the Philharmonic and the NBC Symphony. Although he was not immune to the pull of charismatic politics—he performed in Fiume during d'Annunzio's reign, offering the Prelude and Liebestod by request—he resisted the Fascists when they encroached upon his turf. At Bayreuth, he caused such a sensation that he was talked about as a successor to Siegfried Wagner. But Nazi persecution of Jewish musicians caused Toscanini to withdraw from the 1933 festival. Winifred tried mightily to change his mind: she even cajoled Hitler into sending an obsequious letter, addressed to "Hochverehrter Meister" ("Highly esteemed master"), all but begging the conductor to return. Toscanini was unswayed, and lent his name to anti-Nazi protests.

In the late thirties, as Harvey Sachs observes in his biography of the conductor, Toscanini made a habit of performing in countries bordering Germany. In 1936 and 1937, he led *Meistersinger* at the Salzburg Festival, within sight of Bavaria. Twice in the late thirties, he paid his own way to Palestine to conduct the Palestine Symphony, including the *Lohengrin* preludes on his programs. He knew of the nascent resistance to Wagner in what would become Israel, but maintained that "nothing should interfere with music."

Most conspicuously, in 1938 Toscanini went to Lucerne, Wagner's former place of exile, to lead an orchestra that included refugees from Germany and Austria—an early edition of what would become the Lucerne Festival. One program juxtaposed the *Meistersinger* Act I prelude with Mendelssohn's "Italian" Symphony. The following summer, a few days before Germany invaded Poland, Toscanini led the *Siegfried Idyll* at the old Wagner home in Tribschen. Eva Chamberlain was in attendance; she adored Toscanini's conducting and was distraught when he left Bayreuth. Nonetheless, the former friend of Luranah Aldridge remained loyal to the Nazis. When Eva died, in 1942, her coffin was draped in a Nazi flag, and Hitler sent a wreath.

One member of the family broke away and went into exile. Friedelind Wagner, the twenty-one-year-old daughter of Siegfried and Winifred, wrote to Toscanini in 1940 with a Thomas Mann–like declaration: "Because I am a German I am not in Germany now—because this isn't Germany any more." In 1941, she arrived in the United States, where she made contact with Mann's children Klaus and Erika. As a prize defector, Friedelind was invited to speak on a 1942 *Tannhäuser* broadcast from the Met, one that was sent out to German-speakers in Europe. Erika supplied her with an eloquent, if not entirely persuasive, anti-Nazi script: "Richard Wagner, who loved freedom and justice even more than he loved music itself, could not have breathed in Hitler's Germany . . . My grandfather is dead and cannot fight the abuse. But I, his granddaughter, am speaking in his spirit and sense when I tell you: Senta's pure love, which redeems the wandering Dutchman; Lohengrin's bright figure; and the Christian tolerance of Parsifal are descended from landscapes where no Nazi jackboot has ever trod."

As the thirties gave way to the forties, a very different perspective began to take hold: one that saw Wagner not as a victim of Nazism but as an agent of it. Émigrés played a crucial role in what might be called the Hitlerizing of Wagner. The critic Ludwig Marcuse, who had earlier scorned the Wagnerian left, wrote in 1938 that the Third Reich "has no greater ancestor and no more perfect representative of its ideology" than

Wagner. This formulation was very close to pronouncements emanating from the Third Reich ("*Hitlergeist ist Wagnergeist*"). Nazi Wagnerites and anti-Nazi anti-Wagnerites were essentially in perfect accord about the composer's true nature—a problematic alliance that continues to this day.

Peter Viereck, the most determined proponent of the Hitler-centric view, came from a distinguished and notorious German family. His grandfather Louis was a socialist who knew Marx and Engels; his father, George Sylvester Viereck, a German-American who defended Germany during the First World War and became a Hitler admirer as early as 1923. Viereck renounced his heritage, and did so by castigating the composer whom his father's journal *Fatherland* had called "the greatest artist of modern times in any nation." In 1939, the magazine *Common Sense* published Viereck's two-part article "Hitler and Richard Wagner," which argues that Wagner's blend of socialism, national chauvinism, and antisemitism foretold Nazi philosophy. A promoter of Nietzsche, Viereck is keen to detach his intellectual hero from Nazism, and therefore shifts the onus onto Wagner—a pattern that would recur in postwar intellectual life. Viereck's 1941 book *Metapolitics* presents an expanded version of that thesis, influentially labeling Wagner a "proto-Nazi." This was the real beginning of the "backshadowing" narrative: Wagner as Hitler's precursor.

In the *Common Sense* article, Viereck gently accuses Thomas Mann of clinging to liberal illusions about Wagner. Mann responded in a long letter to the editor—effectively an essay in itself—in which he not only accepted many of Viereck's points but said that he would go further and locate Nazi elements in the operas themselves. At the same time, Mann found Viereck's work lacking in nuance—"the nuance of love, of passionate personal experience." In the same period, Mann said that his attitude toward Wagner "is and remains 'ambivalent,' and I can write about him one way today, another tomorrow." This oscillation continued to the end. In a 1949 letter to his friend Emil Preetorius, Mann wrote, "Certainly, there is much 'Hitler' in Wagner." In almost the same breath, though, he said that the composer had been bound up with Hitler for long enough.

In 1940, the Wagner-to-Hitler thesis reached a much wider readership, that of the *New York Times*. In an article titled "Wagner: Clue to Hitler," the German-American journalist Otto Tolischus identified the composer as the "first totalitarian artist." Three years later, the best-selling émigré author Emil Ludwig, who had once published a book of sycophantic conversations with Mussolini, recommended that the *Ring* should be banned in Germany for at least fifty years. "Around the year 2000 no musical ear will be able to stand this monstrosity, anyway," Ludwig added. Paul Henry Lang wrote a piece on Wagner titled "Background Music for *Mein Kampf*," and Carl Engel entertained the notion that "we should ban and burn every scrap of Wagner's music and writings" in order to "finally extinguish the Wagner-fanned fire of Nazism."

For the time being, such fulminations remained in the minority. During the war, Wagner's popularity in America actually surged. The Met presented the operas as often as ever, making heavy use of the Hungarian-Jewish bass-baritone Friedrich Schorr, whose presence at Bayreuth had struck Hitler as *Rassenschande*, or racial pollution. The composer and radio personality Deems Taylor thought that lumping German composers together with the Nazis was itself a Nazi thing to do—a "refusal to separate the work from the worker, the art from the artist." Tolischus's *Times* piece drew heated rebuttals. A *Times* editorial called the *Ring* "fundamentally a moral, revolutionary document," one that taught "the fatal effects of wealth and overlordship." The *Times* critic Olin Downes wrote that Wagner's operas were "the antithesis of Hitler, and crushing condemnation of all that Hitlerism implies." In the 1941–42 season, Downes later noted, Wagner had been the Met's most often played composer. The company's one concession was to drop *Meistersinger* temporarily from the repertory, having tried out a version in which Hans Sachs's final monologue was cut short.

Toscanini mounted a series of wartime Wagner concerts, effectively conscripting the composer to the Allied cause. In 1941, he led the NBC Symphony in a Wagner program for the benefit of underprivileged families. In 1942, at a gala for the Red Cross, he presented an all-Wagner concert with the New York Philharmonic—an event that Thomas Mann attended. And in 1944, before eighteen thousand people at Madison Square Garden, Toscanini conducted the combined forces of the NBC Symphony and the Philharmonic in another Red Cross benefit, this time pairing Wagner and Verdi, the musical heroes of the enemy powers. "Never has the inherent and indestructible greatness of Wagner's art been more triumphantly demonstrated," Downes wrote. The souvenir booklet emphasized the international dimensions of Wagnerism by reproducing artwork by Henri Fantin-Latour and Salvador Dalí. A note on "The Ride of the Valkyries," evoking "the exultant battle cries of the Valkyries as they galloped through the clouds on their steeds," was paired with a photograph of B-17 bombers surrounded by fighter trails. Wagner was thus commandeered on behalf of the Allied assault on German cities.

I n France, the latest generation of Wagnéristes had to adjust once again to German aggression, as in 1870 and 1914. The composer's reputation had rebounded after the First World War; circa 1933, a quarter of the Opéra's repertory was Wagner. Hitler's appropriation of Bayreuth caused consternation among left-leaning Wagnerites, as the musicologist Rachel Orzech has documented. The novelist Guy de Pourtalès wrote that the Third Reich "wants to ignore Wagner's skeptical and troubled soul, deeply uncertain and uneasy, in a constant search for an imperturbable god." Maurice Bouvier-Ajam asked, "How to react in France against Hitlerian pseudo-Wagnerism?"

The literary polymath Paul Claudel reacted by losing faith in a composer he had once esteemed. The product of a Symbolist-Wagnerian milieu, a Mallarmé disciple like Valéry, Claudel was inclined toward medieval settings and mystical Christian themes. In his 1905 play *Partage de midi* (Break of Noon), he rang variations on *Tristan*. By the late twenties, Claudel was acknowledging Wagner's failings, but could still praise the composer's resistance to scientific materialism, his "accent of lost Paradise." This was in an essay titled "Richard Wagner: Reverie of a French Poet," consciously duplicating Mallarmé's 1885 piece for the *Revue wagnérienne*. A decade later, Claudel joined the opposition. In the 1938 article "The Wagnerian Poison," he speaks of a "ratatouille Boche," of the "endless tossing of a kind of legendary metaphysical salad in which the despair of a lost and irreparable happiness mingles with the most sinister ingredients of paganism." (These dishes could perhaps be served alongside Tristan Tzara's "Wagnerian bouillabaisse.") Events in Germany had clearly sped up Claudel's reevaluation of Wagner. The leitmotif method is likened to *Mein Kampf*: "Hitler says in his book that the entire art of eloquence and propaganda consists in repetition."

Most Wagnéristes on the right were caught in the Fascist web. Camille Mauclair, once an anarchist Symbolist, ended up a reactionary art critic in the Vichy regime. The critic and novelist Lucien Rebatet used categories from "Jewishness in Music" to attack modernist composers. Jean Cocteau, trendily anti-Wagnerian during and after the First World War, turned pro-German in Vichy: his 1943 script for the film *The Eternal Return* is a modern-dress *Tristan*, with Jean Marais cast as an Aryan heartthrob. The saddest case is that of Édouard Dujardin, editor of the *Revue wagnérienne* and progenitor of the interior monologue. Like Mauclair, Dujardin had been a Dreyfusard, and as late as the thirties he was proclaiming himself a Zionist. During the Occupation, though, he suddenly became a Hitler idolater. In 1882, he had sent Wagner a letter regarding anti-German sentiment in Paris, and received a thoughtful reply, in French. Six decades later, he wrote to "Monsieur le Chancelier," mentioning his friendship with Chamberlain, who "came to understand so well" Hitler's greatness. That letter went unanswered.

WAGNER AND THE HOLOCAUST

Wounded soldiers with Winifred Wagner at Bayreuth, 1943

The Bayreuth Festival of 1939 had an atmosphere of déjà vu. As in the summer of 1914, war was imminent, and the tensions of the day crept into the proceedings. Neville Henderson, the British ambassador to Germany, was in attendance, hoping to meet with Hitler and broker a peace. When Winifred Wagner pressed Henderson's case, Hitler rebuffed her. Plans for the invasion of Poland were set, and the would-be conqueror had no interest in negotiations. Hitler did greet two friendly British visitors: Diana Mosley, the wife of Oswald Mosley, the leader of the British Fascists; and her sister Unity Mitford, blessed with the middle name Valkyrie. Mosley, in her autobiography, remembered a lunch with Hitler before *Götterdämmerung*: "Never had the glorious music seemed to me so doom-laden." When the war began, a month later, Unity attempted to kill herself with a pistol that Hitler had supposedly given her for protection.

Winifred Wagner had assumed that the Bayreuth Festival would be shut down in wartime, as had happened in 1914, but Hitler insisted that it proceed. The leisure organization Strength Through Joy (KdF) brought in listeners en masse. Around a hundred thousand "guests of the Führer" visited Bayreuth from 1940 until 1944. Most were from the armed forces. Wounded soldiers had first priority, and they came wrapped in bandages and limping on crutches, sometimes accompanied by nurses. A marine band played as special trains arrived at the Bayreuth station. Introductory lectures were given; Winifred hosted tours of Wahnfried. In 1943 and 1944, only *Meistersinger* was staged, on the grounds that it fit the wartime mood better than the gloomy *Götterdämmerung* or the pacifist *Parsifal*. An orientation pamphlet for the soldiers quotes Sachs's closing peroration— *"Habt Acht!"*—but cautions against retreating into an inner world, into a pure sphere of "holy German art." Only war can stop the enemy's "evil tricks"; only "Nothung, the German sword," can halt the "world flood of ruin."

A scene in Karl Ritter's 1941 film *Stukas* gives a highly idealized, not to say fantastical, impression of how German soldiers might have experienced the War Festivals. It plays like a hideous parody of those Wagner Scenes in which a young person is energized by the Meister's vision. When a dive-bomber pilot named Hans is shot down and wounded, he falls into a depressed, lethargic state. A restorative trip to Bayreuth is prescribed—a sort of Magic Mountain spa treatment for the warrior spirit. At first, Hans seems uninterested, but he perks up when he hears the brass section play Siegfried's horn call from the Festspielhaus balcony. Inside, the sound of "Siegfried's Rhine Journey" electrifies him: he leans forward, his eyes glowing, his mind filled with happy memories of comradeship. The Wagner music acts upon him as a drug—less the dream-inducing narcotic of the fin de siècle than the hyper-energizing methamphetamine that was fed to German soldiers during the Blitzkrieg. Hans returns to battle, his eyes still gleaming as he sings the less sophisticated strains of the "Stuka Song"

Stukas, *1941*

with his comrades: "We are the Black Hussars of the air, / The Stukas, the Stukas, the Stukas . . ."

What did the soldiers really feel? SS intelligence kept tabs on them and gave a generally rosy picture. A 1940 summary says: "All the reports are unanimous in affirming that the great attempt . . . to bring the simple people of the *Volk* to the greatest and in some ways most difficult works of German art proved successful and 'a cultural achievement of the first rank.'" Informants were particularly pleased that manual workers had lost the "inhibitions against serious art" that had supposedly prevailed in the "bourgeois liberal age." One soldier who had been blinded in battle said that he wished he could stay and listen to Wagner forever. Another said, "It is worthwhile to fight to the end for a people that is capable of such cultural events in times of need." On the other hand, as Julia Timpe notes in her book *Nazi-Organized Recreation*, some attendees slept through the proceedings or sold their tickets in exchange for alcohol—the same problems that had surfaced at the Nuremberg rallies. Hitler was attempting to impose on the entire military population his own experience as a soldier, when Wagner had been a balm to him.

In 1955, the city of Bayreuth made the curious decision to install Arno Breker's huge bust of Wagner in the park below the Festspielhaus. The sculpture still gazes stonily at festivalgoers, but in recent years it has been hemmed in by an outdoor exhibition titled Silenced Voices—an array of panels telling of the fates of Jewish musicians who worked at Bayreuth in the pre-Nazi period. A dozen of them perished during the war, whether in ghettos, the "model camp" at Theresienstadt, or the death camps. One panel honors the baritone Karl August Neumann, grandson of Angelo Neumann, the Jewish impresario whom Wagner entrusted with the touring production of the *Ring*. Neumann sang Beckmesser in Hitler's presence in 1933. He was imprisoned on account of supposed resistance contacts but survived the war.

It is possible that a few of Bayreuth's Jewish victims heard Wagner on the eve of their deaths. Several survivors of the Holocaust remember encountering Wagner in the camps. A Polish musician recalled that when he arrived at Auschwitz in 1944 he was greeted by "a full, first-class symphony orchestra" performing *Lohengrin*. Alex Dekel, who as a child was selected for Josef Mengele's medical experiments at Auschwitz, said that he "could hear the blaring music of *Lohengrin* being piped through loudspeakers as I walked through the gates of Auschwitz." A political prisoner at Dachau told of hearing "jingoistic Wagner music" in 1933. Mengele is said to have whistled Wagner, among other composers, as he went about making his selections at Auschwitz.

Yet the vast majority of survivor testimonies make no mention of Wagner. Instead, they indicate that the music of the camps was popular in nature: marches, dance tunes, hits of the day, light classics. If classical music was playing, it was more likely to be Chopin. Szymon Laks, who conducted the men's orchestra at Auschwitz, remembered playing classical potpourris, "one of them based on Schubert melodies, the other on Russian themes." Anita Lasker-Wallfisch and Fania Fénelon, who played in the Auschwitz women's orchestra, spoke of German hits, Strauss waltzes, operetta tunes, bits of Brahms and Beethoven, and opera melodies from *Carmen*, *Madama Butterfly*, and *Tosca*. (Their conductor was Alma Rosé, niece of Gustav Mahler.) Lasker-Wallfisch later said, "We certainly didn't play Wagner"—not least because the music was too difficult for an ensemble that included many amateurs.

Wagner's music was ill suited to the regime of psychological sadism that governed music in the camps. Primo Levi described the routine in his classic 1947 memoir, *If This Is a Man*. On arriving in Auschwitz, in 1944, Levi struggled to make sense not only of what he saw but of what he heard. As prisoners returned to the camp from a day of hard labor, they marched to bouncy popular music: in particular, the polka "Rosamunde." Levi's first reaction was to laugh. He thought that he was witnessing a "colossal farce in Teutonic taste." He later grasped that the juxtaposition of light music and terror was designed to destroy the spirit as surely as the crematoriums destroyed the body. The merry strains of "Rosamunde," which also emanated from loudspeakers during mass shootings of Jews at Majdanek, mocked the suffering of the victims. Laks, too, understood that the music had a numbing effect on the prisoners: it "deepened still further their chronic state of physical and mental prostration."

Nonetheless, the sonic mirage of Wagner at Auschwitz lingers in the popular consciousness. On a strictly historical level, it is misleading; on a psychological level, it gets at a deeper truth. The fact that the Wannsee Conference, the 1942 meeting at which the plan of genocide was formalized, was presided over by a Wagner singer's son—Reinhard Heydrich—speaks to the composer's unavoidable presence in the society that carried out the Holocaust. And in one horrifying instance, Wagner was directly coupled with genocidal imagery. In the fall of 1940, the Propaganda Ministry released an abominable pseudo-documentary titled *The Eternal Jew*. After the opening titles, which are scored with quasi-atonal music meant to inspire revulsion, a spoken prologue accompanies footage of Jews in Polish ghettos. The narration includes these lines: "We recognize that a hotbed of plague lies here, one that threatens the health of the Aryan population. Richard Wagner once said: 'The Jew is the plastic demon of the downfall of humanity.' And these pictures confirm the accuracy of his statement."

The Eternal Jew was a favorite project of Goebbels's. The phrase about the "plastic demon" probably appeared at his instigation, since he quoted it often in his speeches. In 1937, Goebbels described the Jew as the "enemy of the world, the annihilator of civilizations, the parasite among peoples, the son of chaos, the incarnation of evil, the ferment of decomposition, the plastic demon of the downfall of humanity." Six years later, in his 1943 speech declaring a condition of "total war," Goebbels said: "Judaism once again reveals itself as the incarnation of evil, as the plastic demon of downfall, and as the bearer of an international culture-destroying chaos." Moments later, he advised his vociferously cheering audience that the "most total and radical measures" might be needed to bring about the "elimination of *Judentum*." Close listening reveals that Goebbels began to say "*Ausrottung*"—"extermination"—before correcting himself. In these instances, Wagner did not receive credit for the phrase.

Goebbels apparently hoped that *The Eternal Jew* would induce a new level of anti-Jewish loathing in the German people, easing acceptance of the program of genocide. Footage of swarming rats was intended to suggest Jewish infestation—as in the diaries of Cosima Wagner and the poetry of T. S. Eliot—and a slaughter of cows represented Jews' supposed cruelty toward animals. The film then segues to footage of Hitler's January 1939 address to the Reichstag, which essentially announced the onset of the Holocaust: "If international *Finanzjudentum* inside and outside Europe should succeed in plunging the nations once more into a world war, then the result will not be the Bolshevization of the earth, and with it the victory of *Judentum*, but the annihilation of the Jewish race in Europe." The film ends with Riefenstahl footage of shining Aryan faces, accompanied by sub-Wagnerian music.

The Eternal Jew failed to have the desired effect. Some moviegoers reportedly left screenings in distress; a few fainted. Receipts were poor. Still, the film proved to have some usefulness as a training film for concentration camp guards.

As war raged across Europe, operations and fortifications again acquired Wagnerian code names: the Siegfried Line, the Panther-Wotan Line, Operation Brunhild, Operation Magic Fire. A 1941 directive stipulating that captured resistance fighters should vanish without a trace bore the title "Nacht und Nebel" (Night and Fog)—what Alberich says in *Rheingold* when he uses the Tarnhelm to disappear.

On July 20, 1944, one of these Wagner-coded plans was turned against the Führer. Claus von Stauffenberg, formerly a youthful ornament of the poetic circle around Stefan George, set off a bomb in Hitler's headquarters, launching a coup attempt nicknamed Operation Walküre. In 1941, the staff of General Friedrich Fromm, the commander of the home army, had drafted plans titled Walküre and Rheingold, providing for call-ups of reserves in emergency situations. General Friedrich Olbricht, Fromm's deputy, joined Stauffenberg and other members of the resistance in converting Walküre into a blueprint for the overthrow of the Nazi regime. A man of intellectual and liberal bent who avidly attended opera, Olbricht may have savored the ironic code name. He and Stauffenberg were executed immediately after the failure of the July 20 plot.

As the end approached, Hitler stopped listening to Wagner, preferring Lehár's *The Merry Widow* and other operetta fare. Two secretaries who were with him in the bunker in Berlin said that he lost interest in music altogether. Still, he kept Wagnerian artifacts nearby. In 1939, on his fiftieth birthday, he had been given a collection of documents that had once belonged to Ludwig II: the original manuscripts of Wagner's first three operas (*Die Feen, Das Liebesverbot, Rienzi*); fair copies of *Das Rheingold* and *Die Walküre*; and sketches for *The Flying Dutchman, Siegfried*, and *Götterdämmerung*. Winifred later asked that the collection be deposited in Bayreuth for safekeeping, but Hitler said that having Wagner's handwriting in his vicinity meant a great deal to him. As Allied bombings intensified, Winifred and her sons repeatedly attempted to get hold of the trove. As late as April 6, 1945, Wieland and his brother-in-law Bodo Lafferentz— an SS officer who had a lead role in the KdF—drove through the war zone toward Berlin, hoping to retrieve the relics. By telephone, Wieland reached Martin Bormann, Hitler's aide, who assured him that they were safe. They subsequently disappeared. A significant piece of Wagner's legacy therefore went missing: the *Rienzi* manuscript was the only evidence of the uncut original version of the score.

Historical cliché requires Hitler's last days to be described as a Götterdämmerung: so Joachim Fest titled the final chapter of his Hitler biography. The analogy had already begun to circulate before the end of the war. An American publication ran a photo of Hitler, Goebbels, and Göring with the caption "The Nazi Big Three—Their Ending Should Be Wagnerian." Bertolt Brecht clipped out that picture and attached a sneering text, as part of his *War Primer* series:

> Oh Swan Song "You must never ask me"!
> Oh Pilgrim's Chorus! Oh Magic-Fire trick!
> Oh song of Rheingold on the empty stomach!
> I name you the Bayreuth Republic.

Romain Rolland, in 1944, wrote that Hitler was "writing his Wagnerian epic"—a tragedy in which he always intended to die at the end. Albert

Speer placed Brünnhilde's Immolation Scene on the Berlin Philharmonic's last program of the Nazi era, on April 12, 1945.

Yet *Götterdämmerung* is no apocalypse: it envisions a transfer of power, from gods to people. It is also the redress of a wrong, restoring the Ring from the illusory heights to the truthful depths. Wotan, very unlike Hitler, has repented of his megalomania: "I longed in my heart for power . . . I acted unfairly . . . I did not return the ring to the Rhine . . . The curse that I fled will not flee from me now." The conductor Christoph von Dohnányi, whose father, Hans, was part of the anti-Nazi resistance, once told me: "When I really think about Wagner, I don't discover anything that *had* to lead to Hitler. And what happens here"—we were looking at the score of *Walküre*, at Wotan's cries of shame—"is not something that any fascist could have written. Because it is not simplifying. It is a 'giving up' thing. Wagner abused power but hated the state." "Götterdämmerung" is the wrong word for the scenes that unfolded in Berlin during the war's last days: the double suicide of Hitler and Eva Braun, the suicides of Josef and Magda Goebbels, the murder of the Goebbels children, the killing of Hitler's dogs.

Allied bombers spared Bayreuth until April 5, 1945, when a flotilla of B-17s and B-24s, Toscanini's Valkyries, struck the city's industrial facilities. A veteran of the 446th Bombing Group of the U.S. Air Force wryly summarized the action: "Bayreuth, home of the Wagnerian music festivals, heard some hot licks not in the Nazi score when five planes of the Group got through some extremely bad weather to attack its marshalling yards on Mickey equipment." The Festspielhaus was unscathed, presumably because it lay outside the city center. The Wagner villa was not so lucky: a bomb crushed the roof and wrecked much of the interior, though the façade remained intact. Long before, its engraved motto had become a majestic absurdity: "Here where my delusions found peace, let me name this house Wahnfried."

14

RIDE OF THE VALKYRIES

Film from *The Birth of a Nation* to *Apocalypse Now*

D. W. Griffith's The Birth of a Nation

In February 1915, when Adolf Hitler was an anonymous soldier serving on the Western Front, D. W. Griffith's silent film *The Birth of a Nation* opened at Clune's Auditorium in Los Angeles. It was advertised as the most amazing motion picture ever made—the "eighth wonder of the world." Subsequent showings featured orchestras of up to fifty musicians, playing a multi-composer score assembled by the movie-music pioneer Joseph Carl Breil. Set during and after the American Civil War, the film is based on *The Clansman: An Historical Romance of the Ku Klux Klan*, a blatantly racist novel by Thomas Dixon, Jr. In the climactic scene, members of the Klan ride forth on horses to save a Southern town from what the creators perceive to be oppressive African-American rule. The orchestra accompanies these scenes first with Wagner's *Rienzi* overture and then with "The Ride of the Valkyries." At the moment of triumph— "Disarming the blacks" reads the title card—Wagner gives way to "Dixie," the anthem of the South. Another card spells out what kind of nation Griffith wants to see born: "The former enemies of North and South are united again in common defence of their Aryan birthright."

The Birth of a Nation set the pace for a century of Wagnerian aggression on film. More than a thousand movies have the composer on their soundtracks, using him to unleash all manner of rampaging hordes, marching armies, swashbuckling heroes, and scheming evildoers. The "Ride" has figured in a particularly dizzying range of situations. In the Bugs Bunny cartoon *What's Opera, Doc?*, Elmer Fudd pursues his archenemy while chanting "Kill da wabbit." In John Landis's 1980 comedy *The Blues Brothers*, the "Ride" plays while buffoonish neo-Nazis chase the heroes and plunge into oblivion. Arnold Schwarzenegger, trapped on a sadistic reality show in the 1987 movie *The Running Man*, must battle an operatic villain named Dynamo, who sings a cheesy synthesizer version of the "Ride." Most indelibly, Francis Ford Coppola's Vietnam War film *Apocalypse Now*, released in 1979, upends Griffith's racial duality, making white Americans the agents of destruction. A helicopter squadron blares the "Ride" as it launches a brutal raid on a Vietnamese village. Lieutenant Colonel Kilgore, the officer in charge, drops a racist slur as he describes his tactic: "Yeah, I use Wagner—scares the hell out of the slopes. My boys love it."

Action sequences are only one facet of Wagner's celluloid presence. A colorful and often shady array of Wagnerites have appeared on screen, including Dorian Gray (*Penny Dreadful*), F. W. Murnau (*Shadow of the Vampire*), a Nietzschean teenager (*Murder by Numbers*), a diabolical android (*Alien: Covenant*), the psychoanalyst Sabina Spielrein (*A Dangerous Method*), the physicist Stephen Hawking (*The Theory of Everything*), various incarnations of King Ludwig II, and countless Nazis. The composer himself is portrayed in more than a dozen movies, including Tony Palmer's *Wagner* (1983), a nearly eight-hour-long biopic starring Richard Burton. Cinema's integration of image, word, and music promised a fulfillment of the Gesamtkunstwerk ideal. Directors like Sergei Eisenstein, Luis Buñuel, and Abel Gance saw Wagner as a kindred spirit. Film composers adopted the leitmotif system, not to mention the leitmotifs themselves.

A familiar platitude holds that Wagner would have embraced the movies if he had lived to see them. The French critic Émile Vuillermoz wrote in 1927: "If Wagner had been born fifty years later, he would have written his Tetralogy not for the stage but for the screen." Max Steiner, the composer of *King Kong* and *Casablanca*, declared: "If Wagner had lived in this century, he would have been the Number One film composer." Wolfgang Wagner said the same: "If my grandfather were alive today, he would undoubtedly be working in Hollywood." The caveat is that Wagner would have wanted to direct and write as well as to compose. In that regard, Hollywood might have proved less hospitable than Ludwig's Bavaria.

As cinema became Wagnerian, Wagner became cinematic. Popular perceptions of the composer are not easily detached from the visual settings in which he has been assigned—whether the Nazi villainy of *The Boys from Brazil* or the Arthurian fantasy of *Excalibur*. As those associations multiply, though, the music regains its polyvocal power. If "The Ride of the Valkyries" makes people think of both Bugs Bunny and helicopters, it signifies everything and nothing. In the end, film has trouble deciding whether Wagner is an inexhaustible store of wonder or a bottomless well of hate. That uncertainty mirrors Hollywood's own ambiguous role as an incubator of heroic fantasies, which can serve a wide range of political ends. When it talks about Wagner, it is often, consciously or not, talking about itself.

KINO BAYREUTH

When the lights went down at the Bayreuth Festspielhaus in 1876, a kind of cinema came into being. Eduard Hanslick felt that he was looking at a "bright-colored picture in a dark frame," as in a diorama display. Wagner had intended as much, saying that the stage picture should have the "unapproachability of a dream vision." The sound of the orchestra, hidden in the "mystic abyss," wafts through the room, as if transmitted by a speaker system. (Wagner himself likened the orchestra to a "technical apparatus for bringing forth the picture.") The near-blackout of the auditorium was not unprecedented, but it felt revolutionary, particularly in combination with the rumbling, almost subliminal bass E-flats that begin the *Ring*. From the Festspielhaus, the media theorist Friedrich Kittler writes, "the darkness of all our cinemas derives."

Wagner's technical innovations predict cinematic sleights of hand. In the *Ring*, magic-lantern projections evoked the Valkyries on their steeds. The electrically glowing Grail in *Parsifal* was a kind of special effect, as was the rolling panorama that covered the transition to the Grail Temple. Clouds of steam, generated by two locomotive boilers outside the Festspiel-haus, smoothed over changes of scene, in anticipation of the technique of dissolve.

The music itself provides hypnotic continuity. When the action of *Rheingold* shifts from the Rhine to the area around Valhalla, the stage directions say: "Gradually the waves turn into clouds, which resolve into a fine mist." In the score, rushing river patterns give way to shimmering tremolos and then to a more rarefied texture of flutes and violins—what Peter Franklin describes as an "elaborate upward panning shot." In the descent into Nibelheim, the sound of hammering anvils swells in a long crescendo before fading away. This is like a dolly shot: a camera moves in on the Nibelungs at work and then draws back. Sometimes, the equivalent of a jump cut breaks the flow. The interruption of *Tristan*'s central love scene never fails to deliver a visceral shock. Musical close-ups of the lovers are shattered by a loud chord and by a virtual wide shot of Kurwenal rushing in, with King Mark and his courtiers close behind.

The convocation of the nine Valkyries in Act III of *Walküre* is Wagner's finest action sequence—a virtuoso exercise in the massing of forces and the accumulation of energy. At the beginning, winds trill against quick upward swoops in the strings; horns, bassoons, and cellos establish a galloping rhythm, at medium volume; then comes a trickier wind-and-string texture, with staggered entries and downward swooping patterns added; and, finally, horns and bass trumpet lay out the main theme. Successive iterations of the material are bolstered with trumpets, more horns, and four stentorian trombones, but the players are initially held at a dynamic marking of *f*, allowing for a further crescendo to *ff*. When Rossweisse and Grimgerde appear, filling out the Valkyrie ensemble, the contrabass tuba enters fortissimo beneath the trombones, giving the sense of maximum reinforcements arriving.

Just a few years after film history got under way, commentators began touting the medium as a conduit for the Gesamtkunstwerk. The American critic W. Stephen Bush wrote in 1911: "Every man or woman in charge of the music of a moving picture theatre is, consciously or unconsciously, a

disciple or follower of Richard Wagner." Bush quoted the composer's call
for the sister arts to consort in an ideal drama. In the same period, Ric-
ciotto Canudo, in France, promoted a Wagnerian "mimetic representation
of 'total life,'" and Hermann Häfker, in Germany, spoke of a cinematic
Gesamtkunstwerk in which music would play a crucial role. Eisenstein
considered cinema the "genuine and ultimate synthesis of all artistic manifestations that fell to pieces after the peak of Greek culture." A Nazi-era
theorist declared that the Gesamtkunstwerk of sound film would finally
deliver a "true art of the people."

For some observers, though, Hollywood Wagnerism proved no less
oppressive than the German kind. Leftist critics of the Weimar Republic saw an ominous trend in cinema's Wagnerian airs. Siegfried Kracauer
wrote in his 1926 essay "Cult of Distraction" that "a glittering, revue-like
entity has crawled forth from the cinema: the *Gesamtkunstwerk of effects*."
Theodor W. Adorno, Kracauer's protégé, pursued the analogy in the 1944
jeremiad *Dialectic of Enlightenment*, written with Max Horkheimer. Television, then in its infancy, was a "scornfully laughing fulfillment of Wagner's dream of the Gesamtkunstwerk."

Wagner's influence is easily overstated. The film-music scholar Scott
Paulin argues that Hollywood made the composer a kind of "fetish object,"
using him to ennoble an industry that was struggling for respectability. For
Wagner, the Gesamtkunstwerk was ultimately a rubric under which he
negotiated the relationship between text and music, with the former privileged in his radical period and the latter paramount from *Tristan* onward.
In film, by contrast, music almost always plays a subordinate role. That
reversal of priorities makes Hollywood almost the opposite of Bayreuth.
As so often, abstract discussions of Wagner's "system" run up against the
singular fact that composer, dramatist, and director are one and the same.

SILENT WAGNER

In 1895, when the Lumière brothers first presented film to a paying public in Paris and the Skladanowsky brothers did the same in Berlin, Wagnerism was near its height. The composer made his cinematic debut just
three years later, when he was impersonated by the Italian actor Leopoldo
Fregoli, famous for his quick-change routine, in a movie called *Maestri di*

Giuseppe Becce as Wagner, 1913

musica. The earliest attempt to capture the Wagner phantasmagoria on film may have been Kazimierz Prószyński's short *Walkirie* (1903), made for a Warsaw production of *Walküre*; it pictured Valkyries flying through the clouds.

At least a dozen Wagner-themed films were released in the early silent era. One of the more elaborate was the Edison Company's half-hour-long version of *Parsifal* (1904), which tried to capitalize on the sensational Met production of 1903. Ads trumpeted it as "the greatest religious subject that has been produced in motion pictures since the Passion Play was first produced by the Edison Company about eight years ago." The director was Edwin Porter, who had essentially invented narrative filmmaking in *The Great Train Robbery.* His *Parsifal*, shot in Brooklyn, packs fewer thrills. The hero is first seen as a forest lad in a tunic, then as a bearded, Christlike figure. Amfortas writhes in agony and points to his body, as if to say, "Stab me." The Flower Maidens are decorous; Kundry's come-on is discreet. Klingsor skulks about like a stage devil. The large crowds that had been flocking to the Met failed to materialize at the nickelodeons.

The most ambitious Wagner film of the prewar era was *The Life and Works of Richard Wagner*, a German production that was timed to coincide with the Wagner centennial in May 1913. Carl Froelich directed, and the Berlin-based composer Giuseppe Becce played the title role. Originally, Becce had been hired to write a pseudo-Wagnerian score, Bayreuth having asked an exorbitant fee of nearly half a million marks for the use of Wagner's actual music. Then, when the lead actor withdrew, Becce volunteered his services. Although Froelich gives a sanitized, fairy-tale version of the composer's life, Becce's impersonation is eerily persuasive, especially in scenes shot outside Wahnfried and around Bayreuth. At around eighty minutes in length, the film inaugurated the genre of the feature-length biopic.

Movie composers relied on Wagnerian techniques from the outset. The film scholar James Buhler argues that leitmotifs gave viewers a "red thread of orientation" in the unfamiliar landscape of long-form visual narrative. In 1911, Clarence Sinn, the music columnist for *The Moving Picture World*, summarized the system thus: "To each important character, to each important action, motive or idea, and to each important object (Siegmund's sword, for example), was attached a suggestive musical theme." As a rule, the "Ride" was employed for battles and horses, the "Magic Fire" music for flickering flames, the *Flying Dutchman* overture for seas and storms, the *Tannhäuser* Pilgrims' Chorus for church scenes, and, of course, the Bridal Chorus for weddings.

Joseph Carl Breil, a lyric tenor turned theater composer, was probably the first to make a career out of writing and arranging movie music. His score for the 1912 film *Queen Elizabeth* was, in his own words, "built very much upon the motif lines set down by Richard Wagner." Two years later, Breil supervised musical accompaniment for the American release of Giovanni Pastrone's epic *Cabiria*. That spectacle of the Second Punic War drew on a scenario by Gabriele d'Annunzio, who also talked up the cinema's Gesamtkunstwerk potential.

Those projects prepared Breil for his work with David Wark Griffith, the godfather of Hollywood film. The Kentucky-born son of a Confederate Army colonel, Griffith worked as an actor before taking up directing in 1908. Two years later, he shot a short in Hollywood, California, helping to start the movie business there. A technical wizard, Griffith pioneered the alternation of wide shots, medium shots, and close-ups; the intercutting of multiple scenes of action; and kinetic tracking shots for scenes of chase and battle. In *The Birth of a Nation*, his second feature, Griffith used the methods perfected in his short films to sustain a sweeping historical narrative, from the Civil War to the assassination of Lincoln and on to the roiling tensions of the Reconstruction period. That this foundational work of cinema history is racist to the core recapitulates the Wagner problem in an American context. Infamously, President Woodrow Wilson hosted a screening of the film at the White House, giving it an official imprimatur.

When Griffith read Dixon's novel, the ride of the Klan seized his attention: "I could just see these Klansmen in a movie with their white robes flying." The idea of a Wagnerian accompaniment may have occurred to him early on. According to Lillian Gish—who starred as a damsel in distress named Elsie, akin to *Lohengrin*'s Elsa—Breil and Griffith squabbled over the "Ride," with Griffith wanting to make adjustments to the music and Breil saying, "You can't tamper with Wagner! It's never been done!" Griffith apparently won the argument. As the Klan hordes assemble—a famous shot shows hundreds of white-clad horses and riders traversing an open field—we hear a bit of the *Rienzi* overture. Then, as the riders enter the town and engage in combat, the rearranged "Ride" is heard. The effect of all this on audiences of the day can be gauged by a report from a screening in Atlanta: "They are coming, they are coming! / GALLERY GOES WILD / You know it and your spine prickles and in the gallery the yells cut loose with every bugle note." *The Birth of a Nation* is credited with bringing about a revival of the Klan, which had terrorized African-Americans after the Civil War.

Matthew Wilson Smith, in a penetrating essay on the film, concludes: "Griffith's use of Wagner married some of the most reactionary energies of Bayreuth to groundbreaking techniques of filmic integration that proved crucial to the development of classical Hollywood cinema." This is a reasonable assessment, although it bears mentioning that W. E. B. Du Bois's "Of the Coming of John" had employed Wagner in a very different way, as an expression of the yearning inner world of a black man about to be lynched by a horse-riding mob. Du Bois might have pointed out that Dixon and Griffith's racism, like Owen Wister's, had no need for a German antecedent. If anything, the influence moved in the opposite direction. As James Whitman has documented, the Nazis admired and emulated American laws that curtailed the rights of African-Americans and other ethnic minorities. The genocide of Native Americans in the West became a model for the Nazi *Lebensraum* policy in Eastern Europe. The insertion of "The Ride of the Valkyries" into *The Birth of a Nation* tells us more about the cultural arrogance of American white supremacism than it does about the nefarious influence of Wagner.

MURNAU AND LANG

Fritz Lang's Die Nibelungen

In 1917, Erich Ludendorff, the right-wing German general, lamented that native propaganda was inferior to enemy efforts, and championed a national movie studio to correct the imbalance. Government intervention led to the founding of the consortium Universum Film AG, or Ufa, which presided over a golden age of German cinema in the twenties. Ufa fostered the careers of Fritz Lang, F. W. Murnau, Ernst Lubitsch, William Dieterle, G. W. Pabst, and Robert Siodmak, all of whom later worked in Hollywood. It also abetted the rise of Leni Riefenstahl, perhaps the most infernally skilled propagandist in film history. Klaus Kreimeier, in his classic study of Ufa, describes a division between advanced cinematic techniques and a pervasive longing for a pre-industrial world: that contradiction was itself eminently Wagnerian.

In Weimar-era film, the composer looms largest behind Murnau and Lang—the one quasi-Wagnerian in style, the other quasi-Wagnerian in ambition. Murnau was born Friedrich Wilhelm Plumpe, the son of a wealthy textile merchant, and grew up in a *Buddenbrooks* milieu, reading Schopenhauer and Nietzsche by the age of twelve. While studying art and literature in Heidelberg, he befriended—and probably became the lover of—the Expressionist poet Hans Ehrenbaum-Degele, grandson of the Wagner baritone Eugen Degele. When Ehrenbaum-Degele was killed in battle in 1915, the young man's mother, Mary Degele, more or less adopted Murnau as a substitute son. Having joined the acting company of the great Austrian director Max Reinhardt, Murnau chose a stage name in honor of the Bavarian town where Kandinsky, Gabriele Münter, and Franz Marc established an artist colony.

As a filmmaker, Murnau looked toward musical models, speaking of a "symphony of body-melody and space-movement, the play of pure, vitally flowing, streaming movement." Jo Leslie Collier, in her book *From Wagner to Murnau*, tallies parallels between composer and director, some more plausible than others. She is most persuasive in linking *Nosferatu, a Symphony of Horror*, Murnau's 1922 adaptation of *Dracula*, to *The Flying Dutchman*. In both stories, a pure-hearted woman performs an act of self-sacrifice, although in *Nosferatu* the undead wanderer is a pure monster who must be destroyed rather than saved. In one celebrated shot, the vampire's ship glides slowly into view on the right-hand side of the frame, blotting out a vista of an unsuspecting German town. Wagner staged a similar entrance for his ship with blood-red sails. Logically, Hans Erdmann's score for *Nosferatu* drew on the *Dutchman*.

The cool, piercing gaze of Fritz Lang is nearly the antithesis of Murnau's wonderstruck camera eye. Born in Vienna, of partly Jewish descent, Lang was trained as an engineer and architect before turning to painting, writing, and film. In place of Murnau's fluid imagery, Lang offers strict compositions, painting in light and shadow, explosions of action within a tight frame. Lang seemed largely indifferent to music as a free-standing art, though he was crafty about using it on film.

Patrick McGilligan, in his biography of Lang, says that the director "detested Wagner with even more passion than his usual dislike of classical music." It is ironic, then, that the biggest undertaking of Lang's career was *Die Nibelungen*, based on the medieval *Nibelungenlied*. The two parts of the film, *Siegfried* and *Kriemhild's Revenge*, were both released in 1924, each running over two hours. In statements made at the time and in later commentaries, Lang was at pains to differentiate his Nibelung films from the *Ring*. He said that he was bringing the old epic from the operatic elite to the cinematic masses, and claimed that the theater was incapable of delivering the "mystical-magical" mood that the cinema could create. The screenwriter Thea von Harbou, Lang's collaborator and wife, declared that *Die Nibelungen* would liberate the "exhausted brain" of a modern *Volk* that longed to experience great heroic deeds but was too overworked and worn down to imagine them on its own.

In keeping with that national-conservative mission, *Die Nibelungen* returns to the source material of the *Nibelungenlied* and dispenses with psychological, philosophical, and political elaborations. *Siegfried* reenacts the hero's slaying of the dragon, his appropriation of the treasure, his arrival at Gunther's court, and his deception of Brünnhilde. But his true love is not Brünnhilde but Kriemhild, Gunther's sister, who appears in the *Ring* in the smaller role of Gutrune. Furthermore, Hagen is not the villainous son of Alberich but the scheming, dark-minded, but fundamentally loyal figure of the *Nibelungenlied*—the one who inspires the "Nibelung oath" popular in the First World War. In *Kriemhild's Revenge*, Lang enters a part of the story more or less unexplored by Wagner, as the title character marries Attila the Hun and exacts vengeance on Gunther and Hagen. Still, there is an echo of *Götterdämmerung* in the conflagration that ends the film, in the midst of which Attila shouts, à la Wotan, "An end! An end!"

Lang captures the epic razzle-dazzle—dragon, shape-shifting, battles, fires—in ways that Wagner might have envied. Paul Richter, the blond, buff Siegfried, looks the part better than any Heldentenor of the day. Lang's compositions convey almost limitless space. On the other hand, Wagner's *Ring* has Wagner. Despite the director's antipathy, Ufa did apparently try to use music from the *Ring*, only to meet resistance from Bayreuth. So the studio hired an apprentice composer, Gottfried Huppertz, who had trained as an actor and a singer. Although Huppertz made nominal efforts to distance himself from Wagner—"The challenge was to connect an ancient legend with an ancient music," he said—his score depends on a rigid leitmotif technique and luxuriates in post-Wagnerian orchestration, at times almost paraphrasing the *Ring* and *Parsifal*. In 1925, when *Siegfried* was released in America, Huppertz's music gave way to a Wagner mélange.

Lang and Harbou dedicated *Die Nibelungen* to the "German *Volk*." Leftist critics frowned on its reactionary leanings even as they marveled at its technique. Frank Aschau, of *Die Weltbühne*, criticized the rendering of Alberich as a monster straight out of antisemitic caricature—a portrayal probably influenced by the *Ring* illustrations of Arthur Rackham and Franz Stassen. Naturally, the film had admirers on the right; in 1933, Goebbels tried to hire Lang as the head of Ufa. Lang declined, and went into exile soon after. Riefenstahl alludes to Lang's work in *Triumph of the Will*.

When Siegfried arrives at Gunther's court, there is an overhead shot of him walking away from the camera, with soldiers flanking him and comrades following. *Triumph of the Will* has a similar shot, on a vaster scale, of Hitler, Himmler, and Viktor Lutze traversing the Nuremberg parade ground.

For skeptics like Siegfried Kracauer, Lang's impersonal tableaux symbolize the operation of irreversible fate; as such, they double as emblems of totalitarian might. They can be compared to Wagner's grand choral scenes, such as the "Wach auf" in *Meistersinger*. Crowds are seldom a source of wisdom in Wagner, however. The choruses of sailors in the *Dutchman* and *Tristan*, of festive notables in *Lohengrin* and *Tannhäuser*, and of Hagen's vassals in *Götterdämmerung* make an impressive noise, but they embody a conventional mind-set that the heroic individual defies. Furthermore, regimented masses are not in the Bayreuth style. Wagner made clear his aversion to choruses that march about in "militarily ordered rows," and asked for varied, informal, lifelike movement. Nothing in *Die Nibelungen* is more anti-Wagnerian than that cold geometry of manhood on the march.

HOLLYWOOD WAGNER

Marlene Dietrich in The Scarlet Empress

The birth of talkies is usually dated to the release of *The Jazz Singer* in 1927, but in the previous year Warner Brothers presented a series of sound films with the Vitaphone synchronization process. Their inaugural exhibition, on Broadway, opened with footage of Henry Hadley leading the New York Philharmonic in the *Tannhäuser* overture. An introductory homily by the motion-picture administrator Will Hays promised that "the Vitaphone shall carry symphony orchestrations to the town halls of the hamlets." Willa Cather's Aunt Georgiana would no longer need to travel halfway across the country to experience a Wagner matinée. The notion that sound film would serve principally to advance the "national appreciation of good music," in Hays's words, fell by the wayside, but Wagner remained in play.

The lush production values of Golden Age Hollywood invited a kind of sonic carpet from the opening titles to the last frame—endless melody by the yard. Max Steiner, who scored more than three hundred films between 1930 and 1965, developed the leitmotif system to a near-exact science. In *Casablanca*, "As Time Goes By" is not only heard diegetically but also courses through Steiner's score. Erich Wolfgang Korngold, the doyen of the swashbuckler picture, subjected leitmotifs to sophisticated development, variation, combination, and compression. For some critics, admittedly, Hollywood music was more a travesty of Wagner than an homage to him. Hanns Eisler and Theodor W. Adorno, in their 1947 book *Composing for the Films*, said that the mighty, metaphysical leitmotif had been reduced to "a musical lackey, who announces his master with an important air even though the eminent personage is clearly recognizable to everyone."

Wagner's own music rumbled through action-adventure pictures (*The Lion Man*), historical epics (*The Viking*), romantic drama (*The Right to Live*), gangster pictures (*City Streets*), science fiction (*Flash Gordon*), Westerns (*Red River Valley*), screwball comedy (Preston Sturges's *Sullivan's Travels* and *The Lady Eve*), and horror (Tod Browning's *Dracula* and *Freaks*). The Wagner of the Victorian period lived on in Frank Borzage's adaptation of Hemingway's *A Farewell to Arms*, which ends with Gary Cooper holding the lifeless body of Helen Hayes and exclaiming "Peace! Peace!" while the Liebestod swells. Less sentimental is Borzage's nightmarish montage of war scenes, scored to a mishmash of the "Ride" and other *Ring* motifs. From *The Birth of a Nation* onward, the "Ride" almost always signified male derring-do, erasing the femaleness of the Valkyries. One exception is Josef von Sternberg's *The Scarlet Empress*, about the rise of Catherine the Great, where a Valkyrie fantasia accompanies Marlene Dietrich's climactic horse charge into the palace of the tsar.

Comedians like W. C. Fields, Will Hay, and the Marx Brothers treated Wagner with the same sort of irreverence that Carl Sternheim and Frank Wedekind brought to bear at the turn of the century. Carolyn Abbate, in an essay on Wagner in Hollywood, speaks of "sarcastic misapplications of Wagnerian gravitas," which supply a "deflationary corrective." The Marx Brothers' *At the Circus* (1939) delivers the coup de grace. Margaret Dumont, the brothers' infallible foil, has hired a snooty French conductor and his orchestra to perform at her Newport estate. Groucho and company, wishing to eliminate this rival group so their circus act can collect Dumont's paycheck, direct the Frenchmen to a barge at water's edge, then cut them loose. In the closing shot, the musicians play the *Lohengrin* Act III prelude as they float obliviously out to sea—a fine metaphor for the predicament of classical music in a pop-culture age.

The first Wagnerian masterstroke in the suspense genre comes in Alfred Hitchcock's *Murder!* (1930), a breakthrough film from the director's early British period. Sir John Menier, an actor-manager who has recently served on a jury in a murder trial, fears that he and his fellow jurors might have wrongly convicted a young woman. We see him in his apartment, shaving. His butler turns on the radio: the announcer gives a report on the murder trial and then turns to a musical program, which begins with the *Tristan* prelude. A voice-over communicates Sir John's interior monologue: he muses over the trial, wonders if he should have defied the other jurors, admits that he finds the woman attractive. At the first fortissimo in the prelude, he suddenly focuses on an unresolved question about the case: "Who drank that brandy?" The music goes on playing as he decides to intervene and save the woman from execution.

The sequence plays dexterously on Wagner's affiliation with dreamworlds and interior monologues. The groping first phrases of *Tristan* mimic the workings of Sir John's mind as he struggles to make sense of what has happened. At the same time, the slow surge of the love music reveals his growing desire for the accused. In that respect, *Murder!* anticipates Hitchcock's *Vertigo* (1958), in which a retired detective falls in love with a woman apparently possessed by a spirit out of the nineteenth century. The film's scenario is itself haunted by past works: Korngold's opera *The Dead City*, Georges Rodenbach's Symbolist novel *Bruges-la-morte*, and the doomed love triangle of *Tristan*. Bernard Herrmann's matchless score plays upon *Tristan* motifs. This upwelling of half-buried

Romantic obsession raises a modern psychological thriller to the level of the tragic sublime.

EISENSTEIN

From Eisenstein's sketches for Die Walküre, *1940*

"Lenin . . . but he is motionless . . . Lenin . . . but he is silent." The central section of Dziga Vertov's 1934 film *Three Songs of Lenin* is a staggering montage of scenes from Lenin's funeral, some documentary and some staged. Glimpses of the living Lenin—mingling with the people, orating on the podium—are juxtaposed with shots of his corpse. On the soundtrack, we hear the halting drumbeats and upward-slithering figures that introduce Siegfried's Funeral Music, which was indeed played at Lenin's memorial. The people pay homage, shuffling past the camera in a daze. The double-punching entry of the trombones coincides with a shot of a bearded young worker, staring out with wraithlike eyes. As the brass intone the solemn motif of the Wälsungs, Stalin appears—watchful, wary, not visibly distraught. With the music's transition from tragic minor to heroic major, we see hopeful signs reading "The revolution lives on" and "Lenin is our immortality." Images of fires, smoke, and horses make one think that the body is about to be placed upon a pyre. The identification between Siegfried and Lenin is amplified by Yuri Shaporin's muscularly Wagnerian title theme.

This is the great art of Soviet montage: an intricate counterpoint of pictures and sound that seeks not to hypnotize viewers with seamless illusion but to jolt them into a new awareness. Vertov and Sergei Eisenstein were its rival standard-bearers; both drew on the fin-de-siècle Russian avant-garde. Vertov took a more radical approach, flatly rejecting bourgeois narrative; his montages aimed at a direct, though stylized, representation of Bolshevik reality. Eisenstein, by contrast, could not relinquish the sorrows and grandeurs of nineteenth-century art. Wagner was one of his idols, receiving dozens of mentions in his voluminous theoretical writings. Like Meyerhold, with whom he studied, Eisenstein saw himself less as a Wagner apostle than as a liberated successor who strove to realize the composer's frustrated utopian aims. *Alexander Nevsky* and *Ivan the Terrible*, Eisenstein's collaborations with Sergei Prokofiev, are among the cinema's most plausible realizations of the Gesamtkunstwerk concept.

The son of a Russian-Jewish architect who specialized in Art Nouveau style, Eisenstein spent his early years in Riga, Latvia, a city with a long-standing Germanic heritage. Wagner had directed the local opera house early in his career, and the city prided itself on the affiliation. The young Eisenstein took a special interest in myth and legend, attempting at the age of twelve to stage Friedrich Hebbel's 1861 theatrical adaptation of *Die Nibelungen*, one of the principal sources for Lang's *Nibelungen*. The latter were not to Eisenstein's taste. He once wrote: "I have loved the *Nibelung* since childhood, before Fritz Lang's films spoiled it for me."

Eisenstein's theory of montage emerged from the revolutionary tumult of the early Bolshevik period, although it had roots in the aesthetics of modernism and its nineteenth-century precedents. In his 1923 manifesto "The Montage of Attractions," Eisenstein argues for a free arrangement of effects that abandon conventional logic but build to a decisive impression. In "The Montage of Film Attractions," written in the wake of his 1924 feature *Strike*, he holds that schemes of "juxtaposition and accumulation" can lead the audience from purely emotional reactions to a broader intellectual understanding. In *Strike*, when a factory protest is put down with mass shootings, the desperate movements of the crowd are intercut with footage of a bull being slaughtered with a knife. The instinctive disgust caused by those images—uneasily similar to the antisemitic devices of *The Eternal Jew*—prevents the crowd scenes from becoming an abstraction. In the Odessa Steps sequence in *The Battleship Potemkin*, filmed in 1925, a precariously poised baby carriage becomes the focus of the audience's sympathy.

Eisenstein thought more deeply about Wagner as he theorized the use of sound on film. His 1928 "Statement on Sound," cowritten with Vsevolod Pudovkin and Gregori Alexandrov, advocates a "contrapuntal," asynchronous relationship between image and music. Yet Eisenstein seldom adhered strictly to this philosophy, and often sought a more direct synchronization of the sonic and the visual. He enjoyed Disney's "Silly Symphonies," with their split-second choreography of animation and music. In time, he came to speak of this audiovisual fugue as a "unity of opposites," as "unity in variety." Wagner was a recurring point of reference. In Antonio Somaini's words, the composer gave Eisenstein "a model of how one could interpret what he called 'vertical montage': the arrangement of various expressive elements into a powerful, polyphonic, vibrating whole."

When *Potemkin* was released in Germany, it had a score composed by Edmund Meisel, a collaborator of Erwin Piscator's in the political theater of Berlin. Meisel's music is primitive in technique but packs a wallop in the Odessa Steps sequence. Eisenstein planned to work again with Meisel on what was to have been his first synchronized sound film, *The General Line*, also known as *Old and New* (1929). A paean to collectivized agriculture, *The General Line* follows a peasant worker, Marfa, as she finds happiness on a collective farm. Eisenstein's notes ask for "leitmotivs through *all* types (timbres) of sound," including mechanical and animal noises. In the most famous scene, Marfa takes delight in the operation of a cream separator. Milk shoots up in fountains; Marfa lets it run through her fingers; her face fills with awe. Eisenstein wanted the sequence to play like a Soviet *Parsifal*: he spoke of the cream separator as being "lit by an 'inner light,' as if an image of the Holy Grail." Another fantastical sequence depicts a marriage of cows. Here Eisenstein wanted a kind of bovine Liebesnacht: "Moos in industrial theme syncopation, swelling into a gigantic Wagnerian moo as the bull mounts in the sky."

Meisel's score never materialized. *The General Line* was the first of a series of Eisenstein projects that faltered as Bolshevik avant-gardism gave way to socialist realism. In the same period, Wagner was deemed an "ideologically unacceptable product of bourgeois pan-Germanism." Still, Eisenstein kept pondering Wagner. In a 1932 interview, he said: "I would like to create one day, on film, a kind of modern *Götterdämmerung* . . . a kind of dynamic Pergamon frieze, possibly with Richard Wagner's music post-synchronized." In a later account of this project, Eisenstein specified that titans of finance would substitute for gods: "The film was to show the decline of capitalist society, and I proposed to base it on the sensational stories about the recent disappearance of the 'match king' Ivar Kreiger [Kreuger], Loewenstein, the financier who threw himself out of an aeroplane, and a number of other sensational catastrophes that overtook the representatives of big capital."

Although the *Ring* plan came to naught, it gives a tantalizing glimpse of how Eisenstein might have developed Wagner's revolutionary allegory, along the lines of Shaw's *The Perfect Wagnerite*. As Dieter Thomä remarks in a book on Wagner and Eisenstein, these two very different artists are both marked by a productive tension between totalizing and fragmentary visions—between the pageant of community and the agony of the individual subject.

I n August 1939, the signing of the Nazi-Soviet non-aggression pact temporarily returned Wagner to favor in the Soviet Union. Eisenstein, whose *Nevsky* film had been pulled from circulation because of its anti-German message, was asked to direct *Walküre* at the Bolshoi—the first time he had worked in theater since the mid-twenties. Happy to resume his interest in Germanic myth, Eisenstein undertook frenzied research, as his teacher Meyerhold had done when directing *Tristan*. Soon he was sketching ideas not only for *Walküre* but also for *Rheingold* and *Siegfried*. Meyerhold had taken pride in Eisenstein's ascent, saying in 1936 that his disciple's work "had its origins in the laboratory where we once worked together." By the time the rehearsals for *Walküre* began, in the spring of 1940, Meyerhold had fallen victim to Stalin's Terror. As a precaution, Eisenstein had taken possession of his mentor's archives, including the *Tristan* notes. He would preserve them for posterity by hiding them in his dacha.

In an essay titled "The Incarnation of Myth," Eisenstein interpreted

Walküre as a narrative of transition from the primitive to the modern. Wotan incarnates nature in all its anarchic power; rough Hunding marks the earliest stage of human development; Siegmund and Sieglinde are victims of a shift toward the sort of bourgeois morality propounded by Fricka; Brünnhilde represents the future. Civilization overcomes primitive urges, but at the same time it loses the "*original harmony* between man and his surroundings." The Hitler-Stalin Pact notwithstanding, Eisenstein wished to distance himself from the Nazi Wagner. Early in the process, in December 1939, he wrote the following, in a mixture of German and English:

> Our interpretation of the work will probably go from the *unhuman to the human* . . .
>
> The main point of the piece: *Brünnhilde opens herself to human feelings.*
>
> She opens herself up to *love* in *Siegfried.* To *hatred*—in *Gotterdammerung.* But here—the complexity of human feelings—in which she sees how others love one another, also *compassion* and *self-sacrifice.*
>
> (*What is fascistic in this play, wonder?!!!*)

That the production had failed to conform to Nazi aesthetics became clear when officers from the German Embassy dismissed it as "deliberate Jewish tricks."

Eisenstein mobilized various techniques to flesh out his vision of humanity evolving within nature. Cliffs rose and fell; trees bowed and stood. Actors performed pantomimes of Hunding's tribe and Fricka's rams. Papier-mâché figures evoked a Valkyrie horde. The production taxed the Bolshoi's resources, and some cherished ideas fell by the wayside. Eisenstein had wanted the branches of the ash tree in Act I to extend into the auditorium; he also spoke of projecting a film when Siegmund narrates his past and amplifying the "Ride" on loudspeakers arranged around the hall. The siblings were to have made love beneath a wheel representing the Ouroboros, the dragon that eats its own tail. (Eisenstein here drew on the Wagnerian theories of Carl Jung, as Håkan Lövgren has established.) Other effects came off successfully—in particular, a light show for the finale. Eisenstein relished the "*pathos* with which the blue flame grew to the sound of the 'Magic Fire' music in the last act, sometimes repeating it, then conflicting with it, then isolating it, then absorbing it; the blue flame grows, devouring the red, red subduing the blue." This sequence, he said, showed him how to work with color on film.

In his memoirs, Eisenstein associates the Valkyries with pine trees, saying that he had once heard someone play the "Ride" on the piano "among the giant pines in the forests of Finland." Then, falling into a meta-Wagnerian stream of consciousness, he thinks of the "famous redwoods around San Francisco," where he stayed for a week in 1930, bringing with him a copy of *Ulysses*. The novel taught him to appreciate the "structure of leitmotif and counterpoint." While he followed fragmentary phrases across the page, "tiny squirrels hopped about gnawing nuts at the feet of these gigantic trees." The reverie includes a sketch of a scene from Eisenstein's final finished film, the second part of *Ivan the Terrible*. It is the Dionysian dance of the *oprichniki* in Ivan's court, their red, gold, blue, and black robes swirling in a "dance of colors"—shades of Loie Fuller's Fire Dance.

Totalitarian reality encircled Eisenstein's joy in creation. Stalin commissioned *Ivan the Terrible* in the expectation that it would glorify Ivan's ruthlessness and thereby justify his own rule. That the dictator refused to allow the release of *Ivan, Part Two*—in which the tsar experiences Wotanlike spasms of doubt and remorse—does not absolve Eisenstein of having lent his talent to a totalitarian regime. The ideological contradictions at the heart of Eisenstein's work are Wagnerian in every sense. When the director called *Ivan* a fugue on the theme of power, he might as well have been describing the *Ring*.

WAR MOVIES

The Hitlerizing of Wagner in Hollywood began with the onset of the Second World War. For most of the thirties, the studios had shied away from anti-Nazi messages, unwilling to alienate the sizable German market for genre pictures. Warner Brothers' 1939 thriller *Confessions of a Nazi Spy* marked a turning point. When the film was rereleased in 1940 with a semi-documentary epilogue about recent German victories, Max Steiner augmented his score with gratingly harmonized references to Siegfried's principal theme and to "The Ride of the Valkyries." In the same period,

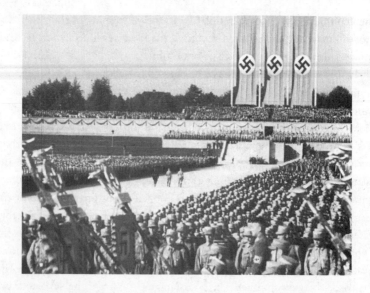

the cliché of the Wagner-loving Nazi started to take hold. In the 1940 drama *Escape*, a Nazi general has an affair with a widowed aristocrat, who grows disenchanted with Wagner as she becomes conscious of the evil of the regime:

NORMA SHEARER: Oh, do play something else, Kurt.
CONRAD VEIDT: I thought *Tristan* was our favorite opera.
NORMA SHEARER: Well, perhaps I've heard it too often.

In *Bombsight Stolen*, Nazi spies play *Meistersinger* to cover their perfidious conversation; in *Secret Mission*, a German armored truck blasts the Pilgrims' Chorus from loudspeakers; in Jean Renoir's *This Land Is Mine*, "The Ride of the Valkyries" heralds Nazi invaders; and in *Reunion in France*, Joan Crawford notes with dismay that *Meistersinger* is "Hitler's favorite melody."

Such associations would have had a familiar ring for filmgoers who had been watching newsreels of Nazis on the march. The 1938 *March of Time* segment "Inside Nazi Germany," an unusually critical look at the regime, explained the idea of *Lebensraum* with the aid of the Dance of the Apprentices from *Meistersinger*. The newsreels, in turn, took their cues from Nazi propaganda—or, at least, from the perception of Nazi propaganda. Many people had the impression that *Triumph of the Will* is awash in Wagner. A correspondent wrote of its opening scene: "To the accompaniment of Wagnerian-like music, Hitler's Junker plane is seen flying above summer clouds en route to Nuremberg." A later book about *Triumph of the Will* claimed that the *Meistersinger* prelude is playing at the outset. In fact, the music is by Herbert Windt, mostly in the style of Richard Strauss. A ninety-second excerpt from *Meistersinger* is heard during the "old Nuremberg" sequence, and Gottfried Sonntag's creaky *Nibelungen-Marsch* appears toward the end, but Wagner is otherwise absent. The historian Celia Applegate calls it a case of "phantom hearing": listeners imagine more Wagner than there is, because he seems to belong in an ode to Hitler.

Nazi film composers, like their American counterparts, drew liberally on Wagnerian techniques. Giuseppe Becce, the former star of *The Life and Works of Richard Wagner*, wrote a Siegfriedish main theme for a German Western titled *The Emperor of California*. For the most part, though, Wagner was "strangely shunned" in Nazi cinema, to quote the scholar Lutz Koepnick. No biopic was made, nor were the music dramas adapted for film. Wagner Scenes like the one in *Stukas*, where an airman recuperates at Bayreuth, were rare. Goebbels's push for a culture of mass distraction— "American hunk," he called it—left little place for Wagner and his complications. Counterintuitively, the composer figured more often in Hollywood films of the thirties and forties than in Nazi ones.

Shortly after America entered the war, Frank Capra, the director of *It Happened One Night* and *Mr. Smith Goes to Washington*, set to work making propaganda films that would explain to young recruits what they were fighting for. As part of his research, Capra watched *Triumph of the Will*, and his first reaction was to think, "We can't win this war." In his memoir, he wrote of Riefenstahl's film: "Though panoplied with all the pomp and mystical trappings of a Wagnerian opera, its message was as blunt and brutal as a lead pipe: We, the Herrenvolk, are the new invincible gods!" The opening sequence sounded to him like *Götterdämmerung*. On reflection, Capra decided that Nazi sound and fury could be turned against itself. The result was *Why We Fight*, a series of seven films that mixed sober history lessons with taunting commentaries on Fascist and Imperial Japanese poses. The project's primary composer was Dimitri Tiomkin, last seen directing music for the Bolshevik mass spectacle *The Mystery of Liberated Labor*.

Less than five minutes into *Prelude to War*, the first episode of *Why We*

Fight, we have heard a musical answer to the series' guiding question. As the narrator speaks of a battle between a free world and an enslaved one, the orchestra quotes Siegfried's theme in muted, menacing form. That theme recurs dozens of times in the opening episodes, in increasingly dissonant variations. These creative manglings serve two distinct purposes. On the one hand, they give the enemy a readily identifiable sonic tag. At the same time, they supply a forward-thrusting energy. Even as Wagner is being painted black, he lends a heroic dimension to the proceedings. Soon enough, we hear patriotic tunes orchestrated à la Wagner. The American side, too, had its *Herrenvolk* mentality. *Why We Fight* opens with a statement to the effect that by war's end the American flag should be "recognized throughout the world as a symbol of freedom on the one hand, of overwhelming power on the other."

Animated films provide a raucous summary of Wagner's overlapping tropes. The movie historian Daniel Ira Goldmark counts well over a hundred Warner Brothers cartoons with the composer on their soundtracks. During the war, cartoons were requisitioned for propaganda purposes, and Wagner quotations in *Der Fuehrer's Face*, *Scrap Happy Daffy*, and *Daffy— The Commando* helped to identify Nazi characters as malicious buffoons. In *Herr Meets Hare*, Bugs Bunny finds himself in the Black Forest, where he confronts a Hermann Göring type. Carl Stalling's score dresses Göring in a frantic cluster of Wagner themes; later, Bugs assumes the bearing of Brünnhilde, riding a white horse to, oddly, the tune of the Pilgrims' Chorus. The Disney cartoon *Education for Death* is even more of a didactic anti-Nazi exercise, teaching how the enemy sullies fairy tales. We see a German child brainwashed into believing that the wicked witch in *Sleeping Beauty* is Democracy; that the princess in distress is Germany; and that the prince who rides to save her is Hitler. A gigantic Valkyrie sings "Heil Hitler" to the music of the "Ride," with glissando trombones jeering her on.

Still, classic cartoons of the forties and fifties were too addicted to Wagner's sonic zest to demonize him entirely. Citations in *Hare We Go* and *Captain Hareblower* bear no trace of Nazi evil. The operatic cetacean in *The Whale Who Wanted to Sing at the Met* essays the love duet from *Tristan*. In one anti-Japanese cartoon—*Bugs Bunny Nips the Nips*—Wagner is actually converted to the Allied cause. Carl Stalling's score uses the Siegfried motif to signify the prospect of Bugs's rescue by an American warship—a rescue he ultimately refuses, in favor of the company of a sexy female rabbit. The film-music historian Neil Lerner has noted the uncomfortable alignment of an Americanized Wagner with a gratuitously racist and dehumanizing depiction of Japanese people.

When Charlie Chaplin watched *Triumph of the Will*, his immediate reaction, according to Luis Buñuel, was to burst into laughter. The orator on screen seemed an insane variation on his own "Little Tramp" persona, down to the toothbrush mustache. The experience unnerved him, though, as it did so many leftist filmmakers who witnessed the technical virtuosity of German cinema being applied to sinister ends. In 1940, Chaplin released *The Great Dictator*, a lavish satire of Hitler's histrionics. Inevitably, Wagner is on the soundtrack, yet Chaplin makes the surprising choice to detach the music from the Nazi context—almost as if he were carrying on the rescue mission of Thomas Mann, his friend in Los Angeles. The prelude to *Lohengrin* is heard twice in the film, serving first to puncture Nazi iconography and then to amplify a message of peace.

Hitler is caricatured as Adenoid Hynkel, a nincompoop of a Führer who jabbers mock-German and is more than a little fey in manner. He clutches his breast, prances about, tinkles on a piano with candelabra all

around, and, at one point, holds a flower in an Oscar Wilde–like pose. When his propaganda minister, Herr Garbitsch, raises the idea of killing all the Jews and making Hynkel "dictator of the world," Hynkel becomes so excited that he scurries up the drapes and exclaims melodramatically, "Leave me, I want to be alone."

Here the *Lohengrin* prelude begins—that high, thin, shining music that Baudelaire greeted as the gateway to another world. Hynkel slides down the drapes and prowls across the floor to an enormous globe. "Emperor of the world," he murmurs. He then plucks the globe from its stand and spins it on his finger, laughing hysterically. A singular ballet ensues, as Chaplin bounces the ball from hand to hand, off his head, off his foot, and so on. Twice he bumps the ball into the air with his butt—a gesture that cannot be described as conventionally masculine. Even as Chaplin ridicules Hitler's pose of manly steeliness, he is exploring his own fluid conception of gender roles. It's almost as if the Wagnerism of Magnus Hirschfeld were stealing in.

A parallel story arc shows the travails of a Jewish barber, identical in appearance to Hynkel. He is consigned to a ghetto and then to a concentration camp. At the climax of the film, the oppressor and the oppressed switch roles: Hynkel is mistaken for the barber and sent to the camp, while the barber finds himself addressing a party rally. His closing speech is a stirring critique of capitalist ruthlessness and a plea for brotherhood. After the crowd cheers, he addresses his girlfriend, Hannah, who is in exile. The music of *Lohengrin* returns as the barber reaches his peroration: "We are coming into a new world, a kindlier world, where men will rise above their hate, their greed and brutality. Look up, Hannah!" Hannah, in a field, gazes in wonder: she has heard the barber on the radio. "Listen!" she exclaims, her eyes shining. *Lohengrin* swells all around her, as if playing from on high.

Chaplin's manipulation of Wagner is at once a dismantling and a rebuilding. As Lutz Koepnick writes, the composer is used both to "condemn the abuse of fantasy in fascism *and* warrant the utopian possibilities of industrial culture." The musicologist Lawrence Kramer, contemplating the same ideological reversal, observes that in Chaplin's retelling of *Lohengrin* "the Grail knight has been replaced by a Jewish exile, and a woman to boot." For some viewers, Chaplin's idealism may seem wincingly naïve, just as his lampoon of Hitler may seem to trivialize the horror of the Nazi regime. Mann himself had doubts about the film's reliance on farce when he saw it. Yet naïveté is at the core of Chaplin's enduring appeal. Eisenstein once called Chaplin "the true and touching 'Holy Innocent,' whose image the aging Wagner dreamed of."

WAGNER NOIR

Hume Cronyn in Brute Force

Chaplin's fantasy of a postwar utopia evaporated in the Cold War era, as the American military machine shifted its attention from Nazi Germany to Soviet Russia. A grim succession of events—the atomic bombing of two Japanese cities, the rise of Red-hunting paranoia, undiminished violence against African-Americans in the South—left marks on Hollywood. The film-noir genre, characterized by hard-boiled plots, acidulous dialogue, and high-contrast Weimar-style cinematography, was symptomatic of the altered national mood. Technicolor epics and musicals provided a countervailing mode of escape. Wagner played his usual ambiguous role, feeding anxiety and fantasy alike. The prominence of Central European émigré directors in Hollywood added to the tension surrounding the composer, as the likes of Fritz Lang, Billy Wilder, and Robert Siodmak examined the Germanic legacy.

The Nazi Wagnerite remained a commonplace. In war and spy movies, a liking for the composer is nearly as reliable an indicator of Nazi affiliations as a swastika armband. In *The Boys from Brazil*, Franklin J. Schaffner's

1978 thriller about the fugitive life of Josef Mengele, Gregory Peck savors the *Siegfried Idyll* as he supervises a scheme to clone Hitler. Laurence Olivier, in the role of a Jewish Nazi-hunter, speaks of Mengele in Auschwitz, "amputating limbs and organs . . . with the strains of Wagner providing an obbligato to the screams of the mutants he was creating!" Such dialogue helped to popularize the idea, not supported by the historical record, that Wagner was an integral part of the soundscape of the death camps. Conversely, when the Franz von Papen character in *Five Fingers* (1952) says, "Wagner makes me ill," we know that he is not wholly evil.

By metaphorical extension, Wagner can be a favorite musical selection for sadists and cold-blooded killers. In Jules Dassin's noir *Brute Force* (1947), a prison guard who follows a pseudo-Nietzschean philosophy of "the weak must die" puts on a recording of the *Tannhäuser* overture as he prepares to torture a prisoner in his office. Modern Hollywood often casts supervillains and serial killers as classical-music fans; the equation of Wagner and Hitler encouraged this durable shorthand, though its roots lie much deeper. Already in the time of Mark Twain, some Americans were spurning European culture as a deviant, unwholesome influence.

During the Cold War, the instinct to vilify the Germans ran up against a rival agenda. Because West Germany had become an ally in the effort to contain the Soviets, *Realpolitik* required a measure of forgiveness. Meanwhile, classical music maintained a high profile in American culture, with Leonard Bernstein explicating Beethoven on television and opera singers making the rounds of talk shows. For these reasons—or perhaps because the music remained so rousingly effective—Wagner kept reverting to older, more innocent functions. The composer of torture music also led countless brides down the aisle, including Marilyn Monroe and Jane Russell in *Gentlemen Prefer Blondes*, where *Lohengrin* morphs into a reprise of "Two Little Girls from Little Rock" and "Diamonds Are a Girl's Best Friend."

The strangest artifact of Hollywood's muddled attitude toward Wagner is William Dieterle's *Magic Fire* (1955), the first full-length biopic about the composer since Carl Fröhlich's film of 1913. Musical biopics became a fad in Hollywood after the surprise success of *A Song to Remember*, a stagey 1945 film about Chopin. Dieterle, a German émigré noted for his adroit handling of prestige pictures, had brushed against Wagner before; in his early years in Germany, he had directed and starred in a film about the last years of Ludwig II. In Los Angeles, he listened to Wagner records in the company of Thomas Mann. *Magic Fire* was to have been the culmination of his career; instead, it proved a fiasco, and the director returned to Europe not long after.

Republic Pictures, a former B-movie studio with upward aspirations, sank considerable resources into the production. In return for a substantial donation, the Wagner family allowed Dieterle to film inside the Festspielhaus—presumably the first such visit since *Stukas* in 1941. Erich Wolfgang Korngold, the production's musical director, condensed the entire *Ring* into a five-minute montage and conducted it on site, wearing a Hans Richter beard. Dieterle's creation suffered from heavy-handed cutting in postproduction, although not even the most artful editing could have redeemed the dialogue, which the director wrote with Bertita Harding:

No doubt you'll notice that there are several themes in the overture which will be repeated again and again throughout the opera. I call them leitmotifs.

An opera by Richard Wagner is not a vaudeville show!

Tristan is dying and you ask me how I am!

Everyone who comes too close to you is consumed by the magic of your fire.

Alan Badel portrays Wagner as a manic Romantic in the grip of a controlling muse. At the end, with *Parsifal* on the soundtrack, a bereft Cosima stumbles through palatial rooms purporting to be the Palazzo Vendramin. She closes the Meister's piano and collapses on his death-sofa as the camera moves past billowing drapes toward a painted Venetian sunset. It is a sad caricature of the woman George Eliot acclaimed as a "genius."

Dieterle was not the only émigré director to take a surprisingly soft-focus approach to Hitler's favorite composer. Curtis Bernhardt's *Interrupted Melody*, also from 1955, tells the story of the Australian-born soprano Marjorie Lawrence, who found fame as a Wagner singer before being struck by polio. Early in the film, she is seen riding her horse across the outback, in a sequence that brings to mind Cather's *The Song of the Lark*. In her Met debut, she uses her horsemanship to make an impressive exit in *Götterdämmerung*. Then, while Lawrence is rehearsing Isolde's Transfiguration, the disease takes hold of her body. For a time, she is on the verge of suicide, but her love of music overcomes her despair. When she makes a triumphant return to the Met, as Isolde, the Liebestod has reversed its fatal effect, guiding her to new life.

One can imagine Billy Wilder, the acerbic master of mid-century Hollywood comedy, smirking at such a rosy scenario. A product of 1920s Vienna and Berlin, Wilder treated Wagner with casual contempt. In *A Foreign Affair* (1948), set in occupied Berlin, American authorities investigate the Nazi past of a cabaret singer played by Marlene Dietrich. They watch a newsreel of a gala performance of *Lohengrin*, at which Hitler is seen kissing the singer's hand. "They certainly fiddled big while Berlin burned," one observer snaps. "*Lohengrin*, you know, swan song," says another. In *Love in the Afternoon* (1957), Wilder stages a performance of *Tristan* in Paris and adds droll commentary. Maurice Chevalier, playing an exceedingly suave private investigator, quips: "*Tristan and Isolde*. Very sad case. Now, if instead of doing all that singing they would have hired a good detective . . ." Fritz Lang, having tussled with Wagner's shadow in *Die Nibelungen*, exacts revenge in his 1953 noir *The Blue Gardenia*, inserting a recording of the Liebestod into a sordid story of sexual predation, jealousy, and murder.

In one classic noir plot, a powerful older man engages a younger, handsomer man on a mission involving a wife, girlfriend, or daughter, triggering an affair between the latter two. Versions of this triangle appear in Jacques Tourneur's *Out of the Past*, Howard Hawks's *The Big Sleep*, Otto Preminger's *Laura*, and Hitchcock's *Vertigo*. Elisabeth Bronfen has plausibly linked such stories to *Tristan*, in which King Mark sends Tristan to fetch Isolde. The difference is that high passion gives way to a cooler, bleaker kind of love-death. In Wilder's incomparable 1944 noir *Double Indemnity*, where Barbara Stanwyck's femme fatale drives the action, Edward G. Robinson says of the lovers: "They're stuck with each other and they've got to ride together all the way to the end of the line. And it's a one-way trip and the last stop is the cemetery." Such fatalism conveys unease within the American psyche at its moment of global triumph.

Jean Negulesco's *Humoresque* (1946), a melodrama with a streak of noir, makes the *Tristan* subtext explicit. A dissipated socialite (Joan Crawford), married to an ineffectual older man, falls in love with a rising violin soloist (John Garfield), who comes from a lower-class immigrant background and speaks a hard-boiled patois. His vacillating responses to her advances send her into terminal despair, and she commits suicide by walking into the ocean. As she goes to her end, the radio is broadcasting a bizarre double-concerto arrangement of Isolde's Transfiguration, which Garfield plays alongside the celebrity pianist Oscar Levant. The female lead has all the characteristics of the femme fatale, and her death is necessary for the maturation of the male protagonist, as the musicologist Marcia Citron has argued. Nonetheless, the disconcerting intensity of Crawford's performance dominates the film, restoring the dire, desperate Romantic aura that tends to fall away when Wagner goes to Hollywood.

The greatest of Wagner noirs—admittedly a limited genre—is Siodmak's *Christmas Holiday* (1944), whose central *Tristan* sequence rivals the most sophisticated Wagner Scenes of fin-de-siècle literature. A native of Dresden, Siodmak came from a cultured German-Jewish family that knew Ernst Toller, Emil Nolde, and Richard Strauss. Siodmak's regard for Thomas Mann would lead him to make a failed attempt at filming *The Magic Mountain*. In *Christmas Holiday*, he settled for a somewhat seedy novel by W. Somerset Maugham. The script was by Herman J. Mankiewicz, the brilliant, erratic screenwriter who wrote *Citizen Kane* for Orson Welles.

The story is, of course, one of fatal passion, although here the overtones of decadence and madness belong to the male. The musical-comedy star

Robert Siodmak's Christmas Holiday

Deanna Durbin ventures the role of Abigail, a naïve young woman who likes nothing more than to go to orchestra concerts. Gene Kelly, also cast against type, plays Robert, a shiftily charming Southerner from a privileged background. They marry, and, this being a noir, the marriage goes south. Robert, an inveterate liar and gambler, kills a bookie and is sentenced to life in prison. Abigail becomes a bar singer, allowing Durbin to trot out numbers like Irving Berlin's "Always." In the bar, Abigail meets a winsome G.I., to whom she tells her woes. In the denouement, Robert, having escaped from prison, is on the point of killing Abigail when the police cut him down.

Like *Citizen Kane*, *Christmas Holiday* is told in flashbacks, one of which shows the moment Abigail and Robert first met. The sequence opens with a long shot of an orchestra in a packed concert hall, seen from a high balcony. The music is Isolde's Transfiguration in its standard orchestral arrangement. It is played straight to the end, without cuts or emendations, for two and a half minutes—an eternity in Hollywood terms. The camera slowly pans to a balcony high on the side, in the cheap seats. It comes to rest on Robert and Abigail, sitting side by side, listening raptly, oblivious to each other. She moves her head slowly from side to side. He stares fixedly, with a certain blank sadness. Where Isolde would be singing "Unconscious, highest bliss," Abigail closes her eyes and then opens them again. The music ends, the crowd applauds. She bumps into him as she is getting ready to leave.

"Oh, excuse me, I guess I just didn't realize it was over," Robert says. "You know, sometimes when a concert's over I get a feeling I've left myself for a long time. Of course, you wouldn't know it, but that's the greatest thing that could happen to me. I'm the most wonderful person in the world to leave. Unfortunately, you can't make a living out of being absorbed in music. You know, sometimes when I listen to it I feel that there's nothing man is capable of that I can't do. Then it stops, and it's over."

"Oh, not for me," Abigail says. "When I hear good music, I feel—well, I feel as if something has been added to my life that wasn't there before." He answers, with a suddenly charming smile: "I'd like that. Think you could teach me?"

Mankiewicz and Siodmak's use of *Tristan* as a marker of tragic love is a defiantly retrograde gesture, falling back on a Gilded Age mode of Wagnerian infatuation and uplift. (The opera does not figure in Maugham's novel.) No one utters Wagner's name beforehand: the music simply materializes. When Abigail introduces the flashback, she lays emphasis on the universality of musical experience: "Those days, anytime I had a half a dollar that didn't belong to the butcher, the landlady, the streetcar company, I'd go to a concert." She could be a future Kronborg, awaiting musical revelation. As in many Wagner Scenes, Abigail's Wagnerism also leaves her vulnerable to predation. Her eyes closed in bliss, she fails to take the measure of the man next to her.

As for Robert, he is a shadowy dreamer, receiving a Glimpse of Future Greatness ("There's nothing man is capable of that I can't do"). Richard Dyer notices that certain traits of Robert's personality—his attachment to a possessive mother, his "inexplicable nocturnal absences"—hint that he is gay, according to the stereotypes of the day. Wagner speaks in different ways to both of these isolated, needful people.

Tristan returns at the end, in a gauzy scene recalling Borzage's *A Farewell to Arms*. When Robert is shot, we hear a bit of the Transfiguration, which gives way to the strains of "Always": "I'll be loving you, always, with a love that's true, always." The Wagnerian connoisseur might hear an echo of the Liebesnacht: "*Ewig einig, / ohne End*'," or "Ever one, without end." Robert says, "You can let go now, Abigail." She sobs. The Transfiguration resumes. Abigail walks to the window, tears streaming down her face. She looks up and sees clouds parting to reveal stars—a sign that Charlie, her new soldier friend, will give her a more stable form of love. As in *The Great Dictator*, Wagner provides a hopeful finish, his score gussied up in high Hollywood style. But the noir atmosphere lingers: the loneliness, the desperation, the Expressionistic grit of Siodmak's black-and-white compositions. Wagner is, finally, an ironic presence in a picture where endless love comes to a quick, dark end.

ART-HOUSE WAGNER

Griffith, Lang, and Eisenstein demonstrated, in their very different ways, that film directors could exert the same world-shaping power that Wagner once wielded in opera. In Hollywood, the rise of the studio curbed their authority; in Europe, especially in the postwar years, they found greater freedom. Italian neorealism, Spanish Surrealism, the French New Wave,

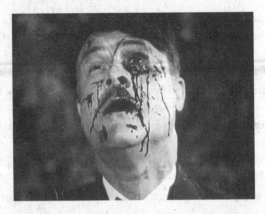

"Mon amour, mon amour . . .": Buñuel's L'Âge d'or

the Japanese avant-garde, and other art-house styles introduced a formidable array of film languages. In that sprawling body of work, Wagner is a frequent visitor, conjuring both the dreamscape of nineteenth-century Romanticism and the nightmare of the century that followed. Variously tormenting, enraging, and inspiring, he is an index of the rise and fall of European culture in an Americanized world.

Wagner's most ardent fans in postwar European cinema were Luis Buñuel and Luchino Visconti—dissimilar figures who shared a propensity for Romantic decadence. Buñuel, cinema's leading Surrealist, featured the composer in his first film, *Un chien andalou* (1929), and in his last, *That Obscure Object of Desire* (1977). He had discovered Wagner during his childhood in a small town in northeast Spain, where, he wrote, "the Middle Ages lasted until World War I." As a teenager, he would entertain his sisters by spinning Wagnerian tales and illustrating them on the violin. Later, he attended performances at the Teatro Real in Madrid, score in hand. Salvador Dalí, a Catalan in Madrid, shared Buñuel's interest. "Wagner, too, was completely surrealist," Dalí said.

In 1929, Buñuel and Dalí collaborated on the scenario for *Un chien andalou*, a short silent film that became a Surrealist landmark. The opening delivers an incomparably disturbing series of images: Buñuel on a balcony, holding a sharpened razor; a thin trail of cloud approaching the moon; the razor being raised to a woman's eye; the cloud cutting across the moon; a dead calf's eye being sliced open. At the premiere, Buñuel stood behind the screen with a phonograph, playing a tango record, and his ad hoc score was replicated for the sound version of the film. The resulting juxtaposition of elements—a Romantic moon, misogynist violence, propulsive tango music—typified Surrealist concerns, for better or worse. The next item on Buñuel's playlist is Isolde's Transfiguration; it accompanies a man dressed in a nun's habit bicycling down nearly empty city streets. The audiovisual dissonance is beyond anything Eisenstein had imagined.

Buñuel had *Tristan* in mind from the beginning. "Stare out the window and look as if you're listening to Wagner," he instructed Pierre Batcheff, who played the bicyclist. For the remainder of the film, the soundtrack alternates between *Tristan* and two Argentinian selections—as if in defiance of Marinetti's manifesto "Down with the Tango and *Parsifal*!" During the first Wagner sequence, the bicyclist falls over, a woman comes to his aid, ants crawl out of a hole in his palm, an androgynous young woman probes a severed hand with a stick, and the androgyne is run over by a car. During the second, another young man, also played by Batcheff, is killed by the first with books that turn into pistols. When Buñuel was asked if this was a case of "comic counterpoint," he replied that he used Wagner simply because he was very fond of him. Indeed, as Torben Sangild writes, *Tristan* gives a tragic continuity to these displaced lovers: "They are no longer metaphysical heroes from a distant past, but confused and immature beings in a chaotic world of desire and violence."

Tristan becomes an anthem of outlaw desire in *L'Âge d'or* (1930), Buñuel's first feature. The film follows the misadventures of a passionate couple at odds with bourgeois convention. In the midst of an outdoor ceremony involving civil servants, soldiers, and clerics—the synopsis claims that this is the founding of Rome—the lovers are discovered thrashing about lustily in the mud. The *Tristan* Prelude begins playing as they are pulled apart. Later, the couple makes love in a garden at night while a nearby orchestra performs Isolde's Transfiguration for a well-dressed crowd. "What joy, what joy, to have murdered our children," the woman says. The man, his face covered in blood, answers, *"Mon amour, mon amour."* At this point, the conductor breaks off, discarding his baton and burying his head in his hands. The crowd murmurs as he staggers away. Soon he is locked in an embrace with the female lover. These anarchic goings-on have a political edge: the conductor might be quitting his podium because he senses the disparity between his bourgeois public and Wagner's revolutionary music. The sequence may be a parable of the artist attaining social independence.

Buñuel returned repeatedly to his beloved Wagner, though never in predictable fashion. *Tristan* drives the climax of *Abismos de pasión*, an adaptation of *Wuthering Heights*. The title and plot of *Tristana*, based on Benito Pérez Galdós's 1892 novel, are implicitly Wagnerian. *The Phantom of Liberty* has dinner-party guests chatting about a new *Tristan* production while sitting on toilets; *The Exterminating Angel* has an opera-singer character nicknamed La Valkyrie. Finally, *That Obscure Object of Desire* transposes Wagner to a modern-day Europe scarred by terrorism. The scenario is taken from Pierre Louÿs's sadomasochistic love story *The Woman and the Puppet*. In the last scene, the lovers, Mathieu and Conchita, stroll through a Paris arcade as a voice-over describes shifting alliances among radical groups, including the Revolutionary Army of the Baby Jesus. "And now, to clear our heads, let's have some music," the voice says. As Mathieu and Conchita watch a woman mend a bloody white garment, Siegmund and Sieglinde sing of their love: "A dream of love / comes to my mind as well: / burning with longing / I have seen you before." Buñuel hints that Wagner's characters undergo an eternal return in the modern world, replaying their fate. A bomb goes off, and the movie ends.

The sexually heretical novelist Henry Miller touched on Buñuel's Wagnerism in a 1931 essay. Remembering that early audiences were shocked by the use of *Tristan* in *L'Âge d'or*, Miller wrote: "Was it possible that the divine music of Wagner could so arouse the sensual appetites of a man and a woman as to make them roll in the graveled path and bite and chew one another until the blood came? Was it possible that this music could so take possession of the young woman as to make her suck the toe of a statued foot with perverted lasciviousness? Does music bring on orgasms, does it entrain perverse acts, does it drive people truly mad? Does this great legendary theme which Wagner immortalized have to do with such a plain vulgar physiological fact as sexual love? The film seems to suggest that it does."

Visconti was the gay scion of an ancient Milanese family whose long decline the director compared to that of Thomas Mann's Buddenbrooks. He grew up on German literature and music. "All my films are

Trevor Howard as Wagner in Visconti's Ludwig

dipped in Mann," he said. In the thirties, he flirted with Nazism, more on erotic than ideological grounds. On a visit to Germany, he saw Hitler speak and attended rallies at which he admired, according to others' recollections, the "discipline and strength of handsome youths," including "blond, sadistic boys in uniform." Although he later turned to the political left, German culture still held him transfixed. Between 1969 and 1973, he produced three films on Germanic themes, moving backward from the Nazi period to Wagner's lifetime: *The Damned* (or *The Fall of the Gods*, in Italian); *Death in Venice*; and *Ludwig*.

The last two are loving, immaculately detailed, glacially slow-moving re-creations of nineteenth-century and fin-de-siècle settings. In *Death in Venice*, the character of Gustav von Aschenbach is changed from a writer to a composer, although an attempt to fuse Mann's doomed Wagnerian vacation with the life and music of Gustav Mahler does no favors either to Mann or to Mahler. *Ludwig* delivers faithful replications of the Mad King's Wagnerian kitsch: a gauzy arrangement of *Tannhäuser*'s Song to the Evening Star accompanies a scene in the king's Venus Grotto, and the same music is heard tinkling from a music box. The prevailing torpor is disrupted by Trevor Howard's flamboyant turn as Wagner. No actor has better captured the composer's clownish vitality. We first see him ensconced in Munich, in the flush of Ludwig's patronage. He strides about, he babbles, he flits from one topic to another, a crafty gleam in his eye all the while. He then starts making woofing noises and wrestling with his dog. A later scene depicts the first performance of the *Siegfried Idyll*, on Christmas Day in 1870—Richard's lavish gift to Cosima. Sadly, a plan to reenact the composer's death and funeral was abandoned.

In *The Damned*, Visconti arrives in territory he knows firsthand: the crossroads of Romanticism, Nazism, and gay desire. A gruesomely vital film results. A German industrialist clan, the Essenbecks, are in business with Nazis. They are a blend of Mann's *Buddenbrooks* and the Krupp armaments dynasty. The paterfamilias, Joachim, symbolizes the lost values of the Kaiser-reich; his son, Konstantin, is an SA leader; Joachim's grandson begins as a cross-dressing Weimar decadent and ends as an icy SS man. The stupefying centerpiece of the film is an all-male SA orgy that gives way to the slaughter of the Night of the Long Knives. Visconti shot the sequence in Bad Wiessee, where, in 1934, Hitler arrested the SA chief Ernst Röhm and many of his henchmen. Just before the purge begins, Konstantin Essenbeck is seen drunkenly howling the Liebestod while a glistening young man dressed in nothing but garters takes a cigarette break. The scene is not entirely ahistorical, since Röhm was a gay Wagnerite of a rough-and-ready sort. But the ensuing bloodbath is invented—most of the killing during the Röhm purge took place elsewhere—and the whole tableau feeds the discredited idea that sexual deviancy lay at the heart of the Nazi phenomenon.

What might be called freak-show Wagnerism figures in several other movies of the postwar period. Federico Fellini's *8½* contains a feverish fantasy sequence scored to the "Ride," in which the film-director protagonist loses control of a harem of women and then regains the upper hand with the aid of a whip. (Fellini also has an orchestra playing the "Ride" at a high-end spa, in a nod to *Magic Mountain* culture.) John Waters's *Mondo Trasho* mixes the "Ride" with the sound of snorting pigs in a ghastly death scene for the drag performer Divine. And Claude Chabrol's New Wave classic *Les Cousins* features a foppish, decadent law student who stages orgiastic parties at his apartment. One evening, he puts on a record of *Tristan*, dons a Nazi officer's cap, and marches around with a candelabra shouting in German. There is no need to specify what music is playing as he meets his inevitable bad end.

The grisliest Liebestod of all—grislier even than the necrophiliac love scene in Marcel Batilliat's *Mystic Flesh* or the doings in *The Damned*—transpires in Yukio Mishima's *Yūkoku*, or *Patriotism: The Rite of Love and Death*, a half-hour-long ode to seppuku. The film has no dialogue, only intermittent handwritten titles; the soundtrack consists entirely of Leopold

Stokowski's "symphonic synthesis" of *Tristan*, recorded in 1932. Mishima made *Patriotism* in 1966; four years later, following a failed attempt to overthrow the Japanese government, he killed himself according to the same procedure, cutting his abdomen open while his beloved acolyte prepared to behead him with a sword.

Wagner had arrived in Japan toward the end of the nineteenth century, in the Meiji period, when the nation began opening itself to ideas from the West and instituted an expansionist nationalist ideology on the Prussian model. Japanese intellectuals detected Germanic values of order and discipline in the operas, while commercial middle-class culture absorbed their legendary motifs. The musicologist Brooke McCorkle has uncovered a 1928 book called *Children's Wagner*, evocatively illustrated in *ukiyo-e* style. An early translation of *Tannhäuser*, by Rofū Akimoto, transmutes the libretto into the style of Japanese epic poetry, infusing it with archaic words and images that parallel Wagner's bygone language.

Mishima took an interest in Wagner at an early date, apparently discovering the composer through Nietzsche, whom he devoured in his teenaged years. He also idolized Thomas Mann, and, like Mann, wallowed in the very Wagnerian decadence that Nietzsche deplored. His 1951–53 novel *Kinjiki*, or *Forbidden Colors*, pays direct homage to *Death in Venice*. Like the young Visconti, Mishima was a gay man attracted to Fascist aesthetics, subscribing to a masculinist conception of gay identity that had something in common with the homoerotic conservatism of Hans Blüher. Ernst Röhm is a character in Mishima's 1968 play *My Friend Hitler*, although the Night of the Long Knives is left offstage. "He should have listened to Wagner more," the Hitler character says, after consigning Röhm to death.

Patriotism is set in 1936, in the wake of an attempted coup by military officers who wanted to cleanse Japan of Western influences. An officer named Lieutenant Takeyama, caught between loyalty to the emperor and loyalty to his comrades, commits seppuku, and his wife, Reiko, dies with him. The film is staged like a Noh play, in a severely stylized domestic setting. Mishima skips the *Tristan* prelude and begins with dark, roiling music from later in Act I, as Isolde orders up the potion that her mother brewed for times of "deepest woe." On screen, we see Reiko in a traditional kimono, writing her will and remembering scenes of past happiness. Placid and pliant, she is nearly the opposite of Wagner's proud, raging Isolde.

When Takeyama appears, Mishima cuts to the introduction to the Act II Liebesnacht. According to the text, Reiko tells her husband, "I will follow you wherever you go." Having sworn to die together, they are "able for the first time in their lives to reveal unabashedly their most secret desires and passions." These formulations draw on the *Tristan* libretto—"Where Tristan now parts, / Will you, Isolde, follow him?"—but the underlying meaning is completely changed. In McCorkle's words, Mishima rewrites Wagner's apolitical drama as "a story of nostalgic nationalism as well as a tale of the melding of Japanese and German aesthetics."

Just as the Liebesnacht is reaching its gentlest phase of ecstasy—"*Lausch Geliebter / Lass mich sterben*," or "Listen, beloved, / Let me die"—the lovemaking ends and the seppuku begins. Takeyama dons military garments, fondles his sword, and exposes his torso. He then inserts the blade into his abdomen. Blood begins to flow just as Stokowski's arrangement arrives at the serene, even-quavered phrase associated with the Liebestod ("*So starben wir, / um ungetrennt*," or "Thus we died / so that, undivided . . ."). His intestines follow—an effect produced by dressing Mishima's body in pig entrails. The final section shows Reiko's suicide. Having lovingly tended to Takeyama's corpse, she takes out a knife and licks its tip at precisely the moment Isolde would be singing "Unconscious, highest bliss." This time we are spared the sight of the blade entering flesh. The last image is of the bodies intertwined in a rock garden, in a pose resembling Jean Delville's mystical drawing of the lovers.

The fetishism of violence in *Patriotism* is foreign to Wagner's world. The lovers in *Tristan* express longing for death, but the surge of the music belies their renunciation of life: as in so much Romantic literature, the salutation to death is a way of metaphorically marking an erotic intensity that cannot be made altogether explicit. *Patriotism*, by contrast, is an eminently twentieth-century work that combines semi-fascist ideology with a narcissistic worship of the body. Not long before his own suicide, Mishima described seppuku as the "ultimate masturbation." The autoerotic atmosphere of *Patriotism* bears out that alarming notion.

Susan Sontag mentions both Mishima and Visconti in her 1975 essay "Fascinating Fascism," which studies the vogue for a kind of Nazi chic in gay pornography and in the broader culture. Sontag speculates that the affluent democracies of the West are reacting against an excess of choice, an "unbearable degree of individuality," in favor of a theater of discipline and mastery. In the same period, punk bands were sporting swastikas; Mick Jagger was paying tribute to Riefenstahl; and David Bowie was issuing provocations along the lines of "Adolf Hitler was one of the first rock stars." Wagner, who understood how crowds long for direction, received dutiful citations in such discussions, although the heroes of stadium rock had devised a far more efficient way of casting a spell over vast numbers of people.

In 1975, Wagner arrived at the scene of the ultimate crime, by way of Lina Wertmüller's black comedy *Seven Beauties*. The Second World War is at its height, and a Neapolitan ruffian named Pasqualino escapes from a troop train bound for the Russian front. He and a companion stumble upon an isolated hunting lodge, where a scantily clad woman of aristocratic bearing is

Ken Russell's Lisztomania

singing Wagner's "Träume" at the piano—a setting of a poem by Mathilde Wesendonck, repurposed in *Tristan*. Moments later, as the runaways are wolfing down stolen food, they are captured by German troops. "The Ride of the Valkyries" strikes up as Pasqualino and his friend are dragged away to a concentration camp that resembles a comic-book Auschwitz. Strutting amid naked bodies and piles of corpses is an obese, sadistic female commandant named Hilde, a Valkyrie gone to seed. Pasqualino must satisfy her needs to survive. He is fed a bowl of sausage and sauerkraut while Hilde smokes a cigar and sings her own croaking version of "Träume". "Tell me, what wondrous dreams are these / That hold my mind in thrall, / Without vanishing like empty bubbles / Into the blank void?"

This appears to be the first sustained cinematic equation of Wagner and the Holocaust, preceding *The Boys from Brazil*. The tone is weirdly satirical. The grotesque Valkyrie commandant seems a projection of male fears of humiliation: she strikes a dominatrix pose while Pasqualino cowers before his bowl of food like a dog. The Wagner citation feels secondhand—a manipulation of prior cinematic practice. Wertmüller, who worked as an assistant director under Fellini, may have been riffing on the harem scene in *8½*, letting a woman wield the whip. This psychedelic Wagnerism matches the changing aesthetic of the sixties and seventies. A generation had come of age for which Wagner was not the threatening soundtrack of wartime newsreels but goofy music for Bugs Bunny.

Wagner, rock 'n' roll, and "Nazi chic" intersect deliriously in Ken Russell's *Lisztomania* (1975), starring Roger Daltrey, the lead singer of the Who. A director who specialized in absurdist biopics—his *Mahler* features Cosima Wagner as a Nazi dominatrix—Russell devotes the first part of *Lisztomania* to a riotous send-up of solemn Hollywood fare like *Magic Fire* and *A Song to Remember*. Wagner shows up as a rascal in a sailor suit and a cap stamped NIETZSCHE. Halfway through, the movie morphs into a horror-schlock homage, with Liszt cast as a vampire hunter and Wagner as his prey. In pitch-perfect Nazi Wagnerese, the Meister pledges to "forge the shattered fragments of this country into a nation of steel."

The final showdown takes place in a castle fit for Dracula, where Wagner romps about in a superhero cape and Aryan children wear a W on their chests. "The Ride of the Valkyries" is outfitted with the lyric "We will be the master race." (Russell also supplied new words for the "Ride" in *Mahler*: "No longer a Jew boy / Winning strength through joy, / You're one of us now, / Now you're a goy.") Wagner is temporarily defeated, then rises from the grave in the form of a Hitler zombie. Up in heaven, Liszt says, "I think we should put him out of his misery. He's giving music a bad name." A sort of pipe-organ spacecraft is launched, with Liszt at the helm. It plays a bit of the "Ride" as it rushes down to blow up the Wagner-Hitler zombie. Evidently, the devil's music can also serve the side of good.

Is Russell endorsing or mocking the demonization of Wagner? One guesses the latter. Contemporary discourse around the composer frames him as a kind of devil, sulfurously consuming everything he touches. Russell accepts that claim at face value and gives it an appropriate staging, whereupon it collapses into nonsense. *Lisztomania* is best enjoyed as a belated exercise in Wagnerian ultra-decadence—a reminiscence of the time when *Tannhäuser* and *Tristan* were the favorite music of vampires and succubi, preaching the "satanism of love."

APOCALYPSE NOW

For decades, aerial warfare had been stirring thoughts of the Valkyries and their "air-horses," as Wagner called them. When Proust's Saint-Loup watched a Zeppelin raid on Paris circa 1916, he exclaimed, "That's it, the music of the sirens was a 'Ride of the Valkyries'!" During the Second World War, Toscanini's performances of the "Ride" were compared to B-17 bombers in flight. The Nazis employed the same conceit: in a German newsreel, the "Ride" underscores a segment documenting a paratrooper assault on Crete. More than one American bomber crew adopted the name Valkyrie for their plane, attaching the customary decal of a scantily dressed female. "Part of the thought was romantic," an airman explained. "We equated ourselves with Odin's battle-watching maidens who picked out the warriors who were to die and took the worthy to Valhalla." When, in the fifties, the U.S. Strategic Air Command began developing the XB-70 long-range bomber, it ran a contest among service members to select a name. Out of twenty thousand entries, the winner was Valkyrie.

Given that history, the "Ride" seems a foreordained choice for the helicopter operation in Coppola's *Apocalypse Now*. The idea of an air cavalry unit blasting Wagner first arose in the mind of the screenwriter John Milius, who finished the first draft of *Apocalypse* in 1969, a decade before the film's release. Milius had heard that American forces in Vietnam were using music as a weapon, to galvanize troops and demoralize the enemy. The American military and intelligence community had long been interested in psychological warfare, and it was also thought that loud music could be used to subject prisoners to "no-touch" torture. Years later, Milius recalled: "I knew that they did have Psy-Ops where they put speakers and played things . . . They didn't play Wagner, they played rock 'n' roll and stuff like that. But I really thought the Wagner would work. I thought that it would be something that fit with helicopters and a helicopter assault."

The dialogue Milius wrote in 1969 appears in the film almost word for word, although Kharnage is renamed Kilgore and Willard's dialogue is given to a champion surfer named Lance, who adds, "Hey! We're gonna play music!"

KHARNAGE
(*to Willard*)

We'll come in low out of the rising sun—We'll put on the music about a mile out.

WILLARD
Music?

KHARNAGE
Yeah I use Wagner—scares hell out of the slopes—the boys love it.

It goes on: "The ocean rushes below as suddenly the loudspeakers BLARE out Wagner's 'Ride of the Valkyries' . . . From on the water we SEE eight-five Hueys—gunships—troop carriers—medevac and recon—roar over low in battle formation BLARING out 'Ride of the Valkyries.'"

Nothing if not ambitious, Milius's *Apocalypse* script gestures toward exalted literary models. The chief point of reference is Conrad's *Heart of Darkness*. Willard, a special-ops soldier, is sent on a mission to track down and kill a renegade officer named Colonel Kurtz, who, like Conrad's villain, has gone mad in the jungle and created a private empire there. Milius also aspired, in Joycean fashion, toward a modernization of Homer's *Odyssey*: Kilgore is the equivalent of the Cyclops. Toward the end, Kurtz recites passages from T. S. Eliot's "The Hollow Men," which has an epigraph from *Heart of Darkness* ("Mistah Kurtz—he dead").

Milius, a Jewish American of politically conservative leanings, did not intend an antiwar message. He was working on *Apocalypse* during the Arab-Israeli War of 1967, and excitedly followed the Israeli advance. He told the journalist and author Lawrence Weschler: "Tracking that victory day by day, I was throbbing to the Doors—'Light My Fire' was the big hit that summer—and of course to Wagner." When Weschler expressed surprise, Milius said, "The Israeli Army prided itself on its Teutonic tactics." Although some scholars have linked the helicopter scene to the Ku Klux Klan assault in *The Birth of a Nation*—the air-cav men style themselves as horsemen—Milius was apparently unaware of Griffith's use of the "Ride."

Coppola, a denizen of the Northern California counterculture, saw *Apocalypse* as a "journey into the surreal." Some of his images are worthy of Buñuel: in one shot, a priest recites the Lord's Prayer while a cow is airlifted behind him. Like Milius, Coppola has no memory of hearing Wagner in *The Birth of a Nation*, but he does remember seeing Wertmüller's *Seven Beauties*—one of very few films in which the "Ride" is heard with a full complement of Valkyrie voices. When the *New Yorker* critic Pauline Kael heard of Coppola's plans to use the "Ride" in *Apocalypse*, she warned him that audiences would be reminded too strongly of *Seven Beauties*. Kael underestimated Coppola's ability to make Wagner his own. The director came from a musical family; his father, the flutist and composer Carmine Coppola, played under Toscanini, and his uncle Anton was both a composer and a conductor.

The version of the "Ride" that we hear in *Apocalypse* comes from the Decca label's celebrated complete recording of the *Ring*, which was begun in 1958 and finished in 1965. The venue for the project was the Sophiensaal in Vienna, where, in 1883, a Wagner memorial had turned into an antisemitic demonstration. Georg Solti's interpretation of the score is notable for its punchy, brass-heavy sonorities. Few renditions of the "Ride" articulate more aggressively its driving rhythms. Coppola took about five minutes of music from the first 143 bars of Act III of *Walküre*, with a few cuts and some telescoping of sections. The sound designer and editor Walter Murch played a crucial role in creating a seamless flow of sound and image.

At the outset of the sequence, Willard and his squad have temporarily joined Colonel Kilgore's air-cav unit on one of its missions. A soldier is heard humming the "Ride" before the operation begins, letting us know that Wagner has been used in this way before. Once the helicopters are in flight, Kilgore gives his order, and a tape machine begins to roll. Shots timed to Wagner's downbeats show speakers affixed to the aircraft. That strict rhythm is broken when the camera focuses on the two African-American members of Willard's company, played by Albert Hall and Laurence Fishburne. Their disbelieving faces point up the subtext of the scene: white Americans are assaulting a non-white village to the music of a racist composer. Another irony is that this pageant of masculine aggression is driven by music that once had feminist connotations.

The entrance of the main Valkyrie motif coincides with a wide shot of fourteen helicopters in flight. The soldiers ready their guns; Kilgore nods to the music. Another wide shot coincides with a gleaming B-major chord, after which the trombones take over the theme. Then comes a brilliant stroke, devised by Murch: one bar before the trombones complete their phrase, the camera cuts away to the Vietnamese village that is about to be struck. The adrenaline rush of men, machines, and music abruptly ceases as the camera lands in a quiet courtyard outside a school. Milius had specified an armed Viet Cong camp in his screenplay, but Coppola paints a more idyllic scene, with children singing as they come out to play. A female soldier runs in, ordering an evacuation, and Wagner seeps in from a distance. The trombones now finish their statement, and the Valkyries enter with their "Hojotoho!" The first missile is fired on Helmwige's sustained high B. Houses explode, and villagers are mowed down from above.

The Wagnerian bravado falters amid the chaos of battle. Copters land, soldiers jump out. A panicked soldier shouts, "I'm not going!" He is yanked out of the helicopter all the same. A young black soldier is badly wounded when a comrade fires into a house and sets off an explosion. He is taken to a helicopter, at which point a Vietnamese woman runs in and explodes a grenade. "Fucking savages," Kilgore says. Tellingly, Wagner drops out at the moment the young soldier falls. The sight of blood gushing from his leg shuts down the Valkyrie fantasy.

A*pocalypse Now* captures an empire in its decadence, to adapt a phrase from Paul Verlaine. The helicopter sequence is one stage of a descent into insanity that will culminate in the rambling, Eliot-quoting monologues of Marlon Brando's Kurtz. (The mad colonel has a copy of *From Ritual to Romance*, Jessie Weston's study of the Grail.) A grand indictment of American hubris is intended, yet the visceral impact of the filmmaking saps its capacity for critique. *Apocalypse* soon became a military fetish object, its Wagner Scene influencing real-life behavior. Black Hawk helicopters blared the "Ride" during the American invasion of Grenada in 1983. In 1991, a psy-ops unit played it at the Battle of 73 Easting, in the Iraqi desert, during the First Gulf War. Loudspeakers mounted on Humvees boomed out the "Ride" at Fallujah in 2004, during the second American invasion of Iraq.

In a Wagnerian mise en abyme, Sam Mendes's 2005 film *Jarhead*, based on Anthony Swofford's memoir of military service during the Gulf War, has a scene in which Marine Corps trainees thrill to a screening of *Apocalypse*, singing along with the "Ride" and pumping their fists in the air. Walter Murch, the mastermind of the *Apocalypse* sequence, also edited *Jarhead*, and found himself in the peculiar position of showing the defeat of his and Coppola's intention—to leave the audience "energized but also upset," in his own words. The cut to the quiet village conspicuously fails to have a sobering effect. When the Wagner resumes, the marines shout, "Shoot that motherfucker!" Swofford, commenting on movie nights with fellow marines, writes that "filmic images of death and carnage are pornography for the military man."

It is an astonishing cultural transformation: the "Ride" made over as an anthem of American supremacy. This displacement is of a piece with troubling historical continuities of the postwar era, as Nazi scientists migrated to America, as Gestapo-style torture techniques resurfaced in Iraq, as the cult of the sculpted body perpetuated Riefenstahl's Aryan ideal. Eric Rentschler, in his book *The Ministry of Illusion*, writes: "Contemporary American media culture has more than a superficial or vicarious relationship with the Third Reich's society of spectacle." Nothing in film history demonstrates that idea as vividly as *Apocalypse Now*, where the German will to power gives way to God-bless-America imperialism.

15

THE WOUND

Wagnerism After 1945

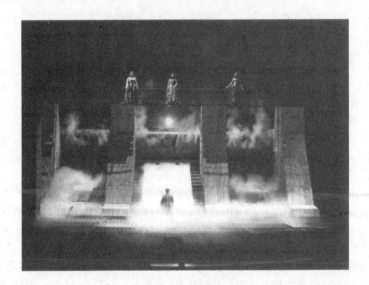

On July 24, 1976, a new production of the *Ring* opened at the Festspielhaus in Bayreuth. On the hundredth anniversary of the Bayreuth Festival, Wolfgang Wagner, the heir to the family business, had entrusted the cycle to an outsider. Having first attempted to engage the film director Ingmar Bergman, Wolfgang settled on the young French actor-director Patrice Chéreau, who joined forces with the composer-conductor Pierre Boulez, a lion of the musical avant-garde. Wolfgang's wish for a bold departure came true. During the *Rheingold* prelude, the mists of prehistory parted to reveal a hydroelectric dam, at the top of which Rhinemaidens frolicked about, costumed as high-class prostitutes. The staging caused a major scandal that first summer: boos and whistles resounded not only after the performances but during them, à la *Tannhäuser* in Paris. "Now the lunatics are really on the loose," Wolfgang's mother, Winifred, was heard to say. By the time of its final run, in 1980, the production had become a modern classic, and the ovations went on for more than an hour.

Chéreau's *Ring*, as recorded for television in its last two summers, gives a panorama of Wagnerism in all its variegated glory. Shaw had proposed that the *Ring* "really demanded modern costumes, tall hats for Tarnhelms, factories for Nibelheims, villas for Valhallas." This is more or less what happens on Chéreau's stage. Nibelheim is a hellishly lit factory floor. The gods are Victorian aristocrats struggling to find their bearings in an industrialized world. Riskily, Alberich, Mime, and Hagen are costumed to look like German-Jewish economic managers: Chéreau accepted that these characters are antisemitic caricatures and tried to humanize them. Time creeps forward as the cycle goes on. Brünnhilde's rock evokes the Symbolist gloom of Arnold Böcklin's *Isle of the Dead*, and the shuffle of mourners past Siegfried's body recalls the funeral sequence in Dziga Vertov's *Three Songs of Lenin*. The philosopher Michel Foucault, one of Chéreau's many admirers, noted the "fragments of utopia, pieces of machinery, elements of engravings, social types, glimpses of dream cities, dragons for children, domestic scenes in the Strindberg manner, the profile of a Jew of the ghetto." By the end, we are nearing the present. Siegfried and Gunther don black tie, Hagen wears a rumpled suit. Part of the outrage in 1976 stemmed from Chéreau's challenge to the elite audience: Wagner's critique of bourgeois society is turned on Bayreuth itself.

The Chéreau *Ring* gave a potent answer to the question that hung in the air as the twentieth century wound down: what can Wagner say to a contemporary culture that seems poised to reject him on both aesthetic and political grounds? The project of renovation moved on many fronts. Stage directors looked for ways either to diminish the Nazi association or to confront it head on. Philosophers from Theodor W. Adorno and Walter Benjamin to Alain Badiou and Slavoj Žižek assessed Wagner as a problem of late-capitalist modernity. Creative figures both inside and outside Germany—the writers Günter Grass and Ingeborg Bachmann; the multimedia artists Joseph Beuys and Anselm Kiefer; the sci-fi novelist Philip K. Dick—wrestled with the implications of the Nazi Wagner. Fantasy and sci-fi epics, from *The Lord of the Rings* to *Star Wars* and *The Matrix*, updated Wagnerian tropes.

Wagner fandom became global and diverse, belying Bayreuth's historic image as an exclusive enterprise. Wagner Societies spread to over forty countries, from Venezuela to Singapore. The *Ring* received stagings in Australia, China, Japan, Thailand, and Brazil. The advent of the long-playing record—and, later, of the compact disc, VHS and DVD, the MP3, and streaming audio—meant that home listeners could immerse themselves in the music dramas without interruption. Georg Solti's Vienna recording of the *Ring*, with such great postwar singers as Hans Hotter, Birgit Nilsson, Christa Ludwig, and Wolfgang Windgassen, was a landmark; John Culshaw, the producer, aimed for a kind of home staging, with special audio effects adding atmosphere. Theatrical productions such as Chéreau's were enshrined on home video. Yet the emergence of a technologically mediated mass-market Wagner failed to resolve the enduring political question. The thoroughgoing Hitlerization of the composer made him Exhibit A for the supposition that German culture had been complicit in the Holocaust. The virtual ban on playing Wagner in Israel has given him a singularly baleful aura.

Alexander Kluge, a major presence in postwar German intellectual life, gives a wry view of the Wagner case in his 1983 film *The Power of Emotions*. A kind of montage essay with fictional episodes, Kluge's work criticizes opera as a "power plant of emotion"—a cultural machine that habitually does violence to women. One sequence tells of a wartime air raid that endangers a German opera house. A fireman is seen running up a narrow staircase. The narrator says: "Since childhood, Schönecke always wondered what was hidden inside the Grail in the opera *Parsifal*. He takes the opportunity to satisfy his curiosity." Schönecke goes into the props room and picks up the Grail. There is nothing inside except a bolt holding the prop together. Wagner seems used up, an empty vessel. Elsewhere in the film, though, *Parsifal* is superimposed on time-lapse shots of glass-and-steel buildings in Frankfurt: night gives way to day, clouds race across the sky, an airplane floats in the distance. Inexplicably beautiful, the sequence suggests how the composer can act in counterpoint to modern life, not the god in Valhalla but the wanderer in disguise.

THE NEW BAYREUTH

Bayreuth's renaissance in the 1950s was a spectacular and unexpected development. In the first few years of the postwar era, a resumption of the festival had appeared unlikely. During the American occupation of Bavaria, the Festspielhaus became an all-purpose variety theater, featuring Jack Benny, the Glenn Miller Orchestra, and the Rockettes. If Bayreuth were to return, anti-Nazi members of the family seemed the most promising candidates to lead it. At the end of 1946, Franz Wilhelm Beidler, son of the familial outcast Isolde von Bülow, drew up a plan for a new festival and approached Thomas Mann about serving as the honorary president of a Bayreuth foundation. The idea struck Mann as the "fantastical fulfillment of a youthful dream and a youthful love." When Beidler's plan foundered, a Social Democratic mayor engineered a solution. Winifred Wagner agreed to step aside, handing the festival to her sons, Wieland and Wolfgang. The Americans assented, and the festival resumed in 1951.

The New Bayreuth, as it was called, transformed Wagner's image. In a feat of sorcery worthy of their grandfather, the brothers convinced the

Wieland Wagner's Siegfried *at Bayreuth*

world that they had decisively broken with the Nazi past. According to their narrative, Wieland's pared-down productions were a repudiation of the traditional styles that had prevailed during the Nazi period. That Hitler had advocated a timeless, abstract approach was not yet known; Wieland kept his quasi-filial relationship with the dictator well hidden. As Beidler bitterly observed, little changed behind the scenes. The conductors at the 1951 festival—Wilhelm Furtwängler, Herbert von Karajan, and Hans Knappertsbusch—had all been active in the Nazi period. Much of the financial support came from industrialists with questionable pasts; former Nazis dotted the audience. No fewer than three Arno Breker sculptures—of Wagner, Cosima, and Liszt—cropped up on the Green Hill in the postwar years. Most gallingly, Winifred generated headlines with frank, fond remarks about Hitler. When the filmmaker Hans-Jürgen Syberberg interviewed her in 1975, she said that if her old friend were to walk through the door "I would be as happy and glad to see him and have him here as ever."

However intractable the family's attitudes, the metamorphosis of the Bayreuth stage was real and profound. In the *Parsifal* of 1951, most of the familiar settings and props vanished. The Grail Temple was reduced to four tall pillars surrounding a circular table. The lighting was kept low, so that it took the eyes some minutes to adjust and pick out shapes in the gloom. This was the theater of suggestion of which Adolphe Appia had dreamed. E. M. Forster, visiting the festival three years later, appreciated the purity of the concept but struggled with its austere execution: "All human life had vanished but on the walls of the Temple what looked like a motor-tyre became visible as the curtain fell."

Wieland's innovations were rooted in years of study. He read Appia, Craig, Freud, and Jung; he caught up on modern art that the Nazis had shelved as degenerate. In 1961, he shocked old-time Wagnerites by assigning the role of Venus in *Tannhäuser* to the African-American soprano Grace Bumbry—sixty-five years after his grandmother cast Luranah Aldridge as a Valkyrie. After the stark simplicity of his "Appia phase," Wieland began to fill the stage with phallic forms, totems, masks. By the mid-sixties, having come to terms with Brecht, he was moving toward a Wagnerian epic theater. Shortly before his early death, in 1966, Wieland made the provocative claim that Wotan, Alberich, and Mime were all proto-fascist figures, and that Nibelheim was the "first concentration camp in history."

When the festival was first revived, the Wagner brothers tried to hide behind the same line from *Meistersinger* that their father had used at Bayreuth in 1925: "Art is what matters here." But the formalist defense was failing. After Wieland's death, Wolfgang carried on alone for a few more years; then, to his credit, he recognized that new voices were needed. He looked first to a group of directors who had come to the fore in the German Democratic Republic, where the theatrical legacy of the Weimar Republic lived on. Stalinist culture had a stifling hold on East Germany, yet when Brecht arrived in Berlin, in 1949, he was able to win a degree of independence for his Berliner Ensemble. Likewise, Walter Felsenstein, the director of the Komische Oper in East Berlin, transcended socialist-realist routine with ferociously naturalistic stagings. Felsenstein, like Brecht, resisted Wagner, but three of his protégés—Götz Friedrich, Harry Kupfer, and Joachim Herz—rose to international fame on the basis of their pathbreaking Wagner productions. Wolfgang inaugurated Bayreuth's new phase by inviting Friedrich—whose father served on the staff of the anti-Nazi general Friedrich Olbricht—to direct *Tannhäuser* in 1972. This, too, caused a scandal. John Neumeier's choreography of the Venusberg, orgiastic and violent, came close to fulfilling Baudelaire's vision of the opera as "satanic religion."

Herz effectively launched this second revolution in Leipzig, Wagner's birthplace. While professing to admire Wieland's "symbolic dreamworld," Herz pointedly added that theater should make spectators think, not dream. His 1960 *Meistersinger* placed the action in an Elizabethan-style theater, with galleries doubling as the balconies of Nuremberg houses and other architectural features. Two years later, at the Komische Oper, he directed *The Flying Dutchman*, and also made a film out of the material. In the film, a silent prologue shows a terrified Senta in her bedroom, watching as a door creaks open and shuts. We sense that she is confined in her father's home, perhaps imperiled. The story of the Dutchman is her fantasy of escape: the overture arises from the whistling of the wind. Scenes of working-class ordinariness, reminiscent of the Kroll Opera's 1929 production, alternate with Expressionistic images of the phantom Dutchman and his crew, recalling Murnau's *Nosferatu*. Montage sequences heighten the tension between imagination and reality. At the end, Senta breaks free, taking the Dutchman's portrait off her wall and walking off into a presumably better future. Kupfer echoed this concept in his 1978 *Dutchman* at Bayreuth, making the entire opera Senta's neurotic dream.

Herz's culminating achievement was his *Ring* in Leipzig (1973–76). Patrick Carnegy describes it at length in his magisterial book *Wagner and the Art of the Theatre.* Two principal sources of inspiration were Shaw's *The Perfect Wagnerite* and "The *Ring* as Bourgeois Parable," an essay by the German-Jewish literary critic Hans Mayer. Costumes and sets suggest a kind of photomontage of historical settings, going back to the feudal period. In *Rheingold*, the gods evolve from primitive people to pompous aristocrats. *Walküre* is set in the high bourgeois period: Valkyries cavort beneath a sculpture of the Roman war goddess Bellona, in a style somewhere between Wilhelmine bombast and Nazi brutality. By the end, the staging has entered the electrified fin de siècle, with intimations of fascist thuggery. Workers in street clothes watch Valhalla collapse, and the stage goes bare. The message is blunt: capitalism tends toward fascism, and must be overturned for a just society to emerge.

Chéreau's *Ring* at Bayreuth made such revisionist conceits emotionally precise and dramatically urgent. Wotan's despairing monologue in *Walküre* is a tour de force in this respect. For much of the act, a pendulum swings from side to side—a symbol of fate in motion. When Donald McIntyre, as Wotan, reaches the line "*Das Ende! Das Ende!*," he stops the pendulum with his hand: that gesture matches the seismic lurch of Wagner's harmony.

The *Ring* underwent many more permutations in the seventies and eighties. A production in Kassel, by Ulrich Melchinger, mounted the Valkyries on motorcycles and rendered the Gibichung court in the style of Albert Speer. Kupfer, at Bayreuth in 1988, removed the cycle to a futuristic wasteland crisscrossed by laser patterns. Friedrich, in a Berlin *Ring* introduced in 1984 and 1985, confined the action to a "time tunnel"—a cavernous underground bunker in which the gods and heroes of a now destroyed civilization endlessly reenact its downfall. In the same period, Ruth Berghaus's *Ring* in Frankfurt cast most of the principal characters as puppetlike, mechanical beings. By the beginning of the twenty-first century, audiences had to be prepared for all manner of perplexities: footage of a decomposing rabbit at the end of *Parsifal* (Christoph Schlingensief in Bayreuth); Tristan and Isolde sipping cocktails on the deck of an ocean liner (Peter Konwitschny in Munich, with shades of Joyce's *Tristan* tales); Brünnhilde depositing the Ring on the prompter's box and slashing her wrists (David Alden in Munich); *Parsifal* staged at Haus Wahnfried (Stefan Herheim in Bayreuth). In one notorious *Tannhäuser*, naked extras were seen entering a gas chamber.

Such deconstructive approaches to Wagner—generally known as *Regietheater*, or director's theater—have elicited howls of indignation from spectators who want to see the operas given in accordance with the composer's scenic instructions. They have been able to take refuge in productions of a more traditional cast, such as the Otto Schenk *Ring* that played at the Met between 1987 and 2009, with Günther Schneider-Siemssen's sets harking back to the Bayreuth of 1876 and 1896. To be sure, such museum decor is equally at odds with Wagner's aesthetic of flux ("Make something *new!*"). The sometimes arduous regime of *Regietheater* is worth enduring because of the extraordinary insights it can yield. Wagner demonstrates again his adhesive power, his capacity to assimilate himself to almost any visual backdrop. The story of Wagner in Hollywood is much the same: it may be no accident that the Chéreau *Ring* and *Apocalypse Now* appeared in the same era.

WAGNERIAN PHILOSOPHY

The proliferation of Wagnerian imagery on stage and screen raises a kind of ontological problem. What irreducible identity lies behind the composer's transformations? What breach in the border between art and life allowed one man to exercise such outsize influence, in aesthetics and politics alike? These questions crop up periodically in philosophical discourse, which has used Wagner to track the crises of Western culture in an age of totalitarianism and total war. The exercise of "taking on Wagner," in Alain Badiou's words, is now a distinct intellectual subgenre. Nietzsche's aphorism from 1888—"Wagner *sums up* modernity"—changes character when the scene shifts from the nineteenth century to the twentieth. After Auschwitz and Hiroshima, modernity's horizon has darkened. An essential issue is whether the composer helped to usher in that modernity or whether he warned against it. Either way, Nietzsche was right to say that "the philosopher is not free to dispense with Wagner."

His persistence as an object of philosophical scrutiny has much to do with Nietzsche's own ascendancy, which began in the 1890s and accelerated as the twentieth century went on. Phenomenologists, existentialists, critical theorists, and poststructuralists all registered Nietzsche's assault on the absolutes of modern Western thought: universal truths, moral norms, the metaphysics of origins and goals. The primal contest between Wagner and his acolyte takes on symbolic significance, with the narrative usually weighted in Nietzsche's favor. Jean-Paul Sartre made a fable out of the clash in his unfinished youthful novel *A Defeat* (c. 1927), which concerns triangular relationships among a famous, aging composer named Richard Organte, his wife, Cosima, and Frédéric, the brilliant young tutor of Cosima's daughters. Organte is revealed to be a feeble, spent old man, a father figure whom Frédéric rejects. The twentieth century surpasses the nineteenth; the incipient existentialist supplants the fading romantic.

A Nietzsche bias colors the work of the young Heidegger, whose explorations of the contingency of human existence strongly influenced Sartre. Having endorsed the Nazi takeover in 1933, Heidegger sided with those who saw Wagner as a decadent detour of the German spirit. Lecturing on Nietzsche in 1936, Heidegger characterizes the Gesamtkunstwerk as "the dissolution of everything solid into a fluid, flexible, malleable state, into a swimming and floundering." This soup of feeling is a poor substitute for a "solidly grounded and articulated position in the midst of beings." Although Heidegger ends up rejecting Nietzsche's will to power as a last gasp of metaphysics, he favors his predecessor's clear, forceful "masculine aesthetics." By uncritically adopting Nietzsche's attack on the "feminine" Wagner, Heidegger exposes the regressive tendencies in his own thought— an ironic outcome, given the widespread perception of Wagner as the more reactionary, Nazi-leaning figure.

Surveying the trajectory of German culture from the vantage point of exile, Theodor W. Adorno saw the Wagner quandary in starkly different terms. He belonged to the cohort of post-Marxist theorists who first achieved prominence during the Weimar Republic, becoming known as the Frankfurt School. They are best remembered for their pioneering dissections of the totalitarian mentality and for their parallel critiques of liberal-democratic culture, which in their eyes was compromised by the domineering logic of late capitalism. Walter Benjamin's famous dictum against bourgeois art-worship—"There is no document of culture that is not at the same time a document of barbarism"—could have been invented for the study of Wagner, although Benjamin had little to say on the topic, leaving such matters to Adorno. A trained composer and sharp-eared critic, Adorno had studied with Alban Berg, who wrested one of the great twentieth-century operas from Frank Wedekind's *Lulu* plays.

At first glance, Adorno's study, which assumed finished form in the 1952 book *Essay on Wagner*, is an act of demolition. Disavowing leftist Wagnerism, Adorno says that the composer never needed to renounce his revolutionary phase because he was never a revolutionary to begin with. He was a bourgeois rebel who acquiesced in the status quo even as he fantasized about laying waste to it. His music encourages the listener to "cast off humanity together with mundane reality"; it mimes the "gesture of hitting." It brings to mind the gesticulations of an agitator who substitutes physical frenzy for intellectual coherence. Adorno repeatedly implies—or says straight out—that Wagner presages Hitler, world war, and genocide. The operas themselves, with their apparent Jewish caricatures, cannot be excluded from the equation. Adorno delivered his most stinging judgment in a 1947 review of Ernest Newman's Wagner biography: "Redemption, in Wagner, is tantamount to annihilation: Kundry is redeemed the same way in which the Gestapo may claim to have redeemed the Jews."

When Walter Benjamin read a draft of Adorno's book, he worried that it was too polemical in style. Adorno protested that he had been true to the intricacy of the Wagner matter, demonstrating the "unity of the progressive and the regressive." Reductive, either-or arguments had bedeviled writing on the subject from the beginning. As Fredric Jameson observes in his book *Late Marxism*, Adorno insists not only on the ideological falsehood of Wagner's work but also on its utopian dimension. The daring instrumental writing augurs musical modernism. Dissonances in *Tristan* destabilize the harmonic order, and, by extension, the social order that music is supposed to prop up. The revolutionary dimension of the *Ring*, with its hostility to private property, remains viable. Even Wagner's decadence gives glimpses of a better future. The composer has "the neurotic's power to look his own downfall in the face, and to transcend it in an image that can withstand the devouring gaze." That "grandiose weakness" might be preferable to Nietzsche's philosophy of health—a conclusion that Thomas Mann had already reached. Adorno closes with an ode to *Tristan* as a protest on behalf of helpless, suffering souls, holding out the promise of "life without fear." Mark Berry is right to say that the *Essay on Wagner* is as much an "inverted panegyric" as Nietzsche's *The Case of Wagner*.

Unlike so many fin-de-siècle youths, Adorno had begun as a Wagner skeptic. Reversing the Nietzsche progression, he became more admiring in his later writings, even rhapsodic. In his 1963 essay "Wagner's Relevance," Adorno asserts that we are still coming to terms with this seemingly overfamiliar figure, scraping away one layer only to discover another underneath. We are ambivalent toward Wagner because we do not fully understand him. We cannot forget the frightening elements in his worldview—the propensity toward violence, mythmaking, domination—but the negative consequences of such ideological strains are made clear in the dramatic context. Nothing is stable, nothing remains fixed: "The feeling of leaving firm ground, of drifting into the unknown, is the thrilling and also compelling aspect of the experience of Wagner's music."

Ernst Bloch, the great leftist philosopher of utopia, arrived at a similar judgment along a less circuitous path. He had loved Wagner from childhood, and right-wing exploitation of the composer during and after the First World War spurred him to fashion an alternative. He was not uncritical, acknowledging in his 1918 work *Spirit of Utopia* that Wagner succeeds all too well in summoning the flow of Schopenhauer's Will, with its unconscious, pathological, and subhuman forces. Carried along like tossing ships, his characters fail to become fully individual. Nonetheless, Bloch is alert to moments where a different spirit breaks through, where utopia appears amid rubble. Act III of *Walküre* follows that trajectory, from the tumult of the "Ride" to the tenderness of Wotan's Farewell. In *The Principle of Hope*, his postwar magnum opus, Bloch singles out the "bliss-making melody" at the end of *Götterdämmerung*—"the opposite of the bombastic entry into Valhalla."

Despite their divergences, Adorno and Bloch both believed that Wagner had a constructive role to play in the fractured culture of modernity. They took heart from the New Bayreuth and other trends in opera production. Bloch had set forth his surrealist, "colportage" philosophy of staging Wagner in 1929, at the time of the Kroll Opera's *Flying Dutchman*. Adorno, in 1963, stated that "only experimental solutions are justifiable today, only that which injures the Wagner orthodoxy is true." In the philosophy of Adorno and Bloch, in the stagings of Herz and Chéreau, in the biographical writing of Hans Mayer and Martin Gregor-Dellin, the Wagner Left was resurgent—to the point that skeptics like the cultural historian Hartmut Zelinsky saw a whitewash of the composer's Nazi legacy. Adorno, at least, could not be accused of concealing the worst. His governing thesis was that this towering, damaged oeuvre mirrors the society that produced it. "Great artworks cannot lie," he writes in his *Aesthetic Theory*, with an eye on Wagner.

For Adorno, the entire project of modernity, rooted in the Reformation, the Enlightenment, and Romantic idealism, had ended in disaster. Hegel held that truth dwells in the whole; Adorno replied, "The whole is the false." The Hegelian paradigm of historical progress collapses into the category that Adorno named Auschwitz, where the World Spirit is pressed into the service of mass death. According to his late work *Negative Dialectic*, thinking that fails to resist totality's grip is "in the mold of the musical accompaniment with which the SS liked to drown out the screams of its victims."

The anthropologist Claude Lévi-Strauss emerged from the war with a much different view of Wagner. Born into a Jewish family, he had fled Vichy France in 1941 and spent most of the remainder of the war in New York, where he worked through the implications of fieldwork he had done in indigenous Brazilian communities. Lévi-Strauss saw universal patterns undergirding the social norms and the mythic narratives of diverse cultures. Appropriating terminology from linguistics, he began to speak of generalizable "structures" that impose order on the world. This insight animated the new philosophical discipline of structuralism. Lévi-Strauss's work was of a piece with the internationalist, central-planning ethos of the postwar era, not to mention the all-encompassing scope of the high-modernist Book of the World. Significantly, it also took a stance against racism and colonialism. By refusing to draw a clear boundary between Western civilization and "so-called primitive peoples," as he put it, Lévi-Strauss took aim at the racial hierarchies that had brought Auschwitz into being.

Some of Lévi-Strauss's readers must have been puzzled to find the thinker publicly declaring his debt to "the god Richard Wagner"—a nod to Mallarmé's sonnet. Lévi-Strauss had fallen for the composer in childhood, going to the Opéra and attending the Pasdeloup and Colonne concerts with his father. He later said, "Wagner played a capital role in my intellectual development and in my taste for myths." In *The Raw and the Cooked*, the first volume of his *Mythologiques* tetralogy, Lévi-Strauss crowned Wagner the godfather of the structural analysis of myth.

Carl Jung had already recognized Wagner as a master of comparative mythology. Lévi-Strauss, like Jung, made an especially close study of incestuous relationships in myth and literature. In the case of the *Ring*, Lévi-Strauss sees the decline of the gods and their progeny as a transition from primitive tribalism to a civilized order: the brother-sister pairing of *Walküre*, in which Wotan invests his hopes, must give way to a more modern community. In various writings on Wagner, Lévi-Strauss shows how the leitmotif system serves to unify the mythic material. He analyzes recurrences of the "renunciation" motif in the *Ring*, noting how it uncovers similarities between Wotan and Alberich. And he recognizes a fundamental link between the leitmotif and his own concept of the "mytheme," the recurring sentence-like constituent unit of legendary stories across many cultures.

Eventually, Lévi-Strauss found his way to the New Bayreuth. The 1975 festival program book featured his analysis of *Parsifal*, which begins by quoting Gurnemanz's line "Here time becomes space." This, Lévi-Strauss writes, is "probably the most profound definition that anyone has ever offered for myth." (In *The Raw and the Cooked*, he says that music and myth are alike in having the ability to eradicate time: in both, historical time disintegrates into an internal continuum.) Parsifal's heroism resides in the way he navigates an incoherent world defined on the one hand by Klingsor's depravity and on the other by the cold silence of the Grail Knights.

The American mythographer Joseph Campbell paid similar tribute to Wagner when he wrote that the composer's work on myth was "far in advance of the allegorical readings suggested by the Orientalists and ethnologists of his time." In his four-volume study *The Masks of God* (1959–68), Campbell credits Wagner with launching a modern art of "creative mythology," in which venerable motifs are filtered through "the unpredictable, unprecedented experience-in-illumination of an object by a subject." Wagner's two great successors, Campbell goes on to say, are James Joyce and Thomas Mann.

The social ferment of the late 1960s coincided with another philosophical upheaval, one that resulted in a further prosecution of the case
of Wagner. In 1966, the French theorist Jacques Derrida, having criticized
Lévi-Strauss's "nostalgia for origins," advanced a radically decentered understanding of the all-powerful medium of language—"the affirmation of
a world of signs without fault, without truth, and without origin." Roland
Barthes, in his 1967 essay "The Death of the Author," wrote that "a text's
unity lies not in its origin but in its destination"—a conclusion that follows naturally from the interpretive pandemonium of Wagnerism. These
and allied thinkers came to be called poststructuralists, although their
project went deeper than a disagreement with Lévi-Strauss. Revisiting
Symbolist terrain, Derrida revered Mallarmé as the poet of undecidability,
of the "excess of syntax over meaning."

Poststructuralism leaned heavily on Nietzsche and Heidegger, both
of whom undermined traditional claims of truth and being. A difficulty
arose: in the wake of Nazism, suspicion had fallen on those thinkers, as
it had on Wagner. The solution devised by Derrida's younger colleagues
Philippe Lacoue-Labarthe and Jean-Luc Nancy was to offer up Wagner as
a kind of sacrifice, assigning him exaggerated responsibility for the general
deterioration of German culture and thought. In their 1980 article "The
Nazi Myth," Lacoue-Labarthe and Nancy supply a sharpened and simplified version of Adorno's critique. The Gesamtkunstwerk becomes not
simply a harbinger of Nazism but a totalitarian political gesture in itself.
Although the authors do not call Auschwitz a Wagnerian performance,
the implication is present between the lines.

Lacoue-Labarthe amplified his critique in his 1991 study *Musica Ficta*,
a deft but often deceptive analysis of the Wagnerisms of Baudelaire, Mallarmé, Heidegger, and Adorno. For Lacoue-Labarthe, all four figures fail
to escape the false religion of art. One problematic passage concerns Heidegger's writing on Nietzsche and Wagner. Like Peter Viereck before him,
Lacoue-Labarthe sees Nietzsche's break with Wagner as a prophetically
anti-Nazi gesture. Thus, when Heidegger affirms that break, he is "tearing
Nietzsche away from the Nazi interpretation"—a highly fanciful notion,
given Heidegger's friendliness toward Nazism in the thirties. Elsewhere in
the same essay, Lacoue-Labarthe recycles Nietzschean figurations of Wagner
as a "hysteric," as insufficiently "virile." Such masculinist language is regres-

sive on its face. In the end, the displacement of proto-Nazism onto Wagner is a transparent attempt at protecting poststructuralism from its own questionable intellectual sources, which are most clearly visible in the collaborationist past of the theorist Paul de Man.

The work of Lacoue-Labarthe and Nancy provoked a response from Alain Badiou, who, like Lévi-Strauss, inherited Wagnerism from his father—a Resistance fighter and socialist politician. The philosophy of Badiou turns away both from the Derridean questioning of fixed truths and from the monolithic modernist paradigms that came before. He proposes an ontology based on the rational operation of mathematics; at the same time, he stresses the infinity of being, defining it in terms of multiplicity. "The one *is not*," he writes, in an echo of Adorno's "The whole is the false." The fields of science, politics, art, and interpersonal love are marked by ruptures, or "events," which reveal limitations in extant paradigms of thinking and precipitate new truths. Retaining a strong political commitment amid postmodern doubt, Badiou believes in the enduring possibility of revolutionary change. Wagner appears to be one such world-altering Event—but not in the form of the oppressive totality perceived by Lacoue-Labarthe.

Badiou's 2010 book *Five Lessons on Wagner* summarizes the accumulated charges against the composer: that he deals in fake salvation and redemption; that his complexities give way to totality; that his religious politics or political religion foreshadows Fascism. Badiou contrasts that familiar critique with his own experience of the operas as a heterogeneous, open-ended, future-oriented corpus. For him, the truth of a work of art does not reside in the work itself or in the author's intention. Rather, it composes a truth as it moves forward in time. This applies especially to a theatrical art such as Wagner's, which is never a static object, like a painting, but changes each time one of the operas is staged. Badiou's aesthetic vision knocks away one credo espoused by rightist and leftist Wagnerites alike: that theater has a special power to form a community. "The public represents humanity in its very inconsistency, in its infinite variety," he writes in his *Handbook of Inaesthetics*. In that sense, the theatrical dimension, which Nietzsche felt to be Wagner's great failing, is what perpetuates his work and allows it to elude the abuse that threatens to consume it. In *Five Lessons*, Badiou paints the *Ring* as a mythological tale that annuls, one by one, the consolations of mythology. Even *Parsifal*, that sacred act in theatrical guise, is not what it seems; for Badiou, it asks "whether a ceremony *without* transcendence is possible."

The ruins of Wagnerian totality have brought out other recuperative readings. For Fredric Jameson, the Gesamtkunstwerk is "an apparatus, a formal device, designed to intensify difference . . . 'Wagner' means multiple positions which are scarcely reducible to each other and which cannot really be synthesized into a single history." Slavoj Žižek approaches Wagner from the perspective of the psychoanalytic theory of Jacques Lacan, with his competing orders of the Imaginary, the Symbolic, and the Real. *Parsifal*, with its phalluses and wounds, lends itself well to such treatment. Like Badiou, Žižek sees in the Grail ritual a complication of existing belief systems rather than a resolution of them. The opera is secretly pagan in orientation, demoting Christ from the Cross and turning him into a fertility god. That analysis contradicts the theological gloss of the Jesuit prelate Jorge Mario Bergoglio, who became Pope Francis in 2013. A longtime Wagnerite, Pope Francis has used Klingsor's magic garden as an analogy for rigidification and self-deception in the Catholic Church.

Susan Sontag, a theorist averse to pure theory, reverted to one of Wagner's older incarnations, that of the artist of erotic danger. In her journals from 1978, Sontag duly records the composer's vulgarity, his kitsch, his "proto-Nazi volkishness." But, she insists, "the music is about sex— eroticism—voluptuousness. That's why one goes on loving Wagner." Extending Nietzsche's insight about Wagner as miniaturist, Sontag locates the music's real power in the intimate, even delicate space that falls between the summits of massed sound. In the gradations of Wagnerian emotion, from euphoria to dejection, from lust to the tenderest love, a new Romantic sublime emerges. Sontag called for an "erotics of art" that would allow us to "*see* more, to *hear* more, to *feel* more." Her musings on *Tristan* raise the possibility that the apogee of artistic eroticism is to be found not in the shameless present but in the shameful past.

HOLY GERMAN ART (II)

Hans-Jürgen Syberberg's Hitler

"The Nuremberg tribunal should have ordered Richard Wagner to be beaten in effigy once a year in the streets of every German town," writes Pascal Quignard in his 1996 book *The Hatred of Music*, an unnerving meditation on music's capacity to serve inhuman ends. Quignard also says, in a variation on Walter Benjamin's aphorism about culture and barbarism: "I am surprised that people are surprised that those among them who love the most refined and complex music, who are capable of crying while listening to it, are at the same time capable of ferocity. Art is not the opposite of barbarity. Reason is not the contradiction of violence." Although no beatings or burnings in effigy took place, Wagner was branded with the swastika in his native land, his work symbolic of the marriage of civilization and barbarism that Adorno mourned.

For many German-speaking artists and writers who came to the fore in the postwar decades, Wagner was the god that failed. Heinrich Böll's 1950 story "Lohengrin's Death," set in the aftermath of the war, tells of an orphaned boy who suffers a fatal fall while trying to steal coal from a moving train. He is named Lohengrin because he was born in 1933, "just when the first photographs of Hitler at the Bayreuth Wagner Festival started flooding all the illustrated weeklies." Lohengrin's pitiful death epitomizes the decrepitude of the Nazi Wagner fantasy. Günter Grass's novel *Dog Years* (1963), which tracks the fate of a half-Jewish boy and his non-Jewish friend under Nazism, features as a supporting character a German shepherd named Prinz, who, as a puppy, was given to Hitler. After the war, in a hallucinatory trial scene modeled on Joyce's "Circe," Prinz is unmasked:

> A BOY: We might as well start right in with *Götterdämmerung*.
> CHORUS: *Göt-ter-dämmerung!*
> *Göt-ter-dämmerung!*
> *(Walli S. puts on the record. The music from* Götterdämmerung *plays at length. The dog howls throughout.)*
> DISCUSSION LEADER: Here we have conclusive proof that the dog Pluto must have belonged to an admirer of Wagner.

If any doubt remains, the dog proceeds to lick a picture of Hitler's face.

For others, Wagner was not entirely a lost cause, although he had to be approached with caution. The charismatic conceptual artist Joseph Beuys believed that art should escape from confined spaces and integrate itself into daily life. Although Beuys vacillated in describing the degree of Wagner's influence on him, the composer typified a politically engaged aesthetic that privileges subjectivity. Prone to esotericism in the Péladan and Rudolf Steiner vein, Beuys took a particular interest in *Parsifal*, repeatedly drawing the image of the Grail and enacting related ceremonies. In the action *Vitex agnus castus* of 1972, he lay on the floor for three hours, representing himself as an androgynous conductor of sacred energy, and a decade later he envisaged a *Parsifal* staging that would consist simply of a staff resting on the stage, pointing in different directions. Reception of Beuys often cast him as a Wagnerian artist, in both a positive and a negative sense. In an article titled "Beuys: The Twilight of the Idol," the art historian Benjamin Buchloh accused Beuys of mimicking Wagner's "collective regressions into Germanic mythology and Teutonic stupor." Similar questions have trailed the Austrian action artist Hermann Nitsch, who stages rituals of "orgy mystery theater" in a Dionysian Gesamtkunstwerk spirit. Nitsch's *Parsifal Action* of 2004 featured a freshly slaughtered bull, various pig carcasses, and a naked Parsifal wielding a thirteen-foot spear.

If Beuys tried to rise above the nightmare of German history, Hans-Jürgen Syberberg marched into the thick of it. Between 1972 and 1982, the filmmaker produced four extended cinematic essays partly or wholly about Wagner: *Ludwig: Requiem for a Virgin King*; *Winifred Wagner and the History of Haus Wahnfried, 1914–1975*; *Hitler: A Film from Germany*; and *Parsifal*. They combine quasi-Brechtian techniques—circus-like tableaux, masks, puppetry, kitsch assemblages—with a somewhat queasy veneration for the German cultural past. The Hitler film, more than seven hours long, attempts the complex maneuver of satirizing the dictator's fetish for Wagner while extracting the music from his grip. Its most memorable image is of a toga-wearing Hitler rising from Wagner's grave—a parody of Nazi propaganda that fails to demystify its target. The *Parsifal*, essentially a filmed *Regietheater* production of the opera, goes deeper into the genealogy of Wagnerism as it explores the theme of androgyny. The role of Parsifal is divided between male and female actors; Kundry and Amfortas are two sides of the same wounded being. The "redemption for the Redeemer" proclaimed at the end is clearly redemption for the composer, released from the Nazi spell.

For the Austrian poet Ingeborg Bachmann, Wagner's ravaged landscapes had a more personal, less historically portentous meaning. In the early sixties, Bachmann underwent a psychological crisis and became addicted to medications. There followed a flood of fragmentary poems, posthumously published as *I Know of No Better World*, in which the seductive fatalism of *Tristan* becomes an idée fixe of Bachmann's hallucinatory state. She echoes Mark's cry of "Dead all, all are dead"; phrases from Isolde's Transfiguration ("Softly and gently," "Do you see it, friends, / do you not see it?"); the lovers' "Thus we died." At times, a lofty Wagnerian phrase is bent toward the mundane or the morbid: "Let me die / Playing cards at night / is not for me . . ." One stark passage incorporates the black flag that flutters in the old *Tristan* legends and in the final tableau of *Death in Venice*:

Don't you see, my friends, don't
you see? For

who wants to live
where he has no
breath, the black
sail always hoisted.

Many of these motifs recur in Bachmann's 1971 novel *Malina*, the first in an unfinished cycle called *Death Styles*. In a section titled "The Third

Man," the female narrator records a series of horrific dreams involving an abusive male whom she identifies as her father, although in the end he seems a personification of Teutonic masculinity. In one scene, the protagonist is performing in an opera composed by her father, one in which she is supposed to act but not sing. Defiantly, she sings familiar fragments of *Tristan*: "Thus we died . . . Dead all. All are dead . . . Do you see it, friends?" She is left alone onstage, and falls into the orchestra pit. "I have rescued the performance, but I lie among the empty stands and chairs with a broken neck."

Historical and personal traumas collide explosively in the paintings of Anselm Kiefer, whose decades-long negotiation with Wagner deserves comparison with that of Thomas Mann. Born in the last weeks of the Second World War, Kiefer came of age with a generation that broke away from the don't-look-back mentality of the immediate postwar years. When he was young, his mother had him listen to a broadcast of *Lohengrin* from Bayreuth. He was smitten at once with the music's sense of longing: "I was attracted to the idea of the holy grail as something far away and enigmatic and a sort of destination where you desperately want to get to, but you know you will never arrive."

A protégé of Beuys, Kiefer won early notoriety with a provocation called *Occupations*, in which he photographed himself mimicking the Hitler salute in front of various public buildings. Controversy erupted, and Kiefer was accused of trivializing the Nazi past. But with these Chaplinesque poses he succeeded in breaking the silence surrounding Germany's recent history. Mock-Hitler poses were subsequently perpetrated by the artist-provocateurs Christoph Schlingensief and Jonathan Meese, both of whom also laid gleeful siege to Wagner. In Schlingensief's 1999 play *The Berlin Republic*, a character purporting to be Chancellor Gerhard Schröder unveils an absurdist project to stage the *Ring* in the former German colony of Namibia, with a hundred Jeeps blaring Wagner in the desert. Later, Schlingensief took that conceit more seriously; at the time of his death, in 2010, he was planning an Opera Village Africa in Burkina Faso, with the aim of fostering native arts in a reformed Gesamtkunstwerk spirit.

In the early seventies, Kiefer began to produce large-scale paintings on mythological, cultural, and historical subjects. He repeatedly used the image of an attic space—modeled on his own studio—as a kind of stage set for a procession of ghosts. In *Germany's Spiritual Heroes* (1973), the elongated attic is empty except for burning torches on the walls. Inscribed on the floor are the names of artists and writers, ranging from Nikolaus Lenau and Caspar David Friedrich to Robert Musil and Joseph Beuys. Wagner's name is on the lower left. A quartet of paintings titled *Parsifal*, also from 1973, resume Wagnerism in the grand manner. The first evokes the hero's birth with a creepy white cot. The second, showing a gleaming sword next to a broken one, suggests his fight with the knight Ither. The third depicts the "wounding-wonderful holy Spear," here a sticklike object spattered with blood. At the center of the last is a wooden stool on which rests a bowl filled with blood. Scrawled in white above it is the *Parsifal* motto: "Highest miracle of salvation! Redemption to the Redeemer!"

The effect of these works is at once overpowering and ambiguous. They crash upon the eyes at first encounter: *Parsifal IV*, at the Kunsthalle in Zurich, fills one's entire field of vision. The canvases, made of wood-chip wallpaper, have the texture of lived-in, weathered spaces; the paint is laid on thick and dark. At the same time, the images have a kind of deliberate tackiness. The swords and spear look like toys. The dripping Grail looks like something out of a low-budget horror movie. In another 1973 work, *Nothung!*, Siegfried's blade takes the form of a charcoal drawing on cardboard, stuck on the painting's surface. As Sabine Schütz writes in a study of Kiefer, the ersatz sword cannot bear the weight of its historical context, and tragedy veers toward farce.

Since then, Kiefer has produced a gallery of Wagneriana: *Tannhäuser Seeing the Grotto of Venus*, *Grotto of Venus*, *Siegfried Forgets Brünhilde*, *My Father Pledged Me a Sword* (namely, Nothung), *Unternehmen Hagenbewegung* (named after Operation Hagen in World War I), *Brünhilde*, *Brünhilde's Death*, *Welt-Esche* (the World Ash Tree of the *Ring*), *Brünhilde and Her Fate*, *Siegfried's Difficult Way to Brünnhilde*, *Herzeleide* (Parsifal's mother), *Johannisnacht* (the holiday celebrated in *Meistersinger*), *Brünhilde Sleeps*, *Brünhilde/Grane*, *Die Meistersinger*, *Klingsor's Garden*, *Walhalla*, *Montsalvat*. Some of these works are playful in tone. The name Brünnhilde is affixed to snapshots of models, porn actors, and Catherine Deneuve. Elsewhere, Wagner motifs converge with furrowed fields, fire-blackened trees and brush, shattered monuments, railway tracks leading to a bleak horizon. In one of the *Meistersinger* paintings, the proud musical tradesmen of Nuremberg are reduced to bunches of straw attached to a canvas, some splotched with red. Numbers are attached, as if marking evidence in a police investigation.

GESAMTKUNSTWERK, INC.

Dalí's Wagner fountain, Castle of Púbol

At the dawn of the twenty-first century, the sculptor and conceptual artist Robert Morris named Anselm Kiefer as a symptom of what he called the "Wagner effect"—a tendency toward "looming icons of dominating presence," toward an artistic style that is "massive, unwieldy, dizzyingly costly, and Wagnerian to its core." Morris's catalogue of gigantism includes the wall-filling canvases of the Abstract Expressionists, the large-scale actions of Beuys and Yves Klein, the lead-and-steel sculptures of Richard Serra, and the earthworks of Michael Heizer. For Morris, all this work suffers from an aesthetic of cheap transcendence, one that mirrors the ambitions of the ruling class that pays for it. Its abstractions show indifference toward twentieth-century terror. It is Wagnerian art that has failed to learn any lessons from Wagner's downfall.

Morris's essay testifies more to the chronic overuse of the adjective "Wagnerian" than to any palpable cultural legacy. The same goes for the ubiquity of the word "Gesamtkunstwerk" in the modern art world. A vast range of interdisciplinary projects, from the happenings of John Cage to the Factory carnivals of Andy Warhol, have been called total works of art. By 1983, enough examples had accumulated that the visionary Zurich curator Harald Szeemann could mount a sprawling exhibition titled *The Tendency Toward the Total Work of Art*. More recently, as Matthew Wilson Smith notes, the Gesamtkunstwerk has figured in the thinking of cyberspace artists like Randall Packer and Roy Ascott. In 1990, amid euphoric predictions about the future of the World Wide Web, Ascott spoke of a "Gesamtdatenwerk," of an "energizing stream of integrated digital images, texts, and sounds," which could constitute "a kind of invisible cloak, a digital noosphere that might contribute to the harmonization of the planet." The metaphor of a virtual Tarnhelm would prove all too apt in the coming Internet age, as tech companies invaded the private sphere and gathered enormous quantities of data.

In some sectors of the art world, the link to Wagner has more specific substance. Robert Rosenblum, in *Modern Painting and the Northern Romantic Tradition*, argues that Abstract Expressionist painters made conscious use of motifs of Romantic sublimity as they attempted to forge "authentic religious experience in a modern world of doubt." Rosenblum likens Jackson Pollock's 1934 *Seascape*—an early, transitional work in the artist's output—to Albert Pinkham Ryder's *Flying Dutchman* picture of the 1880s, in which Wagner's ocean rages to the edge of painterly abstraction. Franz Kline, who liked to blast *Götterdämmerung* in his studio late at night, produced slashing, bold-gestured canvases titled *Wotan*, *Siegfried*, and *Curvinal*—the last a variant of Kurwenal, Tristan's steadfast friend. Cy Twombly listened intermittently to Wagner while working on his ten-painting cycle *Fifty Days at Iliam* (1978), a bloody-hued fantasia on Homeric themes. Nicola Del Roscio, Twombly's longtime partner, recalls that the painter drew on "that perfect, aggressive emotion that Wagner's music radiates, like waves of heat that melt you into frightened tears."

Late-stage Wagnerism most often flourished in communities where the composer was still a vital cultural presence and not merely a free-floating signifier. Barcelona, with its strong Wagner tradition, was one such locale. The Catalan painter and sculptor Antoni Tàpies had a Wagnerite father, who told of the all-night *Parsifal* at the Liceu in the first hours of 1914. Early in his career, in 1950, Tàpies produced cryptically cluttered canvases titled *Wotan's Sleight of Hand* and *The Sorrow of Brünnhilde*, which come across like set designs for future avant-garde productions—"a stage on which nightmares might well play themselves out," to quote the art historian Andreas Franzke. This semi-Surrealist manner soon gave way to a roughly textured mixed-media style, known as "matter painting," which anticipates Kiefer's huge constructions.

Tàpies often listened to and discussed Wagner in the company of the poet and conceptual artist Joan Brossa, who, as it happens, was born on a Barcelona street named Carrer de Wagner. In 1988, Tàpies and Brossa applied the title *Carrer de Wagner* to a limited-edition illustrated book, which combines thirteen Brossa poems on Wagner themes with savage abstractions by Tàpies, featuring imperial gashes of red and black and the scrawled letter W. This concerted fusion of word and image seems an unusually pure homage to Wagner's Gesamtkunstwerk, which, in its original formulation, envisioned a community of artists sharing a dedicated vision. Brossa's poems dwell on the composer's abiding contemporaneity:

> A compact crowd leaves the factories.
> And Wagner presents many things to the spectator that are not confined to
>   the past, like the sulfurous fog
> or the nocturnal uneasiness that extends from one being to the other . . .

Reflecting on his love for the composer, Brossa said: "There's a certain type of Mediterranean who feels strongly attracted to Wagner; it's a curious phenomenon, due, I think, to the fact that people always want what they haven't got. Wagner himself went to Venice to die."

For Salvador Dalí, the gaudy showman of Surrealism, Wagner was a kindred spirit of multimedia extravagance—"a real mountain of mythological images and hallucinations." Dalí, too, was born into the Catalan Wagnerian milieu: his father would sit in front of the family phonograph listening to *Lohengrin*, and his uncle Anselm Domènech was active in the Barcelona Wagner Association. A dozen or so recordings of the operas can be seen at the Dalí castle in Púbol, as well as an eight-track tape of *Wagner's Greatest Hits*. That playlist matched one of the most distinctive features of the Púbol complex: fourteen multicolored Wagner busts overlooking a fountain in the back. Dalí especially loved a scratched old record of *Tristan*, which, he said, made a sizzling sound, "as if one were cooking sardines." Montse Aguer, the director of the Dalí Museums, recalls the playlist: "Satie, tangos, and, always, at the end of the day, *Tristan*." The last was playing on the day Dalí died, in 1989.

Dalí's reworking of Wagner, at once subversive and adoring, has much in common with that of his sometime collaborator Buñuel. At times, the composer is deposited like a kitsch object in pristine landscapes of juxtaposition and dissociation. He makes a majestically absurd appearance in the 1936 painting *A Chemist Lifting with Extreme Precaution the Cuticle of a Grand Piano*, sitting on a beach in full beret-and-robe regalia. (The canvas had the alternate title *Instantaneous Presence of Louis II of Bavaria, Salvador Dalí, Lenin, and Wagner on the Beach at Rosas*, though the other gentlemen are difficult to discern.) A scenario that Dalí composed for Léonide Massine's 1939 ballet *Bacchanale* depicts the *Tannhäuser* Venusberg as Ludwig might have perceived it: "Venus is metamorphosed into a fish, and the fish into a dragon. Louis lifts Lohengrin's sword and skewers the dragon. But this heroism proves a boomerang, for the entrails touch his eye-lid and his sight is further darkened by hypnagogic visions." In a second Massine ballet, *Tristan Fou* (1944), the hero is devoured by Isolde in the manner of the "perverse and tragic nuptial rites of the praying mantis." The poet and critic Edwin Denby reported that during the Liebestod scene a "repulsive mummy is lowered into a vault caressed by white wormlike dismembered living arms." The ballet "murders Wagner, but does it to the hilt."

Dalí also brushed against the tradition of gay Wagnerism. Gay men and lesbians remained a vital part of the operagoing public into the late twentieth century, even as Broadway musicals and dance pop were usurping Wagner's place on questionnaires of gay taste. Dalí's proclivities took a baroque turn when he developed an erotic interest in Hitler, disclosing that a rear view of the Führer gave him a "delicious gustatory thrill," a "Wagnerian ecstasy." Dalí theorized that Hitler secretly wished to lose the war so that he could experience it as a masochistic *Götterdämmerung*: "The end to which Hitler at heart aspires is to feel his enemy's boot crushing his face." This fantasy is of a piece with Visconti's Liebestod orgies in *The Damned* and the outré pornography described by Susan Sontag in "Fascinating Fascism." In the seventies, strains of *Parsifal* are said to have wafted through the New York gay club the Mineshaft, which specialized in extreme sexual practices. The management of that establishment once posted a sign asking patrons not to distract other customers with loud discussions of the *Ring*.

No Wagnerian artwork was more massive or unwieldy, in Robert Morris's terms, than the one the artist David Hockney named *Wagner*

Drive. Yet it cost no more than a tank of gas. In the eighties and nineties, Hockney regularly took friends on sunset drives along twisting Southern California roads, playing carefully timed excerpts from the *Ring* and *Parsifal* on the car stereo. Vistas of canyons, mountains, and ocean aligned with the shifting contours of the music. Wagner had particular power for Hockney during the AIDS plague, which killed thousands of gay men in the world of the arts. In 1987, he created intimately luminous sets for a production of *Tristan* at the Los Angeles Opera, which ended with an image of "transcendental dawn": the Brittany cliffs going black while the sky lit up behind them. "When you suddenly find yourself surrounded by so much suffering, you begin to think of death differently," Hockney told the writer Lawrence Weschler. He spoke of two friends, Nathan Kolodner and René Amrein, who had died of AIDS. "Death ended up joining them really, as they'd both fervently desired," he said. "That's the higher possibility Wagner's music holds out."

GRAIL TEMPLE (II)

At the outset of William Gaddis's 1975 novel *J R*, a colossal satire of postwar America, a junior high school on Long Island is putting on an improbable spring-theater production: *Das Rheingold.* The project is the brainchild of Edward Bast, a would-be Leonard Bernstein who teaches music at the school. Because a driver's-ed class is occupying the school cafeteria, the *Rheingold* rehearsal is moved to a Jewish temple. J R, an eleven-year-old schoolboy, has been cast as Alberich. Unsurprisingly, he is up to no good. The *Rheingold* rehearsal is proceeding fitfully—the bugle player substitutes "Call to the Colors" for the motif of the gold—when it is noticed that a paper bag full of money, representing the gold, has disappeared. On a class trip to the stock exchange, J R begins a precocious round of wheeling and dealing that eventually makes him the chairman of a paper empire, including a chain of Wagner Funeral Homes. At the end, J R's ruses are exposed, but one has the feeling he will rise again.

Gaddis's agile updating of the *Ring*, worthy of Shaw and Upton Sinclair, showed that literature's agon with Wagner had not ended with the spiritual firestorm of *Doctor Faustus.* As in film, the composer's most obvious function is as a signpost of Nazi menace, particularly when authors introduce Hitler himself as a character. Norman Mailer, in his 2007 novel *The Castle in the Forest*, tries to get to the heart of the matter by dramatizing the young Hitler's first experience of *Lohengrin*: "Wagner was a genius. Adolf had come to that opinion instantly . . . But could he say this was also true of himself? Or was he not a genius after all? Not next to Wagner." The protagonist of Harry Mulisch's *Siegfried* (2001) is a Dutch novelist who has written a modern retelling of *Tristan und Isolde*. On a book tour, he comes across a tale of a secret love child of Hitler and Eva Braun, naturally named Siegfried. Hitler operates as an undying, satanic presence, with Wagner hovering as his medium of influence: the final resolution of the Tristan chord is described as a "Harmonic Final Solution."

The shadowy aristocrat Henri de Corinthe, a recurring figure in Alain Robbe-Grillet's novelistic trilogy *Romanesques* (1984–94), is a subtler creation, laying bare the predicament of the unreconstructed Wagnerian aesthete. Corinthe flirts with Fascism and compares the Nuremberg rallies to a *Parsifal* he saw in Bayreuth. Robbe-Grillet modeled the character on French Wagnerites who fell into the Nazi orbit, including Lucien Rebatet, author of the post-Proustian novel *Les Deux Étendards*. Corinthe is not simply a collaborator, however. His quasi-demonic energy stands in for the author's own anarchic politics and aesthetics. Discoursing on the *Ring*, he contends that the real hero of the cycle is Hagen, the "solitary man who says 'no' to the order of things." In this way, as Timothée Picard writes in his *Dictionnaire encyclopédique Wagner*, Corinthe represents the "shipwreck of ideologies and systems" in modern Europe. His active negativity prepares the way for a possible liberation, or at least a banishing of old illusions.

The gnomic French Surrealist author Julien Gracq flatly refused the Hitlerization of Wagner, and did so by holding fast to an older mode of reception: using the composer as a kind of Symbolist intoxicant, a gateway to a netherworld of feeling. Having served in the French army during the first stage of the Second World War—the so-called phony war of 1939–40—Gracq reflected the experience in his slender, haunting 1958 novel *A Balcony in the Forest*, which has as its epigraph Gurnemanz's opening lines from *Parsifal*: "He! Ho! You forest guardians, / or rather guardians of sleep, / at least wake with the morning!" For most of the novel, a lieutenant posted at a blockhouse in the Ardennes wanders about in a pensive haze, listening to the "long, deep rustling" of the forest—imagery echoing Baudelaire and other early Wagnéristes. When the Blitzkrieg begins, the protagonist is reminded of the dragon Fafner and of Wotan's ravens. One might expect this Parsifalian dreamer to awake to cold reality, but he stays in his trance to the end. Even in the face of the German war machine, Wagner remains a meta-historical presence, melting into the murmurs of nature.

The entire torrent of Wagnerian signification—political, psychological, mythological, mystical—runs through the science-fiction novels of Philip K. Dick, whose attachment to the composer approached the feverishness of Joséphin Péladan. Dick first heard *Parsifal* when he was a high-school student in Berkeley, California, in the mid-1940s. "Nothing satisfied me in life thereafter," he wrote. "Q: where do you go next from Act III of *Parsifal*? A: There is only one place, one next step, one answer: *to Christ himself*." He owned a number of recordings of the opera, including Karl Muck's assembly of excerpts from the twenties. Friends recalled him playing Wagner at high volume, to the distress of the neighbors. He named his second child Isolde Freya.

Only in his later work did Dick set his esoteric ecstasies before the public. Early on, Wagner carried a negative charge. In the mordant 1953 story "The Preserving Machine," a music-loving experimenter hopes to immortalize classical music by imprinting characteristics of the great composers onto genetically fabricated organic creatures. Mozart is a bird, Brahms a centipede, Schubert an innocent sheep-like thing. As for the Wagner animal, it is "large and splashed with deep colors," and has a bad temper. "Doc Labyrinth was a little afraid of it, as were the bach bugs." Soon enough, the Schubert animal is found slaughtered: Wagner has run amok. "But it's changed. It's changed. I hardly recognize it," Doc Labyrinth laments, sounding like many a music lover who has pondered Wagner's posthumous reputation.

The dystopias of Dick's classic sci-fi novels, often involving authoritarian regimes on American soil, frequently include the Nazi Wagner. In *The Man in the High Castle* (1962), an alternate-reality narrative in which the Axis powers win the Second World War, Herbert von Karajan is the permanent conductor of the New York Philharmonic, programming "heavy German bombastic Wagner and Orff." In the totalitarian America of *The Simulacra* (1964), an all-powerful First Lady fetches Hermann Göring with a time-travel machine and looks for proper entertainment for him: "We could have the brass band play arrangements of themes from *Parsifal*." And in *Flow My Tears, the Policeman Said* (1974), a music-loving head of police prefers John Dowland and Karlheinz Stockhausen to Wagner, but finds *Walküre* a useful point of reference in justifying an incestuous relationship with his sister: "Sigmund and Siglinde. 'Schwester und Braut.' Sister and bride. And the hell with Hunding."

In 1974, Dick experienced hallucinations in which he felt himself to be in communication with past worlds. In a collection of journals published posthumously as *The Exegesis*, he related these episodes to his old love for *Parsifal*, saying that the opera showed him how one could attain ultimate spiritual clarity through a fusion of Christianity and Buddhism. In the 1981 novel *VALIS*, those *Parsifal* epiphanies assume fictional form. A man with the inimitable name Horselover Fat—"Philip" means "lover of horses" in Greek, "dick" is German for "fat"—becomes aware of an entity known as the Vast Active Living Intelligence System, which seems to be guiding his visions. Trying to make sense of the malleability of space and time, Fat ponders Gurnemanz's line "Here time becomes space," associating it with Hermann Minkowski's theorization of four-dimensional space-time. A subsequent disquisition on *Parsifal* plausibly ties the slogan "Redemption for the Redeemer" to the Gnostic Christian principle of "Salvator salvandus," the Savior saved. Where is the Savior in the present? She turns out to be a two-year-old-girl named Sophia, who does not live long. It is in the nature of Saviors to be born, to die, and to be born again, time after time.

Some of Dick's reflections remain inscrutable, but one passage in *VALIS* neatly captures the hypnotic riddle that Wagner has never ceased to pose. Horselover Fat says: "*Parsifal* is one of those corkscrew artifacts of culture in which you get the subjective sense that you've learned something from it, something valuable or even priceless; but on closer inspection you suddenly begin to scratch your head and say, 'Wait a minute. This makes no sense.'" Dick then conjures the unlikely image of Wagner at the gates of heaven. "'You have to let me in,' he says. 'I wrote *Parsifal*. It has to do with the Grail, Christ, suffering, pity and healing. Right?' And they answer, 'Well, we read it and it makes no sense.' SLAM." Dick goes on: "Wagner is right and so are they . . . What we have here is a Zen paradox. That which makes no sense makes the *most* sense . . . Everybody knows that Aristotelian two-value logic is fucked." The Meister might have agreed, in so many words.

WAGNER IN ISRAEL

The partial rehabilitation of Wagner in the 1960s and '70s, capped by Decca's recording of the *Ring* and worldwide television broadcasts of the Chéreau *Ring* from Bayreuth, faltered in the decades that followed. At a time when consciousness of the enormity of the Holocaust was deepening, both in Germany and abroad, the conversation around Wagner increasingly focused on his antisemitism and his effect on Hitler. The publication of Cosima Wagner's diaries, in 1976 and 1977, revealed that the composer was even more bigoted than his published writings let on. In 1978, Hartmut Zelinsky used the diaries to draw a straight line from Wagner's images of "*Untergang*" and "annihilation" to the Holocaust. In the nineties, scholarly work by Barry Millington, David Levin, and Marc Weiner developed Adorno's thesis that antisemitism resides in the operas themselves. Gottfried Wagner, son of Wolfgang Wagner, wrote that his great-grandfather had prophesied the Final Solution.

In 1981, just as the focus on Wagner's antisemitism was intensifying, Zubin Mehta, the music director of the Israel Philharmonic, tried to break the unofficial Israeli ban on performances of the composer. Mehta said from the stage that the orchestra would play the Prelude and Liebestod from *Tristan* as an encore, and that anyone who preferred not to hear it could leave. Soon after the music began, someone shouted, "You will not play Wagner!" Bedlam ensued. At a subsequent concert, the noise became so loud that Mehta halted the performance. Ben-Zion Leitner, a hero of the 1948 war for Israeli independence, bared his scarred stomach, saying, "Play Wagner over my body." Avraham Melamed, a Holocaust survivor who played in the Philharmonic, spoke of how unexpected encounters with Wagner could be traumatic for Jews: "Some time ago I saw the film *Apocalypse Now*, and in one of the scenes helicopters came down and bombed to the sound of music that made my stomach turn over."

The Wagner moratorium had begun in 1938, when Toscanini agreed to remove the *Meistersinger* prelude from a Palestine Symphony program. News of Kristallnacht prompted the decision. At intervals after the war, conductors attempted to restore Wagner to the repertory. When Mehta first tried, in 1974, a workers' committee declared: "Woe to the Jew in the State of Israel who agrees to play the music that accompanied the six million, the children, women, men and babes, to the death camps." Next into the fray was the Argentine-Israeli pianist and conductor Daniel Barenboim, one of a number of Jewish musicians who pointedly embraced Wagner. In 1991, Barenboim announced a Wagner concert in Tel Aviv, then canceled it. He tried again in 2001, asking an audience in Jerusalem whether they wished to hear the *Tristan* prelude as an encore. During the prolonged debate that followed, protesters shouted "Fascist!" and "Concentration camp music!" The cheers won out, and Barenboim went ahead. In 2012, a planned concert by the Israel Wagner Society at Tel Aviv University fell foul of another media frenzy. Asher Fisch, who was to have conducted the program, had personal reasons for resisting the ban: his mother, who left Vienna in 1939, felt that if her son were to conduct Wagner in Israel it would be a final victory over Hitler. As of this writing, the music remains forbidden.

Na'ama Sheffi, in a study of the Israeli Wagner controversy, finds that the discussion has been driven largely by people who do not attend concerts regularly. (At the time of Mehta's 1981 action, a majority of concertgoers favored playing Wagner.) Sheffi believes that the Wagner ban was at first a kind of compensatory action for normalized relations with the West German state. Later, Sheffi speculates, the abstention from Wagner became symbolic of the very act of Holocaust remembrance: playing him would be tantamount to forgetting. Assisting in this mechanism was the historically shaky but emotionally tenacious idea that Wagner had been heard in the death camps. Films like *The Boys from Brazil* and *Seven Beauties* helped to cement that impression. The Israeli detective novelist Batya Gur capitalized on this tangle of associations in her 1996 novel *Murder Duet*, in which a ruthless Wagner-loving conductor is exposed as a cold-blooded killer.

Some Jewish intellectuals, even those who subject Wagner to strenuous criticism, consider the Israeli ban a problematic mode of cultural politics. The sociologist Moshe Zuckermann has called it an "ideologically pre-formed trivialization of Shoah commemoration." The historian Michael P. Steinberg wonders whether the Wagner taboo is a "symptom of anxiety about the nation itself: in this case, the national self that wishes to equate the Israeli with the Jewish as authentic and equal marks of citizenship."

No matter where it is made, "the claim of cultural purity . . . remains the gravest political danger of all."

W oody Allen made an often-quoted crack about Wagner in his 1993 film *Manhattan Murder Mystery*. As his character walks out of a performance of *The Flying Dutchman* at the Met, he says, "I can't listen to that much Wagner, ya know? I start to get the urge to conquer Poland." It's a joke with a serious undertow. In the minds of many, Wagner still poses a palpable threat. Could the composer somehow stoke new horrors or rouse some future Hitler? In an age when classical music has a marginal role in mainstream culture, the possibility seems remote. Politicians play pop music at their rallies, and, occasional deployments of the "Ride" aside, military operations are fueled by hard-hitting rock and rap. At times, the demonization of Wagner feels like an alibi—an evasion of questions about pop culture's own relationship with misogynist violence, patriotic mythology, and the domination of the many by the few. Allen's joke lost its zing when moral questions encircled his own life and work.

Still, the threat cannot be discounted, especially when authoritarian and neo-fascist politics are gaining ominous new momentum. Wagner does make scattered appearances in white-supremacist literature and propaganda. He has been quoted on the online forum Stormfront ("The Jew is the demon behind the corruption of mankind"). An article featured in the *Daily Stormer*, modeled on *Der Stürmer*, says of "Jewishness in Music" that "the remarkable clarity of its insight retains almost startling relevance." Tellingly, though, some white nationalists lament that Wagner is not as popular with their cohort as he should be. Citations of Nietzsche are much more common—not to mention black-metal bands and the pop star Taylor Swift, hailed as an "Aryan Goddess."

White-supremacist enthusiasm for Wagner is centered on a small group of European and American writers who see no shame in the racism of the Bayreuth Circle. The movement has roots in the politics of post-Gaullist France. Self-identified members of the New Right gathered under the banner of GRECE (*Groupement de recherche et d'études pour la civilisation européenne,* or Research and Study Group for European Civilization), which was founded in 1968, in opposition to multiculturalism. Alain de Benoist and Giorgio Locchi, in particular, reaffirmed Wagner's bond with pagan,

Aryan beliefs. In a 1977 article, "Bayreuth and Wagnerism," Benoist respectfully cites Houston Stewart Chamberlain and dismisses Chéreau's *Ring* as a "vaudeville." In Russia, where the neo-fascist guru Aleksandr Dugin drops Nietzsche and Wagner allusions, a mercenary unit known as the Wagner Group appears to have been named after the composer. Those who monitor the German far right record few Wagner references, although in 2017 a politician linked to the Alternative für Deutschland party adorned an Islamophobic speech with a maladroit mention of a Wagner opera called *Tannenhäuser*.

In America, disciples of the New Right have styled themselves the "alt-right." Although they cite European sources, their white-supremacist thinking stems from the ideology of slavery-era America. In their circles, Wagner is occasionally acclaimed as a cultural hero who has "rich potential to re-emerge as a potent rallying point for White Nationalism." The alt-right leader Richard Spencer spoke of an ambition to become minister of culture and "spend millions of dollars on Wagner." At the University of Chicago, Spencer wrote a master's thesis proposing that Theodor W. Adorno's part-Jewish descent prevented him from fully appreciating Wagner. There is no sign that Donald Trump—whom Spencer welcomed to the presidency with a shout of "Hail Trump!"—shares this interest. After an encounter with the *Ring* at the Met in the 1980s, Trump said to the *Vanity Fair* editor Tina Brown, "Never again."

FANTASY CULTURE

In 1911, a British schoolboy named Clive Staples Lewis, the future author of *The Chronicles of Narnia*, came across a review of a book titled *Siegfried and the Twilight of the Gods*, a translation of the last two parts of the *Ring*. It included an illustration by Arthur Rackham, in which the hero celebrates the forging of Nothung by flinging his arms upward. Lewis immediately felt a passion for Wagner, even before he had heard the music. When he found a record of "The Ride of the Valkyries," he experienced a "new kind of pleasure," a "conflict of sensations without name." He set to work on his own Wagnerian poem, which began, "Descend to earth, descend, celestial Nine / And chant the ancient legends of the Rhine . . ."

Fifteen years later, when Lewis was a young tutor at Oxford, he met

J. R. R. Tolkien, a professor of Anglo-Saxon who was in the process of inventing his own legendary world. Lewis, Tolkien, and like-minded connoisseurs of fantasy began meeting in a circle known as the Inklings. Wagner was a recurring topic on the agenda. In 1934, Lewis and Tolkien spent an evening reading aloud the libretto of *Walküre*, as Lewis's brother Warnie reported in his diaries: "Arising out of the perplexities of Wotan we had a long and interesting discussion on religion which lasted until about half past eleven." In later years, Lewis was quite open about his love of Wagner. Tolkien was considerably cagier. The author of *The Lord of the Rings* knew the composer's work and evidently found some enjoyment in it, but he resisted comparisons between his novels of Middle-earth and the operatic *Ring*.

Tolkien's proprietary attitude toward the Icelandic sagas harks back to that of William Morris, for whom the *Ring* was a theatrical desecration. Like Morris, Tolkien could read Old Norse, and in the thirties he devised his own English-language version of the various Siegfried stories, calling it *The Legend of Sigurd and Gudrún*. That project, which was published posthumously, comes across as an emendation of Wagner's more cavalier composite. As the author and translator Renée Vink points out, Tolkien proceeds to assert his own agenda: his Sigurd is a more sexually virtuous character than the one in the sagas or in Wagner, serving as a kind of Nordic Christ.

Tolkien's tales of Middle-earth cover familiar ground. *The Hobbit* (1937) features a treasure hoard guarded by a dragon, a contest of riddles, a talking bird, and a magic ring that confers invisibility. *The Lord of the Rings* (1954–55), in which that same ring is endowed with ultimate power, has a fratricide for the sake of the ring (as Fafner kills Fasolt, Sméagol kills his cousin Déagol); a sword shattered and reforged (Nothung, Narsil); an ancient tree dying; and a woman losing her immortality (Brünnhilde, Arwen). At the end, evil is subdued with the return of the Ring to its place of origin (the Rhine, Mount Doom), even as one last seeker plunges to his death (Hagen, Gollum). Tolkien fans have sometimes argued that the manifest resemblances to Wagner result from a common use of older sources, but the claim does not withstand scrutiny. The "one Ring to rule them all," which masters its wearer even as it enables mastery over others, has no plausible antecedent except in the *Ring*; the same is true of the restorative ending. When Alberich delivers his curse, he speaks of "the lord of the ring as the slave of the ring." Not just the central idea but the title of Tolkien's saga comes from Wagner.

The Lord of the Rings may have roots in Wagner, but its intent is implicitly anti-Wagnerian. Tolkien began writing it in the wake of the First World War, in which he fought, and he finished it in the wake of the Second. Both wars brought about a wedding of Teutonic mythology to German military might, which he saw as a betrayal of "that noble northern spirit." (Lewis, for his part, hated the naming of German military operations after Alberich and Brünnhilde: "Anything more vulgar than the application of that grand old cycle to the wearisome ugliness of modern war I can't imagine.") *The Lord of the Rings* seems a kind of rescue mission, saving Nordic myth from Wagnerian abuse—a kinder, gentler *Ring*. The "world-redeeming deed," in Wagner's phrase, falls to the little hobbits, who, representative of Britain's self-image as a counterweight to Germanic pomp, have no territorial demands to make in Middle-earth and wish simply to resume their gardening.

Even so, Tolkien cannot resist his own displays of righteous force. In Wagner, the line between hero and villain blurs: Wotan's efforts to expand his overlordship, to take charge of the affairs of others, lead inexorably to his downfall. For Wotan, Alberich, and Fafner alike, the Ring symbolizes the corruption of wealth and power. In Tolkien, by contrast, everything tends toward black and white. The One Ring exists outside of social relations, a cipher of evil. Sex, all-important in Wagner's world, is peripheral in Tolkien's; women tend to stand to the side. One of Tolkien's most Wagnerian moments occurs in the climactic battle of *The Return of the King*, when Éomer, one of the heroes, shouts, "Ride, ride to ruin and the world's ending!" He could be channeling Brünnhilde: "Laughing let us go to our doom." But this is a contest of male destinies. No glorification of the heroine takes place at the end: instead, a hobbit sits down to the meal that his wife has cooked for him. *The Lord of the Rings* spins the fantasy that the world will end and life will go on as before.

T olkien and Lewis helped to create what is often described as fantasy culture: the increasingly vast body of novels, stories, comic books, films, television series, and video games presenting alternative worlds of mythological or legendary character. By the end of the century, fantasy had become an industry of tremendous popularity and power, yielding some of the most successful intellectual properties in history. The cyclone of technological change in twentieth-century life, together with the dismal tone of global politics, fed a new longing to escape into spheres of myth and magic. Some makers of fantasy have deliberately taken Wagner as a model; for others, he is present somewhere in the background.

Many early instances of the fantasy genre had a Germanic stamp. When Walt Disney commissioned a many-towered castle for his Disneyland amusement park, in Anaheim, California, his designers, or Imagineers, took inspiration from Neuschwanstein, Ludwig II's castle in the Alpine foothills of Bavaria. By the fifties, Ludwig's castles and palaces were attracting more than a million visitors a year: they were the prototypical modern theme parks, with Wagner supplying the themes. As Linderhof has its Venus Grotto, Disneyland has its Snow White Grotto. Matthew Wilson Smith, in *The Total Work of Art*, emphasizes Disney's penchant for medieval folktales, often Germanic ones, and for the Romantic vocabulary of magic and dream. "I think we have made the fairy-tale fashionable again," Disney said. For Smith, both Bayreuth and Disneyland present a "mythic time which encourages nostalgia, hope, and fantasy while discouraging present consciousness."

As totalitarian regimes overran Europe and Russia in the twenties and thirties, American comic-book culture countered with the superhero. The cult of the young male body in Communist and Fascist propaganda probably influenced the trend: liberal-democratic societies, derided as weak, summoned warriors of comparable power. The chiseled and buxom torsos of comic-book characters seem descended from Wagner heroes and heroines as sketched by Arthur Rackham, Willy Pogany, and Franz Stassen— the latter a committed Nazi.

Superman made his debut in January 1933, as a bald, telepathic villain in Jerry Siegel and Joe Shuster's illustrated story *The Reign of the Superman*. Hitler became chancellor the same month, and the teenaged creators, both from Jewish families, may have intended an anti-Nazi allegory in their tale of a man bent on "total annihilation." Whether they knew of Nietzsche's *Übermensch* is unclear, although the word "superman" essentially did not exist in the English language before Nietzscheans began using it. Later, Siegel and Shuster reinvented the character as a brawny force for good who disguises himself as the bespectacled Clark Kent. In Slavoj Žižek's ingenious reading, the motif of the concealed identity, which became a staple of comics, recalls Lohengrin, the knight with no name. Like Elsa, girlfriends of Superman and Batman jeopardize the relationship when they ask too many questions. The superhero's powers often depend on Wagnerish potions or amulets. Martin Nodell, the creator of the Green Lantern, said that the character's magic ring was modeled on Wagner's. In some wartime comics, Wagnerian refugees actually battle the enemy. In *Air Fighters*, the Flying Dutchman fights the Nazis; the same series features a femme fatale named Valkyrie, a.k.a. Liselotte von Schellendorf, who was raised by Nazis as a perfect fighting machine but defects to the Allies after receiving a redemptive kiss from the American flyer Airboy.

Modern fantasy began with the release of George Lucas's *Star Wars*, in 1977. Lucas, a New Hollywood comrade of Francis Ford Coppola's, was originally supposed to direct *Apocalypse Now*, but in the early seventies that project temporarily stalled. Instead, Lucas made a "space opera," in homage to the *Flash Gordon* and *Buck Rogers* serials of the thirties. The *Star Wars* saga eventually grew to comprise nine movies, plus spinoffs, a theme park, and a merchandising empire. The project was deemed Wagnerian almost from the outset. Susan Sontag had coined the term "pop-Wagnerian" to describe pro-Nazi films; Pauline Kael applied it to the second *Star Wars* installment, *The Empire Strikes Back*.

Unlike Tolkien, Lucas apparently had little direct acquaintance with the composer, although he did know the Wagner-influenced writings of Joseph Campbell. As in the serials, the sci-fi future of *Star Wars* is given neo-medieval, chivalric features. Light sabers substitute for swords; Darth Vader is a Black Knight with a hidden identity. The critic Mike Ashman has noted various similarities to the *Ring*. When the future hero Luke Skywalker seizes his father's light saber, he is like Siegfried mending Siegmund's sword. When Yoda, the wizened Jedi master, trains Luke in a swampy forest, the scenario recalls Mime and Siegfried, except that Yoda is on the side of good.

At first, Lucas spoke of using preexisting music in place of a freshly composed score, as Stanley Kubrick had done in *2001: A Space Odyssey*. (Kubrick, like Orson Welles, steered clear of Wagner.) The temporary soundtrack for *Star Wars* included an unnamed Wagner piece alongside Bruckner, Dvořák, Holst, Stravinsky, and, strangely, Ravel's *Bolero*. The composer John Williams, on meeting Lucas, made the case that a new score could better deliver a swashbuckling atmosphere. This Williams did, with unfailing brilliance. Reviving techniques of Golden Age Hollywood, he eventually built up a library of some sixty distinct leitmotifs. Although he had no great love for Wagner's music, Williams spoke of accessing "familiar and remembered emotions, which for me as a musician translated into the use of a nineteenth-century operatic idiom, if you like, Wagner and this sort of thing." The method reaches its height in Rian Johnson's *The Last Jedi,* the best of the later *Star Wars* films. at times, characters silently look at each other while leitmotifs articulate their thoughts and feelings.

One particularly Wagnerian moment in the original *Star Wars* comes when young Luke, stuck on a desert planet, looks longingly toward a sky with twin suns. Williams writes a melancholy, expansive G-minor melody for horn, which is then taken up by full strings. Its rising contour brings to mind the noble C-minor theme that Wagner associates with Siegfried. Williams's cue becomes a leitmotif not so much for Luke himself as for the mystical entity known as the Force, which Luke learns to channel. James Buhler comments that the theme is first heard before the Force has been explained; in Wagnerian fashion, it gives us a foreboding of the dramatic future. This is probably the moment at which *Star Wars* steps out of the adolescent-adventure arena and into the realm of myth.

A more unsettling moment comes at the end, when Luke and his comrades Han Solo and Chewbacca, having led the Rebellion to victory over Darth Vader's Empire, are honored at a temple ceremony. Fanfares give way to a vigorous march version of the "Force" theme, in a manner vaguely reminiscent of *Rienzi.* Lucas chooses a curious visual design for this scene. The camera watches from behind as the trio proceeds down a long stone walkway, with troops arranged in rigid rows, toward a dais behind which imposing pillars rise. The shot has two clear cinematic predecessors: Siegfried's entrance into Gunther's court, in Fritz Lang's *Nibelungen*; and Hitler's long march down the Nuremberg parade grounds, in *Triumph of the Will.* Although Lucas subsequently denied any influence from Riefenstahl, the likeness is too close to be accidental. To be sure, his heroes break out in goofy grins, undercutting the solemnity of the tableau. But this quasi-ironic, aw-shucks appropriation of Fascist style makes the allusion no less strange or disturbing. As in *Apocalypse Now,* but without critical distance, American-accented heroes absorb the iconography of the evil empire.

Fantasy films were flooding the global marketplace at the beginning of the twenty-first century. Among them were Peter Jackson's *Lord of the Rings* trilogy (2001–2003); the Harry Potter series, celebrating juvenile British wizardry (2001–11); the television epic *Game of Thrones* (2011–19); sundry Arthurian adventures, including a dreary *Tristan & Isolde*; reanimations of *Superman, Batman,* and *Spider-Man*; and myriad other adaptations of DC Comics and Marvel Comics properties. Susanne Vill, in a survey of Wagnerian elements in the genre, catalogues dozens of variants of such motifs as Venusberg, Holy Grail, magic drink, ring, Tarnhelm, magic sword, dwarf, giant, dragon, Valkyries (Brünnhilde morphs into a Marvel superhero), and the Flying Dutchman (renovated in the *Pirates of the Caribbean* movies). Roy Thomas and Gil Kane adapted the *Ring* itself for DC Comics in 1989 and 1990, staying close to the libretto while sexing up the images. A decade later, P. Craig Russell produced a moodier, more painterly comic-book *Ring*, running to more than four hundred pages.

The trilogy of *Matrix* films (1999–2003), written and directed by the sibling team of Lana and Lilly Wachowski, leans toward mystical Wagnerism in the vein of Philip K. Dick, touching on Parsifalian themes of initiation and enlightenment. A young computer hacker known as Neo is drawn into an underground movement led by a man named Morpheus— Laurence Fishburne, two decades after *Apocalypse Now*—who divulges that the everyday world is an illusion manufactured by a master race of machines. Almost all of humanity sleeps in power-harvesting pods while the dream reality known as the Matrix plays in their heads. Morpheus's summary of the Matrix—"It is the world that has been pulled over your eyes to blind you from the truth"—parallels Schopenhauer's invocation of "Maya, the veil of deception, which covers the eyes of mortals." (A copy of *The World as Will and Representation* is seen on a bookshelf in one of the sequels, *The Matrix Reloaded*.) Žižek, in a 2004 article, was among the first to spot the *Parsifal* subtext. What Morpheus calls the "desert of the real" is equivalent to the waste land that lies behind Klingsor's magic garden. Morpheus is a Gurnemanz figure, leading Neo into a state of secret knowledge. The science-fiction authority Andrew May pinpoints what seems to be the clincher: at the climax of the film, Neo stops bullets in midair, reenacting Parsifal's feat of arresting Klingsor's spear mid-flight.

Democratic mass culture prefers to consider itself exempt from the forces that made Wagner vulnerable to exploitation by the Nazis. Fantasy artists like to believe they are creating allegories of liberal good versus reactionary evil. A scene in the 2011 Marvel Studios film *Captain America: The First Avenger* explicitly inserts Wagner into that binary opposition. Johann Schmidt, a.k.a. the Red Skull, a Nazi operative turned global terrorist, is working away in his mountain laboratory, with bits of the *Ring* playing on a Victrola—first Siegmund's cry of "Wälse!" in *Walküre*, then Siegfried's Funeral Music. As at Hitler's Berghof retreat, a grandiose Alpine view is visible through plate-glass windows. Captain America, by contrast, is a scrawny kid who is magically beefed up to Arno Breker proportions and good-naturedly tours the nation with a troupe of dancing girls. Wagner is a monster from the European past that must be ejected, once the sound designers have obtained a thrill or two from the roar of the *Ring* orchestra—much the same trick that Frank Capra's composers pulled in *Why We Fight*.

Any myth is vulnerable to political simplification and distortion, as Herfried Münkler said of the Wagner case. Superhero narratives in which unheralded individuals acquire exceptional abilities can speak for marginalized communities, but they may also encourage the sort of grandiose self-projection that the Wagner operas inculcated in hordes of fin-de-siècle youth. To borrow Thomas Mann's incisive phrase, they can lend themselves to political abuse. In *The Matrix*, the newly enlightened Neo is given a choice between two pills: a red pill that will make his knowledge permanent and a blue pill that will restore the veil of illusion. Members of the alt-right have made that fable their own: their "red-pill moment" is one in which they cast aside multicultural liberalism. The conceit is tailored to an adolescent mind-set that perceives something profoundly wrong in the extant world and longs for a heroic "*Nothung!*" gesture to cut through the confusion. Above all, fantasy shows that the urge to sacralize culture, to transform aesthetic pursuits into secular religion and redemptive politics, did not die out with the degeneration of Wagnerian Romanticism into Nazi kitsch.

WOUND AND WONDER

Blue sky, white clouds, green tops of trees, reflected in water; the sounds of insects and birds; droplets of rain falling; then, after a credit sequence, three naked female forms in swimming motion, seen from below, the sun gleaming from above, fish darting around them—the opening images of Terrence Malick's 2005 film *The New World* present an idyll of humanity in harmony with nature. The swimmers are members of the Powhatan people, who were living in tidewater Virginia when English settlers arrived to establish the colony of Jamestown, in 1607. For most of this sequence, the eternal E-flat major of the *Rheingold* prelude swells on the soundtrack. A more apt and precise application of Wagner on film is difficult to find. The three female swimmers are Native American versions of Wagner's Rhinemaidens: the gold they guard is unspoiled nature. In the extended cut of the film, a female voice intones, "Dear mother, you fill the land with your beauty. You reach to the end of the world . . . You, the great river that never runs dry." Yves Landerouin notices that the image recalls the Rhinemaidens as painted by Fantin-Latour.

Something else approaches: from the swimmer's perspective, other members of the tribe are seen pointing outward. The camera pans over the water to reveal three ships. These are the settlers, sailing in from Chesapeake Bay. Wagner's music continues playing as the camera switches between native and colonial perspectives, both groups evincing wonder and apprehension. *Rheingold* does an intriguing double duty: it sets up an allegory for the white invasion of the Americas as an act of theft, casting the settlers in the role of Alberich. At the same time, the sailing ships are ennobled by the flow of the music. What follows—the story of Pocahontas and her relations with two men in the settling party—raises the fleeting possibility of a respectful melding of cultures, in harmony with nature. That possibility does not come to pass. Toward the end, after Pocahontas has been transplanted to England as a cultural curiosity, she is seen roaming a well-tended English country estate, with Wagner's primal river sounding once again. There is melancholy irony in the juxtaposition: the fecundity of nature has been constrained and regimented. Still, Pocahontas delights in the residuum of beauty around her. The final shot brings us back to the forest, with the *Rheingold* prelude roaring into silence.

Malick's Native *Rheingold* idyll is emblematic of a mode of Wagnerism that came to the fore in the late twentieth century, in the shadow of environmental crisis. This school of interpretation posits the *Ring* not as a national or racial allegory, nor as an economic parable of the bourgeoisie or of capitalism, but as a story of humanity's suicidal attempt to master nature. It was in the sixties and seventies that environmentalism became a worldwide concern, with such landmark events as the publication of Rachel Carson's *Silent Spring* and the United Nations Conference on the Human Environment. The Chéreau *Ring* offered an indelible image of the scouring of the earth, in the form of the hulking dam of *Rheingold*. Visions of environmental dystopia subsequently appeared in productions by Kupfer, Friedrich, Nikolaus Lehnhoff, Keith Warner, and Francesca Zambello, among others. Thomas Grey calls this approach to the *Ring* an "eco-parable," in which the Twilight of the Gods becomes the twilight of the entire species, the anthropogenic apocalypse.

Wagner, like many of the German Romantics, prefigured modern environmental thinking. He saw industrialization as a corrosive force, condemned cruelty to animals, and espoused vegetarianism. The musicologist Kirsten Paige has drawn attention to the often overlooked 1850 essay "Art and Climate," in which Wagner speaks of a "whole earth-nature" toward which future humanity should turn. His 1860 "Lettre sur la musique" contrasts city noise with forest melody. That spirit is also manifest in the operas—in the image of the sickened World Ash Tree in *Götterdämmerung*, in the young Parsifal's callous killing of a swan. Several early environmental thinkers and animal-rights advocates cited Wagner as a precursor. A monthly periodical published by the pacifist animal-rights activist Magnus Schwantje adopted Wagner's call for a "religion of compassion." At the same time, such progressive-sounding ideas were interwoven with dark fantasies, as the antiracist Schwantje was ruefully aware. Wagner thought that Germans had a special sensitivity to voices of nature, one that Jews supposedly lacked. In Nazi Germany, proto-environmental initiatives coincided with genocide.

Grey, in his survey of ecological readings of the *Ring*, doubts whether *Götterdämmerung* bears any meaningful resemblance to modern-day awareness of environmental crisis. This is, after all, the end of a group of rulers, not the end of the world. It is more plausibly understood as a "mythic trope of beneficial purgation," in line with anarchist thought. Then again, nothing in the *Ring* actively resists readings that see it as a metaphor for the self-destructive conquest of nature. To be sure, the expenses required to stage the work can produce uncomfortable dissonances, as the poet James Merrill perceived at the Met in 1990:

> The very industries whose "major funding"
> Underwrote the production continue to plunder
> The planet's wealth. Erda, her cobwebs beaded
> With years of seeping waste, subsides unheeded
> —Right, Mr. President? Right, Texaco?—
> Into a gas-blue cleft.

Wagnerian fire consumes the earth in the films of Werner Herzog, who, like Anselm Kiefer, belongs to the German generation that had no memory of the war and felt free to reenter forbidden zones of Wagnerian Romanticism. Although Herzog grew up with little exposure to classical music, his early film work triggered comparisons to Wagner, especially when he undertook near-impossible projects in the grip of awesome visions. In *Aguirre, the Wrath of God*, Herzog led actors, extras, and crew deep into the Peruvian rain forest and sent them down rapids on a raft. In *Fitzcarraldo*—the tale of a mad Irish businessman who tries to build an opera house in the Amazonian jungle—Herzog had a steamship dragged over a hill. The same school of criticism that described Kiefer as neo-fascist identified Herzog as a vaguely Hitlerish megalomaniac. But the muddy majesty of the director's images has no relation to Fascist aesthetics in any meaningful sense. Herzog does not stage spectacles of mastery: he is drawn to the solitary struggles of desperate souls.

Werner Herzog's Lessons of Darkness

Wagner enters Herzog's world as a totem of the crushing power of nature. In the documentary *La Soufrière* (1977), the director visits a Caribbean volcano that is on the verge of a violent eruption. The *Parsifal* prelude plays against chillingly beautiful aerial footage of verdant hillsides shrouded in mist and clouds. In the end, the volcano fails to erupt—an eventuality that the director notes with a certain disappointment. Siegfried's Funeral Music surges as Herzog confesses the failure of his death-wish mission: "There was something pathetic for us in the shooting of this picture . . . It has become a report on an inevitable catastrophe that did not take place." Ironic grandiosity also inflects the Wagner sequences of *Nosferatu* (1979), an homage to F. W. Murnau. Klaus Kinski portrays the vampire as an aloof, decadent messenger of chaos and collapse. The *Rheingold* prelude unfolds against the ancient mountain landscape that surrounds Nosferatu's castle. It is later heard alongside the terrifying sight of hundreds of white rats streaming off the vampire's ship and into the streets of a Dutch town.

Herzog's interest in Wagner intensified in the eighties, when Wolfgang Wagner invited him to Bayreuth. The sight and sound of *Parsifal* in rehearsal had a convulsive effect on the director—so much so that he overturned a row of seats at the sound of Kundry's scream. *Lohengrin* also made an impression: "Hearing it for the first time was a moment of complete illumination for me; it was a deep and beautiful shock and I knew this was something very big." In 1987, Herzog directed *Lohengrin* at Bayreuth, and went on to stage *The Flying Dutchman*, *Tannhäuser*, and *Parsifal* at various opera houses. Wagner showed up often on the soundtracks of his fiction films and documentaries, in such diverse contexts as mountain-climbing (*Scream of Stone*), jungle survival (*Wings of Hope*, *Little Dieter Needs to Fly*), aboriginal life (*Where the Green Ants Dream*), and the invention of the Internet (*Lo and Behold*).

The 1992 documentary *Lessons of Darkness* is filled with wounding images of Kuwaiti oil fields burning after the First Gulf War. Refusing to provide political context, Herzog assumes the perspective of an explorer who has happened upon an alien world. Over the *Rheingold* prelude, he intones: "A planet in our solar system. White mountain ranges, clouds, a land shrouded in mist. The first creature we encountered tried to communicate something to us." One sequence is set against the first seven minutes of the *Parsifal* prelude. It begins with the sight of vultures wheeling against blue sky and animal skeletons lying on blackened earth. Then, cued to the entry of the brass, a series of vertiginous tracking shots begins, first from a moving vehicle and then from a helicopter. We see overturned vehicles, trucks piled on top of one another, an airfield studded with bomb craters, mud-caked oil facilities. During the Dresden Amen passage of the prelude, the camera lands on crumpled structures and bombed-out satellite dishes. *Parsifal* gives all this the air of a sacred ruin. Later, Siegfried's Funeral Music accompanies overhead shots of the burning fields: towers of fire and sky-shrouding clouds of smoke justify the director's readings from the book of Revelation. These vistas are like Kiefer's paintings come to life.

Some critics accused *Lessons of Darkness* of aestheticizing war. The director has said in response that his "stylization of the horror" enables him to "penetrate deeper," beyond the numbing familiarity of CNN news footage. Lutz Koepnick elaborates that argument, writing that Herzog opposes the "moralizing gestures of distance and mastery" typical of postwar modernist art. The use of Wagner is "homeopathic": it administers a calculated dose of the old drug of Romantic emotion as a way of overcoming intellectual repression. On a more elemental level, the strains of *Parsifal* and *Götterdämmerung* wrench these images back into the past, giving us a view of our own time from the standpoint of a sorrowing future.

Terrence Malick has an unusual background for a film director. His father, Emil Malick, studied music before going to work as an oil-industry geologist and later as a biotechnology executive. Malick vividly evokes his childhood in *The Tree of Life* (2011), where the father figure plays Brahms records during family dinners. Malick studied philosophy at Harvard under Stanley Cavell, taking an interest in Heidegger. He went on to interview the philosopher and translate his work *The Essence of Reasons*. In the late sixties, Malick abandoned his academic career and began studying film. His debut picture, *Badlands*, is a dark reverie on the American mythology of the open road, with an existentialist undertow. Many of his films seem to address one of Heidegger's fundamental questions: what role is left for art in an age dominated by technology? Heidegger quotes Hölderlin asking, "What are poets for in a destitute time?" Another line from the same source gives solace: "Poetically man dwells upon this earth."

That search for a poetic dwelling pervades *The New World*, where Pocahontas struggles to maintain her relationship with nature under drastically changed circumstances. Malick's *To the Wonder* (2012) pursues the same theme in a modern setting. At the outset, an American man is falling in love with Marina, a Ukrainian in Paris: their romance blossoms against the magic backdrop of the medieval city-island of Mont-Saint-Michel. One part of the Mont-Saint-Michel monastery is called La Merveille, the Wonder. *Wunder* is also a crucial concept in *Parsifal*, and the spacious opening of the *Parsifal* prelude provides apt accompaniment.

Terrence Malick's To the Wonder

The action then shifts to the Great Plains—the oil town of Bartlesville, Oklahoma, where Malick grew up. The lovers marry, settle down, and grow distant. Marina appears lost in a landscape of suburban blandness and reckless development. A nightmare vista of a smelting operation is akin to Herzog's hell on earth in *Lessons of Darkness*. Marina responds to a sexual overture from a repairman and goes with him to a room at a run-down motel. The lovemaking is mechanical, grim, devoid of eros. Marina steals away, walking across acres of asphalt. At this point, more than an hour into the film, the *Parsifal* prelude resumes, with the darkened C-minor variant of the opening theme. On the surface, music and image are cruelly disparate: Wagner's melancholy rapture is set against a run-down nation of strip malls, prefab housing, frustrated lives, impoverished minority communities, and industrial gashes in the land. At bottom, though, the atmosphere of sexual woundedness and spiritual disease is the same.

At the end of the film, Marina finds a provisional escape from the Waste Land of late capitalism. "*L'amour qui nous aime*," she intones—"The love that loves us," a gesture toward the transcendent, selfless love that figures so strongly in Wagner. She is meandering at dusk through an autumnal prairie landscape, flitting across browned meadows and a leafless forest. The *Parsifal* prelude sheds its lambent light again. When she turns to look at the setting sun, a mirage of Mont-Saint-Michel materializes, rising across tidal flats under gray skies. The screen goes black, and *Parsifal* continues playing into the credits. The ending could almost have been scripted by Willa Cather: a female wanderer goes in quest of a world beyond the one that has entrapped her.

The Good Friday Spell is merely a spell, a long moment of perception, in which all living creatures, the wise old Gurnemanz among them, give thanks for the bright instant between birth and death. Another of Heidegger's Hölderlin quotations comes to mind: "Where there is danger, there also grows / That which saves." Or, as Parsifal sings, only the spear that caused the wound can heal it. The spear is art itself: poetry, novels, painting, dance, theater, opera, film, all the mechanisms of distraction that can either obscure our vision or let us see more clearly, depending on the day. The slowness of the music, the ambiguity of it, the radical shiver of its emotions, the disquiet that so many people feel in its face: all this marks Wagner as a contrary voice in modern culture, a warning from the damaged past. "Only down deep is it trusty and true . . ."

POSTLUDE

■ ■

. . . that troubled music, ever-darkening, ever-brightening . . .

—WILLA CATHER, *The Song of the Lark*

Wagner first interested me as a problem. I was indifferent to him throughout my childhood, when the great classical tradition from Bach to Brahms occupied me to the exclusion of almost all other music. I remember borrowing long-playing records of *Lohengrin* from the public library, placing them on my portable turntable, and feeling an almost physical unease. The lack of clear demarcations in the music, the sensation of drift and deliquescence, produced in my ten-year-old self not the otherworldly bliss described by Baudelaire but a kind of auditory seasickness. I returned the records the next day.

In college, I studied the literature, music, and history of the fin de siècle, which became a sort of spiritual homeland. I wrote a thesis about Joyce's *Ulysses*, tracing its imagery of degeneration and decay. Thomas Mann's *Doctor Faustus* had an overwhelming effect on me and led me to begin writing about music. Wagner was the Nosferatu shadow falling on that epoch, and I accepted the idea that he had prophesied Hitler. Nonetheless, I gravitated toward such classic recordings as the Solti *Ring* and Furtwängler's *Tristan*. Two favorite passages were Hagen's call of the vassals in *Götterdämmerung*—the pitch-black voice of Gottlob Frick bellowing "Hoiho!" amid dissonant steerhorns—and the prelude to Act III of *Tristan*, that megalith of melancholy. Wagner's darkness was seductive: it seemed to tell the truth about the world. At the end of my college years, my life veered in a somewhat chaotic, self-destructive direction. It was at this point, naturally, that I began to fall in love with Wagner.

Only when I saw the operas live in the theater, in my twenties, did the drama itself come alive. I realized that Wagner is not simply a phenomenon of sound: the characters assumed sharp profiles in my consciousness, and melded with my own emotional world, stunted as it was. Embarrassingly, I associate early experiences of the *Ring* with the ups and downs of various crushes and love affairs. More than once I sat next to another young man at a Wagner performance, likening myself to Tristan, Isolde, or, on bad days, Alberich. One of these unsuspecting visitors to the unpublishable Mann or Cather story of my life ended our tentative relationship following a performance of *Walküre* at the San Francisco Opera—just after Wotan bade farewell to Brünnhilde and banished her to the ring of fire. This seems comical in retrospect, but it felt like high tragedy at the time.

Another spell of chaos led to a happier phase of life and, unexpectedly, to a deeper connection with Wagner. Recovering from alcoholism, I understood viscerally what it means when Wotan accepts his *Ohnmacht*, his powerlessness. For Alain Badiou, Wotan's monologue is a moment in which "power and impotence are in equipoise"; that paralysis can open a path to a different state of being. Many people have gone away from Wagner feeling uplifted, empowered, aggrandized. For me, he has more often brought revelations of my stupidity, my self-pity, my absurdity— in other words, my humanity. Lévi-Strauss may have had that quality in mind when he wrote that *Parsifal* teaches us to know what we do not know. None of this is interesting except insofar as I am a typical case. My immersion in Wagnerism has led me to realize that I had been reciting a dog-eared script of passionate ambivalence.

My perceptions of the man and his work matured as I thought more deeply about the German cultural tradition in which he took such inordinate pride. Since childhood I had been riveted by that tradition—most of all, by German music. At the same time, I tended to follow the habit, widespread in the Anglophone world, of treating nineteenth- and early twentieth-century German history as an extended preamble to the Nazi calamity. Wagner would seem to be the supreme case study in that dynamic. I came to believe, however, that the backshadowing narrative was too simplistic and, in a way, self-serving. As an American ashamed of my country's recent conduct on the international stage, I reflected on the fact that much devastation has been visited on the world since May 1945, and that very little of it has emanated from Germany. The endlessly relitigated case of Wagner makes me wonder about the less fashionable question of how popular culture has participated in the politics and economics of American hegemony.

No one should talk about Wagner without using the word "perhaps," Nietzsche once said. The accumulated files of Wagnerism permit no clear verdict about the mark that this staggeringly energetic man left upon the world. He played an essential part in the rapid evolution of the modernist arts, from Baudelaire to Mallarmé, from Cézanne to Kandinsky, from Cather to Woolf. He revolutionized theatrical architecture and practice, showing a way beyond naturalism. He mobilized forces across the political spectrum, from the far left to the far right, and if the latter ultimately made the more persuasive claim on him it is a result that can always be contested. Under the protective darkness of Bayreuth, he nurtured dreams of future freedom among oppressed members of the population, even as he emboldened their oppressors. In no way do all these contradictory tendencies cancel one another out. Each has its own obdurate reality. The eternal agon with the old sorcerer—the undergoing of his influence, then the overcoming of it—means that his image is continuously dissolving into rival artistic selves.

In the story of Wagner and Wagnerism, we see both the highest and the lowest impulses of humanity entangled. It is the triumph of art over reality and the triumph of reality over art; it is a tragedy of flaws set so deep that after two centuries they still infuriate us as if the man were in the room. To blame Wagner for the horrors committed in his wake is an inadequate response to historical complexity: it lets the rest of civilization off the hook. At the same time, to exonerate him is to ignore his insidious ramifications. It is no longer possible to idealize Wagner: the ugliness of his racism means that posterity's picture of him will always be cracked down the middle. In the end, the lack of a tidy moral resolution should make us more honest about the role that art plays in the world. In Wagner's vicinity, the fantasy of artistic autonomy falls to pieces and the cult of genius comes undone. Amid the wreckage, the artist is liberated from the mystification of "great art." He becomes something more unstable, fragile, and mutable. Incomplete in himself, he requires the most active and critical kind of listening.

So it goes with all art that endures: it is never a matter of beauty proving eternal. When we look at Wagner, we are gazing into a magnifying mirror of the soul of the human species. What we hate in it, we hate in ourselves; what we love in it, we love in ourselves also. In the distance we may catch glimpses of some higher realm, some glimmering temple, some ecstasy of knowledge and compassion. But it is only a shadow on the wall, an echo from the pit. The vision fades, the curtain falls, and we shuffle back in silence to the world as it is.

CHRONOLOGY OF EVENTS IN
WAGNER'S LIFE

■ ■

1864   Receives patronage from King Ludwig II; moves to Munich

1865   Premiere of *Tristan* in Munich; daughter Isolde born

1866   Settles in Tribschen outside Lucerne; Minna Wagner dies

1867   Completes *Die Meistersinger von Nürnberg*; daughter Eva born

1868   Premiere of *Meistersinger* in Munich; meets Nietzsche

1869   Republishes "Jewishness in Music," with an attack on Eduard Hanslick; begins Act III of *Siegfried*; son Siegfried born; premiere of *Rheingold*

1870   Premiere of *Walküre*; Franco-Prussian War begins; marries Cosima

1871   Founding of German Empire under Wilhelm I

1872   Nietzsche publishes his first book, *The Birth of Tragedy*; Wagner moves to Bayreuth; foundation for Festspielhaus laid

1874   Completes *Götterdämmerung*; moves into Wahnfried in Bayreuth

1876   Premiere of the complete *Ring* at the first Bayreuth Festival

1877   Begins work on *Parsifal*; Wagner Festival in London; meets George Eliot

1878   Nietzsche publishes *Human, All Too Human*, leading to break with Wagner

1880   Writes "Religion and Art" for *Bayreuther Blätter*; other "regeneration writings" follow

1882   Completes *Parsifal* in Palermo; premiere of the opera at the second Bayreuth Festival

1883   Dies in Venice, February 13

NOTES

■ ■

For a bibliographic essay and other auxiliary materials, go to www.therestisnoise.com/wagnerism.

ABBREVIATIONS

BB: *Bayreuther Blätter*, 1878–1938.

BWR: Rosamund Bartlett, *Wagner and Russia* (Cambridge UP, 1995).

CWD: Cosima Wagner, *Die Tagebücher*, 2 vols., ed. Martin Gregor-Dellin and Dietrich Mack (Piper, 1976–77); *Cosima Wagner's Diaries*, 2 vols., trans. Geoffrey Skelton (Harcourt, 1978–80). Entries cited by date; some translations modified.

DEW: Timothée Picard, ed., *Dictionnaire encyclopédique Wagner* (Actes Sud, 2010).

Fremdenlisten: Guest lists for Bayreuth hotels and residences, kept at the National Archives of the Richard Wagner Foundation.

ENRW: Ernest Newman, *The Life of Richard Wagner*, 4 vols. (Cambridge UP, 1976).

GBS: George Bernard Shaw, *The Perfect Wagnerite: A Commentary on the Niblung's Ring*, 4th ed. (Constable, 1923).

HWW: Brigitte Hamann, *Winifred Wagner oder Hitlers Bayreuth* (Piper, 2002).

JM: Jens Malte Fischer, *Richard Wagners "Das Judentum in der Musik": Eine kritische Dokumentation als Beitrag zur Geschichte des Antisemitismus* (Insel, 2000).

MPLT: Marcel Proust, *In Search of Lost Time*, 6 vols., trans. C. K. Scott Moncrieff, Terence Kilmartin, and D. J. Enright (Modern Library, 2003).

MPTP: Marcel Proust, *À la recherche du temps perdu*, 4 vols. (Gallimard Pléiade, 1988).

NAC: Friedrich Nietzsche, *The Anti-Christ, Ecce Homo, Twilight of the Idols, and Other Writings*, ed. Aaron Ridley and Judith Norman, trans. Judith Norman (Cambridge UP, 2005).

NBKG: Giorgio Colli, Mazzino Montinari, et al., eds., *Nietzsche Briefwechsel: Kritische Gesamtausgabe* (De Gruyter, 1975–2004).

NCW: Alan D. Schrift et al., eds., *The Complete Works of Friedrich Nietzsche*, trans. Adrian Del Caro, Richard T. Gray, Gary Handwerk, Brittain Smith, et al. (Stanford UP, 1995–).

NWKG: Giorgio Colli, Mazzino Montinari, et al., eds., *Nietzsche Werke: Kritische Gesamtausgabe* (De Gruyter, 1967–). Nietzsche's published works in German are cited by title and section number;

translations are based on the *Kritische Gesamtausgabe*, which is online at www.nietzschesource.org.

OGB: Oswald Georg Bauer, *Die Geschichte der Bayreuther Festspiele*, 2 vols. (Deutscher Kunstverlag, 2016).

PCW: Patrick Carnegy, *Wagner and the Art of the Theatre* (Yale UP, 2006).

RevW: *Revue wagnérienne* (1885–88).

RWB: Gertrud Strobel et al., eds., *Richard Wagner: Sämtliche Briefe* (Deutscher Verlag für Musik/Breitkopf und Härtel, 1967–).

RWL: Stewart Spencer and Barry Millington, eds. and trans., *Selected Letters of Richard Wagner* (Norton, 1988).

RWSS: Richard Wagner, *Sämtliche Schriften und Dichtungen*, 16 vols. (Breitkopf und Härtel, 1912–14).

SM: Stéphane Mallarmé, *Œuvres complètes*, 2 vols., ed. Bertrand Marchal (Gallimard Pléiade, 1998–2003).

TM: Heinrich Detering et al., eds., *Thomas Mann: Große kommentierte Frankfurter Ausgabe* (Fischer, 2001–).

TMW: Hans Rudolf Vaget, ed., *Im Schatten Wagners: Thomas Mann über Richard Wagner* (Fischer, 1999).

VWD: Anne Olivier Bell and Andrew McNeillie, eds., *The Diary of Virginia Woolf*, 5 vols. (Hogarth, 1977–84).

VWE: Andrew McNeillie and Stuart N. Clarke, eds., *The Essays of Virginia Woolf*, 6 vols. (Hogarth, 1986–2011).

VWL: Nigel Nicolson and Joanne Trautmann, eds., *The Letters of Virginia Woolf*, 6 vols. (Hogarth, 1975–80).

WBY: Richard J. Finneran et al., eds., *The Collected Works of W. B. Yeats* (Scribner, 1996–).

WC: Jeongwon Joe and Sander L. Gilman, eds., *Wagner and Cinema* (Indiana UP, 2010).

WCL: Andrew Jewell and Janis Stout, eds., *The Selected Letters of Willa Cather* (Knopf, 2013).

WECP: David C. Large and William Weber, eds., *Wagnerism in European Culture and Politics* (Cornell UP, 1984).

WW: Thomas S. Grey, ed., *Richard Wagner and His World* (Princeton UP, 2010).

ZRW: Hartmut Zelinsky, *Richard Wagner—Ein deutsches Thema: Eine Dokumentation zur Wirkungsgeschichte Richard Wagners, 1876–1976* (Zweitausendeins, 1976).

PRELUDE: DEATH IN VENICE

3 *"Only down deep"*: Translation adapted from Stewart Spencer and Barry Millington, *Wagner's Ring of the Nibelung: A Companion* (Thames and Hudson, 1993), p. 118. All translations of the *Ring* are based on this source.

3 *"I am fond of them"*: CWD, Feb. 12, 1883. For symphonies, see Feb. 9.

4 *"Nonetheless, the process"*: RWSS12, p. 345. For Wagner's last days and death, see Siegfried Wagner, *Erinnerungen* (Engelhorn, 1923), p. 35; Henry Perl, *Richard Wagner in Venedig: Mosaikbilder aus seinen letzten Lebenstagen* (Reichel, 1883), pp. 92–93, 120–54; Curt von Westernhagen, "Wagner's Last Day," *Musical Times* 120:1635 (1979), pp. 395–97; John W. Barker, *Wagner and Venice* (University of Rochester Press, 2008), pp. 56–57, 89–103, 287–94, 302–307; Oliver Hilmes, *Cosima Wagner: The Lady of Bayreuth*, trans. Stewart Spencer (Yale UP, 2010), pp. 150–56. Stewart Spencer, "'Er starb,—ein Mensch wie alle': Wagner and Carrie Pringle," *Das Festspielbuch 2004* (Bayreuther Festspiele, 2004), pp. 72–85, dismantles a widely retailed story connecting Wagner's death to a supposed argument he had had with Cosima over an alleged affair with Carrie Pringle, one of the Flower Maidens in the 1882 *Parsifal*.

4 *"volcanic eruption"*: Nietzsche, "Richard Wagner in Bayreuth," §9.

4 *"probably the greatest talent"*: TMW, p. 76.

4 *"Richard Wagner dead"*: Perl, *Richard Wagner*, pp. 130–31.

4 *"Deceased yesterday"*: Barker, *Wagner and Venice*, p. 89. For telegrams, see Henry T. Finck, *Wagner and His Works: The Story of His Life*, vol. 2 (Scribner, 1898), p. 450.

5 *"Æschylean music"*: F. W. Hume, "Richard Wagner," Dunedin *Evening Star*, Feb. 17, 1883.

5 *"The life of Richard Wagner"*: "Death of Richard Wagner," *New York Times*, Feb. 14, 1883. See also "Death of Richard Wagner," *New York Daily Tribune*, Feb. 14, 1883.

6 *"None of the newspapers"*: "On Picket Duty," *Liberty*, March 17, 1883.

6 *"the old order"*: Moncure Conway, *Lessons for the Day*, vol. 1 (E. W. Allen, 1882–83), p. 291.

6 "Vagner è morto!!!": Franca Cella et al., eds., *Carteggio Verdi-Ricordi, 1882–1885* (Istituto Nazionale di Studi Verdiani, 1994), p. 86. For Brahms, see Adolphe Jullien, *Richard Wagner: His Life and Works*, vol. 2, trans. Florence Percival Hall (Millet, 1892), p. 356; for Mahler, Kurt and Herta Blaukopf, *Mahler: His Life, Work, and World*, trans. Paul Baker et al. (Thames and Hudson, 1991), p. 44; for Mascagni, Alan Mallach, *The Autumn of Italian Opera: From Verismo to Modernism, 1890–1915* (Northeastern UP, 2007), p. 17.

6 *"He hath ascended"*: W. H. Venable, *Melodies of the Heart, Songs of Freedom, and Other Poems* (Robert Clarke, 1885), p. 61.

6 *"Mourning on earth"*: Algernon Charles Swinburne, *A Century of Roundels* (Chatto & Windus, 1883), p. 28.

7 *"in that sacred hour"*: Nietzsche, *Ecce Homo*, "Zarathustra," §1.

7 *"What a thunderbolt"*: Ben Macintyre, *Forgotten Fatherland: The Search for Elisabeth Nietzsche* (Farrar, Straus and Giroux, 1992), p. 113; CWD, Feb. 9, 1883.

7 *"All the world"*: Lucy Masterman, ed., *Mary Gladstone (Mrs. Drew): Her Diaries and Letters* (Dutton, 1930), p. 283.

7 *Outside the Palazzo Vendramin*: Angelo Neumann, *Erinnerungen an Richard Wagner* (Staackmann, 1907), pp. 301–302; Giacomo Cabasino Renda, "Come Riccardo Wagner conquistò l'Italia," *Teatro illustrato*, June 1907.

7 *"The music had swallowed us"*: [Sarah Butler Wister], "Paris Classical Concerts," *Atlantic Monthly* 53 (1884), p. 746, describing the Feb. 25 program by the Concerts Colonne. For Butler's authorship, see Darwin Payne, *Owen Wister: Chronicler of the West, Gentleman of the East* (Southern Methodist UP, 1985), pp. 54–55.

8 *A friend of Bahr's*: Hermann Bahr, *Selbstbildnis* (Fischer, 1923), pp. 139–40.

8 *"have mercy"*: Ibid., p. 143. See also "Localbericht," *Neue Freie Presse*, March 6, 1883; Eduard Pichl, *Georg Schönerer* (Stalling, 1938), vol. 2, pp. 340–42, 535–36, vol. 3, p. 386; Donald G. Daviau, "Hermann Bahr and the Radical Politics of Austria in the 1880s," *German Studies Review* 5:2 (1982), pp. 170–71.

8 *"developed into"*: Theodor Herzl, *Briefe und Tagebücher*, vol. 1, ed. Johannes Wachten (Propyläen, 1983), pp. 125–26.

9 *"Only on the evenings"*: Herzl, "Selbstbiographie," *Zionistische Schriften*, ed. Leon Kellner (Jüdischer Verlag, 1920), p. 9.

9 *The funeral began at four*: For this and other details, see *Freiburger Zeitung*, Feb. 20, 1883; and Hilmes, *Cosima Wagner*, pp. 155–56.

10 *"wondering band"*: A.E.P., "Bayreuth, 1891," *The Critic* 398 (Aug. 15, 1891), p. 81. For other pilgrimages, see John Philip Sousa, *Through the Year with Sousa* (Crowell, 1910), p. 80; Isabella Stewart Gardner, 1886 travel scrapbook, Isabella Stewart Gardner Museum Archives; Ralph P. Locke, "Leaves from Bayreuth," *Fenway Court*, 1975, pp. 19–26; Anton Bruckner, "Drei Blätter aus Bayreuth," in *Musik-Jahrhundert Wien, 1797–1897: Ausstellung der Musiksammlung der Österreichischen Nationalbibliothek Wien*, ed. Josef Gmeiner and Thomas Leibnitz (Der Apfel, 1997), p. 235; Éric Lacourcelle, *L'Odyssée musicale*

d'*Emmanuel Chabrier (1841–1894): Histoire d'un compositeur insolite* (Harmattan, 2000), p. 331; H. R. Haweis, "Richard Wagner's Grave, 1883," *Longman's Magazine* 2:12 (1883), p. 631; Upton Sinclair, *King Midas: A Romance* (Funk & Wagnalls, 1901), p. 41.

10 "*The musical dramas*": W. E. B. Du Bois, "Forum of Fact and Opinion," *Pittsburgh Courier*, Oct. 31, 1936, in *Newspaper Columns by W. E. B. Du Bois*, vol. 1, ed. Herbert Aptheker (Kraus-Thomson, 1986), p. 129. For Bernstein, see Humphrey Burton, *Leonard Bernstein* (Doubleday, 1994), pp. 513–14.

12 "*The essence of reality*": RWL, p. 302.

12 "*triumph of the Wagnerians*": "Chemnitzer Musik II," *Signale für die musikalische Welt* 5:24 (1847), p. 186; Carl Friedrich Glasenapp, "Stimmen aus der Vergangenheit: Wagnerianer vor vierzig Jahren," BB 10:1–2 (1887), p. 58.

12 "*the most widespread*": Max Nordau, *Entartung*, vol. 1 (Duncker, 1893), p. 378.

13 "*Any attempt*": Adolphe Appia, *Music and the Art of the Theatre*, trans. Robert W. Corrigan and Mary Douglas Dirks (University of Miami Press, 1962), p. 139.

13 "*Gesamtkunstwerk*": For a tally of usages of the word, see Nicholas Vazsonyi, "The Play's the Thing: Schiller, Wagner, and Gesamtkunstwerk," in *The Total Work of Art: Foundations, Articulations, Inspirations*, ed. David Imhoof et al. (Berghahn, 2016), pp. 31–33.

13 "*Enough of that!*": RWB5, 401–402.

13 "*You returned me*": Charles Baudelaire, *Correspondance*, vol. 1, ed. Claude Pichois and Jean Ziegler (Gallimard, 1973), p. 676.

13 "*All the psychologically*": Nietzsche, *Ecce Homo*, "Geburt," §4.

13 "*The incomparable thing*": RWSS4, p. 64.

14 "*There is no path*": Nicholas Vazsonyi, "Reading Right from Left: Hans Mayer and Postwar Wagner Reception," *Opera Quarterly* 30:2–3 (2014), p. 232.

14 *Wagnerisms*: On the need for multiple understandings of the term, see Jean-Jacques Nattiez, "L'Univers wagnérien et les wagnérismes," in *Musiques: Une encyclopédie pour le XXIe siècle*, vol. 4, ed. Nattiez (Actes Sud, 2004), pp. 1221–57.

14 "*proto-fascist*": Alain Badiou, *Five Lessons on Wagner*, trans. Susan Spitzer (Verso, 2010), p. 58.

14 "*backshadowing*": Michael André Bernstein, *Foregone Conclusions: Against Apocalyptic History* (University of California Press, 1994), pp. 9–11, citation via Hans Rudolf Vaget.

14 "*Is Hitler always right*": Eric Bentley, "Wagner, Siegfried, and Hitler: A Study in Ambivalence," *New Mexico Quarterly* 13:2 (1943), p. 178.

15 "*To be devoted*": GBS, p. xxi.

15 "*an absolute shit*": Robert Craft, *Stravinsky: Chronicle of a Friendship* (Vanderbilt UP, 1994), p. 530.

15 "*He believes that*": CWD, Jan. 13, 1869.

1. RHEINGOLD: WAGNER, NIETZSCHE, AND THE *RING*

18 "*somnambulistic state*": Wagner, *My Life*, trans. Andrew Gray, ed. Mary Whittall (Cambridge UP, 1983), p. 499.

18 "*the world's lullaby*": CWD, July 17, 1869.

18 "*Eia popeia*": NBKG II:4, p. 19.

19 "*The tragic hero*": NCW2, p. 329.

19 *criticized monumentality*: RWSS4, p. 237.

19 *fugitive slave*: NCW5, p. 347.

19 "*I actually have it*": Nietzsche, *Ecce Homo*, "Geburt," §1.

19 "*Wagner* sums up": Nietzsche, *Der Fall Wagner*, "Vorwort."

20 *cries of freedom*: RWSS12, p. 358.

20 "*first of the folk*": Ibid., p. 228.

21 "*incontestable father*": Claude Lévi-Strauss, *Mythologiques: Le cru et le cuit* (Plon, 1964), p. 23.

21 "*we still avenge*": RWSS2, p. 144.

22 "*Out of the womb . . . The peace*": Ibid., pp. 156, 157.

22 "*War and always war*": Carl Friedrich Glasenapp, *Das Leben Richard Wagner's*, vol. 2 (Breitkopf und Härtel, 1896), p. 324.

22 "*Herr Kapellmeister*": Wagner, *My Life*, p. 401, translation modified.

23 "*Our god is money*": RWSS3, pp. 27–28.

23 *about eight hundred*: JM, p. 30.

23 "*Works of art . . . enormous desire*": RWL, pp. 184, 171.

24 *only after the Revolution*: Ibid., p. 234.

24 "*great* revolution of humanity": RWSS3, p. 29.

24 "*an immense system*": NCW2, p. 309.

24 *evolutionary fashion*: On Wagner and evolution, see Thomas S. Grey, *Wagner's Musical Prose: Texts and Contexts* (Cambridge UP, 1995), pp. 138–51; for Engels and Kant, Robert C. Tucker, ed., *The Marx-Engels Reader* (Norton, 1978), p. 697.

25 "*ruthlessly radical*": Wagner, *My Life*, p. 430.

25 "*aesthetic state*": Friedrich Schiller, *On the Aesthetic Education of Man*, trans. Reginald Snell (Dover, 2004), p. 137.

25 *artistic mythologies*: See Jürgen Habermas, *The Philosophical Discourse of Modernity: Twelve Lectures*, trans. Frederick G. Lawrence (MIT Press, 1987), pp. 45–50, 88–92.

25 "*primordial chaos*": Friedrich Schlegel, "Rede über die Mythologie," *Sämmtliche Werke*, vol. 5 (Mayer, 1823), p. 272.

25 *Richard Klein*: See his "Wagners plurale Moderne: Eine Konstruktion von Unvereinbarkeiten," in *Richard Wagner, Konstrukteur der Moderne*, ed. Claus-Steffen Mahnkopf (Klett-Cotta, 1999), pp. 189–90.

25 "*charm of individual diversity*": RWSS3, p. 30.

26 "*What is German?*": Dieter Borchmeyer, *Was ist deutsch? Die Suche einer Nation nach sich selbst* (Rowohlt, 2017), p. 13.

26 *Mark Berry*: See his *Treacherous Bonds and Laughing*

Fire: Politics and Religion in Wagner's "Ring" (Routledge, 2016), p. 78.

26 *"poor, rough"*: GBS, p. 9.

27 *"This gloomy place"*: Ibid., p. 18.

27 *"right in his complaints"*: RWSS2, pp. 157–58.

29 *"All that exists"*: RWSS12, p. 248.

29 *"Have your way"*: Richmond Lattimore, trans., *Aeschylus II* (University of Chicago Press, 2013), p. 79.

30 *"If it is presented"*: RWL, p. 351.

31 *Stabreim*: RWSS4, pp. 131–32.

31 *"nothingness"*: Wagner, *My Life*, pp. 509–10.

32 *"innermost nature . . . innermost kernel"*: Arthur Schopenhauer, *The World as Will and Representation*, vol. 1, trans. E. F. J. Payne (Dover, 1969), pp. 260, 263. "We celebrate" is on p. 196.

32 *"Henceforth"*: Nietzsche, *Zur Genealogie der Moral*, §III:5.

32 *"I recognize . . . change his whole nature"*: Schopenhauer, *World as Will*, vol. 1, pp. 258, 392–93.

32 *"only nothingness . . better I"*: Ludwig Feuerbach, *Thoughts on Death and Immortality*, trans. James A. Massey (University of California Press, 1980), pp. 139, 141; "lust for life" on p. 78.

33 *"evil, evil"*: RWL, p. 319.

33 *"His significant movement"*: Bryan Magee, *The Tristan Chord: Wagner and Philosophy* (Metropolitan, 2000), p. 3.

33 *"Wodan under the slipper! . . . It's high time"*: William Ashton Ellis, *Life of Richard Wagner*, vol. 4 (Kegan Paul, 1904), p. 442; Karl S. Guthke, "The Deaf Musician: Arthur Schopenhauer Reads Richard Wagner," *Harvard Magazine* 99:1 (1996), pp. 46–48; David E. Cartwright, *Schopenhauer: A Biography* (Cambridge UP, 2010), pp. 530–33.

33 *"beautiful young man"*: RWSS4, pp. 311–12.

33 *"His origin"*: NAC, pp. 239–40.

34 *"totally unmoral"*: GBS, p. 48.

34 *"resembles us"*: RWL, p. 308.

34 *"The best part"*: CWD, June 4, 1870.

34 *Wesendoncks*: Chris Walton, *Richard Wagner's Zurich: The Muse of Place* (Camden House, 2007), pp. 201–42, concludes that Wagner's relationship with Wesendonck probably was not a sexual one.

35 *"Renunciation of Love"*: On this motif, see Robert Donington, *Wagner's "Ring" and Its Symbols: The Music and the Myth* (Faber, 1974), pp. 60–65, 138–40; and Deryck Cooke, *I Saw the World End: A Study of Wagner's "Ring"* (Oxford UP, 1979), pp. 2–10.

35 *A psychological study*: David J. Baker and Daniel Müllensiefen, "Perception of Leitmotives in Richard Wagner's *Der Ring des Nibelungen*," *Frontiers in Psychology* 8:662 (2017).

35 *"not a musical technique"*: Eric Prieto, *Listening In: Music, Mind, and the Modernist Narrative* (University of Nebraska Press, 2002), p. 16.

37 *"At lunch"*: CWD, May 17, 1869.

37 *"Wagner played"*: NBKG I:2, p. 340.

37 *"He who woke me"*: NBKG II:3, pp. 62, 228.

38 *"quiet and pleasant"*: CWD, May 17, 1869.

38 *"Strictly speaking"*: RWB24, p. 223.

38 *"my only love-affair"*: NWKG IV:4, p. 256; NCW4, p. 447.

38 *"free variation"*: NWKG II:1, p. 282.

38 *"From the musical"*: NBKG II:4, p. 52. For Wagner's mockery of Nietzsche's music, see Carl Friedrich Glasenapp, *Das Leben Richard Wagners*, vol. 5 (Breitkopf und Härtel, 1907), p. 149.

38 *"great deformities"*: NBKG I:2, p. 174. See also I:1, p. 298; NWKG II:4, p. 128.

38 *"the ethical air"*: NBKG I:2, p. 322.

39 *"Every fiber"*: Ibid., p. 332.

39 *taking hashish*: Nietzsche, *Ecce Homo*, "Warum ich so klug bin," §6. For other comparisons, see Baudelaire, *The Painter of Modern Life and Other Essays*, trans. Jonathan Mayne (Phaidon, 1995), p. 117; Feofil Tolstoy, quoted in DEW, p. 1857; Oskar Panizza, "Stoßseufzer aus Bayreuth," *Gesellschaft* 7 (1891), p. 1366.

39 *"more comprehensive"*: RWL, p. 771. On the Apollonian and Dionysian in Wagner and Nietzsche, see M. S. Silk and J. P. Stern, *Nietzsche on Tragedy* (Cambridge UP, 1981), p. 260.

39 *Wagner comments*: RWSS3, pp. 10–11.

39 *"remarkable, even miraculous"*: NBKG II:2, p. 464. For Nietzsche thinking of Genelli, see NBKG II:3, p. 25.

39 *Mutterschooß*: RWSS4, pp. 190–91.

39 *"out of choral song"*: RWSS9, p. 121.

39 *"The choral passages"*: Nietzsche, *Die Geburt der Tragödie*, §8.

40 *"Only as an aesthetic"*: Ibid., §5.

40 *"slavery belongs"*: NWKG III:5/1, p. 147.

40 *Martin Ruehl*: See his *"Politeia* 1871: Nietzsche 'contra' Wagner on the Greek State," *Bulletin of the Institute of Classical Studies* 79 (2003), p. 68. On the slavery question, see Hugo Drochon, *Nietzsche's Great Politics* (Princeton UP, 2016), pp. 49–70; Georges Liébert, *Nietzsche and Music*, trans. David Pellauer and Graham Parkes (University of Chicago Press, 2004), pp. 46–47.

40 *"the gradual awakening . . . the German spirit"*: Nietzsche, *Geburt*, §19, §24.

40 *Benedict Anderson*: See his *Imagined Communities: Reflections on the Origin and Spread of Nationalism* (Verso, 2016), pp. 194–96.

41 *Nietzsche aired*: NCW2, p. 5. See also CWD, Oct. 24, 1870.

41 *"This is the book"*: CWD, Jan. 6, 1872.

41 *"did not recognize"*: NAC, p. 111.

41 *"Everything goes wrong"*: Ibid., p. 240.

41 *"The chief feature"*: Shaw, *London Music in 1888–89* (Constable, 1937), pp. 180–81.

42 *"I would erect"*: RWB3, pp. 425–26.

43 *"nonsensical"*: Wagner, *Das braune Buch: Tagebuchaufzeichnungen 1865 bis 1882* (Atlantis, 1975), p. 83. See also CWD, Jan. 6, 1872.

43 *"Away with the ornaments!"*: Frederic Spotts, *Bayreuth: A History of the Wagner Festival* (Yale UP, 1994), p. 42.

43 *"no more solid"*: RWL, p. 793.

43 *"rambling, no-style"*: Robert Hartford, ed., *Bayreuth: The Early Years* (Gollancz, 1980), p. 95.

43 *gasometer*: Willy [Colette], *Claudine s'en va* (Société d'Éditions Littéraires et Artistiques, 1903), p. 221.

44 *"Once he has taken"*: RWSS9, pp. 337–38.

44 *clairvoyance*: See Schopenhauer, *Parerga and Paralipomena: Short Philosophical Essays*, vol. 1, trans. E. F. J. Payne (Clarendon, 1974), esp. pp. 255–68.

44 *adjustable gas lamps*: Russel Burdekin, "Darkening the Auditorium at Bayreuth in 1876," *Wagner Journal* 14:1 (2020), pp. 49–62. On theatrical darkness, see Noam M. Elcott, *Artificial Darkness: An Obscure History of Modern Art and Media* (University of Chicago Press, 2016), pp. 48–51.

44–45 *"impinge on the impression . . . Bravo!"*: CWD, July 26 and Aug. 11, 1882. For "Did the audience like it," see Martin Gregor-Dellin, *Richard Wagner: Sein Leben, sein Werk, sein Jahrhundert* (Piper, 1980), p. 821.

45 *Abdülaziz, Isma'il Pasha*: Karl Heckel, ed., *Briefe Richard Wagners an Emil Heckel* (Fischer, 1899), p. 100.

46 *"The German will appear"*: NWKG III:2, p. 390.

46 *"bold language"*: CWD, Oct. 31, 1873.

46 *"When on that day"*: NCW2, p. 262; also pp. 269, 303, 324.

46 *"If Goethe"*: NCW11, p. 315; also pp. 318, 319, 323, 326, translations modified: NWKG III:4, pp. 370–79, with abbreviations restored from notebook U.II.5.

47 *"I never thought"*: RWSS10, p. 109. On Wagner's exchanges with a Brazilian intermediary in 1857, see RWB8, pp. 288–89, 320, 356, RWB9, pp. 47, 97; Wagner, *My Life*, p. 548; ENRW2, pp. 519–20; Edgard de Brito Chaves, Jr., *Wagner e o Brasil* (Emebe, 1976), pp. 8–10.

47 *more than two hundred*: Sven Oliver Müller, *Richard Wagner und die Deutschen: Eine Geschichte von Hass und Hingabe* (Beck, 2013), p. 40.

47 *"in a chronic state"*: Joseph Bennett, *Letters from Bayreuth, Descriptive and Critical of Wagner's "Der Ring des Nibelungen"* (Novello, Ewer, 1877), p. 146. The figure of a hundred journalists is the author's estimate, based on the Fremdenlisten and other sources. See also OGB1, p. 123.

47 *"Cutlets, baked potatoes"*: Hartford, *Bayreuth: The Early Years*, p. 53.

47 *tacky merchandise*: Bennett, *Letters from Bayreuth*, pp. 26–27; John R. G. Hassard, *The Ring of the Nibelungs* (Hart, 1877), p. 4.

47 *"Wagner's special skill"*: Nicholas Vazsonyi, *Richard Wagner: Self-Promotion and the Making of a Brand* (Cambridge UP, 2010), p. 204.

48 *"I no longer"*: Nietzsche, *Ecce Homo*, "Menschliches," §2. On Nietzsche at Bayreuth, see Eugen Kretzer, *Friedrich Nietzsche: Nach persönlichen Erinnerungen und aus seinen Schriften* (Kesselring, 1895), pp. 18–19; Julian Young, *Friedrich Nietzsche: A Philosophical Biography* (Cambridge UP, 2010), pp. 211, 223–28; Ronald Hayman, *Nietzsche: A Critical Life* (Oxford UP, 1980), pp. 179–80.

48 *neurological or vascular disorder*: Dimitri Hemelsoet et al., "The Neurological Illness of Friedrich Nietzsche," *Acta Neurologica Belgica* 108:1 (2008), pp. 9–16.

48 *"liquid gold"*: NBKG II:5, p. 105.

48 *"overcome his time"*: Nietzsche, *Fall Wagner*, "Vorwort."

48 *"bored, unmusical"*: Andreas Urs Sommer, *Kommentar zu Nietzsches "Der Antichrist," "Ecce homo," "Dionysos-Dithyramben," und "Nietzsche contra Wagner"* (De Gruyter, 2013), p. 508.

49 *"fantastic gaiety"*: Édouard Schuré, "L'Individualisme et l'anarchie en littérature: Frédéric Nietzsche et sa philosophie," *Revue des deux mondes*, Aug. 15, 1895.

49 *"R. is very sad . . . Never again"*: CWD, Sept. 9, Nov. 5, Oct. 18, 1876.

49 *last meeting*: See Paolo D'Iorio, *Nietzsche's Journey to Sorrento: Genesis of the Philosophy of the Free Spirit*, trans. Sylvia Mae Gorelick (University of Chicago Press, 2016), pp. 24–43. On Rée, see CWD, Nov. 1, 1876; and Richard Du Moulin Eckart, *Cosima Wagner: Ein Lebens- und Charakterbild* (Drei Masken, 1929), p. 842.

50 *"young men . . . unnatural excesses"*: Wagner, *Briefe, 1830–1883*, ed. Werner Otto (Henschel, 1983), p. 412; NBKG III:1, p. 365. Dieter Borchmeyer and Jörg Salaquarda, eds., *Nietzsche und Wagner: Stationen einer epochalen Begegnung*, vol. 2 (Insel, 1994), p. 1238, indicate that Eiser imparted the news only after Wagner's death.

50 *"Sleep of virtue . . . Luke 18:14"*: NCW3, p. 68; "against originals," p. 132.

51 *read Wagner's prose draft*: CWD, Dec. 25, 1869.

51 *"Culture simply cannot . . . temporary relapses"*: NCW3, p. 260.

51 *"Any degree of levity"*: Ibid., p. 86; also pp. 125, 233.

51 *Nietzsche hoped*: NBKG II:5, p. 329.

51 *"At noon arrival"*: CWD, April 25, 1878; also April 27, 29, 30. For "evil," see Du Moulin Eckart, *Cosima Wagner*, p. 842.

51 *lyrical recitation*: CWD, June 29, 1878; NCW3, p. 303.

52 *birthday of Voltaire*: CWD, May 28, 1878.

52 *"great excommunication"*: NBKG II:5, p. 329.

52 *Wagner had originally*: CWD, Jan. 3, 1872.

52 *"unbounded progress . . . astonished"*: RWSS10, pp. 82, 87.

52 *"in such a way"*: CWD, July 21, 1878.

52 *"malice, pleasure"*: CWD, July 24, 1878.

52 *he might have responded*: See Nietzsche, *Menschliches, Allzumenschliches*, §103.

52 *"I know my lot"*: Nietzsche, *Ecce Homo*, "Schicksal," §1.

53 *Nietzsche told friends*: NBKG III:1, p. 157.

53 *"Tell your brother"*: Elisabeth Förster-Nietzsche, *Der einsame Nietzsche* (Kröner, 1914), p. 71.

53 *"The old sorcerer"*: NBKG III:1, p. 234.

53 *"innocence of the highest"*: Nietzsche, *Die fröhliche Wissenschaft*, §99.

53 *"cult of the genius"*: Nietzsche, *Menschliches*, §164.

53–54 *"gods, heroes"*: Nietzsche, *Fröhliche*, §143.

54 *Übermensch*: On the translation issue, see Paul S. Loeb and David F. Tinsley, "Translators' Afterword," NCW14, pp. 748–97.

54 *"Mark well"*: RWL, p. 280.

54 *Hegel's Logic*: Hegel, *Werke*, vol. 6, ed. Eva Moldenhauer and Karl Markus Michel (Suhrkamp, 1969), p. 287.

54 *"Mankind is a rope"*: Nietzsche, *Thus Spoke Zarathustra*, ed. Adrian Del Caro and Robert Pippin, trans. Del Caro (Cambridge UP, 2006) p. 7.

54 *Roger Hollinrake*: See his *Nietzsche, Wagner, and the Philosophy of Pessimism* (Allen & Unwin, 1982), pp. 83–84.

55 *"Up abysmal thought"*: Nietzsche, *Zarathustra*, pp. 173–74.

55 *Zauberer*: Ibid., pp. 203–209.

55 *"I wish that he would"*: NCW4, p. 353.

55 *"And you"*: Nietzsche, *Zarathustra*, p. 256.

56 *"utter disgust"*: CWD, Feb. 3, 1883.

56 *"In the end"*: NBKG III:1, pp. 333–34.

56 *"harshness, violence"*: NCW8, p. 45.

57 *"blond beast"*: Ibid., p. 232.

57 *"What is good?"*: Nietzsche, *Der Antichrist*, §I:2.

57 *"sublime malice"*: Nietzsche, *Genealogie*, §II:24.

57 *"triumphal yes"*: NAC, p. 228.

57 *The Case of Wagner*: Ibid., pp. 235, 242, 237, 236; footnote, p. 235.

57 *"where would he find"*: Nietzsche, *Fall Wagner*, "Vorwort."

58 *"To this day"*: Nietzsche, *Ecce Homo*, "Klug," §6.

59 *"panegyric"*: TMW, p. 94.

59 *"great walls"*: Nietzsche, *Fröhliche*, §87.

59 *"noise about nothing"*: Nietzsche, *Fall Wagner*, §7.

59 *In his 1878 notebooks*: NCW4, pp. 358–59, 363–64.

59 *"phantom"*: NWKG VII:3, pp. 217, 211, 226.

59 *"foreign country . . . condescended"*: Nietzsche, *Ecce Homo*, "Klug," §5.

59 *"Wholesale love . . . He who woke"*: NCW4, pp. 300, 350, 316.

60 *"Homer's Contest"*: Nietzsche, *Fünf Vorreden zu fünf ungeschriebenen Büchern*, §5.

60 *Christa Davis Acampora*: See her *Contesting Nietzsche* (Chicago UP, 2013), pp. 151–97. See also Nietzsche, "Richard Wagner in Bayreuth," §1.

60 *"the only woman"*: NBKG III:5, p. 551.

60 *"Princess Ariadne"*: Ibid., pp. 572–73.

60 *"My wife"*: Raymond J. Benders et al., eds., *Friedrich Nietzsche, Chronik in Bildern und Texten* (Hanser/dtv, 2000), p. 744. For improvisations, see pp. 726, 755; for groans, Harry Kessler, *Journey to the Abyss: The Diaries of Count Harry Kessler, 1880–1918*, ed. and trans. Laird M. Easton (Knopf, 2011), p. 190.

61 *"Thrice sacred"*: CWD, Nov. 21, 1874.

61 *"magnificent love duet"*: GBS, pp. 61–62.

62 *Deciding on the right ending*: See Philip Kitcher and Richard Schacht, *Finding an Ending: Reflections on Wagner's "Ring"* (Oxford UP, 2004), pp. 193–201.

63 *regret of the young Nietzsche*: NBKG II:3, p. 62.

63 *"trumpery"*: GBS, p. 97.

63 *"was to say goodbye"*: NAC, p. 240.

64 *"in which Gretchen"*: Theodor W. Adorno, *Versuch über Wagner* (Suhrkamp, 1952), p. 190.

64 *modern Wagnerites*: Berry, *Treacherous Bonds*, p. 263; Slavoj Žižek, "Afterword: Wagner, Anti-Semitism, and 'German Ideology,'" in Badiou, *Five Lessons*, pp. 196, 222; Badiou, *Five Lessons*, p. 105.

64 *"It is up to you!"*: Jean-Jacques Nattiez, *Tétralogies: Wagner, Boulez, Chéreau* (Bourgois, 1983), p. 84 ("À vous de jouer!").

2. TRISTAN CHORD: BAUDELAIRE AND THE SYMBOLISTS

65 *a staging of* Tristan: RWB12, pp. 27, 43, 79–86.

65 *"Striving to spend"*: Baudelaire, *The Complete Verse*, vol. 1, ed. and trans. Francis Scarfe (Anvil, 1986), p. 235.

66 *"insatiable longing"*: Wagner, *Sämtliche Werke*, vol. 27: *Dokumente und Texte zu "Tristan und Isolde,"* ed. Gabriele E. Meyer and Egon Voss (Schott, 2008), pp. 93–94.

66 *"A breath clouds"*: RWL, p. 486. For the withdrawal of the note, see RWB12, p. 82.

67 *"A chain of fragments"*: David Michael Hertz, *The Tuning of the Word: The Musico-Literary Poetics of the Symbolist Movement* (Southern Illinois UP, 1987), pp. 17–18.

67 *"orgasmic ejaculations"*: Gerhard Winkler, "Christian von Ehrenfels als Wagnerianer," in *Christian von Ehrenfels: Leben und Werk*, ed. Reinhard Fabian (Rodopi, 1986), p. 198.

68 *"Liebestod"*: RWL, pp. 548–49; Robert Bailey, ed., *Richard Wagner: Prelude and Transfiguration from "Tristan und Isolde"* (Norton, 1985), pp. 36–43.

69 *"nihilistic death wish"*: Karol Berger, "A Note on Tristan's Death Wish," in WW, pp. 130–32.

69 *"chromatic moaning"*: Hector Berlioz, *À travers chants* (Lévy, 1872), p. 311.

69 *"You cannot imagine"*: Léon Daudet, "De l'imagination: Dialogue entre mon père et moi," part 2, *Revue du palais* 3 (1897), p. 332.

69 *"first stammerings"*: Camille Mauclair, *Servitude et grandeur littéraires* (Ollendorff, 1922), p. 222.

70 *"Very modern . . . first* intelligent": NAC, pp. 250, 93.

70 *"proper* soil": Nietzsche, *Nietzsche contra Wagner*, "Wohin Wagner gehört."

70 *André Suarès*: See his "Sur Wagner," in *Wagner et la France: Numéro spécial de la Revue musicale*, Oct. 1, 1923, p. 11; and *La Nation contre la race*, vol. 2: *République et barbares* (Émile-Paul, 1917), p. 195.

70 *"By 'modernity'"*: Baudelaire, *Painter of Modern Life*, pp. 12–13.

70 *"passionate energy"*: Ibid., p. 137.

71 *"epoch of decadence"*: Paul Scudo, "Revue musicale: Le Tannhauser, de M. Richard Wagner," *Revue des deux mondes*, Apr. 1, 1861, p. 761.

71 *"unity of the book"*: Paul Bourget, "Psychologie contemporaine: Notes et portraits: Charles Baudelaire," *Nouvelle Revue* 13 (1881), p. 413.

71 *Nietzsche makes the connection*: *Fall Wagner*, §7; NWKG VII:1, p. 688.

71 *"terrorists of music"*: Gustave Bertrand, *Les Nationalités musicales étudiées dans le drame lyrique* (Didier, 1872), p. 350.

71 *"Baudelaire succumbs"*: Walter Benjamin, "Paris, die Hauptstadt des XIX. Jahrhunderts," *Gesammelte Schriften*, vol. 5/1, ed. Rolf Tiedemann (Suhrkamp, 1982), p. 56.

71 *"take back . . . singular challenge"*: SM2, pp. 212, 154. In the original version, Mallarmé wrote "étincelante" in place of "splendide"; see "Richard Wagner: Rêverie d'un poëte français," RevW 1:7, p. 196.

72 *Parisian foray*: On myths surrounding Wagner's first stay in Paris, see Ulrich Drüner, *Richard Wagner: Die Inszenierung eines Lebens* (Blessing, 2016), pp. 126–36.

72 *Freischütz*: Wagner, "Le Freischutz," *Revue et gazette musicale de Paris*, May 23–30, 1841.

72 *The woods of France*: George Sand, *Mouny-Robin* (Lebègue, 1843), pp. 6–10.

72 *"Lohengrin is one of the knights"*: Gérard de Nerval, *Œuvres*, vol. 2, ed. Albert Béguin and Jean Richer (Gallimard, 1956), p. 796. See also vol. 1 (1952), p. 957, and RWB3, p. 434.

73 *"quite related"*: Nerval, *Œuvres*, vol. 1, p. 1103; also p. 1088.

73 *Aurélia*: See Nerval, *Selected Writings*, trans. Richard Sieburth (Penguin, 1999), pp. 265, 269, 306–310, 322–23.

73 *"work full of knowledge"*: Théophile Gautier, "Feuilleton: Théâtres," *Presse*, Dec. 2, 1850. For *"paroxyste,"* see Gautier, "Le Tannhauser de Richard Wagner," *Le Ménestrel*, Oct. 4, 1857.

73 *"aberrations of the spirit"*: Therese Dolan, *Manet, Wagner, and the Musical Culture of Their Time* (Ashgate, 2013), p. 109; François-Joseph Fétis, "Richard Wagner," part 3, *Revue et gazette musicale de Paris*, June 20, 1852.

74 *"second assault"*: ENRW3, p. 3.

74 *"Open all the doors"*: Maxime Leroy, "Les Premiers Amis français de Wagner," in *Wagner et la France* (1923), p. 21.

74 *"subjugated"*: Auguste de Gasperini, *Richard Wagner* (Heugel, 1865), pp. 50–51. See also Gasperini, *De l'art dans ses rapports avec le milieu social* (Guiraudet et Jouaust, 1850).

75 *"a democrat"*: Théodore de Banville, *Critiques*, ed. Victor Barrucand (Charpentier, 1917), p. 179.

75 *"like a fool"*: Delacroix, *Journal de Eugène Delacroix*, vol. 3 (Plon, 1895), p. 90.

75 *Marat of composers*: Hippolyte de Villemessant, *Mémoires d'un journaliste*, vol. 3 (Dentu, 1873), p. 251–52.

75 *"Dresses of yellow satin"*: Pier Angelo Fiorentino, "Théâtre Impérial Italien: M. Richard Wagner," *Constitutionnel*, Jan. 30, 1860.

75 *"mediocre writers"*: Scudo, "Revue musicale," p. 768.

75 *"one of those unfortunates"*: Baudelaire, "Richard Wagner," *Revue européene*, April 1, 1861, p. 461.

75 *the critic died insane*: Hector Berlioz, *Lettres intimes* (Lévy, 1882), pp. 272, 276.

76 *"a dead man"*: Benoît Jouvin, "Théâtres," *Figaro*, Feb. 16, 1860. On Offenbach's *Carnaval des revues*, see Ernest Closson, "À propos de Tannhæuser," *Guide musical*, Oct. 20, 1895, p. 776; Mark Everist, "Jacques Offenbach: The Music of the Past and the Image of the Present," in *Music, Theater, and Cultural Transfer: Paris, 1830–1914*, ed. Annegret Fauser and Everist (University of Chicago Press, 2009), pp. 76–77; Flora Willson, "Future History: Wagner, Offenbach, and 'la musique de l'avenir' in Paris, 1860," *Opera Quarterly* 30:4 (2014), pp. 287–314; Georges Servières, *Richard Wagner jugé en France* (Henry du Parc, 1887), pp. 51–52.

76 *"infallible form"*: Wagner, "Lettre sur la musique," *Quatre poèmes d'opéras traduits en prose française* (Librairie Nouvelle, 1861), p. lxii; RWSS7, p. 130.

76 *Endless melody consists*: Carl Dahlhaus, *Richard Wagner's Music Dramas*, trans. Mary Whittall (Cambridge UP, 1992), pp. 57–61, and "Wagners 'Kunst des Übergangs': Der Zwiegesang in *Tristan und Isolde*," in *Zur musikalischen Analyse*, ed. Gerhard Schuhmacher (Wissenschaftliche Buchgesellschaft, 1974), pp. 475–86.

76 *Gerald Turbow*: See his "Art and Politics: Wagnerism in France," in WECP, pp. 147–49.

77 *"Tannhäuser represents . . . furious song"*: Baudelaire, *Painter of Modern Life*, pp. 125–26, translation modified.

77 *Wagner hoped*: RWL, pp. 489–91.

77 *"Bravo les chiens"*: Wilhelm Ganz, *Memories of a Musician: Reminiscences of Seventy Years of Musical Life* (Murray, 1913), p. 180. See also ENRW 3, p. 107; Dolan, *Manet, Wagner*, pp. 33–34; Ernest Raynaud, *La Bohème sous le Second Empire: Charles Cros et Nina* (L'Artisan du Livre, 1930), pp. 97–98; Adolphe Jullien, *Richard Wagner: Sa vie et ses œuvres* (Librairie de l'Art, 1886), p. 140.

78 *Annegret Fauser*: See her "'Cette musique sans tradition': Wagner's *Tannhäuser* and Its French

Critics," in *Music, Theater, and Cultural Transfer*, pp. 228–55.

79 *"Children! make something"*: RWB4, p. 460. For Baudelaire, see *Complete Verse*, p. 247.

79 *making the horrible beautiful*: Berlioz, *À travers chants*, p. 315.

79 *as early as 1849*: Baudelaire, *Correspondance*, vol. 1, p. 157.

79 *"I dare not speak"*: Ibid., p. 671.

79 *"Before everything"*: Ibid., pp. 672–73.

80 *"extraordinary mind"*: Wagner, *My Life*, p. 606.

80 *"I dream continuously"*: Baudelaire, *Correspondance*, vol. 2, ed. Pichois and Ziegler (Gallimard, 1973), p. 105; also p. 50.

80 *"I propose"*: Baudelaire, *Painter of Modern Life*, p. 111. Other quotations on pp. 114–16, 119, 121, 125, 127.

81 *"From the day"*: Baudelaire, *Correspondance*, vol. 1, p. 674.

82 *"The character of the scene"*: Wagner, "Lettre sur la musique," p. xlix.

82 *adds to everything"*: Baudelaire, "Richard Wagner," p. 484.

82 *"What is Europe"*: Baudelaire, *Richard Wagner et Tannhauser à Paris* (Dentu, 1861), p. 68.

82 *"subjective reappropriation"*: Philippe Lacoue-Labarthe, *Musica Ficta (Figures of Wagner)*, trans. Felicia McCarren (Stanford UP, 1994), p. 21. See also Margaret Miner, *Resonant Gaps: Between Baudelaire and Wagner* (University of Georgia Press, 1995).

83 *"very beautiful . . . which honors"*: Claude and Vincenette Pichois, eds., *Lettres à Charles Baudelaire* (La Baconnière, 1973), p. 398, 399–400. See also RWB13, pp. 116–17 and 107–108, although there the order of the letters is reversed.

83 *"I never believed"*: Baudelaire, *Correspondance*, vol. 2, p. 325.

83 *regular visitors*: Eugène Crépet, "Étude biographique," in Charles Baudelaire, *Œuvres posthumes et correspondances inédites* (Quantin, 1887), pp. xcvi, xcviii.

84 *"half mad"*: NBKG III:5, p. 264.

84 *Concerts Populaires*: Katharine Ellis, "Wagnerism and Anti-Wagnerism in the Paris Periodical Press, 1852–70," in *Von Wagner zum Wagnérisme: Musik, Literatur, Kunst, Politik*, ed. Annegret Fauser and Manuela Schwartz (Leipziger Universitätsverlag, 1999), p. 74; Servières, *Richard Wagner jugé*, p. 116.

84 *"thrown a punch"*: Paul Verlaine, "Épigrammes," XX, *Œuvres complètes de Paul Verlaine*, vol. 3 (Vanier, 1901), p. 265. See also Edmond Lepelletier, *Paul Verlaine: Sa vie—son œuvre* (Mercure de France, 1907), p. 91.

84 *"become like other men"*: Comte de Lautréamont, *Les Chants de Maldoror* (Sirène, 1920), pp. 70–71.

84 *"Bis!"*: Émile Zola, *Correspondance*, vol. 2, ed. B. H. Bakker and Colette Becker (Presses de l'Université de Montréal, 1980), p. 114.

85 *"Oh! Wagner"*: Zola, *L'Œuvre* (Charpentier, 1886), p. 265. On Gagnière, see Michelle Foa, "'One Art

Eating the Other' in Émile Zola's *L'Œuvre*," in *Rival Sisters: Art and Music at the Birth of Modernism, 1815–1915*, ed. James H. Rubin and Olivia Mattis (Ashgate, 2014), pp. 149–63.

85 *"juggler"*: T. J. Clark, *Image of the People: Gustave Courbet and the 1848 Revolution* (University of California Press, 1999), p. 68.

85 *"analogies of sensations"*: Champfleury, *Richard Wagner* (Librairie Nouvelle, 1860), p. 8; "one vast melody" on p. 7.

85 For the chronology of the pamphlet, see Léon Guichard, *La Musique et les lettres en France au temps du Wagnérisme* (Presses universitaires de France, 1963), p. 35; RWB12, p. 80.

86 *"endless diversity"*: RWSS7, p. 131; Wagner, "Lettre sur la musique," pp. lxiv–lxv.

86 *"He always brought"*: SM2, p. 36.

86 *"feverish eyes"*: Edmond and Jules de Goncourt, *Pages from the Goncourt Journals*, ed. and trans. Robert Baldick (New York Review Books, 2007), p. 100.

87 *Villiers's father*: A. W. Raitt, *The Life of Villiers de l'Isle-Adam* (Clarendon, 1981), p. 9; Théophile Janvrais, *Le Berceau des Villiers de l'Isle-Adam: Le Manoir de Penanhoas-l'Isle-Adam* (Champion, 1913), pp. 1–2.

87 *"As for living"*: WBY3, p. 236; Villiers de l'Isle-Adam, *Axël* (Quantin, 1890), p. 283.

87 *"I will play"*: Villiers, *Correspondance générale de Villiers de l'Isle-Adam et documents inédits*, vol. 1, ed. Joseph Bollery (Mercure de France, 1962), p. 46; Raitt, *Life of Villiers*, p. 28.

87 *the two had met*: Maurice Dreyfous, *Ce que je tiens à dire: Un demi-siècle de choses vues et entendues, 1862–1872* (Ollendorff, 1912), p. 90.

88 *"prince of profound music"*: Villiers, "Azrael," *Liberté*, June 26, 1869.

88 *"palmiped . . . cubic!"*: Judith Gautier, *Le Collier des jours: Le Troisième Rang du collier* (Juven, 1909), p. 12; Raitt, *Life of Villiers*, pp. 86–87.

88 *The palmiped met them*: See Gautier, *Collier des jours*, p. 14, and *Richard Wagner et son œuvre poétique* (Charavay, 1882), pp. 24–25.

88 *"fabulous being"*: Jean-Marie Bellefroid, "Villiers de l'Isle-Adam en Bavière (1869)," *Revue d'histoire littéraire de la France* 63:4 (1963), pp. 651–52. For "the very man," see Villiers, *Correspondance*, vol. 1, p. 134.

88 *Mendès has him*: Catulle Mendès, *Richard Wagner* (Charpentier, 1886), pp. 7–9. For the jump, see Villiers, *Correspondance*, vol. 1, p. 135.

88 *"Do you imagine"*: Raitt, *Life of Villiers*, p. 302.

88 *"It is the Nibelungen"*: Villiers, *Correspondance*, vol. 1, pp. 156–57.

89 *"R. demands . . . bombastic style"*: CWD, July 24 and 30, 1870. For Russ, see Villiers, *Correspondance*, vol. 1, pp. 156–57.

89 *broke down in tears*: Raitt, *Life of Villiers*, p. 284.

89 *may have read aloud*: Raitt, "Villiers de l'Isle-Adam in 1870," *French Studies* 13:4 (1959), p. 338. See also Villiers, *Œuvres complètes*, vol. 2, pp. 1413–17.

89 *"utmost pessimism"*: WBY9, p. 236.

89 *The climax of the play*: Villiers, *Axël*, pp. 256, 261, 277, 286, 294–95.

90 *"After the meal"*: Léon Deffoux, *Les Derniers Jours de Villiers de l'Isle-Adam* (Bernard, 1930), pp. 51–52.

90 *Frédéric Bazille*: See John Rewald, *The History of Impressionism* (Museum of Modern Art, 1961), p. 116; Michel Hilaire and Paul Perrin, eds., *Frédéric Bazille (1841–1870) and the Birth of Impressionism* (Flammarion, 2017), pp. 71–72; François Daulte, "A True Friendship: Edmond Maître and Frédéric Bazille," in *Frédéric Bazille and Early Impressionism*, ed. J. Patrice Marandel and François Daulte (Art Institute of Chicago, 1978), pp. 26; also letters on pp. 179, 182.

91 *A Capitulation*: Thomas S. Grey, "Eine Kapitulation: Aristophanic Operetta as Cultural Warfare in 1870," in *WW*, pp. 87–122.

91 *cord around its neck*: Catulle Mendès, *La Légende du Parnasse contemporain* (Brancart, 1884), p. 99.

91 *"À la porte Wagner!"*: Rudolph Aronson, *Theatrical and Musical Memoirs* (McBride, Nast, 1913), p. 17; also "Pasdeloup's Concerts Populaires at Paris," *Monthly Musical Record*, March 1, 1874. For Saint-Saëns, see Stephen Studd, *Saint-Saëns: A Critical Biography* (Cygnus, 1999), p. 93.

91 *rapt silence*: Jann Pasler, *Composing the Citizen: Music as Public Utility in Third Republic France* (University of California Press, 2009), p. 508.

91 *Judith Gautier*: See Joanna Richardson, *Judith Gautier: A Biography* (Franklin Watts, 1987), esp. pp. 138–39 and 170–71; Michał Piotr Mrozowicki, *Richard Wagner et sa réception en France: Première Partie: Le Musicien de l'avenir, 1813–1883* (Presses universitaires de Gdańsk, 2013), pp. 326–27; Myriam Chimènes, "Élites sociales et pratiques wagnériennes: De la propagande au snobisme," in *Von Wagner zum Wagnérisme*, pp. 167–68. For Wotan, see Christophe Beaufils, *Joséphin Péladan (1858–1918): Essai sur une maladie du lyrisme* (Millon, 1993), p. 170; for the bread, Péladan, *Le Théâtre complet de Wagner* (Chamuel, 1894), pp. vi–vii. For the 1898 *Parsifal*, see Remy de Gourmont, *Judith Gautier* (Bibliothèque Internationale d'Édition, 1904), pp. 33–34; Edmond Haraucourt, "Le Petit Théâtre," *Le Gaulois*, May 28, 1898; Mrozowicki, *Richard Wagner et sa réception en France: Du ressentiment à l'enthousiasme, 1883–1893*, vol. 1 (Symétrie, 2016), pp. 524–26.

92 *"Curious people!"*: Modest Tchaikovsky, *The Life and Letters of Peter Ilich Tchaikovsky*, trans. Rosa Newmarch (John Lane, 1906), p. 436.

92 *"Sir, I was singing"*: Adolphe Retté, *Le Symbolisme: Anecdotes et souvenirs* (Vanier, 1903), pp. 65–66; Michael Marlais, *Conservative Echoes in Fin-de-Siècle Parisian Art Criticism* (Pennsylvania State UP, 1992), p. 108. For French visitors, see the Fremdenlisten and Albert Lavignac, *Le Voyage artistique à Bayreuth*, 5th ed. (Delagrave, 1903), pp. 552–54.

92 *toga-wearing art students*: "Chronique du mois," RevW 2:1, pp. 1–2.

92 *Éden-Théâtre*: See Mrozowicki, *Richard Wagner et sa réception en France*, vol. 2 (2016), pp. 901–904; Steven Huebner, *French Opera at the Fin de Siècle: Wagnerism, Nationalism, and Style* (Oxford UP, 1999), pp. 16–18; Pasler, *Composing the Citizen*, pp. 511–20. For *L'Anti-Wagner*, see Martine Kahane and Nicole Wild, eds., *Wagner et la France* (Herscher, 1983), p. 69; for the brick, Jacques Durand, *Quelques souvenirs d'un éditeur de musique* (Durand, 1924), p. 55.

92 *"even I am talking"*: SM2, p. 191.

92 *"Your name"*: Octave Mirbeau, *Correspondance générale*, vol. 1 (L'Âge d'Homme, 2002), pp. 660–61.

93 *"Snicker when you hear"*: Gustave Flaubert, *Bouvard et Pécuchet: Œuvre posthume* (Conard, 1923), pp. 404, 444.

93 *"Wagner's nephew"*: Dolan, *Manet, Wagner*, p. 137; Amédée Pigeon, "Chronique des arts," *Revue des chefs-d'œuvre ancienne et moderne*, Feb. 10, 1884, p. xviii.

93 *Baudelaire reminded him*: Baudelaire, *Lettres, 1841–1866* (Mercure de France, 1906), p. 436.

93 *Tuileries*: Dolan, *Manet, Wagner*, p. 61.

94 *nocturne-symphonies*: CWD, Sept. 29, 1882.

94 *"dancing strokes"*: Jules Laforgue, *Œuvres complètes*, vol. 3, ed. Jean-Louis Debauve et al. (L'Âge d'Homme, 2000), p. 331. See also Anne Holmes, "The 'Music of the Forest': Wagner, Laforgue, Mallarmé," *French Studies Bulletin* 28:104 (2007), pp. 56–58.

94 *sit for a portrait*: Auguste Renoir, "Lettre à un ami," Jan. 14, 1882, in *Les Symbolistes et Richard Wagner/Die Symbolisten und Richard Wagner*, ed. Wolfgang Storch (Hentrich, 1991), pp. 15–16; CWD, Jan. 15, 1882.

94 *Fantin-Latour*: See Xavier Lacavalerie, "Fantin-Latour," in *DEW*, p. 675; Michelle Barbe, "Images du 'Ring': Une vision de Fantin-Latour," in *Richard Wagner, visions d'artistes: D'Auguste Renoir à Anselm Kiefer*, ed. Paul Lang (Somogy, 2005), pp. 29–35; Lisa Norris, "Painting *Around the Piano*: Fantin-Latour, Wagnerism, and the Musical in Art," in *The Arts Entwined: Music and Painting in the Nineteenth Century*, ed. Marsha L. Morton and Peter L. Schmunk (Garland, 2000), pp. 143–75.

94 *"aesthetic of vagueness"*: Corrinne Chong, "Evocations of the 'sonore et voilé': The Scenographic World of *Der Ring* in the Art of Henri Fantin-Latour," in *Scenography and Art History: Performance Design and Visual Culture*, ed. Astrid von Rosen and Viveka Kjellmer (Bloomsbury, 2020), forthcoming).

94 *"You will make"*: Cézanne, *Correspondance*, ed. John Rewald (Grasset, 2006), p. 145. See also Nor-

man Turner, "Cezanne, Wagner, Modulation," *Journal of Aesthetics and Art Criticism* 56:4 (1998), p. 360.

95 *"overwhelming power"*: Raymond Jean, *Cézanne, la vie, l'espace* (Seuil, 1986), p. 29.

95 *Scholars and critics*: André Dombrowski, *Cézanne, Murder, and Modern Life* (University of California Press, 2013), pp. 154–55; Mary Tompkins Lewis, *Cézanne's Early Imagery* (University of California Press, 1989), pp. 144–45, also pp. 186–91.

95 *If Lewis is right*: Ibid., pp. 186–91; "melancholic reverie" on p. 190.

95 *van Gogh*: See Natascha Veldhorst, *Van Gogh and Music: A Symphony in Blue and Yellow*, trans. Di ane Webb (Yale UP, 2018), pp. 43, 62–64; Roland Dorn, "Van Gogh, Gauguin, und Richard Wagner: Eine Etude auf das Jahr 1888," in *Symbolistes et Richard Wagner*, pp. 67–75. Texts of letters numbered 683, 590, 739, 621 taken from www .vangoghletters.org.

96 *"I believe in a last judgment"*: Henri Dorra, "Le 'texte Wagner' de Gauguin," *Bulletin de la Société de l'histoire de l'art français* (1984), p. 281. See also Bogomila Welsh-Ovcharov, "Paul Gauguin's Third Visit to Brittany, June 1889–November 1890," and Robert Welsh, "Gauguin and the Inn of Marie Henry at Le Pouldu," both in *Gauguin's Nirvana: Painters at Le Pouldu, 1889–90*, ed. Eric M. Zafran (Yale UP, 2001), pp. 49, 63.

96 *art historians have linked*: Dorra, "Texte Wagner," p. 284; Ian Hunter, ed., *Gauguin* (Royal Scottish Academy, 1955), p. 27; Philippe Junod, "Paul Gauguin," in *Wagner, visions d'artistes*, p. 226.

96 *Seurat is said*: Michelle Foa, *Georges Seurat: The Art of Vision* (Yale UP, 2015), p. 126; Paul Smith, "Was Seurat's Art Wagnerian? And What If It Was?," *Apollo* 134:353 (1991), pp. 21–28; Peter Vergo, *The Music of Painting: Music, Modernism and the Visual Arts from the Romantics to John Cage* (Phaidon, 2010), pp. 45–53.

96 *"Manet—Zola—Wagner"*: Marina Ferretti-Bocquillon et al., eds., *Signac 1863–1935* (Yale UP, 2001), p. 298.

96 *Denis compared*: Katherine M. Kuenzli, *The Nabis and Intimate Modernism: Painting and the Decorative at the Fin-de-Siècle* (Ashgate, 2010), p. 94. See also Gerard Vaughan, "Maurice Denis and the Sense of Music," *Oxford Art Journal* 7:1 (1984), pp. 38–48.

97 *evolutionary understandings*: See Léon Daudet, *Devant la douleur: Souvenirs des milieux littéraires, politiques, artistiques et médicaux de 1880 à 1905* (Nouvelle Librairie Nationale, 1915), pp. 206–207.

97 *"pure Concept"*: Jean Moréas, *Les Premières armes du symbolisme* (Vanier, 1889), p. 27; also pp. 30, 34.

98 *break the bank at Monte Carlo*: George Moore, *Conversations in Ebury Street* (Boni and Liveright, 1910), pp. 214–15.

98 *tiny swans*: See Henri Régnier, *De mon temps . . .* (Mercure de France, 1933), p. 109; Cécile Leblanc, *Wagnérisme et création en France, 1883–1889* (Champion, 2005), p. 243.

98 *blowing discordantly*: Gilles Candar, ed., *Les Souvenirs de Charles Bonnier: Un intellectuel socialiste européen à la Belle Époque* (Septentrion, 2001), p. 97.

98 *hovered in the Meister's vicinity*: Houston Stewart Chamberlain, *Lebenswege meines Denkens* (Bruckmann, 1919), pp. 236–38.

98 *found a Wagnerian journal*: Elga Liverman Duval, *Téodor de Wyzewa: Critic Without a Country* (Droz/ Minard, 1961), pp. 25–46; Édouard Dujardin, *Rencontres avec Houston Stewart Chamberlain: Souvenirs et correspondance* (Grasset, 1943), pp. 10–11.

98 *"beats a sauce"*: Joris-Karl Huysmans, *À rebours* (Charpentier, 1884), p. 272.

98 *"screams of uncontained desire"*: Huysmans, "L'Ouverture de Tannhæuser," RevW 1:3, p. 60.

99 *"transport men"*: Dujardin, "Les Œuvres théoriques de Richard Wagner," RevW 1:3, p. 73.

99 *"The symbols"*: Edmund Wilson, *Axel's Castle: A Study in the Imaginative Literature of 1870–1930* (Penguin, 1993), p. 20. For a pioneering overview of Wagner and Symbolism, see Grange Woolley, *Richard Wagner et le symbolisme français* (Presses universitaires de France, 1931).

99 *art re-creates life*: Wyzewa, "Notes sur la littérature wagnérienne," RevW 2:5, p. 153; "Notes sur la musique wagnérienne," RevW 2:6, p. 184.

99 *new kind of novel*: Wyzewa, "Notes sur la littérature," pp. 169–70.

99 *"Poetry of painting"*: Wyzewa, "Peinture wagnérienne: Le Salon de 1885," RevW 1:5, pp. 154–55. See also Wyzewa, "Notes sur la peinture wagnérienne et le Salon de 1886," RevW 2:4, pp. 100–113. Degas did not, in fact, care for Wagner.

99 *scores would be read*: Wyzewa, "Notes sur la musique," p. 187.

99 *eight sonnets*: RevW 1:12 (1886), pp. 333–42.

99 *twenty-two Wagner sonnets*: Marjorie Louise Henry, *La Contribution d'un américain au symbolisme français: Stuart Merrill* (Champion, 1927), pp. 75–82; Richard Cándida Smith, *Mallarmé's Children: Symbolism and the Renewal of Experience* (University of California Press, 1999), pp. 191–93.

100 *"scientific correspondences"*: Joseph Acquisto, *French Symbolist Poetry and the Idea of Music* (Ashgate, 2006), p. 1. For the 1886 experience, see Ghil, "Les Fastes, par Stuart Merrill," *Écrits pour l'Art* 5: 4(1891), p. 154.

100 *"A, black . . . In the Brass"*: René Ghil, *Traité du verbe* (Giraud, 1886), pp. 28, 26. Wagner and Mallarmé were later removed from the treatise.

100 *"the organ remained"*: Francis Vielé-Griffin, "Le Symbolisme et la musique," *Le Phalange* 27 (1908), p. 195.

100 *"Because the musical phrase"*: Dujardin, *Les Premiers Poètes du vers libre* (Mercure de France,

1922), p. 63. On *vers libre* and Wagner, see Carl Dahlhaus, *Between Romanticism and Modernism: Four Studies in the Music of the Later Nineteenth Century*, trans. Mary Whittall (University of California Press, 1980), pp. 58–59; Steven Huebner, "Édouard Dujardin, Wagner, and the Origines of Stream of Consciousness Writing," *19th-Century Music* 37:1 (2013), pp. 56–88; Hertz, *The Tuning of the Word*, pp. 38–42.

101 "Weia! Waga!": Dujardin and Houston Stewart Chamberlain, "L'Or du Rhein," RevW 1:8–9, p. 259.

101 *"made symbolist expression"*: Vielé-Griffin, "Le Symbolisme et la musique," p. 198.

101 *"The candles on the mantelpiece"*: Dujardin, *"The Bays Are Sere" and "Interior Monologue,"* trans. Anthony Suter (Libris, 1991), p. 30; *Les Lauriers sont coupés* (Librairie de la Revue Indépendante, 1888), p. 54.

101 *"succession of short sentences"*: Dujardin, *Le Monologue intérieur: Son apparition, ses origines, sa place dans l'œuvre de James Joyce* (Messein, 1931), p. 55.

102 *Such work disconcerted*: A. W. Raitt, *Villiers de l'Isle-Adam et le mouvement symboliste* (Corti, 1965), p. 341. On the end of the *Revue*, see Elwood Hartman, *French Literary Wagnerism* (Garland, 1988), pp. 38–43.

102 *bottle of Riesling*: Graham Robb, *Rimbaud: A Biography* (Norton, 2000), p. 263.

102 *"a face so rosy"*: Moore, *Conversations in Ebury Street*, p. 198.

103 *"uninterrupted series*: Mallarmé, *Œuvres complètes*, ed. Henri Mondor and G. Jean-Aubry (Gallimard, 1945), p. 661.

103 *"I am inventing a language"*: Mallarmé, *Correspondance, 1854–1898*, ed. Bertrand Marchal (Gallimard, 2019), p. 112.

104 *"Everything that is sacred"*: SM2, p. 360.

104 *Heath Lees*: See his definitive *Mallarmé and Wagner: Music and Poetic Language* (Ashgate, 2007), pp. 136–38, 170–71.

104 *stimulated a deeper interest*: SM2, p. 40.

104 *Mallarmé seldom missed*: Vielé-Griffin, "Le Symbolisme et la musique," p. 194; Henri Mondor, *Vie de Mallarmé* (Gallimard, 1946), pp. 757–58; Paul Valéry, *Pièces sur l'art* (Gallimard, 1934), p. 68.

105 *"Nothing has ever seemed"*: Mallarmé, *Correspondance*, p. 561.

105 *"Reverie"*: SM2, pp. 153–59; translations adapted from Mallarmé, *Divagations*, trans. Barbara Johnson (Belknap, 2007), pp. 107–113.

106 *"melancholy of a poet"*: Mallarmé, *Correspondance*, p. 581.

107 *The poem defies explication*: See Wyzewa, "M. Mallarmé: Notes," part 2, *Vogue*, July 12 and 19, 1886, pp. 415–17; Louis Marvick, *Waking the Face That No One Is: A Study in the Musical Context of Symbolist Poetics* (Rodopi, 2004), p. 3; Robert Greer Cohn, *Toward the Poems of Mallarmé* (University

of California Press, 1965), p. 181; Lees, *Mallarmé and Wagner*, p. 230; Gardner Davies, *Les "Tombeaux" de Mallarmé* (Corti, 1950), p. 149; Bertrand Marchal, *Lecture de Mallarmé* (Corti, 1985), pp. 218–19.

107 *"marks the rebirth"*: Acquisto, *French Symbolist Poetry*, p. 72.

107 *"A sort of general"*: SM1, p. 392.

108 *"critical, in some sense"*: Lacoue-Labarthe, *Musica Ficta*, p. 64.

108 *bedside table*: Anne Holmes, "The Last Book Mallarmé Read," *French Studies Bulletin* 25:93 (2004), pp. 6–7, plausibly proposes that Wyzewa's 1898 book *Beethoven et Wagner* is the volume in question.

3 · SWAN KNIGHT: VICTORIAN BRITAIN AND GILDED AGE AMERICA

109 *"Here Comes the Bride"*: Joseph Kaufman's 1915 film *Here Comes the Bride* apparently inspired various English-language lyrics for the Bridal Chorus.

110 *"At half past six"*: Willa Cather, "Under Golden Leaves of Autumn: Marriage of Miss Nell Cochrane to Mr. Frank Woods," *Nebraska State Journal*, Oct. 20, 1894.

110 *"If people are going"*: Willa Cather, "Utterly Irrelevant," *Nebraska State Journal*, Oct. 21, 1894.

110 *The prince loved German music*: Theodore Martin, *The Life of His Royal Highness the Prince Consort*, vol. 1 (Smith, Elder, 1875), pp. 84–87, 405–501.

110 *"A wonderful composition . . . very quiet"*: Stewart Spencer, *Wagner Remembered* (Faber, 2000), p. 93.

111 *"very small"*: RWL, p. 348; dog and parrot on same page.

111 *"politically disreputable"*: RWB7, p. 239.

111 *A festive concert*: "Her Majesty's State Concert," *Morning Post*, Jan. 26, 1858; "Concert at Buckingham Palace," *Musical World*, Jan. 30, 1858. Oliphant's text in "Court Circular," *Standard*, Feb. 11, 1859.

111 *sat in an armchair*: Phyllis Weliver, *Mary Gladstone and the Victorian Salon: Music, Literature, Liberalism* (Cambridge UP, 2017), pp. 244–45.

111 *"After luncheon"*: G. E. Buckle, ed., *The Letters of Queen Victoria, Second Series*, vol. 2 (Murray, 1926), p. 537.

111 *"If you want to read"*: Hannah Pakula, *An Uncommon Woman: The Empress Frederick, Daughter of Queen Victoria, Wife of the Crown Prince of Prussia, Mother of Kaiser Wilhelm* (Simon and Schuster, 1995), p. 394.

112 *"Wagner has found little"*: A Member of the Royal Household, *The Private Life of the Queen* (Appleton, 1897), p. 192.

112 *"Beyond anything beautiful"*: G. E. Buckle, ed., *The Letters of Queen Victoria, Third Series*, vol. 1 (Murray, 1930), p. 513.

112 *"salutary, soothing"*: Alfred Gurney, *"Parsifal," a Festival Play by Richard Wagner: A Study* (Kegan Paul, 1892), p. 6.

112 *veneration of the Germanic*: Matthew Potter, *The Inspirational Genius of Germany: British Art and Germanism, 1850–1939* (Manchester UP, 2012), p. 112.

113 *Arthurian revival*: See Christine Poulson, *The Quest for the Grail: Arthurian Legend in British Art, 1840–1920* (Manchester UP, 1999).

113 *"Alberich's dream"*: CWD, May 25, 1877.

113 *"vast and powerful stream"*: George Henry Lewes, *The Physiology of Common Life*, vol. 2 (Appleton, 1860), pp. 64, 61.

113 *Jacques Barzun*: See his *Darwin, Marx, Wagner: Critique of a Heritage* (Doubleday, 1958), esp. pp. 231–39.

114 *"trail of the serpent"*: Elizabeth Eastlake, *Music and the Art of Dress* (Murray, 1852), p. 62.

114 *free of class strife*: See Ruth Solie, "Music," in *The Cambridge Companion to Victorian Culture*, ed. Francis O'Gorman (Cambridge UP, 2010), pp. 101–18.

114 *"desperate charlatan"*: "Two Songs by Richard Wagner," *Sunday Times* article reprinted in *Musical World*, May 12, 1855.

114 *"Mahomed of modern music"*: [J. W. Davison], "Amateur Musical Society," *Musical World*, April 15, 1854. For "Dagon" and "rank poison," see Davison's *Musical World* column on June 30, 1855; for "man-mermaid," Jan. 20, 1855.

114 *Ferdinand Praeger*: William Ashton Ellis, *Life of Richard Wagner*, vol. 5 (Kegan Paul, 1906), pp. 118–21.

114 *"magnificently Jewish"*: [J. W. Davison], "Philharmonic Concerts," *Musical World*, March 17, 1855. Some sources say that Davison was Jewish, but Leanne Langley doubts that this is the case (communication to author).

115 *eight-month stay in Germany*: Margaret Harris and Judith Johnston, eds., *The Journals of George Eliot* (Cambridge UP, 1998), pp. 26, 28, 233–34.

115 *"propaganda of Wagnerism"*: [George Eliot], "Liszt, Wagner, and Weimar," *Fraser's* 52 (July 1855), p. 49. Other quotations on pp. 50–51, 55.

115 *Spencer held*: Herbert Spencer, *Essays: Scientific, Political, and Speculative*, vol. 2 (Routledge, 1996), p. 426; Delia da Sousa Correa, *George Eliot, Music, and Victorian Culture* (Palgrave, 2003), pp. 12–26.

116 *"found for themselves . . . roar"*: Eliot, *Middlemarch*, ed. David Carroll (Oxford UP, 1996), pp. 3, 182.

116 *"Eliot of music"*: C. Halford Hawkins, "The Wagner Festival at Bayreuth," *Macmillan's* 35 (1876), p. 63.

116 *"meant everything"*: Gordon S. Haight, ed., *The George Eliot Letters*, vol. 6 (Yale UP, 1955), p. 290.

116 *"so vast"*: Henry James, "Daniel Deronda: A Conversation," *Atlantic* 38 (1876), pp. 685–87.

117 *"You sing in tune"*: Eliot, *Daniel Deronda* (Modern Library, 2002), p. 40. Other quotations on pp. 216, 41, 619.

118 *"the prejudiced"*: Eliot, *Miscellaneous Essays* (Estes and Lauriat, 1887), p. 401.

118 *Nicholas Dames*: See his *The Physiology of the Novel: Reading, Neural Science, and the Form of Victorian Fiction* (Oxford UP, 2007), pp. 123–65, esp. p. 158; also Eliot, "Liszt, Wagner, and Weimar," p. 52. On *Deronda* and Wagner, see Correa, *George Eliot*, pp. 130–91, and Ruth Solie, *Music in Other Words: Victorian Conversations* (University of California Press, 2004), pp. 153–86.

118 *"enduring temporality"*: Dames, *Physiology of the Novel*, p. 158.

118 *"tempestuous applause"*: Dan H. Laurence, ed., *Shaw's Music: The Complete Musical Criticism in Three Volumes*, vol. 1 (Bodley Head, 1981), p. 127.

118 *"well up in Wagnerism"*: Rupert Christiansen, *The Visitors: Culture Shock in Nineteenth-Century Britain* (Chatto & Windus, 2000), p. 68.

118 *"Walkers' Ride"*: Masterman, *Mary Gladstone*, pp. 283, 315.

118 *"special trains"*: "For the Master of the Music of the Future," *Punch*, April 28, 1877.

119 *Carl Rosa*: Rosa is identified as Jewish in Erik Levi, "The German-Jewish Contribution to Musical Life in Britain," in *Second Chance: Two Centuries of German-Speaking Jews in the United Kingdom*, ed. Werner E. Mosse et al. (Mohr, 1991), p. 278.

119 *"The Teutonic element"*: "Royal Italian Opera," *Musical Times*, June 1, 1875.

119 *"incontestable success"*: Davison, "The Wagner Festival," *Musical World*, Sept. 9, 1876, reprinted from *The Times*.

119 *"phantasmagoria . . . loftiest"*: Edward Dannreuther, "The Musical Drama," *Macmillan's*, Nov. 1875, pp. 80, 84, 85. See also Solie, *Music in Other Words*, pp. 54–55. On Dannreuther's youth, see Jeremy Dibble, "Edward Dannreuther and the Orme Square Phenomenon," in *Music and British Culture, 1785–1914: Essays in Honor of Cyril Ehrlich*, ed. Christina Bashford and Leanne Langley (Oxford UP, 2000), pp. 276–77.

119 *"firmness . . . middle-class freedom"*: Franz Hueffer, *Richard Wagner and the Music of the Future: History and Aesthetics* (Chapman and Hall, 1874), pp. 58, 86; angels on p. 112. For Nietzsche, see NWKG I:4, p. 518. Ford Madox Hueffer, in *Memories and Impressions: A Study in Atmospheres* (Harper, 1911), pp. 10–11, recounts that his father received anti-Wagnerian death threats.

119 *"TO HER MAJESTY"*: Francis Hueffer, *Half a Century of Music in England, 1837–1887: Essays Towards a History* (Chapman and Hall, 1889), p. vi.

120 *knew Swinburne*: See Michael Craske, "Swinburne, Wagner, Eliot, and the Musical Legacy of *Poems and Ballads*," *Journal of Victorian Culture* 23:4 (2018), pp. 542–55.

120 *organized a dinner*: John Guille Millais, *The Life and Letters of Sir John Everett Millais, President of the Royal Academy*, vol. 2 (Stokes, 1899), p. 422.

120 *"treated the same subjects"*: Fiona MacCarthy, *The Last Pre-Raphaelite: Edward Burne-Jones and the Victorian Imagination* (Harvard UP, 2012), pp. 273–74; Luke Ionides, *Memories* (Dog Rose, 1925), p. 22; CWD, June 1, 1877. For unpublished letters from Burne-Jones to Cosima, see Barry Millington, "Edward Burne-Jones, George Eliot and Richard Wagner: A Collision of Like-Minded Souls," *Wagner Journal* 10:1 (2016), pp. 26–44.

120 *"Art is long"*: Oscar Wilde, "The Grosvenor Gallery," *Dublin University Magazine*, July 1877, p. 118. On the Spinning Chorus and Wilde's probable non-attendance, see Yvonne Ivory, "Wagner Without Music: The Textual Rendering of Parsifal's Pity in Oscar Wilde's 'The Young King,'" in *Wilde's Worlds: Oscar Wilde in International Contexts*, ed. Michael Davis and Petra Dierkes-Thrun (Routledge, 2018), pp. 180–81. For Cosima at the reception, see George Henry Lewes, diary, May 9, 1877, George Eliot and George Henry Lewes Collection, MS Vault Eliot, VI.11A, Beinecke Library, Yale; and Charles Larcom Graves, *Hubert Parry: His Life and Works*, vol. 1 (Macmillan, 1926), p. 178.

120 *reportedly wept*: Moncure Conway, *Autobiography*, vol. 2 (Houghton Mifflin, 1904), p. 372; Graves, *Hubert Parry*, vol. 1, p. 178; K. K. Collins, ed., *George Eliot: Interviews and Recollections* (Palgrave, 2010), pp. 136–37.

120 *Wagner read aloud*: George Henry Lewes, diary, May 17, 1877; Dibble, "Edward Dannreuther," p. 284.

120 *"épicier . . . genius"*: Charles Villiers Stanford, *Pages from an Unwritten Diary* (Edward Arnold, 1914), p. 180. For "rare person," see *George Eliot Letters*, vol. 6, p. 368; for "noble and pleasant," CWD, May 6, 1877; for Wagner yelling, Graves, *Hubert Parry*, vol. 1, p. 179.

121 *George Eliot und das Judenthum*: William Baker, ed., *Letters of George Henry Lewes*, vol. 2 (English Literary Studies, 1995), p. 233. The pamphlet was by David Kaufmann.

121 *"I heard Wagner's Parsifal"*: Georgiana Burne-Jones, *Memorials of Edward Burne-Jones*, vol. 2 (Macmillan, 1904), p. 43.

121 *"appeal to Heaven"*: William Holman Hunt, *Pre-Raphaelitism and the Pre-Raphaelite Brotherhood*, vol. 1 (Macmillan, 1905), p. 114.

121 *"degradation of the operative"*: John Ruskin, *On the Nature of Gothic Architecture* (Smith, Elder, 1854), p. 9.

122 *"The leading passion"*: William Morris, *How I Became a Socialist* (Twentieth Century Press, 1896), p. 11.

122 *Fantin-Latour's rendering*: Jean Overton Fuller, *Swinburne: A Biography* (Schocken, 1971), p. 82.

122 *"I would never have believed"*: Cecil Y. Lang, ed., *The Swinburne Letters*, vol. 1 (Yale UP, 1959), p. 87. For the non-mailing of the letter, see Nadar, *Charles Baudelaire intime: Le Poète vierge* (Blaizot, 1911), p. 108; for the mailing of the essay, Swinburne, *Notes on Poems and Reviews* (Hotten, 1866), p. 16.

123 *"Asleep or waking"*: Swinburne, *Major Poems and Selected Prose*, ed. Jerome McGann and Charles L. Sligh (Yale UP, 2004), p. 71. For Baudelaire, see *Painter of Modern Life*, p. 126.

123 *"It has the languid"*: Swinburne, *Major Poems*, p. 343.

123 *"fallen goddess"*: Swinburne, *Notes on Poems and Reviews*, p. 16.

123 *"Greek depravity"*: Clyde K. Hyder, ed., *Algernon Swinburne: The Critical Heritage* (Routledge, 1970), pp. 23, 29.

124 *"For this, for this"*: *The Collected Works of William Morris*, vol. 6 (Longmans, Green, 1911), p. 294.

124 *Icelandic sources*: See Árni Björnsson, *Wagner and the Volsungs: Icelandic Sources of "Der Ring des Nibelungen"* (Viking Society for Northern Research, 2003).

124 *"the Great Story"*: Eiríkr Magnússon and William Morris, trans., *Völsunga Saga: The Story of the Volsungs and Niblungs, with Certain Songs from the Elder Edda* (Ellis, 1870), p. xi.

124 *"nothing short of desecration"*: J. W. Mackail, *The Life of William Morris*, vol. 1 (Longmans, Green, 1901), p. 299.

124 *"clumsy, blundering"*: E. T. Cook and Alexander Wedderburn, eds., *The Letters of John Ruskin*, vol. 2 (Allen, 1909), p. 402.

124–25 *"would have been very different"*: Jane Susanna Ennis, *A Comparison of Richard Wagner's "Der Ring des Nibelungen" and William Morris's "Sigurd the Volsung"* (Ph.D. diss., University of Leeds, 1993), p. 23.

125 *"Long have I slept"*: Magnússon and Morris, *Völsunga Saga*, p. 70. Compare *The Poetic Edda*, trans. Carolyne Larrington (Oxford UP, 1996), pp. 166–67.

126 *"But therewith"*: Morris, *The Story of Sigurd the Volsung and the Fall of the Niblungs* (Ellis and White, 1877), p. 159. Other quotations on pp. 1, 312. For Hueffer and Shaw, see Ennis, *A Comparison*, p. 8.

127 *"I have managed"*: George W. E. Russell, ed., *Letters of Matthew Arnold, 1848–1888*, vol. 2 (Macmillan, 1895), p. 374.

127 *"this fool passion"*: Kenneth Allott, ed., *The Poems of Matthew Arnold* (Longman, 1979), p. 234.

128 *"He rose, he turn'd"*: Alfred Tennyson, "The Last Tournament," *Contemporary Review* 19 (1871), p. 22. The book edition changed the wording somewhat.

128 *"degraded and debased"*: Cecil Y. Lang, ed., *The Swinburne Letters*, vol. 4 (Yale UP, 1960), p. 260.

128 *Gasperini*: Cecil Y. Lang, ed., *The Swinburne Letters*, vol. 2 (Yale UP, 1959), p. 38. The book in

question is Gasperini's *Richard Wagner* (Heugel, 1865).

128 *Powell had tea*: Terry L. Meyers, ed., *Uncollected Letters of Algernon Charles Swinburne*, vol. 2 (Pickering & Chatto, 2005), pp. 86–87.

128 *"Love, that is first"*: Swinburne, *Major Poems*, p. 206. Other quotations on pp. 207, 208, 231–32, 311–12. See also Francis Jacques Sypher, Jr., "Swinburne and Wagner," *Victorian Poetry* 9:1–2 (1971), pp. 165–83.

129 *"herald soul"*: Swinburne, *Century of Roundels*, p. 25. Other poems on pp. 30, 31–32.

130 *"The Wagner-cultus"*: William Beatty-Kingston, "Our Musical-Box," *The Theatre*, Dec. 1, 1881.

130 *Prince of Wales*: Neumann, *Erinnerungen*, pp. 226–27. For Gladstone, see Weliver, *Mary Gladstone*, pp. 82–86.

130 *"bathed the listener"*: Anne Dzamba Sessa, *Richard Wagner and the English* (Fairleigh Dickinson UP, 1979), p. 139.

130–31 *"regenerative life-force . . . never composed one bar"*: *The Meister* 1:1 (1888), pp. 2, 3.

131 *commemorative poems*: See *Meister* 1:1, p. 32; 6:21, p. 1; 1:2, p. 53; 1:1, p. 20.

131 *"Fitly . . . To drown"*: Alfred Forman, trans., *The Nibelung's Ring* (Schott, n.d.), p. 348; Forman, trans., *Tristan and Isolde* (Reeves and Turner, 1891), p. 76. See also John Collins, "A Short Note on Alfred William Forman (1840–1925)," *Book Collector* 23:1 (1974), pp. 69–77.

132 *"tall and very fair"*: Anna Alice Chapin, *Wonder Tales from Wagner: Told for Young People* (Harper, 1898), p. 103. Other quotations on pp. 111, 125.

132 *"the emotional contents"*: "New Publications," *New York Times*, Oct. 21, 1894.

132 *"brave friend"*: Grace Edson Barber, *Wagner Opera Stories* (Public-School Publishing, 1901), p. 62.

132 *"They loved each other"*: Anna Alice Chapin, *The Story of the Rhinegold (Der Ring des Nibelungen): Told for Young People* (Harper, 1897), p. 34.

132 *"The transformation is coming!"*: Barber, *Wagner Opera Stories*, pp. 151–52.

132 *"hurry, worry"*: Florence Akin, *Opera Stories from Wagner: A Reader for Primary Grades* (Houghton Mifflin, 1915), p. 106.

132 *"Probably no stupider"*: Dolores Bacon, *Operas Every Child Should Know* (Doubleday, 1911), p. 163.

133 *"commanding tones"*: Constance Maud, *Wagner's Heroines* (Edward Arnold, 1896), pp. 130–35.

133 *spoke of selling Wahnfried*: Hans von Wolzogen, ed., "Richard Wagner an Friedrich Feustel," BB 26 (1903), pp. 207–208.

133 *"America??"*: CWD, May 11, 1877.

134 *"unconquerable vigor"*: Wagner, "The Work and Mission of My Life," Part I, *North American Review* 129 (1879), p. 109. For Wolzogen's authorship, see ENRW4, p. 600; CWD, May 1, 1879.

134 *"Washington for art"*: Carl Friedrich Glasenapp, ed., *Bayreuther Briefe von Richard Wagner* (Schuster & Loeffler, 1907), p. 270.

134 *"Again and again"*: CWD, Feb. 1, 1880.

134 *"some State of the Union"*: Newell Sill Jenkins, *Reminiscence* (privately printed, 1924), pp. 486–87. For Minnesota, see CWD, Feb. 1, 1880.

134 *"proper German"*: CWD, March 22, 1880.

135 *"Your roses"*: Ludwig II and Wagner, *Briefwechsel*, vol. 3, ed. Otto Strobel (Braun, 1936), p. 104. See also ENRW4, p. 566.

135 *despite occasional calls*: "Remove Wagner Statue from Park," letter to *Cleveland Jewish News*, Sept. 8, 2016; Ernest F. Imhoff, "A Statue Without Limitations," *Baltimore Sun*, July 22, 2001. Parsifal Places can be found in the Bronx, Albuquerque, Las Vegas, and Apex, N.C.

135 *"coarseness . . . rude forcefulness"*: Joseph Horowitz, *Wagner Nights: An American History* (University of California Press, 1994), p. 147. See also Joann P. Krieg, "The Ring in America," in *Inside the Ring: Essays on Wagner's Opera Cycle*, ed. John DiGaetani (McFarland, 2006), pp. 189–204; Burton W. Peretti, "Democratic Leitmotivs in the American Reception of Wagner," *19th-Century Music* 13:1 (1989), pp. 28–38; Anne Dzamba Sessa, "At Wagner's Shrine: British and American Wagnerians," in WECP, pp. 246–77.

135 *"paroxysms"*: Henry Adams, *The Education of Henry Adams: An Autobiography* (Houghton Mifflin, 1918), pp. 404–405.

136 *"I would rather listen"*: See *The Works of Robert G. Ingersoll*, vol. 2 (Dresden, 1901), p. 435.

136 *"produce a finer type"*: Kathleen Pyne, *Art and the Higher Life: Painting and Evolutionary Thought in Late Nineteenth-Century America* (University of Texas Press, 1996), p. 31.

136 *"loose and sloppy talk"*: Theodore Roosevelt, "The Foundations of the Nineteenth Century," *Outlook* 98 (1911), p. 729.

137 *"communism was . . . enflame and stimulate"*: Nancy Newman, *Good Music for a Free People: The Germania Musical Society in Nineteenth-Century America* (University of Rochester Press, 2010), pp. 25–26.

137 *"Strange, original"*: Samuel Longfellow, ed., *Life of Henry Wadsworth Longfellow*, vol. 2 (Houghton Mifflin, 1891), p. 261.

137–38 *"Wagner, the man of the liberal arts"*: Hoplit [Richard Pohl], "Ein Blick nach dem 'fernen Westen,'" *Neue Zeitschrift für Musik*, June 17, 1853. See also Newman, *Good Music*, p. 145.

138 *"In Boston they are"*: RWB6, p. 74.

138 *small and grubby*: "Musical Correspondence," *Dwight's Journal of Music* 15:4 (1859), pp. 29–30. See also John Koegel, *Music in German Immigrant Theater: New York City, 1840–1940* (University of Rochester Press, 2009), pp. 35–39.

138 *"Verily here"*: "Concerts at Hand," *Dwight's Journal of Music* 4:9 (1853), p. 70.

138 *"ignoble and small-minded"*: "Wagner Versus Judaism in Music," *Dwight's Journal of Music* 29:5 (1869), p. 33.

139 *"The people jumped"*: George P. Upton, ed., *Theodore Thomas: A Musical Autobiography*, vol. 1 (McClurg, 1905), p. 62.

139 *intermittent disapproval*: See Robert Bailey, "Wagner's Musical Sketches for *Siegfrieds Tod*," in *Studies in Music History: Essays for Oliver Strunk*, ed. Harold Powers (Princeton UP, 1968), pp. 467–68; also CWD, Jan. 25 and March 28, 1871, Dec. 25, 1872.

139 *"feminine loveliness"*: Ezra Schabas, *Theodore Thomas: America's Conductor and Builder of Orchestras, 1835–1905* (University of Illinois Press, 1989), p. 74; Lieselotte Z. Overvold, "Wagner's American Centennial March: Genesis and Reception," *Monatshefte* 68:2 (1976), pp. 179–87. For the Flower Maidens connection, see William Kinderman, *Wagner's "Parsifal"* (Oxford UP, 2013), p. 91; CWD, Feb. 9, 1876.

139 International Congress Fantasy: Paul E. Bierley, *The Works of John Philip Sousa* (Integrity, 1984), p. 145; Patrick Warfield, *Making the March King: John Philip Sousa's Washington Years, 1854–1893* (University of Illinois Press, 2013), p. 82.

139 *"brass band man"*: Anon., "Sousa and His Mission," *Music* 16 (1899), p. 275.

139 *serenaded Hayes*: Peter Hannaford, *Presidential Retreats: Where the Presidents Went and Why They Went There* (Threshold, 2012), p. 104. For Cleveland, see Elise K. Kirk, *Musical Highlights from the White House* (Krieger, 1992), pp. 72–73; "The President Married," *National Republican*, June 3, 1886.

140 *seventy-four Wagner concerts*: Schabas, *Theodore Thomas*, pp. 129–37; "The Wagner Artists' Return," *Montreal Gazette*, July 2, 1884; for eight thousand, "Festival Music," *Daily Inter Ocean*, May 30, 1884.

140 "THE GREATEST": Horowitz, *Wagner Nights*, p. 142; *St. Louis Post-Dispatch*, May 5, 1889. For Rex, see Edmee F. Reel and Jerome V. Reel, "King Arthur Comes to New Orleans," *Arthuriana* 12:2 (2002), pp. 120–21.

141 *Brooklyn Bayreuth*: Diane Sasson, *Yearning for the New Age: Laura Holloway-Langford and Late Victorian Spirituality* (Indiana UP, 2012), p. 185. For Festspielhaus replicas, see "Wagner's Operas: They Will Be Presented During the World's Fair," *Los Angeles Herald*, Nov. 13, 1891; "Nordica Off to Plan Her Music Temple," *New York Times*, June 6, 1907.

141 Wagner et al. v. Conried et al.: *Federal Reporter* 125 (West, 1904), pp. 798–801; Katherine R. Syer, "*Parsifal* on Stage," in *A Companion to Wagner's "Parsifal,"* ed. William Kinderman and Syer (Camden House, 2005), pp. 281–84.

141 *"stupid sacrilege ... witnesses"*: Charles Henry Meltzer, ed., "*Parsifal": The Story of This Solemn Festival Play* (Ogilvie, 1903), p. 103; Washington Gladden, *Witnesses of the Light* (Houghton Mifflin, 1903), pp. 191–236. See also Frederick Hale, "American

Christians For and Against *Parsifal*: Debating the Holy Grail Opera in New York," *In die Skriflig* 51:1 (2017), www.scielo.org.za.

141 *$186,000*: "'Parsifal' Receipts Have Been $186,000," *New York Times*, Feb. 26, 1904.

141 *"Mrs. Vanderbilt was in black velvet"*: "Among the Spectators," *New York Times*, Dec. 25, 1903. For other quotations, see "In the Topmost Gallery," same page.

141 *"Mother came back"*: Joseph Bucklin Bishop, ed., *Theodore Roosevelt's Letters to His Children* (Scribner, 1919), p. 93.

142 *"I envy you Bayreuth"*: Elting E. Morison, ed., *The Letters of Theodore Roosevelt*, vol. 2 (Harvard UP, 1951), p. 1049. For Marcius-Simons, see "President in an Art Gallery," *New York Sun*, Feb. 20, 1904; and *The Parsifal Tone Pictures: Marcius Simons* (Williams & Everett, 1904). For Alice Roosevelt, see Carol Felsenthal, *Princess Alice: The Life and Times of Alice Roosevelt Longworth* (St. Martin's, 1988), p. 105.

142 *"I worked"*: Elliott Daingerfield, "Albert Pinkham Ryder, Artist and Dreamer," *Scribner's* 63:3 (1918), p. 380. See also Diane Chalmers Johnson, "*Siegfried and the Rhine Maidens*: Albert Pinkham Ryder's Response to Richard Wagner's *Götterdämmerung*," *American Art* 8:1 (1994), pp. 22–31.

143 *"overwhelming energies"*: Robert Rosenblum, *Modern Painting and the Northern Romantic Tradition: Friedrich to Rothko* (Harper & Row, 1975), pp. 204, 225.

143 *Wagner inspired paintings*: On these artists, see Charles C. Eldredge, *American Imagination and Symbolist Painting* (Grey Art Gallery and Study Center, 1979).

143 *"American Nibelungenlied"*: Henry T. Finck, ed., *Anton Seidl: A Memorial by His Friends* (Scribner, 1899), p. 139; Horowitz, *Wagner Nights*, pp. 169–70.

143 *Sidney Lanier*: For his musical background, see Jane Gabin, *A Living Minstrelsy: The Poetry and Music of Sidney Lanier* (Mercer UP, 1985); Patricia Harper and Paula Robison, eds., *The Sidney Lanier Collection* (Universal Edition, 1997); Robison's recording, *By the Old Pine Tree: Flute Music by Stephen Foster and Sidney Lanier* (Pergola, 1996); Aubrey H. Starke, "Sidney Lanier as a Musician," *Musical Quarterly* 20:4 (1934), pp. 384–400.

144 *"well-nigh universal"*: Sidney Lanier, *The Science of English Verse* (Scribner, 1880), p. 145. For more, see Jack Kerkering, "'Of Me and of Mine': The Music of Racial Identity in Whitman and Lanier, Dvořák and Du Bois," *American Literature* 73:1 (2001), pp. 147–84.

144 *"unbroken march"*: Sidney Lanier, *Centennial Edition*, vol. 8, ed. Charles R. Anderson and Aubrey H. Starke (Johns Hopkins Press, 1945), p. 99.

144 *"Of the Rhine-maiden's Gold"*: Sidney Lanier Papers, Special Collections, Milton S. Eisenhower

Library, Johns Hopkins University. See also Lanier, *Centennial Edition*, vol. 9, p. 112.

144 *"immeasurable profounds"*: "Notes on Music," Lanier Papers, Ms. 7, Series 4, Writings. See also Lanier, "The Truth About Wagner" and "Wagner's Beethoven," *Centennial Edition*, vol. 2, pp. 336–40.

144 *"old voices... Wave the world's"*: Mary Day Lanier, ed., *Poems of Sidney Lanier* (Scribner, 1899), pp. 257, 259.

144 *"early Wagner pamphlets"*: Dudley Buck to Lanier, May 29, 1876, Lanier Papers, Ms. 7, Series 2, Correspondence.

145 *"I saw a sky"*: Lanier, "To Richard Wagner," *Galaxy* 21.5 (1077), pp. 652–53. See also "To Richard Wagner," Lanier Papers, Ms. 7, Series 4, Writings.

146 *"indecorous and scandalous"*: Payne, *Owen Wister*, p. 38. For the Hasty Pudding, see Owen Wister, "The First Operetta," in *The Thirteenth Catalogue & A History of the Hasty Pudding Club*, ed. Hermann Hagedorn, Jr. (Riverside, 1907), pp. 28, 32; Wister, *Roosevelt: The Story of a Friendship, 1880–1919* (Macmillan, 1930), p. 14.

146 *"looking rather cross"*: Owen Wister to Sarah Butler Wister, Aug. 29, 1882, Owen Wister Papers, Manuscript Division, Library of Congress. For "*talent prononcé*," see Wister, "Strictly Hereditary," *Musical Quarterly* 22:1 (1936), p. 4.

147 *"The remains of the moon"*: Wister, Journal, "His First Trip to Wyoming, July–August 1885," July 3, Owen Wister Papers, American Heritage Center, University of Wyoming, digitalcollections.uwyo .edu. For the Wagner scores, see Wister to Sarah Butler Wister, July 15, 1885, Wister Papers, Library of Congress.

147 *"when the whole orchestra"*: Fanny Kemble Wister, ed., *Owen Wister Out West: His Journals and Letters* (University of Chicago Press, 1958), p. 128.

147 *"crystal silence"*: Leslie T. Whipp, "Owen Wister: Wyoming's Influential Realist and Craftsman," *Great Plains Quarterly* 10 (1990), p. 256. For Wister's later ambivalence, see "Musical Matters Abroad," *New York Times*, Feb. 25, 1900.

147 *"In personal daring"*: Wister, "The Evolution of the Cow-Puncher," *Harper's* 91 (1895), p. 606.

148 *"inferior race"*: Wister, introduction to *Done in the Open* (Collier, 1904), n.p.

148 *"Lounging there... creation's first morning"*: Wister, *The Virginian: A Horseman of the Plains* (Macmillan, 1902), pp. 4, 9, 12. Gerald Thompson, "Musical and Literary Influences on Owen Wister's *The Virginian*," *South Atlantic Quarterly* 85:1 (1986), pp. 40–55, discusses the *Lohengrin* theme.

148 *"It was through"*: Wister, *The Virginian*, p. 147.

149 *"The very masonry"*: Paul Rosenfeld, *Musical Portraits: Interpretations of Twenty Modern Composers* (Harcourt, 1920), pp. 6–7.

150 *"rhythmical, deep"*: Louis Sullivan, "The Tall Office Building Artistically Considered," *Lippincott's Magazine* 57 (1896), p. 409.

150 *"a thing rising"*: Sullivan, *The Autobiography of an Idea* (Press of the American Institute of Architects, 1924), p. 314.

150 *"lively rendition of 'The Ride'"*: Harriet Monroe, *John Wellborn Root: A Study of His Life and Work* (Houghton Mifflin, 1896), p. 202.

150 *"symphony of color... complete unification"*: Donald Hoffmann, ed., *The Meanings of Architecture: Buildings and Writings by John Wellborn Root* (Horizon, 1967), p. 186. For the funeral, see Thomas S. Hines, *Burnham of Chicago: Architect and Planner* (University of Chicago Press, 1979), p. 360.

150 *"He saw arise"*: Sullivan, *Autobiography of an Idea*, pp. 208–209.

150 *"He would often"*: Frank Lloyd Wright, *An Autobiography* (Faber, 1945), pp. 95–96.

151 *Joseph Siry*: See his "Chicago's Auditorium Building: Opera or Anarchism," *Journal of the Society of Architectural Historians* 57:2 (1998), p. 139.

151 *Festspielhaus model*: Roula Mouroudellis Geraniotus, "German Design Influence in the Auditorium Theater," in *The Midwest in American Architecture*, ed. John S. Garner (University of Illinois Press, 1991), pp. 43–75; Mark Clague, "The Industrial Evolution of the Arts: Chicago's Auditorium Building (1889–) as Cultural Machine," *Opera Quarterly* 22:3–4 (2006), pp. 477–511.

151 *"dissolve enveloping surfaces"*: Lauren S. Weingarden, "The Colors of Nature: Louis Sullivan's Architectural Polychromy and Nineteenth-Century Color Theory," *Winterthur Portfolio* 20:4 (1985), p. 254.

151 *"The architects of the building"*: *The Dream City: A Portfolio of Photographic Views of the World's Columbian Exposition* (Thompson, 1893), n.p.

151 *"color symphony"*: Larry Millett, *The Curve of the Arch: The Story of Louis Sullivan's Owatonna Bank* (Minnesota Historical Society Press, 1985), p. 85.

152 *"besotted Wagnerite"*: Ralph Adams Cram, *My Life in Architecture* (Little, Brown, 1936), p. 8.

152 *"look more like"*: Christine Smith, *St. Bartholomew's Church in the City of New York* (Oxford UP, 1988), p. 76.

152 *Riverside Church*: For more, see Alex Ross, "A Walking Tour of Wagner's New York," newyorker.com, May 13, 2013, based on research at the Rockefeller Family Archives.

152 *"Wagner fever"*: William Dean Howells, *A Hazard of New Fortunes*, vol. 1 (Boni and Liveright, 1889), p. 204.

153 *"Oh, I love"*: Victor Herbert and Harry B. Smith, *Miss Dolly Dollars* (Witmark, 1905), pp. 159–66. The song is titled "American Music ('Tis Better Than Old Parsifal to Me)."

153 *"Some people rave"*: Scott Joplin and Joe Snyder, *Pine Apple Rag* (Seminary Music, 1910).

153 *"Wagner's music is better"*: Harriet Elinor Smith et al., eds., *Autobiography of Mark Twain*, vol. 1 (University of California Press, 2010), p. 288.

153 *"We went to Mannheim"*: Mark Twain, *A Tramp Abroad* (Chatto & Windus, 1889), pp. 83–84.

153 *"Mark Twain at Bayreuth"*: Quotations are taken from the version printed in the *Chicago Daily Tribune*, Dec. 6, 1891, which varies slightly from later editions.

155 *"If I could have"*: Benjamin Griffin and Harriet Elinor Smith, eds., *Autobiography of Mark Twain*, vol. 2 (University of California Press, 2013), p. 294. Dictated 1906.

155 *"But for the opera"*: John Townsend Trowbridge, "Reminiscences of Walt Whitman," *Atlantic Monthly* 89 (1902), p. 166.

155 *"I have got rather"*: Horace Traubel, *With Walt Whitman in Camden*, vol. 2 (Mitchell Kennerley, 1915), p. 116.

155 *"What indeed is finally beautiful"*: Walt Whitman, *Complete Poetry and Collected Prose*, ed. Justin Kaplan (Library of America, 1982), p. 269.

155 *"So many of my friends"*: Traubel, *With Walt Whitman*, vol. 2, p. 116. For Conway, see Kenneth M. Price, ed., *Walt Whitman: The Contemporary Reviews* (Cambridge UP, 1996), p. 106. For Dannreuther, see his *Richard Wagner: His Tendencies and Ideas* (Augener, 1873), pp. 6, 19, 37; for William Sloane Kennedy, see his *Reminiscences of Walt Whitman* (Gardner, 1896), pp. 164–65.

156 *"constructed on my lines"*: Traubel, *With Walt Whitman in Camden*, vol. 4, ed. Sculley Bradley (University of Pennsylvania Press, 1959), p. 48.

156 *"arouse and initiate . . . music of the present"*: Whitman, "The Poetry of the Future," *North American Review* 132 (1881), p. 202; "verbal melody" on p. 197.

156 *"Do you figure out Wagner"*: Traubel, *With Walt Whitman*, vol. 2, p. 116.

4. GRAIL TEMPLE: ESOTERIC, DECADENT, AND SATANIC WAGNER

158 *"annihilation"*: "The First Steamer from Europe," *New York Morning Herald*, April 17, 1838; Karl Marx, *Grundrisse: Foundations of the Critique of Political Economy*, trans. Martin Nicolaus (Penguin, 1973), p. 539.

159 *mistaken for a vampire*: For more, see Slavoj Žižek, "Why Is Wagner Worth Saving?," *Journal of Philosophy and Scripture* 2:1 (2004), p. 26.

159 *"Savior on the Cross"*: CWD, Feb. 27, 1880.

159 *"Children, tomorrow"*: Friedrich Eckstein, *Alte, unnennbare Tage: Erinnerungen aus siebzig Lehr- und Wanderjahren* (Severus, 2013), p. 198.

159 *"What is Parsifal"*: James Huneker, "The Supreme Sin," *Forum* 55 (1916), p. 302.

160 *"one could say"*: RWSS10, p. 211. For "renunciation," see ibid., p. 223; for "new religion," RWSS3, p. 123.

160 *"If Wagner takes up"*: NWKG IV:1, pp. 279–80.

160 *"Unfortunately, all"*: RWB11, p. 106.

161 *Ronald Perlwitz*: See his "Indien in der Literatur des 19. Jahrhunderts und seine Rezeption bei Richard Wagner," *wagnerspectrum* 13:1 (2017), p. 56.

161 *Kaaba at Mecca*: RWB11, p. 106. See also Meihui Yu, "Kundry, Blumenmädchen, Klingsors Zaubergarten: Das Arabische im *Parsifal*," *wagnerspectrum* 13:1 (2017), p. 101. On the Persian connection, see Kinderman, *Wagner's "Parsifal,"* pp. 72–73.

161 *"Christian-Buddhist"*: Ernst Bloch, "Paradoxa und Pastorale bei Wagner," *Literarische Aufsätze* (Suhrkamp, 1965), p. 315.

161 *"metaphors for poetry"*: WBY14, p. 7.

162 *"revolt against rationalism"*: Holbrook Jackson, *The Eighteen Nineties: A Review of Art and Ideas at the Close of the Nineteenth Century* (Mitchell Kennerley, 1914), pp. 159–60.

162 *"eternal rebel"*: Mikhail Bakunin, *God and the State*, ed. Max Nettlau (Freedom, 1910), p. 2.

162 *"fallen Lucifer . . . the greatest unconscious"*: Édouard Schuré, *Souvenirs sur Richard Wagner: La Première de Tristan et Iseult* (Perrin, 1900), p. 54; Schuré, *L'Évolution divine du sphinx au Christ* (Perrin, 1912), p. 430.

162 *"world of enchantments"*: Papus, *Traité méthodique de science occulte* (Carré, 1891), p. xi.

162 *"That there is in Wagner"*: Rudolf Steiner, "Parsifal: The Secret of the Grail in the Works of Richard Wagner, Parsifal, Arthur," 1906 lecture, wn .rsarchive.org.

162 *"O MASTER of the ring"*: Aleister Crowley, "To Richard Wagner," *The Works of Aleister Crowley*, vol. 1 (Society for the Propagation of Religious Truth, 1905), p. 179. For Reuss, see Crowley, *The Book of Thoth: A Short Essay on the Tarot of the Egyptians* (Weiser, 1974), p. 59; for order membership, "Liber LII: Manifesto of the O.T.O.," *Equinox* 3:1 (1919), pp. 198–99. Reuss obviously had nothing to do with the genesis of *Parsifal*, which was first conceived when he was an infant.

163 *"access the divine"*: Michelle Facos and Thor J. Mednick, "Introduction," in *The Symbolist Roots of Modern Art*, ed. Facos and Mednick (Routledge, 2016), pp. 1–8.

163 *John Bramble*: See his *Modernism and the Occult* (Palgrave, 2015), p. 14.

163 *less than full houses*: OGB1, pp. 182–227; Susanna Großmann-Vendrey, *Bayreuth in der deutschen Presse*, vol. 3/1 (Bosse, 1983), p. 49.

164 *Péladan habitually*: Robert Pincus-Witten, *Occult Symbolism in France: Joséphin Péladan and the Salons de la Rose-Croix* (Garland, 1976), p. 2.

164 *"The renovation of the Rose + Croix"*: Péladan, "Les Héroïnes de Wagner," autograph manuscript quoted in Roland Van der Hoeven, "L'Idéalisme musical: Musique et musiciens autour du Sâr Péladan," *Revue de la Société liégeoise de musicologie* 2 (1995), p. 6. See also Péladan, *Le Théâtre complet de Wagner*, p. xii.

164 *"one goes in search"*: Péladan, *La Victoire du mari* (Slatkine, 1979), pp. 74–75.

164 *family steeped in esoterica*: Beaufils, *Péladan*, pp. 9–36. On Péladan's father, see Vincent Lajoinie,

Erik Satie (L'Âge d'Homme, 1985), p. 23, and Jean-Pierre Laurant and Victor Nguyen, *Les Péladan* (Les Dossiers H, 1990); on the brother, see Jennifer Birkett, "Fetishizing Writing: The Politics of Fictional Form in the Work of Remy de Gourmont and Joséphin Péladan," in *Perennial Decay: On the Aesthetics and Politics of Decadence*, ed. Liz Constable et al. (University of Pennsylvania Press, 1999), p. 274.

164 *"I believe . . . What he paints"*: Péladan, *La Décadence esthétique*, vol. 1: *L'Art ochlocratique: Salons de 1882 & de 1883* (Dalou, 1888), pp. 45, 48.

165 *"Man puppet of woman"*: Ibid., p. 50.

165 *"seeing and hearing . . . reforged Nothing"*. Péladan, *La Prométhéide: Trilogie d'Eschyle en quatre tableaux* (Chamuel, 1895), pp. vii, 149. For "People of Nîmes," see Ambroise Vollard, *Souvenirs d'un marchand de tableaux* (Albin Michel, 1937), p. 282.

165 *"greetings and glory"*: Péladan, *Victoire du mari* p. xxi. Other quotations on pp. 38, 87, 91, 236.

166 *other Péladan novels*: Péladan, *Le Panthée* (Dentu, 1892), pp. 12–13; *L'Androgyne* (Dentu, 1891), pp. 70–71; *La Gynandre* (Dentu, 1891), pp. 323–26.

166 *"bizarre but of great distinction"*: Verlaine, *Œuvres complètes*, vol. 5 (Vanier, 1904), p. 277.

166–67 *"religion of modern art"*: Bramble, *Modernism and the Occult*, p. 63. See also Vivien Greene, "The Salon de la Rose+Croix: The Religion of Art," in *Mystical Symbolism: The Salon de la Rose+Croix in Paris, 1892–1907*, ed. Vivien Greene (Guggenheim, 2017), p. 30.

167 *"superhuman Wagner . . . a priest"*: Péladan, *Panthée*, p. 298; Péladan, *Geste esthétique: Catalogue du Salon de la Rose+Croix* (Durand-Ruel, 1892), p. 11.

167 *"there will unfold"*: Péladan, *Panthée*, p. 312.

167 *Solemn Mass*: Beaufils, *Péladan*, p. 222; *Figaro*, March 11, 1892. For brass players, see Léonce de Larmandie, *L'Entr'acte idéal: Histoire de la Rose+Croix* (Chacornac, 1903), p. 25.

167 *Mallarmé and Verlaine*: Beaufils, *Péladan*, p. 221.

167 *restrictions and regulations*: Péladan, *La Rose+Croix: Organe trimestriel de l'Ordre* (Commanderie de Tiphereth, 1893), pp. 23–30. For Puvis, see Beaufils, *Péladan*, p. 211; for Gautier, Mary Slavkin, *Dynamics and Divisions at the Salons of the Rose-Croix: Statistics, Aesthetic Theories, Practices, and Subjects* (Ph.D. diss. City University of New York, 2014), p. 208.

168 *"a felon, a coward"*: "Wagner chez l'archonte," *Le Temps*, April 7, 1892.

168 *Sotaukrack*: Willy [Jean de Tinan], *Maîtresse d'esthètes* (Empis, 1897).

168 *"The artist is a 'king'"*: Kandinsky, *Über das Geistige in der Kunst, insbesondere in der Malerei* (Piper, 1912), p. 119. On ties to modernism, see Kenneth Silver, "Afterlife: The Important and Sometimes Embarrassing Links Between Occultism and the Development of Abstract Art, ca. 1909–13," in Greene, *Mystical Symbolism*, pp. 46–53.

168 *"Monsalvat restored"*: *IIe Geste esthétique: Catalogue officiel du second Salon de la Rose+Croix* (Nilsson, 1893), p. xxvi; Péladan, *Constitutions de la Rose+Croix, le Temple et le Graal* (Secrétariat, 1893), p. 8.

169 *"Wagner alone"*: Péladan, *Comment on devient artiste: Esthétique* (Chamuel, 1894), pp. xv–xx.

169 *Wagner was still scarce*: On the eventual acceptance of the composer, see Katharine Ellis, "How to Make Wagner Normal: *Lohengrin*'s 'Tour de France' of 1891–92," *Cambridge Opera Journal* 25:2 (2013), pp. 121–37.

170 *"shifted the setting"*: Katherine M. Kuenzli, *Henry van de Velde: Designing Modernism* (Yale UP, 2019), pp. 32–33. See also Michèle Goslar, *Victor Horta, 1861–1947: L'Homme, l'architecte, l'art nouveau* (Fonds Mercator, 2012), p. 373; and Robert Michael Brain, "Protoplasmania: Huxley, Haeckel, and the Vibratory Organism in Late Nineteenth-Century Science and Art," in *The Art of Evolution: Darwin, Darwinisms and Visual Culture*, ed. Barbara Larson and Fae Brauer (University Press of New England, 2009), pp. 105–107.

170 *"It may be necessary"*: Maurice Maeterlinck, "Menus Propos: Le Théâtre," *Jeune Belgique* 9:9 (1890), p. 335. For Maeterlinck and music, see Marie Rolf, "Mauclair and Debussy: The Decade from 'Mer belle aux îles sanguinaires' to *La Mer*," *Cahiers Debussy* 11 (1987), p. 11.

170 *"valiant Wagnerian army"*: "Le Mouvement wagnérien," *L'Art moderne* 3:6 (1883), p. 43. On Rops, see Edmond Bailly, "La Musique dans l'œuvre de Félicien Rops," *La Plume* 172 (1896), p. 436.

171 *Alma Mahler-Werfel*: See her *Diaries, 1898–1902*, ed. Antony Beaumont and Susanne Rode-Breymann, trans. Beaumont (Cornell UP, 1999), pp. 263–64.

172 *"The destiny of the Wagnerian"*: Sébastien Clerbois, *L'Ésotérisme et le symbolisme belge* (Pandora, 2012), p. 103.

172 *"animastic union"*: Brendan Cole, *Jean Delville: Art Between Nature and the Absolute* (Cambridge Scholars, 2015), p. 269. An 1890 charcoal drawing of a young man's head resting on a platter was long labeled *Parsifal*, but Cole does not believe that it is connected to Wagner's opera (communication to author).

173 *"leave you shivering"*: Jules Destrée, "Odilon Redon," *Jeune Belgique* 5:2 (1886), p. 143. For Jean Lorrain, see his *Sensations et souvenirs* (Charpentier, 1895), pp. 217–18.

173 *"pale and soft sketches"*: Odilon Redon, *À soi-même: Journal (1867–1915): Notes sur la vie, l'art et les artistes* (Floury, 1922), p. 149. For other comments on Wagner, see *Lettres d'Odilon Redon*

(1878–1916), publiées par sa famille (van Oest, 1923), pp. 27, 25.

173 *"terrifying"*: Wyzewa, "Peinture wagnérienne," p. 155. For Mallarmé's copy, see *De la bibliothèque Stéphane Mallarmé*, catalogue for Sotheby's auction, Oct. 15, 2015, p. 182.

173 *"His head is anointed"*: Ernest Verlant, "Chronique artistique: Exposition Meunier," *Jeune Belgique* 11 (1892), p. 92. See also Dario Gamboni, *"Parsifal/ Druidess*: Unfolding a Lithographic Metamorphosis by Odilon Redon," *Art Bulletin* 89:4 (2007), pp. 766–96.

174 *Debora Silverman*: See her "Art Nouveau, Art of Darkness: African Lineages of Belgian Modernism, Part I," *West 86th* 18:2 (2011), pp. 139–81, and two subsequent articles.

174 *"I glimpsed"*: James Ensor, *Lettres*, ed. Xavier Tricot (Labor, 1999), p. 124. For *Indignant Bourgeois*, see Tricot, "James Ensor," in *Wagner, visions d'artistes*, p. 132; and Émile Verhaeren, *James Ensor* (van Oest, 1908), p. 116. On Ensor and politics, see Patricia G. Berman, *James Ensor: Christ's Entry into Brussels in 1889* (J. Paul Getty Museum, 2002), pp. 52–70.

175 *"sathanisme"*: Péladan, *L'Androgyne*, p. ix. For Garrigues, see ENRW4, p. 22; for Ander, Hilde Strell-Anderle, *Alois Ander: Aus dem Leben eines grossen Tenors* (Berger, 1996), pp. 65–76.

176 *"My Tristan!"*: Wagner, *Das braune Buch*, p. 50. For the danger of insanity, see RWL, p. 452.

177 *"son of a race"*: Élémir Bourges, *Le Crépuscule des dieux* (Giraud, 1884), p. 13.

177 *"From exalted mysticism"*: Huysmans, *Là-bas: A Journey into the Self*, trans. Brendan King (Dedalus, 2001), p. 62.

177 *"The Succubus"*: Camille Lemonnier, *La Vie secrète* (Ollendorff, 1898), pp. 137–48.

178 *Rubén Darío*: See his *Selected Writings*, ed. Ilan Stavans, trans. Andrew Hurley et al. (Penguin, 2005), pp. 379, 291; and Lysander Kemp, trans., *Selected Poems of Rubén Darío* (University of Texas Press, 1965), p. 55.

178 *"Those twenty minutes"*: Horacio Quiroga, *Cuentos completos*, vol. 1 (Ediciones de la Plaza, 1987), p. 292.

178 *"reviving the divine loves"*: Marcel Batilliat, *Chair mystique* (Séguier, 1995), p. 75. Other quotations on pp. 61, 143, 208–209, 211–12.

180 *"Such a handling"*: Helena Blavatsky, *Collected Writings*, vol. 4 (Theosophical Publishing House, 1966), p. 333. For Ellis, see Constance Wachtmeister, *Reminiscences of H. P. Blavatsky and "The Secret Doctrine"* (Theosophical Publishing Society, 1893), pp. 72–78; and David Cormack, "Faithful, All Too Faithful: William Ashton Ellis and the Englishing of Richard Wagner," *Wagner* 14 (1993), pp. 104–37.

180 *"mystic as well as a musician"*: Anon. [Blavatsky?], "The Meister," *Lucifer* 2:7 (1888), p. 76.

181 *"one of the most accomplished"*: Peter Washington, *Madame Blavatsky's Baboon: A History of the Mystics, Mediums, and Misfits Who Brought Spiritualism to America* (Schocken, 1995), p. 83.

181 *"Divine Wisdom"*: William Ashton Ellis, "A Glance at *Parsifal?*," *Lucifer* 3:14 (1888), pp. 106–109.

181 *"the essential elements"*: Alice Leighton Cleather and Basil Crump, *Parsifal, Lohengrin, and the Legend of the Holy Grail* (Schirmer, 1904), p. 103. On *Tristan*, see Cleather and Crump, *Tristan and Isolde: An Interpretation Embodying Wagner's Own Explanations* (Methuen, 1905), pp. 7, 72, 116–17. For the Wahnfried library, see Sessa, *Richard Wagner and the English*, p. 131.

182 *excerpts from the music dramas*: Christopher Scheer, "Theosophy and Wagner Reception in England and the United States, 1886–1911: Some Preliminary Findings," in *The Legacy of Richard Wagner: Convergences and Dissonances in Aesthetics and Reception*, ed. Luca Sala (Brepols, 2012), pp. 251–54; "Third Annual Convention," T.S.A., *Theosophical Forum* 3:1 (1897), p. 1.

182 *new aspect of Theosophy*: Crump, "The Wagner Lectures," *Theosophical Forum* 3:2 (1897), p. 28. See also "Hopes of Theosophists in Point Loma Mysteries," *San Francisco Call*, March 13, 1898.

182–83 *"A second Bayreuth!"*: Bertha Damaris Knobe, "The Point Loma Community," *Munsey's Magazine* 29:3 (1903), p. 361. For Melba, see "Statement of Facts," *Theosophical Path* 14 (1918), p. 210.

183 *Reginald Machell*: One reproduction appears in Katherine Tingley, *The Wine of Life* (Women's International Theosophical League, 1925), p. 34; another, with the quotation "Every conqueror," in *The New Way* 1:5 (1912), p. 3. For more, see Massimo Introvigne, "Reginald W. Machell (1854–1927): Blavatsky's Child, British Symbolist, American Artist," *Aries* 14 (2014), pp. 165–89.

183 *"psychic development"*: Harry Collison, "Introduction," in Rudolf Steiner, *Four Mystery Plays* (Putnam, 1920), p. iii.

183 *"strange and deep connection"*: Rudolf Steiner, "Das Gralsgeheimnis im Werk Richard Wagners," July 29, 1906, Rudolf Steiner Archive, fvn-rs.net. For subsequent Steiner quotations, see *Die Geschichte und die Bedingungen der anthroposophischen Bewegung im Verhältnis zur Anthroposophischen Gesellschaft* (Steiner Verlag, 1981), pp. 16–20; "Richard Wagner im Lichte der Geisteswissenschaft," *Die okkulten Wahrheiten alter Mythen und Sagen* (Steiner Verlag, 1999), p. 129; "Richard Wagner und sein Verhältnis zur Mystik," *Die okkulten Wahrheiten*, p. 177. For entrance music, see Irène Diet, *Jules et Alice Sauerwein et l'anthroposophie en France* (Steen, 1999), p. 102.

184 *"We have been thinking"*: Rudolf Grosse, *The Christmas Foundation: Beginning of a New Cosmic Age* (Steiner Book Centre, 1984), p. 26.

185 *"the theater was to be"*: Adrian Frazier, *Behind the Scenes: Yeats, Horniman, and the Struggle for the Abbey Theatre* (University of California Press, 1990), p. 114. For Horniman's costumes, see Edward Malins, "Annie Horniman, Practical Idealist," *Canadian Journal of Irish Studies* 3:2 (1977), p. 21.

185 *"cult of liturgical aestheticism"*: Edward Martyn, "Wagner's *Parsifal*, or the Cult of Liturgical Æstheticism," *Irish Review* 3:34 (1913), pp. 535–40.

185 *"strange solemn harmonies"*: Edward Martyn, *The Heather Field and Maeve* (Duckworth, 1899), p. 83.

185 *"art for everybody"*: George Moore, *Hail and Farewell*, vol. 1: *Ave* (Appleton, 1912), p. 206. For more, see William Blissett, "George Moore and Literary Wagnerism," *Comparative Literature* 13:1 (1961), pp. 52–71.

185 the Meisterin deems: Moore, *Evelyn Innes* (Appleton, 1898), p. 349. Other quotations on pp. 269, 296, 162–63, 139, 376.

186 *"unmusical"*: Moore, *Hail and Farewell*, vol. 1, p. 62.

186 delved into Nietzsche: See Otto Bohlmann, *Yeats and Nietzsche: An Exploration of Major Nietzschean Echoes in the Writings of William Butler Yeats* (Macmillan, 1982).

187 *"The Celtic Element in Literature"*: WBY4, pp. 130, 132, 137, 138.

187 *"ecstasy of Parsifal"*: WBY9, p. 390.

187 *"attains to puberty"*: Crowley, *The Book of Thoth*, p. 59.

187 *"The soul of the Obscene"*: *The Works of Aleister Crowley*, vol. 1, p. 239.

187 *"worth travelling round"*: Anna MacBride White and A. Norman Jeffares, eds., *The Gonne-Yeats Letters, 1893–1938* (Syracuse UP, 1994), p. 142. On Gonne, see Adrian Frazier, *The Adulterous Muse: Maud Gonne, Lucien Millevoye, and W. B. Yeats* (Lilliput, 2016), pp. 26, 125–26; and Maud Gonne, *A Servant of the Queen: Reminiscences* (Purnell, 1938), p. 287.

188 speak confidently: WBY4, p. 75.

188 public debate: John Eglinton, W. B. Yeats, A. E., and William Larminie, *Literary Ideals in Ireland* (Fisher Unwin, 1899), pp. 17, 24–25, 31–32.

188 inspiration from Bayreuth: R. F. Foster, *W. B. Yeats: A Life*, vol. 1: *The Apprentice Mage, 1865–1914* (Oxford UP, 1998), p. 210.

188 *"The darkness is broken"*: WBY2, pp. 62–63. On Wagner in *Diarmuid*, see W. B. Yeats and George Moore, *Diarmuid and Grania: Manuscript Materials*, ed. J. C. C. Mays (Cornell UP, 2005), p. xl; and Herbert Howarth, *The Irish Writers, 1880–1940* (Hill and Wang, 1959), p. 26.

188 *"dressed like Wagner's"*: Michael J. Sidnell et al., eds., *Druid Craft: The Writing of "The Shadowy Waters"* (University of Massachusetts Press, 1971), p. 191. See also John Kelly and Ronald Schuchard, eds., *The Collected Letters of W. B. Yeats*, vol. 3

(Oxford UP, 1994), p. 338: "Wagner's period more or less." For the first version of *The Shadowy Waters*, see *North American Review* 170:522 (1900), pp. 711–29.

189 *"Parsifal symbolises"*: WBY10, p. 257.

189 Yeats was criticized: Ian Mör, "From a Student's Easy Chair," *Theosophical Review* 36:216 (1905), pp. 550–51.

189 *"needless symbols"*: John Kelly and Ronald Schuchard, eds., *The Collected Letters of W. B. Yeats*, vol. 4 (Oxford UP, 2005), p. 133.

189 *"The Wagnerian essay"*: Ibid., p. 175.

189 *"Has he not led us"*: WBY1, p. 409. Other quotations on pp. 424, 428, 413.

190 visit to Palermo: John P. Frayne and Colton Johnson, eds., *Uncollected Prose by W. B. Yeats*, vol. 2 (Macmillan, 1975), pp. 485–86; also WBY10, p. 212.

5. HOLY GERMAN ART: THE KAISERREICH AND FIN-DE-SIÈCLE VIENNA

192 *"Many a habit"*: Wagner, *Sämtliche Werke*, vol. 28: *Dokumente und Texte zu "Die Meistersinger von Nürnberg,"* ed. Egon Voss (Schott, 2013), p. 267; "half ironic" on p. 125.

192 in the middle of the night: Cosima Wagner and Ludwig II, *Briefe: Eine erstaunliche Korrespondenz*, ed. Martha Schad (Lübbe, 1996), pp. 348–49. See also Wagner, *Sämtliche Werke*, vol. 28, p. 275.

192 *"wälsch"*: Adelbert von Keller, *Hans Sachs: Werke*, vol. 2 (Laupp, 1870), p. 382.

193 *"the incarnation"*: "Reichsminister Dr. Goebbels huldigt Richard Wagner," *Musik* 25:12 (1933), p. 953.

193 *"I can think of no other"*: Karol Berger, *Beyond Reason: Wagner contra Nietzsche* (University of California Press, 2017), p. 291.

194 *"I am the most German . . . My own artistic"*: Wagner, *Das braune Buch*, p. 86; RWL, p. 686.

194 *"deep-cultural teleology"*: Geoff Eley, *Nazism as Fascism: Violence, Ideology, and the Ground of Consent in Germany, 1930–1945* (Routledge, 2013), p. 199.

195 *"not as a static"*: Richard J. Evans, *Rethinking German History: Nineteenth-Century Germany and the Origins of the Third Reich* (HarperCollins, 1987), p. 2. See also Geoff Eley and David Blackbourn, *The Peculiarities of German History: Bourgeois Society and Politics in Nineteenth-Century Germany* (Oxford UP, 1984); Thomas Nipperdey, *Deutsche Geschichte 1866–1918* (Beck, 1998); Pieter M. Judson, *The Habsburg Empire: A New History* (Harvard UP, 2016).

195 seventeen thousand: Michael Walter, *Hitler in der Oper: Deutsches Musikleben 1919–1945* (Metzler, 1995), pp. 132–33.

195 Erwin Koppen: See his *Dekadenter Wagnerismus: Studien zur europäischen Literatur des Fin de siècle* (De Gruyter, 1973), p. 83.

195 *"nineteenth-century imaginary"*: Andreas Huyssen, "Monumental Seduction," *New German Critique* 69 (1996), p. 193.

195 *"The Wagnerian artwork"*: Hermann Broch, *Hofmannsthal und seine Zeit: Eine Studie* (Suhrkamp, 1974), p. 35.

196 *"distorted world"*: Sigmund Freud, *Studienausgabe*, vol. 2: *Die Traumdeutung* (Fischer, 1969), p. 421.

196 *"the spot is one"*: Ludwig II and Wagner, *Briefwechsel*, vol. 2, p. 225.

197 *"Believe me"*: RWB12, p. 260. Compare "Mann Finds U.S. Sole Peace Hope," *New York Times*, Feb. 22, 1938.

198 *"On State and Religion"*: RWSS8, p. 12.

198 *"lust for power"*: RWSS10, p. 40; Ludwig II and Wagner, *Briefwechsel*, vol. 4, pp. 29–30. See also ENRW3, pp. 475–81.

198 *Constantin Frantz*: Wagner read Frantz's *Föderalismus* in the summer of 1879: see CWD, June 30 to July 14, 1879. See also Hannu Salmi, *Imagined Germany: Richard Wagner's National Utopia* (Lang, 1999), pp. 57–61.

199 *made oblique overtures*: Salmi, *Imagined Germany*, pp. 124–26.

199 *"Perhaps she can influence"*: CWD, Jan. 19, 1869.

199 *"It appears"*: RWB22, p. 240.

199 *Georg Herwegh*: CWD, Aug. 7, 1879.

199 *"armored Monitors"*: RWSS10, p. 252.

199 *"the King's castle"*: CWD, Jan. 30, 1883.

199–200 *"Ludwig's passion . . . had everything"*: PCW, pp. 67, 55.

200 *"private mystery"*: Dieter Borchmeyer, *Drama and the World of Richard Wagner*, trans. Daphne Ellis (Princeton UP, 2003), p. 262.

200 *"A friend of Richter's"*: CWD, Nov. 20, 1870.

201 *"guttural shouts"*: See Huebner, *French Opera*, p. 17, citing Lonlay, *Français et Allemands*, vol. 1, p. 699. See also Jules Huret, *Tout yeux, tout oreilles* (Fasquelle, 1901), p. 98; and Theodor Fontane, *Kriegsgefangen: Erlebtes 1870* (Fontane, 1910), pp. 329–30.

201 *twenty-six seats*: "Abreise des deutschen Kaisers," *Neuigkeits-Welt-Blatt*, Aug. 13, 1876. Bernhard von Bülow, *Denkwürdigkeiten*, vol. 4 (Ullstein, 1931), p. 308, describes Wilhelm's reluctance. For "dreadful," see Sommer, *Kommentar zu Nietzsches "Der Antichrist,"* p. 508.

201 *"spoiled, pampered"*: Friedrich III, *Tagebücher, 1866–1888*, ed. Winfried Baumgart (Schöningh, 2012), p. 382; *Parsifal* on p. 426.

201 *"chauvinistic and ultra Prussian"*: John C. G. Röhl, *Young Wilhelm: The Kaiser's Early Life, 1859–1888*, trans. Jeremy Gaines and Rebecca Wallach (Cambridge UP, 1998), p. 409. For the uniform, see Müller, *Wagner und die Deutschen*, p. 58. The car horn is notated as C-E-G-C in Henry F. Urban, "Der Kaiser," *Jugend* 16 (1911), p. 1384.

201 *"ennobling effect"*: Röhl, *Young Wilhelm*, p. 715. See also Lamar Cecil, *Wilhelm II*, vol. 1 (University of North Carolina Press, 1989), p. 65.

201 *"I don't like Wagner"*: Arthur Seidl, "Vom kaiserlichen Wagner-Enthusiasmus," *Gesellschaft* 18 (1902), p. 135; Bernhard von Bülow, *Denkwürdigkeiten*, vol. 1 (Ullstein, 1930), p. 149.

202 *Salmi has assembled*: Salmi, *Imagined Germany*, p. 181. On the Patrons' Association, see Stephan Mösch, *Weihe, Werkstatt, Wirklichkeit: Wagners "Parsifal" in Bayreuth 1882–1933* (Bärenreiter, 2009), pp. 154–58; and Veit Veltzke, *Vom Patron zum Paladin: Wagnervereinigungen im Kaiserreich von der Reichsgründung bis zur Jahrhundertwende* (Brockmeyer, 1987).

202 *"eternal idea . . . epoch of servitude"*: Thomas S. Grey, "Wagner's *Die Meistersinger* as National Opera (1868–1945)," in *Music and German National Identity*, ed. Celia Applegate and Pamela Potter (University of Chicago Press, 2002), pp. 86–87.

202 *"showed us what we were"*: Franz Merloff, *Richard Wagner und das Deutschthum* (Wurm, 1873), p. 3.

202 *John Deathridge*: See his "Living with Wagner," paper delivered at the WagnerWorldWide:America conference, University of South Carolina, Jan. 31, 2013.

203 *Hans Makart*: See Thomas S. Grey, "Wagner and the 'Makart Style,'" *Cambridge Opera Journal* 25:3 (2013), pp. 225–60.

203 *Franz Stassen*: See Stephen C. Meyer, "Illustrating Transcendence: *Parsifal*, Franz Stassen, and the Leitmotif," *Musical Quarterly* 92 (2009), pp. 9–32; Udo Bermbach, *Richard Wagner in Deutschland: Rezeption—Verfälschungen* (Metzler, 2011), pp. 331–39; Rudolf Herzog, *Siegfried der Held: Der deutschen Jugend erzählt* (Ullstein, 1912).

203 *Siegfried Schnitzel*: Rudolf Sabor, *The Real Wagner* (Deutsch, 1987), p. 282.

203 *military bands*: Celia Applegate, *The Necessity of Music: Variations on a German Theme* (University of Toronto Press, 2017), p. 217.

203 *he expressed horror*: CWD, May 31, 1882.

204 *Antichrist, Heliogabalus*: Wilhelm Tappert, *Richard Wagner im Spiegel der Kritik* (Siegel, 1903).

204 *"musical savior"*: Johannes Scherr, *Michel: Geschichte eines Deutschen unserer Zeit*, vol. 2 (Kober, 1858), pp. 143–44. On early Wagner-themed novels, see Anna Jacobson, *Nachklänge Richard Wagners im Roman* (Carl Winter, 1932), pp. 9–19.

204 *Friedrich Theodor Vischer*: See his *Auch einer: Eine Reisebekanntschaft*, vol. 1 (Hallberger, 1879), pp. 308–35.

205 *"I was bored"*: Fritz Stern, *The Politics of Cultural Despair: A Study in the Rise of the Germanic Ideology* (University of California Press, 1974), p. 89. For "The *Volk* cannot travel," see Paul de Lagarde, *Le opere italiane di Giordano Bruno*, vol. 2 (Dieterichsche Universitätsbuchhandlung, 1888), p. 792.

205 *"out-Meyerbeered"*: Julius Langbehn, *Rembrandt als Erzieher: Von einem Deutschen* (Hirschfeld, 1890), pp. 268–69.

205 *Wilhelm Heinrich Riehl*: See his *Kulturgeschicht-liche Charakterköpfe* (Cotta, 1891), pp. 516–17, 520–21.

205 *"As a half-Magyar"*: *Rheinisch-Westfälische Zeitung*, July 28, 1894, quoted in Großmann-Vendrey, *Bayreuth in der deutschen Presse*, vol. 3/1, p. 117.

205 *widespread complaints*: Ibid., pp. 114–23.

206 *"kind of limbo"*: Applegate, *Necessity of Music*, pp. 55–56.

206 *"Parsifal, though"*: Theodor Fontane, *Briefe*, vol. 3, ed. Walter Keitel et al. (Wissenschaftliche Buchge-sellschaft, 1980), pp. 706–707. Other quotations on pp. 715, 706, 713.

206 *"not to intoxication"*: TM14, p. 257.

206 *defended the opera*: Fontane, "Otto Reinsdorff: Rich-ard Wagners *Meistersinger von Nürnberg*," *Sämtliche Werke*, vol. 21 (Nymphenburger, 1974), p. 175.

207 *"childish"*: Fontane, *Briefe*, vol. 3, p. 152; mention of librettos in *Tagebücher, 1866–1882, 1884–1898*, ed. Gotthard and Therese Erler (Aufbau, 1995), pp. 127–28.

207 *"there are more Wogelindes"*: Ernst Heilborn, ed., *Das Fontane-Buch*, vol. 2 (Fischer, 1919), p. 88.

207 *three major Wagner Scenes*: Fontane, *Two Novellas: The Woman Taken in Adultery and The Poggenpuhl Family*, trans. Gabrielle Annan (Penguin, 1995), pp. 27, 41–42, translation modified; Fontane, *Cécile*, trans. Stanley Radcliffe (Angel, 1992), pp. 156–58, 163; Fontane, *Effi Briest*, trans. Hugh Rorrison and Helen Chambers (Penguin, 2000), p. 75.

208 *"the artificial"*: Isabel Nottinger, *Fontanes Fin de Siècle: Motive der Dekadenz in "L'Adultera," "Cécile," und "Der Stechlin"* (Königshausen & Neumann, 2003), p. 186.

209 *"Munich shone"*: Thomas Mann, *"Death in Venice" and Other Stories*, trans. David Luke (Bantam, 1988), pp. 75–77, translation modified; TM2, pp. 222–25. For numbers of artists, see Maria Makela, *The Munich Secession: Art and Artists in Turn-of-the-Century Munich* (Princeton UP, 1990), p. 14.

209 *Makela notes*: See her *Munich Secession*, pp. 31–32.

209 *Michael Georg Conrad*: Peter Jelavich, *Munich and Theatrical Modernism: Politics, Playwriting, and Performance, 1890–1914* (Harvard UP, 1985), pp. 27–28.

210 *"From the Gesamtkunstwerk"*: Michael Georg Con-rad, "Angewandte Kunst," *Gesellschaft* 20 (1898), pp. 73–74.

210 *"Lament be silent!"*: Robert E. Norton, *Secret Ger-many: Stefan George and His Circle* (Cornell UP, 2002), pp. 91–92; Stefan George, *Sämtliche Werke in 18 Bänden*, vol. 2 (Klett-Cotta, 1987), p. 44.

210 *"bad actor . . . dragging"*: Norton, *Secret Germany*, p. 236; Kurt Hildebrandt, *Erinnerungen an Stefan George und seinen Kreis* (Bouvier, 1965), p. 108. See also Wolfgang Osthoff, *Stefan George und "les deux musiques": Tönende und vertonte Dichtung im Ein-klang und Widerstreit* (Steiner, 1989), pp. 252–57.

211 *Friedrich Huch*: See his *Tristan und Isolde, Lohen-grin, Der fliegende Holländer: Drei groteske Komö-dien* (Mörike, 1911), pp. 111, 124.

211 *variously irritating and engrossing*: For a range of opinions, see Artur Kutscher, *Frank Wedekind: Sein Leben und seine Werke*, vol. 1 (Müller, 1922), p. 117.

212 *"irresistibly beautiful . . . Love for my art"*: Frank Wedekind, *Prosa, Dramen, Verse* (Langen Müller, 1960), p. 749.

212 *"Good God!"*: Ibid., p. 548. Other quotations on pp. 562, 565, 578, 580.

213 *In the view of Eric Bentley*: Wedekind, *The First Lulu*, ed. and trans. Eric Bentley (Applause, 1994), pp. 27–29. On Wedekind's youthful interest in *Tannhäuser*, see Rolf Kieser, *Benjamin Franklin Wedekind: Biographie einer Jugend* (Arche, 1990), p. 209; and Kieser, *Olga Plümacher-Hünerwadel: Eine gelehrte Frau des neunzehnten Jahrhunderts* (Lenzburger Druck, 1990).

214 *"No, no"*: Ludwig Speidel, "Briefe aus Baireuth," in Susanna Großmann-Vendrey, *Bayreuth in der deutschen Presse*, vol. 1 (Bosse, 1977), p. 229. On Speidel and Hanslick's politics, see David Brod-beck, *Defining Deutschtum: Political Ideology, German Identity, and Music-Critical Discourse in Liberal Vienna* (Oxford UP, 2014), esp. pp. 25–52, 126–34.

214 *"diverse imaginings"*: Kevin C. Karnes, *A Kingdom Not of This World: Wagner, the Arts, and Utopian Visions in Fin-de-Siècle Vienna* (Oxford UP, 2013), p. 2.

214 *"The city was a dream"*: Broch, *Hofmannsthal*, p. 82.

214 *Camillo Sitte*: Michael Mönninger, "Sitte und Wagner," in *Camillo Sitte Gesamtausgabe*, vol. 1, ed. Klaus Semsroth et al. (Böhlau, 2008), pp. 89–90.

214 *"translated Wagner's idea"*: Carl E. Schorske, *Fin-de-Siècle Vienna: Politics and Culture* (Vintage, 1981), p. 71.

215 *Max Klinger*: Karnes, *Kingdom*, pp. 101–105.

216 *"flag of the Secession"*: Stephen Carlton Thursby, *Gustav Mahler, Alfred Roller, and the Wagnerian Gesamtkunstwerk: "Tristan" and Affinities Between the Arts at the Vienna Court Opera* (Ph.D. diss., Florida SU, 2009), p. 132. See also PCW, pp. 157–70.

216 *"Rushing waves"*: Hugo von Hofmannsthal, "Zu-kunftsmusik," *Sämtliche Werke*, vol. 2, ed. Andreas Thomasberger and Eugene Weber (Fischer, 1988), p. 49. See also Dieter Borchmeyer, "Der Mythos als Oper: Hofmannsthal und Richard Wagner," *Hofmannsthal-Forschungen* 7 (1983), pp. 19–65. For Chandos, see Hofmannsthal, "Ein Brief," *Sämtliche Werke*, vol. 31, ed. Ellen Ritter (Fischer, 1991), p. 54.

218 *Cronaca Wagneriana*: Axel Körner, *Politics of Cul-ture in Liberal Italy: From Unification to Fascism* (Routledge, 2008), p. 238.

218 *"He wanted to hear"*: Saverio Procida, "Ricordi intimi su Arturo Colautti," *Lettura* 15:2 (1915), p. 141. See also Annamaria Andreoli, *Il vivere inimitabile: Vita di Gabriele D'Annunzio* (Mondadori, 2000), p. 230.

218 *"In articulating"*: Gabriele d'Annunzio, *Il caso Wagner*, ed. Paola Sorge (Editori Laterza, 1996), pp. 76–77. See also a commentary and translation in Thomas S. Grey and James Westby, "Gabriele d'Annunzio's 'Il caso Wagner' (The Case of Wagner): Reflections on Wagner, Nietzsche, and *Wagnerismo* from *Fin-de-Siècle* Italy," *Leitmotive*, Fall 2012, pp. 7–26; and Bettina Vogel-Walter, "D'Annunzios Wagner," *wagnerspectrum* 6:1 (2010), pp. 206–208.

218 *"oblivion, supreme intoxication"*: D'Annunzio, *The Triumph of Death*, trans. Arthur Hornblow (Page, 1896), p. 57. Other quotations on pp. 376–77, 380, 412.

220 *"violent action"*: D'Annunzio, *The Flame of Life*, trans. Kassandra Vivaria (Page, 1900), p. 33. Other quotations on pp. 127, 111, 147, 148, 196. See also William Blissett, "D. H. Lawrence, D'Annunzio, Wagner," *Wisconsin Studies in Contemporary Literature* 7:1 (1966), pp. 21–46.

221 *"an affair"*: TMW, p. 43.

222 *Júlia Mann*: Hans Rudolf Vaget, *Seelenzauber: Thomas Mann und die Musik* (Fischer, 2012), p. 60.

222 *"hard to digest"*: TM14, p. 24. See also Mann, "Erinnerungen ans Lübecker Stadttheater," *Gesammelte Werke*, vol. 11 (Fischer, 1960), p. 418.

222 *"In the accompaniment"*: Heinrich Mann, *In einer Familie* (Fischer, 2000), p. 179. For more, see Ulrich Weisstein, "Satire und Parodie in Heinrich Manns Roman *Der Untertan*," in *Heinrich Mann 1871–1971: Bestandsaufnahme und Untersuchung, Ergebnisse der Heinrich-Mann-Tagung in Lübeck*, ed. Klaus Matthias (Fink, 1973), pp. 125–46; and Matthias, "Heinrich Mann und die Musik," in ibid., pp. 235–362.

222 *"bad little Wagner imitator"*: TM21, p. 385

223 *"I have no interest"*: Ibid., p. 269.

223 *seldom missing a chance*: Ibid., p. 121.

223 *"The violins sang"*: Mann, *"Death in Venice" and Other Stories*, p. 13.

223 *suppressed Dionysian desires*: On this theme, see Vaget, *Seelenzauber*, pp. 86–87.

223 *"considerable epic effect"*: TM21, pp. 179–80.

224 *extended backward*: Mann, "Lübeck als geistige Lebensform," *Gesammelte Werke*, vol. 11, p. 381.

224 *"There should be no"*: Mann, *Buddenbrooks*, trans. John E. Woods (Knopf, 1993), pp. 41–42. Other quotations on pp. 436–37, 537, 606, 640, 443, 644, some translations modified.

224 *as Mann pointed out*: TM14, p. 74.

225 *"Doctor Bieber's Temptation"*: Heinrich Mann, *Haltlos: Sämtliche Erzählungen*, vol. 1 (Fischer, 1995), pp. 501, 524, 527.

226 *Arthur Holitscher*: On his connection to Spinell, see Andrew Barker, "'Bloss aus Lemberg gebürtig': Detlev Spinell, the Austrian Jewish Aesthete in Thomas Mann's *Tristan*," *Modern Language Review* 102:2 (2007), pp. 440–50. Excerpts from *The Poisoned Well* are in Raymond Furness, ed., *The Dedalus Book of German Decadence: Voices of the Abyss*, trans. Furness and Mike Mitchell (Dedalus, 1994), pp. 82–120.

226 *opera glasses*: Arthur Holitscher, *Lebensgeschichte eines Rebellen* (Fischer, 1924), pp. 218–21.

226 *"merry noise"*: Mann, *"Death in Venice" and Other Stories*, p. 112. Other quotations on pp. 108, 116–18. On the d'Annunzio connection, see Nachum Schoffman, "D'Annunzio and Mann: Antithetical Wagnerisms," *Journal of Musicology* 11:4 (1993), pp. 517–24; and Stevie Anne Bolduc, "A Study of Intertextuality: Thomas Mann's *Tristan* and Richard Wagner's *Tristan und Isolde*," *Rocky Mountain Review of Language and Literature* 37 (1983), pp. 82–90.

228 *"shields and swords"*: Heinrich Mann, *The Loyal Subject*, trans. Ernest Boyd and Daniel Theisen (Continuum, 1998), p. 250. Other quotations on pp. 256, 342, 344.

229 *"exterminated root"*: Mann, *Der Untertan* (Wolff, 1918), pp. 504–505.

6. NIBELHEIM: JEWISH AND BLACK WAGNER

230 *"Of the Coming of John"*: W. E. B. Du Bois, *Writings*, ed. Nathan Huggins (Library of America, 1986), pp. 521–35. "This sense" on p. 364.

232 *"secondary attributes"*: Russell A. Berman, "Du Bois and Wagner: Race, Nation, and Culture Between the United States and Germany," *German Quarterly* 70:2 (1997), p. 129.

232 *"incompatibility"*: Sieglinde Lemke, "Of the Coming of John," in *The Cambridge Companion to W. E. B. Du Bois*, ed. Shamoon Zamir (Cambridge UP, 2008), p. 43.

233 *Larry David*: "Trick or Treat," episode of *Curb Your Enthusiasm*, aired Oct. 7, 2001.

233 *"one stylized essence"*: Laurence Dreyfus, "Hermann Levi's Shame and *Parsifal*'s Guilt: A Critique of Essentialism in Biography and Criticism," *Cambridge Opera Journal* 6:2 (1994), pp. 125–26.

234 *"Judaism is not really . . . We will tolerate"*: Léon Poliakov, *The History of Anti-Semitism*, vol. 3, trans. Miriam Kochan (Vanguard, 1975), pp. 178, 162.

234 *"sad privilege"*: Jean-Jacques Nattiez, *Wagner antisémite: Un problème historique, sémiologique et esthétique* (Bourgois, 2015), p. 228.

234 *in the 1830s*: Drüner, *Wagner*, p. 83.

234 *"On the Jewish Question"*: See Friedrich Dieckmann, *Richard Wagner in Venedig: Eine Collage* (Luchterhand, 1983), p. 183; Arnold Ruge to Karl Marx, March 1843, in *Deutsch-Französische Jahrbücher*, ed. Ruge and Marx (Bureau des Annales, 1844), p. 21; RWSS9, p. 334; Udo Bermbach, *Der Wahn des Gesamtkunstwerks: Richard Wagners politisch-*

ästhetische Utopie (Metzler, 2004), pp. 276–78; Marx, *Zur Judenfrage* (Rowohlt, 1919), p. 49.

235 *"This rancor"*: RWB3, p. 544.

235 *Drüner has shown*: See his *Wagner*, pp. 293–99.

235 *"it is all made for them"*: RWB5, p. 189.

235 Judenmusik: Theodor Uhlig, "Zeitgemäße Betrachtungen, VI: Außerordentliches," *Neue Zeitschrift für Musik*, July 23, 1850.

235 *"fantasy derived"*: Ludwig Bischoff, "TU: hoc intrivisti: tibi omne est exedendum," *Rheinische Musik-Zeitung*, Aug. 10, 1850, p. 45. On these exchanges, see Sinéad Dempsey-Garratt, "Mendelssohn's 'Untergang': Reconsidering the Impact of Wagner's 'Judaism in Music,'" in *Mendelssohn Perspectives*, ed. Nicole Grimes and Angela R. Mace (Routledge, 2016), p. 39.

236 *"The Jew has never had"*: JM, p. 158. Other quotations on pp. 149, 151, 159–60, 172–73.

236 *"feeling his way"*: Thomas S. Grey, "The Jewish Question," in *The Cambridge Companion to Wagner*, ed. Grey (Cambridge UP, 2008), p. 207.

236 "Verjüdung": JM, p. 147. For two usages of "verjudet," see *Der freie Staatsbürger* 55 (1848), pp. 213, 232. For an earlier example, see *Deutscher Sprachschatz*, 1691, p. 903. For the claim that Wagner invented the term, see JM, p. 81.

237 *"rebirth through self-annihilation"*: JM, p. 173.

237 *"I wish to go under"*: RWB5, p. 189.

237 *"old Italian painting"*: Hanslick, "Richard Wagner's 'Meistersinger von Nürnberg,'" part 2, *Neue Freie Presse*, June 25, 1868.

238 *had been exposed*: JM, p. 31.

238 *"delicately hidden . . . I cannot judge"*: Ibid., pp. 177, 196.

238 *Cosima recorded*: CWD, March 13, April 3, May 24, 1869.

238 *elicited much ridicule*: See Richard Schmidt-Cabanis, attrib., *Hepp, hepp! oder Die Meistersinger von Nürnberg: Große confessionell-socialdemokratische Zukunftsoper in 3 gegenwärtigen Acten* (Erbe, 1872). For Mauthner, see Dieter Borchmeyer and Stephen Kohler, eds., *Wagner Parodien* (Insel, 1983), pp. 141–47. See also Thomas S. Grey, "Masters and Their Critics: Wagner, Hanslick, Beckmesser, and *Die Meistersinger*," in *Wagner's "Meistersinger": Performance, History, Representation*, ed. Nicholas Vazsonyi (University of Rochester Press, 2002), pp. 186–87.

238 *"Jewishness here"*: Moritz Anton Grandjean and Josef Koch von Langentreu, *Das Judenthum in der Musik*, op. 36 (Bösendorfer, 1870?).

239 *survey by Annette Hein*: See her *"Es ist viel 'Hitler' in Wagner": Rassismus und antisemitische Deutschtumsideologie in den "Bayreuther Blättern" (1878–1938)* (Niemeyer, 1996), p. 113.

239 *"ferocious joke"*: CWD, Dec. 18, 1881. For a debate about the meaning of such passages, see Derek Hughes, "Wagner, the Pogrom, and the Critics,"

Wagner Journal 10:1 (2016), pp. 4–25; and Barry Emslie, "The Volk That Wagner Loved to Hate: A Reply to Derek Hughes," *Wagner Journal* 11:3 (2017), pp. 27–34.

239 *"Israel must"*: Adolf Stoecker, *Christlich-Sozial: Reden und Aufsätze* (Velhagen and Klasing, 1885), p. 153.

239 *"I read a very good"*: CWD, Oct. 11, 1879.

239 *suitable reading material*: CWD, Jan. 29 and 31, 1875.

239 *"seven-day silence"*: CWD, Jan. 25, 1875. For more, see Wolf-Daniel Hartwich, *Romantischer Antisemitismus: Von Klopstock bis Richard Wagner* (Vandenhoeck & Ruprecht, 2005), pp. 229–45.

240 *disputed many of its findings*: See Éric Eugène, *Wagner et Gobineau: Existe-t-il un racisme wagnérien?* (Cherche midi, 1998). For the American translation, see *The Moral and Intellectual Diversity of Races*, trans. Henry Hotz, ed. Josiah Nott (Lippincott, 1856).

240 *"might raise the very lowest"*: RWSS10, p. 283; "blood of the Savior" on p. 280; objections to Jewish lineage on p. 83.

240 *"plastic demon"*: RWSS10, p. 272. Other quotations on pp. 264, 268, 274.

241 *Ruth HaCohen*: See her *The Music Libel Against the Jews* (Yale UP, 2011), pp. 248–51, 461–62. For "heartless," see JM, p. 154.

241 *"I hate the Jews"*: Johann Christian Lobe, "Das Judentum in der Musik," 1851, in JM, p. 227.

241 *"The gold-grabbing"*: Adorno, *Versuch über Wagner*, pp. 23–24; also "Fragmente über Wagner," *Zeitschrift für Sozialforschung* 8 (1939–40), p. 11.

241 *"aesthetics of anti-Semitism"*: David J. Levin, *Richard Wagner, Fritz Lang, and the Nibelungen: The Dramaturgy of Disavowal* (Princeton UP, 1998), p. 88. See also Paul Lawrence Rose, *Wagner: Race and Revolution* (Yale UP, 1992); Marc A. Weiner, *Richard Wagner and the Anti-Semitic Imagination* (University of Nebraska Press, 1995); Barry Millington, "Nuremberg Trial: Is There Anti-Semitism in 'Die Meistersinger'?," *Cambridge Opera Journal* 3:3 (1991), pp. 247–60; David J. Levin, "Reading Beckmesser Reading: Antisemitism and Aesthetic Practice in *The Mastersingers of Nuremberg*," *New German Critique* 69 (1996), pp. 127–46; Ulrich Drüner, "Judenfiguren bei Richard Wagner," in *Judenrollen: Darstellungsformen im europäischen Theater von der Restauration bis zur Zwischenkriegszeit*, ed. Hans-Peter Bayerdörfer and Jens Malte Fischer (Niemeyer, 2008), pp. 143–64.

241 *"pendant to the riot scene"*: JM, p. 314.

242 *hisses went up*: Ludwig Nohl, "Correspondenz: Die 'Meistersinger' in Wien," *Neue Zeitschrift für Musik*, March 11, 1870.

242 *"Hepp, hepp!"*: CWD, July 4, 1869. For Berlin, see NBKG II:7/1, pp. 615–16.

242 *"have put it about"*: CWD, March 14, 1870. See also NBKG II:2, p. 166.

242 *mock Jewish singing*: Millington, "Nuremberg Trial," pp. 151–54. For critical responses, see Dieter David Scholz, *Richard Wagners Antisemitismus: Jahrhundertgenie im Zwielicht—Eine Korrektur* (Parthas, 2000), pp. 95–100; Magee, *Tristan Chord*, pp. 371–80; Borchmeyer, *Drama and the World of Richard Wagner*, pp. 196–211. For other readings of Beckmesser, see Thomas S. Grey and Kirsten Paige, "The Owl, the Nightingale and the Jew in the Thorn-bush: Relocating Anti-Semitism in *Die Meistersinger*," *Cambridge Opera Journal* 28:1 (2016), pp. 1–35; and Hughes, "Wagner: The Pogrom and the Critics," pp. 22–25.

242 *David Dennis*: See his "'The Most German of All German Operas': *Die Meistersinger* Through the Lens of the Third Reich," in Vazsonyi, *Wagner's "Meistersinger,"* pp. 101–103.

243 *Hans Rudolf Vaget*: See his "'Du warst mein Feind von je': The Beckmesser Controversy Revisited," in ibid., p. 203.

243 *dwarves in the Ring*: See Jean-Jacques Nattiez, *Wagner Androgyne: A Study in Interpretation*, trans. Stewart Spencer (Princeton UP, 1998), pp. 60–73; and Nattiez, *Wagner antisémite*, pp. 283–90.

243 *"burrow with restless"*: RWSS2, p. 156. Compare JM, pp. 171–72.

243 *associated them with Mongols*: CWD, Nov. 17, 1882.

243 *"intended by Wagner"*: Herbert Killian, ed., *Gustav Mahler in den Erinnerungen von Natalie Bauer-Lechner* (Wagner, 1984), p. 122.

243 *Paul Gisbert*: See his *Der Ring der nie gelungen* (Wedekind & Schwieger, 1877); also Veit Veltzke, *Der Mythos des Erlösers: Richard Wagners Traumwelten und die deutsche Gesellschaft, 1871–1918* (Arnoldsche Verlagsanstalt, 2002), p. 109.

243 *"Kundry lives"*: Wagner, *Das braune Buch*, p. 62.

244 *liberal and Jewish critics*: See Paul Lindau, *Bayreuther Briefe vom reinen Thoren: "Parsifal" von Richard Wagner* (Schottlaender, 1883), p. 7; Max Kalbeck, *Richard Wagner's Parsifal: Erste Aufführung am 26. Juli 1882 zu Bayreuth* (Schletter, 1883), p. 64; Ludwig Speidel, "'Parsifal' in Bayreuth," in Susanna Großmann-Vendrey, *Bayreuth in der deutschen Presse*, vol. 2 (Bosse, 1977), p. 186. In his review of the *Ring* (*Bayreuth in der deutschen Presse*, vol. 1, p. 226), Speidel had said that the part of Mime had the sound of "Mauscheln." Rose comments in *Wagner: Race and Revolution*, pp. 168–69.

244 *"a-Jehovah"*: Ludwig Schemann, "Die Gral- und die Parzival-Sage in ihren hauptsächlichsten dichterischen Verarbeitungen," part 4, BB 2:4 (1879), p. 113; CWD, April 27, 1879. See also Arthur Seidl, "R. Wagner's 'Parsifal' und Schopenhauer's 'Nirwâna,'" BB 11:9 (1888), p. 300.

244 *the composer was Jewish*: On Wagner's paternity,

see ENRW2, pp. 608–13, and Drüner, *Wagner*, pp. 40–43. Nietzsche's "Geyer" comment is in NAC, p. 255. For the Nazi rebuttal, see Walter Lange, *Richard Wagners Sippe* (Beck, 1942). For cartoons, see Nattiez, *Wagner antisémite*, pp. 110–12; Karl Storck, *Musik und Musiker in Karikatur und Satire* (Stalling, 1911), pp. 403, 406; Ernst Kreowski and Eduard Fuchs, *Richard Wagner in der Karikatur* (Behr, 1907), p. 58.

244 *"he himself appears"*: Gustav Freytag, "Der Streit über das Judenthum in der Musik," *Grenzboten* 28:22 (1869), p. 336. See also Larry Ping, *Gustav Freytag and the Prussian Gospel: Novels, Liberalism, and History* (Peter Lang, 2006), p. 140.

244 *"Talmud-sniffing . . . abounds"*: Daniel Spitzer, *Wiener Spaziergänge*, vol. 3 (Klinkhardt, 1881), p. 351; Spitzer, *Wiener Spaziergänge*, vol. 5 (Klinkhardt, 1882), pp. 59–60.

245 *"felt every sympathy"*: CWD, March 2, 1878. On Wagner's height, see Pascal Bouteldja, *Un patient nommé Wagner* (Symétrie, 2014), pp. 161–62.

246 *Theodor Fritsch*: See his *Antisemiten-Katechismus: Eine Zusammenstellung des wichtigsten Materials zum Verständniss der Judenfrage* (Beyer, 1893).

246 *"purification"*: Rudolf Wellingsbach, "Wolzogen, Baron Hans Paul von," in *The Cambridge Wagner Encyclopedia*, ed. Nicholas Vazsonyi (Cambridge UP, 2013), p. 723.

246 *originated at Bayreuth*: Peter Pulzer, *The Rise of Political Anti-Semitism in Germany & Austria* (Harvard UP, 1988), p. 91.

246 *he has already done*: CWD, June 16, 1880.

246 *might frighten away*: Hans von Wolzogen, "Patriotische Randglossen eines Idealisten zu der vorstehenden Abhandlung," BB 8:3–4 (1885), pp. 113–14. For Frantz, see ZRW, pp. 58–59.

246 *Wolzogen recast him*: "Vorwort" to *Bayreuther Taschenbuch mit Kalendarium für das jahr 1889*, reproduced in ZRW, p. 71.

246 *"pious, patriotic"*: David C. Large, "Wagner's Bayreuth Disciples," in WECP, p. 103.

247 *"something inalienable"*: CWD, Jan. 17, 1883. See also Carl Friedrich Glasenapp, *Das Leben Richard Wagners*, vol. 6 (Breitkopf und Härtel, 1911), pp. 761–62, for a paraphrase of the diary. Hannu Salmi notes in *Imagined Germany*, p. 44, that Wagner used the word "Aryan" only once.

247 *"make all the ideas"*: CWD, Feb. 9, 1883.

247 *nor did all antisemites*: For Lagarde and Langbehn, see Stern, *The Politics of Cultural Despair*: pp. 63, 141; for Eugen Dühring, *Der Ersatz der Religion durch Vollkommeneres und die Ausscheidung alles Judäerthums durch den modernen Völkergeist* (Kufahl, 1897), p. 112; for Heinrich Pudor, "Deutsche Musik," *Das Zwanzigste Jahrhundert* 2:1 (1891–92), pp. 533–34.

247 *denigrating Jewish culture*: See Beaufils, *Péladan*, pp. 394–95; also Péladan, "Tribune publique," *Archives israélites*, Oct. 3 1901, p. 273. On Merrill, Mau-

clair, and others, see Smith, *Mallarmé's Children*, pp. 48, 189–90.

248 *"He would have known"*: Jean Laporte, "Wagneriana," *Revue musicale* 9 (1913), p. 32.

248 *"The German and German-Jewish"*: Léon Daudet, *L'Entre-deux-guerres: Souvenirs des milieux littéraires, politiques, artistiques et médicaux de 1880 à 1905*, third series (Nouvelle Librairie Nationale, 1915), pp. 310–11. See Daudet, *Devant la douleur*, pp. 201–24, for an account of his early Wagnerism.

248 *"a woman who was"*: MPTP3, p. 146; "Dreyfusard" on p. 1390.

249 *four or five hundred*: Hein, *"Es ist viel 'Hitler' in Wagner,"* pp. 52–53.

250 *"honest Jew . . . only great"*: Chamberlain, *Lebenswege meines Denkens*, pp. 195, 194.

250 *"expression of sterility"*: Dietrich Mack, ed., *Cosima Wagner: Das zweite Leben: Briefe und Aufzeichnungen, 1883–1930* (Piper, 1980), pp. 363–64, 820.

250 *equally plausible opposing view*: Roger Allen, "'All Here Is Music': Houston Stewart Chamberlain and *Der Ring des Nibelungen*," *wagnerspectrum* 2:1 (2006), p. 175.

250 *"the Jews themselves"*: Chamberlain, *Richard Wagner* (Bruckmann, 1904), pp. 227–29.

250 *"awakening of the Teutonic"*: Chamberlain, *Die Grundlagen des Neunzehnten Jahrhunderts*, vol. 1 (Bruckmann, 1900), p. 8; "downright ridiculous" and "Jewish peril" on p. 18.

251 *"Not just the Jew"*: Chamberlain, *Grundlagen*, vol. 2 (Bruckmann, 1900), p. 935.

251 *began a vigorous correspondence*: Chamberlain, *Briefe, 1882–1924: Und Briefwechsel mit Kaiser Wilhelm II*, vol. 2 (Bruckmann, 1928).

251 *Roger Allen*: See his *"Die Weihe des Hauses* (The Consecration of the House): H. S. Chamberlain and the Early Reception of *Parsifal*," in *Companion to Wagner's "Parsifal,"* pp. 264–72; also Chamberlain, *Grundlagen*, 3rd ed. (Bruckmann, 1903), pp. xv, xx, xxv.

252 *Blandine and Isolde*: Oliver Hilmes, *Cosimas Kinder: Triumph und Tragödie der Wagner-Dynastie* (Siedler, 2009), pp. 102–103.

252 *"alter ego"*: Dreyfus, "Hermann Levi's Shame," p. 131; Eckart Kröplin, *Richard Wagner-Chronik* (Metzler, 2016), p. 571. For "most Christian," see Ludwig II and Wagner, *Briefwechsel*, vol. 3, p. 158. Dreyfus, on p. 129, points out, citing John Deathridge, that no specific directive forcing Wagner to use Levi is documented; Mösch, *Weihe, Werkstatt, Wirklichkeit*, p. 266, is more inclined to see pressure on Wagner.

253 *"a man who seizes"*: Julia Bernhardt, ed., *Der Briefwechsel zwischen Paul Heyse und Hermann Levi: Eine kritische Edition* (Kovač, 2007), p. 116.

253 *"He is the best"*: ZRW, p. 28.

253 *"salvation through participation"*: CWD, March 7, 1872.

253 *Many other Jews*: See Elaine Brody, "The Jewish Wagnerites," *Opera Quarterly* 1:3 (1983), pp. 66–80; Eric Werner, "Jews Around Richard and Cosima Wagner," *Musical Quarterly* 71:2 (1985), pp. 172–99; James Loeffler, "Richard Wagner's 'Jewish Music': Antisemitism and Aesthetics in Modern Jewish Culture," *Jewish Social Studies* 15:2 (2009), pp. 2–36.

253 *"If I have friendly"*: RWL, p. 918.

253 *paragons of self-loathing*: See Theodor Lessing, *Der jüdische Selbsthass* (Jüdischer Verlag, 1930), pp. 106–107; Peter Gay, *Freud, Jews, and Other Germans: Masters and Victims in Modernist Culture* (Oxford UP, 1979), pp. 189–230; Dreyfus, "Hermann Levi's Shame," pp. 132–33. See also Jacob Katz, *The Darker Side of Genius: Richard Wagner's Anti-Semitism* (Brandeis UP, 1986), pp. 97–98.

254 *coughing fit*: John C. G. Röhl, ed., *Philipp Eulenburgs politische Korrespondenz*, vol. 2 (Boldt, 1976), p. 817. See also Norman Domeier, *The Eulenburg Affair: A Cultural History of Politics in the German Empire*, trans. Deborah Lucas Schneider (Camden House, 2015), p. 171.

254 *Howard Winant*: See his "Dialectics of the Veil," *The New Politics of Race: Globalism, Difference, Justice* (University of Minnesota Press, 2004), p. 26.

254 *"Huge success"*: CWD, April 7, 1869.

254 *pamphleteers debated*: See Julius Lang, *Zur Versöhnung des Judenthums mit Richard Wagner* (Stilke und van Muyden, 1869); and E. Liéser, *Die modernen Judenhasser, und der Versuch von Julius Lang, das Judenthum mit Richard Wagner zu versöhnen* (Hallmann, 1869).

254 *"one could hear"*: Daniel Spitzer, *Wiener Spaziergänge: Neue Sammlung* (Rosner, 1873), p. 82.

254 *"we can gain"*: M. S. Sarca, "By the Way," *Jewish Criterion*, Jan. 11, 1901.

254 *"There was a gallery"*: Fritz Stern, *Gold and Iron: Bismarck, Bleichröder, and the Building of the German Empire* (Vintage, 1979), p. 478.

255 *"Lowengreen's"*: "Mock Wedding at the Highland Hotel," *Jewish Criterion*, Aug. 7, 1914.

255 *For some German Jews*: See Adalbert Horawitz, *Richard Wagner und die nationale Idee* (Gutmann, 1874), pp. 18–19; Friedrich Eckstein, *Alte, unnennbare Tage*, p. 195; Anna Stoll Knecht, "Mahler's *Parsifal*," *Wagner Journal* 11:3 (2017), p. 7.

255 *Alfred Pringsheim*: See Egon Voss, ed., *Alfred Pringsheim, der kritische Wagnerianer* (Königshausen & Neumann, 2013). For arrangements, see Pringsheim, *Musikalische Bilder aus R. Wagner's Tristan und Isolde* (Breitkopf und Härtel, 1877).

255 *"No thought of Jewishness"*: TM21, p. 271.

255 *"Blood of the Wälsungs"*: TM2, pp. 463, 461. See also Cristina Herbst's commentary in Hedwig Pringsheim, *Tagebücher*, vol. 4, ed. Herbst (Wallstein, 2015), pp. 39–44, and pp. 135–50 of the

diaries; Hans Rudolf Vaget, *"Wehvolles Erbe": Richard Wagner in Deutschland: Hitler, Knappertsbusch, Mann* (Fischer, 2017), pp. 369–99; Sander Gilman, "Sibling Incest, Madness, and the 'Jews,'" *Social Research* 65:2 (1998), pp. 401–33.

257 *"I am no longer"*: Spitzer, *Verliebte Wagnerianer* (Klinkhardt, 1880), pp. 97–98. For more, see Leon Botstein, "German Jews and Wagner," in WW, p. 158.

257 Die Hose: Sternheim, *Gesammelte Werke*, vol. 2, ed. Fritz Hofmann (Aufbau, 1963), pp. 22, 23. For tears over *Meistersinger*; see Sternheim, *Briefe I: Briefwechsel mit Thea Sternheim, 1904–1906*, ed. Wolfgang Wendler (Luchterhand, 1988), p. 633.

257 *"Worries"*: Arthur Schnitzler, *Tagebücher, 1903–1908* (Verlag der Österreichschen Akademie der Wissenschaften, 1991), p. 237. *Tristan* on pp. 103–106.

257 *"Music for Schnitzler"*: Marc A. Weiner, *Arthur Schnitzler and the Crisis of Musical Culture* (Winter, 1986), p. 16.

257 *"a future full . . . Wherever he went"*: Schnitzler, *Der Weg ins Freie* (Fischer, 1978), pp. 83, 33.

258 *"weary ocean waves"*: Ibid., pp. 292–93.

258 Marc Weiner: See his *Undertones of Insurrection: Music, Politics, and the Social Sphere in the Modern German Narrative* (University of Nebraska Press, 1993), pp. 1–4.

259 *"I am now"*: David Abrahamsen, *The Mind and Death of a Genius* (Columbia UP, 1946), p. 215. For *Meistersinger*, see p. 204.

259 *"leaves behind"*: Otto Weininger, *Über die letzten Dinge* (Braumüller, 1904), p. 87

259 chapter on *"Judentum"*: All quotations from Weininger, *Geschlecht und Charakter: Eine prinzipielle Untersuchung* (Braumüller, 1919), pp. 402–404, except "greatest man," p. 456.

260 *"The devil is"*: Weininger, *Über die letzten Dinge*, p. 183.

260 *"he took his own"*: Henry Picker, *Hitlers Tischgespräche im Führerhauptquartier, 1941–1942*, ed. Percy Ernst Schramm (Seewald, 1965), p. 152.

262 *"O Jews"*: Desmond Stewart, *Theodor Herzl: Artist and Politician: A Biography of the Father of Modern Israel* (Doubleday, 1974), p. 151. For "learn to die," see CWD, Nov. 12, 1880.

262 *"There was a time . . . strong Jews"*: Schnitzler, *Briefe, 1875–1912*, vol. 1, ed. Therese Nickl and Heinrich Schnitzler (Fischer, 1981), pp. 237, 239.

262 *"Wagner-experts"*: Theodor Herzl, "Feuilleton: Pariser Theater," *Neue Freie Presse*, May 14, 1895.

262 In his diaries: Herzl, *Briefe und Tagebücher*, vol. 2, ed. Johannes Wachten and Chaya Harel (Propyläen, 1983), pp. 69, 74.

263 *"Heine says"*: Herzl, "Selbstbiographie," p. 9.

263 Music from Tannhäuser: Erwin Rosenberger, *Herzl as I Remember Him* (Herzl Press, 1959), p. 158, referring to *"Fantasie* from Wagner's *Tannhäuser."*

263 *"the heart against the head"*: Schorske, *Fin-de-Siècle Vienna*, p. 163. See also Steven Beller, "Herzl's *Tannhäuser*: The Redemption of the Artist as Politician," in *Austrians and Jews in the Twentieth Century: From Franz Joseph to Waldheim*, ed. Robert S. Wistrich (St. Martin's, 1992), pp. 41–42, 52–53.

263 *"folk ideal"*: *Stenographisches Protokoll der Verhandlungen des II. Zionisten-Congresses* (Verlag des Vereines Erez Israel, 1898), p. 24. On Herzl and the masculine idea, see Daniel Boyarin, *Unheroic Conduct: The Rise of Heterosexuality and the Invention of the Jewish Man* (University of California Press, 1997), pp. 75–76. On Wagnerian elements in Lilien, see Amos Elon, *Herzl* (Holt, Rinehart and Winston, 1975), p. 259; Milly Heyd, "Lilien and Beardsley: To the Pure All Things Are Pure," *Journal of Jewish Art* 7 (1980), pp. 60–63; Lynne Swarts, "Lilien's Sensual Beauties: Discovering Jewish Orientalism in Ephraim Moses Lilien's Biblical Women," *Nashim* 33 (5779/2018), p. 100.

263 a few positive mentions: Fritz Leinhard, "Der Zionismus," *BB* 18 (1895), p. 331; Adolf Wahrmund, "Rabbinismus und Zionismus," *BB* 21 (1898), p. 310.

264 *Thalia*: Arthur Holitscher, *Amerika heute und morgen: Reiseerlebnisse* (Fischer, 1912), p. 415.

264 Daniela Smolov Levy: See her *"Parsifal* in Yiddish? Why Not?," *Musical Quarterly* 97:2 (2014), pp. 160–61. "Happily the author" comes from Levy's communication to author.

264 Heinrich York-Steiner: Daniel Jütte, "'Mendele Lohengrin' and the Kosher Wagner," in *Gefühlskraftwerke für Patrioten: Wagner und das Musiktheater zwischen Nationalismus und Globalisierung*, ed. Arne Stollberg et al. (Königshausen & Neumann, 2017), pp. 177–91. The story appeared in *Welt* on April 22, April 29, and May 6, 1898.

266 *"free, strong"*: Arthur de Gobineau, *The Inequality of Human Races*, trans. Adrian Collins (Putnam's, 1915), p. 59.

267 *"my first Italian"*: CWD, March 31, 1878. For Weber, see Sept. 1, 1879.

267 *"taking sides"*: CWD, Feb. 27, 1882. Other quotations from July 13, 1879, Oct. 8, 1882, July 21, 1871, Dec. 10 and June 22, 1879.

267 *"sage, controlled"*: Théophile Gautier, *Voyage en Russie*, vol. 1 (Charpentier, 1867), p. 255. For Budapest, see *Illustrirte Zeitung*, Jan. 14, 1854. For more on the Aldridges, see Herbert Marshall and Mildred Stock, *Ira Aldridge: The Negro Tragedian* (Rockcliff, 1958); and Bernth Lindfors, *Ira Aldridge*, 4 vols. (University of Rochester Press, 2011–15).

268 *"Everything thought through"*: Bruno Kaiser, ed., *Der Freiheit eine Gasse: Aus dem Leben und Werk Georg Herweghs* (Volk und Welt, 1948), p. 298. For Keller, see Jakob Baechtold, *Gottfried Kellers Leben: Seine Briefe und Tagebücher*, vol. 2 (Wilhelm Herz, 1894), p. 412.

268 *"Wednesday"*: Othello": RWB9, p. 65. Aldridge performed in Zurich on Nov. 18, 1857, which was a Wednesday.

268 *remarked on it*: James Weldon Johnson, *Black Manhattan* (Da Capo, 1991), pp. 85–86; Langston Hughes, "Ira Aldridge: A Star Who Never Came Home," *The Collected Works of Langston Hughes*, vol. 12, ed. Dolan Hubbard (University of Missouri Press, 2001), p. 31.

268 *Three of the actor's children*: Marshall and Stock, *Ira Aldridge*, pp. 295–309. On Luranah, see Alex Ross, "Othello's Daughter," *New Yorker*, July 29, 2013. For the casting, see *Le Ménestrel*, Jan. 19, 1896, p. 24.

268 *"strong-willed, dominating"*: Marshall and Stock, *Ira Aldridge*, p. 296.

268 *"vigorous masculinity"*: Review by "R. D." [Raymond Duval-Den'lex], *Guide musical*, Nov. 25, 1900. For various appearances, see *Wiener Zeitung*, March 28, 1890; *Musikalisches Wochenblatt*, Nov. 13, 1890; *Neue Zeitschrift für Musik*, April 22, 1891.

268 *"strong, dark-colored"*: Johannes Flach, "Theater und Musik: Konzert Luranah Aldridge," *Hamburger Anzeiger*, Oct. 29, 1891, in Aldridge Collection, Charles Deering McCormick Special Library of Collections, Northwestern University.

268 *"Do you want to hear"*: Charles Gounod to Augustus Harris, Aug. 16, 1892, Aldridge Collection.

268 *Wagner figured*: Program for Grand Wagner Concert from Aldridge Collection; John Snelson, *The Ring: An Illustrated History of Wagner's "Ring" at the Royal Opera House* (Oberon Books, 2006), pp. 164–66. Litvinne: photo marked "Bruxelles, 1901," Aldridge Collection.

269 *Cosima apparently invited*: Marshall and Stock, *Ira Aldridge*, p. 296, evidently drawing on interviews with Amanda Aldridge.

269 *"To dear Miss Aldridge"*: Eva Wagner to Luranah Aldridge, Aldridge Collection. On the Hôtel Kurhaus, see Lothar Schnabel, "Rupprechtstegen und sein ehemaliges Kurhotel," *Altnürnberger Landschaft* 27 (1978), pp. 8–13.

269 *"Mama and we"*: Eva Wagner to Luranah Aldridge, May 30, 1896, Aldridge Collection.

269 *"A name that may"*: Friedrich Wild, ed., *Bayreuth 1896: Praktisches Handbuch für Festspielbesucher* (Constantin Wilds, 1896), p. 17.

270 *"My dear Miss Aldridge"*: Cosima Wagner to Luranah Aldridge, May 24, 1897, Aldridge Collection. For Cosima's command of English, see Allen C. Hinckley, "An American Singer at Bayreuth," *Munsey's Magazine* 43:3 (1910), p. 406. Oliver Hilmes believes that, signature aside, the letter is not in Cosima's own hand, nor is it in Eva's; it was probably dictated to an unknown person (communication to author).

270 *"Schmerzen"*: Program for recital of June 7, 1913, Aldridge Collection. For her death, see a copy of the death certificate dated April 30, 1954, Aldridge Collection.

271 *"The Negroes have surprised me"*: Paul Pretzsch, ed., *Cosima Wagner und Houston Stewart Chamberlain im Briefwechsel, 1888–1908* (Reclam, 1934), p. 451.

271 *"She is surely"*: W. E. B. Du Bois to Amanda Aldridge, March 9, 1933, W. E. B. Du Bois Papers, Special Collections and University Archives, University of Massachusetts Amherst Libraries. For correspondence, see Aldridge to Du Bois, Oct. 4, 1923; Aldridge to Du Bois, Aug. 27, 1921; and Du Bois to Aldridge, June 1, 1908, all in the Du Bois Papers. On Du Bois and the Aldridges, see Jeffrey Green, *Black Edwardians: Black People in Britain, 1901–1914* (Frank Cass, 1998), p. 249; for Gautier, see "Gautier on Aldridge," Du Bois Papers.

272 *Kwame Anthony Appiah*: See his "Ethics in a World of Strangers: W. E. B. Du Bois and the Spirit of Cosmopolitanism," *Berlin Journal* 11 (2005), pp. 24, 25; and *Lines of Descent: W. E. B. Du Bois and the Emergence of Identity* (Harvard UP, 2014), pp. 45–82.

272 *Paul Gilroy*: See his *The Black Atlantic: Modernity and Double Consciousness* (Verso, 1993), esp. pp. 111–45.

272 *"master of masters"*: "What the Colored People Are Doing," *Nashville American*, Jan. 23, 1900. On Freeman, see Kira Thurman, "Wagnerian Dreams, Grandiose Visions: Lawrence Freeman's *Voodoo* at the Miller Theater at Columbia University," *Opera Quarterly* 32:2–3 (2016), pp. 226–32; and David J. Gutkin, "The Modernities of H. Lawrence Freeman," *Journal of the American Musicological Society* 72:3 (2019), pp. 719–79.

272 *"Afro-Wagnerism"*: Samuel Dwinell, "Afro-Wagnerism in Imperial London: Samuel Coleridge-Taylor's 'Thelma' and the Endless Melody of Interracial Dreams," talk given at the *Current Musicology* 50th Anniversary Conference, Columbia University, March 29, 2015.

272 *point of reference*: For black colleges, see Kira Thurman, *A History of Black Musicians in Germany and Austria, 1870–1961: Race, Performance, and Reception* (Ph.D. diss., University of Rochester, 2013), p. 30. For Alain Locke, see his "The New Negro," in *The New Negro*, ed. Locke (Touchstone, 1997), p. 3. For Hughes, see Stanley J. Kunitz and Howard Haycraft, eds., *Twentieth-Century Authors: A Biographical Dictionary of Modern Literature* (Wilson, 1942), p. 684. For Ralph Ellison, see his *Shadow and Act* (Random House, 1964), pp. 12, 116–17; and Maryemma Graham and Amritjit Singh, eds., *Conversations with Ralph Ellison* (University of Mississippi Press, 1995), p. 181. For King, see *The Papers of Martin Luther King, Jr.*, vol. 6, ed. Clayborne Carson et al. (University of California Press, 2007), p. 297; for bel canto, James M. Washington, ed., *A Testament of Hope: The Essential Writings and Speeches of Martin Luther King, Jr.* (HarperCollins, 1990), p. 418.

273 *"bickering peoples"*: David Levering Lewis, *W. E. B. Du Bois: Biography of a Race, 1868–1919* (Holt, 1993), pp. 76–77.

273 *"one of the sorrows"*: Du Bois, "A Woman," dated May 22, 1893, W. E. B. Du Bois Papers. See also Lewis, *W. E. B. Du Bois: Biography of a Race*, p. 129; and Du Bois, *The Autobiography of W. E. B. Du Bois: A Soliloquy on Viewing My Life from the Last Decade of Its First Century* (International Publishers, 1968), p. 156.

273 *"I had a very, very interesting"*: Kenneth Barkin, "Introduction: Germany on His Mind: 'Das Neue Vaterland,'" *Journal of African American History* 91:4 (2006), p. 448, quoting from William Ingersoll's oral history.

273 *"We are Negroes"*: Du Bois: *Writings*, p. 822; Lewis, *W. E. B. Du Bois: Biography of a Race*, pp. 161–74. For his later reconsideration of the Kaiserreich, see Du Bois, *Autobiography*, pp. 106, 154–55, 169, 175.

273 *his colleagues wondered*: David Levering Lewis, *W. E. B. Du Bois: The Fight for Equality and the American Century, 1919–1963* (Holt, 2000), pp. 388–89; Du Bois to Wilbur K. Thomas, Oct. 17, 1934, Nina Du Bois to W. E. B. Du Bois, Sept. 2, 1936, Du Bois Papers.

274 *"surpasses in vindictive . . . I have not suffered"*: Du Bois, *Newspaper Columns*, vol. 1, pp. 143, 148.

274 *"Men need places"*: Ibid., pp. 124–26. Other quotations on pp. 129–31.

274 *"He thought how"*: Du Bois, *Worlds of Color* (Mainstream, 1961), p. 51.

274 *Tom-Tom*: See Shirley Graham Du Bois Papers, Schlesinger Library, Radcliffe Institute, Harvard University; Sarah Schmalenberger, "Debuting Her Political Voice: The Lost Opera of Shirley Graham," *Black Music Research Journal* 26:1 (2006), pp. 39–87; Bettina Aptheker, "The Passion and Pageantry of Shirley Graham's Opera Tom-Tom," *Souls* 18:2–4 (2016), pp. 263–70.

275 *"Now, that is something"*: Shirley Graham to W. E. B. Du Bois, Jan. 11, 1935, Du Bois Papers. See also Gerald Horne, *Race Woman: The Lives of Shirley Graham Du Bois* (New York UP, 2000), p. 125.

275 Deep Rivers: A copy of the text, published in *Arts Quarterly* in Sept. 1939, was kindly supplied to the author by Lucy Caplan.

275 *"fetishized black"*: Paul Allen Anderson, *Deep River: Music and Memory in Harlem Renaissance Thought* (Duke UP, 2001), p. 49. See also Du Bois, *Newspaper Columns*, vol. 1, p. 114.

275 *"nascent practice"*: Dwinell, "Afro-Wagnerism in Imperial London."

276 *Samuel Delany*: See his "*A Lost Lady* and Modernism, a Novelist's Overview," *Critical Inquiry* 41:3 (2015), pp. 573–95; and "Wagner/Artaud: A Play of 19th and 20th Century Critical Fictions," *Longer Views* (Wesleyan UP, 1996), pp. 1–86.

276 *Charlie Parker*: See "Cool Blues," Sept. 22, 1953,

at Storyville, Boston, and two takes of "Chi Chi," Aug. 4, 1953, in New York.

276 *"go back to Africa"*: Ijoma Mangold, *Das deutsche Krokodil: Meine Geschichte* (Rowohlt, 2017), p. 287.

7. VENUSBERG: FEMINIST AND GAY WAGNER

277 *"Ride of the Walküre"*: Aldred Scott Warthin, "Some Physiologic Effects of Music in Hypnotized Subjects," *Medical News* 65:4 (1894), pp. 89–92.

278 *incite hysteria in women*: Frank Parsons Norbury, "Nervousness in Young Women: Its Mechanism, and Some of Its Causes," *Medical Fortnightly* 9:4 (1896), p. 112; James Kennaway, *Bad Vibrations: The History of the Idea of Music as a Cause of Disease* (Ashgate, 2012), p. 73.

278 *"Music can vicariously"*: Otto Weininger, *Eros und Psyche: Studien und Briefe, 1899–1902*, ed. Hannelore Rodlauer (Verlag der Österreichischen Akademie der Wissenschaften, 1990), p. 148. For Peter Altenberg, see his *Prodromos* (Fischer, 1906), p. 90; for Bloy, Jennifer Birkett, *The Sins of the Fathers: Decadence in France 1870–1914* (Quartet, 1986), p. 152; for Joyce, Oscar Schwarz to Richard Ellmann, Aug. 16, 1955, Richard Ellmann Papers, University of Tulsa Special Collections, p. 3.

278 *"a sickness that required"*: Laurence Dreyfus, *Wagner and the Erotic Impulse* (Harvard UP, 2010), p. 117.

279 *"first and last . . . just look"*: Nietzsche, *Jenseits von Gut und Böse*, §239; *Fall Wagner*, §8.

279 *Daniel Pick*: See his *Faces of Degeneration: A European Disorder, c. 1848–c. 1918* (Cambridge UP, 1989), pp. 37–73; also Barbara Spackman, *Decadent Genealogies: The Rhetoric of Sickness from Baudelaire to D'Annunzio* (Cornell UP, 1989).

279 *"moral degeneration"*: Theodor Puschmann, *Richard Wagner: Eine psychiatrische Studie* (Behr, 1873), p. 59.

279 *"tendency to stupid puns"*: Nordau, *Entartung*, vol. 1, pp. 304–78, esp. 305; Thomas S. Grey, "Wagner the Degenerate: Fin de Siècle Cultural 'Pathology' and the Anxiety of Modernism," *Nineteenth-Century Studies* 16 (2002), pp. 73–92.

280 *"Are you peculiarly fond"*: Xavier Mayne, *The Intersexes: A History of Similisexualism as a Problem in Social Life* (privately printed, 1908), p. 633.

280 *"puritanical hypocrisy"*: RWSS1, p. 21.

281 *"The most orgastic"*: Herbert Marcuse, *Eros and Civilization: A Philosophical Inquiry into Freud* (Beacon, 1966), p. 119.

281 *"The father is there"*: CWD, Aug. 8, 1869. For a revealing account of Wagner's first marriage, see Eva Rieger, *Minna und Richard Wagner: Stationen einer Liebe* (Artemis & Winkler, 2003).

282 *a form of cross-dressing*: Dreyfus, *Wagner and the Erotic Impulse*, pp. 147–50.

282 *"This trimming"*: RWL, p. 713.

282 *"create a furor"*: Daniel Spitzer, "Briefe Richard Wagner's an eine Putzmacherin," *Neue Freie Presse,* June 16, 1877, p. 4.

282 *"Frou-Frou Wagner"*: Storck, *Musik und Musiker in Karikatur und Satire,* p. 407. Originally in *Der Floh,* 1877.

282 *"When R. now talks"*: CWD, June 22–23, 1877.

283 *"androgynous being"*: Nattiez, *Wagner Androgyne,* p. 40.

283 *"so that the effect"*: CWD, June 27, 1880.

283 *"deadly pale"*: Louise Otto, *Mein Lebensgang: Gedichte aus fünf Jahrzehnten* (Moritz Schäfer, 1093), p. 171. For Wagner declining, see RWL, pp. 123–24. Otto is not named, but she must be the "verehrte Dichterin" in question. See also Johanna Ludwig and Rita Jorek, *Louise Otto-Peters: Ihr literarisches und publizistisches Werk* (Leipziger Universitätsverlag, 1995), p. 37; and Laurie McManus, "Feminist Revolutionary Music Criticism and Wagner Reception: The Case of Louise Otto," *19th-Century Music* 37:3 (2014), pp. 161–87.

283 *"My proud freedom is all gone"*: Otto, "Die Nibelungen, Oper in fünf Acten" (last part), *Neue Zeitschrift für Musik,* Dec. 5, 1845, p. 182. For "In Brunhilde," see Otto, *Die Nibelungen* (Hofmeister, 1852), p. 4.

283 *their voices are exalted*: Catherine Clément, *Opera, or the Undoing of Women,* trans. Betsy Wing (University of Minnesota Press, 1988), p. 53.

284 *"typically Wagnerian . . . everything that is actively"*: Eva Rieger, *Richard Wagner's Women,* trans. Chris Walton (Boydell, 2011), pp. 35, 54.

284 *"murderous fanaticism"*: RWB4, pp. 273–74.

284 *"deeper and far more complicated"*: Nila Parly, *Vocal Victories: Wagner's Female Characters from Senta to Kundry* (Museum Tusculanum Press, 2011), p. 55.

284 *"full essence of love"*: RWSS4, p. 301.

285 *"self-annihilation"*: Ibid., p. 63.

285 *"intoxication or madness"*: Carolyn Abbate, *Unsung Voices: Opera and Musical Narrative in the Nineteenth Century* (Princeton UP, 1991), pp. 248–49. For the Valkyrie motif, see Bailey, "Wagner's Musical Sketches for *Siegfrieds Tod,*" pp. 464–69.

286 *Emma Sutton*: See her *Aubrey Beardsley and British Wagnerism in the 1890s* (Oxford UP, 2002), p. 100.

286 *"writhe on her chair"*: Weiner, *Undertones of Insurrection,* p. 14.

287 *"I found myself"*: Arnold Bennett, *Sacred and Profane Love* (Tauchnitz, 1906), p. 59.

287 *"You like Wagner"*: Eugène Brieux, *Les Trois Filles de M. Dupont* (Stock, 1899), pp. 51, 56–57.

288 *"The handsome Erik"*: Pierre Louÿs, "Le Trophée des vulves légendaires," *L'Œuvre érotique,* ed. Jean-Paul Goujon (Sortilèges, 1994), p. 779: "Le bel Erik est trop faible, ô Vierge! / Tu l'avalerais d'un coup de con; / Tu veux qu'on ait les reins durs,

et qu'on / Bande en avant dix pouces de verge." For "the greatest man," see Henri Borgeaud, ed., *Correspondance de Claude Debussy et Pierre Louÿs (1893–1904)* (Corti, 1945), p. 34.

288 *"the elemental untrammeled"*: Emma Goldman, "Dear Dr. Hirschfeld," 1923 draft of a letter to be published in Magnus Hirschfeld's *Jahrbuch für sexuelle Zwischenstufen,* Emma Goldman Papers, International Institute of Social History, search .iisg.amsterdam. Goldman is contesting the description of the French anarchist Louise Michel as a lesbian.

288 *"Utterly unsettled . . . Isa & Edith"*: Daniel Cavicchi, *Listening and Longing: Music Lovers in the Age of Barnum* (Wesleyan UP, 2011), pp. 109, 118.

288 *"the ratio of tourists"*: Joe Mitchell Chapple, "The Wagner Festival at Bayreuth," *National Magazine* 7:1 (1897), p. 14. On female tourists from the Nordic countries, see Hannu Salmi, *Wagner and Wagnerism in Nineteenth-Century Sweden, Finland, and the Baltic Provinces: Reception, Enthusiasm, Cult* (University of Rochester Press, 2005), pp. 189–90.

289 *"plain and unvarnished"*: R. Milner Barry, *Bayreuth and Franconian Switzerland* (Swan Sonnenschein, 1887), p. 2.

289 *Goldener Anker*: Fremdenlisten, Aug. 1, 1912. A few of the names were garbled in transmission; "Miss Sirinne" probably hailed from the prominent Sirrine family of Greenville, South Carolina.

289 *"My own impression"*: Lisle March-Phillipps and Bertram Christian, eds., *Some Hawarden Letters, 1878–1913, Written to Mrs. Drew (Miss Mary Gladstone), Before and After Her Marriage* (Dodd Mead, 1918), p. 233.

290 *"secret pact"*: Horowitz, *Wagner Nights,* p. 216.

290 *"A clamorous sea"*: Ella Wheeler Wilcox, "The Prelude to 'Tristan und Isolde,'" *Munsey's* 12:3 (1894), p. 288.

290 *"only place where men and women"*: "Maude Adams Makes Pilgrimage to Ireland," *Louisville Courier-Journal,* July 10, 1910.

290 *suffragist pageants*: "Suffragette Parade Attracted Thousands," *Lead Daily Call,* March 3, 1913; "Suffragists' Big Night," *New York Times,* April 23, 1913; "Roosevelt Centre of Suffrage Host," *New York Times,* May 3, 1913.

291 *Charlotte Teller*: See her *The Cage* (Appleton, 1907), p. 98.

291 *Hamlin Garland*: See his *The Rose of Dutcher's Coolly* (Harper, 1899), pp. 235–36, 333.

292 *"Such crudeness"*: Applegate, *Necessity of Music,* p. 244; Huch on p. 250.

292 *Elena Lindholm Narvdez*: See her "The Valkyrie in a Bikini: The Nordic Woman as Progressive Media Icon in Spain, 1891–1975," in *Communicating the North: Media Structures and Images in the Making of the Nordic Region,* ed. Jonas Harvard and Peter Stadius (Routledge, 2016), pp. 206–207.

292 *"as seen by a woman in love"*: Colette, *Claudine s'en va* (1903), p. 157. Other quotations on pp. 173, 205, 206, 143–44, 315.

293 *"To confirm my faith"*: Colette, *Claudine à Paris*, pp. 171–72. Compare Georges Eekhoud, *Escal-Vigor* (Société du Mercure de France, 1899), p. 202. The aside about Eekhoud is omitted in *The Complete Claudine*, trans. Antonia White (Farrar, Straus and Giroux, 2001).

294 *"sexual nature opposed"*: Gladius furens [Karl Heinrich Ulrichs], *Das Naturräthsel der Urningsliebe und der Irrthum als Gesetzgeber: Eine Provocation an den deutschen Juristentag* (Württenberger, 1868), p. 4. See also Robert Beachy, *Gay Berlin: Birthplace of a Modern Identity* (Knopf, 2014), pp. 3–30.

295 *"Expel nature"*: Schopenhauer, *The World as Will and Representation*, vol. 2, trans. E. F. J. Payne (Dover, 1966), p. 562. For Ulrichs quoting Schopenhauer, see Hubert Kennedy, *Karl Heinrich Ulrichs: Pioneer of the Modern Gay Movement* (Peremptory Publications, 2002), p. 66.

295 *"This love"*: RWSS3, pp. 134–35.

295 *"my adored"*: Barry Millington, *The Sorcerer of Bayreuth: Richard Wagner, His Work and His World* (Oxford UP, 2012), p. 163.

295 *"I was so gripped"*: Dreyfus, *Wagner and the Erotic Impulse*, p. 200.

295 *"It is something"*: CWD, Feb. 25, 1881.

295–96 *inducing giggles*: On *Parsifal*'s sexual imagery, see Richard D. Mohr, *Gay Ideas: Outing and Other Controversies* (Beacon, 1992), pp. 135–39; and Linda Hutcheon and Michael Hutcheon, *Opera: Desire, Disease, Death* (University of Nebraska Press, 1996), pp. 61–93.

296 *"I much prefer Siegfried"*: Clyde Fitch, *The Smart Set: Correspondence & Conversations* (Stone, 1897), p. 120.

296 *"the demon of hidden sin"*: Wagner, *Das braune Buch*, pp. 62, 54.

297 *"That is a terrible secret"*: RWL, p. 664.

297 *"Strong is the magic"*: ENRW3, pp. 245–46; Ludwig II, *Tagebuch-Aufzeichnungen von Ludwig II., König von Bayern*, ed. Edir Grein (Quaderer, 1925), p. 23. Compare *Das braune Buch*, p. 70.

297 *"Lolo Montez"*: Josefa Dürck-Kaulbach, ed., *Erinnerungen an Wilhelm von Kaulbach und sein Haus* (Delphin, 1918), p. 343; Eduard Hanslick, *Die moderne Oper*, vol. 5 (Allgemeiner Verein für Deutsche Literatur, 1889), p. 278.

297 *Albert Moll*: Rainer Herrn, "Ein historischer Urning: Ludwig II. von Bayern im psychiatrisch-sexualwissenschaftlichen Diskurs und in der Homosexuellenbewegung den frühen 20. Jahrhunderts," in *"Ein Bild von einem Mann": Ludwig II. von Bayern, Konstruktion und Rezeption eines Mythos*, ed. Katharina Sykora (Campus, 2004), pp. 48–52.

297 *"virgin king"*: Verlaine, *Œuvres poétiques complètes* (Gallimard, 1962), p. 1405. The last phrase could be interpreted either as "only for men" or as "for the solitary man." On Verlaine and gay themes, see

297 *"beautiful hermaphrodite"*: Robert de Montesquiou, *Les Chauves-souris: Clairs-obscurs* (Richard, 1907), pp. 258, 266.

298 *"Seeking young bicyclist"*: Oskar Panizza, "Bayreuth und die Homosexualität: Eine Erwägung," *Gesellschaft* 11 (1895), pp. 88–92.

298 *"feminized"*: Huneker, "Bayreuth," *Musical Courier*, Aug. 20, 1896, p. 104. For "pert and primping," see Peretti, "Democratic Leitmotivs," p. 33.

299 *"he was seen"*: Henry Gauthier-Villars, "Bayreuth et la homosexualité," *Revue blanche*, March 1, 1896. Gauthier-Villars also claimed that Ludwig was an "unbridled onanist but not at all a pederast."

299 *"stupid boy"*: Peter D. G. Brown, *Oskar Panizza and "The Love Council": A History of the Scandalous Play on Stage and in Court, with the Complete Text in English and a Biography of the Author* (McFarland, 2010), pp. 108–109. For "You in Germany," see Panizza, *Parisjana: Deutsche Verse aus Paris* (Zürcher Diskussionen, 1899), p. 32–33.

299 *"In general, my whole"*: Richard von Krafft-Ebing, *Psychopathia sexualis*, trans. Charles Gilbert Chaddock (F. A. Davis, 1894), p. 291.

300 *"popular gathering place"*: Magnus Hirschfeld, *Die Homosexualität des Mannes und des Weibes* (Marcus, 1914), p. 689; ad on p. 695. For his attendance at Bayreuth, see Fremdenlisten, 1911.

300 *Edward Carpenter*: See his *Homogenic Love, and Its Place in a Free Society* (Labour Press Society Limited, 1894), pp. 38–40. Carpenter included both the *Männerliebe* passage and the Ludwig letters in his book *Iolaus: An Anthology of Friendship* (Swan Sonnenschein, 1902), pp. 153–57.

300 *Sappho and Socrates*: Th. Ramien [Magnus Hirschfeld], *Sappho und Sokrates oder Wie erklärt sich die Liebe der Männer und Frauen zu Personen des eigenen Geschlechts?* (Spohr, 1896), pp. 25–26.

300 *"Heaven is descending"*: "Zeitungsmitteilungen," *Jahrbuch für sexuelle Zwischenstufen* 2 (Spohr, 1900), p. 476. See also "Briefe König Ludwigs II. von Bayern an Richard Wagner," *Die Wage* 2:11 (1899), p. 168.

300 *Hanns Fuchs*: See his *Richard Wagner und die Homosexualität* (Barsdorf, 1903), pp. 270, 261, 269, and "Parsifal and Eroticism in Wagner's Music," trans. John Urang, *Opera Quarterly* 22:2 (2006), pp. 334–44.

301 *Mitchell Morris*: See his "Tristan Wounds: On Homosexual Wagnerians at the Fin-de-Siècle," in *Queer Episodes in Music and Modern Identity*, ed. Sophie Fuller and Lloyd Whitesell (University of Illinois Press, 2002), pp. 283–89.

301 *"deepest poetry"*: Weininger, *Geschlecht und Charakter*, p. 456.

301 *"the transsexual and the sexual"*: Weininger, *Über die letzten Dinge*, p. 90; also p. 45.

302 *"feminine element"*: Hirschfeld, *Die Transvestiten: Eine Untersuchung über den erotischen Verkleidungstrieb* (Pulvermacher, 1910), pp. 218–19. See also "Die Bibliographie der Homosexualität für das Jahr 1899," *Jahrbuch für sexuelle Zwischenstufen* 2 (Spohr, 1900), p. 377.

302–303 *"It is all metaphysics . . . commit any 'follies'"*: TM21, p. 160.

303 *"The teachers tolerated it"*: *Buddenbrooks*, pp. 618–19, 636–37; TM1, pp. 793, 820–21.

303 *"The music sounded light"*: Hermann Hesse, *Peter Camenzind*, trans. Michael Roloff (Picador, 2003), p. 52.

303 *"true German art . . . hysterical woman"*: Catulle Mendès, *Le Roi vierge* (Dentu, 1881), pp. 301, 299–300.

304 *Mikhail Kuzmin*: See his *Wings*, trans. Hugh Aplin (Hesperus, 2007), pp. 75, 89–90.

304 *"I like Wagner's . . . in his box"*: Wilde, *The Picture of Dorian Gray: An Annotated, Uncensored Edition*, ed. Nicholas Frankel (Harvard UP, 2011), pp. 113, 196.

304 *"Sometimes, when I listen"*: Wilde, "The Critic as Artist," *The Complete Works of Oscar Wilde*, vol. 4: *Criticism*, ed. Josephine M. Guy (Oxford UP, 2007), p. 158.

305 *"In his elaborately folded"*: Sutton, *Aubrey Beardsley*, pp. 36–37.

306 *"feverish insistent . . . As the boy"*: Aubrey Beardsley, *Under the Hill*, ed. John Glassco (Grove Press, 1959), pp. 60–62.

306 *"transparent hands"*: Gleeson White, "Aubrey Beardsley: In Memoriam," *International Studio* 4 (1898), p. 260.

307 *Victor Chan*: See his "Aubrey Beardsley's Frontispiece to 'The Comedy of the Rhinegold,'" *Arts Magazine* 57 (1983), p. 94.

307 *"unsung history"*: Terry Castle, *The Apparitional Lesbian: Female Homosexuality and Modern Culture* (Columbia UP, 1993), p. 203.

307 *"Captivated by the music"*: Anna Livia, ed. and trans., *A Perilous Advantage: The Best of Natalie Clifford Barney* (New Victoria, 1992), p. 42. See also Suzanne Rodriguez, *Wild Heart: A Life—Natalie Clifford Barney and the Decadence of Literary Paris* (Ecco, 2003), pp. 164–65.

307 *"the most glorious"*: Horowitz, *Wagner Nights*, p. 227. See also Helen Lefkowitz Horowitz, *The Power and Passion of M. Carey Thomas* (University of Illinois Press, 1999), pp. 215–16.

307 *"I cannot let you go"*: Michael Field, *The Tragedy of Pardon: Diane* (Sidgwick and Jackson, 1911), p. 62.

308 *"that seemed to scale"*: Gertrude Stein, *Writings, 1903–1932* (Library of America, 1998), p. 39. For Stein's love for *Tristan* in her youth, see Kimberly Rose Fairbrother Canton, *The Operatic Imperative in Anglo-American Literary Modernism: Pound, Stein, and Woolf* (Ph.D. diss., University of Toronto, 2009), p. 141 (1913 letter to Mabel Dodge Luhan).

308 *"All excess"*: Richard Ellmann, *Oscar Wilde* (Vintage, 1988), p. 321.

308 *Italian destinations*: See Robert Aldrich, *The Seduction of the Mediterranean: Writing, Art, and Homosexual Fantasy* (Routledge, 1993).

308 *"knew Venice like a book"*: Hughes, *The Big Sea* (Hill and Wang, 1993), p. 189. See also Arnold Rampersad, *The Life of Langston Hughes*, vol. 1 (Oxford UP, 1986), p. 93; and Jeffrey C. Stewart, *The New Negro: The Life of Alain Locke* (Oxford UP, 2018), pp. 439–43.

309 *"Attentive or inattentive"*: Vernon Lee, "The Religious and Moral Status of Wagner," *Fortnightly Review* 89 (1911), pp. 877–80.

309 *"A Wicked Voice"*: Lee, *Hauntings: Fantastic Stories* (John Lane, 1906), pp. 195–237.

310 *"persecutes Wagner"*: Carlo Caballero, "'A Wicked Voice': On Vernon Lee, Wagner, and the Effects of Music," *Victorian Studies* 35:4 (1992), p. 401.

310 *"I did not avail"*: Leon Edel, ed., *The Letters of Henry James*, vol. 2 (Belknap Press, 1975), pp. 283, 287–88. See also Fred Kaplan, *Henry James: The Imagination of Genius: A Biography* (Morrow, 1992), pp. 171–72; and Emma Sutton, "Too Close for Comfort: Henry James, Richard Wagner, and *The Sacred Fount*," *Nineteenth-Century Music Review* 6:2 (2009), pp. 3–17.

310 *"Did Bayreuth come off?"*: Henry James, *Letters to Isabella Stewart Gardner*, ed. Rosella Mamoli Zorzi (Pushkin Press, 2009), p. 191. For Cram, see Douglass Shand-Tucci, *Ralph Adams Cram: Life and Architecture*, vol. 1 (University of Massachusetts Press, 1995), p. 60.

310 *"held down as by a hand"*: Henry James, *The Finer Grain* (Scribner, 1910), pp. 10–12.

311 *"great sustained sea-light"*: James, *Novels 1901–1902: The Sacred Fount, The Wings of the Dove* (Library of America, 2006), p. 291. Other quotations on pp. 591, 261, 565, 689.

311 *homosexual atmosphere*: Vaget, *Seelenzauber*, pp. 307–308. "Siehst du, Kind, ich liebe dich" appeared in the January 1895 issue of *Die Gesellschaft*.

311 *"in terms of ambience"*: TM21, pp. 427–28.

312 *"Auseinandersetzung mit Wagner"*: Mann's essay appeared in *Der Merker* 2:19 (1911), pp. 21–23. For the disclaimer, see "Nachschrift der Redaktion," p. 23.

312 *"very charming"*: Katia Mann, *Meine ungeschriebenen Memoiren*, ed. Elisabeth Plessen and Michael Mann (Fischer, 1983), p. 71.

312 *"Obviously someone"*: Mann, *Tagebücher, 1918–1921*, ed. Peter de Mendelssohn (Fischer, 1979), p. 11. See also Frederic Spotts, *Cursed Legacy: The Tragic Life of Klaus Mann* (Yale UP, 2016), pp. 18–19.

312 *"nothing is invented"*: Mann, *Essays*, vol. 3: *Ein Appell an die Vernunft*, ed. Hermann Kurzke and Stephen Stachorski (Fischer, 1994), p. 202.

313 *"The writer's joy"*: TM2, pp. 555–56.

314 *"The weather had suddenly"*: Wagner, *Mein Leben*, ed. Martin Gregor-Dellin (List, 1969), p. 586.

314 *"Venice pulls me in"*: Georg von Laubmann and Ludwig von Scheffler, eds., *Die Tagebücher des Grafen August von Platen*, vol. 2 (Cotta, 1900), p. 684. Other Platen quotations from *Gedichte*, ed. Carl Fischer (Schneider, 1958), pp. 167, 43.

315 *"most secret lust"*: TM2, p. 555.

315 *"imperious, surveying"*: TM2, p. 503.

315 *"black cloth"*: Raymond Furness, *Wagner and Literature* (St. Martin's, 1982), p. 47; TM2, p. 590.

315 *"Since I have never"*: RWL, pp. 323–24.

315 *"To him it was"*: TM2, p. 592. For more, see William Kinderman, "The Motif of the Gaze (*Blick*) in Thomas Mann's *Der Tod in Venedig* and Wagner's *Tristan und Isolde*," *German Studies Review* 41:2 (2018), pp. 313–33.

316 *associated with gay desire*: TM21, p. 160.

316 *"Pederasty is made"*: Ehrhard Bahr, *Thomas Mann, "Der Tod in Venedig": Erläuterungen und Dokumente* (Reclam, 1991), p. 141.

316 *"I chose homosexual"*: Volkmar Hansen und Gert Heine, eds., *Frage und Antwort: Interviews mit Thomas Mann, 1909–1955* (Knaus, 1983), p. 36.

316 *Kurt Hiller*: See his "Wo bleibt der homoerotische Roman?," reprinted in Jules Siber, *Seelenwanderung* (Männerschwarm, 2011), p. 155.

316 *"The degree and kind"*: Nietzsche, *Jenseits*, §75. On Nietzsche and sublimation, see Luke Phillips, "Sublimation and the Übermensch," *Journal of Nietzsche Studies* 46:3 (2015), pp. 349–66.

316 *Sexual love is at the core*: RWL, p. 303.

317 *"very peculiar intuitive affinity"*: TMW, p. 20. For Magee, see *Aspects of Wagner*, p. 36; for Thomas S. Grey and Adrian Daub, "Wagner After Freud: Stages of Analysis," *Opera Quarterly* 31:1–2 (2015), p. 128; for Patrick Süskind, *Der Kontrabaß* (Diogenes, 1984), p. 20, translation by Leo Carey.

317 *"real ideas are set"*: Sigmund Freud, *Aus den Anfängen der Psychoanalyse: Briefe an Wilhelm Fliess, Abhandlungen und Notizen aus den Jahren 1887–1902* (Imago, 1950), p. 253. The Hofoper presented *Meistersinger* on Nov. 23 and Dec. 12, 1897.

318 *quote lines from memory*: Freud, *Studienausgabe*, vol. 2, p. 293: "Dazwischen Tannhäuser: Weil du von böser Lust beseelt" (should be "Hast du so böse Lust geteilt"); Freud and Carl Jung, *Briefwechsel*, ed. William McGuire and Wolfgang Sauerländer (Fischer, 1974), p. 206: "Mein Vater zeugte mich und starb" (should be "Da er mich zeugt' und starb").

318 *a kind of repression*: Grey and Daub, "Wagner After Freud," p. 122.

318 *"Where they love . . . renunciation and sorrow"*: Sigmund Freud, *Beiträge zur Psychologie des Liebeslebens* (Internationaler Psychoanalytischer Verlag, 1924), pp. 19, 28.

318 *Many of Freud's colleagues*: Otto Rank, *Die Lohengrinsage: Ein Beitrag zu ihrer Motivgestaltung*

und Deutung (Deuticke, 1911), p. 138; Rank, *Das Inzest-Motiv in Dichtung und Sage: Grundzüge einer Psychologie des dichterischen Schaffens* (Deuticke, 1912), pp. 639–48; Max Graf, *Richard Wagner im "Fliegenden Holländer": Ein Beitrag zur Psychologie künstlerischen Schaffens* (Kraus, 1970). For more, see Isolde Vetter, "Wagner in the History of Psychology," in *Wagner Handbook*, ed. Ulrich Müller and Peter Wapnewski, trans. John Deathridge (Harvard UP, 1992), pp. 118–55.

319 *Carl Jung*: See his *Symbols of Transformation: An Analysis of the Prelude to a Case of Schizophrenia*, trans. R. F. C. Hull (Princeton UP, 1976), p. 361; Nattiez, *Wagner Androgyne*, p. 222.

320 *"What distinguishes Wagner"*: Aldo Carotenuto, *A Secret Symmetry: Sabina Spielrein Between Jung and Freud*, trans. Arno Pomerans et al. (Pantheon, 1982), p. 100; "planted the demon," p. 107, "Aoles," pp. 86–87. See also Sabine Richebächer, *Sabina Spielrein: Eine fast grausame Liebe zur Wissenschaft* (BTB, 2008), pp. 139–41; and John Launer, *Sex Versus Survival: The Life and Ideas of Sabina Spielrein* (Overlook Duckworth, 2014), pp. 97–98.

320 *Freud admitted*: See his *Jenseits des Lustprinzips* (Internationaler Psychoanalytischer Verlag, 1920), p. 54.

320 *figurative, spiritual destruction*: On this point, see Spielrein, "Unedited Extracts from a Diary," trans. Pramila Bennett and Barbara Wharton, in *Sabina Spielrein: Forgotten Pioneer of Psychoanalysis*, ed. Coline Covington and Barbara Wharton (Brunner-Routledge, 2003), p. 21.

320 *"With Wagner, death"*: Spielrein, "Die Destruktion als Ursache des Werdens," *Jahrbuch für Psychoanalytische und psychopathologische Forschungen* 4:1 (1912), p. 495; *Untergang* on p. 503.

321 *Later in life*: On Spielrein's last years and death, see Richebächer, *Sabina Spielrein*, pp. 268–303; and Launer, *Sex Versus Survival*, pp. 235–43.

8. BRÜNNHILDE'S ROCK: WILLA CATHER AND THE SINGER-NOVEL

322 *"Fricka knows"*: Willa Cather, *The Song of the Lark*, ed. Ann Moseley and Kari A. Ronning (University of Nebraska Press, 2012), pp. 487–88. All quotations from this edition.

323 *"Whenever somebody asks"*: Author's interview with Stephanie Blythe, March 25, 2011. See also Alex Ross, "Secret Passage," *New Yorker*, April 25, 2011.

325 *scorned feminists*: See Cather's review of Elizabeth Cady Stanton's *The Woman's Bible* in *The World and the Parish: Willa Cather's Articles and Reviews, 1893–1902*, vol. 2, ed. William M. Curtin (University of Nebraska Press, 1970), pp. 538–41.

325 *"world's masters . . . beauty-making"*: World and the Parish, vol. 2, pp. 952, 951.

325 *"It was so gigantic"*: World and the Parish, vol. 2, p. 518.

326 *David Porter*: See his *On the Divide: The Many Lives of Willa Cather* (University of Nebraska Press, 2008), pp. 255–56.

327 *"That hour always had"*: Cather, *My Ántonia*, ed. Charles Mignon et al. (University of Nebraska Press, 1994), p. 39.

327 *"I felt a good deal"*: L. Brent Bohlke, ed., *Willa Cather in Person: Interviews, Speeches, and Letters* (University of Nebraska Press, 1986), p. 10. On the Wieners, see James Woodress, *Willa Cather: A Literary Life* (University of Nebraska Press, 1987), pp. 52–55.

327 *"Questions!"*: Mildred Bennett, *The World of Willa Cather* (Dodd, Mead, 1951), pp. 153–54.

328 *He was born Albert Gustav*: Communication to author from Anke Leonhardt, Darmstadt Stadtarchiv. Schindelmeisser's arrival is documented in a passenger manifest for the *Prussia*, Feb. 20, 1862. For activity at Lawrence, see *Eighteenth Annual Catalogue of the Lawrence University of Wisconsin*; A. Schindelmeisser, "Music," *Lawrence Collegian*, May 1868. For subsequent wanderings, see *Appleton Post*, June 16, 1870; *Quad-City Times* (Davenport, Iowa), March 11, 1872; *Leavenworth Times*, Oct. 6, 1872; *Abilene Weekly Chronicle*, April 14, 1876; *Wichita Weekly Beacon*, Jan. 8, 1879; *Daily Evening News* (Lincoln), Dec. 7, 1883; *Nebraska State Journal*, Dec. 8, 1882, and April 7, 1883. For Red Cloud, see *Red Cloud Chief*, Aug. 8, 1884, May 15, 1885. For last sightings, see *Topeka State Journal*, July 30, 1886; "Letters List," *Kansas City Gazette*, Jan. 3, 1890; "Advertised Letter List," *Macon Times*, June 26, 1891; Nashville *Directory*, 1898.

329 *H. R. Haweis*: See his *My Musical Memories* (Funk & Wagnalls, 1887), p. 145.

329 *"the place where his dramas"*: Philip Kennicott, "Wagner, Place, and the Growth of Pessimism in the Fiction of Willa Cather," *Cather Studies* 5 (2003), p. 193.

329 *"White Birch in Wyoming"*: Cather, *April Twilights* (Gorham, 1903), p. 31.

329 *fell sick with pneumonia*: *Lincoln Courier*, March 23, 1895.

330 *"The first measures"*: Cather, *Lucy Gayheart*, ed. David Porter et al. (University of Nebraska Press, 2015), p. 111.

330 *"It was a great day"*: WCL, p. 216.

330 *"feeling of the mystical . . . let the eternal conflict"*: *World and the Parish*, vol. 1, pp. 401, 402, 408.

331 *Nevin adored Wagner*: Vance Thompson, *The Life of Ethelbert Nevin: From His Letters and His Wife's Memories* (Boston Music Company, 1913), pp. 69–70.

331 *"Suddenly, in the low cut"*: Sharon O'Brien, ed., *Willa Cather: Stories, Poems, and Other Writings* (Library of America, 1992), pp. 234–35.

331 *"How much more terrible"*: *World and the Parish*, vol. 2, p. 625. Other quotations on pp. 625, 622, 626, 624.

332 *"kindling the latent"*: Bernice Slote, ed., *The Kingdom of Art: Willa Cather's First Principles and Critical Statements, 1893–1896* (University of Nebraska Press, 1966), p. 116. For Bernhardt and Duse, see pp. 117, 118; for Calvé, see *World and the Parish*, vol. 1, p. 410.

332 *"the diva's passion"*: Castle, "In Praise of Brigitte Fassbaender," p. 49.

333 *"Perhaps it was"*: Cather, *The Troll Garden: Short Stories*, ed. James Woodress (University of Nebraska Press, 1983), pp. 54–55.

333 *John H. Flannigan*: See his "Issues of Gender and Lesbian Love: Goblins in 'The Garden Lodge,'" *Cather Studies* 2 (1993), pp. 31–33.

333 *"Paul's Case"*: Cather, *Troll Garden*, pp. 111, 117, 106. For more, see John P. Anders, *Willa Cather's Sexual Aesthetics and the Male Homosexual Literary Tradition* (University of Nebraska Press, 2001).

334 *Victor Herbert*: "Last of the Concerts," *Pittsburgh Weekly Gazette*, March 20, 1903.

334 *"The story was all worked out"*: WCL, p. 80.

334 *"A Wagner Matinée"*: *Everybody's Magazine* 10:3 (1904), pp. 325–28.

335 *Pastor Baehr*: L. Brent Bohlke and Sharon Hoover, eds., *Willa Cather Remembered* (University of Nebraska Press, 2002), p. 12.

336 *"leaving the stage"*: Cather, *Troll Garden*, p. 101.

336 *Joseph C. Murphy*: See his "Wagnerism and American Modernism: Rereading Willa Cather's 'A Wagner Matinée,'" *Forum for Modern Language Studies* 50:4 (2014), pp. 407, 409, 417.

337 *"there are only two"*: Cather, *O Pioneers!*, ed. Susan J. Rosowski et al. (University of Nebraska Press, 1992), p. 110.

337 *"Eric Hermannson's Soul"*: *Cather: Stories, Poems*, pp. 22–45.

337 *having given a copy*: Now at the archive at the National Willa Cather Center, Red Cloud, Nebraska. It is signed "To Auntie Sister"—Sarah Ellen Boak Seymour Andrews.

337 *"cow-puncher's experience"*: WCL, p. 211.

337 *"spoke for the Middlewestern"*: Susie Thomas, *Willa Cather* (Macmillan, 1990), p. 64.

338 *"tall, strong girl"*: All quotations from *O Pioneers!*, ed. Susan J. Rosowski et al. (University of Nebraska Press, 2002).

338 *Cather let drop*: Cather, "Preface," in Gertrude Hall, *The Wagnerian Romances* (Knopf, 1923), p. ix; "cloudless" on p. 285.

338 *Mary Jane Humphrey*: See her "'The White Mulberry Tree' as Opera," *Cather Studies* 3 (1996), pp. 51–66.

339 *"I went up to see"*: WCL, p. 177.

339 *"Three American Singers"*: *McClure's* 42:2 (Dec. 1913), pp. 33–48.

341 *"My one aim"*: "Fremstad Gets Rousing Farewell," *New York Times*, April 24, 1914.

342 *"felt like . . . buffer"*: Mary Watkins Cushing, *The Rainbow Bridge* (Putnam, 1954), pp. 17, 4.

342 *met many times*: Fremstad to Cather, Nov. 16, 1913, Willa Cather Archive, UNL.

342 *"the greatest artist... She fished"*: WCL, pp. 191–92.

342 *"The woods are so strong"*: Fremstad to Cather, May 13, 1913, Willa Cather Archive.

342 *"the arrogant Valkyrie"*: Vicente Blasco Ibáñez, *Entre naranjos* (Sempere, 1901), pp. 160–61. See also Henry Céard, *Terrains à vendre au bord de la mer* (Charpentier, 1906); Gertrude Atherton, *Tower of Ivory* (Macmillan, 1910).

343 *"Our Olive deserved"*: James Huneker, "Bayreuth," *The Musical Courier*, Aug. 20, 1896, p. 106.

343 *"Venus or Valkyr"*: Huneker, *Bedouins* (Scribner, 1920), pp. 225–46.

343 *"harps, anvils"*: Huneker, *Painted Veils* (Boni and Liveright, 1920), p. 293.

343 *"no human love"*: Marcia Davenport, *Of Lena Geyer* (Scribner, 1936), p. 349. Other quotations on pp. 225, 208; Cather on p. 380.

344 *"I hate most"*: WCL, p. 216.

344 *"first completely serious"*: Joan Acocella, *Willa Cather and the Politics of Criticism* (University of Nebraska Press, 2000), p. 2.

346 *"The most beautiful country"*: WCL, p. 151.

348 *"wish-maiden"*: *World and the Parish*, vol. 2, p. 625.

348 *"historic imagination"*: WCL, p. 205.

348 *"destroy the composition"*: WCL, p. 218; Moseley, "Historical Essay," pp. 604–605.

349 H. L. Mencken: See his "Partly About Books," *Smart Set* 48:1 (1916), pp. 306–307; Mencken, Introduction to *The Nietzsche-Wagner Correspondence*, ed. Elizabeth Förster Nietzsche, trans. Caroline V. Kerr (Boni and Liveright, 1921), p. xii.

349 *"the vanishing point"*: WCL, p. 218.

349 *Jonathan Goldberg*: See his *Willa Cather and Others* (Duke UP, 2001), pp. 52, 81. See also Robin Heyeck and James Woodress, "Willa Cather's Cuts and Revisions in *The Song of the Lark*," *Modern Fiction Studies* 25 (1979–80), pp. 651–58; and Cather to Ferris Greenslet, Feb. 15, 1932, Willa Cather Archive, discussing talk of Fremstad's influence.

350 *"a young girl's awakening"*: Cather, "Preface to the 1932 Jonathan Cape Edition," *Song of the Lark*, p. 617.

351 *"Trust and truth"*: *Cather: Stories, Poems*, p. 432.

351 *"blue air... emotional effect"*: Hall, *Wagnerian Romances*, pp. x, viii.

352 *"I had all my life"*: *Cather: Stories, Poems*, p. 960.

352 *Klaus P. Stich*: See his "Cather's 'Midi Romanesque': Missionaries, Myth, and the Grail in 'Death Comes for the Archbishop,'" *Studies in the Novel* 38:1 (2006), p. 66.

352 *"golden chalice"*: Cather, *Death Comes for the Archbishop*, ed. John H. Murphy et al. (University of Nebraska Press, 1999), p. 216. Other quotations on pp. 48, 246.

352 *"great portal"*: Hall, *Wagnerian Romances*, p. 11.

352 *Susan Rosowski*: See her *The Voyage Perilous: Willa Cather's Romanticism* (University of Nebraska Press, 1986), pp. 165, 167.

353 *"As long as every"*: Cather, *The Professor's House*, ed. James Woodress et al. (University of Nebraska Press, 2002), pp. 68–69.

9. MAGIC FIRE: MODERNISM, 1900 TO 1914

356 *"on or about December 1910"*: VWE3, p. 421.

356 *"the world broke in two"*: *Cather: Stories, Poems*, p. 812.

356 *"both as a model"*: Emma Sutton, *Virginia Woolf and Classical Music: Politics, Aesthetics, Form* (Edinburgh UP, 2013), p. 28.

357 *"the spasmodic"*: VWE3, p. 436.

357 *Michael Levenson*: See his *Modernism* (Yale UP, 2011), p. 3.

357 *"make something new!"*: RWB4, p. 460; Guillaume Pauthier, *Les Livres sacrés de l'Orient* (Panthéon Littéraire, 1852), p. 156. For Wagner's ownership of the book, see the inventory of the Wahnfried library, National Archives of the Richard Wagner Foundation; for Pound's, see John Driscoll, *The China Cantos of Ezra Pound* (Ubsaliensis S. Academiae, 1983), p. 21.

358 *"horror and elation"*: T. J. Clark, *Farewell to an Idea: Episodes from a History of Modernism* (Yale UP, 1999), pp. 7–8.

358 *Gesamtkunstwerk*: On its surfacing, see Sanna Pederson, "From Gesamtkunstwerk to Music Drama," in Imhoof, *Total Work of Art*, p. 43.

358 *Juliet Koss*: See her *Modernism After Wagner* (University of Minnesota Press, 2010), pp. xi–xxix. On the Gesamtkunstwerk and modernism, see Harald Szeemann, ed., *Der Hang zum Gesamtkunstwerk: Europäische Utopien seit 1800* (Sauerländer, 1983); Anke Finger, *Das Gesamtkunstwerk der Moderne* (Vandenhoeck & Ruprecht, 2006); Matthew Wilson Smith, *The Total Work of Art: From Bayreuth to Cyberspace* (Routledge, 2007); Finger and Danielle Follett, eds., *The Aesthetics of the Total Artwork: On Borders and Fragments* (Johns Hopkins UP, 2011); Hilda Meldrum Brown, *The Quest for the Gesamtkunstwerk and Richard Wagner* (Oxford UP, 2016).

358 *"sea of emotions"*: Wyzewa, "Notes sur la littérature wagnérienne," pp. 169–70.

359 *"on that Paris night"*: Nancy Reynolds and Malcolm McCormick, *No Fixed Points: Dance in the Twentieth Century* (Yale UP, 2003), p. 5.

360 *"As the orchestra began"*: Caroline J. Kappel, *Labyrinthine Depictions and Tempting Colors: The Synaesthetic Dances of Loïe Fuller as Symbolist Choreography* (Ph.D. diss., Ohio University, 2007), p. 201.

360 *concealed bulb*: Smith, *Total Work of Art*, pp. 43–44.

360 *"She dreams"*: Jules Claretie, *La Vie à Paris, 1907* (Charpentier, 1908), p. 71.

360 *"Brunehilde, it is you"*: Georges Rodenbach, "La Loïe Fuller," *Revue illustrée*, May 1, 1893. Translation

from Rhonda K. Garelick, *Electric Salome: Loie Fuller's Performance of Modernism* (Princeton UP, 2007), p. 163.

361 *"does not burn"*: Dee Reynolds, "The Dancer as Woman: Loïe Fuller and Stéphane Mallarmé," in *Impressions of French Modernity: Art and Literature in France 1850–1900*, ed. Richard Hobbs (Manchester UP, 1998), p. 161.

361 *"Future decor"*: SM2, p. 313. *National Observer* article, May 13, 1893.

361 *"Isadora Duncan est dionysiaque"*: Conférence au Trocadéro, 1913, Mary Desti Papers, UCLA Library, Department of Special Collections.

361 *Cather disliked*: Cather, "Training for the Ballet," *McClure's*, Oct. 1913. For more, see Wendy K. Perriman, *Willa Cather and the Dance: "A Most Satisfying Elegance"* (Fairleigh Dickinson UP, 2009), pp. 37–46.

361 *"glorious far-seeing"*: Roger Copeland and Marshall Cohen, eds., *What Is Dance?: Readings in Theory and Criticism* (Oxford UP, 1983), p. 266.

361 *"Dance of the Future"*: Isadora Duncan, *Der Tanz der Zukunft (The Dance of the Future)* (Diederichs, 1903), pp. 11–26.

362 *"seductively wild"*: RWSS5, p. 148.

362 *David Breckbill*: See his "Cosima Wagner's Bayreuth," in WW, p. 466.

362 *"bare feet, sandals"*: Sandy Sturges, ed., *Preston Sturges by Preston Sturges* (Simon and Schuster, 1990), p. 30. For chatter, see Alfred Holzbock, "Aus der Stadt Richard Wagners," in Großmann-Vendrey, *Bayreuth in der deutschen Presse*, vol. 3/1, p. 193.

362 *"A single gesture"*: Duncan, *My Life* (Liveright, 2013), p. 124.

362 *"chaste Venusberg"*: Heinrich Chevalley, "Review of 1904 Bayreuth Festival," in WW, pp. 467–68. On Duncan in Bayreuth, see Peter Kurth, *Isadora: A Sensational Life* (Little, Brown, 2001), pp. 118–23; Victor Seroff, *The Real Isadora* (Dial Press, 1971), pp. 63–68; Mary Desti, *The Untold Story: The Life of Isadora Duncan, 1921–1927* (Da Capo, 1981), pp. 33–41.

363 *"Superwoman in America"*: Benjamin De Casseres, *The Superman in America* (University of Washington Book Store, 1929), p. 18. For 1911 program, see [Carl Van Vechten], "Miss Duncan Dances to Wagner Music," *New York Times*, Feb. 16, 1911; programs from the Howard Holtzman Collection on Isadora Duncan, UCLA Library Special Collections.

363 *"clear, soft beauty"*: Mary Simonson, "Dancing the Future, Performing the Past: Isadora Duncan and Wagnerism in the American Imagination," *Journal of the American Musicological Society* 65:2 (2012), p. 542.

363 *"dead immobility"*: Ernest Newman, "The Dances of Isadora Duncan," *Living Age*, June 4, 1921.

363 *"Her legs are motionless"*: André Levinson, "The

Art and Meaning of Isadora Duncan," in *What Is Dance?*, p. 443.

363 *Mary Simonson*: See her "Dancing the Future," p. 525.

363 *"The Master made"*: Duncan, *My Life*, pp. 130–31.

364 *"The Wagnerian contradiction"*: PCW, p. 176.

364 *"Now that I"*: CWD, Sept. 23, 1878.

364 *Martin Puchner*: See his *Stage Fright: Modernism, Anti-Theatricality, and Drama* (Johns Hopkins UP, 2002), p. 9.

365 *"Wagner has taken the place"*: Walther Volbach, *Adolphe Appia, Prophet of the Modern Theatre* (Wesleyan UP, 1968), p. 45. See also Richard C. Beacham, *Adolphe Appia: Artist and Visionary of the Modern Theatre* (Harwood, 1994), pp. 7–8.

365 *"Characters in scrupulously historic"*: Appia, *Music and the Art of the Theatre*, p. 62. Other quotations on pp. 18, 74.

365 *Mariano Fortuny*: See Paolo Bolpagni, ed., *Fortuny e Wagner: Il wagnerismo nelle arti visive in Italia* (Skira, 2012); Wendy Ligon Smith, "Mariano Fortuny and His Wagnerian Designs," *Wagner Journal* 11:3 (2017), pp. 35–50; Smith, "Wagner and Fortuny: Designs for the Bayreuth Theatre," in *Music Theater as Global Culture: Wagner's Legacy Today*, ed. Anno Mungen et al. (Königshausen & Neumann, 2017), pp. 371–92; Smith, *Reviving Fortuny's Phantasmagorias* (Ph.D. diss., University of Manchester, 2015), pp. 40–41; "Lettre de Milan," *Le Gaulois*, Jan. 3, 1901, citation via Smith.

366 *"the world's foremost"*: Eduard Hanslick, *Aus dem Opernleben der Gegenwart: Neue Kritiken und Studien*, vol. 3 (Allgemeiner Verein für deutschen Literatur, 1889), p. 324.

366 *"With the Word-Tone Drama"*: Appia, *Œuvres complètes*, vol. 2, ed. Marie L. Bablet-Hahn (L'Âge d'Homme, 1986), p. 73.

366 *"All this has no meaning"*: Beacham, *Adolphe Appia*, p. 37; also PCW, pp. 147–48.

366 *Tristan at La Scala*: Beacham, *Adolphe Appia*, pp. 143–44.

367 *Denis Bablet*: See his *Edward Gordon Craig*, trans. Daphne Woodward (Theatre Arts Books, 1966), p. 32; for *Vikings* and *Parsifal*, p. 60.

367 *"I said to Frau Cosima"*: Gordon Craig, *Index to the Story of My Days: Some Memoirs of Edward Gordon Craig, 1872–1907* (Hulton, 1957), p. 272. See also Kessler, *Journey to the Abyss*, p. 341; and L. M. Newman, ed., *The Correspondence of Edward Gordon Craig and Count Harry Kessler, 1903–1937* (Maney, 1995), p. 53. For lighting at Bayreuth, see William F. Apthorp, "Wagner and Scenic Art," *Scribner's Magazine*, November 1887, pp. 524–26.

367 *Georg Fuchs*: See Koss, *Modernism After Wagner*, pp. 118–31.

368 *"I wonder if"*: Jan van Holt [Craig], "Richard Wagner, Revolution, and the Artist," *The Mask* 1:2 (1908), pp. 1–2. For the pseudonym, see Christo-

pher Innes, *Edward Gordon Craig: A Vision of Theatre* (Harwood, 1998), pp. 210–11.

369 *Clement Greenberg*: See his "Towards a Newer Laocoon," in *Art in Theory, 1900–2000: An Anthology of Changing Ideas*, ed. Charles Harrison and Paul Wood (Blackwell, 2003), pp. 562–68.

369 *"breaking down"*: Irving Babbitt, *The New Laokoon: An Essay on the Confusion of the Arts* (Houghton Mifflin, 1910), pp. 105–106.

369 *"I got everything"*: See Silver, "Afterlife: The Important and Sometimes Embarrassing Links Between Occultism and the Development of Abstract Art, ca. 1909–13," pp. 46–53; and Carel Blotkamp, *Mondrian: The Art of Destruction* (Reaktion, 2001), p. 111.

369 *"stamped my whole life"*: Kenneth C. Lindsay and Peter Vergo, eds., *Kandinsky: Complete Writings on Art* (Da Capo, 1994), pp. 363–64. See also Kandinsky, "Rückblicke," in *Kandinsky: 1901–1913* (Der Sturm, 1913), p. ix.

370 *"nightmare of materialistic . . . not only by theatrical"*: Kandinsky, *Über das Geistige* (1912), pp. 4, 30.

370 *Sixten Ringbom*: See his "Art in 'The Epoch of the Great Spiritual': Occult Elements in the Early Theory of Abstract Painting," *Journal of the Warburg and Courtauld Institutes* 29 (1966), p. 405. See also Annie Besant and C. W. Leadbeater, *Thought-Forms* (Theosophical Publishing Society, 1905), pp. 82–84.

371 *Chris Short*: See his *The Art Theory of Wassily Kandinsky, 1909–1928: The Quest for Synthesis* (Peter Lang, 2010), pp. 52–55.

371 *"The inner sound"*: *Kandinsky: Complete Writings*, p. 261; Kandinsky, "Über Bühnenkomposition," in *Der blaue Reiter*, ed. Kandinsky and Franz Marc (Piper, 1914), p. 108. For "inner necessity," see RWSS3, p. 44.

372 *"symbols for their own time"*: Marc, "Die 'Wilden' Deutschlands," *Der blaue Reiter*, pp. 5–7. For *Götterdämmerung*, see Klaus Lankheit, *Franz Marc im Urteil seiner Zeit* (Schauberg, 1960), p. 24.

372 *Yggdrasil*: Frederick S. Levine, *The Apocalyptic Vision: The Art of Franz Marc as German Expressionism* (Icon, 1979), pp. 76–103.

372 *Parsifal Series*: See Briony Fer, "Hilma af Klint: The Outsider Inside Herself," in *Hilma af Klint: Seeing Is Believing*, ed. Kurt Almqvist and Louise Belfrage (Koenig, 2017), pp. 96–98.

373 *"The men and women . . . All human relations"*: VWE3, pp. 427, 432, 422.

374 *"dreadful eyes"*: Ford Madox Ford, *Mightier Than the Sword* (Allen & Unwin, 1938), p. 266. For Ford as composer, see Sondra J. Stang and Carl Smith, "'Music for a While': Ford's Compositions for Voice and Piano," *Contemporary Literature* 30:2 (1989), pp. 183–223.

374 *"the putting of certain realities"*: *Collected Poems of Ford Madox Hueffer* (Secker, 1916), p. 17.

374 *Ezra Pound*: For an early positive comment on

Wagner, see A. David Moody, *Ezra Pound: Poet—A Portrait of the Man and His Work*, vol. 1 (Oxford UP, 2007), p. 41.

374 *"Wagner is a bum"*: Mary de Rachewiltz et al., eds., *Ezra Pound to His Parents: Letters 1895–1929* (Oxford UP, 2010), p. 371. Pound saw Thomas Beecham conduct *Tristan* in 1916. For the *Tristan* play, see Pound, *Plays Modelled on the Noh*, ed. Donald Gallup (Friends of the University of Toledo Libraries, 1987), pp. 32–37.

374 *"you confuse the spectator"*: Pound, *Antheil and the Treatise on Harmony* (Covici, 1927), p. 44.

375 *"ends with a long"*: Frederick Karl and Laurence Davies, eds., *The Collected Letters of Joseph Conrad*, vol. 1 (Cambridge UP, 1983), p. 156.

375 *"abysmal ignorance"*: Laurence Davies et al., eds., *The Collected Letters of Joseph Conrad*, vol. 9 (Cambridge UP, 2007), p. 208. For Frederick Karl, see *Joseph Conrad: The Three Lives—A Biography* (Farrar, Straus and Giroux, 1978), p. 268.

375 *"I am modern"*: Frederick Karl and Laurence Davies, eds., *The Collected Letters of Joseph Conrad*, vol. 2 (Cambridge UP, 1986), p. 418.

375 *Heart of Darkness*: Quotations taken from the edition by D. C. R. A. Goonetilleke (Broadview, 2003).

375 *John DiGaetani*: See his *Richard Wagner and the Modern British Novel* (Associated University Presses, 1978), p. 56. On Conrad and Wagner, see also Furness, *Wagner and Literature*, pp. 78–80.

375 *"fierce Wagner music"*: Conrad, "Freya of the Seven Isles," *The Collected Works of Joseph Conrad*, vol. 13 (Doubleday, Page, 1925), p. 152.

376 *"Every human being knows"*: Conrad and Ford, *The Nature of a Crime*, in *The Collected Works of Joseph Conrad*, vol. 22 (Doubleday, Page, 1926), pp. 17–18.

376 *"The curse attached"*: Paul Wiley, *Conrad's Measure of Man* (Gordian Press, 1966), p. 99.

376 *"immense occult influence"*: Conrad, *Nostromo: A Tale of the Seaboard*, vol. 8 of *The Collected Works of Joseph Conrad* (Doubleday, Page, 1925), p. 117. Other quotations on pp. 52, 533, 539, 554, 531, 560, 563.

377 *"authentic projections"*: Ford, *Mightier Than the Sword*, p. 103.

377 *"wanted their sons"*: Ford, *Return to Yesterday* (Liveright, 1932), p. 377. See also John Worthen, *D. H. Lawrence: The Early Years, 1885–1912* (Cambridge UP, 1992), p. 171. For Carpenter, see Jane Heath, "Helen Corke and D. H. Lawrence: Sexual Identity and Literary Relations," *Feminist Studies* 11:2 (1985), pp. 317–42.

378 *Welsh singers*: "Welsh News Notes," *The Cambrian* 20:9 (1900), p. 430.

378 *"long, feeble"*: James T. Boulton, ed., *The Letters of D. H. Lawrence*, vol. 1 (Cambridge UP, 1979), p. 140. Other quotations on p. 247.

378 *"hurricane of music"*: Helen Corke, *In Our Infancy: An Autobiography, Part I: 1882–1912* (Cambridge UP, 1975), p. 157. On Corke's lesbianism, see

Heath, "Helen Corke and D. H. Lawrence," pp. 325–31.

378 *"Siegmund, in an irresponsible"*: Corke, *In Our Infancy*, p. 233.

378 *"sleeping in her large"*: Lawrence, *The Trespasser*, ed. Elizabeth Mansfield (Viking, 1983), p. 86. Other allusions on pp. 28, 30, 162, 220–21.

378 *"ecstasy of the* Untergang*"*: TM22, p. 92. For Lawrence's review of *Death in Venice*, see *Introductions and Reviews*, ed. N. H. Reeve and John Worthen (Cambridge UP, 2005), pp. 205–12; see also a critique of *Tristan* in Lawrence, *Reflections on the Death of a Porcupine and Other Essays*, ed. Michael Herbert (Cambridge UP, 1988), p. 10.

379 *"understand Wagner"*: Lawrence, *The Trespasser*, p. 245. Compare Corke studying German with Lawrence in Corke, *D. H. Lawrence: The Croydon Years* (University of Texas Press, 2014), pp. 4–5; *In Our Infancy*, pp. 177–78.

379 *Ascona*: See Martin Green, *Mountain of Truth: The Counterculture Begins, Ascona, 1900–1920* (University Press of New England, 1986), pp. 122–23.

379 *"ancient spirit"*: Lawrence, "Letter from Germany," *Phoenix: The Posthumous Papers of D. H. Lawrence*, ed. Edward D. McDonald (Viking, 1936), p. 109.

379 *"like a Nibelung"*: Lawrence, *Women in Love*, ed. David Farmer et al. (Cambridge UP, 1987), p. 47. Other quotations on pp. 223, 222, 394.

379 *god in decline*: Stoddard Martin, *Wagner to "The Waste Land": A Study of the Relationship of Wagner to English Literature* (Barnes and Noble, 1982), p. 176.

379 *Hugh Stevens*: See his "From Genesis to the *Ring*: Richard Wagner and D. H. Lawrence's *Rainbow*," *Textual Practice* 28:4 (2014), pp. 611–30.

380 *"She let the flames . . . And the rainbow stood"*: Lawrence, *The Rainbow*, ed. Mark Kinkead-Weekes (Cambridge UP, 1989), pp. 448, 452, 458–59.

381 *"Music flowed past him"*: E. M. Forster, *The Longest Journey* (Penguin, 2006), p. 40.

381 *"Wagner proves a siren song"*: Michelle Fillion, *Difficult Rhythm: Music and the Word in E. M. Forster* (University of Illinois Press, 2010), p. 43. See also DiGaetani, *Wagner and the Modern British Novel*, pp. 90–108; and Elizabeth Heine, "Afterword," in Forster, *Longest Journey*, pp. 297–98.

381 *"his wound might heal"*: Forster, *The Longest Journey*, p. 153. Other quotations on pp. 257, 272–73.

382 *"Every now and then . . . building"*: Forster, *Howards End* (Everyman's Library, 1991), pp. 40–41, 194.

383 *"egotistic anti-hero"*: Hermione Lee, *Virginia Woolf* (Knopf, 1997), p. 433.

383 *"In this series"*: May Sinclair, "The Novels of Dorothy Richardson," *Egoist* 5:4 (1918), p. 58. On problems with the term "stream of consciousness," see Allen McLaurin, "Consciousness and Group Consciousness in Virginia Woolf," in *Virginia Woolf:*

A Centenary Perspective, ed. Eric Warner (Macmillan, 1984), pp. 28–40.

383 *ubiquity of music*: Dorothy Richardson, *Pilgrimage: Pointed Roofs* (Knopf, 1919), p. 53.

384 *performance of* Walküre: Margaret Scott, ed., *The Katherine Mansfield Notebooks*, vol. 1 (Lincoln UP, 1997), p. 107.

384 *"A bird—large . . . Oh, the sea"*: Mansfield, *The Urewera Notebook*, ed. Anna Plumridge (Edinburgh UP, 2015), p. 103; *Mansfield Notebooks*, vol. 1, p. 151.

384 *"dreaming exquisite"*: Margaret Scott, ed., *The Katherine Mansfield Notebooks: The Complete Edition* (University of Minnesota Press, 2002), p. 50. Other quotations on pp. 52, 61, 62.

385 *Delia da Sousa Correa*: See her "Katherine Mansfield and Nineteenth-Century Musicality," in *Words and Notes in the Long Nineteenth Century*, ed. Phyllis Weliver and Katharine Ellis (Boydell, 2013), pp. 103–18. On Mansfield as modernist, see Sydney Janet Kaplan, *Katherine Mansfield and the Origins of Modernist Fiction* (Cornell UP, 1991).

385 *"Ah-Aah!"*: Mansfield, *The Collected Stories of Katherine Mansfield* (Wordsworth, 2006), p. 165.

385 *"Aunt Anne"*: Margaret Scott, ed., *The Katherine Mansfield Notebooks*, vol. 2 (Lincoln UP, 1997), p. 297.

385 *Woolf once said*: VWD2, p. 227.

385 *"I felt within"*: VWL1, p. 406.

386 *"Like Shakespeare, Wagner"*: VWE1, p. 290.

386 *Valkyrie costume*: David Garnett, *Great Friends: Portraits of Seventeen Writers* (Atheneum, 1980), p. 118.

386 *"My eyes are bruised"*: VWL2, p. 26.

386 *"I went to Tristan"*: VWL3, p. 56.

386 *singing the spring music*: VWD2, p. 233. For *Meistersinger*, see VWD4, p. 107.

386 *only sixteen*: VWL1, p. 17.

386 *"sacrifice my Richter"*: VWL1, p. 312. Other quotations on pp. 294, 308.

386 *"we go almost nightly"*: VWL1, p. 331.

386 *"Wagner cult"*: Leonard Woolf, *Beginning Again: An Autobiography of the Years 1911 to 1918* (Harcourt, 1963), p. 49; Leonard Woolf, *An Autobiography*, vol. 1 (Oxford UP, 1980), pp. 66–67.

387 *possible that both writers*: On the chronology of Mann's visit, see Rainer-Maria Kiel, "Thomas Mann—Bayreuth—Karl Würzburger," *Thomas Mann Jahrbuch* 20 (2007), pp. 237–60.

387 *"very deep . . . One is fired"*: VWE1, p. 289. "From the hill" on p. 290.

388 *"sit for hours playing"*: Woolf, *The Voyage Out* (Doran, 1920), p. 33. Other quotations on pp. 35, 45–48, 280–89.

389 *"immense vagueness"*: Woolf, *Melymbrosia: An Early Version of "The Voyage Out*,*"* ed. Louise A. DeSalvo (New York Public Library, 1982), p. 20.

390 *"sinking and sinking . . . No two people"*: Ibid.,

p. 231; *The Voyage Out*, pp. 353–54. For Sutton, see her *Virginia Woolf and Classical Music*, p. 41.

391 *Louise DeSalvo*: See her "'A View of One's Own: Virginia Woolf and the Making of *Melymbrosia*," in *Melymbrosia*, p. xl.

392 *"solidified what has always"*: VWL2, p. 566.

392 *Jean-Jacques Nattiez*: See his *Proust as Musician*, trans. Derrick Puffett (Cambridge UP, 1989), pp. 19–23.

392 *"all of a sudden"*: MPLT5, p. 208.

392 *"matter of musical memory"*: Thomas S. Grey, "Leit-motif, Temporality, and Musical Design in the *Ring*," in *Cambridge Companion to Wagner*, p. 114.

392 *"I shall present"*: Nattiez, *Proust as Musician*, p. 31.

393 *though he disapproved*: Proust, "About Baudelaire," *Marcel Proust: A Selection from His Miscellaneous Writings*, ed. and trans. Gerard Hopkins (Allan Wingate, 1948), p. 193.

393 *great women of society*: On Greffulhe, see Jann Pasler, *Writing Through Music: Essays on Music, Culture, and Politics* (Oxford UP, 2008), pp. 285–317; on Polignac, Sylvia Kahan, *Music's Modern Muse: A Life of Winnaretta Singer, Princesse de Polignac* (University of Rochester Press, 2003), pp. 47–50.

393 *"The more legendary"*: Proust, *Correspondance*, vol. 1, ed. Philip Kolb (Plon, 1970), p. 382.

393 *"The Grail"*: Ibid., p. 325.

393 *"can read Lamartine"*: Proust, *Les Plaisirs et les jours* (Calmann-Lévy, 1896), p. 63.

393 *"revolutionary if ever . . . will always be"*: Ibid., pp. 91–92, 94.

394 *"The Melancholy Summer"*: Ibid., pp. 109, 111, 115–16.

394 *"Really, it oughtn't . . . too violent"*: MPLT1, pp. 265–66.

394–95 *"secret, murmuring, detached"*: Ibid., p. 298.

395 *Saint-Saëns*: MPTP1, pp. 909, 911, 913, 918, 935, 941. For other sources, see Proust, *Correspondance*, vol. 17 (Plon, 1989), p. 194.

395 *"Below the delicate line"*: MPLT1, p. 294.

395 *"national anthem"*: Quotations in this section from MPLT1, pp. 308, 335, 375, 491. For Bayreuth, see pp. 427–28.

395 *"Sound can reflect"*: MPLT2, p. 146.

396 *"the sensual and the anxious"*: Quotations in this section from MPLT5, pp. 204–206.

396 *"filles-fleurs"*: MPLT3, pp. 746, 579; MPTP2, p. 716.

397 *"Supernatural beings"*: Nattiez, *Proust as Musician*, p. 28; MPTP4, p. 825; "seul livre" on p. 824.

397 *"What exactly"*: Nattiez, *Proust as Musician*, p. 28; MPTP4, p. 826.

397 *"purely frivolous"*: MPLT6, p. 253.

398 *"order of supernatural . . . It was still there"*: MPLT1, pp. 498, 500–501.

398 *"boldest approximation . . . invisible being"*: MPLT5, pp. 347, 340, 346.

398 *"experience his revelation"*: Nattiez, *Proust as Musician*, p. 30.

399 *"giants plunged"*: MPLT6, p. 532.

10. NOTHUNG: THE FIRST WORLD WAR AND HITLER'S YOUTH

400 *New Year's Day*: Syer, "*Parsifal* on Stage," pp. 291–94. For vote, see Hilmes, *Cosima Wagner*, pp. 226–31.

401 *"Montserrat-Montsalvat"*: Manuel Muntadas y Rovira, *Balades Wagnerianes* (Francesch Puig, 1910), pp. 87–95. See also his *Probable Origen Català de les Llegendes del Sant Graal* (L'Avenç, 1910).

401 *sets for the Liceu*: Catharine Macedo, "Between Opera and Reality: The Barcelona 'Parsifal,'" *Cambridge Opera Journal* 10:1 (1998), pp. 102–103, 108–109.

401 *actually began at 10:25 p.m.*: Joan Matabosch's communication to author. See also Alfonsina Janés, "Wagner al Liceu," in *Wagner al Liceu* (Gran Teatre del Liceu, 2004), p. 68.

401 *"interpenetration of the art"*: Juan José Lahuerta, *Antoni Gaudí, 1852–1926: Architecture, Ideology, and Politics*, trans. Graham Thompson (Electra/Phaidon, 2003), p. 276.

401 *most extreme Wagnerites*: Macedo, "Between Opera and Reality," pp. 103–106; Lahuerta, *Gaudí*, p. 181. See also Francesc Fontbona, "Richard Wagner et l'art catalan," in *Wagner, visions d'artistes*, pp. 48–55.

402 *"It was Gaudí"*: Cèsar Martinell i Brunet, *Gaudí: His Life, His Theories, His Work*, trans. Judith Rohrer (MIT Press, 1975), p. 184. See also Jan Molema, "The Labours of Gaudí: Foreign Influences," in *Gaudí 2002: Miscellany*, ed. Daniel Giralt-Miracle (Planeta, 2002), p. 109. For Güell and *Parsifal*, see Dorothy Noyes, "Breaking the Social Contract: El Comte Arnau, Violence, and Production in the Catalan Mountains at the Turn of the Century, *Catalan Review* 14.1–2 (2000), p. 151; and Lahuerta, *Gaudí: Architecture, Ideology, Politics*, p. 117. For the Nibelung comparison, see Robert Hughes, *Barcelona* (Vintage, 1993), p. 455.

402 *"Gaudí's love"*: Hughes, *Barcelona*, p. 455.

402 *Catalans were not the only ones*: See Marion S. Miller, "Wagnerism, Wagnerians, and Italian Identity," in WECP, pp. 177–78; Mário Vieira de Carvalho, "Parsifal Versus Siegfried: Aspects of the Reception of Wagner in Portugal," in *Portugal e o mundo: O encontro de culturas na música*, ed. Salwa El-Shawan Castelo-Branco (Dom Quixote, 1997), pp. 149–50; Curuppumullagê Jinarājadāsa, *Theosophy and Modern Thought* (Theosophical Publishing House, 1915), p. 107; "The New York Fashion Letter," *Tacoma Times*, Feb. 27, 1904; "Through the Lorgnette," *New York Press*, Jan. 31, 1904.

403 *"savior from a different-colored box"*: Maximilian Harden, "Tutte le Corde: Siegfried und Isolde," *Zukunft*, June 27, 1914.

403 *"we straightway forgot . . . The day before"*: Clare Benedict, *Six Months: March–August 1914* (Crist, 1914), pp. 40–42.

404 *"Glances became insolent"*: Péladan, *La Guerre des idées* (Flammarion, 1916), p. 94.

404 *"One could imagine"*: RWSS10, p. 252.

404 *"victorious struggle"*: Spotts, *Bayreuth*, p. 135; Reinhold von Lichtenberg, "Die Bayreuther Festspiele 1911," *Grenzboten* 70 (1911), p. 318.

404 *88 percent*: Lichtenberg, "Die Bayreuther Festspiele 1911," p. 320.

405 *"The wonderful acoustics"*: ZRW, p. 138.

405 *"Now the strong German"*: Jonas Karlsson, "Wagnerian Iconography in the *Kladderadatsch*, 1914–1944," *Wagner Journal* 10:3 (2016), p. 42.

405 *"After the holy German war"*: Richard Sternfeld, *Richard Wagner und der heilige deutsche Krieg* (Stalling, 1915), p. 63.

405 *Operation Alberich*: Erich Ludendorff, *Meine Kriegserinnerungen, 1914–1918* (Mittler, 1919), p. 113; Kronprinz Rupprecht von Bayern, *Mein Kriegstagebuch*, vol. 3 (Deutscher National Verlag, 1929), pp. 126–37; Jeremy Black, *The Great War and the Making of the Modern World* (Continuum, 2011), p. 144.

405 *"There is always someone"*: Walther Rathenau, *An Deutschlands Jugend* (Fischer, 1918), p. 83.

406 *"heart-pounding enthusiasm"*: Chamberlain, *Briefe*, vol. 2, p. 246.

406 *"struggle between 2"*: John C. G. Röhl, *Kaiser, Hof und Staat: Wilhelm II. und die deutsche Politik* (Beck, 1995), p. 217.

406 *swan motorcar*: Marion Schmid, "'À bas Wagner!': The French Press Campaign Against Wagner During World War I," in *French Music, Culture, and National Identity, 1870–1939*, ed. Barbara L. Kelly (University of Rochester Press, 2008), pp. 81–82. See also Esteban Buch, "'Les Allemands et les Boches': La Musique allemande à Paris pendant la Première Guerre mondiale," *Le Mouvement social* 208 (2004), pp. 45–69.

406 *"machine of war"*: Camille Saint-Saëns, "Germanophilie," *L'Écho de France*, Oct. 16, 1914.

406 *"German poison"*: Léon Daudet, *Hors du joug allemand: Mesures d'après-guerre* (Nouvelle Librairie Nationale, 1915), p. 85. For Pierre Lasserre, see his *L'Esprit de la musique française* (Payot, 1917), p. 237.

406 *"the state must de-Germanicize"*: Charles Maurras, *La France se sauve elle-même* (Nouvelle Librairie Nationale, 1916), p. 362.

406 *Louis Aragon*: See his *Chroniques de la pluie et du beau temps* (Français Réunis, 1979), p. 249.

407 *"Even at the height"*: André Suarès, *La Nation contre la race, I: La Fourmilière* (Émile-Paul, 1916), pp. 67–68. On *Parsifal*, see pp. 221–22, 232–34.

407 *"Das Rheingold begins"*: Péladan, *La Guerre des idées* (Flammarion, 1916), pp. 151–52. For "Valkyries," see p. 311.

407 *"prodigious fertilization . . . imbecilic"*: Proust, *Correspondance*, vol. 13, ed. Philip Kolb (Plon, 1985), pp. 334, 351.

407 *"If Saint-Loup had occasion"*: MPLT6, p. 93.

408 *"For the dead of Padua!"*: Harvey Sachs, *Toscanini: Musician of Conscience* (Liveright, 2017), p. 310.

408 *Vienna heard Verdi's operas*: Steven Beller, "The Tragic Carnival: Austrian Culture in the First World War," in *European Culture in the Great War: The Arts, Entertainment and Propaganda, 1914–1918*, ed. Aviel Roshwald and Richard Stites (Cambridge UP, 1999), p. 380.

408 *"that drama of peace"*: Giulio Gatti-Casazza, *Memories of the Opera* (Vienna House, 1973), p. 180.

408 *"personally I should hate"*: Arthur S. Link, ed., *The Papers of Woodrow Wilson*, vol. 42 (Princeton UP, 1983), p. 8, April 7, 1917.

408 *"Kill Muck!"*: Melissa D. Burrage, *The Karl Muck Scandal: Classical Music and Xenophobia in World War I America* (University of Rochester Press, 2019), p. 153. See also E. Douglas Bomberger, *Making Music American: 1917 and the Transformation of Culture* (Oxford UP, 2018), pp. 164–77.

408 *"favorite composer"*: Thomas Beecham, *A Mingled Chime: An Autobiography* (Putnam, 1943), p. 270. For *Tristan* on leave, see John Lucas, *Thomas Beecham: An Obsession with Music* (Boydell, 2008), p. 133. For more, see Gordon Williams, *British Theatre in the Great War: A Revaluation* (Continuum, 2003).

408 *"sub-conscious prophecy"*: Glyn Philpot, *Die Hohenzollern-Dämmerung: Eine Welt-Tragödie / The Twilight of the Hohenzollerns: A World Tragedy* (Cecil Palmer & Hayward, 1917), p. 13. For Sandeman, see *The Collected Letters of Joseph Conrad*, vol. 9, p. 208.

409 *"The creation of Empire"*: Camille Mauclair, *La Religion de la musique* (Fischbacher, 1928), p. 331.

410 *Rebekah Lockyer*: See her "Ford Madox Ford's Musical Legacy: *Parade's End* and Wagner," *Forum for Modern Language Studies* 50:4 (2014), p. 431.

410 *"There was a crash . . . immense tea-tray"*: Ford, *Parade's End* (Everyman's Library, 1992), pp. 149, 313.

411 *"polyphonic simultaneity"*: Lockyer, "Ford's Musical Legacy," p. 434.

411 *"She was humming"*: Ford, *Parade's End*, pp. 477–78. Other quotations on pp. 608, 604–605.

412 *"Go on playing"*: Lockyer, "Ford's Musical Legacy," p. 439. For more on Ford and Wagner, see Angus Wrenn, "Wagner's *Ring* Cycle and *Parade's End*," in *Ford Madox Ford's "Parade's End": The First World War, Culture, and Modernity*, ed. Ashley Chantler and Rob Hawkes (Rodopi, 2014), pp. 67–80.

412 *"I loved the Walküre"*: Valéry, *Cahiers I*, ed. Judith Robinson (Gallimard, 1973), p. 307. For despair, see Valéry, *Cahiers II*, ed. Robinson (Gallimard, 1974), p. 979; for "uselessness," Valéry, *Œuvres*, vol. 1, ed. Jean Hytier (Gallimard, 1957), p. 1615.

413 *"somewhat remarkable"*: Valéry, *Cahiers I*, p. 307. For Shakespeare and Beethoven, see p. 303.

413–14 *"This body . . . sweet and strong"*: Valéry, *Œuvres*, vol. 1, pp. 109, 110.

414 *Theodor W. Adorno*: See his "Valéry's Deviations," *Notes to Literature*, vol. 1, trans. Shierry Weber Nicholsen (Columbia UP, 1991), pp. 139–40.

414 *"You wouldn't have made"*: WCL, p. 328.

415 *"The people that sing"*: All quotations from Cather, *One of Ours*, ed. Frederick M. Link and Kari A. Ronning (University of Nebraska Press, 2006).

416 *"God's soldiers"*: WCL, p. 261.

416 *"Parsifal heals"*: Rosowski, *Voyage Perilous*, p. 106.

416 Hon. Mrs. Assheton Harbord: "A Lady Balloon Owner," *Bystander*, Oct. 2, 1907; "Exciting Balloon Adventure," *Quarterly Journal of the Royal Meteorological Society*, April 1908, pp. 156–58.

417 *"Perhaps a hundred yards"*: H. G. Wells, *The War in the Air* (Bell, 1908), p. 265.

417 *Aeronautical Syndicate*: "'Valkyries' and the Government," *Flight*, July 8, 1911.

417 *"Those that I fight"*: WBY1, pp. 135–36.

417 *Robert Gregory*: James Pethica, ed., *Lady Gregory's Diaries, 1892–1902* (Colin Smythe, 1996), p. 261.

417 *"There is no nobler bond"*: D'Annunzio, *Notturno*, trans. Stephen Sartarelli (Yale UP, 2011), p. 21.

417 *"all my blood trembles"*: D'Annunzio, *Taccuini*, ed. Enrica Bianchetti and Roberto Forcella (Mondadori, 1965), p. 1028; "had the rhythm" on p. 1035.

418 *"Just as you have got"*: MPLT6, p. 99.

418 *closing door . . . ringing telephone*: MPLT3, p. 536, MPLT4, p. 177.

419 *"Vulcan-like skill"*: MPLT5, pp. 209–10.

419 *"Down with the Tango"*: F. T. Marinetti, *Critical Writings*, ed. Günter Berghaus, trans. Doug Thompson (Farrar, Straus and Giroux, 2006), pp. 132–33.

420 *"bit"*: Guillaume Apollinaire, "Futurist Anti-Tradition," in *Futurism: An Anthology*, ed. Lawrence Rainey et al. (Yale UP, 2009), p. 154.

420 *"There is no longer"*: Guillaume Apollinaire, *Œuvres en prose complètes*, vol. 2, ed. Pierre Caizergues and Michel Décaudin (Gallimard, 1991), p. 945.

420 *"Wagnerian bouillabaisse"*: Tristan Tzara, *Œuvres complètes*, vol. 1, ed. Henri Béhar (Flammarion, 1975), p. 417.

420 *"unending, futile"*: Marinetti, *Critical Writings*, p. 15; compare RWL, p. 210.

421 Peter Bürger: See his *Theory of the Avant-Garde*, trans. Michael Shaw (University of Minnesota Press, 1984), pp. 27–34, 48–50.

421 *"greatest decadent genius"*: Günter Berghaus, *Futurism and Politics: Between Anarchist Rebellion and Fascist Reaction, 1909–1944* (Berghahn, 1996), p. 18.

421 *"frenetic exuberance"*: Ibid., p. 18. For Marinetti, Wagner, and Nietzsche, see Luca Somigli, *Legitimizing the Artist: Manifesto Writing and European Modernism, 1885–1915* (University of Toronto Press, 2003), pp. 106–107.

421 *"reintegrate art"*: Bürger, *Theory of the Avant-Garde*, p. 22.

421 *"stillness, rapture"*: Marinetti, *Critical Writings*, p. 13.

421 *"We support unconditionally"*: Ibid., p. 189.

422 *"Marcia del cannoneggiamento"*: Éanna Ó Ceallacháin, ed. *Twentieth-Century Italian Poetry: A Critical Anthology (1900 to the Neo-Avantgarde)* (Troubadour, 2007), p. 34.

422 *"glorious and revolutionary"*: *Futurism: An Anthology*, pp. 76, 80. On Pratella's opera, see Giovanni Lista, "Futurist Music," in *Italian Futurism, 1909–1944: Reconstructing the Universe*, ed. Vivien Greene (Guggenheim, 2014), pp. 116–17.

422 Ramón Gómez de la Serna: See his "Futurist Proclamation to the Spaniards" (1910), trans. Mary Ann Caws, in *Manifesto: A Century of Isms*, ed. Mary Ann Caws (University of Nebraska Press, 2001), p. 372.

423 *"The Futurists wanted"*: Günter Berghaus, "The Futurist Conception of Gesamtkunstwerk and Marinetti's Total Theatre," in *"Sul fil di ragno della memoria": Studi in onore di Ilona Fried*, ed. Franciska Hervai d'Elhoungne and Dávid Falvay (Ponte Alapítvány, 2012), p. 286.

423 *"Total Theater"*: Marinetti, *Critical Writings*, p. 405.

423 Peter Dayan: See his "Zurich Dada, Wagner, and the Union of the Arts," *Forum for Modern Language Studies* 50:4 (2014), p. 456. Hugo Ball, *Flight out of Time: A Dada Diary*, ed. John Elderfield, trans. Ann Raimes (University of California Press, 1996), p. 233, compares Kandinsky to Parsifal's "purity and pathos."

423 Maria Stavrinaki: See her "Total Artwork vs. Revolution," trans. Nils Schott, in *Aesthetics of the Total Artwork*, pp. 267–74; Kurt Schwitters, "Ich und meine Ziele," *Merz* 21 (1931), p. 114.

423 *"romantic in their conviction"*: Badiou, *Handbook of Inaesthetics*, trans. Alberto Toscano (Stanford UP, 2005), p. 8.

424 *"A truly beautiful Germanic"*: Albrecht von Thaer, *Generalstabsdienst an der Front und in der OHL: Aus Briefen und Tagebuchaufzeichnungen 1915–1919*, ed. Siegfried A. Kaehler (Vandenhoeck & Ruprecht, 1958), p. 234. For a particularly gruesome *Dolchstoß* cartoon, see Gérard Silvain, *La Question juive en Europe, 1933–1945* (Lattès, 1985), p. 326.

424 *"We were at the end!"*: Paul von Hindenburg, *Aus meinem Leben* (Hirzel, 1920), p. 403.

425 George Mosse: See his *Fallen Soldiers: Reshaping the Memory of the World Wars* (Oxford UP, 1990). For the opposing view, see Robert Gerwarth, *The Vanquished: Why the First World War Failed to End* (Farrar, Straus and Giroux, 2016), pp. 1–15, 120–32.

426 *A neighbor in Linz remembers him*: Franz Jetzinger, *Hitler's Youth*, trans. Lawrence Wilson (Hutchinson, 1958), pp. 85–86.

426 *"I was captivated"*: Hitler, *Mein Kampf* (NSDAP, 1936), p. 15.

426 *"We who stood"*: Hitler, *Monologe im Führer-Hauptquartier, 1941–1944*, ed. Werner Jochmann (Knaus, 1980), p. 224.

426 Sebastian Werr: See his *Heroische Weltsicht: Hitler und die Musik* (Böhlau, 2014), p. 50; and "Romantische Traumwelten und Alldeutsche Politik: Linzer Wagner-Aufführungen in Adolf Hitlers Jugend (1901–1908)," *wagnerspectrum* 8:1 (2012), pp. 119–21.

427 *"Powerful waves of sound"*: Hitler, *Sämtliche Aufzeichnungen 1905–1924*, ed. Eberhard Jäckel with Axel Kuhn (Deutsche Verlags-Anstalt, 1980), p. 44. For Roller's letter, see Hitler, *Monologe*, p. 200.

427 *"pale light"*: Billy Price, *Adolf Hitler als Maler und Zeichner: Ein Werkkatalog der Ölgemälde, Aquarelle, Zeichnungen und Architekturskizzen* (Gallant, 1983), no. 542; Brigitte Hamann, *Hitler's Vienna: A Dictator's Apprenticeship*, trans. Thomas Thornton (Oxford UP, 1999), p. 61.

427 *first twelve lines*: Price, *Adolf Hitler*, no. 56; Hitler, *Sämtliche Aufzeichnungen*, p. 1254. An often-cited sketch of Siegfried with the legend "Wagner's work showed me for the first time what Blutmythos [blood-myth] is" is a forgery; see Eberhard Jäckel, Axel Kuhn, and Hermann Weiß, "Neue Erkenntnisse zur Fälschung von Hitler-Dokumenten," *Vierteljahrshefte für Zeitgeschichte* 32 (1984), p. 164.

427 *"conjured up in magnificent"*: August Kubizek, *Adolf Hitler war mein Jugendfreund* (Stocker, 1953), pp. 140–42. See also Albert Speer, *Spandauer Tagebücher* (Propyläen, 1994), p. 136; and Henry Picker, *Hitlers Tischgespräche im Führerhauptquartier* (Seewald, 1976), p. 95.

427 *"A. H. und Rienzi"*: Hanfstaengl Nachlass, Handschriften, Bayerischer Staatsbibliothek, Ana 405, box 25.

427 *Otto Wagener*: See his *Hitler: Memoirs of a Confidant*, ed. Henry Ashby Turner, Jr., trans. Ruth Hein (Yale UP, 1985), p. 217.

428 *partly or wholly fabricated*: Werr, "Romantische Traumwelten," pp. 122–30; Jonas Karlsson, "'In That Hour It Began'?: Hitler, *Rienzi*, and the Trustworthiness of August Kubizek's *The Young Hitler I Knew*," *Wagner Journal* 6:2 (2012), pp. 33–47. For a contrary view, see Ben Novak, "Hitler's *Rienzi* Experience: Factuality," *Revista de Historia Actual* 5:5 (2007), pp. 105–16. For more questions about Kubizek, see Frederic Spotts, *Hitler and the Power of Aesthetics* (Overlook Press, 2003), pp. xv–xviii.

428 *"hymns, processions"*: RWSS4, p. 259.

428 *Karl Lueger*: On Hitler's attitudes toward Schönerer and Lueger, see Hamann, *Hitler's Vienna*, pp. 236–303.

428 *testimony of Hanisch and others*: Volker Ullrich, *Hitler: Ascent, 1889–1939*, trans. Jefferson Chase (Knopf, 2016), pp. 43–45; Hamann, *Hitler's Vienna*, pp. 164–68.

428 *"patent normality"*: Hans Rudolf Vaget, "Wagnerian Self-Fashioning: The Case of Adolf Hitler," *New German Critique* 101 (2007), p. 114.

429 *humming the music*: Hans Severus Ziegler, *Adolf Hitler, aus dem Erleben dargestellt* (Schütz, 1964), p. 70.

429 *"will not only smash"*: Hitler, *Sämtliche Aufzeichnungen*, p. 69.

429 *"ever purer"*: Ernst Jünger, *In Stahlgewittern* (Klett, 1961), p. 155. Other quotations on pp. 279, 222.

429 *"very persuaded"*: Kessler, *Journey to the Abyss*, p. 692; Kessler, *Das Tagebuch 1880–1937*, vol. 5, ed. Günter Riederer and Ulrich Ott (Klett-Cotta, 2008), p. 364.

11. RING OF POWER: REVOLUTION AND RUSSIA

431 *William Archer noticed*: Michael Holroyd, *Bernard Shaw*, vol. 1 (Vintage, 1990), p. 135; Peter Whitebrook, *William Archer: A Biography* (Methuen, 1993), pp. 1–2.

431 *"frightfully real . . . predestined end"*: GBS, pp. 10, 102.

432 *"originated where Wagner"*: Frank Trommler, "The Social Politics of Musical Redemption," in *Re-Reading Wagner*, ed. Reinhold Grimm and Jost Hermand (University of Wisconsin Press, 1993), p. 133.

433 *James Garratt*: See his *Music, Culture, and Social Reform in the Age of Wagner* (Cambridge UP, 2010), pp. 160–61.

433 *"A tremendous movement"*: Gregor-Dellin, *Richard Wagner*, p. 290; RWSS12, p. 278. For the 1849 date, see Kröplin, *Wagner-Chronik*, pp. 167–68.

433 *"transforms loyalty"*: Marx, *Ökonomisch-philosophische Manuskripte aus dem Jahre 1844*, 3.4; Borchmeyer, *Drama and the World of Richard Wagner*, pp. 173–74. For monetary metamorphosis, see Marx, *Das Kapital*, vol. 1 (Meissner, 1883), p. 81.

434 *"sacrifices the lusts"*: Marx, *Das Kapital*, vol. 1, p. 107. In *Rheingold*, Woglinde sings; "Nur wer der Minne / Macht versagt." Wagner appears to have wavered between "entsagt" and "versagt," deciding on the latter during rehearsals for the 1876 première; see Wagner, *The Ring of the Nibelung*, ed. and trans. John Deathridge (Penguin, 2018), p. 729.

434 *"muddled people"*: CWD, May 31, 1878. On Wagner's later leftward shift, see Eckart Kröplin, *Richard Wagner und der Kommunismus: Studie zu einem verdrängten Thema* (Königshausen & Neumann, 2013), pp. 219–41.

434 *"He is becoming"*: CWD, June 17, 1879.

434 *"festivals seem absurd"*: CWD, Feb. 9, 1883.

434 *"Bayreuth fool's festival"*: Karl Marx and Friedrich Engels, *Werke*, vol. 34 (Dietz, 1966), p. 23.

434 *"The activities of this group"*: Ibid., p. 193.

434 *long footnote*: Engels, *Der Ursprung der Familie, des Privateigenthums und des Staats*, 5th ed. (Dietz, 1892), pp. 19–20.

435 *Alexander Herzen*: BWR, p. 13.

435 *"I am still in endless"*: Ferdinand Lassalle, *Nachgelassene Briefe und Schriften*, vol. 5 (Deutsche Verlags-Anstalt, 1925), p. 24.

435 *"like a Nordic bard"*: David Footman, *Ferdinand Lassalle: Romantic Revolutionary* (Yale UP, 1947), p. 122.

435 *"Germanic-Judaic"*: RWB16, p. 298.

435 *Marches from Rienzi*: Garratt, *Music, Culture*, p. 206.

435 *"society of the future . . . entirely socialistic"*: August Bebel, *Die Frau und der Sozialismus* (Dietz, 1891), pp. 324–27.

435 *Siegfried thrusting his sword*: Veltzke, *Mythos des Erlösers*, p. 79.

435 *Later socialist literature*: Quotations from Rudolf Franz, "Wagner der Erlöser," *Neue Zeit* 30 (1912), p. 783.

436 *"strong, beautiful man"*: Clara Zetkin, *Über Literatur und Kunst*, ed. Emilia Zetkin-Milowidowa (Henschel, 1955), p. 107.

436 *William McGrath*: See his *Dionysian Art and Populist Politics in Austria* (Yale UP, 1974) p. 203, and "Student Radicalism in Vienna," *Journal of Contemporary History* 2:3 (1967), p. 193. See also Wolfgang Maderthaner, "Victor Adlers Wagner: Zur Wagnerrezeption im Austromarxismus," *wagnerspectrum* 3:2 (2007), p. 170; and Johann Wilhelm Seidl, *Musik und Austromarxismus: Zur Musikrezeption der österreichischen Arbeiterbewegung im späten Kaiserreich und in der Ersten Republik* (Böhlau, 1989), pp. 19–15.

436 *"For us in Austria"*: McGrath, *Dionysian Art*, p. 222.

436 *Wolfgang Maderthaner*: "Victor Adlers Wagner," p. 173.

436 *"man of the people"*: Engelbert Pernerstorfer, "Richard Wagner und der Sozialismus," *Deutsche Worte* 11 (1891), p. 167. Other quotations on pp. 187, 189.

437 *"never went to America"*: Franz, "Wagner der Erlöser," part 2, p. 815.

437 *Wilhelm Ellenbogen*: See his *Ausgewählte Schriften*, ed. Norbert Leser and Georg G. Rundel (Österreichischer Bundesverlag, 1983), pp. 356–63.

437 *"revealed to Wagner"*: Jean Jaurès, "L'Art et le socialisme," *Revue socialiste* 31 (1900), p. 524.

437 *at once deeply traditional*: Maurice Pottecher, "Jean Jaurès et Richard Wagner," *Grande Revue*, July 1932, pp. 35–45.

437 *"cults of force"*: Harvey Goldberg, *The Life of Jean Jaurès* (University of Wisconsin Press, 1962), p. 400. For Jaurès and Dreyfus, see *Souvenirs de Charles Bonnier*, pp. 214–18.

437 *"superhuman" characters*: Romain Rolland, *Le Théâtre du peuple* (Cahiers de la Quinzaine, 1903), pp. 47–49. For more, see David Roberts, *The Total Work of Art in European Modernism* (Cornell UP, 2011) p. 191.

437 *"if we had* life": Rolland, *Théâtre du peuple*, p. 149. See also RWL, p. 246.

438 *"the mob becomes"*: WBY10, p. 88.

438 *Katerina Clark*: See her *Petersburg: Crucible of Cultural Revolution* (Harvard UP, 1995), pp. 79–80.

438 *"our seats"*: Margaret Cole, *Beatrice Webb* (Harcourt, 1946), p. 63; also Norman and Jeanne Mackenzie, eds., *The Diary of Beatrice Webb*, vol. 3 (Virago, 1984), p. 199. For Shaw and the Fabians, see May Morris, *William Morris, Artist, Writer, Socialist*, vol. 2 (Basil Blackwell, 1936), p. 98.

439 *"the evil of deliberately"*: Shaw, *London Music in 1888–89* (Constable, 1937), p. 177.

439 *"a garden scene"*: William Irvine, *The Universe of G.B.S.* (Whittlesey, 1949), p. 155; Shaw, *Widowers' Houses* (Henry, 1893), p. x.

439 *Scholars have detected*: See William Blissett, "Bernard Shaw: Imperfect Wagnerite," *University of Toronto Quarterly* 27:2 (1958), pp. 185–99; J. L. Wisenthal, "The Underside of Undershaft: A Wagnerian Motif in *Major Barbara*," *Shaw Review* 15:2 (1972), pp. 56–64; Robert Coskren, "Wagner and Shaw: *Rheingold* Motifs in *Major Barbara*," *Comparative Drama* 14:1 (1980), pp. 70–73; Christopher Innes, "The (Im)perfect Wagnerite: Bernard Shaw and Richard Wagner," in *Text & Presentation, 2009*, ed. Kiki Gounaridou (McFarland, 2010), pp. 22–31.

439 *"cultured, leisured . . . There is a moon"*: Shaw, *Complete Plays with Prefaces*, vol. 1 (Dodd, Mead, 1962), pp. 449, 561.

440 *"the real"*: *Complete Plays with Prefaces*, vol. 3 (Dodd, Mead, 1962), p. 649.

440 *Wagner is, at least half*: Blissett, *Bernard Shaw*, p. 198.

440 *"drama of today"*: GBS, p. 1. Other quotations on pp. 5, 90–91, 68, 87, 117.

441 *Herr Battler*: Michael Holroyd, *Bernard Shaw*, vol. 3 (Random House, 1991), p. 403.

441 *Upton Sinclair*: See his *Prince Hagen: A Phantasy* (Kerr, 1910).

442 *"The Valkyries fly"*: Translation by Rosamund Bartlett.

443 *"the aesthetic-cultural"*: Bernice Glatzer Rosenthal, "Wagner and Wagnerian Ideas in Russia," in WECP, p. 199.

443 *"suspicious and politically suspect"*: BWR, p. 19.

443 *Nicholas II*: Aleksandr Mossolov, *At the Court of the Last Tsar* (Methuen, 1935), p. 20.

443 *"full of noble aims"*: BWR, pp. 50–51.

443 *"stupid puppet show"*: Ibid., p. 53.

443 *"model work of counterfeit art"*: Leo Tolstoy, *What Is Art?*, trans. Aylmer Maude (Crowell, 1899), p. 114. On Tolstoy and Wagner, see Bartlett, *Tolstoy: A Russian Life* (Houghton Mifflin, 2011), pp. 372–74.

443 *"the mistake Wagner"*: Tolstoy, *Anna Karenina*, trans. Rosamund Bartlett (Oxford UP, 2014), p. 688.

443 *"naturalistic power"*: TMW, p. 87.

444 *"The very first chords"*: Alexandre Benois, *Reminiscences of the Russian Ballet*, trans. Mary Britnieva (Da Capo, 1977), p. 114. For wandering the woods, see Benois, *Memoirs*, vol. 2, trans. Moura Budberg (Chatto & Windus, 1964), p. 56.

444 *"Wagner fanatic . . . Until I've heard"*: Sjeng Scheijen, *Diaghilev: A Life*, trans. Jane Hedley-Prôle and S. J. Leinbach (Profile, 2009), pp. 57–58, 62; death on pp. 439–40.

444 *Russian Parsifal*: Ibid., p. 112.

445 *"the idea for which"*: Benois, *Reminiscences*, pp. 370–71. See also Janet Kennedy, *The "Mir iskusstva" Group and Russian Art, 1898–1912* (Ph.D. diss., Columbia University, 1976), p. 343.

445 *"the very closest fusion"*: PCW, pp. 210–11.

445 *"alliance of dancing"*: Cyril Beaumont, *Michel Fokine and His Ballets* (Dance Horizons, 1981), p. 147.

445 *Juliet Bellow*: See her *Modernism on Stage: The Ballets Russes and the Parisian Avant-Garde* (Ashgate, 2013), pp. 13, 248–49.

445 *"Periodicals are commemorating"*: Author's translation from *Montjoie*, as reproduced in Richard Taruskin, *Stravinsky and the Russian Traditions: A Biography of the Works Through "Mavra,"* vol. 2 (University of California Press, 1996), p. 1000.

445 *twentieth-century Wagner*: Annegret Fauser, "Le Sacre du Printemps: Un ballet . . . français?," paper at "Reassessing the *Rite*; A Centennial Conference," University of North Carolina at Chapel Hill, Oct. 28, 2012.

445–46 *Nijinsky, who could play*: Vera Krasovskaya, *Nijinsky*, trans. John E. Bowlt (Schirmer, 1979), p. 45. For staging ideas, see Romola Nijinsky, *Nijinsky and the Last Years of Nijinsky* (Simon and Schuster, 1980), p. 304. For Bayreuth, see Scheijen, *Diaghilev*, p. 235; Bronislava Nijinska, *Early Memoirs*, ed. and trans. Irina Nijinska and Jean Rawlinson (Duke UP, 1992), p. 441.

446 *"unseemly and sacrilegious"*: Stravinsky, *An Autobiography* [*Chroniques de ma vie*] (Norton, 1962), pp. 38–39. For "great art," see Stephen Walsh, *Stravinsky: A Creative Spring: Russia and France, 1882–1934* (Knopf, 1999), p. 183.

446 *Roerich*: See Taisiya Pugachev, "N. K. Roerich and R. Wagner: The Opera *Walküre*," *Culture into Life*, Sept. 29, 2012, culture-into-life.ru; Jacqueline Decter, *Nicholas Roerich: The Life and Art of a Russian Master* (Thames and Hudson, 1989), pp. 39–40; BWR, pp. 67–68.

446 *"do the stage setting"*: Mary Fanton Roberts, "Roerich: A Master of Modern Russian Art," *Touchstone* 8:5 (1921), p. 333.

446 *rocks seemed to sing Wagner*: Roerich, *Altai-Himalaya: A Travel Diary* (Stokes, 1929), p. 107.

446 *"Long have I been aware"*: John C. Culver and John Hyde, *American Dreamer: A Life of Henry A. Wallace* (Norton, 2001), p. 135.

447 *goblet supposedly filled*: Robert Bird, *The Russian Prospero: The Creative Universe of Viacheslav Ivanov* (University of Wisconsin Press, 2006), p. 12; Kristi A. Groberg, "'The Shade of Lucifer's Dark Wing': Satanism in Silver Age Russia," in *The Occult in Russian and Soviet Culture*, ed. Bernice Glatzer Rosenthal (Cornell UP, 1997), pp. 99–101.

447 *"first forerunner"*: Rebecca Mitchell, *Nietzsche's Orphans: Music, Metaphysics, and the Twilight of the Russian Empire* (Yale UP, 2015), p. 48.

447 *sobornost'*: See BWR, p. 125; Bird, *Russian Prospero*, pp. 27–30.

447 *"The spectator must"*: Vyacheslav Ivanov, "Presentiments and Portents," *Selected Essays*, ed. Michael Wachtel, trans. Robert Bird (Northwestern UP, 2001), p. 104. See also BWR, pp. 117–38; and Simon Morrison, *Russian Opera and the Symbolist Movement* (University of California Press, 2019), pp. 147–50.

447 *"mystical anarchism"*: Bernice Glatzer Rosenthal, "The Transmutation of the Symbolist Ethos: Mystical Anarchism and the Revolution of 1905," *Slavic Review* 36:4 (1977), pp. 608–27.

448 *Emil Medtner*: See BWR, pp. 145–46; Magnus Ljunggren, *The Russian Mephisto: A Study of the Life and Work of Emilii Medtner* (Almqvist & Wiksell, 1986), p. 25.

448 *"the first musician"*: Andrey Bely, *The Dramatic Symphony and The Forms of Art*, trans. Roger and Angela Keys and John Elsworth (Grove, 1986), p. 181.

448 *Ada Steinberg*: See his *Word and Music in the Novels of Andrey Bely* (Cambridge UP, 1982), p. 31; "with phrases" on p. 41.

448 *"1. A season"*: Bely, *Dramatic Symphony*, p. 19. Other quotations on pp. 90, 91, 102, 105, 110, 127, 95, 137. For Siegfried and Brünnhilde in the symphonies, see BWR, p. 160.

449 *"borrowed heroism"*: BWR, p. 162. For Palermo, see p. 174.

449 *"We wait for Parsifal"*: Bernice Glatzer Rosenthal, "Revolution as Apocalypse: The Case of Bely," in *Andrey Bely: A Critical Review*, ed. Gerald Janacek (University Press of Kentucky, 1978), p. 183. See also David N. Wells, "The Symbolic Structure of Belyi's 'Pervoe svidanie': Echoes of Wagner and Steiner," *Slavonic and East European Review* 81:2 (2003), pp. 201–16.

449 *"from the leaden expanses"*: Bely, *Petersburg*, trans. David McDuff (Penguin, 2011), p. 17.

450 *"intended to study meloplastics"*: Ibid., p. 75.

450 *"Black sword broke"*: Alexander Blok, "Valkiria," *Sobranie sochinenii*, vol. 1 (Khudozhestvennaya Literatura, 1960), pp. 349–50.

451 *"The whole horizon"*: Blok, *The Twelve and Other Poems*, trans. Jon Stallworthy and Peter France (Oxford UP, 1970), p. 44. See also Lyubov Mendeleeva-Blok's commentary on Brünnhilde in Lucy Vogel, ed. and trans., *Blok: An Anthology of Essays and Memoirs* (Ardis, 1982), p. 23; Blok, *The*

Rose and the Cross, in *The Russian Symbolist Theatre: An Anthology of Plays and Critical Texts*, ed. and trans. Michael Green (Ardis, 1986), pp. 59–107; Morrison, *Russian Opera*, pp. 14–24.

451 *"Every time I hear him"*: Avril Pyman, *The Life of Aleksandr Blok*, vol. 2 (Oxford UP, 1979), p. 67.

451 *"Wagner is still both alive"*: Blok, "Iskusstvo i revoliutsiia," *Sobranie sochinenii*, vol. 6 (Khudozhestvennaya Literatura, 1962), pp. 24–25.

451 *"The great bell of anti-humanism"*: Translations taken from Rosenthal, "Wagner and Wagnerian Ideas," p. 229, and Isaiah Berlin's 1931 translation of "The Collapse of Humanism," Isaiah Berlin Virtual Library, berlin.wolf.ox.ac.uk.

451 *"Only down deep"*: BWR, p. 197.

452 *Parsifal*: BWR, p. 223, says that there was a *Parsifal* at the Theatre of Musical Drama in March 1918; Pauline Fairclough, *Classics for the Masses: Shaping Soviet Musical Identity Under Lenin and Stalin* (Yale UP, 2016), p. 243, has trouble verifying this.

452 *"He liked Wagner"*: Tamás Krausz, *Reconstructing Lenin: An Intellectual Biography* (Monthly Review, 2015), p. 463. See also Robert Service, *Lenin: A Biography* (Macmillan, 2000), p. 30; Fairclough, "Wagner Reception in Stalinist Russia," in Sala, *Legacy of Richard Wagner*, p. 310; Gerda and Hermann Weber, *Lenin: Life and Works*, ed. and trans. Martin McCauley (Macmillan, 1980), p. 117.

453 *"It is as if"*: BWR, p. 235. See also Fairclough, *Classics for the Masses*, p. 26. For the memorial, see Simon Morrison, *Bolshoi Confidential: Secrets of the Russian Ballet from the Rule of the Tsars to Today* (Liveright, 2016), p. 231.

453 *"The Party must be"*: Sheila Fitzpatrick, *The Commissariat of Enlightenment: Soviet Organization of Education and the Arts Under Lunacharsky, October 1917–1921* (Cambridge UP, 1970), p. 245.

453 *"The revolutionary movement"*: Rosenthal, "Wagner and Wagnerian Ideas," p. 234.

453 *"first significant"*: Lars Kleberg, "'People's Theater' and the Revolution," in *Art, Society, Revolution: Russia, 1917–1921*, ed. Nils Åke Nilsson (Almqvist & Wiksell, 1979), p. 189. See also Kleberg, *Theatre as Action: Soviet Russian Avant-Garde Aesthetics* (NYU Press, 1993); Anatoly Lunacharsky, "Richard Wagner," *On Literature and Art* (Progress, 1965), pp. 340–54.

453 *"close fraternity"*: Stefan Aquilina, "Platon Kerzhentsev and His Theories on Collective Creation," *Journal of Dramatic Theory and Criticism* 28:2 (2014), p. 33.

454 *Kingdom of Freedom*: Clark, *Petersburg*, p. 130.

454 *"orgiastic exultation"*: James Von Geldern, *Bolshevik Festivals, 1917–1920* (University of California Press, 1993), p. 33.

454 *Vladimir Tatlin*: See Flora Syrkina, "Tatlin's Theatre," in *Tatlin*, ed. Larissa Zhadova (Rizzoli, 1988), p. 160; BWR, pp. 221–23. For Mikhail Kolesnikov, see his "The Russian Avant-Garde and the Theatre of

the Artist," in *Theatre in Revolution: Russian Avant-Garde Stage Design, 1913–1935*, ed. Nancy Van Norman Baer (Thames and Hudson, 1991), p. 85.

454 *read in their entirety*: Paul Schmidt, "Discovering Meyerhold: Traces of a Search," *October* 7 (1978), p. 78.

455 *"I want to burn"*: Edward Braun, *Meyerhold: A Revolution in Theatre* (Methuen Drama, 1995), p. 13.

455 *"convention, generalization . . . cold coining"*: Ibid., pp. 35, 38.

455 *"bench where Venus"*: Blok, "The Puppet Show," in Green, *Russian Symbolist Theatre*, pp. 51, 48.

455 *seventy-one pages*: BWR, p. 97.

455 *"First Attempts"*: Edward Braun, ed. and trans., *Meyerhold on Theatre* (Hill and Wang, 1969), pp. 49, 55–56, 51.

456 *"The world of the soul"*: Ibid., p. 83. Other quotations on pp. 81, 89.

456 *Carney points out*: PCW, pp. 214–17.

456 *"Tristan and Isolde writhe"*: Konstantin Rudnitsky, *Meyerhold the Director*, ed. Sydney Schultze, trans. George Petrov (Ardis, 1981), p. 144.

457 *Wagnerian-Nietzschean agenda*: Clark, *Petersburg*, pp. 74–99.

457 *"Bolshevized"*: BWR, p. 239.

457 *"symphony of color"*: BWR, p. 248. For other radical productions, see pp. 224–25, 241–47. For Meyerhold's regret, see his *Écrits sur le théâtre*, vol. 4, ed. and trans. Béatrice Picon-Vallin (L'Âge d'Homme, 1992), p. 340. For more on Yakulov's *Rienzi*, see Huntley Carter, *The New Theatre and Cinema of Soviet Russia* (Chapman and Hall, 1924), p. 144.

458 *"retreat from"*: Clark, *Petersburg*, p. 151.

458 *"Catholic," "mystical"*: BWR, pp. 250–51; "self-affirming aspirations" on p. 261.

459 *"Johannistag!"*: Rosa Luxemburg, *Gesammelte Briefe*, vol. 5 (Dietz, 1984), pp. 249–50. See also *Gesammelte Briefe*, vol. 3 (Dietz, 1982), p. 193; *Gesammelte Briefe*, vol. 2 (Dietz, 1982), p. 395.

459 *conversant with Wagner's work*: Bernhard Grau, *Kurt Eisner, 1867–1919: Eine Biographie* (Beck, 2001), pp. 38, 42; Kurt Eisner, *Gesammelte Schriften*, vol. 2 (Cassirer, 1919), p. 327.

459 *"sunk below"*: Mann, *Tagebücher, 1918–21*, p. 160. After reading the papers the day after Eisner's funeral, Mann wrote, "The Wagner music appears to have been canceled" (p. 163). It is not clear whether it was. "Die Totenfeier für Kurt Eisner," *Rosenheimer Anzeiger*, Feb. 28, 1919, mentions an "orchestral piece" but does not name it. For the announcement of Wagner, see Reinhart Hoffmeister, *Schatten über München: Wahrheit und Wirklichkeit in Lion Feuchtwangers Roman "Erfolg": Eine Dokumentation* (Langen Müller, 1981), p. 61.

460 *"Today the arts exist"*: Anton Kaes et al., eds., *The Weimar Republic Sourcebook* (University of California Press, 1994), p. 435.

460 *Lyonel Feininger*: Reproduced in Charles W. Haxthausen, "Walter Gropius and Lyonel Feininger:

Bauhaus Manifesto, 1919," in *Bauhaus 1919–1933: Workshops for Modernity*, ed. Barry Bergdoll and Leah Dickerman (Museum of Modern Art, 2009), p. 65.

460 *"appeal to primordial"*: Smith, *Total Work of Art*, p. 49; "multifarious complexities" on p. 65.

460 *"What we need"*: László Moholy-Nagy, *Painting, Photography, Film*, trans. Janet Seligman (MIT Press, 1969), p. 17. See also his "Theater, Circus, Variety," trans. Arthur S. Wensinger, in *The Theater of the Bauhaus*, ed. Walter Gropius and Arthur S. Wensinger (Wesleyan UP, 1961), pp. 62–64.

461 *Rudolf Laban*: See Valerie Preston-Dunlop, *Rudolf Laban: An Extraordinary Life* (Dance Books, 1998), pp. 69, 106–107, 157–59; Rudolf Laban, *Ein Leben für den Tanz: Erinnerungen* (Reissner, 1935), p. 210; Karl Toepfer, *Empire of Ecstasy: Nudity and Movement in German Body Culture, 1910–1935* (University of California Press, 1997).

461 *"Wagner's program"*: Gertrud Bäumer, *Die soziale Idee in den Weltanschauungen des 19. Jahrhunderts: Die Grundzüge der modernen Sozialphilosophie* (Salzer, 1910), p. 309. See also Kevin Repp, *Reformers, Critics, and the Paths of German Modernity* (Harvard UP, 2000), p. 320.

461 *Stella Junker-Weissenberg*: See Andrea Winklbauer, ed., *Euphorie und Unbehagen: Das jüdische Wien und Richard Wagner* (Metroverlag, 2013), p. 177.

463 *"Wagner was himself"*: Hermann Hesse, *Klingsors letzter Sommer: Erzählungen* (Fischer, 1920), p. 120.

463 *"plunged berserk"*: Hugo Ball, *Hermann Hesse: Sein Leben und sein Werk* (Suhrkamp, 1977), p. 149.

463 *"Intermittent waves"*: Robert Musil, *The Man Without Qualities*, vol. 1, ed. Burton Pike, trans. Sophie Wilkins (Vintage, 1996), p. 47.

464 *"herrlich"*: Brecht, *Werke*, vol. 19, ed. Werner Hecht et al. (Aufbau/Suhrkamp, 1997), p. 12. For "nicht Wagner," see *Werke*, vol. 28, ed. Günter Glaeser (Aufbau/Suhrkamp, 1981), pp. 20–21.

464 *"bound together"*: Joy H. Calico, *Brecht at the Opera* (University of California Press, 2008), p. 2.

464 *hurdy-gurdy is heard playing*: Tristan was introduced in the 1922 version. See Brecht, *Collected Plays*, vol. 1, ed. and trans. John Willett and Ralph Manheim (Methuen, 1970), p. 375.

464 *"Siegfried Had Red Hair"*: Brecht, *Werke*, vol. 13, ed. Werner Hecht et al. (Aufbau/Suhrkamp, 1993), p. 255.

464 *He admired*: Gunnar Decker, *Hesse: The Wanderer and His Shadow*, trans. Peter Lewis (Harvard UP, 2018), p. 211.

465 *"radical separation of the elements"*: John Willett, ed. and trans., *Brecht on Theatre: The Development of an Aesthetic* (Hill and Wang, 1964), pp. 37–38; Calico, *Brecht at the Opera*, pp. 52–53; Brecht, *Werke*, vol. 24, ed. Werner Hecht et al. (Aufbau/Suhrkamp, 1991), p. 79.

465 *"Brecht, like Wagner"*: Smith, *Total Work of Art*, p. 78. See also Christiane Heibach, "Avant-Garde Theater as Total Artwork?: Media-Theoretical Reflections on the Historical Development of Performing Art Forms," in *Aesthetics of the Total Artwork*, pp. 222–23.

465 *"both gist and gesture"*: Willett, *Brecht on Theatre*, p. 42.

466 *"primacy of the body"*: Calico, *Brecht at the Opera*, p. 53. See also Hilda Meldrum Brown, *Leitmotiv and Drama: Wagner, Brecht, and the Limits of "Epic" Theatre* (Clarendon, 1991), p. 82; and Mary Ann Smart, *Mimomania: Music and Gesture in Nineteenth-Century Opera* (University of California Press, 2004), pp. 28–29.

466 *Wagner's attacks*: RWSS9, p. 204.

466 *"Who bears the greatest"*: Bernhard Diebold, *Der Fall Wagner: Eine Revision* (Frankfurter Societäts-Druckerei, 1928), p. 11. For Gustav Stresemann, see his *Vermächtnis*, vol. 3: *Von Thoiry bis zum Ausklang* (Ullstein, 1933), p. 514.

466 *Many leftist intellectuals*: Ludwig Marcuse, "Fortschrittliche Reaktion," *Weltbühne*, Nov. 6, 1928; Peter Panter [Kurt Tucholsky], "Oh you my sweet evening-star," *Weltbühne*, Aug. 28, 1928; Carl von Ossietzky, "Richard Wagner," *Weltbühne*, Feb. 21, 1933; Paul Bekker, *Wagner: Das Leben im Werke* (Deutsche Verlags-Anstalt, 1924), p. 536; Alfred Einstein, "Der Jude in der Musik," *Der Morgen* 6 (1927), p. 599.

467 *"expressionist color-light-music"*: Oswald Georg Bauer, *Richard Wagner: Die Bühnenwerke von der Uraufführung bis heute* (Propyläen, 1982), p. 234. For Weimar-era productions, see Bauer, *Richard Wagner*, pp. 74–75, 77, 276–77, 248–49; Christian Bührle, "Scénographie wagnérienne et peinture," in *Wagner, visions d'artistes*, pp. 70–71.

467 *"unparalleled cultural shamelessness"*: Peter Heyworth, *Otto Klemperer: His Life and Times*, vol. 1 (Cambridge UP, 1983), p. 279.

467 *Dülberg*: Peter W. Marx, ed., *Dülberg Meets Wagner* (Wienand, 2013), pp. 24–27.

468 *Alfred Einstein*: His commentaries and those of Beidler and Diebold quoted from Hans Curjel, *Experiment Krolloper, 1927–1931* (Prestel, 1975), pp. 253, 58, 255.

468 *Karl May*: See Hans-Werner Schmidt, ed., *Weltenschöpfer: Richard Wagner, Max Klinger, Karl May* (Hatje Cantz, 2013).

468 *"kitsch-mythology"*: Ernst Bloch, *Erbschaft dieser Zeit* (Suhrkamp, 1969), p. 373; other quotations on pp. 374, 377.

468 *"big singers, big arias"*: Heyworth, ed., *Conversations with Klemperer* (Faber and Faber, 1985), p. 80. See also John Rockwell, "Idealism and Innocence: The Failure of Opera Reform in the Late Weimar Republic," in *Late Thoughts: Reflections on Artists and Composers at Work*, ed. Karen Painter and Thomas Crow (Getty, 2006), pp. 195–200.

468 *"modern question"*: Bloch, *Erbschaft*, p. 372.

12. FLYING DUTCHMAN: *ULYSSES*, *THE WASTE LAND*, *THE WAVES*

470 *"the wanderings of Ulysses"*: William Ashton Ellis, trans., *Richard Wagner's Prose Works*, vol. 1 (University of Nebraska Press, 1993), p. 307; Timothy Martin, *Joyce and Wagner: A Study of Influence* (Cambridge UP, 1991), pp. 55–57, 69–70 (marking of text). For the original, see RWSS4, p. 265. Quotations from *Ulysses* are based on the Hans Walter Gabler edition (Vintage, 1986).

470 *"the great Work"*: Fredric Jameson, *Postmodernism; or, The Cultural Logic of Late Capitalism* (Duke UP, 1991), p. 305.

470 *"destroyed the whole"*: VWD2, p. 203.

471 *"I've always told him"*: Richard Ellmann, *James Joyce: New and Revised Edition* (Oxford UP, 1982), p. 561.

472 *quintet from* Meistersinger: Ibid., p. 269.

472 *"a more serious"*: Martin, *Joyce and Wagner*, p. 6.

472 *"and, unlike Joyce"*: Sylvia Beach, *Shakespeare and Company* (University of Nebraska Press, 1991), p. 162.

472 *"As we grew older"*: J. F. Byrne, *Silent Years: An Autobiography with Memoirs of James Joyce and Our Ireland* (Farrar, Straus and Young, 1953), p. 65.

472 *on the Valkyrie"*: Stanislaus Joyce, *My Brother's Keeper: James Joyce's Early Years* (Viking, 1958), pp. 86, 171.

472 *Carl Rosa*: Seamus Reilly, "James Joyce and Dublin Opera, 1888–1904," in *Bronze by Gold: The Music of Joyce*, ed. Sebastian D. G. Knowles (Garland, 1999), pp. 21–22.

472 *remarkable mixture*: John P. Jackson, "Introduction," in *The Flying Dutchman*, trans. Jackson (Carl Rosa Opera Company, 1876), p. x.

472–73 *"Every race has made . . . Lohengrin, the drama"*: Ellsworth Mason and Richard Ellmann, eds., *The Critical Writings of James Joyce* (Cornell UP, 1989), pp. 43, 45. "The Day of the Rabblement" is on pp. 68–72.

473 *both terms appear*: George Bernard Shaw, *The Sanity of Art: An Exposure of the Current Nonsense About Artists Being Degenerate* (New Age, 1908), pp. 38, 25.

473 *"In Wagner's Ring"*: Jelavich, *Munich and Theatrical Modernism*, pp. 24–25.

473 *"majestic-sclerotic"*: TMW, p. 88. For the swan, see *Critical Writings of James Joyce*, p. 58.

473 *"Tell Stannie"*: Richard Ellmann, ed., *Letters of James Joyce*, vol. 2 (Viking, 1966), p. 25. For the dragon, see *L'Illustration*, Jan. 4, 1902.

473 *the passage that Joyce marked*: Martin, *Joyce and Wagner*, pp. 69–70. See also *Richard Wagner's Prose Works*, vol. 1, p. 310; RWSS4, p. 268.

474 *"When I play Wagner"*: Ellmann, *James Joyce*, p. 112.

474 *"the sensation of swimming"*: Richard Ellmann, ed., *Letters of James Joyce*, vol. 3 (Viking, 1966), pp. 191–92.

474 *"a sudden spiritual manifestation"*: Joyce, *Stephen Hero*, ed. Theodore Spencer (New Directions, 1963), p. 211.

474 *Paul Devine*: See his "Leitmotif and Epiphany: George Moore's *Evelyn Innes* and *The Lake*," in *Moments of Moment: Aspects of the Literary Epiphany*, ed. Wim Tigges (Rodopi, 1999), pp. 155–75.

474 *"I go to encounter"*: Joyce, *A Portrait of the Artist as a Young Man* (Penguin, 1976), p. 253.

474 *William Blissett*: See his "James Joyce in the Smithy of His Soul," in *James Joyce Today: Essays on the Major Works*, ed. Thomas F. Staley (Indiana UP, 1966), pp. 101–102; also George Moore, *Hail and Farewell*, vol. 3 (Appleton, 1914), p. 306.

475 *"lived in the public"*: Wagner's Prose Works, vol. 1, pp. 51–52; Martin, *Joyce and Wagner*, pp. 49–50. In Michael Patrick Gillespie, *James Joyce's Trieste Library: A Catalogue of Materials at the Harry Ransom Humanities Research Center, the University of Texas at Austin* (HRHRC, 1986), p. 251, markings are specified as beginning with "adequate expression of the public conscience."

475 *attended three or four performances*: Alessandro Francini Bruni to Richard Ellmann, July 1954, Richard Ellmann Papers, University of Tulsa Special Collections. On Wagner in Trieste, see Ute Jung, *Die Rezeption der Kunst Richard Wagners in Italien* (Bosse, 1974), p. 130. For the Good Friday Spell in French, see Francini Bruni to Ellmann, July 1954, Ellmann Papers.

475 *"nothing in the opera"*: Letters of James Joyce, vol. 2, p. 214. For "pretentious stuff," see Stuart Gilbert, ed., *Letters of James Joyce*, vol. 1 (Viking, 1957), p. 67; for "despised Wagner," Oscar Schwarz to Richard Ellmann, Aug. 16, 1955, Ellmann Papers. Similar comments appear in Willard Potts, ed., *Portraits of the Artist in Exile: Recollections of James Joyce by Europeans* (University of Washington Press, 1979), pp. 168, 195, 248.

476 *d'Annunzio's Wagner-themed novels*: John McCourt, *The Years of Bloom: James Joyce in Trieste, 1904–1920* (University of Wisconsin Press, 2000), pp. 76, 155.

476 *"hard-won acceptance"*: Vicki Mahaffey, "Joyce's Shorter Works," in *The Cambridge Companion to James Joyce*, 2nd ed., ed. Derek Attridge (Cambridge UP, 2004), p. 192.

476 *befriended Leopoldo*: Vicki Mahaffey, "Fascism and Silence: The Coded History of Amalia Popper," *James Joyce Quarterly* 32:3–4 (1995), p. 504.

476 *read Otto Weininger*: McCourt, *Years of Bloom*, pp. 228–29; see also II.i.1. Notebook, the Joyce Papers, National Library of Ireland, catalogue .nli.ie. On Joyce and Weininger, see Ralph Robert Joly, "Chauvinist Brew and Leopold Bloom: The Weininger Legacy," *James Joyce Quarterly* 19:2 (1982), pp. 194–98; and Wim Van Mierlo, "The Subject Notebook: A Nexus in the Composition History of Ulysses—A Preliminary Analysis," *Genetic Joyce Studies* 7 (2007), www.geneticjoycestudies.org.

476 *"Jewishness in Music"*: For its inclusion in Joyce's Trieste library, see Gillespie, *Joyce's Trieste Library*, p. 250.

476 *Neil Davison*: See his *James Joyce, "Ulysses," and the Construction of Jewish Identity: Culture, Biography, and "The Jew" in Modernist Europe* (Cambridge UP, 1996), p. 151. See also Ira Nadel, *Joyce and the Jews: Culture and Texts* (University of Iowa Press, 1989), pp. 16–17.

476 *"The Jew converses"*: Wagner, *Judaism in Music*, trans. Edwin Evans (Reeves, 1910), p. 11.

477 *Joyce walked out*: Ellmann, *James Joyce*, p. 460.

477 *"Wagner was a fantasist"*: Eric Bentley, "The Theatres of Wagner and Ibsen," *Kenyon Review* 6:4 (1944), p. 568.

479 *spurred much debate*: See Michael Seidel, "*Ulysses'* Black Panther Vampire," *James Joyce Quarterly* 13:4 (1976), pp. 415–27; John Gordon, "Notes in Response to Michael Seidel's "*Ulysses'* Black Panther Vampire," *James Joyce Quarterly* 15:3 (1978), pp. 229–35; John Gordon, "Haines and the Black Panther," *James Joyce Quarterly* 27:3 (1990), pp. 587–94.

479 *"black dog . . . the annihilation"*: Weininger, *Über die letzten Dinge*, pp. 122–23.

480 *"Vieille ogresse"*: Édouard Drumont, *Le Testament d'un antisémite* (Dentu, 1891), p. 162. Citation first identified in Alex Ross, *The Archconspirators of the Age: Outlaws and Outcasts in Conan Doyle's Sherlock Holmes Stories and in Joyce's "Ulysses"* (B.A. thesis, Harvard University, 1990).

481 *standard explanation*: Don Gifford, in *"Ulysses" Annotated: Notes for James Joyce's "Ulysses,"* 2nd ed. (University of California Press, 1988), p. 62.

481 *"She dreams him"*: II.ii.1.a. Notebook, the Joyce Papers, National Library of Ireland, catalogue.nli.ie.

481 *Stuart Gilbert*: See his *James Joyce's "Ulysses": A Study* (Faber and Faber, 1930), p. 133.

481 *"eternal Jew of the ocean"*: Heine, *Gesammelte Werke*, vol. 4, ed. Gustav Karpeles (Grote, 1887), p. 293.

482 *Bram Stoker*: Robert Eighteen-Bisang and Elizabeth Miller, eds., *Bram Stoker's Notes for "Dracula": A Facsimile Edition* (McFarland, 2008), pp. 94–95. On Bloom as vampire, see Lori B. Harrison, "Bloodsucking Bloom: Vampirism as a Representation of Jewishness in *Ulysses*," *James Joyce Quarterly* 36:4 (1999), pp. 781–97.

484 *Matthew Hodgart*: See his *James Joyce: A Student's Guide* (Routledge, 1978), p. 99. On *Ulysses* leitmotifs, see Gilbert, *James Joyce's "Ulysses,"* p. 243; and Zack Bowen, *Musical Allusions in the Works of James Joyce: Early Poetry Through "Ulysses"* (State University of New York Press, 1974), pp. 52–53.

484 *"my favorite Wagnerian"*: Recollection of George Borach, in Potts, *Portraits of the Artist in Exile*, p. 72. For more, see Martin, *Joyce and Wagner*, pp. 245–46.

485 *"this industry that kills"*: RWSS3, p. 49.

488 *"No writer tried"*: Bryan Cheyette, *Constructions of "the Jew" in English Literature and Society: Racial Representations, 1875–1945* (Cambridge UP, 1993), p. 233.

488 *"The rats are underneath"*: Christopher Ricks and Jim McCue, eds., *The Poems of T. S. Eliot*, vol. 1 (Faber & Faber, 2015), p. 35. The "j" in "jew" is capitalized in this edition, but Eliot originally used lowercase.

488 *"reasons of race"*: T. S. Eliot, *After Strange Gods: A Primer of Modern Heresy* (Faber, 1934), p. 20.

489 *"I have also heard"*: Eliot, *Selected Essays, 1917–1932* (Faber and Faber, 1932), p. 54.

489 *"Eliot's Wagner nostalgia"*: Igor Stravinsky and Robert Craft, *Themes and Episodes* (Knopf, 1966), p. 125.

489 *admirers on the faculty*: George Santayana, *The Life of Reason; or, The Phases of Human Progress*, vol. 2 (Scribner's, 1919), p. 11; William Henry Schofield, *English Literature from the Norman Conquest to Chaucer* (Macmillan, 1921), pp. 203, 214.

489 *"Love me on a low fire"*: Jules Laforgue, *Moralités légendaires* (Vanier, 1901), pp. 100–103.

490 *"the intellectualising"*: Eliot, *The Varieties of Metaphysical Poetry*, ed. Ronald Schuchard (Harvest, 1996), pp. 213, 215.

490 *"a breadth and power"*: "Grand Opera Season Ends," *Boston Globe*, April 12, 1908.

490 *"crazy over Wagner"*: Journals of Haniel Long, March 31, 1909, UCLA Library Special Collections. Eliot saw *Tristan* at the Boston Opera in 1913 and saved a program from the occasion; see Robert Crawford, *Young Eliot: From St. Louis to "The Waste Land"* (Farrar, Straus and Giroux, 2015), p. 198. John J. Soldo, in *The Tempering of T. S. Eliot* (UMI Research Press, 1983), p. 58, states that a *Tristan* ticket stub can be found in the Houghton collection. Lyndall Gordon, *T. S. Eliot: An Imperfect Life* (Norton, 2000), pp. 38, 77, says that Eliot saw *Tristan* at the Boston Opera in 1909, as does Nancy Duvall Hargrove in *T. S. Eliot's Parisian Year* (University Press of Florida, 2009), p. 190; but that company did not stage the opera until 1912.

490 *swan-boat rides*: Lorraine Lauzon, "It's Officially Spring in Boston When the Swan Boats Float Out," *Berkshire Eagle*, April 5, 1979.

490 *"Tristan and Isolde"*: *Poems of T. S. Eliot*, vol. 1, p. 236.

491 *"suffocating cloud"*: Jacques Rivière, *Études* (Nouvelle Revue Française, 1911), pp. 145, 148, 147.

491 *Jean Verdenal*: See James E. Miller, Jr., *T. S. Eliot: The Making of an American Poet, 1888–1922* (Pennsylvania State UP, 2005), pp. 117–35; and Claudio Perinot, "Jean Verdenal, an Extraordinary Young Man: T. S. Eliot's *mort aux Dardanelles*," *South Atlantic Review* 76:3 (2011), pp. 33–50.

491 *"fallen completely"*: Colleen Lamos, "The Love Song of T. S. Eliot: Elegiac Homoeroticism in the Early Poetry," in *Gender, Desire, and Sexuality in*

T. S. Eliot, ed. Cassandra Laity and Nancy K. Gish (Cambridge UP, 2004), p. 23. On the boat trip, see Miller, *T. S. Eliot*, pp. 128–31.

492 *"Try, if possible"*: Valerie Eliot and Hugh Haughton, eds., *The Letters of T. S. Eliot*, vol. 1 (Yale UP, 2011), p. 24. Other quotations on pp. 29, 37.

492 *"Now can you understand"*: *Poems of T. S. Eliot*, vol. 1, p. 372.

493 *Anthony Julius*: See his *T. S. Eliot, Anti-Semitism, and Literary Form* (Cambridge UP, 1996), pp. 48, 124.

493 *T. Sturge Moore*: "The Story of Tristram and Isolt in Modern Poetry, Part I: Narrative Versions," *Criterion* 1:1 (1922), p. 38.

493 *"synthetic type"*: Martin, *Wagner to "The Waste Land,"* p. 199.

494 *Mann may have been thinking*: Ernst Braches, *Kommentar zum "Tod in Venedig"* (Overveen, 2015), p. 920.

494 *"April is the cruellest"*: All quotations from *The Waste Land* are from *Poems of T. S. Eliot*, vol. 1.

495 *Marie Larisch*: See her *My Past* (Eveleigh Nash, 1913), pp. 154–57.

496 *"presumptive evidence"*: William Blissett, "Wagner in *The Waste Land*," in *The Practical Vision: Essays in English Literature in Honour of Flora Roy*, ed. Jane Campbell and James Doyle (Wilfrid Laurier UP, 1978), p. 71. In the *Criterion* publication, "Öd'" is missing the umlaut; later editions, including *Poems of T. S. Eliot*, vol. 1, have "Oed'." For the manuscript, see Valerie Eliot, ed., *T. S. Eliot: "The Waste Land": A Facsimile and Transcript of the Original Drafts, Including the Annotations of Ezra Pound* (Faber and Faber, 1971).

496 *"implosion of Wagnerian"*: Josh Epstein, *Sublime Noise: Musical Culture and the Modernist Writer* (Johns Hopkins UP, 2014), pp. 91–98; quotation on p. 94.

497 *"the whole"*: Stephen Spender, *T. S. Eliot* (Penguin, 1976), p. 206.

497 *could have seen the opera*: The Metropolitan Opera presented *Parsifal* in Boston on Jan. 15, 1910, with Fremstad as Kundry.

498 *"bogus scholarship"*: *Poems of T. S. Eliot*, vol. 1, p. 570.

498 *In his youth he read*: Crawford, *Young Eliot*, p. 61.

498 *Jessie Weston*: See Janet Grayson, "In Quest of Jessie Weston," *Arthurian Literature* 11 (1992), pp. 1–61; Leon Surette, "*The Waste Land* and Jessie Weston: A Reassessment," *Twentieth Century Literature* 34:2 (1988), pp. 223–44; Patricia Sloane, "Richard Wagner's Arthurian Sources, Jessie L. Weston, and T. S. Eliot's *The Waste Land*," *Arthuriana* 11:1 (2001), pp. 30–53.

498 *Vienna-based Indologist*: Jessie L. Weston, *From Ritual to Romance* (Peter Smith, 1941), p. v. See also Leopold von Schroeder, *Die Vollendung des arischen Mysteriums in Bayreuth* (Lehmann, 1911); and Stefan Arvidsson, *Aryan Idols: Indo-European*

Mythology as Ideology and Science (University of Chicago Press, 2006), pp. 149–50, 162.

498 *"great Aryan family"*: Jessie L. Weston, *The Legends of the Wagner Drama: Studies in Mythology and Romance* (Nutt, 1896), p. 93.

498–99 *"close connection . . . divine"*: Weston, *From Ritual to Romance*, pp. 21, 58.

499 *Pound talked Eliot out of it*: Julius, *T. S. Eliot, Anti-Semitism*, p. 132.

499 *"crystallizes the hidden"*: Spender, *T. S. Eliot*, pp. 114, 111.

499 *discordant memories*: Miller, *T. S. Eliot*, pp. 126–30; "waving a branch" on p. 116.

500 *no moment of salvation*: Martin, *Wagner to "The Waste Land,"* pp. 231–33.

501 *"poetry for ladies"*: Ellmann, *James Joyce*, p. 495.

501 *"The thing is"*: Woolf, "Modern Novels (Joyce)," ed. Suzette A. Henke, in *The Gender of Modernism: A Critical Anthology*, ed. Bonnie Kime Scott (Indiana UP, 1990), p. 643.

501 *"spasms of wonder"*: VWD5, p. 353. For "great beauty," see VWD2, p. 178.

502 *"The autumn season"*: Woolf, *Jacob's Room* (Oxford UP, 1999), pp. 89–98.

503 *"critically, intently"*: Woolf, *The Years* (Harcourt, 1937), p. 184.

503 *"He lay very high"*: Woolf, *Mrs. Dalloway* (Harcourt, 1981), pp. 68–69. For Bach, see p. 176. See also Jamie Alexander McGregor, *Myth, Music, and Modernism: The Wagnerian Dimension in Virginia Woolf's "Mrs. Dalloway" and "The Waves" and James Joyce's "Finnegans Wake"* (Ph.D. diss., Rhodes University, 2009), pp. 104–41; and Emma Sutton, "Flying Dutchmen, Wandering Jews: Romantic Opera, Anti-Semitism, and Jewish Mourning in *Mrs. Dalloway*," in *Virginia Woolf and Music*, ed. Adriana Varga (Indiana UP, 2014), pp. 161–64. On Woolf's hallucinations, see Lee, *Virginia Woolf*, pp. 186–92.

504 *"Virility has now"*: Woolf, *A Room of One's Own* (Hogarth, 1935), p. 152; "woman-manly" on p. 157. For "purely human," see RWSS4, p. 102.

504 *"some desire still unsatisfied"*: VWE5, pp. 83–84.

504 *"confined and shut in"*: VWE4, p. 162.

505 *"saturate every atom . . . continuous stream"*: VWD3, pp. 209, 139.

505 *"life of anybody . . . vast undifferentiated"*: J. W. Graham, ed., *Virginia Woolf, "The Waves": The Two Holograph Drafts* (University of Toronto Press, 1976), Draft 1, pp. 1, 9, 155.

505 *"the most Wagnerian"*: William Blissett, "Wagnerian Fiction in English," *Criticism* 5:3 (1963), p. 257.

505 *A half-dozen other commentators*: DiGaetani, *Wagner and the Modern British Novel*, pp. 118–24; Tracey Sherard, "'Parcival in the Forest of Gender': Wagner, Homosexuality, and *The Waves*," in *Virginia Woolf: Turning the Centuries*, ed. Ann Ardis and Bonnie Kime Scott

(Pace UP, 2000), pp. 62–69; Gyllian Phillips, "Re(de)composing in the Novel: *The Waves*, Wagnerian Opera and Percival/Parsifal," *Genre* 28:1–2 (1995), pp. 119–44; Kimberly Fairbrother Canton, *The Operatic Imperative in Anglo-American Literary Modernism: Pound, Stein, and Woolf* (Ph.D. diss., University of Toronto, 2009), pp. 202–205.

505 "*The sun had not yet risen*": Woolf, *The Waves* (Harcourt, 1931), pp. 7–9.

506 "*The six characters*": Lee, *Virginia Woolf*, p. 612.

506 *a version of T. S. Eliot*: Doris Eder, "Louis Unmasked: T. S. Eliot in *The Waves*," *Virginia Woolf Quarterly* 2:1–2 (1973), pp. 13–27.

506 "*My shattered mind*": Woolf, *Waves*, p. 39. "My roots," p. 12; "ring of steel," p. 40. For Sutton, see her *Virginia Woolf and Classical Music*, p. 147.

506 "*I then cursed Percival*": Woolf, "*The Waves*," Draft 1, p. 372. For "pagan" and "commander," see Woolf, *Waves*, pp. 36, 37.

507 *blood-filled chalice*: McGregor, *Myth, Music*, p. 187.

507 "*I do not believe*": Woolf, *Waves*, p. 67. "Let me cast," p. 294; St. Paul's, pp. 281–82; "eternal renewal," p. 297.

507 *revisions to the draft*: Woolf, "*The Waves*," Draft 1, pp. 366–67. The Verlaine allusion is noticed by Julia Briggs in *Virginia Woolf: An Inner Life* (Harcourt, 2005), p. 253, and picked up by McGregor, *Myth, Music*, p. 180.

508 "*unshakable affirmation*": McGregor, *Myth, Music*, p. 181.

508 "*One cannot live*": Woolf, *Waves*, p. 154.

508 *read* The Voyage Out: *Letters of James Joyce*, vol. 1, p. 115.

508 "*poverty of the writer's mind*": VWE4, p. 161. Compare Joyce, *Finnegans Wake* (Penguin, 1976), p. 192; Dirk Van Hulle, *James Joyce's "Work in Progress": Pre-Book Publications of "Finnegans Wake" Fragments* (Routledge, 2016), p. 5.

508 "*river Rhine . . . A way*": Matthew J. C. Hodgart and Ruth Bauerle, *Joyce's Grand Operoar: Opera in Finnegans Wake* (University of Illinois Press, 1997), pp. 115, 236.

509 "*pressed into service*": Martin, *Joyce and Wagner*, p. 117.

509 "*unconscious memory*": Joyce, *Scribbledehobble: The Ur-Workbook for Finnegans Wake*, ed. Thomas E. Connolly (Northwestern UP, 1961), p. 104.

509 *One sketch*: Joyce, *A First-Draft Version of Finnegans Wake*, ed. David Hayman (University of Texas Press, 1963), pp. 208–12, digicoll.library.wisc.edu. See also Hayman, "Tristan and Isolde in *Finnegans Wake*: A Study of the Sources and Evolution of a Theme," *Comparative Literature Studies* 1:2 (1964), pp. 93–112; and Joyce, *Scribbledehobble*, pp. 75–83.

509 "*Three quarks*": Text quoted from *Finnegans Wake*, p. 383, slightly different from the Tristan tale.

509 *listening constantly to Wagner*: Potts, *Portraits of the Artist in Exile*, p. 64.

509 "*is exactly the behavior*": Martin, *Wagner to "The Waste Land*,*"* p. 137.

510 *Martin's count*: Martin, *Joyce and Wagner*, pp. 185–221. See also Harry White, *Music and the Irish Literary Imagination* (Oxford UP, 2008), p. 183.

510 *one notebook shows*: Joyce, *The "Finnegans Wake" Notebooks at Buffalo: VI.B.3*, ed. Vincent Deane et al. (Brepols, 2001), pp. 59–67; Geert Lernout, "Richard Wagner's *Tristan und Isolde* in the Genesis of *Finnegans Wake*," *James Joyce Quarterly* 38:1–2 (2000–2001), p. 147.

510 "*No, it's pure music*": Ellmann, *James Joyce*, p. 703.

510 *at least a thousand*: Clive Hart, *Structure and Motif in Finnegans Wake* (Northwestern UP, 1962), pp. 161, 211–47.

511 "*unintelligible*": Stephen Barkway, ed., "The Letters of Virginia Woolf to Christabel McLaren," *Virginia Woolf Bulletin* 15 (2004), p. 29.

511 "*I am thunderstruck!*": *Letters of James Joyce*, vol. 3, p. 491.

511 "*about a fortnight*": VWD5, pp. 352–53.

13. SIEGFRIED'S DEATH: NAZI GERMANY AND THOMAS MANN

513 "*half-Bolshevik*": Joseph Wulf, *Musik im Dritten Reich: Eine Dokumentation* (Mohn, 1963), p. 286. See also press reports included in Thomas Mann, *Richard Wagner: Vortrag (1933): Edition und Dokumentation*, ed. Dirk Heißerer and Egon Voss (Königshausen & Neumann, 2017), pp. 167–78.

513 "*cosmopolitan-democratic . . . inexpert*": TMW, pp. 232–33. On the Munich protest, see Vaget, "Wehvolles Erbe," pp. 258–65.

513 "*romantic purity . . . thoroughly anarchic*": TMW, pp. 133–34. Other quotations on pp. 129, 140, 141. For *Kulturbolschewist* in the lectures, see Mann, *Richard Wagner: Vortrag 1933*, pp. 33–34, 76.

514 "*Stay in Switzerland!*": Donald Prater, *Thomas Mann: A Life* (Oxford UP, 1995), p. 204.

515 "*single-bullet theory*": Ron Rosenbaum, *Explaining Hitler: The Search for the Origins of His Evil* (Random House, 1998), p. 140.

515 "*perhaps the most important*": Peter Viereck, "Hitler and Richard Wagner," part 1, *Common Sense* 8:11 (1939), p. 3.

515 "*campaign to exterminate*": Joachim Köhler, *Wagner's Hitler: The Prophet and His Disciple*, trans. Ronald Taylor (Polity, 2000), p. 293.

515 "*the composer's influence*": Richard J. Evans, *The Third Reich in Power* (Penguin, 2005), p. 199.

515 *Joachim Fest*: See his *Hitler*, trans. Richard and Clara Winston (Harcourt, 1974), pp. 47–51; and "Richard Wagner—Das Werk neben dem Werk," in *Richard Wagner im Dritten Reich: Ein Schloss Elmau-Symposion*, ed. Saul Friedländer and Jörn Rüsen (Beck, 2000), pp. 24–25. For Köhler's re-

traction, see "Wagner's Acquittal," *Wagner Journal* 8:2 (2014), pp. 43–51.

515 *concept of influence*: Vaget, "*Wehvolles Erbe*," pp. 51–55.

516 "*We need a dictator*": Hitler, *Sämtliche Aufzeichnungen*, p. 127. For "self-styling," see Vaget, "*Wehvolles Erbe*," p. 73.

516 "*the politician Hitler*": Wolfram Pyta, *Hitler: Der Künstler als Politiker und Feldherr: Eine Herrschaftsanalyse* (Siedler, 2015), p. 16.

516 "*consummation of l'art pour l'art*": Walter Benjamin, "Das Kunstwerk im Zeitalter seiner technischen Reproduzierbarkeit," *Gesammelte Schriften*, vol. 1/2, ed. Rolf Tiedemann and Hermann Schweppenhäuser (Suhrkamp, 1974), p. 469.

516 "*overestimation of genius*": NWKG IV:3, p. 410; NCW4, p. 359.

516 *Carl Schmitt*: See his "Richard Wagner und eine neue 'Lehre vom Wahn,'" BB 35 (1912), pp. 239–41.

516 "*narrative context*": Herfried Münkler, "Mythischer Sinn: Der Nibelungen-Mythos in der politischen Symbolik des 20. Jahrhunderts," in *In der Trümmern der eigenen Welt: Richard Wagners "Ring des Nibelungen,"* ed. Udo Bermbach (Reimer, 1989), p. 255.

516 "*Horrible oil paintings*": Mann, *Tagebücher, 1937–1939*, ed. Peter de Mendelssohn (Fischer, 1980), p. 115.

516 *The German spirit . . . malicious abuse*": TMW, pp. 173, 150.

518 "*co-religionist . . . realization of the unreal*": Lincoln Kirstein, *Mosaic: Memoirs* (Farrar, Straus and Giroux, 1994), pp. 65–67. See also Martin Duberman, *The Worlds of Lincoln Kirstein* (Knopf, 2007), p. 26; and Kirstein, *Thirty Years: Lincoln Kirstein's The New York City Ballet* (Knopf, 1978), pp. 87–88.

518 *Cosima called*: Mack, *Cosima Wagner: Die zweite Leben*, p. 744.

518 *heard of the Nazi Party*: HWW, pp. 61–62. On Cerny, see Othmar Plöckinger, *Geschichte eines Buches: Adolf Hitlers "Mein Kampf," 1922–1945* (Oldenbourg, 2006), pp. 130–32.

518 *Guido von List*: Nicholas Goodrick-Clarke, *The Occult Roots of Nazism: Secret Aryan Cults and Their Influence on Nazi Ideology* (Tauris Parke, 2004), p. 41.

519 "*The ceremony began*": Ibid., p. 130. The original document, "Ein Einführung in den Untergrad," can be found in NS 26/852, Bundesarchiv Berlin-Lichterfelde.

519 "*Is that human?*": ZRW, p. 165.

519 "*we have nothing*": HWW, p. 121.

519 "*instinctively the most violent*": Hans Alfred Grunsky, "Der Ring des Nibelungen," in *Offizieller Bayreuther Festspielführer 1924*, ed. Karl Grunsky (Niehrenheim, 1924), p. 99. For

"*pure, strong will*," see Grunsky, "Parsifal," p. 128.

520 "*guide toward national socialism*": Erwin Geck, "Richard Wagner und der Staat," in ibid., p. 175.

520 *festival of 1924*: Karl Holl, "Bayreuth 1924," ZRW, p. 187; Hannes Heer, "Geschichte der Festspiele 1924," in *verstummte stimmen: Die Bayreuther Festspiele und die "Juden," 1876 bis 1945*, ed. Heer et al. (Metropol, 2012), pp. 133–63; OGB1, pp. 404–15; Olin Downes, "Wagner a Political Storm Centre," *New York Times*, Aug. 24, 1924. For the flag, see HWW, p. 128.

520 "*Jews have been spat at*": HWW, p. 132.

520 *use "Wagner*": Ibid., p. 162.

521 "*Thoughts in War*": TM15, pp. 27–28.

522 "*not a very proper German*": Thomas Mann, *Reflections of a Nonpolitical Man*, trans. Walter D. Morris (Ungar, 1983), pp. 48–49. Other quotations on pp. 52, 55, 289–90. See also TM13, pp. 77, 84, 83, 88, 431–32.

522 "*feelings of hate*": Mann, *Tagebücher, 1918–1921*, p. 427, also p. 275.

522 "*poisoned emotions*": Heinrich Mann, *Macht und Mensch* (Wolff, 1919), p. 228.

523 "*all-embracing kingdom*": TM15, pp. 555–56; *Meistersinger* on p. 529. On the erotic dimension of "On the German Republic," see Anthony Heilbut, *Thomas Mann: Eros and Literature* (Knopf, 1996), pp. 375–82.

524 "*Hörselberg idea*": Hans Rudolf Vaget, "The Making of *The Magic Mountain*," in *Thomas Mann's "The Magic Mountain": A Casebook*, ed. Vaget (Oxford UP, 2008), p. 18.

524 "*domain of sickness*": Mann, *Tagebücher, 1918–1921*, pp. 303–304.

524 *Howard Nemerov*: See Mann, *Tagebücher, 1937–1939*, p. 401; Mann to Nemerov, May 14, 1939, Howard Nemerov Papers, Washington University Libraries, Department of Special Collections. Hélène Vuillet, *Thomas Mann, ou Les Métamorphoses d'Hermès* (PUPS, 2007), p. 244, tells of Mann underlining his copy of Nemerov's thesis.

524–25 "*politically suspect . . . Literature must precede*": Mann, *The Magic Mountain*, trans. John E. Woods (Knopf, 1995), pp. 112, 111.

525 "*Fullness of Harmony*": A catalogue of Mann's 1920s-era record collection is at the Deutsches Rundfunkarchiv. See also Volker Mertens, "'Elektrische Grammophonmusik' im *Zauberberg* Thomas Manns," in "*Der Zauberberg*": Die Welt der Wissenschaften in Thomas Manns Roman, ed. Dietrich von Engelhardt and Hans Wißkirchen (Schattauer, 2003), pp. 174–202.

525 "*spiritual backsliding*": Mann, *Magic Mountain*, p. 97; TM5, pp. 152, 989.

525 "*In the solitude of night*": Mann, *Magic Mountain*, p. 643; TM5, p. 990.

526 *"magic song of death"*: TM15, pp. 790–91.

526 *émigrés ironically referred*: Konrad Heiden, *Hitler: Eine Biographie*, vol. 1 (Europa, 1936), p. 206; Lion Feuchtwanger, *Exil* (Aufbau, 1993), p. 188.

527 *Vaget observes*: See his "'Politically Suspect': Music on the Magic Mountain," in *Thomas Mann's "The Magic Mountain,"* pp. 133–34.

527 *"And out of this worldwide"*: Mann, *Magic Mountain*, p. 706.

527 *"Embarrassingly enough"*: Mann, "Ein Bruder," *Essays*, vol. 2, ed. Hermann Kurzke (Fischer, 1977), p. 224. See also Mann, "That Man Is My Brother," *Esquire* 11 (March 1939), pp. 31, 132–33.

528 *"subjugating the world . . . Wagnerish"*: Mann, "Ein Bruder," p. 224.

528 *"a sea of red flags"*: Hitler, *Mein Kampf* (NSDAP, 1936), p. 552.

528 *Hamann surmised*: See her *Hitler's Vienna*, p. 176.

528 *Dietrich Eckart*: See Margarete Plewnia, *Auf dem Weg zu Hitler: Der "völkische" Publizist Dietrich Eckart* (Schünemann, 1970), p. 146, for Eckart's 1894 writing on *Parsifal*. For "wonderful," see *Hitlers Tischgespräche* (1965), p. 187.

528 *"hour of retribution"*: Eckart, "Geduld," *Auf gut deutsch*, Dec. 5, 1919.

529 *"A fire was kindled"*: Hitler, *Mein Kampf*, p. 406.

529 *"period in which . . . all wretchedness"*: Reginald H. Phelps, "Hitlers 'grundlegende' Rede über den Antisemitismus," *Vierteljahrshefte für Zeitgeschichte* 16:4 (1968), pp. 405, 413. For Wagner excerpts, see David Dennis, *Inhumanities: Nazi Interpretations of Western Culture* (Cambridge UP, 2012), p. 325.

529 *Hitler's Munich apartment*: For Hitler's ownership of Chamberlain's book on Wagner, see Ernst Hanfstaengl, *The Unknown Hitler* (Gibson Square, 2005), p. 52. For records and Wagner writings, see Antonie Reichert's testimony, June 20, 1952, Institut für Zeitgeschichte, Archivdatenbank Online, ZS 287, p. 2.

529 *"He knew the thing"*: Hanfstaengl, *Unknown Hitler*, p. 53. For T. S. Eliot, see p. 28.

530 *iconography of Fascism*: Lucy Hughes-Hallett, *Gabriele d'Annunzio: Poet, Seducer, and Preacher of War* (Knopf, 2013), pp. 5–6.

530 *"anchored in the works"*: Hans Schemm, "Richard Wagner," *Reichszeitung der deutschen Erzieher* 2 (1934), p. 2. For "Heil!," see HWW, p. 80; for the veranda, Udo Bermbach, *Houston Stewart Chamberlain: Wagners Schwiegersohn—Hitlers Vordenker* (Metzler, 2015), pp. 557–58; for trembling hands, Martin Schramm, "'Im Zeichen des Hakenkreuzes': Der Deutsche Tag in Bayreuth am 30. September 1923," *Jahrbuch für fränkische Landesforschung* 65 (2005), p. 267. For Cosima's nonappearance, see Elke Fröhlich, ed., *Die Tagebücher von Joseph Goebbels*, II:4 (Saur, 1995), p. 408. Berta Geissmar, *The Baton and the Jackboot: Recollections of Musical Life* (Columbus, 1988), p. 206, reports that Cosima "refused to receive" Hitler.

530 *"We feel the artist"*: Heinz Preiß, ed., *Adolf Hitler in Franken: Reden aus der Kampfzeit* (c. 1939), p. 26.

530 *"coming man"*: HWW, p. 91.

530 *"first through the Master"*: Hitler, *Sämtliche Aufzeichnungen*, p. 1232.

531 *lost in thought*: Report by Karl Fiehler in *Quellen und Dokumente zur Geschichte von "Mein Kampf," 1924–1945*, ed. Othmar Plöckinger (Steiner, 2016), p. 112. On Hitler and the Bruckmanns, see Wolfgang Martynkewicz, *Salon Deutschland: Geist und Macht, 1900–1945* (Aufbau, 2009), p. 409.

531 *"Parsifal nature"*: HWW, p. 119.

531 *tended to blurt out*: Joseph Chapiro, "Zum 'höheren Zwecke der Kunst,'" in Großmann-Vendrey, *Bayreuth in der deutschen Presse*, vol. 3/2, p. 191. See also "Mrs. Siegfried Wagner Aids Royalist Cause," *New York Times*, Jan. 18, 1924.

531 *"the ones who come"*: HWW, p. 136.

531 *he kept a low profile*: Heinz Linge, *Bis zum Untergang: Als Chef des persönlichen Dienstes bei Hitler* (Herbig, 1980), p. 103.

531 *arriving after dark*: Friedelind Wagner and Page Cooper, *The Royal Family of Bayreuth* (Eyre and Spottiswoode, 1948), p. 30.

531 *"Hitler, Adolf, writer"*: HWW, p. 139.

531–32 *"inner Jewification"*: Hitler, *Mein Kampf*, p. 349. For "never had," see JM, p. 158; "never called," *Mein Kampf*, pp. 332–33; "swarming," JM, pp. 171–72; "parasite," *Mein Kampf*, p. 334.

532 *"Alberichs-Herrschaft"*: Klaus A. Lankheit, ed., *Hitler: Reden, Schriften, Anordnungen, Februar 1925 bis Januar 1933*, III:2 (Saur, 1994), p. 124.

532 *"The World War in the* Ring*"*: Dennis, *Inhumanities*, pp. 208–13; Joseph Stolzing [Josef Stolzing-Cerny], "Der Weltkrieg im Ring des Nibelungen," *Völkischer Beobachter*, Aug. 7–9, 1923. For "the German people," see Bermbach, *Richard Wagner in Deutschland*, p. 367, quoting Fridolin Riedel's *Der Ring des Nibelungen*, 1945 edition. For similar readings, see Karl Grunsky, *Richard Wagner und die Juden* (Deutscher Volksverlag, 1920), p. 9; Karl Gäbler, *Richard Wagners Ringdichtung als deutsches Erleben* (Fritsch, 1940), p. 63; Rudolf Grisson, *Beiträge zur Auslegung von Richard Wagners "Ring des Nibelungen"* (Klein, 1934), pp. 134–35.

532 *nowhere in the entire corpus*: Saul Friedländer, "Bayreuth und der Erlösungsantisemitismus," in *Richard Wagner und die Juden*, ed. Dieter Borchmeyer et al. (Metzler, 2000), pp. 17–18; Dina Porat, "'Zum Raum wird hier die Zeit': Richard Wagners Bedeutung für Adolf Hitler und die nationalsozialistische Führung," in ibid., p. 208.

532 *"When I hear Wagner"*: Hitler, *Monologe*, p. 234.

533 *Hitler's third day in office*: Karl-Heinz Minuth, ed., *Akten der Reichskanzlei: Regierung Hitler, 1933–38*, I: (Boldt, 1983), p. 31.

533 *two memorial events*: HWW, pp. 231–32; H. F. Peters, *Zarathustra's Sister: The Case of Elisabeth and Friedrich Nietzsche* (Crown, 1977), p. 220.

534 *"the savior who sat above"*: Hugo Rasch, "Die Festvorstellung in der Staatsoper," *Völkischer Beobachter*, March 23, 1933. See also Dennis, *Inhumanities*, pp. 376–77.

534 *"there is no more glorious"*: OGB1, p. 497.

534 *"mistaken this year's"*: Anson Rabinbach and Sander L. Gilman, eds., *The Third Reich Sourcebook* (University of California Press, 2013), p. 536.

534 *intermission talk*: "Reichsminister Dr. Goebbels huldigt Richard Wagner," *Musik* 25:12 (Sept. 1933), pp. 952–54.

534 *"protest of a genius"*: Max Domarus, ed., *Hitler: Reden und Proklamationen, 1932–1945*, vol. 1/1 (Pamminger, 1988), pp. 292–93.

534 *"leaning forward"*: Gunter d'Alquen, "Richard Wagner zum Gedächtnis," *Völkischer Beobachter*, Aug. 15, 1933.

535 *"our movement is nothing less"*: Frederick T. Birchall, "Nazi Legions Mass at Greatest Rally," *New York Times*, Aug. 31, 1933.

535 *Strains of* Meistersinger: Birchall, ibid.; Birchall, "Nazis Pledge Jobs; Hitler Places Art on a 'Nordic' Basis," *New York Times*, Sept. 2, 1933; Stephen Brockmann, *Nuremberg: The Imaginary Capital* (Camden House, 2006), pp. 133–46. For the evening *Meistersinger*, see Daniel Reupke, "Mit 'Musik und offenen Fahnen' auf den NS-Reichsparteitagen: Eine Quellenstudie als Historische Aufführungsforschung," *Moderne Stadtgeschichte* 1 (2017), p. 74.

535 *Benno von Arent*: See Tobias Reichard, Anno Mungen, and Alexander Schmidt, eds., *Hitler. Macht. [Oper]. Propaganda und Musiktheater in Nürnberg* (Imhof, 2018), pp. 24–27.

535 *Wilhelm Rode*: See footage included in the DVD *Great Conductors of the Third Reich* (Bel Canto Society, 2005).

535 *Wagner and Hitler were often mentioned*: Quotations from Siegfried Scheffler, "Bayreuth im Dritten Reich" (1933), in Berndt W. Wessling, *Bayreuth im Dritten Reich: Richard Wagners politische Erben—Eine Dokumentation* (Beltz, 1983), p. 175; Johann Hahn, "Tannenberg—Bayreuth," BB 59 (1936), p. 60; Hermann Seeliger, "Der deutsche Seher: Die nationalsozialistische Idee bei Richard Wagner," BB 57 (1934), p. 159.

535 *Party posters*: See *Wochenspruch* posters for Feb. 15–21, 1942, and July 16–22, 1939, in Randall Bytwerk's German Propaganda Archive, research.calvin.edu/german-propaganda-archive/wochenspruch-index.htm, accessed Dec. 25, 2019. The first quotation is a paraphrase; see RWSS8, pp. 96–97, for the original.

535 *"nation's most precious"*: Manuela Jahrmärker, "Wagners Aufsatz 'Das Judenthum in der Musik' im Spiegel zeitgenössischer Reaktionen," in *Meyerbeer, Wagner: Eine Begegnung*, ed. Gunhild Oberzaucher-Schüller et al. (Böhlau, 1998), p. 125.

536 *Nazi propaganda*: Hubert Lanzinger's "Der Bannerträger," Karl Stauber's "Es lebe Deutschland!"

See also William Kinderman, "From *Death in Venice* to *The Magic Mountain*: Thomas Mann's Ironic Response to Wagner," *Wagner Journal* 12:2 (2018), pp. 56–73.

536 *"the art of sculpture"*: Elke Fröhlich, ed., *Die Tagebücher von Joseph Goebbels*, I:4 (Saur, 1987), p. 99.

536 *Berghof refuge*: See Albert Speer, *Inside the Third Reich*, trans. Richard and Clara Winston (Simon & Schuster, 1970), p. 90; Despina Stratigakos, *Hitler at Home* (Yale UP, 2015), pp. 56, 66, 89, 249.

536 *Winifred Wagner pasted*: "Architects' drawings and models of the Festspielhaus in Bayreuth, Germany," album in the Prints and Photographs Division, Library of Congress. One page is inscribed: "In die Hände des Führers gelegt, Bayreuth 15 August 1942." It seems impossible for the album to have been given to Hitler on that date, since he was at the Werwolf headquarters in Ukraine.

537 *American-style media landscape*: See Thomas Saunders, "How American Was It? Popular Culture from Weimar to Hitler," in *German Pop Culture: How "American" Is It?*, ed. Agnes C. Mueller (University of Michigan Press, 2004), pp. 52–65.

537 *"whole devil's brood"*: Georges Motschan, *Thomas Mann—von nahem erlebt* (Matussek, 1988), p. 119. All these signatures except Hitler's can be seen in the guestbook of the Hotel Goldener Anker, which Mann also signed.

537 *Heydrich's father*: Lina Heydrich, *Leben mit einem Kriegsverbrecher* (Ludwig, 1976), pp. 16–17; Robert Gerwarth, *Hitler's Hangman: The Life of Heydrich* (Yale UP, 2011), pp. 15–19.

537 *Fanget an!*: Egon Fein, *Hitlers Weg nach Nurnberg: Verführer, Täuscher, Massenmörder* (Nürnberger Presse, 2002), p. 20.

537 *Adolf Bartels*: See his *Die deutsche Dichtung von Hebbel bis zur Gegenwart: Die Alten und die Jungen* (Avenarius, 1901), p. 188.

537 *"strongly church-inflected"*: Alfred Rosenberg, *Der Mythus des 20. Jahrhunderts: Eine Wertung der seelisch-geistigen Gestaltenkämpfe unserer Zeit* (Hoheneichen, 1939), p. 434.

537 *"already had his triumph"*: Jürgen Matthäus and Frank Bajohr, eds., *The Political Diary of Alfred Rosenberg and the Onset of the Holocaust* (United States Holocaust Memorial Museum / Rowman and Littlefield, 2015), pp. 113–14.

537 *churchly trappings*: Hans Frank, *Im Angesicht des Galgens* (Beck, 1953), p. 213, and Hermann Rauschning, *Gespräche mit Hitler* (Europa, 1940), pp. 216–17, report similar Hitler remarks about *Parsifal*, though the reliability of these sources is in question.

537 *"timeless Grail temple," "to have Parsifal"*: HWW, p. 441.

538 *"into the mystical"*: Eva Rieger, *Friedelind Wagner: Richard Wagner's Rebellious Granddaughter*, trans. Chris Walton (Boydell, 2013), p. 115.

538 *"Jewish-Oriental spirit"*: Otto Daube, "Richard Wagner und die deutsche Schule," part 1, *Deutscher Erzieher* 11 (1942), pp. 299–300.

538 *"We are not here"*: Elke Fröhlich, ed., *Die Tagebücher von Joseph Goebbels*, II:2 (Saur, 1996), p. 498; also Heinz Guderian, *Erinnerungen eines Soldaten* (Vowinckel, 1951), p. 242.

538 *"Gentlemen"*: Klaus-Peter Friedrich, ed., *Die Verfolgung und Ermordung der europäischen Juden durch das nationalsozialistische Deutschland, 1933–1945*, vol. 9: *Polen: Generalgouvernement August 1941–1945* (Oldenbourg, 2014), pp. 159–60.

538 "Mitleid ist Schwäche": Hermann Langbein, *People in Auschwitz*, trans. Harry Zohn (University of North Carolina Press, 2004), p. 282. For Nietzsche, see *Antichrist*, §7.

538 *"He had patrols"*: Albert Speer, *Erinnerungen* (Propyläen, 1969), p. 73. Speer dates this incident to 1933, but 1935 is more likely, since he mentions Furtwängler conducting.

538 *"1. the wife of the dentist"*: Reichard, *Hitler. Macht. Oper.*, p. 18.

539 *"only by those visitors"*: Werr, *Heroische Weltsicht*, p. 196. For hotel guests, see Fritz Wiedemann, *Der Mann der Feldherr werden wollte* (Blick + Bild, 1964), p. 207; for sleeping underlings, Traudl Junge, *Bis zur letzten Stunde: Hitlers Sekretärin erzählt ihr Leben* (Ullstein, 2004), p. 93.

539 *Opera houses should hold*: Hitler: *Reden und Proklamationen*, vol. 1/2, pp. 983–84.

539 *Wagner's popularity*: Erik Levi, *Music in the Third Reich* (Palgrave, 1994), pp. 192–93; Henry Bair, "National Socialism and Opera: The Berlin Opera Houses, 1933–1939, Part 2," *Opera* 35:2 (1984), pp. 129–30.

539 *"typical agent of liberalism"*: Karl Hermann, "Bayreuth und Deutschlands junge Generation," *Bayreuther Festspielführer 1936* (Niehrenheim, 1936), pp. 83–84.

539 *"a large proportion"*: Benjamin Korstvedt, "Resistance, Satire, and Strange Enthusiasm: Progressive Responses to Wagner During the First World War Era," in *Von Grenzen und Ländern, Zentren und Rändern': Der Erste Weltkrieg und die Verschiebungen in der musikalischen Geographie Europas*, ed. Christa Brüstle et al. (Argus, 2006), p. 202.

539 *Hitler Youth circles*: Hans Rudolf Vaget, "Otto Strobel und die Richard-Wagner-Forschungsstätte," *wagnerspectrum* 13:1 (2017), pp. 184–86.

539 *Michael Kater*: See his *Culture in Nazi Germany* (Yale UP, 2019), pp. 83–84.

539 *"The soldier who is fighting"*: Luke Brian Berryman, *Richard Wagner's "Die Meistersinger von Nürnberg" in Nazi Propaganda* (Ph.D. diss., King's College, 2014), p. 133. See also Brian Currid, *A National Acoustics: Music and Mass Publicity in Weimar and Nazi Germany* (University of Minnesota Press, 2006), pp. 133–35.

539 *Duke Ellington, Louis Armstrong*: Nancy Drechsler, *Die Funktion der Musik im deutschen Rundfunk, 1933–1945* (Centaurus, 1988), p. 42. On Nazi pop culture, see also Michael Kater, "The Impact of American Popular Culture on German Youth," in *The Arts in Nazi Germany: Continuity, Conformity, Change*, ed. Jonathan Huener and Francis R. Nicosia (Berghahn, 2006), pp. 31–62; and Pamela Potter, *Art of Suppression: Confronting the Nazi Past in Histories of the Visual and Performing Arts* (University of California Press, 2016), p. 179.

540 *"proclivity for the employment . . . primal power"*: Ernst Jünger, *Sämtliche Werke*, vol. 7 (Klett-Cotta, 1980), pp. 133, 135.

540 *"free of the pressure"*: Speer, *Erinnerungen*, p. 164.

540 *Hitler's chauffeur*: HWW, p. 311.

540 *"The ten days"*: Hitler, *Monologe*, p. 225. For retirement, see HWW, pp. 424–25.

541 *personal archive of Craig*: Spotts, *Hitler*, p. 207; Edward Craig, *Gordon Craig: The Story of His Life* (Gollancz, 1968), pp. 345–47.

541 *"politicization"*: Rieger, *Friedelind Wagner*, p. 57. On Roller's *Parsifal*, see OGB1, pp. 526–48.

541 *Hitler stepped in*: OGB1, p. 493.

541 *Winifred periodically agitated*: For the Pringsheims, see HWW, p. 381; for Lorenz, see Heinz Boberach, ed., *Meldungen aus dem Reich, 1938–1945: Die geheimen Lageberichte des Sicherheitsdienstes der SS*, vol. 15 (Pawlak, 1984), pp. 5807–808.

541 *Richard Wagner Research Center*: Walter Lange, *Richard Wagners Sippe* (Beck, 1938). See also Vaget, "Otto Strobel," pp. 190–91.

542 *"Jewish concern"*: Werr, "Die Bayreuther Festspiele—eine 'jüdische Angelegenheit'? Winifred Wagner gegen wagnerfeindliche Tendenzen im Nationalsozialismus," *Musikforschung* 65:3 (2012), pp. 259–62; Werr, *Heroische Weltsicht*, p. 202. For "Wagner craze," see HWW, p. 293.

542 *"Where I am"*: "Mann Finds U.S. Sole Peace Hope," *New York Times*, Feb. 22, 1938.

543 *Georg Lukács*: See his *Essays on Thomas Mann*, trans. Stanley Mitchell (Merlin, 1965), pp. 155–56.

543 *"was only strengthened"*: Mann, *Joseph and His Brothers*, trans. John E. Woods (Everyman's Library, 2005), pp. xxxvii–xxxviii.

543 *"Deep is the well . . . The essence of life"*: Ibid., pp. 3, 39.

544 *Eckhard Heftrich*: See his *Geträumte Taten: "Joseph und seine Brüder"* (Klostermann, 1993), pp. 17–32, etc.

544 *Mann himself pointed out*: Thomas Mann, *Briefe*, vol. 2, ed. Erika Mann (Fischer, 1963), p. 484. For Potiphar's Wife, see Dorothea Kirschbaum, "Kundry in Ägypten: Mut-em-enet, das Weib des Potiphar: Muster und Abwandlung in Thomas Manns *Joseph und seine Brüder*," *wagnerspectrum* 13:1 (2017), pp. 61–81.

544 *"Unique Friend"*: Mann, *Joseph*, p. 1252.

544 *"the racial instinct rebels"*: Eugen Kalkschmidt in *Deutsches Volkstum*, July 1934, quoted in Hans

Wißkirchen, ed., *Die Beleuchtung, die auf mich fällt, hat . . . oft gewechselt: Neue Studien zum Werk Thomas Manns* (Königshausen & Neumann, 1991), p. 89.

544 *"psychologically smeared"*: Joachim Wecker in *Die literarische Welt*, Oct. 1933, excerpted in Klaus Schröter, ed., *Thomas Mann im Urteil seiner Zeit: Dokumente 1891–1955* (Klostermann, 2000), p. 219.

545 *"Mann has made something"*: Cather: *Stories, Poems*, p. 859. For meetings between Cather and Mann, see Mann, *Tagebücher, 1937–1939*, pp. 186, 244. The "angesehene Schriftstellerin" mentioned in Mann, *Tagebücher, 1933–1934*, ed. Peter de Mendelssohn (Fischer, 1977), p. 436, is probably Cather. For Cather on *The Magic Mountain*, see her letter to Fanny Butcher, Oct. 16, 1936, text communicated to author by Andrew Jewell, University of Nebraska, Lincoln.

545 *"It will be my* Parsifal*"*; Mann, *Briefe*, vol. 2, p. 309.

545 *May 1943*: See TM10/2, p. 174, for discussion of the date, which is given as May 23 in some editions and May 27 in others.

546 *"sordid abuse"*: Thomas Mann, *Doctor Faustus*, trans. John E. Woods (Knopf, 1997), p. 186. Compare TM10/1, p. 256 ("schmierenhaften Mißbrauch") to TMW, p. 150 ("feindseligen Mißbrauch").

546 *"skilled rabble-rouser . . . long-range plan"*: Mann, *Doctor Faustus*, pp. 68, 174.

546–47 *"quickly sated . . . urge to laugh"*: Ibid., pp. 141–43.

547 *Mann later revealed*: *The Story of a Novel: The Genesis of Doctor Faustus*, trans. Richard and Clara Winston (Knopf, 1961), p. 103.

547 *"bourgeois-moderate . . . fusty Wagnerism"*: Mann, *Doctor Faustus*, pp. 246, 217, translation modified.

547 *"in an utterly destructive . . . first-name basis"*: Ibid., pp. 337, 339.

547 *"pandemonium of laughter"*: Ibid., p. 397.

549 *"I still love the opera"*: WCL, p. 645.

549 *"strong are so stupid"*: E. M. Forster, *What I Believe* (Hogarth, 1939), pp. 11–12.

549 *Elizabeth Enright*: See her *The Saturdays* (Holt, 2002), p. 57.

549 *Arturo Toscanini*: For his performance in Fiume, see Mimmo Franzinelli, *Fiume: L'ultima impresa di d'Annunzio* (Mondadori, 2009), p. 181. For the Liebestod request, see d'Annunzio to Toscanini, Nov. 21, 1920, Toscanini Legacy Papers, Music Division, New York Public Library for the Performing Arts. On Bayreuth, see Sachs, *Toscanini: Musician of Conscience*, pp. 486–93, 544–48.

549 *Harvey Sachs observes*: Sachs, *Toscanini*, p. 700.

550 *"nothing should interfere"*: "Toscanini, Huberman Citizens of Tel Aviv," report from the Jewish Telegraphic Agency, reprinted in *The Jewish Post* (Indiana), April 29, 1938.

550 *her coffin was draped*: Hilmes, *Cosimas Kinder*, pp. 269–71.

550 *"Because I am a German"*: Rieger, *Friedelind Wagner*, p. 150.

550 *"Richard Wagner, who loved"*: Friedelind Wagner, broadcast on Feb. 14, 1942, included in the audiobook for Hans Sarkowicz, *Geheime Sender: Der Rundfunk im Widerstand gegen Hitler* (Hörverlag, 2016).

550 *"has no greater"*: Quoted in Klaus-Uwe Fischer, "Von Wagner zu Hitler: Annahme oder Ablehnung einer These von Ludwig Marcuse," *Musik–Konzepte 5: Richard Wagner: Wie antisemitisch darf ein Künstler sein?* (text+kritik, 1978), p. 34. See also Berthold Hoeckner, "Wagner and the Origin of Evil," *Opera Quarterly* 23:2–3 (2007), pp. 151–83.

551 *"the greatest artist"*: Frederick Schrader, open letter, *The Fatherland*, Oct. 7, 1914.

551 *two-part article*: Viereck's "Hitler and Richard Wagner" appeared in *Common Sense* 8:11 (1939), pp. 3–6; and 8:12, pp. 20–22. For "proto-Nazi," see Viereck, *Metapolitics: The Roots of the Nazi Mind* (Capricorn, 1965), p. 91.

551 *"the nuance of love"*: TMW, p. 181.

551 *"is and remains"*: Mann and Agnes E. Meyer, *Briefwechsel 1937–1955*, ed. Hans Rudolf Vaget (Fischer, 1992), p. 372.

551 *"there is much 'Hitler'"*: TMW, p. 204.

551 *"first totalitarian artist"*: Otto Tolischus, "Wagner: Clue to Hitler," *New York Times Magazine*, Feb. 25, 1940. This article attributes to Hitler the statement "Whoever wants to understand National Socialist Germany must know Wagner"—a declaration that has become part of the standard literature, even though no source is given. Other quotations from Emil Ludwig, *How to Treat the Germans* (Hutchinson, 1943), p. 66; Paul Henry Lang, "Background Music to 'Mein Kampf,'" *Saturday Review of Literature*, Jan. 20, 1945, pp. 5–9; Carl Engel, "Views and Reviews," *Musical Quarterly* 27:2 (1941), p. 245.

552 Rassenschande: Picker, *Hitlers Tischgespräche* (1965), p. 187.

552 *"refusal to separate"*: Annegret Fauser, *Sounds of War: Music in the United States During World War II* (Oxford UP, 2013), p. 71.

552 *"fundamentally a moral"*: "Wagner and Hitler," *New York Times*, Feb. 26, 1940.

552 *"the antithesis of Hitler"*: Downes, "On Misrepresenting Wagner," *New York Times*, March 3, 1940. See also Downes, "Season in Review," March 15, 1942; Downes, "Leinsdorf Directs Wagnerian Opera," Dec. 3, 1939; Mark A. Schubart, "'Meistersinger' Returns," Jan. 7, 1945.

552 *Mann attended*: See his *Tagebücher, 1940–1943*, ed. Peter de Mendelssohn (Fischer, 1982), p. 503.

552 *"Never has the inherent"*: Downes, "Toscanini Directs 2 Orchestras, 600-Voice Chorus for Red Cross," *New York Times*, May 26, 1944.

552 *souvenir booklet*: New York Philharmonic Leon Levy Digital Archives, archives.nyphil.org. The photograph, by Sgt. Stanley M. Smith, is from a 1943 mission by the 390th Bombardment Group.

553 *"wants to ignore . . . How to react"*: Rachel Orzech, "'How to React in France Against Hitlerian Pseudo-Wagnerism': The Reception of Richard Wagner in Paris, 1933," *Context* 39 (2014), pp. 17, 18. The one-quarter statistic is on p. 13.

553 *Paul Claudel*: On the writer's relationship with Wagner, see Timothée Picard, "Claudel," in DEW, pp. 374–80, also p. 2145.

553 *"accent of lost Paradise"*: Claudel, "Richard Wagner; Rêverie d'un poète français," *Œuvres complètes de Paul Claudel*, vol. 16 (Gallimard, 1959), p. 322.

553 *"The Wagnerian Poison"*: Claudel, "Le Poison wagnérien," *Figaro*, March 26, 1938.

553 *Lucien Rebatet*: Jane Fulcher, *The Composer as Intellectual: Music and Ideology in France, 1914–1940* (Oxford UP, 2005), pp. 249–50.

554 *modern-dress* Tristan: Claude Arnaud, *Jean Cocteau: A Life*, trans. Lauren Elkin and Charlotte Mandell (Yale UP, 2016), p. 682. See also pp. 227–28, 664–67.

554 *"Monsieur le Chancelier"*: Dujardin to Hitler, June 28, 1943, Dujardin Papers, Harry Ransom Center, University of Texas at Austin. On Dujardin's later history, see Simon Epstein, *Les dreyfusards sous l'Occupation* (Michel, 2001), pp. 151–52.

555 *"Never had the glorious"*: Diana Mosley, *A Life of Contrasts: The Autobiography* (Hamish Hamilton, 1977), p. 160.

555 *Strength Through Joy*: For an overview, see Julia Timpe, *Nazi-Organized Recreation and Entertainment in the Third Reich* (Palgrave, 2017), pp. 73–75; for band, lectures, and tours, see Richard Wilhelm Stock, ed., *Richard Wagner und seine Meistersinger: Eine Erinnerungsgabe zu den Bayreuther Kriegsfestspielen 1943* (Karl Ulrich, 1943), pp. 172, 175, 177.

555 *"holy German art"*: Hauptmann Dr. Lorenz, "Deutschlands Kampf und Richard Wagner," in *Kriegsfestspiele 1943: Bayreuth: Die Stadt Richard Wagners grüsst die Soldaten des Führers*, ed. Fritz Kempfler (Bayreuth, 1943), pp. 3–4.

555 *Stukas*: See Hans Rudolf Vaget, "Bayreuth and the German War Effort: Karl Ritter's *Stukas*," in *Music Theater as Global Culture*, pp. 41–50. For SS reports, see *Meldungen aus dem Reich*, vol. 5, p. 1508, vol. 8, p. 2675, and vol. 15, pp. 5808–809.

556 *some attendees slept*: Timpe, *Nazi-Organized Recreation*, p. 76.

557 *Silenced Voices*: For full documentation, see Heer, *Verstummte stimmen*, pp. 320–72. For Breker's bust, see OGB2, pp. 16, 78.

557 *"full, first-class symphony"*: Michael Kater, *Different Drummers: Jazz in the Culture of Nazi Germany* (Oxford UP, 1992), p. 180. For Alex Dekel, see Lucette Matalon Lagnado and Sheila Cohn Dekel,

Children of the Flames: Dr. Josef Mengele and the Untold Story of the Twins of Auschwitz (Penguin, 1992), p. 34; for Dachau, Guido Fackler, *"Des Lagers Stimme": Musik im KZ* (Temmen, 2000), p. 153. For Mengele whistling, see Gerald L. Posner and John Ware, *Mengele: The Complete Story* (Cooper Square, 2000), p. 13; Olga Lengyel, *Five Chimneys: The Story of Auschwitz* (Ziff-Davis, 1947), pp. 144–45; and Alan Levi, *Wanted: Nazi Criminals at Large* (Berkley, 1962), p. 53.

557 *more likely to be Chopin*: Yehudi Lindeman, ed., *Shards of Memory: Narratives of Holocaust Survival* (Praeger, 2007), p. 27.

557 *"one of them based"*: Szymon Laks, *Music of Another World*, trans. Chester A. Kisiel (Northwestern UP, 1989), p. 70.

557 *Auschwitz women's orchestra*: See Anita Lasker-Wallfisch, *Inherit the Truth, 1939–1945: The Documented Experiences of a Survivor of Auschwitz and Belsen* (Giles de la Mare, 1996), p. 79; and Fania Fénelon and Marcelle Routier, *Playing for Time*, trans. Judith Landry (Atheneum, 1977), pp. 106, 171–72. Fénelon's memoir is controversial, now considered partly fictional.

557 *"We certainly didn't"*: Stephen Fry's interview with Lasker-Wallfisch, for the documentary *Wagner & Me* (BBC, 2012).

558 *"colossal farce"*: Primo Levi, *If This Is a Man*, trans. Stuart Woolf, in *The Complete Works of Primo Levi*, vol. 1, ed. Ann Goldstein (Liveright, 2015), p. 26.

558 *"deepened still further"*: Laks, *Music of Another World*, pp. 117–18. For Majdanek, see Paul Trepman, *Among Men and Beasts* (Barnes, 1978), pp. 141–43; Łukasz Posłuszny and Joanna Posłuszna, "The Aural Landscape of Majdanek," in *Music and Genocide*, ed. Wojciech Klimczyk and Agata Świerzowska (Peter Lang, 2015), pp. 116–19.

558 The Eternal Jew: On the film's genesis and reception, see Yizhak Ahren, Stig Hornshøj-Møller, and Christoph B. Melchers, *"Der ewige Jude": Wie Goebbels hetzte: Untersuchungen zum nationalsozialistischen Propagandafilm* (Alano, 1990); and David Culbert, "The Impact of Anti-Semitic Film Propaganda on German Audiences: *Jew Süss* and *The Wandering Jew* (1940)," in *Art, Culture, and Media Under the Third Reich*, ed. Richard A. Etlin (University of Chicago Press, 2002), pp. 150–57.

558 *"plastic demon"*: See *Ausgewählte Reden des Führers und seiner Mitarbeiter, 1937* (Eher, 1937), p. 132. For other Goebbels citations of the phrase, see Herbert Michaelis and Ernst Schraepler, eds., *Ursachen und Folgen: Vom deutschen Zusammenbruch 1918 und 1945 bis zur staatlichen Neuordnung Deutschlands in der Gegenwart*, vol. 7 (Wendler, 1956), p. 216, and vol. 18 (Wendler, 1959), p. 114.

559 *"Ausrottung"*: Randall L. Bytwerk, ed. and trans., *Landmark Speeches of National Socialism* (Texas A&M UP, 2008), p. 121. For the use of *Der ewige*

Jude during the Holocaust, see Stefan Mannes, *Antisemitismus im nationalsozialistischen Propagandafilm: "Jud Süss" und "Der ewige Jude"* (Teiresias, 1999), p. 115; and Fotini Tzani, *Zwischen Karrierismus und Widerspenstigkeit: SS-Aufseherinnen im KZ-Alltag* (Lorbeer, 2011), p. 43. Hitler's phrase about the "Bolshevization of the earth" was edited out of the film on account of the Hitler-Stalin pact.

559 *Operation Walküre*: See Helena Schrader, *Codename Valkyrie: General Friedrich Olbricht and the Plot Against Hitler* (Haynes, 2009), pp. 222–24; Helena Page, *General Friedrich Olbricht: Ein Mann des 20. Juli* (Bouvier, 1994), pp. 186–87; Carl Dirks and Karl Heinze Janßen, *Der Krieg der Generäle: Hitler als Werkzeug der Wehrmacht* (Berlin: Propyläen, 1999), pp. 161–79. For Olbricht's musical interests, see Page, *Olbricht*, p. 88; for his support for Weimar, Joachim Fest, *Plotting Hitler's Death: The Story of the German Resistance*, trans. Bruce Little (Metropolitan Books, 1994), pp. 187–88.

560 *operetta fare*: See HWW, p. 431; Hans Wollschläger, "Der kleine Mann als ironische Hohlform," *Frankfurter Allgemeine Zeitung*, Oct. 6, 1998; Rochus Misch, *Hitler's Last Witness: The Memoirs of Hitler's Bodyguard* (Frontline, 2014), pp. 95–96. For Hitler's loss of interest in music, see Christa Schroeder, *Er war mein Chef: Aus dem Nachlaß der Sekretärin von Adolf Hitler*, ed. Anton Joachimsthaler (Langen Müller, 1985), p. 130; and Junge, *Bis zur letzten Stunde*, p. 184.

560 *Wagner's handwriting*: Henriette von Schirach, "Die verschollenen Wagner-Partituren," May 19, 1984, Institut für Zeitgeschichte, Archivdatenbank Online, ZZ 2238, p. 8. For attempts to retrieve the manuscripts, see letters from Wieland Wagner to Hans-Heinrich Lammers and Martin Bormann, both dated Feb. 9, 1945, National Archives of the Richard Wagner Foundation, Bayreuth; and Wolfgang Wagner, *Acts: The Autobiography of Wolfgang Wagner*, trans. John Brownjohn (Wiedenfeld, 1994), pp. 72–73; HWW, p. 502. On the disappearance, see Holger Reiner Stunz, "Richard Wagners Partituren als Spielball der Zeitgeschichte: Eine Spurensuche," *wagnerspectrum* 4:2 (2008), pp. 175–207.

560 *"Oh Swan Song"*: Brecht, *Kriegsfibel* manuscript, USC Libraries Special Collections, digitallibrary .usc.edu, p. 60. For Romain Rolland, see *Journal de Vézelay, 1938–1944* (Bartillat, 2012), p. 1036; for Speer, see his *Inside the Third Reich*, p. 463.

561 *"When I really think"*: Author's interview with Christoph von Dohnányi, Jan. 17, 2011.

561 *"hot licks not in the Nazi score"*: Albert F. Pishioneri, *Me, Mom, and World War II* (AuthorHouse, 2008), p. 370.

14. RIDE OF THE VALKYRIES: FILM FROM *THE BIRTH OF A NATION* TO *APOCALYPSE NOW*

562 *up to fifty musicians*: Martin Miller Marks, *Music and the Silent Film: Contexts and Case Studies, 1895–1924* (Oxford UP, 1997), p. 276.

563 *more than a dozen movies*: For an overview, see John C. Tibbetts, *Composers in the Movies: Studies in Musical Biography* (Yale UP, 2005), pp. 62–68, 71–76, 222–30; Peter Jammerthal, "Richard Wagner als Filmfigur," in *Wagner Kino: Spuren und Wirkungen Richard Wagners in der Filmkunst*, ed. Jan Drehmel et al. (Junius, 2013), pp. 12–19.

563 *Abel Gance*: See Paul Cuff, *Abel Gance and the End of Silent Cinema: Sounding Out Utopia* (Palgrave, 2016), pp. 27–31.

564 *"If Wagner had been born"*: Émile Vuillermoz, "La Musique des images," *L'Art cinématographique*, vol. 3, ed. André Maurois et al. (Félix Alcan, 1927), p. 56. For Max Steiner, see Tony Thomas, *Music for the Movies* (Silman-James, 1997), p. 157; for Wolfgang Wagner, Tony Palmer, "Foreword," in WC, p. x.

564 *"bright-colored picture"*: Eduard Hanslick, *Musikalische Stationen* (Hofmann, 1880), p. 228.

564 *"technical apparatus"*: RWSS9, p. 336.

564 *"the darkness"*: Friedrich Kittler, "World-Breath: On Wagner's Media Technology," in *The Truth of the Technological World: Essays on the Genealogy of Presence*, trans. Erik Butler (Stanford UP, 2013), p. 122.

565 *Clouds of steam*: See Gundula Kreuzer, *Curtain, Gong, Steam: Wagnerian Technologies of Nineteenth-Century Opera* (University of California Press, 2018), pp. 180–81.

565 *"elaborate upward panning shot"*: Peter Franklin, "Underscoring Drama—Picturing Music," in WC, p. 55.

565 *"Every man or woman"*: W. Stephen Bush, "Giving Musical Expression to the Drama," *Moving Picture World*, Aug. 12, 1911. See also Bush, "Possibilities of Musical Synchronization," *Moving Picture World*, Sept. 2, 1911.

566 *"mimetic representation"*: Canudo, "The Birth of the Sixth Art," in *Film Theory: Critical Concepts in Media and Cultural Studies*, vol. 1, ed. Philip Simpson et al. (Routledge, 2004), p. 29. See also Laurent Guido, *L'Âge du rythme: Cinéma, musicalité et culture du corps dans les théories françaises des années 1910–1930* (Payot, 2007), pp. 215–24. For Häfker, see Helmut H. Diederichs, "Naturfilm als Gesamtkunstwerk: Hermann Häfker und sein 'Kinetographie'-Konzept,'" *Augenblick* 8 (1990), pp. 37–60.

566 *"genuine and ultimate"*: Sergei Eisenstein, "Achievement" (1939), in *Film Form: Essays in Film Theory*, ed. and trans. Jay Leyda (Harcourt, 1977), p. 181.

566 *"true art of the people"*: Carolyn Birdsall, *Nazi Soundscapes: Sound, Technology and Urban Space*

in Germany, 1933–1945 (Amsterdam UP, 2012), pp. 145–46.

566 "glittering, revue-like": Siegfried Kracauer, Das Ornament der Masse: Essays (Suhrkamp, 1977), p. 312.

566 "scornfully laughing": Max Horkheimer and Theodor W. Adorno, Dialektik der Aufklärung: Philosophische Fragmente (Fischer, 1988), p. 132.

566 "fetish object": Scott D. Paulin, "Richard Wagner and the Fantasy of Cinematic Unity: The Idea of the Gesamtkunstwerk in the History and Theory of Film Music," in Music and Cinema, ed. James Buhler et al. (Wesleyan UP, 2000), p. 59.

567 Kazimierz Prószyński: Bartosz Staszczyszyn, "Kazimierz Prószyński: Edison of the Tenth Muse," Dec. 20, 2018, culture.pl/en/article/kazimierz-proszynski-edison-of-the-tenth-muse, accessed Dec. 25, 2019.

567 At least a dozen: See Tobias Plebuch, "Richard Wagner im Film bis 1945," wagnerspectrum 4:2 (2008), pp. 126–27.

567 "the greatest religious subject": "New Edison Films," Billboard, Nov. 30, 1907. The film seems to have been rereleased in 1907. For more, see Charles Musser, Before the Nickelodeon: Edwin S. Porter and the Edison Manufacturing Company (University of California Press, 1991), pp. 287–89.

567 The Life and Works: Paul Fryer, "The Life and Works of Richard Wagner (1913): Becce, Froelich, and Messter," in WC, pp. 65–84; Ennio Simeon, "Giuseppe Becce and Richard Wagner: Paradoxes of the First German Film Score," in A Second Life: German Cinema's First Decades, ed. Thomas Elsaesser and Michael Wedel (Amsterdam UP, 1996), pp. 219–24.

568 "red thread": James Buhler, "Wagnerian Motives: Narrative Integration and the Development of Silent Film Accompaniment, 1908–1913," in WC, p. 35.

568 "To each important character": Clarence E. Sinn, "Music for the Picture," Moving Picture World, Jan. 21, 1911. Ernő Rapée says much the same in his Encyclopedia of Music for Pictures (Arno Press, 1970), p. 8. On early uses of Wagner, see Christoph Henzel, "Wagner und die Filmmusik," Acta Musicologia 76:1 (2004), pp. 108–109; Plebuch, "Richard Wagner im Film bis 1945," p. 133.

568 "built very much": Marks, Music and the Silent Film, p. 103. For d'Annunzio and film, see Andrea Mirabile, Multimedia Archaeologies: Gabriele D'Annunzio, Belle Époque Paris, and the Total Artwork (Rodopi, 2014), pp. 157–82.

568 White House: On the screening, see Mark E. Benbow, "Birth of a Quotation: Woodrow Wilson and 'Like Writing History with Lightning,'" Journal of the Gilded Age and Progressive Era 9:4 (2010), pp. 509–33.

569 "I could just see": James Hart, ed., The Man Who Invented Hollywood: The Autobiography of D. W. Griffith (Touchstone, 1972), p. 88.

569 "You can't tamper": Marks, Music and the Silent Film, p. 140.

569 "They are coming": Matthew Wilson Smith, "American Valkyries: Richard Wagner, D. W. Griffith, and the Birth of Classical Cinema," Modernism/modernity 15:2 (2008), p. 238.

569 "Griffith's use of Wagner": Smith, "American Valkyries," p. 238.

569 James Whitman: See his Hitler's American Model: The United States and the Making of Nazi Race Law (Princeton UP, 2017), pp. 9–10, 28.

570 Ludendorff . . . lamented: Klaus Kreimeier, The Ufa Story: A History of Germany's Greatest Film Company 1918–1945, trans. Robert and Rita Kimber (Hill and Wang, 1996), p. 8.

570 Klaus Kreimeier: Ibid., pp. 45, 108–109.

570 reading Schopenhauer: Lotte H. Eisner, Murnau (University of California Press, 1973), pp. 15–16. On Murnau's youth, see Fred Gehler and Ullrich Kasten, Friedrich Wilhelm Murnau (Henschel, 1990), pp. 14–21.

571 "symphony of body-melody": Gehler and Kasten, Murnau, p. 141.

571 Jo Leslie Collier: See her From Wagner to Murnau: The Transposition of Romanticism from Stage to Screen (UMI Research Press, 1988), p. 135. On Hans Erdmann's score, see Berndt Heller, "La Musique de la 'Fête de Nosferatu,'" Cinémathèque Française 15 (1986), p. 11.

571 "detested Wagner": Patrick McGilligan, Fritz Lang: The Nature of the Beast (University of Minnesota Press, 2013), p. 103.

571 "mystical-magical": Hans-Michael Bock and Michael Töteberg, eds., Das Ufa-Buch: Kunst und Krisen, Stars und Regisseure, Wirtschaft und Politik (Zweitausendeins, 1992), p. 143. See also Lotte Eisner, Fritz Lang (Oxford UP, 1977), p. 76.

571 "exhausted brain": Thea von Harbou, "Vom Epos zum Film," Die Woche 26:6 (1924), p. 139. See also Levin, Richard Wagner, Fritz Lang, pp. 130–31.

572 "The challenge was to connect": Adeline Mueller, "Listening for Wagner in Fritz Lang's Die Nibelungen," in WC, p. 87. For Bayreuth's resistance, see p. 86; for the American release, pp. 94–95. On Huppertz's leitmotifs, see Henzel, "Wagner und die Filmmusik," pp. 95–97.

572 Frank Aschau: "Nibelungen-Film," Weltbühne, Feb. 28, 1924.

572 irreversible fate: Siegfried Kracauer, From Caligari to Hitler: A Psychological History of the German Film (Princeton UP, 1947), pp. 93–95.

572 "militarily ordered rows": RWSS5, p. 147.

573–74 inaugural exhibition: Hannah Lewis, "'The Realm of Serious Art': Henry Hadley's Involvement in Early Sound Film," Journal of the Society for American Music 8:3 (2014), pp. 288–92.

574 "As Time Goes By": See Peter Wegele, Der Filmkomponist Max Steiner (1888–1971) (Böhlau, 2012), pp. 182–87; David Neumeyer, "The Resonances of

Wagnerian Opera and Nineteenth-Century Melodrama in the Film Scores of Max Steiner," in WC, pp. 111–30.

574 *"a musical lackey"*: Theodor W. Adorno and Hanns Eisler, *Composing for the Films* (Athlone, 1994), pp. 5–6.

575 *"sarcastic misapplications"*: Carolyn Abbate, "Wagner, Cinema, and Redemptive Glee," *Opera Quarterly* 21:4 (2005), p. 599.

575 Murder!: For more, see Jack Sullivan, *Hitchcock's Music* (Yale UP, 2006), pp. 11–12. On *Vertigo* and *Tristan*, see Robert J. Yanal, *Hitchcock as Philosopher* (McFarland, 2005), pp. 52–58.

576 Three Songs of Lenin: Description based on the 1938 revision of *Three Songs of Lenin*, as released in the DVD compilation *Dziga Vertov: Tri pesni o Lenine* (Edition Filmmuseum, 2014). On the different versions, see John MacKay, "Allegory and Accommodation: Vertov's *Three Songs of Lenin* (1934) as a Stalinist Film," *Film History* 18:4 (2006), pp. 376–91; Lilya Kaganovsky, *The Voice of Technology: Soviet Cinema's Transition to Sound, 1928–1935* (Indiana UP, 2018), pp. 178–226.

577 *"I have loved the Nibelung"*: Eisenstein, *Selected Works*, vol. 4: *Beyond the Stars: The Memoirs of Sergei Eisenstein*, ed. Richard Taylor, trans. William Powell (BFI, 1995), p. 593. For childhood interests, see Yon Barna, *Eisenstein*, trans. Lise Hunter (Indiana UP, 1973), p. 34.

577 *"The Montage of Film Attractions"*: Eisenstein, *Selected Works*, vol. 1: *Writings, 1922–1934*, ed. and trans. Richard Taylor (BFI, 1988), p. 35, "Juxtaposition and accumulation" on p. 41.

578 *"unity of opposites"*: Eisenstein, *Nonindifferent Nature*, trans. Herbert Marshall (Cambridge UP, 1987), p. 84; comparison to music on p. 57.

578 *"a model of how"*: Antonio Somaini, "Cinema as 'Dynamic Mummification': History as Montage: Eisenstein's Media Archaeology," in Eisenstein, *Notes for a General History of Cinema*, ed. Naum Kleiman and Antonio Somaini (Amsterdam UP, 2016), p. 48.

578 *"leitmotivs through all types"*: Jay Leyda and Zina Voynow, *Eisenstein at Work* (Pantheon, 1982), pp. 38–40. For *Parsifal* comparison, see Eisenstein, *Nonindifferent Nature*, p. 39.

578 *"Moos in industrial theme"*: Fiona Ford, *The Film Music of Edmund Meisel (1894–1930)* (Ph.D. diss., University of Nottingham, 2011), p. 253.

579 *"ideologically unacceptable"*: BWR, p. 261.

579 *"I would like to create"*: Barna, *Eisenstein*, p. 141.

579 *"The film was to show"*: Eisenstein, *Selected Works*, vol. 3: *Writings 1934–1947*, ed. Richard Taylor, trans. William Powell (BFI, 1996), p. 147.

579 Dieter Thomä: See his *Totalität und Mitleid: Richard Wagner, Sergej Eisenstein und unsere ethisch-ästhetische Moderne* (Suhrkamp, 2006), p. 246.

579 frenzied research: Rosamund Bartlett, "The Embodiment of Myth: Eizenshtein's Production of *Die Walküre*," *Slavonic and East European Review* 70:1 (1992), p. 55. See *Eisenstein at Work*, pp. 114–15, for other *Ring* sketches.

579 *"had its origins"*: *Meyerhold on Theatre*, p. 311.

579 *"Incarnation of Myth"*: Eisenstein, *Selected Works*, vol. 3, pp. 142–69, quotation on p. 164.

579 *"Our interpretation"*: Ulrich Krempel, ed., *Beispiel Eisenstein: Zeichnung, Theater, Film* (Städtische Kunsthalle Düsseldorf, 1983), p. 17; Bartlett, "Embodiment of Myth," pp. 64–65.

580 *"deliberate Jewish tricks"*: Leyda and Voynow, *Eisenstein at Work*, p. 114.

580 Håkan Lövgren: See his "Sergei Eisenstein's Gnostic Circle," in *The Occult in Russian and Soviet Culture*, ed. Bernice Glatzer Rosenthal (Cornell UP, 1997), pp. 283–93.

580 *"pathos with which"*: Eisenstein, *Nonindifferent Nature*, p. 109; *Beyond the Stars*, p. 660.

581 *"among the giant pines"*: Eisenstein, *Beyond the Stars*, pp. 662–63, 670.

581 theme of power: Eisenstein, *Nonindifferent Nature*, p. 324.

581 the studios had shied away: See Thomas Doherty, *Hollywood and Hitler, 1933–1939* (Columbia UP, 2013), pp. 335–45.

582 March of Time: Scott D. Paulin, "Piercing Wagner: The *Ring* in *Golden Earrings*," WC, pp. 228–29, 247, cites usage of Wagner in the newsreels "Hitler Sets the Stage for His Coup," Feb. 17, 1938, and "Hitler Takes Austria—Is Czechoslovakia Next?," March 17, 1938.

583 *"To the accompaniment"* "Nazi Party Congress Film," *Observer*, March 31, 1935. For the *Meistersinger* claim, see Linda Deutschmann, *Triumph of the Will: The Image of the Third Reich* (Longwood, 1991), p. 32.

583 *"phantom hearing"*: Applegate, *Necessity of Music*, p. 294. See also Reimar Volker, *"Von oben sehr erwünscht": Die Filmmusik Herbert Windts im NS-Propagandafilm* (WVT, 2003), pp. 72–77; Stefan Strötgen, "'I Compose the Party Rally . . .': The Role of Music in Leni Riefenstahl's *Triumph of the Will*," *Music & Politics* 2:1 (2008), pp. 1–14.

583 The Emperor of California: See Lutz Koepnick, *The Dark Mirror: German Cinema Between Hitler and Hollywood* (University of California Press, 2002), pp. 114–25.

583 *"strangely shunned"*: Koepnick, *Dark Mirror*, p. 40. See also Volker, "Verfilmet mir den Meister nicht: Wagner im NS-Film," in *Wagner Kino*, pp. 62–71.

583 *"American bunk"*: Koepnick, *Dark Mirror*, p. 11. On Goebbels's admiration for Hollywood, see Ben Urwand, *The Collaboration: Hollywood's Pact with Hitler* (Belknap, 2013), pp. 112–14.

583 *"We can't win this war"*: Mark Harris, *Five Came Back: A Story of Hollywood and the Second World War* (Penguin, 2014), p. 141.

583 *"Though panoplied"*: Frank Capra, *The Name Above the Title: An Autobiography* (Macmillan, 1971),

p. 328. On Wagner in *Why We Fight*, see Paulin, "Piercing Wagner," p. 229.

584 *"recognized throughout the world"*: In *Prelude to War*, this statement is ascribed to Henry L. Stinson, the secretary of war, but it seems to originate in a 1942 speech by George C. Marshall.

584 *well over a hundred*: Daniel Ira Goldmark, *Tunes for 'Toons: Music and the Hollywood Cartoon* (University of California Press, 2005), p. 141.

584 *Nips the Nips*: Neil Lerner, "Reading Wagner in *Bugs Bunny Nips the Nips*," in WC, pp. 221–22.

585 *burst into laughter*: Luis Buñuel, *My Last Breath*, trans. Abigail Israel (Flamingo, 1985), p. 180.

586 *"condemn the abuse"*: Koepnick, *The Dark Mirror*, p. 141. For Lawrence Kramer, see "Contesting Wagner: The Lohengrin Prelude and Anti-anti-Semitism," *19th-Century Music* 25:2–3 (2001–2002), p. 205. For Mann's doubts, see Mann and Meyer, *Briefwechsel*, p. 243.

587 *"the true and touching 'Holy Innocent'"*: Eisenstein, *Selected Works*, vol. 3, p. 262.

587 *The Nazi Wagnerite*: See, among others, *The Stranger* (1946), *Golden Earrings* (1947), *Appointment in London* (1953), *Young Lions* (1958), *Verboten!* (1959), *The Night of the Generals* (1967), and *The Last Escape* (1970).

588 *William Dieterle*: For background, see Marta Mierendorff, *William Dieterle: Der Plutarch von Hollywood* (Henschel, 1993), pp. 15–16, 156, 191–94.

590 *Elisabeth Bronfen*: See her "Nocturnal Wagner: The Cultural Survival of *Tristan und Isolde* in Hollywood," in WC, pp. 315–32; "Hollywood's Wagner: The Return to/of the Ordinary," in *Jenseits von Bayreuth: Richard Wagner heute*, ed. Stefan Börnchen et al. (Fink, 2014), pp. 239–62; and "Isoldes Liebestod in Hollywood: Eine transmediale Affäre," in *Wagner, Gender, Mythen: Wagner in der Diskussion*, ed. Christine Fornoff and Melanie Unseld (Königshausen & Neumann, 2015), pp. 231–57.

591 *Marcia Citron*: See her "'Soll ich lauschen?': Love-Death in *Humoresque*," in WC, pp. 167–85.

591 *A native of Dresden*: For background, see Deborah Lazaroff Alpi, *Robert Siodmak: A Biography, with Critical Analysis of His Film Noirs and a Filmography of All His Works* (McFarland, 1998), pp. 11, 126–30, 298; Joseph Greco, *The File on Robert Siodmak in Hollywood, 1941–1951* (Ph.D. diss., State University of New York, Stony Brook, 1995).

593 *Richard Dyer*: See his *The Culture of Queers* (Routledge, 2002), p. 95.

594 *"the Middle Ages lasted"*: Buñuel, *My Last Breath*, p. 8. For his teenage Wagnerism, see J. Francisco Aranda, "Out of Innocence," in *The World of Luis Buñuel: Essays in Criticism*, ed. Joan Mellen (Oxford UP, 1978), p. 39. For Wagner in Madrid, see Max Aub, *Conversations with Buñuel: Interviews with the Filmmaker, Family Members, Friends and Collaborators*, ed. and trans. Julie Jones (McFarland, 2017), p. 76; Dalí's comment on p. 243.

594 *At the premiere*: Aub, *Conversations with Buñuel*, pp. 42–43.

595 *"Stare out the window"*: Buñuel, *My Last Breath*, p. 104. For "comic counterpoint," see Aub, *Conversations with Buñuel*, p. 76. For Torben Sangild, see "Buñuel's Liebestod: Wagner's *Tristan* in Luis Buñuel's Early Films: *Un chien andalou* and *L'Âge d'or*," *Journal of Music and Meaning* 13 (2014/2015), p. 38.

596 *"Was it possible"*: Henry Miller, "The Golden Age," in *Film: An Anthology*, ed. Daniel Talbot (University of California Press, 1969), p. 382.

596 *Visconti*: For the *Buddenbrooks* comparison, see Henry Bacon, *Visconti: Explorations of Beauty and Decay* (Cambridge UP, 1998), p. 146; for "all my films," p. 140. For Nazi youths, see Gaia Servadio, *Luchino Visconti: A Biography* (Franklin Watts, 1983), p. 47.

597 *reenact the composer's death*: Servadio, *Visconti*, p. 203.

598 *Ernst Röhm*: On Röhm and Wagner, see HWW, pp. 278–29; Röhm, *Die Geschichte eines Hochverräters* (Eher, 1933), p. 356. On Visconti and Wagner, see David Huckvale, *Visconti and the German Dream: Romanticism, Wagner and the Nazi Catastrophe in Film* (McFarland, 2012).

599 *"symphonic synthesis"*: On Mishima's use of Stokowski, see Donald Richie, *The Japan Journals, 1947–2004* (Stone Bridge, 2005), p. 147.

599 *Meiji period*: See Toru Takenaka, "Wagner-Boom in Meiji-Japan," *Archiv für Musikwissenschaft* 62:1 (2005), pp. 13–31; Brooke McCorkle, "Was ist Japanisch?: Wagnerism and Dreams of Nationhood in Modern Japan," in *Dreams of Germany: Musical Imaginaries from the Concert Hall to the Dance Floor*, ed. Neil Gregor and Thomas Irvine (Berghahn, 2019), pp. 169–93. *Children's Wagner* comes from McCorkle's communication to author. For Rofū Akimoto, see McCorkle, *Searching for Wagner in Japan* (Ph.D. diss., University of Pennsylvania, 2015), pp. 38–44.

599 *Mishima took an interest*: See McCorkle, *Searching for Wagner in Japan*, p. 145. For *Death in Venice*, see Yukio Mishima, *Forbidden Colors*, trans. Alfred H. Marks (Perigee, 1980), pp. 20–23; Irmela Hijiya-Kirschnereit, "Thomas Mann's Short Novel *Der Tod in Venedig* and Mishima Yukio's novel *Kinjiki*: A Comparison," in *European Studies on Japan*, ed. Ian Nish and Charles Dunn (Norbury, 1979), pp. 312–17.

600 *"He should have listened"*: Hiroaki Sato, trans., *"My Friend Hitler" and Other Plays of Yukio Mishima* (Columbia UP, 2002), p. 156.

600 *"deepest woe"*: The Stokowski excerpt begins at the marking "Gedehnt und langsam" and Isolde's line "für tieftes Weh."

600 *"a story of nostalgic"*: McCorkle, *Searching for Wagner in Japan*, p. 160.

601 *"ultimate masturbation"*: Henry Scott-Stokes, *The Life and Death of Yukio Mishima* (Farrar, Straus and Giroux, 1974), p. 308.

601 *"unbearable degree of individuality"*: Sontag, "Fascinating Fascism," *New York Review of Books*, Feb. 6, 1975.

601 *"Hitler was one of the first"*: Cameron Crowe, "Playboy Interview: David Bowie," *Playboy*, September 1976.

603 *German newsreel*: Wochenschau, June 4, 1941; Müller, *Wagner und die Deutschen*, pp. 180–81.

604 *"Part of the thought"*: Ian McLachlan, *Flight into History: Final Missions Retold by Research and Archaeology* (History Press e-book, 2013), chapter 7. For the XB-70, see "B-70 to Be Called Valkyrie," *New York Times*, July 3, 1958.

604 *"I knew that they did have"*: Milius in conversation with Coppola, documentary material for *Apocalypse Now Redux* (Paramount, 2001). On the weaponization of music, see Alex Ross, "The Sound of Hate," *New Yorker*, July 4, 2016.

605 *"Tracking that victory"*: Lawrence Weschler, "Valkyries over Iraq," *Harper's*, Nov. 2005, p. 72. For the link to *The Birth of a Nation*, see Smith, "American Valkyries," esp. pp. 221–22.

605 *"journey into the surreal"*: James M. Welsh et al., eds., *The Francis Ford Coppola Encyclopedia* (Scarecrow, 2010), p. 10.

605 *Coppola has no memory*: Francis Ford Coppola's communication to author, Oct. 16, 2017.

606 *Walter Murch*: See his "How I Tried to Transplant the Musical Heart of *Apocalypse Now*," *Nautilus* 30, Nov. 12, 2015. For a detailed account of the sequence, see Christina Zenk, "Ausdiskutiert?: Die *Walküren* in *Apocalypse Now*," (Schott Campus, 2016). See also Richard Klein, "Walkürenritt in Vietnam," in *Richard Wagner und seine Medien: Für eine kritische Praxis des Musiktheaters*, ed. Johanna Dombois and Richard Klein (Klein-Cotta, 2012), pp. 394–408.

606 *devised by Murch*: Author's interview with Murch, May 17, 2019.

607 *military fetish object*: For Grenada, see Herbert A. Friedman, "United States Psyop in Grenada," www .psywarrior.com/GrenadaHerb.html, accessed Dec. 25, 2019; Mark Whitaker et al., "We Will Not Be Intimidated," *Newsweek*, Nov. 14, 1983. For 73 Easting, Douglas Macgregor, *Warrior's Rage: The Great Tank Battle of 73 Easting* (Naval Institute Press, 2009), pp. 63–64. For Fallujah, James Janega, "'Ghost 3' Keeps Wary Watch for Snipers," *Chicago Tribune*, Nov. 10, 2004.

607 *"energized but also upset"*: Author's interview with Murch.

607 *"filmic images"*: Anthony Swofford, *Jarhead: A Marine's Chronicle of the Gulf War and Other Battles* (Scribner, 2003), pp. 6–7.

608 *Eric Rentschler*: *The Ministry of Illusion: Nazi Cinema and Its Afterlife* (Harvard UP, 1996), p. 6.

15. THE WOUND: WAGNERISM AFTER 1945

609 *Ingmar Bergman*: OGB2, p. 267.

610 *"Now the lunatics"*: "Der 'Ring'-Kampf von Bayreuth," *Spiegel*, Aug. 2, 1976.

610 *"really demanded"*: GBS, p. 91.

610 *"fragments of utopia"*: Michel Foucault, "L'Imagination du XIXe siècle," *Dits et écrits, 1954–1988*, vol. 4, ed. Daniel Defert and François Ewald (Gallimard, 1994), p. 114.

612 *Jack Benny . . . the Rockettes*: OGB1, p. 649.

612 *"fantastical fulfillment"*: Franz Wilhelm Beidler, *Cosima Wagner: Ein Porträt: Richard Wagners erster Enkel: Ausgewählte Schriften und Briefwechsel mit Thomas Mann*, ed. Dieter Borchmeyer (Königshausen & Neumann, 2011), p. 357.

613 *Much of the financial support*: Müller, *Wagner und die Deutschen*, pp. 189–91, 261–67; Gottfried Wagner, *Twilight of the Wagners: The Unveiling of a Family's Legacy*, trans. Della Couling (Picador, 1999), p. 45.

613 *"All human life"*: E. M. Forster, "Revolution at Bayreuth," *Listener*, Nov. 4, 1954, p. 755.

613 *Wieland's innovations*: Geoffrey Skelton, *Wieland Wagner: The Positive Sceptic* (St. Martin's, 1971), pp. 72, 89.

613 *Grace Bumbry*: On this complex episode, see Kira Thurman, "Black Venus, White Bayreuth: Race, Sexuality, and the Depoliticization of Wagner in Postwar West Germany," *German Studies Review* 35:3 (2012), pp. 60–76.

613 *"first concentration camp"*: Antoine Goléa, *Entretiens avec Wieland Wagner* (Belfond, 1967), p. 115. Fascist comparisons on pp. 115–20.

614 *whose father served*: See Friedrich's introduction to Page, *General Friedrich Olbricht*, pp. xi–xv.

614 *"symbolic dream-world"*: PCW, p. 319; Joachim Herz, "Richard Wagner und das Erbe—Möglichkeiten des Musiktheaters an einer Repertoirebühne," *Theater—Kunst des erfüllten Augenblicks: Briefe, Vorträge, Notate, Gespräche, Essays*, ed. Ilse Kobán (Henschel, 1989), p. 129.

615 *Herz's culminating achievement*: For descriptions of Herz's *Ring*, see PCW, pp. 331–40; Alexander K. Rothe, *Staging the Past: Richard Wagner's Ring Cycle in Divided Germany During the 1970s and 1980s* (Ph.D. diss., Columbia University, 2015), pp. 71–129; Bauer, *Richard Wagner*, p. 257. For Hans Mayer, see "Wagners 'Ring' als bürgerliches Parabelspiel" in *Anmerkungen zu Richard Wagner* (Suhrkamp, 1966), pp. 100–110.

615 *many more permutations*: For an overview, see Mike Ashman, "Producing Wagner," in *Wagner in Performance*, ed. Barry Millington and Stewart Spencer (Yale UP, 1992), pp. 29–47. On Melchinger, see Rothe, *Staging the Past*, pp. 101–102,

174; on Berghaus, PCW, pp. 364–74; on the gas-chamber *Tannhäuser*, Udo Badelt, "*Tannhäuser* in der Gaskammer," *Tagesspiegel*, May 9, 2013, reporting on Burkhard C. Kosminski's production at the Deutsche Oper am Rhein.

616 "*taking on Wagner*": Badiou, *Five Lessons*, p. 55.

616 "*the philosopher is not free*": Nietzsche, *Fall Wagner*, "Vorwort."

617 *Jean-Paul Sartre*: See his *Écrits de jeunesse*, ed. Michel Contat and Michel Rybalka (Gallimard, 1990), pp. 189–286; Terry Keefe and Simon P. Keefe, "Sartre's Wagner," *Musical Times* 137:1846 (1996), pp. 9–11.

617 "*the dissolution . . . masculine aesthetics*: Martin Heidegger, *Nietzsche*, vols. 1–2, trans. David Farrell Krell (HarperCollins, 1991), pp. 87, 88, 70.

617 "*There is no document*": Benjamin, *Gesammelte Schriften*, vol. 1/2, p. 696.

618 "*cast off . . . gesture of hitting*": Adorno, *Versuch über Wagner*, pp. 154, 33.

618 "*Redemption, in Wagner*": Adorno, "Wagner, Nietzsche, and Hitler," *Kenyon Review* 9:1 (1947), p. 161.

618 "*unity of the progressive*": Adorno and Benjamin, *Briefwechsel, 1928–1940*, ed. Henri Lonitz (Suhrkamp, 1994), pp. 336–37, 345.

618 *Fredric Jameson*: See his *Late Marxism: Adorno; or, The Persistence of the Dialectic* (Verso, 2007), p. 221.

618–19 "*neurotic's power . . . life without fear*": Adorno, *Versuch über Wagner*, pp. 196, 198. For private property, see p. 180.

619 "*inverted panegyric*": Mark Berry, "Adorno's *Essay on Wagner*: Rescuing an Inverted Panegyric," *Opera Quarterly* 30:2–3 (2014), pp. 205–27.

619 *Adorno had begun*: Adorno and Benjamin, *Briefwechsel*, pp. 344–45.

619 "*The feeling of leaving*": Adorno, "Wagners Aktualität," *Gesammelte Schriften*, vol. 16 (Suhrkamp, 1978), p. 551.

619 *Spirit of Utopia*: Ernst Bloch, *Geist der Utopie* (Duncker & Humblot, 1918), pp. 151–53.

619 "*bliss-making melody*": Bloch, *Das Prinzip Hoffnung*, vol. 2: *Kapitel 38–55* (Suhrkamp, 1959), p. 974. On Bloch and Wagner, see Adrian Daub, "'An All-Too-Secret Wagner': Ernst Bloch the Wagnerian," *Opera Quarterly* 30:2–3 (2014), pp. 188–204; Benjamin Korstvedt, *Listening for Utopia in Ernst Bloch's Musical Philosophy* (Cambridge UP, 2010), pp. 97–124.

619 "*only experimental solutions*": Adorno, "Wagners Aktualität," p. 562. For a recent critique of leftist readings of Wagner, see Drüner, *Wagner*, esp. pp. 30–32.

620 "*Great artworks cannot lie*": Adorno, *Ästhetische Theorie* (Suhrkamp, 1970), p. 196.

620 "*in the mold of*": Adorno, *Negative Dialektik* (Suhrkamp, 1966), p. 356.

620 "*so-called primitive peoples*": Emmanuelle Loyer,

Lévi-Strauss: A Biography, trans. Ninon Vinson-neau and Jonathan Magidoff (Polity, 2018), p. 250.

620 "*the god Richard Wagner*": Lévi-Strauss, *Le cru et le cuit* (1964), p. 23.

620 *fallen for the composer*: Patrick Wilcken, *Claude Lévi-Strauss: The Poet in the Laboratory* (Bloomsbury, 2010), p. 24; Loyer, *Lévi-Strauss*, p. 43.

621 "*Wagner played a capital role*": Didier Eribon, *Conversations with Claude Lévi-Strauss*, trans. Paula Wissing (University of Chicago Press, 1991), p. 176.

621 *In the case of the* Ring: Lévi-Strauss, "A Note on the Tetralogy," *The View from Afar*, trans. Joachim Neugroschel and Phoebe Hoss (University of Chicago Press, 1992), pp. 235–39. For "mytheme," see Eribon, *Conversations*, p. 176. See also Jean-Jacques Nattiez, *Lévi-Strauss musicien: Essai sur la tentation homologique* (Actes Sud, 2008), pp. 73–87.

621 "*probably the most profound*": Lévi-Strauss, "From Chrétien de Troyes to Richard Wagner," *View from Afar*, p. 219; Parsifal's heroism on pp. 233–34. For myth and music, see *Le cru et le cuit*, pp. 23–24.

621 "*far in advance*": Joseph Campbell, *The Masks of God: Primitive Mythology* (Viking, 1959), p. 17. For "experience-in-illumination," see *The Masks of God: Creative Mythology* (Penguin, 1976), p. 40.

622 "*nostalgia for origins . . . without origin*": Jacques Derrida, *Writing and Difference*, trans. Alan Bass (University of Chicago Press, 1978), p. 292. For Roland Barthes, see his *Image, Music, Text*, ed. and trans. Stephen Heath (Noonday, 1977), p. 148. For "excess of syntax," see Derrida, *Dissemination*, trans. Barbara Johnson (Athlone, 1981), p. 231.

622 "*The Nazi Myth*": Philippe Lacoue-Labarthe and Jean-Luc Nancy, *Le Mythe nazi* (Éditions de l'Aube, 1991), p. 48. See also Lacoue-Labarthe, *La Fiction du politique* (Bourgois, 1988), p. 59.

622 "*tearing Nietzsche away . . . virile*": Lacoue-Labarthe, *Musica Ficta*, pp. 90, 105, 106.

623 *inherited Wagnerism*: Badiou, *Five Lessons*, p. ix.

623 "*The one is not*": Badiou, *Being and Event*, trans. Oliver Feltham (Continuum, 2007), p. 23.

623 *Wagner appears to be*: On Badiou and Wagner, see Kenneth Reinhard, "Badiou and the Subject of *Parsifal*," *Opera Quarterly* 29:3–4 (2013), pp. 361–67.

623 "*The public represents humanity*": Badiou, *Handbook of Inaesthetics*, p. 74.

624 "*whether a ceremony*": Badiou, *Five Lessons*, p. 147. On the "destruction of *all* mythologies" in the *Ring*, see pp. 105–106.

624 *other recuperative readings*: Fredric Jameson, "Wagner as Dramatist and Allegorist," *Modernist Cultures* 8:1 (2013), p. 11; Slavoj Žižek and Mladen Dolar, *Opera's Second Death* (Routledge, 2002); Žižek, "Brünnhilde's Act," *Opera Quarterly* 23:2–3 (2007), pp. 199–216.

624 *Pope Francis*: Antonio Spadaro, "A Big Heart Open

to God: An Interview with Pope Francis," *America*, Sept. 30, 2013.

624 *"proto-Nazi volkishness"*: Susan Sontag, *As Consciousness Is Harnessed to Flesh: Journals and Notebooks, 1964–1980*, ed. David Rieff (Farrar, Straus and Giroux, 2012), p. 452.

624 *new Romantic sublime*: Sontag, *Where the Stress Falls: Essays* (Farrar, Straus and Giroux, 2001), pp. 206–207. For "erotics," see Sontag, *Against Interpretation and Other Essays* (Picador, 2001), p. 14.

625 *"The Nuremberg tribunal . . . I am surprised"*: Pascal Quignard, *The Hatred of Music*, trans. Matthew Amos and Fredrik Rönnbäck (Yale UP, 2016), pp. 148, 146.

625 *"Lohengrin's Death"*: Heinrich Böll, *The Collected Stories*, trans. Leila Vennewitz and Breon Mitchell (Melville, 2011), p. 118.

626 *"We might as well start"*: Günter Grass, *Dog Years*, trans. Ralph Manheim (Harcourt, 1965), p. 501.

626 *the composer typified*: Jürgen Geisenberger, *Joseph Beuys und die Musik* (Tectum, 1999), p. 50. See also "Joseph Beuys im Gespräch mit Antje von Graevenitz: 'Im Wanderer steckt stets ein neuer Mensch,'" in *Der Raum Bayreuth: Ein Auftrag aus der Zukunft*, ed. Wolfgang Storch (Suhrkamp, 2002), pp. 199–208. For the *Parsifal* staging, see Graevenitz, "Erlösungskunst oder Befreiungspolitik: Wagner und Beuys," in *Unsere Wagner: Joseph Beuys, Heiner Müller, Karlheinz Stockhausen, Hans Jürgen Syberberg: Essays*, ed. Gabriele Förg (Fischer, 1984), pp. 18–19.

626 *"collective regression" | Benjamin Buchloh*, "Beuys: The Twilight of the Idol," in *Joseph Beuys: The Reader*, ed. Claudia Mesch and Viola Michely (MIT Press, 2007), p. 115.

626 *"orgy mystery theater"*: Aaron Levy, ed., *Blood Orgies: Hermann Nitsch in America* (Slought, 2008); Carl Abrahamsson, "Hermann Nitsch: Prinzendorf Is My Bayreuth!," carlabrahamsson.blogspot.com/2013/01/hermann-nitsch-prinzendorf-is-my.html, accessed Dec. 25, 2019.

626 *Hans-Jürgen Syberberg*: On Syberberg and Wagner, see PCW, pp. 375–94, and essays by Susan Sontag and Hans Rudolf Vaget in *Hans-Jürgen Syberberg, the Film Director as Critical Thinker: Essays and Interviews*, ed. R. J. Cardullo (Sense, 2017).

627 *Ingeborg Bachmann*: Quotations from *Darkness Spoken: The Collected Poems*, trans. Peter Filkins (Zephyr, 2006), pp. 473–503; longer passage on p. 479. See also Áine McMurty, "Reading *Tristan* in Ingeborg Bachmann's *Ich weiss keine bessere Welt* and *Malina*," *German Life and Letters* 60:4 (2007), pp. 534–53. "Tot ist alles, alles tot" is a slight variation on Marke's "Tot denn Alles! Alles tot!"

627 *"Thus we died"*: Ingeborg Bachmann, *Malina* (Suhrkamp, 1980), pp. 195–97.

628 *"I was attracted"*: Nicholas Wroe, "A Life in Art: Anselm Kiefer," *Guardian*, March 21, 2011.

628 *Christoph Schlingensief*: On these projects, see Fabian Lehmann et al., eds., *Art of Wagnis: Christoph Schlingensief's Crossing of Wagner and Africa* (Verlag für moderne Kunst, 2017), esp. Anna Teresa Scheer, "The Berlin Republic—or the *Ring* in Africa," pp. 62–76, and Koku G. Nonoa, "Christoph Schlingensief's Theatre and the African Opera Village," pp. 169–74.

629 *Sabine Schütz*: See her *Anselm Kiefer: Geschichte als Material: Arbeiten, 1969–1983* (Dumont, 1999), p. 181.

630 *"Wagner effect"*: Robert Morris, "Size Matters," *Critical Inquiry* 26:3 (2000), pp. 474–87.

630 *Andy Warhol*: See Smith, *Total Work of Art*, pp. 134–56; Annette Michelson, "'Where Is Your Rupture?': Mass Culture and the Gesamtkunstwerk," *October* 56 (1991), pp. 42–63; Simon Shaw-Miller, *Visible Deeds of Music: Art and Music from Wagner to Cage* (Yale UP, 2002), pp. 13–14.

631 *"Gesamtdatenwerk"*: Roy Ascott, "Is There Love in the Telematic Embrace?," in *Multimedia: From Wagner to Virtual Reality*, ed. Randall Packer and Ken Jordan (Norton, 2001), p. 335. For Smith, see his *Total Work of Art*, pp. 165–66.

631 *"authentic religious experience"*: Rosenblum, *Modern Painting and the Northern Romantic Tradition*, p. 216; Ryder on p. 204. On Kline and Wagner, see Harry F. Gaugh, *The Vital Gesture: Franz Kline* (Abbeville, 1985), pp. 94, 118–19, 177. On Twombly, see Nicola Del Roscio, "Cy Twombly and the Making of *Fifty Days at Iliam*," in *Cy Twombly: Fifty Days at Iliam*, ed. Carlos Basualdo (Yale UP, 2019), p. 161, and Mary Jacobus, *Reading Cy Twombly: Poetry in Paint* (Princeton UP, 2016), p. 120.

631 *Wagnerite father*: Antoni Tàpies, *Complete Writings, Volume 1: A Personal Memoir, Fragments for an Autobiography*, trans. Josep Miquel Sobrer (Indiana UP, 2009), pp. 85, 90.

631 *"a stage on which"*: Andreas Franzke, *Tàpies* (Prestel, 1992), p. 58.

632 *Carrer de Wagner*: Joan Brossa and Antoni Tàpies, *Carrer de Wagner* (Edicions T, 1989), pamphlet. See also Deborah Wye, *Antoni Tàpies in Print* (MoMA, 1991), pp. 45–46.

632 *"There's a certain type"*: Marta Nadal, "Joan Brossa: An Atypical Poet," trans. Graham Thomson, *transcript* 3, www.transcript-review.org.

632 *"a real mountain"*: Dawn Adès and Michael R. Taylor, eds., *Dalí* (Rizzoli, 2004), p. 316.

632 *Anselm Domènech*: Caroline Barbier de Reulle, "Salvador Dalí et la musique: Dissonances entre le discours et l'œuvre," *Cahiers du MNAM* 121 (2012), p. 37.

632 *"cooking sardines"*: Ibid., p. 51.

632 *"Satie, tangos"*: Author's interview with Montse Aguer, March 5, 2013.

632 *The last was playing*: Meredith Etherington-Smith, *The Persistence of Memory: A Biography of Dalí* (Da Capo, 1995), p. 431.

633 *alternate title*: A. Reynolds Morse and Michel Tapié, *Dalí: A Study of His Life and Work* (New York Graphic Society, 1958), p. 42.

633 *"Venus is metamorphosed"*: Program booklet for Ballet Russe de Monte Carlo, 1939–1940 season, University of Florida Digital Collections, ufdc.ufl.edu.

633 *"perverse and tragic"*: Leslie Norton, *Léonide Massine and the 20th Century Ballet* (McFarland, 2004), p. 283.

633 *"repulsive mummy . . . murders Wagner"*: Edwin Denby, *Looking at the Dance* (Pellegrini & Cudahy, 1949), pp. 263–64.

633 *"delicious gustatory thrill"*: Dalí and André Parinaud, *The Unspeakable Confessions of Salvador Dalí*, trans. Harold J. Salemson (William Morrow, 1976), p. 125.

633 *"The end to which"*: Dalí, *Hidden Faces*, trans. Haakon Chevalier (William Morrow, 1974), p. 30.

633 *strains* of Parsifal: Adam Gopnik, "The Last Living Bohemian in Chelsea Tells All," newyorker.com, June 17, 2015. For the *Ring* sign, see Mark Thompson, *Leatherfolk: Radical Sex, People, Politics, and Practice* (Alyson, 1991), p. 198.

634 *"When you suddenly . . . Death ended up"*: Lawrence Weschler, "The Colors of Silence," *Los Angeles*, Feb. 1997. For "dawn," see Christopher Sykes, *David Hockney: The Biography, 1975–2012: A Pilgrim's Progress* (Doubleday, 2014), pp. 260–61.

634 Rheingold *rehearsal*: William Gaddis, *J R* (Dalkey Archive, 2016), pp. 17–37; "Call to the Colors" on p. 33.

635 *"Wagner was a genius"*: Norman Mailer, *The Castle in the Forest* (Random House, 2007), pp. 424–25.

635 *"Harmonic Final Solution"*: Harry Mulisch, *Siegfried*, trans. Paul Vincent (Penguin, 2004), p. 33.

635 *compares the Nuremberg rallies*: Alain Robbe-Grillet, *Le Miroir qui revient* (Éditions de Minuit, 1984), p. 218.

635 *"solitary man who says"*: Robbe-Grillet, *Angélique, ou l'Enchantement* (Éditions de Minuit, 1987), pp. 22–23. For "shipwreck," see Picard, "Robbe-Grillet, Alain," in DEW, p. 1833.

635 *"long, deep rustling"*: Julien Gracq, *Un balcon en forêt* (Corti, 1970), p. 100; Fafner on p. 141, Wotan on p. 230.

636 *"Nothing satisfied me"*: Pamela Jackson and Jonathan Lethem, eds., *The Exegesis of Philip K. Dick* (Houghton Mifflin, 2011), p. 663. For Karl Muck, see Don Herron, ed., *The Selected Letters of Philip K. Dick, 1977–1979* (Underwood-Miller, 1993), p. 66. For loud Wagner, see Anne R. Dick, *The Search for Philip K. Dick* (Tachyon, 2010), pp. 246, 255–56.

636 *"The Preserving Machine"*: *The Collected Stories of Philip K. Dick*, vol. 1: *The Short Happy Life of the Brown Oxford* (Citadel Twilight, 1990), pp. 149–56.

636 *frequently include the Nazi Wagner*: Dick, *The Man in the High Castle* (Vintage, 1992), p. 156; *The Simulacra* (Mariner, 2011), pp. 84–85; *Flow My Tears, the Policeman Said* (Vintage, 1993), p. 188.

637 *the opera showed him*: Dick, *Exegesis*, p. 876.

637 *"Here time becomes space"*: Dick, *VALIS* (Mariner, 2011), p. 38; *Parsifal* analysis on pp. 141–44.

637 *"Parsifal is one of those . . . is fucked"*: Ibid., p. 144.

638 *"Untergang" and "annihilation"*: Hartmut Zelinsky, "Die 'feuerkur' des Richard Wagner oder die 'neue religion' der Erlösung durch 'Vernichtung,'" in *Musik-Konzepte* 5, pp. 79–112. For Gottfried Wagner, see his *Twilight of the Wagners*, pp. 64–65; and Alex Ross, "The Unforgiven," *New Yorker*, Aug. 10, 1998.

638 *"You will not play Wagner!"*: Zubin Mehta and Renate Gräfin Matuschka, *The Score of My Life*, trans. Anu Pande (Amadeus, 2009), pp. 106–107.

638 *"Play Wagner over my body"*: Karin Laub, "Israel Takes a Step to End Ban on Wagner's Music," Associated Press, April 1, 1990.

638 *"Some time ago"*: Na'ama Sheffi, "A Strident Silencing: The Ban on Richard Wagner in Israel," in *The Oxford Handbook of Music Censorship*, ed. Patricia Hall (Oxford UP, 2018), p. 140.

639 *"Woe to the Jew"*: Sheffi, *The Ring of Myths: The Israelis, Wagner, and the Nazis* (Sussex Academic Press, 2001), p. 90.

639 *"Fascist!"*: Ewen MacAskill, "Barenboim Stirs Up Israeli Storm by Playing Wagner," *Guardian*, July 9, 2001. For Asher Fisch, see David Weininger, "Bringing Wagner to Tanglewood, and One Day to Israel," *Boston Globe*, July 20, 2012; and Dan Ephron, "What's Behind Israel's Unofficial Ban on Wagner?," *TheDailyBeast.com*, June 20, 2012.

639 *compensatory action*: Sheffi, *Ring of Myths*, pp. 113, 116, 140; Sheffi, "Between Collective Memory and Manipulation: The Holocaust, Wagner, and the Israelis," *Journal of Israeli History* 23:1 (2004), pp. 65–77.

639 *Batya Gur*: See her *Murder Duet: A Musical Case*, trans. Dalya Bilu (HarperCollins, 1999).

639 *"ideologically preformed"*: Moshe Zuckermann, "The Wagner Syndrome: Aspects of a German-Israeli Symbiosis," in Winklbauer, *Euphorie und Unbehagen*, p. 194.

639 *"the claim"*: Michael P. Steinberg, *The Trouble with Wagner* (University of Chicago Press, 2018), p. 136.

640 *"remarkable clarity"*: Andrew Joyce, "On Contemporary Opera and Wagner's 'Jewry in Music,'" www.theoccidentalobserver.net, Sept. 26, 2015. For Taylor Swift, see Zachary Woolfe, "We Never Go out of Style," *Even* 6 (2017). For laments about Wagner's lack of popularity, see Collin Cleary, "Wagner's Place in the Germanic Tradition, Part 1," www.counter-currents.com, May 31, 2013.

640 *reaffirmed Wagner's bond*: Catherine Coquio, "Völkisch," in DEW, pp. 2197–98.

641 *"vaudeville"*: Alain de Benoist, *Vu de droite: Anthologie critique des idées contemporaines* (Copernic, 1979), pp. 529–38.

641 *Wagner Group*: Mike Giglio, "Inside the Shadow War Fought by Russian Mercenaries," *Buzzfeed News*, April 17, 2019. For Dugin, see Mark Sedgwick, *Against the Modern World: Traditionalism and the Secret Intellectual History of the Twentieth Century* (Oxford UP, 2004), p. 233.

641 *Tannenhäuser*: "'Entsorgen!' AfD-Chef Meuthen legt noch einen drauf," *Merkur*, Sept. 9, 2017. Wenzel Michalski, of Human Rights Watch, reports little Wagnerism on the German far right (communication to author).

641 *"rich potential"*: Brenton Sanderson, "Evil Genius: Constructing Wagner as Moral Pariah, Part 4," www.counter-currents.com, May 2013.

641 *"spend millions of dollars"*: Julia Ioffe, "Scenes from the Trump Hotel," *Politico*, Nov. 9, 2016. For Spencer and Adorno, see Josh Harkinson, "Meet the White Nationalist Trying to Ride the Trump Train to Lasting Power," *Mother Jones*, Oct. 27, 2016; and "Frankfurt School Revisionism," podcast conversation between Spencer and Jonathan Bowden, February 16, 2012, published at www.counter-currents.com, June 3, 2016.

641 *"Never again"*: Tina Brown, *The Vanity Fair Diaries: 1983–1992* (Holt, 2017), p. 260.

641 *review of a book*: Algernon Tassin, "Old Spirits and New Seas," part 1, *Bookman* 34:4 (1911), pp. 383, 385. For C. S. Lewis's memories, see his *Surprised by Joy: The Shape of My Early Life* (Harcourt, 1955) pp. 72–76.

642 *"Arising out of"*: Warren Lewis, *Brothers and Friends: The Diaries of Major Warren Hamilton Lewis* (Harper & Row, 1982), pp. 145–46. See also Walter Hooper, ed., *The Collected Letters of C. S. Lewis*, vol. 2 (HarperCollins, 2004), pp. 137–39.

642 *he resisted comparisons*: For one widely quoted remark—"Both Rings were round, and there the resemblance ceases"—see Humphrey Carpenter and Christopher Tolkien, eds., *The Letters of J. R. R. Tolkien* (Houghton Mifflin, 1981), p. 306. Renée Vink, *Wagner and Tolkien: Mythmakers* (Walking Tree, 2012), pp. 6–14, casts doubt on whether this passage really expresses hostility to Wagner and notes scattered evidence of Tolkien's liking for the composer.

642 *Renée Vink: Wagner and Tolkien*, pp. 262–64. See also J. R. R. Tolkien, *The Legend of Sigurd and Gudrún*, ed. Christopher Tolkien (Houghton Mifflin, 2009); Tom Shippey, "The Legend of Sigurd and Gudrún (review)," *Tolkien Studies* 7 (2010), pp. 306–308; J. P. E. Harper-Scott, "Wagner and the Königsproblem," in Sala, *Legacy of Richard Wagner*, pp. 131–36.

642 *cover familiar ground*: For a list of twenty-eight resemblances, see Vink, *Wagner and Tolkien*, pp. 15–28. See also Susanne Vill, "Wagners

Visionen—Motive aus Werken Richard Wagners in Fantasyfilmen," *wagnerspectrum* 4:2 (2008), pp. 49–70; Tom Shippey, *The Road to Middle-Earth* (Houghton Mifflin, 2003), pp. 343–44; Edward Haymes, "The Two Rings," lecture to the Wagner Society of New York, Jan. 14, 2004.

643 *"noble northern spirit"*: Letters of J. R. R. Tolkien, pp. 55–56.

643 *"Anything more vulgar"*: Walter Hooper, ed., *The Collected Letters of C. S. Lewis*, vol. 1 (HarperCollins, 2004), pp. 405–406.

643 *"Ride, ride to ruin"*: Tolkien, *The Lord of the Rings* (Houghton Mifflin, 1955), p. 826.

644 *"I think we have made"*: Smith, *Total Work of Art*, pp. 119–20; "mythic time" on p. 125. For Ludwig tourism in the fifties, see Rudy Koshar, *Germany's Transient Pasts: Preservation and National Memory in the Twentieth Century* (University of North Carolina Press, 1998), p. 263.

645 *Superman*: On the origins of the character, see Gerard Jones, *Men of Tomorrow: Geeks, Gangsters, and the Birth of the Comic Book* (Basic, 2004), pp. 78–86.

645 *Žižek's ingenious reading*: Slavoj Žižek, "'The Wound Is Healed Only by the Spear That Smote You': The Operatic Subject and Its Vicissitudes," in *Opera Through Other Eyes*, ed. David J. Levin (Stanford UP, 1994), pp. 199–200.

645 *Martin Nodell*: "Green Lantern: 60th Anniversary Panel," *Alter Ego* 3:148 (Sept. 2017), pp. 45–47. For *Air Fighters*, see Donald D. Markstein's entries for Airboy and Valkyrie at www.toonopedia.com, accessed Dec. 25, 2019.

645 *"pop-Wagnerian"*: Susan Sontag, "Fascinating Fascism"; Pauline Kael, "Fun Machines," *New Yorker*, May 30, 1983.

645 *Mike Ashman*: See his "The Ring in Later Mythologies," essay accompanying the two-CD set *Twilight of the Gods* (Deutsche Grammophon, 2012).

645 *spoke of using*: For Wagner in *Star Wars*, see Charles Champlin, *George Lucas: The Creative Impulse: Lucasfilm's First Twenty-Five Years* (Abrams, 1997), pp. 49–51. For other cues, see J. W. Rinzler, *The Making of "Star Wars": The Definitive Story Behind the Original Film* (Ballantine, 2007), pp. 238, 243, 246; Emilio Audissino, *John Williams's Film Music: "Jaws," "Star Wars," "Raiders of the Lost Ark," and the Return of the Classical Hollywood Music Style* (University of Wisconsin Press, 2014), p. 71; and, for *Bolero*, Richard Dyer, "Making 'Star Wars' Sing Again in a London Studio," *Boston Globe*, March 28, 1999.

646 *sixty distinct leitmotifs*: Frank Lehman, "Complete Catalogue of the Musical Themes of *Star Wars*," franklehman.com/starwars, accessed Dec. 25, 2019.

646 *"familiar and remembered"*: Craig L. Byrd, "Interview with John Williams," in *Celluloid Symphonies: Texts and Contexts in Film Music History*, ed. Julie

Hubbert (University of California Press, 2011), p. 416. Williams distanced himself from Wagner in an interview with the author, Feb. 5, 2020.

646 *James Buhler*: See his *"Star Wars*, Music, and Myth," in *Music and Cinema*, p. 44. On Williams, see Frank Lehman, *Hollywood Harmony: Musical Wonder and the Sound of Cinema* (Oxford UP, 2018); and Matthew Bribitzer-Stull, *Understanding the Leitmotif: From Wagner to Hollywood Film Music* (Cambridge UP, 2015).

646 *Lucas subsequently*: Rinzler, *The Making of "Star Wars,"* pp. 296–97.

647 *dozens of variants*: Vill, "Wagners Visionen," pp. 9–95. See also Alex Ross, "Wagner, Incest, and *Game of Thrones*," newyorker.com, Aug. 29, 2017; and David Ng, "Richard Wagner's Cycle Has Made Its Mark on Comic Books," *Los Angeles Times*, April 11, 2010.

648 *among the first to spot*: Žižek, "Why Is Wagner Worth Saving?," p. 22.

648 *Neo stops bullets*: Andrew May, "Parsifal as Proto-SF," lecture from 2005, www.andrew-may.com /parsifal.htm, accessed Dec. 25, 2019. See also Vill, "Wagners Visionen," pp. 89–91.

649 *Yves Landerouin*: See his "La Réception contemporaine de la musique de Richard Wagner au cinéma," in *Verdi/Wagner: Images croisées, 1813–2013: Musique, histoire des idées, littérature et arts*, ed. Jean-François Candoni et al. (Presses universitaires de Rennes, 2018), p. 417.

650 *"eco-parable"*: Thomas S. Grey, "Wagner's *Ring* as Eco-Parable," in *Music Theater as Global Culture*, pp. 183–98.

650 *"whole earth-nature"*: Wagner, "Kunst und Klima," *Deutsche Monatsschrift für Politik, Wissenschaft, Kunst und Leben*, April 1850, p. 8. See also Kirsten Paige, "'Art and Climate,' *Parsifal*, and the Atmospheric Politics of Wagnerian Theater," *Opera Quarterly* 33:3–4 (2019), pp. 1–32; Paige, "Wagnerian Climatic Fantasies: Sound, Space, and Breath," *European Romantic Review* 28:3 (2017), pp. 343–48; Paige, *Richard Wagner's Political Ecology* (Ph.D. diss., University of California, 2018).

650 *animal-rights advocates*: See, for example, "Wagner's Dog Friends," *Zoophilist and Animals'*

Defender, Oct. 1, 1901, p. 147, citation via Kirsten Paige. On Wagner and dogs, see Kerstin Decker, *Richard Wagner: Mit den Augen seiner Hunde betrachtet* (Berenberg, 2013); and Franziska Polanski, *Richard Wagners Hunde: Da lernt' ich wohl, was Liebe sei* (Implizit, 2017).

650 *"religion of compassion"*: See front pages of Schwantje's *Ethische Rundschau* (1912–15), www.magnus-schwantje-archiv.de. For awareness of Wagner's racism, see Schwantje, *Ueber Richard Wagner's ethisches Wirken* (Bund für radikale Ethik, 1919), pp. 17–18.

651 *"mythic trope"*: Grey, "Wagner's *Ring* as Eco-Parable," p. 193.

651 *"The very industries"*: James Merrill, *Collected Poems*, ed. J. D. McClatchy and Stephen Yenser (Knopf, 2002), p. 612.

652 *overturned a row*: Author's interview with Herzog, Jan. 26, 2018.

652 *"Hearing it"*: Paul Cronin, ed., *Herzog on Herzog* (Faber, 2002), p. 259.

653 *"stylization"*: Ibid., p. 245. For Koepnick, see his "The Sound of Ruins," in *German Postwar Films: Life and Love in the Ruins*, ed. Wilfried Wilms and William Rasch (Palgrave, 2008), p. 204. See also Laurent Guido, "Dans les 'abysses du temps': Echos wagnériens dans l'œuvre documentaire de Werner Herzog," *Décadrages* 25 (2013), pp. 53–54.

654 *Terrence Malick*: Background derived from Paul Maher, Jr., *All Things Shining: An Oral History of the Films of Terrence Malick* (Lulu, 2017), and author's conversations with Malick.

654 *"What are poets for . . . Poetically man dwells"*: Heidegger, "Wozu dichter?," *Gesamtausgabe* I:5: *Holzwege* (Klostermann, 1977), pp. 269–320; Heidegger, ". . . dichterisch wohnet der Mensch . . . ," *Gesamtausgabe* I:7: *Vorträge und Aufsätze* (Klostermann, 2000), pp. 189–208.

655 *"Where there is danger"*: Heidegger, "Die Frage nach der Technik," *Gesamtausgabe* I:7, pp. 29–30.

POSTLUDE

658 *"power and impotence"*: Badiou, *Five Lessons*, p. 120.

658 *teaches us to know*: Lévi-Strauss, *View from Afar*, p. 234.

659 *"perhaps"*: NWKG VII:3, p. 309.

ACKNOWLEDGMENTS

■ ■

Among the hundreds of sympathetic souls who led me through the Wagnerian labyrinth, I wish first to thank Kristina Unger, Tanja Dobrick, and their colleagues at the National Archives of the Richard-Wagner-Stiftung Bayreuth. It was an eerie pleasure to spend several days browsing in the old Wagner library. Peter and Friederike Emmerich, at the Bayreuther Festspiele press department, were attentive hosts during my visits to the Green Hill. Eva Graf graciously showed me the guest ledger of the Hotel Goldener Anker. Alessandra Althoff Pugliese of the Associazione Richard Wagner di Venezia gave me a tour of the Wagner quarters at the Palazzo Vendramin, where the story begins.

I could not have written *Wagnerism* without the benevolent support of the MacArthur Foundation, the John Simon Guggenheim Memorial Foundation, and the American Academy in Rome. I am especially grateful to Martin Brody for arranging a Roman idyll, which allowed me to follow Wagner's tracks in Venice and Sorrento.

The following facilitated archival research and answered inquiries: D. J. Hoek, Music Library, Bienen School of Music, Northwestern University; Scott Krafft, Charles Deering McCormick Library of Special Collections, Northwestern University; Pauline Wolstencroft, Balch Art Research Library, LACMA; Nancy Adgent, Rockefeller Archive Center; Richard Leab, Berkshire Athenaeum; Lisa Long Feldmann, Isabella Stewart Gardner Museum; Leslie A. Morris, Houghton Library, Harvard University; Laura Russo, Howard Gotlieb Archival Research Center, Boston University; Anne Moore, Special Collections, University of Massachusetts Amherst; Erin K. Dix, Lawrence University; Kate Goldkamp, Washington University Libraries; James Stimpert, Special Collections, Sheridan Libraries, Johns Hopkins University; Peter H. Hassrick, Buffalo Bill Center of the West; Kristina Warner, Norwegian-American Historical Association; Will Thackara, Theosophical Society, Pasadena; Alison Greenlee and Milissa Burkart, McFarlin Library, University of Tulsa; Heather Oswald, Baker Library Special Collections, Harvard Business School; Catherine Broad, Humanist Library, Conway Hall Ethical Society; Jean-Michel Vinciguerra,

Bibliothèque-musée de l'Opéra; Frédéric Delmotte, Archives de la Ville de Bruxelles; Joseph Saunders and Wenzel Michalski, Human Rights Watch; Klaus-Peter Möller, Theodor-Fontane-Archiv, Universität Potsdam; Katrin Keller, Thomas-Mann-Archiv, ETH Zürich; Michael Schwarz, Walter Benjamin Archiv, Akademie der Künste, Berlin; Benjamin Ortmeyer, Forschungsstelle NS-Pädagogik, Goethe-Universität Frankfurt am Main; Annemarie Kaindl, Bayerischer Staatsbibliothek; Kerstin Stremmel, Theaterwissenschaftliche Sammlung, Universität zu Köln; Anno Mungen and Daniel Reupke, Forschungsinstitut für Musiktheater, Universität Bayreuth; Karola Wagner, Bundesarchiv Berlin-Lichterfelde; Maria Canelles, Fundació Joan Brossa; Ulf Wagner, Hilma af Klint Foundation; Ksenia Yakovleva, Russian State Archive; Eva König, Atelier Anselm Kiefer.

I also received valuable assistance during several visits to the Rare Book and Special Collections, Prints and Photographs, and Manuscript Divisions at the Library of Congress. The Manhattan Research Library Initiative (MaRLI) enabled access to materials at the New York Public Library and at the Columbia and NYU libraries. I later relied on the resources of the Los Angeles Public Library, the Brand Library & Art Center, and the library system at the University of California, Los Angeles.

No part of my Wagner immersion gave as much delight as my visits to Red Cloud and Lincoln, Nebraska, on the trail of Willa Cather. For their aid and hospitality, I thank Guy Reynolds, Andrew Jewell, Beth Burke, Josh Caster, and Kari Ronning at the University of Nebraska–Lincoln; Ashley Olson and Tracy Tucker at the National Willa Cather Center; and Jay Yost and Wade Leak at the five-star Kaley House. Joseph Murphy shared his thinking about the Cather-Wagner nexus. Melissa Homestead undertook a close reading of the Cather chapter. Anke Leonhardt, at the Darmstadt Stadtarchiv, and Ursula Kramer, at the Institut für Kunstgeschichte und Musikwissenschaft in Mainz, helped me reconstruct the career of Albert Schindelmeisser.

Francis Ford Coppola, Werner Herzog, Terrence Malick, Walter Murch, and John Williams were kind enough to answer questions about their work. Stephanie Blythe, Justin Brown, Christoph von Dohnányi, Esa-Pekka Salonen, Yuval Sharon, and Simone Young spoke to me about singing, conducting, and directing Wagner. Some years ago, Gottfried Wagner told me of his troubled relationship with his great-grandfather. Frido Mann shared memories of his grandfather, the supreme Wagnerite. Steven Lavine and Nikolai Blaumer welcomed me into the community of the Thomas Mann House in L.A. During visits to Barcelona, Joan Matabosch, Marc Busquets Figuerola, and Montse Aguer gave me insight into Catalan Wagnerism, and Elena Ramirez, my marvelous publisher at Seix Barral, arranged for me to see Dalí's Púbol castle during the off-season.

Scholars and experts in various disciplines magnanimously replied to out-of-the-blue queries. These include Kwame Anthony Appiah, Robert Baldwin, Tim Barringer, Eric Bentley, Mark Berry, Leah Branstetter, Lucy Caplan, Corrinne Chong, Brendan Cole, Jeremy Coleman, Adam Crane, Robert Crawford, Samuel Dwinell, Brent Edwards, Jeremy Eichler, Hermann Grampp, Mark Harris and Tony Kushner, Chris Herbert, Claire Hirshfield, Jeffery Howe, Steven Huebner, Daniel Jütte, Leanne Langley, Aleksander Laskowski, John LeBourgeois, Frank Lehman, Rex Levang, James Leverett, John Mackay, Brooke McCorkle, Hans-Peter Messmer, Theresa Muir, Klara Naszkowska, Nancy Newman, Kirsten Paige, Othmar Plöckinger, Jadranka Ryle, William Scott, Brendan Simms, Wendy Ligon Smith, Frederic Spotts, Lynne Swarts, Kira Thurman, Sarah Tomlinson, Kristen Turner, Marc Weiner, and Douglas Wolk. Absorbing the impact of Timothée Picard's monumental Wagner dictionary delayed the book for at least a year. For the opportunity to try out Wagnerian material in scholarly settings, I am grateful to Walter Frisch and Mark Anderson at Columbia University; W. Anthony Sheppard at Williams College; Andrew Motion at Johns Hopkins University; Robert Faggen at Claremont McKenna College; Robert Elias at the Colburn School; Suzannah Clark at Harvard University; Nicholas Vazsonyi and Julie Hubbert at the University of South Carolina; Annegret Fauser and Tim Carter at the University of North Carolina at Chapel Hill; Robert Scafe and Sanna Pederson at the University of Oklahoma; Paul Fahy at the Galway Arts Festival; and Ian McNeely at the University of Oregon. Alan Hollinghurst devised a Belgian Symbolist itinerary; Arthur Kolat shared maps of David Hockney's Wagner Drives; Jason Schwartzman relayed an *Apocalypse Now* query; David Simon joined me at the Goetheanum; Annie Gosfield sent along movie leads. Roman Pashutin helped with Roerich images, Tom Artin with Wagnerian jazz, Dave Robinson with Valkyrie planes. Tammy Hepps gave me "Lowengreen's Wedding March."

Hans Rudolf Vaget was the first person to read the monstrous rough draft. Long before he did me that service, I had come to rely upon his vast knowledge and sagacity. Vivien Greene, Tom Grey, Michael Kater, Heath Lees, Jean-Jacques Nattiez, Peter Schjeldahl, and Nicholas Vazsonyi also read complete drafts, making incisive comments on nearly every page. Rosamund Bartlett,

Sydney Boyd, Joy Calico, Ken Collins, Kevin Dettmar, Leland de la Durantaye, Marina Harss, Elizabeth Kendall, Glenn Kenny, Jonathan Lethem, Andrew Marantz, John Plotz, Kenneth Reinhard, Emma Sutton, and Chris Walton provided crucial notes and corrections on individual chapters. I have no idea how to repay all this generosity.

When I embarked on this project, in 2008, Will Robin was an undergraduate; now he is a professor who has finished his first book. Early on, he assisted me with research; toward the end, he supplied wise advice. He calls me a mentor, but now I more often learn from him. Emre Tetik spent several years tracking down cryptic tomes in libraries and fine-tuning translations. Matthew Aucoin, Alexander Devereux, Miles Graham, and Emily Shyr also contributed to the research phase.

Laurent Slaars and Luis Gago, my impeccable French and Spanish translators, offered guidance in their respective languages. Ann Goldstein reviewed passages in Italian; Alex Abramovich and David Shengold fashioned Russian translations; Roger Evans gave pointers on Catalan matters; Jens Laurson weighed in on German questions. Cyril Kuhn, a brilliant artist who doubles as my German tutor, spent countless hours reviewing translations and discussing the book's themes. His friendship was another unexpected gift of this long process. I hardly know how to acknowledge Fergus McIntosh, Hélène Werner, and Madeleine Baverstam, who had the near-hopeless task of checking the manuscript. However much they privately cursed me and my blurry scans, they were a joy to work with, and they saved me from myriad stupidities.

Years passed; youth gave way to middle age; twilight settled over the land; and Eric Chinski, my editor at Farrar, Straus and Giroux, waited with Erda-like patience as my manuscript grew menacingly large. He then set to work with colossal dedication, coaxing the book toward readability and coherence. If it falls short, it is not for lack of his mighty efforts. John McGhee again achieved wonders as an eagle-eyed copy editor. Scott Auerbach, the meticulous production editor, patiently handled a slew of frantic last-minute inserts, not excluding this sentence. Julia Ringo amiably addressed a year-long barrage of authorial anxieties. Steve Weil threw himself into the improbable task of publicizing the book. Alex Merto and Gretchen Achilles produced a beautiful cover and design. I also thank Jonathan Galassi, Deborah Ghim, Sarita Varma, and Sheila O'Shea for their labors on behalf of the "Wagner animal."

At *The New Yorker*, David Remnick maintains a writer's utopia in which I am lucky to have a place. Daniel Zalewski, my overperson of an editor, is also an extraordinary friend. Henry Finder, Pam McCarthy, and Dorothy Wickenden have steered the magazine through strange seas. I raise a coffee mug to my colleagues Michael Agger, Richard Brody, Leo Carey, Bruce Diones, David Grann, Rebecca Mead, and Emily Nussbaum (source of *The Saturdays*). Dorothy Vincent, Cullen Stanley, and Zoë Nelson looked after me at Janklow & Nesbit. Tina Bennett, my agent, has offered more than twenty years of astute, steadfast, buoyant counsel.

The friendship of Alex Star, Paula Puhak, Liberty Aldrich, Jason Shure, Michael Miller, Sean O'Toole, Tim Arango, Marc Geelhoed, Amanda Ameer, Will again, and the Goldstine clan—Josh, Stephanie, Danny, Hilary, Eli, and Theo—kept me partly tethered to reality. My brother, Christopher, has been kind and selfless beyond measure. Bea, Minnie, and the dearly missed Maulina provided wry commentary. My magnificent husband, Jonathan Lisecki, has lovingly endured a decade of Wagnerian madness.

Lastly, I remember with gratitude my mother, Daphne Ross, to whom I owe my love of words and music, and Andrew Patner, wisest of friends.

INDEX

∎ ∎

Page numbers in *italics* refer to illustrations.

ILLUSTRATION CREDITS

page 180   The Goetheanum in Dornach: Photograph by author
page 182   Reginald Machell, *The Holy Grail*, undated: Reproduced by permission, Archives, The Theosophical Society, Pasadena
page 191   Adolf von Werner, *Enthüllung des Richard-Wagner-Denkmals im Tiergarten*, 1908: Berlinische Galerie
page 196   Singers' Hall, Neuschwanstein: Courtesy of the Library of Congress
page 200   Hans Thoma, *Kopf Wotans*, c. 1896: From Henry Thode, ed., *Hans Thoma's Kostümentwürfe zu Richard Wagner's Ring des Nibelungen* (Breitkopf und Härtel, 1897), courtesy of e-rara / Universitätsbibliothek Basel
page 204   Franz Stassen, *"Nothung trägst du im Herzen,"* 1914: ©: Ketterer Kunst GmbH und Co. KG
page 214   Gustav Klimt, *Beethovenfrieze*, 1902: Erich Lessing / Art Resource, NY
page 217   Gabriele d'Annunzio: Courtesy of Polona, National Library of Poland
page 221   Heinrich and Thomas Mann: Photograph from Hofatelier Elvira, 1900, courtesy of ETH-Bibliothek Zürich, Thomas-Mann-Archiv
page 230   W, E, B, Du Bois's ticket to *Lohengrin* at Bayreuth, 1936: Special Collections and University Archives, W. E. B. Du Bois Library, University of Massachusetts Amherst
page 234   Wagner as a Jew: Theodor Zajaczkowski, "Darwinistische Entwicklungslehre," *Der Floh*, undated; from Karl Storck, *Musik und Musiker in Karikatur und Satire* (Stalling, 1911)
page 237   "Der Untergang!": From "Das Judenthum in der Musik," *Neue Zeitschrift für Musik*, Sept. 6, 1850
page 249   Houston Stewart Chamberlain: Bundesarchiv
page 252   Otto Weininger: Frontispiece of Weininger's *Geschlecht und Charakter* (Braumüller, 1919)
page 256   Klaus and Katia Pringsheim: Photogtaph from Atelier Jaeger & Goergen, circa 1900, courtesy of ETH-Bibliothek Zürich, Thomas-Mann-Archiv
page 261   Theodor Herzl in Basel: Photograph by Ephraim Moses Lilien, 1901; courtesy of the National Library of Israel
page 266   Luranah Aldridge: Aldridge Collection, Charles Deering McCormick Library of Special Collections, Northwestern University Libraries
page 270   Cosima Wagner's letter to Luranah Aldridge, May 24, 1897: Aldridge Collection, Charles Deering McCormick Library of Special Collections, Northwestern University Libraries
page 271   W. E. B. Du Bois: Courtesy of the Library of Congress
page 277   Pulse rates of Wagner listeners: From Aldred Scott Warthin, "Some Physiologic Effects of Music in Hypnotized Subjects," *Medical News* (1894)
page 281   Cosima Wagner: Courtesy of ETH-Bibliothek Zürich, Thomas-Mann-Archiv
page 282   Frou-Frou Wagner: Illustration by Friedrich Graetz for *Der Floh*, 1877; from Karl Storck, *Musik und Musiker in Karikatur und Satire* (Stalling, 1911)
page 286   Aubrey Beardsley, *The Wagnerites*, 1894: V&A Images, London / Art Resource, NY
page 290   Lillian Nordica: Courtesy of the Library of Congress
page 293   Fidus [Hugo Höppener], *Parzival*, 1900: From *Der Jugend* 39 (1900)
page 302   Franz Stassen, *Siegfried badet im Blut des Drachens*: From Rudolf Herzog, *Siegfried, der Held: Der deutschen Jugend erzählt* (Ullstein, 1912)
page 306   Aubrey Beardsley, *Siegfried, Act II*, c. 1892–93: V&A Images, London / Art Resource, NY
page 308   The Lido of Venice: Courtesy of ETH-Bibliothek Zürich, Thomas-Mann-Archiv
page 317   Sabina Spielrein: Les Archives Institut J.-J. Rousseau
page 322   Olive Fremstad as Isolde: Archives & Special Collections, University of Nebraska–Lincoln Libraries
page 326   The Willa Cather Memorial Prairie: Photograph by author
page 332   Willa Cather in a field in Jaffrey, New Hampshire, early 1920s: Archives & Special Collections, University of Nebraska–Lincoln Libraries
page 341   Olive Fremstad at Little Walhalla in Maine, 1915: Courtesy of the Library of Congress
page 345   Jules Breton, *The Song of the Lark*, 1884: Courtesy of the Art Institute of Chicago
page 351   Acoma, New Mexico: Photograph by author
page 355   Adolphe Appia, design for *Die Walküre*, 1896: Courtesy of the Beinecke Library
page 359   Jules Chéret, poster for Loie Fuller's *La Danse du feu*, 1897: Bibliothèque nationale de France
page 364   Adolphe Appia, design for *Das Rheingold*, 1892: Courtesy of the Beinecke Library
page 368   *Music of Wagner*, from Annie Besant and C. W. Leadbeater's *Thought-Forms* (Theosophical Publishing Society, 1905)
page 368   Wassily Kandinsky, *Landscape with Red Spots II*, 1913: Guggenheim Venice
page 400   Poster for *Parsifal* in Barcelona, 1914: Courtesy of Joan Matabosch
page 404   Franz Stassen, *Auf nach Walhall!*: Historische Bildpostkarten, Universität Osnabrück, Sammlung Prof. Dr. Sabine Giesbrecht, www.bildpostkarten.uos.de